Everywhere You Loo

Chapter 10: A Brand Image for Guinness Beer
Chapter 11: Controversial Uses of LeBron James in Singapore and China
Chapter 12: Is What's Good for Vodka Good for Tequila?
Chapter 13: Searching for Media Options Around the Globe
Chapter 14: The (Sorry) State of Radio Advertising in China
Chapter 15: Nescafé's Viral E-mail Effort in Argentina
Chapter 16: Dubbing in Brands to Fit the Needs of Different Countries
Chapter 17: Driving Sales for Fiat in Brazil
Chapter 18: M&M's Global Color Vote
Chapter 19: Barq's Root Beer and Russian Knickknacks
Chapter 20: Negative Publicity for Coca-Cola's Dasani in the United Kingdom

imc focus

Chapter 1: An Authority Delcares That Positioning Is Out of Date
Chapter 2: Neuromarketing and the Case of Why Coca-Cola Outsells Pepsi
Chapter 3: An Adman's Struggle with Joe Camel and Free Speech
Chapter 3: A Rigged Promotion for Frozen Coke
Chapter 4: Tweens and Materialism
Chapter 4: A Special Beverage for Latino Consumers, Clamato
Chapter 5: Diamonds (Given to Yourself) Are Forever
Chapter 6: The Cat(fight) Is a Dog
Chapter 7: Selecting a Name for a New Airline
Chapter 7: Illustrations of Workable Packages
Chapter 8: ABC, CBS, Fox, NBC, and Now Wal-Mart TV Network
Chapter 9: B2B Advertising on Television
Chapter 10: How Well Do You Know Advertising Slogans?
Chapter 11: Selection of the "Mark" Character in Holiday Inn's Campaign
Chapter 12: Testing TV Commercials in Prefinished Form
Chapter 13: Esuvee and SUV Safety
Chapter 14: The Rising Cost of Super Bowl Advertising
Chapter 15: Enhancing Brand Equity via Search Engine Advertising
Chapter 16: The Human Body as an Ad Medium
Chapter 17: Pay-for-Performance at Nestlé
Chapter 18: Sampling Toilet Tissue
Chapter 19: The Use of Rebates by an Enterprising Realtor
Chapter 20: Georgia Pacific's Quilts of Inspiration CRM Program

SEVENTH EDITION

Advertising, Promotion,

and Other Aspects of Integrated Marketing Communications

Terence A. Shimp
University of South Carolina

THOMSON
SOUTH-WESTERN

Australia · Brazil · Canada · Mexico · Singapore · Spain · United Kingdom · United States

THOMSON
SOUTH-WESTERN

Advertising, Promotion, and Other Aspects of Integrated Marketing Communications, 7th Edition
Terence A. Shimp

VP/Editorial Director:
Jack W. Calhoun

VP/Editor-in-Chief:
Dave Shaut

Sr. Publisher:
Melissa Acuña

Executive Editor:
Neil Marquardt

Sr. Developmental Editor:
Susanna C. Smart

Marketing Manager:
Nicole C. Moore

Sr. Marketing Communications Manager:
Terron Sanders

Sr. Production Project Manager:
Emily S. Gross

Manager of Technology, Editorial:
Vicky True

Technology Project Editor:
Pam Wallace

Web Coordinator:
Karen Schaffer

Manufacturing Coordinator:
Diane Lohman

Production House:
Stratford Publishing Services

Printer:
Quebecor World Dubuque
Dubuque, IA

Art Director:
Stacy Shirley

Internal and Cover Designer:
Craig LaGesse Ramsdell
www.ramsdelldesign.com

Cover Images:
© Getty Images

Photography Manager:
John Hill

Photo Researcher:
Susan Van Etten

Printed in the United States of America

1 2 3 4 5 10 09 08 07 06

ISBN 0-324-40807-2

Library of Congress Control Number:
2005936424

For more information about our products, contact us at:

Thomson Learning
Academic Resource Center

1-800-423-0563

Thomson Higher Education
5191 Natorp Boulevard
Mason, OH 45040
USA

Dedication

To my dear wife, Judy, who has been my number-one supporter over the years, and who helped me on this edition by locating advertising illustrations and other visuals. Since the previous edition, I have been blessed with two additional grandsons, John Parker and Spencer James—now the twenty-first-century version of a basketball team is in place (my brothers know what I refer to). Also, to all of my family members, past and present, to whom I owe whatever positive character traits I may possess, a heartfelt word of appreciation and love.

BRIEF CONTENTS

CONTENTS

Advantages

Advertising in Action. Promotion with Purpose. Marketing in Motion. The Message is Clear.

Advertising, Promotion, and Other Aspects of Integrated Marketing Communications provides a contemporary view of the role and importance of marketing communications. Integrated marketing communications (IMC) enhances the equity of brands, and provides a thorough coverage of all aspects of an IMC program: advertising, promotions, packaging and branding strategies, point-of-purchase communications, marketing-oriented public relations, word-of-mouth buzz creation, and event- and caused-oriented sponsorships. These topics are made even more accessible in this edition through expanded use of examples and applications.

Some of the highlights of this edition include:

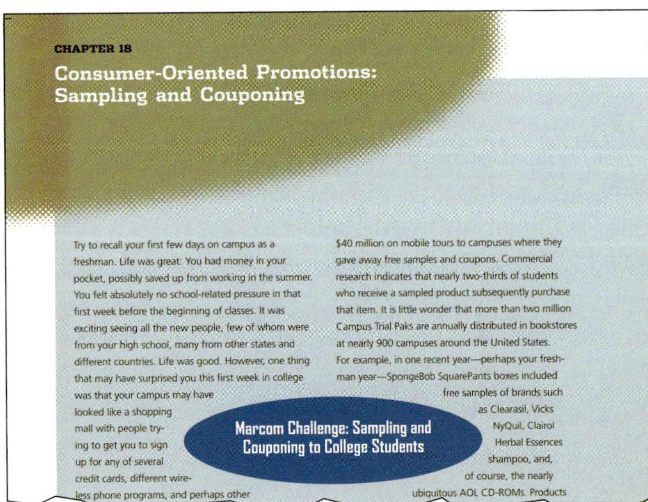
CHAPTER 18

Consumer-Oriented Promotions: Sampling and Couponing

Try to recall your first few days on campus as a freshman. Life was great: You had money in your pocket, possibly saved up from working in the summer. You felt absolutely no school-related pressure in that first week before the beginning of classes. It was exciting seeing all the new people, few of whom were from your high school, many from other states and different countries. Life was good. However, one thing that may have surprised you this first week in college was that your campus may have looked like a shopping mall with people trying to get you to sign up for any of several credit cards, different wireless phone programs, and perhaps other

Marcom Challenge: Sampling and Couponing to College Students

$40 million on mobile tours to campuses where they gave away free samples and coupons. Commercial research indicates that nearly two-thirds of students who receive a sampled product subsequently purchase that item. It is little wonder that more than two million Campus Trial Paks are annually distributed in bookstores at nearly 900 campuses around the United States. For example, in one recent year—perhaps your freshman year—SpongeBob SquarePants boxes included free samples of brands such as Clearasil, Vicks NyQuil, Clairol Herbal Essences shampoo, and, of course, the nearly ubiquitous AOL CD-ROMs. Products

IMC Focus — These features illustrate key IMC concepts within each chapter by using real-company situations that showcase how various aspects of marketing communications are put into practice.

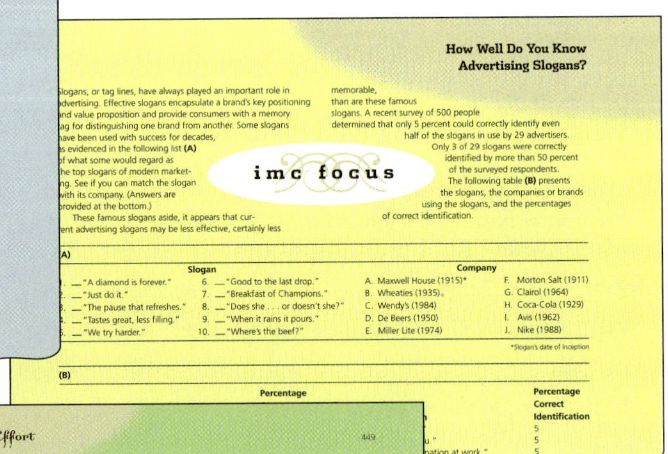
How Well Do You Know Advertising Slogans?

imc focus

Slogans, or tag lines, have always played an important role in advertising. Effective slogans encapsulate a brand's key positioning and value proposition and provide consumers with a memory tag for distinguishing one brand from another. Some slogans have been used with success for decades, as evidenced in the following list (A) of what some would regard as the top slogans of modern marketing. See if you can match the slogan with its company. (Answers are provided at the bottom.) These famous slogans aside, it appears that current advertising slogans may be less effective, certainly less memorable, than are these famous slogans. A recent survey of 500 people determined that only 5 percent could correctly identify even half of the slogans in use by 29 advertisers. Only 3 of 29 slogans were correctly identified by more than 50 percent of the surveyed respondents. The following table (B) presents the slogans, the companies or brands using the slogans, and the percentages of correct identification.

(A)

Slogan		Company	
__"A diamond is forever."	6. __"Good to the last drop."	A. Maxwell House (1915)*	F. Morton Salt (1911)
__"Just do it."	7. __"Breakfast of Champions."	B. Wheaties (1935)	G. Clairol (1964)
__"The pause that refreshes."	8. __"Does she . . . or doesn't she?"	C. Wendy's (1984)	H. Coca-Cola (1929)
__"Tastes great, less filling."	9. __"When it rains it pours."	D. De Beers (1950)	I. Avis (1962)
__"We try harder."	10. __"Where's the beef?"	E. Miller Lite (1974)	J. Nike (1988)

*Slogan's date of inception

(B)

	Percentage	Percentage Correct Identification
		5
u."		5
nation at work."		5

Marcom Challenge — Each chapter opens with a factual anecdote about a real company that relates to the coverage within the chapter. Marcom Challenges serve to pique students' interest and set the stage for the chapter ahead.

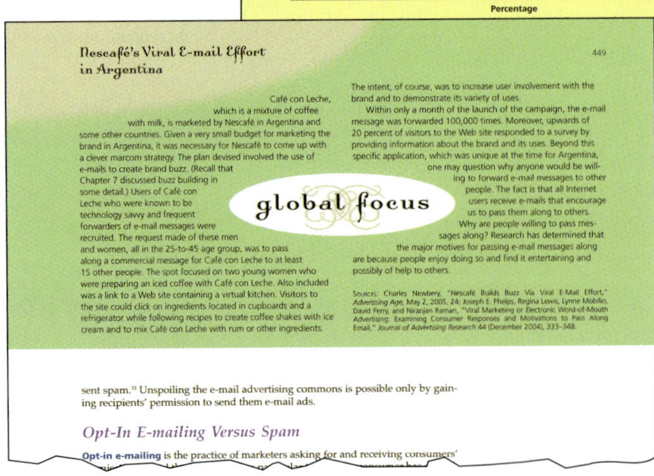
Nescafé's Viral E-mail Effort in Argentina

449

global focus

Café con Leche, which is a mixture of coffee with milk, is marketed by Nescafé in Argentina and some other countries. Given a very small budget for marketing the brand in Argentina, it was necessary for Nescafé to come up with a clever marcom strategy. The plan devised involved the use of e-mails to create brand buzz. (Recall that Chapter 7 discussed buzz building in some detail.) Users of Café con Leche who were known to be technology savvy and frequent forwarders of e-mail messages were recruited. The request made of these men and women, all in the 25-to-45 age group, was to pass along a commercial message for Café con Leche to at least 15 other people. The spot focused on two young women who were preparing an iced coffee with Café con Leche. Also included was a link to a Web site containing a virtual kitchen. Visitors to the site could click on ingredients located in cupboards and a refrigerator while following recipes to create coffee shakes with ice cream and to mix Café con Leche with rum or other ingredients.

The intent, of course, was to increase user involvement with the brand and to demonstrate its variety of uses.

Within only a month of the launch of the campaign, the e-mail message was forwarded 100,000 times. Moreover, upwards of 20 percent of visitors to the Web site responded to a survey by providing information about the brand and its uses. Beyond this specific application, which was unique at the time for Argentina, one may question why anyone would be willing to forward e-mail messages to other people. The fact is that all Internet users receive e-mails that encourage us to pass them along to others.

Why are people willing to pass messages along? Research has determined that the major motives for passing e-mail messages along are because people enjoy doing so and find it entertaining and possibly of help to others.

Sources: Charles Newbery, "Nescafé Builds Buzz Via Viral E-Mail Effort," *Advertising Age*, May 2, 2005, 24; Joseph E. Phelps, Regina Lewis, Lynne Mobilio, David Perry, and Niranjan Raman, "Viral Marketing or Electronic Word-of-Mouth Advertising: Examining Consumer Responses and Motivations to Pass Along Email," *Journal of Advertising Research* 44 (December 2004), 333–348.

sent spam.[10] Unspoiling the e-mail advertising commons is possible only by gaining recipients' permission to send them e-mail ads.

Opt-In E-mailing Versus Spam

Opt-in e-mailing is the practice of marketers asking for and receiving consumers'

Global Focus — These features enhance the text's global perspective and spotlight the international application of Marcom principles.

Everywhere You Look.

Catch the Latest Developments in Advertising & Promotion

The text retains the same number of chapters (20) as in the prior edition, but some chapters have been substantially rewritten or rearranged to reflect a more logical progression of material coverage. Here is a sample of just some of the chapter changes to this edition:

Chapter 1, "Overview of Integrated Marketing Communications and the Marcom Process," expands its coverage of IMC fundamentals and provides a model of the Marcom process in a framework for comprehending the strategic and tactical aspects of marketing communications.

Chapter 3, "Ethical, Regulatory, and Environmental Issues in Marketing Communications" provides in-depth coverage of ethical issues in marketing communications. This chapter is moved front and center in this edition to stress its importance in this area.

NEW Chapter 8, "On- and Off-Premise Signage and Point-of-Purchase Communications" explores the role of on- and off-premises signage, out-of-home advertising, and point-of-purchase communications—in setting this book apart from most advertising and Marcom texts.

Coverage of Internet advertising (Chapter 15 "Employing the Internet for Advertising") is greatly expanded and completely current in its treatment of search engine advertising, wireless forms of Internet advertising, and the role of blogs and podcasts.

Contemporary Ads — Approximately 90% of the ads are new to this edition. These contemporary ads illustrate concepts and provide examples to the reader of effective advertising as part of a successful IMC campaign.

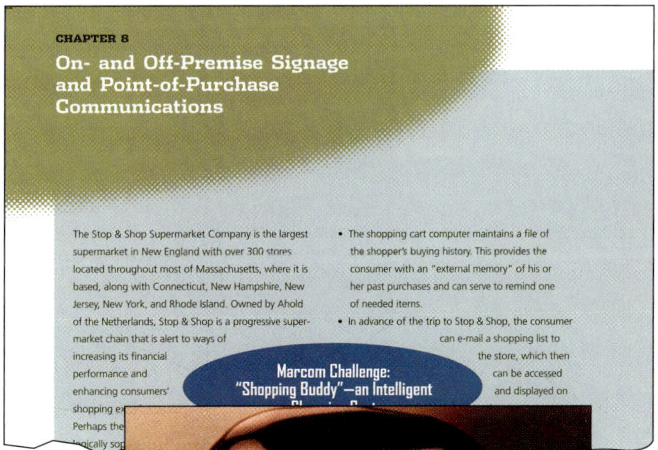

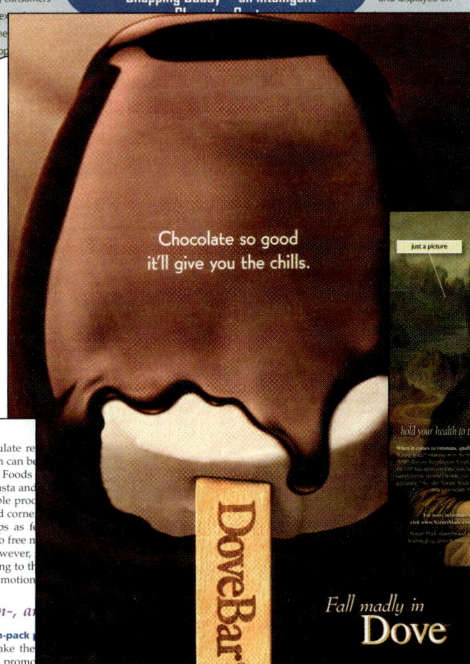

7th Edition Advantages

Technology That Makes A Difference.

This edition offers a variety of high-quality and technologically advanced supplements to bring a contemporary, real-world feel to the study of advertising, promotion, and integrated marketing communications.

- **Xtra!** is an interactive product that provides additional support for students such as Xtra! Quizzing, Video Clips, and a MarComm Plan template. Xtra! is provided at no charge with the purchase of a new textbook.

http://shimpxtra.swlearning.com

- **JoinIn™ on TurningPoint®** is the only classroom response software tool that gives you true PowerPoint® integration and real-time results while turning your classroom into a fully interactive experience for your students. You can walk about your classroom as you lecture, showing PowerPoint slides and displaying responses with ease.

http://turningpoint.thomsonlearningconnections.com

- **Business & Company Resource Center** delivers up-to-the-minute articles from over 4,000 journals and periodicals along with access to online company and industry information including market share date, company history, and more.

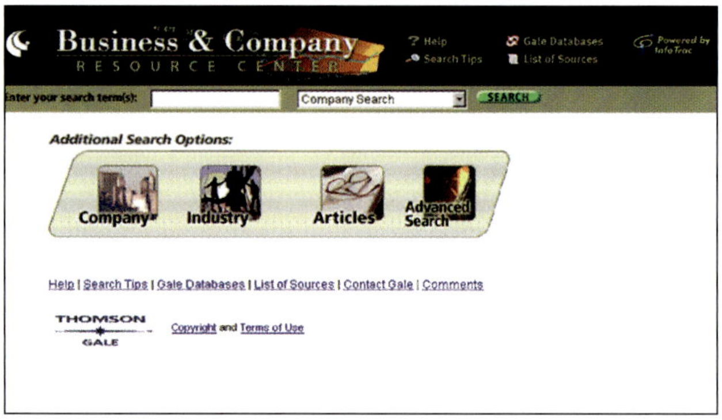

http://bcrc.swlearning.com

- **1Pass** eliminates the need of multiple logon passwords and URLs by providing a single point of access to Business & Company Resource Center and Xtra!

Everywhere You Look.

Top-Rated Tools Ease Your Workload.

- The **Instructor's Manual** is a comprehensive and valuable teaching aid which includes the Resource Integration Guide, a list of chapter objectives, chapter summaries, detailed chapter outlines, teaching tips, and answers to discussion questions. The *Instructor's Manual* for this edition is revised by Laurie A. Babin of the University of Southern Mississippi.
- A **Resource Integration Guide (RIG)** helps instructors coordinate all of the text's resources—helping instructors plan, teach and facilitate their students' coursework. The RIG can be found online as well as in the *Instructor's Manual*.
- **Test Bank**, revised by Laurie A. Babin, contains over 1,500 multiple choice, true/false, and essay questions in varying levels of difficulty.
- **ExamView® Testing Software** is a computerized testing program that contains all the questions in the printed test bank. It is an easy-to-use test creation software that allows instructors to add or edit questions, instructions, and answers, and choose questions by previewing them on the screen; selecting them randomly
- **Video Package** provides a relevant and interesting visual teaching tool for the classroom. Each video segment gives students the opportunity to apply what they are learning to real-world situations viewing companies such as Timberland, Tower Records, Pfizer, and Radio Shack.
- **Clio Award Videos** are award-winning video clips designed to show students how advertising works in the real world, showing the creative examples of advertising worldwide.
- **PowerPoint® Presentation on CD-ROM**, completely updated for this edition, covers all of the material found in the text in addition to outside supplemental examples found in radio, television, and print media. It also contains nearly two hours of videos, numerous still pictures, animations, build slides, and viewers.

PREFACE

Responding to a Dynamic World

The field of marketing communications is ever-changing. Brand managers continually attempt to gain advantage over competitors and endeavor to achieve larger market shares and profits for the brands they manage. Marketing communications, or *marcom,* is just one element of the marketing mix, but advertising, promotions, marketing-oriented public relations, and other marcom tools perform increasingly important roles in firms' quests to achieve financial and nonfinancial goals. Marcom practitioners are confronted with the rising costs of placing ads in traditional advertising media (television, magazines, and so on) and are aggravated by the ever-growing clutter when advertising in these media. For these reasons, advertising and promotion budgets are beginning to shift away from traditional media and toward the Internet, which in recent years has become an important advertising medium both as a means of accessing difficult-to-reach groups (such as college-age consumers) and in providing numerous options for presenting advertising messages and promotional offers to these groups.

Marketing communicators realize now more than ever that their advertising, promotion, and other marcom investments must be held financially accountable. Companies continually seek more effective ways of communicating effectively and efficiently with their targeted audiences. Marketing communicators are challenged to use communication methods that will break through the clutter, reach audiences with interesting and persuasive messages that enhance brand equity and drive sales, and assure that marcom investments yield an adequate return on investment. In meeting these challenges, companies increasingly embrace a strategy of integrated marketing communications whereby all marcom elements must be held accountable for delivering consistent messages and influencing action.

Focus of the Text

Whether a student is taking this course to learn more about the dynamic nature of this field or to make a career in advertising, promotions, or some other aspect of marketing, *Advertising, Promotion, and Other Aspects of Integrated Marketing Communications* will provide him or her with a contemporary view of the role and importance of marketing communications. The text emphasizes the role of integrated marketing communications (IMC) in enhancing the equity of brands and provides thorough coverage of all aspects of an IMC program: advertising, promotions, packaging and branding strategies, point-of-purchase communications, marketing-oriented public relations, word-of-mouth buzz creation, and event- and cause-oriented sponsorships. These topics are made even more accessible in this edition through expanded use of examples and applications. Appropriate academic theories and concepts are covered in the text to provide formal structure to the illustrations and examples.

Advertising, Promotion, and Other Aspects of Integrated Marketing Communications is intended for use in undergraduate or graduate courses in marketing communications, advertising, promotion strategy, promotion management, or other courses with similar concentrations. Professors and students should find this book substantive but highly readable, eminently current but also appreciative of the evolution of the field. Above all, marketing communications practice in its varied forms is blended with research and theory. Throughout its previous six editions, this book has always attempted to balance its coverage by examining marketing communications from both the consumer's and marketer's vantage points. This edition, however, represents a slight shift of emphasis to focus more than ever on managerial aspects of marketing communications. Business-to-business (B2B) oriented marketing communications also receives greater attention in this edition than before.

Changes and Improvements in the Seventh Edition

The seventh edition of *Advertising, Promotion, and Other Aspects of Integrated Marketing Communications* reflects many changes beyond those described so far. The entire textbook has been thoroughly updated and reflects the following emphasis:

- The text provides state-of-the-art coverage of major academic literature and practitioner writings on all aspects of marketing communications. These writings are presented at an accessible level to students and illustrated with copious examples and special inserts—Marcom Challenge vignettes, IMC Focus boxes, and Global Focus inserts.
    - *Marcom Challenge*—Each chapter opens with a factual anecdote that corresponds with the thematic coverage of the chapter and serves to pique students' interest and illustrate the type of material to follow.
    - *IMC Focus*—These features have been updated to further illustrate key IMC concepts within each chapter by using real-company situations that showcase how various aspects of marketing communications are put into practice.
    - *Global Focus*—These updated boxed features enhance the text's global perspective and spotlight the international application of marcom principles.
- The text retains the same number of chapters (20) as in the sixth edition, but some chapters have been substantially rewritten or rearranged to reflect a more logical progression of material covered. The following updates and improvements are reflected in this new edition:
- Chapter 1 expands its coverage of IMC fundamentals and also provides a model of the marcom process that makes a useful framework for comprehending the strategic and tactical aspects of marketing communications.
- Marcom's role in enhancing brand equity and influencing behavior receives expanded coverage in Chapter 2. The most important addition to this chapter is increased emphasis on achieving marcom accountability, including discussion of return on marketing investment and efforts to measure marcom effectiveness.
- In view of the growing importance of ethical issues, Chapter 3 provides in-depth coverage of ethical issues in marketing communications along with marcom-related regulatory and environmental issues. This chapter is moved front and center in this edition to better stress its importance.

- Chapters 4 through 6 focus on the fundamental marcom decisions that are based on the marcom-process model introduced in Chapter 1. These chapters include detailed coverage of marcom targeting (Chapter 4), positioning (Chapter 5), and objective setting and budgeting (Chapter 6). Chapter 4 includes a thorough update of demographic facts and figures, Chapter 5 integrates the coverage of positioning with fundamentals of consumer behavior and the concept of meaning creation, and Chapter 6 augments discussion of marcom budgeting.
- Chapter 7 combines material previously covered in two chapters that discusses marcom's role in facilitating product adoption and the importance of brand naming and packaging.
- Chapter 8 is a new and unique chapter that explores the role of on- and off-premises signage, out-of-home advertising, and point-of-purchase communications—all of which generally are neglected or receive minimal coverage in most advertising and marcom texts.
- In its overview of advertising management, Chapter 9 examines the role of messages, media, and measurement. Added coverage is given to the relation between share of voice and share of market and the role of advertising elasticity.
- Chapter 10 lays out the fundamentals and importance of advertising creativity, and Chapter 11 then deals with the message and endorser factors that influence message processors' motivation, opportunity, and ability to process ad messages.
- Expanded and improved coverage of measures of advertising effectiveness is the focus of Chapter 12.
- Chapter 13 provides detailed treatment of media planning and analysis. Importantly, this chapter is presented before coverage of specific advertising media, whereas in previous editions it was presented after that coverage. By presenting the media planning and analysis material first, it is possible to employ a common set of concepts, terms, and metrics in describing the specific media covered in the chapters that follow.
- Chapters 14 (traditional ad media), 15 (Internet advertising), and 16 (other ad media) offer in-depth coverage of all forms of advertising media. The material is thoroughly updated with numerous applications and illustrations.
- Coverage of Internet advertising (Chapter 15) is greatly expanded and updated in view of the profound changes that have transpired since the previous edition. This new chapter is especially current in its treatment of search engine advertising, wireless forms of Internet advertising, and the role of blogs and podcasts.
- Chapter 16 expands its coverage of other forms of ad media, including material related to direct mail and database marketing, videogame advertising (adver-gaming), brand placements in movies and TV programs, and cinema advertising.
- Chapter 17 introduces sales promotions and covers trade-oriented promotions in detail. However, the treatment of trade promotions is scaled back in comparison to the previous edition as it looks primarily at the most important and troubling form of trade promotion: trade allowances.
- Chapters 18 and 19 deal with consumer-oriented forms of sales promotions. Whereas all forms of consumer-oriented promotions were covered in a single chapter in the previous edition, these topics are included as two separate chapters in the seventh edition. Chapter 18 covers only sampling and couponing, and Chapter 19 examines all remaining forms of consumer promotions.
- Chapter 20 provides updated coverage of marketing-oriented public relations along with event- and cause-oriented sponsorships.

A Premier Instructional Resource Package

The resource package provided with *Advertising, Promotion, and Other Aspects of Integrated Marketing Communications,* seventh edition, is specifically designed to meet the needs of instructors facing a variety of teaching conditions and to enhance students' experience with the subject. We have addressed both the traditional and the innovative classroom environments by providing an array of high-quality and technologically advanced items to bring a contemporary, real-world feel to the study of advertising, promotion, and integrated marketing communications.

- ***Instructor's Manual.*** This comprehensive and valuable teaching aid includes the Resource Integration Guide, a list of chapter objectives, chapter summaries, detailed chapter outlines, teaching tips, and answers to discussion questions. The *Instructor's Manual* for this edition is revised by Laurie A. Babin of the University of Southern Mississippi.
- ***Test Bank.*** The Test Bank, also revised by Laurie A. Babin, provides testing items for instructors' reference and use. It has been thoroughly revised and contains over 1,500 multiple-choice, true/false, and essay questions in varying levels of difficulty.
- ***ExamView™ Testing Software.*** ExamView is a computerized testing program that contains all of the questions in the printed test bank. **ExamView™ Testing Software** is an easy-to-use test creation software compatible with Microsoft Windows. Instructors can add or edit questions, instructions, and answers, and select questions by previewing them onscreen; select them randomly, or select them by number. Instructors can also create and administer quizzes online, whether over the Internet, a local area network (LAN), or a wide area network (WAN).
- ***PowerPoint Presentation CD.*** This edition includes an updated and improved PowerPoint presentation. The presentation contains award-winning Clio video clips, numerous still pictures, and animations. This powerful software is easily adaptable for instructors who wish to introduce additional material. The presentation covers all of the material found in the textbook in addition to outside supplemental examples and materials from various media.
- ***Video Package.*** The video package provides a relevant and interesting visual teaching tool for the classroom. Each video segment gives students the opportunity to apply what they are learning to real-world situations and enables instructors to better illustrate concepts. Companies such as Timberland, Tower Records, Pfizer, and Radio Shack are featured.
- ***Clio Awards Videos.*** These award-winning video clips on DVDs are designed to show students how advertising works in the real world, and shows creative examples of advertising worldwide.
- ***JoinIn™ on TurningPoint.*** **JoinIn on TurningPoint** is the only classroom response software tool that gives you true PointPoint integration. With **JoinIn**, you are no longer tied to your computer . . . you can walk about your classroom as you lecture, showing slides and collecting and displaying responses with ease. There is simply no easier or more effective way to turn your lecture hall into a personal, fully interactive experience for your students. If you can use PowerPoint, you can use **JoinIn on TurningPoint**!

Comprehensive Web Site

Visit the text Web site at *http://shimp.swlearning.com* to find instructor's support materials and study resources to help students practice and apply the concepts they learned in class.

Instructor Resources

- Downloadable **Instructor's Manual** files available in Microsoft Word and Adobe Acrobat format.
- Downloadable **PowerPoint Presentations** prepared by Elizabeth Hurley of Editors, Inc. (Available for download without embedded videos only.)
- A **Resource Integration Guide** helps instructors coordinate all of the print and online resources available for each chapter to help in their teaching and to facilitate their students' coursework.
- The **Business & Company Resource Center** provides online access to a wide variety of global business information including current articles and business journals, detailed company and industry information, investment reports, stock quotes, and much more. Unlike other online resources, this comprehensive database offers ever-changing research results, providing accurate and up-to-date company and industry intelligence for thousands of companies. View a guided tour of the Business & Company Resource Center at http://bcrc.swlearning.com. *For college and university adopters only.*

Student Resources

Product Support Site (http://shimp.swlearning.com)

- **Online Interactive quizzes** for each chapter are available to those students who would like extra study material. After each quiz is submitted, automatic feedback tells the students how they scored and what the correct answers are to the questions they missed. Students are then able to email their results directly to their instructor.
- **Flashcards** pulled from the key terms in the text help students study the vocabulary covered in the text.

1pass™

Simplify your lives with **1pass**, a single point of access to all the text's media resources. 1pass provides students with the ability to access a wide range of media using a single, personalized username and password—no more multiple URLs and login information to remember! Shimp 1pass at http://1pass.thomson.com includes access to Shimp Xtra! and Business & Company Resource Center (BCRC).

- ***Shimp Xtra!* (http://shimpxtra.swlearning.com)**
  This interactive product provides additional support for students and special insights into the field of advertising that are not offered in the main text. Components include: Xtra! Quizzing designed to prepare students for exams; award-winning Clio video clips designed to show students how advertising works in the real world with the creative examples of advertising worldwide; PowerPoint slides; and other materials. Shimp Xtra! is provided at no charge with the purchase of a new textbook. Used book buyers can purchase access by visiting http://shimpxtra.swlearning.com.
- **Business & Company Resource Center (http//bcrc.swlearning.com)**
  The Business & Company Resource Center provides online access to a wide variety of global business information including current articles and business journals, detailed company and industry information, investment reports, stock quotes, and much more. Unlike other online resources, this comprehensive database offers ever-changing research results, providing accurate and up-to-date company and industry intelligence for thousands of companies. View a guided tour of the Business & Company Resource Center at http://bcrc.swlearning.com.

Get Started Today at http://1pass.thomson.com!

If an access card came with this book, you can start using many of these resources right away by following the directions on the card.

Acknowledgments

I sincerely appreciate the thoughtful comments from the colleagues who critiqued the sixth edition and recommended changes and improvements. Previous editions also have benefited from the many useful comments from the following reviewers, friends, and acquaintances, whose affiliations may have changed since reviewing this text:

Craig Andrews
Marquette University

Guy R. Banville
Creighton University

Barbara M. Brown
San Jose State University

Newell Chiesl
Indiana State University

Denise Essman
Drake University

James Finch
University of Wisconsin, LaCrosse

Clayton Hillyer
American International College

Robert Harmon
Portland State University

Stewart W. Husted
Lynchburg College

Russell Laczniak
Iowa State University

Monle Lee
Indiana University, South Bend

Wendy Macias
University of Georgia

John McDonald
Market Opinion Research

Gordon G. Mosley
Troy State University

John Mowen
Oklahoma State University

Kent Nakamoto
Virginia Tech University

Jayanthi Rajan
University of Connecticut

Edward Riordan
Wayne State University

Stanley Scott
Boise State University

Jeff Stoltman
Wayne State University

John A. Taylor
Brigham Young University

Kate Ternus
Century College

Josh Wiener
Oklahoma State University

Charles S. Areni
Texas Tech University

M. Elizabeth Blair
Ohio University

Gordon C. Bruner II
Southern Illinois University

Robert Dyer
George Washington University

P. Everett Fergenson
Iona College

Linda L. Golden
University of Texas, Austin

Stephen Grove
Clemson University

Ronald Hill
Villanova University

Patricia Kennedy
University of Nebraska, Lincoln

Geoffrey Lantos
Bentley College

J. Danile Lindley
Bentley College

Therese A. Maskulka
Lehigh University

Darrel D. Muehling
Washington State University

D. Nasalroad
Central State University

Alan Sawyer
University of Florida

Douglas Stayman
Cornell University

Linda Swayne
University of North Carolina, Charlotte

Carolyn Tripp
Western Illinois University

Karen Faulkner Walia
Long Beach City College

Liz Yokubison
College of DuPage

My appreciation extends to a number of former Ph.D. students, my friends, who have shared their experiences in using the textbook and have provided valuable suggestions for change: Avery Abernethy, Auburn University; Craig Andrews, Marquette University; Mike Barone, Iowa State University; Paula Bone, West Virginia University; Tracy Dunn, Benedict College; Ken Manning, Colorado State University; David Sprott, Washington State University; Elnora Stuart, American University of Cairo; and Scott Swain, Boston University.

I also appreciate the work of several MBA students who were of considerable assistance on the present or previous editions: Andrew Johnson, Yenseob (Cklio) Lee, Michael Shipe, Barbara Yale, and Yun J. Yang.

Appreciation is extended to two special friends. First, though not involved in this edition, Professor Jack Lindgren, University of Virginia, developed the multimedia supplements that served in prior editions to create an exciting, dynamic, and enjoyable teaching environment for adopters of the text. Second, sincere appreciation is extended to my colleague, Professor Satish Jayachandran, for his invaluable suggestions regarding chapter sequencing and material coverage.

Further appreciation goes out to my friends at the Dryden Press who I worked with for nearly 20 years during the first five editions. I am grateful to Mary Fisher, Rob Zwettler, Lyn Hastert, Lise Johnson, and Bill Schoof.

Finally, I very much appreciate the excellent work of the Thomson/South-Western team for their outstanding efforts in bringing this seventh edition to fruition. I especially appreciate the support and guidance of Susan Smart; the encouragement of Neil Marquardt and Melissa Acuña; the extensive production management by Emily Gross; the marketing efforts of Nicole Moore; the professional editing by Heather Savage; the work by permissions and photo researchers John Hill, Susan van Etten, and Diana Fleming; and the creativity of the technology group in preparing the Web site and its contents.

Terence A. Shimp
University of South Carolina
August 2005

About the Author

Terence A. Shimp received his doctorate from the University of Maryland and taught for four years at Kent State University before moving to the University of South Carolina, where he has been a faculty member for 29 years. He is Professor of Marketing, the W. W. Johnson Distinguished Foundation Fellow, and Chair of the Marketing Department in the Moore School of Business, University of South Carolina, Columbia. Professor Shimp teaches courses in marketing communications and research philosophy and methods. He has earned a variety of teaching awards, including the Amoco Foundation Award that named him the outstanding teacher at the University of South Carolina in 1990.

He has published widely in the areas of marketing, consumer behavior, and advertising. His work has appeared frequently in outlets such as the *Journal of Consumer Research, Journal of Marketing Research, Journal of Marketing, Journal of Advertising, Journal of Advertising Research, Journal of Consumer Psychology,* and the *Journal of Public Policy and Marketing.* "Endorsers in Advertising: The Case of Negative Celebrity Information," co-authored with Brian Till, was named the outstanding article published in the *Journal of Advertising* in 1998. "A Critical Appraisal of Demand Artifacts in Consumer Research," published with Eva Hyatt and David Snyder in the *Journal of Consumer Research* received that journal's award for the top article published during the period 1990–1992. In 2001 he was the recipient of the American Academy of Advertising's lifetime award for outstanding contributions to research in advertising. The Society for Consumer Psychology elected him a Fellow of the Society in 2003.

Professor Shimp is past president of the Association for Consumer Research and past president of the *Journal of Consumer Research* policy board. He has served on the editorial policy boards of many premier journals, including the *Journal of Consumer Research, Journal of Consumer Psychology, Journal of Marketing, Marketing Letters, Journal of Public Policy & Marketing,* and the *Journal of Advertising.* He has represented the Federal Trade Commission and various state agencies as an expert witness in issues concerning advertising deception and unfairness.

PART 1
Integrated Marketing Communications: Processes, Brand Equity, and the Marcom Environment

Part One introduces students to the fundamentals of integrated marketing communications (IMC). *Chapter 1* overviews IMC and discusses the importance of marketing communications (marcom). The chapter emphasizes the need for integrating the various marketing communication elements (advertising, sales promotions, event marketing, etc.) rather than treating them as separate and independent tools. The payoff from an IMC approach is synergy—multiple tools working together achieve more positive communication results than do the tools used individually. The chapter describes five key IMC features: (1) the customer is the starting point for all marcom decisions; (2) brand managers and their agencies should be amenable to using various marcom tools; (3) multiple messages delivered by different marcom tools must be unified; (4) the objective is to build relationships with customers; and (5) marcom's ultimate objective is to affect customer behavior.

A model of the marcom decision-making process also is introduced in Chapter 1. This integrative framework postulates the marcom program as consisting of a set of fundamental decisions (about targeting, positioning, etc.) and a series of implementation decisions that determine program outcomes with regard to enhancing brand equity and affecting behavior. The final model component is program evaluation, which entails measuring the results of communications activities, providing feedback, and taking corrective action.

Chapter 2 explains how IMC enhances brand equity, influences behavior, and achieves accountability. A brand equity model conceptualizes brand equity from the customer's perspective and shows how equity is enhanced by elevating brand awareness and creating brand associations. It is explained that marcom's eventual challenge is to influence customer behavior and to ultimately affect a brand's sales volume and revenue, and the return on marketing investment, or ROMI is discussed.

Chapter 3 provides a critical transition between the first two chapters and subsequent chapters. It is important that ethical, regulatory, and environmental issues be examined so as to fully appreciate that marketing communicators operate under constraints that limit certain actions yet ultimately benefit free markets and the businesses and customers who participate in them. The ethical issues discussed included targeting vulnerable groups, deceptive advertising, and other types of unethical marcom practices. Also covered are governmental regulations, industry self-regulation of marcom practices and environmental issues relevant to marcom decisions are explored.

CHAPTER 1

Overview of Integrated Marketing Communications and the Marcom Process

Marcom Challenge: B2C and B2B Applications of IMC

All firms employ marketing communications to one degree or another, and it doesn't matter whether their efforts are directed at people like you and me in our day-to-day consumption activities or focused on other businesses. In short, marketing communications play an important role for *all* companies. This vignette provides examples of two integrated marketing communications programs, the first in a business-to-consumer (B2C) context and the second in a business-to-business (B2B) environment. Though most readers of this text are thoroughly acquainted with B2C applications by virtue of frequent exposure to advertisements and other forms of marketing communications, relatively few have acquired experience in B2B situations. Hence, it is important to appreciate at the outset that marcom concepts and practices are applicable universally, regardless of the type of organization involved.

Marcom in a B2C Context. When Buick introduced its Rainier sports utility vehicle (SUV), it needed a marketing communications program that would create awareness for the Rainier and enhance the image of the Buick name. These tasks were accomplished with an integrated program combining online and TV advertising along with appealing sales promotions. The job was made easier by hiring Tiger Woods as endorser of the Buick line of vehicles. A series of five-minute films featuring this famous golfer were available at Buick's Web site (http://www.buick.com). With a 30-second commercial that was widely aired on network and cable stations, Buick encouraged consumers to visit its Web site. Visitors to the site were able to enter a contest that provided winners an opportunity to play a round of golf with Tiger Woods and a chance to win a Rainier vehicle. Only two months after initiating this program, two million unique visitors were drawn to Buick's Web site, awareness of the Rainer SUV increased by 70 percent, and positive perceptions of Buick rose by 122 percent.[1]

Marcom in a B2B Environment. According to a recent study, four out of five B2B marketers use some form of integrated marketing communications. In fact, over three-fourths of those firms using integrated campaigns employ three or more different communication elements, such as, for example, using a magazine advertising campaign along with TV advertising, an online presence, and a direct mail program.[2]

An integrated communications program undertaken by General Electric (GE) illustrates a successful B2B application of integrated marketing communications.[3] To raise awareness of GE's products beyond its well-known lighting and appliance offerings, GE initiated an integrated campaign titled "Imagination at Work" to establish that it also is successful in producing wind power, security systems, and jet engines, among other products. Working with its advertising agency (BBDO New York), GE's objective was to increase awareness that GE is a company that does more than manufacture lightbulbs and appliances. Using a combination of TV, print (magazine ads in business publications such as *BusinessWeek, Forbes,* and *Fortune*), and online advertising, GE and its ad agency undertook an intensive campaign to improve businesspeople's understanding of GE's diverse product offerings. For example, a clever TV advertisement dramatically illustrated that GE produces jet engines by showing a vintage Wright Brothers-era airplane equipped with a modern GE jet engine.

General Motors Corp. Used with permission. GM Media Archives

CHAPTER OBJECTIVES

After reading this chapter you should be able to:

1. Introduce the topic of marketing communications (marcom) and identify the tools used by practitioners.
2. Describe the philosophy and practice of integrated marketing communications (IMC).
3. Present the five key features of IMC.
4. Identify obstacles to implementing IMC.
5. Introduce a framework that illustrates the activities involved in developing an integrated communications program.
6. Distinguish some of the important trade associations in the marcom field.

The integrated campaign, which was conducted in Europe as well as in the United States, was fabulously successful in changing perceptions about GE. Post-campaign research revealed that perceptions of GE as an innovative company increased by 35 percent, opinions of GE as offering high-tech solutions increased by 40 percent, and perceptions of GE as being dynamic increased by 50 percent. By any standard, this was a successful integrated campaign that combined multiple communication elements to positively alter perceptions of GE.

The Nature of Marketing Communications

Marketing communications is a critical aspect of companies' overall marketing missions and a major determinant of their successes or failures. The importance of the marketing communications component of the marketing mix has increased dramatically in recent decades. Indeed, it has been claimed that marketing and communications are virtually inseparable.[4] All organizations—whether firms involved in B2B exchanges, companies engaged in B2C marketing, or organizations delivering not-for-profit services (museums, symphony orchestras, charitable organizations, etc.)—use various forms of marketing communications to promote their offerings and achieve financial and nonfinancial goals.

JOB OUTLOOK

A National Association of Colleges and Employers survey found that starting salaries for marketing majors graduating in 2003 averaged $34,038; starting salaries for advertising majors averaged $29,495, but salaries for experienced analysts and managers range from $65,000 into the six figures. *(Occupational Outlook Handbook, 2004–05 Edition, U.S. DOL, http://www.bls.gov/oco/home.htm)*

The primary forms of marketing communications include traditional mass media advertising (TV, magazines, etc.); online advertising (Web sites, opt-in e-mail messages, text messaging, and so on); sales promotions (such as samples, coupons, rebates, and premium items); store signage and point-of-purchase communications; direct-mail literature; marketing-oriented public relations and publicity releases; sponsorships of events and causes; presentations by salespeople; and various collateral forms of communication devices. (See Table 1.1 for a listing of various marketing communication elements.) Collectively, these communication tools and media constitute what traditionally has been termed the *promotion* component of the marketing mix. (You will recall from your introductory marketing course that the so-called marketing mix includes four sets of interrelated decision areas: *product, price, place, and promotion.*) Although the "4P" characterization has led to widespread use of the term *promotion* for describing communications with prospects and customers, the term *marketing communications* is preferred by most marketing practitioners as well as by many educators. In this text we use *marketing communications* to refer to the collection of advertising, sales promotions, public relations, event marketing, and other communication devices; comparatively, we reserve *promotions* as a shorthand reference to sales promotions. The text devotes coverage to all of these topics except personal selling, which is a subject that is better treated in a stand-alone course devoted exclusively to that topic.

Marketing Communications at the Brand Level

Marketing communicators in their various capacities (as advertisers, sales promotion specialists, salespeople, public relations professionals, etc.) develop and deliver messages regarding different types of marketing topics: products, services, stores, events, and even people. Although these terms capture different forms of marketing foci, one term will suffice as a summary means for describing *all* forms of marketing focus. That term is *brand.* The Buick Rainier is a brand. So are Red Bull, Evian, Guinness, McDonald's, Levi's, Motorola, Sony, Intel, Microsoft, MasterCard, Amazon.com, Kodak, IBM, Dell, Honda, Mercedes-Benz, and the list goes on. The point that deserves particular emphasis is that most marketing communications occurs at the brand level.

Table 1.1

The Tools of Marketing Communications

1. Media Advertising • TV • Radio • Magazines • Newspapers 2. Direct Response and Interactive Advertising • Direct mail • Telephone solicitation • Online advertising 3. Place Advertising • Billboards and bulletins • Posters • Transit ads • Cinema ads 4. Store Signage and Point-of-Purchase Advertising • External store signs • In-store shelf signs • Shopping cart ads • In-store radio and TV	5. Trade- and Consumer-Oriented Promotions • Trade deals and buying allowances • Display and advertising allowances • Trade shows • Cooperative advertising • Samples • Coupons • Premiums • Refunds/rebates • Contests/sweepstakes • Promotional games • Bonus packs • Price-off deals	6. Event Marketing and Sponsorships • Sponsorship of sporting events • Sponsorship of arts, fairs, and festivals • Sponsorship of causes 7. Marketing-Oriented Public Relations and Publicity 8. Personal Selling

SOURCE: Adapted from Figure 1 in Kevin Lane Keller, "Mastering the Marketing Communications Mix: Micro and Macro Perspectives on Integrated Marketing Communication Programs," *Journal of Marketing Management*, 2001, 17, 823–851.

Discussion throughout this text focuses on *brand-level* marketing communications. It is critical for students to fully appreciate that the term *brand* is a convenient (and appropriate) label for describing any object of concerted marketing efforts. It could be a product, a service, a retail outlet, a media company, or even a person.

A well-known and respected brand is an invaluable asset. Brands perform a critical strategic role by providing a key means for differentiating one company's offering from those of competitive brands. From the consumer's perspective, respected brands offer an assurance of consistent performance and provide a signal of whatever benefits consumers seek when making purchase decisions in particular product categories. More than this, a brand is a covenant with the consumer whereby the mere mention of the name triggers expectations about what the brand will deliver in terms of quality, convenience, status, and other critical buying considerations.[5] Consider what a senior marketing executive at Procter & Gamble (P&G)—historically one of the world's best marketing organizations—has to say about the roles performed by several of P&G's respected brands:

When you [the consumer] have a brand like Tide [detergent], you don't have to think a lot about it. You know that it's going to give you the best performance, the best value and get the job done without question. Great brands bring an element of simplicity to what is a very complex world. I believe as strongly as I possibly could that we're [i.e., P&G] going to be selling Tide and Crest and Pampers and Folgers and Downy 50 years from now, and they're going to be bigger and better than they are today.[6]

The Integration of Marketing Communications

Mountain Dew is a well-known brand that is consumed by millions of predominately young consumers. On the market for more than 30 years, Mountain Dew is positioned as a brand that stands for fun, exhilaration, and energy—FEE for short. Brand managers have been consistent over time and across communication

AP Topic Gallery

media in maintaining the FEE theme that represents the brand's core meaning—its positioning. Various advertising media, event sponsorships, and consumer promotions have been employed over the years to trumpet the brand's core meaning. Advertisements placed during the Super Bowl, which reaches in excess of 90 million people, as well as local TV and radio spots, are used to appeal to the brand's primary and secondary targets. Event sponsorships provide a major communication medium for Mountain Dew, which has sponsored leading alternative sports competitions such as ESPN's X Games and NBC's Gravity Games. In addition to these prominent sponsorships, Mountain Dew also hosts a variety of smaller events that draw audiences as small as 5,000 people. Appealing giveaway items (T-shirts, videos, branded snowboards and mountain bikes, etc.) are distributed at these events to generate excitement and foster positive connections between the Mountain Dew brand and its loyal consumers.

Much of Mountain Dew's success over the years is attributable to its brand managers having dedicated themselves to presenting consistent messages about the brand, both over time and across communication media. By contrast, many companies treat the various communication elements—advertising, sales promotions, public relations, and so on—as virtually separate activities rather than as integrated tools that work together to achieve a common goal. Personnel responsible for advertising sometimes fail to adequately coordinate their efforts with individuals in charge of sales promotions or publicity. The lack of integration was more prevalent in the past than currently, but many brands still suffer from poorly integrated marketing communications programs.

Current marketing philosophy holds that integration is absolutely imperative for success. *Integrated marketing communications,* or simply IMC, is the philosophy and practice of carefully coordinating a brand's sundry marketing communications elements. The logic underlying integration seems so crystal clear and compelling that the student may be wondering: Why is this such a big deal? Why haven't firms practiced IMC all along? Why is there reluctance to integrate? Good questions, all, but what sounds reasonable in theory is not always easy to put into practice.[7] Organizations traditionally have handled advertising, sales promotions, point-of-purchase displays, and other communication tools as virtually separate practices because different units within organizations have specialized in separate aspects of marketing communications—advertising, *or* sales promotions, *or* public relations, and so on—rather than having generalized knowledge and experience with all communication tools. Furthermore, outside suppliers (such as advertising agencies, public relations agencies, and sales promotion agencies) also have tended to specialize in single facets of marketing communications rather than to possess expertise across the board.

There has been a reluctance to change from this single-function, specialist model due to managerial parochialism (e.g., advertising people sometimes view the world exclusively from an advertising perspective and are blind to other communication traditions) and for fear that change might lead to budget cutbacks in their areas of control (such as advertising) and reductions in their authority and power. Advertising, public relations, and promotion agencies also have resisted change due to reluctance to broaden their function beyond the one aspect of marketing communications in which they have developed expertise and built their reputations.

However, in recent years a number of advertising agencies have expanded their roles by merging with other companies or creating new departments that specialize in the growth areas of sales promotions, marketing-oriented public relations, event sponsorship, and direct marketing. Many firms, including suppliers of marketing communication services, along with their brand-manager clients, have increasingly adopted an integrated approach to their communication activities.[8] Although IMC received its primary initial acceptance by manufacturers of consumer packaged goods, the practice has also been adopted by numerous retail and service marketers.[9]

Skeptics have suggested that IMC is little more than a management fashion that is short lived,[10] but evidence to the contrary suggests that IMC is not fleeting but rather has become a permanent feature of the marketing communications landscape around the world and in many different types of marketing organizations.[11] As an IMC pioneer describes it, "Integration just plain makes sense for those planning to succeed in the 21st century marketplace. Marketers, communicators, and brand organizations simply have no choice."[12] In the final analysis, the key to successfully implementing IMC is that brand managers, who represent the client side, must closely link their efforts with outside suppliers of marketing communications services (such as ad agencies), and both parties must be committed to assuring that all communication tools are carefully and finely integrated.[13]

Although there is movement toward increased implementation of IMC, not all brand managers or their firms are equally likely to have adopted IMC. In fact, experienced managers are more likely than novice managers to practice IMC. Firms involved in marketing services (rather than products) and B2C (versus B2B) companies are more likely to practice IMC. More sophisticated companies also are likely adherents to IMC.[14] All said, though achieving integration is easier said than done, it is a goal worth pursuing.[15]

What Exactly Is IMC?

Proponents of IMC have provided slightly different perspectives on this management practice. Not all educators or practitioners are in perfect agreement regarding the precise meaning of IMC. Notwithstanding these differences, a working definition is in order. The following definition reflects this text's position on the topic.

IMC *is a communications process that entails the planning, creation, integration, and implementation of diverse forms of marcom (advertisements, sales promotions, publicity releases, events, etc.) that are delivered over time to a brand's targeted customers and prospects. The goal of IMC is ultimately to influence or directly affect the behavior of the targeted audience. IMC considers all touch points, or sources of contact, that a customer/prospect has with the brand as potential delivery channels for messages and makes use of all communications methods that are relevant to customers/prospects. IMC requires that all of a brand's communication media deliver a consistent message. The IMC process further necessitates that the customer/prospect is the starting point for determining the types of messages and media that will serve best to inform, persuade, and induce action.*[16]

The Payoff from IMC: The Value of Synergy

We will shortly identify the key aspects of IMC that are contained in the foregoing definition. First, however, it will be useful to examine the "bottom line" of IMC. What is the payoff from using multiple communication tools and developing consistent, integrated messages? The payoff is that by closely integrating multiple communication tools and media, brand managers achieve **synergy**—that is, multiple methods in combination with one another yield more positive communication results than do the tools used individually. This value of synergy was illustrated in a study of Levi Strauss' Dockers brand of khaki pants.[17] Using sophisticated analytical techniques, researchers determined that the use of both TV and print advertisements produced a synergistic effect on sales of pants that was significantly additional to the individual effects of each advertising medium. Another study demonstrated that TV and online advertising used in conjunction produced positive synergistic effects that were additional to each medium's individual effects. TV and online advertising used together produced more attention, more positive thoughts, and higher message credibility than did either medium alone.[18]

Table 1.2
Five Key Features of IMC

1. Start with the customer or prospect.
2. Use any form of relevant contact or touch point.
3. Speak with a single voice.
4. Build relationships.
5. Affect behavior.

Key IMC Features

Though the preceding definition of IMC is long-winded and certainly not worth committing to memory, inherent in the definition are several essential features that provide the philosophical foundation for this practice. These features are listed in Table 1.2 and require detailed discussion hereafter. It is important to note before proceeding that these elements are interdependent and that there is no particular order of importance suggested by the listing in Table 1.2. It also is essential that students recognize that all five features are critical to both understanding the philosophy of IMC and appreciating what must be accomplished to implement this philosophy into practice. These five features do merit commitment to memory.

1. The Customer Represents the Starting Point for All Marketing Communications Activities. An initial key feature of IMC is that the process should *start with the customer or prospect* and then work back to the brand communicator in determining the most appropriate messages and media for informing, persuading, and inducing customers and prospects to act favorably toward the communicator's brand. The IMC approach avoids an "inside-out" approach (from company to customer) in identifying communication vehicles and instead starts with the customer ("outside-in") to determine those communication methods that will best serve the customers' information needs and motivate them to purchase the brand.

The point of this feature is that brand managers and their agencies should not restrict themselves to only one or a select number of communication media. Rather, the IMC mind-set calls for considering any of numerous options that might be appropriate for reaching and influencing any particular target audience. Moreover, the communication media that are best for any one brand and its target audience are not necessarily best for another brand / target audience combination. Additionally, the best communication media at the present time in light of the competitive environment will not necessarily be the best media in subsequent periods. In short, brand managers and agencies that practice IMC must be nimble and avoid a one-size-fits-all solution to marketing communications problems. This can be accomplished by using the customer's information needs as the touchstone for all marketing communication decisions rather than using past practice or management preference as the default option when selecting communications methods and media. The most important question to pose is this: "what is the communications supposed to do or accomplish?"[19] The choice of appropriate marketing communications tools and media naturally flows from the answer to this key question.

2. Brand Managers and Their Agencies Should Be Amenable to Using Various Marketing Communication Tools. This second element naturally extends from the first and its emphasis on starting with the customer. To fully appreciate this second key feature of IMC, it will be useful to draw an analogy between the tools available to marketing communicators (advertising, sales promotions, sponsorships, etc.) and those used by people in craft industries such as carpentry, plumbing, and automobile repair. Each of these craftsmen possesses a toolbox that is filled with a variety of tools. Consider, for example, a car-

Figure 1.2 Coffee Sleeve Advertising

Courtesy, BriteVision Media.

Baby Carriages as Touch Points

global focus

An outdoor media company in Denmark devised a creative way to reach consumers with advertising messages. The company gives parents of newborn babies free use of high-quality baby carriages (a.k.a. buggies). However, as always, there is no free lunch: parents receive free buggies only by agreeing to have a corporate sponsor's name applied to the side of the carriage. Advertisers pay a one-time fee of $750 per baby carriage to have their corporate or brand names displayed. When accepting the free baby carriage deal, parents also agree to have their names and addresses released to companies that market baby products and services. From the advertiser's perspective, there would seem to be little downside to this form of advertising unless carriages displaying their logos are wheeled around by people whose characteristics fail to match the sponsor's desired image.

Source: Adapted from Gerard O'Dwyer, *Advertising Age,* August 19, 2002, 27.

fierce criticism and is in the throes of major change due to the fact that many marketers consider traditional advertising, especially network television, too fragmented and excessively expensive—not to mention the threat of personal video recorders of the TiVo variety, which have reduced consumers' exposure to advertisements inasmuch as skipping commercials is possible with this technology.[28] Hence, professional communicators must be receptive to using whatever touch points are most efficient and effective for accomplishing the job. For a final example of an alternative type of touch point, see the *Global Focus.*

3. Multiple Messages Must Speak with a Single Voice. Inherent in the philosophy and practice of IMC is the demand that a brand's assorted communication elements (advertisements, point-of-purchase signage, sales promotions, event sponsorships, etc.) must all strive to present the same message and convey that message consistently across diverse message channels, or points of contact. Marketing communications must, in other words, *speak with a single voice.* Coordination of messages and media is absolutely critical to achieving a strong and unified brand image and moving consumers to action.[29]

The failure to closely coordinate all communication elements can result in duplicated efforts or—worse yet—contradictory brand messages. A vice president of marketing at Nabisco fully recognized the value of speaking with a single voice when describing her intention to integrate all the marketing communication contacts for Nabisco's Oreo brand of cookies. This executive captured the essential quality of "single voicing" when stating that, under her leadership, "whenever consumers see Oreo, they'll be seeing the same message."[30] A general manager at Mars, Inc., maker of candy products, expressed a similar sentiment when stating, "We used to look at advertising, PR, promotion plans, each piece as separate. Now every piece of communication from package to Internet has to reflect the same message."[31]

In general, the single-voice principle involves selecting a specific positioning statement for a brand. A **positioning statement** is the key idea that encapsulates what a brand is intended to stand for in its target market's mind and then consistently delivers the same idea across all media channels. IMC practitioners, such as Oreo's vice president of marketing and Mars, Inc.'s general manager, know it is critical that they continually convey the same message on every occasion where the brand comes into contact with the target audience. A framework presented later in the chapter will further discuss the important role of positioning, and Chapter 5 will cover the topic of positioning in detail as it applies in an advertising context. It is important to note that some marketers rail against the idea that a brand should have a single positioning. Indeed, the *IMC Focus* presents an alternate view, termed "brand journalism," that was propounded by food giant McDonald's global chief marketing officer.

4. Build Relationships Rather Than Engage in Flings. A fourth characteristic of IMC is the belief that successful marketing communication requires building relationships between brands and their consumers/customers. A **relationship** is an enduring link between a brand and its customers.[32] It can be argued, in fact, that relationship building is the key to modern marketing and that IMC is one of the keys to relationship building.[33] Successful relationships between customers and brands lead to repeat purchasing and perhaps even to loyalty toward a brand. The importance of relationship building has spawned the growth of an entire industry of consultants and software suppliers who are involved in the practice of customer relationship management, or CRM. Companies that hire these consultants and use their software programs have learned that it is more profitable to build and maintain relationships than it is to continuously search for new customers. The value of customer retention has been compared to a "leaky bucket," the logic of which is nicely captured in the following quote:

As a company loses customers out of the leak in the bottom of the bucket, they have to continue to add new customers to the top of the bucket. If the company can even partially plug the leak, the bucket stays fuller. It then takes fewer new customers added to the top of the bucket to achieve the same level of profitability. It's less expensive and more profitable to keep those customers already in the bucket. Smart business people realize that it costs five to 10 times more to land a new customer than to keep a customer they already have. They also recognize that increasing the number of customers they keep by a small percentage can double profits.[34]

There are myriad ways to build brand/customer relationships. One well-known method is the use of frequent-flyer and other so-called frequency, loyalty, or ambassador programs. All these programs are dedicated to creating customers who are committed to a brand and encouraging them to satisfy most of their product or service needs from offering organizations.[35] Airlines, hotels, supermarkets, and many other businesses provide customers with bonus points—or some other form of accumulated reward—for their continued patronage.

Relationships between brand and customer also are nurtured by creating brand experiences that make positive and lasting impressions. This is done by creating special events or developing exciting venues that attempt to build the sensation that a sponsoring brand is relevant to the consumer's life and lifestyle. For example, Toronto-based Molson beer conducted the Molson Outpost campaign that took 400 sweepstakes winners on a weekend escapade of outdoor camping and extreme activities such as mountain climbing. Lincoln automobiles, a sponsor of the U.S. Open tennis tournament, converted an unused building at the USTA National Tennis Center into a complex that immersed visitors into the history of tennis. The building featured soundstages, faux docks with real water, and images of the evolution of tennis around the world. Some 30,000 leads were obtained from people interested in Lincoln automobiles, prompting Lincoln's marketing communications coordinator to comment that "experiential marketing is permeating our entire marketing mix."[36]

5. Don't Lose Focus of the Ultimate Objective: Affect Behavior. A final IMC feature is the goal to *affect the behavior* of the target audience. This means that marketing communications must do more than just influence brand awareness or enhance consumer attitudes toward the brand. Instead, successful IMC requires that communication efforts be directed at encouraging some form of behavioral response. The objective, in other words, is to *move people to action.* We must be careful not to misconstrue this point. An IMC program must be judged, *ultimately,* in terms of whether it influences behavior; but it would be simplistic and unrealistic to expect an action to result from every communication effort. Prior to purchasing a new brand, consumers generally must be made aware of the

An Authority Declares That Positioning Is Out of Date

imc focus

At important conferences among marketing and advertising practitioners in 2004, Larry Light, McDonald's global chief marketing officer, declared that "the days of mass marketing as we know it are over." Light challenged the prevailing view that brands must have a single message appeal, or positioning. He declared that it is passé and out of touch to employ a single brand positioning in a world where audiences are fragmented and brands possess multiple attributes and benefits. "A brand is multidimensional. No one communication, no one message can tell a whole brand story."

This heretical viewpoint is not particularly surprising coming from an executive of a company with a global marketing budget exceeding $1 billion and which has nearly 50 million consumers spread over 119 countries where its fast-food outlets are located. Obviously, the identical message likely would not be equally successful in different countries with diverse cultures and varying attitudes regarding the role of fast food.

Light has offered an alternative approach to brand marketing that he refers to as "brand journalism." Using journalism as a metaphor for advertising, his point essentially is that brand marketers can tell different stories about their brands, just like journalists tell different stories about the same basic topic. For example, a journalist might write a series of several articles about a politician, with each article telling a different story about the politician's background, philosophy, and likelihood of being elected. In a similar vein, many stories about a complex brand such as McDonald's can be presented to the same audience, and different stories told to different audiences.

Though portraying the concept of "brand journalism" as antithetical to the well-established practice of positioning, it would seem that McDonald's global chief marketing officer really is not claiming that developing a unified message is a bad idea. Surely, a brand would suffer in the marketplace if it told multiple stories that were inconsistent or conflicting. Rather, as I interpret Light's argument, a brand needs to come up with a big creative idea and then deliver the essence of that idea by presenting different stories to the same or different audience—but all stories should be based on conveying the "big idea." Light calls this "brand journalism" and distinguishes it from positioning, but the difference between these concepts is nuanced at best. Both are based on the philosophy that consistency is important. The traditional concept of brand positioning surely does not demand that just a single story be told about a brand.

Sources: Mercedes M. Cardona, "Mass Marketing Meets Its Maker," *Advertising Age,* June 21, 2004, 1, 31; Hilary Chura, "McDonald's Pulls Further Away from Mass Marketing," *AdWatch: Outlook 2004,* http://www.adage.com (accessed July 14, 2004); Danielle Veldre, "CMO Light Out to Tell the McDonald's Story," *http://www.bandt.com.au* (accessed July 14, 2004).

brand and its benefits and be influenced to have a favorable attitude toward it. Communication efforts directed at accomplishing these intermediate, or prebehavioral, goals are fully justified. Yet eventually—and preferably sooner than later—a successful marketing communications program must accomplish more than encouraging consumers to like a brand or, worse yet, merely familiarizing them with its existence. This partially explains why sales promotions and direct-to-consumer advertising are used so extensively—both practices typically yield quicker results than other forms of marketing communications such as advertising.

To better understand IMC's behavior-affecting objective, consider the situation faced by producers of natural food products. Research conducted to gauge consumers' feelings about 10 natural products (free-range chickens, organic fruits, and so on) revealed that natural products had a good image but not many people were buying them. Only 6 percent of the sampled consumers had purchased free-range chickens during the year preceding the survey, yet 43 percent thought that free-range chickens were superior to conventional chickens.[37] This is a classic illustration of buyer behavior not following directly from attitudes. In a case such as this, the goal of marketing communications would be to convert these good feelings toward natural products into product consumption—it does little good to have consumers like your product but not to buy it.

A similar challenge confronts antismoking proponents. Although most people understand intellectually that smoking causes cancer, emphysema, and other ailments, these same people often think that cancer and other problems will happen to other smokers but not to them. Hence, antismoking ads may serve to make people aware of the problems associated with smoking, but such campaigns are ineffective if people continue to smoke. The IMC goal in such a case is to develop more compelling advertisements that influence smokers to discontinue this practice. A creative approach other than the standard smoking-is-bad-for-you message is needed to redirect behavior. Appeals to normative influences (e.g., "smoking is uncool" or "only losers smoke") may represent a superior tack in the antismoking initiative to reduce this unhealthy practice, particularly among teenagers.

Changes in Marketing Communication Practices

The adoption of an IMC mind-set necessitates some fundamental changes in the way marketing communications have traditionally been practiced. The following interrelated changes are particularly prominent.

Reduced Dependence on Mass Media Advertising

Many marketing communicators now realize that communication methods other than media advertising often better serve the needs of their brands. As noted previously, the objective is to contact customers and prospects effectively; media advertising is not always the most effective or cost-efficient medium for accomplishing this objective. But of course this does not mean that media advertising is unimportant or in threat of extinction. The point instead is that other communication methods should receive careful consideration *before* mass media advertising is automatically assumed to be *the* solution. In other words, it is easy to argue that cheaper, alternative means of communication should be the default option rather than defaulting to mass media advertising.

As alluded to previously, many brand managers and their agencies have reduced the role of TV advertising, especially during network (versus cable) programs, in their marcom budgeting. Part of this is simply due to the fact that TV advertising is not as effective or cost-efficient as it once was due to audience fragmentation and the availability of many alternative entertainment options. Moreover, other advertising and non-advertising communication tools often are superior to TV in achieving brand managers' objectives. Consider, for example, Unilever's brand of Wisk detergent. This brand was historically advertised heavily on TV. Recently, however, Wisk's brand managers devised a media plan that reaches people at "the point of dirt." This approach calls for using billboard advertising directing consumers to a Wisk Web site and placing messages near ballparks, playgrounds, and other touch points where kids get dirty.[38] TV advertising is minimized with this approach, though only time will tell whether the point-of-dirt approach is an effective alternative.

In the spirit of reducing dependence on TV advertising, McCann Worldgroup, a highly respected advertising agency, has developed the concept of a *media-neutral approach* when counseling its clients in selecting appropriate marcom tools. This approach requires that the brand marketer first identify the goal(s) a marcom program is designed to accomplish (building brand awareness, creating buzz, influencing behavior, etc.) and then identify the best way to allocate the marketer's budget.[39] This media-neutral approach is perfectly in accord with our earlier discussion about selecting the most appropriate communication tool given the task at hand. Analogously, a hammer may be the best tool for a carpenter when driving nails but not for fastening screws.

Increased Reliance on Highly Targeted Communication Methods

Direct mail, opt-in (permission) e-mailing, specialty interest magazines, cable TV, and event sponsorships are just some of the contact methods that enable pinpointed communications that often are less expensive and more effective than mass media advertising. Targeting messages is especially feasible today with the large, up-to-date databases of customers that are maintained by many organizations.

Heightened Demands on Suppliers

Marketing communication suppliers such as advertising agencies, sales promotion firms, and public relations agencies have historically offered a limited range of services. Now it is increasingly important for suppliers to offer multiple services—which explains why some major advertising agencies have expanded their offerings beyond just advertising services to include sales promotion assistance, public relations, direct marketing, and event marketing support. In fact, brand managers can turn to "full-service" agencies that supply all forms of marcom and not just advertising, sales promotion, or publicity per se.

Increased Efforts to Assess Communications' Return on Investment

A final key feature of IMC is that it demands that systematic efforts be undertaken to determine whether communication programs yield a reasonable return on their investment. All managers—and marketing communicators are no exception—must increasingly be held financially accountable for their actions. The investment in marketing communications must be assessed in terms of the profit-to-investment ratio to determine whether changes are needed or whether other forms of investment might be more profitable.[40] It is imperative in a world where shareholder value is the touchstone for assessing the prudence of investments that marketing communicators be ever mindful of whether their investments are garnering an adequate return on investment, or ROI. The following chapter discusses in some detail the importance of efforts to demonstrate marcom's ROI.

Obstacles to Implementing IMC

Brand managers typically use outside suppliers, or specialized services, to assist them in managing various aspects of marketing communications. These include advertising agencies, public relations firms, sales promotion agencies, direct-advertising firms, and special-event marketers. Herein is a major reason why marketing communication efforts often do not meet the ideals described in this chapter. Integration requires tight coordination among all elements of a communications program. However, this becomes complicated when different specialized services operate independently of one another.

Perhaps the greatest obstacle to integration is that few providers of marketing communication services have the far-ranging skills to plan and execute programs that cut across all major forms of marketing communications. Advertising agencies, which traditionally have offered a greater breadth of services than do other specialists, are well qualified to develop mass media advertising campaigns; most, however, do not also have the ability to conduct direct-to-customer advertising, and even fewer have departments for sales promotions, special events, and publicity campaigns. Although many advertising agencies have expanded their services and full-service agencies have emerged, IMC awaits major changes in the culture of marketing departments and service providers before it becomes a reality on a large scale. In the final analysis, although most marketers consider themselves proponents of IMC, a major challenge facing brand marketers and their agencies is assuring that all marcom tools used in a particular marketing execution are consistently executed.[41]

A Model of the Marketing Communications Decision-Making Process

To this point in the chapter we have discussed the importance of tightly integrating all marcom such that a unified message is delivered wherever the customer or prospect comes into contact with the brand. This section presents a framework that will provide a useful conceptual and schematic structure for thinking about the types of practical decisions that marketing communicators make. The framework is presented in Figure 1.3 and described hereafter. It is very important at this time that you scan and achieve a basic understanding of the model components in preparation for the following discussion, which fleshes out the model's skeleton.

Figure 1.3 conceptualizes the various types of brand-level marcom decisions and the outcomes desired from those decisions. It will be noted that the model consists of a set of fundamental decisions, a set of implementation decisions, and program evaluation. The model in Figure 1.3 shows that *fundamental decisions* (targeting, positioning, setting objectives, and budgeting) influence *implementation decisions* regarding the mixture of communications elements and the determination of messages, media, and momentum. The expected *outcomes* from these decisions are enhancing brand equity and affecting behavior. Subsequent to the implementation of the marcom decisions, *program evaluation*—in the form of measuring the results from marcom efforts, providing feedback (see dashed arrow in Figure 1.3), and taking corrective action—is essential to determining whether outcomes match objectives. Corrective action is required when performance falls below expectations.

Figure 1.3

Making Brand-Level Marcom Decisions and Achieving Desired Outcomes

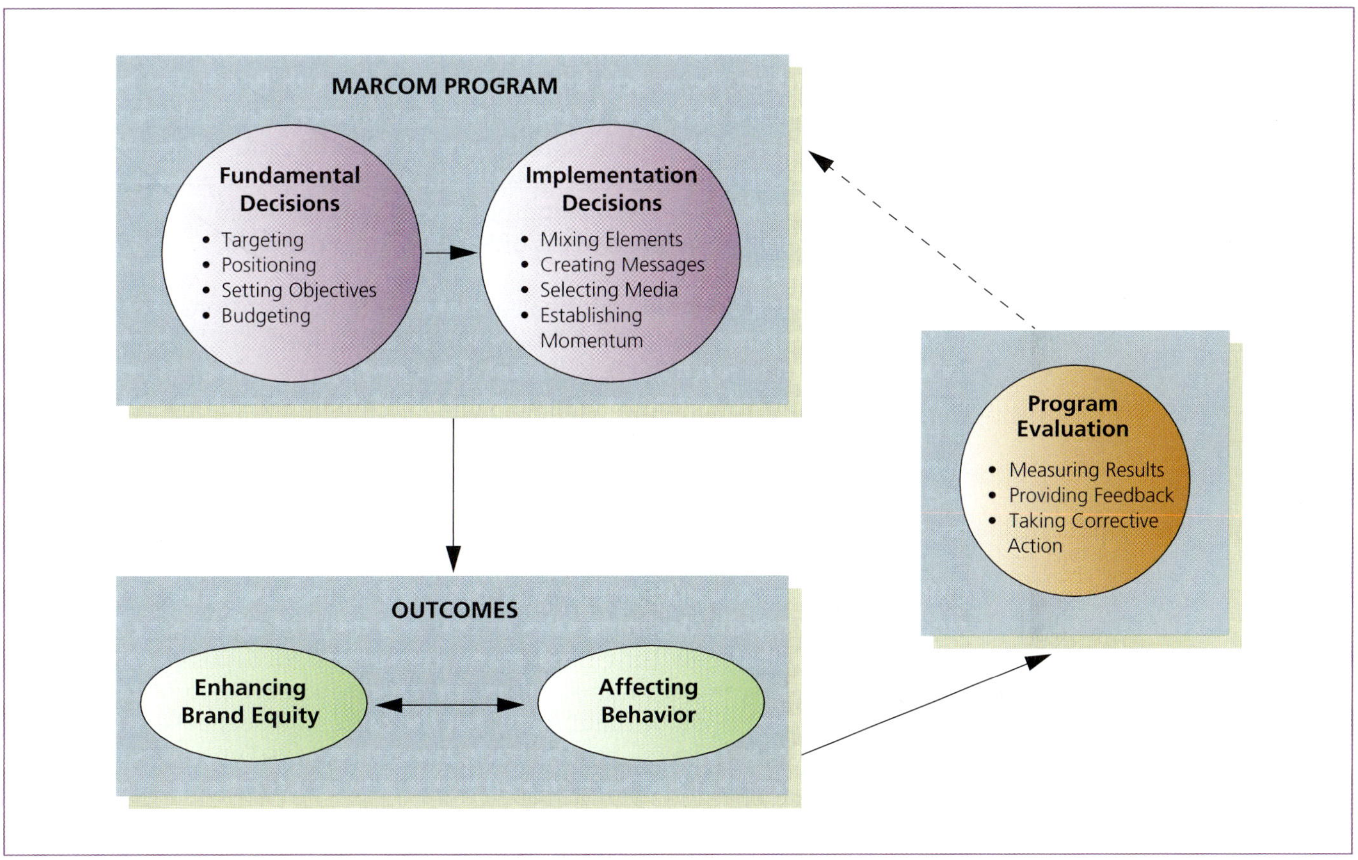

The objective of marketing communications is to enhance *brand equity* as a means of moving customers to *favorable action toward the brand*—that is, trying it, repeat purchasing it, and, ideally, becoming loyal toward the brand. Enhancing equity and affecting behavior depend, of course, on the suitability of all marketing-mix elements. Marcom efforts nonetheless play a pivotal role by informing customers about new brands and their relative advantages and by elevating brand images. As will be fully developed in the following chapter, brand equity is enhanced when consumers become familiar with the brand and hold favorable, strong, and perhaps unique associations in memory about the brand.[42] A brand has no equity if consumers are unfamiliar with it. Once consumers have become aware of a brand, the amount of equity depends on how favorably they perceive the brand's features and benefits as compared to competitive brands and how strongly these views are held in memory.

Fundamental Marcom Decisions

Targeting

Targeting allows marketing communicators to deliver messages more precisely and to prevent wasted coverage to people falling outside the intended audience. Hence, selection of target segments is a critical step toward effective and efficient marketing communications.

Companies identify potential target markets in terms of demographics characteristics, lifestyles, product usage patterns, and geographic considerations. It is important to recognize, however, that most profitable segments are not based on a single characteristic (such as gender, age, ethnicity, etc.). Rather, meaningful market segments generally represent consumers who share a *combination of characteristics* and demonstrate similar behavior.

Consider, for example, the segmentation implications of a new brand of premium-priced low carbohydrate ice cream that has hitchhiked on the low-carb diet craze based on the widely known Atkins and South Beach diet books. The market segment for this new brand is not just women, not just men, not just younger people or older people, and, in general, not any group of people sharing any single characteristic. Rather, a meaningful segment would possess several or more shared characteristics—for example, people who live in urban or suburban areas, earn annual incomes in excess of $50,000, are older than 35, and are health and weight conscious.

B2B marketing communicators also make targeting decisions. For example, Gateway, a computer company best known as a consumer (B2C) brand, undertook a campaign to reach the B2B market. The campaign, dubbed "Humanology," was targeted toward technologically sophisticated decision makers and designed to broadcast the human touch behind the company's hardware and software. This human touch was graphically demonstrated by visual representations of products and people morphing, such as an ear transforming into a server and an eye becoming a computer monitor (see Figure 1.4).[43]

Another illustration of B2B targeting is an advertising effort by the National Cattlemen's Beef Association that was designed to increase sales of veal. Beef ranchers faced rapidly declining sales of veal as a result of advertising by animal rights activists that had convinced many consumers to bypass veal because, according to the activists' claims, calves are raised in cruel circumstances. The activists' argument is not without merit, but the cattle ranchers believe they have a legitimate right to raise calves. The trade association's challenge was to counter anti-veal sentiment that had been created by the activist advertising effort. But the association had a budget of only slightly more than $1 million. Surely such a small budget could not reach many consumers nor allow sufficient momentum (as discussed later in the chapter) to have much impact. What to do? The decision: use the small ad budget by targeting advertising efforts at chefs rather than toward consumers. Attractive ads were placed in magazines read by chefs, magazines such as *Restaurant Business Magazine* and *Bon Appétit*. This campaign increased veal consumption by 20 percent, which is a substantial increase under the circumstances.[44]

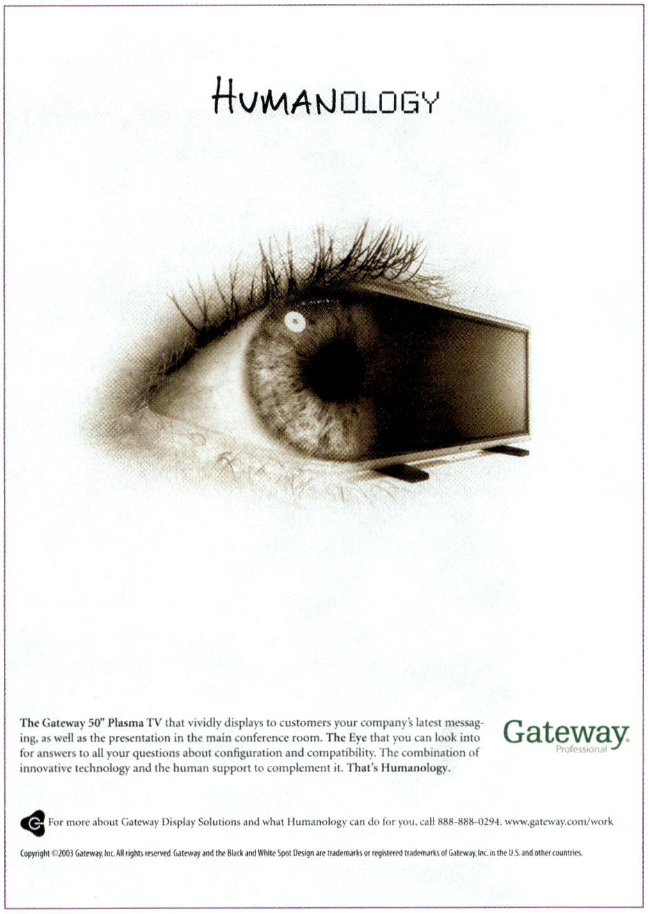

Courtesy, Gateway

Figure 1.4
A Targeted B2B Advertisement

Positioning

A brand's position represents the key feature, benefit, or image that it stands for in the target audience's collective mind. Brand communicators and the marketing team in general must decide on a brand positioning statement, which is the central idea that encapsulates a brand's meaning and distinctiveness vis-à-vis competitive brands in the product category. It should be obvious that positioning and targeting decisions go hand in hand: positioning decisions are made with respect to intended targets, and targeting decisions are based on a clear idea of how brands are to be positioned and distinguished from competitive offerings. A separate chapter (Chapter 5) covers the topic of positioning in considerable detail.

Setting Objectives

Marketing communicators' decisions are grounded in the underlying goals, or objectives, to be accomplished for a brand. Of course, the content of these objectives varies according to the form of marketing communications used. For example, whereas mass media advertising is ideally suited for creating consumer awareness of a new or improved brand, point-of-purchase communications are perfect for influencing in-store brand selection, and personal selling is unparalleled when it comes to informing B2B customers and retailers about product improvements. Specific chapters later in the text detail the objectives that each component of the marcom mix is designed to accomplish.

Budgeting

Financial resources are budgeted to specific marcom elements to accomplish desired objectives. Companies use different budgeting procedures in allocating funds to marketing communications managers and other organizational units. At one extreme is *top-down budgeting (TD)*, in which senior management decides how much each subunit receives. At the other extreme is *bottom-up budgeting (BU)*, in which managers of subunits (such as at the product category level) determine how much is needed to achieve their objectives; these amounts are then combined to establish the total marketing budget. Most budgeting practices involve a combination of top-down and bottom-up budgeting. For example, in the *bottom-up/top-down process (BUTD)*, subunit managers submit budget requests to a chief marketing officer (say, a vice president of marketing), who coordinates the various requests and then submits an overall budget to top management for approval. The *top-down/bottom-up process (TDBU)* reverses the flow of influence; top managers first establish the total size of the budget and then divide it among the various subunits. Research has shown that combination budgeting methods (BUTD and TDBU) are used more often than the extreme methods (TD or BU). The BUTD process is by far the most frequently used, especially in firms where marketing departments have greater influence than finance units.[45]

A Concluding Mantra

Mantra is a Hindu word meaning incantation or recitation (of a song, word, statement, or passage). The following statement serves as a mantra to summarize the preceding discussion of fundamental marcom decisions. This mantra should be committed to memory and used as a hallmark when formulating marcom strategies. For example, is your brand clearly positioned? Is your communication directed at a specific target?

All marketing communications should be: (1) directed to a particular ***target market****, (2) clearly* ***positioned****, (3) created to achieve a* ***specific objective****, and (4) undertaken to accomplish the objective* ***within budget constraint****.*

Marcom Implementation Decisions

The fundamental decisions just described are conceptual and strategic. Comparatively, the implementation decisions are practical and tactical. Here is where the proverbial rubber hits the road. Marcom managers must make a variety of implementation decisions in the pursuit of accomplishing brand-level objectives and achieving the brand's positioning and targeting requirements. Initially they must choose how best to integrate, or mix, the various communications elements to achieve objectives toward the target market and within budget constraint. Then they must decide what types of messages will accomplish the desired positioning, which media are appropriate for delivering messages, and what degree of momentum is needed to support the media effort. Please refer again to Figure 1.3 to obtain a view of the "forest" prior to examining specific "trees."

Mixing Elements

A fundamental issue confronting all companies is deciding exactly how to allocate resources among the various marketing communications tools. For B2B companies, the mixture typically emphasizes personal selling with supplementation from trade advertising, technical literature, and trade shows.[46] For consumer goods manufacturers, mixture decisions are, in many respects, more complicated because greater options are available. The issue boils down in large part to a decision of how much to allocate to advertising and to sales promotions. (Note: In keeping with practitioner convention, the word *promotion* hereafter will be used interchangeably with *sales promotion*.) The trend during the past two decades has been toward greater expenditures on promotions and fewer on advertising.

Is there an *optimum mixture* of expenditures between advertising and promotion? There is not, unfortunately, because the marketing communications-mix decision constitutes an *ill-structured problem*.[47] This means that for a given level of expenditure, there is no way of determining the mathematical optimum allocation between advertising and promotion that will maximize revenue or profit. Two major factors account for this inability to determine a mathematically optimum mix. First, advertising and promotions are somewhat interchangeable—both tools can accomplish some of the same objectives. Hence, it is impossible to know exactly which tool or combination of tools is better in every situation. Second, advertising and promotions produce a synergistic effect—their combined results are greater than what they would achieve individually. This makes it difficult to determine the exact effects that different combinations of advertising and sales promotion might generate.

Although it is impossible to determine a mathematically optimum mixture of advertising and promotion expenditures, a satisfactory mixture can be formulated by considering the differing purposes of each of these marcom tools. A key strategic consideration is whether short- or long-term schemes are more important given a brand's life-cycle stage. An appropriate mixture for mature brands is likely to be different from the mixture for brands recently introduced. New brands require larger investment in promotions such as couponing and sampling to generate trial purchases, whereas mature brands might need proportionately greater advertising investment to maintain or enhance a brand's image.

Brand equity considerations also play a role in evaluating a satisfactory combination of advertising and promotions. Poorly planned or excessive promotions can damage a brand's equity by cheapening its image. If a brand is frequently placed on sale or if some form of deal (price-offs, discounts) is regularly offered, consumers will delay purchasing the brand until its price is reduced. This can cause the brand to be purchased more for its price discount than for its nonprice attributes and benefits.

The matter of properly mixing advertising and promotion is aptly summarized in the following quote:

As one views the opportunities inherent in ascertaining the proper balance between advertising and promotion, it should be quite clear that both should be used as one would play a pipe organ, pulling out certain stops and pushing others, as situations and circumstances change. Rigid rules, or continuing application of inflexible advertising-to-promotion percentages, serve no real purpose and can be quite counterproductive in today's dynamic and ever-changing marketing environment. A short-term solution that creates a long-term problem is no solution at all.[48]

The "short-term solution" refers to spending excessive amounts on promotion to create quick sales while failing to invest sufficiently in advertising to build a brand's long-term equity. That is, excessive promotions can rob a brand's future. An appropriate mixture involves spending enough on promotions to ensure sufficient sales volume in the short term while simultaneously spending enough on advertising to ensure the growth or preservation of a brand's equity position.

Creating Messages

A second implementation decision is the creation of messages in the form of advertisements, publicity releases, promotions, package designs, and any other form of marcom message. Subsequent chapters will address specific message issues relating to each marcom tool. Suffice it to say at this point that systematic (versus ad hoc) decision making requires that message content be dictated by the brand's positioning strategy and aligned with the communications objective for the designated target audience.

Selecting Media

All marketing communications messages require an instrument, or medium, for transmission. Though the term *media* is typically applied to advertising (television, magazines, radio, Internet, etc.), the concept of *media* is relevant to all marcom tools. For example, personal sales messages can be delivered via face-to-face communications or by telemarketing; these media alternatives have different costs and effectiveness. Point-of-purchase materials are delivered via in-store signs, electronically, musically, and otherwise. Each represents a different medium.

Detailed discussions of media are reserved for specific chapters that follow. Advertising media are discussed in particular detail, and considerable attention also is devoted to the media of consumer promotions. At the risk of redundancy it is important to again note that media decisions are determined in large measure by the fundamental decisions previously made regarding choice of target audience, positioning strategy, type of objectives to be achieved, and how much is to be budgeted to a brand during each budgeting period.

Establishing Momentum

The word *momentum* refers to an object's force or speed of movement—its impetus. A train has momentum as it races down the tracks, a spacecraft has momentum as it is launched into orbit, a hockey player has momentum when skating past the defensive opposition, a student has momentum when making good progress on a term paper after delaying getting started. Marketing communications programs also have, or lack, momentum. Simply developing an advertising message, personal sales presentation, or publicity release is insufficient. The effectiveness of each of these message forms requires both a sufficient amount of effort and continuity of that effort. This is the meaning of momentum as it relates to marketing communications. Insufficient momentum is ineffective at best and a waste of money at worst.

Critical to the concept of momentum is the need to sustain an effort rather than starting advertising for a while, discontinuing it for a period, reinstating the advertising, stopping it again, and so on. In other words, some companies never create nor sustain momentum because their marketplace presence is inadequate. "Out of sight, out of mind" is probably more relevant to brands in the marketplace than to people. We generally do not forget our friends and family, but today's brand friend is tomorrow's stranger unless it is kept before our consciousness. Because consumers make hundreds of purchase decisions in many different product categories, they require continual reminders of brand names and their benefits if these brands are to stand a strong chance of becoming serious purchase candidates.

dpa/Landov

A few years ago Toyota Motor Corporation had only a 16-day supply of the fast-selling Camry. Yet it launched a major advertising campaign aggressively encouraging consumers to purchase Camrys. Some marketing observers were critical of this campaign, saying that it was unwise to advertise when insufficient product was available to fulfill orders. In response, the vice president of Toyota Motor Sales, USA asserted that even when demand is strong, it is important "to keep your momentum in the marketplace going."[49] This executive obviously appreciates the value of achieving and maintaining a brand's momentum. Many marketing communicators and higher-level managers don't. For example, advertising is one of the first items cut during economic downturns.

Marcom Outcomes

Referring back to our conceptual framework for marketing communications decisions, it can be seen that the outcomes from a marcom program are twofold: enhancing brand equity and affecting behavior. Figure 1.3 displays a double-headed arrow between these outcomes, which signifies that each outcome influences the other. If, say, an advertising campaign for a new brand generates brand awareness and creates a positive brand image, consumers may be inclined to try the new brand. In such a situation, the brand's equity has been enhanced, and this in turn has affected consumer behavior toward the brand. In similar fashion, a promotion for the new brand, such as a free sample, may encourage consumers to initially try and then subsequently purchase the brand. A positive experience in using the brand may lead to positive brand perceptions. In this situation, a promotion affected consumer behavior, which in turn enhanced the promoted brand's equity.

As established previously, a fundamental IMC principle is that marcom efforts must ultimately be gauged by whether they affect behavior. Sales promotion is the marcom tool most capable of directly affecting consumer behavior. However, excessive reliance on promotions can injure a brand's reputation by creating a low-price and perhaps low-quality image. It is for this reason that marketing communicators often seek to first enhance a brand's equity as a foundation to influencing behavior. It indeed can be argued that much if not most marcom efforts are designed to enhance brand equity. We thus need to fully explore the concept of brand equity and understand what it is and how it can be influenced by marcom efforts. We will examine this topic in detail in the following chapter.

Program Evaluation

After marketing communications objectives are set, elements selected and mixed, messages and media chosen, and programs implemented and possibly sustained, program evaluation must take place. This is accomplished by measuring the results of marcom efforts against the objectives that were established at the outset. For a local advertiser—say, a sporting goods store that is running an advertised special on athletic shoes for a two-day period in May—the results are the number of Nike, Reebok, Adidas, and other brands sold. If you tried to sell an old automobile through the classified pages, the results would be the number of phone inquiries you received and whether you ultimately sold the car. For a national manufacturer of a branded product, results typically are not so quick to occur. Rather, a company invests in point-of-purchase communications, promotions, and advertising and then waits, often for weeks, to see whether these programs deliver the desired sales volume.

Regardless of the situation, it is critical to evaluate the results of marcom efforts. Throughout the business world there is increasing demand for *accountability*, which requires that research be performed and data acquired to determine whether implemented marcom decisions have accomplished the objectives they were expected to achieve. Results can be measured in terms of behavioral impact (such as increased sales) or based on communication outcomes.

Measures of *communication outcomes* include brand awareness, message comprehension, attitude toward the brand, and purchase intentions. All of these are communication (rather than behavioral) objectives in the sense that an advertiser has attempted to communicate a certain message argument or create an overall impression. Thus, the goal for an advertiser of a relatively unknown brand may be to increase brand awareness in the target market by 30 percent within six months of starting a new advertising campaign. This objective (a 30 percent increase in awareness) would be based on knowledge of the awareness level prior to the campaign's debut. Post-campaign measurement would then reveal whether the target level was achieved.

It is essential to measure the results of all marcom programs. Failure to achieve targeted results prompts corrective action (see the dashed arrow in Figure 1.3). Corrective action might call for greater investment, a different combination of communications elements, revised creative strategy, different media allocations, or a host of other possibilities. Only by systematically setting objectives and measuring results is it possible to know whether marcom programs are working as well as they should and how future efforts can improve on the past.[50]

Summary

This opening chapter has overviewed the fundamentals of IMC and provided a framework for thinking about all aspects of marcom decision making. IMC is an organization's unified, coordinated effort to promote a consistent brand message through the use of multiple communication tools that "speak with a single voice." One of several key features of IMC is the use of all sources of brand or company contacts as potential message delivery channels. Another key feature is that the IMC process starts with the customer or prospect rather than the brand communicator to determine the most appropriate and effective methods for developing persuasive communications programs. The use of database marketing and highly pinpointed communication methods (such as direct mail and opt-in, or permission, e-mailing) to affect behavioral responses, along with attempts to measure the impact of marketing communications, are significant developments associated with the growing practice of IMC.

This chapter has provided a model of the marcom process to serve as a useful integrative device for better structuring and understanding the topics covered throughout the remainder of the text. The model (Figure 1.3) includes three components: a marcom program consisting of fundamental and implementation decisions, outcomes (enhancing brand equity and affecting behavior), and program evaluation. Fundamental decisions include choosing target markets, establishing a brand positioning, setting objectives, and determining a marcom budget. Implementation decisions involve determining a mixture of marketing communications tools (advertising, promotions, events, point-of-purchase efforts, etc.) and establishing message, media, and momentum plans. These decisions are evaluated by comparing measured results against brand-level communications objectives.

As author of seven editions of this text for over two decades, it is my sincere hope that this introductory chapter has piqued your interest and provided you with a basic understanding of the many topics you will be studying throughout the reading of this text and participating in classroom lectures and discussions. Marketing communications truly is a fascinating and dynamic subject. It combines art, science, and technology and allows the practitioner considerable latitude in developing effective ways to skin the proverbial cat. It will serve you well throughout your studies and into your marketing career to remain ever mindful of the key elements of IMC described in this chapter. Organizations that truly succeed in their marcom pursuits must accept and practice these key elements.

Because the field of marketing communications involves many forms of practice, a number of specialty trade associations have evolved over time. The following appendix overviews, in alphabetical order, a subset of some of the more influential associations in the United States.[51] Internet sites are provided to facilitate your search for additional information about these organizations. (Many countries other than the United States have similar associations. Interested students might want to conduct an Internet search to identify similar associations in a country of interest.)

Appendix

Some Important U.S. Trade Associations in the Marketing Communications Field

Advertising Research Foundation (ARF, http://www.arfsite.org)—ARF is a nonprofit association dedicated to increasing advertising effectiveness by conducting objective and impartial research. ARF's members consist of advertisers, advertising agencies, research firms, and media companies.

American Association of Advertising Agencies (AAAA, http://www.aaaa.org)—The Four *A*s, as it is referred to in speaking, has the mission of improving the advertising agency business in the United States by fostering professional development, encouraging high creative and business standards, and attracting first-rate employees to the advertising business.

Association of Coupon Professionals (ACP, http://www.couponpros.org)—This coupon-redemption trade association strives to ensure coupons as a viable promotional tool and to improve coupon industry business conditions.

Association of National Advertisers (ANA, http://www.ana.net)—Whereas the AAAA serves primarily the interests of advertising agencies, ANA represents the interests of business organizations that advertise regionally and nationally. ANA's members collectively represent over 80 percent of all advertising expenditures in the United States.

The Marketing Agencies Association Worldwide (MAAW, http://www.maaw.org)—This worldwide industry association represents full-service sales promotion agencies and serves to educate members of the promotion agency's strategic role in distinction from that of advertising and direct marketing agencies.

Direct Marketing Association (DMA, http://www.the-dma.org)—DMA is dedicated to encouraging and advancing the effective and ethical use of direct marketing. The association represents the interests of direct marketers to the government, media, and general public.

Incentive Manufacturers and Representatives Alliance (IMRA, http://www.imra1.org)—Members of IMRA are suppliers of premium merchandise. The association serves these members by promoting high professional standards in the pursuit of excellence in the incentive industry.

Point-of-Purchase Advertising International (POPAI, http://www.popai.org)—This trade association serves the interests of advertisers, retailers, and producers/suppliers of point-of-purchase products and services.

Promotional Products Association International (PPAI, http://www.ppa.org)—PPAI serves the interests of producers, suppliers, and users of promotional products. The businesses PPAI represents used to be referred to as the specialty advertising industry, but promotional products is the term of current preference.

Promotion Marketing Association (PMA, http://www.pmalink.org)—PMA's mission is to foster the advancement of promotion marketing and facilitate better understanding of promotion's role and importance in the overall marketing process.

Discussion Questions

1. Assume that your college or university is currently undertaking a huge marketing communications campaign targeted to high school students. Explain how your school might "partner" advertisements and sales promotions to increase enrollment.
2. Offer your views on the following statement: "the basic reason for IMC is that marcom is the only sustainable competitive advantage of marketing organizations."
3. Given your understanding of IMC and its fundamental characteristics, describe the probable outcome of practicing nonintegrated, rather than integrated, marketing communications.
4. One key feature of IMC is the emphasis on affecting behavior and not just its antecedents (such as brand awareness or favorable attitudes). For each of the following situations, indicate the specific behavior(s) that marketing communications might attempt to affect: (a) your university's advertising efforts, (b) a professional baseball team's promotion for a particular game, (c) a not-for-profit organization's efforts to recruit more volunteers, and (d) Gatorade's sponsorship of a volleyball tournament.
5. IMC also emphasizes using all economically effective contact methods as potential message delivery channels. Assume you are advertising a product that is marketed specifically to high school seniors. Identify seven contact methods (include no more than two forms of mass media advertising) you might use to reach this audience.
6. Early in the chapter it was claimed that the partnering of communication tools—for example, advertising along with promotions—generally yields better results than using the tools in isolation. Provide an explanation of what this claim means to you, and support your explanation with an example of a specific brand of your choosing.
7. Objectives and budgets are necessarily interdependent. Explain this interdependency and provide an example to support your point.
8. Brand positioning and targeting also are necessarily interdependent. Explain this interdependency and provide an example to support your point.
9. When discussing changes in marketing communications that are occasioned with the adoption of IMC, it was stated that marketing communicators might

consider defaulting to cheaper, alternative media as their initial solution to a communications problem rather than defaulting to mass media advertising. Offer an explanation of what this means and build an argument in favor of defaulting to alternative (versus mass) advertising media.

10. What is the distinction between top-down (TD) and bottom-up (BU) budgeting? Why is BUTD used in companies that are more marketing oriented, whereas TDBU is found more frequently in finance-driven companies?
11. Why do you think that the trend in marcom budgeting is toward increased expenditures on promotions and reduced advertising spending?
12. Explain the concept of *momentum,* and offer an account as to why momentum is important for a brand such as Red Bull.
13. Assume you are in charge of fund-raising for an organization on your campus—a social fraternity or sorority, a business fraternity, or any other suitable organization. It is your job to identify a suitable project and to manage the project's marketing communications. For the purpose of this exercise, identify a fund-raising project idea and apply the subset of the model involving fundamental decisions. In other words, explain how you would position your fund-raising project, whom you would target, what objective(s) you would set, and how much (ballpark figure) you would budget for marcom efforts.
14. Compare the concepts of brand positioning and brand journalism and explain, in your own words, how they are similar or different.

ENDNOTES

1. This description is adapted from Jean Halliday, "Buick Builds Buzz for SUV On-, Off-Line," *Advertising Age,* August 11, 2003, 34.
2. Kate Maddox, "Special Report: Integrated Marketing Success Stories," BtoBonline.Com, June 7, 2004 http://www.btobonline.com (accessed June 7, 2004).
3. This description is adapted from ibid.
4. Don E. Schultz, Stanley I. Tannenbaum, and Robert F. Lauterborn, *Integrated Marketing Communications* (Lincolnwood, Ill.: NTC Publishing Group, 1993), 46.
5. Jacques Chevron, "Of Brand Values and Sausage," *Brandweek,* April 20, 1998, 22.
6. Robert Wehling, cited in *Marketing Science Institute Review* (spring 1998), 7.
7. Bob Hartley and Dave Pickton, "Integrated Marketing Communications Requires a New Way of Thinking," *Journal of Marketing Communications* 5 (June 1999), 97–106.
8. Fred Beard, "IMC Use and Client-Ad Agency Relationships," *Journal of Marketing Communications* 3 (December 1997), 217–230; Patricia B. Rose, "Practitioner Opinions and Interests Regarding Integrated Marketing Communications in Selected Latin American Countries," *Journal of Marketing Communications* 2 (September 1996), 125–140.
9. Glen J. Nowak, Glen T. Cameron, and Denise Delorme, "Beyond the World of Packaged Goods: Assessing the Relevance of Integrated Marketing Communications for Retail and Consumer Service Marketing," *Journal of Marketing Communications* 2 (September 1996), 173–190.
10. Joep P. Cornelissen and Andrew R. Lock, "Theoretical Concept or Management Fashion? Examining the Significance of IMC," *Journal of Advertising Research* 40 (September/October 2000), 7–15. For counter positions, see Don E. Schultz and Philip J. Kitchen, "A Response to 'Theoretical Concept or Management Fashion?,'" *Journal of Advertising Research* 40 (September/October 2000), 17–21; Stephen J. Gould, "The State of IMC Research and Applications," *Journal of Advertising Research* 40 (September/October 2000), 22–23.
11. Don E. Schultz and Philip J. Kitchen, "Integrated Marketing Communications in U.S. Advertising Agencies: An Exploratory Study," *Journal of Advertising Research* 37 (September/October 1997), 7–18; Philip J. Kitchen and Don E. Schultz, "A Multi-Country Comparison of the Drive for IMC," *Journal of Advertising Research* 39 (January/February 1999), 21–38.
12. Don E. Schultz, "Integration Is Critical for Success in 21st Century," *Marketing News,* September 15, 1997, 26.
13. Stephen J. Gould, Andreas F. Grein, and Dawn B. Lernan, "The Role of Agency-Client Integration in Integrated Marketing Communications: A Complementary Agency Theory-Interorganizational Perspective," *Journal of Current Issues and Research in Advertising* 21 (spring 1999), 1–12.

14. These findings are based on research by George S. Low, "Correlates of Integrated Marketing Communications," *Journal of Advertising Research* 40 (May/June 2000), 27–39.
15. Howard Draft, "Putting It All Together," *Advertising Age,* August 25, 2003, 16.
16. This definition is the author's adaptation of one developed by members of the marketing communications faculty at the Medill School, Northwestern University. The original definition was reprinted in Don E. Schultz, "Integrated Marketing Communications: Maybe Definition Is in the Point of View," *Marketing News,* January 18, 1993, 17.
17. Prasad A. Naik and Kalyan Raman, "Understanding the Impact of Synergy in Multimedia Communications," *Journal of Marketing Research* 40 (November 2003), 375–388.
18. Yuhmiin Chang and Esther Thorson, "Television and Web Advertising Synergies," *Journal of Advertising* 33 (summer 2004), 75–84.
19. Don E. Schultz, "Relax Old Marcom Notions, Consider Audiences," *Marketing News,* October 27, 2003, 8.
20. David Sable, "We're Surrounded," *Agency* (spring 2000), 50–51.
21. The practitioner is Shelly Lazarus, whose career at Ogilvy & Mather advertising agency has extended over a quarter century. Lazarus was quoted by Laurie Freeman, "Internet Fundamentally Changes Definition," *Marketing News,* December 6, 1999, 15.
22. Maureen Tkacik, "Puma to Serve Up Soccer Cleats on Tables in Sushi Restaurants," *The Wall Street Journal Online,* May 9, 2002, http://online.wsj.com (accessed May 9, 2002).
23. Vanessa O'Connell, "Fictional Hershey Factory Will Send Kisses to Broadway," *The Wall Street Journal Online,* August 5, 2002, http://online.wsj.com (accessed August 5, 2002).
24. Bruce Orr, "Dew Gets Personal: Brand-Building with Beepers," *Marketing News,* July 6, 1998, 13.
25. This quote and the accompanying description are adapted from Shelley Emling, *Cox News Service,* posted on July 14, 2004.
26. Merissa Marr, "Fox to Pitch Its Movies at the Mall," *The Wall Street Journal Online,* July 15, 2004, http://online.wsj.com (accessed July 15, 2004).
27. Peter A. Georgescu, "Looking at the Future of Marketing," *Advertising Age,* April 14, 1997, 30.
28. Devin Leonard, "On Madison Avenue," *Fortune,* June 28, 2004, 93–108; "The Harder Hard Sell," *Economist.com,* June 24, 2004, http://www.economist.com (accessed July 6, 2004).
29. This one-voice perspective is widely shared by various writers on the topic of IMC. See Schultz, Tannenbaum, and Lauterborn, *Integrated Marketing Communications;* Tom Duncan, "Integrated Marketing? It's Synergy," *Advertising Age,* March 8, 1993, 22; and Glen J. Nowak and Joseph Phelps, "Conceptualizing the Integrated Marketing Communications' Phenomenon: An Examination of Its Impact on Advertising Practices and Its Implications for Advertising Research," *Journal of Current Issues and Research in Advertising* 16 (spring 1994), 49–66.
30. Judann Pollack, "Nabisco's Marketing VP Expects 'Great Things,'" *Advertising Age,* December 2, 1996, 40.
31. Stephanie Thompson, "Busy Lifestyles Force Change," *Advertising Age,* October 9, 2000, s8.
32. For an insightful discussion of different forms of consumer-brand relationships, see Susan Fournier, "Consumers and Their Brands: Developing Relationship Theory in Consumer Research," *Journal of Consumer Research* 24 (March 1998), 343–373.
33. Schultz, Tannenbaum, and Lauterborn, *Integrated Marketing Communications,* 52–53.
34. This quote is from author Vicki Lenz as cited in Matthew Grimm, "Getting to Know You," *Brandweek,* January 4, 1999, 18.
35. The importance of creating committed customers is verified empirically in Peter C. Verhoef, "Understanding the Effect of Customer Relationship Management Efforts on Customer Retention and Customer Share Development," *Journal of Marketing* 27 (October 2003), 30–45.
36. Dan Hanover, "Are You Experienced?" *Promo,* February 2001, 48.
37. Leah Rickard, "Natural Products Score Big on Image," *Advertising Age,* August 8, 1994, 26.
38. Jack Neff, "Making Soil Selling Point," *Advertising Age,* June 14, 2004, 12.
39. Lisa Sanders, "'Demand Chain' Rules at McCann," *Advertising Age,* June 14, 2004, 6.
40. Peter Doyle, *Value-Based Marketing: Marketing Strategies for Corporate Growth and Shareholder Value* (Chichester, England: John Wiley & Sons, 2000); Don E. Schultz, "Trying to Determine ROI for IMC," *Marketing News,* January 3, 1994, 18; and Don E. Schultz, "Spreadsheet Approach to Measuring ROI for IMC," *Marketing News,* February 28, 1994, 12.
41. A survey of over 200 marketing professionals found that both brand marketers and agencies consider consistency of execution the major challenge to integrating Marcom strategies. See Claire Atkinson, "Integration Still a Pipe Dream for Many," *Advertising Age,* March 10, 2003, 1, 47.
42. Kevin Lane Keller, "Conceptualizing, Measuring, and Managing Customer-Based Brand Equity," *Journal of Marketing* 57 (January 1993), 2.
43. Todd Wasserman, "Gateway Reboots B2B Effort After 3-Year Layoff," *Brandweek,* September 8, 2003, 8.
44. "Veal Industry Focuses on Chefs in Countering Animal-Rights Ads," *The Wall Street Journal Online,* March 18, 1998, http://online.wsj.com.
45. Nigel F. Piercy, "The Marketing Budgeting Process: Marketing Management Implications," *Journal of Marketing* 51 (October 1987), 45–59.
46. Donald W. Jackson, Jr., Janet E. Keith, and Richard K. Burdick, "The Relative Importance of Various Promotional Elements in Different Industrial Purchase Situations," *Journal of Advertising* 16, no. 4 (1987), 25–33.

47. Thomas A. Petit and Martha R. McEnally, "Putting Strategy into Promotion Mix Decisions," *The Journal of Consumer Marketing* 2 (winter 1985), 41–47.
48. Joseph W. Ostrow, "The Advertising/Promotion Mix: A Blend or a Tangle," *AAAA Newsletter,* August 1988, 7.
49. Quoted in Sally Goll Beatty, "Auto Makers Bet Campaigns Will Deliver Even If They Can't," *The Wall Street Journal Online,* October 13, 1997, http://online.wsj.com.
50. Tim Ambler, *Marketing and the Bottom Line: The New Metrics of Corporate Wealth* (London: Pearson Education Limited, 2000), especially Appendix A.
51. Adapted from "Directory of Marketing Industry Associations," *Promo's 8th Annual Sourcebook 2001,* 255–256.

CHAPTER 2

Marcom's Challenges: Enhancing Brand Equity, Influencing Behavior, and Being Accountable

Marcom Challenge: Harley-Davidson—An Iron Horse for Rugged Individualists

Brand managers at Harley-Davidson Motor Co. ran a magazine ad several years ago that captured the essence of this company's famous motorcycles. The ad depicted a driver-less Harley-Davidson motorcycle on an open road in the American West in a fashion reminiscent of a wild mustang in a similar scene. The ad's headline declared, "Even Cows Kick Down the Fence Once in a While," and was supported with copy stating:

It's right there in front of you, Road, wind, country. A Harley-Davidson motorcycle. In other words, freedom. A chance to live on your own terms for a while . . . Anyone who's been there knows: Life is better on the outside.

This ad did not tout product features for which the Harley-Davidson is known or functional benefits such as power and performance. It simply represented the sense of freedom, independence, and even rebelliousness ("Life is better on the outside") that a prospective purchaser might desire in owning this brand and driving the open roads. The message was subtle but clear: if you cherish freedom, independence, and perhaps a sense of being a kindred spirit with others of like mind, then Harley-Davidson is the motorcycle for you. The cowboy spirit was encapsulated in this positioning, which tacitly equated Harley motorcycles with horses. (Harley-Davidson equals "iron horse.") Potential purchasers of Harley motorcycles probably as youngsters envisioned themselves riding horses in America's Old West.[1]

What makes Harley-Davidson motorcycles such a unique and strong brand, indeed a brand of virtual iconic status? Informed observers and students of brand marketing would suggest that Harley, more so than most brands, has a deep emotional connection with present and prospective owners.[2] As captured in the previous description of a Harley advertisement, the brand has been marketed as and has virtually become synonymous with American culture and values of personal freedom, rebelliousness, and rugged individualism.[3] This reputation is not due to any single advertisement but rather has been cultivated for decades by Harley's marketing people when using multiple touch points (recall discussion in Chapter 1) and telling a consistent brand story. For example, during World Wars I and II, much of Harley's production was dedicated to supplying U.S. and allied troops with motorcycles. This served to establish the company's reputation for producing high-quality and reliable products and situated the brand securely in mainstream American culture when returning troops, who had a strong affinity for this uniquely American brand, passed along their feelings to fellow Americans.

Harley also has created a sense of brand community among owners of its brand, who share strong comradeship.[4] Harley-Davidson has created this sense of community through a variety of efforts that have touched its customers in many ways: by conducting special events and races, through offering tours of production facilities, by holding bike rallies, through licensing its brand name on various other products (e.g., a Barbie Biker doll), and, perhaps most of all, by forming the Harley Owners Group (H.O.G.) that counts among its membership 650,000 people worldwide. In fact, when Harley celebrated its 100th anniversary in 2003, over 250,000 individuals from around the world came to Milwaukee, Wisconsin, to participate in the big party. Needless to say, there are few brands anywhere in the world that have such loyal and devoted followers. This following translates into a level of brand equity that places Harley-Davidson in the top 25 of 1,000 brands rated by business leaders.[5]

CHAPTER OBJECTIVES

After reading this chapter you should be able to:

1

Explain the concept of brand equity from both the company's and the customer's perspectives.

2

Describe the positive outcomes that result from enhancing brand equity.

3

Present a model of brand equity from the customer's perspective.

4

Examine how marcom efforts must influence behavior and achieve financial accountability.

Desired Outcomes of Marcom Efforts

The previous chapter introduced the philosophy and practice of integrated marketing communications (IMC) and then presented a framework for thinking about all aspects of the marcom process. You will recall that this framework included four components: (1) a set of fundamental decisions (targeting, positioning, etc.), (2) a group of implementation decisions (mixing elements, creating messages, etc.), (3) two types of outcomes resulting from these decisions (enhancing brand equity and affecting behavior), and (4) a regimen for evaluating marcom results and taking corrective action. This chapter focuses on the third component in this framework, namely, the desired outcomes of marcom efforts.

The basic issues addressed in this chapter are these: What can marketing communicators do to enhance the equity of their brands and, beyond this, affect the behavior of their present and prospective customers? Also, how can marketing communicators justify their investments in advertising, promotions, and other marcom elements and demonstrate financial accountability? As described in the *Marcom Challenge,* Harley-Davidson has created tremendous equity for it motorcycles. But having people think favorable thoughts about this brand and harbor warm feelings is not enough. The marketing people at Harley-Davidson must encourage non-owners to purchase Harley cycles rather than other brands. And, it is critical that first-time purchasers of Harley motorcycles later become repeat purchasers when again in the market for a newer, perhaps bigger, more expensive "hog." The present chapter first discusses the concept of brand equity and explores this topic from both company and customer perspectives. A following section then devotes treatment to the importance of affecting behavior. As part of this latter topic, discussion is devoted to the concept of accountability introduced in the previous chapter and to measures, or metrics, to assess marcom performance.

The Concept of Brand Equity

The term "brand" is at the root of brand equity. A **brand** represents a "name, term, sign, symbol, or design, or a combination of them intended to identify the goods and services of one seller or group of sellers and to differentiate them from those of competition."[6] A brand thus exists when a product, retail outlet, or service receives its own name, term, sign, symbol, design, or any particular combination of these elements. Without a recognizable brand, a product is but a mere commodity. Many marcom experts are of the mind-set that all products and services can be branded. One observer has even claimed that the word "commodity" is an open admission of marketing bankruptcy.[7]

But a brand is more than *just* a name, term, symbol, and so on. A brand is everything that one company's particular offering stands for in comparison to other brands in a category of competitive products. A brand represents a set of values that its marketers, senior company officials, and other employees consistently embrace and communicate for an extended period.[8] For example, Volvo is virtually synonymous with safety; Crayola crayons stand for fun; Absolut vodka encapsulates hipness; Harley-Davidson embodies freedom and rugged individualism; Sony represents high quality and dependability; Chanel No. 5 means eloquence; and Rolex watches represent master craftsmanship and sophistication. Each of these brands has embraced and communicated a particular set of values for many years. All of these brands possess high equity because consumers believe these brands have the ability and willingness to deliver on their brand promises.[9]

Brand equity has been defined in different ways, and various approaches have been developed to measure it.[10] The concept of brand equity can be considered either from the perspective of the organization that owns a brand or from the vantage point of the customer. We will devote more discussion to brand equity from the customer perspective, but it will be useful to first examine the concept from the point of view of the marketing organization that owns a brand. Although many organizations own and market brands, including not-for-profit organizations as well as business firms, for convenience we will refer hereafter to firms rather than organizations in toto.

© Susan Van Etten

A Firm-Based Perspective on Brand Equity

The firm-based viewpoint of brand equity focuses on outcomes extending from efforts to enhance a brand's value to its various stakeholders. As the value, or equity of a brand increase, various positive outcomes result. These include (1) achieving a higher market share, (2) increasing brand loyalty, (3) being able to charge premium prices, and (4) earning a revenue premium.[11] The first two outcomes are straightforward and require no further discussion. Simply put, higher equity brands earn greater levels of customer loyalty and achieve higher market shares. The third outcome, being able to charge premium prices, means that a brand's elasticity of demand becomes less elastic as its equity increases. Phrased differently, brands with more equity can charge higher prices than brands with less equity. Consider household brands of paint, such as Sears brand versus Martha Stewart or Ralph Lauren brands. The quality differential between the Sears brand and the "designer" brands likely is considerably less than is the premium-price differential that the designer brands command. This is brand equity in action.

The fourth outcome, namely, earning a revenue premium, is an especially interesting result of achieving higher levels of brand equity. **Revenue premium** is defined as the revenue differential between a branded item and a corresponding private labeled item. With revenue equaling the product of brand's net price × volume, a branded good enjoys a revenue premium over a corresponding private labeled item to the degree it can charge a higher price and/or generate greater sales volume. In equation form, the revenue premium for brand *b* compared to a corresponding private labeled item, *pl*, is as follows:

$$\text{Revenue premium}_b = (\text{volume}_b)(\text{price}_b) - (\text{volume}_{pl})(\text{price}_{pl}) \tag{2.1}$$

It has been demonstrated that grocery brands possessing higher equity generate higher revenue premiums. In turn, there is a strong positive correlation between the revenue premiums brands enjoy and the market shares they realize.[12] The ability to charge higher prices and generate greater sales volume is due in large part to marcom efforts that build favorable images for well-known brands. In other words, many private-label products—which are items that carry the names of retail outlets—possess levels of quality that are equivalent to manufacturers' national brands; nevertheless, many consumers prefer the more expensive national brands and buy them regularly rather than switching to private brands. These national brands thus enjoy a revenue premium because they possess higher equity, which is a tribute to effective marcom efforts.

A Customer-Based Perspective on Brand Equity

From the perspective of the customer—whether a B2B customer or a B2C consumer—a brand possesses equity to the extent that customers/consumers are familiar with the brand and have stored in their memory warehouses favorable, strong, and unique brand associations.[13] That is, brand equity from the customer's perspective consists of two forms of brand-related knowledge: *brand awareness* and *brand image*. For example, Adidas, the German brand of athletic shoes and apparel, substantially increased its advertising budget one year by a whopping 25 percent over the previous year's budget. Adidas' director of sales and marketing explained that this increase was designed to raise consumer awareness of the Adidas name and pound home the message that Adidas is an authentic and high-performance athletic shoe.[14] You will note that he does not refer to brand equity per se, but this is precisely what he's talking about in reference to raising awareness and conveying a desired performance image for the Adidas brand.

Figure 2.1 graphically portrays the two dimensions of brand knowledge—awareness and image—and then delineates each dimension into its specific components. The subsequent discussion describes each dimension in detail. It will be useful before reading on to thoroughly examine this figure.

Brand Awareness

Brand awareness is an issue of whether a brand name comes to mind when consumers think about a particular product category and the ease with which the name is evoked. Stop reading for a moment and consider all the brands of toothpaste that come immediately to your mind. (Now stop reading.) Probably Crest and Colgate came to mind, because these brands are the market share leaders among American brands of toothpaste. Perhaps you also thought of Aquafresh, Mentadent, and Arm & Hammer insofar as these brands also obtain a large share of toothpaste purchases. But did you consider Close-Up, Pepsodent, or Aim? Maybe so; probably not. These brands are not nearly as widely known or frequently purchased as are their more successful counterparts. As such, they have

Figure 2.1

A Customer-Based Brand Equity Framework

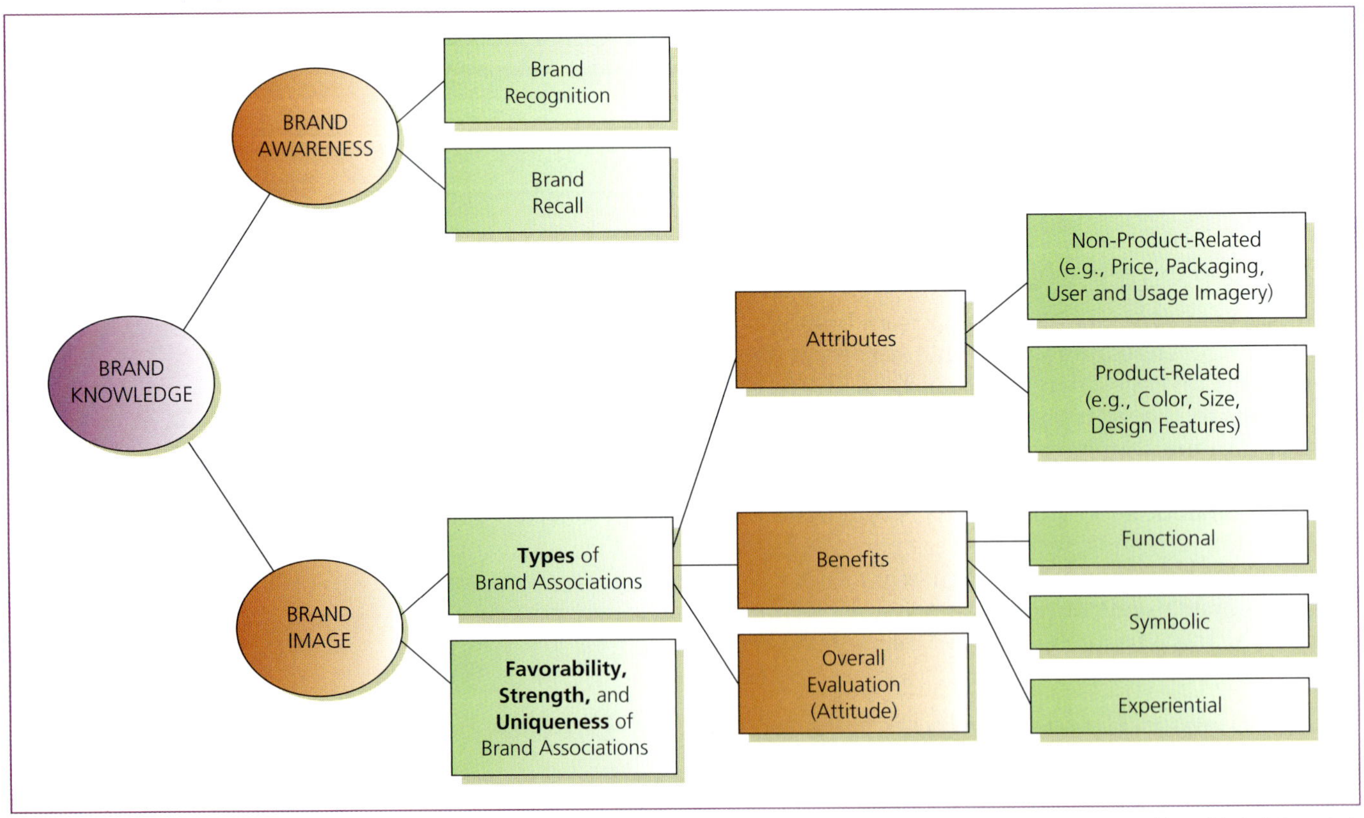

Source: Adapted from Kevin Lane Keller, "Conceptualizing, Measuring, and Managing Customer-Based Brand Equity," *Journal of Marketing* 57 (January 1993), 7.

less brand equity than, say, Colgate and Crest. Now repeat the same exercise for brands of athletic footwear. Your short list probably contains Nike, Reebok, Adidas, and maybe New Balance. What about K-Swiss, Vans, Converse, and Asics? Again, these latter brands possess lower levels of awareness for most people and, as such, have less equity vis-à-vis a brand such as Nike.

Brand awareness is the basic dimension of brand equity. From the vantage point of an individual consumer, a brand has no equity unless the consumer is at least aware of the brand. Achieving brand awareness is the initial challenge for new brands. Maintaining high levels of brand awareness is the task faced by all established brands.

Figure 2.1 shows two levels of awareness: brand recognition and recall. *Brand recognition* reflects a relatively superficial level of awareness, whereas *brand recall* indicates a deeper form of awareness. Consumers may be able to identify a brand if it is presented to them on a list or if hints/cues are provided. However, fewer consumers are able to retrieve a brand name from memory without any reminders. It is this deeper level of brand awareness—recall—to which marketers aspire. Through effective and consistent marcom efforts, some brands are so well known that virtually every living person of normal intelligence can recall the brand. For example, if asked to mention names of luxury automobiles, most people would include Mercedes-Benz on the list. Asked to name brands of athletic footwear, most people would mention Nike, Reebok, and perhaps Adidas. The marcom imperative is thus to move brands from a state of unawareness, to recognition, on to recall, and ultimately to top-of-mind awareness (TOMA). This pinnacle of brand-name awareness (i.e., TOMA status) exists when your company's brand is the first brand that consumers recall when thinking about brands in a particular product category. Figure 2.2 illustrates this brand-awareness progression.

It is important to note that it is not just consumer-oriented (B2C) firms that must be concerned with building brand awareness. A survey of B2B marketing personnel determined that the vast majority of these practitioners consider the

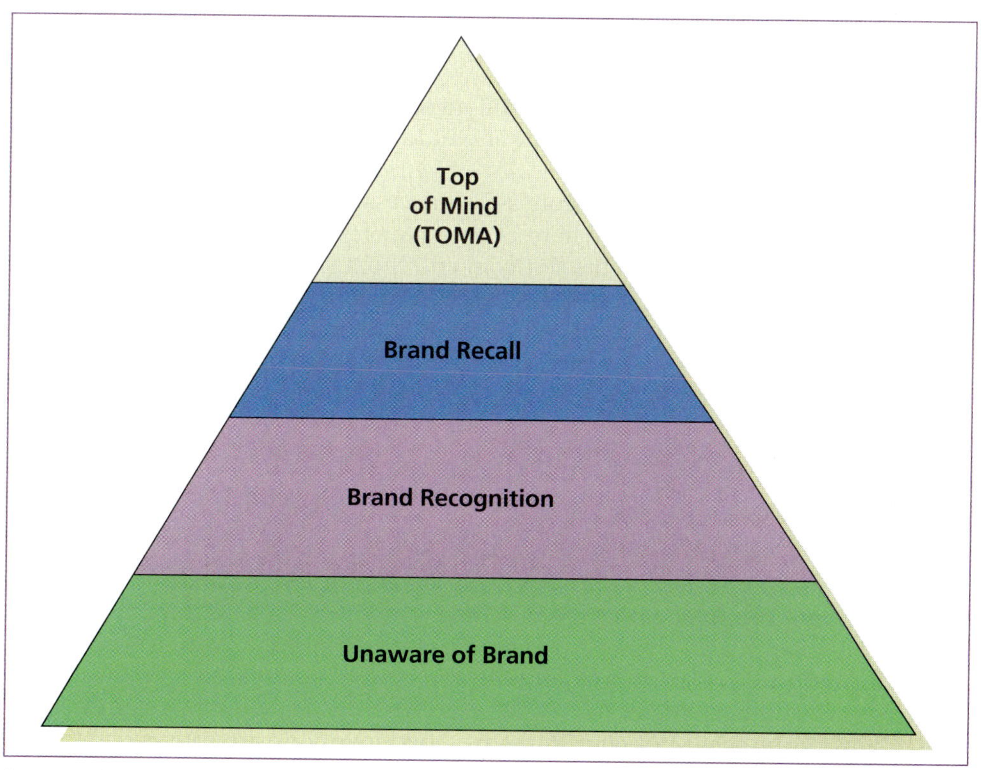

Figure 2.2
The Brand Awareness Pyramid

Source: David A. Aaker, Managing Brand Equity (New York: Free Press, 1991), 62.

When Brand Marketers Must Deal with Unfavorable Country Images

global focus

Brands are marketed by companies that typically are identified with the identities and images of the countries in which they originate. For example, Volkswagen markets an automobile under the brand name Passat. Consumers' images of the Passat are affected by Passat's own product features and also by Volkswagen's reputation and of Germany's. Because Volkswagen mostly has a positive image, stemming in large part from the historical success of the Beetle, and Germany is known as a country of fine craftsmen and sophisticated industry, Passat benefits from these positive associations. But what about a brand that is associated with a country that does not possess a favorable image for manufacturing and marketing products in general or those in a specific category?

Consider the case of China. Though China is well known and much admired for making low-cost and good-quality products that are outsourced by companies in other countries, China is not known for its domestic companies that produce and market branded products of their own. Think for a moment: can you identify a single brand that you purchase which carries a Chinese brand name? I suspect you're having difficulty naming a single brand. Comparatively, if you were asked to name well-known brands marketed by Japanese companies, you could easily bring to mind the names of quite a few brands.

Many Chinese companies are in process of dealing with their country's image problem and attempting to market products globally under their own brand names. Consider the case of TCL Corp., which is a large electronics firm that manufactures TV sets marketed under the names of many well-known companies. TCL is in process of beginning to manufacture and market products under its own brand name. It desires to turn itself into a household name first in Indonesia, where entry barriers for new products are relatively minimal, and then elsewhere in Asia and around the world. Successful TV brands in Indonesia include Japan's Sony and Sharp brands and Korea's Samsung. Though all of these brands are respected, price-conscious Indonesian consumers are receptive to alternative brands offering good value for the money.

This represents the opportunity for TCL. Rather than spending heavily on advertising, officials at TCL decided they could be most successful in Indonesia by bypassing retailers and selling directly to consumers. The company offers a three-year warranty, which is the longest on the market, and provides excellent customer service. For example, repairmen are at customers' homes within 24 hours of being contacted and, if necessary, provide a loaner TV until the damaged model can be repaired. These strategies seem to be working, and TCL is making inroads on its Japanese and Korean competitors. However, it may be many years before a Chinese company can successfully market its brands in countries such as Japan, France, Canada, and the United States. Yet, older readers of this book (translation: professors) can recall with great surprise the ascendancy of Japanese brands. It has only been 40 years or so since Japan was known for little else than producing trinkets and low-quality products. Now, numerous Japanese brands are world renowned, and the one brand with the greatest equity in the world may be Japan's own Sony.

SOURCE: Adapted from Chris Prystay, "Can China Sell the World On Its Own Brands?" *The Wall Street Journal Online*, December 18, 2003, http://online.wsj.com (accessed December 18, 2003).

major goal of B2B advertising is to create awareness of a new product or brand. These same practitioners also believe that building brand image is another goal of B2B marcom efforts.[15]

Although building brand awareness is a necessary step toward brand equity enhancement, it is insufficient. There is no better testament to this claim than a short history lesson relating to the dot-com craze that started in the late 1990s and basically came to a crash by the early 2000s. Who could forget the go-go days of the Internet "land rush" that extended from about 1998 until early 2000.[16] During the Internet's heyday, it seemed that every Tom, Dick, and Harry came up with an idea for a new form of e-tailing. Coming into existence was one dot-com company after another, most of which eventually went belly up.

What was the model for forming these dot-com businesses? At the risk of oversimplification, it was something like the following. A businessperson—or, as likely, a businessperson wanna-be who had little experience in "old-economy" business—came up with the idea of marketing on the Internet a product or service that heretofore was available only from a brick-and-mortar retailer. This individual then sought capitalization from a venture capitalist. Gobs of money in hand, the new e-tailer realized that success required primarily two achievements: being the first (or second) to market with the new e-tailing idea and spending a lot on advertising to create brand awareness. We thus observed huge advertising expenditures from these dot-com start-ups, often involving advertising on expensive programs such as the Super Bowl. (A large percentage of all commercials placed on the 2000 Super Bowl were for dot-com companies. But by 2001 only a few dot-com companies advertised on this hugely expensive extravaganza.) You might be thinking, what's wrong with this approach?

The problem, in short, is that most of the dot-com companies spent large sums of money on advertising (not a problem per se), but they didn't invest adequately in building a brand (this *is* a problem). Investing in and building a brand is a matter of identifying a reason for the brand's being—its underlying positioning statement and point of distinction from competitive offerings—and then promoting that point of distinction on a consistent basis. In other words, many of the dot-com companies spent heavily on advertising to create awareness, but they failed to build strong and favorable brand images. A spokesman from Briefing.com, an investment site, characterized a fatal flaw that he observed with most dot-coms' approach to business:

Because the marketing budget is only driving short-term name recognition and site traffic rather than building an established brand, sales growth is highly correlated with growth in the marketing budget. But a marketing budget cannot remain at a dollar of ads for each dollar of sales indefinitely. The business model assumes that the initial marketing drive builds self-sustaining growth in sales, which eventually overtake the marketing budget.[17]

The failed brand-building efforts by dot-com companies is stated even more compellingly by marketing consultant Kevin Clancy in the following passage:

For a long time, etailers believed that marketing and brand building were relatively easy. Go "first to market" with a rave new Internet concept and "grab land." Create a site so cool that the viral marketing—efforts that spread information about a company like a virus—goes wild. Then mix it up with requisite brand juice—edgy brand names, beautiful logos, clever tag lines, big-ticket promotions to lure people to Web sites, rave launch parties, non-stop publicity, and lots and lots of advertising. But drinking brand juice gets you about as close to building a brand as reading bumper stickers gets you to spiritual enlightenment. Style over substance cannot build a brand. Simply put, a brand is ultimately based on more than marketing communications alone. Product quality, customer service, employee communications, management vision and leadership, and social responsibility all influence a brand's reputation.[18]

Brand Image

The second dimension of consumer-based brand knowledge is a brand's image. *Brand image* can be thought of in terms of the types of associations that come to the customer's or consumer's mind (for reading ease, just *consumer* hereafter) when contemplating a particular brand. An *association* is simply the particular thoughts and feelings that a consumer has about a brand, much in the same fashion that we have thoughts and feelings about other people. For example, what thoughts/feelings come immediately to mind when you think of your best friend? You undoubtedly associate your friend with certain features, strengths, and perhaps frailties. Likewise, brands are linked in our memories with specific thought-and-feeling associations. As shown in Figure 2.1, these associations can be conceptualized in terms of *type, favorability, strength,* and *uniqueness.*

To illustrate these points, it will be helpful to consider a specific brand and the associations that a particular consumer has stored in memory for this brand. (It will be instructive to refer back to Figure 2.1 before reading the following description.) Consider the case of Henry and the McDonald's fast-food chain. Now a 27-year-old college graduate living in Chicago, Henry has been eating at McDonald's since he was only two years old. He can be described as a life-long lover of fast-food and McDonald's in particular. His mouth virtually salivates (à la Pavlov's dog) when the name McDonald's is mentioned. He vividly remembers going to a McDonald's in his home town with his parents and siblings. Nothing was more enjoyable than going to their local McDonald's on a cool autumn day after raking leaves and doing other chores. Ronald McDonald, the golden arches, and the pungent smell of burgers and fries are some of the thoughts that immediately enter his mind. He especially loves McDonald's fries and considers them superior to those available in other chains. He also likes the simple décor that is common to McDonald's. And he can't forget all of the good times that he and his high school friends had when enjoying each other's company after school or following football and basketball games. To this day Henry loves McDonald's. About the only thing he dislikes is the fact that clerks sometimes are poorly trained, inefficient, and not particularly friendly.

All of these thoughts and feelings represent *types* of associations in Henry's memory about McDonald's. All of these associations, with the exception of occasional mediocre service, represent *favorable* links with McDonald's as far as Henry is concerned. These associations are held *strongly* in Henry's memory. Some of the associations are *unique* in comparison to other fast-food chains. Only McDonald's has golden arches and Ronald McDonald. No other fast-food chain has, in Henry's mind, fries that taste nearly as good as McDonald's.

We can see from this illustration that Henry associates McDonald's with various *attributes* (e.g., golden arches), *benefits* (e.g., great tasting fries), and that he possesses an overall favorable evaluation, or *attitude,* toward this brand. These associations for Henry are held strongly and are favorable and somewhat unique. McDonald's would love to have millions of Henrys in its market, which it undoubtedly does. To the extent that Henry is prototypical of other consumers, it can be said that McDonald's has high brand equity. In contrast to McDonald's, many brands have relatively little equity. This is because consumers are (1) only faintly aware of these brands or, worse yet, are completely unaware of them or (2) even if aware, do not hold strong, favorable, and unique associations about these brands.

Figure 2.3

Illustration of a Sincere Brand

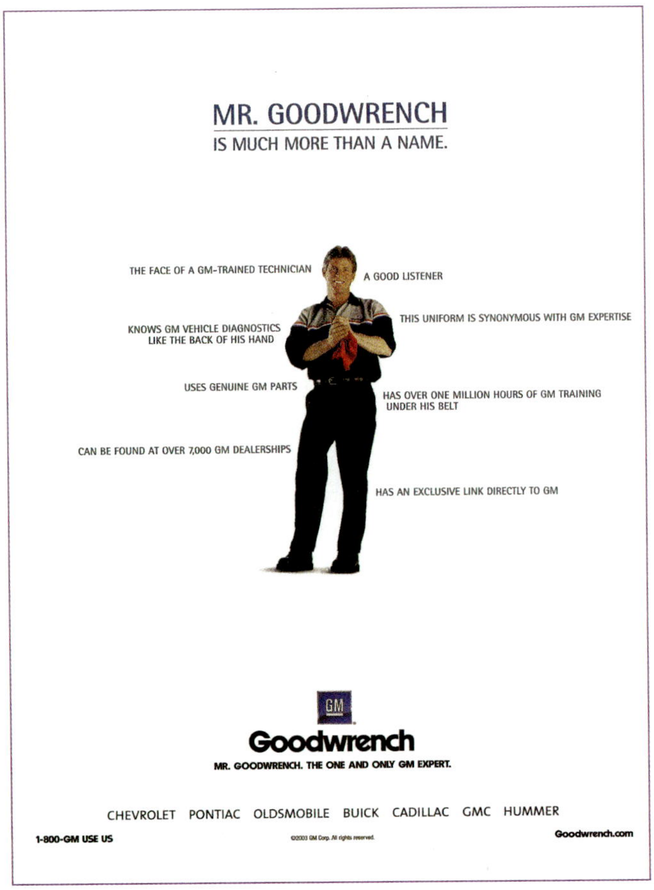

Although a brand's image is based on a variety of associations that consumers have developed over time, brands—just like people—can be thought of as having their own unique personalities. Research has identified five personality dimensions that describe most brands: sincerity, excitement, competence, sophistication, and ruggedness.[19] That is, brands can be described as possessing some degree of each of these dimensions, ranging from "the dimension doesn't describe the brand at all" to "the dimension captures the brand's essence." For example, one brand may be regarded as high in sincerity and competence but low in sophistication, excitement, and ruggedness. Another brand may be considered to epitomize sophistication and excitement but regarded as lacking on all other dimensions. The five brand-related personality dimensions are now described and illustrated. Bear in mind that each illustration attempts to capture a single personality dimension when in fact brands are multidimensional with respect to their personality characteristics—just like people.

1. **Sincerity**—This dimension includes brands that are down-to-earth, honest, wholesome, and cheerful. Sincerity is precisely the personality that General Motors (GM) has attempted to create for its repair services as personified by the hypothetical "Mr. Goodwrench," who represents the name and "face," the sincere persona of the trained technicians who work in thousands of GM dealerships (Figure 2.3).
2. **Excitement**—Brands scoring high on the excitement dimension are perceived as daring, spirited, imaginative, and up-to-date. The Hummer (Figure 2.4) typifies

Figure 2.4 Illustration of an Exciting Brand

an exciting brand. Of course, it also is a rugged brand, which suggests that it, like most brands, has a multidimensional personality.

3. **Competence**—Brands scoring high on this personality dimension are considered reliable, intelligent, and successful. In the automobile category, there are few brands perceived as more competent than Toyota (Figure 2.5). Toyotas are not particularly exciting or rugged, but consumers regard them as sincere and competent. J. D. Power, an organization that surveys automobile owners to assess levels of satisfaction, annually reports that Toyota is at or near the top of satisfaction ratings. This, of course, is due to the brand's overall success and reliability.
4. **Sophistication**—Brands that are considered upper class and charming score high on the sophistication dimension. Rolex watches (Figure 2.6) typify sophistication, which accounts for why people who wish to convey a sophisticated image often proudly wear Rolexes on their wrists.
5. **Ruggedness**—Rugged brands are thought of as tough and outdoorsy. Timberland (Figure 2.7) represents such a brand.

Figure 2.5
Illustration of a Competent Brand

How Can Brand Equity Be Enhanced?

In general, efforts to enhance a brand's equity are accomplished through the initial choice of positive brand identity (that is, via the selection of a good brand name and logo) but mostly through marketing and marcom programs that forge favorable, strong, and unique associations with the brand in the consumer's mind. It is impossible to overstate the importance of efforts to enhance a brand's equity. Brands that are high in quality and represent good value potentially possess high equity, but effective and consistent marcom efforts are needed to build on and maintain brand equity.

A favorable brand image does not happen automatically. Sustained marketing communications are generally required to create favorable, strong, and perhaps unique associations about the brand. For example, it could be claimed that one of the world's greatest brands, Coca-Cola, is little more than colored sugar water. This brand, nevertheless, possesses immense brand equity because its managers are ever mindful of the need for continual advertising executions that sustain the Coca-Cola story and build the image around the world. In the United States alone, the Coca-Cola Company in a recent year commanded 44 percent of the carbonated soft-drink market, which totals over $50 billion in revenue. Coke Classic (Coke) held an individual brand share of nearly 19 percent, whereas its nearest competitor, Pepsi, had about a 12 percent share.[20] Consumers don't buy this "colored sugar water" merely for its taste; they instead purchase a lifestyle and an image when selecting Coke over other available brands. It is effective advertising, exciting sales promotions, creative sponsorships, and other forms of marketing communications that are responsible for Coca-Cola's positive image and massive market share. For a fascinating review of a new technology called neuromarketing and an application to Coke and its major competitor, Pepsi, see the *IMC Focus* on page 42.

What actions can be taken to enhance a brand's equity? Because a brand's equity is a function of the favorability, strength, and uniqueness of associations held in consumers' memories, the simple answer is to forge stronger, more favorable, and unique associations. But this begs the question of how this is to be accom-

Figure 2.6
Illustration of a Sophisticated Brand

plished. In actuality, associations are created in a variety of ways, some of which are initiated by marketers (e.g., via advertising) and others that are not.[21] The following discussion identifies three ways by which brand equity is enhanced and labels these the (1) speak-for-itself approach, (2) message-driven approach, and (3) leveraging approach.

On the one hand, favorable (or perhaps unfavorable) associations are built merely by allowing the brand to "speak for itself." That is, by trying and using brands consumers learn how good (or bad) they are and what benefits they are (in)capable of delivering. Secondly, marcom practitioners in their various capacities can build (or attempt to build) advantageous associations via the dint of repeated claims about the features a brand possesses and/or the benefits it delivers. Such a tact is effective if the marcom message is creative, attention getting, and believable. This second brand-equity-building strategy can be thought of as the "message-driven approach." Needless to say, the "speak-for-itself" and "message-driven" approaches need not be independent; that is, consumers' associations related to a particular brand result both from what they've learned firsthand about a brand through usage and what they've acquired through exposure to the brand's marcom messages. There is a third equity-building strategy that is being used in increasingly competitive marketplaces. This is the "leveraging" strategy.[22]

Figure 2.7
Illustration of a Rugged Brand

Brand associations can be shaped and equity enhanced by leveraging positive associations already contained in the world of people, places, and "things" that are available to consumers. The culture and social systems in which marketing communications take place are loaded with meaning. Through socialization, people learn cultural values, form beliefs, and become familiar with the physical manifestations, or artifacts, of these values and beliefs. The artifacts of culture are charged with meaning, which is transferred from generation to generation. For example, the Lincoln Monument and Ellis Island are signs of freedom to Americans. To Germans and many other people throughout the world, the now-crumbled Berlin wall signified oppression and hopelessness. Comparatively, yellow ribbons signify crises and hopes for hostage release and the safe return of military personnel. Pink ribbons signal support for breast cancer victims. Red ribbons have grown into an international symbol of solidarity on AIDS. The Black Liberation flag with its red, black, and green stripes—representing blood, achievement, and the fertility of Africa—symbolizes civil rights.

Marketing communicators draw meaning from the *culturally constituted* world (i.e., the everyday world filled with artifacts such as the preceding examples) and transfer that meaning to consumer goods. Advertising is an especially important instrument of meaning transfer. The role of advertising in transferring meaning has been described in this fashion:

Advertising works as a potential method of meaning transfer by bringing the consumer good and a representation of the culturally constituted world together within the frame of a particular advertisement. . . . The known properties of the culturally constituted world thus come to reside in the unknown properties of the consumer good and the transfer of meaning from world to [consumer] good is accomplished.[23]

Stated alternatively, this account says that advertisers (as well as practitioners in other marcom capacities) can *leverage* meaning, or associations, for their brands by connecting them with other objects that already possess well-known meaning.

Neuromarketing and the Case of Why Coca-Cola Outsells Pepsi

imc focus

Coca-Cola (Coke) and Pepsi are two well-known carbonated beverages that have been marketed for over 100 years. These brands for decades have been locked in fierce battle, described sometimes as "the cola wars." One sensational battle began in 1975 when Pepsi sponsored a national taste test to determine which brand, Coke or Pepsi, is regarded as better tasting. Following this testing, Pepsi undertook an advertising campaign (called the "Pepsi Challenge") that directly compared Pepsi with Coke and claimed the research evidence (i.e., so-called "blind" taste tests) revealed that consumers prefer Pepsi over Coke. If in fact Pepsi is a better tasting beverage than Coke, why is Coca-Cola the higher selling and more popular beverage? For an answer, let's enter the world of neuromarketing and the technology of brain imaging.

Neuromarketing is a specific application of the field of brain research called neuroscience. Neuroscientists study activation of the brain to outside stimuli with the use of brain scanning machines that take functional magnetic resonance images (fMRIs) when individuals visually or otherwise employ their various senses (sight, taste, touch, etc.) upon exposure to stimuli. Brain scans with fMRI machines reveal which areas of the brain are most activated in response to external stimuli. With this brief description in mind, we can describe research conducted by a neuroscientist at the Baylor College of Medicine in Texas that might be described as the "21st Century Pepsi Challenge."

The scientist, Read Montague, performed this new-fangled Pepsi Challenge by scanning the brains of 40 study participants after they tasted intermittent squirts of Pepsi and Coke. When "blind" as to which brand they were tasting, Pepsi came out the clear winner. That is, the reward center of the brain, the ventral putamen, revealed a much stronger preference for Pepsi versus Coke when study participants were unaware of which brand they had tasted. However, this result flip flopped when Montague altered the testing procedure by informing participants the name of the brand they were about to taste. Now a different region of the brain was more activated and Coca-Cola was the winner in this non-blind taste test. In particular, activation in the medial prefrontal cortex—an area of the brain associated with cognitive functions such as thinking, judging, preference, and self-image—revealed that participants now preferred Coke. In short, with blind taste tests, Pepsi was the winner. With non-blind tests, Coke prevailed. What's going on?

The apparent answer is a difference in brand images, with Coke possessing the more attractive image earned through years of effective marketing and advertising effort. When participants knew they were tasting Coke, their preference for that brand was mediated by past experiences and positive associations of the brand matching their self-images—as reflected in the activation of the medial prefrontal cortex. When clueless of brand identity, the "raw" reward center of the brain, the ventral putamen, revealed Pepsi to be the winner, presumably because it is a somewhat better tasting soft drink. Most interesting is the fact that Coca-Cola's marcom efforts have enabled that brand to rise to the top. Past ad campaigns such as "It's the Real Thing," "I'd Like to Buy the World a Coke," and "Have a Coke and a Smile" have possibly resonated more positively with consumers than has Pepsi's marketing, which has concentrated more on aligning that brand with celebrities such as Michael Jackson and Britney Spears. In sum, this "21st century Pepsi Challenge" further demonstrates the importance of effective marcom efforts and the role that a positive brand image plays in determining brand equity and influencing consumer choices.

Sources: Edwin Colyer, "The Science of Branding," *Brandchannel,* March 15, 2004, http://brandchannel.com (accessed March 22, 2004); Clive Thompson, "There's a Sucker Born in Every Medial Prefrontal Cortex," The *New York Times,* October 26, 2003, http://rickross.com (accessed July 20, 2004); David Wahlberg, "Advertisers Probe Brains, Raise Fears," *The Atlanta Journal-Constitution,* February 1, 2004, http://cognitiveliberty.org (accessed July 20, 2004); Melani Wells, "In Search of the Buy Button," *Forbes.com,* September 1, 2003, http://forbes.com (accessed July 20, 2004); "The Cola Wars: Over a Century of Cola Slogans, Commercials, Blunders, and Coups," http://geocities.com/colacentury (accessed July 21, 2004).

Figure 2.8 provides an account of how a brand can leverage associations by connecting itself with (1) other brands, (2) places, (3) things, and (4) people. For example, a brand leverages positive associations when it is identified with a particular country that is known for, say, fine craftsmanship or when it employs an endorser that has an image that the brand itself would like to be known for. There are numerous ways for leveraging favorable brand associations, and Figure 2.8 is a good starting point for appreciating these options.

Among other forms of leveraging, Figure 2.8 shows how a brand can leverage associations from other brands. In recent years there have been a number of occurrences where two brands enter into an alliance that potentially serves to enhance both brands' equity and profitability. You need only look at your bank card (e.g., Visa) to see that it likely carries the name of an organization such as your college or university. The two have entered into an alliance, or a *co-branding relation,* for their mutual benefit. Rayovac (flashlights) is in partnership with Harley-Davidson (motorcycles) with a line of flashlights carrying the Harley-Davidson logo. Ocean Spray, the well-known marketer of cranberry products, has entered

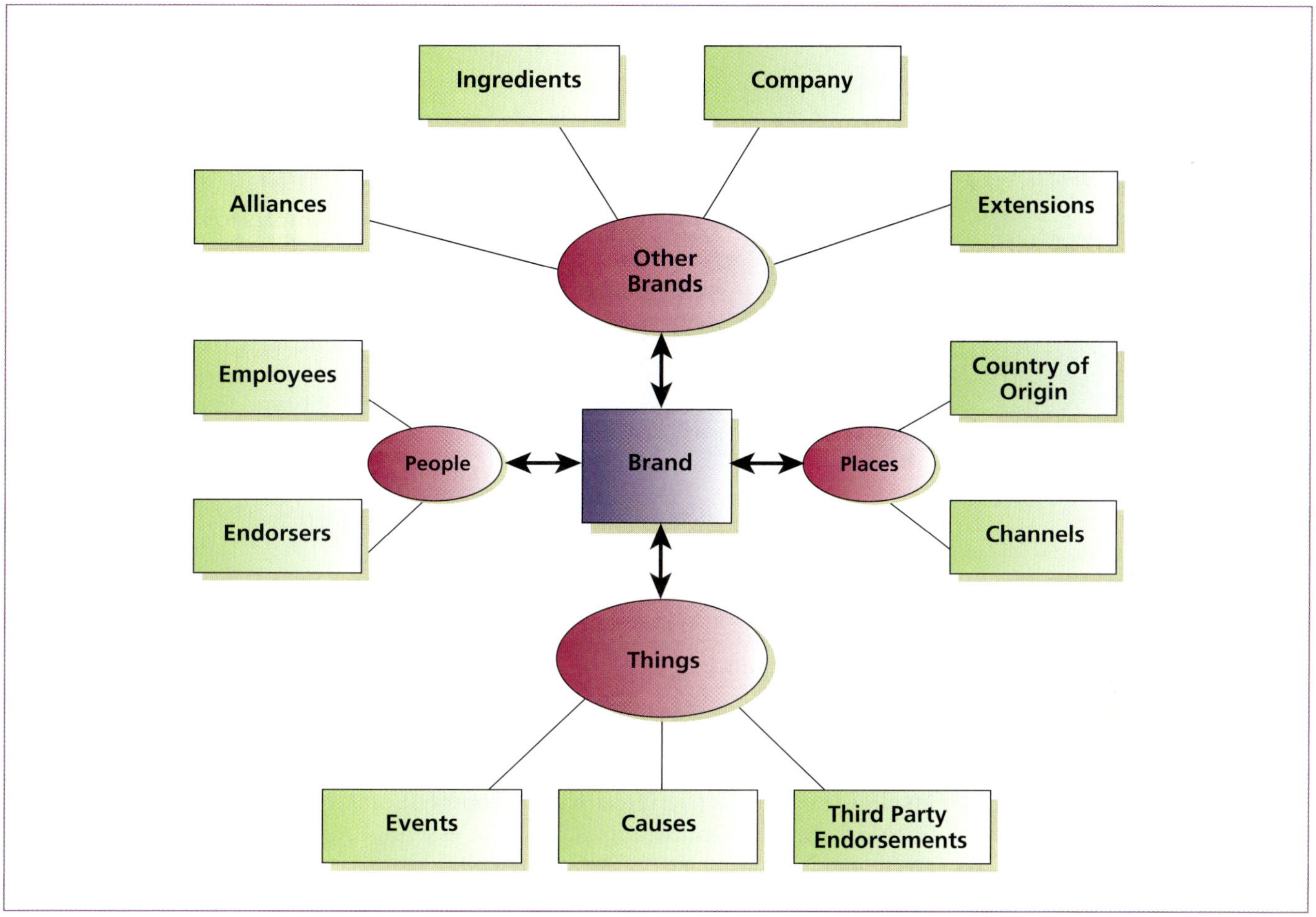

Source: Kevin Lane Keller, "Brand Synthesis: The Multidimensionality of Brand Knowledge," Journal of *Consumer Research* 29 (March 2003), 598. By permission of the University of Chicago Press.

Figure 2.8

Leveraging Brand Meaning from Various Sources

into branding alliances with a number of other famous branded products, including Post's Cranberry Almond Crunch cereal, Nabisco's Cranberry Newtons (cookies), and Kraft's Stove Top Stuffing with Cranberries.

The examples are virtually endless, but the common theme is that brands that enter into alliances do so on grounds that their images are similar, that they appeal to the same market segment, and that the co-branding initiative is mutually beneficial. The most important requirement for successful co-branding is that brands possess a common fit and that the combined marcom efforts maximize the advantages of the individual brands while minimizing the disadvantages.[24]

Ingredient branding is a special type of alliance between branding partners. For example, Lycra, a brand of spandex from DuPont, initiated a $10 million to $12 million global advertising effort to increase consumer ownership of jeans made with Lycra. Along the lines of the "Intel Inside" campaign, Lycra's advertising featured Lycra jeans by Levi Strauss, Diesel, DKNY, and other jean manufacturers. DuPont began this campaign in an effort to differentiate itself from cheaper unbranded spandex from Asia.[25] Other well-known instances of ingredient branding include various ski-wear brands that prominently identify the Gore-Tex fabric from which they are made and cookware makers that tout the fact that their skillets and other cookware items are made with DuPont's Teflon nonstick coating. Although ingredient branding is in many instances beneficial for both the ingredient and "host" brands, a potential downside for the host brand is that the equity of the ingredient brand might be so great that it overshadows the host brand. This situation would arise, for example, if skiers knew that their ski jacket was made of

© Susan Van Etten

Gore-Tex fabric but they had no awareness of the company that actually manufactured their jacket.

What Benefits Result from Enhancing Brand Equity?

One major by-product of efforts to increase a brand's equity is that consumer *brand loyalty* might also increase.[26] Indeed, long-term growth and profitability are largely dependent on creating and reinforcing brand loyalty. The following quote from two respected marketing practitioners sums up the nature and importance of brand loyalty:

While marketers have long viewed brands as assets, the real asset is brand loyalty. A brand is not an asset. Brand loyalty is the asset. Without the loyalty of its customers, a brand is merely a trademark, an ownable, identifiable symbol with little value. With the loyalty of its customers, a brand is more than a trademark. A trademark identifies a product, a service, a corporation. A brand identifies a promise. A strong brand is a trustworthy, relevant, distinctive promise. It is more than a trademark. It is a trustmark of enormous value. Creating and increasing brand loyalty results in a corresponding increase in the value of the trustmark.[27]

Research has shown that when firms communicate unique and positive messages via advertising, personal selling, promotions, events, and other means, they are able to differentiate their brands effectively from competitive offerings and insulate themselves from future price competition.[28]

Marketing communications plays an essential role in creating positive brand equity and building strong brand loyalty. However, this is not always accomplished with traditional advertising or other conventional forms of marketing communications. For example, Starbucks, the virtual icon for upscale coffee, does very little advertising, yet this brand has a near cult-like following. To a lesser degree, the same can be said for Red Bull energy drink. With worldwide sales exceeding $1 billion, the marketers of Red Bull rely more on word-of-mouth buzz and events than advertising for brand-building purposes.[29]

Roger Enrico, ex-CEO and chairman of PepsiCo, provides us with a fitting section conclusion in the following implicit description of the importance of that company's efforts to build the equity of its brands:

In my mind the best thing a person can say about a brand is that it's their favorite. That implies something more than simply they like the package, or the taste. It means they like the whole thing—the company, the image, the value, the quality, and on and on. So as we think about the measurements of our business, if we're only looking at this year's bottom line and profits, we're missing the picture. We should be looking at market share, but also at where we stand vis-à-vis our competitors in terms of consumer awareness and regard for our brands. You always know where you stand in the [profit and loss statement] because you see it every month. But what you need to know, with almost the same sense of immediacy, is where you stand with consumers and your customers.[30]

Characteristics of World-Class Brands

Some brands have such exceptional brand equity that they deserve the label "world class." The well-known EquiTrend survey by market research firm Harris Interactive is conducted biannually and includes responses from consumers who collectively, not individually, rate over 1,000 brands.[31] This survey asks respondents to rate a number of brands in terms of two dimensions: quality and salience.

Respondents rate a brand's *quality* by selecting a score ranging from 0 to 10, where 0 equals unacceptable/poor quality and 10 equals outstanding/extraordinary quality. *Salience,* which is a measure of brand awareness, represents the percentage of people who feel sufficiently well informed about a brand to rate it. A brand's salience score thus ranges between 0 percent to 100 percent. An *equity* score is determined by multiplying the quality and salience scores and dividing the product by 10 so that equity scores range between 0 and 100. Brands receiving high equity scores are both well known and perceived as high quality, whereas those receiving lower scores are either less known or are well known but have received low quality scores.

The most recent EquiTrend survey (at the time of this writing), reveals the 10 brands in Table 2.1 as the overall highest equity brands. Note carefully in Table 2.1 that the rankings are based on "quality" scores and not overall "equity" scores. Hence, Smithsonian Institution is ranked number 1 in terms of quality, but Hershey's Kisses have the top equity score at 79.6. Many of these brands (e.g., Craftsman tools, Discovery Channel, M&M's candies, Crayola crayons and markers, Bose stereo and speaker systems, and WD-40 spray lubricant) regularly appear in EquiTrend's top-10 rankings. Brands that receive high equity scores based on EquiTrend's measure tend to make straightforward promises to consumers and deliver on these promises over extended periods.[32] In other words, these brands are well known, possess strong and favorable associations in consumers' memories, and thus possess high brand equity.

Beyond these particular survey results, a thought leader in the area of branding and brand equity has identified 10 traits shared by the world's strongest brands:[33]

1. **The brand excels at delivering the benefits customers truly desire.** Consumers buying stereo equipment and speakers want a brand they can depend on for delivering impeccably clear music. Bose stereo and speaker systems unsurprisingly rates extremely high in quality (8.12), though its overall equity score suffers from a relatively low salience score (only 72 percent). It is little wonder that Bose regularly appears on EquiTrend's top-10 list.
2. **The brand stays relevant.** "Relevant" brands stay in touch with consumers' changing tastes, desire for change and excitement, and need for product improvements. For example, M&M's candies and Crayola crayons are continually introducing new colors, and the Discovery Channel regularly produces creative and exciting programs.
3. **The pricing system is based on consumers' perceptions of value.** Craftsman tools are not inexpensive compared to cheaper brands that can be purchased at many stores other than Sears, but the product price is justified in light of the high quality and dependability.
4. **The brand is properly positioned.** M&M's candies are positioned well against other candies. Only M&M's come in a variety of colors and have the unique

Table 2.1

Top Ten World-Class Brands Overall (Among 1,152 total brands included in the Spring 2003 survey)

Brand	Rank	Quality	Salience	Equity
Smithsonian Institution	1	8.23	79	64.9
Craftsman Tools	2	8.17	88	71.6
Crayola Crayons & Markers	3	8.12	94	76.2
Bose Stereo & Speaker Systems	4	8.12	72	58.7
Hershey's Kisses	5	8.08	99	79.6
Reynolds Wrap Aluminum Foil	6	8.08	97	78.6
M&M's Chocolate Candies	7	8.05	98	79.3
Discovery Channel	8	8.02	93	74.9
WD-40 Spray Lubricant	9	8.01	90	72.4
Ziploc Food Bags	10	7.98	98	77.9

Source: Spring 2003 EquiTrend® brand study by Harris Interactive®

shape. M&M's virtually stands for fun, and it is for this reason that children of all ages (from 3 to 83) love this simple little product.

5. **The brand is consistent.** A consistent brand is one that is not continually changing its positioning and always reinventing itself. Consumers learn to depend on the brand because it remains unchanged—a dependable old friend. All 10 brands in the EquiTrend survey personify consistency.
6. **The brand portfolio and hierarchy make sense.** Most brands are part of a company's brand portfolio. For example, automobile manufacturers market multiple models of BMWs, Toyotas, Fords, and so on. Successful brands are well coordinated such that the various offerings under the brand umbrella are not inconsistent with one another or in conflict.
7. **The brand makes use of and coordinates a full repertoire of marketing activities to build equity.** The essential point in this regard is that successful brands employ whatever marcom tools are needed in order to satisfy the brand's positioning strategy. This characteristic is very much in harmony with the IMC principles established in Chapter 1.
8. **The brand's managers understand what the brand means to consumers.** "If it's clear what customers like and don't like about a brand, and what core associations are linked to the brand, then it should also be clear whether any given action will dovetail nicely with the brand or create friction."[34] In other words, knowing the customer is essential to knowing your brand and determining which marcom efforts are needed to best position the brand. The managers of WD-40 spray lubricant know what consumers like about this brand and what they expect from it; thus, they are able to maximize sales volume primarily by simply advertising the brand as having innumerable household uses.
9. **The brand is given proper support, and that support is sustained over the long run.** In a word, world-class brands maintain their *momentum.* (Recall the discussion in Chapter 1 of momentum in context of the various implementation decisions.)
10. **The company monitors sources of brand equity.** Ongoing studies (brand audits, tracking studies) are essential for monitoring a brand's health. The need for such studies can be likened to the importance of middle-aged and older individuals having annual medical examinations. Annual exams determine whether changes have occurred in, say, one's heart condition compared to baseline measures from prior exams. An attending physician can thus determine whether a problem exists and whether corrective action is needed. Brand managers must in similar fashion expose their brands to annual (or more frequent) exams to detect potential problems and identify needed changes.

Affecting Behavior and Achieving Marcom Accountability

When discussing in Chapter 1 the principles underlying IMC, one major point of emphasis was that marcom efforts should be directed, ultimately, at affecting behavior rather than stopping with enhancing equity. Creating brand awareness and boosting brand image serve little positive effect unless individuals ultimately make purchases or engage in some other form of desired behavior—by "behavior" we mean that the customer takes some action such as contributing to a charitable organization, discontinuing smoking, voting for a political candidate, staying on a diet plan, attending a concert, and so on. All of these behaviors, or acts, contrast with pre-behavioral cognitions or emotions whereby one merely thinks that doing something is a good idea or feels good about the prospect of doing something. The proof of the behavioral pudding is in the *action.*

Marcom's eventual challenge is to influence behavior, whatever the nature of that behavior might be. To simplify the following discussion we will hereafter refer to behavior only in context of business organizations rather than talking about many different forms of behavior. From this perspective, behavior essentially equates to purchase behavior. Purchase behavior is, of course, a customer-based concept (i.e., customers buy, or purchase products and services). From the marketer's standpoint, desired behavior from customers corresponds to sales volume and revenue, with revenue representing the monetized equivalent of sales volume (i.e., volume × net price = revenue). Looked at in this manner, marcom's objective is to ultimately affect sales volume and revenue.

The effect of marcom, or of its specific elements such as advertising, can thus be gauged in terms of whether it generates a reasonable revenue return on the marcom investment. This idea of return on investment, which is well known to anyone who has taken a basic course in accounting, finance, or managerial economics, is referred to in marketing circles as **ROMI**, or *return on marketing investment.* In a world of increased accountability, as discussed in Chapter 1, it is imperative that marketing people in all capacities, including marcom practitioners, demonstrate that additional investments in, say, advertising yield returns that meet or exceed alternative applications of corporate funds. Chief executive officers (CEOs) as well as chief marketing officers (CMOs) and chief financial officers (CFOs) are increasingly asking, "What's my ROMI?"[35] The vast majority of marketing executives consider the measurement of marketing performance an important priority, and marketing academics along with practitioners are actively involved in devising ways to measure marketing performance so as to achieve financial accountability for marketing actions.[36] Two primary motivations underlie this increased focus on measuring marketing performance, as explained in the following quote:

First, greater demands for accountability on the marketing function from the CEO, the Board, and other executives mandate a greater focus on measurement. For a CMO to truly command an equal seat at the executive table, a CMO must define and deliver quantitative measurements for the corporation. And these metrics must be clearly and convincingly communicated to the appropriate audiences. A second, perhaps equally important driver is the imperative for a CMO to get better at what they do. As the budget battles become more frequent and uncomfortable, a CMO can make marketing a more effective organization only by measuring and understanding what is working and what isn't.[37]

JOB OUTLOOK

Market and survey researchers and analysts held close to 300,000 jobs in 2002. Private industry provided about 97 percent of salaried market research analyst jobs; because of the applicability of market research to many industries, market research analysts are employed in most industries. (*Occupational Outlook Handbook, 2004–05 Edition, U.S. DOL, http://www.bls.gov/oco/home.htm*)

Difficulty of Measuring Marcom Effectiveness

Though most marketing executives agree that measuring marketing performance is critically important, at the present time relatively few organizations are doing a sophisticated job. This is not because marketing executives are uninterested in determining what aspects of their marcom efforts are or are not working most effectively; rather, the problem resides with the difficulty of measuring marcom effectiveness. Several reasons account for this complexity: (1) obstacles in identifying an appropriate measure, or metric, of effectiveness; (2) complications with getting people throughout the organization to agree that a particular measure is the most appropriate; (3) snags with gathering accurate data to assess effectiveness; and (4) problems with determining the exact effect that specific marcom elements have on the measure that has been selected to indicate effectiveness.

Choosing a Metric

An initial problem is one of determining which specific measures (also called *metrics*) should be used to judge marcom effectiveness. Consider, for example, the case of an automobile company that has increased its annual marcom budget for a particular model by 25 percent over last year's budget. The company will advertise this particular model using a combination of TV, magazine, and online advertising. It also will sponsor a professional golf tournament and have a presence at several other sporting and entertainment events. It, moreover, will use an attractive rebate program to encourage consumers to buy sooner rather than postponing purchases. What metric(s) should the company use to gauge the effectiveness of its marcom efforts? Possible options include changes in *brand awareness* before and after the aggressive marcom program is undertaken, improved *attitudes* toward the automobile model, increased *purchase intentions,* and larger *sales volume* compared to last year's performance. None of these options is without problems. For example, awareness is a good measure of marcom effectiveness only if increases in awareness translate in some known proportion to sales increases; likewise, improved attitudes and purchase intentions are suitable measures only if they predictably turn into increased sales in this or subsequent accounting periods. And sales itself is an imperfect measure insofar as marcom efforts in the current accounting period may not improve sales volume measurably until a later period. In short, there typically is no magic bullet by which marcom effectiveness can be judged unambiguously and perfectly. All measures/metrics are flawed in some way.

The difficulty of determining how best to measure marketing's return on investment is illustrated by a recent study conducted of its membership by the Association of National Advertisers (ANA).[38] In response to a key question asking respondents to identify which metric is closest to their company's definition of marketing ROI, more than 15 versions of ROMI were revealed. It is evident from this study that companies differ widely in their concept of how to measure ROMI. The five metrics in most frequent usage are these: (1) incremental sales revenue generated by marketing activities (66 percent of respondents identified this metric), (2) changes in brand awareness (57 percent), (3) total sales revenue generated by marketing activities (55 percent), (4) changes in purchase intention (55 percent), and (5) changes in attitudes toward the brand (51 percent).[39] You will note that these percentages sum to greater than 100 because some companies use multiple metrics. It also is noteworthy that three of the leading metrics do not even involve sales revenue but instead are based on pre-sales diagnostics: changes in brand awareness, attitudes, and purchase intentions.

Gaining Agreement

As generally is the case when intelligent people representing different organizational interests are asked to settle in on a particular solution to a problem, there generally is no consensus. This is not because people are necessarily uncooperative; rather, individuals from different backgrounds and with varied organizational interests often see the "world" differently or operate with varying ideas of what best indicates suitable performance. Whereas finance people are inclined to view things in terms of *discounted cash flows* and *net present values* of investment decisions, marketing executives have historically tended to use measures of brand awareness, image, and equity to indicate success.[40] Hence, arriving at a suitable system for measuring marcom performance requires agreement as to how performance is to be assessed.

Collecting Accurate Data

Whatever the measure chosen, any effort to meaningfully assess marcom performance necessitates having data that are reliable and valid. Returning to the automobile illustration, suppose that sales volume is the metric used to judge the effectiveness of this year's marcom efforts. It would seem a simple matter to accurately assess how many units of the automobile model have been sold during the present fiscal period. However, some of the units sold this year are residual orders from last. Also, a number of the units sold are fleet sales to companies that are entirely independent of the marcom efforts directed to consumers. It also is problematic as to how sales should be calculated, whether in terms of units sold in to dealers or units moved through to end-user consumers. All in all, collecting accurate data is no slam dunk.

Calibrating Specific Effects

Our hypothetical automobile company will employ several marcom tools (various advertising media, several events, and periodic rebates) to "move" automobiles to consumers. Ultimately, brand managers and other marketing executives are interested in knowing more than just how effective the overall marcom program was. They also need to identify the relative effectiveness of individual program elements so that even better decisions can be made in the future as to how best to allocate resources. This is, perhaps, the most complicated problem of all. How much relative effect does each program element have on, say, sales volume compared to the effects of other elements? A technique called *marketing-mix modeling* is increasingly being used for this purpose.

Assessing Effects with Marketing-Mix Modeling

To understand and appreciate the nature and role of marketing-mix modeling, let's return to our example of the automobile marketer that increased its marcom budget for a particular model by 25 percent over last year's budget. To advertise and promote the brand, the following individual activities, or elements, will be used: (1) advertising via TV, magazine, and online media; (2) sponsorship of a professional golf tournament along with several other sporting and entertainment events; and (3) use of an attractive rebate program to encourage consumers to buy now rather than later.

Each of these activities can be thought of as individual elements constituting the brand's marketing mix. The issue that marketing-mix modeling addresses is this: what effect does each element have in affecting this automobile model's sales volume? Marketing-mix modeling employs well known statistical techniques (e.g., multivariate regression analysis) to estimate the effects that the various advertising and promotion elements have in driving sales volume. Though it is beyond the scope of this text to offer a technical explanation of regression analysis or of other more sophisticated analytic techniques used in marketing-mix modeling, the conceptual underpinnings are straightforward. Let us demonstrate this approach using the following multivariate regression equation:

$$Y = \beta_0 + \beta_1 X_1 + \beta_2 X_2 + \beta_3 X_3 + \beta_4 X_4 + \beta_5 X_5 + \beta_6 X_6 \quad (2.2)$$

where:

Y = Estimated sales of the particular automobile model in a specific period.
X_1 = TV advertising
X_2 = Magazine advertising
X_3 = Online advertising
X_4 = Sponsorship of golf tourney
X_5 = Sponsorship of other, minor events
X_6 = Rebate program
–0 = Baseline sales without any advertising or promotions
–1, –2, –3, –4, –5, –6 = Parameter estimates of the individual effects the various advertising and promotion elements have on sales

In order to employ marketing-mix modeling, a relatively long series of longitudinal data—say, for a two-year period—is required. The data for each period would include the level of sales during that period (Y) along with corresponding advertising and promotion expenditures for each program element (X_1 through X_6). Imagine, for example, that our hypothetical automobile company records weekly sales and has meticulous records of precisely how much is spent weekly on each advertising and promotion element. Records of this sort would produce a set of 104 observations (52 weeks × 2 years), which would provide a sufficient number of observations to produce reliable parameter estimates for the various program elements.

Resulting from the analytic aspect of marketing-mix modeling is statistical evidence regarding the relative effects that each program element has had in driving automobile sales. Managers learn from such analysis which elements are outperforming others and can use this statistical information to shift budgets from program element to element. Obviously, more effective elements (as revealed by larger parameter estimates) would in the future receive relatively larger budgets vis-à-vis the less effective elements.

Marketing-mix modeling has been used off and on for nearly a quarter century, but current use is at a high point with leading marketers such as Procter & Gamble (P&G) and the Clorox Company benefiting greatly from the use of this analytic approach. In one recent year, for example, P&G's application of marketing-mix modeling resulted in that firm's changing how it spent more than $400 million of its advertising and promotion budget.[41] Based on its modeling, P&G substantially increased its advertising budget. Comparatively, Clorox's use of marketing-mix modeling led it to shift some money away from advertising into promotions. The important point is that each application of marketing-mix modeling is based on a unique set of marketing circumstances. What's good for the goose (say, P&G) is not necessarily good for the gander (say, Clorox). One solution does not, in other words, fit all.

Marketing-mix modeling is widely used by consumer package good companies (CPGs) such as P&G and Clorox, but it also is being used increasingly by non-CPG companies in the B2C environment and also by B2B companies. Any company can employ the techniques of marketing-mix modeling provided it maintains (or can purchase from syndicated sources) sales data on a period-by-period basis and also has meticulous records of its expenditures on a period-by-period basis for all of its advertising and promotion elements. The example we've been working with for the automobile model is actually simplistic in that a full marketing-mix analysis would consider not just expenditures on, say, a particular advertising medium such as television but would disaggregate the data for specific types of TV expenditures (e.g., network TV versus cable) and even different day parts (daytime, prime time, etc.). The finer, or more disaggregated, the data, the better the analysis can be in determining which specific marketing-mix elements are most and least effective in driving sales.

Summary

This chapter discussed the nature and importance of brand equity. The concept of brand equity is described as the value in a brand resulting from high brand-name awareness and strong, favorable, and perhaps unique associations that consumers have in memory about a particular brand. Marcom efforts play an important role in enhancing brand equity. Enhanced equity, in turn, bolsters consumer brand loyalty, increases market share, differentiates a brand from competitive offerings, and permits charging relatively higher prices. The chapter also discussed the importance of not restricting the assessment of marcom performance to brand equity measures only, but should also consider whether marcom efforts have influenced behavior. By examining the effect that marcom has on behavior, it is possible to gauge financial accountability and thus better equip marketing communicators when they request increased budgets from CFOs. The technique of marketing-mix modeling provides an analytic method for assessing the effectiveness of individual marcom elements and for determining how budgets should be shifted among program elements.

Discussion Questions

1. Tom Peters, author and management consultant, describes a brand as "passion made palpable."[42] What do you think he means by this expression. Provide a couple of personal examples that support Peters's characterization of brands.
2. Using the framework in Figure 2.1, describe all personal associations that the following brands hold for you: (a) Harley-Davidson motorcycles, (b) Hummer vehicles, (c) Red Bull energy drink, (d) *The Wall Street Journal*, and (e) movie star Nicole Kidman.
3. Roger Enrico, CEO of PepsiCo, was quoted in the text as saying, "In my mind the best thing a person can say about a brand is that it's their favorite." Identify two brands that you regard as your favorites. Describe the specific associations that each of these brands holds for you and thus why they are two of your favorites.
4. Provide examples of brands that in your opinion are positioned in such a way as to reflect the five personality dimensions: sincerity, excitement, competence, sophistication, and ruggedness.
5. Provide several examples of co-branding or ingredient branding other than those presented in the chapter.
6. When discussing brand equity from the firm's perspective, it was explained that as the equity of a brand increases, various positive outcomes result: (1) a higher market share, (2) increased brand loyalty, (3) ability to charge premium prices, and (4) capacity to earn a revenue premium. Select a brand you are particularly fond of and explain how its relatively greater equity compared to a lesser brand in the same product category is manifest in terms of each of these four outcomes.
7. Brand awareness is a necessary but insufficient condition toward building positive brand equity. Explain what this statement means to you and provide a couple of examples of brands that you are aware of but that, for you, do *not* possess positive brand equity.
8. Select a brand of vehicle (automobile, truck, motorcycle, SUV, etc.) and with this brand illustrate the meaning to you personally of type, favorability, strength, and uniqueness of brand associations.
9. What are your reactions to the application of neuroscience to marketing (neuromarketing) that was described in the *IMC Focus*? Do you consider this technique ethical? Do you fear that with the knowledge obtained from its application marketers will be able to manipulate consumers?
10. Describe the leveraging strategy for enhancing brand equity. Take a brand of your choice and, with application to Figure 2.8, explain how that brand could build positive associations, thereby enhancing its equity, by linking itself to (a) places, (b) things, (c) people, and (d) other brands. Be specific.
11. A certain brand, Brand X, receives an average quality score of 8.3 and a salience score of 68 percent. What is this brand's equity score based on the EquiTrend procedure?
12. Why is demonstrating financial accountability an imperative for marcom practioners?
13. Assume that your college or university has had difficulty getting nonstudent residents in the local community to attend football games. Your school's athletic

director requests that an organization you belong to (say, a local chapter of the American Marketing Association) develop an advertising program that is to be targeted to local residents to encourage them to attend football games. What measures/metrics could you use to assess whether the advertising program you developed has been effective? How might you assess the ad campaign's ROMI?

ENDNOTES

1. For a fascinating ethnographic analysis of Harley-Davidson owners and more detail on the Harley-as-horse metaphor, see John W. Schouten and James H. McAlexander, "Subcultures of Consumption: An Ethnography of the New Bikers," *Journal of Consumer Research* 22 (June 1995), 43–61.
2. Some of the following comments are adapted from James D. Speros, chief marketing officer at Ernst & Young and chair of the Association of National Advertisers, in "Why the Harley Brand's So Hot," *Advertising Age,* March 15, 2004, 26.
3. For an interesting treatment of rugged individualism in a marketing/advertising context, see Elizabeth C. Hirschman, "Men, Dogs, Guns, and Cars," *Journal of Advertising* 32 (spring 2003), 9–22.
4. For further reading on brand communities, see Albert M. Muniz Jr. and Thomas C. O'Guinn, "Brand Community," *Journal of Consumer Research* 27 (March 2000), 412–432.
5. Johathan Fahey, "Tribal Knowledge," *Forbes.com,* April 13, 2004, http://forbes.com (accessed July 20, 2004).
6. Cited in Kevin Lane Keller, *Strategic Brand Management: Building, Measuring, and Managing Brand Equity* (Upper Saddle River, NJ: Prentice Hall, 1998), 2.
7. Statement made by Terry O'Connor as cited in Bob Lamons, "Brand Power Moves BASF Past Commodity," *Marketing News,* March 15, 2004, 6.
8. Jacques Chevron, "Unholy Grail: Quest for the Best Strategy," *Brandweek,* August 11, 2003, 20.
9. Brand credibility includes dimensions of expertise, or ability, and trustworthiness, or willingness, to consistently deliver on brand promises. See Tülin Erdem and Joffre Swait, "Brand Credibility, Brand Consideration, and Choice," *Journal of Consumer Research* 31 (June 2004), 191–198.
10. Highly readable and insightful discussions of brand equity are provided in two excellent books written by David A. Aaker: *Managing Brand Equity* (New York: The Free Press, 1991) and *Building Strong Brands* (New York: Free Press, 1996).
11. Arjun Chaudhuri and Morris B. Holbrook, "The Chain of Effects from Brand Trust and Brand Affect to Brand Performance: The Role of Brand Loyalty," *Journal of Marketing* 65 (April 2001), 90; Peter Doyle, *Value-Based Marketing: Marketing Strategies for Corporate Growth and Shareholder Value* (Chichester, England: John Wiley & Sons, Ltd., 2000), 300.
12. Kusum L. Ailawadi, Donald R. Lehmann, and Scott A. Neslin, "Revenue Premium as an Outcome Measure of Brand Equity," *Journal of Marketing* 67 (October 2003), 1–17.
13. Keller, "Conceptualizing, Measuring, and Managing Customer-Based Brand Equity," 2.
14. Terry Lefton, "Adidas Goes to Image Pitch with '98 $$ Boost," *Brandweek,* January 26, 1998, 37.
15. Matthew Martinez, "Reed Study Sees Where Ad Dollars Go," *Advertising Age's Business Marketing,* October 1997, 46.
16. The land rush metaphor is an expression used to describe homesteading practices in 19th-century America when government policy encouraged individuals to settle the vast American West by making land available at low prices or at no cost. Settlers could lay claim to a parcel of land simply by first occupying it, which inspired a virtual frenzy, a land rush.
17. Gregory A. Jones, "The Big Lie," from Briefing.com's subscriber service, http://briefing.com (accessed June 29, 2000).
18. Kevin J. Clancy, "Getting Serious about Building Profitable Online Retail Brands," *Retailing Issues Letter* 12 (November 2000)—a publication of Texas A&M University's Center for Retailing Studies.
19. Jennifer L. Aaker, "Dimensions of Brand Personality," *Journal of Marketing Research* 34 (August 1997), 347–356. See also, Jennifer Aaker, Susan Fournier, and S. Adam Brasel, "When Good Brands Do Bad," *Journal of Consumer Research* 31 (June 2004), 1–16.
20. *Beverage Digest* press release, March 4, 2004.
21. This and subsequent comments in this section are adapted from Kevin Lane Keller, "Brand Synthesis: The Multidimensionality of Brand Knowledge," *Journal of Consumer Research* 29 (March 2003), 595–600.
22. The concept of leveraging is fully treated in *ibid.*
23. Grant McCracken, "Culture and Consumption: A Theoretical Account of the Structure and Movement of the Cultural Meaning of Consumer Goods," *Journal of Consumer Research* 13 (June 1986), 74.
24. Keller, *Strategic Brand Management,* 285. For excellent theoretical treatments of this issue, see C. Whan Park, Sung Youl Jun, and Allan D. Shocker, "Composite Branding Alliances: An Investigation of Extension and Feedback Effects," *Journal of Marketing Research* 33 (November 1996), 453–466; and Bernard L. Simonin and Julie A. Ruth, "Is a Company Known by the Company It Keeps? Assessing the Spillover Effects of Brand Alliances on Consumer Brand Attitudes," *Journal of Marketing Research* 35 (February 1998), 30–42.
25. Sandra Dolbow, "DuPont Lycra Stretches Out Into Jeans," *Brandweek,* July 2, 2001, 8.
26. For sophisticated discussions of the relationship between brand equity and brand loyalty, consult the following sources: Tülin Erdem and Joffre Swait, "Brand Equity as a Signaling Phenomenon," *Journal of Consumer Psychology* 7 2 (1998), 131–158; Chaudhuri and Holbrook, "The Chain of Effects from Brand Trust and Brand Affect to Brand Performance: The Role of Brand Loyalty."

27. Larry Light and Richard Morgan, *The Fourth Wave: Brand Loyalty Marketing* (New York: Coalition for Brand Equity, 1994), 11.
28. William Boulding, Eunkyu Lee, and Richard Staelin, "Mastering the Mix: Do Advertising, Promotion, and Sales Force Activities Lead to Differentiation?" *Journal of Marketing Research* 31 (May 1994), 159–172.
29. Kenneth Hein, "A Bull's Market," *Brandweek,* May 28, 2001, 21–24.
30. "The PepsiCo Empire Strikes Back," *Brandweek,* October 7, 1996, 60.
31. Press release from Harris Interactive, August 28, 2003, http://www.harrisinteractive.com.
32. Kenneth Hein, "Can't Buy Me Love," *Brandweek,* June 4, 2001, S22.
33. Kevin Lane Keller, "The Brand Report Card," *Harvard Business Review,* January/February 2000, 147–157.
34. Ibid., 154.
35. "Managing Marketing Assets for Sustained Returns," undated executive summary of report from the Advertising Research Foundation.
36. For example, see Sunil Gupta, Donald R. Lehmann, and Jennifer Ames Stuart, "Valuing Customers," *Journal of Marketing Research* 41 (February 2004), 7–18; Roland T. Rust, Katherine N. Lemon, and Valarie A. Zeithaml, "Return on Marketing: Using Customer Equity to Focus Marketing Strategy," *Journal of Marketing* 68 (January 2004), 109–127; "Measures and Metrics: The Marketing Performance Measurement Audit," The CMO Council, June 9, 2004.
37. The CMO Council, "Measures and Metrics: The Marketing Performance Measurement Audit," June 9, 2004, 3.
38. Hillary Chura, "Advertising ROI Still Elusive Metric," *Advertising Age,* July 26, 2004, 8.
39. Ibid.
40. The *net present value (NPV)* of an investment represents the present, or discounted, value of future cash inflows minus the present value of the investment. The related concept of *discounted cash flow* expresses the value of future cash flows in present dollars. For example, if a firm's cost of borrowing money is 10 percent, then $100 that will not be received for three years is worth in current value only about $75. That is, if you invested $75 today and received 10 percent interest on this investment, in three years it would grow in value to $100. The concept of discounted cash flow simply reverses this logic and examines what a future flow of cash is worth in today's dollars. If this remains unclear, please go online and identify a source that discusses the concept of *time value of money.*
41. Jack Neff, "P&G, Clorox Rediscover Modeling," *Advertising Age,* March 29, 2004, 10.
42. "Great Age of the Brand," *Advertising Age,* November 8, 1999, s10.

CHAPTER 3

Ethical, Regulatory, and Environmental Issues in Marketing Communications

Marcom Challenge: Trans Fat Labeling

If you're like many consumers, at least occasionally you examine the Nutrition Facts information that is printed on packages of food products. By federal requirement in the United States, this information is mandatory. Food manufacturers must report information on the number of grams per serving (and the amount these grams represent as a percentage of recommended daily values) for total fat, cholesterol, sodium, total carbohydrates, and protein.

Figure 3.1 presents a Nutrition Facts label for a brand of soy-based chips named EatSmart Soy-Crisps. You will see on the label that, among other ingredients, a single serving size of this brand (about 20 chips) contains 9 grams of "total fat," which includes 1 gram of saturated fat and 0grams of trans fats. Both saturated and trans fats are considered unhealthy, or "bad" forms of fat, which means that most of the fat (8 grams) contained in Soy-Crisps is "good" fat. A particularly interesting aspect of the Nutrition Facts label for Soy-Crisps is that it includes a listing for trans fat. In late 2004, food manufacturers were *not* required to list the amount of trans fat contained in their products. The maker of Soy-Crisps (Snyder's of Hanover) was willing to do this for obvious reasons—that brand contains *zero* trans fats.

Snyder's of Hanover EatSmart All Natural Snacks

Figure 3.1
An Illustrative Nutritional Facts Label

It was not until January 1, 2006 that food manufacturers were required by the U.S. Food and Drug Administration (FDA) to indicate the number of grams of *trans fats* contained in a serving size. What are trans fats? Trans fats are fats that increase levels of bad cholesterol and reduce the amount of good cholesterol; in short, trans fats, if consumed excessively, can lead to clogged arteries.

Trans fats occur naturally in meat and some dairy items, but the real culprits are many dessert and snack products. These products typically are fried in hydrogenated cooking oil, which is vegetable oil that has been infused with hydrogen so that the oil remains more stable and longer lasting under intense cooking temperatures. Hydrogenated cooking oil makes food products more appealing (e.g., makes pastries flakier) and better tasting, which explains why food makers turned en masse to this cooking method. The result: people are consuming increasingly higher levels of trans fats than ever, but until January 1, 2006, consumers had no idea how many trans fat grams were contained in a single serving of their favorite products.

The FDA issued a requirement in 2003 that trans fat information would be required reporting on Nutrition Facts labels by 2006. This is a problem for some companies who either are not able to produce foods that taste as good when cooked without hydrogenated oil, or will continue making products loaded with trans fats and be required to report this information on nutrition labels.

On the other hand, consumers are better informed when they pick up, say, a box of cookies and learn precisely how many trans fat grams they will be consuming per serving. The FDA's trans-fat regulation influenced companies' behaviors even prior to its implementation.

CHAPTER OBJECTIVES

After reading this chapter you should be able to:

1
Appreciate the ethical issues in marketing communications.

2
Understand why the targeting of products and marketing communications is a heatedly debated practice.

3
Explore the ethical issues associated with advertising, sales promotions, and other marcom practices.

4
Explain the role and importance of governmental efforts to regulate marketing communications.

5
Understand deceptive advertising and the elements that guide the determination of whether a particular advertisement is potentially deceptive.

6
Explain the regulation of unfair business practices and the major areas where the unfairness doctrine is applied.

7
Recognize the role of the states in regulating unfair or deceptive marketing communications practices.

8
Know the process of advertising self-regulation.

9
Appreciate the role of marketing communications in environmental (green) marketing.

10
Recognize the principles that apply to all green marketing efforts.

For example, Frito-Lay eliminated trans fats from six of its major snack brands—Cheetos, Doritos, Fritos, Lays, Rold Gold pretzels, Ruffles, and Tostitos. The net result of trans fat labeling is that consumers are able to make wiser choices, which should lead to reduced levels of trans-fat consumption.[1]

Overview

This chapter represents an appropriate point in the text to investigate ethical issues and governmental regulations that have considerable relevance to marketing communicators, consumers, and society at large. It is important that we examine these topics now so as to fully appreciate that marketing communicators, as well as all marketing actors, operate under constraints—governmental, competitive, and moral—that limit certain actions but which ultimately benefit free markets and the competitors and consumers who participate in them.

To appreciate the importance of these topics and their interrelatedness, consider the following scenario. Though this set of circumstances pales in comparison to the bevy of major accounting and financial scandals that occurred in recent years (e.g., Enron, Arthur Andersen, Adelphia Communications, and Tyco), it nonetheless reflects a situation that is similar to the decisions many businesspeople make on a regular basis.

Imagine you are the vice president of marketing and sales for the consumer products division of a large chemical company. One of your products, plastic trash bags, is likely to experience lost sales because your competitors are promoting their brands as degradable. To nontechnical consumers, the word *degradable* implies that these trash bags literally disintegrate within a relatively short period after they leave the consumer's curbside and are buried in a landfill. Although these bags *are* photo-degradable (i.e., they will degrade if left out in the sun and rain for an extended period), you know they will not disintegrate when placed in landfills; rather, like most everything else that is buried in landfills, these "degradable" bags will remain intact for decades.

You know your own yet-to-be introduced brand is not truly degradable. However, your regular brand of nondegradable trash bags is likely to lose sales because environmentally conscious consumers think they are serving the environment better by using your competitors' "degradable" bags. You could introduce a photodegradable bag, but you know that it, like the competitors' bags, is not truly degradable and will not solve the solid waste problem. If you introduce a new bag labeled "degradable," you can prevent potential lost sales to competitors. However, you will be misleading consumers into thinking they are purchasing truly degradable bags.

The situation just described is not hypothetical. Something very similar to this confronted the Mobil Chemical Company at a time when American consumers' concerns about environmental protection were at their peak. Concurrently, many marketers were beginning to respond to consumers' concerns, sometimes in exploitative ways. Mobil's brand of regular Hefty trash bags was, in fact, losing supermarket shelf space and sales to brands such as First Brands' "degradable" Glad bags. Nonetheless, Mobil fully recognized that photo-degradable bags were no panacea to solving the landfill problem.

Bowing to the pressure of potential lost sales, Mobil nevertheless introduced its own line of "degradable" trash bags. No media advertising was undertaken; rather, the communications burden fell entirely on the Hefty package itself. The package was labeled *Hefty Degradable**, with the asterisk qualifying the degradable property as photodegradable ("*Activated by Exposure to the Elements"). The package front included a scene of a pine tree with bright sunlight shining through and an osprey preparing to land on the tree—all presumably chosen as emblematic of the implied claim that Hefty bags are themselves compatible with the environment. The back of the package made additional claims about the degradability of Hefty trash bags.

Shortly after Mobil introduced Hefty Degradable, the Federal Trade Commission (FTC) requested both Mobil and First Brands (Glad bags) to provide substantiation for the degradability claims. Within a year Mobil voluntarily discontinued using degradability claims on its trash bag packages. Nonetheless, several months later the attorneys general of seven states (California, Massachusetts, Minnesota, New York, Texas, Washington, and Wisconsin) brought suits against Mobil on grounds that it had engaged in deceptive communications and consumer fraud by falsely claiming that trash bags degrade in landfills. Although refusing to admit wrongdoing, Mobil settled the suits out of court and arranged to pay the states an agreed-on sum to fund environmental educational programs.[2]

The preceding scenario encapsulates much of the material covered in this chapter. In particular, the chapter addresses three major topics: (1) *ethical issues* in marketing communications, (2) the *regulation* of marcom practices, and (3) *environmental matters* and their implications for marketing communications. All three topics are interrelated: ethical issues confronting contemporary marketing communicators sometimes occur over environmental marketing efforts (as with Mobil's trash bags), and regulation (from federal and state governments and by industry self-regulators) is needed due in large part to some unethical marketing communications practices.[3]

Ethical Issues In Marketing Communications

Marketing communicators in their various capacities—as advertisers, sales promoters, package designers, public relations representatives, point-of-purchase designers, and so on—regularly make decisions that have ethical ramifications. Ethical lapses and moral indiscretions sometimes occur under pressures of trying to meet business goals and attempting to satisfy the demands of the financial community. Although the behavior of executives at Enron was repugnant—and devastating to the thousands of employees and stockholders who thought they were dealing with an honest business—it probably is safe to say that the moral training of Enron executives was about the same as that of any of their employees, or ours.

With an understanding of how marketing communications is ripe for assertions of unethical actions—because marcom practitioners sometimes *do* engage in unacceptable behaviors, though probably not more so than practitioners engaged in other noble pursuits—you will be better prepared to assess your own planned actions by taking a moral check and resisting the temptation to do something that may be expedient and rewarding in the short run, but inappropriate and potentially costly in the long run. Carolyn Yoo, a respected educator, has framed the importance of examining ethical issues in the following terms:

I think most people—and [college] students are no different—know right from wrong. I believe they care about doing right. But even those of us with a rudimentary moral sensibility aren't always able to evoke those basic principles when dealing with fairly routine business decisions. For instance, we may do an enthusiastic sales pitch and promise things our company isn't quite ready to deliver, or we might highlight the positive aspects of our products and downplay the negative ones. We might formulate financial projections to favor the outcome we advocate. We might overstep the boundaries when advertising to children or go overboard when we use personal data to target customers . . . Ethical dilemmas do not arrive bathed in red lights. There is no sign that says, 'You're about to enter an ethical zone.' Therefore, ethics education is not about defining for students what is right and what is wrong. Ethics education should aim to raise our students' antennae for recognizing ethical implications, conflicts of interest, and exercises of asymmetric power when such dilemmas pop up without warning.[4]

Ethics in our context involves matters of right and wrong, or *moral*, conduct pertaining to any aspect of marketing communications. For our purposes, the terms ethics and morality will be used interchangeably and considered synonymous with societal notions of *honesty, honor, virtue,* and *integrity.* Though it is relatively easy to define ethics, there is a lack of consensus throughout the field of marketing—as well as elsewhere in society—about what ethical conduct actually entails.[5] We nonetheless can identify marketing communications practices that are especially susceptible to ethical challenges. The following sections examine, in order, ethical issues in (1) targeting marketing communications, (2) advertising, (3) public relations, (4) packaging communications, (5) sales promotions, and (6) Internet marketing.

The Ethics of Targeting

According to widely accepted dictates of sound marketing strategy, firms should direct their offerings at specific segments of customers rather than use a scatter or shotgun approach. Nevertheless, ethical dilemmas are sometimes involved when special products and corresponding marketing communications efforts are directed at particular segments. Especially open to ethical debate is the practice of targeting products and communications efforts to segments that, for various psychosocial and economic reasons, are vulnerable to marketing communications—such as children and economically disadvantaged groups.[6]

Targeting to Children and Teens

In-school marketing programs, advertisements in traditional media, and messages on the Internet continually urge children to desire various products and brands. In fact, one study has estimated that U.S. businesses spent $15 billion in a recent year advertising and marketing their brands to children ages 12 and under.[7] Critics contend that many of the products targeted to children are unnecessary and that the communications are exploitative. Because it would involve debating personal values to discuss what children do or do not need, the following examples present the critics' position and allow you to draw your own conclusions.

© Yellowdog Productions/ The Image Bank/Getty Images

Consider a past advertising campaign that targeted Gatorade to children. Advertisements claimed that Gatorade is the "healthy alternative for thirsty kids." Nutritionists and other critics charged that Gatorade is unnecessary for children and no better than water—no harm or benefit arises from its consumption.[8] If indeed Gatorade does not benefit kids, is it ethical to urge them to encourage a parent to purchase this product?

The issue of childhood obesity and the marketing of food products to children is an especially hotly debated topic. Obesity is a major problem with America's children. According to the Centers for Disease Control and Prevention, nearly 1 in 6 children is considered obese, a rate that compares to only 1 in 16 cases of childhood obesity only about 25 years ago.[9] Many critics consider it unethical to market food products to children, perhaps especially through practices using cartoon characters to sell sugared cereals and non-nutritious snacks.[10]

Now consider targeting efforts by the famous food company, Campbell Soup. Campbell historically marketed its soup and pasta brands primarily to mothers with the expectation that they would make appropriate choices for their children. But the company has learned that direct appeals to children can effectively increase sales volume. In efforts to reach older children, Campbell has used well-known rapper Bow Wow and soccer phenom Freddy Adu as product spokespersons. To reach younger children, Campbell advertises its products during TV programs such as *Dora the Explorer* and *Jimmy Neutron*.[11] Soup and pasta are pretty good products in the nutritional scheme of things, so is targeting these products to children unethical?

Now let's examine an advertising effort by the Subway sandwich chain, which, as you may recall, achieved much success along with considerable publicity when using spokesman Jared Fogle, a once morbidly obese man who supposedly lost nearly 250 pounds by dieting on Subway sandwiches. Subway more recently extended the campaign in an effort directed at children. In one commercial a preteen boy is overheard in the background saying, "When my brother had friends over, I would, like, stay up in my room because I was afraid they'd call me fat, or something. Now I'm not afraid of that at all. I started running and eating better stuff. I'm Cody. I'm twelve years old." After the child bares his soul, Jared Fogle comes before the camera and declares, "More than anything, we [Subway] want your children to lead long and healthy lives." By implication, eating at Subway rather than at nutritionally challenged fast-food outlets is one means for children to reduce weight and increase the quality of their lives. Critics have suggested this campaign is exploitive.[12] Defenders of Subway's advertising could readily counter that this type of advertising serves to raise children's awareness of the importance of eating more nutritious foods and undertaking exercise regimens. Has Subway crossed the exploitation line?

Another criticized aspect of children-directed marketing communications is the practice of using posters, book covers, free magazines, advertising, and other so-called learning tools. Disguised as educational materials, these communications often are little more than attempts to persuade schoolchildren to want the promoted products and brands. Critics contend these methods are unethical because they use children's trust in educational materials as a deceptive means of hawking merchandise.

In addition to classroom tactics, critics also question the ethics of practices such as product placements in movies and TV programs. Longstanding consumer activist Ralph Nader has proposed listing companies on the Internet that go overboard in targeting children and encouraging consumers to boycott their brands.[13]

Marketers also have been criticized for targeting adult products to teens and college students. The Miller Brewing Company, for example, was criticized for running a television commercial for its Molson Ice brand that focused on a label displaying 5.6 percent alcoholic content at the same time that an off-camera announcer uttered that Molson Ice is a "bolder" drink. A spokesperson for the Center for Science in the Public Interest asserted that the Molson Ice commercial appealed to children because they "drink to get drunk" and higher alcohol content is "what they want in a beer."[14] The beer industry itself would be expected to be opposed to such advertising inasmuch as one of the brewing industry's advertising guidelines explicitly states that beer advertisements "should neither state nor carry any implication of alcohol strength."[15]

In general, there is considerable concern regarding the marketing of beer and other alcoholic beverages to teens and young adults. A study by a watchdog group at Georgetown University reported that one-quarter of alcohol advertising was more likely seen by youths than adults.[16] Lawsuits have been filed against major brewers and other companies that market alcohol products on the basis that their advertising and marketing practices increase underage drinking.[17] A consumer advocacy group, the Center for Science in the Public Interest, has initiated an effort to reduce the amount of alcohol advertising on televised sports. Coaching legends Dean Smith (ex-basketball coach at the University of North Carolina) and Tom

Osborne (ex-football coach at the University of Nebraska and now a U.S. Congressman) participated in the program, and Ohio State University (OSU) was the first major school to get involved when it curbed its local media partners from airing any alcohol ads during the broadcast of OSU sporting events.[18]

By far the greatest controversy to erupt in many years involves claims of unfair targeting of cigarettes to children via advertisements and product placements in movies. This issue is of considerable concern to many parents, consumer advocates, and academic researchers who have suggested that exposure to cigarette advertising leads youth to view cigarettes as a positive consumption symbol and to be more likely to smoke.[19] (Other researchers have challenged whether the scientific evidence does in fact permit the conclusion that advertising increases teenage smoking.)[20] Investigators also have studied whether antismoking campaigns are effective in lowering teenagers' attitudes toward smoking and their likelihood of beginning to smoke or discontinuing once the habit is started.[21]

Alarm regarding the impact of cigarette advertising directed to youth is best reflected by an advertising campaign for Camel cigarettes that used a man-like camel popularly known as "Joe Camel." The campaign—which consistently portrayed Joe as a swank character in various social settings always with a cigarette hanging from his lips or dangling from his fingertips—was widely criticized as responsible for increased smoking among teenagers.[22] With cigarette smoking among teenagers on the rise, many parties urged a ban on Joe Camel advertisements, and research was performed to determine whether the Joe Camel advertising campaign was indeed responsible for more positive smoking attitudes and increased smoking among youth.[23] Under pressure from antismoking activists, the U.S. Congress, and the FTC, R. J. Reynolds ultimately discontinued its use of the Joe Camel advertising campaign, although the character still appears in advertising outside the United States.

Has the Joe Camel campaign targeted nonadults? Is it partially responsible for increased rates of smoking? Is it unethical? These are complicated questions and simple answers are not possible. The issues need to be debated both in and outside the classroom. The *IMC Focus* includes a provocative position on the topic. It is presented here *not* as the final statement on the issue but rather as an intelligent and sobering statement that should serve to spark further discussion regarding the inevitable clash between advertisers' free-speech rights and their societal obligation to be moral citizens. Though billboards advertising cigarettes are a thing of the past in the United States, the commentary in the *IMC Focus* is as compelling today as when in the 1990s it was composed with considerable apprehension over the power of cigarette advertising on America's youth.

Critics also are up in arms over the marketing of adult-oriented entertainment products to children and teens. The FTC has issued a regular series of reports, titled *Marketing Violent Entertainment to Children,* that criticize the entertainment industry for targeting children with advertisements for violent films, video games, and music. However, the FTC believes that its authority in regulating such advertising is limited in that it would have difficulty proving that such ads are deceptive or unfair, which, as we will cover in a subsequent section, are the two doctrines under which the FTC regulates advertising. The FTC has called on the entertainment industry to self-regulate and rigorously apply its own codes of conduct, though there are serious concerns that the industry is not much motivated or even capable of cleaning its own house.[24] An editor of *Advertising Age,* a publication widely read by advertising practitioners and a voice of reason in the ad industry, offers the following appropriate conclusion to this discussion:

This publication's editors—myself included—almost always side with the advertising industry in preferring self-regulation to government intervention. But self-regulation is a privilege earned with responsible behavior and voluntary restraint. In the marketing of

An Adman's Struggle with Joe Camel and Free Speech

imc focus

Last week, just over the Howard Street Bridge, I crossed a camel's path. Stopped at a traffic light on my way to a business meeting, I glanced up and saw the camel rising above the brick building tops in vibrant, unnatural hues, stretching, it seemed, far into the sky.

I thought he saw me, too; he winked at me with a grin. And there was an understanding between us—camel and man, man and camel.

But his wink and grin were not meant for me alone.

I am a local advertising professional, and the camel is the symbol for Camel cigarettes. He speaks to the city from high atop Howard Street and North Avenue on his billboard perch. As an "adman," I am impressed by the camel. The cartoonish, humanistic depiction of the desert beast in a jazz jam session with his camel buddies is intriguing. It doesn't ask for your attention, it grabs it. And once you are hooked, as it were, on the visual, the message is clear: camels are cool; they're fun; they make you part of the desirable crowd. All of this, conveyed in just a glance.

More than that, the cartoons speak most persuasively to the "target market" the company wishes to reach. All in all, it is an expert use of the medium and an excellent piece of advertising.

As a man, as a father, I am appalled by the camel. To me, he is perverse, a distortion. Strip away his sleek, tan exterior and what is left? Not a camel, but a purplish, black-plumed raven forlornly whispering to the children of the streets when their parents and teachers are not looking. He beckons the poor, preying upon their weaknesses and panhandling their few coins.

The spectacle leaves me between a rock and a camel's hump—and not only for selfish reasons. Of course, being a glad participant in the free-enterprise system, I am all for the aggressive manufacturing and marketing of any legal product. Beyond that, I believe that free speech, even for ignoble, detestable causes, should be protected without reservation.

But is it free speech to lure children with images they've been taught to trust, cartoon images, to a product the surgeon general has called an addiction that can lead to death? In fact, *The New York Times Magazine* recently reported that "the product kills more than 420,000 Americans a year—surpassing the combined deaths from homicide, suicide, AIDS, automobile accidents, alcohol and drug abuse."

I came to the conclusion that, yes, it is free speech. People are, and should be, allowed to convey whatever message they choose. That is the American way. But freedom of expression also includes the freedom not to express one's self. No one forces an advertising agency to devise strategies and create images for a tobacco company targeting an inappropriate market. No one forces the media outlets to provide them a forum. And finally, no one should overlook them when it comes time to pass out blame.

But it is not enough, either, to merely ignore the camel. Those of us in the marketing business know exactly what he's up to; we should be the first to denounce him. Even in public and professional life, there is a place for personal morality and common decency.

These meager thoughts passed through my head as I sat at that light just over the Howard Street Bridge. When the signal turned green, I waited for a group of school kids to cross the street, then I gently pulled away. A couple of blocks later, I was stopped again at a light. This time, under a billboard for malt liquor.

SOURCE: George Des Roches, "An Adman's Struggle with Joe Camel and Free Speech," *Advertising Age*, September 26, 1994, v65 23n40 p/(1). © 1994 by Crain Communications, Inc. Reprinted by permission.

entertainment products to children, marketers have shown little restraint. If they continue to act irresponsibly, they will have invited the regulation they so desperately want to avoid.[25]

Targeting Economically Disadvantaged Consumers

Makers of alcohol and tobacco products frequently employ billboards and other advertising media in targeting brands to economically disadvantaged consumers. Although billboard advertising of tobacco products is restricted under the Master Settlement Agreement between the federal government and firms in the tobacco industry, in the past billboards advertising tobacco and alcohol were disproportionately more likely to appear in inner-city areas.[26]

Two celebrated cases illustrate the concerns.[27] A national uproar ensued when R. J. Reynolds (RJR) was preparing to introduce Uptown, a brand of menthol cigarette aimed at African-Americans and planned for test marketing in Philadelphia, where African-Americans make up 40 percent of the population. Because African-Americans have more than a 50 percent higher rate of lung cancer than whites, many critics, including the U.S. government's secretary for Health and Human Services, were incensed by the product launch. In response to the public outcry, RJR canceled test marketing, and the brand died.[28]

Following in the wake of Uptown's demise, critics challenged another firm, the Heileman Brewing Company, for introducing its PowerMaster brand of high-alcohol malt liquor targeted to inner-city residents—a brand containing 5.9 percent alcohol compared with the 4.5 percent content of other malt liquors.[29] Brewing-industry supporters claimed that rather than being exploitive, PowerMaster and other malt liquors merely meet the demand among African-Americans and Hispanics, who buy the vast majority of malt liquor.[30] Nonetheless, the U.S. Treasury Department's Bureau of Alcohol, Tobacco, and Firearms (ATF), which regulates the brewing and liquor industries, would not permit the Heileman Brewing Company to market malt liquor under the name PowerMaster. The ATF arrived at this decision because it considered the name PowerMaster as promoting the brand's alcoholic content in violation of federal regulations.

The R. J. Reynolds tobacco company was again widely criticized when preparing to introduce its Dakota brand of cigarettes to young, economically downscale women. RJR's plans to test market Dakota in Houston were squashed when critics created an outcry in response to what was considered to be exploitive marketing.[31]

Is Targeting Unethical or Just Good Marketing?

The foregoing discussion points out instances where advertising and other forms of marketing communications are criticized because they are directed at specific target markets. Proponents of targeting respond to such criticisms by arguing that targeting benefits rather than harms consumers. Targeting, according to the proponents, provides consumers with products best suited to their particular needs and wants. Not to be targeted, according to the advocates' position, is to have to choose a product that better accommodates someone else's needs.[32]

The issue is, of course, more complicated than whether targeting is good or bad. Sophisticated marketing practitioners and students fully accept the strategic justification for target marketing. There is the possibility, however, that some instances of targeting are concerned not with fulfilling consumers' needs and wants but rather with exploiting consumer vulnerabilities—so that the marketer gains while society loses. Herein rests the ethical issue that cannot be dismissed with a mere claim that targeting is sound marketing.[33]

Ethical Issues in Advertising

The role of advertising in society has been debated for centuries. Advertising ethics is a topic that has commanded the attention of philosophers, practitioners, scholars, and theologians. Even advertising practitioners are mixed in terms of their awareness of and concern for ethical issues in the day-to-day conduct of advertising.[34] The following is a succinct yet eloquent account of why advertising is so fiercely criticized:

> *As the voice of technology, [advertising] is associated with many dissatisfactions of the industrial state. As the voice of mass culture it invites intellectuals' attack. And as the most visible form of capitalism it has served as nothing less than a lightning-rod for social criticism.*[35]

A variety of ethical criticisms have been leveled against advertising. Because the issues are complex, it is impossible to treat each criticism in great detail. Thus, the following discussion introduces some illustrative issues with the expectation that each will prompt more in-depth thought and perhaps class discussion.[36]

Advertising Is Untruthful and Deceptive

Roughly two-thirds of Americans think that advertising often is untruthful.[37] As will be discussed in a subsequent section on advertising regulation, deception occurs when an advertisement falsely represents a product and consumers believe the false representation. By this definition it is undeniable that some advertising *is* deceptive—the existence of governmental regulation and industry self-regulation attests to this fact. It would be naïve, however, to assume that *most* advertising is deceptive. The advertising industry is not much different than other institutions in a pluralistic society. Lying, cheating, and outright fraud are universal, occurring at the highest levels of government and in the most basic human relationships. Advertising is not without sin, but neither does it hold a monopoly on it.

Advertising Is Manipulative

The criticism of manipulation asserts that advertising has the power to influence people to do things they would not do if they were not exposed to advertising. Taken to the extreme, this suggests that advertising is capable of moving people against their free wills. The fact is that people, when *consciously aware* that attempts are being made to persuade or influence them, have the cognitive capacity to resist efforts to motivate them in a direction they wish not to be moved. That is, consumers have insight about how marketing communicators attempt to persuade them and possess cognitive defenses for protecting themselves from being coerced into doing something against their free wills.[38] This is not to say that as consumers we never make bad decisions or are not sometimes led into buying things later regretted; however, being susceptible to persuasive influences and making bad decisions is not tantamount to being manipulated. We can thus conclude that individuals *who are cognitively aware* that an attempt is being made to persuade them are pretty good at protecting themselves from doing things that are counter to their best interests.

However (and it's a big however) there is growing evidence that much human behavior *is not under conscious control.* Many of our actions occur virtually automatically (without cognitive intervention) as if we were on autopilot. Communicators can, for example, activate—or prime—subconscious thoughts in people using subtle techniques and subliminal messages. For example, people can be primed with the thought of "being cooperative," and without conscious awareness, people so primed are inclined to act more cooperatively, at least temporarily, in comparison to an equivalent group of people who have not been primed with the cooperation thought. For subconscious priming to be effective, the primed topic must be compatible with the individual's current need states. In other words, one cannot be subliminally induced to act more cooperatively unless she or he has a need to cooperate.[39]

It is important to qualify the preceding comments on two counts. First, priming, or activating a certain thought in individuals, is possible only if that thought represents a present need state. For example, if being considered attractive is salient to an individual, then one's attractiveness need can be activated with subtle commands or subliminal primes suggesting that a certain product will enhance attractiveness. Second, a primed goal state does not remain an active driver of judgments and behavior over the long run, but is limited in its length of influence. Hence, an advertiser may activate a certain thought but the consumer would not act on that thought if she or he is not presently in the market to purchase a product that relates to that thought. It would be expected that mass-media advertising would have little effectiveness in this regard given that exposure to ads and purchase decisions typically are separated in time. Perhaps, however, point-of-purchase advertising (e.g., in-store radio programming) would provide an opportune (albeit unethical) medium for subliminally priming consumers into purchasing products and brands.

In sum, advertising practitioners (along with communicators in all other aspects of life) *do* have the ability to influence consumers in very subtle ways. It is unknown whether advertisers are indeed employing the subtle priming techniques that are known to modern psychologists, but techniques exist to influence consumers in ways unbeknownst to them. In short, advertising practitioners have the wherewithal to manipulate if they so choose. Although marketing communicators theoretically can use subliminal cues and primes to influence consumer behavior in a subtle way, it is important to recognize that priming is not like brainwashing or the embedding of electronic computer chips in brains and controlling people's behavior as if they were automatons. The *Manchurian Candidate,* in the event you saw that movie or read the book, is *not* the type of power that marketing communicators have at their command (thankfully).

Advertising Is Offensive and in Bad Taste

Advertising critics contend that advertisements sometimes are insulting to human intelligence, vulgar, and generally offensive to the tastes of many consumers. The critics have in mind such practices as sexual explicitness or innuendo, outlandish humor, and excessive repetition of the same advertisements.

Undeniably, quite a lot of advertising is disgusting and offensive.[40] Yet the same can be said for all forms of mass media presentations. For example, many network television programs verge on the idiotic, and movies are often filled with inordinate amounts of sex and violence. This certainly is not to excuse advertising for its excesses, but a balanced view demands that critical evaluations of advertising be conducted in a broader context of popular culture and other forms of mass media presentations. Interestingly, the widespread backlash resulting from singer Janet Jackson's baring her breast (with the "help" of Justin Timberlake) during halftime of the 2004 Super Bowl led some advertisers to take a more cautious approach in using sex appeal and off-color humor for fear of public condemnation.[41]

Advertising Creates and Perpetuates Stereotypes

At the root of this criticism is the contention that advertising tends to portray certain groups in a very narrow and predictable fashion. For example, minorities have historically been portrayed disproportionately in working-class roles rather than in the full range of positions they actually occupy; women have been stereotyped as sex objects; and senior citizens sometimes are characterized as feeble and forgetful people. Though advertising *has* been guilty of perpetuating stereotypes, it would be unfair to blame advertising for creating these stereotypes, which, in fact, are perpetuated by all elements of society. Spreading the blame does not make advertising any better, but it does show that advertising is probably not any worse than the rest of society.

People Buy Things They Do Not Really Need

A frequently cited criticism suggests that advertising causes people to buy items or services they do not need. This criticism is a value-laden judgment. Do you need another pair of shoes? Do you need a college education? Who is to say what you or anyone else needs? Advertising most assuredly influences consumer tastes and encourages people to undertake purchases they may not otherwise make, but is this unethical?

Advertising Plays on People's Fears and Insecurities

Some advertisements appeal to the negative consequences of not buying and using certain products—rejection by others, bad breath, failure to have provided for the family if one should die without proper insurance coverage, not saving starving children in third world countries, and so on. Some advertisers must plead guilty to this charge when attempting to influence consumer behavior by appealing to negative emotions such as fear, guilt, and humiliation. However, once again, advertising possesses no monopoly on this transgression.

In sum, the institution of advertising is certainly not free of criticism. What should be clear, however, is that advertising reflects the rest of society, and any indictment of advertising probably applies to society at large. It is doubtful that advertisers and other marketing practitioners are any less ethical in their practices than are other elements of society.[42] Responsible advertising practitioners, knowing that their practice is particularly susceptible to criticism, have a vested interest in producing legitimate advertisements. The advertising industry has an important stake in its members acting ethically so as to ward off public criticism and governmental regulation. Accordingly, advertising practitioners typically operate under ethical codes of conduct.

Presented in this section is the American Association of Advertising Agencies (AAAA) standard on ethics in advertising. The AAAA is the national trade association that represents advertising agencies in the United States. Its members are responsible for creating approximately three-quarters of the total advertising volume placed nationwide by ad agencies. The mission of the AAAA organization is to improve and strengthen the ad agency business, to advocate advertising, to influence public policy, to resist advertising-related legislation that it regards as unwise or unfair, and to work with government regulators to achieve desirable social and civic goals. The AAAA promulgated a code of high ethical standards in 1924 and updated the code in 1990. It is presented here in verbatim form because it represents, on the one hand, a set of lofty goals for the advertising industry and, on the other, a framework for evaluating whether television commercials and other forms of advertisements produced by these agencies meet these high standards.

We, the members of the American Association of Advertising Agencies, in addition to supporting and obeying the laws and legal regulations pertaining to advertising, undertake to extend and broaden the application of high ethical standards. Specifically, we will not knowingly create advertising that contains:

a. *False, or misleading statements or exaggerations, visual or verbal*
b. *Testimonials that do not reflect the real opinion of the individual(s) involved*
c. *Price claims that are misleading*
d. *Claims insufficiently supported or that distort the true meaning or practicable application of statements made by professional or scientific authority*
e. *Statements, suggestions, or pictures offensive to public decency or minority segments of the population.*

We recognize that there are areas that are subject to honestly different interpretations and judgment. Nevertheless, we agree not to recommend to an advertiser, and to discourage the use of, advertising that is in poor or questionable taste or that is deliberately irritating through aural or visual content or presentation.

Comparative advertising shall be governed by the same standards of truthfulness, claim substantiation, tastefulness, etc., as apply to other types of advertising.

These Standards of Practice of the American Association of Advertising Agencies come from the belief that sound and ethical practice is good business. Confidence and respect are indispensable to success in a business embracing the many intangibles of agency service and involving relationships so dependent upon good faith.

Clear and willful violations of these Standards of Practice may be referred to the Board of Directors of the American Association of Advertising Agencies for appropriate action, including possible annulment of membership as provided by Article IV, Section 5, of the Constitution and By-Laws.[43]

Ethical Issues in Public Relations

Publicity, the aspect of public relations that relates primarily to marketing communications, involves disseminating positive information about a company and its products and handling negative publicity when things go wrong. Because publicity is like advertising in that both are forms of mass communications, many of the same ethical issues apply and need not be repeated. The one distinct aspect worthy of separate discussion is the matter of *negative publicity.*

A number of celebrated cases have surfaced in recent years in which companies have been widely criticized for marketing unsafe products. One example is the case of Firestone tires that were claimed responsible for a raft of Ford Explorer rollover accidents. The way firms confront negative publicity has important strategic as well as ethical ramifications. The primary ethical issue concerns whether firms confess to product shortcomings and acknowledge problems or, instead, attempt to cover up the problems.

Consider, for example, the case of Tylenol capsules. Seven people in the Chicago area died after purchasing and ingesting Tylenol capsules that had been spiked with cyanide at a time (back in the early 1980s) prior to the implementation of government regulations that thereafter required tamper-proof packages for over-the-counter drug items. The publicity people at Johnson & Johnson (J&J), the makers of Tylenol, could have claimed that the problem was not of their making but rather was the fault of an isolated lunatic in Chicago. Such a position would have led J&J to continue selling Tylenol in all markets except Chicago. However, because it was unknown at the time whether the capsules had been poisoned at the factory or by a deranged person in retail outlets, the cautionary and ethical response was to remove Tylenol from store shelves throughout the country. This is precisely what J&J chose to do in taking the moral high road. It turned out the problem was restricted to Chicago, but the ethics of the situation required caution to prevent the possibility of widespread deaths around the country. Not only was J&J's action ethically correct, but Tylenol quickly regained its market share upon return to store shelves, which shocked observers who predicted the cyanide incident would mortally wound the brand.

Ethical Issues in Packaging and Branding

Four aspects of packaging involve ethical issues: (1) label information, (2) packaging graphics, (3) packaging safety, and (4) environmental implications of packaging.[44] *Label information* on packages can mislead consumers by providing exaggerated information or by unethically suggesting that a product contains more of desired attributes (for instance, nutrition) or less of undesired attributes (such as trans fat) than is actually the case. *Packaging graphics* are unethical when the picture on a package is not a true representation of product contents (as when a children's toy is made to appear much bigger on the package than it actually is). Another case of unethical packaging is when a store brand is packaged so that it looks virtually identical to a well-known national brand. *Unsafe packaging* problems are particularly acute when packaging is not tamper-proof and contain dangerous products that are unsafe for children. *Environmental issues* in packaging are typified by the discussion of Hefty trash bags earlier in the chapter. Packaging information is misleading and unethical when it suggests environmental benefits that cannot be delivered.[45]

Related to packaging ethics is that of *brand naming*. A marketer's choice of brand name engages ethical considerations when the chosen name suggests the brand possesses product features that it doesn't, or will deliver benefits that it cannot. In other words, the brand is incapable of living up to the expectations signaled by the name and thus is potentially misleading. Consider, for example, a hypothetical children's toy carrying the name "PowerGlider." Because this name suggests that the toy (a plastic airplane) has an actual power source such as an engine, consumers would be deceived when purchasing the brand if in fact the only source of power is the person who has to throw it.

Another ethical violation occurs when a company borrows (or steals) a brand name from a better known and established brand. In effect, by using another company's well-known brand for its own product, the violator is capitalizing on the power of *leveraging* as described in the previous chapter. Stealing another company's established brand name is not only unethical but also illegal. However,

Is the Use of the "SOR" Brand Logo Too Similar to "SCR"?

Honda, a well-known Japanese company, produces automobiles, motorcycles, motor scooters, and other vehicles. It began making motor scooters in China in 1982 and commands a substantial share of the large Chinese market. Honda markets its scooters using the "SCR" logo, which it places on each side of the motor at the back. As with all brands that possess positive equity, it is important to prevent other companies from pirating a well-known logo. This, however, is precisely what Honda has accused a Chinese company of doing. The Chinese company in question is Chongqing Lifan Industry Group Co., or Lifan for short. Lifan is China's biggest private maker of motorcycles and scooters.

What's the complaint? Honda alleges that its "SCR" logo has been pirated by Lifan, which is using the highly similar "SOR" logo on its own motor scooters. Not only do the letters look alike, but Lifan places the logo at exactly the same locations on the motor where Honda places its logo. Lifan denies that it copied Honda's logo.

In another case between these same two companies, Honda alleges that Lifan's use of the name "Hongda" on its products is too similar to the Honda name. Both cases were under review in Chinese courts in early 2005.

global focus

SOURCES: "Honda, Lifan Locked in Trademark Disagreement," *China Daily,* June 3, 2004, http://www.chinadaily.com (accessed August 5, 2004); Elaine Kurtenbach, "Honda Sues Chinese Motorcycle Maker for Logo Piracy," *The Detroit News Autos Insider,* June 5, 2004, http://www.detnews.com/autoinsider (accessed August 5, 2004); "Chinese Motorcycle Maker Is Sued by Honda Over Logo," *The Wall Street Journal Online,* June 7, 2004, http://online.wsj.com (accessed June 7, 2004).

brand name piracy takes place when marketers in one country use brand names for their products that are virtually the same as the names of established brands from another country. The *Global Focus* describes one such situation in China.

Ethical Issues in Sales Promotions

Ethical considerations are involved with all facets of sales promotions, including manufacturer promotions directed at wholesalers and retailers and to consumers. As will be detailed in a later chapter, retailers have gained considerable bargaining power vis-à-vis manufacturers. One outcome of this power shift has been retailers' increased demands for deals. *Slotting allowances* illustrate the power shift. This practice (thoroughly discussed in Chapter 17) requires manufacturers to pay retailers a per-store fee for their willingness to handle a new stock unit from the manufacturer. Critics of slotting allowances contend this practice represents a form of bribery and is therefore unethical.

Consumer-oriented sales promotions (including practices such as coupons, premium offers, rebates, sweepstakes, and contests) are unethical when the sales promoter offers consumers a reward for their behavior that is never delivered—for example, failing to mail a free premium object or to provide a rebate check. Sweepstakes and contests are potentially unethical when consumers think their odds of winning are much greater than they actually are.[46]

As a matter of balance, it is important to note that marketers are not the only ones guilty of unethical behavior in the area of sales promotions. Consumers also engage in untoward activities such as submitting coupons at the point of checkout for items not purchased or tendering phony rebate claims. For example, one individual obtained in excess of $700,000 from manufacturers by submitting thousands of rebate claims using fictitious names and addresses. She paid people to steal proofs-of-purchase from products in stores or from discarded packages in trash receptacles and then mailed these in for rebates.[47] The woman eventually was sentenced to 20 years in prison and levied $1 million in fines.

Ethical Issues in Online Marketing

Ethical issues abound in the use of the Internet as a marcom medium, many of which overlap with the prior, general discussions involving the ethics of advertising and promotions. Aside from the general ethical issues already discussed,

© Susan Van Etten

privacy is probably the most important ethical issue that is unique to the online medium.

Because online marketers are able to collect voluminous information about people's personal characteristics, online shopping behavior, and use of information, it is easy to invade individuals' privacy rights by selling information to other sources and divulging information that should be confidential. It would take us too far afield to get into a detailed discussion of all the issues surrounding privacy invasion, but there will be more coverage of Internet advertising in Chapter 15; in the meantime, interested readers are directed to the articles listed in the endnote.[48] Also worth reviewing are the self-regulatory principles espoused by the Network Advertising Initiative (http://www.networkadvertising.org), a trade association of online media companies.

Fostering Ethical Marketing Communications

Primary responsibility for ethical behavior resides within each of us when we are placed in any of the various marketing communicator roles. We can take the easy route and do what is expedient, or we can pursue the moral high road and treat customers in the same honest fashion we expect to be treated. In large part it is a matter of our own personal integrity. *Integrity* is perhaps the pivotal concept of human nature. Although difficult to precisely define, integrity generally means being honest and not acting in a deceptive or purely expedient manner.[49] Hence, marketing communications itself is not ethical or unethical—it is the degree of integrity exhibited by communications practitioners that determines whether their behavior is ethical or unethical. As a case in point, see the *IMC Focus* dealing with a rigged promotion for Frozen Coke.

Placing the entire burden on individuals is perhaps unfair, because how we behave as individuals is largely a function of the organizational culture in which we operate. Businesses can foster ethical or unethical cultures by establishing *ethical core values* to guide marketing communications behavior. Two core values that would go a long way toward enhancing ethical behavior are (1) treating customers with respect, concern, and honesty—the way you would want to be treated or the way you would want your family treated—and (2) acting toward the environment as though it were your own property.[50]

Firms can foster ethical marcom behavior by encouraging their employees to apply each of the following tests when faced with an ethical predicament:[51]

(1) Act in a way that you would want others to act toward you (the *Golden Rule test*);
(2) take only actions that would be viewed as proper by an objective panel of your professional colleagues (the *professional ethic test*); and
(3) always ask, "Would I feel comfortable explaining this action on television to the general public?" (the *TV test*).

It is important to commit these three tests to memory. During your business career (and otherwise in life), you undoubtedly will be confronted with times of moral/ethical predicament calling for one decision versus another. Thoughts such as these will enter your mind: "My supervisor wants me to do such and such (fill in the blanks), but I'm not sure it is the right thing to do." "I could increase my brand's sales and profits if I were to (fill in the blanks), but though doing that would be expedient, I'm concerned that it is not the right thing to do." When confronted with such dilemmas, stop before you act. Apply the three tests. Imagine

A Rigged Promotion for Frozen Coke

Imagine yourself in the following situation: your firm is trying to increase its business with a major customer. To expand the business you have to convince the customer that it should run a nationwide contest featuring one of your products. This contest, if successful, will increase sales of your product and boost your customer's profits. However, the customer isn't convinced the promotion will be effective and wants to conduct a trial run prior to undertaking the promotion nationally. The test will be conducted by comparing sales in a city where the promotion is run (the "test" city) against sales in another city that isn't offering the promotion (the "control" city). Initial test results reveal your customer's business does not much increase in the test versus control city. The nationwide promotion is in jeopardy. Your job status is threatened. What to do?

This hypothetical situation actually occurred several years ago. The protagonists were Coke and its customer, Burger King. Mid-level executives at Coca-Cola Co. pitched the idea to Burger King to run a promotion offering a free Frozen Coke (a product consisting of crushed ice blended with Coke) when customers bought a "value meal" at a Burger King outlet. The argument presented to Burger King was that by offering free Frozen Cokes it could significantly increase customer traffic and thus the sales of value meals. Burger King's executives were unwilling to commit to an expensive, nationwide promotion until they had some evidence that it would significantly increase sales. They decided to run a test in Richmond, VA (the test city), where free Frozen Cokes would be offered when a value meal was purchased at Burger King, and compare the number of value meal purchases in Richmond during the test period against value meal volume in Tampa, FL (the control city) where free Frozen Cokes would *not* be provided when consumers purchased value meals. This test involved, in other words, a simple field experiment where the presence (Richmond) or absence (Tampa) of free Frozen Cokes was the experimental treatment.

Unfortunately, initial sales results at the start of the Richmond promotion were disappointing, as value meal volume in Richmond was not much different than in Tampa. Under pressure that Burger King might reject the concept of a nationwide promotion, which would have adverse effects for sales of Frozen Coke, a couple of mid-level Coca-Cola executives hatched a scheme to boost sales of value meals in Richmond during the remainder of the test. They hired a free-lance consultant and gave him $9,000 to distribute to Boys & Girls Clubs in the Richmond area. The free lancer distributed cash to leaders of these clubs, who were instructed to treat children to value meals at Burger King.

imc focus

Although this $9,000 in cash contributed less than 1 percent of the total number of value meals purchased in Richmond during the test period, it played a role in demonstrating that sales of value meals in Richmond increased by 6 percent during the test period in comparison to a Tampa sales increase of only 2 percent. On the basis of this differential, Burger King decided to take the promotion nationwide.

Needless to say, the rigged promotion eventually came to Burger King's attention, but only after the fast-food chain had invested in the nationwide Frozen Coke promotion. Coca-Cola's corporate office acknowledged that its employees improperly influenced the test results in Richmond, but the company denied any corporate wrongdoing and laid the blame on the mid-level employees who devised the rigged sales results. Coca-Cola agreed to pay Burger King up to $21 million to compensate it and its franchises for any financial losses.

In explaining his behavior to a supervisor, one of the mid-level executives rationalized that the monetary giveaway was necessary in Richmond to "deseasonalize the data in order to have an accurate measure [of sales response]." His justification, in other words, was that the weather was warmer in Tampa compared to Richmond at the time of the test, which would, according to his logic, have biased business in favor of greater value meal sales in Tampa than Richmond. In short, this executive rationalized what appears to be unethical behavior, but his argument is self-serving and disingenuous. If he truly thought that seasonal differences would have biased test results, then he should have convinced Burger King's executives to pick a control city where the weather would have been comparable to Richmond's rather than selecting Tampa.

In sum, the mid-level executives at Coca-Cola got caught with their proverbial pants down. They engaged in what appears to be unethical behavior and were exposed. The corporation claims no wrongdoing, but the executives apparently felt pressure to do whatever was necessary to produce results. This case is minor in comparison to the financial scandals at Enron and elsewhere, but it demonstrates yet again that businesspeople eventually pay for their (unethical) mistakes.

Sources: Christina Cheddar Berk, "Executive at Coke Gives Up His Post in Scandal's Wake," *The Wall Street Journal Online,* August 26, 2003, http://online.wsj.com (accessed August 26, 2003); Chad Terhune and Richard Gibson, "Coke Agrees to Pay Burger King $10 Million to Resolve Dispute," *The Wall Street Journal Online,* August 4, 2003, http://online.wsj.com (accessed August 4, 2003); Chad Terhune, "How Coke Officials Beefed Up Results of a Marketing Test," *The Wall Street Journal Online,* August 20, 2004, http://online.wsj.com (accessed August 20, 2004).

yourself standing before a television camera and justifying your behavior. Ask if this is how you would want someone to treat you. Ponder whether other professionals would endorse your behavior. In short, think before you act. Business can be tough. Living with your own bad decisions (those reflecting anything other than high integrity) can be miserable. There is absolutely no substitute for integrity.

We conclude this section by presenting the thoughts of a marketing practitioner who has urged his fellow practitioners to conduct their marcom activities in a manner that lifts the human spirit rather than appeals to human nature's most base instincts. Toward achieving this goal, he urges marcom practitioners to contemplate four questions before creating and transmitting messages.[52] These questions deserve our careful consideration.

- *What lasting impact will this message have on our brand if we continue to communicate it over the long run?*
- *What lasting impact, if any, will my message have on society at large?*
- *Does my message appeal to the best in people and attempt to life the human spirit?*
- *What response am I trying to elicit and what macro message does that send about our society?*

Regulation of Marketing Communications

Advertisers, sales promotion managers, and other marcom practitioners are faced with a variety of regulations and restrictions that influence their decision-making latitude. The history of the past century has shown that regulation is necessary to protect consumers and competitors from unethical, fraudulent, deceptive, and unfair practices that some businesses choose to perpetrate. In market economies there is an inevitable tension between the interests of business organizations and the rights of consumers. Regulators attempt to balance the interests of both parties while ensuring that an adequate level of competition is maintained.

When Is Regulation Justified?

Strict adherents to the ideals of free enterprise would argue that government should rarely if ever intervene in the activities of business. More moderate observers believe that regulation is justified in certain circumstances, especially when consumer decisions are based on *false or limited information*.[53] Under such circumstances, consumers are likely to make decisions they would not otherwise make and, as a result, incur economic, physical, or psychological injury. For example, it can be expected that consumers' choice of which foods to purchase is altered as of 2006 when nutritional labeling of trans fat content was required. Competitors also are harmed because they lose business they might have otherwise enjoyed when companies against whom they compete present false or misleading information. In theory, regulation is justified if the *benefits realized exceed the costs*. What are the benefits and costs of regulation?[54]

Benefits

Regulation offers three major benefits. First, *consumer choice* among alternatives is improved when consumers are better informed in the marketplace. For example, consider the Alcoholic Beverage Labeling Act, which requires manufacturers to place the following warning on all containers of alcoholic beverages:

GOVERNMENT WARNING: (1) According to the Surgeon General, women should not drink alcoholic beverages during pregnancy, due to the risk of birth defects. (2) Consumption of alcoholic beverages impairs your ability to drive a car or operate machinery, and may cause health problems.[55]

This regulation serves to inform consumers that drinking has negative consequences. Pregnant women can help themselves and especially their unborn children by heeding this warning to refrain from drinking alcoholic beverages, though it is unlikely that warning labels alone have a major impact in curbing drinking among pregnant women.[56]

A second benefit of regulation is that when consumers become better informed, *product quality tends to improve* in response to consumers' changing needs and preferences. For example, when consumers began learning about the dangers of fat and cholesterol, manufacturers started marketing healthier food products that now are widely available in grocery stores. The same can be expected to occur in restaurants with pending legislation in some states that will require restaurants to make available nutritional information for the levels of calories, fat, and sodium contained in menu items.[57]

A third regulatory benefit is *reduced prices* resulting from a reduction in a seller's "informational market power." For example, prices of used cars undoubtedly would fall if dealers were required to inform prospective purchasers about a car's defects, because consumers would not be willing to pay as much for automobiles with known problems.

Costs

Regulation is not costless. Companies often incur the *cost of complying* with a regulatory remedy. For example, U.S. cigarette manufacturers are required to rotate over the course of a year four different warning messages for three months each. This obviously is somewhat more costly than the previously required single warning message. *Enforcement costs* incurred by regulatory agencies and paid for by taxpayers represent a second cost category.

The *unintended side effects* that might result from regulations represent a third cost to both buyers and sellers. There are a variety of potential side effects that are unforeseen at the time legislation is written. For example, a regulation may unintentionally harm sellers if buyers switch to other products or reduce their level of consumption after regulation is imposed. The cost to buyers may increase if sellers pass along, in the form of higher prices, the costs of complying with a regulation. Both of these prospects are possible when food makers either choose to switch from hydrogenated oil or continue to make their products with hydrogenated oil, with the requirement that they must reveal the high levels of trans fat in their labeling. In sum, regulation is theoretically justified only if the benefits exceed the costs.

When regulation is justified, federal and state agencies, along with the industry, work to oversee the integrity of marketing communications. The following sections examine the two forms of regulation that affect many aspects of marketing communications: governmental regulation and industry self-regulation.

Regulation of Marketing Communications by Federal Agencies

Governmental regulation takes place at both the federal and state levels. All facets of marketing communications are subject to regulation, but advertising is the one area in which regulators have been most active. This is because advertising is the most conspicuous aspect of marketing communications. The discussion that follows examines federal governmental regulation of advertising in the United States as performed by two agencies: the FTC and the FDA. Readers who wish to know more about advertising regulation in European Union countries are directed to the source cited in this endnote.[58]

The FTC is the U.S. government agency with primary responsibility for regulating advertising at the federal level. The FTC's regulatory authority cuts across three broad areas that directly affect marketing communicators: deceptive advertising, unfair practices, and information regulation.

Deceptive Advertising

In a general sense, consumers are deceived by an advertising claim or campaign when (1) the impression left by the claim or campaign is false—that is, there is a *claim-fact discrepancy;* and (2) the false claim or campaign is *believed* by consumers. The important point is that a false claim is not necessarily deceptive by itself. Rather, consumers must believe a claim to be deceived by it: "a false claim does not harm consumers unless it is believed, and a true claim can generate harm if it generates a false belief."[59]

Although the FTC makes deception rulings case by case, it does employ some general guidelines in deciding whether deceptive advertising has occurred. Under current deception policy, the FTC will find a business practice deceptive if, to the consumer's detriment, an advertised claim has been made or an important fact is omitted, either of which is likely to mislead consumers who are acting reasonably under the circumstances. Thus there are three elements that provide the essence of the FTC's deception policy:[60]

1. Misleading. There must be a representation, omission, or a practice that is likely to mislead the consumer. A *misrepresentation* is defined by the FTC as an express or implied statement contrary to fact. For example, if a pharmaceutical company claimed that one of its prescription drugs did not contain a substance that it actually did, this would be considered a misrepresentation. A *misleading omission* is said to occur when qualifying information necessary to prevent a practice, claim, representation, or reasonable expectation or belief from being misleading is *not* disclosed. A misleading omission would exist, for example, if the same pharmaceutical company failed to disclose an important side effect of using its prescription drug.

2. Reasonable consumer. The act or practice must be considered from the perspective of the "reasonable consumer." The FTC's test of reasonableness is based on the consumer's interpretation or reaction to an advertisement—that is, the commission determines the effect of the advertising practice on reasonable members of the group to which the advertising is targeted. The following quote indicates that the FTC evaluates advertising claims case by case in view of the target audience's unique position—its education level, intellectual capacity, mental frame, and so on.

For instance, if a company markets a cure to the terminally ill, the practice will be evaluated from the perspective of how it affects the ordinary member of that group. Thus, terminally ill consumers might be particularly susceptible to exaggerated cure claims. By the same token, a practice or representation directed to a well-educated group, such as a prescription drug advertisement to doctors, would be judged in light of the knowledge and sophistication of that group.[61]

3. Material. To be considered deceptive, the representation, omission, or practice must be "material." A *material representation* involves information that is important to consumers and that is likely to influence their *choice* or *conduct* regarding a product. In general, the FTC considers information to be material when it pertains to the central characteristics of a product or service (including performance features, size, and price). Hence, if an athletic-shoe company falsely claimed that its brand possesses the best shock absorption feature on the market, this would be a material misrepresentation to the many runners who make purchase choices based on this factor. On the other hand, if this same company were to falsely claim it has been in business for 28 years—when in fact it has been in business for only 25 years—this would not be regarded as material because most consumers would not be swayed much differently whether the company had been in business 25 or 28 years.

An important case involving the issue of materiality was brought by the FTC against Kraft Foods and its advertising of Kraft Single American cheese slices. The FTC challenged Kraft on grounds that advertisements for Kraft Singles falsely claimed that each slice contains the same amount of calcium as *five* ounces of milk. In fact, each slice of Kraft Singles begins with five ounces of whole milk, but during processing 30 percent, or 1.5 ounces of milk, is lost. In other words, each slice contains only 70 percent of the amount of calcium claimed in Kraft's advertisements.[62] Kraft responded that its $11 million advertising campaign did not influence consumer purchases. Kraft's legal counsel argued that the advertisements (1) did not convey the misleading representation claimed by the FTC, but (2) even if this representation had been conveyed, it would not have mattered because calcium is a relatively unimportant factor in consumers' decision to purchase Kraft Singles. (Out of nine factors rated by consumers in a copy test, calcium was rated no higher than seventh.)

Whereas the FTC's position was that Kraft's advertising *was* likely to mislead consumers, Kraft's defense was that its calcium claim, whether false or not, is nondeceptive because the difference between 5 ounces of milk and 3.5 ounces is an immaterial difference to consumers. Kraft's defense, in other words, amounted to the following: yes, we (Kraft) made claims about the calcium benefits of Kraft Singles, but the issue of deceptiveness is moot because the difference in calcium content between what we claimed (a single slice contains the calcium equivalency of 5 ounces of milk) and what is reality (a single slice contains the calcium equivalency of 3.5 ounces of milk) is immaterial to consumers and hence not deceptive.

After hearing detailed testimony on the matter and following an appeal process, the commissioners of the FTC determined that Kraft's advertising claim was indeed material.[63] Accordingly, the FTC ordered Kraft to cease and desist (literally, "stop and go no more," or discontinue) further misrepresentations of Kraft Singles' calcium content. The Kraft case generated much discussion and controversy. The articles cited in the endnote are worthwhile reading for this particular case, as well as for their broader significance to advertising practice and public policy involving deceptive advertising.[64]

Unfair Practices

The FTC has legal authority to regulate unfair as well as deceptive acts or practices in commerce. Unlike deception, a finding of unfairness to consumers may go beyond questions of fact and relate merely to public values.[65] The criteria used to evaluate whether a business act is unfair involve such considerations as whether the act (1) offends public policy as it has been established by statutes, (2) is immoral, unethical, oppressive, or unscrupulous, and (3) causes substantial injury to consumers, competitors, or other businesses.[66]

The FTC's right to regulate unfair advertising was a matter of considerable dispute for years, because the precise meaning of "unfair" was not clear.[67] The dispute ended when Congress devised a definition of unfairness that is satisfactory to all parties. **Unfair advertising** is defined as "acts or practices that cause or are likely to cause *substantial injury to consumers,* which is *not reasonably avoidable* by consumers themselves and *not outweighed by countervailing benefits to consumers or competition*" (emphasis added).[68] The italicized features of the definition point out Congress's intention to balance the interests of advertisers with those of consumers and to prevent capricious applications of the unfairness doctrine by the FTC.

The FTC has applied the unfairness doctrine in instances where questionable advertisements are aimed at children. Because children are more credulous and less well-equipped than adults to protect themselves, public-policy officials are especially concerned with protecting youngsters. The unfairness doctrine is especially useful in cases involving children because many advertising claims are not deceptive per se but are nonetheless potentially unethical, unscrupulous, or inherently dangerous to children. For example, the FTC considered one company's use of Spider-Man vitamin advertising unfair because such advertising was judged capable of inducing children to take excessive and dangerous amounts of vitamins.[69]

In recent years, the FTC has most actively applied the unfairness doctrine to numerous instances of telemarketing scams and Internet fraud.[70] Both technologies are ripe for fraudulent behavior by unscrupulous marketers, and such behavior can readily injure consumers (as well as competitors) because the tricks and scams cannot reasonably be avoided by consumers themselves. E-mail fraud is the most widely practiced abuse, and the FTC has brought over 200 enforcement actions under its unfairness power against such fraudulent behavior.[71]

Information Regulation

Although the primary purpose of advertising regulation is the prohibition of deceptive and unfair practices, regulation also is needed at times to provide consumers with information they might not otherwise receive. The corrective advertising program is the most important of the FTC's information provision programs.[72]

Corrective advertising is based on the premise that a firm that misleads consumers should have to use future advertisements to rectify the deceptive impressions it has created in consumers' minds. Corrective advertising is designed to prevent a firm from continuing to deceive consumers rather than to punish the firm.

The most prominent corrective advertising order issued by the FTC to date involved advertising over 30 years ago for Warner-Lambert's Listerine mouthwash. According to the FTC, Warner-Lambert misled consumers for a number of years; the FTC accordingly required Warner-Lambert to run this corrective statement: "Listerine will not help prevent colds or sore throats or lessen their severity." The corrective campaign ran for 16 months at a cost of $10.3 million to Warner-Lambert, most of which was spent on television commercials. Several studies evaluated the effectiveness of the Listerine corrective advertising order. The FTC's own study revealed only partial success for the Listerine corrective campaign. On the positive side, there was a 40 percent drop in the amount of mouthwash used for the misconceived purpose of preventing colds and sore throats; on the negative side, 57 percent of Listerine users continued to rate cold and sore throat prevention as a key factor in their purchasing decision (only 15 percent of Scope users reported a similar goal), and 39 percent of Listerine users reported continued use of the mouthwash to relieve or prevent a cold or sore throat.[73]

In one of the first major applications of corrective advertising since the Listerine case, the FTC issued a corrective order against the Novartis Corporation and its Doan's Pills. Doan's advertisements referred to the brand's special or unique ingredients, called itself the "back specialist," and depicted the brand against packages of competitors Advil, Bayer, and Tylenol. The FTC concluded that the advertising campaign created the false impression that Doan's was more effective than other over-the-counter drugs for combating back pain. The FTC ordered Novartis to undertake an $8 million advertising campaign to correct the misimpression that Doan's Pills outperform other over-the-counter analgesics in treating back pain. This order required Doan's packaging and advertising to carry the message, "Although Doan's is an effective pain reliever, there is no evidence that Doan's is more effective than other pain relievers for back pain." Novartis' legal counsel claimed the order was excessive, whereas others have appraised the order as an inadequate remedy in the face of compelling evidence that Doan's advertising was deceptive.[74]

The FTC walks a fine line when issuing a corrective advertising order and specifying the remedial action a deceptive advertiser must take. The objective is to restore the marketplace to its original position prior to the deceptive advertising so that a firm does not continue to reap the rewards from its past deception. However, there is always the possibility that the corrective advertising effort may go too far and severely damage the firm and perhaps, unintentionally, hurt other companies in the industry.[75]

Product Labeling

The FDA is the federal body responsible for regulating information on the packages of food and drug products. As described in the chapter opening feature, the FDA has become very active in regulating the type of nutritional information that must appear on food labels, as, for example, the requirement that labels must include the amount of trans fats contained in a single serving.

Prescription Drug Advertising

Whereas the FTC is responsible for regulating deceptive and unfair advertising for all products (including over-the-counter drugs), the FDA is charged with regulating advertisements for *prescription drugs.* This has been a major challenge in recent years with the onset of direct-to-consumer (DTC) advertising. As the name suggests, this form of advertising involves messages for prescription drugs that are directed toward consumers. Pharmaceutical companies expect DTC ads to motivate consumers to urge their physicians to prescribe advertised drug brands. The FDA's role is, in this regard, to police the truthfulness of DTC ads and to ensure that any claims made are supported by scientific evidence.

The FDA requires prescription drug advertisers to present a *balanced perspective* when advertising drugs. That is, in addition to touting product benefits, they must also identify the side effects and risks of using particular drugs. You may have noticed that TV commercials for DTC drugs show how wonderful a drug is in treating arthritis, cholesterol levels, weight problems, or other health issues. It is only at the end of the commercial that consumers are informed that in using the drug one may experience nausea, diarrhea, reduced sexual functioning, or any of a number of other undesirable consequences. Drug companies would prefer not to mention these side effects, but doing so is required—for the protection of consumers in the best spirit of regulation.

In magazine ads, pharmaceutical companies provide detailed information about their products' undesirable side effects, but this information typically is placed on the back pages of ads and in very small print. Critics have questioned the value of such information on grounds that it is too technical, too detailed, and difficult to read because it typically is printed in very small print. Accordingly, the FDA recently proposed that drug makers present less-detailed information about side effects in print ads, but that they explain the most serious problems in language accessible to typical consumers.[76]

State Agencies' Regulation of Marketing Communications

Individual states have their own statutes and regulatory agencies to police the marketplace from fraudulent business practices. Most, if not all, states have departments of consumer affairs or consumer protection. The National Association of Attorneys General (NAAG), which includes attorneys general from all 50 states, has played a particularly active role. In one instance, for example, attorneys general from 22 states filed a complaint against Honda of America, alleging that Honda's three-wheel, all-terrain vehicles were "rolling death traps."[77]

An especially interesting case involved a lawsuit filed by the Texas attorney general against Volvo North America. Volvo had produced a television commercial showing Bear Foot, a monster truck with huge wheels, running over a string of automobiles. All the automobiles collapsed except the Volvo station wagon. An investigation revealed, however, that the Volvo had been reinforced with steel and wood, while the other cars had their roof supports severed.[78]

There is every indication that states will remain active in their efforts to regulate advertising deception and other business practices, which poses a potentially significant problem for many national advertisers who might find themselves subject to multiple, and perhaps inconsistent, state regulations.[79] It is somewhat ironic that many national companies would prefer to see a stronger FTC inasmuch as these companies are better off with a single regulatory agency that institutes uniform national guidelines and keeps the marketplace as free as possible from the fly-by-night operators that tarnish the image of all businesses.

Advertising Self-Regulation

Self-regulation, as the name suggests, is undertaken by the advertising community itself (i.e., advertisers, industry trade associations, and ad media) rather than by governmental bodies. Self-regulation is a form of *private government* whereby peers establish and enforce voluntary rules of behavior.[80] Advertising self-regulation has flourished in countries such as Canada, France, the United Kingdom, and the United States.[81]

Media Self-Regulation

The *advertising clearance process* is a form of self-regulation undertaken by ad media that takes place behind the scenes before a commercial or other advertisement reaches consumers. A magazine advertisement or television commercial undergoes a variety of clearance steps prior to its actual printing or airing, including (1) advertising agency clearance, (2) approval from the advertiser's legal department and perhaps also from an independent law firm, and (3) media approval (such as television networks' guidelines regarding standards of taste).[82] A finished ad that makes it through the clearance process and appears in advertising media is then subject to the possibility of post hoc regulation from federal (e.g., the FTC), state (e.g., NAAG), and self-regulators (e.g., the National Advertising Review Council).

The National Advertising Review Council

Self-regulation by the National Advertising Review Council (NARC) has been the most publicized and perhaps most effective form of self-regulation. NARC is an organization formed via a partnership among the Association of National Advertisers, the American Association of Advertising Agencies, the American Advertising Federation, and the Council of Better Business Bureau's National Advertising Division (NAD).

NARC consists of three review units: the Children's Advertising Review Unit (CARU), NAD, and the National Advertising Review Board (NARB). CARU monitors children's television programming and commercials, whereas the NAD and NARB were established to sustain standards of truth and accuracy in national advertising to adults. NARB is the umbrella-like term applied to the combined NAD/NARB self-regulatory mechanism; however, by strict definition, NARB is a court consisting of 50 representatives who are formed into five-member panels to hear appeals of NAD cases when an involved party is dissatisfied with the initial verdict.[83] NAD is the investigative arm of NARB and is responsible for evaluating, investigating, and holding initial negotiations with an advertiser on complaints involving truth or accuracy of national advertising.

The number of cases investigated and resolved varies, but NAD often becomes involved in as many as 150 cases a year. Cases are brought to the NAD by competitors, initiated by the NAD staff itself, or originate from local Better Business Bureaus, consumer groups, and individual consumers. For example, Bayer AG, the German company that invented aspirin, took exception to an ad by competitor St. Joseph, known for its baby aspirin formulated at 81 milligrams per tablet, when a St. Joseph ad claimed that taking "too much aspirin just isn't a good idea for anybody." Bayer brought the case to the NARB, which ruled in Bayer's favorite and requested that St. Joseph's revise its commercial.[84]

Another NAD case involved an advertisement by Tropicana for its Light'n Healthy brand that contains one-third less sugar and calories than orange juice. The issue in dispute in this ad involved Tropicana's use of the rhetorical question, "Counting carbs?" An NAD investigation concluded that this query could reasonably be interpreted by consumers as suggesting that Light'n Healthy is a low carbohydrate beverage. The NAD therefore recommended that Tropicana discontinue any advertisements that included the "counting carbs?" question or, alternatively, disclose that a single serving of Light'n Healthy contains 17 carbohydrate grams. In response, Tropicana respectfully disagreed with NAD that the question suggests that its brand is low in carbs but it agreed to NAD's recommendation to incorporate a disclosure of the actual carb count. Had Tropicana refused, there is nothing the NAD could have done other than perhaps refer the case to the FTC.[85]

In conclusion, advertising self-regulation reduces the need for government regulation and maintains the general integrity of advertising and, in so doing, protects both consumers and competitors. A president of NARC has succinctly captured self-regulation's value:

Self-regulation is smart business. It provides a level playing field. Continuing NAD improvements provide the quickest, least expensive and most effective way for advertisers to challenge one another's claims. A court case can take over a year (vs. NAD's 60 business days) and cost 10 times as much as a NAD case.[86]

Environmental, or "Green," Marketing Communications

People around the world are concerned with the depletion of natural resources and the degradation of the physical environment. Some companies have responded to environmental concerns by introducing environmentally oriented products and undertaking marcom programs to promote them. These actions are referred to as *green marketing*.[87] Unfortunately, there is relatively little evidence that many consumers are much interested in paying more for environmentally friendly products. In concept tests of new product ideas, American consumers have rated environmental issues as no more important than about a 6 on a 10-point scale; ratings as low as these simply do not motivate purchase decisions.[88] Nonetheless, it is clear that the green movement is here to stay to one degree or another.

Green Marketing Initiatives

Motivated for reasons such as achieving regulatory compliance, gaining competitive advantage, being socially responsible, and following the commitment of top management, some companies have made legitimate responses to environmental

American Honda Motor Co., Inc.

Figure 3.3

The Honda Civic Hybrid Automobile

problems.[89] These responses mostly have been in the form of *new* or *revised products*. Illustrative green products include the following:

- Personal computers are now equipped with energy-efficient features and are made with some recycled materials.
- Batteries used in laptops, cell phones, camcorders, PDAs, and other products are increasingly being recycled, and consumers are urged to take "dead" batteries to participating retailers for recycling purposes (see Figure 3.2 on page 79).
- Furniture manufacturers make environmentally friendly furniture from recycled wood, plastic, and even recycled newspaper mixed with wood and wax.[90]
- Perhaps the major environmentally responsive product initiative has been the electric-gas hybrid automobile marketed under brand names such as the Honda Civic (Figure 3.3) and the Toyota Prius (Figure 3.4). These hybrids run on a combination of gas and electric power, which delivers higher MPG than conventional transport. The Prius has been in such great demand, partially due to rising gas prices and the fact that hybrid autos get much better mileage per gallon than conventional autos, that Toyota has had difficulty filling orders. In the summer of 2004, demand was so great that Toyota had to more than double the number of vehicles allocated to the United States.[91]

Although these product innovations are important, of more direct relevance to this text are the marcom efforts that appeal to environmental sensitivities. The major green communications efforts involve advertisements that promote green products, environmentally friendly packaging, seal-of-approval programs that promote green products, cause-oriented communication efforts that support green products, and point-of-purchase display materials that are environmentally efficient.

Figure 3.4

The Toyota Prius Hybrid Automobile

Toyota Motor/North America, Inc.

Green Advertising

Environmental appeals in advertising were commonplace in American advertising for a short period in the early to mid-1990s, but the initial fervor toward the deteriorating physical environment has waned. In fact, it is difficult to find many examples of environmentally oriented advertising.

There are three types of green advertising appeals when this form of advertising occasionally surfaces: (1) ads that address a relationship between a product/service and the biophysical environment (such as that for Shell in Figure 3.5 on page 80); (2) those that promote a green lifestyle without highlighting a product or service; and (3) ads that present a corporate image of environmental responsibility (see Figure 3.6 for BP on page 81).[92]

Packaging Responses

Various efforts have been initiated to improve the environmental effectiveness of packaging materials. Illustrative programs include packaging soft drinks and many other products in recyclable plastic bottles; switching from polystyrene clamshell containers to paperboard packages for burgers and other sandwiches; and introducing concentrated laundry detergents as a way of achieving smaller packages and thus less waste disposal to be placed in already crowded landfills.

Figure 3.2 Recyclable Batteries

Courtesy of the Rechargeable Battery Recycling Corporation (RBRC)

Shell Oil Company

Figure 3.5

Green Advertising Addressing the Biophysical Environment

As counter to these positive packaging developments, there is evidence that package materials often are wasted due to a practice called *short filling*. For example, over 40 percent of juice containers, milk cartons, and other dairy products contain a smaller amount of product—from 1 to 6 percent less—than the package labels promise.[93] This short-filling problem is partially due to profit skimming and also results, more innocently, from poorly calibrated packing machines. Whatever the reason, the fact remains that short filling results annually in thousands of tons of wasted packaging materials.

Seal-of-Approval Programs

Organizations around the world have designed programs to assist consumers in identifying environmentally friendly products and brands. In Germany, for example, the Blue Angel seal represents a promise to consumers that a product carrying an environmental claim is in fact legitimate. Green Seal, a Washington, D.C., nonprofit organization, has developed standards and awarded seals to companies that meet environmental standards—which fewer than 20 percent of all products in the category are able to satisfy. General Electric, for example, received a seal for developing compact fluorescent light bulbs. In addition to Green Seal, there are various product-category-specific seal programs. For example, the 100% Recycled Paperboard Alliance—a group of North American recycled paperboard manufacturers—allows participating members to identify their products with a logo that consists of a semicircle of 10 small arrows pointing to the words *100% Recycled Paperboard*.[94] Programs such as these provide consumers with assurance that the products carrying these seals legitimately are environmentally friendly.

Cause-Oriented Programs

Cause-oriented marketing is practiced when companies sponsor or support worthy environmental or social programs. In doing so, the marketing communicator anticipates that associating the company and its brands with a worthy cause will generate goodwill. It is for this reason that companies sponsor various environmental causes. At one time General Motors planted a tree for every Chevrolet Geo car sold. Evian, a company that markets mineral water, had representatives visit college campuses to raise environmental awareness and recruit new members for the World Wildlife Fund. Cause-oriented programs can be effective if they are not overused and if consumers perceive a company's involvement in an environmental cause is sincere and not just naked commercialism.

Point-of-Purchase Programs

Billions of dollars are invested in plastic, wood, metal, paper, and other display materials. Many of the displays sent by manufacturers to retailers are never used and simply end up in landfills. Closer consultations with retailers regarding their point-of-purchase needs would lead to fewer unused and discarded displays, and increased use of permanent displays (those engineered to last at least six months) would substantially reduce the number of temporary displays that are quickly discarded. As a result, this would mean a major conservation effort and substantial savings to manufacturers.

Guidelines for Green Marketing

The significance of the environmental problem demands that marketing communicators do everything possible to ensure that green claims are credible, realistic, and believable. To assist companies in knowing what environmental claims can and cannot be communicated in advertisements, on packages, and elsewhere, the FTC promulgated guides for environmental marketing claims.[95] These guides outline four general principles that apply to all environmental marketing claims: (1) qualifications and disclosures should be sufficiently clear and prominent to prevent deception; (2) claims should make clear whether they apply to the product, the package, or a component of either; (3) claims should not overstate an environmental attribute or benefit, either expressly or by implication; and (4) comparative claims should be presented in a manner that makes the basis for the comparison sufficiently clear to avoid consumer deception.

In addition to these general guidelines, marcom practitioners are offered four general recommendations for making appropriate environmental claims: (1) make the claims specific, (2) use claims that reflect current disposal options, (3) make the claims substantive, and (4) only use supportable claims.[96]

BP North America/Ogilvy & Mather

Figure 3.6

Green Advertising Promoting an Image of Environmental Responsibility

1. **Make Specific Claims.** This guideline is intended to prevent marketing communicators from using meaningless claims such as "environmentally friendly" or "safe for the environment." The use of specific environmental claims enables consumers to make informed choices, reduces the likelihood that claims will be misinterpreted, and minimizes the chances that consumers will think that a product is more environmentally friendly than it actually is. In general, it is recommended that environmental claims be as specific as possible—not general, vague, incomplete, or overly broad. For example, a claim that a brand of washing detergent is "fully biodegradable" is more precise than an expression that this brand is "good for the environment."
2. **Reflect Current Disposal Options.** This recommendation is directed at preventing environmental claims that are technically accurate but practically unrealizable due to local trash-disposal practices. For example, most communities dispose of trash by burying it in public landfills. Because paper and plastic products do not degrade when buried, it is misleading for businesses to make environmental claims that their products are degradable, biodegradable, or photodegradable.
3. **Make Substantive Claims.** Some marketing communicators use trivial and irrelevant environmental claims to convey the impression that a promoted brand is environmentally sound. An illustration of a nonsubstantive claim is a company promoting its polystyrene foam cups as "preserving our trees and forests." Another trivial claim is when single-use products such as paper plates are claimed to be "safe for the environment." Clearly, a paper plate is not unsafe to the environment in the same sense that a toxic chemical is unsafe; however, paper plates and other throwaways do not actually benefit the environment but rather exacerbate the landfill problem.
4. **Make Supportable Claims.** This recommendation is straightforward: environmental claims should be supported by competent and reliable scientific

evidence. The purpose of this recommendation is to encourage businesses to make only those environmental claims that can be backed by facts. The injunction to businesses is clear: don't claim it unless you can support it.

Summary

This chapter examined a variety of issues related to ethical marcom behavior, the regulation of marketing communications, and green marcom initiatives. The first major section looked at ethical marketing communications behavior. The ethics of each of the following marcom activities were discussed: the targeting of marketing communications efforts, advertising, public relations, packaging communications, sales promotions, and online marketing communications. A concluding discussion examined how firms can foster ethical behavior.

The second section examined the regulation of marcom activities. The regulatory environment was described with respect to both government regulation and industry self-regulation. The FTC's role was explained in terms of its regulation of deception and unfair practices. Self-regulation by the Council of Better Business Bureaus' National Advertising Division (NAD) and National Advertising Review Board (NARB) were discussed.

In the final section, environmental, or *green,* marketing was described, and implications for marketing communications were elaborated. Marketing communicators have responded to society's environmental interests by developing more environmentally friendly packaging and undertaking other communications initiatives. Recommendations provided to marketing communicators for making appropriate environmental claims are to (1) make the claims specific, (2) have claims reflect current disposal options, (3) make the claims substantive, and (4) make supportable claims.

Discussion Questions

1. With regard to the Hefty trash bag description at the beginning of the chapter, answer the following questions: What would you have done if you were placed in this position? Would you have introduced your own brand of nondegradable trash bag, or would you be willing to suffer the consequences of lost sales to unethical competitors? What other alternatives may have been available other than the choice between "introducing versus not introducing" a nondegradable bag?
2. Has Subway crossed the exploitation line in targeting its food products to obese children?
3. What is your opinion regarding the ethics of product placements in movies targeted to children? Identify the arguments on both sides of the issue, and then present your personal position.
4. Is targeting unethical or just good marketing? Identify the arguments on both sides of the issue, and then present your personal position.
5. What is your view regarding Anheuser-Busch's use in the early to mid 1990s of humorous TV commercials that portrayed animated characters Frank and Louie, and an accompanying cast of lizard and frog characters? Is this form of advertising simply a marvelous creative execution, or is it insidious in its potential to encourage children to like the concept of drinking beer, and perhaps Budweiser in particular? (Note: If you don't recall these commercials, ask your professor to provide a description.)
6. Several years ago during the holiday season Philip Morris Companies introduced a new cigarette brand named "M" and promoted it as "A Special Blend for a Special Season." Convenience stores and other retailers displayed signs with

the appearance of gift-wrapping paper in green and red paisley backgrounds and the message, "Season's Greetings from Marlboro Country." The president of the Campaign for Tobacco-Free Kids exclaimed that the marketing effort behind M "is selling cancer for Christmas."[97] What are your views on Philip Morris' marketing of M? Is it unethical or a case of smart marketing behavior?

7. Are you in favor of the federal government requiring nutritional labeling (such as the trans fat requirement described in the *Marcom Challenge*), or do you consider such requirements an unnecessary intrusion into the free marketplace? Justify your position on this matter.
8. What is the distinction between a deceptive and an unfair business practice?
9. Give examples of advertising claims that, if found false, probably would be considered material and those that probably would be evaluated as immaterial.
10. What is your opinion of the defense Kraft used in claiming that calcium is an immaterial product attribute?
11. When discussing the criticism that advertising is manipulative, a distinction was made between persuasion efforts of which consumers are cognitively aware and those that fall below their conscious radar screens. First, explain in your own words the distinction between the potential for advertisers to cognitively and unconsciously manipulate consumers. Second, express your thoughts about the ethical ramifications of say, retailers' potential use of in-store advertising to air subliminal messages.
12. What is your view of a proposal by Senator Hillary Clinton (Democrat, New York) that would ban all advertising and marketing in elementary schools?
13. In theory, corrective advertising represents a potentially valuable device for regulating deceptive advertising. In practice, however, corrective advertising must perform a very delicate balancing act by being strong enough without being too forceful. Explain the nature of this dilemma.
14. In the late 1990s, the Distilled Spirits Council of the United States voted to lift its voluntary ban on advertising "hard" liquor on television and radio, a self-imposed ban that had been in effect for nearly a half-century. In your opinion, what are the arguments on both sides of the issue regarding the removal of this ban? If you were an executive employed by the Distilled Spirits Council, would you have urged a return to the airways? Is this return to advertising distilled spirits via electronic media unethical or, alternatively, is it a matter of a gutsy business decision by the Distilled Spirits Council that was long overdue?
15. Some consumers are more concerned about the physical environment than others. Provide a specific profile of what in your opinion would be the socioeconomic and psychographic (i.e., lifestyle) characteristics of the "environmentally concerned" consumer.

ENDNOTES

1. Ideas and facts for this vignette are from Leila Abboud, "The Truth about Trans Fats: Coming to a Label Near You," *The Wall Street Journal Online,* July 10, 2003, http://online.wsj.com; Patricia Odell, "Let There Be Lite," *Promo,* March 2004, 14–17.
2. Jennifer Lawrence and Christy Fisher, "Mobil, States Settle Degradability Suits," *Advertising Age,* July 1, 1991, 4.
3. For an interesting discussion of the interrelation between ethical issues and regulation, see George M. Zinkhan, "Advertising Ethics: Emerging Methods and Trends," *Journal of Advertising* 23 (September 1994), 1–4.
4. Carolyn Y. Yoo, "Personally Responsible," *BizEd,* May/June 2003, 24.
5. O. C. Ferrell and Larry G. Gresham, "A Contingency Framework for Understanding Ethical Decision Making in Marketing," *Journal of Marketing* 49 (summer 1985), 87–96.
6. A provocative and informative discourse on the issue of consumer vulnerability is presented in N. Craig Smith and Elizabeth Cooper-Martin, "Ethics and Target Marketing: The Role of Product Harm and Consumer Vulnerability," *Journal of Marketing* 61 (July 1997), 1–20.
7. Sara Schaefer Munoz, "Nagging Issue: Pitching Junk to Kids," *The Wall Street Journal Online,* November 11, 2003, http://online.wsj.com (accessed November 11, 2003).
8. Laura Bird, "Gatorade for Kids," *Adweek's Marketing Week,* July 15, 1991, 4–5.
9. Matthew Grimm, "Is Marketing to Kids Ethical?" *Brandweek,* April 5, 2004, 44–48.
10. Joseph Pereira and Audrey Warren, "Coming Up Next. . . ," *The Wall Street Journal Online,* March 15, 2004, http://online.wsj.com (accessed March 15, 2004).

11. Stephanie Thompson, "Campbell Aims Squarely at Kids with Push for Pastas and Soups," *Advertising Age,* May 31, 2004, 62.
12. Janet Whitman, "Subway Weighs Television Ads on Childhood Obesity," *The Wall Street Journal Online,* June 16, 2004, http://online.wsj.com (accessed June 17, 2004); Bob Garfield, "Subway Walks Line between Wellness, Child Exploitation," *Advertising Age,* July 26, 2004, 29.
13. Claire Atkinson, "Nader on Advertising," *Advertising Age,* March 1, 2004, 35.
14. Eben Shapiro, "Molson Ice Ads Raise Hackles of Regulators," *The Wall Street Journal,* February 25, 1994, B1, B10.
15. Guideline 8 in the Industry Advertising Code. Published in an undated pamphlet distributed by the Department of Consumer Awareness and Education, Anheuser-Busch, Inc., St. Louis, MO.
16. Brian Steinberg and Suzanne Vranica, "Brewers Are Urged to Tone Down Ads," *The Wall Street Journal Online,* June 23, 2003, http://online.wsj.com (accessed June 23, 2003).
17. Christopher Lawton, "Lawsuits Allege Alcohol Makers Target Youths," *The Wall Street Journal Online,* February 5, 2004, http://online.wsj.com (accessed February 5, 2004).
18. Stefan Fatsis and Christopher Lawton, "Beer Ads on TV, College Sports: Explosive Mix?" *The Wall Street Journal Online,* November 12, 2003, http://online.wsj.com (accessed November 12, 2003).
19. See, for example, Cornelia Pechmann and Susan J. Knight, "An Experimental Investigation of the Joint Effects of Advertising and Peers on Adolescents' Beliefs and Intentions about Cigarette Consumption," *Journal of Consumer Research* 29 (June 2002), 5–19; Marvin E. Goldberg, "American Media and the Smoking-related Behaviors of Asian Adolescents," *Journal of Advertising Research* 43 (March 2003), 2–11; Marvin E. Goldberg, "Correlation, Causation, and Smoking Initiation among Youths," *Journal of Advertising Research* 43 (December 2003), 431–440; Kathleen J. Kelly, Michael D. Slater, and David Karan, "Image Advertisements' Influence on Adolescents' Perceptions of the Desirability of Beer and Cigarettes," *Journal of Public Policy & Marketing* 21 (fall 2002), 295–304.
20. See, for example, Robert N. Reitter, "Comment: 'American Media and the Smoking-related Behaviors of Asian Adolescents,'" *Journal of Advertising Research* 43 (March 2003), 12–13; Charles R. Taylor and P. Greg Bonner, "Comment on 'American Media and the Smoking-related Behaviors of Asian Adolescents,'" *Journal of Advertising Research* 43 (December 2003), 419–430.
21. For an insightful review of the literature and a provocative study on this issue, see J. Craig Andrews, Richard G. Netemeyer, Scot Burton, D. Paul Moberg, and Ann Christiansen, "Understanding Adolescent Intentions to Smoke: An Examination of Relationships among Social Influence, Prior Trial Behavior, and Antitobacco Campaign Advertising," *Journal of Marketing* 68 (July 2004), 110–123.
22. For opposing positions on this issue, see Joel B. Cohen "Playing to Win: Marketing and Public Policy at Odds over Joe Camel," *Journal of Public Policy & Marketing,* 19 (fall 2000), 155–167; John E. Calfee, "The Historical Significance of Joe Camel," *Journal of Public Policy & Marketing,* 19 (fall 2000), 168–182.
23. For reviews of this research and alternative perspectives, see Jean J. Boddewyn, "Where Should Articles on the Link between Tobacco Advertising and Consumption Be Published?" *Journal of Advertising* 22 (December 1993), 105–107; Lawrence C. Soley, "Smoke-filled Rooms and Research: A Response to Jean J. Boddewyn's Commentary," *Journal of Advertising* 22 (December 1993), 108–109; Richard W. Pollay, "Pertinent Research and Impertinent Opinions: Our Contributions to the Cigarette Advertising Policy Debate," *Journal of Advertising* 22 (December 1993), 110–117; Claude R. Martin, Jr., "Ethical Advertising Research Standards: Three Case Studies," *Journal of Advertising* 23 (September 1994), 17–29; and Claude R. Martin, Jr., "Pollay's Pertinent and Impertinent Opinions: 'Good' versus 'Bad' Research," *Journal of Advertising* 23 (March 1994), 117–122.
24. See Ira Teinowitz, "Filmmakers: Give Ad-practice Shifts a Chance to Work," *Advertising Age,* October 2, 2000, 6; David Finnigan, "Pounding the Kid Trail," *Brandweek,* October 9, 2000, 32–38; Betsy Spethmann, "Now Showing: Federal Scrutiny," *Promo,* November 2000, 17.
25. Scott Donaton, "Why the Kids Marketing Fuss? Here's Why Parents Are Angry," *Advertising Age,* October 16, 2000, 48.
26. "Fighting Ads in the Inner City," *Newsweek,* February 5, 1990, 46.
27. For further reading about these and other controversial cases, see Smith and Cooper-Martin, "Ethics and Target Marketing."
28. Dan Koeppel, "Insensitivity to a Market's Concerns," *Adweek's Marketing Week,* November 5, 1990, 25; "A 'Black' Cigarette Goes Up in Smoke," *Newsweek,* January 29, 1990, 54; "RJR Cancels Test of 'Black' Cigarette," *Marketing News,* February 19, 1990, 10.
29. Laura Bird, "An 'Uptown' Remake Called PowerMaster," *Adweek's Marketing Week,* July 1, 1991, 7.
30. "Fighting Ads in the Inner City."
31. For more discussion of this case, see Smith and Cooper-Martin, "Ethics and Target Marketing."
32. See John E. Calfee, "'Targeting' the Problem: It Isn't Exploitation, It's Efficient Marketing," *Advertising Age,* July 22, 1991, 18.
33. For additional insight on the issue, see Smith and Cooper-Martin, "Ethics and Target Marketing."
34. For an insightful treatment of practitioners' views of advertising ethics, see Minette E. Drumwright and Patrick E. Murphy, "How Advertising Practitioners View Ethics," *Journal of Advertising* 33 (summer 2004), 7–24.
35. Ronald Berman, "Advertising and Social Change," *Advertising Age,* April 30, 1980, 24.
36. The interested reader is encouraged to review the following three articles for an extremely thorough, insightful, and provocative debate over the social and ethical role of advertising in American society. Richard W. Pollay, "The Distorted Mirror: Reflections on the Unintended Consequences of Advertising," *Journal of Marketing* 50 (April 1986), 18–36; Morris B. Holbrook, "Mirror, Mirror on the Wall, What's Unfair in the Reflections of Advertising?" *Journal of Marketing* 51 (July 1987), 95–103; Richard W. Pollay, "On the Value of Reflections on the Values in 'The Distorted Mirror,'" *Journal of Marketing* (July 1987), 104–109. Professors Pollay and Holbrook present alternative views of whether advertising is a "mirror" that merely reflects societal attitudes and values or a "distorted mirror" that is responsible for unintended and undesirable social consequences.
37. John E. Calfee and Debra Jones Ringold, "The 70% Majority: Enduring Consumer Beliefs about Advertising," *Journal of Public Policy & Marketing* 13 (fall 1994), 228–238.
38. Marian Friestad and Peter Wright, "The Persuasion Knowledge Model: How People Cope with Persuasion Attempts," *Journal of Consumer Research* 21 (June 1994), 1–31; Marian Friestad and Peter Wright, "Persuasion Knowledge: Lay People's and Researchers' Beliefs about the Psychology of Advertising," *Journal of Consumer Research* 22 (June 1995), 62–74.
39. For an accessible treatment on the issue of automatic, or non-controlled motivation and behavior, see John A. Bargh, "Losing Consciousness: Automatic Influences on Consumer

Judgment, Behavior, and Motivation," *Journal of Consumer Research* 29 (September 2002), 280–285. See also John A. Bargh and Tanya L. Chartrand, "The Unbearable Automaticity of Being," *American Psychologist* 54 (July 1999), 462–479.

40. Terence A. Shimp and Elnora W. Stuart, "The Role of Disgust as an Emotional Mediator of Advertising Effects," *Journal of Advertising* 33 (spring 2004), 43–54.
41. Brian Steinberg and Suzanne Vranica, "Anheuser Ponders Approach to Ads," *The Wall Street Journal Online,* April 16, 2004, http://online.wsj.com (accessed April 16, 2004).
42. Stephen B. Castleberry, Warren French, and Barbara A. Carlin, "The Ethical Framework of Advertising and Marketing Research Practitioners: A Moral Development Perspective," *Journal of Advertising* 22 (June 1993), 39–46.
43. American Association of Advertising Agencies, http://www.aaaa.org.
44. These issues were identified by Paula Fitzgerald Bone and Robert J. Corey, "Ethical Dilemmas in Packaging: Beliefs of Packaging Professionals," unpublished working paper, West Virginia University Department of Marketing, 1991. The following discussion is guided by this paper. The authors identified a fifth ethical aspect of packaging (the relationship between a package and a product's price) that is not discussed here.
45. For an interesting discussion of perceptual differences among packaging professionals, brand managers, and consumers on the issue of packaging ethics, see Paula Fitzgerald Bone and Robert J. Corey, "Packaging Ethics: Perceptual Differences among Packaging Professionals, Brand Managers and Ethically-interested Consumers," *Journal of Business Ethics* 24 (April 2000), 199–213.
46. For an insightful discussion of sales promotion practices and related consumer psychology that result in exaggerated expectations of winning, see James C. Ward and Ronald Paul Hill, "Designing Effective Promotional Games: Opportunities and Problems," *Journal of Advertising* 20 (September 1991), 69–81.
47. Bob Gatty, "Atlanta Woman Guilty of Rebate Fraud," *Promo,* February 1994, 18.
48. A special issue of the *Journal of Public Policy & Marketing* 19 (spring 2000) is devoted to privacy and ethical issues in online marketing. See the articles on pages 1 through 73 by the following authors: George R. Milne; Eve M. Caudill and Patrick E. Murphy; Mary J. Culnan; Joseph Phelps, Glen Nowak and Elizabeth Ferrell; Ross D. Petty; Anthony D. Miyazaki and Ana Fernandez; and Kim Bartel Sheehan and Mariea Grubbs Hoy.
49. Jeffrey P. Davidson, "The Elusive Nature of Integrity: People Know It When They See It, but Can't Explain It," *Marketing News,* November 7, 1986, 24.
50. Donald P. Robin and R. Eric Reidenbach, "Social Responsibility, Ethics, and Marketing Strategy: Closing the Gap between Concept and Application," *Journal of Marketing* 51 (January 1987), 44–58. In this context, two additional articles that discuss ethical responsibilities of marketing practitioners are Rhoda H. Karpatkin, "Toward a Fair and Just Marketplace for All Consumers: The Responsibilities of Marketing Professionals," *Journal of Public Policy & Marketing* 18 (spring 1999), 118–122; Gene R. Laczniak, "Distributive Justice, Catholic Social Teaching, and the Moral Responsibility of Marketers," *Journal of Public Policy & Marketing* 18 (spring 1999), 125–129.
51. Based on Gene R. Laczniak and Patrick E. Murphy, "Fostering Ethical Marketing Decisions," *Journal of Business Ethics* 10 (1991), 259–271.
52. Dave Dolak, "Let's Lift the Human Spirit," *Brandweek,* April 28, 2003, 30.
53. Michael B. Mazis, Richard Staelin, Howard Beales, and Steven Salop, "A Framework for Evaluating Consumer Information Regulation," *Journal of Marketing* 45 (winter 1981), 11–21.
54. The following discussion is adapted from Mazis, et al.
55. *Alcohol Beverage Labeling Act of 1988,* S.R. 2047.
56. A thorough review of research pertaining to warning labels is provided by David W. Stewart and Ingrid M. Martin, "Intended and Unintended Consequences of Warning Messages: A Review and Synthesis of Empirical Research," *Journal of Public Policy & Marketing* 13 (spring 1994), 1–19. See also Janet R. Hankin, James J. Sloan, and Robert J. Sokol, "The Modest Impact of the Alcohol Beverage Warning Label on Drinking During Pregnancy Among a Sample of African-American Women," *Journal of Public Policy & Marketing* 17 (spring 1998), 61–69.
57. Shirley Leung, "Two States Ready Bills Requiring Nutrition Data from Restaurants," *The Wall Street Journal Online,* February 13, 2003, http://online.wsj.com (accessed February 13, 2003).
58. Ross D. Petty, "Advertising Law in the United States and European Union," *Journal of Public Policy & Marketing* 16 (spring 1997), 2–13.
59. J. Edward Russo, Barbara L. Metcalf, and Debra Stephens, "Identifying Misleading Advertising," *Journal of Consumer Research* 8 (September 1981), 120. For a thorough review of advertising deception, see also David M. Gardner and Nancy H. Leonard, "Research in Deceptive and Corrective Advertising: Progress to Date and Impact on Public Policy," *Current Issues & Research in Advertising* 12 (1990), 275–309.
60. For a more thorough discussion of these elements and other matters surrounding FTC deception policy, see Gary T. Ford and John E. Calfee, "Recent Developments in FTC Policy on Deception," *Journal of Marketing* 50 (July 1986), 82–103.
61. Public copy of a letter dated October 14, 1983 from FTC Chairman James C. Miller III to Senator Bob Packwood, Chairman of Senate Committee on Commerce, Science, and Transportation.
62. These facts are offered by Jacob Jacoby and George J. Szybillo, "Consumer Research in FTC Versus Kraft (1991): A Case of Heads We Win, Tails You Lose?" *Journal of Public Policy & Marketing* 14 (spring 1995), 2.
63. Ruling of the Federal Trade Commission, Docket No. 9208, January 30, 1991.
64. Jef I. Richards and Ivan L. Preston, "Proving and Disproving Materiality of Deceptive Advertising Claims," *Journal of Public Policy & Marketing* 11 (fall 1992), 45–56; Jacoby and Szybillo, "Consumer Research in FTC Versus Kraft," 1–14; David W. Stewart, "Deception, Materiality, and Survey Research: Some Lessons from Kraft," *Journal of Public Policy & Marketing* 14 (spring 1995), 15–28; Seymour Sudman "When Experts Disagree: Comments on the Articles by Jacoby and Szybillo and Stewart," *Journal of Public Policy & Marketing* 14 (spring 1995), 29–34.
65. Dorothy Cohen, "The Concept of Unfairness as It Relates to Advertising Legislation," *Journal of Marketing* 38 (July 1974), 8.
66. Cohen, "Unfairness in Advertising Revisited," 8.
67. The nature of the dispute is clearly played out in alternative positions presented by the president of the American Advertising Federation and the legal affairs director for the Center for Science in the Public Interest. See alternative positions argued by Wally Snyder (AAF) and Bruce A. Silverglade (CSPI) in "Does FTC Have an 'Unfair' Future?" *Advertising Age,* March 28, 1994, 20.

68. Christy Fisher, "How Congress Broke Unfair Ad Impasse," *Advertising Age,* August 22, 1994, 34.
69. Cohen, "Unfairness in Advertising Revisited," 74.
70. J. Howard Beales III, "The FTC's Use of Unfairness Authority: It's Rise, Fall, and Resurrection," *Journal of Public Policy and Marketing* 22 (fall 2003), 192–200.
71. Ibid.
72. The following discussion borrows liberally from the excellent review article by William L. Wilkie, Dennis L. McNeill, and Michael B. Mazis, "Marketing's 'Scarlet Letter': The Theory and Practice of Corrective Advertising," *Journal of Marketing* 48 (spring 1984), 11. See also Gardner and Leonard, "Research in Deceptive and Corrective Advertising."
73. For review, see Wilkie, et al., "Marketing's 'Scarlet Letter'."
74. See Michael B. Mazis, "FTC v. Novartis: The Return of Corrective Advertising?" *Journal of Public Policy & Marketing* 20 (spring 2001), 114–122; Bruce Ingersoll, "FTC Orders Novartis to Run Ads to Correct 'Misbeliefs' about Pill," *The Wall Street Journal Online,* May 28, 1999, http://online.wsj.com.
75. A study evaluating the effects of a corrective advertising order against STP oil additive determined that corrective advertising action in this case worked as intended: False beliefs were corrected without injuring the product category or consumers' overall perceptions of the STP Corporation. See Kenneth L. Bernhardt, Thomas C. Kinnear, and Michael B. Mazis, "A Field Study of Corrective Advertising Effectiveness," *Journal of Public Policy & Marketing* 5 (1986), 146–162. This article and the one by Mazis in the previous endnote are essential reading for anyone interested in learning more about corrective advertising.
76. Anna Wilde Mathews and Brian Steinberg, "FDA Proposes Drug Ads without the Fine Print," *The Wall Street Journal Online,* February 5, 2004, http://online.wsj.com (accessed February 5, 2004).
77. Paul Harris, "Will the FTC Finally Wake Up?" *Sales and Marketing Management,* January 1988, 57–59.
78. David Kiley, "Candid Camera: Volvo and the Art of Deception," *Adweek's Marketing Week,* November 12, 1990, 4–5; Raymond Serafin and Gary Levin, "Ad Industry Suffers Crushing Blow," *Advertising Age,* November 12, 1990, 1, 76–77; Raymond Serafin and Jennifer Lawrence, "Four More Volvo Ads Scrutinized," *Advertising Age,* November 26, 1990, 4.
79. Andrew J. Strenio, Jr., "The FTC in 1988: Phoenix or Finis?" *Journal of Public Policy & Marketing* 7 (1988), 21–39.
80. Jean J. Boddewyn, "Advertising Self-Regulation: True Purpose and Limits," *Journal of Advertising* 18, no. 2 (1989), 19–27.
81. Jean J. Boddewyn, "Advertising Self-Regulation: Private Government and Agent of Public Policy," *Journal of Public Policy & Marketing* 4 (1985), 129–141.
82. Avery M. Abernethy and Jan LeBlanc Wicks, "Self-regulation and Television Advertising: A Replication and Extension," *Journal of Advertising Research* 41 (May/June 2001), 31–37; Avery M. Abernethy, "Advertising Clearance Practices of Radio Stations: A Model of Advertising Self-Regulation," *Journal of Advertising* 22 (September 1993), 15–26; Herbert J. Rotfeld, Avery M. Abernethy, and Patrick R. Parsons, "Self-Regulation and Television Advertising," *Journal of Advertising* 19 (December 1990), 18–26; Eric J. Zanot, "Unseen but Effective Advertising Regulation: The Clearance Process," *Journal of Advertising* 14, no. 4 (1985), 44–51, 59.
83. Eric J. Zanot, "A Review of Eight Years of NARB Casework: Guidelines and Parameters of Deceptive Advertising," *Journal of Advertising* 9, no. 4 (1980), 20.
84. Scott Hensley, "J&J Ad for St. Joseph Aspirin Draws Complaints from Bayer," *The Wall Street Journal Online,* April 4, 2002, http://online.wsj.com (accessed April 4, 2002).
85. "Tropicana Products, Inc. Participate in the NAD Process," *NAD News,* June 24, 2004.
86. Jim Guthrie, "Give Self-regulation a Hand," *Advertising Age,* October 15, 2001, 16.
87. The concept of green marketing has various dimensions beyond this general explanation. For a review of the nuances, see William E. Kilbourne, "Green Advertising: Salvation or Oxymoron?" *Journal of Advertising* 24 (summer 1995), 7–20.
88. Jack Neff, "It's Not Trendy Being Green," *Advertising Age,* April 10, 2000, 16.
89. Subhabrata Bobby Banerjee, Easwar S. Iyer, and Rajiv K. Kashyap, "Corporate Environmentalism: Antecedents and Influence of Industry Type," *Journal of Marketing* 67 (April 2003), 106–122; Pratima Bansal and Kendall Roth, "Why Companies Go Green: A Model of Ecological Responsiveness," *Academy of Management Journal,* 43 (No. 4, 2000), 717–736.
90. Lauren Mechling, "'Green' Furniture's New Terrain," *The Wall Street Journal Online,* December 12, 2003, http://online.wsj.com (accessed December 12, 2003).
91. Sholnn Freeman, "Forget Rebates: The Hybrid-Car Markup," *The Wall Street Journal Online,* June 10, 2004, http://online.wsj.com (accessed June 10, 2004).
92. This classification is based on Subhabrata Banerjee, Charles S. Gulas, and Easwar Iyer, "Shades of Green: A Multidimensional Analysis of Environmental Advertising," *Journal of Advertising* 24 (summer 1995), 21–32. For additional discussion of the types of environmental advertising claims and their frequency of use, see Les Carlson, Stephen J. Grove, and Norman Kangun, "A Content Analysis of Environmental Advertising Claims: A Matrix Method Approach," *Journal of Advertising* 22 (September 1993), 27–39.
93. For review of a report on the short-filling problem, see http://www.ftc.gov/opa/1997/07/milk.htm.
94. Queena Sook Kim, "Recycling Alliance Wants Symbol with Chasing Arrows Scrapped," *The Wall Street Journal Online,* March 6, 2002, http://online.wsj.com (accessed March 6, 2002).
95. Published in the *Federal Register* on August 13, 1992 [57 FR 36,363 (1992)]. These guides also available online at http://www.ftc.gov/bcp/grnrule/green02.htm. See also, Jason W. Gray-Lee, Debra L. Scammon, and Robert N. Mayer, "Review of Legal Standards for Environmental Marketing Claims," *Journal of Public Policy & Marketing* 13 (spring 1994), 155–159.
96. Julie Vergeront (principal author), *The Green Report: Findings and Preliminary Recommendations for Responsible Environmental Advertising* (St. Paul: Minnesota Attorney General's Office, November 1990). The following discussion is a summary of the recommendations in *The Green Report.* The Federal Trade Commission's guidelines are similar in stating that environmental claims should (1) be substantiated; (2) be clear as to whether any assumed environmental advantage applies to the product, the package, or both; (3) avoid being trivial; and (4) if comparisons are made, make clear the basis for the comparisons.
97. Gordon Fairclough, "Philip Morris Launches 'M,' New Holiday Tobacco Blend," *The Wall Street Journal Online,* December 4, 2001, http://online.wsj.com (accessed December 4, 2001).

PART 2
The Fundamental Marcom Decisions: Targeting, Positioning, Objective Setting, and Budgeting

Part Two builds a foundation for understanding the nature and function of marketing communications by providing practical and theoretical overviews of four fundamental marcom decisions: targeting, positioning, objective setting, and budgeting. *Chapter 4* introduces targeting as the key element in effective marketing communications. The chapter focuses on four sets of audience-defining characteristics that singularly or in combination influence how people respond to marcom programs: behaviorgraphics, psychographics, demographics, and geodemographics. Each of these characteristics is discussed in detail, with major emphasis on: (1) the population age structure, (2) the changing household composition (e.g., increases in the number of single-person households), and (3) ethnic population developments.

Chapter 5 deals with brand positioning from the marcom practitioner's vantage point and examines positioning from the consumer's perspective. The positioning statement is described as the central idea that encapsulates a brand's meaning and distinctiveness and explains that a good positioning statement must reflect a brand's competitive advantage and motivate customers to action. Potential starting points for developing positioning statements then are discussed as well as the topic of brand repositioning. Detailed attention is devoted to how consumers process marcom information. Particular detail is applied to describing the marcom activites necessary to promote consumer attention, comprehension, and learning of marcom messages.

Chapter 6 completes the treatment of fundamental marcom decisions by examining objective setting and budgeting. The importance of setting objectives is initially discussed and a framework called the hierarchy of effects explains how the choice of marcom objective rests with knowing where on the hierarchy members of the target audience are located. Requirements for setting suitable marcom objectives are detailed. Then addressed is the issue of whether marcom objectives should be formulated based on sales or presales (communication) goals. Marcom budgeting is next covered with treatment of how budgets should be established in theory and practical budgeting methods are discussed in detail. Separate sections cover four budgeting methods: percentage-of-sales budgeting, objective-and-task budgeting, budgeting via the competitive parity method (with detailed treatment of share of voice and share of market assessments), and budgeting via the affordability method.

CHAPTER 4
Marcom Targeting

Marcom Challenge: Esprit and Gap—No Longer Just for Youth

Esprit is a brand name that's been around since the mid-1960s. Started in a San Francisco apartment by a young couple in their mid-twenties, the Esprit brand—with its readily identifiable triple-bar-E logo—became a favorite around the world, especially among millions of teens and young adults who purchased clothing items from the Esprit and Esprit Sport collections. Esprit's business thrived with heavy catalog sales and customers galore in retail outlets. By the late 1990s the company's official headquarters had moved from the United States to Hong Kong under the name Esprit Holdings Limited.[1]

A fascinating shift in marcom strategy occurred during the early 2000s. The Esprit brand, which historically catered to the whims of teens and young adults, shifted its targeting. Starting in Europe and moving to the United States, the company repositioned the brand from one virtually synonymous with youthful exuberance to a mature fashion brand aimed at consumers between the ages of 25 and 40. Whereas sales of fashion items to teens had declined—not just sales of Esprit but those also of brands such as Abercrombie & Fitch and American Eagle Outfitters—purchases of fashion items by young and middle-aged adults were experiencing substantial growth.[2]

Because the demographic tide changes, firms have to be prepared to alter marketing actions when effectiveness declines. Managers at Esprit, realizing that growth could not be sustained by focusing its efforts primarily on teens and young adults, altered the company's course by targeting an older demographic group. Only time will tell whether this strategy is effective, but in terms of sheer numbers alone, the 25 to 40 age group is huge with millions of Europeans, Asians, and Americans occupying this age range.

A similar development has occurred at Gap Inc. This huge retailer with annual revenues around $16 billion includes three well-known chains: Banana Republic, Gap, and Old Navy. Though Gap Inc. has a commanding market share—about 7 percent of all U.S. apparel sales—it only garners about 3 percent of female baby boomers' apparel spending. So, what would you do if you were CEO at Gap Inc.? Well, you'd probably encourage some action that would reach out to female baby boomers whose apparel needs remain unfulfilled. That's precisely what Gap Inc. is in process of doing. In 2005 it opened a new chain of stores designed specifically to appeal to the apparel needs of female baby boomers. Gap Inc. initially opened 10 test stores—with a new name—in an appeal to women over 35—a group of nearly 40 million in the United States with annual apparel purchases around $15 billion.[3]

AP Photo/David Paul Morris/Wide World Photos

CHAPTER OBJECTIVES

After reading this chapter you should be able to:

1. Discuss the importance of targeting marketing communications to specific consumer groups and realize that the targeting decision is the initial and most fundamental of all marcom decisions.
2. Understand the role of behaviorgraphics in targeting consumer groups.
3. Describe the nature of psychographic targeting and the VALS system.
4. Appreciate major demographic developments such as changes in the age structure of the population and ethnic population growth.
5. Explain the meaning of geodemographics and understand the role for this form of targeting.
6. Recognize that any single characteristic of consumers—whether their age, ethnicity, or income level—likely is *not* a sufficient basis alone for sophisticated marcom targeting.

Targeting Customers and Prospects

This chapter expands the discussion of targeting that was introduced in Chapter 1. You will recall that Chapter 1 provided a model of the marcom process and described various forms of "fundamental" and "implementation" decisions. The section on fundamental decisions concluded with the following mantra:

All marketing communications should be: (1) directed to a particular ***target market****, (2) clearly* ***positioned****, (3) created to achieve a* ***specific objective****, and (4) undertaken to accomplish the objective* ***within budget constraint****.*

Targeting specific audiences can be considered the starting point for all marcom decisions. Thus, the purpose of this chapter is to describe how marcom practitioners target prospective customers. Targeting allows marketing communicators to more precisely deliver their messages and prevent wasted coverage to people falling outside the targeted market. Targeting thus implies efficiency of effort. Not to target is equivalent to shooting a basketball wildly in the air without directing it toward the hoop. It is difficult enough to connect on a shot from a 20-foot distance when that is one's intent. Imagine how unlikely you are to make a shot if you don't consciously concentrate on a specific target. Such is the case when marcom efforts fail to concentrate on a specific audience.

The chapter focuses on four sets of consumer characteristics that singularly or in combination influence what people consume and how they respond to marketing communications: behaviorgraphics, psychographics, demographics, and geodemographics. Note that "graphics," the suffix for each of these consumer characteristics, is a term that refers to *measurable characteristics* of target audiences. The prefix to each type of targeting represents *how* the audience is measured. Specifically, *behavior*graphics represents information about the audience's behavior—in terms of past purchase behavior or online search activity—in a particular product category or set of related categories. *Psycho*graphics captures aspects of consumers' psychological makeups and lifestyles including their attitudes, values, and motivations. *Demo*graphics reflect measurable population characteristics such as age, income, and ethnicity. And *geodemo*graphics is based on demographic characteristics of consumers who reside within geographic clusters such as zip code areas and neighborhoods.

Subsequent sections are devoted to all four groups of audience-defining characteristics. First, however, it will be useful to distinguish the four general targeting methods in terms of two considerations: (1) how easy or difficult it is to obtain data (i.e., *measure*) the characteristic on which a targeting decision is to be made, and (2) how *predictive* the characteristic is of consumer choice behavior. The graph presented in Figure 4.1 lays these two considerations out as the vertical (measurement ease/difficulty) and horizontal (behavior predictability) dimensions. It thus can be seen that demographic data is relatively easy to obtain but that demographic information is the least predictive of consumer choice behavior. At the other extreme, behaviorgraphic data are relatively difficult or are expensive to procure but are highly predictive of choice behavior. Geodemographic and psychographic data fall between these extremes. The discussion proceeds from the most (behaviorgraphics) to the least predictive indicator of behavior (demographics).

Behaviorgraphic Targeting

Let's move forward 15 years and imagine that you are a successful entrepreneur who owns a really cool clothing store located in a trendy area. Your establishment appeals primarily to professionals and white-collar workers. From the very start

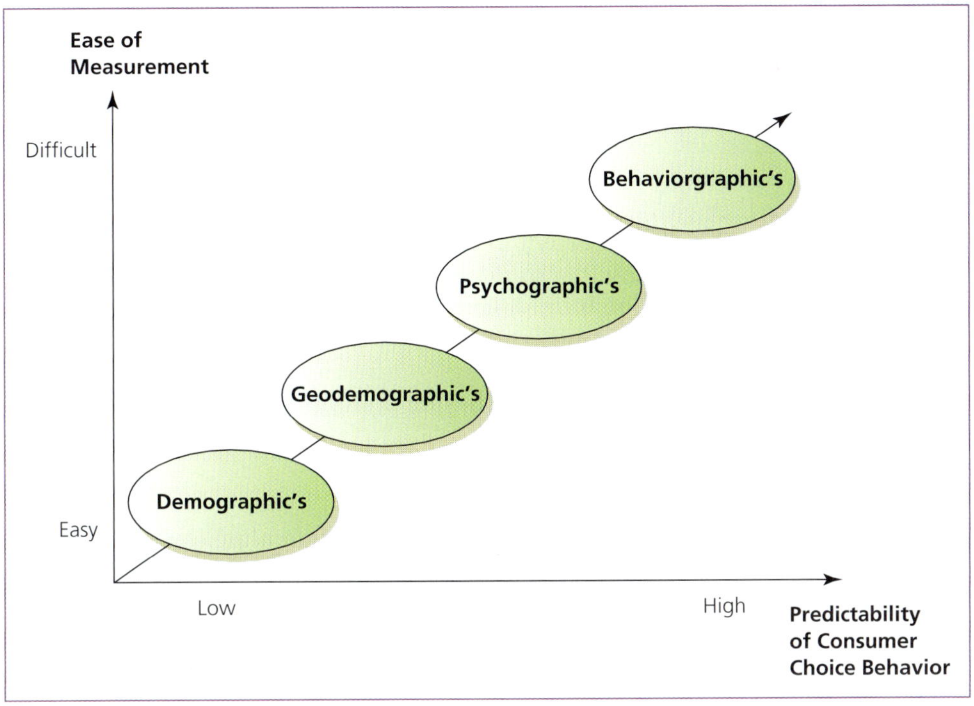

Figure 4.1

Classification of Four General Targeting Characteristics

of your business five years ago you have maintained impeccable records on every customer's purchases. You know precisely when they have purchased, what items they have selected, and how much they have spent. Now let us suppose that you are going to run a sale on a certain line of merchandise and will announce this sale via a combination of direct (postal) mail and e-mail. Though you could send postal announcements to all of your customers, you want to be more efficient in your selection so as to not waste money in reaching less viable prospects.

How would you make the targeting decision? In actuality, you have no need to target based on customers' demographic characteristics (say, by selecting just those between the ages of 25 and 39) or their psychographic profiles because you have an even better basis for making the selection decision. In particular, you know whether they have made past purchases of the specific merchandise line that you are discounting. Thus, based on customers' past behavior profiles you know which people are likely to be responsive to a sale on items that they have or have not previously purchased. Accordingly, you send flyers (sales announcement) to all customers who have previously purchased the merchandise in question. By focusing on their past behavior, you have increased the odds that your direct mail advertising will receive a good ROMI and that you will not have wasted ad dollars by directing sale announcements to prospects unlikely to respond to discounts on merchandise they typically do not purchase.

The previous scenario, albeit simplistic, describes the essence of behaviorgraphic targeting: namely, that this form of targeting is based on how people behave (with respect to a particular product category or class of related products) rather than in terms of their attitudes and lifestyles (psychographics), their age, income, or ethnicity (demographics), or where they live (geodemographics). Behaviorgraphics provide the best basis for targeting marcom messages to customers insofar as the best predictor of one's future behavior is his or her past behavior. Frankly, there is little need to target customers using any of the nonbehavioral bases for targeting if behaviorgraphic details are available. However, in some marcom situations behaviorgraphic information is *not* available, and marketing communicators resort to the "inferior" bases for targeting as a matter of necessity. For example, marketers of truly innovative new products have no past behavior information on which to identify the best prospective customers. Similarly, many manufacturers of products that are sold in retail outlets where optical scanning machines are unavailable have no way of tracking customer purchase behavior. On the other hand, mass marketers of CPG items (i.e., consumer package goods) do have detailed records on consumer purchase behavior that is available from firms that track—via optical scanners in supermarkets and other retail outlets—the specific items people purchase and the conditions under which purchases are made (e.g., with or without a coupon). Information Resource Inc. (IRI) is a well-known company that tracks retail sales via its InfoScan service. (See the Web site in the endnote for access to information about the InfoScan service.)[4] Likewise, most B2B marketers have detailed records on customer purchase behavior and thus are in an ideal situation to target future communications toward "best" prospects based on their past purchasing patterns.

Online Behavioral Targeting

In addition to behavior-based targeting in conventional retailing contexts, an even more ideal venue for this form of targeting is the Internet. Web sites increasingly are tracking their users' online site-selection behavior so as to enable advertisers to serve targeted ads. Known as *audience management systems,* companies such as Revenue Science and Tacoda Systems track Internet users' surfing behaviors and provide this information to advertisers that wish to target prospective customers based on their online search behavior. For example, suppose the Calloway Golf Company wishes to reach the best prospects for purchasing its newest driver—a club likely to cost $400 or more. Turning to a company such as Revenue Science or Tacoda Systems, Calloway would request either provider to identify prospective customers who spend a lot of time visiting golf-related Web sites. With knowledge of these individuals, it is technologically simple (by inserting "cookies" on computers that identify Web users' site-selection behavior) to place ads for Calloway's new driver on sites visited by these "golf surfers"—golf-related or otherwise. The essence of online behavioral targeting is thus a matter of directing online advertisements to just those individuals who most likely are interested—as indicated by their online site-selection behavior—in making a purchase decision for a particular product category.

A basic axiom of targeted marketing communications is to "aim where the ducks are flying." In other words, rather than shooting a gun wildly in the air and hoping that a duck might pass by, a duck hunter increases his or her odds of downing a duck if she or he refrains from shooting until flying ducks have been identified. But not all marcom practitioners heed this advice. Behaviorgraphics is a targeting approach that embodies the aim-where-the-ducks-are-flying axiom.

American Airlines employed the service of Revenue Science to identify best prospects for placing online ads. People who visited Web sites containing travel articles were pinpointed on the assumption that these individuals likely traveled on business at least occasionally. Ads for American Airlines were accordingly placed on the Web site of *The Wall Street Journal* (http://online.wsj.com) whenever individuals identified as business travelers visited this Web site. This behavioral targeting campaign enjoyed considerable success.[5]

Snapple Beverage Corp. wanted to reach women who are concerned about health, fitness, and dieting. With this target in mind, its online research consultant identified individuals who visited the diet and fitness channel of iVillage three or more times in the previous 45 days. Advertisements for Snapple's cleverly named Snapple-a-Day—a new meal-replacement product aimed at diet-conscious consumers—were then served to these individuals whenever they visited iVillage sites. This precise targeting, which cost far less than a mass-media campaign would have, generated extremely high scores on key indicators of ad performance: brand awareness (76 percent), brand favorability (36 percent), and purchase intent (37 percent).[6]

Privacy Concerns

As is typically the case, technological advances in marketing bring with them increased ability to serve consumers but also at the risk of invading privacy. Applied in the context of online behavior targeting, Web surfers are increasingly more likely to be served with ads for products that are most relevant to their interests. However, this advantage comes at the expense that companies such as Revenue Science and Tacoda Systems have access to our Internet search behavior *without our approval or knowledge.* What's the harm? It's easy to argue on either side of the issue, very much in the same fashion as was suggested when in the previous chapter the general issue of targeting was discussed. On the plus side, to be targeted with only those ads that we are most likely interested in is a good thing. However, on the other side, who wants Big Brother overlooking what we do? Would you want someone observing, if they could, every TV program you viewed during the course of a year? Probably not. Here then is the same issue as it applies to the Internet. Do you want commercial firms tracking your surfing behavior? As always in life, there are tradeoffs to be made.

Psychographic Targeting

It is important to place the role of psychographic targeting in context of demographics, the form of targeting that historically preceded it and which now is practiced in conjunction with psychographics. Marketers for many years based their targeting decisions almost exclusively on their audiences' demographic characteristics—considerations such as the market's age group, gender, income level, and race/ethnicity. However, sophisticated practitioners eventually realized that demographic information tells only part of the story about consumers' buying preferences and purchase behaviors. It is for this reason that marketing communicators also began investigating consumers' psychographic characteristics as a means of obtaining a richer understanding of consumer behavior and how best to influence consumers to respond positively to marcom efforts.

Consider, for example, how you might go about identifying target customers if you were marketing to prospective cruise-line travelers. Demographic information such as age and income undoubtedly would play some role in defining appropriate audiences to direct your marcom efforts; that is, you might expect somewhat older individuals (35-plus) and those with average or higher incomes to be prime prospects. But not everyone in the same age or income categories would be equally responsive to, say, advertisements for cruises to the Caribbean. Not all baby boomers and elderly consumers are good candidates for cruises, but rather only those boomers and elders who are members of two particular psychographic segments—"pampered relaxers" and "global explorers"—are the prime prospects for cruising.[7]

© Taxi/Getty Images

In general, **psychographics** refers to information about consumers' attitudes, values, motivations, and lifestyles as they relate to buying behavior in a particular product category. For example, a psychographic study of SUVs would assess the types of activities owners of such vehicles participate in (e.g., camping and fishing, tailgating at sporting events, hauling lawn care items and do-it-yourself building materials) and measure their values and attitudes toward issues related to owning or not owning an SUV (e.g., how much value they place on safety, their views toward the environment, and their need for being in control). This information would be useful in designing advertising messages and selecting appropriate media vehicles.

JOB OUTLOOK

Aspiring market and survey researchers should gain experience gathering and analyzing data, conducting interviews or surveys, and writing reports on their findings while in college. The experience can be invaluable in obtaining a full-time position in the field. (*Occupational Outlook Handbook, 2004–05 Edition*, U.S. DOL, *http://www.bls.gov/oco/home.htm*)

Numerous marketing research firms conduct psychographic studies for individual clients. These studies are typically *customized* to the client's specific product category. In other words, the questionnaire items included in a psychographics study are selected in view of the unique characteristics of the product category. Table 4.1 presents a set of illustrative statements that were included in a psychographic study of consumers' banking practices. Survey respondents answered these statements in terms of how strongly they agreed or disagreed with each. Researchers then analyzed the results and determined that the responses from more than 1,000 consumers grouped into four psychographic segments—"worried traditionalists," "bank loyalists," "secured investors," and "thrifty bankers"—and that people classified into these segments differed substantially in terms of various banking behaviors.[8] The regional bank that sponsored this study used these results to better serve all four segments by providing new services appropriate for each and communicating differently to customers in the various segments. For example, communications aimed at "worried traditionalists" emphasized safety and security, whereas rate of return received greater emphasis in communications targeted to "secured investors."

In addition to psychographic studies that are customized to a client's particular needs, brand managers can purchase "off-the-shelf" psychographic data from services that develop psychographic profiles of people independently of any particular product or service. One of the best known of these is the Yankelovich MindBase psychographic segmentation scheme. Yankelovich's MindBase consists of eight general segments and 32 specific subsegments. Table 4.2 summarizes the eight general MindBase segments. To appreciate the types of questions used to identify individuals' segment membership, it will be informative to answer the questions at the following Web site: http://www.yankelovich.com/shortform2_p01.asp. Upon answering these questions, you'll learn to which of the eight MindBase segments you belong.

A second well-known psychographic segmentation scheme is SRI Consulting Business Intelligence's (SRIC-BI's) VALS™ system. The U.S. VALS segmentation

Table 4.1

Illustrative Statements Used in a Banking-Related Psychographic Study

• A local bank is more likely to lend me money. • Bankers don't know as much as brokers about investments. • I rely on a banker's advice about managing money. • My debt is too high. • I'd never consider an account at a bank that doesn't have an ATM.	• A long-term relationship with a bank is more important than price. • All banks are the same. • I prefer a fixed price for all services provided to me. • I always shop around for the best deal. • I enjoy going to the lobby to do my banking business.	• There is never enough time to study all the financial alternatives. • I worry about saving enough money for the future. • I'd rather invest in Mutual Funds than CDs.

SOURCE: James W. Peltier, John A. Schibrowsky, Don E. Schultz, and John Davis, "Interactive Psychographics: Cross-Selling in the Banking Industry," *Journal of Advertising Research*, 42 (March/April 2002), Table 1. Reprinted from the Journal of Advertising Research, © Copyright 2002, by the Advertising Research Foundation.

Table 4.2

Yankelovich MindBase Segments

I am Expressive my motto is *Carpe Diem* I live life to the fullest and I'm not afraid to express my personality. I'm active and engaged and I embody a true "live in the now" attitude with a firm belief that the future is limitless and that I can be or do anything I put my mind to.
I am Driven my motto is *Nothing Ventured, Nothing Gained* I'm ambitious with a drive to succeed both personally and professionally. I think of myself as self-possessed and resourceful, and I'm determined to show the world I'm on top of my game in all I do, from career ambitions to family, home, and my social life.
I am At Capacity my motto is *Time is of the Essence* My life is very busy and I'm looking for control and simplification. I am a demanding and vocal consumer, and I'm looking for convenience, respect, and a helping hand so I can devote more of my time to the important things in life.
I am Rock Steady my motto is *Do the Right Thing* I think of myself as a positive individual. I draw energy from my home and family. I'm dedicated to living an upstanding life and I listen to my own instincts in terms of making thoughtful decisions in my personal life and in the marketplace.
I am Down to Earth my motto is *Ease on Down the Road* I'm cruising down life's path at my own pace, seeking satisfaction where I can. I'm looking to enhance my life, stretch myself to try new things, and treat myself through novel experiences and products along the way.
I am Sophisticated my motto is *Sense and Sensibility* I am intelligent, upstanding and I have an affinity for the finer things in life. I also have high expectations both for myself and for the companies I give my business. I am dedicated to doing a stellar job at work but I balance my career dedication with a passion for enriching experiences.
I Measure Twice my motto is *An Ounce of Prevention* I'm a mature individual and I like to think of myself on a life path to actualization and fulfillment. I live a healthy, active life. I'm dedicated to ensuring that my future is both secure and highly rewarding and vitalized.
I am Devoted my motto is *Home is Where the Heart is* I'm traditional and rooted in the comforts of home. Some would say my beliefs are conventional, but they make sense to me. I'm spiritual and content with my life. I like things the way they have always been and I don't need novelty for novelty's sake or newfangled technology.

SOURCE: Yankelovich MindBase /Segments, http://www.yankelovich.com/shortform2_p01.asp. Yankelovich ©2005.

scheme places American adult consumers into one of eight segments based on psychological characteristics that are related to purchase behavior and several key demographics. Japan VALS and U.K. VALS are available for understanding consumers in those countries. (You can determine your segmentation grouping by answering the questions on a survey available at http://www.sric-bi.com/VALS/presurvey.shtml.)

Figure 4.2 presents the eight VALS segments. The horizontal dimension in this figure represents individuals' *primary motivations,* whether in terms of their pursuit of ideals, their need for achievement, or drive to self-express. The vertical dimension reflects individuals' *resources* as based on their educational accomplishments, income levels, health, energy, and consumerism. For example, as can be gleaned from Figure 4.2, "Thinkers" and "Believers" both are motivated by the pursuit of ideals, but "Thinkers" have greater resources than "Believers." Similarly, both "Experiencers" and "Makers" are driven by the need for self-expression, but

Figure 4.2
The 8 VALS Segments

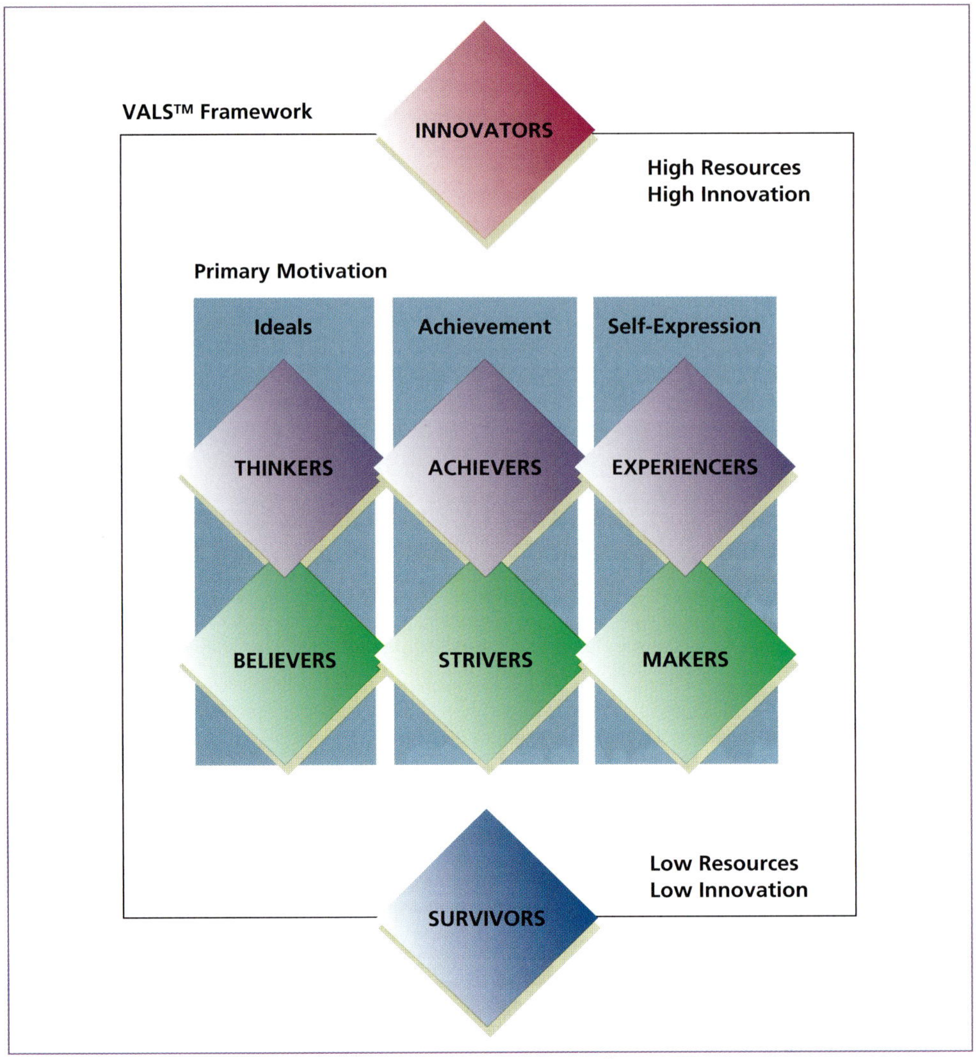

SOURCE: SRI Consulting Business Intelligence, http://www.sric-bi.com/VALS/types.shtm.

"Makers" have fewer resources than "Experiencers." Each of the eight segments in the VALS framework is now described.[9]

Innovators *are successful, sophisticated, take-charge people with high self-esteem. Because they have such abundant resources, they exhibit all three primary motivations (i.e., ideals, achievement, and self-expression) in varying degrees. They are change leaders and are the most receptive to new ideas and technologies. Innovators are very active consumers, and their purchases reflect cultivated tastes for upscale, niche products and services.*

Thinkers *are motivated by ideals. They are mature, satisfied, comfortable, and reflective people who value order, knowledge, and responsibility. They tend to be well educated and actively seek out information in the decision-making process. They are well informed about world and national events and are alert to opportunities to broaden their knowledge. Thinkers have a moderate respect for the status quo institutions of authority and social decorum, but are open to consider new ideas. Although their incomes allow them many choices, Thinkers are conservative, practical consumers; they look for durability, functionality, and value in the products they buy.*

Believers*, like Thinkers, are motivated by ideals. They are conservative, conventional people with concrete beliefs based on traditional, established codes: family, religion, community, and the nation. Many Believers express moral codes that are deeply rooted and literally interpreted. They follow established routines, organized in large part around home, family, community, and social or religious organizations to which they belong. As* *consumers, Believers are predictable; they choose familiar products and established brands. They favor American products and are generally loyal customers.*

***Achievers**, who are motivated by the desire for achievement, have goal-oriented lifestyles and a deep commitment to career and family. Their social lives reflect this focus and are structured around family, their place of worship, and work. Achievers live conventional lives, are politically conservative, and respect authority and the status quo. They value consensus, predictability, and stability over risk, intimacy, and self-discovery. With many wants and needs, Achievers are active in the consumer marketplace. Image is important to Achievers; they favor established, prestige products and services that demonstrate success to their peers. Because of their busy lives, they are often interested in a variety of time-saving devices.*

***Strivers** are trendy and fun loving. Because they are motivated by achievement, Strivers are concerned about the opinions and approval of others. Money defines success for Strivers, who don't have enough of it to meet their desires. They favor stylish products that emulate the purchases of people with greater material wealth. Many see themselves as having a job rather than a career, and a lack of skills and focus often prevents them from moving ahead. Strivers are active consumers because shopping is both a social activity and an opportunity to demonstrate to peers their ability to buy. As consumers, they are as impulsive as their financial circumstance will allow.*

***Experiencers** are motivated by self-expression. As young, enthusiastic, and impulsive consumers, Experiencers quickly become enthusiastic about new possibilities but are equally quick to cool. They seek variety and excitement, savoring the new, the offbeat, and the risky. Their energy finds an outlet in exercise, sports, outdoor recreation, and social activities. Experiencers are avid consumers and spend a comparatively high proportion of their income on fashion, entertainment, and socializing. Their purchases reflect the emphasis they place on looking good and having "cool" stuff.*

***Makers**, like Experiencers, are motivated by self-expression. They express themselves and experience the world by working on it—building a house, raising children, fixing a car, or canning vegetables—and have enough skill and energy to carry out their projects successfully. Makers are practical people who have constructive skills and value self-sufficiency. They live within a traditional context of family, practical work, and physical recreation and have little interest in what lies outside that context. Makers are suspicious of new ideas and large institutions such as big business. They are respectful of government authority and organized labor, but resentful of government intrusion on individual rights. They are unimpressed by material possessions other than those with a practical or functional purpose. Because they prefer value to luxury, they buy basic products.*

***Survivors** live narrowly focused lives. With few resources with which to cope, they often believe that the world is changing too quickly. They are comfortable with the familiar and are primarily concerned with safety and security. Because they must focus on meeting needs rather than fulfilling desires, Survivors do not show a strong primary motivation. Survivors are cautious consumers. They represent a very modest market for most products and services. They are loyal to favorite brands, especially if they can purchase them at a discount.*

To determine the best prospective customer target for a new product or service, the design team could work with the SRIC-BI consulting team. Imagine, for example, that an automobile manufacturer is interested in gauging receptivity to an innovative new automobile design. A series of focus groups could be held where each group is composed of just one VALS type (for example, one group comprised of Innovators, another group comprised of Achievers, etc.). Generally, each VALS type responds differently to different feature and benefit sets. Getting focus group feedback by VALS type would allow the new product team to select as the target the consumer group that responds most positively to the new design concept. Having a clearly defined target and a clear understanding of their preferences and needs enables the design team to effectively focus its work. Later in the process, knowledge of the VALS target can direct marketers in product positioning and advertising.

Geodemographic Targeting

The word geodemographic is a conjunction of *geography* and *demography,* which beautifully describes this form of targeting. The premise underlying geodemographic targeting is that people who reside in similar areas, such as neighborhoods or postal zip code zones, also share demographic and lifestyle similarities. Hence, knowing where people live also provides some information regarding their general marketplace behaviors. Several companies have developed services that delineate geographical areas into common groups, or clusters, wherein reside people with similar demographic and lifestyle characteristics. These companies (and their services, in parentheses) include CACI (ACORN), Donnelly Marketing (ClusterPlus), National Decision Systems (Vision), Experian (MOSAIC), Claritas (PRIZM_{NE}), and SRIC-BC (GeoVALS™). The following section describes Claritas's PRIZM_{NE} system of geodemographic profiling. Geodemographic clustering systems have been developed in many countries other than the United States, including Canada, most countries in Western Europe, some African countries, Australia, and Japan.[10]

PRIZM_{NE} is an acronym in which PRIZM stands for *P*otential *R*ating *I*ndex by *Z*ip *M*arkets and NE represents the "new evolution" of Claritas' original segmentation system. The PRIZM_{NE} classification system delineates every neighborhood in the United States into one of 66 clusters based on an analysis of neighborhoods' demographic characteristics. These characteristics include variables such as educational attainment, race/ethnicity, predominant age range, occupational achievement, and type of housing (e.g., owned versus rented). Sophisticated statistical analysis of these demographic characteristics has enabled Claritas to identify 66 groups, or clusters, of neighborhoods that share similar demographic profiles. Each cluster is labeled with a colorful and descriptive term. Illustrative names include "Upper Crust"; "Big Fish, Small Pond"; "Bohemian Mix"; "Country Casuals"; "White Picket Fences"; "Heartlanders"; "Suburban Pioneers"; and "City Roots." Let us briefly characterize three of these clusters.[11]

Bohemian Mix captures a collection of young, mobile urbanites who represent the nation's most liberal lifestyles. Bohemian Mixers are a blend of young singles and couples, students and professionals, Hispanics, Asian-Americans, African-Americans, and whites. They are disproportionately likely to be early adopters who are quick to attend the latest movie, frequent the newest nightclub, or adopt the most up-to-date laptop. Bohemian Mix households represent nearly 2 percent of all U.S. households. The average occupant of a Bohemian Mix household is less than 35 years old; has an income of about $50,000; likely is unmarried; rents an apartment or lives in a high-rise; is college educated; and is employed as a professional or in a white-collar position. He or she is not defined by any particular race or ethnicity.

White Picket Fences represents those households at the middle of the United States' socioeconomic ladder. People living in these households are predominantly young, middle-class, and married with children—a stereotypical American household of previous generations. Now, however, rather than being almost exclusively white, "White Picket Fencers" reflect ethnic diversity with large numbers of African-American and Hispanic households. Households such as these represent slightly over 1 percent of all U.S. households. The average occupant of a White Picket Fence household falls in the age range of 25 to 44, has an income of around $48,000, is married with children, has some college education, and works in a variety of jobs ranging from blue- to white-collar occupations.

Suburban Pioneers includes neighborhoods where occupants live eclectic lifestyles and includes a mix of young singles, recently divorced and single parents who have moved into older, inner-ring suburbs. They reside in aging homes and garden-style apartment buildings. The mix of African-American, Latino, and white residents work in mostly blue-collar jobs and live a working-class lifestyle.

The average occupant of Suburban Pioneer households is under age 45, earns an income around $33,000, and has a high school education or less. Just over 1 percent of U.S. households fall into this cluster.

Many major marketers use $PRIZM_{NE}$, Donnelly's ClusterPlus, or another geodemographic clustering service to help them with important marcom decisions. Selecting geographical locales for narrowcasting television advertisements and identifying candidates for direct mailing are just two marcom decisions that are facilitated by the availability of geodemographic data. Needless to say, geodemographic data are extremely useful for other marketing purposes such as deciding where to locate new stores.

If you would like to know how the neighborhood in which you grew up or resided would be classified by the $PRIZM_{NE}$ system, go to http://www.claritas.com. Once into this site, click on the "You Are Where You Live" button. You will be directed to submit a five-digit zip code, and following this you will see the major clusters that characterize your own neighborhood. For foreign nationals studying in the United States, you might want to enter your college or university's zip code to identify how the surrounding neighborhood is classified. Students in countries outside the United States should go online to identify whether your country has a PRIZM system in place. Finally, interested students are strongly encouraged to read the works of Michael Weiss, who has popularized geodemographic clustering via his books, such as the one cited in Endnote 10.

Demographic Targeting

This section examines three major demographic aspects that have considerable relevance for marcom practitioners: (1) the age structure of the population (e.g., children, Generations X and Y, and baby boomers); (2) the changing household composition (e.g., the increase in the number of single-person households); and (3) ethnic population developments. The focus is, as a matter of necessity, exclusively on characteristics of the U.S. population. Although the same considerations are relevant elsewhere, the particulars are country specific. Interested readers from countries outside the United States can obtain detailed demographic information from a government agency that is equivalent to the U.S. Census Bureau, which is a division of the Department of Commerce. Before examining features of the U.S. population, it will be helpful to place these topics in context by first examining population growth and geographic distribution of the world and U.S. populations.

At the time of this writing, the total population of human beings on the earth is estimated to be approximately 6.4 billion people. (For a daily update on the projected world and U.S. populations, go to http://www.census.gov/main/www/popclock.html.) The world population is expected to grow to approximately 8 billion people by the year 2025 and 9 billion by 2050. Table 4.3 provides a list of the world's 25 largest countries as of 2004, where it can be seen that both China and India have populations exceeding 1 billion people with a huge drop off to the next largest country—the United States—with an estimated population of approximately 293 million. (Please note that projections of population size vary somewhat depending on the source, because estimators use slightly different assumptions about fertility rates, longevity levels, and other factors that enter into the equation.)

A particularly interesting aspect of the U.S. population is the ancestral diversity of its residents. Known as a melting pot, the United States has attracted immigrants from throughout the world, thus making the country an amalgam of people whose ancestors had different cultures and backgrounds. Many immigrants to the United States now arrive from Latin America, Asia, and Eastern Europe, though historically most came from Western European countries. This is

Table 4.3

World's 25 Largest Countries as of 2004

Rank	Country	Population	Rank	Country	Population
1.	China	1,298,847,624	14.	Germany	82,424,609
2.	India	1,065,070,607	15.	Egypt	76,117,421
3.	United States	293,027,571	16.	Turkey	68,893,918
4.	Indonesia	238,452,952	17.	Ethiopia	67,851,281
5.	Brazil	184,101,109	18.	Iran	67,503,205
6.	Pakistan	159,196,336	19.	Thailand	64,865,523
7.	Russia	143,782,338	20.	France	60,424,213
8.	Bangladesh	141,340,476	21.	United Kingdom	60,270,708
9.	Nigeria	137,253,133	22.	Congo, Dem. Rep. of	58,317,930
10.	Japan	127,333,002	23.	Italy	58,057,477
11.	Mexico	104,959,594	24.	Korea, South	48,598,175
12.	Philippines	86,241,697	25.	Ukraine	47,732,079
13.	Vietnam	82,689,518			

Source: http://www.infoplease.com/ipa/a0004391.html, U.S. Census Bureau, International Database, Information Please® Database,

shown in Table 4.4, which portrays the percentage of the U.S. population claiming their ancestral roots. Interestingly, slightly over 7 percent of the U.S. population now refer to themselves simply as "Americans," which is up from 5 percent in 1990.[12] In other words, many American residents do not acknowledge any particular ancestry—possibly in part due to pride and also in view of the hybrid character of Americans' ancestries.

The Changing Age Structure

One of the most dramatic features of the American population is its *relentless aging*. The median age of Americans was 28 in 1970, 30 in 1980, 33 in 1990, 36 in 2000, and is projected to be about 38 by 2025. Table 4.5 presents population figures distributed by age group. The following sections examine major age groupings of the U.S. population and the implications these hold for marcom efforts. Discussion proceeds from the youngest age cohort, preschoolers, to the elderly. First, however, it will be helpful to overview the epochal event—namely, the baby boom—that has affected future generations and the general trend toward an ever-aging population.

Demographers (people who study demographic trends) termed the birth of around 77 million Americans between 1946 and 1964 the **baby boom** generation. This population-boom period following the end of World War II (in 1945) persisted for nearly two decades. Using 2005 as a point of reference, the youngest person classified as a "boomer" would be 41, and the oldest baby boomer would be 59. Effects of the baby boom (and subsequent bust) have been manifested in the following major population developments:

1. The original baby boomers created a *mini baby boom* as they reached childbearing age. As shown in Table 4.5, the number of children and teenagers in the United States totaled about 80 million in 2005.
2. Due to a low birthrate from the mid-1960s through the 1970s (prior to the time when most baby boomers were of childbearing age), relatively few babies were born. There now are proportionately fewer young adults (ages 20 to 34) than there were in prior generations.
3. The number of middle-agers (ages 35 to 54) has increased dramatically, totaling nearly 85 million Americans as of 2005. This maturing of the baby boomers has been one of the most significant demographic developments faced by marketers.

Table 4.4

Largest Ancestral Groups of U.S. Residents

Ancestry	Percentage of U.S. Population
German	15.2%
Irish	10.8
African-American	8.8
English	8.7
American	7.2
Mexican	6.5
Italian	5.6
Polish	3.2
French	3.0
American Indian	2.8
Scottish	1.7
Dutch	1.6
Norwegian	1.6
Scotch-Irish	1.5
Swedish	1.4

SOURCE: "A County-by-County Look at Ancestry," *USA Today,* July 1, 2004, 7A. Reprinted with permission.

Table 4.5

Population of the United States by Age Group, as of 2005 (estimated)

Age	Population (millions)	Percent of Total
Children and Teens (<20)		
Under 5	19.21	6.7
5–9	19.12	6.6
10–14	20.63	7.2
15–19	20.99	7.3
Total	**79.95**	**27.8**
Young Adults (20–34)		
20–24	20.16	7.0
25–29	18.35	6.4
30–34	18.58	6.5
Total	**57.09**	**19.8**
Middle-Agers (35–54)		
35–39	20.08	7.0
40–44	22.63	7.9
45–49	22.23	7.7
50–54	19.66	6.8
Total	**84.60**	**29.4**
Olders (55–64)		
55–59	16.84	5.9
60–64	12.85	4.5
Total	**29.69**	**10.3**
Elders (65–74)		
65–69	10.09	3.5
70–74	8.38	2.9
Total	**18.47**	**6.4**
The Very Old (75+)		
75–79	7.43	2.6
80–84	5.51	1.9
85+	4.97	1.7
Total	**17.91**	**6.2**
Total U.S. Population	**287.71**	**100%**

SOURCE: Projections of the Total Resident Population by 5-Year Age Groups, Middle Series, 2001–2005, Population Projections Program, U.S. Census Bureau.

Children and Teenagers

The group of young Americans age 19 and younger has fallen dramatically from 40 percent of the population in 1965 (during the baby-boom heyday) to approximately 28 percent of the population in 2005. Yet this remains a substantial group, with about 80 million occupants in 2005. (See Table 4.5 for specific breakouts by age group—i.e., under 5, 5 to 9, 10 to 14, and 15 to 19.)

Marketers typically refer to children ages 4 through 12 as "kids" to distinguish this cohort from toddlers and teenagers. It is estimated that children in this broad grouping either directly spend or influence the spending of billions of dollars worth of purchases each year. Aggregate spending by children ages 4 through 12 or in behalf of this age group roughly doubled every decade in the 1960s, 1970s, and 1980s. Spending in the 1990s tripled. Spending by or for this age group in one recent year totaled more than $24 billion.[13]

Preschoolers. Preschool-age children, age 5 or younger, represent a cohort that has grown substantially in recent years. More babies were born in the United States in 1990 (4.2 million) than at any time since the baby boom peak of 4.3 million babies born in 1957.[14] Toys, furniture items, and other products and services appealing to the family and home have increased to cater to this mini baby boom. For example, 5 million LeapPads—the educational toy that allows specially designed books to speak at the touch of small antennae disguised as a pen—were sold in a recent year at a price of $49.99.[15] Figure 4.3 on page 103 is an ad for Orajel Toddler Training Toothpaste—shown in the ad being used by a preschooler.

Elementary-school-age children. This group includes children ages 6 to 11. These children directly influence product purchases (e.g., toys, records) and indirectly influence what their parents buy. Children in this group are influential in their parents' choice of clothing and toys and even the brand choice of products such as toothpaste and food products. Advertising and other forms of marketing communications aimed at young children, or their families, have increased substantially in recent years. Numerous new products annually hit the shelves to cater to kids' tastes. For example, Mattel, which is known for its line of Hot Wheels toy cars, has extended the brand into the area of marketing skateboards, snowboards, and extreme-sports apparel under the Hot Wheels name.[16] The Walt Disney Company introduced the Disney Dream Desk PC, a computer and monitor combo where the monitor is shaped in the form of Mickey Mouse ears (Figure 4.4) and will be priced at about $900.[17] Among other features, the Disney Dream PC contains special software that blocks hate, violence, and pornographic content. (For a sophisticated but readable treatment of how children are socialized as consumers and learn to understand advertising, the reader is encouraged to examine two articles identified in this Endnote.)[18]

Figure 4.4
The Disney Dream Desk PC

AP/Topic Gallery

Tweens. A category of children that marketers have dubbed "tweens"—not quite kids nor yet teenagers—is an age cohort actively involved in consumption. *Tweens* are usually classified as children between the ages of 8 and 12. One specialist in the area of marketing to children estimates that tweens in a recent year had a yearly average income of $22.68 or, collectively, a total annual income of around $23 billion.[19] Retailers such as Limited Too gear much of their marcom efforts at garnering tweens' growing desire for fashionable clothing items (https://www.limitedtoo.com). See the *IMC Focus* insert on page 105 for an interesting study about tweens' levels of materialism.

Figure 4.3 Orajel Advertisement

Courtesy, Del Laboratories, Inc.

© Taxi/Getty Images

Teenagers. Consumers in this age group, totaling in the United States over 25 million 13- to 19-year-olds, have tremendous earning power and considerable influence in making personal and household purchases.[20] Teenagers often are referred to as the *Millennial Generation* or *Generation Y* (in contrast to the generation that preceded it, *Generation X*). Technically speaking, **Generation Y** (Gen Y) consists of individuals born between 1979 and 1994, but to avoid overlap with the generation that preceded it, Generation X (Gen X), in this book we will consider Gen Y as the generation born between *1982 to 1994*. Thus, as of 2005, Gen Yers include all people between the ages of 11 and 23, approximately 50 million Americans. The present discussion focuses just on the subset of teenagers who comprise this generation.

A study by Teenage Research Unlimited, which follows teen trends and attitudes, estimated that American teenagers spend over $150 billion annually.[21] Teenagers have purchasing influence and power far greater than ever, which accounts for the growth of marcom programs aimed at this group. For example, Coca-Cola has substantially increased its marcom efforts directed at teenagers. Among other initiatives, the company has tested "red lounges" in suburban shopping malls. These lounges are equipped with curvy red couches that allow teens to hang out while watching music videos, charging their cellphones, and, of course, buying Coke.[22] Sea-Doo, a manufacturer of jet skis, is actively marketing its 3D brand, which retails at around $7,000, to the Gen Y market. The advertisement for Skechers in Figure 4.5 is a notable appeal to teens who are interested in fashionable casual footwear.

Figure 4.5

Skechers Advertisement

Skecher's USA, Inc.

Teenagers are noted for being highly conformist, narcissistic, and fickle consumers. These characteristics pose great opportunities and yet challenges for marketing communicators. An accepted product can become a huge success when the teenage bandwagon selects a brand as a personal mark of the in-crowd. However, today's accepted product or brand can easily become tomorrow's passé item.

It is said that teenagers don't like to be "marketed to." As with all consumers, it is important that marketing communicators provide useful information, but teens would rather acquire the information themselves—such as on the Internet or from friends—rather than having it imposed on them. Marcom personnel thus walk a precarious plank in communicating useful information to teens while at the same time avoiding being overbearing. The Internet is an obvious communication medium for reaching teens, who, it is estimated, represent over 11 million online users.[23]

Young Adults

Scholarly treatment of this age cohort, commonly referred to as **Generation X**, identifies it as Americans born between 1961 and 1981.[24] However, to avoid overlap with the baby boomer generation (1946 to 1964) and Gen Y (1982 to 1994), it is convenient to define this age cohort as people born between *1965 and 1981*. Hence, as of 2005,

Tweens and Materialism

imc focus

An important recent study of tweens (including also some teens age 13 and 14) examined their materialistic values and how materialism relates to a variety of demographic variables, purchase-related behaviors, and involvement with advertisements and promotions. To measure *materialism*—which includes the desire to buy and own products, the enjoyment of these items, and the desire for money that enables the acquisition of products—the researchers developed a measure called the "youth materialism scale" (YMS). The YMS consists of the following 10 items that youths responded to using options ranging from "disagree a lot" to "agree a lot" in reaction to each statement:

1. I'd rather spend time buying things than doing almost anything else.
2. I would be happier if I had more money to buy more things for myself.
3. I have fun just thinking of all the things I own.
4. I really enjoy going shopping.
5. I like to buy things my friends have.
6. When you grow up, the more money you have, the happier you are.
7. I'd rather not share my snacks with others if it means I'll have less for myself.
8. I would love to be able to buy things that cost lots of money.
9. I really like the kids that have very special games or clothes.
10. The only kind of job I want when I grow up is one that gets me a lot of money.

Based on a national sample of U.S. households, nearly 1,000 youths between the ages of 9 and 14 completed the YMS and answered a number of other questions. The researchers then statistically correlated the YMS and the other questions and produced the following set of illustrative findings:

- Boys are more materialistic than girls.
- Youths from lower income households are more materialistic.
- Highly materialistic youths shop more frequently.
- Highly materialistic youths show a greater interest in new products.
- Highly materialistic youths are: (a) more likely to watch TV commercials, (b) ask parents to buy products because they've seen them on TV, (c) more responsive to celebrity endorsements, (d) more likely to exert pressure on their parents to purchase products, (e) inclined to want more spent on them for Christmas and birthdays, and (f) prone to like school less and to have somewhat poorer grades.

Though it has been speculated that people who are more materialistic are less happy, the present research determined that highly materialistic youth are no more or less happy than less materialistic youth. However, highly materialistic youth expect in the future to be better off financially than their parents.

SOURCE: Marvin E. Goldberg, Gerald J. Gorn, Laura A. Peracchio, and Gary Bamossy, "Understanding Materialism Among Youth," *Journal of Consumer Psychology* 13 (No. 3, 2003), 278–288.

Gen X constituted over 50 million Americans in the age category from 24 to 40. Because Gen Xers were born immediately after the baby boom, which ended in 1964, this group also is referred to as *baby busters* and *twentysomethings*—the latter label reflecting the fact that most people in this cohort are in their 20s. The labels do not end there, however; indeed, Gen X has been subjected to more clichés than any group in history, most of which are deprecatory: slackers, cynics, whiners, grunge kids, and hopeless. As is typically the case when a group is stereotyped, these labels characterize only a subset of Gen Xers and are much too general to begin to capture the complexity of this group and the differences among its occupants.

One well-known marketing research firm has classified Gen Xers into four groups based on their attitudinal profiles: Yup & Comers, Bystanders, Playboys, and Drifters. *Yup & Comers* have the highest levels of education and income and account for approximately 28 percent of Gen Xers. They tend to focus on intangible rewards rather than material wealth and are confident about themselves and their futures. This clearly is not a group of people who fit the stereotypical labels attached to Gen X. *Bystanders* represent nearly 37 percent of Gen Xers and consist predominantly of female African-Americans and Hispanics. Although their disposable income is relatively low, this subsegment of Gen Xers has a flair for fashion and loves to shop. *Playboys* is a predominantly white, male group accounting for almost 19 percent of the Gen X cohort. Playboys adhere to a "pleasure before duty" lifestyle and are self-absorbed, fun loving, and impulsive. *Drifters* constitute the smallest subset at 16 percent of Gen Xers. This group is closest to the Gen X

Can Renault Develop a Hip Image?

global focus

In late 2004 Renault introduced a new vehicle to European consumers that looks something like a minivan, a little like a station wagon, but not what most consumers would regard as especially hip. What makes the introduction so interesting, however, is the company's two-pronged approach in targeting the vehicle. On the one hand, TV ads appealed to parents in their 30s and 40s. This age group is the primary target in that a vehicle such as the Modus is bigger than a compact car and provides the necessary room for hauling children and various objects that don't fit into a car's trunk. The other target, surprisingly, is the group of younger consumers known as Gen X, or "twentysomethings." Why would someone in that age group want a Modus?

Well, officials at Renault are not convinced they will. Yet, an aggressive marcom effort was designed to enhance Renault's image with the younger group and rejuvenate the brand, even if that effort does not translate into immediate sales of the Modus or other Renault products. Using a viral advertising approach, Renault's ad agency created humorous online films with the hopes of generating positive word-of-mouth buzz about the Modus. In one film clip, for example, Renault's CEO is shown at his desk playing with a red car, and a tagline reads "Grow up. What for?" A similar tagline appears in TV commercials, with the expectation that TV viewers will remember the same tagline from their online viewing. A potential downside to this viral marketing effort is that rather than enhance Renault's image, online viewers may instead make fun of the film vignettes and create an undesired form of buzz wherein Renault becomes the butt of jokes.

Source: Adapted from Erin White, "Renault Gets Hip with Minivan Ads," *The Wall Street Journal Online*, http://online.wsj.com (accessed August 26, 2004).

stereotype. They are frustrated with their lives, are among the least educated, seek security and status, and choose brands that offer a sense of belonging and self-esteem.[25]

These groupings make it apparent that contrary to their stereotypical portrayal, Gen Xers are *not* monolithic. The generalizations are incorrect and generally unfair. As a group they are no more cynical, disenfranchised, or inclined to whine than most people. Marketing communications directed to twentysomethings must use appeals targeted to specific subgroups such as Yup & Comers rather than stereotypes that do not adequately reach any subsegment.

Once again it is important to emphasize that the Gen X age cohort, however labeled, is not a unified group in terms of demographics or lifestyle preferences and should not be misconstrued as a single group for targeting marcom messages. Indeed, the four groupings just described are themselves simplifications, but they do offer some refinement of the general differences among the over 50 million Americans who have been simplistically collapsed into a single category.

It is not only marketers in the United States who are interested in appealing to the huge group of Gen X consumers. The *Global Focus* insert describes an interesting campaign undertaken by French automobile maker Renault to appeal to young adults.

Middle-Aged and Mature Consumers

Although somewhat arbitrary, we can think of **middle age** as starting at age 35 and ending at 54, at which point maturity is reached. Actually, there is some disagreement over the dividing point between middle age and maturity. Sometimes a 65-and-over classification is used, because age 65 normally marks retirement. In this text we will use the U.S. Census Bureau's designation, which classifies **mature people** as those who are *55 and older.*

Middle-aged. As of 2005 there were roughly 85 million Americans between the middle ages of 35 and 54 (see Table 4.5). Most of these individuals constitute the previously described *baby boomers* born between 1946 and 1964. The baby-boom generation offers tremendous potential for many marketers. What makes boomers such an attractive target is that this age category is relatively affluent and thus represents a good general target for second homes, quality vehicles, investments (insurance, real estate, and securities), travel, self-help products, cosmetic surgery, and grown-up "toys" like golfing equipment, automobiles with convertible tops (the average convertible buyer is 50 years old),[26] and motorcycles—Harley-Davidson's best customers are middle-aged men, and the typical buyer has an average age of 46 (see Figure 4.6).[27] Given their relative affluence, baby boomers also represent an attractive target for a variety of "luxury" goods. For example, appliance maker Whirlpool appeals to affluent boomers who want the very best appliance quality with a line of items named Whirlpool Gold. And luxury skin-care marketers have experienced revenue growth by introducing high-priced anti-aging products such as L'Oreal's Absolue.

Moreover, just because baby boomers are aging does not necessarily mean they are getting psychologically old or are significantly altering their consumption patterns from a younger age. Rather, there are indications that baby boomers are retaining many of their more youthful consumption habits and, in a sense, are taking longer to grow up or are unwilling to change. For example, the rather dramatic increase in purchases of hair-color products by baby boomers reflects this tendency for boomers to prolong youth and to gravitate toward products that support their youth obsession. Manufacturers of health-care items, exercise machines, and food products have actively appealed to baby boomers' passion for remaining in youthful shape. Because boomers represent the "epicenter of society," advertisers will march in lockstep with this group and continue to reflect their characteristics and appeal to their purchase interests and needs.[28] For example, athletic-footwear makers such as New Balance cater to baby boomers by offering shoes that come in wider widths than just the medium-size option offered in the past. Even the makers of the high-energy drink, Red Bull, well known for its appeal to twentysomethings and teens, is now targeting British golfers—many of whom are 40 or older—by making the product available in course shops, restaurants, and hotels across Britain.[29]

Figure 4.6
Harley-Davidson Advertisement

Courtesy, Harley-Davidson: Photograph © 2005 Chris Whimpey

An important point of clarification is needed before concluding this section and moving on to the next age group. In particular, it is tempting to think of baby boomers as a monolithic group of people who think alike, act the same, and purchase identical products. Such an impression would be erroneous. Baby boomers do *not* represent a true market segment in the strictest sense of this term. That is, just because millions of Americans share one commonality (being born between 1946 and 1964), this does not mean they are virtual clones of one another. Within this age cohort, there are distinct differences among people with respect to age, income, ethnicity, lifestyle choices, and product/brand preferences. Hence, although it is convenient to speak of baby boomers as a single group, it would be a mistake to conclude they represent an actionable market segment. It is important to appreciate the fact that meaningful and profitable marcom targeting efforts typically require that audience members share a combination of demographic, lifestyle, and possibly geographical characteristics; broad groupings such as "baby boomers" are much too crude to satisfy the characteristics of a meaningful market segment.

In sum, baby boomers are a significant age cohort and en masse represent a powerful economic force, but they do *not* constitute a sufficient basis for targeting marcom programs. Thus, for example, the marketers of L'Oreal Absolue should not consider their target to be all boomers

From V103 Senior Lifestyles/Getty Images

but rather only the subset of people in this age category who have indulgent personalities (a psychographic trait) and sufficient incomes to afford an expensive product.

Mature Consumers. Turning to **mature consumers** (also called *seniors*), in 2005 there were approximately 66 million U.S. citizens *age 55 or older*, representing about 23 percent of the total U.S. population. In other words, nearly one quarter of all Americans are senior citizens. Historically, many marketers have ignored mature consumers or have treated this group in unflattering ways by focusing on "repair kit products" such as dentures, laxatives, and arthritis remedies.[30] Not only are mature consumers numerous, but they also are wealthier and more willing to spend than ever before. Mature Americans control nearly 70 percent of the net worth of all U.S. households.

People age 65 and older are particularly well off, having the highest *discretionary income* (i.e., income unburdened by fixed expenses) and the most assets of any age group. The number of people in this 65-plus age category is huge, totaling over 36 million in 2005, which represents nearly 13 percent of the total population.

A variety of implications accompany marcom efforts directed at mature consumers. In advertising aimed at this group, it is advisable to portray them as active, vital, busy, forward looking, and concerned with looking attractive and being romantic. Levitra, Cialis, and Viagra advertisements often exemplify advertisers' recognition that romance is not the sole province of youth. Advertisers now generally appeal to seniors in a flattering fashion as typified by the use of attractive models to represent clothing, cosmetics, and other products that had been the exclusive advertising domain of youthful models.

Advertisers that use the Internet cannot neglect appeals to seniors, who represent one of the fastest growing groups on the Web. Investments, health and travel research, genealogy, and gambling are the most popular online activities with seniors.[31] Seniors spend an average 700 minutes online per month, which exceeds any other group's use of the Internet.[32]

It is important to again point out that just because mature consumers share a single commonality (i.e., age 55 or older), they by no means represent a homogeneous market segment. Indeed, the Census Bureau divides people age 55 and older into three distinct age segments: 55 to 64 (*olders*); 65 to 74 (*elders*); and 75 and over (*the very old*) (see Table 4.5). On the basis of age alone, consumers in each of these groups differ—sometimes dramatically—in terms of lifestyles, interest in the marketplace, reasons for buying, and ability to spend. Moreover, it is important to realize that age alone is not the best indicator of how an individual lives or what role consumption plays in that lifestyle. In fact, research has identified four groups of mature consumers based on a combination of health and self-image characteristics. Based on a national mail survey of over 1,000 people age 55 and older, respondents were classified into the following groups: Healthy Hermits, 38 percent; Ailing Outgoers, 34 percent; Frail Recluses, 15 percent; and Healthy Indulgers, 13 percent.[33] Brief descriptions follow.

- *Healthy Hermits*, though in good health, are psychologically withdrawn from society. They represent a good market for various services such as tax and legal advice, financial services, home entertainment, and do-it-yourself products. Direct mail, the Internet, and print advertising are the best media for reaching this group.
- *Ailing Outgoers* are diametrically opposite to Healthy Hermits. Though in poor health, they are socially active, health conscious, and interested in learning to do new things. Home health care, dietary products, planned retirement com-

munities, and entertainment services are some of the products and services most desired by this group. They can be reached via the Internet and through select mass media tailored to their positive self-image and active, social lifestyle.

- *Frail Recluses* are withdrawn socially and are in poor health. Various health and medical products and services, home entertainment, and domestic assistance services (e.g., lawn care) can be successfully marketed to this group via mass media advertising.
- *Healthy Indulgers* are vigorous, relatively wealthy, and socially active. They are independent and want the most out of life. Mature consumers in this group represent a good market for financial services, leisure/travel entertainment, clothes, luxury goods, and high-tech products and services. They are accessible via in-store promotions, direct mail, specialized print media, and the Internet.

The Ever-Changing American Household

A household represents an independent housing entity, either rental property (e.g., a single room or an apartment) or owned property (a mobile home, condominium, or house). As of 2002, there were *109.3 million* households in the United States, of which 74.3 million (68 percent) were family households (i.e., two or more related people occupying the household) and 35 million (32 percent) nonfamily households. The average household size across all 109.3 million American households was 2.6 people.[34]

Households are growing in number, shrinking in size, and changing in character. The traditional American family—that is, married couples with children younger than 18—represents less than one-fourth of all U.S. households, whereas in 1960 such families constituted nearly 50 percent. The number of new households has grown twice as fast as the population, while household size has declined. In 1950, families constituted nearly 90 percent of all households, whereas in 2002 fewer than 70 percent were family units.[35]

The changing composition of the American household has tremendous implications for marketing communicators, perhaps especially advertisers. Advertising has to reflect the widening range of living situations that exist. This is particularly true in the case of households with a single occupant. Singles and unrelated couples or friends living together represent a large and ever-growing group. Many advertisers make special appeals to the buying interests and needs of singles, appealing in food ads, for example, to such needs as ease and speed of preparation, maintenance simplicity, and small serving sizes. Reaching singles requires special media-selection efforts because singles tend not to be big prime-time television viewers but are skewed instead toward the late fringe hours (after 11 P.M.), are disproportionately more likely than the rest of the population to view cable television, and are disproportionately heavy magazine readers. Many magazines cater to the interests of singles, and TV programs are produced to represent their actual or idealized lifestyles—programs such as *Friends* and *Sex and the City*, both of which remain on TV in syndication but no longer are being produced.

Ethnic Population Developments

America has always been a melting pot. It became even more so in recent decades. The largest ethnic groups in the United States are Hispanics and African-Americans. Ethnic minorities now represent nearly one of three people in the United States. In recognition of the growing role of ethnic groups, the following sections examine population developments and marcom implications for African, Hispanic, and Asian-Americans.

A few background statistics will be helpful to set the stage for these discussions. First, at the time of the last 10-year census (in 2000), the American population was distributed in roughly the following fashion:[36]

White, not Hispanic	71%
Black, not Hispanic	12
Hispanic, of any race	12
Asian and Pacific Islanders	4
American Indians, Eskimos, and Aleut	1
Total	100%

Non-Hispanic whites' share of the U.S. population is projected to decline from 71 percent to 65 percent of the total population by the year 2010 and just 50 percent by 2050.[37] The implication is obvious: marketers and marketing communicators need to do a better job developing products and marcom strategies that are designed to meet the unique needs of ethnic groups because ethnicity plays an important role in directing consumer behavior.[38] Table 4.6 provides a useful picture of the major ethnic groups' population representation in the United States from 2000 through 2050. The following sections provide more details for the three major ethnic groups: African-Americans, Hispanics (Latinos), and Asians. Remaining ethnic groups (e.g., American Indians and Pacific Islanders) are important to the cultural fiber of the United States but represent relatively limited economic forces due to their relative small sizes.

African-Americans

Non-Hispanic African-Americans are projected to constitute approximately 40.5 million individuals as of 2010, or slightly more than 13 percent of the U.S. population.[39] African-Americans are characterized more by their common heritage than by skin color—a heritage based on a beginning in slavery, a history of discrimination, limited housing opportunities, and, historically, only partial participation in many aspects of the majority culture.[40]

Table 4.6

Ethnic Groups' Population Representation in the United States, 2000–2050 (in millions)

Ethnic Group	2000	2010	2020	2030	2040	2050
African-American	35.82* (12.7%)	40.45 (13.1%)	45.37 (13.5%)	50.44 (13.9%)	55.88 (14.3%)	61.36 (14.6%)
Hispanic**	35.62 (12.6%)	47.76 (15.5%)	59.76 (17.8%)	73.06 (20.1%)	87.59 (22.3%)	102.56 (24.4%)
Asian	10.68 (3.8%)	14.24 (4.6%)	17.99 (5.4%)	22.58 (6.2%)	27.99 (7.1%)	33.43 (8.0%)
Total population (major ethnic groups)	82.12 (29.1%)	102.45 (33.2%)	123.12 (36.7%)	146.1 40.2%)	171.5 (43.7%)	197.4 (47.0%)
Total U.S. Population	282.13	308.94	335.81	363.58	391.95	419.85

*To be read: there were 35.82 million African-Americans in the United States as of 2000, which constituted approximately 12.7 percent of the total population.

**Includes Hispanics of any race.

Source: U.S. Census Bureau, 2004, "U.S. Interim Projections by Age, Sex, Race, and Hispanic Origin," http://www.census.gov/ipc/www/usinterimproj.

© Yellowdog Productions/The Image Bank/Getty Images

Several notable reasons explain why African-Americans are attractive consumers for many companies: (1) the average age of black Americans is considerably younger than that for whites; (2) African-Americans are geographically concentrated, with approximately three-fourths of all blacks living in just 16 states (California, Texas, Illinois, Louisiana, Alabama, Georgia, Florida, South Carolina, North Carolina, Maryland, Michigan, Ohio, Pennsylvania, Virginia, New York, and New Jersey);[41] and (3) African-Americans tend to purchase prestige and name-brand products in greater proportion than do whites.

These impressive figures notwithstanding, many companies make no special efforts to communicate with African-Americans. This is unwise considering that research indicates blacks are responsive to advertisements placed in black-oriented media and that make personalized appeals by using African-American models and contexts with which blacks can identify. Major corporations are increasingly developing marcom programs for communicating with black consumers. In recent years, for example, Sears, Roebuck & Co. launched an ad campaign that targeted African-Americans; Jaguar Cars North America embarked on a major direct marketing effort to African-Americans by mailing about 1 million advertising brochures to middle-aged African-Americans who had annual incomes of $75,000 or more; General Motors launched a magazine campaign that spotlighted its prominent African-American executives; and various automobile makers, including GM, have begun targeting black consumers via hip-hop magazines and other media that reach hip-hop fans.

Although greater numbers of companies are realizing the importance of directing special marcom efforts to African-Americans, it is important to emphasize that black consumers do *not* constitute a single market any more than whites do. African-Americans exhibit diverse purchasing behaviors according to their lifestyles, values, and demographics. Therefore, companies must use different advertising media, distribution channels, advertising themes, and pricing strategies as they market to the various subsegments of the African-American population.

Hispanic Americans (Latinos)

The U.S. Latino[42] population grew from only 4 million in 1950 to an expected population of nearly 48 million in 2010 and now is America's largest minority with a slight edge over African-Americans in share of the total U.S. population.[43] Latinos in the United States will constitute about one-quarter of the total population by 2050 (see Table 4.6) and presently constitute a population of nearly 40 million residents—a population larger than that of all of Canada. The largest percentage of Latinos are Mexican Americans, but large numbers of Puerto Rican Americans, Latin Americans from Central and South America, and Cuban Americans also reside in the United States.

Hispanic Americans have historically been concentrated in a relatively few states such as California, Texas, New York, Florida, Illinois, Arizona, and New Jersey. However, Latinos are becoming increasingly mobile and have begun to fan out from the few states in which they originally concentrated. Table 4.7 provides information pertinent to the top 10 Hispanic markets in the United States.

Marketing communicators in the past did not devote sufficient attention to Hispanic Americans, but their attention has increased substantially since the Census Bureau announced a 58 percent increase in the number of Hispanic Americans between 1990 and 2000. Yet companies advertise to Latinos much less

Table 4.7

Top 10 U.S. Hispanic Markets (estimates as of 2004)

Rank	Market	Hispanic Population	Hispanic % of Total Market Population
1	Los Angeles	7,811,100	44.5
2	New York	4,316,400	20.5
3	Chicago	1,838,000	19.0
4	Miami	1,836,800	43.1
5	Houston	1,822,600	33.4
6	Dallas–Fort Worth	1,509,700	23.5
7	San Francisco	1,491,800	21.3
8	San Antonio	1,293,700	60.3
9	Phoenix	1,208,000	27.2
10	McAllen, Texas	1,142,000	94.8

SOURCE: "Hispanic Fact Pack, 2004 Edition," *Advertising Age's Annual Guide to Hispanic Advertising & Marketing.* Reprinted with permission from *Advertising Age.* Copyright, Crain Communications.

than their market size would justify. Research has shown that the frequency of Hispanics' appearances in television advertising is considerably less than their proportion of the population.[44] Many companies are increasingly shifting more of their budgets into media that reach Latino consumers, but it would appear that marketers in large part are underspending in efforts targeted toward this large and growing element of the U.S. population.[45]

Marketing communicators need to be aware of several important points when attempting to reach Latino consumers: because a large percentage of Hispanics use primarily Spanish media, it is important to target messages to some (but not all) Latinos using Spanish-speaking media. A key in designing effective advertising for Hispanics is to advertise to them in their *dominant language.*[46] Because approximately half of Hispanic Americans speak only or mostly Spanish at home, reaching these consumers requires the use of Spanish. The ad in Figure 4.7 acknowledges this fact. However, for Hispanics who are English dominant, as are many younger Latinos, it obviously makes greater sense to use English in advertising copy that reflects their values and culture.

It is absolutely critical to recognize that Latinos do *not* represent a single, unified market. There are strong intraethnic differences among Cubans, Mexicans, and Puerto Ricans, which thus necessitate unique appeals be directed to each Latino group. Moreover, as with all general groupings, there are huge differences within each group in terms of English-speaking ability, length of residence in the United States (and thus degree of acculturation), level of income, and so on. It is erroneous to speak of a Hispanic market, a Mexican market, or any other crude lumping of people who share their descent as a single defining factor.

Some prominent companies—Coca-Cola, Pepsi, Procter & Gamble, Sears, McDonald's, Dunkin' Donuts, and Best Buy to name a few—are now investing heavily in Hispanic-oriented advertising and event sponsorships that reach Latinos in their local communities and often in joyous moods. Sponsoring Cinco de Mayo events, for example, is beginning to take on the same proportion as putting commercial support behind St. Patrick's Day celebrations. For an interesting appeal to the Latino market, see the *IMC Focus* insert about the marketing of Clamato.

Asian-Americans

Asians in the United States include many nationalities: Asian Indians, Chinese, Filipino, Japanese, Korean, Vietnamese, and others. Asian-Americans have been heralded as the newest "hot" ethnic market. The demographics support this optimistic outlook. As of the year 2000, approximately 10.7 million Asians were living

A Special Beverage for Latino Consumers, Clamato

imc focus

Clamato, the name representing the conjoining of clam and tomato, is a tomato juice containing a hint of clam along with celery, onions, and spices. Many American consumers have never tried the product or dislike it due to the difficulty of drinking juice tinged with clams. Though available on supermarket shelves for over 25 years, the brand basically languished until its marketer, Mott's, concentrated its entire marketing budget on the Latino market. Why? Because Latino consumers somehow have the impression that Clamato juice is an aphrodisiac. Although Mott's makes no claims as to Clamato's powers, advertising refers obliquely to the brand's appeal with the tagline "Clamato le pone sabor al momento" (Clamato adds flavor to the moment).

Leveraging this (mis)perception among Latino consumers, Mott's undertook an integrated campaign that involved TV and radio advertisements, outdoor signage, and in-store promotions in major Hispanic markets. In a special appeal to Mexican Americans, who constitute about 60 percent of U.S. Latinos, Mott's developed a phone card promotion whereby cards with free minutes for calls to Mexico were given away when consumers purchased 64-ounce bottles of Clamato. These IMC efforts have driven a substantial sales increase since Mott's began the Hispanic initiative for Clamato.

Source: Adapted from Gabriel Sama, "Appeal of Clamato Isn't Just Its Taste," *The Wall Street Journal Online,* October 21, 2003, http://online.wsj.com (accessed October 21, 2003).

in the United States. By 2010 that number will increase to over 14 million and more than 33 million by 2050 (see Table 4.6). Though Chinese Americans at 2.4 million are the largest group of Asians residing in the United States, Asian Indians grew the fastest during the decade from 1990 to 2000, with that population doubling and now totaling 1.7 million.[47]

Asian-Americans on average are better educated, have higher incomes, and occupy more prestigious job positions than any other segment of American society. The median household income for Asian-Americans in one recent year was $52,285 compared with median incomes of $46,900, $33,103, and $29,177 for whites, Hispanics, and African-Americans, respectively.[48]

It is important to emphasize that just as there is no single African-American or Hispanic market, there certainly does not exist a single Asian-American market. Moreover, unlike other ethnic groups, such as Hispanics, who share a similar language, Asian-Americans speak a variety of uniquely different languages. Among Asian nationalities there are considerable differences in product choices and brand preferences. Even within each nationality there are variations in terms of English-language skills and financial well-being. Many Asian-Americans do not speak English fluently, and quite a few live in homes where no adults speak any English.

Some firms have been successful in marketing to specific Asian groups by customizing marketing programs to their values and lifestyles rather than merely translating Anglo programs. For example, Metropolitan Life, an insurance company, conducted research that determined that Asian parents' top priority was their children's security and education. Metropolitan translated this finding into a successful campaign targeted to Korean and Chinese Americans. Reebok's sales among Asian-Americans increased substantially after that company used past tennis star Michael Chang in its advertisements.

Mainstream marketers have available various media options for targeting Asian-Americans: Asian-language radio

Figure 4.7

Recognition of Importance of Advertising in Spanish

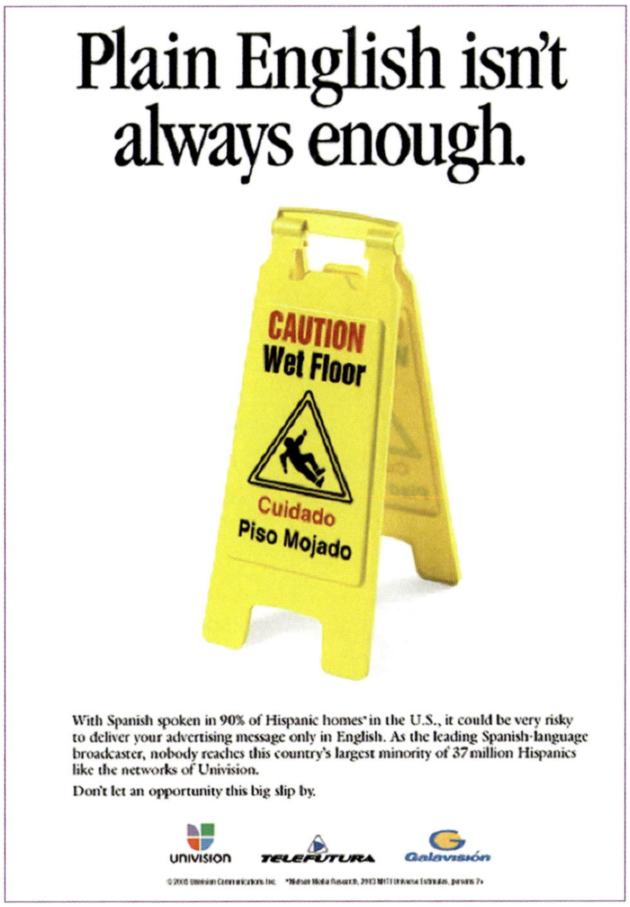

stations are now burgeoning in areas where large concentrations of Asians live, and direct marketing via the mail is an outstanding medium for micromarketing to specific groups of Asian-Americans. The Internet also is a valuable medium for reaching Asian-Americans inasmuch as this group represents a disproportionately high group of online users in comparison to other groups of Americans, including the majority white population.

Summary

This chapter has emphasized the importance of targeting marcom messages. Determining how a brand's marcom efforts should be directed toward specific groups of consumers—based on behaviorgraphic, psychographic, demographic, or geodemographic considerations—is the initial and most fundamental of all marcom decisions. All subsequent marcom decisions (positioning, setting objectives, and determining budgets) are inextricably intertwined with this initial, targeting decision. Hence, the targeting decision is of critical importance.

Perhaps the most diagnostic basis upon which to target consumers is to identify their past purchase behavior in the product category for which a brand manager is making a targeting decision. Armed with *behaviorgraphic* information about how customers have behaved in the past, it is possible to project with considerable accuracy how they will behave in the future. Marcom programs can thus be aimed toward those consumers whose behavioral profiles indicate they are prime candidates to receive and act upon advertisements and other messages. Also, knowledge of consumers' online search behavior enables the targeting of advertisements for brands that match the characteristics of consumers who visit those sites.

Marketing communicators also target customers using knowledge about their activities, interests, and opinions (or, collectively, their lifestyles) to better understand what people want and how they are likely to respond to advertising, direct mail, and other forms of marketing communications. The term *psychographics* describes this form of targeting. Customized studies are conducted to identify psychographic segments directly applicable to the marketer's product category and brand, but syndicated research systems such as SRI's VALS system also provide useful information for making important marcom decisions. The VALS system classifies people into one of eight groups based on a combination of their self-orientation and resources.

Another basis for targeting consumers is that of geodemographics. This form of targeting basically identifies clusters of consumers who reside in neighborhoods where residents share similar demographic characteristics and related lifestyles. Donnelly's ClusterPlus and Claritas's PRIZM_{NE} are two well-known and respected clustering systems that identify meaningful groupings of geographical units such as zip code areas. The section on geodemographics covered the PRIZM_{NE} and indicated that this clustering system delineates the population into 66 groups that are labeled with catchy names such as Bohemian Mix, Country Casuals, Suburban Pioneers, and City Roots. Geodemographic information is especially useful when making direct marketing decisions, selecting retail outlets, or spotting broadcast advertisements in select markets.

A final section of the chapter reviewed three major demographic developments: (1) the age structure of the U.S. population, (2) the changing American household, and (3) ethnic population developments. Some of the major demographic developments discussed include (1) the progressive aging of the U.S. population from an average age of 33 in 1990 to nearly 36 years old in 2000 and to an expected average age of 38 by 2025, (2) the increase in the percentage of single American adults, and (3) the explosive growth of ethnic minorities, particularly Latinos.

Discussion Questions

1. In what sense is behaviorgraphic information about customers more diagnostic of their future purchase behavior than is, say, demographic information?
2. In your own words, explain how online behavioral targeting works.
3. In what sense is online behavioral targeting a potential invasion of one's privacy?
4. If you were to design a psychographic study for a new chain of lower-priced coffee stores that are planned to compete against Starbucks, what lifestyle characteristics (i.e., people's interests, values, and activities they participate in) might you consider as indicative of whether they might be interested in your new stores?
5. To which of Yankelovich's eight MindBase segments do you belong? (Go to http://www.yankelovich.com/shortform2_p01.asp.)
6. To which of the VALS segments do you belong? (Go to http://www.sric-bi.com/VALS/presurvey.shtml.)
7. Having read the section on the size of the world and U.S. populations, update the figures presented in the text, which were current as of late 2004, by going to http://www.census.gov/main/www/popclock.html.
8. Demographers tell us that households in the United States are growing in number, shrinking in size, and changing in character. Assume that you are the vice president of marketing for a corporation that manufactures chairs and sofas, say La-Z-Boy Corporation. What specific implications do these changes hold for your company?
9. Most readers of this text fall either in the Gen X or Gen Y age categories. Just because you share this one commonality with all other Gen Xers or Gen Yers, does this one piece of information about you and your cohorts represent a sufficient basis on which a marcom practitioner might aim its advertising efforts?
10. African-American, Latinos, and Asian-American consumers do not signify three homogeneous markets; rather, they represent many markets composed of people who merely share a common race and/or language. Explain.
11. Explain the reasons for the relentless aging of the U.S. population, and discuss some implications this will have on marketing and marketing communications in the foreseeable future.
12. Due to rather dramatic changes in the population composition of the United States, one could argue that advertising in earlier decades, say the 1970s and 1980s, was a lot easier than it is today. From your reading of the chapter, provide two or three reasons to support this argument.
13. Assume you are brand manager of a food product that is consumed by all Americans—blacks, whites, Hispanics, Asians, and others. You are considering running an extended advertising campaign on prime-time television that uses Latino actors and appeals to Latino consumers. Aside from cost considerations, what reservations might you have about this type of campaign?
14. When the mature market was discussed, it was noted that advertising aimed at this group should portray them as vital, busy, forward looking, and attractive or romantic. Interview several mature consumers and coalesce their views on how they perceive advertising directed at them and their peers. Your interview results along with those from fellow students should lead to an interesting class discussion.
15. What are your views on the targeting of products to children? Aside from your personal views, discuss the issue of targeting to children from two additional perspectives: first, that of a brand manager who is responsible for the profitability of a child-oriented product, and second, from the viewpoint of an

ethicist. Imagine what each of these parties might say about the practice of targeting products to children.

16. Based on your personal background and using the VALS system, how would you categorize most of the adults with whom you and your family associate?
17. Identify magazine advertisements that reflect appeals to at least three of the eight VALS groups. Describe in as much detail as possible the neighborhood in which you were raised. Come up with a label (similar to the $PRIZM_{NE}$ cluster names) that captures the essence of your neighborhood.

ENDNOTES

1. Details summarized from http://www.esprit.com.
2. Cynthia H. Cho, "Esprit Tries to Shed Its Youth Image," *The Wall Street Journal Online,* September 3, 2004, http:/online.wsj.com.
3. Amy Merrick, "Gap's Greatest Generation? *The Wall Street Journal Online,* September 15, 2004, http://online.wsj.com.
4. http://www.infores.com/public/us/content/infoscan.
5. Kris Oser, "Targeting Web behavior pays, American Airlines study finds," *Advertising Age,* May 17, 2004, 8.
6. Kris Oser, "Snapple Effort Finds Women As They Browse," *Advertising Age,* May 3, 2004, 22.
7. Carol M. Morgan and Doran J. Levy, "Targeting to Psychographic Segments," *Brandweek,* October 7, 2002, 18–19.
8. James W. Peltier, John A. Schibrowsky, Don E. Schultz, and John Davis, "Interactive Psychographics: Cross-Selling in the Banking Industry," *Journal of Advertising Research* 42 (March/April 2002), 7–22.
9. These descriptions are from http://www.sric-bi.com/VALS/types.shtml.
10. Michael J. Weiss, *The Clustered World: How We Live, What We Buy, and What It All Means About Who We Are* (Boston: Little, Brown and Company, 2000).
11. The following descriptions and data are based on documentation provided by Claritas, Inc. in materials sent to the author by Susan Fuller, Account Executive, dated June 16, 2004.
12. "A County-by-County Look at Ancestry," *USA Today,* July 1, 2004, 7A.
13. Lisa Bannon, "For Toys and Clothes, the Six-to-12 Set Is Showing Teenage Purchasing Habits," *The Wall Street Journal Online,* October 13, 1998, http://online.wsj.com.
14. Christy Fisher, "Wooing Boomers' Babies," *Advertising Age,* July 22, 1991, 3, 30.
15. Miguel Helft, "Leapfrogging the Competition," *The Industry Standard,* April 9, 2001, 68–75.
16. Queena Sook Kim, "Hot Wheels Chases Extreme Look," *The Wall Street Journal Online,* June 8, 2004, http://online.wsj.com.
17. Peter Sanders, "Disney Lends Its Ears to Kiddie PC," *The Wall Street Journal Online,* August 5, 2004, http://online.wsj.com; Kris Oser, "Parental PC Market Is Child's Play for Disney, *Advertising Age,* August 9, 2004, 4, 23.
18. Deborah Roedder John, "Consumer Socialization of Children: A Retrospective Look at Twenty-Five Years of Research," *Journal of Consumer Research* 26 (December 1999), 183–213; Elizabeth S. Moore and Richard J. Lutz, "Children, Advertising, and Product Experiences: A Multimethod Inquiry," *Journal of Consumer Research* 27 (June 2000), 31–48.
19. James U. McNeal, "It's Not Easy Being Tween," *Brandweek,* April 16, 2001, 22.
20. For an academic treatment on the topic, see Sharon E. Beatty and Salil Talpade, "Adolescent Influence in Family Decision Making: A Replication with Extension," *Journal of Consumer Research* 21 (September 1994), 332–341; and Kay M. Palan and Robert E. Wilkes, "Adolescent-Parent Interaction in Family Decision Making," *Journal of Consumer Research* 24 (September 1997), 159–169.
21. Becky Ebenkamp, "Youth Shall Be Served," *Brandweek,* June 24, 2002, 21.
22. Betsy McKay and Chad Terhune, "Coke Pulls TV AD After Some Call It the Pits," *The Wall Street Journal Online,* June 8, 2004, http://online.wsj.com.
23. Carrie LaFerle, Steven M. Edwards, and Wei-Na Lee, "Teens' Use of Traditional Media and the Internet," *Journal of Advertising Research* 40 (May/June 2000), 55.
24. William Strauss and Neil Howe, *Generations: The History of America's Future, 1584–2069* (New York: William Morrow and Company, Inc., 1991). For a less technical treatment written by an advertising person, see Karen Ritchie, *Marketing to Generation X* (New York: Lexington Books, 1995).
25. Yankelovich Partners, cited in "Don't Mislabel Gen X," *Brandweek,* May 15, 1995, 32, 34.
26. Michelle Higgins, "Cushier Convertibles for Aging Boomers," *The Wall Street Journal Online,* September 1, 2004, http://online.wsj.com.
27. Margaret G. Zackowitz, "Harley's Midlife Crisis," *National Geographic,* August 2003.
28. The "epicenter of society" expression is attributed to Fred Elkind, an executive with the Ogilvy & Mather advertising agency, and cited in Christy Fisher, "Boomers Scatter in Middle Age," *Advertising Age,* January 11, 1993, 23.
29. Hannah Karp, "Red Bull Aims at an Older Crowd," *The Wall Street Journal Online,* June 7, 2004, http://online.wsj.com.
30. The expression "repair kit" is from Charles D. Schewe, "Marketing to Our Aging Population: Responding to Physiological Changes," *The Journal of Consumer Marketing* 5 (summer 1988), 61–73.
31. John Dodge, "Seniors Often Are Overlooked by Websites, Hardware Firms," *The Wall Street Journal Online,* October 3, 2000, http://online.wsj.com; Sara Teasdale Montgomery, "Senior Surfers Grab Web Attention," *Advertising Age,* July 10, 2000, s4.
32. Dodge, "Seniors Often Are Overlooked by Websites, Hardware Firms."

33. The research was performed by George P. Moschis and is reported in "Survey: Age Is Not Good Indicator of Consumer Need," *Marketing Communications,* November 21, 1988, 6. See also George P. Moschis and Anil Mathur, "How They're Acting Their Age," *Marketing Management* 2, no. 2 (1993), 40–50.
34. All statistics in this paragraph are from the U.S. Bureau of the Census, Tables HH-1 and HH-6, Internet release date: June 12, 2003.
35. Ibid., Table HH-1.
36. http://www.census.gov/population/estimates/nation/intfile3-1.txt.
37. U.S. Census Bureau, 2004, "U.S. Interim Projections by Age, Sex, Race, and Hispanic Origin," http://www.census.gov/www/usinterimproj.
38. See Douglas M. Stayman and Rohit Deshpande, "Situational Ethnicity and Consumer Behavior," *Journal of Consumer Research* 16 (December 1989), 361–371; and Cynthia Webster, "Effects of Hispanic Ethnic Identification on Marital Roles in the Purchase Decision Process," *Journal of Consumer Research* 16 (September 1994), 319–331.
39. U.S. Census Bureau, 2004, "U.S. Interim Projections by Age, Sex, Race, and Hispanic Origin," http://www.census.gov/ipc/www/usinterimproj.
40. This characterization is based on James F. Engel, Roger D. Blackwell, and Paul W. Miniard, *Consumer Behavior,* 8th ed. (Fort Worth: The Dryden Press, 1995), 647.
41. Bob Woods, "Urban Sprawl," *Promo,* September 2000, 29.
42. *Hispanic* is a government-invented term that encompasses people of Spanish or Latin American descent or Spanish-language background. Many people of Latin American descent prefer to be referred to as *Latinos.*
43. U.S. Census Bureau, 2004, "U.S. Interim Projections by Age, Sex, Race, and Hispanic Origin."
44. "Hispanic Characters Remain Scarce on Prime-Time TV," *The Wall Street Journal Online,* June 24, 2003, http://online.wsj.com.
45. Dana James, "Many Companies Underspend in Segment," *Marketing News,* October 13, 2003, 6.
46. Sigfredo A. Hernandez and Larry M. Newman, "Choice of English vs. Spanish Language in Advertising to Hispanics," *Journal of Current Issues and Research in Advertising* 14 (fall 1992), 35–46.
47. Nicholas Kulish, "U.S. Asian Population Increased and Diversified," *The Wall Street Journal Online,* May 15, 2001, http://online.wsj.com.
48. *Income in the United States: 2002,* Current Population Reports (Washington: The U.S. Census), September 2003, Table A-1.

CHAPTER 5
Marcom Positioning

Marcom Challenge: Tango to Success

MeadWestvaco Corporation is a huge, Connecticut-based company that generates annual sales in the neighborhood of $8 billion and is a leading producer of packaging products, coated and specialty papers, and other items. The company operates in 33 countries and employs more than 30,000 people worldwide. One of its many products is a printing paper that at one time was branded under the name TexCover II. Though an excellent product providing consistent performance, TexCover II held just the fifth largest market share in its category and generated annual revenues of less than $40 million. Marketing folks at MeadWestvaco knew the brand was under-performing in view of its excellent quality and reputation for dependable performance. The product did not require improvements, but it was time to get serious about the marcom program.

Enter the Chicago-based advertising agency, Mobium Creative Group. Mobium's staff went to work devising an IMC strategy to jump-start TexCover II's performance.

A few words about the Mobium Creative Group will be helpful prior to describing the strategy the group devised for repositioning TexCover II. Unlike most B2B agencies, which are known for being relatively un-exciting, if not outright boring, Mobium prizes itself on being a rather wacky creative shop. For example, its opening Web page (http://www.mobium.com) states, "buddy, can you paradigm," which is a clever takeoff on the depression-era expression—"buddy, can you spare a dime?"—that captures the plea of the impoverished asking for a little help from their more well-off brethren. Mobium's paradigm expression suggests that this is what this creative agency is all about, creating new paradigms for its clients. In fact, the agency's fundamental value system and business model is captured on its Web site (http://www.mobium.com/thework/theworkFlash.asp) in terms that characterizes business customers as driven by emotions as well as logic. The Mobium Creative Group is, in other words, positioning its creative work as out of the ordinary compared to other B2B-oriented advertising and branding agencies.

> *Deep down, business buyers are people. They're moved by emotion as well as by logic. They always have been. Ever since we stopped dragging our knuckles on the ground and started using them to give each other noogies. And they always will be. We believe that to break through to them you have to make human contact. You have to stop thinking that your communications is about your products or services. Because it's not. It's about one person who can help, talking to one person who has a need.*

With this backdrop in mind, Mobium set about the task of repositioning the line of TexCover II printing paper. A major strategic shift was made by changing the brand name to the catchy name Tango and positioning the brand as "always performing." The name Tango is easy to remember though it is not naturally related to the attributes or benefits of printing paper. The newly named brand's positioning strategy ("always performing") was reinforced through a series of attention-gaining advertisements that cleverly illustrated this positioning in a humorous and captivating manner.

These marcom innovations resulted in a first-year revenue increase of 27 percent. Despite an industry-wide recession, Tango's revenues continued to climb—doubling in fact—and now the brand has the number two position in its category. In a period of only four years, this B2B brand increased its total revenue by $126 million on a marcom investment of only $2 million! This obviously represents a huge return (greater than 6000 percent) on a modest marcom investment and demonstrates how success can be achieved when a brand is properly positioned, cleverly named, and adequately supported.[1]

CHAPTER OBJECTIVES

1

Introduce the concept and practice of brand positioning.

2

Explain that positioning involves the creation of meaning and that meaning is a constructive process involving the use of signs and symbols.

3

Give details about how brand marketers position their brands by drawing meaning from the culturally constituted world.

4

Describe how brands are positioned in terms of various types of benefits and attributes.

5

Explicate two perspectives that characterize how consumers process information and describe the relevance of each perspective for brand positioning.

Positioning in Theory: A Matter of Creating Meaning

This chapter is about brand positioning. A brand's **positioning** represents the key feature, benefit, or image that it stands for in the target audience's collective mind. Brand communicators and the marketing team in general must identify a *positioning statement,* which is the central idea that encapsulates a brand's meaning and distinctiveness vis-à-vis competitive brands. MeadWestvaco and its advertising agency understood that they had to give Tango a clear meaning (see Marcom Challenge). It should be obvious that positioning and targeting decisions—the subject of Chapter 4—go hand in hand: positioning decisions are made with respect to intended targets, and targeting decisions are based on a clear idea of how brands are to be positioned and distinguished from competitive offerings.

Fundamental to the concept and practice of positioning is the idea of *meaning.* This section discusses the nature of meaning using a perspective known as semiotics. **Semiotics**, broadly speaking, is the study of signs and the analysis of meaning-producing events.[2] The important point of emphasis is that the semiotics perspective sees meaning as a *constructive process.* That is, meaning is determined both by the message source's choice of communication elements and, just as importantly, by the receiver's unique social-cultural background and mind-set at the time he or she is exposed to a message. In other words, meaning is not thrust upon consumers; rather, consumers are actively involved in constructing meaning from marcom messages, meaning that may or may not be equivalent to what the communicator intended to convey. The marcom goal is, of course, to do everything possible to increase the odds that consumers will interpret messages exactly as they are intended.

The fundamental concept in semiotics is the *sign,* the noun counterpart to the verb *signify.* (Singers sing; runners run; dancers dance; and signs signify!) Marketing communications in all its various forms uses signs in the creation of messages. When reading the word *sign,* you probably think of how this word is used on an everyday basis—such as with respect to road signs (stop, yield, danger, or directional signs), store signs, signs announcing a car or home for sale, and signs of less tangible concepts such as happiness (the happy face sign). The general concept of sign encompasses these everyday notions but includes many other types of signs, including words, visualizations, tactile objects, and anything else that is perceivable by the senses and has the potential to communicate meaning to the receiver, or interpreter.

Figure 5.1
The Thumbs-Up Sign

Formally, a **sign** is something physical and perceivable that signifies something (the *referent*) to somebody (the *interpreter*) in some *context.*[3] The dollar sign ($), for example, is understood by many people throughout the world as signifying the currency of the United States (as well as the currencies of Australia, Canada, Hong Kong, New Zealand, and several other countries). The thumbs-up sign (Figure 5.1) signifies a positive reaction to or appraisal of an action or event. For example, movie critics sometimes signify that they like a new movie by displaying an upward thumb sign. Parents can be seen displaying the thumbs-up when their children perform well in artistic or athletic events. Interestingly, the upward thumb in the Middle East signifies an entirely different meaning than in the West; it represents a crass expression not unlike the middle-finger sign in the West. This difference in sign usage anticipates the following discussion which explains that meaning is contained in the person and not the sign per se; in other words, meaning is both idiosyncratic and context dependent.

The Meaning of Meaning

Although we use signs to share meaning with others, the two terms (*signs* and *meanings*) are not synonymous.[4] Signs are simply stimuli that are used to evoke an intended meaning in another person. But words and nonverbal signs do not have meanings per se; instead, *people have meanings for signs.* Meanings are internal responses people hold for external stimuli. Many times people have different meanings for the same words or gestures, as all of us have experienced when, say, attempting to explain something to someone from a different background or culture. It follows from these points that meanings are *not* contained in a marcom message per se but rather are perceived by the message receiver. Thus, the challenge when positioning a brand is to make sure that the signs used by the marketing communicator are interpreted as intended by consumers.

This desirable outcome is most likely accomplished when signs are common to both the sender's and the receiver's fields of experience. A field of experience, also called the *perceptual field,* is the sum total of a person's experiences that are stored in memory. The larger the overlap, or commonality, in their perceptual fields, the greater the likelihood that signs will be interpreted by the receiver in the manner intended by the sender. Effective communication is severely compromised when, for example, marketing communicators use words, visualizations, or other signs that customers do not understand. This is especially problematic when developing communication programs for consumers in other cultures.

Up to this point we have referred to meaning in the abstract. Now a definition is in order. **Meaning** can be thought of as *the perceptions (thoughts) and affective reactions (feelings)* that are evoked within a person when presented with a sign in a particular *context.*[5] It should be clear at this point that meaning is internal, rather than external, to an individual. Meaning, in other words, is subjective and highly context dependent.

Meaning Transfer: From Culture to Object to Consumer

The culture and social systems in which marketing communications take place are loaded with meaning. Through socialization, people learn cultural values, form beliefs, and become familiar with the physical manifestations, or artifacts, of these values and beliefs. The artifacts of culture are charged with meaning, which is transferred from generation to generation. For example, the Lincoln Memorial and Ellis Island are signs of freedom to Americans. To Germans and many other people throughout the world, the now-crumbled Berlin wall signified oppression and hopelessness. Comparatively, yellow ribbons signify crises and hopes for hostage release and the safe return of military personnel. Pink ribbons signal support for breast cancer victims. Red ribbons have grown into an international symbol of solidarity on AIDS. The Black Liberation flag with its red, black, and green stripes—representing blood, achievement, and the fertility of Africa—symbolizes civil rights.

Marketing communicators, when in the process of positioning their brands, draw meaning from the *culturally constituted world* (i.e., the everyday world filled with artifacts such as the preceding examples) and transfer that meaning to their brands. Advertising is an especially important instrument of meaning transfer and positioning. The role of advertising in transferring meaning has been described in this fashion:

Advertising works as a potential method of meaning transfer by bringing the consumer good and a representation of the culturally constituted world together within the frame of a particular advertisement. . . . The known properties of the culturally constituted world thus come to reside in the unknown properties of the consumer good and the transfer of meaning from world to [consumer] good is accomplished.[6]

When exposed to an advertisement (or any other form of marcom message), the consumer is not merely drawing information from the ad but is actively involved in assigning meaning to the advertised brand.[7] Stated alternatively, the consumer approaches advertisements as texts to be interpreted.[8] (Note that the term *text* refers to any form of spoken or written words and images, which clearly encompasses advertisements.) To demonstrate the preceding points, take into account the following advertising illustrations.

Figure 5.2

Advertisements Illustrating Contextual Meaning

Courtesy of Tropicana Products, Inc.

Courtesy of Tropicana Products, Inc.

Consider first an advertisement for the Honda Accord that was created some years ago when American consumers were suspicious of Japanese-made automobiles and perhaps even considered it un-American to buy something other than an American model. Shortly after the Honda Motor Company began producing automobiles in the United States, it undertook a print advertising campaign to convey the point that four out of five Accords sold in America are manufactured in the United States. Beyond stating this fact in the ad copy, the two-page advertisement presented large photos of five icons of American culture: a hamburger, cowboy boots, an oversized bicycle (not like the sleek, Asian or European racing bikes), a baseball, and a jazz ensemble. By associating itself with these well-known symbols of American consumer culture, Honda pulled meaning from the "culturally constituted world" of the consumers in its target audience, most of whom would immediately recognize the five icons as uniquely American. The obvious intent was to subtly convey the meaning to consumers that the Accord, embedded as it was among the five icons of American popular culture, is made in America and thus is itself American. If Honda's advertising agency had made such a claim in stark, verbal form ("Honda *is* an American automobile!"), most readers likely would have doubted the claim, fully realizing that the Honda is of Japanese origin. But by presenting the message at a nonverbal level and merely via association with American icons, consumers probably were somewhat inclined to accept the Honda Accord as at least quasi-American.

Consider also the two advertisements for Tropicana Light 'n Healthy in Figure 5.2 that embed this brand in the context of fitness symbols—one ad showing an orange "working out" on a stair stepper and the other displaying an orange wrapped in a tape measure. The suggestion is that Tropicana Light 'n Healthy, which is made with one-third less sugar and calories than orange juice, will enable the consumer to get into better shape and maintain a healthy regimen. Thus, once again the advertiser is drawing meaning from the "culturally constituted world" and attempting to transfer that meaning to the advertised brand.

Positioning in Practice: The Nuts and Bolts

Brand positioning is an essential preliminary activity, or fundamental decision, to developing a successful marcom program. By having a clear positioning statement, the brand management team is committed to conveying a clear and consistent message in all forms of marcom messages. Positioning is both a useful conceptual notion and an invaluable strategic tool. Conceptually, the term *positioning* suggests two interrelated ideas. First, the marketing communicator wishes to create a specific meaning for the brand and have that meaning clearly lodged in the consumer's memory (think of this as "positioned in" the consumer's mind). Second, the brand's meaning in consumers' memories stands in comparison to what they know and think about competitive brands in the product or service category (think of this as "positioned against" the competition).

Strategically and tactically, positioning is a short statement—even a word—that represents the message you wish to imprint in customers' minds.[9] This statement tells how your brand differs from and is superior to competitive brands. It gives a reason why consumers should buy your brand rather than a competitor's and promises a solution to the customer's needs or wants. As noted earlier, a brand's *positioning statement* represents how we want customers and prospects to think and feel about the brand. These thoughts and feelings should stand out in comparison to competitive offerings and motivate the customer or prospect to want to try our brand. In other words, a good positioning statement should satisfy two requirements: (1) it should reflect a brand's *competitive advantage* (vis-à-vis competitive offerings in the same product category) and, (2) it should *motivate* consumers to *action*.[10]

Figure 5.3 captures these two requisites by posing whether a proposed positioning strategy reflects a competitive advantage and motivates action. Considering,

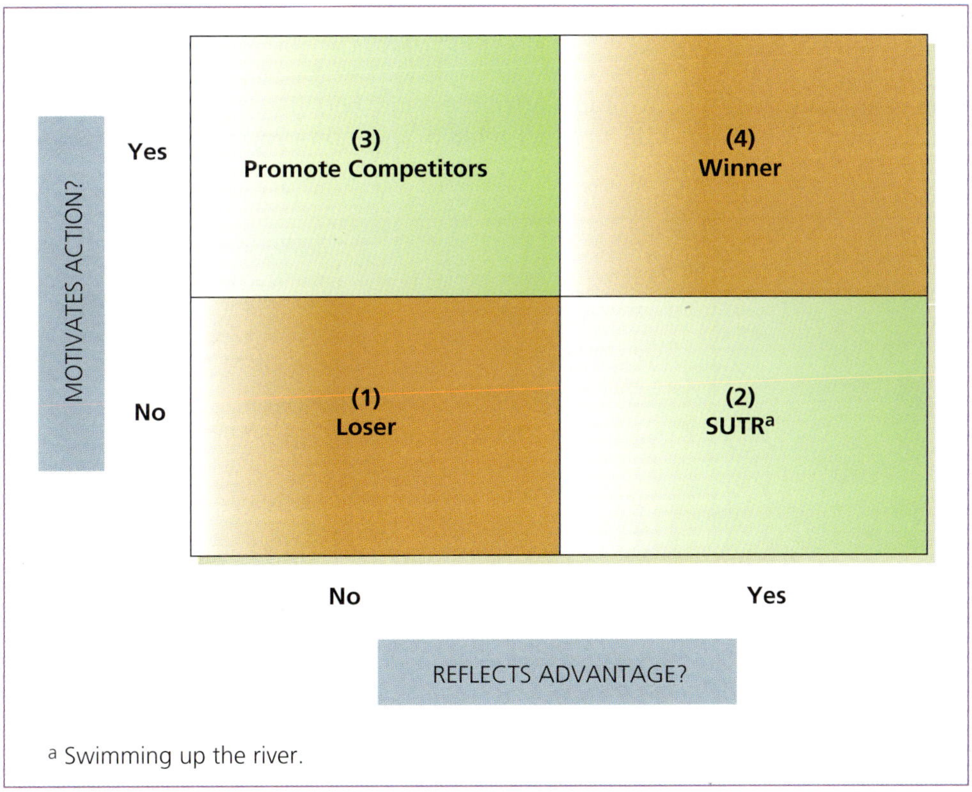

Figure 5.3 Outcomes of Proposed Positioning

simplistically, that the answer to each query is "no" or "yes," four conclusions about a proposed positioning are possible: (1) it is a *Loser* prospect (No / No quadrant); (2) a *Swimming-up-the-river*, or SUTR, decision (Yes / No quadrant); (3) a *Promote-competitors* option (No / Yes quadrant); or (4) a *Winner* (Yes / Yes quadrant).

Brief explanations of each are in order. First, the "Loser" label characterizes a proposed positioning wherein the brand possesses no competitive advantage and the basis for the positioning is not sufficiently important to motivate consumers to want to purchase the brand. Second, the "SUTR" situation occurs when a proposed positioning represents a competitive advantage for a trivial product feature or benefit, but does not represent something that would give consumers compelling reasons to select the brand positioned as such. Hence, any effort to promote a brand on this basis would be tantamount to attempting to swim up the river (i.e., against the current)—hard work will be expended but little progress will be made. Third, the "Promote Competitors" description characterizes a positioning statement that does not reflect a competitive advantage but does represent an important reason for making brand selection decisions in the product category. Hence, any effort to position "our" brand on this basis would essentially serve to aid other brands that do have a competitive advantage. Finally, the "Winner" label characterizes a prospect where we have positioned our brand on a product feature or benefit for which we have an advantage over competitors and which gives consumers a persuasive reason for trying our brand. When considering how best to position a brand, it is essential to objectively and hypercritically appraise whether a proposed positioning affords "your" brand a competitive advantage and whether this advantage is important enough to encourage consumers to at least make a trial purchase of your brand.

To make this idea of positioning even more concrete, let us call on the customer-based brand equity framework that you read about in Chapter 2. For present purposes, it will be useful to reproduce the *brand image* part of the brand equity framework as a useful graphic for expanding our discussion of brand positioning. As can be seen in Figure 5.4, a brand's image consists of types, favorability, strength, and uniqueness of brand associations. Our focus for present purposes will be limited to the *types* of brand associations. Please notice in Figure 5.4 that types of associations include brand attributes, benefits, and an overall evaluation, or attitude, toward the brand.

Let us talk more about brand attributes and benefits. Notice in Figure 5.4 that brand *attributes* include product-related and non-product-related features.

Figure 5.4

A Framework for Brand Positioning

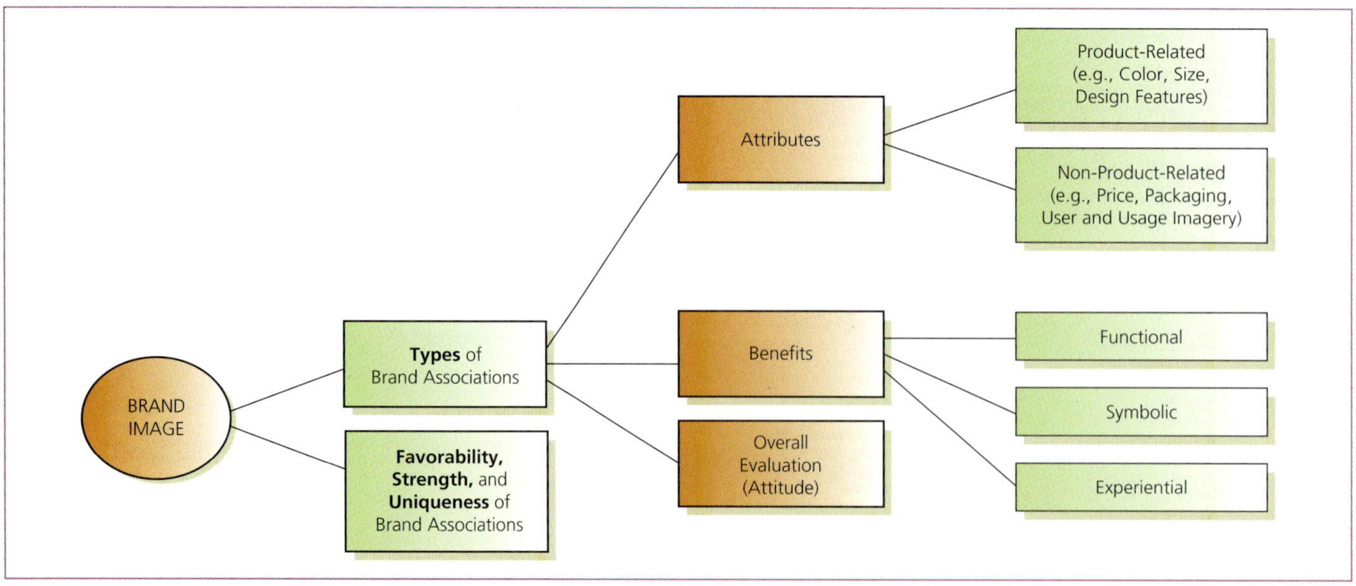

SOURCE: Adapted from Kevin Lane Keller, "Conceptualizing, Measuring, and Managing Customer-Based Brand Equity." *Journal of Marketing* 57 (January 1993), 7.

For example, Sharp's Viewcam Z camcorder possesses features such as swiveling action to allow maximum comfort for recording and a screen that gets brighter in the sunlight to facilitate high-resolution outdoor viewing. These are its product-related attributes. Non-product-related attributes would include, for example, the Viewcam Z's price and consumer perceptions of the type of people who own this brand of camcorder (user imagery) and the occasions when it would be appropriately used (usage imagery). Brand *benefits* consist of ways by which a brand satisfies customers' needs and wants and can be classified as functional, symbolic, or experiential.

With Figure 5.4 and the previous terminology in mind, we now can pursue the options available to marketing communicators for positioning their brands. Generally speaking, we can position a brand by focusing on product *attributes* or *benefits*. Because benefits provide B2C consumers or B2B customers with more compelling reasons for selecting a particular brand than do product attributes per se, we will first look at positioning via product benefits and then via attributes.

© Digital Vision/Getty Images

Benefit Positioning

Positioning with respect to brand benefits can be accomplished by appealing to any of three categories of basic consumer *needs:* functional, symbolic, or experiential.[11] Upon a quick review of the consumer-based brand equity framework (Figure 5.4), you will see that these three categories are shown as a specific type of association termed *benefits*. Please note that the distinction between benefits and needs simply involves a matter of perspective. That is, consumers have needs and brands have features that satisfy those needs. Thus, benefits are the need-satisfying features provided by brands. In short, needs and benefits can be thought of as flip sides of the same coin.

Positioning Based on Functional Needs. A brand positioned in terms of **functional needs** attempts to provide solutions to consumers' current consumption-related problems or potential problems by communicating that the brand possesses specific benefits capable of solving those problems. In B2B marketing, for example, salespeople typically appeal to their customers' functional needs for higher-quality products, faster delivery time, or better service. Consumer goods marketers also regularly appeal to consumers' needs for convenience, safety, good health, cleanliness, and so on, all of which are functional needs that can be satisfied by brand benefits. The advertisement for Timberland outerwear (Figure 5.5) appeals to the consumer's need for protection from the elements when suggesting that the Timberland Outdoor Performance Waterproof jacket not only is water-resistant but also breathable and lightweight. In harmony with its rugged image, Timberland's positioning statement says "Make it better." In general, appeals to functional needs are the most prevalent form of brand benefit positioning.

Positioning Based on Symbolic Needs. Other brands are positioned in terms of their ability to satisfy non-functional, or symbolic, needs. Positioning in terms of symbolic needs attempts to associate brand ownership with a desired group, role, or self-image. Appeals to **symbolic needs** include those directed at consumers' desire for self-enhancement, group membership, affiliation, altruism, and other abstract need states that involve aspects of consumption not solved by practical product benefits. (See the *Global Focus* insert for discussion of the growing impor-

The Symbolism of Certifying Products as Fair Traded

global focus

Most consumers know that agricultural commodities often are imported from other countries rather than grown and harvested domestically. Yet, most people go to their local grocery stores or supermarkets with little awareness that agricultural workers in other countries often are paid dreadfully low wages and farm owners have difficulty earning a profit. Poor wage rates and minuscule profits, if not losses, are largely due to the economics of growing commodity products. Coffee, for example, is grown in Latin American countries such as Brazil and Colombia and also is harvested in African countries and, ever increasingly, Vietnam. In most years, coffee supply exceeds demand, and anyone familiar with basic economics knows that the effect of this imbalance is falling prices. Intense competition has forced prices and wages down to the point where growers have difficulty making a living and workers are hard-pressed to feed their families. On the other hand, low coffee prices benefit retailers and consumers in countries that import low-priced coffee. The situation, in other words, is not win-win but rather one where businesses and consumers in economically advantaged economies gain at the expense of growers and workers in developing economies. Is there a resolution to this imbalance? Yes there is; please read on.

The resolution is *not* the competitive marketplace, because the economics of supply-demand disequilibrium inevitably lead to further lowering of commodity prices. Hence, the only way possible for commodity growers and workers to receive higher profits and wages is some form of "artificial" intervention—that is, for forces other than the economics of supply and demand to come into play. This has happened, in fact, because many consumers in advanced economies are willing to pay higher prices so poor workers and growers are able to survive. These consumers have been given the label "LOHAS" consumers, which stands for "lifestyles of health and sustainability." About one-third of adults in the United States are classified as LOHAS according to a recent study.

But even if a consumer is LOHAS inclined, how does one know which products to purchase? Increasingly, commodity products such as coffee, grapes, mangos, pineapples, and others are labeled with stickers bearing "Fair Trade Certified." This label means that workers in developing economies receive higher wages and benefits for their efforts than the supply-demand disequilibrium would normally dictate. Large retail chains such as Dunkin' Donuts and Starbucks offer fair-traded coffee, and many supermarkets are carrying more commodity products with the fair-trade label. Another label being used to signify fair trading is "Rainforest Alliance Certified." Procter & Gamble's coffee products carry this label.

The LOHAS movement reveals that consumers' symbolic needs—the sense of being fair and socially responsible—sometimes trump their functional need to pay the lowest possible prices. This form of altruism enables workers and farm owners in poor countries to sustain an existence and to continue to grow and harvest products their economies depend on. Fair trading achieves more of a win-win outcome than the rich-countries-win/poor-countries-lose situation previously prevailing.

SOURCE: Adapted from Katy McLaughlin, "Is Your Grocery List Politically Correct?" *The Wall Street Journal Online*, February 17, 2004, http://online.wsj.com.

tance of appeals to consumers using claims that agricultural products are "fair traded.") Marketers in categories such as personal beauty products, jewelry, alcoholic beverages, cigarettes, and motor vehicles frequently appeal to symbolic needs.

The DeBeers diamond ad (Figure 5.6) illustrates an exemplary appeal to symbolic needs. This magazine ad asks the reader to imagine the happiness his wife or girlfriend will experience when he presents her with a luxurious diamond, and implicitly suggests that he will reap the benefits of the recipient's abiding appreciation for such a generous gesture ("Oh Michael. You shouldn't have. Oh Michael."). DeBeers' positioning statement—"A Diamond Is Forever"—is a claim not so much about the obvious fact that diamonds are virtually indestructible, but rather a statement about the enduring bond between giver and receiver that is symbolized by the gift of a precious diamond. See the *IMC Focus* on page 130 for another discussion about diamonds.

Positioning Based on Experiential Needs. Consumers' **experiential needs** represent their desires for products that provide sensory pleasure, variety, and, in a few product circumstances, cognitive stimulation. Brands positioned toward experiential needs are promoted as being out of the ordinary and high in sensory value (looking elegant, feeling wonderful, tasting or smelling great, sounding divine, being exhilarating, and so on) or rich in the potential for cognitive stimulation (exciting, challenging, mentally entertaining, and so on). The DoveBar advertisement (Figure 5.7) represents this brand's traditional positioning as an especially flavorful ice cream bar ("Chocolate so good it'll give you the chills"). Consumers are promised the experience of tasting a product so special that it will make them "fall madly in Dove."

It is important to recognize that brands often offer a mixture of functional, symbolic, and experiential benefits. It has been argued that successful positioning requires a communication strategy that entices a *single type* of consumer need (functional, symbolic, or experiential) rather than attempting to be something for everyone.[12] According to this argument, a brand with a generic (multiple-personality) image is difficult to manage because it: (1) competes against more brands (those with purely functional, purely symbolic, purely experiential, and mixed images); and (2) may be difficult for consumers to readily understand what it stands for and what its defining characteristics are. This argument, though based on sound logic, is *not* irrefutable. In fact, a reasonable counterargument holds that a brand positioned as having, say, both functional qualities and symbolic appeal has the potential of recruiting potential users who desire different things from the product category. Hence, according to this counter-perspective, a "multi-personality" positioning allows consumers to read into the brand precisely what they are seeking.

Which argument is more correct? The only viable conclusion is that whether a single or multi-type positioning is more effective depends on the competitive circumstances and consumer dynamics that are involved in a particular situation. What works best for a brand in one product category does not necessarily work as well for another brand in a different category. As academics like to say, it's an empirical issue, which means that no single logical account or theoretical explanation is available to resolve the issue. Trial and error experience and marketing research evidence are the final arbiters.

Figure 5.5

Advertisement Illustrating Positioning Based on Functional Needs

Attribute Positioning

A brand can be positioned in terms of a particular attribute or feature, provided that the attribute represents a competitive advantage and can motivate customers to purchase that brand rather than a competitive offering. Product attributes, as shown in Figure 5.4, can be distinguished as either *product-related* or *non-product-related*.

Figure 5.6

Advertisement Illustrating Positioning Based on Symbolic Needs

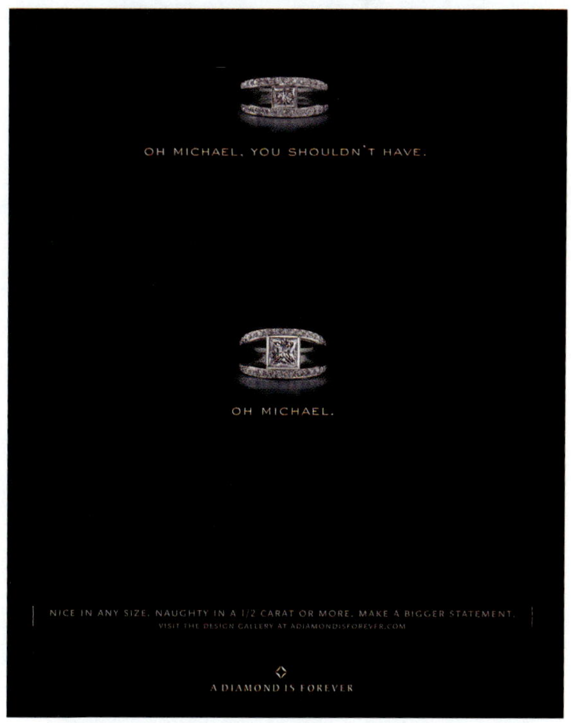

Product-Related

Sleeker product design, superior materials, and more color options are just a few of the virtually endless list of attributes that can provide the foundation for positioning a brand. If your brand has a product advantage, flaunt it, especially if the advantage is something that consumers truly desire in the product category and will motivate them to action. For example, in an appeal to people with hearing problems, Duracell hearing aid batteries are advertised (Figure 5.8) on the basis of an "EasyTab" device that makes changing hearing aid batteries "easier than ever." This is a distinct product-related positioning to the predominantly elderly users whose dexterity often is reduced by arthritis and other ailments that accompany aging.

Non-Product-Related: Usage and User Imagery

Brands can be positioned in terms of their unique usage symbolism or with respect to the kinds of people who use them. A brand positioned according to the image associated with how it

Figure 5.7 Advertisement Illustrating Positioning Based on Experiential Needs

is used, its *usage imagery*, depicts the brand in terms of specific, and presumably unique, usages that become associated with it. For example, advertisers sometimes position SUVs and passenger trucks in terms of their seemingly unique ability to go "off road" and traverse rough terrain. Such advertisements create the impression that only the advertised brand is capable of forging streams, climbing hills, and navigating other tough-to-travel areas. The Jeep Liberty Renegade (Figure 5.9) is positioned as a vehicle in which people working in stressful business and professional positions—as symbolized by the yellow "power" tie—can unwind and "leave the [workday] world behind."

Similarly, brands can be positioned in terms of the kind of people who use them. This *user imagery* thus becomes the brand's hallmark; the brand and the people who are portrayed as using it become virtually synonymous. Positioning a brand via user imagery thus amounts to associating the brand with icon-like representations of the kind of people who are portrayed in advertisements as typical users of the brand. Consider for example an advertisement for Acqua Di Giò cologne marketed by Giorgio Armani. The ad, which is not displayed here, simply mentions the brand name along with the name of the retailer where it is available (Nordstrom) and presents a bottle of the product. But the main feature of the ad is a prominent facial portrayal of an attractive man in his early 20s. The ad says absolutely nothing about brand benefits. Rather, the ad associates this brand with the prominently featured user, who himself is symbolic of the brand's target class. Plain and simple, Acqua Di Giò's meaning (what it stands for) is inseparable from the user who serves to signify the brand's desired users. Hence, this brand is being positioned *not* in terms of what it has (its features) or what needs it satisfies (its benefits) but in terms of the type of man who uses the brand (its user imagery).

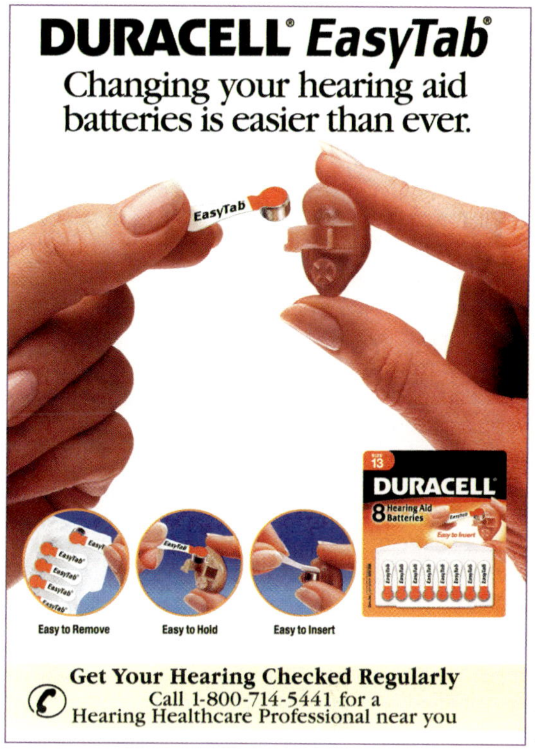

The Gillette Company

Figure 5.8

Advertisement Illustrating Positioning Based on Product-Related Features

Figure 5.9

Advertisement Illustrating Positioning Based on Usage Imagery

Courtesy, Daimler Chrysler Company; Ad Agency: BBDO Detroit.

Repositioning a Brand

As competitive and customer dynamics change, managers must evaluate whether their brands remain appropriately positioned. Revising a brand's positioning is termed, naturally, *repositioning*. For example, the Burger King fast-food chain slightly altered its positioning when it advertised that its burgers are cooked using "fire grilling" rather than the old claim of "flame broiling." This repositioning was based on consumer research that determined fire grilling elicits a more positive reaction than flame broiling, perhaps because fire grilling suggests the good taste and fun atmosphere of outdoor barbecues.[13]

Another instance of repositioning involves Oil of Olay, a line of skin-care products that has been on retail shelves for decades. Created in World War II as a lotion to treat burns, Procter & Gamble (P&G) purchased the brand from Richardson-Vicks in 1985 and developed the brand into a major line of skin-care products with revenues exceeding $500 million annually. However, over the years the brand eventually became a bit outdated. P&G's consumer research revealed that many young women considered the brand more appropriate for older women than for themselves. Young women also did not like the idea of using what they considered to be a greasy skin-care product. Although in actuality Oil of Olay is not greasy, apparently the word *oil* in the Oil of Olay brand name suggested just such an unpleasant product

Diamonds (Given to Yourself) Are Forever

imc focus

The Diamond Trading Company is a London-based organization responsible for selling and marketing diamonds supplied by DeBeers, the world's largest supplier of diamonds. In concert with its advertising agency, J. Walter Thompson (JWT) of New York, the Diamond Trading Company embarked on an ambitious program to create demand for right-hand diamond rings. Unlike "left-hand diamond rings," which traditionally are purchased by men for women to whom they are engaged to be married, right-hand diamond rings were designed to be purchased by women for themselves. As such, whereas the traditional engagement ring symbolizes love between two people, right-hand diamond rings are an expression of a woman's individuality and style. Women have always purchased rings for themselves to be worn on their right hands, but a right-hand diamond ring is a rather dramatic move in its juxtaposition against the traditional engagement ring. The purchase of such a ring effectively represents a statement that "I'm important," "I'm worth it," "I don't need to depend on anyone else," or "I can indulge myself."

Right-hand diamond rings were introduced in 2003 with an ad campaign in upscale magazines (e.g., *Elle, Vogue,* and *Vanity Fair*). All of the ads compared the symbolism of right versus left hands, and each ended with the statement: "Women of the world, raise your right hand." In addition to the highly creative ad campaign, efforts were made to create enthusiasm and generate word-of-mouth buzz by giving free rings to celebrities (e.g., Faith Hill, Jennifer Lopez, and Julia Roberts) who were shown wearing them at special events such as the Oscars. The left-hand diamond (engagement) ring is a lasting symbol of love between two people. What are the odds that right-hand diamond rings will have similar staying power in their symbolic tribute to self-love and individualism?

Source: Adapted from Sandra O'Loughlin, "Sparkler on the Other Hand," *Brandweek,* April 19, 2004, 18–19.

characteristic to young women who had never actually tried the brand. Based on this invaluable research evidence, P&G's brand management team decided to reposition Oil of Olay to make it more appealing to younger women. Several steps were undertaken. First, without any fanfare so as not to bring attention to the change, P&G modified the brand name from Oil of Olay to simply Olay. They also altered the logo to look more modern and reduced the amount of writing on the package to make it more appealing to younger consumers. The new name and look appealed to younger women without alienating baby boomers and older women who had been Oil of Olay's core consumers.

The moral of this story is that brands sometimes must be repositioned in order to grow and prosper. Oil of Olay's mature image was unappealing to millions of younger consumers who also were turned off by the thought of using what they imagined to be a greasy, oily product. By dropping *Oil* from the name and updating the packaging, P&G breathed new life into this old, successful brand. Interestingly, the name Olay, which originally was made up by the chemists who developed the product, is a surprisingly good name when marketing the product globally. The word is easily pronounced in most languages and hints at being of Spanish origin with its similar pronunciation to the Spanish word *olé,* which is a shout of approval to a bullfighter or other performer.[14]

Implementing Positioning: Know Thy Consumer

Marketing communicators direct their efforts toward influencing consumers' brand-related *beliefs, attitudes, emotional reactions,* and *choices.* Ultimately, the objective is to encourage consumers to choose "our" brand rather than a competitive offering. To accomplish this goal, marketing communicators design advertising messages, promotions, packages, brand names, sales presentations, and other forms of brand-related messages—all of which are designed to drive home the brand's meaning, its positioning. This section examines positioning from the consumer's perspective by examining how individuals process marcom messages.

The discussion is based on different perspectives about how consumers process marcom information and ultimately use this information to choose from among the alternatives available in the marketplace. We will label these the *consumer processing model (CPM)* and the *hedonic, experiential model (HEM).* From a consumer-processing perspective (CPM), information processing and choice are seen as rational, cognitive, systematic, and reasoned.[15] The hedonic, experiential perspective, on the other hand, views consumer processing of marcom messages and behavior as driven by emotions in pursuit of fun, fantasies, and feelings.[16]

A very important point needs to be emphasized before discussing each framework. Specifically, it must be recognized that consumer behavior is much too complex and diverse to be captured perfectly by two extreme models. You should think of these as bipolar perspectives that anchor a continuum of possible consumer behaviors—ranging, metaphorically speaking, from the "icy-blue cold" CPM perspective to the "red-hot" HEM perspective (see Figure 5.10). At the CPM end of the continuum is consumer behavior that is based on *pure reason*—cold, logical, and rational. At the HEM end is consumer behavior based on *pure passion*—hot, spontaneous, and perhaps even irrational. Between these extremes rests the bulk of consumer behavior, most of which is not based on pure reason or pure passion and is neither icy blue cold nor red hot. Rather, most behavior ranges, again in metaphorical terms, from cool to warm. In the final analysis, we will examine the rather extreme perspectives of consumer behavior but recognize that often both perspectives are applicable to understanding how and why consumers behave as they do.

The Consumer Processing Model (CPM)

The information-processing situation faced by consumers and the corresponding communication imperatives for marketing communicators have been described in these terms:

The consumer is constantly being bombarded with information which is potentially relevant for making choices. The consumer's reactions to that information, how that information is interpreted, and how it is combined or integrated with other information may have crucial impacts on choice. Hence, [marketing communicators'] decisions on what information to provide to consumers, how much to provide, and how to provide that information require knowledge of how consumers process, interpret, and integrate that information in making choices.[17]

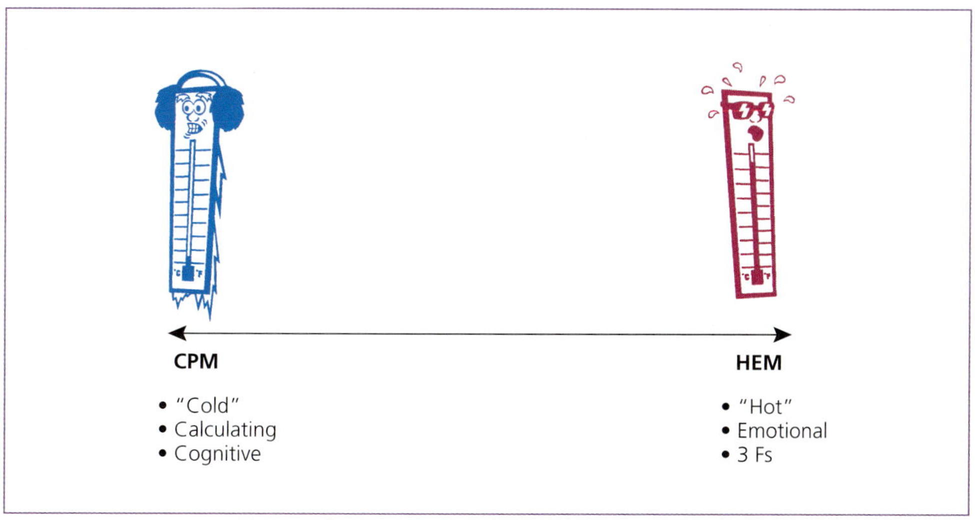

Figure 5.10

Comparison of the CPM and HEM Models

The following sections discuss consumer information processing in terms of a set of interrelated stages.[18] Although marcom efforts play an important role in affecting all stages of this process, we will focus exclusively on the first six stages because the last two (decision making and action) are determined by all marketing-mix elements and not by marketing communications per se:

Stage 1: Being *exposed* to information
Stage 2: Paying *attention*
Stage 3: *Comprehending* attended information
Stage 4: *Agreeing* with comprehended information
Stage 5: *Retaining* accepted information in memory
Stage 6: *Retrieving* information from memory
Stage 7: *Deciding* from alternatives
Stage 8: *Acting* on the basis of the decision

Stage 1: Being Exposed to Information

The marketing communicator's fundamental task is to deliver messages to consumers, who, it is expected, will process the messages, understand the brand positioning, and, if the positioning is congenial with the consumer's preference structure, undertake the course of action advocated by the marketer. By definition, **exposure** simply means that consumers come in contact with the marketer's message (they see a magazine ad, hear a radio commercial, notice an Internet banner, and so on). Although exposure is an essential preliminary step to subsequent stages of information processing, the mere fact of exposing consumers to the marketing communicator's message does not ensure the message will have any impact. Gaining exposure is a *necessary* but *insufficient* condition for communication success. Ultimate success generally depends upon message quality and frequency. The preceding sentence added a qualifier in saying that ultimate success "generally" depends on message quality along with frequency. The reason for this qualification is there is some evidence that the mere fact of being repeatedly exposed to a message increases the likelihood that the receiver will judge that message to be true. This is called the *truth effect.*[19]

In practical terms, exposing consumers to a brand's message is a function of two key managerial decisions: (1) establishing a sufficient marcom budget, and (2) selecting appropriate media and vehicles with which to present a brand message. In other words, a high percentage of a targeted audience will be exposed to a brand's message if adequate funds are allocated and wise choices of media outlets are made; insufficient budget and poor media selection invariably result in low levels of exposure.

Stage 2: Paying Attention

Laypeople use the expression "paying attention" in reference to whether someone is really listening to and thinking about what a speaker (such as a teacher) is saying, or whether his or her mind is wandering off into its own world of thought. For psychologists, the term *attention* means fundamentally the same thing. **Attention**, in its formal use, means to focus cognitive resources on and think about a message to which one has been exposed. Actually, consumers pay attention to only a small fraction of marcom messages. This is because the demands placed on their attention are great (we are virtually bombarded with advertisements and other commercial messages), but information-processing *capacity is limited.* Effective utilization of limited processing capacity requires that consumers selectively allocate mental energy (processing capacity) only to messages that are *relevant and of interest to current goals.*

For example, once their initial curiosity is satisfied, most people who do *not* do a lot of printing would, on exposure to the ad in Figure 5.11, pay relatively little attention to the detailed comments about HP printers because the product has little relevance to them. On the other hand, small business owners and individuals who run businesses from their homes could be expected to devote *conscious attention* to the advertisement because it holds a high level of relevance to their interests. Please notice that "conscious attention" is emphasized in the previous sentence. This is to distinguish this deliberate, controlled form of attention from an *automatic* form of relatively superficial attention that occurs when, for example, an individual reacts to a loud noise even when a message holds little personal relevance.[20]

Hewlett Packard; Ad Agency, Creative-I, Inc. Palo Alto, CA

Figure 5.11

Illustration of an Ad Likely to Encounter Selective Attention

How can attention selectivity be avoided? The short answer is that marketing communicators can most effectively gain the consumer's attention by creating messages that truly appeal to their needs for product-relevant information. The likelihood that consumers will pay attention to an advertisement or other form of marcom message also is increased by creating messages that are novel, spectacular, aesthetically appealing, eye catching, and so forth. We will delay further discussion of these attention-gaining strategies until a subsequent chapter, at which point we will describe in detail ways to augment consumers' motivation to attend brand messages.

In sum, attention involves allocating limited processing capacity in a selective fashion. Effective marketing communications are designed to activate consumer interests by appealing to those needs that are most relevant to the target audience. This is no easy task; marcom environments (stores, advertising media, noisy offices during sales presentations) are inherently cluttered with competitive stimuli and messages that also vie for the prospective customer's attention. Research shows that *clutter* reduces message effectiveness.[21]

Stage 3: Comprehension of What Is Attended

To comprehend is to understand and create meaning out of stimuli and symbols. Communication is effective when the meaning, or positioning, a marketing communicator intends to convey matches what consumers actually extract from a message. The term **comprehension** often is used interchangeably with *perception;* both terms refer to *interpretation.* Because people respond to their perceptions of the world and not to the world as it actually is, the topic of comprehension, or perception, is one of the most important subjects in marketing communications.[22]

The perceptual process of interpreting stimuli is called **perceptual encoding**. Two main stages are involved. **Feature analysis** is the initial stage whereby a receiver examines the basic features of a stimulus (such as size, shape, color, and angles) and from this makes a preliminary classification. For example, we are able to distinguish a motorcycle from a bicycle by examining features such as size, presence of an engine, and the number of controls. Lemons and oranges are distinguishable by their colors and shapes. The second stage of perceptual encoding, **active synthesis**, goes beyond merely examining physical features. The *context* or situation in which information is received plays a major role in determining what is perceived and interpreted, or, in other words, what meaning is acquired. Interpretation results from combining, or synthesizing, stimulus features with expectations of what should be present in the context in which a stimulus is perceived. For example, a synthetic fur coat placed in the window of a discount clothing store (the context) is likely to be perceived as a cheap imitation; however, the same coat, when attractively merchandised in an expensive boutique (a different context) might now be considered a high-quality, stylish garment.

A humorous way to better understand the difference between feature analysis and active synthesis is by examining cartoons. Witty cartoonists often use humor in subtle ways. They insert characters and props in cartoons that require the

Figure 5.12

Humorous Illustration of Selective Perception

reader to draw from his or her own past experiences in order to perceive (comprehend) the humor.

The important point in the preceding discussion is that consumers' comprehension of marketing stimuli is determined by stimulus features and by characteristics of the consumers themselves. Expectations, needs, personality traits, past experiences, and attitudes toward the stimulus object all play important roles in determining consumer perceptions. Due to the subjective nature of the factors that influence our perceptions, comprehension is oftentimes idiosyncratic, or peculiar to each individual. Figure 5.12 provides a humorous, albeit revealing, illustration of the idiosyncrasy of perception. *The Investigation* illustrates that each individual's personal characteristics and background influence how he or she perceives the man in the middle.

A classic statement regarding the idiosyncratic nature of perception is offered in the following quote:

> *We do not simply "react to" a happening or to some impingement from the environment in a determined way (except in behavior that has become reflexive or habitual). We [interpret and] behave according to what we bring to the occasion, and what each of us brings to the occasion is more or less unique.*[23]

This quote is from an analysis of fan reaction to a heatedly contested football game between Dartmouth and Princeton universities way back in 1951. The game was highly emotional and arguments and fights broke out on both sides. Interestingly, fan reaction to the dirty play divided along team loyalties. Dartmouth fans perceived Princeton players as the perpetrators, and vice versa. That is, what fans experienced and how they interpreted events depended on their view of who the "good guys" were prior to the game. In short, our individual uniqueness conditions what we see!

An individual's *mood* also can influence his or her perception of stimulus objects. Research has found that when people are in a good mood they are more likely to retrieve positive rather than negative material from their memories; are more likely to perceive the positive side of things; and, in turn, are more likely to respond positively to a variety of stimuli.[24] Advertisers are well aware of this, at least intuitively, when they use techniques such as humor and nostalgia to put message receivers in a good mood.

Miscomprehension. People sometimes *misinterpret* or *miscomprehend* messages so as to make them more consistent with their existing beliefs or expectations. This typically is done without conscious awareness; nonetheless, distorted perception and message miscomprehension are common. Miscomprehension of marcom messages occurs primarily for three reasons: (1) messages are themselves sometimes misleading or unclear, (2) consumers are biased by their own preconceptions and thus "see" what they choose to see, and (3) processing of advertisements often takes place under time pressures and noisy circumstances. The moral is clear: marketing communicators cannot assume that consumers interpret messages in the manner intended. It is for this reason that message testing (also called *copy testing*) is absolutely imperative before investing in print space, broadcast time, or other media outlets. Also, it is important that marcom messages be repeated so as to assure that most viewers and readers eventually understand the marketer's intended meaning.

Stage 4: Agreement with What Is Comprehended

A fourth information-processing stage involves the matter of whether the consumer *agrees with* (i.e., accepts) a message argument that he or she has comprehended. It is crucial from a marcom perspective that consumers not only comprehend a message but that they also agree with the message (as opposed to countering it or rejecting it outright). Comprehension by itself does not ensure that the message will change consumers' attitudes or influence their behavior. Understanding that an advertisement is attempting to position a brand in a certain way is not tantamount to accepting that message. For example, we may clearly understand when a retailer advertises itself as providing outstanding service, but we would not agree with that positioning if we personally have experienced something less than this level of service from that retailer.

Agreement depends on whether the message is *credible* (i.e., believable, trustworthy) and whether it contains information and appeals that are *compatible with the values* that are important to the consumer. For example, a consumer who is more interested in the symbolic implications of consuming a particular product than in acquiring functional value is likely to be persuaded more by a message that associates the advertised brand with a desirable group than one that talks about mundane product features. Using endorsers who are perceived as trustworthy is another means of enhancing message credibility. Credibility also can be boosted by structuring believable messages rather than making unrealistic claims.

Stages 5 and 6: Retention and Search and Retrieval of Stored Information

These two information-processing stages, *retention* and *search and retrieval,* are discussed together because both involve *memory* factors. The subject of memory is a complex topic, but these complexities need not concern us here, because our interest in the topic is considerably more practical.[25]

From a marcom perspective, memory involves the related issues of what consumers remember (recognize and recall) about marketing stimuli and how they access and retrieve information when in the process of choosing among product alternatives. The subject of memory is inseparable from the process of learning, so the following paragraphs first discuss the basics of memory, then examine learning fundamentals, and finally, emphasize the practical application of memory and learning principles to marketing communications.

Elements of memory. Memory consists of long-term memory *(LTM);* short-term, or working, memory *(STM);* and a set of sensory stores *(SS).* Information is received by one or more sensory receptors (sight, smell, touch, and so on) and passed to an appropriate SS, where it is rapidly lost (within fractions of a second) unless attention is allocated to the stimulus. Attended information is then transferred to STM, which serves as the center for current processing activity by integrating information from the sense organs and from LTM. *Limited processing capacity* is the most outstanding characteristic of STM; individuals can process only a finite amount of information at any one time. An excessive amount of information will result in reduced recognition and recall. Furthermore, information in STM that is not thought about or rehearsed will be lost from STM in about 30 seconds or less.[26] (This is what happens when you get a phone number from a telephone directory but then are distracted before you have an opportunity to dial the number. You must refer to the directory a second time and then repeat the number to yourself—rehearse it—so that you will not forget it again.)

Information is transferred from STM to LTM, which cognitive psychologists consider to be a virtual storehouse of unlimited information. Information in LTM is organized into coherent and associated cognitive units, which are variously called *schemata, memory organization packets,* or *knowledge structures.* All three terms

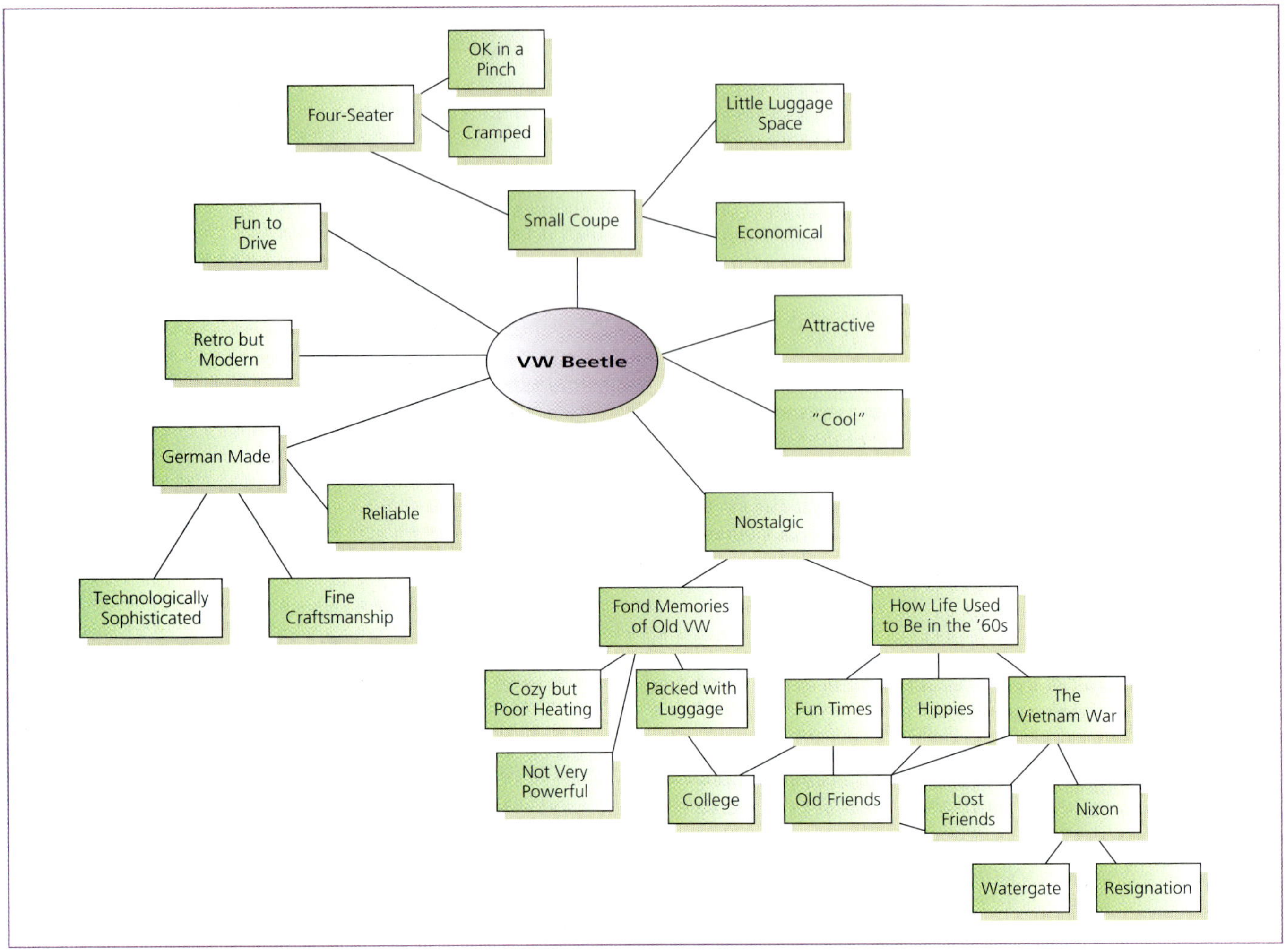

Figure 5.13

Consumer's Knowledge Structure for the VW Beetle

reflect the idea that LTM consists of associative links among related information, knowledge, and beliefs. A diagram of the concept of a knowledge structure is illustrated in Figure 5.13. This representation captures one baby boomer's memory structure for the Volkswagen Beetle, a car she first owned during her college years in the late 1960s and repurchased in 2005 to celebrate her 58th birthday.

The marketing communicator's challenge is to provide positively valued information that consumers will store in LTM and that will be used at some later time to influence the choice of "our" brand over competitive options. There is a good reason why information communicated about a brand *must* achieve long-term memory storage and be readily retrievable from memory. Namely, the point at which a consumer is exposed to information about a brand typically is separated in time—sometimes by months—from the occasion at which the consumer needs to access and use the information to make a purchase decision. Marketing communicators continually attempt to alter consumers' long-term memories, or knowledge structures, by facilitating consumer *learning* of information that is compatible with the marketer's interest.

Types of learning. Two primary types of learning are relevant to marcom efforts.[27] One form is *strengthening of linkages* between the marketer's brand and some feature or benefit of that brand. Metaphorically, the marketing communicator wishes to build mental "ropes" (rather than flimsy strings) between a brand and its positive features and benefits. The objective, in other words, is to securely position the brand's essence in the consumer's memory. In general, linkages are strengthened by *repeating* claims, being *creative* in conveying a product's features, and presenting claims in a *concrete* fashion. For example, the ad for Purex laundry detergent (Figure 5.14) displays a miner's hat on top of the container as a concrete instantiation of the claim that Purex laundry detergent removes dirt and odors by penetrating clothing "deep down"—just like miners go deep down into shafts.

Marketing communicators facilitate a second form of learning by *establishing entirely new linkages.* Returning to our discussion of brand equity back in Chapter 2, the present notion of establishing new linkages is equivalent to the previously discussed idea of enhancing brand equity by building strong, favorable, and perhaps unique associations between the brand and its features and benefits. Hence, the terms *linkage* and *association* are interchangeable in this context. Both involve a relation between a brand and its *features and benefits that are stored in a consumer's memory.*

Courtesy, The Dial Corporation/Purex Division

Figure 5.14

An Effort to Strengthen a Brand Linkage Using a Concrete Illustration

Search and retrieval of information. Information that is learned and stored in memory only impacts consumer choice behavior when it is searched and retrieved. Precisely how retrieval occurs is beyond the scope of this chapter. Suffice it to say that retrieval is facilitated when a new piece of information is linked, or associated, with another concept that is itself well known and easily accessed. This is precisely what Purex's brand management and ad agency team has attempted to accomplish by using the miner's hat to illustrate deep-down cleaning ability. It is much easier for people to retrieve the concrete idea of a miner's hat as emblematic of going "deep down" than it is to salvage from memory the abstract semantic concept of deep penetration. *Dual-coding theory* offers an explanation.

According to **dual-coding theory**, pictures are represented in memory in verbal as well as visual form, whereas words are less likely to have visual representations.[28] In other words, pictures and visuals (versus words) are better remembered because pictures are especially able to elicit mental images. Research has shown that information about product attributes is better recalled when the information is accompanied with pictures than when presented only as prose.[29] The value of pictures is especially important when verbal information is itself low in imagery.[30]

A CPM Wrap-Up

A somewhat detailed account of consumer information processing has been presented. As noted in the introduction, the CPM perspective provides an appropriate description of consumer behavior when that behavior is deliberate, thoughtful, or, in short, highly cognitive. Much consumer behavior is of this nature. On the other hand, behavior also is motivated by emotional, hedonic, and experiential considerations. Therefore, we need to consider the HEM perspective and the implications this model holds for marketing communicators and brand positioning.

The Hedonic, Experiential Model (HEM)

It again is important to emphasize that the *rational* consumer processing model (CPM) and the *hedonic, experiential* model (HEM) are *not* mutually exclusive. Indeed, there is impressive evidence that individuals comprehend reality by these rational and experiential processes operating interactively with one another, with their relative influence contingent on the nature of the situation and the amount of

© Mark Richards/PhotoEdit, Inc.

emotional involvement—the greater the emotional involvement, the greater the influence of experiential processes.[31] Hence, the HEM model probably better explains how consumers process information when they are carefree and happy and confronted with positive outcomes.[32]

Whereas the CPM perspective views consumers as pursuing such objectives as "obtaining the best buy," "getting the most for their money," and "maximizing utility," the HEM viewpoint recognizes that people often consume products for the sheer fun of it or in the pursuit of amusement, fantasies, or sensory stimulation.[33] Product consumption from the hedonic perspective results from the *anticipation* of having fun, fulfilling fantasies, or having pleasurable feelings. Comparatively, choice behavior from the CPM perspective is based on the thoughtful evaluation that the chosen alternative will be more functional and provide better results than will the alternatives.

Thus, viewed from an HEM perspective, products are more than mere objective entities (a bottle of perfume, a stereo system, a can of soup, etc.) and are, instead, subjective symbols that precipitate *feelings* (e.g., love and pride) and promise *fun* and the possible realization of *fantasies*. Products most compatible with the hedonic perspective include the performing arts (e.g., opera and modern dance), the so-called plastic arts (e.g., photography and crafts), popular forms of entertainment (e.g., movies and rock concerts), fashion apparel, sporting events, leisure activities, and recreational pursuits.[34] It is important to realize, however, that any product—not just these examples—may have hedonic and experiential elements underlying its choice and consumption. For example, a lot of pleasant feelings and fantasizing are attached to thinking about purchasing a product such as skis, an automobile, a bicycle, or furniture. Even Procter & Gamble, which historically has been noted for its matter-of-fact advertising style, altered its emphasis on performance claims for Tide detergent and focused more on the emotions associated with clean, fresh laundry.

Figure 5.15

Illustration of a CPM-Oriented Advertisement

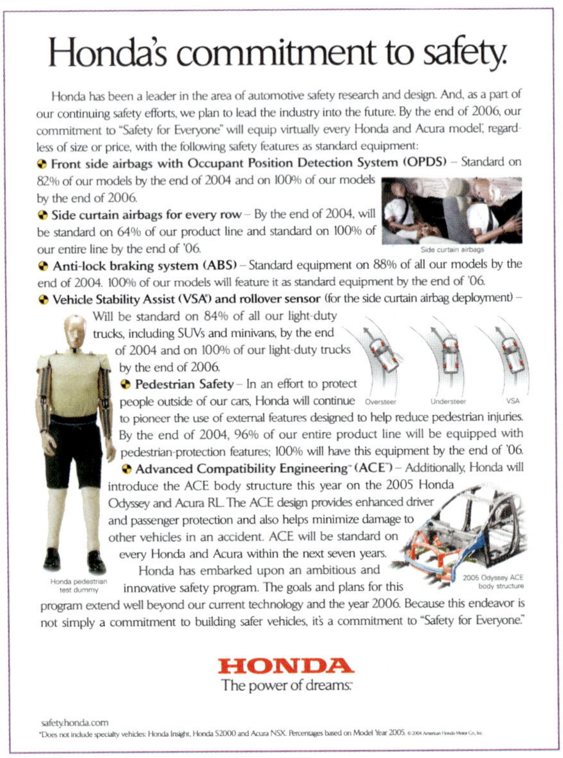

American Honda Motor Co., Inc.

The differences between the HEM and CPM perspectives hold meaningful implications for marcom practice. Whereas verbal stimuli and rational arguments designed to position a brand and to affect consumers' product knowledge and beliefs are most appropriate in CPM-oriented marcom efforts, the HEM approach emphasizes nonverbal content or emotionally provocative words and is intended to generate images, fantasies, and positive emotions and feelings.

A vivid contrast between the CPM and HEM orientations is illustrated in the differences in the advertisements for Honda automobiles (Figure 5.15) and the BMW 6 Series (Figure 5.16). The former ad uses verbal content to explain in some detail Honda's commitment to safety, which is a relatively new positioning for this brand. The ad exemplifies the CPM approach in that it attempts to move the consumer through all the CPM stages discussed previously. Honda's ad agency expects that consumers will think of that company and its automobiles in a slightly different light than in the past: Honda products not only are high performing and dependable (well-established associations for Honda), but they also are superb in safety (a new positioning).

Comparatively, the BMW ad (Figure 5.16) provides little information about product attributes and functional benefits. Rather, the ad in its striking simplicity appeals directly to the emotions of fun and exhilaration. The consumer in seeing this ad need not expend any thought; emotion and fantasy are front and center—you owe yourself this indulgence ("U.O.U." according to the ad's headline).

The prior discussion and examples have emphasized advertising, but it should be apparent that the differences between the CPM and HEM perspectives apply as well to other forms of marketing communications. A salesperson, for example, may emphasize product features and tangible benefits in attempting to make a sale (CPM approach), or he or she may attempt to convey the fun, fantasies, and pleasures that prospective customers can enjoy with product ownership. Successful salespersons employ both approaches and orient the dominant approach to the consumer's specific personality and needs. That is, successful salespersons know how to adapt their presentations to different customers—it is hoped, of course, that they are doing it honestly and maintaining standards of morality.

Finally, no single positioning strategy, whether aimed at CPM or HEM processing, is effective in all instances. What works best depends on the specific nature of the product category, the competitive situation, and the character and needs of the target audience. Returning to the fundamentals of positioning, brands can be positioned to appeal to *functional* needs, which is congenial with the CPM perspective, or to *symbolic* or *experiential* needs, which is more harmonious with the HEM approach.

Courtesy, BMW of North America, LLC; Advertising Agent: Fallon Minneapolis

Figure 5.16

Illustration of an HEM-Oriented Advertisement

Summary

This chapter introduced the concept and practice of brand positioning and described it as representing the key feature, benefit, or image that a brand stands for in the target audience's collective mind. A positioning statement is the central idea that encapsulates a brand's meaning and distinctiveness vis-à-vis competitive brands. Because meaning is fundamental to positioning, the chapter introduced the notion of semiotics and described meaning production as a process in which consumers are actively involved in constructing meaning from marcom messages, meaning that may or may not be equivalent to what the communicator intended to convey. It was further described that the fundamental concept in semiotics is the sign, which is something physical and perceivable that signifies something (the referent) to somebody (the interpreter) in some context. It further was explained that marcom practitioners, when in the process of positioning their brands, draw meaning from the culturally constituted world (i.e., the everyday world filled with artifacts) and transfer that meaning to their brands.

It was made clear that a good positioning statement must satisfy two requirements: (1) reflect a brand's competitive advantage (vis-à-vis competitive offerings in the same product category), and (2) motivate consumers to action. In the context of these two considerations, four possible outcomes from an attempted brand positioning were identified, namely, that the positioning is a potential "loser," a "winner," a "swimming-up-the-river" proposition, or a "promotes-competitors" prospect.

Detailed discussion was devoted to the various ways brands can be positioned. The options included benefit positioning—where a brand is positioned in terms of functional, symbolic, or experiential needs—and attribute positioning. This latter form includes positioning based on product-related features or in terms of usage or user imagery.

The chapter also described the fundamentals of consumer-choice behavior. Two relatively distinct perspectives on choice behavior were presented: the consumer processing model (CPM) and the hedonic, experiential model (HEM). The CPM approach views the consumer as an analytical, systematic, and logical decision maker. According to this perspective, consumers are motivated to achieve desired goals. The CPM process involves attending to, encoding, retaining, retrieving, and integrating information so that a person can achieve a suitable choice among consumption alternatives. Brands positioned to be in tune with the CPM process emphasize logical arguments and functional features over emotion and symbolism. Comparatively, the HEM perspective views consumer-choice behavior as resulting from the pursuit of fun, fantasy, and feelings. Thus, some consumer behavior is based predominantly on emotional considerations rather than on objective, functional, and economic factors. The distinction between the CPM and HEM views of consumer choice is an important one for marketing communicators. The techniques and creative strategies for affecting consumer-choice behavior clearly are a function of the prevailing consumer orientation.

Discussion Questions

1. Meaning creation, according to the semiotics perspective, is a constructive process. Explain what this means and illustrate your understanding with a personal example.
2. In Chapter 2 you read about "leveraging" (refer to Figure 2.8) as one of the ways by which brand associations are created. Relate that discussion to the concept of imbuing a brand with meaning by pulling existing meaning from the "culturally constituted world."
3. As a brand manager, assume you have decided to promote your brand on the basis of an attribute that is very important to consumers but for which your brand has no advantage over competitive offerings. In the context of Figure 5.3, explain the likely outcome of this positioning effort.
4. How does your college or university position itself? If you were responsible for coming up with a new positioning, or repositioning, for your college or university, what would that be? Justify your choice.
5. How is your favorite brand of athletic footwear (Adidas, Nike, Reebok, etc.) positioned?
6. A reality of marketing communications is that the same sign often means different things to different people. Provide an example from your own personal experience in which the same sign has had different meanings for diverse people. What are the general implications for marketing communications?
7. Some magazine advertisements show a picture of a product and mention the brand name, but have virtually no verbal content except, perhaps, a single statement about the brand. Locate an example of this type and explain what

meaning you think the advertiser is attempting to convey. Ask two friends to offer their interpretations of the same ad, and then compare their responses to determine the differences in meaning that these ads have for you and your friends. Draw a general conclusion from this exercise.

8. When discussing exposure as the initial stage of information processing, it was claimed that gaining exposure is a necessary but insufficient condition for success. Explain.
9. Explain why attention is highly selective and what implication selectivity holds for brand managers and their advertising agencies.
10. All marketing communications environments are cluttered. Explain what this means and provide several examples. Do not restrict your examples just to advertisements.
11. Explain each of the following related concepts: perceptual encoding, feature analysis, and active synthesis. Using a consumer packaged good of your choice, explain how package designers for this brand have used concepts of feature analysis in designing the package.
12. Figure 5.13 presents a consumer's knowledge structure for the VW Beetle. Construct your knowledge structure for the one automobile you most covet owning. If you have no automobile ownership desires, construct your knowledge structure for the Beetle.
13. Some experts claim that countries, states, and municipalities can be positioned just like other "products" for purposes of attracting tourism dollars. If you are a U.S. resident, explain how you would position your home state to enhance its ability to attract more tourists. If you are a foreign national, explain how you would promote your country, or a region of your country, to attract more tourists.

ENDNOTES

1. This description is based on Bob Lamons, "Marcom Proves Itself a Worthy Investment," *Marketing News*, June 9, 2003, 13.
2. For in-depth treatments of semiotics in marketing communications and consumer behavior, see David Glen Mick, "Consumer Research and Semiotics: Exploring the Morphology of Signs, Symbols, and Significance," *Journal of Consumer Research* 13 (September 1986), 196–213; Eric Haley, "The Semiotic Perspective: A Tool for Qualitative Inquiry," in *Proceedings of the 1993 Conference of the American Academy of Advertising*, ed. Esther Thorson (Columbia, Mo.: The American Academy of Advertising, 1993), 189–196; and Birgit Wassmuth et al., "Semiotics: Friend or Foe to Advertising?" in *Proceedings of the 1993 Conference of the American Academy of Advertising*, ed. Esther Thorson (Columbia, Mo.: The American Academy of Advertising, 1993), 271–276. For interesting applications of a semiotic analysis, see Morris B. Holbrook and Mark W. Grayson, "The Semiology of Cinematic Consumption: Symbolic Consumer Behavior in *Out of Africa*," *Journal of Consumer Research* 13 (December 1986), 374–381; Edward F. McQuarrie and David Glen Mick, "On Resonance: A Critical Pluralistic Inquiry into Advertising Rhetoric," *Journal of Consumer Research* 19 (September 1992), 180–197; Linda M. Scott, "Understanding Jingles and Needledrop: A Rhetorical Approach to Music in Advertising," *Journal of Consumer Research* 17 (September 1990), 223–236; and Teresa J. Domzal and Jerome B. Kernan, "Mirror, Mirror: Some Postmodern Reflections on Global Advertising," *Journal of Advertising* 22 (December 1993), 1–20. For an insightful treatment on "deconstructing" meaning from advertisements and other marketing communications, see Barbara B. Stern, "Textual Analysis in Advertising Research: Construction and Deconstruction of Meanings," *Journal of Advertising* 25 (fall 1996), 61–73.
3. This description is based on John Fiske, *Introduction to Communication Studies* (New York: Routledge, 1990), and Mick, "Consumer Research and Semiotics," 198.
4. The subsequent discussion is influenced by the insights of David K. Berlo, *The Process of Communication* (San Francisco: Holt, Rinehart & Winston, 1960), 168–216.
5. This interpretation is adapted from Roberto Friedmann and Mary R. Zimmer, "The Role of Psychological Meaning in Advertising," *Journal of Advertising* 17, no. 1 (1988), 31; and Robert E. Klein III and Jerome B. Kernan, "Contextual Influences on the Meanings Ascribed to Ordinary Consumption Objects," *Journal of Consumer Research* 18 (December 1991), 311–324.

6. Grant McCracken, "Culture and Consumption: A Theoretical Account of the Structure and Movement of the Cultural Meaning of Consumer Goods," *Journal of Consumer Research* 13 (June 1986), 74.
7. For further discussion, see Grant McCracken, "Advertising: Meaning or Information," in *Advances in Consumer Research,* vol. 14, ed. Melanie Wallendorf and Paul F. Anderson (Provo, Utah: Association for Consumer Research, 1987), 121–124.
8. Edward F. McQuarrie and David Glen Mick, "Visual Rhetoric in Advertising: Text-Interpretive, Experimental, and Reader-Response Analyses," *Journal of Consumer Research* 26 (June 1999), 37–54; Linda M. Scott, "The Bridge from Text to Mind: Adapting Reader-Response Theory to Consumer Research," *Journal of Consumer Research* 21 (December 1994), 461–480.
9. Kevin J. Clancy and Peter C. Krieg, *Counter-Intuitive Marketing: Achieve Great Results Using Uncommon Sense* (New York: Free Press, 2000), 110.
10. Ibid., 111.
11. C. Whan Park, Bernard J. Jaworski, and Deborah J. MacInnis, "Strategic Brand Concept-Image Management," *Journal of Marketing* 50 (October 1986), 136. The following discussion of functional, symbolic, and experiential needs/benefits adheres to Park et al.'s conceptualizations.
12. For further discussion of this point, see ibid.
13. Aaron Baar and Kenneth Hein, "Grillin' Time," *Brandweek,* May 12, 2003, 5.
14. Adapted from Emily Nelson, "Procter & Gamble Tries to Hide Wrinkles in Aging Beauty Fluid," *The Wall Street Journal Online,* May 16, 2000, http://online.wsj.com.
15. What is being called the *consumer processing model* (CPM) is more conventionally called the *consumer information processing* (CIP) model. CPM is chosen over CIP for two reasons: (1) it is nominally parallel to the HEM label and thus simplifies memory, and (2) the term *information* is too limiting inasmuch as it implies that only verbal claims (information) are important to consumers and that other forms of communications (e.g., nonverbal statements) are irrelevant. This latter point was emphasized by Esther Thorson, "Consumer Processing of Advertising," *Current Issues & Research in Advertising* 12, ed. J. H. Leigh and C. R. Martin, Jr. (Ann Arbor: University of Michigan, 1990), 198–199.
16. Elizabeth C. Hirschman and Morris B. Holbrook, "Hedonic Consumption: Emerging Concepts, Methods, and Propositions," *Journal of Marketing* 46 (summer 1982), 92–101; Morris B. Holbrook and Elizabeth C. Hirschman, "The Experiential Aspects of Consumption: Consumer Fantasies, Feelings, and Fun," *Journal of Consumer Research* 9 (September 1982), 132–140.
17. James B. Bettman, *An Information Processing Theory of Consumer Choice* (Reading, Mass.: Addison-Wesley, 1979), 1.
18. William J. McGuire, "Some Internal Psychological Factors Influencing Consumer Choice," *Journal of Consumer Research* 4 (March 1976), 302–319.
19. Scott A. Hawkins and Stephen J. Hoch, "Low-Involvement Learning: Memory without Evaluation," *Journal of Consumer Research* 19 (September 1992), 212–225.
20. For an excellent treatment of this distinction as well as a broader perspective on factors determining consumer attention, comprehension, and learning of advertising messages, see Klaus G. Grunert, "Automatic and Strategic Processes in Advertising Effects," *Journal of Marketing* 60 (October 1996), 88–102.
21. Paul Surgi Speck and Michael T. Elliott, "The Antecedents and Consequences of Perceived Advertising Clutter," *Journal of Current Issues and Research in Advertising* 19 (fall 1997), 39–54. In addition to being disliked by consumers, advertising clutter has also been shown to have undesirable effects for the advertising community, at least in the case of magazine circulation. See Louisa Ha and Barry R. Litman, "Does Advertising Clutter Have Diminishing and Negative Returns?" *Journal of Advertising* 26 (spring 1997), 31–42.
22. A thorough discussion of comprehension processes is provided by David Glen Mick, "Levels of Subjective Comprehension in Advertising Processing and Their Relations to Ad Perceptions, Attitudes, and Memory," *Journal of Consumer Research* 18 (March 1992), 411–424.
23. Albert H. Hastorf and Hadley Cantril, "They Saw a Game: A Case Study," *Journal of Abnormal & Social Psychology* 49 (1954), 129–134.
24. Alice M. Isen, Margaret Clark, Thomas E. Shalker, and Lynn Karp, "Affect, Accessibility of Material in Memory, and Behavior: A Cognitive Loop," *Journal of Personality and Social Psychology* 36 (January 1978), 1–12; Meryl Paula Gardner, "Mood States and Consumer Behavior: A Critical Review," *Journal of Consumer Research* 12 (December 1985), 281–300.
25. Several valuable sources for technical treatments of memory operations are available in the advertising and marketing literatures. See Bettman, "Memory Functions," *An Information Processing Theory of Consumer Choice,* chap. 6; James B. Bettman, "Memory Factors in Consumer Choice: A Review," *Journal of Marketing* 43 (spring 1979), 37–53; Andrew A. Mitchell, "Cognitive Processes Initiated by Advertising," in *Information Processing Research in Advertising,* ed. R. J. Harris (Hillsdale, N.J.: Lawrence Erlbaum Associates, 1983), 13–42; Jerry C. Olson, "Theories of Information Encoding and Storage: Implications for Consumer Research," in *The Effect of Information on Consumer and Market Behavior,* ed. A. A. Mitchell (Chicago: American Marketing Association, 1978), 49–60; Thomas K. Srull, "The Effects of Subjective Affective States on Memory and Judgment," in *Advances in Consumer Research,* vol. 11, ed. T. C. Kinnear (Provo, Utah: Association for Consumer Research, 1984); and Kevin Lane Keller, "Advertising Retrieval Cues on Brand Evaluations," *Journal of Consumer Research* 14 (December 1989), 316–333.
26. Richard M. Shiffrin and R. C. Atkinson, "Storage and Retrieval Processes in Long-Term Memory," *Psychological Review* 76 (March 23, 1969), 179–193.
27. Mitchell, "Cognitive Processes Initiated by Advertising."
28. Allan Paivio, "Mental Imagery in Associative Learning and Memory," *Psychological Review* 76 (May 1969), 241–263; John R. Rossiter and Larry Percy, "Visual Imaging Ability as a Mediator of Advertising Response," in *Advances in Consumer*

Research, vol. 5, ed. H. Keith Hunt (Ann Arbor: Association for Consumer Research, 1978), 621–629.
29. Michael J. Houston, Terry L. Childers, and Susan E. Heckler, "Picture-Word Consistency and the Elaborative Processing of Advertisements," *Journal of Marketing Research* 24 (November 1987), 359–369.
30. H. Rao Unnava and Robert E. Burnkrant, "An Imagery-Processing View of the Role of Pictures in Print Advertisements," *Journal of Marketing Research* 28 (May 1991), 226–231.
31. Veronika Denes-Raj and Seymour Epstein, "Conflict between Intuitive and Rational Processing: When People Behave against Their Better Judgment," *Journal of Personality and Social Psychology* 66, no. 5 (1994), 819–829.
32. Ibid.
33. Hirschman and Holbrook, "Hedonic Consumption."
34. Ibid., 91.

CHAPTER 6

Marcom Objective Setting and Budgeting

Marcom Challenge: Brands with the Most Loyal Customers

Gaining loyal customers is a goal that brand managers work diligently to achieve. It is no easy task, however, as consumers often have high expectations for their brands that are difficult to satisfy. A New York research firm, Brand Keys, conducts an annual survey to identify companies in a variety of product and service categories that have the most loyal customers. Brand Keys surveys a sample of 16,000 men and women between the ages of 21 and 60. The survey asks frequent consumers of brands in each category to rate, in order of importance, those choice factors (termed *drivers*) that most ensure their loyalty to a particular brand. In the airline category, for example, the top four drivers are safety, boarding and booking efficiency, overall experience, and in-flight comfort. In early 2005, Brand Keys' most recent survey identified airline company JetBlue as the top brand in

Product/Service Category	Brand Winner
Airlines	JetBlue
Athletic footwear	Skechers/New Balance (tie)
Light beer	Miller Lite
Regular beer	Miller Genuine Draft
Bottled water	Poland Spring
Car rental	Avis
Computers	Apple
Credit cards	Discover Card
Hotels	Hyatt
Long-distance phone service	Verizon
Mobile phone	Samsung
Online travel	Expedia
Parcel delivery	FedEx
Pizza	Pizza Hut/Papa John's (tie)
Quick-service food	Subway
Retail	Wal-Mart
Search engine	Google
Soft drinks	Pepsi

terms of overall brand loyalty.[1] This young airline is noted for its new planes, leather seats, low fares, and in-flight DirecTV. One respondent offered this explanation for his loyalty to JetBlue: "You can't beat the service you get from them. It's like traveling business class for a tenth of the price." In addition to JetBlue, the customer loyalty winners in other product and service categories are as shown in this list.

CHAPTER OBJECTIVES

1
Understand the process of marcom objective setting and the requirements for good objectives.

2
Describe the hierarchy-of-effects model and its relevance for setting marcom objectives.

3
Understand the role of sales as a marcom objective and the logic of vaguely right versus precisely wrong thinking.

4
Understand the nature and importance of marcom budgeting.

5
Explain the relation between a brand's share of market (SOM) and its share of voice (SOV).

6
Explain the various rules of thumb, or heuristics, that guide practical budgeting.

Overview

Returning again to the model of the marcom process provided in Chapter 1, you will recall that the framework described various forms of "fundamental" and "implementation" decisions. We continue with this theme as it relates specifically to advertising objective setting and budgeting. These activities, along with targeting (the subject of Chapter 4) and positioning (Chapter 5), are the bedrock of all subsequent marcom decisions. Marcom strategy built on a weak foundation is virtually guaranteed to fail. Intelligent objectives and an adequate budget are critical for success. Let us not forget the mantra introduced in Chapter 1:

All marketing communications should be (1) directed to a particular ***target market****, (2) clearly* ***positioned****, (3) created to achieve a* ***specific objective****, and (4) undertaken to accomplish the objective* ***within budget constraint****.*

This chapter culminates the discussion of fundamental marcom decisions by examining both objective setting and budgeting. Both topics have been treated in the past mostly from the perspective of advertising rather than marcom in general. However, because the issues are similar regardless of the form of marketing communications, in this chapter we will pull from the advertising literature and apply it to all forms of marketing communications.

The key argument to be made is that objective setting and budgeting decisions must be formal and systematic rather than unplanned. Both topics represent key decisions that set the stage for the subsequent set of "implementation" decisions, which include the choice of messages, media, mixture of marcom elements, and the achievement of a continuous message presence, or momentum. (Please note that these four "implementation" decisions, along with the "fundamental" decisions, were introduced in the model of the marcom process in Chapter 1. It would be useful to review this model in Figure 1.3 to reacquaint yourself with the overall scope of marcom strategy.)

Setting Marcom Objectives

Marcom objectives are goals that the various marcom elements aspire to individually or collectively achieve during a scope of time such as a business quarter or fiscal year. Objectives provide the foundation for all remaining decisions. Specific chapters later in the text detail the objectives that each component of the marcom mix is designed to accomplish; for present purposes it will suffice merely to list an illustrative set of objectives that communicators hope to accomplish using different marcom tools. Alongside each objective, in brackets, are the marcom tools most suitable for accomplishing that objective:

- Facilitate the successful introduction of new brands [brand naming and packaging, advertising, sales promotions, word-of-mouth buzz generation, and point-of-purchase (P-O-P) displays].
- Build sales of existing brands by increasing the frequency of use, the variety of uses, or the quantity purchased [advertising and sales promotions].
- Inform the trade (wholesalers, agents or brokers, and retailers) and consumers about brand improvements [personal selling and trade-oriented advertising].
- Create brand awareness [advertising, packaging, and P-O-P messages].
- Enhance a brand's image [brand naming and packaging, advertising, event sponsorship, cause-oriented marketing, and marketing-oriented PR].
- Generate sales leads [advertising].

- Persuade the trade to handle the manufacturer's brands [trade-oriented advertising and personal selling].
- Stimulate point-of-purchase sales [brand naming and packaging, P-O-P messages, and external store signage].
- Increase customer loyalty [advertising and sales promotions].
- Improve corporate relations with special interest groups [marketing-oriented PR].
- Offset bad publicity about a brand or generate good publicity [marketing-oriented PR].
- Counter competitors' communications efforts [advertising and sales promotions].
- Provide customers with reasons for buying immediately instead of delaying a purchase [advertising and sales promotions].

The objectives that marketing communications in its various forms must accomplish are varied, but regardless of the substance of the objective, there are three major reasons why it is essential that objectives be established *prior to* making the all-important implementation decisions regarding message selection, media determination, and how the various marcom elements should be mixed and maintained:[2]

1. The process of setting objectives literally forces top marketing executives and marcom personnel to agree on the course that a brand's marcom strategy will take for the following planning period as well as the tasks it is to accomplish for a specific brand. As such, objectives provide a formalized expression of *management consensus.*
2. Objective setting *guides* the budgeting, message, and media aspects of a brand's marcom strategy. Objectives determine how much money should be spent and provide guidelines for the kinds of message strategy and media choice needed to accomplish a brand's marketing communications objectives.
3. Objectives provide *standards* against which results can be measured. As will be detailed later, good objectives set precise, quantitative yardsticks of what a marcom program hopes to accomplish. Subsequent results can then be compared with these standards to determine whether the effort accomplished what it was intended to do.

The Hierarchy of Marcom Effects

A full appreciation of marcom objective setting requires that we first look at the process of communications from the customer's perspective. A framework called the *hierarchy of effects* is appropriate for accomplishing this understanding. The hierarchy framework reveals that the choice of marcom objective depends on the target audience's degree of experience with the brand prior to commencing a marcom campaign.[3]

The **hierarchy-of-effects** metaphor implies that for marketing communications to be successful, the various marcom elements must advance consumers through a series of psychological stages, much in the way a person climbs a ladder—one step, then another, and another, until the top of the ladder is reached. A variety of hierarchy models have been formulated, all of which are predicated on the idea that the marcom elements, if successful, move people from an initial state of unawareness about a brand to eventually purchasing that brand.[4] Intermediate stages in the hierarchy represent progressively closer steps to brand purchase. The hierarchy in Figure 6.1 goes a step further by establishing brand loyalty as the

Figure 6.1
Hierarchy of Marcom Effects

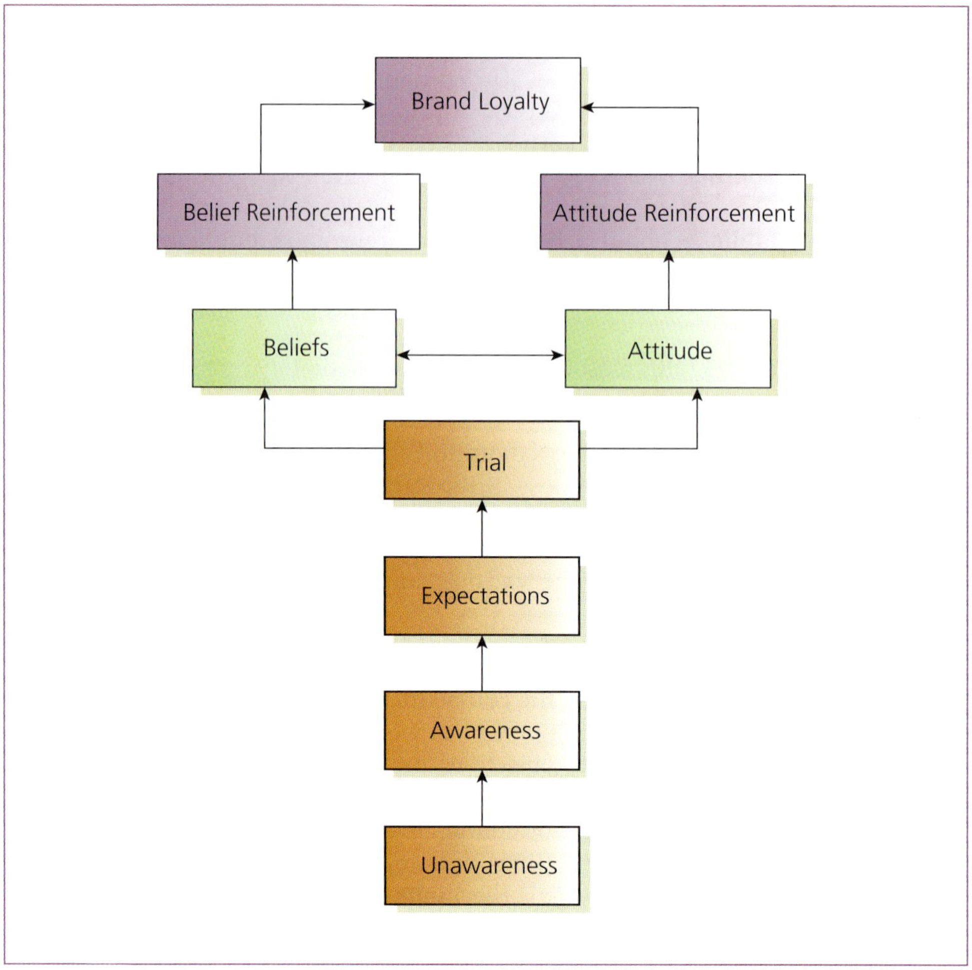

top step on the ladder.[5] Please examine Figure 6.1 carefully before reading on. The meaning of each of these stages, or hierarchy steps, is best understood by examining an actual advertisement. Consider the ad in Figure 6.2 for a brand called *Beano.* A glance at this ad quickly indicates that this product somehow is related to beans. It is a simple product indeed, but it provides us with an apt illustration of how the various marcom elements can work in concert to move consumers through the hierarchy stages.

Advancing Consumers from Unawareness to Awareness

When first introduced to the market, consumers were initially *unaware* of Beano's existence and of its special features (many no doubt remain unaware). The initial marcom imperative, therefore, is to make consumers *aware* that there is a product such as Beano. In general, creating awareness is essential for new or unestablished brands. Unless consumers are aware of a brand, that brand cannot be a member of their set of viable purchase alternatives. Of all the marcom tools, advertising (via mass media or otherwise) generally is the most effective and efficient method for quickly creating brand awareness. Sometimes advertising agencies place excessive emphasis on building brand awareness by creating zany ads with offbeat humor or using blatant sex appeals. However, as described in the *IMC Focus,* creating awareness does not assure that consumers will move further up the hierarchy toward purchasing the brand and potentially becoming loyal repeat purchasers.

Figure 6.2 Advertisement Illustrating Hierarchy of Marcom Effects

Glaxo Smith Kline

This Cat(fight) Is a Dog

imc focus

In response to diet fads eschewing the intake of carbohydrates (e.g., the Atkins and South Beach diets), the Miller Brewing Company, starting in 2004, undertook an aggressive ad campaign by comparing Miller Lite against Anheuser-Busch's Bud Light. Using humorous but hard-hitting TV ads, Miller Lite's advertisements attempted to persuade consumers that that brand should be their preferred choice because it contains only one-half the carbohydrate content of Bud Light. This campaign had a substantial impact on Miller Lite's market share, which rose while Bud Light's share declined.

But prior to this campaign, Miller had attempted to boost sales of Miller Lite by running a campaign with blatant sex appeal. The campaign was dubbed "Catfight" based on the campaign's initial spot in which two scantily clad women fought and shed clothing over whether Miller Lite tastes great or is less filling. (Older readers will recall 1970s advertising for Miller Lite that advertised the brand as both tasting great and being less filling.) A series of additional spots presented sexy women in confrontational scenes arguing over Miller Lite's relative merits. The campaign generated considerable buzz as well as controversy in feminist circles and elsewhere for its treatment of women as sex objects.

However, of primary relevance in the context of the present discussion is the fact that, although brand awareness of Miller Lite increased during the Catfight campaign, actual sales declined by 3 percent. In a meeting with financial analysts who track the performance of Miller's various brands, the president of Miller Lite had this to say about the ad campaign in a retrospective analysis: "Awareness is not the problem, but actual [purchase] consideration is the problem and challenge and opportunity. We want to ensure that the [advertising] spend we put behind the brand is leading toward actual consideration and not just continuing to build awareness."

SOURCE: Hillary Chura, "Miller Loses 'Catfight,' Buzz Doesn't Lift Lite," *Advertising Age,* June 2, 2003, 3, 51. Reprinted with permission from the June 2, 2003 issue of *Advertising Age.* Copyright, Crain Communications, Inc.

Creating an Expectation

Mere brand name awareness generally is not sufficient to get people to buy a brand, particularly when consumers already possess a solution to a consumption-related problem or remain unaware that a solution is available. Advertising and other marcom elements must instill in consumers an *expectation* of what product benefit(s) they will obtain from buying and experiencing a brand. It should be noted that an expectation from the consumer's perspective is based on how the brand has been positioned, which was the subject of Chapter 5. In the case of Beano, consumers are basically promised that if they take Beano just before eating gassy products (beans, broccoli, cauliflower, etc.), gas buildup will be prevented. This is how Beano has been positioned, and this is the expectation that Beano's brand management team wishes to implant in the target audience's collective mind. To the extent consumers develop this expectation, they may undertake *trial* purchases of Beano to learn for themselves whether it lives up to its promise.

Encouraging Trial Purchases

Sales promotions and advertisements sometimes work together to encourage *trial purchases,* often by influencing consumers to switch from brands they currently are purchasing. As the name suggests, a trial purchase is just that: the consumer tries a brand for the first time. Because most advertisements can simply hope to entice, enthuse, and whet one's appetite—or, in general, create expectations—a more compelling mechanism is required for generating trial purchases. And, indeed, this is the role of the *sales promotions* component of marketing communications. Free samples and coupons are particularly effective devices for getting consumers to try new brands of packaged goods. In the case of expensive durable products, major price discounts and rebate offers are effective in encouraging a form of trial behavior such as test-driving automobiles or hitting golf balls with so-called demonstrator golf clubs.

Forming Beliefs and Attitudes

Upon trying a brand for the first time, the consumer will form *beliefs* about its performance. With respect to Beano, the beliefs may be thoughts such as, "It does prevent gas buildup, but I don't like its taste." These beliefs, in turn, form the basis for developing an overall *attitude* toward the brand. Beliefs and attitudes are mutually reinforcing, as illustrated by the double-headed arrow linking these two elements in Figure 6.1. If Beano lives up to the consumer's expectations about preventing gas buildup, the attitude toward that brand most likely will be positive; on the other hand, the attitude can be expected to be somewhat ambivalent or even negative if the brand fails to satisfy the expected benefit that motivated the trial purchase.

Reinforcing Beliefs and Attitudes

Once brand-specific beliefs and attitudes are formed as the outcome from firsthand product usage experience, subsequent marketing communications serve merely to *reinforce* the consumers' beliefs and attitudes that resulted from trying the product. In Figure 6.1 this is referred to as *belief reinforcement* and *attitude reinforcement*. The reinforcement objective is accomplished when a marketing communicator sticks with a particular promise and promotes this point repeatedly over time.

Accomplishing Brand Loyalty

As long as the brand continues to satisfy expectations and a superior brand is not introduced, the consumer may become a *brand-loyal* purchaser. This indeed is the ultimate objective, because, as has been mentioned, it is much cheaper to retain present customers than it is to continuously prospect for new ones.[6] The Marcom Challenge provided illustrations of brands in different product and service categories where customer loyalty is particularly high.

Brand loyalty is the top rung on the hierarchy of marcom effects (Figure 6.1). Loyalty is not a guaranteed outcome, however. Strong brand loyalty occasionally develops. For example, some consumers always purchase the same brand of cola; others forever smoke the same brand of cigarette; and there are those who use the same brand of deodorant, toothpaste, shampoo, or even automobile. In many other instances, however, the consumer never forms a strong preference for any brand. Rather, the consumer continually shifts his or her allegiance from one brand to the next, constantly trying, trying, and trying but never developing a strong commitment to any particular brand. Consumer behavior can be like dating; some people continue to "play the field" but never become committed to anyone.

Brand loyalty is a goal that the marketing communicator aspires to achieve. Obtaining the consumer's loyalty necessitates meeting the consumer's needs better than competitive brands and continuing to communicate the brand's merits to reinforce the consumer's brand-related beliefs and attitudes. (See Figure 6.1 as a graphic reminder of this point.) It is interesting to note, however, that the various marcom elements may be in conflict toward the goal of accomplishing brand loyalty. Whereas advertising has the desirable long-run effect of making consumers less price sensitive and more brand loyal, sales promotions can reduce loyalty by effectively "training" consumers to be price sensitive and thus inclined to switch among brands to avail themselves of price discounts.[7]

Section Summary

It should be apparent from this discussion of marcom's hierarchy of effects that the objective for a brand's marcom program at any point in time depends on where in the hierarchy consumers are located. Although individual consumers inevitably will be at different levels of the hierarchy, the issue is one of where *most* consumers are located. For example, if research reveals that the vast majority of the target audience remains unaware of the brand, then creating awareness is of uppermost importance. If, however, most members of the target audience know of the brand but they're not clear what it stands for, then the marcom task becomes one of designing messages that build an expectation capable of motivating consumers to try the brand.

Requirements for Setting Suitable Marcom Objectives

A marcom objective is a specific statement about a planned execution in terms of what a marcom program is intended to accomplish at a point in time. That goal is based on knowledge of where on the hierarchy of effects members of the target audience are located and knowledge of the current, or anticipated, competitive situation in the product category and on the problems that the brand must confront or the opportunities that are available.

The specific content of a marcom objective depends entirely on the brand's unique situation. Hence, it is not feasible to discuss objective content without having current details (such as those provided by marketing research) about the competitive context. We can, however, describe the requirements that all good objectives must satisfy. Let us start by making it clear that not all objectives are well stated. Consider the following examples:

Example A: *The objective next business quarter for Brand X is to realize increased sales.*
Example B: *The objective next business quarter for Brand X is to elevate overall brand awareness from the present level of 60 percent to 80 percent.*

These extreme examples differ in two important respects. First, example B is obviously more specific. Second, whereas example A deals with a sales objective, example B involves a presales goal (increase awareness). The sections that follow describe the specific criteria that good objectives must satisfy.[8] We will return to examples A and B in the process of presenting these criteria, which are listed in Figure 6.3.

Objectives Must Include a Precise Statement of Who, What, and When

Objectives must be stated in precise terms. At a minimum, objectives should specify the target audience (who), indicate the specific goal—such as awareness level—to be accomplished (what), and indicate the relevant time frame over which the objective is to be achieved (when). For example, the marcom campaign for Beano (Figure 6.2) might include objectives such as: (1) "Within six months from the beginning of the campaign, research should show that 40 percent of all adults are aware of the Beano name"; (2) "Within six months from the begin-

Figure 6.3
Criteria That Good Marcom Objectives Must Satisfy

- Include a precise statement of who, what, and when
- Be quantitative and measurable
- Specify the amount of change
- Be realistic
- Be internally consistent
- Be clear and in writing

ning of the campaign, research should show that at least 30 percent of the target audience knows that Beano prevents gas buildup from eating beans and other foods"; or (3) "Within one year from the beginning of the campaign, at least 10 million consumers should have tried Beano."

Returning to the hypothetical objectives (A versus B) for Brand X, example B represents the desired degree of specificity and, as such, would give brand managers something meaningful to direct their efforts toward and provide a clear-cut benchmark for assessing whether the marcom campaign has accomplished its objective. Example A, by comparison, is much too general. Suppose sales have actually increased by 2 percent during the course of the campaign. Does this mean the campaign was successful since sales have in fact increased? If not, how much increase is necessary for the campaign to be regarded as a success?

Objectives Must Be Quantitative and Measurable

This requirement demands that ad objectives be stated in quantitative terms so as to be measurable. A nonmeasurable objective for Beano would be a vague statement such as, "Marketing communications should enhance consumers' knowledge of Beano." This objective lacks measurability because it fails to specify the product benefit of which consumers are to possess knowledge.

Objectives Must Specify the Amount of Change

In addition to being quantitative and measurable, objectives must specify the amount of change they are intended to accomplish. Example A (to increase sales) fails to meet this requirement. Example B (to increase awareness from 60 percent to 80 percent) is satisfactory because it clearly specifies that anything less than a 20 percent awareness increase would be considered unsuitable performance.

Objectives Must Be Realistic

Unrealistic objectives are as useless as having no objective at all. An unrealistic objective is one that cannot be accomplished in the time allotted to the proposed marcom campaign. For example, a brand that has achieved only 15 percent consumer awareness during its first year on the market could not realistically expect a small marcom budget to increase the awareness level to, say, 45 percent next year.

Objectives Must Be Internally Consistent

Objectives set for a particular element of a marcom program must be compatible (internally consistent) with objectives set for other marcom components. It would be incompatible for a manufacturer to proclaim a 25 percent reduction in sales force while simultaneously stating that the advertising and sales promotion objective is to increase retail distribution by 20 percent. Without adequate sales force effort, it is doubtful that the retail trade would give a brand more shelf space.

Objectives Must Be Clear and in Writing

For objectives to accomplish their purposes of fostering communication and permitting evaluation, they must be stated clearly and in writing so that they can be disseminated to marcom personnel who will be held responsible for seeing that the objectives are accomplished.

Should Marcom Objectives Be Stated in Terms of Sales?

We can broadly distinguish two types of marcom objectives: sales versus presales objectives. *Presales objectives* are commonly referred to as *communication objectives*, with the term *communication* derived from efforts to communicate outcomes that will increase the target audience's brand awareness, enhance their attitudes toward the brand, shift their preference from competitors' brands to our brand, and so on. Comparatively, using *sales* as the goal for a particular advertising campaign means that the marcom objective literally is to increase sales by a specified amount. Marcom practitioners and educators since the early 1960s have traditionally rejected the use of sales as an appropriate objective. On the other hand, a relatively recent perspective asserts that influencing sales should *always* represent the objective of any marcom effort.

The following discussion first presents the traditional view on this matter (favoring a presales objective) and then introduces the heretical position (preferring a sales objective). In the manner of Hegelian dialectic—that is, stating a thesis, identifying its opposite (antithesis), and then offering a synthesis of positions—we will present the traditional and heretical views as thesis and antithesis, respectively, and follow these with a synthesis of positions.

The Traditional View (Thesis)

This point of view asserts that using sales as the objective for a branded product's marcom effort is unsuitable for two major reasons. First, a brand's sales volume during any given period is the consequence of a host of factors in addition to advertising, sales promotions, and other elements of the program. These include the prevailing economic climate, competitive activity, and all the marketing mix variables used by a brand—its price level, product quality, distribution strategy, and so forth. It is virtually impossible, according to the traditional view, to determine precisely the role advertising or other marcom elements have had in influencing sales in a given period, because marketing communications is just one of many possible determinants of sales.

A second reason that sales response is claimed to represent an unsuitable objective is that marcom's effect on sales is typically delayed, or *lagged.* For example, advertising during any given period does not necessarily influence sales in the current period but may influence sales during later periods. The advertising of a particular automobile model this year may have limited effect on some consumers' purchasing behavior because these consumers are not presently in the market for a new automobile. On the other hand, this year's advertising can influence consumers to select the advertised model next year when they *are* in the market. Thus, advertising may have a decided influence on consumers' brand awareness, product knowledge, expectations, attitudes, and, ultimately, purchase behavior, but this influence may not be evident during the period when the effect of advertising on sales is measured.

Advocates of the traditional view thus argue that it is misguided to use sales as the goal for a particular marcom effort. Their view, fundamentally, is that it is idealistic to set sales as the objective because marcom's exact impact on sales cannot be accurately assessed.

A Heretical View (Antithesis)

On the other hand, some specialists contend that marketing communicators should always state objectives in terms of sales or market share gains and that failure to do so is a cop-out. The logic of this nontraditional, or heretical, view is that marcom's purpose is not just to create brand awareness, convey copy points, influence expectations, or enhance attitudes but rather to generate sales. Thus, according to this position it is always possible to measure, if only vaguely and imprecisely, marcom's effect on sales. Presales, or communication, objectives such as increases in brand awareness are claimed to be "precisely wrong," in contrast to sales measures that are asserted to be "vaguely right."[9]

To better understand the logic of this *vaguely right versus precisely wrong* thinking (or VR versus PW for short), we need to examine closely the constituent oppositional elements: wrong versus right and precise versus vague (see Figure 6.4).

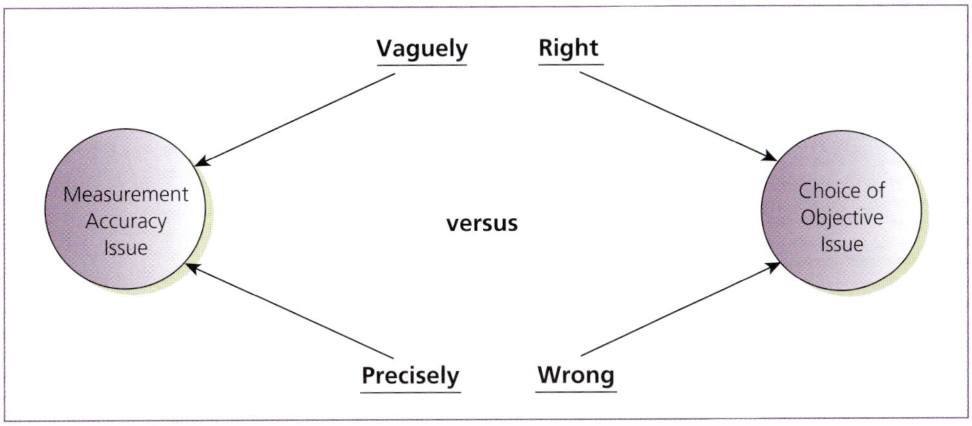

Figure 6.4
The Logic of Vaguely Right versus Precisely Wrong Thinking

First, the issue of *right* versus *wrong* concerns the marcom objective. The heretical view contends that a sales objective is the right objective and that any other objective is wrong. Second, the issue of *precise* versus *vague* refers to the ability to determine whether the marcom program has accomplished its objective. With a communication objective such as brand awareness, it can be determined with relative certainty that any registered change in brand awareness that has occurred since the onset of a marcom campaign is due primarily to the marcom effort. Hence, the amount of influence that, say, advertising has had on brand awareness can be measured *relatively precisely*. However, as described previously, because many factors influence a brand's sales level, the effect that advertising and the other marcom tools have had on sales can be measured only somewhat crudely, imprecisely, or, in other words, *vaguely*.

Thus, the VR versus PW perspective makes the very important point that marketing communicators, and perhaps especially their agencies, might be deceiving themselves into thinking that, say, advertising is effective when it leads to increases in consumer awareness or some other presales objective. Adherents to the vaguely right versus precisely wrong perspective argue that marcom is not accomplishing its job unless sales and market share are increasing. If marcom's sole accomplishment is to create higher awareness levels or bolster brand images, but not to increase sales or market share, then such effort is ineffective according to this nontraditional viewpoint.

An Accountability Perspective (Synthesis)

Although there is no simple resolution as to whether the traditional or heretical view is more correct, one thing is certain: companies and their chief executives and financial officers are increasingly demanding greater *accountability* from marcom programs. Increasing pressure has been placed on agencies to develop campaigns that produce bottom-line results—increases in sales, market share, and return on investment (ROI).[10] Although it is difficult to measure the precise effect marketing communications have on sales, in a climate of increased demands for accountability, it is critical that advertisers and other marketing communicators measure, as best they can, marcom's effect on augmenting a brand's sales, market share, and ROI.

This is not to say that efforts should not also be made to assess whether marcom affects presales goals such as improving brand awareness, driving home copy points, and augmenting attitudes and intentions. The point, instead, is that the measurement of effects should not stop with these measures. Awareness, for example, is a suitable substitute for sales only if there is a direct transformation of enhanced awareness levels into increased sales. This, unfortunately, is rarely the case. A marcom campaign may increase brand awareness by a substantial amount but have limited impact on sales. As such, brand managers should not permit agencies to mislead them into thinking that a campaign has been successful just because brand awareness has improved. Returning to the hierarchy of marcom effects, increased awareness will lead to sales gains only if other rungs on the ladder have been traversed. In sum, the assessment of effectiveness should include, but not be restricted to, presales goals. Setting sales as the objective of a marcom campaign ensures that this ultimate goal will not be neglected.

Marcom Budgeting

Establishing a budget is, in many respects, the most important marcom decision. Budgeting is a critical decision inasmuch as marcom endeavors such as advertising are typically very expensive. (The substantial investment in marketing communications is illustrated in the *Global Focus* insert, which identifies advertising spending by the top-25 global marketers.) Moreover, the implications of spending too little or too much are considerable. If too little is invested in marketing communications, sales volume will not achieve its potential and profits will be lost. If too much is spent, unnecessary expenses will reduce profits. Of course, the dilemma faced by brand managers is determining what spending level is "too little" or how much is "too much." As with most marketing and business decisions, the "devil is in the doing"! Budgeting not only is one of the most important marcom decisions, it also is one of the most complicated, as will be demonstrated in the following discussion of how—in theory—advertising budgets should be set if the objective is to maximize profits. In order to simplify the following discussion, we will restrict the focus just to advertising. It should be realized, however, that the comments about budgeting for advertising apply, in principle, to all marcom elements.

Budgeting in Theory

Budgeting for advertising or other marcom elements is, in theory, a simple process, provided one accepts the premise that the best (optimal) level of any investment is the level that *maximizes profits.* This assumption leads to a simple rule for establishing advertising budgets: continue to invest in advertising as long as the marginal revenue from that investment exceeds the marginal cost.

Some elaboration is needed on this clear-cut rule. According to basic economics, marginal revenue (MR) and marginal cost (MC) are the changes in the total revenue and total cost curves, respectively, that result from a change in a business factor (such as advertising) that affects the levels of total revenue and cost. The profit-maximization rule is a matter of straightforward economic logic: profits are maximized at the point where MR = MC. At any investment level below this point (where MR > MC), profits are not maximized because at a higher level of advertising investment more profit can be earned. Similarly, at any level above this point (where MC > MR), there is a marginal loss. In practical terms, this means that advertisers should continue to increase their advertising investments as long as every dollar of investment yields more than a dollar in revenue.

It is evident from this simple exercise that setting the advertising budget is a matter of answering a series of *if-then* questions—*if* $X are invested in advertising, *then* what amount of revenue will be generated? Because

The Top-25 Global Marketers' Advertising Spending

global focus

Advertising expenditures around the globe are huge. As the following table shows, the top-25 global marketers alone spent over $42 billion on advertising in a recent year. These are all well-known companies whose products and services are available around the world. The huge American company, Procter & Gamble, leads the way with global advertising expenditures of nearly $4.5 billion, but even the smallest advertiser among these top 25 (Viacom) spent over $800 million advertising its services.

Rank	Advertiser	Headquarters	Ad Spending (in $ million)
1	Procter & Gamble	Cincinnati, OH	4,479
2	Unilever	London, UK/Rotterdam, Netherlands	3,315
3	General Motors	Detroit, MI	3,218
4	Toyota Motor Corp.	Toyota City, Japan	2,405
5	Ford Motor Co.	Dearborn, MI	2,387
6	Time Warner	New York, NY	2,349
7	DaimlerChrysler	Auburn Hills, MI/Stuttgart, Germany	1,800
8	L'Oreal	Paris, France	1,683
9	Nestlé	Vevey, Switzerland	1,547
10	Sony Corp.	Tokyo, Japan	1,513
11	Johnson & Johnson	New Brunswick, NJ	1,453
12	Walt Disney Co.	Burbank, CA	1,428
13	Altria Group	New York, NY	1,425
14	Honda Motor Co.	Tokyo, Japan	1,383
15	Volkswagen	Wolfsburg, Germany	1,349
16	Nissan Motor Co.	Tokyo, Japan	1,280
17	Coca-Cola Co.	Atlanta, GA	1,199
18	McDonald's Corp.	Oak Brook, IL	1,183
19	Vivendi Universal	Paris, France	1,176
20	GlaxoSmithKline	Greenford, UK	1,157
21	PepsiCo	Purchase, NY	1,096
22	Pfizer	New York, NY	1,075
23	PSA Peugeot Citroën	Paris, France	904
24	Mars, Inc.	McLean, VA	870
25	Viacom	New York, NY	827
			42,501

Source: "Top 100 Global Marketers," *Advertising Age,* November 10, 2003, 28.

budgets are set before the actual observance of how sales respond to advertising, this requires that the if-then questions be answered before the fact. (Analogously, this would be equivalent to predicting how many fish one would catch on a given day based simply on knowing the number of lures in one's fishing box.) But this is where the complications begin. To employ the profit-maximization rule for budget setting, the advertising decision maker must know the *sales-to-advertising response function* for every brand for which a budgeting decision will be made. Because such knowledge is rarely available, theoretical (profit-maximization) budget setting is an ideal that is generally impractical in the real world of advertising decision making. To fully appreciate this point we need to elaborate on the concept of a sales-to-advertising (S-to-A) response function.

The **sales-to-advertising response function** refers to the relationship between money invested in advertising and the response, or output, of that investment in terms of revenue generated. As with any mathematical function, the S-to-A function maps the relationship between an "output" (in this case, sales revenue) to each meaningful level of an "input" (advertising expenditures). Table 6.1

Table 6.1

Hypothetical Sales-to-Advertising Response Function

(A) Advertising Expenditures ($)	(B) Sales Response ($)	(C) Marginal Cost ($)	(D) Marginal Revenue ($)	(E) Marginal Profit (MR–MC)
1,000,000	5,000,000	NA	NA	NA
1,500,000	5,750,000	500,000	750,000	250,000
2,000,000	6,500,000	500,000	750,000	250,000
2,500,000	7,500,000	500,000	1,000,000	500,000
3,000,000	10,000,000	500,000	2,500,000	2,000,000
3,500,000	10,600,000	500,000	600,000	100,000
4,000,000	11,100,000	500,000	500,000	0
4,500,000	11,500,000	500,000	400,000	–100,000
5,000,000	11,800,000	500,000	300,000	–200,000

demonstrates a hypothetical S-to-A response function by listing a series of advertising expenditures and the corresponding revenue yielded at each ad-expenditure level. Marginal costs, revenues, and profits also are presented in columns C through E of Table 6.1.

Consider that our hypothetical decision maker is contemplating spending anywhere between $1,000,000 and $5,000,000 in advertising a brand during a particular period. Column A in Table 6.1 lists a range of possible advertising expenditures that increase in $500,000 increments starting at $1,000,000 and ending at $5,000,000. Assume, for convenience sake, that it is somehow possible to know precisely how much revenue will be generated at each level of advertising. Column B presents the various levels of sales in response to advertising. If you were to graph the relation between columns A and B, it could be seen that sales respond slowly to advertising until ad expenditures increase above $2,000,000, at which point sales revenue jumps considerably, especially at $3,000,000 invested in advertising. Thereafter, sales response to advertising tapers off substantially. It is easy to determine the level of marginal profit by simply subtracting the marginal cost at each level of advertising from the corresponding marginal revenue. The point of profit maximization is realized at an advertising investment of $4,000,000 where MR = MC = $500,000. Any ad investment below that amount continues to yield marginal profit, whereas any investment above $4,000,000 results in a marginal loss.

If in fact marcom personnel could accurately estimate the S-to-A response function (columns A and B in Table 6.1), then setting the advertising budget to maximize profits would represent the proverbial "piece of cake." However, because the S-to-A response function is influenced by a multitude of factors (such as the creativity of advertising execution, the intensity of competitive advertising efforts, the overall quality of the brand's marketing mix, the state of the economy at the time advertising is undertaken, etc.) and not solely by the amount of advertising investment, it is difficult to know with any certainty what amount of sales a particular level of advertising expenditure will generate. In other words, under most circumstances it is extremely difficult, if not impossible, to derive anything approximating an accurate S-to-A response function.

Hence, if an S-to-A response function is unknown prior to when a budgeting decision is to be made, then a total revenue curve cannot be constructed, and, in turn, marginal revenue cannot be derived at each level of ad investment. In short, applying profit-maximization budgeting requires information that rarely is available. This approach to budgeting represents a theoretical ideal but an infeasible tactic. Necessarily, marcom budget setters turn to more practical approaches for establishing budgets—methods that do not assure profit maximization but that are easy to work with and have the semblance, if not the substance, of being "correct."

Practical Budgeting Methods

In view of the difficulty of accurately predicting sales response to advertising, companies typically set budgets by using judgment, applying experience with analogous situations, and using rules of thumb, or *heuristics*.[11] Although criticized because they do not provide a basis for advertising budget setting that is directly related to the profitability of the advertised brand, these heuristics continue to be widely used.[12] The practical budgeting methods most frequently used by both B2B companies and consumer goods firms in the United States and Europe are the percentage-of-sales, objective-and-task, competitive parity, and affordability methods.[13]

Percentage-of-Sales Budgeting

In using the **percentage-of-sales method**, a company sets a brand's advertising budget by simply establishing the budget as a fixed percentage of *past* (e.g., last year's) or *anticipated* (e.g., next year's) sales volume. Assume, for example, that a company allocates 3 percent of anticipated sales to advertising and that the company projects next year's sales for a particular brand to be $100,000,000. Its advertising budget would be set at $3,000,000.

A survey of the top 100 consumer goods advertisers in the United States found that slightly more than 50 percent employ the percentage-of-anticipated-sales method and 20 percent use the percentage-of-past-sales method.[14] This is to be expected, since budget setting should logically correspond to what a company expects to do in the future rather than being based on what it accomplished in the past.

What percentage of sales revenue do most companies devote to advertising? Actually, the percentage is highly variable. For example, among 200 different categories of products and services, the highest percentage of sales devoted to advertising in a recent year was the miscellaneous publishing industry, which invested 46.3 percent of sales on advertising. Some other categories with double-digit advertising-to-sales ratios were sugar and confectionary products (18.1 percent); cleaners and polish preparations (15.7 percent); wine and brandy (15.6 percent); distilled and blended liquor (15.1 percent); watches, clocks, and parts (15.1 percent); agricultural chemicals (13.7 percent); dolls and stuffed tools (12.9 percent); amusement parks (12.8 percent); and perfume, cosmetics, and toilet preparations (11.2 percent). Most product categories average less than 5 percent advertising-to-sales ratios. These, of course, are industry averages, and advertising-to-sales ratios vary considerably across firms within each industry.[15]

The percentage-of-sales method is frequently criticized as being illogical. Criticism is based on the argument that the method reverses the logical relationship between sales and advertising. That is, the true ordering between advertising and sales is that advertising causes sales, meaning that the level of sales is a function of advertising: *Sales = f (Advertising)*. Contrary to this logical relation, implementing the percentage-of-sales method amounts to reversing the causal order by setting advertising as a function of sales: *Advertising = f (Sales)*.

By this logic and method, when sales are anticipated to increase, the advertising budget also increases; when sales are expected to decline, the budget is reduced. Applying the percentage-of-sales method leads many firms to reduce advertising budgets during economic downswings. However, rather than decreasing the amount of advertising, it may be wiser during these times to increase advertising to prevent further sales erosion. When used blindly, the percentage-of-sales method is little more than an arbitrary and simplistic rule of thumb substituted for what needs to be a sound business judgment. Used without justification, this budgeting method is another application of precisely wrong (versus vaguely right) decision making, as was discussed in the context of setting marcom objectives.[16]

In practice, most sophisticated marketers do *not* use percentage of sales as the sole budgeting method. Instead, they employ the method as an initial pass, or first cut, for determining the budget and then alter the budget forecast depending on the objectives and tasks that need to be accomplished, the amount of competitive ad spending, and the availability of funds.

The Method of Objective-and-Task Budgeting

The **objective-and-task method** is generally regarded as the most sensible and defendable advertising budgeting method. In using this method, advertising decision makers—or those in any other marcom capacity—must specify what role they expect advertising (or some other marcom element) to play for a brand and then set the budget accordingly. The role is typically identified in terms of a communication objective (e.g., increase brand awareness by 20 percent) but could be stated in terms of expected sales volume or market share (e.g., increase market share from 15 to 20 percent).

The objective-and-task method is the advertising budget procedure used most frequently by both B2C and B2B companies. Surveys have shown that over 60 percent of consumer goods companies and 70 percent of B2B companies use this budgeting method.[17] The following steps are involved when applying the objective-and-task method: [18]

1. The first step is to establish specific *marketing objectives* that need to be accomplished, such as sales volume, market share, and profit contribution.

   Consider the marketing and advertising challenge in the United States that faced Volkswagen (VW). Although this once-vaunted automobile company had achieved huge success in the 1960s and 1970s with its VW "Beetle," by the mid-1990s VW was confronted with what perhaps was its final opportunity to recapture the American consumer, who had turned to other imports and domestic models because VW had not kept up with what Americans wanted.[19] Sales of its two leading brands, the Golf and Jetta, had dropped by about 50 percent each compared with sales in prior years. VW's marketing objective (not to be confused with its specific advertising objective, which is discussed next) was, therefore, to substantially increase sales of the Golf and Jetta models and its overall share of the U.S. automobile market—from a low of only about 21,000 Golfs and Jettas to a goal of selling 250,000 VW models in the near future.
2. The second step in implementing the objective-and-task method is to assess the *communication functions* that must be performed to accomplish the overall marketing objectives.

   VW had to accomplish two communication functions to realize its rather audacious marketing objective. First, it had to substantially increase U.S. consumers' awareness of the Golf and Jetta brand names, and, second, it had to establish an image for VW as a company that offers "honest, reliable, and affordable cars." In short, VW had to enhance the Golf's and Jetta's brand equities.
3. The third step is to determine *advertising's role in the total communication mix* in performing the functions established in step 2.

   Given the nature of its products and communication objectives, advertising was a crucial component in VW's mix.
4. The fourth step is to establish specific advertising goals in terms of the levels of *measurable communication response* required to achieve marketing objectives.

   VW might have established goals such as (1) increase awareness of the Jetta from, say, 45 percent of the target market to 75 percent; and (2) expand the percentage of survey respondents who rate VW products as high quality from, say, 15 percent to 40 percent. Both objectives are specific, quantitative, and measurable.

5. The final step is to establish the *budget* based on estimates of expenditures required to accomplish the advertising goals.

   In view of VW's challenging objectives, the decision was made to invest approximately $100 million in an advertising campaign in hopes of gaining higher brand awareness, enhancing the company's image among American consumers, and, ultimately, substantially increasing sales of VW products. The chief executive officer of VW's advertising agency explained that the advertising challenge was "to come up with hard, clear, product-focused ads that give car buyers the kind of information they need to make an intelligent choice."

Budgeting via the Competitive Parity Method

The **competitive parity method** (also called the **match-competitors method**) sets the budget by examining what competitors are doing. A company may learn that its primary competitor is devoting 10 percent of sales to advertising and then adjust its percentage of advertising for its own brand. Armed with information on competitors' spending, a company may decide not merely to match but to exceed the expenditures that competitors are committing to advertising.

Consider the case of Minnesota Mining and Manufacturing (3M) when it introduced the Scotch-Brite Never Rust Soap Pads to compete against the entrenched S.O.S and Brillo brands. Based on research revealing that consumers despised rusty steel wool pads, 3M introduced its Never Rust brand as the first major innovation in the soap pad category since Brillo entered the market in 1917. Knowing it had a super product, 3M greatly outspent its rival brands during the product's introductory year by investing an estimated $30 million on advertising in a category that totaled just $120 million in sales potential. The Scotch-Brite Never Rust brand quickly acquired a major market share against its competitors who, according to one critic, were essentially doing nothing.[20]

The importance of paying attention to what competitors are spending on advertising (or on any other marcom element) cannot be overemphasized. To fully appreciate this point, it is necessary to understand the concepts of share of market (SOM) and share of voice (SOV) and their relationship. These concepts relate to a single product category and consider each brand's revenues (ad expenditures) during, say, a fiscal year compared to the total revenues (ad expenditures) in the category. The ratio of one brand's revenue to total category revenue is that brand's **SOM**. Similarly, the ratio of a brand's advertising expenditures (its "ad spend") to total category advertising expenditures is that brand's **SOV**.

SOV and SOM generally are correlated: brands having larger SOVs also generally realize larger SOMs. For example, Tables 6.2 and 6.3 list the advertising expenditures, SOVs, and SOMs for the top-10 wireless phone brands (Table 6.2)

Table 6.2

Advertising Spend, SOV, and SOM for Top-10 Wireless Phone Brands

Brand	Ad Spend (in $ million)	SOV	SOM
Verizon	$644.2	25.94	24.3
Cingular	411.3	16.56	18.4
AT&T	522.4	21.04	14.8
Sprint	477.9	19.24	9.5
Nextel	160.0	6.44	6.4
Alltell	53.3	2.15	5.6
VoiceStream	203.7	8.20	4.7
U.S. Cellular	8.6	0.35	2.9
Leap	1.9	0.08	0.3
Western	0	0.00	1.0
Totals	$2,483.3	100.00	87.9*

*SOM does not sum to 100 because these data include just the top-10 wireless phone brands.

SOURCE: Reprinted with permission from the June 24, 2002 special edition of Advertising Age. Copyright, Crain Communication Inc., 2002.

Table 6.3

Advertising Spend, SOV, and SOM for Top-10 Beer Brands

Brand	Ad Spend (in $ million)	SOV	SOM
Bud Light	$ 93.6	16.64	16.7
Budweiser	131.7	23.41	16.3
Coors Light	121.4	21.58	8.1
Miller Lite	102.9	18.29	7.7
Natural Light	0.1	0.02	4.0
Busch	9.4	1.67	3.7
Corona Extra	31.9	5.67	3.0
Busch Light	0.1	0.02	2.7
Miller High Life	21.8	3.87	2.6
Miller Genuine Draft	49.7	8.83	2.6
Totals	$562.6	100.00	67.4*

*SOM does not sum to 100 because these data include just the top-10 beer brands.

SOURCE: Reprinted with permission from the June 24, 2002 special edition of *Advertising Age*. Copyright, Crain Communications Inc., 2002.

and the top 10 beer brands (Table 6.3). The correlation between the shares of market and voice for these brands is apparent. That is, brands with larger shares of market typically have larger shares of voice. This does not mean, however, that SOV causes SOM. In fact, the relationship between SOV and SOM is bidirectional: a brand's SOV is partially responsible for its SOM. At the same time, brands with larger SOMs can afford to achieve higher SOVs, whereas smaller-share brands often are limited to relatively small SOVs.

The SOM-SOV relationship is a jousting match of sorts between competitors. If large-market-share brands reduce their SOVs to levels that are too low, they are vulnerable to losing market share to aggressive competitors (such as VoiceStream Wireless in Table 6.2). On the other hand, if brands with relatively small market shares (such as Coors Light and Miller Lite in Table 6.3) become too aggressive, the leading brands (i.e., Anheuser-Busch's Bud Light and Budweiser) are forced to increase their advertising expenditures to offset the competitive challenge.

Figure 6.5 provides a framework for evaluating whether a brand should increase or decrease its advertising expenditures in view both of its share of market (horizontal axis) and of the competitor's share of voice (vertical axis).[21] Although there are numerous possible relations in this two-dimensional space, we can simplify the discussion by considering just four general situations, which in Figure 6.5 are the quadrants, or cells, labeled *A, B, C,* and *D*. Advertising budgeting implications for each situation are as follows:

Figure 6.5

The SOV Effect and Ad Spending Implications

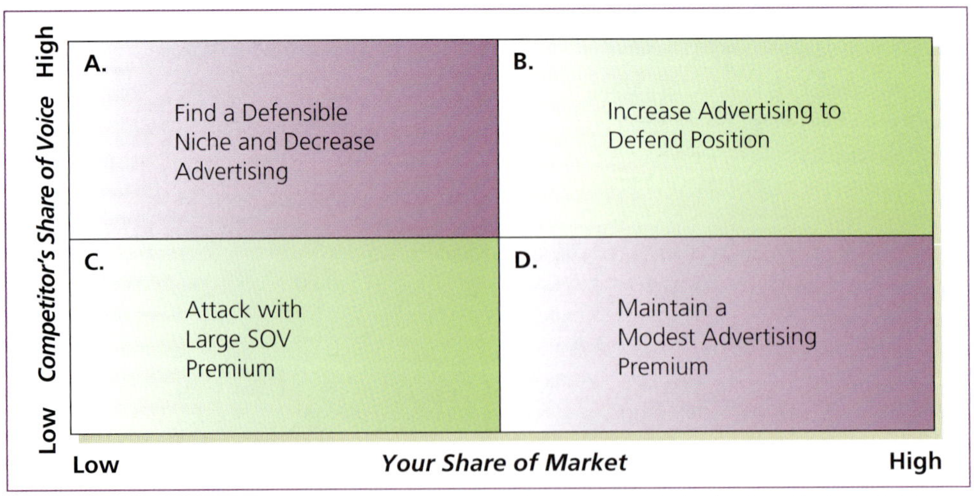

SOURCE: Reprinted by permission of *Harvard Business Review* from, "Ad Spending: Growing Market Share," by James C. Schoer (January–February 1990), p. 48. © 1990 by The Harvard Business School Publishing Corporation; all rights reserved.

- *Cell A:* In this situation, your brand's SOM is relatively low and your competitor's SOV is relatively high. Corona Extra in Table 6.3 exemplifies this situation when compared with Budweiser. The recommendation in such a situation is that the advertiser should consider *decreasing* ad expenditures and find a niche that can be defended against other small-share brands.
- *Cell B:* Your SOM in this situation is relatively high and your competitor has a high SOV. This characterizes Bud Light in Table 6.3 vis-à-vis Coors Light and Miller Lite. Bud Light probably should *increase* its advertising expenditures to defend its present market share position. Failure to do so likely would result in a share loss to these aggressive competitors.
- *Cell C:* In this situation your SOM is low and your competitor's SOV also is low. Nextel and Alltell in Table 6.2 appear to occupy such a relationship. The general recommendation in such a situation is to aggressively attack the low-SOV competitor with a *large SOV premium* vis-à-vis that competitor. This appears to be the tact that Nextel has taken by spending three times more than Alltell. In other words, this is a good opportunity to wrest market share from a moribund or complacent competitor.
- *Cell D:* In this situation you have the attractive position of holding a high market share, but your competitor is nonaggressive and has a relatively low SOV. Hence, it is possible for you to retain your present large share by *maintaining only a modest advertising spending premium* over your competitor.

These simply are guidelines for determining a brand's advertising budget rather than hard-and-fast rules. The general point to be stressed is that advertising budgets—as well as budgets for all other marcom elements—must be set with knowledge of what competitors are doing.[22] This is because the opportunity for growth in market share or the challenge to maintain an existing share position depends in large part on the quality and effectiveness of competitive efforts. Moreover, brand managers should generally set budgets on a market-by-market basis, rather than nationally, because the competitive warfare actually takes place in the individual markets.

It is absolutely essential that advertising budgets be set with an eye to the actions of competitors. This is especially important in view of the fact that a brand's advertising must compete for the consumer's recall with the advertising from competitive brands, a situation of potential *competitive interference.* If "your" brand were the only one advertising in a particular product category, it probably could get by with a substantially smaller ad budget than what is necessitated when competitors also are aggressively advertising their brands. The mere fact of increasing advertising expenditures is *not* guaranteed to have a substantial impact on augmenting a brand's sales volume.[23]

There are reasons to expect that established brands in a product category are less susceptible to the interference from competitive advertising than are less-established and relatively unfamiliar brands. This explains why established brands' SOMs tend to exceed their advertising SOVs, whereas unestablished brands' SOVs often exceed their SOMs.[24] Unfamiliar brands that compete in an environment of advertising clutter are, in effect, at a competitive disadvantage in conveying their points of uniqueness vis-à-vis established brands, though even established brands themselves suffer from the effects of competitive interference.[25] It follows from this discussion that because relatively small-share brands are disadvantaged by competitive advertising, they need to avoid heavily cluttered, traditional media and perhaps turn to alternative marcom tools—such as by using event marketing (discussed in Chapter 20), buzz-generating methods (as discussed in Chapter 7), or any of a number of nontraditional (alternative) advertising media.

Overcoming competitive interference is not just a matter of spending more but rather one of *spending more wisely.* A psychological theory called the *encoding variability hypothesis* explains how advertisers can be smarter spenders.[26] (The term *encoding* refers to transferring information into memory.) The **encoding variability hypothesis**, in its barest details, contends that people's memory for information is enhanced when multiple *pathways*, or connections, are created between the object to be remembered and the information about the object that is to be remembered.

In the case of advertising, the brand represents the object to be remembered, and the brand's attributes and benefits designate the object's information. Advertising can create multiple pathways and thus enhance memory for the advertised information by varying (recall the name *encoding variability hypothesis*) at least two aspects of the advertising execution: (1) the advertising *message* itself, and (2) the advertising *media* in which the message is placed. That is, altering how the ad is presented (its message) and where the ad is placed (its media) should enhance memory for the advertised information and hence mitigate the effect of competitive interference. This results because multiple pathways are created when the same brand is advertised with varied messages or in multiple media. In other words, when Brand X is advertised with a single message in a single medium, just a single pathway is established in memory. When, however, Brand X is advertised in two media, there are two potential pathways established in memory whereby consumers can retrieve information about Brand X. Increasing both the number of message executions and the number of media to convey these messages serves to increase the number of pathway permutations. Increased as well is the probability that consumers will be able to retrieve key information about Brand X when they are in the market for the product category in which that brand competes.

This completes the discussion of the competitive parity "method" of setting advertising budgets. Comments have been somewhat extensive because the effectiveness of your brand's advertising is directly affected by the magnitude and quality of competitive efforts. Larger market share brands tend to gain more from their advertising efforts than do their small-share counterparts, who have difficulty overcoming the competitive clutter of their bigger adversaries. Regardless of a brand's SOM situation, it is absolutely imperative to constantly "scope out" competitive marcom spending to ensure the competition is not increasing its foothold and that you are investing adequately in your own brand.

Budgeting via the Affordability Method

In the so-called **affordability method**, a firm spends on advertising only those funds that remain after budgeting for everything else. In effect, when this "method" is used, advertising, along with other marcom elements, are relegated to a position of comparative insignificance (vis-à-vis other investment options) and are implicitly considered relatively unimportant to a brand's present success and future growth. There are times when marcom funds simply are in short supply due to extreme sales slowdowns. At such times product and brand managers behave rationally when severely cutting back on their advertising spending or other marcom investments. Yet, in many competitive marketing situations it is critical that marcom personnel fight the tendency of financial planners to treat marcom expenditures as an unnecessary evil. The challenge is for brand managers to demonstrate that advertising and other marcom initiatives do, in fact, produce results. Absent compelling evidence, it is understandable when financial officials allocate funds for advertising as a virtual afterthought.

Section Summary

In the final analysis, most advertising budget setters combine two or more methods rather than depending exclusively on any one heuristic. For example, an advertiser may have a fixed percentage-of-sales figure in mind when starting the budgeting process but subsequently adjust this figure in light of anticipated competitive activity, funds availability, and other considerations.

Moreover, brand managers often find it necessary to adjust their budgets during the course of a year, keeping them in line with sales performance. Many advertisers operate under the belief that they should "shoot when the ducks are flying." In other words, advertisers spend most heavily during periods when products are hot and cut spending when funds are short.

Summary

This chapter detailed marcom objective setting and budgeting. Advertising objective setting depends on the pattern of consumer behavior and information that is involved in the particular product category. Toward this end, an introductory section presented a hierarchy-of-effect model of how consumers' respond to marcom messages and discussed the implications for setting objectives. Requirements for developing effective objectives were discussed. A final section described the arguments both promoting and opposing the use of sales volume as the basis for setting objectives.

The chapter concluded with an explanation of the marcom budgeting process. The budgeting decision is one of the most important decisions and also one of the most difficult. The complication arises with the difficulty of determining the sales-to-advertising response function. In theory, budget setting is a simple matter, but the theoretical requirements are generally unattainable in practice. For this reason, practitioners use various rules of thumb (heuristics) to assist them in arriving at satisfactory, if not optimal, budgeting decisions. Percentage-of-sales budgeting and objective-and-task methods are the dominant budgeting heuristics, though maintaining competitive parity and not exceeding funds availability are other relevant considerations when setting budgets.

Discussion Questions

1. It can be argued that creating an expectation is the most important function performed by many advertisements and other marcom messages. Provide examples of two magazine advertisements that illustrate attempts on the part of the advertisers to create expectations. Offer explanations of what expectations the advertisers are attempting to forge in their audiences' minds.
2. Chapter 5 was devoted to the topic of marcom positioning. Offer an explanation of the similarity between the concepts of positioning and creating expectations.
3. Apply the hierarchy-of-marcom-effects framework (Figure 6.1) to explain the evolution of a relationship between two people, beginning with dating and culminating in a wedding.
4. Now do the same thing as in question 3, but use a relatively obscure brand as the basis for your application of Figure 6.1. Along the lines of the Beano illustration (Figure 6.2), identify a relatively unknown brand and explain how marcom efforts must attempt to move prospective customers through the various hierarchy stages.
5. What reasons can you give for certain industries investing considerably larger proportions of their sales in advertising than other industries?
6. Compare the difference between precisely wrong and vaguely right advertising objectives. Give an example of each.
7. Some critics contend that the use of the percentage-of-sales budgeting technique is illogical. Explain.
8. Explain how an advertising budget setter could use two or more budgeting heuristics in conjunction with one another?
9. In your own words, explain why it is extremely difficult to estimate sales-to-advertising response functions.
10. Established brands' shares of market tend to exceed their advertising shares of voice, whereas unestablished brands' SOVs often exceed their SOMs. Using the concept of competitive interference as your point of departure, explain these relationships.
11. Construct a picture to represent your understanding of how the encoding variability hypothesis applies in an advertising context. Use an actual brand for illustration purposes.

ENDNOTES

1. Kenneth Hein, "The Consumer Loyalty Conundrum," *Brandweek*, May 24, 2004, 24–27.
2. Charles H. Patti and Charles F. Frazer, Advertising: *A Decision-Making Approach* (Hinsdale, Ill.: Dryden Press, 1988), 236.
3. It has been claimed that hierarchy models poorly represent the advertising process. See William M. Weilbacher, "Point of View: Does Advertising Cause a 'Hierarchy of Effects'?" *Journal of Advertising Research* 41 (November–December 2001), 19–26; William M. Weilbacher, "Weilbacher Comments on 'In Defense of Hierarchy of Effects,'" *Journal of Advertising Research* 42 (May–June 2002), 48–49; and William M. Weilbacher, "Point of View: How Advertising Affects Consumers," *Journal of Advertising Research* 43 (June 2003), 230–234. For an alternative view, see Thomas E. Barry, "In Defense of the Hierarchy of Effects: A Rejoinder to Weilbacher," *Journal of Advertising Research* 42 (May–June 2002), 44–47. Though the hierarchy model attributes excessive influence to advertising per se, the model does represent a reasonable representation of the effects that all marcom elements have working collectively.
4. For thorough discussions, see Demetrios Vakratsas and Tim Ambler, "How Advertising Works: What Do We Really Know," *Journal of Marketing* 63 (January 1999), 26–43; Thomas E. Barry, "The Development of the Hierarchy of Effects: An Historical Perspective," *Current Issues and Research in Advertising*, vol. 10, ed. James H. Leigh and Claude R. Martin, Jr. (Ann Arbor: Division of Research, Graduate School of Business Administration, University of Michigan, 1987), 251–296; Ivan L. Preston, "The Association Model of the Advertising Communication Process," 11, no. 2 (1982), 3–15; and Ivan L. Preston and Esther Thorson, "Challenges to the Use of Hierarchy Models in Predicting Advertising Effectiveness," in *Proceedings of the 1983 Convention of the American Academy of Advertising*, ed. Donald W. Jugenheimer (Lawrence, Kans.: American Academy of Advertising, 1983).
5. Adapted from Larry Light and Richard Morgan, *The Fourth Wave: Brand Loyalty Marketing* (New York: Coalition for Brand Equity, American Association of Advertising Agencies, 1994), 25.
6. For further reading on the nature and role of brand loyalty, see Richard L. Oliver, "Whence Consumer Loyalty?", *Journal of Marketing* 63 (special issue 1999), 33–44; and Arjun Chaudhuri and Morris B. Holbrook, "The Chain of Effects from Brand Trust and Brand Affect to Brand Performance: The Role of Brand Loyalty," *Journal of Marketing* 65 (April 2001), 81–93.
7. Carl F. Mela, Sunil Gupta, and Donald R. Lehmann, "The Long-Term Impact of Promotion and Advertising on Consumer Brand Choice," *Journal of Marketing Research* 34 (May 1997), 248–261.
8. The following discussion is influenced by the classic work on advertising planning and goal setting by Russell Colley. His writing, which came to be known as the DAGMAR approach, set a standard for advertising objective setting. See Russell H. Colley, *Defining Advertising Goals for Measured Advertising Results* (New York: Association of National Advertisers, 1961).
9. Leonard M. Lodish, *The Advertising and Promotion Challenge: Vaguely Right or Precisely Wrong?* (New York: Oxford University Press, 1986), chap. 5.
10. For example, Kevin J. Clancy and Peter C. Krieg, *Counter-Intuitive Marketing: Achieve Great Results Using Uncommon Sense* (New York: Free Press, 2000), chap. 18; and Kevin J. Clancy, "The Coming Revolution in Advertising: Ten Developments Which Will Separate Winners from Losers," *Journal of Advertising Research* (February/March 1990), 47–52.
11. Gary L. Lilien, Alvin J. Silk, Jean-Marie Choffray, and Murlidhar Rao, "Industrial Advertising Effects and Budgeting Practices," *Journal of Marketing* 40 (January 1976), 21.
12. J. Enrique Bigné, "Advertising Budgeting Practices: A Review," *Journal of Current Issues and Research in Advertising* 17 (fall 1995), 17–32; Fred S. Zufryden, "How Much Should Be Spent for Advertising a Brand?" *Journal of Advertising Research* (April/May 1989), 24–34.
13. The extensive use of the percentage-of-sales and objective-and-task methods in an industrial context has been documented by Lilien et al., "Industrial Advertising Effects," while support in a consumer context is provided by Kent M. Lancaster and Judith A. Stern, "Computer-Based Advertising Budgeting Practices of Leading U.S. Consumer Advertisers," *Journal of Advertising* 12, no. 4 (1983), 6. A thorough review of the history of advertising budgeting research is provided in Bigné, "Advertising Budget Practices."
14. Lancaster and Stern, "Computer-Based Advertising."
15. All ratios are based on "2001 Advertising-to-Sales Ratios for the 200 Largest Ad Spending Industries," *Advertising Age*, September 17, 2001, 20. These data are based on research by Schonfeld & Associates and published by that company in "Advertising Ratios & Budgets," 2001.
16. See Lodish, *The Advertising and Promotion Challenge*, chap. 6.
17. Charles H. Patti and Vincent J. Blasko, "Budgeting Practices of Big Advertisers," *Journal of Advertising Research* 21 (December 1981), 23–29; Vincent J. Blasko and Charles H. Patti, "The Advertising Budgeting Practices of Industrial Marketers," *Journal of Marketing* 48 (fall 1984), 104–110. See also C. L. Hung and Douglas C. West, "Advertising Budgeting Methods in Canada, the UK and the USA," *International Journal of Advertising* 10, no. 3 (1991), 239–250.
18. Adapted from Lilien et al., "Industrial Advertising and Budgeting," 23.
19. This description is based on Kevin Goldman, "Volkswagen Has a Lot Riding on New Ads," *The Wall Street Journal*, January 31, 1994, B5.
20. Eben Shapiro, "Minnesota Mining's Wool Pads Grab Sizable Chunk of Business," *The Wall Street Journal*, January 13, 1994, B6.
21. Adapted from James C. Schroer, "Ad Spending: Growing Market Share," *Harvard Business Review* 68 (January/February 1990), 48. See also John Philip Jones, "Ad Spending: Maintaining Market Share," *Harvard Business Review* 68 (January/February 1990), 38–42.
22. For a slightly different perspective on how the relationship between competitors affects ad budgeting, see Boonghee Yoo and Rujirutana Mandhachitara, "Estimating Advertising Effects on Sales in a Competitive Setting," *Journal of Advertising Research* 43 (September 2003), 310–321.
23. Leonard M. Lodish, Magid Abraham, Stuart Kalmenson, Jeanne Livelsberger, Beth Lubetkin, Bruce Richardson, and Mary Ellen Stevens, "How T.V. Advertising Works: A Meta-Analysis of 389 Real World Split Cable T.V. Advertising Experiments," *Journal of Marketing Research* 32 (May 1995), 125–139.
24. Jones, "Ad Spending: Maintaining Market Share."
25. Robert J. Kent and Chris T. Allen, "Competitive Interference Effects in Consumer Memory for Advertising: The Role of Brand Familiarity," *Journal of Marketing* 58 (July 1994), 97–105; Robert J. Kent, "How Ad Claim Similarity and Target Brand Familiarity Moderate Competitive Interference Effects in Memory for Advertising," *Journal of Marketing Communications* 3 (December 1997), 231–242. For evidence that established brands suffer from competitive interference, see Anand Kumar and Shanker Krishnan, "Memory Interference in Advertising: A Replication and Extension," *Journal of Consumer Research* 30 (March 2004), 602–611.
26. H. Rao Unnava and Deepak Sirdeshmukh, "Reducing Competitive Ad Interference," *Journal of Marketing Research* 31 (August 1994), 403–411.

PART 3
Marcom for New Products, Store Signage, and Point-of-Purchase Communications

The chapters in Part Three deal with the role of marketing communications in successfully introducing new products, and the functions of brand names, packages, store signage, and point-of-purchase communications in introducing new products and facilitating the growth of mature products. Chapter 7 looks at marcom's role in achieving acceptance for new products: how marketing communicators facilitate product adoption and diffusion. Also covered is the role of marketing communications in stimulating word-of-mouth influence and creating "buzz."

Chapter 7 also provides detailed descriptions of the initial elements responsible for a brand's image: brand name, logo, and package. This section explores the requirements for a good brand name, the steps involved in arriving at a good name, and the role of logos. Also presented is a useful framework—the VIEW model—that describes the visual, informational, emotional, and functional features that determine packaging success.

Chapter 8 examines two important aspects of firms' marcom programs that typically receive little coverage in marketing communications texts: out-of-store signage (both off- and on-premises signage) and in-store signage in the form of point-of-purchase communications. Billboard advertising is the major OOH medium, and chapter coverage presents the various strengths and limitations of this form of advertising. Also described is how OOH audience size and characteristics are measured along with a case study of billboard effectiveness. A unique section devoted to on-premises business signage describes an important but overlooked topicæthe use of store signage to attract attention and draw customers to retail businesses.

The final topic treated in Chapter 8 is point-of-purchase (P-O-P) advertising. The point-of-purchase is the critical point where the brand name, logo, and package come face to face with the customer. Expanded investment in this marcom component is explained in terms of the valuable functions that P-O-P performs for consumers, manufacturers, and retailers. The chapter devotes considerable attention to the various forms of P-O-P communications, presents results from the POPAI Consumer Buying Habits Study, and provides evidence regarding the impact displays can have in increasing a brand's sales volume.

CHAPTER 7

Facilitation of Product Adoption, Brand Naming, and Packaging

Marcom Challenge: Absolut Wanna Be Becomes Absolute Flop

Vodka is a distilled spirit that traditionally has been associated with eastern European countries such as Poland and Russia. Until the late 1970s the famous Russian brand Stolichnaya (a.k.a. Stoli) was the only premium-priced vodka brand that most non–eastern European consumers considered buying. But then, around 1980, an unknown brand from Sweden named Absolut literally revolutionized vodka marketing. This brand had a radical package design (a clear bottle with blue lettering) compared with traditional vodka brands, which typically were cylinidrically shaped. Moreover, it was considerably higher priced than all brands except the classic Stoli. On top of this, it was from Sweden, a country not known for vodka! Yet largely driven by an excellent brand name (Absolut, which sounds and reads like the word *absolute*, suggests a product that is complete, perfect, pure, and supreme), a unique and memorable package design, and an outstanding advertising campaign (see Figure 7.1 for a montage of Absolut advertisements), Absolut became a category leader. And it held this position for nearly two decades.

An interesting development in the vodka category started in the mid-1990s and continues to this day: a number of vodka companies began stealing market share from Absolut. They did this by developing quality products that had interesting brand names (e.g., Belvedere, Grey Goose, Ketel One, Three Olives), appealing and eye-catching bottles, and super-premium prices as much as twice that of Absolut. Some of Absolut's loyal users began switching to the new brands. Executives at Swedish-based V&S Vin & Sprit AB (the parent company of Absolut vodka) and its North America distributor, Seagrams, knew it was time to develop a new brand to capture lost sales and profits.

The V&S–Seagram team launched a new brand that sold at retail for $30 a bottle. Executives knew that the brand name and package design for this new brand would play instrumental roles in its successful launch and profitability. Numerous English and Swedish words were placed before focus group participants. The name ultimately selected was Sundsvall, which is the name of a small town in Sweden. The packaging decision entailed numerous meetings conducted over several months and high-level give-and-take sessions between the V&S and Seagram participants. V&S executives favored an understated, clear-bottle design, whereas Seagram's representatives preferred a sleek, frosted bottle. The eventual selection was a bottle with a clear barrel and an orange shrink-wrapped top.

With the name and package selected and the price strategy determined, Sundsvall was ready for launch. This required generating buzz for the brand (as will be discussed later in the chapter) by appealing to innovators (entertainment celebrities, food and beverage writers, etc.) and gaining the support of influential bartenders in major markets who determine where on store shelves to place different brands and which brands to recommend to customers. Unfortunately for the V&S–Seagram team, a "tipping point" (a concept discussed later in the chapter) never occurred for Sundsvall. In addition to not achieving adequate retail distribution and having to compete in an overcrowded product category at the time of launch, could it be that the brand name, Sundsvall, simply did not register positively with either bartenders or consumers and thus did not facilitate spontaneous "bar calls" ("I'll have a Sundsvall vodka") or resonate positively with customers while making brand selection decisions from retail outlets? And was the bottle sufficiently eye-catching and appealing to attract attention and generate positive brand associations? Perhaps not. One executive characterized the package design as "difficult to see. It wasn't invisible, but it was too discrete where it was competing."

After months of disappointing sales, Sundsvall was eventually yanked from the market. As with many other new-product failures, no single factor can fully explain why the brand did not achieve its financial objectives. However, it is more than a remote possibility that the brand name and package may have been poorly chosen. Because hindsight always is better than foresight, it is only fair to conclude that the rationale underlying the introduction of the Sundsvall brand probably was sound but that the marketing execution was perhaps not up to the challenging requirements for product success in a somewhat saturated and highly competitive product category.[1]

Figure 7.1

A Montage of Absolut Advertisements

CHAPTER OBJECTIVES

1. Appreciate marcom's role in facilitating the introduction of new products.
2. Explain the innovation-related characteristics that influence adoption of new products.
3. Understand efforts employed by marketing communicators to manage the diffusion process.
4. Appreciate word-of-mouth communications in facilitating new-product adoption.
5. Be familiar with the role of "buzz" in facilitating product adoption.
6. Understand the role of brand naming and the requirements for developing effective brand names.
7. Explain the activities involved in the brand-naming process.
8. Appreciate the role of logos.
9. Describe the various elements underlying the creation of effective packages.
10. Explain the VIEW model for evaluating package effectiveness.
11. Describe a five-step package design process.

Overview

Introducing a stream of new products is absolutely essential to most companies' success and long-term growth. Despite the huge investments and concerted efforts required to introduce new products and services, many are never successful. Though it is impossible to pinpoint the exact percentage of new ideas and products that eventually flop, failure rates typically range between 35 to 45 percent, and the rate may be increasing.[2] This chapter's purpose is to explain marcom's role in facilitating successful new-product introductions and in reducing the product failure rate. Brand names, logos, and packages are critical to all these efforts, and proactive efforts by brand marketers to stimulate word-of-mouth influence (buzz) are critical to new product success.

This chapter starts by examining general factors that influence the likelihood that new products will be rapidly adopted and diffused among markets of potential customers. A separate section is devoted to the role of word-of-mouth influence and the proactive efforts by brand marketers to stimulate enthusiasm for new products. Next, examined in separate sections, are considerations involved in developing brand names and designing packages, both of which play key roles in influencing new product success.

Marcom and New Product Adoption

This section explores factors that determine product adoption rates for low-tech as well as high-tech products and describes actions marcom personnel can take to manage the diffusion of new product adoption. It is appropriate to initiate this discussion by conceptualizing the process by which final consumers of marketers' efforts (B2C marketing) and the customers of B2B marketing activities become aware of new products and subsequently try and repetitively purchase these products.[3] The notions of trial and repeat-purchase are particularly apt for inexpensive consumer packaged goods, but even expensive durable goods like automobiles are tried via test-drives and repeat-purchased at longer inter-purchase rates than characterizes consumer goods. Likewise, products purchased by B2B customers also are subject to being tried and repeat-purchased.

The New-Product Adoption Process Model in Figure 7.2 indicates with circles the three main stages through which an individual becomes an adopter of a new or even an established product. These stages are the awareness, trier, and repeater classes, with the term *class* referring to a group, or category, of consumers and customers who occupy the same stage with respect to whether they are simply aware of a brand, have tried it, or are repeat purchasers of that brand. The blocks surrounding the circles are mostly marcom tools that play a role in moving consumers from initial awareness, through trial, and ultimately to becoming repeat purchasers. Please note these tools are designated (in parentheses) as being used primarily in the B2C or B2B domains, or both. The advertisement in Figure 7.3 for DHL, a company that delivers packages and serves the shipping needs of businesses, will facilitate the subsequent discussion.

The first step in facilitating adoption is to make consumers aware of a product's existence. Figure 7.2 illustrates four determinants of the **awareness class**: free samples and coupons, trade shows and personal selling, advertising, and distribution. The first three of these are distinctly marcom activities, and the fourth, distribution, is closely allied in that point-of-purchase materials and shelf placement are aspects of a brand's distribution. Successful introduction of new products typically requires an effective advertising campaign, widespread product distribution backed up with point-of-purchase materials, and, in the case of inexpen-

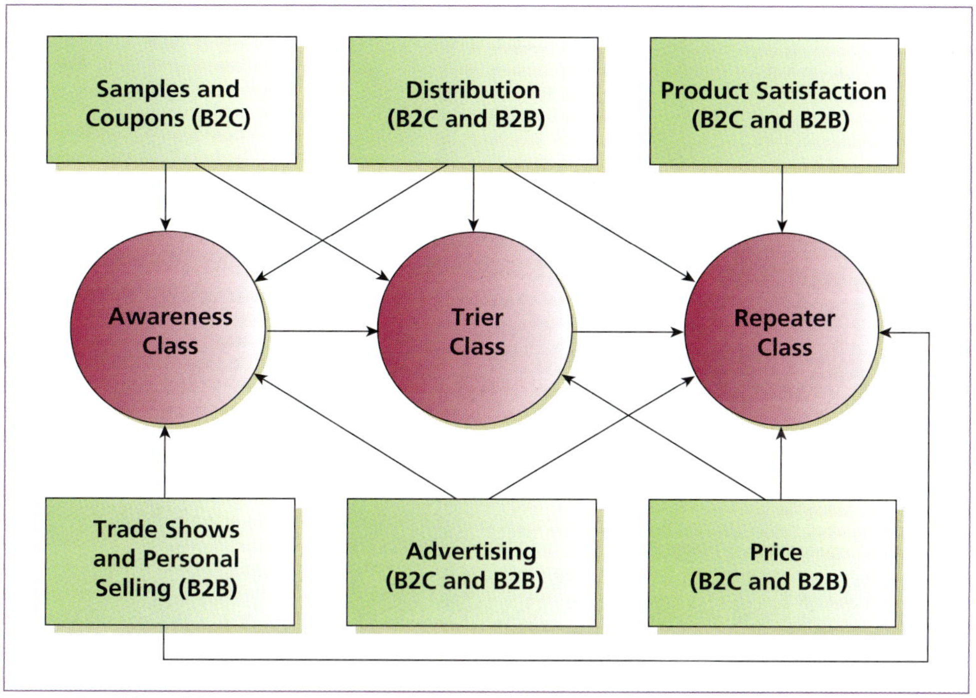

Figure 7.2

New-Product Adoption Process Model

SOURCE: Adapted from Chakravarthi Narasimhan and Subrata K. Sen, "New Product Models for Test Market Data," *Journal of Marketing* 47 (Winter 1983), 13, 14, with permission from the Marketing Association.

sive packaged goods, extensive sampling and couponing. In B2B marketing, trade shows and personal sales efforts are invaluable means of making prospective customers aware of new offerings. Though not shown in the New-Product Adoption Process Model, word-of-mouth communication, a form of free advertising, also plays a significant role in facilitating product awareness. A later section will describe, in detail, efforts by marketing communicators to build buzz surrounding the introduction of new products.

Once customers and consumers become aware of a new product or brand, there is an increased probability they will actually try the new offering.[4] Coupons, distribution, and price are the factors that affect the **trier class** (see Figure 7.2). That is, the availability of cents-off coupons, wide product distribution on retailer shelves and displays, and lower prices (such as introductory, low-price offers) all facilitate trial of new products. For durable goods, trial may involve test-driving a new automobile or visiting an electronics store to acquire hands-on experience with, say, a new digital camera, music player, or computer. In the case of inexpensive packaged goods, trial more likely involves purchasing a new brand to test its performance characteristics—its taste, cleaning ability, or whatever attributes and benefits are pertinent to the product category. A business may try DHL's shipping service (see Figure 7.3) on an experimental basis to learn whether this company is easy to deal with, its offering is priced appropriately, and it outperforms competitors in terms of delivery time and shipping services.

Repeat purchasing, demonstrated by the **repeater class**, is a function of five primary forces: personal selling, advertising, price, distribution, and product satisfaction. That is, customers and consumers are more likely to continue to purchase a particular brand if personal sales efforts and advertising continue to remind them about the brand, if the price is considered reasonable, if the product or service is easily accessed, and if product quality is deemed satisfactory. On this last point, it is undeniable that marcom efforts are critical to boosting repeat purchasing but cannot make up for poor product performance. This is to say that consumer satisfaction with a brand is *the* major determinant of repeat purchasing. Consumers typically will not stick with brands that fail to live up to expectations.

Figure 7.3 Advertisement Illustrating the Product Adoption Process

Product Characteristics That Facilitate Adoption

Discussion to this point has identified several marcom activities that affect product adoption. Explanation now turns to five product-related characteristics that influence consumers' attitudes toward new products and hence their likelihood of adopting new products. These are a product's: (1) relative advantage(s), (2) compatibility, (3) complexity, (4) trialability, and (5) observability.[5] Each of these characteristics is discussed in detail in the following sections.

Relative Advantage

This represents the degree to which consumers perceive a product innovation as being better than existing alternatives with respect to a specific attribute or benefit. **Relative advantage** is a function of consumer perception and is *not* a matter of whether a product is actually better by objective standards.

Relative advantage is positively correlated with an innovation's adoption rate: the greater an innovation's relative advantage(s) compared to existing offerings, the more rapid the rate of adoption, all other considerations held constant. (Conversely, a new brand's relative *dis*advantage(s)—high price, difficulty of learning how to use a new product, and so on—will retard the rate of adoption.) In general, a relative advantage exists to the extent that a new product offers (1) better performance compared to other options, (2) savings in time and effort, or (3) immediacy of reward.

Consider the following illustrations of relative advantages (also see the *Global Focus* for another illustration of relative advantages for washing machines in developing countries):

- Digital cameras allow photographers the opportunity to view images prior to committing them to hard-copy photographs. Moreover, these images can be transmitted electronically in digitized form, thus avoiding the expense, hassle, and time associated with snail mailing photographs.
- Pfizer's Listerine PocketPaks are dissolving mouthwash strips. In addition to the advantage of portability, PocketPaks kill germs that cause bad breath (unlike breath mints and gum).
- The sweetener product Splenda affords consumers the distinct relative advantage of tasting like sugar but being calorie free.
- Hybrid automobiles (such as discussed in Chapter 3) offer meaningful relative advantages in the form of being more fuel efficient and environmentally friendly than conventional, fully gasoline-fueled automobiles.
- Flat-screen, plasma TVs take up less space, weigh less, and provide better resolution than conventional televisions. This technology is expensive for most consumers, which explains the slow rate of adoption in households, but bars and restaurants have shifted in droves from conventional to flat-screen TVs.[6]
- Low-carbohydrate food and beverage products allow dieting consumers to restrict their intake of carbs, but these products typically don't taste as good as the "real" item.
- Products in the so-called quick clean category have exploded in recent years. This includes items such as Procter & Gamble's Swiffer, which is a home mopping system that allows the consumer to easily mop hard surfaces by placing dirt-grabbing electrostatic sheets on pads that are attached to mop handles. The most recent Swiffer product is called Swiffer Sweep+Vac, which includes a small vacuum attached to a regular Swiffer for purposes of capturing bigger objects like dry cereal.
- Innovations such as Rio Audio's MP3 player and Apple's iPod offer huge music storage capacity and portability. It is little wonder that MP3's and iPod's successes have generated a slew of competitors including offerings from the likes of Samsung Electronics and Sony.

global focus

Washing Machines for the Masses in Brazil, China, and India

Millions of people throughout the developing world wash clothes the old-fashioned way: either with washboards and soap or with machines that are not fully automatic. (Most readers of this text never have seen such a machine, but the author and his contemporaries remember seeing their mothers wash the laundry in electric-powered machines that required individual items be manually "fed" through rollers to remove excess water prior to hanging the items on lines for drying.) This still is how it is done in much of the world. But Whirlpool Corp. has designs on changing the model of how people do their laundry. The secret to success is one of designing fully automatic washing machines that are functional and aesthetically appealing, yet inexpensive enough so that the masses can afford to purchase them. These relative advantages over traditional (non-automatic washer) solutions to doing the laundry will likely yield huge profits for Whirlpool in its global undertaking to alter laundry-washing behavior.

Whirlpool has designed a machine named Ideale for distribution in Brazil, China, India, and other developing countries. The retail price is in the range of \$150–\$200, which compares to the average automatic washer in the United States, priced at nearly \$500. About one-quarter of Brazilian households have automatic washing machines, whereas the penetration levels in China and India are less than 10 percent. Importantly, Whirlpool has designed its washing machines to uniquely fit the consumption habits and preferences in each country. For example, in Brazil consumers are in the habit of washing floors beneath furniture and appliances; accordingly, the Ideale for Brazil was made to stand high on four legs. Also, because Brazilian homemakers want to see the machine operate, Whirlpool equipped the Ideale with a transparent, acrylic lid. In China, families often have shelves above their washers, so the tops of Whirlpool machines for that country were designed to be foldable. Also, because space constraints in China mean that many families locate their appliances in the living room, it was important that the washing machine for consumers in that country be aesthetically appealing. In India, washers often are placed in a position of pride in the home but are moved around the house; thus, washing machines for that market have caster wheels for easy mobility. Color preferences also vary from country to country. In Brazil, the Ideale comes only in white because Brazilians associate white with cleanliness. But Chinese dislike white appliances because they show dirt and grime, so Whirlpool produces light blue and gray machines for consumers in that country. Consumers in India can choose among white, blue, or green machines.

Source: Adapted from Miriam Jordan and Jonathan Karp, "Machines for the Masses," *The Wall Street Journal Online*, December 9, 2003, http://online.wsj.com.

- Finally, consider the case of children's consumption of milk in fast-food restaurants. Outlets such as Wendy's, McDonald's, and Denny's have experienced huge increases in milk sales. These increases have resulted, in large part, because dairy companies have begun packaging milk in colorful plastic containers rather than in the traditional paper cartons. Children are increasingly switching from soft drinks to milk when frequenting fast-food outlets.

Compatibility

The degree to which an innovation is perceived to fit into a person's way of doing things is termed **compatibility**. In general, a new product is more compatible to the extent that it matches consumers' needs, personal values, beliefs, and past consumption practices. Incompatible products are those that are perceived as incongruent with how customers and consumers have learned to satisfy their consumption needs. For example, although horse meat is an alternative to beef in European countries such as Belgium, France, Italy, and Spain, it is hard to imagine North American consumers converting from their deeply ingrained preference for beef to this lean, sweet-tasting alternative.

Consider also the traditional manner by which wine bottles have been "corked." For hundreds of years real cork—which is the outer bark of oak trees—has provided the stopper material for wine bottles. Alternatives to real cork now are beginning to serve as substitutes, including plastic stoppers and even twist-off metal caps. Although these newer types of stoppers are as effective as cork (and may even be superior because they cannot contaminate wine with the sometimes musty smell of cork), many traditionalists consider non-cork stoppers unacceptable. In short, in many people's minds, cork stands for fine wine, whereas wines plugged with non-cork stoppers are considered cheap substitutes.

Generally speaking, adoption rapidity is increased with greater compatibility. Innovations that are compatible with consumers' existing situations are less risky, are more meaningful, and require less effort to incorporate into one's consumption lifestyle. Hybrid automobiles probably will experience a relatively slow rate of adoption because the idea of a gasoline-electric hybrid automobile is somewhat incompatible with consumers' concept of how an automobile should be energized.

Sometimes the only way to overcome perceptions of incompatibility is through heavy advertising to convince consumers that a new way of doing things truly is superior to an existing solution. Consider the case of ultra-high-temperature (UHT) milk, which is a heat-treated product that lasts up to six months on the shelf and tastes the same as "regular" milk. Shelf-stable milk is standard fare throughout much of Europe and Latin America with market shares of well over 50 percent in many countries. In the United States, however, sales of UHT are negligible. Italy's Parmalat brand entered the massive U.S. market with plans of changing America's preference to shelf-stable milk. However, after more than a decade on the U.S. market, Parmalat's market share pales in comparison to sales of refrigerated milk. The problem is one of incompatibility: Americans are wedded to refrigerated milk. Parmalat, along with other UHT producers, will have to advertise heavily to stand any chance of large numbers of American consumers regularly purchasing UHT milk instead of the conventional refrigerated variety. Of course, because success breeds further success, products that suffer from images of incompatibility often do not have sufficient funds to overcome their status.

Makers of soy "milk" also have recognized that they must advertise aggressively to overcome incompatibility problems. Although soy drinks possess the relative advantage of being healthier than traditional cow's milk, many consumers eschew purchasing soy drinks due to thoughts that a product made from a vegetable would probably taste strange and ruin, rather than enhance, the taste of milk-related products such as cereal. In an attempt to overcome incompatibility problems, makers of soy milk brands such as Silk and Great Awakenings have substantially increased their ad budgets in the hopes of attracting new users to the category.

At the time of this writing it was recently announced that German footwear manufacturer Adidas–Salomon AG was in process of launching a new line of running shoes called Adidas 1, which were to be priced at approximately $250 per pair. This high-tech shoe contains a microprocessor under the arch of the shoe to measure compression of the runner's stride. Using software that calculates whether a shoe is too firm or too soft, messages are sent to cables in the shoe to make appropriate adjustments around the foot. In effect, the runner obtains customized cushioning depending on the running terrain and his or her size and speed. This obvious relative advantage is offset by the disadvantage of high price. Yet, the factor that may most retard rapid and extensive product adoption is that this technology requires extra work from runners. That is, runners can either run the microprocessor, which requires battery replacements after approximately 100 hours, or he or she can adjust the cushioning manually by pushing buttons located under Adidas's famous three-stripes design. In either event, extra "work" is required. An industry expert who doubts the product will be a big success claims that "runners just want to put the shoe on and go; they don't want to think about what to do with it."[7] His claim, in other words, is that this new technology is incompatible with the low-tech running shoes that experienced runners are used to wearing.

Complexity

Complexity refers to an innovation's degree of perceived difficulty. The more difficult an innovation is to understand or use, the slower the rate of adoption. Home computers were adopted slowly because many homeowners perceived them too difficult to understand and use. The adoption of programmable TVs with hard drives (e.g., TiVo) also has been slower than expected, likely because many consumers fear they will be unable to successfully use the technology.

The success of Apple's iMac in the late 1990s attests to the value of making product use simple. The iMac was virtually an instant success upon its introduction, selling about one-quarter of a million units in the first six weeks after launch and becoming one of the hottest products on the market during the holiday season. Although a very good personal computer, the iMac's retail price at $1,299 was, if anything, at a premium level compared to functionally competitive PCs. Indeed, in terms of specifications, the original iMac was nothing exceptional, with only 32MB of RAM, a 4GB hard drive, and a 233-MHz processing chip. However, the iMac's design *was* special. With a choice of five novel colors, translucent case, one-piece unit, rounded (versus angular) shape, and pre-installed software, the iMac was unlike any personal computer that consumers had seen. Beyond its unique design, the iMac was perhaps the most user-friendly computer to ever hit the market. Essentially, the user simply had to plug it in and turn it on—no setup, no hassle. This perhaps explains why nearly one-third of the iMac buyers were first-time computer owners who apparently believed that the iMac did not exceed their threshold for complexity.[8]

Trialability

The extent to which an innovation can be used on a limited basis prior to making a full-blown commitment is referred to as **trialability**. In general, products that lend themselves to trialability are adopted at a more rapid rate. Trialability is tied closely to the concept of *perceived risk.* Test-driving new automobiles, eating free items of food products at local supermarkets, and consuming mail-delivered samples of new grocery products all represent instances of consumers trying new products on an experimental basis. The trial experience serves to reduce the consumer's risk of being dissatisfied with a product after having permanently committed to it through an outright purchase. As will be discussed in detail in Chapter 18, sampling is an incomparable promotional method for encouraging trial by reducing the risk that accompanies spending money on a new, untried product.

Facilitating trial is typically more difficult with durable products than with inexpensive packaged goods. Automobile companies allow consumers to take test-drives, but what do you do if you are, say, a computer manufacturer or a lawn mower maker? If you are creative, you do what companies like Apple Computer and John Deere did in novel efforts to give people the opportunity to try their products. Apple developed a "Test Drive a Macintosh" promotion that gave interested consumers the opportunity to try the computer in the comfort of their own homes for 24 hours at no cost. John Deere offered a 30-day free test period during which prospective mower purchasers could try the mower and then return it, no questions asked, if not fully satisfied. Ford Motor Company, the owner of British-based Land Rover, initiated a unique money-back offer to encourage purchases of Land Rover's Discovery Series II model of SUV. Prospective buyers could drive the new SUV for 30 days or 1,500 miles and then return it for a full refund if they were dissatisfied with its performance.

Observability

Observability is the degree to which the product user or other people can observe the positive effects of new-product usage. The more a consumption behavior can be sensed (seen, smelled, etc.), the more observable, or *visible,* it is said to be. Thus, wearing a new perfume with a subtle fragrance is less "visible" than adopting an avant-garde hairstyle, and driving an automobile with a new type of engine is less visible than driving one with a unique body design such as a BMW Mini Cooper or a Hummer. In general, innovations that are high in observability lend themselves to rapid adoption if they also possess relative advantages, are compatible with consumption lifestyles, and so on. Products whose benefits lack observability are generally slower in adoptability.[9]

The important role of product observability is illustrated by Nike's long-standing use of showing the technology in its athletic shoes. One version of this practice is the Nike Shox. Highly visible inserts in the heel of the shoe convey the product benefits of stability, cushioning, and increased lift through tiny shock absorbers ("shox") that provide spring. Nike could have designed its shoes so that the shock absorbers were concealed from observation; instead, the company made the feature conspicuous by "exposing the technology" and, in so doing, provided itself with the easily communicable point that Nike shoes enable greater leaping ability than do competitive brands. Nike's exposing-the-technology practice recognizes the basic fact that consumers are more likely to adopt a new product when its advantages are observable.

Because status from brand ownership is one form of consumption advantage, albeit an advantage high in symbolism rather than functionality, it perhaps is not surprising that many well-known brands of fashion wear plaster the outside of clothing with prominent brand names and logos that are observable to the world. Consumers have become walking billboards for designer brands, a case of observability incarnate. This trend has now been extended to the vehicle tire category where tires display university names such as the Florida Gators. Hey, if fans are willing to paint their faces during game days with Gators, Tiger Paws, Dogs, or whatever their mascot is, why not emblazon tires with school names?

Quantifying the Adoption-Influencing Characteristics

To this point we have described each of the five factors that influence the likelihood that a new product will be adopted and the rate at which it will occur. It would be useful to go beyond mere description and have a procedure whereby the five characteristics could be quantified on a case-by-case basis to determine whether a proposed product concept stands a good chance of being successful. Figure 7.4 illustrates a procedure for accomplishing this goal. Each of the five characteristics is rated, first in terms of its *importance* in determining the success of the proposed new product and then with respect to how well the new product performs on each characteristic, its *evaluation* score.

For illustration purposes, consider the issue of hair removal. Many women (and some men) go to doctors and salons to have unwanted hair removed by a laser procedure. Hair removal via this procedure stunts the growth of hair follicles by using light at a frequency and wavelength that is absorbed by the follicles but not by the surrounding skin tissue. Imagine how popular such a procedure would be if a product were available for in-home use. Or would it? Well, Gillette, a company famous for its razors and blades is betting that such a product will be highly demanded. Gillette has teamed up with a small company to develop an in-home laser-based hair-removal product.[10] With this product in mind, let's apply the model in Figure 7.4 to quantify the success potential of such a product.

Figure 7.4
Hypothetical Illustration of Quantifying the Adoption-Influencing Characteristics

Characteristic	Importance (I)*	Evaluation (E)**	I x E
Relative advantage(s)	5	5	25
Compatibility	3	3	9
Complexity	4	–2	–8
Trialability	5	–1	–5
Observability	1	0	0
Total Score	NA	NA	21

*Importance is rated on a scale with values ranging from zero to five. A rating of zero would indicate that a specific characteristic has no importance in this particular case. Higher positive values indicate progressively increasing levels of importance.

**Evaluation is rated on a scale with values ranging from minus five to five. A rating of zero, the midpoint of the scale, would indicate that the proposed new product performs neither favorably or unfavorably on the characteristic at hand; negative values indicate poor performance, with minus five representing the worst possible performance; positive values indicate favorable performance, with five representing the best possible performance.

As shown in Figure 7.4, relative advantages and trialability are judged to be the most important considerations in determining the success of this new laser product, both with importance ratings of five. This in-home hair-removal product must compete against conventional hair-removal procedures (e.g., shaving legs with blades or applying a chemical substance) in terms of ease of hair removal, length of effectiveness, and amount of effort and pain involved. The proposed new product (let's call it LaserGillette, for convenience) must possess these *relative advantages* vis-à-vis existing hair-removal products if it stands any chance of succeeding. Likewise, it is maximally important that potential purchasers be able to try the product in advance of actually purchasing it, so *trialability* also receives an importance score of five. *Compatibility*, on the other hand, is considered to be of only moderate importance (a score of three) insofar as potential users of LaserGillette may be willing to adopt a somewhat radical new method of removing hair if the procedure has distinct relative advantages. *Complexity* of use, with an importance score of four, is considered a very important determinant of product adoption inasmuch as many potential users would be reluctant to switch from their present hair-removal procedure, say shaving, if the laser procedure is perceived as being difficult to use. Finally, *observability* receives an importance score of only one in that product adoption does not involve others seeing how well the product works because this is a private matter that is best ascertained by the product user.

With importance ratings determined, we can turn to the evaluation of LaserGillette on each of the five adoption-influencing characteristics. On relative advantages, this new product is assessed to have the highest possible score, a five. The arithmetic product of its importance rating multiplied by its evaluation score results in LaserGillette receiving a combined relative advantage score ($I \times E$) of 25 points. Because the product is not drastically different than other hair-removal procedures (all involve moving an object, such as a razor, over the skin), its compatibility evaluation score is a three, which thus produces a combined $I \times E$ score of nine. It can be seen in Figure 7.4, however, that LaserGillette scores on the negative side with respect to both complexity and trialability. The product is perceived as being somewhat difficult to learn to use and cannot be tried prior to actually purchasing it other than by viewing a CD-ROM that is available at the point of purchase. Because observability is not really at issue, LaserGillette's $I \times E$ score on this dimension is 0. The total score, as shown in Figure 7.4, is a 21. Based on its past new-product introduction efforts, let us assume that Gillette has learned that all products with scores of 15 or higher typically are successful when introduced to the market. Hence, with a total score of 21, it is likely that LaserGillette will be a successful new product.

Although this illustration is hypothetical, the point to be made is that it is possible to quantify the five adoption determining factors and arrive at a total score that indicates the likelihood that a new product will succeed. Models such as this are invariably somewhat subjective, but a brand management team along with its various marcom agencies should be able to make these judgments with some degree of reliability. Obviously, consumer research also can be applied to determine how prospective members of the target audience rate a proposed new product on each characteristic and how important they consider each characteristic to be in their decision to adopt a new product. Brand managers can build spreadsheets and play around with the numbers in the process of ascertaining what changes may be needed in order to increase the odds that a new product will succeed. For example, because LaserGillette is not evaluated favorably in terms of its trialability, the brand management team may seriously consider devising an in-store procedure that allows prospective users to try the product in a safe and hygienic manner.

Managing the Diffusion Process

The foregoing discussion examined marcom activities and product characteristics that influence whether *individual* consumers and customers are likely to adopt a new product innovation. Emphasis now is directed at the broader issue of how an innovation is communicated and adopted *throughout the marketplace.* This is termed the **diffusion process**, in contrast to the individual-level adoption process just described. Diffusion is, in simple terms, the process of spreading out. In a marcom sense this means that as time passes a new product is adopted by increasingly greater numbers of people. By way of analogy, consider what happens when gas is released into a room: the fumes eventually spread throughout the entire room. Similarly, product innovations spread ideally to all parts of a potential market. The word *ideally* is used because, unlike the physical analogy, the communication of an innovation in the marketplace often is impeded by factors such as unsuitable communication channels, competitive maneuverings, and other imperfect conditions.

JOB OUTLOOK

The media director oversees planning groups that select the communication media—for example, radio, television, newspapers, magazines, Internet, or outdoor signs—to disseminate the advertising. *(Occupational Outlook Handbook, 2004–05 Edition, U.S. DOL, http://www.bls.gov/oco/home.htm)*

When a product does spread through the marketplace over time, it is adopted by different types of consumers. These different types, or groups, are termed *innovators, early adopters, early majority, late majority,* and *laggards.* Because you likely have been introduced to these various groups in an introductory marketing or consumer behavior course, we will not spend time here describing the various groups and their identifying characteristics. We instead will focus on the issue of how the diffusion process can be managed.

Toward this end, consider an interesting product innovation—an antidepressant drug that was marketed under the brand name Clomicalm. You might think, "What's so innovative about an antidepressant drug?" Well, the drug was marketed not for individuals' personal use but for their dogs! Apparently, about 7 million dogs in the United States suffer from a syndrome called *separation anxiety,* manifested by the dog destroying furniture, howling, or eliminating inappropriately when its owners are away from home. Clomicalm is a meat-flavored pill designed to be taken for a minimum treatment length of two to three months.

What did Novartis, the maker of this doggy antidepressant pill, do to facilitate successful product diffusion? Answers are shortly forthcoming, but, in general, firms attempt to manage the diffusion process so that a new product or service accomplishes the following objectives:[11]

1. Secure initial sales as quickly as possible (*rapid takeoff*).
2. Achieve cumulative sales in a steep curve (*rapid acceleration*).
3. Secure the highest possible sales potential in the targeted market segment (*maximum penetration*).
4. Maintain sales for as long as possible (*a long-run franchise*).

How do marketing communicators accomplish these objectives? First, *rapid takeoff* can be facilitated by having a marcom budget that is sufficiently large to permit (1) the aggressive sales-force efforts needed to secure trade support for new products, (2) intensive advertising to create high brand-awareness levels among the target market, and (3) sufficient sales promotion activity to generate desired levels of trial-purchase behavior. Novartis embarked on a major marketing campaign to persuade pet owners to take their anxious dogs to see a veterinarian. Millions of dollars were invested in radio and magazine advertising, including ad placements in *Parade, Reader's Digest,* and *People.* Advertisements

Novartis Animal Health US, Inc.

Figure 7.5
Clomicalm Advertisement

portrayed a sad-looking dog with an emotional appeal in the headline reading, "Some dogs just hate to be alone" (see Figure 7.5). In addition to the consumer-oriented advertising, a major promotional campaign was aimed at training vets and encouraging them to prescribe Clomicalm to separation-anxious dogs. All in all, this was an earnest effort to secure a rapid takeoff.

Second, *rapid acceleration* may be accomplished by (1) ensuring that product quality is suitable and will promote positive word-of-mouth communication, (2) continuing to advertise heavily to reach later adopter groups, (3) ensuring that the sales force provides reseller support, and (4) using sales promotion creatively so that incentives are provided for repeat-purchase behavior. Following the introduction of Clomicalm, Novartis continued supporting its resellers' (i.e., vets) selling efforts and offered attractive promotional deals to consumers to accelerate the adoption rate.

Third, *maximum penetration* can be approached by (1) continuing the same strategies that stimulated rapid acceleration and, where appropriate, (2) revising the product and advertising strategies as necessary to appeal to the needs of later adopters.

Finally, a *long-run franchise* can be maintained by ensuring that: (1) a mature product continues to meet the target audience's needs, (2) distribution is suitable to continue reaching the audience, and (3) advertising continues to remind consumers and customers about the product. Only time will tell whether Clomicalm achieves a long-run franchise. Continued advertising and promotional effort assuredly will be required to offset competitive efforts and position Clomicalm as the best brand for treating Fido's separation anxiety. Ultimately, it will be the brand's effectiveness and relative price that will determine its long-run success.

Stimulating Word-of-Mouth Influence

People in all buying capacities—consumers buying automobiles, purchasing agents buying maintenance materials, physicians ordering drug products, hospitals purchasing supplies, athletic teams acquiring equipment, and so on—rely on two major sources of information to assist them in making decisions: impersonal and personal sources. *Impersonal sources* include information received from television, magazines, the Internet, and other mass media sources. *Personal sources,* the subject of this section, include word-of-mouth influence from friends and acquaintances, and from business associates in the case of organizational buying decisions.[12] Research has shown that the more favorable information a potential product adopter has received from peers, the more likely that individual is to adopt the new product or service.[13] This section begins with some theoretical ideas about *word-of-mouth* influence, or WOM, and then discusses the practice of *buzz building*—also referred to as *viral marketing, guerilla marketing, diffusion marketing,* and *street marketing.*

Strong and Weak Ties

People are connected in what can be referred to as *networks* of interpersonal relationships. Family members and friends interact on a regular basis; people also intermingle with work associates daily. There also are interaction patterns that are less frequent and less strong. We thus can think of social relations in terms of *tie strength*. Consumers' interpersonal relations range along a continuum from very strong ties (such as frequent and often intimate communications between friends) to weak ties (such as rare interactions between casual acquaintances).[14] It is through these ties, both weak and strong, that information flows about new products, new restaurants, recently released movies and albums, and myriad other new products and services.[15]

The important point to conclude from this brief discussion is that marcom efforts (especially through traditional as well as alternative advertising media) are critical for getting the information-dissemination ball rolling, but thereafter it is social interactions via both strong and weak ties between B2C consumers or B2B customers that drive the flow of information about new products. Hence, marketing communicators need to orchestrate the flow of information about products using advertising and "buzz" efforts (as discussed in a later section) and then the information ball will be propelled at an accelerating rate by social networks of people interacting with one another—via online chat rooms and Web logs (blogs) or through more traditional venues of social intercourse. Opinion leaders play a crucial role in this process.

Opinion Leaders and Market Mavens

An **opinion leader** is a person who frequently influences other individuals' attitudes and behavior.[16] Opinion leaders perform several important functions: they inform other people (followers) about new products, they provide advice and reduce the follower's perceived risk in purchasing a new product, and they offer positive feedback to support or confirm decisions that followers have already made. Thus, an opinion leader is an informer, persuader, and confirmer. Consider the phenomenon of movie critiques and the role of the critic. These individuals preview movies before the general public and write reviews, which then are aired on TV or printed in newspapers. The critics' comments serve to influence moviegoers' choice of movies and possibly confirm their own opinions about the movies they have seen.[17]

Opinion leadership influence is typically restricted to one or several consumption topics rather than applying universally across many consumption domains. That is, a person who is an opinion leader with respect to issues and products in one consumption area—such as, movies, computers, skiing, or cooking—is not generally influential in other unrelated areas. It would be very unlikely, for example, for one person to be respected for his or her knowledge and opinions concerning all four of the listed consumption topics. Moreover, opinion leaders are found in every social class. In most instances, opinion leadership influence moves *horizontally* through a social class instead of vertically from one class to another.

Opinion leader profiles are distinctly different from profiles of followers. In general, opinion leaders: (1) are more *cosmopolitan* and have greater contact with the mass media than do followers; (2) are usually more *gregarious* than the general population and have more social contacts—and thus more opportunity for discussing and conveying information—than followers; (3) have slightly *higher socioeconomic status* than followers; (4) are more *innovative* than followers; and (5) are willing to act differently than other people, can withstand criticism and rejection, and have a *need to be unique*.[18]

What motivates opinion leaders to give information? It seems that opinion leaders are willing to participate in word-of-mouth communications with others because they derive satisfaction from sharing their opinions and explaining what they know about new products and services. Opinion leaders thus continually strive (and often feel obligated) to keep themselves informed. In general, *prestige* is at the heart of word-of-mouth influence, whether that influence is from opinion leaders or from those who follow in the information dissemination process. "We like being the bearers of news. Being able to recommend gives us a feeling of prestige. It makes us instant experts."[19]

Being an expert in marketplace matters does bring prestige. Researchers have referred to the marketplace expert as a *maven*. (In dictionary terms, a *maven*, is considered an expert in everyday matters.) **Market mavens** have information about many kinds of products, stores, and other facets of markets, and initiate discussions with consumers and respond to requests from others for market information.[20] In other words, the market maven is looked upon as an important source of information and receives prestige and satisfaction from supplying information to friends and others. Opinion leaders are mavens!

The key to generating good WOM is by finding *cheerleaders*—that is, consumers who will start talking about a new product. Usually this is a carefully selected target group that is most likely to love a new movie, a new book, or other product or service. In the publishing industry, cheerleading is stimulated by giving free copies of a new book to a select group of opinion leaders. This practice is suitably referred to as "seeding" the market. For example, teenage girls in Japan play an extremely important cheerleading role (called *kuchikomi*) that has been recognized and cultivated by Japanese firms.

Kuchikomi refers to the swift network of word-of-mouth advertising that connects teenage girls in Japan. Never was *kuchikomi* more apparent than in the success of the Tamagotchi craze that first hit Japan and then spread globally. Because there is little space in Japan for people to own pets, the Tamagotchi toy provided a substitute outlet for the desire to own an animal. Meaning "cute little egg," Tamagotchi is a plastic toy with an embedded electronic chip that emits chirps of affection based on the owner's behavior. After an extraterrestrial creature hatches from the toy "egg," the owner presses select buttons on a tiny screen to feed, clean, and care for the virtual pet. Proper care is rewarded with affectionate chirps. Bandai Company Ltd., the innovator of this product, estimated initial sales of about 300,000 Tamagotchi at $16 each. However, without any advertising and relying primarily on the WOM generated by teenage girls and other owners, sales volume reached 23 million units in Japan in slightly over one year. Since then Bandai has exported the Tamagotchi to over 25 other countries.

The Tamagotchi is just one example of the *kuchikomi* power of Japan's teenage girls. Many Japanese consumer product companies do not just wait for Japanese girls to engage in word-of-mouth behavior but solicit their opinions during new-product development. *Girl guides*, as they are called, are recruited by Japanese companies to test proposed new products and provide feedback on preliminary television commercials. They also are paid to "cheerlead" new products. For example, Dentsu Eye, a marketing consultancy, paid schoolgirls to talk up a previously unknown product at their schools. Brand awareness quickly grew to 10 percent of high school students. Dentsu Eye's executives estimated that using television advertising to achieve a comparable level of brand awareness would have cost at least $1.5 million compared with less than $100,000 actually paid to the schoolgirls.[21]

Avoid Negative Information

Positive word-of-mouth communication is a critical element in the success of a new product or service. Unfavorable WOM, on the other hand, can have devastating effects on adoption, because consumers seem to place more weight on negative information in making evaluations than on positive information.[22]

Marketing communicators can do several things to minimize negative word of mouth.[23] At a minimum, companies need to show customers that they are responsive to legitimate complaints. Manufacturers can do this by providing detailed warranty and complaint-procedure information on labels or in package inserts.

Retailers can demonstrate their responsiveness to customer complaints through employees with positive attitudes, store signs, and inserts in monthly billings to customers. Companies also can offer toll-free numbers and e-mail addresses to provide customers with an easy way to voice their complaints and provide suggestions. By being responsive to customer complaints, companies can avert negative—and perhaps even create positive—WOM.

Creating "Buzz"

The preceding section applied traditional concepts such as opinion leadership to describe the process of word-of-mouth communication. That section may have given the impression that WOM is something that just happens and that marketing communicators are like spectators in a sporting event who passively enjoy the action but are not involved in its creation. The present section makes it clear that marketing communicators—now more than ever—are active participants in the WOM process rather than merely idle spectators.

Because interpersonal communications play such a key role in affecting consumers' attitudes and actions, brand marketers have found it essential to proactively influence what is said about their brands rather than merely hoping that positive word of mouth is occurring. Marketing practitioners refer to this proactive effort as creating the buzz. By definition, we can think of **buzz creation** as the systematic and organized effort to encourage people to talk favorably about a particular item (a product, service, or specific brand) and to recommend its usage to others who are part of their social network. The terms *guerrilla marketing, viral marketing, diffusion marketing,* and *street marketing* also are used to refer to proactive efforts to spread positive WOM information and to encourage product usage. Let's explore these practices and understand why they are being used extensively, even now to the point that major advertising agencies have created buzz-generating units.

Some Anecdotal Evidence

Before formally examining the topic of buzz creation, it will be useful to first examine some illustrations of this practice:

- Microsoft's Halo2 game reached retail shelves in November 2004. However, prior to that time more than 1.5 million orders had already been placed. This early success and widespread buzz were accomplished by creating a Web site (http://halo2.com) that whetted the appetites of people who play games such as Halo2. The fascinating thing about the Web site is that it was written in the language of and from the viewpoint of aliens (the Covenant) who, in Halo2's story line, are prepared to attack Earth. Without a single word of English or any other Earth language, "gamers" were able to crack the Covenant's language within 48 hours, which was about two weeks quicker than Microsoft personnel had anticipated. Apparently gamers worked as a community and divvied up responsibilities until the language code was broken. Intense excitement was created by this unique Web site, which generated enthusiasm for the new Microsoft game and stimulated early ordering.[24]
- In an effort to get young trendsetters to become brand evangelists, Toyota used guerilla tactics in launching its Scion model in 2003. So-called street teams were formed to distribute promotional items to large gatherings of young consumers in cities across the United States. People had the opportunity to test-drive Scion models fitted with video cameras and then e-mail copies of the drives to friends.[25]
- Mel Gibson produced a religious film, *The Passion of the Christ,* that chronicled the last 12 hours of Jesus' life. Gibson invested around $25 to $30 million of his

own money in producing the movie. *The Passion* stirred intense controversy due to its vivid violence, along with charges of anti-Semitism in allegedly casting Jews in a negative light. Gibson spent months on the road prior to the movie's launch, meeting with church leaders and giving speeches about the film. His production company advised theologians as to how to use the movie to promote churches and recruit new members. The huge amount of buzz resulted in a film that was highly successful at the box office.[26]

- Another movie, *Crouching Tiger, Hidden Dragon*—the Chinese-language martial arts film directed by Ang Lee—had earlier used buzz-building techniques to achieve box office success. This film was a sensation during the 2000–2001 movie season and an Academy Award winner as best foreign film. With a limited budget for promoting the film, the studio decided that word of mouth would be critical to the film's box-office success. In an effort to generate "cheerleading" by movie aficionados, special screenings of the film were presented to a variety of audiences deemed likely to spread positive commentary about the film. These screenings included audiences such as graduates of a women's leadership institute, an assemblage of female athletes, advertising agency executives, and representatives of magazines and television. It was expected that these various groups would subsequently share their delight with others and thus get the WOM "ball" rolling for the movie.[27]
- Lee jeans needed a way to encourage consumers to visit stores where they might try on and purchase the Lee brand. Toward this end, Fallon, the brand's advertising agency, created an online game that featured characters from an accompanying ad campaign. To move to level two of the game, consumers needed a special code they could obtain only by checking out a price tag for Lee jeans. To generate enthusiasm for the game, Fallon sent e-mail messages to 200,000 consumers who were targeted with the intent of directing them to a video clip designed to interest them in the game characters. These messages, described as "hip" and "intriguing," were widely disseminated by the original recipients to their friends, who in turn, in the best spirit of viral marketing passed the messages along to their friends, who forwarded it to their friends, and so on.[28]
- New York–based JetBlue Airways began operations in 2000. This innovative airline features attractive planes with leather seats, live television, and low prices. In an effort to establish Long Beach, a suburb of Los Angeles, as a hub for West Coast flights, the marketing personnel at JetBlue undertook a buzz-building campaign. The campaign was designed to reach influential customers such as bartenders and hotel concierges in hopes that they would spread the word about JetBlue Airways and its flights from the Long Beach airport. College interns were employed to visit bars, hotels, and other locales and to talk up JetBlue and provide "influentials" with bumper stickers, buttons, and tote bags that served as visible reminders of JetBlue's daily flights from the Long Beach airport. To generate further interest in JetBlue and initiate buzz, interns drove Volkswagen Beetles, painted in JetBlue's signature blue color, around the streets of Long Beach.[29]
- During the opening show of the 2004 season of Oprah Winfrey's popular daytime television program, every audience member—276 in total—received a new Pontiac G6 automobile worth over $28,000. Oprah didn't provide these gifts from the goodness of her heart; rather, the cars were donated by the Pontiac division of General Motors in an effort to generate gobs of free publicity about the new G6. Ms. Winfrey devoted a half hour of airtime to the Pontiac G6 and described the car as being "so cool!" Of course, this stunt was arranged by Pontiac's marketing people in coordination with producers of *The Oprah Winfrey Show*. As part of the arrangement, the G6 became sole sponsor of Winfrey's Web site (http://oprah.com) for 90 days. Pontiac's marketing director claimed that the car giveaway generated $20 million in unpaid media coverage and public relations—quite a bargain considering that the actual cost to Pontiac of the donated automobiles likely was less than $5 million.[30]

Formal Perspectives on Buzz Creation

To now more fully appreciate the concept of buzz, it will be useful to introduce the concepts of *networks, nodes,* and *links.* These concepts apply not just to buzz creation, but to any type of network—including brains (nerve cells connected by axons), the World Wide Web (Internet sites linked with other sites), transportation systems (cities linked with other cities via roads, highways, and interstate systems), societies (people linked with other people), and so on.[31] More specifically, consider, for example, a transportation *network* such as the airline system. The *nodes* in an airline system are the various airports that are located in cities served by airlines; these cities, in turn, are *linked* by the airline routes that emanate in one city and culminate in another. Most nodes (airports) in an airline system are linked to relatively few other nodes. However, some large airports (e.g., Chicago O'Hare, Atlanta Hartsfield, and New York JFK) are *hubs* (another name for large nodes) that are linked with numerous other airports.

The notion of an airline network is applicable to social systems. Each person within his or her own social system can be considered a node. Each person (node) is potentially linked with every other person (additional nodes). Most of us are linked with relatively few other people; however, some people are linked with numerous others. Due to the large number of contacts these highly connected people have, they sometimes are referred to as *influentials.* In comparison to major hubs in airline networks, influentials represent the hubs in social networks. It obviously follows that if you, as a marketing communicator, wanted people to disseminate positive WOM about your brand, then getting your message to influentials would be critical to your success. This, by the way, explains in large part how the Bush Administration got its "morality" message disseminated during the 2004 presidential election campaign: they sent communiqués to theologians urging their support; the theologians in turn spread the word to their congregations. Theologians are influentials because they come in contact with hundreds of others and have the capacity to influence religious beliefs and sway public opinion.

Hereafter, we will describe two perspectives on the notion of creating buzz. One is based on the insightful observations of a journalist, Malcolm Gladwell, in his book *The Tipping Point.* The other originates from principles derived by the renowned consulting firm McKinsey & Company and is called *explosive self-generating demand.* Frankly, there is some redundancy in these perspectives. Yet, each perspective is sufficiently unique to warrant separate treatment.

Creating an Epidemic

Marketplace buzz can be compared to an epidemic. By analogy, consider how the common influenza (flu) virus spreads. A flu epidemic starts with a few people, who interact with other people, who in turn spread it to others until eventually, and generally quickly, thousands or even millions of people have the malady. Needless to say, flu epidemics could not occur unless people—such as school children—were in close contact with one another. For an epidemic to occur there must be a *tipping point,* which is the moment of critical mass at which enough people are infected so that the epidemic diffuses rapidly throughout the social system.[32]

It has been conjectured that epidemics in a social context, including the spread of information about new products and their adoption, can be accounted for by three straightforward rules—the *law of the few,* the *stickiness factor,* and the *power of context:*[33]

Law of the Few. The first rule, the *law of the few,* suggests that it only takes a few well-connected people to start an epidemic. These people are variously referred to as *connectors, influentials, opinion leaders,* or *market mavens.* Whatever they may be called, the important point is that connected people start "commercial epidemics"—such as the widespread adoption of new ideas and products—because they know a lot of people and are innately persuasive.

In short, buzz-building efforts for new products (new-product epidemics) require *messengers* who are willing to talk about the products and share their usage experiences with others and who, by virtue of their inherent persuasiveness, influence others to also become product users and perhaps "apostles." Paid advertising could never accomplish the results that informal social networks achieve. Advertising might inform, but it is common people who legitimize new-product usage. Indeed, whereas advertisements lack credibility—because people realize that ads are designed to influence their behavior—personal messages from friends and acquaintances are readily accepted because no vested interest is involved.

Stickiness Factor. The second rule, the stickiness factor, deals with the nature of the *message,* whereas the first rule involves the messenger. Messages about new products that are attention catching and memorable (i.e., "sticky" messages) enable more rapid diffusion. This explains why rumors and urban legends fly through the social system. Such messages are inherently interesting and thus are passed along with lightning speed.

The point is that not all messages diffuse rapidly, just those that are *innately interesting* and *memorable.* Millions of people talked about the giveaway of hundreds of Pontiacs on *The Oprah Winfrey Show* mentioned earlier, because that was a newsworthy and exciting event. Tens of millions of people discussed Janet Jackson's breast-baring that occurred during the halftime program of the 2004 Super Bowl. The capture of Iraqi leader Saddam Hussein was widely chatted about due to both his notoriety and his disheveled appearance as he was removed literally from a hole in the ground. In general, people must want to talk about a product or brand-related idea if it is to spread. Hence, it is through clever advertising and viral-marketing efforts that otherwise mundane news can be made interesting, even exciting, and thus worthy of sharing with other people who are connected via strong or weak social ties.

Power of Context. The third rule of epidemics, the power of context, simply indicates that the circumstances and conditions have to be right for a persuasive message conveyed by a connector to have its impact and initiate an epidemic. It doesn't sound very scientific to say it, but sometimes the "stars have to be properly aligned" for epidemics to occur. In other words, there is a chance factor involved that is difficult to predict or control, or even to explain. But whatever the exact reason, sometimes the circumstances are just right for word-of-mouth dissemination. Imagine, for example, that a student on your campus got arrested for driving under the influence. This wouldn't be particularly exciting news that would be worthy of discussion among the student body. However, envision that this student was the son or daughter of the university president. In this context, discussion about his or her behavior would be rampant. When the context is right, WOM epidemics can occur.

Igniting Explosive Self-Generating Demand

The foregoing account has simply described the conditions that are congenial to the spread of epidemics. The present account will examine how buzz generation can be managed to get the message about a brand rapidly diffused throughout a social network.

The well-known management consulting firm, McKinsey & Company, has formulated a set of principles for igniting positive WOM momentum for new brands. McKinsey's associates refer to word-of-mouth momentum as explosive self-generating demand, or ESGD for short. Key principles underlying ESGD are as follows:[34]

1. **Design the product to be unique or visible.** Products and brands that are most likely to experience ESGD have two distinguishing characteristics. First, they are *unique* in some respect—in terms of appearance (e.g., vehicles such as the Hummer, the PT Cruiser, and the Mini Cooper), functionality (e.g., Viagra pills for erectile dysfunction and the high-fat Atkins diet), or in any other

attention-gaining manner. Second, they are *highly visible* or *confer status* on opinion leaders and connectors, who are among the first to know about new products and services. For example, being among the first to attend an exciting new bar or restaurant, or to attend a provocative movie, can confer a sense of status on the innovator, which thus explains why these topics command much time in our day-to-day discourse.

In general, not all products are worthy of buzz. Rather, people are interested in talking only about those products and brands that have some uniqueness, excitement, or some inherent "wow" factor.[35]

2. **Select and seed the vanguard.** Every new product and service has a group that is out in front of the crowd in terms of the speed at which the group adopts the product. This group, earlier termed *innovators,* is called the *vanguard* by McKinsey & Company. The challenge for the marketer of a new brand is identifying which consumer group will have the greatest influence over other consumers and then doing whatever it takes to get your brand accepted by that group, the vanguard. Athletic shoe companies often launch new brands by supplying advance pairs to local basketball heroes, the vanguard for this product. In general, vanguards include basketball stars, Hollywood divas, the most popular kids in high schools, the coolest kids in "the hood," and so on. The vanguard for new business books are business leaders, such as those occupying corner offices in major corporations. When they read a new book and consider it relevant to their organization, it is only a short time before they encourage their subordinates to read the same book, and they, in turn, instruct their underlings to do the same, and so on.
3. **Ration supply.** Scarcity is a powerful force underlying influencers' efforts to persuade. This is because people often want what they can't have. Automobile companies frequently exploit this reality by not producing sufficient supplies to meet immediate demand when the product is launched. The BMW Z3, the DaimlerChrysler PT Cruiser, Ford's retro Thunderbird roadster, and the Hummer all experienced demand far outstripping supply. The thinking is that people will talk more about those things they cannot immediately have. Thus, by rationing supply at the outset of product introduction, the excitement level increases and the WOM network is set into action.
4. **Use celebrity icons.** Perhaps there is no better means to generate excitement about a new product than to first get it into the hands of a celebrity. Hairstyles, clothing fashions, and product choices that celebrities adopt are often accepted by large numbers of people who emulate their behavior. In the world of golf, for example, celebrities often appear in advertisements or infomercials and tout the benefits of new balls, clubs, and self-help products. Oprah Winfrey's endorsement of new books and many other products (such as the Pontiac G6) virtually assures product success.
5. **Tap the power of lists.** The media disseminate many kinds of lists that are designed to influence consumer behavior and direct action. For example, aspiring college students and their parents read magazines such as *U.S. News & World Report's* annual lists of top colleges and universities. Newspapers regularly provide lists of the best mutual funds. Radio stations often announce the top-drawing movies over the weekend. It has been claimed that "lists are potent tools for creating buzz because they're effective road signs for information-besieged consumers who don't know where to focus their attention."[36]
6. **Nurture the grass roots.** Similar to the concept of cheerleading described earlier, this tactic is based on the idea of getting adopters of a product to convert other people into users. Naturally, people who are satisfied with a product oftentimes will encourage others to use the same product. But rather than "letting it happen" (or fail to happen) the notion of nurturing the grass roots involves—as do all buzz-building tactics—some form of proactive effort to get present product adopters to recruit new members or customers. People who have achieved success with a new form of diet or exercise program, for

example, can be encouraged with incentives to recruit others to adopt this same form of behavior. Exercise clubs sometimes provide discounts to current members when they attract additional members to the club. Brand communities can be formed (online or otherwise) so that present adopters of a product can share their enthusiasm and hopefully spread the word to others. In short, nurturing the grass roots involves a proactive effort to get existing customers more involved with the product and thus willing to become product disciples.

This section hopefully has provided you with an appreciation that WOM momentum can be managed in a proactive fashion rather than accepted as a *fait accompli.* Also, it should be clear that not all products and brands are appropriate for buzz-creation efforts. The principles identified here offer insight into when and why buzz creation is particularly likely and most effective. Growing numbers of firms are turning to buzz creation as a low-cost and effective supplement for (or even an alternative to) mass media advertising. Hence, it will serve you well to study this topic in greater detail than has been possible in this text. A number of books on the topic have been written in recent years. Please see endnote 37 for a list of several informative and well-written books on the topic.[37] (This list, in line with ESGD principle #5, should further generate buzz for these books about buzz building.)

Using the Internet for Creating Buzz

Before departing the topic of buzz, brief commentary is needed about the role of the Internet in buzz-creation efforts. Of course, word-of-mouth communications is at the heart of buzz creation, and the Internet is possibly the most effective and efficient medium in the history of the world for disseminating information rapidly and widely. Chat rooms and blogs are the two online instruments via which WOM information is disseminated about new products. Everyone knows about chat rooms, so no commentary is needed here. Blogs, by comparison, are relatively new and have been defined as follows:

It's a Web-based journal powered by a self-publishing tool that enables the author(s) to regularly and easily update the content. The log consists of commentary along with links to other blogs or online resources. Blog posts are always presented in reverse chronological order. Each entry is time- and date-stamped.[38]

Blogs, in other words, present the ideas, thoughts, and opinions of "bloggers." Blogs often foster spirited discussion and debate among communities of individuals who share common viewpoints. It is estimated that there were approximately 8 million blogs on the Web at the time of this writing and that as many as 20 million people read blogs.[39]

In a marketing context, bloggers often have strong, even passionate, opinions about product categories and brands. Consider the case of a product introduced by Procter & Gamble (P&G) called Mr. Clean AutoDry, which is a car-washing product that dries spot free. Prior to the formal launch of the product, marketing folks at P&G detected that auto enthusiasts were discussing the product in auto blogs and chat rooms. In an effort to seed further discussion, P&G gave free AutoDry samples to bloggers and requested their honest reviews. By the time the product was on store shelves several months later, brand awareness had already reached 25 percent among consumers and 45 percent among car enthusiasts.[40]

P&G's AutoDry enjoyed a positive experience from blogging directed at that brand. However, the distinct possibility exists that Internet driven WOM will not always be positive. Because negative information is more salient than positive, the reality is that negative information about products—mature as well as new—will spread even faster than positive information. And because blogs are written by "real people" rather than by public relations personnel and advertisers, the reality is that information disseminated via blogs can have a devastating impact if that information is anything other than positive.

Finally, although the previous discussion has focused on what may be referred to as independent blogs—those emanating from individuals who have no vested interest in a company or its products—many companies have started their own blogs. These formal, corporate blogs represent instruments for fostering better relations with customers, enhancing brand loyalty, gaining feedback, and keeping the company's fingers on the pulse of the marketplace. Because credibility always reigns supreme in determining how consumers and customers judge companies and their offerings, it goes without saying that corporate-sponsored blogs will serve only to hurt brands if they are perceived as disseminating hyped news and false testimonials rather than delivering factual information.

Brand Naming

A brand is a company's unique designation, or trademark, which identifies a company's offering and distinguishes it from other product category entries. Many executives regard brand naming to be one of the most important aspects of marketing management. Product and brand managers consider it critical to choose an appropriate brand name, largely because that choice can influence early trial of a brand and affect sales volume. A brand's name is crucially important—indeed, names have been described as the "cerebral switches" that activate images in target audiences' collective minds.[41] Research has shown that even children (as young as 3 or 4) are aware of brand names and that by the age of 10 or so the brand name takes on conceptual significance whereby children think about brand names as more than simply another product feature. In other words, the name takes on a "life of its own," and children judge brands on the basis of their acquired reputations and evaluate people in terms of what brands they own.[42] In short, a product's brand name plays a major role in determining its immediate success upon introduction and its sustained prosperity as it matures.

It is worth mentioning at this point that the name chosen for a new brand is an especially important decision. A new brand can succeed in spite of being saddled with a "bad" name, but the odds of success are boosted if the brand has an effective name. Good brand names evoke feelings of trust, confidence, security, strength, durability, speed, status, and many other desirable associations. The name chosen for a brand: (1) affects the speed with which consumers become aware of the brand, (2) influences the brand's image, and (3) thus plays a major role in brand equity formation. Achieving consumer awareness of a brand name is the critical initial aspect of brand equity enhancement. Brand name awareness has been characterized as the "gateway" to consumers' more complicated learning and retention of associations that constitute a brand's image.[43] Through brand names, a company can create excitement, elegance, exclusiveness, and influence consumers' perceptions and attitudes.[44]

What Constitutes a Good Brand Name?

This is a complex question that precludes a straightforward answer. To gain perspective, let's twist the question around and pose it in these terms: what determines whether a person's name is a good name? (Please think about this for a moment before reading on.) As you pondered this question, you likely arrived quickly at the conclusion that people's names differ dramatically and that no simple rule can answer whether a person's name is good. Perhaps you also entertained the notion that whether a person's name is "good" depends in large part on whether it "fits" the person's size, personality, and demographic characteristics. Quite simply, there are many ways to have a good name, either for a person or for a brand.

Complexity aside, researchers have attempted to specify the factors that determine brand name quality. Although the accumulated knowledge is nowhere close to the point of specifying scientific principles, there is general agreement that brand names should satisfy several fundamental requirements. First, a good brand name should distinguish the brand from competitive offerings. Second, it should describe the brand and its attributes or benefits. Third, it is important that the name achieve compatibility with the brand's desired image and with its product design or packaging. Fourth, it is useful for the name to be memorable and easy to pronounce and spell.[45] Finally, though not discussed subsequently as a fifth requirement, another important consideration when selecting a brand name is the suitability of that name for marketing that brand in multiple countries. Ideally, a brand name would satisfy requirements one through four equally well in all countries in which the brand is marketed. Needless to say, most brand names fail to satisfy this ideal.

Requirement 1: Distinguish the Brand from Competitive Offerings

It is desirable for a brand to have a unique identity, something that clearly differentiates it from competitive brands. Failure to distinguish a brand from competitive offerings creates consumer confusion and increases the chances that consumers will not remember the name or mistakenly select another brand. Clinique selected the name Happy to suggest precisely that feeling for its perfume brand, a name choice that is striking in its differentiation from the usually sexually suggestive names chosen for perfumes such as Passion, Allure, and Obsession. This brand quickly achieved the top market share in the category.

In the low-fare airline category, brand marketers have come up with unique names such as Ted Airlines, Song, Spirit Airlines, and JetBlue Airways—unique names all that provide each airline with an identity distinct from its competitors. Compare these names with the stodgy monikers that historically dominated the U.S. airline industry, names such as United, Continental, TWA, Delta, American, Northwest, Southwest, and so on. The new airline names seem intent on conveying brand personalities that suggest these airlines deliver something more than mere functionality. Moreover, all are memorable and easy to pronounce (see requirement #4).

Some marketers attempt to hitchhike on the success of other brands by using names similar to better-known and more respected brands. However, the Federal Trademark Dilution Act of 1995 protects owners of brand names and logos from other companies using the identical or similar names. (In legal terms, brand names and logos are referred to as *trademarks.*) The objective of this legislation is to protect trademarks from losing their distinctiveness.[46] Trademark infringement cases occur with some regularity in the United States, and stealing well-known brand names is widely practiced in some newly emerging market economies. Chinese marketers have been accused of using facsimiles of famous brand names on their own domestically manufactured products. For example, a toothpaste is packaged under the Colgate-sounding name Cologate, and a Chinese brand of sunglasses is named Ran Bans, which is obviously similar to Bausch & Lomb's well-known Ray Ban brand.[47]

Requirement 2: Describe the Brand and Its Attributes or Benefits

A name that clearly describes a brand's attributes and benefits enables consumers to make informed buying decisions—by letting them know what to expect from the brand—and also performs the all-important function of enabling consumers to recall important information about the brand. In other words, brand names serve as memory cues that facilitate recall of product attributes and benefits and also predict product performance.[48] Post-it (notepads), I Can't Believe It's Not Butter (margarine), I Can't Believe It's Not Chicken (a faux-chicken soy-based product), Healthy Choice (low-fat foods), and Huggies (diapers) illustrate brand names that do outstanding jobs in describing their respective products' attributes or benefits.

Transmeta Corp., a manufacturer of computer chips that competes against the much larger Intel and its Pentium class of products, introduced a super-efficient chip designed for laptop computers. This new chip promised to extend laptop usage without battery recharge for many hours beyond the standard two or three hours enabled by conventional chips. Transmeta named the new chip "Crusoe" after the famous fictional character Robinson Crusoe. This brand name suggests (to anyone familiar with the Robinson Crusoe story) that a laptop powered with a Crusoe chip permits a "stranded" user to continue working for many hours without access to an electrical outlet. Though the name-benefit relation is a bit abstract in this case, it would be expected that Crusoe readily suggests a stranded-usability benefit to most prospective laptop purchasers.

Researchers have carefully examined the issue of brand name suggestiveness. *Suggestive brand names* are those that imply particular attributes or benefits in the context of a product category. Crusoe is a suggestive brand name. So is Healthy Choice for food products, intimating that this brand is low in fat content and calories. The name Outback for Subaru's SUV suggests a product that is durable and rugged—capable of taking on the challenge of the famous Australian outback. Ford Explorer is a name that suggests adventure for prospective purchasers of pickup trucks seeking the thrill of off-road driving.

Research has demonstrated that suggestive brand names facilitate consumer recall of advertised benefit claims that are consistent in meaning with the brand names.[49] Suggestive brand names reinforce in consumers' memories the association between the name and the semantically related benefit information about the brand.[50] On the other hand, these same suggestive names may reduce the recallability of benefit claims after a brand has been repositioned to stand for something different than its original meaning.[51]

Brand names sometimes are *made-up names* (i.e., created or fabricated) rather than selected from actual words found in dictionaries. Many automobile brand names currently in use or used in the past are made-up names, including Acura, Altima, Geo, Lexus, Lumina, and Sentra. These names were created from *morphemes,* which are the semantic kernels of words. For example, Compaq, which now has merged with Hewlett-Packard, combined two morphemes (com and paq) and in so doing suggested the product benefit of a compact computer. The automobile name Acura is a derivative of "accurate" and suggests precision in product design and engineering. The name Lexus, by comparison, appears to have been an entirely made-up name.

Research is increasingly showing that *sound symbolism* plays a major role in determining how consumers react to brand names and form judgments about brands.[52] Individual sounds, called *phonemes,* are the basis for brand names. Not only do phonemes serve to form syllables and words, they also provide meaning about a brand through a process of sound symbolism.[53] Consider, for example, the use of "front" vowels in brand names (i.e., vowels such as ē as in "bee" and ā as in "ate") compared to "back" vowels (vowels such as ü as in "food" and ō as in "home"). Research has demonstrated that brand names that include front vowels (versus back vowels) convey attribute qualities such as smallness, lightness, mildness, thinness, femininity, weakness, and prettiness.[54]

A study using ice cream as the target product created the names Frosh and Frish for an allegedly new brand in this category. These names differ only with respect to their phonetic sounds, with Frosh and Frish based on *ä* (a back vowel) and *i* (a front vowel) sounds, respectively. The study determined that the name Frosh conveyed more positive brand attribute associations and more favorable brand evaluations than did Frish. It further was learned from this study that the effect of brand name sound symbolism occurred in an effortless, automatic fashion without cognitive involvement. In other words, these brand names had differential effects on perceptions and evaluations of allegedly new brands of ice cream, but participants in the research were unaware that their judgments were based on sound symbolism. Nonetheless, it was this sound symbolism that led research participants to more favorably evaluate Frosh versus Frish ice cream.

Requirement 3: Achieve Compatibility with a Brand's Desired Image and with Its Product Design or Packaging

Again, Healthy Choice is an ideal name for a category of fat-free and low-fat food items that are targeted toward weight- and health-conscious consumers. The name suggests that the consumer has an alternative and that Healthy Choice is the right choice. Another name that is perfectly compatible with the brand's desired image is Second Nature, which is the brand name for a line of recycled tablets and legal pads. The *o* in *Second* is formed from three chasing arrows that symbolize recyclability, and the words *Second* and *Nature* are colored in environmentally congruent green against a woodsy-brown background. Second Nature is an excellent name that suggests that writing pads carrying this name are not made from virgin wood but rather are recycled—hence, the rebirth of nature, or Second Nature. The name also serves as a subtle injunction to the consumer that using recycled writing materials should be virtually an automatic decision, as implied by the vernacular expression "It's second nature."

Another name that fits well with the desired brand image is Swerve, which is Coca-Cola's milk-based drink aimed at children and teens. The dictionary meaning of the word *swerve* is to make an abrupt turn in movement or direction. Prospective users of Swerve are thus promised a drink that is out of the ordinary and which permits users to be part of a "movement"—perhaps away from ordinary soft drinks. In a sense, this name may suggest that drinking milk is a "cool" thing. Swerve's packaging graphics reinforce the name by displaying a grinning cow in dark glasses, again suggesting that this is a hip brand for young people who desire their own identity and perhaps march to their own drummer.

Because marketplaces are dynamic and consumer preferences and desires change over time, some brand names lose their effectiveness and have to be changed to avoid negative images. A case in point is Kentucky Fried Chicken. This name was compatible with the product for well over two decades, but a name change was needed when health consciousness swept the nation. A change from Kentucky Fried Chicken to simply KFC was undertaken with hopes of preventing the negative implications associated with the word *fried*. Then, in 2005, after using the KFC name for nearly a decade, executives at KFC decided that being associated with fried food is not necessarily a negative and switched the company name back to the original Kentucky Fried Chicken. In Egypt, there have been protests against Procter & Gamble's Ariel brand of soap powder with activists falsely charging that it is named after Israel's controversial prime minister, Ariel Sharon.

Company names are being changed with increasing frequency due to mergers, acquisitions, and other factors. For example, the company name Verizon Communications was created from the merger of Bell Atlantic and GTE. The name Verizon was formed by combining the words *veritas* and *horizon*, the former word suggesting the quality of truth.[55] The company now known as Accenture had to change its name after a split with its sister company. Arthur Andersen introduced the Accenture name and logo in 2001, which features a greater-than sign over the letter *t* (see Figure 7.6). The name is a made-up word that conjoins two real words, *accent* and *future*, thus suggesting an accent on the future. Interestingly, in the process of selecting this new name, the company employed the services of a company, Landor Associates, that specializes in name selection. Landor's name selection process considered 5,500 different names, half of which were generated by Accenture employees who participated in an internal naming initiative.

Figure 7.6
The Accenture Name

Courtesy of Accenture

Requirement 4: Be Memorable and Easy to Pronounce

Finally, a good brand name is one that is easy to remember and pronounce. Though shortness is not an essential ingredient for a good name, many brand names are short, one-word names that facilitate ease of memory and pronunciation (Tide, Bold, Shout, Edge, Bounce, Cheer, Swatch, Smart, and so on). Probably few words are as memorable as those learned in early childhood, and among the first words learned are animal names. This likely explains marketers' penchant for using animals as brand names; for example, automobile companies have used names such as Mustang, Thunderbird, Bronco, Cougar, Lynx, Skyhawk, Skylark, Firebird, Jaguar, and Ram. In addition to their memorability, animal names also conjure up vivid images. This is very important to the marketing communicator because concrete and vivid images facilitate consumer information processing. Dove soap, for example, suggests softness, grace, gentleness, and purity. Ram (for Dodge trucks) intimates strength, durability, and toughness.

In coming up with memorable names, companies often take liberties with standard dictionary spellings. For example, Campbell's (of soup fame) introduced a line of energy drinks aimed at young adults. The name chosen for the brand was Invigor8. This name obviously is a derivative of *invigorate,* which literally means to feel with life and energy. This is an excellent name for the desired brand image (requirement #3) and is also memorable and easy to pronounce. The spelling, which substitutes the numeral *8* for the suffix *ate* gives the name a special distinctiveness and yet enables easy pronunciation. Interestingly, it also is likely that Campbell's, which makes the well-known juice drink, V8, is attempting to leverage off the equity in that mature brand in a very subtle way. Whatever the case, Invigor8 is a captivating brand name. The use of this name is supported by research showing that names with unusual spellings enhance consumer recall and recognition.[56]

Some Exceptions to the "Rules"

The foregoing discussion has identified four guidelines for brand naming. The observant student will note, however, that some successful brand names seem entirely at odds with the "rules." First, some brands become successful in spite of their names. (Analogously, some people achieve prominence even though their names may not be the ones they personally would have chosen or that a "name meister" would have selected as more ideal.) The first brand in a new product category can achieve tremendous success regardless of its name if the brand offers customers distinct advantages over alternative solutions to their problems. Second, in all aspects of life there are exceptions to the rules, and this certainly is the case in brand naming.

A third major exception to the "rules" is that brand managers and their brand name consultants sometimes intentionally select names that, at inception, are virtually meaningless. For example, the word *lucent* in Lucent Technologies was selected because for most people this word has relatively little meaning and few associations—the *empty-vessel philosophy* of brand naming. The empty-vessel expression implies that when a name does not have much preexisting meaning, subsequent marketing communications are able to create the exact meaning desired without contending with past associations already accumulated in people's memories. In other words, rather than selecting a name already rich in meaning and filled with associations, there are advantages to using a relatively neutral name that a marcom campaign can endow with intended meaning.

The Brand-Naming Process

Brand naming involves a rather straightforward process as determined by a survey of over 100 product and brand managers who represent both B2C and B2B products. Figure 7.7 lists the steps, and the following discussion describes each.

Step 1: Specify Objectives for the Brand Name

As with all managerial decisions, the initial step is to identify the objectives to be accomplished. Most managers are concerned with selecting a name that will

Figure 7.7
The Brand-Naming Process

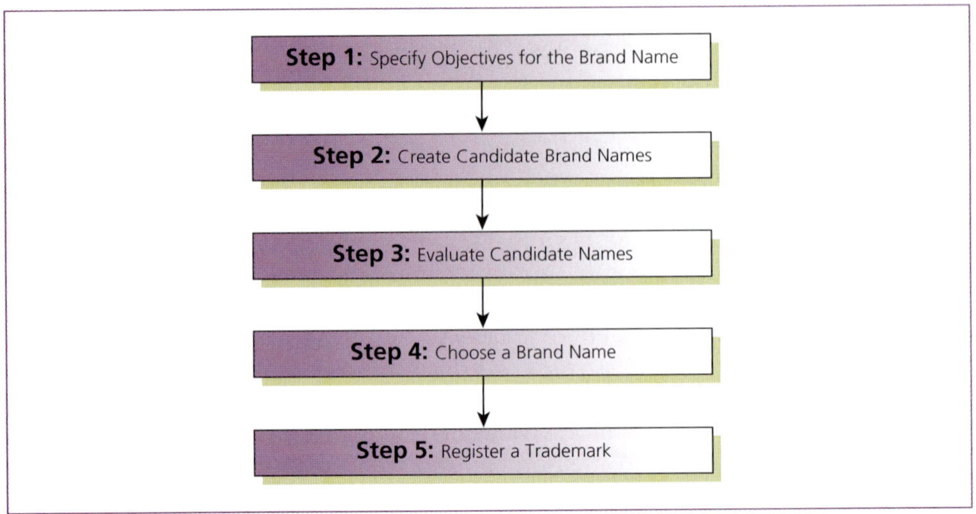

Source: "The Brand-Naming Process," adapted from Chiranjeev Kohli and Douglas W. LaBahn, "Observations: Creating Effective Brand Names: A Study of the Naming Process," *Journal of Advertising Research* 37 (January/February 1997), p. 69. Reprinted by permission.

successfully position the brand in the minds of the target audience, provide an appropriate image for the brand, and distinguish it from competitive brands.[57]

Step 2: Create Candidate Brand Names

Brand name candidates often are selected using creative-thinking exercises and brainstorming sessions. Companies frequently use the services of naming consultants to generate candidate names, as was the case in the selection of JetBlue, Verizon, Accenture, and Lucent. The survey of product and brand managers noted previously determined that nearly 50 candidate names were created for each brand-naming assignment.[58]

Step 3: Evaluate Candidate Names

The many names generated are evaluated using criteria such as relevance to the product category, favorability of associations conjured up by the name, and overall appeal. Product and brand managers consider it critical that names be easily recognized and recalled.

Step 4: Choose a Brand Name

The criteria noted in steps 1 and 3 are used by managers to select a final name from the candidate field. In many firms this choice is a matter of subjective judgment rather than the product of rigorous marketing research. For example, the airline name JetBlue was chosen subjectively based on hunch and insight. (See the *IMC Focus* about JetBlue Airways for a description of how the airline arrived at that particular name.)

Step 5: Register a Trademark

Most companies apply for trademark registration. Some companies submit only a single name for registration, whereas others submit multiple names (on average, five names). One survey found that three names are rejected for every registered name.[59] A brand-naming consultant indicated that the number of rejections is even higher, noting that about 75 percent of the names his firm generates are already taken upon searching federal registrations.[60]

Selecting a Name for a New Airline

imc focus

Previously we mentioned a buzz-building effort in Long Beach, California, by the new airline, JetBlue Airways. Let's learn a little more about this company and how it selected its interesting name. The company's chief executive officer is a guy named David Neeleman, who had been involved in the early 1990s with a successful start-up airline that eventually was sold to Southwest Airlines. Neeleman described his new JetBlue Airways in these terms: "We're a new kind of low-fare airline, with deep pockets, new planes, leather seats with more legroom, great people, and innovative thinking. With our friendly service and hassle-free technology, we're going to bring humanity back to air travel." JetBlue is based at New York's JFK International Airport. The airline is positioned as both being less expensive and providing greater comforts compared with established airlines. In short, JetBlue wants to be known as a low-fare but classy airline.

But how and why did it select the name JetBlue? Initially, Neeleman and his associates were uncertain what they wanted in a name for their new airline, but they were absolutely certain what they did *not* want—namely, they didn't want (1) a geographic destination such as Southwest or Northeast; or (2) a made-up word such as brand names popular in automobile marketing (e.g., Lexus and Acura). The marketing team at "New Air," which was the operating name for the airline while awaiting the selection of a permanent name, considered numerous name possibilities, including New York Air, Gotham, Taxi, the Big Apple, Imagine Air, Yes!, and Fresh Air. Taxi was the name that had the greatest appeal to a top marketing executive, who thought that the name had "a New York feel" and would enable a unique plane design with yellow and black checkering on the tails of planes (reminiscent of the look of New York City's Checker Cabs). The name Taxi eventually was rejected, however, because in its verb usage, *taxi* describes what planes do on runways, and the Federal Aviation Administration rejected this usage for a brand name. Also, some feared that New York City taxi cabs had a negative image associated with high prices, poor service, and unsafe rides.

New Air's marketing executives then considered other name possibilities, such as Blue, It, and Egg (what were they thinking?). All three names were rejected, and as a last resort the company employed the services of Landor Associates, a firm that specializes in brand naming. Landor eventually came up with six candidate names that were presented to Chief Executive Officer Neeleman and his colleagues at a gathering in Landor's San Francisco headquarters. The slate of finalists (and their reasons for rejection) were: Air Avenues (too suggestive of New York's swank Park Avenue, which is an inappropriate association for a budget airline); Hiway Air (a made-up word that Neeleman eschewed, and silly at that); Air Hop (another silly name); Lift Airways (ultimately rejected for being suggestive of the emergency situation embodied in the similar sounding "airlift"); Scout Air (rejected because it implied an adventure destination and suggested the name of scouting organizations such as the Girl Scouts); and True Blue.

True Blue was the name selected at this important meeting in San Francisco. A key member of the marketing team shared these views: "The *blue* has a good visual aspect to it. It's the sky, it's friendship, it's loyalty." A long and arduous process was finally completed, and the new airline was prepared to trumpet its engaging name, True Blue. But just two weeks before launching public relations and advertising campaigns, the company learned that the True Blue name was already owned by Thrifty-Rent-A-Car, which had copyrighted the name for use in a customer service program. (Parenthetically, the fact that the name was already owned had escaped Landor's legal analysis, much to the dismay of this respected brand-naming company.) Just one week before announcing the new airline, a member of the marketing team recommended the name JetBlue. Everyone agreed that the name would work, and New Air became JetBlue Airways—a fledgling airline that may become a mainstay of American airline service.

SOURCES: Adapted from Rebecca Johnson, "Name That Airline," *Travel & Leisure*, October 1999, 159–164; "JetBlue Airways Open for Business" (Company Press Release), January 11, 2000, http://www.jetblue.com/learnmore/pressDetail.asp?newsId=10; Bonnie Tsui, "JetBlue Soars in First Months," *Advertising Age*, September 11, 2000, 26.

The Role of Logos

Related to the brand name is a graphic design element called a brand *logo*. These design elements, or logos, can be thought of as a shorthand way of identifying a brand. For purposes of identifying their brands, companies use logos with or without brand names.[61] Not all brand names possess a distinct logo, but many do. Figure 7.8 presents a collection of six famous logos, ones that are readily recognizable to millions of people around the globe. For example, the Nike swoosh is virtually as famous as the company name, as are the logos for Shell Oil, Coca-Cola, and the other brands shown in Figure 7.8. Consumers learn these logos and easily recognize the brands on which the logos are emblazoned. (To test this, take a moment and visualize the logos for each of the following well-known brands:

Figure 7.8
Famous Logos

Courtesy of (clockwise): General Motors, General Motors, © MasterCard International Incorporated. Used with permission, "Coca-Cola" is a registered trademark of The Coca-Cola Company, AP Topic Gallery, AP Topic Gallery.

Pepsi, Ralph Lauren's Polo, Tommy Hilfiger clothing, Starbucks coffee, Mercedes-Benz automobiles, Toyota automobiles, Arm & Hammer baking soda, and Cracker Jack popcorn.)

Figure 7.9
Cingular's Logo

Cingular Wireless www.cingular.com

Logo designs are incredibly diverse, ranging from highly abstract designs to those that depict nature scenes and from very simple to complex depictions. Generally, good logos are (1) recognized readily, (2) convey essentially the same meaning to all target members, and (3) evoke positive feelings.[62] Although logos undoubtedly perform valuable communication roles and influence brand equity via their effect both on brand awareness and image, published research on logos is surprisingly absent. However, an important study determined that the best strategy for enhancing the likeability of a logo is to choose a design that is *moderately elaborate* rather than one that is too simple or too complex. Also, natural designs (as opposed to abstract illustrations) were found to produce more favorable consumer responses.[63] Cingular's heavily advertised logo perhaps represents an illustration of a logo that achieves the goal of being neither too simple nor too complex. Cingular, a major company in the wireless industry, invested heavily in selecting the simple yet distinct icon shown in Figure 7.9. Company personnel refer affectionately to the Cingular icon as Jack, apparently due to its similarity to the object in the old-fashioned children's game of jacks.

Packaging

A brand's package is, of course, the container that both protects and helps sell the product. Products available on store shelves are most always bottled, boxed, or packaged in some other manner. As the term *package* is used in the present context, beverage bottles and cereal boxes are packages; so are the jewel box for a CD and Gateway's Holstein cow box, and so on. Growing numbers of marcom specialists appreciate the crucial role performed by brand packaging. The increasingly important communications role of packaging has given rise to expressions such as, "Packaging is the least expensive form of advertising," "Every package is a five-second commercial," "The package is a silent salesman," and "The package is the product."[64] Packaging performs key communication and salesmanship roles at the point of purchase inasmuch as shoppers spend an incredibly short amount of time—on the order of 10 to 12 seconds—viewing brands before moving on or selecting an item and placing it in the shopping cart.[65]

The growth of supermarkets, mass merchandisers (such as Wal-Mart and Target) and other self-service retail outlets has necessitated that the package perform marketing functions beyond the traditional role of merely containing and protecting the product. The package also serves to (1) draw attention to a brand, (2) break through competitive clutter at the point of purchase, (3) justify price and value to the consumer, (4) signify brand features and benefits, (5) convey emotionality, and (6) ultimately motivate consumers' brand choices. Packaging is particularly important for differentiating homogenous or unexciting brands from available substitutes. Packaging accomplishes this by working uninterruptedly to say what the brand is, how it is used, and what it can do to benefit the user.[66] In short, packages perform a major role in enhancing brand equity by creating or fortifying brand awareness and building brand images via conveying functional, symbolic, and experiential benefits (recall the brand equity model presented in Chapter 2).

Packaging Structure

There is a tendency for consumers to impute characteristics from a package to the brand itself, a tendency termed *sensation transference*.[67] A package communicates meaning about a brand via its various symbolic components: color, design, shape, size, physical materials, and information labeling. These components taken together represent what is referred to as the *packaging structure*.[68] These structural elements must interact harmoniously to evoke within buyers the set of meanings intended by the brand marketer. The notion underlying good packaging is *gestalt*. That is, people react to the unified whole—the gestalt—not to the individual parts.

The following sections describe various package structure components. Although these descriptions are more anecdotal than scientific, you should find these characterizations thought provoking though certainly not definitive. Serious students also will want to add personal examples to the lists of illustrations for each of the following packaging components.

The Use of Color in Packaging

Packaging colors have the ability to communicate various cognitive and emotional meanings to prospective buyers.[69] Research has convincingly demonstrated the important role that color plays in affecting our senses. For example, in one study researchers altered the shade of pudding by adding food colors to create dark brown, medium brown, and light brown "flavors." In actuality, the pudding was identical in all three versions, namely vanilla flavor. However, the research revealed that all three brown versions were perceived as tasting like chocolate. Moreover, the dark brown pudding was considered to have the best chocolate flavor and to be the thickest. The light brown pudding was perceived to be the creamiest, possibly because cream is white in color.[70] This study, though not conducted in a packaging context per se, certainly holds implications for the use of color in package design.

The strategic use of colors in packaging is effective because colors affect people emotionally. For example, the so-called high-wavelength colors of red, orange, and yellow possess strong excitation value and induce elated mood states.[71] *Red* is often described in terms such as *active, stimulating, energetic,* and *vital.* Brands using this as their primary color include Close-Up (toothpaste), Tylenol (medicine), Coca-Cola (soft drink), and Pringles (potato chips). *Orange* is an appetizing color that is often associated with food. Popular food brands using orange packaging include Wheaties (cereal), Uncle Ben's (rice), Sanka (coffee), Stouffer's (frozen dinners), and Kellogg's Mini-Wheats (cereal). *Yellow,* a good attention getter, is a warm color that has a cheerful effect on consumers. Cheerios (cereal), Kodak (film), Mazola (corn oil), and Pennzoil (motor oil) are just a few of the many brands that use yellow packages.

Green connotes abundance, health, calmness, and serenity. Green packaging is sometimes used for beverages (e.g., Heineken beer, Seven-Up, Sprite, and Mountain Dew), often for vegetables (e.g., Green Giant), most always for mentholated products (e.g., Salem cigarettes), and for many other products (Irish Spring deodorant soap, Fuji film, etc.). Green also has come to stand for environmentally friendly products and as a cue to consumers of reduced-fat, low-fat, and fat-free products (e.g., Healthy Choice products). *Blue* suggests coolness and refreshment. Blue is often associated with laundry and cleaning products (e.g., Downy fabric softener and Snuggle dryer sheets) and skin products (e.g., Nivea skin lotion, Noxzema skin cream). Finally, *white* signifies purity, cleanliness, and mildness. Gold Medal (flour), Special K (cereal), Dove (body lotion), and Pantene (shampoo) are a few brands that feature white packages.

In addition to the emotional impact that color brings to a package, elegance and prestige can be added to products by the use of polished reflective surfaces and color schemes using white and black or silver and gold. Cosmetic packages often use gold (e.g., Revlon's MoistureStay Lipcolor) or metallic silver packages (e.g., Almay Sheer makeup).

It is pertinent to note that the meaning of color varies from culture to culture. The comments made here are based on North American culture and are not necessarily applicable elsewhere. Readers from other cultures should identify exceptions to these comments and illustrate packages that do not adhere to North American color usage. It is interesting to note that a site on the Internet has since 1997 conducted a global survey of what meanings are conveyed by particular colors. At the time of this writing, over 30,000 people from around the world have taken the survey and identified the colors they associate with particular meanings. For example, what colors suggest the following meanings or emotions to you: dignity, happiness, dependability, high quality, and power? To take the survey and see what others think, go to http://express.colorcom.com/colorsurvey.

Design and Shape Cues in Packaging

Design refers to the organization of the elements on a package. An effective package design is one that permits good eye flow, provides the consumer with a point of focus, and conveys meaning about the brand's attributes and benefits. Package designers bring various elements together to help define a brand's image. These elements include—in addition to color—shape, size, and label design.

One way of evoking different feelings is through the choice of the slope, length, and thickness of lines on a package. *Horizontal lines* suggest restfulness and quiet, evoking feelings of tranquillity. There appears to be a physiological reason for this reaction—it is easier for people to move their eyes horizontally than vertically; vertical movement is less natural and produces greater strain on eye muscles than horizontal movement. *Vertical lines* induce feelings of strength, confidence, and even pride. Energizer (batteries), Aquafresh (toothpaste), and Jif (peanut butter) all feature vertical lines in their package designs. One can even think of an athletic uniform as a package of sorts, and vertical lines sometimes appear on uniforms (think, for example, of the New York Yankees' uniform with its famous pinstripes). *Slanted lines* suggest upward movement to most people in the Western world, who read from left to right and thus view slanted lines as ascending rather than descending. Armor All (automobile polish), Gatorade (power drink), and Dr. Pepper (soft drink) use slanted lines in their package designs.

Shapes, too, arouse certain emotions and have specific connotations. Generally, round, curving lines connote femininity, whereas sharp, angular lines suggest masculinity. A package's shape also affects the apparent volume of the container. In general, if two packages have the same volume but a different shape, the taller of the two will appear to hold a greater volume inasmuch as height is usually associated with volume.

Packages also can be shaped to convey information about their product contents. An interesting example of this is the package for the now retired Whipper Snapple brand of fruit drinks. Whipper Snapple, from Triarc Beverage, was a packaged "smoothie," a thick fruit drink made from fresh fruit blended with milk or another dairy product. Whipper Snapple was itself a clever brand name derived from the word *whippersnapper,* which is an expression referring to a young, presumptuous person. Testing revealed that the name appealed to consumers from all age groups and geographic regions of the United States. The packaging objective was to design a container that would signal Whipper Snapple's dairy content in an unmistakable way at the point of purchase. After much deliberation, it was decided to mold an ice cream–style swirl into the bottle to convey the impression that Whipper Snapple mixes fruit and dairy products in a smoothie-drink fashion.[72]

Packaging Size

Many product categories are available in several product sizes. Soft drinks, for example, come in 8-, 12- and 24-ounce bottles, 1-, 1.5-, and 2-liter containers, and in 6-, 12-, and 24-unit packs. Manufacturers offer different-sized containers to satisfy the unique needs of various market segments, to represent different usage situations, and to gain more shelf space in retail outlets. An interesting issue arises from the consumer's perspective with regard to the size of the container. In particular, does the amount of product consumption vary depending on the size of the container? For example, do consumers consume more content from a large package than a smaller version? Preliminary research on this matter reveals a tendency for consumers to indeed consume more content from larger packages. One reason for this behavior is that consumers perceive they gain lower unit prices from larger than smaller packages.[73] This finding is not universal across all products, however, because consumption for some products (such as laundry bleach or vitamins) is relatively invariant. Research also has revealed that packages with unusual shapes are perceived as containing larger quantities compared to more conventional packages, even when these latter packages are taller. The reason is that the unusual- or irregular-shaped packages draw more attention from consumers, and because there also is a tendency for larger packages to draw more attention than smaller ones, consumers' judgments of volume are biased when attending to irregularly shaped packages. That is, because both larger packages and irregularly shaped ones command greater attention, consumers somehow subconsciously associate irregular shapes with containing larger quantities.[74]

Physical Materials in Packaging

Another important consideration is the materials that make up a package. Increased sales and profits often result when upgraded packaging materials are used to design more attractive and effective packages. Packaging materials can arouse consumer emotions, usually subconsciously. Packages constructed of *metal* evoke feelings of strength, durability, and, perhaps undesirably, coldness. *Plastic* packages connote lightness, cleanliness, and perhaps cheapness. Materials that are *soft*, such as velvet, suede, and satin are associated with femininity. *Foil* can be used to convey a high-quality image and provoke feelings of prestige. Beverage products such as beers and sparkling wines often use foil with the apparent intent of appearing "high class." Finally, *wood* sometimes is used in packages to arouse feelings of masculinity.

Evaluating the Package: The VIEW Model

A number of individual features have been discussed in regard to what a package communicates to buyers, but what exactly constitutes a good package? Although, as always, no single response is equally suitable across all packaging situations, four general features can be used to evaluate a particular package. These are visibility, information, emotional appeal, and workability, which are conveniently remembered with the acronym **VIEW**.[75]

V = Visibility

Visibility signifies the ability of a package to attract attention at the point of purchase. The objective is to have a package stand out on the shelf yet not be so garish that it detracts from a brand's image. Brightly colored packages are especially effective at gaining the consumer's attention. Novel packaging graphics, sizes, and shapes also enhance a package's visibility and thus serve to draw the consumer's attention.

Many brands in product categories such as soft drinks, cereal, and candy alternate packages throughout the year with special seasonal and holiday packaging as a way of attracting attention. By aligning the brand with the shopping mood fitting the season or holiday, companies provide consumers with an added reason for selecting the specially packaged brand over more humdrum brands that never vary their package design. The heart-shaped package for Reese's peanut butter cups (Figure 7.10) is an attractive, attention-gaining, and romance-conveying package design that is perfect for Valentine's Day.

Figure 7.10
An Effective Seasonal Package Design

I = Information

This second element of the VIEW model deals with various forms of product information that are presented on packages (e.g., product ingredients, usage instructions, claimed benefits, nutritional information, and product warnings). The objective is to provide the right type and quantity of information without cluttering the package with excessive information that could interfere with the primary message or cheapen the look of the package. As discussed in the Marcom Challenge back in Chapter 3, information about the amount of trans fat contained in food products became required information on food products starting in 2006. Trans fats raise the level of "bad" cholesterol in the body and lower the level of "good" cholesterol. Frito-Lay—the maker of salted snacks such as Lay's, Ruffles, Doritos, and Tostitos—preempted the FDA's mandate by adding the "Smart Snack" label to the front of its baked-snack packages (see Figure 7.11). This information undoubtedly will influence purchase decisions among the segment of health-conscious consumers.

In some instances, putting a short, memorable slogan on a package is a wise marketing tactic. Slogans on packages are best used when a strong association has been built between the brand and the slogan through extensive and effective advertising. The slogan on the package, a concrete reminder of the brand's advertising, can facilitate the consumer's retrieval of advertising content and thereby enhance the chances of a trial purchase. (When discussing point-of-purchase advertising in Chapter 8, we will refer to this practice of putting an advertising slogan on a package as utilizing the *encoding specificity principle.*)

Courtesy FRITO-LAY, INC.

Figure 7.11
Frito Lay's Smart Snack Label

E = Emotional Appeal

The third component of the VIEW model, *emotional appeal,* is concerned with a package's ability to evoke a desired feeling or mood. Package designers attempt to arouse feelings such as elegance, prestige, cheerfulness, and fun through the use of color, shape, packaging materials, and other devices. Packages for some brands contain virtually no emotional elements and emphasize instead informational content, whereas packages of other brands emphasize emotional content and contain very little information. The emotional value of packaging is well illustrated by the relatively new packaging of Heinz ketchup. Heinz, like other brands in this category, had always been packaged in glass bottles. Then the company began packaging ketchup in plastic containers. Both the bottles and the plastic containers were relatively blah, however. In an appeal to children, who consume 55 percent of all ketchup in the United States, Heinz eventually designed an emotionally appealing, fun-oriented package with bright coloring and a multihued, striped design. Children love the different ketchup colors (red, green, and purple) and the similarly colored packages that convey these various hues.

What determines whether information or emotion is emphasized in a brand's package? The major determinant is the nature of the product category and the underlying consumer behavior involved. Recognizing the distinction drawn in Chapter 5 between the consumer processing model (CPM) and the hedonic, experiential model (HEM), it should be expected that greater informational influence in packaging would go along with CPM-oriented consumer behavior, whereas more emotional influence would be associated with HEM-oriented behavior. In other words, if consumers make brand-selection decisions based on objectives such as obtaining the best buy or making a prudent choice (CPM-type objectives), then packaging must provide sufficient concrete information to facilitate the consumer's selection. When, however, product and brand selections are made in the pursuit of amusement, fantasies, or sensory stimulation (HEM-type objectives), packaging must contain the requisite emotional content to activate purchase behavior.

This discussion should not be taken as suggesting that all packaging emphasizes either information or emotion. Although the packaging of brands in some categories does emphasize one or the other, there are many product categories where it is necessary for packaging to blend informational and emotional content so as to simultaneously appeal to consumers' rational and symbolic needs. Cereal is a case in point. Consumers require nutritional information to intelligently select from among the dozens of available brands, and research indicates that consumer

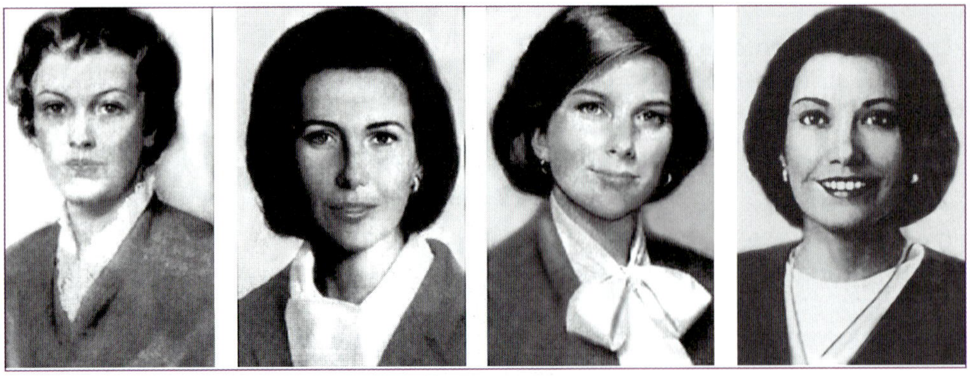

Courtesy of General Mills

Figure 7.12
The Changing Faces of Betty Crocker

choice in the cereal category is indeed influenced by nutritional components such as protein, fat, fiber, sodium, sugar, and vitamins and minerals.[76] Cereal choice also is driven by emotional factors—wholesomeness, nostalgia, excitement, and so on. General Mills, for example, has used pictures of fictitious Betty Crocker on its boxes for over 50 years. This virtual icon on the supermarket shelves symbolizes family values and wholesomeness. Over the years, General Mills has periodically changed the photo of Betty Crocker to keep in step with the times. Several years ago General Mills introduced the most recent Betty Crocker—a digitally morphed amalgam of the photos of 75 women in celebration of General Mills's 75th birthday (see Figure 7.12).

W = Workability

The final component of the VIEW model, *workability,* refers to how a package functions rather than how it communicates. Several workability issues are prominent: (1) does the package protect the product contents, (2) does it facilitate easy storage on the part of both retailers and consumers, (3) does it simplify the consumer's task in accessing and using the product, (4) does it protect retailers against unintentional breakage from consumer handling and from pilferage, and (5) is the package environmentally friendly?

Numerous packaging innovations in recent years have enhanced workability. These include pourable-spout containers for motor oil and sugar; easy-pour containers (such as for Heinz ketchup); microwaveable containers for many food items; zip-lock packaging for cheese and other food items; single-serving bags and boxes; food in tubes (e.g., yogurt, applesauce, and pudding); slimmer 12 packs of beer and soft drinks that take up less room in refrigerators; and easy-to-hold/open/pour paint containers (see Figure 7.13). Some additional examples of "workable" packages are described in the *IMC Focus.*

Figure 7.13
Dutch Boy's Easy-to-Hold/Open/Pour Paint Container

Courtesy Dutch Boy Paints

The introduction of Go-Gurt yogurt for children is a fascinating illustration of how a "workable" package altered consumer behavior and increased sales. Because eating yogurt from a standard container minimally requires the availability of a spoon, children and teens were not consuming yogurt at school. Hence, standard yogurt packaging essentially restricted sales of yogurt to adults and to the relatively few children and teens willing to take a spoon to school. Marketing executives at General Mills' Yoplait division developed a fascinatingly simple but profitable solution to this problem when it introduced the Go-Gurt brand of yogurt in a tube. In its first year after introduction, Go-Gurt garnered national sales in excess of $100 million and nearly doubled the proportion of yogurt users under the age of 19 to about one in six. The choice of Go-Gurt as the brand name facilitated product adoption by signifying that the tube contained yogurt and suggesting that the brand was to be consumed on the go.[77] Yoplait has also developed a similar yogurt-in-a-tube product for adults called Yoplait Express.

Companies also have developed "smart packages" that include magnetic strips, bar codes, and electronic chips that can

Illustrations of Workable Packages

imc focus

Various examples of packaging workability were mentioned in this chapter. Following are three additional illustrations that are interesting due to their novelty and potential to alter consumer behavior. Consider first a new type of package container for wine. Of course, wine has traditionally been packaged in glass bottles. But now Francis Ford Coppola (the famous Hollywood filmmaker) has introduced Sofia Blanc de Blancs sparkling wine packaged in a 4-pack of 6.35-ounce cans. The cans for Sofia wine come with pop-tops and attached straws that can be inserted for drinking wine in a ladylike fashion rather than guzzling it in the manner some guys do when drinking beer. It is a matter of time whether this novel package design will catch on and be adopted by consumers and other wine makers. Interestingly, some critics are concerned that this new package design has ethical implications in its targeting of young women. (Refer to the discussion of the ethics of targeting in Chapter 3.)

Also in the wine category, Canandaigua Wine Co. has introduced a new Tetra Pak wine container reminiscent of juice boxes for kids. The container is about the size of a large soda or beer can and is designed for easy holding. Needless to say, critics also are concerned that this package design will appeal to novice drinkers and blur the line between alcoholic and non-alcoholic beverages.

A further innovation in the alcoholic beverages category is aluminum bottles for beer, which first was introduced by Pittsburgh Brewing Co. for packaging its Iron City brand. Aluminum beer bottles offer the relative advantages of being lighter than glass, unbreakable, more portable, faster chilling, and cheaper to recycle. Though it would seem strange for traditional beer drinkers to drink beer from a long-neck aluminum bottle rather than a glass container, familiarity with drinking beer from aluminum cans should make this a relatively smooth transition.

Sources: Margaret Menge, "Wine in Translation," *U.S. News & World Report,* May 24, 2004, D13 (Sophia wine can); Alice Z. Cuneo, "Single-serve Wine Boxes Raise Watchdogs' Eyebrows," *Advertising Age,* April 19, 2004, 8 (Tetra Park wine container); Paul Glader and Christopher Lawton, "Beer, Wine Makers Use Fancy Cans to Court New Fans," *The Wall Street Journal Online,* August 24, 2004, http://online.wsj.com (aluminum beer bottles).

communicate with appliances, computers, and consumers. For example, packages of microwaveable foods eventually will be programmed to "tell" microwaves how long the food item should be cooked. Upjohn, maker of the hair-loss product Rogaine, developed packaging to prevent consumer pilferage of this relatively expensive product. This packaging contains electronic sensors that require deactivation at the store register. Procter & Gamble (P&G) is testing a smart-package program that is designed to send information about a product sale to a computer database as soon as a customer removes a P&G brand from the shelf. Small computer chips attached to the package send a signal to the store shelf, which contains printed circuit boards. The objective is, of course, to provide the company with immediate sales data that will facilitate its supply chain management.[78]

A host of environmentally safe packaging innovations have served to increase what might be called *societal workability.* Many of the changes have involved moves from plastic to recyclable paper packages; for example, many fast-food chains eliminated the use of foam packaging, and other firms have transformed their packages from plastic to cardboard containers. Another significant environmental initiative has been the increase in spray containers as substitutes for ozone-harming aerosol cans.

Workability is, of course, a relative matter. The objective is to design a package that is as workable as possible yet economical for the retailer and consumer. For example, consumers prefer food packages that completely prevent food from getting stale or spoiling, but the manufacturer's ability to provide this degree of workability is limited by cost. At the other extreme, some marketers skimp in package design and use inexpensive packages that are unsuitable because they are difficult to use and frustrate consumers.

Quantifying the VIEW Components

In conclusion, most packages do not perform well on all the VIEW criteria, but packages need not always be exemplary on all four VIEW components because the relative importance of each criterion varies from one product category to another. Emotional appeal dominates for some products (e.g., perfume), information is most important for others (e.g., staple food items), while visibility and workability are generally important for all products in varying degrees. In the final analysis, the relative importance of packaging requirements depends, as always, on the particular market and the competitive situation.

Though we have simply provided straightforward descriptions of the four VIEW components, it would be useful to go beyond mere description and have a procedure whereby the four components could be quantified on a case-by-case basis to determine whether a new package proposal stands a good chance of being successful. Figure 7.14 illustrates a procedure for accomplishing this goal and applies it to the new type of paint container that was presented in Figure 7.13. In a manner similar to what was done previously in quantifying the five adoption-determining characteristics (Figure 7.4), each VIEW component could be rated, first, in terms of its *importance* in determining the suitability of a proposed new package and then with respect to how well the new package performs on each component, its *evaluation* score. Applying this straightforward multiplicative model to the Dutch Boy paint container generates a hypothetical set of importance and evaluation scores. Because workability is considered the most important VIEW component for this particular packaging application and because the new container for Dutch Boy paint is evaluated as performing "at the max" on this component, this new packaging design receives a highly adequate total score of 49. It should be apparent that the importance scores for each packaging component will change from packaging situation to situation, and that the evaluation scores will differ for different prototype package designs that are under consideration. A simple model of this sort is not intended to make what ultimately is a subjective decision but rather to structure one's thinking in arriving at such a decision.

Designing a Package

Because package design is so critical to a brand's success, a systematic approach is recommended. Figure 7.15 provides a five-step package design process. The subsequent discussion describes each of these stages.[79]

Step 1: Specify Brand-Positioning Objectives

This initial stage requires that the brand management team specify how the brand is to be positioned in the consumer's mind and against competitive brands. What identity or image is desired for the brand? For example, when Pfizer Inc. developed Listerine PocketPaks, which is a dissolvable breath-strip product containing Listerine mouthwash, the objective was to design a package that was both functional and aesthetically appealing. Specifically, the package was designed such

Figure 7.14

Hypothetical Illustration of Quantifying the VIEW Model Components

VIEW Component	Importance (I)*	Evaluation (E)**	I x E
Visibility	3	4	12
Information	2	5	10
Emotional Appeal	2	1	2
Workability	5	5	25
Total Score	NA	NA	49

*Importance is rated on a scale with values ranging from zero to five. A rating of zero would indicate that a specific packaging component has no importance in this particular case. Higher positive values indicate progressively increasing levels of importance.

**Evaluation is rated on a scale with values ranging from minus five to five. A rating of zero, the midpoint of the scale, would indicate that the proposed new package performs neither favorably or unfavorably on the characteristic at hand; negative values indicate poor performance, with minus five representing the worst possible performance; positive values indicate favorable performance, with five representing the best possible performance.

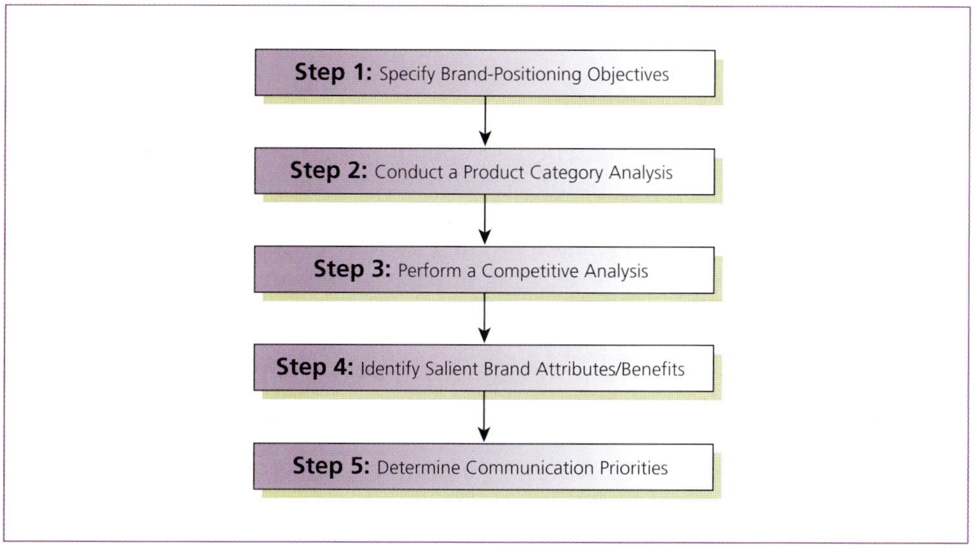

Figure 7.15
The Package Design Process

that oral care could be provided outside the home, be easily transportable, and be accessible by men as well as women in a variety of situations.[80] The brand name, PocketPaks, describes perfectly how the package was designed to literally fit in a person's pants or jacket pocket.

Step 2: Conduct a Product Category Analysis

Having established what the brand represents (step 1) and thus what the packaging must convey, it is essential to study the product category and related categories to determine relevant trends or anticipated events that would influence the packaging decision. The point, in other words, is that to be forewarned is to be forearmed.

Step 3: Perform a Competitive Analysis

Armed with knowledge about competitors' use of packaging colors, shapes, graphical features, and materials, the package designer is thus prepared to create a package that conveys the desired image (step 1) yet is sufficiently unique and differentiating (step 2) to capture consumer attention.

Step 4: Identify Salient Brand Attributes or Benefits

As noted earlier, research reveals that shoppers spend an incredibly short amount of time—on the order of 10 to 12 seconds—viewing brands before moving on or selecting an item and placing it in the shopping cart. It is imperative, therefore, that the package not be too cluttered with information and that it feature benefits that are most important to consumers. A general rule for identifying packaging benefits is "The fewer, the better."[81]

Step 5: Determine Communication Priorities

Having identified the most salient brand benefits (step 4), the package designer at this phase of the process must establish verbal and visual priorities for the package. Although perhaps three benefits may have been identified in step 4 as essentially equal in importance, the designer must prioritize which of the three is to capture the greatest visual or verbal attention on the package. This is a very tough decision because it is tempting to devote equal attention to all important brand benefits. It is critical that the package designer acknowledge that the package "advertisement" at the point of purchase occurs in an incredibly cluttered environment for a very short duration. Acknowledging this fact makes it much easier to devote package space to the most important brand benefit.

Summary

The continual introduction of new products and services is critical to the success of most business organizations. The concepts of adoption and diffusion explain the processes by which new products and services are accepted by increasing numbers of customers as time passes. Marketing communications can facilitate the process by communicating a new product's relative advantages, showing how it is compatible with consumers' existing purchase preferences and values, reducing real or perceived complexity, enhancing the product's communicability, and making it easy to try.

Opinion leadership and word-of-mouth influence are important elements in facilitating more rapid product adoption and diffusion. Opinion leaders are individuals who are respected for their product knowledge and opinions. Opinion leaders inform other people (followers) about new products and services, provide advice and reduce the follower's perceived risk in purchasing a new product, and confirm decisions that followers have already made. Compared with followers, opinion leaders are more cosmopolitan, are more gregarious, have higher socioeconomic status, and are more innovative. Positive word-of-mouth influence is often critical to new-product success. It appears that people talk about new products and services because they gain a feeling of prestige from being the bearer of news. Marketing communicators can take advantage of this prestige factor by stimulating cheerleaders, who will talk favorably about a new product or service.

Buzz creation—also called *viral marketing, guerrilla marketing,* and *street marketing*—is a relatively recent phenomenon as a proactive marketing practice. Firms employ the services of buzz-creation units to generate new–product adoption by recruiting the efforts of connected people (opinion leaders and market mavens) who will both adopt and talk about new products. Indeed, buzz creation can be compared to a social epidemic. Online buzz generation is occurring at an increasingly rapid pace with the advent of chat rooms and blogs.

The brand name is the single most important element found on a package. The brand name works with package graphics and other product features to communicate and position the brand's image. The brand name identifies the product and differentiates it from others on the market. A good brand name can evoke feelings of trust, confidence, security, strength, durability, speed, status, and many other desirable associations. A good brand name must satisfy several fundamental requirements: it must describe the product's benefits, be compatible with the product's image, and be memorable and easy to pronounce. A major section in this chapter was devoted to a five-step process for selecting a brand name. Another section discussed the nature and role of brand logos.

The package is perhaps the most important component of the product as a communications device. It reinforces associations established in advertising, breaks through competitive clutter at the point of purchase, and justifies price and value to the consumer. Package design relies on the use of symbolism to support a brand's image and to convey desired information to consumers. A number of package cues are used for this purpose, including color, design, shape, brand name, physical materials, and product information labeling. These cues must interact harmoniously to evoke within buyers the set of meanings intended by the marketing communicator. Package designs can be evaluated by applying the VIEW model, which contains the elements of visibility, information, emotional appeal, and workability. A concluding section described a five-step process for package design.

Discussion Questions

1. Sugar-substitute products have been available for years. The two historically leading brands in this category are Equal (blue package) and Sweet'N Low (pink package). More recently, a yellow-packaged product named Splenda was introduced. The company that markets this brand claims that it is "made from sugar, so it tastes like sugar." Using Splenda for illustration, explain the process by which marketing variables can influence consumers to become part of the awareness, trier, and repeater classes for this brand (refer to Figure 7.2).
2. Based on what you now know about factors that facilitate the adoption process (relative advantages, compatibility, etc.), what is the likelihood that Splenda will receive widespread consumer acceptance and become a major competitor to the older and better-known brands in this product category?
3. What determines whether a new product or service has relative advantages over competitive offerings? Identify the relative advantages of each of the following: disposable cameras, hybrid automobiles, plasma TVs. Given that each of these products also has relative disadvantages compared to competitive products, present a general statement (i.e., a statement with universal applicability) that would explain why consumers are willing to adopt new products even though they almost invariably have relative disadvantages.
4. Pick a new product or service of your choice, and describe in detail how that product or service satisfies, or fails to satisfy, the following success requirements: relative advantages, compatibility, communicability, trialability, and observability.
5. Suppose you are the manager of a new restaurant located in your college or university community that caters primarily to the campus population. Your fledgling restaurant cannot yet afford media advertising, so the promotional burden rests on stimulating positive word-of-mouth communications. Present a specific strategy for how you might go about stimulating positive WOM.
6. With thoughts of the Toyota Prius in mind, if you were the brand manager for this brand, what would you do to generate explosive self-generating demand?
7. BMW employed the services of top film directors to develop five-minute short films with a BMW vehicle as the subject of each "short." These films are available for viewing on the Web (http://www.bmwfilms.com). Apparently this site has attracted an enormous number of viewers. With reference to pertinent material in the chapter about word-of-mouth influence and buzz-building efforts, explain why this alternative marcom effort may be effective for BMW's featured brands.
8. The researchers who conceived the concept of the market maven devised a scale to measure consumers' responses to the following six items:
   (1) I like introducing new brands and products to my friends.
   (2) I like helping people in providing them with information about many kinds of products.
   (3) People ask me for information about products, places to shop, or sales.
   (4) If someone asked where to get the best buy on several types of products, I could tell him or her where to shop.
   (5) My friends think of me as a good source of information when it comes to new products or sales.
   (6) Think about a person who has information about a variety of products and likes to share this information with others. This person knows about new products, sales, stores, and so on, but does not necessarily feel he or she is an expert on one particular product. This description fits me well.

   Respondents are asked to rate each item on a 7-point scale, from strongly disagree (1) to strongly agree (7); thus, total scores range from a low of 6 (strongly disagrees to all six items) to 42 (strongly agrees to all items). Administer the scale to two friends whom you regard as market mavens and to two friends who are not market mavens. See if the mavens receive predictably higher scores than the non-mavens. Also, comment on whether you think these six items do a good job of measuring market mavenness. What additions or deletions, if any, would you make?

9. Explain how you would go about seeding a new music CD in a particular market of your choice. Be specific regarding the nature of the target audience toward which your seeding efforts would be directed and the techniques and methods you would employ to seed the vanguard among your target audience.
10. In your view, why do marketing practitioners use the terms *guerilla marketing*, *viral marketing*, and *street marketing* in reference to efforts to create buzz for new products and brands?
11. With reference to the discussion of explosive self-generating demand, describe a current movie that *would* lend itself to buzz-creation efforts and another that would *not*. What's the difference between these movies that makes only one amenable to buzz-building efforts?
12. Assume you have just started a new company that is in the business of creating brand names for clients. Your first client is a company that plans to go into business to compete against Dunkin' Donuts. However, the company's unique advantage is that its donuts are made with a fat substitute and hence are fat free. The client wants a name for its future donut shops to convey that its donuts are fat free but tasty. Create two names you consider appropriate and justify the logic underlying each.
13. Perform the same exercise as in question 12, but now develop a brand name for a new brand of soy milk. Perhaps the best-known brand in this category is Silk, which obviously is a conjunction of soy and milk.
14. Select a product category of personal interest and analyze the brand names for three competitive brands in that category. Analyze each brand name in terms of the fundamental requirements that were described in the text. Order the three brands according to which has the best, next best, and worst brand name. Support your ranking with specific reasons.
15. A Boston diamond wholesaler developed a special way for cutting diamonds that gives diamonds perfect symmetry and extra sparkle. The wholesaler developed a viewing device (called the *proportion scope*) that allows consumers to see a diamond with eight perfect hearts and eight arrows when they peer through the scope. The inventor of this specially cut diamond gave his gems the brand name Hearts on Fire. Evaluate this name by applying concepts from the chapter. Propose an alternative name.
16. What are your views regarding the Sundsvall brand name for vodka as described in the Marcom Challenge?
17. SUVs have names such as the Ford Explorer, Chevy Blazer, Mercury Mountaineer, Lincoln Navigator, Subaru Forester, Mazda Navajo, Infinity QX-4, Honda Passport, Jeep Wrangler, Dodge Dakota, Olds Bravada, and so on. Several years ago the Ford Motor Company purchased the Volvo Motor Company of Sweden. Assume that Ford executives decide to add an upscale Volvo SUV to their expanded product line. What would you name this new vehicle? What is your rationale for this name?
18. Select a packaged-goods product category, and apply the VIEW model to three competitive brands within that category. Define all four components of the model, and explain how each applies to your selected product. Then use the following procedures to weigh each component in the model in terms of your perception of its relative packaging importance in your chosen product category:
    a. Distribute 10 points among the four components, with more points signifying more importance and the sum of the allocated points totaling exactly 10. (This weighting procedure involves what marketing researchers refer to as a *constant sum scale*.)

b. Next, evaluate each brand in terms of your perception of its performance on each packaging component by assigning a score from 1 (does not perform well) to 10 (performs extremely well). Thus, you will assign a total of 12 scores: four for each VIEW component for the three different brands.
c. Combine the scores for each brand by multiplying the brand's performance on each component by the weight of that component (from step a) and then summing the products of these four weighted scores.

The summed score for each of your three chosen brands will reflect your perception of how good that brand's packaging is in terms of the VIEW model—the higher the score, the better the packaging in your opinion. Summarize the scores for the three brands for an overall assessment of each brand's packaging.

ENDNOTES

1. Adapted from Shelly Branch, "This High End Vodka Brand Turns into an Absolut Flop," *The Wall Street Journal Online,* December 21, 2000, http://online.wsj.com
2. William Boulding, Ruskin Morgan, and Richard Staelin, "Pulling the Plug to Stop the New Product Drain," *Journal of Marketing Research* 34 (February 1997), 164.
3. The following discussion is adapted from Chakravarthi Narasimhan and Subrata K. Sen, "New Product Models for Test Market Data," *Journal of Marketing* 47 (winter 1983), 13, 14.
4. A sophisticated and thorough empirical analysis of factors influencing the probability the people will undertake trial purchases of consumer packaged goods is provided by Jan-Benedict E. M. Steenkamp and Katrijn Gielens, "Consumer and Market Drivers of the Trial Probability of New Consumer Packaged Goods," *Journal of Consumer Research* 30 (December 2003), 368–384.
5. Everett M. Rogers, *Diffusion of Innovations,* 5th ed. (New York: Free Press, 2003).
6. Jennifer Saranow, "Cold Beer, Hot Plasma," *The Wall Street Journal Online,* May 25, 2004, http://online.wsj.com.
7. This quote and details about Adidas 1 are from Stephanie Kang, "Adidas's New Running Shoe to Outpace Rivals—in Price," *The Wall Street Journal Online,* May 6, 2004, http://online.wsj.com.
8. "iMac's Success Spawns Imitators of Translucent Product Casing," *The Wall Street Journal Online,* January 4, 1999, http://onine.wsj.com.
9. For further discussion of the role of observability, see Robert J. Fisher and Linda L. Price, "An Investigation into the Social Context of Early Adoption Behavior," *Journal of Consumer Research* 19 (December 1992), 477–486.
10. Charles Forelle, "Razors to Lasers: Gillette Pursues In-Home System," *The Wall Street Journal Online,* February 20, 2003, http://online.wsj.com.
11. This section is adapted from Thomas S. Robertson, Joan Zielinski, and Scott Ward, *Consumer Behavior* (Glenview, Ill.: Scott, Foresman and Company, 1984), 380–382.
12. For discussion of adoption of innovations in organizations, see Rogers, *Diffusion of Innovations,* chapter 10, and R. Bruce Money, Mary C. Gilly, and John L. Graham, "Explorations of National Culture and Word-of-Mouth Referral Behavior in the Purchase of Industrial Services in the United States and Japan," *Journal of Marketing* 62 (October 1998), 76–87.
13. Johan Arndt, "Role of Product-Related Conversation in the Diffusion of a New Product," *Journal of Marketing Research* 4 (August 1967), 291–295; Dorothy Leonard-Barton, "Experts as Negative Opinion Leaders in the Diffusion of a Technological Innovation," *Journal of Consumer Research* 11 (March 1985), 914–926.
14. For further discussion, see Rogers, *Diffusion of Innovations,* chapter 8, and Jacqueline Johnson Brown and Peter H. Reingen, "Social Ties and Word-of-Mouth Referral Behavior," *Journal of Consumer Research* 14 (December 1987), 350–362.
15. In addition to Brown and Reingen's findings, ibid., see also Jacob Goldenberg, Barak Libai, and Eitan Muller, "Talk of the Network: A Complex Systems Look at the Underlying Process of Word-of-Mouth," *Marketing Letters* 12 (August 2001), 211–224.
16. Rogers, *Diffusion of Innovations.*
17. Jehoshua Eliashberg and Steven M. Shugan, "Film Critics: Influencers or Predictors?" *Journal of Marketing* 61 (April 1997), 68–78.
18. This fifth point is based on research by Kenny K. Chan and Shekhar Misra, "Characteristics of the Opinion Leader: A New Dimension," *Journal of Advertising* 19, no. 3 (1990), 53–60.
19. This quote is from the famous motivational researcher Ernest Dichter, in Eileen Prescott, "Word-of-Mouth: Playing on the Prestige Factor," *The Wall Street Journal,* February 7, 1984, 1.
20. Lawrence F. Feick and Linda L. Price, "The Market Maven: A Diffuser of Marketplace Information," *Journal of Marketing* 51 (January 1987), 83–97.
21. Aki Maita, "Tamagotchi," *Ad Age International,* December 1997, 10; Norihiko Shirouzu, "Japan's High-School Girls Excel in the Art of Setting Trends," *The Wall Street Journal Online,* April 24, 1998, http://online.wsj.com.
22. Paul M. Herr, Frank R. Kardes, and John Kim, "Effects of Word-of-Mouth and Product-Attribute Information on Persuasion: An Accessibility-Diagnosticity Perspective," *Journal of Consumer Research* 17 (March 1991), 454–462; Richard J. Lutz, "Changing Brand Attitudes through Modification of Cognitive Structure," *Journal of Consumer Research* 1 (March 1975), 49–59; Peter Wright, "The Harassed Decision Maker: Time Pressures, Distractions, and the Use of Evidence," *Journal of Applied Psychology* 59 (October 1974), 555–561.
23. Marsha L. Richins, "Negative Word-of-Mouth by Dissatisfied Consumers: A Pilot Study," *Journal of Marketing* 47 (winter 1983), 76.
24. Kris Oser, "Microsoft's Halo2 Soars on Viral Push," *Advertising Age,* October 25, 2004, 46.

25. Jean Halliday, "Toyota Goes Guerilla to Roll Scion," *Advertising Age,* August 11, 2003, 4; Norihiko Shirouzu, "Scion Plays Hip-Hop Impresario to Impress Young Drivers," *The Wall Street Journal Online,* October 5, 2004, http://online.wsj.com.
26. T. L. Stanley, "Gibson on Mission to Market 'Passion,'" *Advertising Age,* February 16, 2004, 27; Merissa Marr, "Publicity, PR and 'Passion,'" *The Wall Street Journal Online,* February 20, 2004, http://online.wsj.com.
27. John Lippman, "Sony's Word-of-Mouth Campaign Creates Buzz for 'Crouching Tiger,'" *The Wall Street Journal Online,* January 11, 2001, http://online.wsj.com.
28. Ellen Neuborne, "Ambush," *Agency,* spring 2001, 22–25.
29. Chris Woodyard, "JetBlue Turns to Beetles, Beaches, Bars," *USA Today,* August 22, 2001, 3B.
30. Sholnn Freeman, "Oprah's GM Giveaway Was Stroke of Luck for Agency, Audience," *The Wall Street Journal Online,* September 14, 2004, http://online.wsj.com; Jean Halliday and Claire Atkinson, "Pontiac Gets Major Mileage Out of $8 Million 'Oprah' Deal," *Advertising Age,* September 20, 2004, 12.
31. Albert-László Barabási and Eric Bonabeau, "Scale-free Networks," *Scientific American,* May 2003, 60–69.
32. The idea of a "tipping point" is based on the popular book by journalist Malcolm Gladwell, *The Tipping Point* (Boston: Little, Brown and Company, 2000).
33. Ibid.
34. Renée Dye, "The Buzz on Buzz," *Harvard Business Review* (November/December 2000), 139–146.
35. This expression was attributed to a marketing practitioner and cited in Justin Kirby, "Online Viral Marketing: The Strategic Synthesis in Peer-to-Peer Brand Marketing," Brand Channel White Paper, 2004.
36. Dye, "The Buzz on Buzz."
37. Emanuel Rosen, *The Anatomy of Buzz: How to Create Word-of-Mouth Marketing* (New York: Doubleday, 2000); Marian Salzman, Ira Matathia, and Ann O'Reilly, *Buzz: Harness the Power of Influence and Create Demand* (New York: Wiley, 2003); Jon Berry and Ed Keller, *The Influentials: One American in Ten Tells the Other Nine How to Vote, Where to Eat, and What to Buy* (New York: Free Press, 2003).
38. Debbie Weil, "5 Key Questions (You've Been Dying) to Ask about Business Blogs," July 8, 2003, http://www.marketingprofs.com/3/weil7.asp.
39. Kris Oser, "More Marketers Test Blogs to Build Buzz," *Advertising Age,* September 14, 2004, 3, 49.
40. Ibid.
41. Rob Osler, "The Name Game: Tips on How to Get It Right," *Marketing News,* September 14, 1998, 50.
42. Gwen Bachmann Achenreiner and Deborah Roedder John, "The Meaning of Brand Names to Children: A Developmental Investigation," *Journal of Consumer Psychology* 13 no. 3 (2003), 205–219.
43. Joseph W. Alba, J. Wesley Hutchinson, and John G. Lynch, "Memory and Decision Making," in *Handbook of Consumer Behavior,* ed. Thomas S. Robertson and Harold H. Kassarjian (Englewood Cliffs, NJ: Prentice Hall, 1991), 1–49.
44. France Leclerc, Bernd H. Schmitt, and Laurette Dubé, "Foreign Branding and Its Effects on Product Perceptions and Attitudes," *Journal of Marketing Research* 31 (March 1994), 263–270.
45. These requirements represent a summary of views from a variety of sources, including Kevin Lane Keller, *Strategic Brand Management: Building, Measuring, and Managing Brand Equity* (Upper Saddle River, NJ: Prentice Hall, 1998), 136–140; Daniel L. Doden, "Selecting a Brand Name That Aids Marketing Objectives," *Advertising Age,* November 5, 1990, 34; and Walter P. Margulies, "Animal Names on Products May Be Corny, but Boost Consumer Appeal," *Advertising Age,* October 23, 1972, 77.
46. For excellent coverage of trademark infringement, review the following sources: Jeffrey M. Samuels and Linda B. Samuels, "Famous Marks Now Federally Protected Against Dilution," *Journal of Public Policy & Marketing* 15 (fall 1996), 307–310; Daniel J. Howard, Roger A. Kerin, and Charles Gengler, "The Effects of Brand Name Similarity on Brand Source Confusion: Implications for Trademark Infringement," *Journal of Public Policy & Marketing* 19 (fall 2000), 250–264.
47. Marcus W. Brauchli, "Chinese Flagrantly Copy Trademarks of Foreigners," *The Wall Street Journal,* June 20, 1994, B1, B2.
48. Chris Janiszewski and Stijn M. J. Van Osselaer, "A Connectionist Model of Brand-Quality Associations," *Journal of Marketing Research* 37 (August 2000), 331–350.
49. Kevin Lane Keller, Susan E. Heckler, and Michael J. Houston, "The Effects of Brand Name Suggestiveness on Advertising Recall," *Journal of Marketing* 62 (January 1998), 48–57. See also J. Colleen McCracken and M. Carole Macklin, "The Role of Brand Names and Visual Clues in Enhancing Memory for Consumer Packaged Goods," *Marketing Letters* 9 (April 1998), 209–226; and Richard R. Klink, "Creating Brand Names with Meaning: The Use of Sound Symbolism," *Marketing Letters* 11, no. 1 (2000), 5–20.
50. Sankar Sen, "The Effects of Brand Name Suggestiveness and Decision Goal on the Development of Brand Knowledge," *Journal of Consumer Psychology* 8 no. 4 (1999), 431–454.
51. Keller et al., "The Effects of Brand Name Suggestiveness on Advertising Recall." However, for an alternative perspective see Sen "The Effects of Brand Name Suggestiveness and Decision Goal."
52. For example, Richard R. Klink, "Creating Brand Names with Meaning: The Use of Sound Symbolism," *Marketing Letters* 11 (February 2000), 5–20; and Eric Yorkston and Geeta Menon, "A Sound Idea: Phonetic Effects of Brand Names on Consumer Judgments," *Journal of Consumer Research* 31 (June 2004), 43–51.
53. Yorkston and Menon, "A Sound Idea," 43.
54. Klink, "Creating Brand Names with Meaning."
55. Steve Jarvis, "What Changing a Name Involves Today," *Marketing News,* March 26, 2001, 1, 11, 12.
56. Tina M. Lowrey, L. J. Shrum, and Tony M. Dubitsky, "The Relation Between Brand-Name Linguistic Characteristics and Brand-Name Memory," *Journal of Advertising* 32 (fall 2003), 7–18. See also Dawn Lerman and Ellen Garbarino, "Recall and Recognition of Brand Names: A Comparison of Word and Nonword Name Types," *Psychology & Marketing* 19 (July/August 2002), 621–639. This latter article provides preliminary evidence that brand names that are created (i.e., nonword names) generate higher recognition scores than brand names based on actual words.
57. Chiranjeev Kohli and Douglas W. LaBahn, "Observations: Creating Effective Brand Names: A Study of the Naming Process," *Journal of Advertising Research* 37 (January/February 1997), 67–75.
58. Ibid., 69.

59. Ibid., 73.
60. Osler, "The Name Game."
61. When brand names are used, logos are set in any of a multitude of typefaces. Typeface design can have a substantial impact on the impressions formed when viewing a logo. Fascinating research on this issue is provided by Pamela W. Henderson, Joan L. Giese, and Joseph A. Cote, "Impression Management Using Typeface Design," *Journal of Marketing* 68 (October 2004), 60–72.
62. Pamela W. Henderson and Joseph A. Cote, "Guidelines for Selecting or Modifying Logos," *Journal of Marketing* 62 (April 1998), 14–30. This article is must reading for anyone interested in learning more about logos.
63. Henderson and Cote, "Guidelines for Selecting or Modifying Logos."
64. Some of these phrases were mentioned in Michael Gershman, "Packaging: Positioning Tool of the 1980s," *Management Review* (August 1987), 33–41.
65. Peter R. Dickson and Alan G. Sawyer, "The Price Knowledge and Search of Supermarket Shoppers," *Journal of Marketing* 54 (July 1990), 42–53; John Le Boutillier, Susanna Shore Le Boutillier, and Scott A. Neslin, "A Replication and Extension of the Dickson and Sawyer Price-Awareness Study," *Marketing Letters* 5 (January 1994), 31–42.
66. John Deighton, "A White Paper on the Packaging Industry," Dennison Technical Papers, December 1983, 5.
67. An interesting article about package meaning is available in Robert L. Underwood and Julie L. Ozanne, "Is Your Package an Effective Communicator? A Normative Framework for Increasing the Communicative Competence of Packaging," *Journal of Marketing Communications* 4 (December 1998), 207–220.
68. Herbert M. Meyers and Murray J. Lubliner, *The Marketer's Guide to Successful Package Design* (Chicago: NTC Business Books, 1998), 2.
69. For an in-depth treatment of the role of color in packaging and other forms of marketing communications, see Lawrence L. Garber, Jr. and Eva M. Hyatt, "Color as a Tool for Visual Persuasion," in *Persuasive Imagery: A Consumer Response Perspective,* Linda M. Scott and Rajeev Batra, eds. (Mahwah, NJ: Lawrence Erlbaum, 2003), 313–336.
70. Gail Tom, Teresa Barnett, William Lew, and Jodean Selmants, "Cueing the Consumer: The Role of Salient Cues in Consumer Perception," *The Journal of Consumer Marketing* 4 (spring 1987), 23–27.
71. This comment and parts of the following discussion are based on statements appearing in Joseph A. Bellizzi, Ayn E. Crowley, and Ronald W. Hasty, "The Effects of Color in Store Design," *Journal of Retailing* 59 (spring 1983), 21–45.
72. Gerry Khermouch, "Triarc's Smooth Move," *Brandweek,* June 22, 1998, 26–32.
73. Brian Wansink, "Can Package Size Accelerate Usage Volume?" *Journal of Marketing* 60 (July 1996), 1–14.
74. Valerie Folkes and Shashi Matta, "The Effect of Package Shape on Consumers' Judgments of Product Volume: Attention as a Mental Contaminant," *Journal of Consumer Research* 31 (September 2004), 390–401.
75. Dik Warren Twedt, "How Much Value Can Be Added through Packaging," *Journal of Marketing* 32 (January 1968), 61–65.
76. George Baltas, "The Effects of Nutrition Information on Consumer Choice," *Journal of Advertising Research* 41 (March / April 2001), 57–63.
77. Sonia Reyes, "Groove Tube." *Brandweek's* Marketers of the Year insert, October 16, 2000, M111–M116.
78. Greg Dalton, "If These Shelves Could Talk," *The Industry Standard,* April 2, 2001, 49–51.
79. This discussion is adapted from Meyers and Lubliner, *The Marketer's Guide to Successful Package Design,* 55–67.
80. Catherine Arnold, "Way Outside the Box," *Marketing News,* June 23, 2003, 13, 15.
81. Meyers and Lubliner, *The Marketer's Guide to Successful Package Design,* 63.

CHAPTER 8

On- and Off-Premise Signage and Point-of-Purchase Communications

Marcom Challenge: "Shopping Buddy"—an Intelligent Shopping Cart

The Stop & Shop Supermarket Company is the largest supermarket in New England with over 300 stores located throughout most of Massachusetts, where it is based, along with Connecticut, New Hampshire, New Jersey, New York, and Rhode Island. Owned by Ahold of the Netherlands, Stop & Shop is a progressive supermarket chain that is alert to ways of increasing its financial performance and enhancing consumers' shopping experiences. Perhaps the most technologically sophisticated move in Stop & Shop's history is the recent introduction of an intelligent shopping cart, affectionately referred to as "Shopping Buddy." Stop & Shop is introducing the intelligent shopping carts to its stores on a planned schedule and should have intelligent carts operational in over 20 stores by the end of 2005.[1]

Each Shopping Buddy cart is equipped with a wireless touch-screen IBM computer with a laser scanner to enable shoppers to check prices and then to scan purchased products. The carts maintain a running total of how much the shopper is spending, which enables rapid self-checkout at the end of the shopping trip. In addition to these fundamental services, here are some additional advantages of shopping with an intelligent shopping cart:

- The shopping cart computer maintains a file of the shopper's buying history. This provides the consumer with an "external memory" of his or her past purchases and can serve to remind one of needed items.
- In advance of the trip to Stop & Shop, the consumer can e-mail a shopping list to the store, which then can be accessed and displayed on the computer screen. This prevents the hassle of carrying (and possibly losing) a hard-copy list.
- As the shopper approaches items in the aisle, the intelligent shopping cart alerts him or her to which items are on sale and for which items shelf-dispensed coupons are available.
- Shoppers can place deli orders from the cart while shopping and then pick up the order when the deli counter sends a computer message notifying the shopper that the order is ready.
- Equipped with RFID (radio frequency identification) technology, the consumer can query Shopping Buddy as to where any item is located in the store and be directed via a path displayed on the computer screen to the exact location of that item.

Needless to say, intelligent shopping carts represent an exciting new technology that can serve the interests of all parties to marketing transactions: consumers, retailers, and manufacturers. The point of purchase is perhaps the ideal time to influence buying decisions, and intelligent shopping carts along with a variety of low-tech forms of signage are used by retailers and their manufacturer partners precisely for this purpose.

© Susan Van Etten

CHAPTER OBJECTIVES

1
Appreciate the role and importance of out-of-home, or off-premise, advertising.

2
Understand billboard advertising's strengths and limitations.

3
Appreciate the role and importance of on-premise business signage.

4
Review the various forms and functions of on-premise signage.

5
Appreciate the role and importance of point-of-purchase advertising.

6
Examine the tasks that P-O-P advertising accomplishes.

7
Review evidence of P-O-P's role in influencing consumers' in-store decision making.

8
Examine empirical evidence revealing the effectiveness of P-O-P displays.

9
Appreciate the importance of measuring audience size and demographic characteristics for out-of-home as well as in-store advertising messages.

Overview

The next major part of the text covers the subject of advertising management in considerable detail, focusing on topics such as creating ad messages, selecting media, and measuring results. The emphasis in that section is mostly on traditional advertising media (print and broadcast) along with the emerging role of online advertising.

The present chapter deals with topics that also represent a form of advertising but not in the same sense typically thought of when considering media such as television, radio, magazines, newspapers, and the Internet. Rather, the material covered in this chapter examines communicating with consumers at the point of purchase or close to it. In particular, we explore in this chapter three general forms of marketing communications: out-of-home advertisements (e.g., billboards), on-premise signage, and in-store point-of-purchase messages. All of these communication modes attempt to influence consumers' store- or brand-selection decisions. Out-of-home ads, on-premise store signage, and P-O-P messages represent important forms of communications that serve in very important ways to influence consumers' awareness and images of retail outlets and the brands they carry.

Topical coverage in this chapter first examines forms of message delivery that literally are located *outside* retail stores. We distinguish two general forms of "outside" marcom messages and refer to these as (1) out-of-home advertisements, or *off*-premise ads; and (2) *on*-premise business signage. The difference between on-premise business signage and out-of-home advertising (off-premise signage) is that the former communicates information about products and services in close proximity to the store, whereas the latter provides information about goods and services that are available somewhere else.[2] Following this coverage of "outside" communications, we then turn attention to "inside" forms of message presentation, which are referred to as point-of-purchase advertising, or, for short, P-O-P.

Out-of-Home (Off-Premise) Advertising

Though out-of-home (OOH) advertising pales in significance compared to media such as television and is regarded as a supplementary, rather than primary, advertising medium, OOH is nonetheless a very important form of marketing communications. The Outdoor Advertising Association of America, the industry's trade association, estimates that OOH advertising expenditures in the United States exceed $5 billion annually.[3] Out-of-home, or *outdoor,* advertising is the oldest form of advertising with origins dating back literally thousands of years. Although billboard advertising is the major aspect of out-of-home advertising, outdoor media encompasses a variety of other delivery modes: advertising on bus shelters and street furniture (e.g., benches), giant inflatables (blimps), various forms of transit advertising (including ads on buses, taxis, and trucks), shopping-mall displays, campus kiosks, advertising on public bicycle racks, skywriting, and so on.

The one commonality among these is that they are seen by consumers outside of their homes (hence the name) in contrast to television, magazines, newspapers, and radio, which typically are received in the home (or in other indoor locations). And reaching consumers with ad messages outside their homes is especially important when considering that most people spend much of their daily time at work or otherwise away from their homes. Americans report traveling an average of slightly over 300 miles in a vehicle during a typical week with an average round-trip commute totaling about 55 minutes.[4] It is obvious from these statistics that outdoor media reach millions of people in the United States—as well as around the globe.

Billboard Advertising

Billboard advertising is the major outdoor medium. Interestingly, the term *billboard* originates from the custom in colonial America of attaching a paper poster containing a message (known as a "bill") on a board for conveyance around town.[5] There are approximately 400,000 billboards in the United States.[6] Advertising on billboards is designed with name recognition as the primary objective. The major forms of billboard advertising are poster panels and painted bulletins.

Poster Panels

These billboards are what we regularly see alongside highways and in other heavily traveled locales. Posters are silk-screened or lithographed and then pasted in sheets to the billboard. The billboard industry in the United States is dominated by a few media conglomerates (e.g., Clear Channel Outdoor and Viacom Outdoor) that essentially control the industry. These companies typically sell billboard space on a monthly basis. Posters can be either 8-sheet or 30-sheet, literally designating the number of sheets of paper required to fill the allotted billboard space. An *8-sheet poster* is 6 feet, 2 inches high by 12 feet, 2 inches wide, although the actual viewing area is slightly smaller—5 feet by 11 feet (in other words, 55 square feet of viewing space). The much larger *30-sheet poster* is 12 feet, 3 inches high by 24 feet, 6 inches wide, with a viewing area of 9 feet, 7 inches by 21 feet, 7 inches (roughly 207 square feet).

Painted Bulletins

Painted bulletins are hand painted directly on the billboard by artists hired by the billboard owner. Standard bulletins measure 14 feet high by 48 feet wide and represent a total viewing space of 672 square feet. These bulletins are generally repainted every several months to provide a fresh look. Advertisers typically purchase these large bulletins for a one- to three-year period with the objective of achieving a consistent and relatively permanent presence in heavily traveled locations.

Buying Out-of-Home Advertising

Outdoor advertising is purchased through companies that own billboards, called *plants*. Plants are located in all major markets throughout the nation. To simplify the national advertiser's task of buying outdoor space in multiple markets, buying organizations, or agents, facilitate the purchasing of outdoor space at locations throughout the country.

Plants have historically sold poster-advertising space in terms of so-called showings. A *showing* is the percentage of the population that is theoretically exposed to an advertiser's billboard message. Showings are quoted in increments of 25 and are designated as #25, #50, #75, and #100. The designation #50, for example, means that 50 percent of the population in a particular market is expected on any given workday to pass the billboards on which an advertiser's message is posted. A showing of #100 is equivalent to saying that the entire population in a given market has an opportunity to see (referred to as an *OTS*) an advertiser's message in that particular market.

In recent years plants have converted to *gross rating points* (GRPs) as the metric for quoting poster prices. GRPs represent the percentage and frequency of an audience being reached by an advertising vehicle. Specifically, one outdoor GRP means reaching 1 percent of the population in a particular market a single time. Outdoor GRPs are based on the daily duplicated audience (meaning that some people may be exposed on multiple occasions each day) as a percentage of the total potential market. For example, if four billboards in a community of 200,000 people achieve a daily exposure to 80,000 persons, the result is 40 gross rating points. As with traditional showings, GRPs are sold in blocks of 25, with 100 and 50 being the two levels purchased most.

Billboard Advertising's Strengths and Limitations

Billboard advertising presents marketing communicators with several unique strengths and problems.

Strengths

A major strength of billboard advertising is its *broad reach and high frequency levels.* Billboards are effective in reaching virtually all segments of the population. The number of exposures is especially high when signs are strategically located in heavy traffic areas. Automobile advertisers are heavy users of outdoor media because they can reach huge numbers of potential purchasers with high frequency. The same can be said for fast-food advertisers.

Another advantage is *geographic flexibility.* Outdoor advertising can be strategically positioned to supplement other advertising efforts (e.g., TV, radio, and newspaper ads) in select geographic areas where advertising support is most needed.

Low cost per thousand is a third advantage. The cost-per-thousand metric (abbreviated as CPM, where *M* is the Roman numeral for 1,000) is literally the cost, on average, of exposing 1,000 people to an advertisement. It is estimated that the 8- and 30-sheet poster CPMs are $0.85 and $1.78, respectively. Comparatively, a full-page four-color magazine ad has an average CPM of $9.62, and a 30-second advertisement during prime time on network TV has an average CPM of $11.31.[7] It is obvious that outdoor advertising is the least expensive advertising medium on a cost-per-thousand basis. However, as will be emphasized in Chapter 14 when discussing the relative advantages of traditional advertising media, CPM comparisons across different media can be misleading. In other words, because the various media perform different functions, it is inappropriate to use CPM as the sole basis of evaluation.

Figure 8.1
Humans Playing Soccer on a Japanese Billboard

TBWA/Japan

Because outdoor advertising is literally bigger than life, *brand identification is substantial.* The ability to use large representations offers marketers excellent opportunities for brand and package identification. Also, billboard companies are becoming quite ingenious in designing billboards that attract viewers' attention. See the *Global Focus* insert for a description of a creative billboard approach used in advertising Adidas's athletic footwear in Japan (Figure 8.1).

Billboard advertising also provides an excellent opportunity to reach consumers as a *last reminder before purchasing.* This explains why products such as beer and restaurants are among the heaviest users. (Tobacco advertisers in the United States also used to be heavy outdoor advertisers, but as part of a legal settlement with the state attorneys general, tobacco brands stopped advertising in outdoor media in 1999.)

Live Soccer Players on Japanese Billboards

global focus

In Japanese cities such as Tokyo, outdoor media play a more prominent role than in countries such as the United States. It is estimated, in fact, that advertisers in Japan spend proportionately three to four times as much on out-of-home media as do American advertisers. Neon signs and electronic video billboards are ubiquitous in large Japanese cities. One reason for this widespread usage of OOH media is because the average Tokyo resident has a 70-minute commute to work, which makes billboards and other outdoor media an attractive and relatively inexpensive way of reaching them.

However, the heavy spending on outdoor ads has created a major clutter problem. How does an advertiser break through the clutter and capture consumers' attention? Sports-equipment and apparel maker Adidas came up with a novel solution: it designed faux soccer fields on billboards and suspended (via dangling ropes; see Figure 8.1) two soccer players and a ball 12 stories above the ground. The players participated in brief matches in Japan's two largest cities, Osaka and Tokyo. The two dangling soccer players played 10- to 15-minute matches at one-hour intervals during afternoons, while hundreds of pedestrians gathered below to watch. Of course, while they watched the soccer "matches," they were continuously exposed to the Adidas name and logo along with a message overlaid on the soccer "field" proclaiming, "Own the passion and you own the game." It is difficult imagining a more attention-gaining billboard than Adidas's use of live soccer players.

SOURCES: Geoffrey A. Fowler and Sebastian Moffett, "Adidas's Billboard Ads Give Kick to Japanese Pedestrians," *The Wall Street Journal Online,* August 29, 2003, http://online.wsj.com; Normandy Madden, "Adidas Introduces Human Billboards," *Advertising Age,* September 1, 2003, 11.

Limitations

A significant problem with outdoor advertising is *nonselectivity.* Outdoor advertising can be geared to general groups of consumers (such as inner-city residents) but cannot pinpoint specific market segments (say, professional African-American men between the ages of 25 and 39). Advertisers must turn to other advertising media (such as magazines) to better pinpoint audience selection. However, with newer technology that is under development, outdoor advertising is in the process of improving its ability to target customers. For example, a California company, Smart Sign Media, introduced technology that adjusts digital billboards to the radio stations playing inside passing vehicles. Using radio-station selection as an indicator of income, Smart Sign's technology calculates the average income of passersby and then changes the message to target the biggest cluster of people who drive by a particular billboard location.[8]

Short exposure time is another drawback. "Now you see it, now you don't" appropriately characterizes the fashion in which outdoor advertising engages the consumer's attention. For this reason, outdoor messages that have to be read are less effective than predominantly visual ones.

A final outdoor advertising limitation involves *environmental concerns.* Billboards, the so-called litter on a stick, have been banned in some manner by several U.S. states and hundreds of local governments. Although some would argue that attractive billboards can enliven and even beautify neighborhoods and highways with attractive messages, others consider this advertising medium to be ugly and intrusive. This largely is a matter of personal taste. The articles cited in the following endnote explore the issue in some depth, including a discussion of the value and potential hazards attendant to the growing use of *changeable message signs*—that is, billboards that vary the advertising message on a schedule of every 4 to 10 seconds.[9]

Measuring OOH Audience Size and Characteristics

When placing ads in print (newspapers and magazines) and broadcast media (radio and TV), advertisers have access to so-called syndicated data sources that inform them about (1) the size of the audience to be reached when using these media, and (2) the demographic characteristics of audiences reached by media vehicles such as individual magazines (e.g., *Cosmopolitan*) or TV programs (e.g., *Saturday Night Live*). (Audience measurement techniques for the print and broadcast media are described in detail in Chapter 14.) This information is invaluable when planning for and making media buying decisions. In advance of making a media buy, an advertiser can estimate what percentage of a target audience is likely to be reached and the average frequency audience members will have an OTS (opportunity to see—or read or hear) an ad message during, say, a four-week media planning period. Print and broadcast media are, in other words, *measurable*, and advertisers have quite a lot of faith in the accuracy of the audience data for these media.

Comparatively, there has been no equivalent measurable audience data available for the out-of-home advertising industry. Historically, the outdoor industry has relied on traffic data collected by the Traffic Audit Bureau that simply indicates how many people pass by an outdoor site such as a billboard. However, no information has been available regarding the demographic characteristics of the people who have an opportunity to see advertising messages on billboards. The lack of verified data regarding audience characteristics is widely regarded as a significant impediment that must be overcome if outdoor advertising is to become a more widely used advertising medium. Although traffic-flow data indicate the number of people who may have an opportunity to see a billboard message, it provides absolutely no information about people's demographic characteristics, which is the type of information needed by advertisers to make intelligent *targeting* decisions. (Recall again the mantra introduced in Chapter 1: all marketing communications should be (1) directed to a particular target market, (2) clearly positioned, (3) created to achieve a specific objective, and (4) undertaken to accomplish the objective within budget constraint.)

This lack of information has retarded the growth of the OOH industry and has prevented many advertisers from investing heavily in out-of-home media. Relatively few national advertisers spend large percentages of their advertising budgets on OOH advertising. This situation is unlikely to change until the OOH industry somehow develops accurate measures of audience size and demographic characteristics. To place ads in media without accurate knowledge of audience characteristics is equivalent to, in farmer's language, "purchasing a pig in a poke [a bag or sack]." In other words, it is unwise to purchase something that has been concealed without knowing in advance what you're acquiring.

Fortunately, a company that specializes in the measurement of advertising audiences—namely, Nielsen Media Research—is making substantial strides toward developing ways to determine the demographic characteristics of outdoor audiences. Nielsen's service involves selecting a demographically representative set of individuals, collecting relevant demographic information from them, and equipping them with battery-operated meters called Npods (for Nielsen Personal Outdoor Devices). Using global positioning satellite (GPS) technology, these Npod meters automatically track individuals' movements from the time they leave their homes until they return. With knowledge of the demographic characteristics of sample members and knowing literally their geographical whereabouts, it is possible to connect these two data sets and draw conclusions about the demographic characteristics of the people who have had an opportunity to see an ad carried on any particular billboard location. Armed with verifiable knowledge about the demographic characteristics of people who pass particular billboard locations or the sites of other outdoor ads, it is likely that advertisers will increase their use of OOH advertising.

A Case Study of Billboard Effectiveness

Adams Outdoor Advertising, a large Atlanta-based firm, undertook a creative campaign to demonstrate the effectiveness of billboard advertising. With the assistance of Cognetix—an advertising agency located in Charleston, South Carolina—a scheme was hatched to test the effectiveness of billboard advertising. Adams and Cognetix ran a billboard campaign for a fictitious brand of bottled water that they named Outhouse Springs. Playing on the concept of incongruity (a bottled water named Outhouse Springs?) and using potty-type humor, billboard advertisements for Outhouse Springs were located throughout the Charleston, South Carolina market and achieved a 75 showing at a monthly cost of approximately $25,000. Messages on the billboards included amusing, albeit incredulous, statements such as "America's First Recycled Water"; "Originally in Cans . . . Now in Bottles"; "L-M-N-O- . . ."; and "It's #1, Not #2" (see Figure 8.2 for illustrations). To assess campaign effectiveness, brand awareness, perceptions, and purchase intentions were measured in weekly intervals. By week three, 67 percent of a large sample of consumers indicated awareness of the hypothetical Outhouse Springs brand, 77 percent had neutral or favorable perceptions of this bottled water brand, and 85 percent indicated an intention to purchase the product. In light of this success, Adams Outdoor extended the campaign to markets in North Carolina, Virginia, Pennsylvania, Michigan, and Wisconsin.

Though admittedly a highly unique and buzzable product (recall the discussion in Chapter 7), this campaign for a fictitious brand of bottled water reveals that large numbers of people are exposed to billboard ads and can be favorably influenced. Part of the success was no doubt due to the fact that widespread buzz generated stories on TV, radio, and in newspaper articles.[10] Nonetheless, this test of a hypothetical brand does illustrate that people are alert to billboard messages that are attention catching and memorable.

On-Premise Business Signage

This section deals with a topic—on-premise signage—that is commonplace and may therefore be considered trivial. We are indeed surrounded by store signs of one variety or another. Every reader of this text has been exposed to literally thousands of signs—many, if not most, of which have not much captured your attention or

Figure 8.2
Illustration from the Outhouse Springs Billboard Campaign

Cognetix Advertising/Adams Outdoor

interest. However, we can place this topic in perspective when noting that *on-premise signs* (i.e., those located on or near retail stores) are considered the most cost-effective and efficient form of communication available to retail businesses. Beyond this generalization, the value of on-premise signs has been described in these optimistic terms:

> *No amount of money spent on other forms of communication media will equal the investment return of the well-designed and optimally visible on-premise sign. Surveys of new customers/clients disclose over and over that the on-premise business sign either: (1) provided the new customer with their first knowledge of the company, or (2) provided the new customer with their first impression of the company. This is true even if the customer originally learned of the business through some other communication medium, such as the Yellow Pages or 'word of mouth.' It is no longer [an] overstatement to assert that legible, conspicuous place-based signage, easily detectable and readable within the cone of vision of the motoring public, is essential to small business survival.*[11]

Types of Signs

Although on-premise signs include an incredible diversity of signage that is limited only by designers' creativity and governmental regulations, we can identify two general categories, either free-standing or building-mounted.[12] *Free-standing* signs include monument signs, pole signs, A-frame (a.k.a. sandwich-board) signs, portable signs, inflatable signs, and other forms of signs that are unattached to a retail building (see Figure 8.3 for illustrations). *Building-mounted signs* include projecting signs, wall signs, roof signs, banners, murals, and canopy or awning signs (see Figure 8.4 for illustrations).

Figure 8.3
Illustrations of Free-Standing Signs

Courtesy, The Signage Foundation for Communication Excellence, Inc.

The ABCs of On-Premise Signs

On-premise signs enable consumers to identify and locate businesses and can influence their store-choice decisions and prompt impulse purchasing. These functions are conveniently referred to as the ABCs of store signage. That is, an effective sign should minimally perform the following functions:[13]

- Attract new customers
- Brand the retail site in consumers' minds
- Create impulse purchases

Of course, the specific functions performed and the importance of having eye-catching and attractive signs depend on the nature of the business, whether it is a small retailer with a relatively fixed clientele—in which case, signage is relatively less critical—or a business that must constantly attract new customers. In this latter situation, signage performs a critical function because for retailers to stay in business and potentially thrive they must capture travelers, who are one-time or occasional customers.

Attracting new customers requires first and foremost that a store sign capture the consumer's attention. This is no small feat when considering that the retail landscape often is dense with competing signs that are attempting to achieve the same outcome, namely, to capture attention and make a positive impression. Experts in the design of store signage use a concept, termed *conspicuity,* that refers to the ability of a sign to capture attention. By definition, **conspicuity** involves those signage characteristics that enable walkers or drivers and their passengers to distinguish a sign from its surrounding environment.[14] This requires that a sign be of sufficient size and the information on it be clear, concise, legible, and distinguishable from competing signage.

Don't Be a Fool

This section has merely touched on the topic of on-premise signage. Although the material presented is basic and descriptive, it cannot be overemphasized how important signage is to retail success. Signs perform an extremely important communication function, and one is well advised to seek the assistance of professionals when making such determinations as where best to locate a sign, how large it should be, and what colors and graphics are best employed. The old saying "He who represents himself has a fool for a lawyer" is likely as applicable to making an on-premise sign-selection decision as it is in all matters legal. Fortunately, a tremendous amount of experience and expertise has accumulated in the off-premise sign industry, and retailers can turn to professional sign companies for needed assistance. Large retail chains include professionals on their staffs who specialize in signage, but small retailers don't have this luxury and should seek the assistance of professionals. A wealth of accumulated information is available for ready access (see endnotes in this section).

Courtesy, The Signage Foundation for Communication Excellence, Inc.

Figure 8.4

Illustrations of Building-Mounted Signs

Point-of-Purchase Advertising

Brand names and packages, topics of Chapter 7, confront head on at the point of purchase the ultimate arbiter of their effectiveness, the consumer. The point of purchase, or store environment, provides brand marketers with a final opportunity to affect consumer behavior. Brand managers recognize the value of point-of-purchase (P-O-P) advertising; indeed, marketers in the United States annually spend in excess of $17 billion on various forms of point-of-purchase communications.[15]

The point of purchase is an ideal time to communicate with consumers because this is the time at which many product and brand-choice decisions are made. It is the time and place at which all elements of the sale (consumer, money, and product) come together.[16] The consumer's in-store behavior has been described in the following terms that highlight the importance of point-of-purchase advertising:

Shoppers are explorers. They're on safari, hunting for bargains, new products and different items to add excitement to their everyday lives. Three of every four are open to new experiences as they browse the aisles of supermarkets and search for bargains at drugstores and mass merchandisers.[17]

This translates into an opportunity to make a measurable impact just when shoppers are most receptive to new product ideas and alternative brands. Savvy marketers realize that the in-store environment is the last best chance to make a difference. P-O-P advertising often represents the culmination of a carefully integrated IMC program—at the point of purchase, consumers are reminded of previously processed mass media advertisements and now have the opportunity to realize the benefits of a sales promotion offer.

The Spectrum of P-O-P Materials

Point-of-purchase materials include various types of signs, mobiles, plaques, banners, shelf ads, mechanical mannequins, lights, mirrors, plastic reproductions of products, checkout units, full-line merchandisers, various types of product displays, wall posters, floor advertisements (Figure 8.5), in-store radio and TV advertisements, electronic billboard advertising, and other items.[18]

Industry representatives classify P-O-P materials into four categories:

- *Permanent displays:* These are displays intended for use for six months or more. (Note that the six-month dividing line is an arbitrary convention established by Point-of-Purchase Advertising International, which is known by its abbreviation, POPAI.) An illustration of an award-winning permanent display is presented in Figure 8.6.[19]
- *Semipermanent displays:* Semipermanent P-O-P displays have an intended life span of less than six but more than two months. An illustration of an award-winning semipermanent display is presented in Figure 8.7.
- *Temporary displays:* Temporary P-O-P displays are designed for fewer than two months' usage. An illustration of an award-winning temporary display is presented in Figure 8.8.
- *In-store media:* In-store media include advertising and promotion materials, such as in-store radio and TV advertising, shopping cart advertisements, shelf advertisements (called *shelf talkers*), floor graphics (advertisements placed on store floors), coupon dispensers, and other in-store materials. A third-party company (i.e., a company other than the brand manufacturer or retailer) executes these in-store media. For example, ActMedia, a company well known in the P-O-P industry, provides a variety of in-store services, including in-store radio programs that carry commercials in thousands of stores nationwide, shopping carts with signs that are available nationwide, and shelf extensions that promote brands in stores nationwide. Brand marketers pay ActMedia advertising rates to secure in-store radio time or shopping-cart and shelf-talker space on a nationwide basis or in specific markets.

© Susan Van Etten

Figure 8.5

Illustration of a Floor Advertisement

Figure 8.6

Illustration of an Award-Winning Permanent Display

POPAI

What Does P-O-P Accomplish?

Companies are increasingly investing in point-of-purchase advertising materials. As mentioned earlier, P-O-P advertising expenditures in the United States exceed $17 billion annually. This investment is justified inasmuch as in-store materials provide useful services for all participants in the marketing process: manufacturers, retailers, and consumers.

Accomplishments for Manufacturers

For manufacturers, P-O-P keeps the company's name and the brand name before the consumer and reinforces a brand image that has been previously established through mass-media advertising or other outlets. P-O-P signage and displays also call attention to sales promotions and stimulate impulse purchasing.

Service to Retailers

P-O-P serves retailers by attracting the consumer's attention, increasing his or her interest in shopping, and extending the amount of time spent in the store—all of which lead to increased retail revenue and profits. Furthermore, P-O-P materials perform a critical merchandising function in aiding retailers in using available space to the best advantage when, for example, various products are displayed in the same unit. P-O-P displays also enable retailers to better organize shelf and floor space and to improve inventory control and stock turnover.

Value to Consumers

Consumers are served by point-of-purchase units that deliver useful information and simplify the shopping process. Permanent, semipermanent, and temporary P-O-P units provide this value to consumers by setting particular brands apart from similar items and simplifying the selection process. Also, in-store radio and TV advertisements serve to inform consumers of new products and brands. (See the *IMC Focus* for further discussion of in-store TV advertising.)

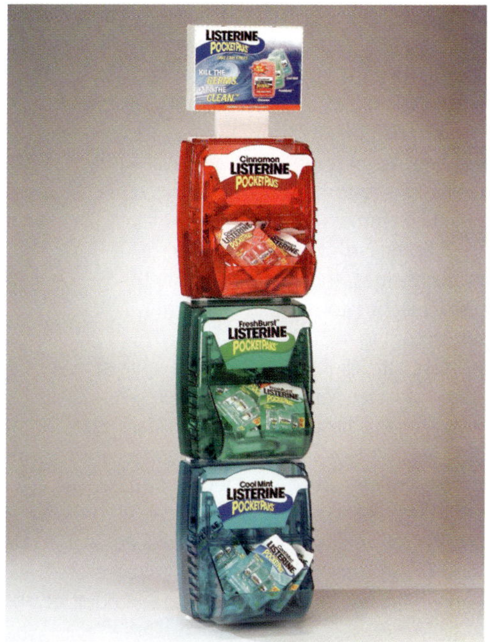

POPAI

Figure 8.7

Illustration of an Award-Winning Semipermanent Display

However, there is a downside to the growing use of in-store displays and advertising materials, namely, consumers sometimes are overwhelmed with excessive P-O-P stimuli. A marketing commentator has even compared the widespread usage of in-store advertising materials with online spam.[20] In other words, like all advertising media, the in-store environment suffers from ad clutter, which can irritate consumers and reduce the effectiveness of brand marketers' advertising efforts.

In addition to benefiting all participants in the marketing process, point-of-purchase plays another important role: it serves as the capstone for an IMC program. P-O-P by itself may have limited impact, but when used in conjunction with mass-media advertisements and promotions, P-O-P can create a synergistic effect. Indeed, research has shown that when P-O-P reinforces a brand's advertising message, the increase in sales volume can average more than 100 percent compared to advertising alone.[21] Illustrations of this synergism appear in a later section that presents empirical evidence of P-O-P's effectiveness.

Figure 8.8

Illustration of an Award-Winning Temporary Display

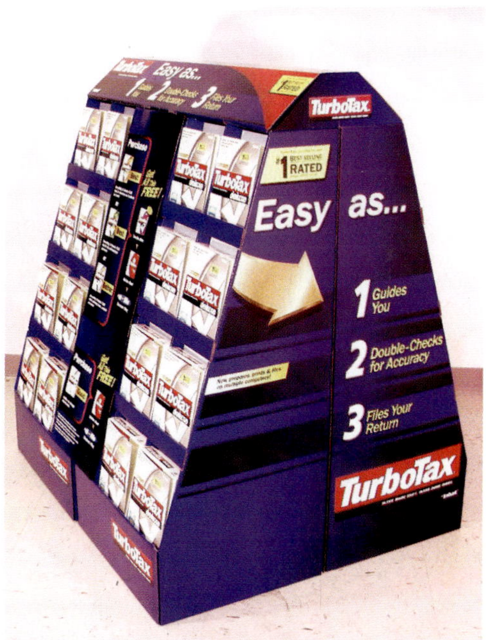

POPAI

P-O-P's Influence on Consumer Behavior

P-O-P materials influence consumers in three general ways: (1) by *informing* them about specific items; (2) by *reminding* them of information acquired from other advertising media; and (3) by *encouraging*, or directing, their brand-choice decisions.

Informing

Informing consumers is P-O-P's most basic communications function. Signs, posters, displays, in-store advertisements, and other P-O-P materials alert consumers to specific items and provide potentially useful information.

Motion displays are especially effective for this purpose. Motion displays, though typically more expensive than static displays, represent a sound business investment because they attract significantly higher levels of shopper attention. Evidence from three studies shows that motion displays are often worth the extra expense.[22]

Researchers tested the relative effectiveness of motion and static displays for Olympia beer, a once successful but now bygone brand, by placing the two types of displays in a test sample of California liquor

ABC, CBS, Fox, NBC, and Now Wal-Mart TV Network

imc focus

There are four major TV networks in the United States: ABC, CBS, Fox, and NBC. Each of these networks has affiliated stations throughout the country, thus representing attractive media for reaching millions of viewers for TV programs and the commercials carried therein. And now there is another major network for carrying television commercials, the Wal-Mart TV network. Unlike the four major TV networks, which reach consumers in the comfort of their homes or at bars and other public venues, the Wal-Mart TV network reaches consumers while they are shopping in Wal-Mart stores. This in-store television network is available in over 80 percent of Wal-Mart's 3,000 U.S. stores. Nielsen Media Research estimates that the Wal-Mart network reaches 133 million viewers in a typical four-week period, which represents about one-third of Wal-Mart's customers during the same period.

What advertising content is carried on the Wal-Mart TV network? You might think just ads placed by Wal-Mart itself. In actuality, the ads are placed by national advertisers who hope to reach consumers as close as possible to the point at which they make purchasing decisions. For example, Kellogg Co. reported a significant increase in sales from advertising two new products on Wal-Mart TV, Cheez-It Twists and Corn Flakes with bananas.

TV spots on Wal-Mart TV cost anywhere from $50,000 to $300,000 per four-week period, with the actual cost depending on the frequency with which the ads appear. Advertisers have learned that it is best to customize ads just for in-store TV rather than merely running the identical ads shown on conventional television. In-store ads must be particularly attention grabbing in order to divert consumers' attention away from the primary reason they are in the store, namely to shop rather than watch TV.

Sources: Erin White, "Look Up for New Products in Aisle 5," *The Wall Street Journal Online,* March 23, 2004, http://online.wsj.com; Ann Zimmerman, "Wal-Mart Adds In-store TV Sets, Lifts Advertising," *The Wall Street Journal Online,* September 22, 2004, http://online.wsj.com.

stores and supermarkets. Each of the sampled stores was stocked with either static or motion displays. Another sample of stores, serving as the control group, received no displays. More than 62,000 purchases of Olympia beer were recorded during the four-week test period. Static displays in liquor stores increased Olympia sales by 56 percent over stores with no displays (the control group). In supermarkets, static displays improved Olympia sales by a considerably smaller, though nonetheless substantial, amount (18 percent). More dramatic, however, was the finding that motion displays increased Olympia sales by 107 percent in liquor stores and by 49 percent in supermarkets.

A second test of the effectiveness of motion displays used S. B. Thomas' English muffins as the focal product. Two groups of 40 stores each were matched by store volume and customer demographics. One group was equipped with an S. B. Thomas' English muffin post sign that moved from side to side. The other 40 stores used regular floor displays with no motion. Records of product movement revealed that sales in the stores stocked with motion displays were more than 100 percent greater than in stores with static displays.

Researchers conducted a study of motion displays for Eveready batteries in Atlanta and San Diego. Studied in each city were six drugstores, six supermarkets, and six mass merchandise stores. The stores were divided into two groups, like the English muffin study. For mass merchandisers, the static displays increased sales during the test period by 2.7 percent over the base period, but surprisingly sales in the drug and food outlets using the static displays were slightly less (each 1.6 percent lower) than those not using the static displays. By comparison, the motion displays uniformly increased sales by 3.7 percent, 9.1 percent, and 15.7 percent in the drugstore outlets, supermarkets, and mass merchandisers, respectively.

All three sets of results demonstrate the effectiveness of motion displays. The consumer information-processing rationale (see Chapter 5) is straightforward: motion displays attract attention. Attention, once attracted, is directed toward salient product features, including recognition of the displayed brand's name. Brand name information activates consumers' memories pertaining to brand attributes previously processed from media advertising. Information on brand attributes, when recalled, supplies a reason for the consumer to purchase the displayed brand. It also is possible that the mere fact of seeing a display suggests the prospect that the displayed brand is on sale, whether in fact it is.[23]

Hence, a moving display performs the critical in-store function of bringing a brand's name to active memory. The probability of purchasing the brand increases, perhaps substantially (as in the case of S. B. Thomas' English muffins), if the consumer is favorably disposed toward the brand. The Eveready display was less effective apparently because the selling burden was placed almost exclusively on the display. Without prior stimulation of demand through advertising, the static display was ineffective, and the motion display was not as effective as it might have been.

Reminding

A second point-of-purchase function is reminding consumers of brands they have previously learned about via broadcast, print, or other advertising media. This reminder role serves to complement the job already performed by advertising before the consumer enters a store.

To fully appreciate the reminder role served by point-of-purchase materials, it is important at this point to address a key principle from cognitive psychology: the **encoding specificity principle**. In simple terms, this principle states that information recall is enhanced when the context in which people attempt to retrieve information is the same as or similar to the context in which they originally encoded the information. (*Encoding* is the placing of informational items into memory.)

A non-marketing illustration—one that may bring back some unpleasant memories—will serve to clarify the exact meaning and significance of the encoding specificity principle. Remember back to a time when you were studying for a crucial exam that required problem-solving skills. You may have been up late at night trying to solve a particularly difficult problem, perhaps in accounting, calculus, or statistics. Eventually, the solution came to you, and you felt well prepared for the next day's exam. Sure enough, the exam had a problem very similar to the one you worked on the night before. However, to your dismay, your mind went blank, and you were unable to solve the problem. But after the exam, back in your room, the solution hit you like the proverbial ton of bricks.

Encoding specificity is the "culprit." Specifically, the context (your room) in which you originally encoded information and formulated a solution to the problem was different from the context (your classroom) in which you subsequently were asked to solve a similar problem. Hence, contextual retrieval cues were unavailable in the classroom to readily facilitate your recall of how you originally solved the problem.

Returning to the marketplace, consider the situation in which consumers encode television commercial information about a brand and its unique features and benefits. The advertiser's expectation is that consumers will be able to retrieve this information at the point of purchase and use it to select the advertiser's brand over competitive offerings. It doesn't always work like this, however. Our memories are fallible, especially since we are exposed to an incredible amount of advertising information. Hence, although we may have encoded advertising information at one time, we may not be able to retrieve it subsequently without a reminder cue at the point of purchase.

Consider, for example, the pink-bunny-pounding-a-drum advertising campaign. Most everyone is aware of this campaign, but many consumers have difficulty remembering the advertised brand. (Think for a moment; which brand is it?) When facing brands of Duracell, Eveready, and Energizer on the shelf, the consumer may not connect the pink-bunny advertising with any specific brand. Here is where point-of-purchase materials can perform a critically important role. Energizer (the pink-bunny brand) can facilitate encoding specificity by using shelf signs or packaging graphics that present the bunny and the Energizer name together (just as they appeared together in advertisements). Accordingly, by providing consumers with encoding-specific retrieval cues, chances are that consumers will recall from earlier advertisements that Energizer is the battery brand that powers the unceasing drum-pounding bunny.

The crucial point is that media advertising and P-O-P communications must be tightly integrated so that in-store reminder cues can capitalize on the background work accomplished by media advertising. Signs, displays, and in-store media provide the culmination for an IMC campaign and increase the odds that consumers will select a particular brand over alternatives.

Encouraging

Encouraging consumers to buy a specific item or brand is P-O-P's third function. Effective P-O-P materials influence product and brand choices at the point of purchase and encourage impulse buying.

A Vital Result of P-O-P: Increased In-Store Decision Making

Studies of consumer shopping behavior have shown that a high proportion of all purchases are unplanned, especially in supermarkets, drugstores, and mass merchandise outlets (such as Wal-Mart and Target). *Unplanned purchasing* means that many product and brand choice decisions are made while the consumer is in the store rather than beforehand. Point-of-purchase materials play a role—perhaps the major role—in influencing unplanned purchasing and in increasing sales. The following section discusses research on unplanned purchasing, and a subsequent section then presents impressive evidence on the role of P-O-P displays in increasing sales volume.

The POPAI Consumer Buying Habits Study

This study, conducted by POPAI, is the most recent of a series of studies conducted by this trade association.[24] The study confirms that in-store media, signage, and displays heavily influence consumers' purchase decisions. In conducting the study, researchers obtained purchase data and other information from 4,200 consumers who were shopping in the stores of 22 leading supermarket chains and 4 mass merchandisers—Bradlees, Kmart, Target, and Wal-Mart—located in 14 major markets throughout the United States.

The Consumer Buying Habits Study was conducted in the following manner:[25] shoppers age 16 or older were screened by researchers to determine that they were on a "major shopping trip." Researchers then interviewed qualified shoppers both before they began their shopping (*entry* interviews) and after they had completed their shopping trips (*exit* interviews). During the pre-shopping entry interviews, researchers used an unaided questioning format to ask shoppers about their planned purchases on that particular occasion and probed for brand buying intentions. Then, during post-shopping exit interviews, researchers gathered supermarket shoppers' register tapes or physically inventoried shoppers' carts at the mass merchandise stores. Interviews were conducted during all times of the day and every day of the week.

By comparing shoppers' planned purchases obtained during entry interviews with actual purchases during exit interviews, it was possible to classify every brand purchase into one of four types of purchase behaviors:

1. **Specifically planned:** This category represents purchases of a brand that the consumer had indicated an intention to buy. For example, the purchase of Diet Pepsi would be considered a specifically planned purchase if during the entry

Table 8.1

Results from the POPAI Consumer Buying Habits Study

Type of Purchase	Supermarket	Mass Merchandising Store
1. Specifically planned	30%	26%
2. Generally planned	6	18
3. Substitute	4	3
4. Unplanned	60	53
In-store decision rate (2 + 3 + 4)	70%	74%

SOURCE: The 1995 POPAI Consumer Buying Habits Study, p. 18 (Washington, D.C.: Point-of-Purchase Advertising International). Reprinted by permission.

interview a consumer mentioned her or his intention to purchase that brand and in fact bought Diet Pepsi. According to the Consumer Buying Habits Study (see Table 8.1), 30 percent of supermarket purchases and 26 percent of mass merchandise purchases were specifically planned.

2. **Generally planned:** This classification applies to purchases for which the shopper indicated an intention to buy a particular product (say, a soft drink) but had no specific brand in mind. The purchase of Diet Pepsi in this case would be classified as a generally planned purchase rather than a specifically planned purchase. Generally planned purchases constituted 6 percent of those in supermarkets and 18 percent in mass merchandise stores (see Table 8.1).
3. **Substitute purchases:** Purchases where the shopper does not buy the product or brand he or she indicated in the entry interview constitute substitute purchases. For example, if a consumer said she or he intended to buy Diet Pepsi but actually purchased Diet Coke, that behavior would be classified as a substitute purchase. These represented just 4 percent of supermarket purchases and 3 percent of mass merchandise purchases.
4. **Unplanned purchases:** Under this heading are purchases for which the consumer had no prior purchase intent. If, for example, a shopper buys Diet Pepsi without having informed the interviewer of this intent, the behavior would be recorded as an unplanned purchase. Sixty percent of the purchases in supermarkets and 53 percent of those in mass merchandise stores were classified as unplanned.

© Susan Van Etten

Notice in Table 8.1 that the summation of generally planned, substitute, and unplanned purchases constitutes the *in-store decision rate.* In other words, the three categories representing purchases that are not specifically planned all represent decisions influenced by in-store factors. The in-store decision rates are 70 and 74 percent for supermarkets and mass merchandise stores, respectively. These percentages indicate that approximately 7 out of 10 purchase decisions are influenced by in-store factors. It is apparent that P-O-P materials represent a very important determinant of consumers' product and brand choice behaviors!

A technical point needs to be addressed at this time. It is important to recognize that not all purchases recorded as unplanned by interviewers are truly unplanned. Rather, some purchases are recorded as unplanned simply because shoppers are unable or unwilling during the entry interview to inform interviewers of their exact purchase plans. This is not to imply that the POPAI research is seriously flawed but rather that the measurement of unplanned purchases probably is somewhat overstated due to the unavoidable bias just described. Other categories may be biased also. For example, by the same logic, the percentage of specifically planned purchases is probably somewhat understated. In any event, POPAI's findings are important even if they are not precisely correct.

Table 8.2

Product Categories with the Five Highest and Five Lowest In-Store Decision Rates: Supermarket Purchases

Category	In-Store Decision Rate
Highest in-store decision rate	
First aid	93%
Toys, sporting goods, crafts	93
Housewares/hardware	90
Stationery	90
Candy/gum	89
Lowest in-store decision rate	
Produce	33
Meat, seafood	47
Eggs	53
Coffee	58
Baby food/formula	58

SOURCE: "Product Categories with the Five Highest and Five Lowest In-Store Decision Rates: Supermarket Purchases," p. 19. The 1995 POPAI Consumer Buying Habits Study (Washington, D.C.: Point-of-Purchase Advertising International). Reprinted by permission.

Table 8.3

Product Categories with the Five Highest and Five Lowest In-Store Decision Rates: Mass Merchandise Purchases

Category	In-Store Decision Rate
Highest in-store decision rate	
Apparel accessories	92%
Foils, food wraps	91
Hardware, electric, plumbing	90
Infant/toddler wear	90
Garbage bags	88
Lowest in-store decision rate	
Disposable diapers	35
Baby food	35
Eyedrops and lens care	52
Prerecorded music, videos	54
Coffee, tea, cocoa	55

SOURCE: "Product Categories with the Five Highest and Five Lowest In-Store Decision Rates: Mass Merchandise Purchases," p. 20. The 1995 POPAI Consumer Buying Habits Study (Washington, D.C.: Point-of-Purchase Advertising International). Reprinted by permission.

The summary statistics in Table 8.1 represent types of purchases aggregated over literally hundreds of product categories. It should be apparent that in-store decision rates vary greatly across product categories. To emphasize this point, Tables 8.2 and 8.3 present categories with the highest and lowest in-store decision rates for supermarkets (Table 8.2) and mass merchandise stores (Table 8.3).

The data presented in Tables 8.2 and 8.3 make it clear that in-store decision rates vary substantially. Supermarket products that are virtual staples (e.g., produce) and mass merchandise products that are essential and regularly purchased items (e.g., disposable diapers) have the lowest in-store purchase rates because most consumers know they are going to purchase these items when they go to the store. On the other hand, nonnecessities and items that generally do not occupy top-of-the-mind thoughts (e.g., first-aid supplies and garbage bags) are especially susceptible to the influence of in-store stimuli. It is clear that for these types of products, brand marketers must have a distinct presence at the point of purchase if they hope to sway purchase decisions toward their brands.

Factors Influencing In-Store Decision Making

Two academic researchers were provided access to data from POPAI's Consumer Buying Habits Study.[26] The researchers' objective was to determine what effect a variety of shopping-trip factors (e.g., size of shopping party, use of a shopping list, number of aisles shopped) and consumer characteristics (e.g., deal proneness, compulsiveness, age, gender, and income) have on unplanned purchasing.

Among other findings, they determined that the rate of unplanned purchasing is elevated when consumers are on a major (versus fill-in) shopping trip, when they shop more of a store's aisles, when the household size is large, and when they are deal prone. Perhaps the major practical implication from this research is that retailers benefit from having consumers shop longer and traverse more of the store while shopping, thus increasing the odds of purchasing unintended items. One way of accomplishing this is by locating frequently purchased items (e.g., items such as bread and milk) in locations that require consumers to pass as many other items as possible.[27]

The Brand Lift Index

POPAI and its research collaborator (the Meyers Research Center) have developed a measure—called the *brand lift index*—to gauge the average increase of in-store purchase decisions when P-O-P is present versus when it is not.[28] (The term *lift* is used in reference to increasing, or lifting, sales in the presence of P-O-P materials.) This index simply indicates how in-store P-O-P materials affect the likelihood that customers will buy a product that they had not specifically planned to buy. Table 8.4 shows the products sold in supermarkets and mass merchandise stores that enjoy the highest brand lift indexes from displays. For example, the index of 47.67 for film and photofinishing products in mass merchandise stores indicates that shoppers are nearly 48 times more likely to make in-store purchase decisions for these products when advertised with displays than if there were no displays. (Note that the index of 47.67 does *not* mean that sales of film and other photofinishing items are over 47 times greater when a display is used. Rather, this index merely reveals that consumers are nearly 48 times more likely to make in-store decisions in the presence versus absence of displays.) And supermarket shoppers are 6.47 times more likely to make in-store decisions to purchase butter or margarine when these items are displayed compared to when they are not displayed. Needless to say, displays can have incredible influence on consumer behavior.

Table 8.4

Supermarket and Mass Merchandise Product Categories with Highest Average Brand Lifts from Displays

	Brand Lift Index
Supermarket categories	
Butter/margarine	6.47
Cookies	6.21
Soft drinks	5.37
Beer/ale	4.67
Mixers	4.03
Sour cream/cream cheese	3.79
Cereal	3.73
Hand and body soaps	3.62
Packaged cheese	3.57
Canned fish	3.55
Salty snacks	3.50
Mass merchandise categories	
Film/photofinishing	47.67
Socks/underwear/panty hose	29.43
Cookies/crackers	18.14
Small appliances	8.87
Foils, food wraps, and bags	7.53
Adult apparel	7.45
Pet supplies	5.55
Packaged bread	5.01

SOURCE: "Supermarket and the Mass Merchandise Product Categories with Highest Average Brand Lifts from Displays," p. 24. The 1995 POPAI Consumer Buying Habits Study (Washington, D.C.: Point-of-Purchase Advertising International). Reprinted by permission.

Evidence of Display Effectiveness

Practitioners are vitally interested in knowing whether the cost of special P-O-P displays is justified. It has only been in recent years that good research evidence has been available to provide answers to this question. Two particularly important studies have examined the impact of displays on a brand's temporary sales.

The POPAI/Kmart/P&G Study

This notable study was conducted by a consortium of a trade association (POPAI), a mass merchandiser (Kmart), and a consumer-goods manufacturer (Procter & Gamble [P&G]).[29] The study investigated the impact that displays have on sales of P&G brands in six product categories: paper towels, shampoo, toothpaste, deodorant, coffee, and fabric softener. The test lasted for a period of four weeks, and P&G's brands were sold at their regular prices throughout this period. Seventy-five Kmart stores in the United States were matched in terms of brand sales, store volume, and shopper demographics and then assigned to three panels of 25 stores each:

Control panel. The 25 stores in this group contained the advertised brands in their normal shelf position with no display or other advertising present.

Test panel 1. These 25 stores carried the advertised brands on display.

Test panel 2. These stores contained the advertised brands either on a different display or on the same display as in test panel 1 but at a different location in the store.

Specific differences in displays/locations between test panels 1 and 2 are shown in Table 8.5. For example, paper towels were displayed in a mass waterfall display at two different (but undisclosed) store locations; shampoo was displayed in either a special shelf unit display or a floorstand display; and coffee was displayed either on a quarter pallet outside the coffee aisle or a full pallet at the end of the coffee aisle—called an *endcap* display.

Most importantly, the last column in Table 8.5 compares the percentage sales increase in each set of test stores (with displays) against the control stores where P&G brands were sold in their regular (non-display) shelf locations. It is readily apparent that positive sales increases materialized for all products and both test conditions; in some instances the increases were nothing short of huge. P&G's brands of shampoo and deodorant experienced modest increases during the four-week test of only about 18 percent (test panel 1), whereas paper towels and coffee experienced triple-digit increases in both display conditions—sales increases of 773.5 percent for paper towels (test panel 2) and 567.4 percent for coffee (test panel 2)!

Table 8.5
Display Information for POPAI/Kmart/P&G Study

Product Category	Test Panels and Displays	Test Panel Sales versus Control Panel Sales (percentage increase)
Paper towels	Test 1: Mass waterfall (MW) display	447.1%
	Test 2: MW display in a different location	773.5
Shampoo	Test 1: Shelf unit	18.2
	Test 2: Floorstand	56.8
Toothpaste	Test 1: Floorstand in toothpaste aisle	73.1
	Test 2: Quarter pallet outside toothpaste aisle	119.2
Deodorant	Test 1: Powerwing	17.9
	Test 2: Powerwing in a different store location	38.5
Coffee	Test 1: Quarter pallet outside coffee aisle	500.0
	Test 2: Full pallet on endcap of coffee aisle	567.4
Fabric softener	Test 1: Full pallet on endcap of laundry aisle	66.2
	Test 2: Quarter pallet outside laundry aisle	73.8

SOURCE: "Display Information for POPAI/Kmart/P&G Study," from POPAI/Kmart/Procter & Gamble Study of P-O-P Effectiveness in Mass Merchandising Stores, p. 20. The 1995 POPAI Consumer Buying Habits Study (Washington, D.C.: Point-of-Purchase Advertising International). Reprinted by permission.

The POPAI/Warner-Lambert Benylin Study

Another important study extends the POPAI/Kmart/P&G findings obtained from mass merchandise stores in the United States to drugstores in Canada.[30] POPAI and Warner-Lambert Canada jointly investigated the effectiveness of P-O-P displays on sales of health items in drugstores. Eighty stores from four major drugstore chains participated (Shoppers Drug Mart, Jean Coutu, Cumberland, and Pharmaprix), and testing was conducted in three major cities: Toronto, Montreal, and Vancouver. Two brands were involved in the testing: Benylin cough syrup and Listerine mouthwash. This section discusses the Benylin study, and the following section describes the Listerine study.

For the Benylin test, stores were divided into four groups: one group offered regularly priced Benylin in its normal shelf position; a second group merchandised Benylin in the normal shelf position but at a feature (i.e., discounted) price; a third group of stores displayed Benylin at a feature price on endcap displays; and the final group employed in-aisle floorstand displays of Benylin at a feature price. Sales data were captured during a two-week period in each store to gauge display effectiveness.

The effectiveness of both feature pricing and displays is determined simply by comparing sales volume during the test period in store groups 2 through 4 with sales in group 1—the baseline group. These comparisons reveal the following:

- Stores in group 2 (Benylin located at its regular shelf position but feature priced) enjoyed 29 percent greater sales volume of Benylin than the stores in group 1 (Benylin at both its regular price and shelf location). This 29 percent increment reflects simply the effect of feature pricing inasmuch as both store groups sold Benylin from its regular shelf location.
- Stores in group 3 (Benylin on an endcap display and feature priced) enjoyed 98 percent greater sales of Benylin than did stores in group 1. This increment reflects the substantial impact that the endcap display and feature price combination had on the number of units sold. The large percentage increase in comparison to group 2 (i.e., 98 percent versus 29 percent) reflects the incremental impact of the endcap display location over the effect of feature pricing per se.
- Stores in group 4 (Benylin displayed in-aisle and feature priced) realized 139 percent greater sales volume than the baseline stores, which indicates that this location, at least for this product category, is more valuable than is the endcap location.

The POPAI/Warner-Lambert Listerine Study

Stores were divided into four groups for this test: one group offered regularly priced Listerine in its normal shelf position; a second group of stores offered Listerine in the normal shelf position but at a feature price; a third group displayed Listerine at a feature price on endcap displays at the rear of the store; and the fourth group displayed Listerine at a feature price on endcap displays at the front of the store. Sales data were captured during a two-week period in each store to gauge display effectiveness.

Again, the effectiveness of displays can be determined simply by comparing sales volume of groups 2 through 4 with sales in baseline group 1:

- Stores in group 2 (Listerine located at its regular shelf position but feature priced) enjoyed 11 percent greater sales volume of Listerine than the stores in group 1 (where Listerine was regular priced and located in its regular shelf position).
- Stores in group 3 (Listerine at a rear endcap display and feature priced) experienced 141 percent greater sales of Listerine than the stores in group 1.
- Stores in group 4 (Listerine at a front endcap display and feature priced) enjoyed 162 percent greater sales volume than the baseline stores.

Both sets of results reveal that these two drugstore brands, Benylin and Listerine, benefited greatly when feature priced and merchandised from prized locations. The Listerine study results came as a bit of surprise to industry observers, however, who expected the advantage of the front endcap location to be substantially greater in comparison to the rear endcap location. The premium price that manufacturers pay for front endcap placement (versus rear endcap positioning) may not be fully justified in light of these results. Additional research with other product categories is needed before any definitive answer is possible.

The Use and Nonuse of P-O-P Materials

Although P-O-P materials can be very effective for manufacturers and perform several desirable functions for retailers, the fact remains that perhaps as much as 40 to 50 percent of all P-O-P materials supplied by manufacturers are never used by retailers.[31]

Reasons Why P-O-P Materials Go Unused

Five major reasons explain why retailers choose not to use P-O-P materials. First, there is no incentive for the retailer to use certain P-O-P materials because these materials are inappropriately designed and do not satisfy the retailer's needs. Second, some displays take up too much space for the amount of sales generated. Third, some materials are too unwieldy, too difficult to set up, too flimsy, or have other construction defects. A fourth reason many signs and displays go unused is because they lack eye appeal. Finally, retailers are concerned that displays and other P-O-P materials simply serve to increase sales of a particular manufacturer's brand during the display period, but that the retailer's sales and profits for the entire product category are not improved. In other words, a retailer has little incentive to erect displays or use signage that merely serves to transfer sales from one brand to another but that does not increase the retailer's overall sales and profits for the product category.

Encouraging Retailers to Use P-O-P Materials

Encouraging retailers to use P-O-P materials is a matter of basic marketing. Persuading the retailer to enthusiastically use a display or other P-O-P device means that the manufacturer must view the material from the retailer's perspective. First and foremost, P-O-P materials must satisfy the retailer's needs and the needs of the retailer's customers (i.e., consumers) rather than just those of the manufacturer. This is the essence of marketing, and it applies to encouraging the use of P-O-P materials just as much as promoting the acceptance of the manufacturer's own brands. Hence, manufacturers must design P-O-P materials to satisfy the following requirements:

- They are the right size and format.
- They fit the store decor.
- They are user friendly—that is, easy for the retailer to attach, erect, or otherwise use.
- They are sent to stores when they are needed (e.g., at the right selling season).
- They are properly coordinated with other aspects of the marcom program (i.e., they should tie into a current advertising or sales promotion program).
- They are attractive, convenient, and useful for consumers.[32]

Measuring In-Store Advertising's Audience

Earlier in the chapter we concluded the section on OOH advertising by discussing the measurement of that medium's audience size and characteristics and noting that, unfortunately, accurate data have in the past been unavailable regarding OOH's audience characteristics. Historically, the same could be said for P-O-P advertising. However, in recent years the P-O-P's trade association—the Point of Purchase Advertising International (POPAI)—has undertaken a major initiative to develop a means of measuring in-store advertising media.[33] It would take us too far afield at this point in the text to go into the methodology that has been developed, but let it simply suffice to say that a procedure has been devised for acquiring standard diagnostics (reach, frequency, gross ratings, etc.) for in-store media. Advertisers can now plan and evaluate in-store advertising using the same procedures and discipline that they have used for decades in planning for and evaluating print and broadcast media.

Summary

This chapter covers three relatively minor (vis-à-vis mass-media advertising) forms of marcom communications: out-of-home, or off-premise, advertising; on-premise business signage; and point-of-purchase advertising. The first two topics are covered somewhat briefly compared to P-O-P advertising, but the argument is made that both off- and on-premise messages perform important functions and are capable of influencing consumers' awareness of and perceptions of stores and brands. The various forms of off- and on-premise messages are described and illustrations provided.

Major chapter coverage is devoted to P-O-P advertising. The point of purchase is an ideal time to communicate with consumers. Accordingly, anything that a consumer is exposed to at the point of purchase can perform an important communications function. A variety of P-O-P materials—signs, displays, and various in-store media—are used to attract consumers' attention to particular brands, provide information, affect perceptions, and ultimately influence shopping behavior. P-O-P displays—which are distinguished broadly as permanent, semipermanent, or temporary—perform a variety of useful functions for manufacturers, retailers, and consumers.

Research has documented the high incidence of consumers' in-store purchase decision making and the corresponding importance of P-O-P materials in these purchase decisions. POPAI's Consumer Buying Habits Study classified all consumer purchases into four categories: specifically planned, generally planned, substitutes, and unplanned decisions. The combination of the last three categories represent in-store decisions that are influenced by P-O-P displays and other store cues. Importantly, it is estimated that in-store decisions represent as much as 70 percent of supermarket purchase decisions and 74 percent of the decisions in mass merchandise stores. Research on the effectiveness of displays—such as the joint undertaking by POPAI, Kmart, and Procter & Gamble—provides evidence that displayed brands sometimes enjoy gigantic, triple-digit increases in sales volume during the display period.

Discussion Questions

1. What are your personal views about the advantages and disadvantages of supermarket shopping with "Shopping Buddy" (see *Marcom Challenge*)?
2. During past decades, cigarette advertisements were responsible for a very large percentage of all billboard advertising in the United States. What explanation can you offer for why this product used to dominate the billboard medium? In other words, what is it about consumer behavior related to this product that would make billboards an especially attractive advertising medium?

3. Changeable message signs are billboards that vary the advertising message on a schedule of every 4 to 10 seconds. What, in your opinion, is the value of this technology to the advertiser, and what are the potential hazards to society?
4. The Outhouse Springs bottled water case illustrated an effective application of billboard advertising. With reference to the material on "buzz generation" covered in Chapter 7, what is it about this particular campaign that may make these results atypical and thus unrepresentative of more mundane products advertised via billboards?
5. Conduct an informal audit of on-premise business signage in your college or university community. Specifically, select five examples of on-premise signage that you regard as particularly effective. Using material from Chapter 5 on the CPM and HEM models, explain why your chosen illustrations likely stand a good chance of attracting consumer attention and influencing their behavior.
6. What functions can point-of-purchase materials accomplish that mass media advertising cannot?
7. Explain why the POPAI Consumer Buying Habits Study probably overestimates the percentage of unplanned purchases and underestimates the percentage of specifically planned and generally planned purchases.
8. Although not presented in the chapter, the POPAI Consumer Buying Habits Study revealed that the percentage of in-store decisions for coffee was 57.9 percent, whereas the comparable percentage for salsa, picante sauce, and dips was 87.1 percent. What accounts for the 29.2 percent difference in in-store decision making for these two products? Go beyond these two product categories and offer a generalization as to what product categories likely have high and low proportions of in-store decision making.
9. The POPAI Consumer Buying Habits Study also revealed that the highest average brand lift index from signage (rather than displays) in mass merchandise stores was dishwashing soaps, with an index of 21.65. Provide an exact interpretation of this index value.
10. The discussion of the S. B. Thomas' English muffin study pointed out that in stores using motion displays, sales increased by more than 100 percent. By comparison, sales of Eveready batteries, when promoted with motion displays, increased anywhere from 3.7 percent to 15.7 percent, depending on the type of store in which the display was placed. Provide an explanation that accounts for the tremendous disparity in sales impact of motion displays for English muffins compared with batteries.
11. Why were motion and static displays considerably more effective at increasing Olympia beer sales in liquor stores than in supermarkets?

ENDNOTES

1. This description is based on the following sources: "We 'Check Out' Latest Supermarket 'Smart' Cart," MSNBC.com, July 20, 2004, http://www.msnbc.com; "Stop & Shop to Roll Out New Intelligent Shopping Carts from IBM and Cuesol," *Yahoo! Finance,* October 13, 2004; Kelly Shermach, "IBM Builds High-Tech Grocery Cart," *CRMBuyer,* November 16, 2004.
2. R. James Claus and Susan L. Claus, *Unmasking the Myths about Signs* (Alexandria, VA: International Sign Association, 2001), 16.
3. "Outdoor," special advertising section of *Advertising Age,* June 9, 2003, C1.
4. Pierre Bouvard and Jacqueline Noel, "The Arbitron Outdoor Study," *Arbitron,* 2001, http://www.arbitron.com.
5. Claus and Claus, *Unmasking the Myths about Signs,* 17.
6. "The Great Outdoors," special advertising insert in *Agency* 11 (fall 2001).
7. Estimates by the Media Edge as reprinted in "The Great Outdoors."
8. Kimberly Palmer, "Highway Ads Take High-Tech Turn," *The Wall Street Journal Online,* September 12, 2003, http://online.wsj.com.
9. Myron Laible, "Changeable Message Signs: A Technology Whose Time Has Come," *Journal of Public Policy & Marketing* 16 (spring 1997), 173–176; Frank Vespe, "High-Tech Billboards: The Same Old Litter on a Stick," *Journal of Public Policy & Marketing* 16 (spring 1997), 176–179; Charles R. Taylor, "A

Technology Whose Time Has Come or the Same Old Litter on a Stick? An Analysis of Changeable Message Boards," *Journal of Public Policy & Marketing* 16 (spring 1997), 179–186.
10. One of my graduate students, Ms. Brie Morrow, informed me of the Outhouse Springs billboard campaign. Brie and two of her colleagues, Jason Darby and Erin Vance, performed background work in writing a term paper for another class. I have referred to their term paper as well as additional source materials such as Jeremy D'Entremont, "Outhouse Springs and Piggly Wiggly Help Save the Light," *Lighthouse Digest*, http://www.lighthousedepot.com.
11. Claus and Claus, *Unmasking the Myths about Signs*, 9.
12. This distinction and the following details are from *The Signage Sourcebook: A Signage Handbook* (Washington, DC: U.S. Small Business Administration, 2003), 193.
13. Darrin Conroy, *What's Your Signage?* (Albany, NY: The New York State Small Business Development Center, 2004), 8.
14. Ibid., 20.
15. "Retail Details," *Promo*, April 2004, AR31.
16. John A. Quelch and Kristina Cannon-Bonventre, "Better Marketing at the Point-of-Purchase," *Harvard Business Review* (November/December 1983), 162–169.
17. "Impact in the Aisles: The Marketer's Last Best Chance," *Promo*, January 1996, 25.
18. An inventory of P-O-P advertising materials is provided in Robert Liljenwall and James Maskulka, Marketing's Powerful Weapon: Point-of-Purchase Advertising (Washington, DC: Point-of-Purchase Advertising International, 2001), 177–180.
19. This and the following examples are drawn from resources provided by the Point-of-Purchase Advertising International at its Web site available to members only (http://www.popai.com).
20. Kate Fitzgerald, "In-store Media Ring Cash Register," *Advertising Age*, February 9, 2004, 43.
21. Doug Leeds, "Accountability Is In-Store for Marketers in '94," *Brandweek*, March 14, 1994, 17.
22. The Effect of Motion Displays on the Sales of Beer; The Effect of Motion Displays on Sales of Baked Goods; The Effect of Motion Displays on Sales of Batteries (Englewood, N.J.: Point-of-Purchase Advertising Institute, undated).
23. J. Jeffrey Inman, Leigh McAlister, and Wayne D. Hoyer, "Promotion Signal: Proxy for a Price Cut," *Journal of Consumer Research* 17 (June 1990), 74–81.
24. Measuring the In-Store Decision Making of Supermarket and Mass Merchandise Store Shoppers (Englewood, N.J.: Point-of-Purchase Advertising Institute, 1995). Please note that POPAI has since changed its name from the Point-of-Purchase Advertising *Institute* to Point-of-Purchase Advertising *International*.
25. This and all following details are according to the 1995 POPAI Consumer Buying Habits Study, ibid.
26. J. Jeffrey Inman and Russell S. Winer, "Where the Rubber Meets the Road: A Model of In-store Decision Making," *Marketing Science Institute Report* No. 98–122 (October 1998).
27. Ibid., 26.
28. Measuring the In-Store Decision Making of Supermarket and Mass Merchandise Store Shoppers, 23.
29. POPAI/Kmart/Procter & Gamble Study of P-O-P Effectiveness in Mass Merchandising Stores (Englewood, N.J.: Point-of-Purchase Advertising Institute, 1993).
30. POPAI/Warner-Lambert Canada P-O-P Effectiveness Study (Englewood, N.J.: The Point-of-Purchase Advertising Institute, 1992).
31. John P. Murry, Jr. and Jan B. Heide, "Managing Promotion Program Participation within Manufacturer-Retailer Relationships," *Journal of Marketing* 62 (January 1998), 58. POPAI/Progressive Grocer Supermarket Retailer Attitude Study (Englewood, N.J.: Point-of-Purchase Advertising Institute, 1994), 2.
32. Adapted from Don E. Schultz and William A. Robinson, *Sales Promotion Management*, 278–279. For further insights on gaining retailer participation in P-O-P programs, see Murry, Jr. and Heide (1998), "Managing Promotion Program Participation within Manufacturer-Retailer Relationships."
33. Doug Adams and Jim Spaeth, "In-store Advertising Audience Measurement Principles" (Washington, DC: Point-of-Purchase Advertising International, July 2003).

PART 4
Advertising Management

Part Four includes eight chapters that examine various facets of advertising management. *Chapter 9* presents fundamentals about the role and importance of advertising, provides advertising-to-sales ratios for various industries, and describes the functions that advertising performs. The chapter then overviews the advertising management process from the perspective of clients, and examines the role of advertising agencies in assisting clients. The chapter also presents arguments both for investing and disinvesting in advertising, compares the relative effectiveness of increasing advertising expenditures versus reducing prices, and describes share of market and share of voice relationships as input into deciding whether to increase, maintain, or decrease advertising expenditures.

Chapter 10 delves into the creative aspect of the advertising management process. Discussed are general requirements for producing effective advertising messages and the role of creativity, with emphasis on originality and appropriateness. A formal framework for developing advertising plans and strategy is presented, and the features of a creative brief are explained. Alternative styles of creative advertisements are described, and means-end chains and laddering are presented as formal frameworks for understanding how knowledge of consumer values provides a starting point for creating advertising messages. Corporate image and issue advertising is the final topic covered in this chapter.

Chapter 11 expands the coverage of advertising message creation by examining the use of various message appeals in advertising and the role of endorsers. Initial coverage focuses on efforts by advertisers to enhance consumers' motivation, opportunity, and ability to process ad messages. The role of endorsers in advertising receives detailed treatment, and considerations used in selecting endorsers are described. Coverage then turns to treatment of six types of appeals/formats that are widely used in designing advertising messages.

Chapter 12 deals with the assessment of ad message effectiveness, discussing industry standards for message research and the types of information a brand management team and its ad agency desire from this form of research. Coverage then turns to four general categories of message-based research: (1) brand recognition and recall measurement: (2) indicators of emotional reactions; (3) measures of persuasion; and (4) measures of sales response. The chapter concludes with discussion of major research-based conclusions about television advertising.

Chapter 13 provides thorough treatment of the four major activities involved in media planning and analysis: target audience selection, objective specification, media and vehicle selection, and media-buying activities. In-depth discussion focuses on media selection considerations, and also explored are advertising continuity considerations. Another topic covered in this chapter is cost considerations in media planning. The chapter continues with an in-depth discussion of the various tradeoffs that media planners make among the various media-planning objectives. The chapter culminates with discussion of several actual media plans.

Chapter 14 provides an analysis of traditional advertising media. The chapter devotes primary attention to evaluating the unique characteristics and strengths/weaknesses of four major media: newspapers, magazines, radio, and television. Discussion is devoted to how advertising space or time is purchased for each of these ad media. The chapter also describes media-based research methods such as audience measurement for magazines, radio, and television.

Chapter 15 is devoted exclusively to the use of the Internet as an advertising medium. First comes coverage of the magnitude of online advertising and the medium's dramatic growth potential, and then topical coverage turns to the wide variety of online advertising methods. The chapter culminates with discussion of the tracking of online advertising performance and the choice of metrics for assessing effectiveness.

Chapter 16 covers a variety of other advertising media and distinguishes between direct and indirect forms of ad media. Initial coverage is devoted to direct, postal-mail advertising (p-mail), which is the offline equivalent of e-mail. P-mail's distinctive features are described, and the roles of database marketing, lifetime value analysis, and data mining are explored. Coverage of indirect forms of advertising include yellow-pages advertising, videogame advertising, brand placements in movies and other media, cinema advertising and Web films, virtual signage, and additional forms of alternative media. The general point emphasized in this chapter is that advertisers have many available media options that can complement or even substitute for mass-media advertising.

CHAPTER 9

Overview of Advertising Management: Messages, Media, and Measurement

Marcom Challenge: Is Advertising Rocket Science?

With reference to performing a simple task, people often use the expression "It's not rocket science." Rocket science serves as a comparison point to other activities because for many of us it represents the epitome of complexity. How scientists are able to propel rockets and their passengers to the moon, for example, literally boggles the mind. The enormity of this feat and its essential confluence of mathematical brilliance, mechanical sophistication, and computer wizardry is nothing short of amazing. The complexity of getting people safely into outer space and back exceeds the ordinary person's ability to grasp this accomplishment. Rocket science is not an undertaking fit for those who are ill trained to participate in the pursuit of overcoming the forces of nature and the limits of science.

What does this have to do with advertising? Well, a marketing and advertising practitioner, Sam Hill, has made the bold claim that "advertising *is* rocket science."[1] In keeping with the rocket science analogy, it is tempting to summarily dismiss this assertion and label its claimant a "space cadet." But let's evaluate whether there is any truth to Mr. Hill's statement.

His contention, more specifically, is that advertising, like rocket science, is itself a very complex activity. It is tempting to immediately retort, "Anyone can create an advertisement, so in what sense is advertising complex?" Unlike rocket science—which necessitates that its practitioners receive advanced academic degrees in physics, mathematics, computer science, and engineering—people with no formal training in advertising can create ads. If anyone can do it, how complex can it be?

The complexity is not in creating an ad per se; rather, it is in creating a *successful* advertising campaign. A successful campaign requires a confluence of the right message delivered to a targeted audience via appropriate advertising media. But accomplishing this is no easy task in view of the ever-changing competitive situation and evolving consumer tastes and preferences. The advertising milieu is, in short, more dynamic than the environment confronted by rocket scientists. In other words, the workings of gravity, mechanics, and computing can be reduced to highly predictable accounts and captured in mathematical equations. Comparatively, the landscape for advertising is continually shifting with numerous factors coming into play. And the target of any advertising effort—that is, the consumer—is inherently complex and unpredictable. According to Sam Hill, "The customer is pulling one way, the client is pushing another and the competitors are shifting this way or that. One little mistake and hundreds of millions of dollars of advertising becomes nothing more than a bathroom break during halftime."[2] The complexity of advertising is nicely summed up as follows:

The truth is that in many ways advertising is harder than rocket science. It's news when a rocket launch fails. *It's news when an ad campaign launch* succeeds.[3]

CHAPTER OBJECTIVES

1

Understand the magnitude of advertising and the percentage of sales revenue companies invest in this marcom tool.

2

Recognize that advertising can be extraordinarily effective but that there is risk and uncertainty when investing in this practice.

3

Appreciate the various functions advertising is capable of performing.

4

Explore the advertising management process from the perspective of clients and their agencies.

5

Understand the functions agencies perform and how they are compensated.

6

Explore the issue of when investing in advertising is warranted and when disinvesting is justified.

7

Examine advertising elasticity as a means for understanding the contention that "strong advertising is an investment in the brand equity bank."

Overview

This chapter presents an introduction to the fundamentals of advertising management. The initial section looks at the magnitude of advertising in the United States and elsewhere. The second major section explores the advertising management process, describes the functions advertising performs, and examines the role of advertising agencies. A concluding section provides a detailed discussion of the arguments favoring investments in advertising and counterarguments regarding circumstances when it is advisable to disinvest. This section also explores the concept of advertising elasticity and compares it with price elasticity to determine the circumstances when a brand manager should either increase advertising expenditures or reduce prices.

First, however, it will be useful to specifically define the topic of this and the seven subsequent chapters so as to clearly distinguish advertising from other forms of marketing communications.

Advertising is a paid, mediated form of communication from an identifiable source, designed to persuade the receiver to take some action, now or in the future.[4]

The word *paid* in this definition distinguishes advertising from a related marcom tool, public relations, that secures unpaid space or time in media due to the news value of the public relations content. The expression *mediated communication* is designed to distinguish advertising, which typically is conveyed (mediated) via print and electronic media, from person-to-person forms of communication, including personal selling and word of mouth. Finally, the definition emphasizes that advertising's purpose is to influence action, either presently or in the future. The idea of influencing action is in keeping with the fifth key IMC feature presented back in Chapter 1, namely, that the ultimate objective of any form of marketing communications is to increase behavior rather than merely its precursors such as brand awareness and attitudes.

Most advertising is undertaken by companies that market their brands to final consumers (B2C advertising). Consumer packaged goods companies are especially heavy advertisers in the B2C arena, but service providers (e.g., wireless telephone service) and consumer durables (e.g., automobiles) are heavy advertisers as well. Some companies that market to other companies rather than directly to consumers also are heavy advertisers (B2B advertising). Much of their advertising takes place in trade magazines that appeal to the special interests of practitioners who are prospects for the B2B advertiser's products. Interestingly, however, B2B advertisers also use traditional consumer media (e.g., television) to reach audiences that do not typically subscribe to trade publications. The *IMC Focus* describes two such instances of B2B advertising.

The Magnitude of Advertising

Advertising is big business, to say the very least. Ad expenditures in the United States alone totaled approximately $280 billion in 2005.[5] This amounts to more than $900 in advertising for each of the nearly 290 million men, women, and children in the United States. Advertising spending is also considerable in other major industrialized countries but not nearly to the same magnitude as in the

B2B Advertising on Television

imc focus

When most people think of television as an advertising medium, they think of it being used by B2C companies that advertise their goods and services to the ultimate users of these products, namely, end-user consumers. However, B2B advertisers also find TV a useful medium for reaching customers, as illustrated by the following examples for Nortel and Parker Hannifin.

Nortel's "This Is the Way" Campaign

Nortel is a Toronto-based company that competes against better-known companies such as Cisco in the area of Internet-related products. Lacking in corporate and brand awareness, Nortel undertook an advertising campaign on television and in print to enhance *C* people's (i.e., chief executive officers, chief information officers, and chief financial officers) awareness of its products and applications. The ad campaign was positioned around the idea that Nortel's products are widely used and have numerous applications. This concept was made tangible with the tag line "This is the way. This is Nortel." One advertisement, for example, featured children singing the nursery rhyme lyrics, "This is the way we sweep the floor" while showing images of people using Nortel networks for a variety of purposes. TV spots were aired on network and cable channels including Fox, CNN, CNBC, and MSNBC—all outlets expected to reach the desired executive audience. Supplementary print ads were placed in outlets such as *Business Week, Financial Times, Fortune,* and the *Wall Street Journal.*

Parker Hannifin's Campaign

Marketing folks at Parker Hannifin—an industrial company that manufactures hoses, valves, and other such products—recently introduced the first television campaign in the company's 85-year history. Advertisements were placed on cable television programs that appeal to engineers. These included the Learning Channel's *Junkyard Wars* (a program showing clever people building machines from discarded items) and the History Channel's *Modern Marvels* (a program focusing on technology feats). The campaign was designed to increase engineers' awareness of the Parker Hannifin name and to make the name more salient such that Parker Hannifin would come to mind when a valve- or hose-purchasing need arose.

Interestingly, the campaign used humor to convey its point, which is an atypical appeal in B2B advertising. In one TV spot, for example, two engineer-type characters are seated at a sushi bar and appear to be flirting with two attractive women at the other end of the bar. As one of the women uses chopsticks to lift a piece of sushi to her lips, an engineer asks his colleague, "Do you see what I see?" And the other responds, "Oh yeah." This brief dialogue is punctuated by the scene changing to a research lab where a robotic arm is shown lifting a lobster out of a tank. The connection between the sushi bar scene and the research lab is made clear when the campaign's tag line appears on the screen: "Engineers see the world differently." Parker Hannifin's campaign celebrates engineers and engineering feats, and in so doing hopes to increase the odds that real (not TV) engineers will be more likely to recommend the use of the company's products.

SOURCES: The Nortel description is adapted from Kate Maddox, "Nortel Dials Up Brand Campaign," *B2B,* December 13, 2004, 12. The Parker Hannifin illustration is adapted from Timothy Aeppel, "For Parker Hannifin, Cable TV Is the Best," *Wall Street Journal Online,* August 7, 2003, http://online.wsj.com.

United States. Worldwide ad spending in 2005 is estimated to total slightly over $550 billion, which indicates that over half of worldwide ad spending takes place in the United States, albeit not exclusively by American companies; many firms from other countries advertise heavily in the United States in attempting to capture the loyalty of American consumers.[6]

Some American companies invest more than $2 billion annually on domestic advertising. In a recent year General Motors spent $3.43 billion; Procter & Gamble, $3.32 billion; Time Warner, $3.1 billion; Pfizer, $2.84 billion; DaimlerChrysler, $2.32 billion; Ford Motor Company, $2.23 billion; and Walt Disney, $2.13 billion.[7] Table 9.1 lists the 100 top-spending U.S. advertisers in a recent year. As can be seen, even the U.S. government (ranked number 28) advertised to the tune of $1.1 billion. The government's advertising goes to such efforts as drug control, the Postal Service, Amtrak rail services, antismoking campaigns, and military recruiting. Advertising expenditures aimed at military recruiting alone totaled about $592 million in 2003![8]

Table 9.1

Top-100 Spenders in U.S. Advertising, 2003

Rank	Advertiser	Headquarters	Total U.S. Ad Spending (in millions)
1	General Motors Corp.	Detroit, MI	$3,429.9
2	Procter & Gamble Co.	Cincinnati, OH	3,322.7
3	Time Warner	New York, NY	3,097.3
4	Pfizer	New York, NY	2,838.5
5	DaimlerChrysler	Auburn Hills, MI/Stuttgart, Germany	2,317.5
6	Ford Motor Co.	Dearborn, MI	2,233.8
7	Walt Disney Co.	Burbank, CA	2,129.3
8	Johnson & Johnson	New Brunswick, NJ	1,995.7
9	Sony Corp.	Tokyo, Japan	1,814.8
10	Toyota Motor Corp.	Toyota City, Japan	1,682.7
11	Verizon Communications	New York, NY	1,674.2
12	Sears, Roebuck & Co.	Hoffman Estates, IL	1,633.6
13	General Electric Co.	Fairfield, CT	1,575.7
14	GlaxoSmithKline	Greenford, Middlesex, U.K.	1,553.7
15	SBC Communications	San Antonio, TX	1,511.0
16	McDonald's Corp.	Oak Brook, IL	1,368.3
17	Unilever	London/Rotterdam	1,332.1
18	Altria Group	New York, NY	1,311.0
19	Nissan Motor Co.	Tokyo, Japan	1,300.7
20	Merck & Co.	Whitehouse Station, NJ	1,264.4
21	Viacom	New York, NY	1,248.8
22	L'Oréal	Paris, France	1,239.4
23	PepsiCo	Purchase, NY	1,212.2
24	Home Depot	Atlanta, GA	1,149.9
25	Microsoft Corp.	Redmond, WA	1,147.2
26	Honda Motor Co.	Tokyo, Japan	1,143.7
27	Nestlé	Vevey, Switzerland	1,112.7
28	U.S. Government	Washington, DC	1,102.3
29	Target Corp.	Minneapolis, MN	1,083.3
30	Sprint Corp.	Westwood, KS	1,069.3
31	AT&T Wireless	Redmond, WA	1,034.9
32	News Corp.	Sydney, Australia	1,031.8
33	J. C. Penney Co.	Plano, TX	1,024.8
34	Novartis	Basel, Switzerland	966.5
35	General Mills	Minneapolis, MN	955.6
36	Estée Lauder Cos.	New York, NY	905.6
37	Hewlett-Packard Co.	Palo Alto, CA	898.9
38	IBM Corp.	Armonk, NY	862.0
39	Best Buy Co.	Eden Prairie, MN	837.5
40	Wyeth	Madison, NJ	821.4
41	Mars Inc.	McLean, VA	813.4
42	Bristol-Myers Squibb Co.	New York, NY	778.1
43	Anheuser-Busch Cos.	St. Louis, MO	776.4
44	Cendant Corp.	Parsippany, NJ	773.1
45	ConAgra Foods	Omaha, NE	764.8
46	Yum! Brands	Louisville, KY	761.1
47	Diageo	London, England	748.2
48	Federated Department Stores	Cincinnati, OH	707.2
49	Wal-Mart Stores	Bentonville, AR	677.9
50	American Express Co.	New York, NY	673.1

Rank	Advertiser	Headquarters	Total U.S. Ad Spending (in millions)
51	May Department Stores Co.	St. Louis, MO	$630.0
52	Gillette Co.	Boston, MA	611.7
53	Kroger Co.	Cincinnati, OH	611.5
54	Schering-Plough Corp.	Madison, NJ	609.0
55	Volkswagen	Wolfsburg, Germany	608.2
56	Sara Lee Corp.	Chicago, IL	582.7
57	Kellogg Co.	Battle Creek, MI	569.7
58	Dell	Austin, TX	564.8
59	Nike	Beaverton, OR	559.0
60	Clorox Co.	Oakland, CA	553.4
61	Safeway	Pleasanton, CA	533.3
62	Burger King Corp.	Miami, FL	524.5
63	Deutsche Telekom	Bonn, Germany	517.6
64	MCI	Ashburn, VA	517.0
65	Lowe's Cos.	North Wilkesboro, NC	503.7
66	Mattel	El Segundo, CA	487.8
67	Gap Inc.	San Francisco, CA	485.8
68	AT&T Corp.	Basking Ridge, NJ	478.7
69	Coca-Cola Co.	Atlanta, GA	472.7
70	Albertson's	Boise, ID	466.8
71	Visa International	San Francisco, CA	462.1
72	InterActiveCorp.	New York, NY	460.9
73	Aventis	Strasbourg, France	459.1
74	Kohl's Corp.	Menomonee Falls, WI	451.7
75	MasterCard International	New York, NY	439.5
76	Bayer	Leverkusen, Germany	434.5
77	SABMiller	London, England	432.9
78	Berkshire Hathaway	Omaha, NE	430.9
79	Nextel Communications	Reston, VA	423.5
80	Citigroup	New York, NY	420.2
81	Kmart Corp.	Troy, MI	413.1
82	Campbell Soup Co.	Camden, NJ	412.3
83	Doctor's Associates	Milford, CT	407.9
84	AstraZeneca	London, England	404.3
85	Limited Brands	Columbus, OH	396.5
86	Intel Corp.	Santa Clara, CA	393.8
87	Reckitt Benckiser	Windsor, Berkshire, England	392.8
88	Wendy's International	Dublin, OH	385.8
89	Mitsubishi Motors Corp.	Tokyo, Japan	381.5
90	BellSouth Corp.	Atlanta, GA	375.6
91	Kimberly-Clark Corp.	Irving, TX	347.6
92	Kia Motors Corp.	Seoul, Korea	347.3
93	Cadbury Schweppes	London, England	340.8
94	United Parcel Service	Greenwich, CT	339.8
95	Adolph Coors Co.	Golden, CO	339.5
96	Hyundai Motor Co.	Seoul, Korea	332.8
97	Colgate-Palmolive Co.	New York, NY	331.7
98	Philips Electronics	Eindhoven, Netherlands	318.7
99	S. C. Johnson	Racine, WI	318.2
100	Canon	Tokyo, Japan	317.2

SOURCE: "100 Leading National Advertisers," *Advertising Age,* June 28, 2004, S–2, 4. Reprinted with permission from the *Advertising Age*. Copyright, Crain Communications Inc. 2004.

Advertising-to-Sales Ratios

Table 9.2 provides another interesting portrayal of advertising expenditures in the United States. In particular, the table presents advertising-to-sales ratios for various companies in select product categories: automotive, computers and software, drugs, food, personal care items, and telephone service. These figures indicate that advertising as a percentage of sales for these select product categories ranges between 1.4 and 30.7 percent, with most ad-to-sales ratios in the vicinity of 2 to 10 percent.

Perusal of this table also reveals that smaller competitors in each industry typically have to invest relatively larger percentages of their sales revenues in advertising. This is because they have to spend heavily on advertising in order to be competitive, and thus the ad-to-sales ratios are higher because the sales base is relatively small compared to bigger competitors. A final notable observation is that the category average ad-to-sales ratio for personal care products is substantially higher than the corresponding averages for the remaining product categories.

Table 9.2

Advertising-to-Sales Ratios for Select Product Categories

Industry & Company	U.S. Revenue ($)*	U.S. Advertising ($)*	Ad/Sales Ratio
Automotive			
Ford	103,435	2,234	0.022
General Motors	133,897	3,430	0.026
Honda	40,306	1,144	0.028
DaimlerChrysler	72,814	2,317	0.032
Toyota	52,323	1,683	0.032
Volkswagen	16,701	608	0.036
Nissan	29,028	1,301	0.045
Mitsubishi	5,247	382	0.073
Kia	3,131	347	0.111
Category Average			**0.045**
Computers & Software			
Dell	28,603	565	0.020
IBM	33,762	862	0.026
Hewlett-Packard	29,200	899	0.031
Intel	7,644	394	0.052
Microsoft	22,100	1,147	0.052
Category Average			**0.036**
Drugs			
AstraZeneca	9,835	404	0.041
Aventis	9,096	459	0.050
Bayer	7,567	434	0.057
Bristol-Myers Squibb	12,897	778	0.060
Johnson & Johnson	25,274	1,996	0.079
Wyeth	9,581	821	0.086
Merck	13,321	1,264	0.095
GlaxoSmithKline	15,481	1,554	0.100
Pfizer	26,844	2,838	0.106
Novartis	6,568	967	0.147
Schering-Plough	3,559	609	0.171
Category Average			**0.090**

Industry & Company	U.S. Revenue ($)*	U.S. Advertising ($)*	Ad/Sales Ratio
Food			
Altria Group	40,298	1,311	0.033
ConAgra Foods	17,739	765	0.043
Nestlé	20,527	1,113	0.054
Sara Lee	10,662	583	0.055
Campbell Soup	4,549	412	0.091
Kellogg	5,629	570	0.101
General Mills	9,144	956	0.105
Category Average			**0.069**
Personal Care			
Kimberly-Clark	8,657	348	0.040
Unilever	11,155	1,332	0.119
Colgate-Palmolive	2,356	332	0.141
Procter & Gamble	21,853	3,323	0.152
Gillette	3,448	612	0.177
L'Oréal	4,318	1,239	0.287
Estée Lauder	2,953	906	0.307
Category Average			**0.175**
Telephone Service			
AT&T	34,529	479	0.014
BellSouth	20,337	376	0.018
MCI	20,186	517	0.026
Verizon	65,303	1,674	0.026
SBC	40,843	1,511	0.037
Sprint	26,197	1,069	0.041
Nextel	9,892	423	0.043
Deutsche	8,464	518	0.061
AT&T Wireless	16,695	1,035	0.062
Category Average			**0.036**

*In millions of dollars, 2003.

SOURCE: Adapted from "U.S. Company Revenue Per 2003 Advertising Dollar," *Advertising Age*, June 28, 2004, S–10. Reprinted with permission from *Advertising Age*. Copyright, Crain Communications Inc. 2004.

This is because personal care items often are sold less on the basis of product performance and more in terms of image, which requires greater advertising support to convey the desired impression. As an industry practitioner once claimed, "In the factory we make cosmetics; in the store [as well as in advertisements], we sell hope."[9]

Advertising Effects Are Uncertain

Advertising is costly and its effects often uncertain. It is for these reasons that many companies think it appropriate occasionally to reduce advertising expenditures or to eliminate advertising entirely. Marketing managers—and perhaps especially chief financial officers and chief executive officers—sometimes consider it unnecessary to advertise when their brands already are enjoying great success. Companies find it particularly seductive to pull funds out of advertising during economic downturns—every dollar not spent on advertising is one more dollar added to the bottom line. During the economic downturn in 2001 and the impending recession late that year—propelled in part by the economic fallout from the unimaginable terrorist attacks on the World Trade Center and the Pentagon—advertising expenditures in the United States declined between 4 percent and 6 percent. Declines of this magnitude had not been seen in the United States since the Great Depression of the late 1920s and early 1930s.[10]

Such behavior implicitly fails to consider the fact that advertising is not just a current expense (as the term is used in accounting parlance) but rather is an investment. Although businesspeople fully appreciate the fact that building a more efficient production facility or purchasing a new computer system is an investment in their company's future, many of these same people often think advertising is an expense that can be reduced or even eliminated when financial pressures call for cost-cutting measures.

However, an ex–chief executive officer at Procter & Gamble—one of the world's largest advertisers—aptly draws an analogy between advertising and exercise in that both provide long-term benefits. Moreover, like exercise, it is easy to stop advertising or postpone it because there is no immediate penalty for the interruption.

If you want your brand to be fit, it's got to exercise regularly. When you get the opportunity to go to the movies or do something else instead of working out, you can do that once in a while—that's [equivalent to] shifting funds into [sales] promotion. But it's not a good thing to do. If you get off the regimen, you will pay for it later.[11]

This viewpoint is captured further in the advice of a vice president at Booz Allen Hamilton, a major marketing consultant, when asked what great companies such as Procter & Gamble, Kellogg, General Mills, Coca-Cola, and PepsiCo have in common. All these companies, in his opinion, are aware that *consistent investment spending* is the key factor underlying successful advertising. "They do not raid their budgets to ratchet earnings up for a few quarters. They know that advertising should not be managed as a discretionary variable cost."[12] This point should remind you of our discussion back in Chapter 1 where we discussed the importance of establishing momentum for marcom efforts. Advertising *momentum* is like exercise. Stop exercising, and you will lose conditioning and probably gain weight. Stop advertising, and your brand likely will lose some of its equity and market share as well.

Advertising Functions

Many business firms as well as not-for-profit organizations have faith in advertising. In general, advertising is valued because it is recognized as performing five critical communications functions: (1) informing, (2) influencing, (3) reminding and increasing salience, (4) adding value, and (5) assisting other company efforts.[13]

Informing

One of advertising's most important functions is to publicize brands.[14] That is, advertising makes consumers *aware* of new brands, *educates* them about a brand's distinct features and benefits, and facilitates the creation of positive *brand images.* Because advertising is an efficient form of communication capable of reaching mass audiences at a relatively low cost per contact, it facilitates the introduction of new brands and increases demand for existing brands, largely by increasing consumers' *top-of-mind awareness (TOMA)* for established brands in mature product categories.[15] Advertising performs another valuable information role—both for the advertised brand and the consumer—by teaching new uses for existing brands. This practice, termed *usage expansion advertising*, is typified by the following illustrations:[16]

- Campbell's soup, which is typically eaten for lunch and during other informal eating occasions, was advertised as being suitable for eating during formal family dinners or even at breakfast.
- Gatorade, which originally was used during heavy athletic activity, was advertised for replenishing liquids during flu attacks.
- Special K, a breakfast cereal, was advertised for afternoon or late-night snacking.

Courtesy First Street On Line

Figure 9.1

An Illustrative Advertising Effort to Influence

Influencing

Effective advertising influences prospective customers to try advertised products and services. Sometimes advertising influences *primary demand*—that is, creating demand for an entire product category. More frequently, advertising attempts to build *secondary demand*, the demand for a company's brand. Advertising by both B2C and B2B companies provides consumers and customers with reasoned arguments and emotional appeals for trying one brand versus another. Figure 9.1 represents an advertising effort that presents one straightforward argument after another (low price, energy efficiency, brilliant lighting) in attempting to influence consumers to purchase a Balanced Spectrum floor lamp. Because this product is direct marketed and not available in stores, frequent and effective advertising are absolutely critical to sales success.

Reminding and Increasing Salience

Advertising keeps a company's brand fresh in the consumer's memory. When a need arises that is related to the advertised product, past advertising impact makes it possible for the advertiser's brand to come to the consumer's mind as a purchase candidate. This has been referred to as making a brand more *salient*, that is, enriching the memory trace for a brand such that the brand comes to mind in relevant choice situations.[17] Effective advertising also increases the consumer's *interest* in mature brands and thus the likelihood of purchasing brands that otherwise might not be chosen.[18] Advertising has been demonstrated, furthermore, to influence *brand switching* by reminding consumers who have not recently purchased a brand that the brand is available and that it possesses favorable attributes.[19] See the *Global Focus* insert for an illustration of a global advertising campaign that serves to remind consumers of a well-known brand of gasoline and petroleum products.

Adding Value

There are three basic ways by which companies can add value to their offerings: innovating, improving quality, and altering consumer perceptions. These three value-added components are completely interdependent as astutely captured in the following quote:

Innovation without quality is mere novelty. Consumer perception without quality and/or innovation is mere puffery. And both innovation and quality, if not translated into consumer perceptions, are like the sound of the proverbial tree falling in the empty forest.[20]

Advertising adds value to brands by influencing perceptions. Effective advertising causes brands to be viewed as more elegant, more stylish, more prestigious, of higher quality, and so on. Indeed, research involving over 100 brands drawn

A Global Advertising Campaign for Exxon Mobil

global focus

Exxon and Mobil are two major gasoline and oil companies that merged to form Exxon Mobil. This huge enterprise markets its portfolio of brands—Exxon, Esso, and Mobil—in more than 100 countries around the globe. Success requires effective advertising that positions these brands in a similar fashion throughout the world so as to accomplish Exxon Mobil's objectives for brand equity and market share. All global companies confront a key advertising issue: should they prepare different advertising campaigns in each country or develop a similar, or even identical, advertising message for use around the globe? Many marketers hold the view that local (versus global) advertising campaigns are most effective. Other marketing and advertising executives are of the viewpoint that local campaigns have the notable disadvantage of creating diverse brand images in different countries rather than building a uniform positioning. Moreover, with local ad campaigns the advertising production expense is compounded compared with producing a uniform (also known as *global*) campaign.

Exxon Mobil decided on a global advertising campaign for use in all countries. A $150 million campaign included advertisements with the same look and feel for placement in every country in which Exxon Mobil operates. This may seem a simple task but is actually quite complicated when considering the diversity of language and other cultural differences. To achieve its goal, Exxon Mobil and its advertising agency produced five hours of commercial footage that was to be used as a library for unique selection in each local market. Some scenes were videotaped using up to six different casts of actors, with each cast acting out essentially the same story line. Managers in local markets could then pick from the library those vignettes most suitable for their region.

As a result, the advertising story line for Exxon Mobil's brands is virtually identical around the globe. The same message is acted out in all commercials, and casting selections reflect local people who act out situations but don't have speaking roles. The audio portion of the commercials is restricted to background statements (voice-over) from an announcer who speaks in one of twenty-five languages to reflect local language customs.

Source: Adapted from Vanessa O'Connell, "Exxon Mobil 'Centralizes' a New Global Campaign," *Wall Street Journal Online*, July 11, 2001, http://online.wsj.com.

from five nondurable products (e.g., paper towels and shampoo) and five durable products (e.g., televisions and cameras) has demonstrated that greater ad spending influences consumers to perceive advertised brands as higher in quality.[21] Effective advertising, then, by influencing perceived quality and other perceptions, can lead to increased market share and greater profitability.[22]

By adding value, advertising can generate for brands more sales volume, revenue, and profit and reduce the risk of unpredictable future cash flows. In finance parlance, all of this can be captured in the concept of discounted cash flow (DCF). By making a brand more valuable, advertising generates incremental DCF. One advertising practitioner eloquently captures advertising's value-adding role with this claim: "Advertising builds brands. Brands build the business. Let the discounted cash flow!"[23] And, in a world of accountability (see Chapter 2), it is absolutely imperative that advertising deliver positive financial results.

Assisting Other Company Efforts

Advertising is just one member of the marcom team. Advertising's primary role is at times to facilitate other marcom efforts. For example, advertising may be used as a vehicle for delivering coupons and sweepstakes and attracting attention to these and other promotional tools. Another crucial role is to assist sales representatives. Advertising presells a company's products and provides salespeople with valuable introductions prior to their personal contact with prospective customers. Sales effort, time, and costs are reduced because less time is required to inform prospects about product features and benefits. Moreover, advertising legitimizes or makes more credible the sales representative's claims.[24]

Advertising also enhances the effectiveness of other marcom tools. For example, consumers can identify product packages in the store and more readily recognize a brand's value following exposure to advertisements for it on television or in a magazine. Advertising also can augment the effectiveness of price deals. Customers are known to be more responsive to retailers' price deals when retailers advertised that fact compared to when retailers offer a deal absent any advertising support.[25]

The Advertising Management Process

As intimated in the *Marcom Challenge,* people sometimes suggest that creating advertisements is a simple act and that anyone can do it. That viewpoint is, in a sense, not entirely incorrect. Any literate person can construct an advertisement. Of course, any literate person also can write a story or craft a poem. But not all storytellers or poets are particularly good, and the outcome of their efforts often is ineffective. So it is with advertising: the issue is not just doing it, but doing it well, really well so that the advertising gains attention and ultimately influences purchase choices. The challenge of advertising goes beyond the act of creating messages and involves also the task of placing ads in the right advertising media and selecting appropriate measures to assess whether an advertising campaign has achieved its goals.

Advertising management can thus be thought of as the process of creating ad messages, selecting media in which to place the ads, and measuring the effects of the advertising efforts: messages, media, and measures. This process generally involves at least two parties, the organization that has a product or service to advertise—the client—and the independent agency, or agencies, responsible for creating ads, making media choices, and measuring results—the agency or agencies. The following sections first examine advertising management from the client's perspective and then the agent's. Because most advertising is undertaken for specific brands, the client typically is represented by an individual who works in a brand- or product-management position. This individual and his or her team are responsible for marcom decisions that affect the brand's welfare.

JOB OUTLOOK

Advertising managers determine the demand for products and services, identify potential markets, develop marketing and pricing strategy, develop promotion strategy, and monitor trends that indicate the need for new products and services. (Occupational Outlook Handbook, 2004–05 Edition, U.S. DOL, http://www.bls.gov/oco/home.htm)

Managing the Advertising Process: The Client Perspective

Figure 9.2 graphically illustrates the advertising management process. It can be seen that this process consists of three sets of interrelated activities: advertising strategy, strategy implementation, and assessing ad effectiveness.

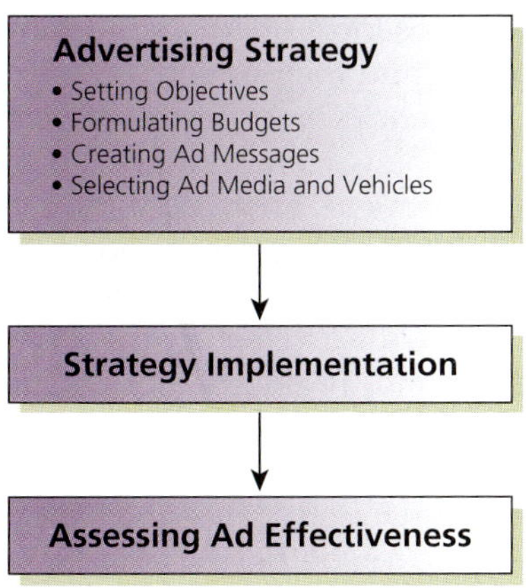

Figure 9.2
The Advertising Management Process

Dennis Sabangan/EPA/Landov

Formulating and Implementing Advertising Strategy

Advertising strategy formulation involves four major activities (see the top box in Figure 9.2). The first two, setting objectives and devising budgets, were described in Chapter 6 when discussing these activities in the context of all marcom elements. Message creation, the third aspect of formulating advertising strategy, is the subject of Chapters 10 and 11. The fourth element, media strategy, the topic of Chapters 13 through 16, involves the selection of media categories and specific vehicles to deliver advertising messages. (The term *vehicle* is used in reference to, say, the specific TV program in which an advertisement is to be placed—TV is the medium, the program is the vehicle.)

Implementing Advertising Strategy

Strategy implementation deals with the tactical, day-to-day activities that must be performed to carry out an advertising campaign. For example, whereas the decision to emphasize television over other media is a strategic choice, the selection of specific types of programs and times at which to air a commercial is a tactical implementation matter. Likewise, the decision to emphasize a particular brand benefit is a strategic message consideration, but the actual way the message is delivered is a matter of creative implementation. This text focuses more on strategic than tactical issues.

Measuring Advertising Effectiveness

Assessing effectiveness is a critical aspect of advertising management—only by evaluating results is it possible to determine whether objectives are being accomplished. This often requires that baseline measures be taken before an advertising campaign begins (to determine, for example, what percentage of the target audience is aware of the brand name) and then afterward to determine whether the objective was achieved. Because research is fundamental to advertising control, Chapter 12 explores a variety of measurement techniques that are used for evaluating advertising effectiveness.

The Role of Advertising Agencies

Message strategies and decisions most often are the joint enterprise of the companies that advertise (the clients) and their advertising agencies. This section examines the role of advertising agencies and describes how agencies are organized. Table 9.3 lists the top-25 advertising agencies in the United States according to revenue. Two observations are pertinent. First, all of these agencies were at one time independent businesses; now, due to mergers and acquisitions, most are owned by large marketing organizations such as Omnicom Group (New York), WPP Group (London), Interpublic Group (New York), Publicis Groupe (Paris), and Havas (Suresnes, France). Second, it is apparent that most of the major U.S. ad agencies are located in New York City, which for many years has been the world's major advertising center. Needless to say, there literally are thousands of advertising agencies throughout the United States and worldwide, though most generate revenues only a small fraction of those shown in Table 9.3.

Table 9.3

Top-25 U.S. Advertising Agencies in Ad Revenue, 2003

Rank	Agency	Parent Organization	Headquarters	Advertising Revenue (in millions)
1	J. Walter Thompson	WPP Group	New York	$456.2
2	Leo Burnett Worldwide	Publicis	Chicago	404.2
3	McCann Erickson Worldwide	Interpublic	New York	300.4
4	BBDO Worldwide	Omnicom	New York	279.1
5	Grey Worldwide	Grey	New York	270.5
6	DDB Worldwide	Omnicom	New York	252.3
7	Ogilvy & Mather Worldwide	WPP Group	New York	235.6
8	Foote, Cone, & Belding Worldwide	Interpublic	New York	221.6
9	Y&R Advertising	WPP Group	New York	215.7
10	Publicis Worldwide	Publicis	New York	200.9
11	Saatchi & Saatchi	Publicis	New York	195.6
12	Euro RSCG Worldwide	Havas	New York	194.1
13	Deutsch	Interpublic	New York	167.2
14	Arnold Worldwide	Havas	Boston	150.2
15	Campbell-Ewald	Interpublic	Warren, Mich.	146.3
16	Lowe & Partners Worldwide	Interpublic	New York	133.8
17	TBWA Worldwide	Omnicom	New York	125.6
18	Donner	NA	Southfield, Mich.	122.7
19	Richards Group	NA	Dallas	114.5
20	Hill, Holliday, Connors, Cosmopulos	Interpublic	Boston	102.6
21	Campbell Mithun	Interpublic	Minneapolis	95.7
22	RPA	NA	Santa Monica	92.6
23	Dailey & Associates	Interpublic	West Hollywood	89.2
24	Zimmerman & Partners	Omnicom	Fort Lauderdale	85.6
25	Fallon Worldwide	Publicis	Minneapolis	82.2

SOURCE: "Top 25 U.S. Agency Brands by Core Advertising Revenue," *Advertising Age*, April 19, 2004, S–2. Most revenue amounts have been estimated. Reprinted with permission from *Advertising Age*. Copyright, Crain Communications Inc. 2004.

To appreciate why a company would use an ad agency, it is important to recognize that businesses routinely employ outside specialists: lawyers, financial advisors, management consultants, tax specialists, and so on. By their very nature, these "outsiders" bring knowledge, expertise, and efficiencies that companies do not possess within their own ranks. Advertising agencies can provide great value to their clients by developing highly effective and profitable advertising campaigns. The relationship between ad agency and client sometimes lasts for decades. Of course, client-agency relationships also can be short lived and volatile if the client evaluates the agency as underperforming and failing to enhance the equity and market share of the client's brand. Research has demonstrated that agencies are fired shortly after clients experience declines in their brands' market shares.[26]

In general, advertisers have three alternative ways to perform the advertising function: use an in-house advertising operation, purchase advertising services on an as-needed basis from specialized agencies, or select a full-service advertising agency. First, a company can choose not to use an advertising agency but rather maintain its own *in-house advertising operation.* This necessitates employing an advertising staff and absorbing the overhead required to maintain the staff's operations. Such an arrangement is unjustifiable unless a company does a large amount of continual advertising. Even under these conditions, most businesses choose instead to use the services of advertising agencies.

A second way for a client to accomplish the advertising function is to purchase advertising services à la carte. That is, rather than depending on a single full-service agency to perform all advertising and related functions, an advertiser may recruit the services of a variety of firms with particular specialties in creative work, media selection, production, advertising research, and so on. This arrangement's advantages include the ability to contract for services only when they are needed and potential cost efficiencies. On the downside, specialists (so-called boutiques) sometimes lack financial stability and may be poor in terms of cost accountability.

Third, *full-service advertising agencies* perform at least four basic functions for the clients they represent (1) creative services, (2) media services, (3) research services, and (4) account management. They also may be involved in the advertiser's total marketing process and, for a fee, perform other marcom functions, including sales promotion, publicity, package design, strategic marketing planning, and sales forecasting. Why would an advertiser want to employ the services of a full-service agency? The primary advantages include acquiring the services of specialists with in-depth knowledge of advertising and obtaining negotiating leverage with the media. The major disadvantage is that some control over the advertising function is lost when it is performed by an agency rather than in house.

Creative Services

Advertising agencies have staffs of copywriters, graphic artists, and creative directors who create advertising copy and visualizations. Advertising agencies on occasion create brilliant advertising campaigns that enhance brand equity and increase a brand's sales volume, market share, and profitability. Oftentimes, however, advertisements are not sufficiently clever or novel to break through the clutter of surrounding advertising.

Media Services

This unit of an advertising agency is charged with the task of selecting the best advertising media for reaching the client's target market, achieving ad objectives, and meeting the budget. *Media planners* are responsible for developing overall media strategy (where to advertise, how often, when, etc.), and *media buyers* then procure specific vehicles within particular media that have been selected by media planners and approved by clients. The complexity of media buying requires the use of sophisticated analysis and continual research of changing media costs and availability. Experts in media and vehicle selection are able to make more effective decisions than are brand managers on the client side who have no particular expertise in media and vehicle selection.

Research Services

Full-service advertising agencies employ research specialists who study their clients' customers' buying habits, purchase preferences, and responsiveness to advertising concepts and finished ads. Focus groups, mall intercepts, ethnographic studies by trained anthropologists, and acquisition of syndicated research data are just some of the services performed by agencies' research specialists.

Account Management

This facet of a full-service advertising agency provides the mechanism to link the agency with the client. Account managers act as liaisons so that the client does not need to interact directly with several different service departments and specialists. In most major advertising agencies, the account management department includes account executives and management supervisors. *Account executives* are involved in tactical decision making and frequent contact with brand managers and other client personnel. Account executives are responsible for seeing that the client's interests, concerns, and preferences have a voice in the advertising agency and that the work is being accomplished on schedule. Account executives report to *management supervisors,* who are more involved in actually getting new business for the agency and working with clients at a more strategic level. Account executives are groomed for positions as management supervisors.

Agency Compensation

There are three basic methods by which clients compensate agencies for services rendered (1) receiving commissions from media, (2) being compensated based on a fee system, and (3) earning compensation based on outcomes.

1. *Commissions from media* for advertisements aired or printed on behalf of the agency's clients provided the primary form of ad agency compensation in the past. Historically, U.S. advertising agencies charged a standard commission of 15 percent of the gross amount of billings.[27] To illustrate, suppose the Creative Advertising Agency buys $200,000 of space in a certain magazine for its client, ABC Company. When the invoice for this space comes due, Creative would remit payment of $170,000 to the magazine ($200,000 less Creative's 15 percent commission); bill ABC for the full $200,000; and retain the remainder, $30,000, as revenue for services rendered. The $30,000 revenue realized by Creative was, in the past, regarded as a fair amount of compensation to the agency for its creative expertise, media-buying insight, and ancillary functions performed in behalf of its client, ABC Company.

   The 15 percent compensation system has, as one may suppose, been a matter of some controversy between client marketing executives and managers of advertising agencies. The primary area of disagreement is the matter of whether 15 percent compensation is too much (the marketing executives' perspective) or too little (the ad agencies' perspective). The disagreement has spurred the growth of alternative compensation systems. Indeed, today only a fraction of advertisers still pay a 15 percent commission. Although there are alternatives to the commission system, it probably will not vanish entirely. Rather, a *reduced commission system,* by which the ad agency is compensated with a flat fee that is less than 15 percent, has experienced increased usage.
2. The most common compensation method today is a *labor-based fee system* by which advertising agencies are compensated much like lawyers, tax advisors, and management consultants. That is, agencies carefully monitor their time and bill clients an hourly fee based on time commitment. This system involves price negotiations between advertisers and agencies such that the actual rate of compensation is based on mutual agreement concerning the worth of the services rendered by the advertising agency.
3. *Outcome- or performance-based programs* represent the newest approach to agency compensation. Ford Motor Company, for example, uses a compensation system whereby it negotiates a base fee with its agencies to cover the cost of services provided, and additionally offers incentive payments that are tied to brand performance goals such as targeted revenue levels. Procter & Gamble (P&G) employs a sales-based model whereby ad agencies are compensated based on a percentage of sales that a P&G brand obtains. The agency's compensation rises with sales increases and falls with declines. Needless to say, this incentive-based system encourages, indeed demands, agencies to use whatever IMC programs are needed to build brand sales. P&G's best interest (growth in brand sales and market share) and the agency's best interest (increased compensation) are joined by this compensation system in a hand-in-glove fashion. In addition to these companies, many others are turning away from the historical commission-based system and toward some form of outcome-based compensation program. The success of outcome-based programs will depend on demonstrating that advertising and other marcom efforts initiated by agencies do indeed translate into enhanced brand performance.[28]

Ad-Investment Considerations

To this point in the chapter we have introduced the topic of advertising, presented facts illustrating its magnitude, discussed its functions, provided an overview of the advertising management process from the client's perspective, and described the functioning and compensation of advertising agencies. It is pertinent to ask at this point whether the billions of dollars invested in advertising are warranted. Or, framing the question more precisely, when is it justifiable to invest in advertising and when is it appropriate to disinvest?

We can better appreciate the issues surrounding this complex question by examining a few equations that will put things into crisper perspective. These equations deal with the relations among sales volume (or simply volume), sales revenue (or simply revenue), and profit.

(9.1) Profit = Revenue – Expenses
(9.2) Revenue = Price × Volume
(9.3) Volume = Trial + Repeat

We see first with Equation 9.1 that a brand's profit during any accounting period—such as a business quarter or an entire year—is a function of its revenue minus expenses. Because advertising is an expense, total profit during an accounting period can be increased by reducing advertising expenses. At the same time, an undesirable effect of reducing advertising is that revenue may decline because fewer units can be sold or the price per unit has to be reduced in the absence of adequate advertising support (see Equation 9.2). We can further note from Equation 9.3 that sales volume (i.e., number of units sold) is obtained by a combination of recruiting more *trial*, or first-time, users to a brand and encouraging users to continue purchasing the brand—that is, to remain *repeat* purchasers.

Whether one chooses to invest or disinvest in advertising a brand depends largely on expectations about how advertising will influence a brand's sales volume (Equation 9.3) and revenue (Equation 9.2). Let us look at arguments first for investing and then for disinvesting.

The Case for Investing in Advertising

In terms of profitability, investing in advertising is justified only if the incremental revenue generated from the advertising exceeds the advertising expense. In other words, if the advertising expense is $*X*, then over the long term (i.e., not necessarily immediately) revenue attributable to the advertising must be more than $*X* to justify the investment. On what grounds might one expect that the revenue will exceed the advertising expense? In terms of Equation 9.3, it might be expected that effective advertising will attract new triers to a brand and encourage repeat purchasing. (Obviously, advertising is not the only marcom tool able to generate trial and repeat purchasing; indeed, sales promotions perform both roles in conjunction with advertising.) Hence, effective advertising should build sales volume by enhancing brand equity—both by increasing brand awareness and by enhancing brand image (recall the discussion in Chapter 2).

Equation 9.2 shows that the other determinant of revenue besides sales volume is the unit price at which a brand is sold. Advertising has the power to enhance a brand's perceived quality and thus the ability of brand managers to charge higher prices; that is, consumers are willing to pay more for brands they perceive as higher quality. Taken together, then, the case for investing in advertising is based on the belief that it can increase profitability by increasing sales volume, enabling higher selling prices, and thus increasing revenue beyond the incremental advertising expense.

The Case for Disinvesting

As previously noted, firms often choose to reduce advertising expenditures either when a brand is performing well or during periods of economic recession. This is a seductive strategy because a reduction in expenses, everything else held constant, leads to increased profits (Equation 9.1). But is "everything else held constant" when advertising budgets are cut or, worse yet, severely slashed? The implicit assumption is that revenue (and revenue's constituent elements, volume and price) will *not* be affected adversely when ad budgets are diminished. However, such an assumption is based on Pollyanna-like thinking that past advertising will continue to positively affect sales volume even when advertising in the current period is curtailed or reduced. The assumption also is somewhat illogical. On the one hand, it presumes that past advertising will carry over into the future to maintain revenue; on the other hand, it neglects to acknowledge that the absence of advertising in the present period will have an adverse effect on revenues in subsequent periods!

Which Position Is More Acceptable?

The profit effect of reducing advertising expenses is relatively certain: for every dollar not invested in advertising, there is a dollar increase in short-term profit—assuming, of course, that the reduction in advertising does not adversely affect revenue. It is far less certain, however, that maintaining or increasing advertising expenditures will increase profits. This is because it is difficult to know with certainty whether advertising will build brand volume or enable higher prices; either outcome or both will lead to increased revenues. Yet, and it is a big *yet,* most sophisticated companies are willing to place their bets on advertising's ability to boost revenues and thus enhance profits from the *revenue-increase side* rather than from the *expense-reduction side.*

An Investment in the Brand Equity Bank

The reason many marketing executives continue to invest in advertising, even during economic downturns, is because they believe advertising will enhance a brand's equity and increase sales. You will recall from the discussion in Chapter 2 that marcom efforts enhance a brand's equity by creating brand awareness and forging favorable, strong, and perhaps unique associations in the consumer's memory between the brand and its features and benefits. When advertising and other forms of marketing communications create unique and positive messages, a brand becomes differentiated from competitive offerings and is relatively insulated from future price competition.

Advertising's long-term role has been described in these terms: "Strong advertising represents a deposit in the brand equity bank."[29] This clever expression nicely captures the advertising challenge. It also correctly notes that not all advertising represents a deposit in the brand equity bank, only advertising that is *strong*—that is, different, unique, clever, and memorable.

Advertising Versus Pricing Elasticity

Returning more directly to the issue of investing or disinvesting in advertising, we have to grapple with the following challenge: what are the alternative ways by which brand managers can grow their brands' sales volume, revenue, and profits? Increasing advertising is one option; reducing price—via outright price cuts or through promotional dealing—is another. Which option is more promising? The answer requires we have a common measure, or metric, for comparing the effects of increasing advertising versus decreasing prices. The concept of *elasticity* provides just such a metric.

Elasticity, as you will recall from a basic economics or marketing course, is a measure of how responsive the demand for a brand is to changes in marketing variables such as price and advertising. We can calculate elasticity coefficients for price (E_P) and advertising (E_A), respectively, based on the following equations:

(9.4) E_P = Percentage change in quantity ÷ Percentage change in price
(9.5) E_A = Percentage change in quantity ÷ Percentage change in advertising

To illustrate these concepts, consider the situation faced by a recent college graduate, Aubrey, who sells T-shirts imprinted with thematic messages. (Students well familiar with the concept of elasticity are encouraged to skip this basic treatment, at least to the point where advertising and price elasticities are compared.) Let's assume that Aubrey is doing a pretty good business but thinks he can increase revenues and profits by lowering the price at which he sells imprinted T-shirts. (The "law" of inverse demand says that sales volume, or quantity, typically increases when prices are reduced, and vice versa.)

Last week (let's refer to this as week 1) Aubrey priced T-shirts at $10 and sold 1,500 shirts (P1 = $10; Q1 = 1,500). He decided the following week, week 2, to reduce the price to $9, and then sold 1,800 shirts (P2 = $9; Q2 = 1,800). Applying Equation 9.4, we quickly see that the percentage change in quantity is 20 percent. That is, (1,800 – 1,500) ÷ 1,500 = 20 percent. Thus, with an 11 percent decrease in price—that is, (10 – 9) ÷ 9—he realized a 20 percent increase in quantity sold. The price elasticity (E_P) expressed as an absolute value is 1.82 (i.e., 20 ÷ 11). (Refer to Equation 9.4 to see how the elasticity coefficient for price, E_P, is calculated.) Aubrey was pleased with this result because total revenue in week 2 was $16,200 (P2 × Q2 = $9 × 1,800 = $16,200) compared with the $15,000 revenue obtained in week 1 ($10 × 1,500). Thus, although he reduced the price of T-shirts, he enjoyed an 8 percent increase in revenue—that is, ($16,200 – $15,000) ÷ $15,000.

Let us now consider the possibility that, rather than reducing price, Aubrey decided to increase the amount of advertising from week 1 to week 2. Suppose that in week 1 he had spent $1,000 advertising in the local newspaper. As before, he obtained $15,000 revenue in week 1 from selling 1,500 T-shirts at a price of $10 each. Suppose in week 2 he increased the level of advertising to $1,500 (a 50 percent increase over week 1) and sold 1,600 shirts at $10 each. In this case, the percentage change in quantity is 6.67 percent. That is, (1,600 – 1,500) ÷ 1,500 = 6.67 percent. This increase in quantity sold was enjoyed with a 50 percent increase in ad expenditures. Thus, applying Equation 9.5, the advertising elasticity (E_A) is 6.67 ÷ 50 = 0.133. Whereas Aubrey received $15,000 in week 1 revenue (P1 = $10; Q1 = 1,500), revenue increased in week 2 by $1,000 (P2 = $10; Q2 = 1,600). This increased revenue ($1,000) was obtained with a $500 increase in advertising, so Aubrey enjoyed a $500 increase in profit—not a bad week's work for a young entrepreneur!

You might be thinking, "Where are we going with this?" Well, let's take this simple example and relate it to a more general point that tells us something about how advertising works and whether increases in advertising can be justified, especially when juxtaposed against the alternative possibility of merely reducing prices. We know a lot about advertising and price elasticities. An important study determined that the average price and advertising elasticities for 130 brands of durable and nondurable products were 1.61 and 0.11, respectively.[30] (The price elasticity is presented here as an absolute value, though technically it should have a negative sign insofar as price increases result in volume decreases, and vice versa.) A price elasticity of 1.61 is to be interpreted as meaning that a 1 percent reduction in price leads to a 1.61 percent increase in sales volume; similarly, the ad elasticity coefficient of 0.11 indicates that a 1 percent increase in ad expenditures increases volume by only 0.11 percent.

Hence, sales volume is about 14.6 times (1.61 ÷ 0.11) more responsive, on average, to changes in price than to changes in advertising. For just *durable* goods, the average price and advertising elasticities are 2.01 and 0.23, which indicates that sales volume for these goods is, on average, 8.7 times more responsive to price discounts than advertising increases. Comparatively, for *nondurable* goods, the average price and advertising elasticities are 1.54 and 0.09, respectively, indicating that, on average, sales volume is 17 times more responsive to price cuts than advertising increases.

Do these results indicate that brand managers should always discount prices and never increase advertising? Absolutely not! As you have learned from this text and elsewhere, every situation is unique. Pat answers ("This is how you should do it.") are flat out wrong and misleading! The fact is that every brand does not experience the same price and advertising elasticities as presented here. "On average," as used in our discussion, means that some brands are at the average, whereas others are above or below the average; there is, in other words, a distribution of elasticity coefficients around the average. In general, we can consider four combinations of advertising and price elasticities. For each situation we will identify the appropriate strategy, whether to increase advertising or reduce price, for increasing profit:[31]

- *Situation 1* (*maintain status quo*): Consider a situation where consumers have well-established brand preferences such as during the decline stage of a product's life cycle or in established niche markets. In such a situation, the market would not be very price elastic or advertising elastic; consequently, profits would be maximized by basically adhering to the status quo and maintaining the present price and advertising levels. In short, facing a situation such as this, brand managers should neither discount prices nor increase levels of advertising.
- *Situation 2* (*build image via increased advertising*): In a situation where the market is more advertising elastic than price elastic, it is advisable to spend relatively more on advertising increases than price discounts. This situation is likely for new products, luxury goods, and products characterized by symbolism and imagery (cosmetics, designer labels in apparel and home furnishings, expensive brands of vodka and other distilled spirits, etc.). The profit-increasing strategy in a situation such as this is to build a brand's image by increasing advertising.
- *Situation 3* (*grow volume via price discounting*): This third situation is characterized by mature consumer goods markets where consumers have complete information about most brands in the category and brand switching is frequent. Because brands are little differentiated, the market is more price than advertising elastic. Profit increases are obtained more from price discounts than advertising investments.
- *Situation 4* (*increase advertising and/or discount prices*): This is a situation where the market is both price elastic and advertising elastic. This would be expected when brands in the product category are inherently differentiable (cereals, automobiles, appliances, etc.) and for products that are seasonal (e.g., lawn products, seasonal clothing, and special holiday gift items). In situations such as these, informative advertising can influence consumers' beliefs about product attributes (e.g., Scotts fertilizer is longer-lasting than competitive brands), but because brands are similar, consumers also are eager to compare prices.

Given knowledge of the price and advertising elasticities that exist in a particular situation, it is possible to mathematically determine whether it is more profitable to increase advertising or discount price. The mathematics are beyond the scope of this text, but the interested reader is referred to additional sources.[32] It is hoped that this section conveyed the point that the choice to invest (increase) or disinvest (decrease) in advertising can be made only after determining the relative advertising and price elasticities that confront a brand in a particular market situation. We have provided some general guidelines in the previously mentioned situations as to when it might be advisable to increase advertising expenditures or discount prices. It is critical to appreciate that every situation is unique. It is important to understand that "on average" applies to all brands in a product category but that particular brands may distinguish themselves by developing really clever advertising that serves to create an appealing advertising image or present functional information in an especially compelling manner.

Your job as a brand manager is to work with your advertising agency and other marcom suppliers (e.g., public relations specialists and event marketers) to develop campaigns that distinguish your brand from the crowd of competitors. Please note, by comparison, that the average professional basketball player scores only around, say, 5 to 10 points per game. But players such as Kobe Bryant, Allen Iverson, Dirk Nowitzki, Kevin Garnett, and Lebron James average more than 20 points per game. Perhaps your brand can also perform above the average with effective advertising. If it cannot, and the average advertising elasticity in your product category is low, then the appropriate strategy is probably *not* to invest in additional advertising but to maintain or even lower prices. In other words, do not waste money on advertising if the circumstances (such as situations 1 and 3) dictate against further advertising investment. However, if the market is responsive to advertising (such as situations 2 or 4), then be prepared to invest in developing creative and effective (i.e., "strong") advertising campaigns so that your advertising represents an investment in the brand equity bank!

Ad Spending, Advertising Elasticity, and Share of Market

The effect of advertising for a brand on its sales volume, revenue, and market share—that is, its proportional representation of total product category revenue—is determined both by how much it spends relative to other brands in the category (its share of voice, or SOV) and how effective its advertising is. It earlier was mentioned that *strong* advertising is an investment in the brand equity bank. Full appreciation of this statement requires that we explore the concept of advertising "strength." We have, in fact, a measure of advertising strength, and that measure is the familiar concept we've been discussing, namely, advertising elasticity. Table 9.4 presents real data for the top-10 airlines from a recent year as a basis for illustrating advertising elasticity and the concept of strength. However, before proceeding, it is necessary to introduce a final equation, Equation 9.6.

$$(9.6) \qquad SOM_i = A_i^e \Big/ \sum_{j=1}^{n} A_j^e$$

Equation 9.6 indicates that a brand's predicted market share (i.e., the SOM for the *i*th brand in a product category) depends on its level of advertising (A_i) raised to the power of its advertising elasticity (*e*) in comparison to the total level of

Table 9.4

The Effect of Advertising Elasticity on Share of Market

Airline	Ad Spend ($ million) (A)	Hypothetical Elasticity Coefficients (B)	(A) ^ (B)* (C)	Predicted SOM (1) (D)	(A) ^ (B)** (E)	Predicted SOM (2) (F)
United	$ 57.3	.1	1.499	11.8	1.499	11.3
American	71.7	.1	1.533	12.1	1.533	11.6
Delta	32.1	.1 OR .2	1.415	11.2	2.001	15.1
Northwest	41.5	.1	1.451	11.4	1.451	10.9
Continental	22.2	.1	1.363	10.8	1.363	10.3
US Airways	17.0	.1	1.328	10.5	1.328	10.0
Southwest	112.8	.1	1.606	12.7	1.606	12.1
American West	9.4	.1	1.251	9.9	1.251	9.4
TWA	0.0	.1	0.000	0.0	0.000	0.0
Alaska	8.0	.1	1.231	9.7	1.231	9.3
SUM (_)	$373	NA	12.677	100%	13.264	100%

* All elasticity coefficients equal .1

** All elasticity coefficients equal .1 except Delta; Delta's coefficient equals .2

SOURCE: "Top 10 U.S. Airlines," *Advertising Age*, June 24, 2002, S–13.

advertising for all brands in the category (brands j = 1 to n, where n is the total number of brands in the category) raised to the power of their elasticity coefficients.[33] This may seem a little abstract, but Table 9.4 brings this formulation to life with a straightforward example drawn from the airline industry.

The first column of data, column A, indicates the advertising expenditures in a recent year for each of the top-10 U.S. airlines. United Airlines, for example, spent $57.3 million. Column B makes the simplifying assumption that each airline's advertising is equally strong (or equally weak), as indicated by identical elasticity coefficients of 0.1. (Please note that two coefficients are presented for Delta Air Lines; we'll return, subsequently, to the second coefficient, with a value of 0.2.) In column C the ad spend is raised to the power of the elasticity coefficient, with the symbol ^ indicating a power function. Thus, 57.3 raised to the power of 0.1 equals 1.499. The summation of all of the values in column C is 12.677. Thus, following Equation 9.6, each value in column C is divided by the summation of all values to yield, in column D, predicted market shares for all 10 airlines. Of course, Equation 9.6 makes the simplifying assumption that advertising is the sole determinant of market share. If that were the case, then the market shares in column D should correlate strongly with actual market shares. In fact, though not shown in Table 9.4, the correlation between actual and predicted market shares is slightly over 0.5, which indicates that advertising is an important determinant of shares in the airline industry.

Column E provides a new set of values that have been derived by assuming that all elasticity coefficients remain equal at 0.1 with the exception of Delta's, which is 0.2. The assumption, in other words, is that Delta's advertising is "stronger" than its competitors', due perhaps to more creative advertising content or a novel and compelling ad message. If this in fact were the case, then predicted market shares would look like those in column F. Note carefully that Delta's predicted market share has increased by nearly four share points (from 11.2 to 15.1), whereas the shares for all other airlines have declined by about one-half a share point each. Delta's gain (due to hypothetically superior advertising) has come at the expense of its competitors.

In sum, this exercise has shown how it is possible to translate the idea of advertising "strength" into numerical values by capitalizing on the concept of advertising elasticity. Equation 9.6 is based on the simplifying assumption that advertising alone influences market share, but, simplification aside, it enables us to see the effect of creating better, more creative, and stronger advertising: namely, stronger advertising vis-à-vis competitors' efforts can lead to increased market shares. The following two chapters will go into much greater detail in developing the concept of advertising creativity and ad message strategies.

Summary

This chapter offered an introduction to advertising. First, advertising was defined as a paid, mediated form of communication from an identifiable source that is designed to persuade the receiver to take some action, either now or in the future. We then looked at the magnitude of advertising in the United States and elsewhere. For example, ad expenditures in the United States totaled approximately $280 billion in 2005, and worldwide ad spending in the same year was slightly over $550 billion. Also discussed in this context were advertising-to-sales ratios for several illustrative product categories.

Next explored were the functions advertising performs, which include informing, influencing, reminding and increasing salience, adding value, and assisting other company efforts. Following this, the advertising management process was examined from the perspectives of clients. The role of advertising agencies then was discussed, and methods of compensation were reviewed.

A concluding section provided a detailed discussion of the arguments favoring investment in advertising and counterarguments regarding circumstances when it is advisable to disinvest. In the context of this discussion, considerable attention was devoted to the issue of advertising versus pricing elasticities. It was pointed out that sales volume is about 14.6 times more responsive, on average, to changes in price than to changes in advertising. Though this would seem to suggest that revenue is best grown by reducing prices rather than increasing ad spending, the point was made that not all advertisers are "average" and not all advertising situations are the same. Thus, whether increasing advertising or reducing price is a better strategy depends entirely on the situation facing each particular product category and competitor in that category. In conclusion we examined the role of advertising expenditures and elasticity coefficients in determining market shares.

Discussion Questions

1. Describe circumstances when each of the five advertising functions described in the chapter might be more important than the others.
2. Advertising is said to be an "investment in the brand equity bank," but only if the advertising is "strong." Explain.
3. Provide two examples of usage expansion advertising other than those illustrated in the chapter.
4. Present arguments for and against using advertising agencies.
5. Ad agency compensation is increasingly turning to performance- or outcome-based compensation. Explain how this form of ad agency compensation works and why it potentially is superior to alternative methods of compensating ad agencies.
6. Using Equations 9.1 through 9.3, explain the various means by which advertising is capable of influencing a brand's profitability.
7. In the context of the discussion of price and advertising elasticities, four situations were presented by comparing whether price or advertising elasticity is stronger. Situation 2 was characterized as "build image via increased advertising." In your own terms, explain why in this situation it is more profitable to spend relatively more on advertising rather than reduce a brand's price.
8. Research results were presented showing that sales volume is about 14.6 times more responsive, on average, to changes in price than to changes in advertising. Explain exactly what this means for the brand manager of a brand who is considering whether to grow sales by increasing advertising expenditures or lowering the price.
9. Data in this same section indicated that nondurable goods (versus durables) are relatively more responsive to price cuts than advertising increases. Offer an explanation for this differential.
10. Show your understanding of Equation 9.6 and the data presented in Table 9.4 by constructing a spreadsheet (using, for example, Microsoft Excel) and altering the elasticity coefficients for different airlines. For example, just as Delta's elasticity coefficient was changed from 0.1 to 0.2 while holding all the others constant at 0.1, you may want to vary the coefficient for, say, Southwest Airlines, which for this particular year was by far the major investor in advertising.

ENDNOTES

1. Sam Hill, "Advertising Is Rocket Science," *Advertising Age,* January 26, 2004, 18.
2. Ibid.
3. Ibid.
4. Jef I. Richards and Catharine M. Curran, "Oracles on 'Advertising': Searching for a Definition," *Journal of Advertising* 31 (summer 2002), 63–77.
5. Based on an estimate by advertising authority Robert Cohen. See Hillary Chura, "Cohen: 2005 Ad Spending Will Increase to $280 Billion," *Advertising Age,* June 28, 2004, 8.
6. Brian Steinberg, "Media Forecaster Sees More Ad Money, Challenges in 2005," *Wall Street Journal Online,* December 7, 2004, http://online.wsj.com.
7. "100 Leading National Advertisers," *Advertising Age,* June 28, 2004, S–2.
8. Tim Parry, "Selling Brand USA," *Promo,* December 2004, 13–15.
9. This oft-repeated quote is attributed to Revlon's founder, Charles Revson, though the source is unknown.
10. Laurel Wentz and Mercedes M. Cardona, "Ad Fall May Be Worst Since Depression," *Advertising Age,* September 3, 2001, 1, 24.
11. Jennifer Lawrence, "P&G's Artzt on Ads: Crucial Investment," *Advertising Age,* October 28, 1991, 1, 53.
12. Bernard Ryan, Jr., *It Works! How Investment Spending in Advertising Pays Off* (New York: American Association of Advertising Agencies, 1991), 11.
13. These functions are similar to those identified by the noted advertising pioneer James Webb Young. For example, "What Is Advertising, What Does It Do," *Advertising Age,* November 21, 1973, 12.
14. The idea of publicizing brands is based on the ideas of Andrew Ehrenberg and colleagues who regard advertising as a form of creative publicity. See Andrew Ehrenberg, Neil Barnard, Rachel Kennedy, and Helen Bloom, "Brand Advertising as Creative Publicity," *Journal of Advertising Research* 42 (August 2002), 7–18.
15. Giles D'Souza and Ram C. Rao, "Can Repeating an Advertisement More Frequently than the Competition Affect Brand Preference in a Mature Market?" *Journal of Marketing* 59 (April 1995), 32–42. See also A. S. C. Ehrenberg, "Repetitive Advertising and the Consumer," *Journal of Advertising Research* (April 1974), 24–34; Stephen Miller and Lisette Berry, "Brand Salience Versus Brand Image: Two Theories of Advertising Effectiveness," *Journal of Advertising Research* 28 (September/October 1998), 77–82.
16. The term *usage expansion advertising* and the examples are from Brian Wansink and Michael L. Ray, "Advertising Strategies to Increase Usage Frequency," *Journal of Marketing* 60 (January 1996), 31–46.
17. Ehrenberg et al., "Brand Advertising as Creative Publicity," 8.
18. Karen A. Machleit, Chris T. Allen, and Thomas J. Madden, "The Mature Brand and Brand Interest: An Alternative Consequence of Ad-Evoked Affect," *Journal of Marketing* 57 (October 1993), 72–82.
19. John Deighton, Caroline M. Henderson, and Scott A. Neslin, "The Effects of Advertising on Brand Switching and Repeat Purchasing," *Journal of Marketing Research* 31 (February 1994), 28–43.
20. *The Value Side of Productivity: A Key to Competitive Survival in the 1990s* (New York: American Association of Advertising Agencies, 1989), 12.
21. Sridhar Moorthy and Hao Zhao, "Advertising Spending and Perceived Quality," *Marketing Letters* 11 (August 2000), 221–234.
22. *The Value Side of Productivity,* 13–15. See also, Larry Light and Richard Morgan, *The Fourth Wave: Brand Loyalty Marketing* (New York: Coalition for Brand Equity, American Association of Advertising Agencies, 1994), 25.
23. Jim Spaeth, "Lost Lessons of Brand Power," *Advertising Age,* July 14, 2003, 16.
24. The synergism between advertising and personal selling does not always equate to a one-way flow from advertising to personal selling. In fact, one study has demonstrated a reverse situation, in which personal sales calls sometimes pave the way for advertising. See William R. Swinyard and Michael L. Ray, "Advertising-Selling Interactions: An Attribution Theory Experiment," *Journal of Marketing Research* 14 (November 1977), 509–516.
25. Albert C. Bemmaor and Dominique Mouchoux, "Measuring the Short-Term Effect of In-Store Promotion and Retail Advertising on Brand Sales: A Factorial Experiment," *Journal of Marketing Research* 28 (May 1991), 202–214.
26. Mukund S. Kulkarni, Premal P. Vora, and Terence A. Brown, "Firing Advertising Agencies," *Journal of Advertising* 32 (Fall 2003), 77–86.
27. The 15 percent rate was for advertisements placed in newspapers and magazines, and on television and radio. The discount paid to advertising agencies for outdoor advertising has historically been slightly higher at 16.67 percent.
28. A theoretical treatment of outcome-based compensation programs is provided by Deborah F. Spake, Giles D'Souza, Tammy Neal Crutchfield, and Robert M. Morgan, "Advertising Agency Compensation: An Agency Theory Explanation," *Journal of Advertising* 28 (Fall 1999), 53–72.
29. John Sinisi, "Love: EDLP Equals Ad Investment," *Brandweek,* November 16, 1992, 2.
30. Raj Sethuraman and Gerard J. Tellis, "An Analysis of the Tradeoff Between Advertising and Price Discounting," *Journal of Marketing Research* 28 (May 1991), 160–174. A recent study reveals that the average price elasticity based on an analysis of over 1,800 elasticity coefficients is even larger than previously thought. In fact, compared to Sethuraman and Tellis' estimated price elasticity of –1.61, this more complete and recent study yielded a mean price elasticity coefficient of –2.62. See Tammo H. A. Bijmolt, Harald J. van Heerde, and Rik G. M. Pieters, "New Empirical Generalizations on the Determinants of Price Elasticity," *Journal of Marketing Research* 42 (May 2005), 141–156.
31. Adapted from ibid., especially Figure 1, p. 163, and the surrounding discussion.
32. See ibid., p. 164.
33. This formulation is based on an Internet posting by Gerard Tellis on ELMAR-AMA, June 4, 2003, http://elmar.ama.org.

CHAPTER 10

Creating Effective and Creative Advertising Messages

Like everything else in life, the concept of "advertising quality" has a statistical distribution. That is, most ads are of average quality, not really bad or very good, and then at the extremes of the distribution are ads that are really bad or exceptionally good. Some ads, though relatively few, are so dreadful that we almost want to gag when seeing or hearing them. Then, at the opposite end of the ad-quality distribution, are a small number of fabulous advertisements. Following are descriptions of two advertisements that many advertising pundits would regard as among the best advertising executions of all time.

Marcom Challenge: Two of the Greatest Ads in the History of Advertising

Miss Clairol: "Does She . . . or Doesn't She?" Imagine yourself employed as a copywriter in a New York advertising agency in 1955. You have just been assigned creative responsibility for a product that heretofore (as of 1955) had not been nationally marketed or advertised. The product: hair coloring. The brand: Miss Clairol. Your task: devise a creative strategy that will convince millions of American women to purchase Miss Clairol hair coloring—at the time called Hair Color Bath. This challenge occurred, by the way, in a cultural context where it was considered patently inappropriate for respectable women to smoke in public, wear long pants, or color their hair.

The person actually assigned this task was Shirley Polykoff, a copywriter for the Foote, Cone & Belding agency. Her story of how she came up with the famous line "Does she . . . or doesn't she?" provides a fascinating illustration of the creative process in advertising. At the time of the Miss Clairol campaign, there was no hair-coloring business. In fact, according to Ms. Polykoff, at-home hair-coloring jobs invariably turned out blotchy. Women were ashamed to color their own hair at home. A product that provided a natural look stood a strong chance of being accepted, but women would have to be convinced that an advertised hair-coloring product would, in fact, give them that highly desired natural look.

Shirley Polykoff explains the background of the famous advertising line that convinced women Miss Clairol would produce a natural look.

In 1933, just before I was married, my husband had taken me to meet the woman who would become my mother-in-law. When we got in the car after dinner, I asked him, "How'd I do? Did your mother like me?" and he told me his mother had said, "She paints her hair, doesn't she?" He asked me, "Well, do you?" It became a joke between my husband and me; anytime we saw someone who was stunning or attractive we'd say, "Does she, or doesn't she?" Twenty years later [at the time she was working on the Miss Clairol account], I was walking down Park Avenue talking out loud to myself, because I have to hear what I write. The phrase came into my mind again. Suddenly, I realized, "That's it. That's the campaign." I knew that [a competitive advertising agency] couldn't find anything better.

I knew that immediately. When you're young, you're very sure about everything.[1]

The advertising line "Does she . . . or doesn't she?" actually was followed with the tag line "Hair color so natural only her hairdresser knows for sure!" The headline grabbed the reader's attention, whereas the tag line promised a conclusive benefit: the product works so well that only an expert would recognize that the at-home application was not performed at a beauty salon. This brilliant advertising persuaded millions of American women to become product users and led to dramatically increased sales of Miss Clairol.[2]

Macintosh Computer: "1984" Apple Computer had just developed the world's most user-friendly computer and needed break-through advertising to introduce its new Macintosh brand, which was a revolution in computing technology. Steve Jobs, the co-founder of Apple, who was only 29 at the time of the Macintosh

CHAPTER OBJECTIVES

1
Appreciate the factors that promote effective and creative advertising.

2
Understand a five-step program used in formulating advertising strategy.

3
Describe the features of a creative brief.

4
Explain alternative creative styles that play a role in the development of advertising messages.

5
Understand the concept of means-end chains and their role in advertising strategy.

6
Appreciate the MECCAS model and its role in guiding message formulation.

7
Describe the laddering method that provides the data used in constructing a MECCAS model.

8
Recognize the role of corporate image and issue advertising.

introduction, instructed his advertising agency, Chiat/Day, to create an explosive television commercial that would portray the Macintosh as a truly revolutionary machine. The creative people at Chiat/Day faced a challenging task, especially since Macintosh's main competitor was the powerful and much larger "Big Blue" (IBM). (In 1984, Compaq, Dell, and Gateway were nonexistent. It was only Apple versus IBM in the personal computer business, and IBM was the well-established leader known for its corporate computers.) However, Chiat/Day produced a commercial in which IBM was obliquely caricatured as the much-despised and feared institution reminiscent of the Big Brother theme in George Orwell's book *1984.* (In the book, political power is controlled by Big Brother, and individual dignity and freedom are superseded by political conformity.) The one-minute commercial created in this context, dubbed "1984," was run during the Super Bowl XVIII on January 22, 1984, and was never repeated on commercial television. This was not because it was ineffective; to the contrary, its incredible word-of-mouth-producing impact negated the need for repeat showings.

The commercial . . . opens on a room of zombie-like citizens staring at a huge screen where Big Brother is spewing a relentless cant about "information purification . . . unprincipled dissemination of facts" and "unification of thought."

Against this ominous backdrop, a woman in athletic wear [a white jersey top and bright red running shorts, which was the only primary color in the commercial] runs in and hurls a sledgehammer into the screen, causing a cataclysmic explosion that shatters Big Brother. Then the message flashes on the TV screen: "On January 24th, Apple Computer will introduce Macintosh. And you'll see why 1984 won't be like '1984.'"[3]

This remarkable advertising is considered by some to be the greatest TV commercial ever made.[4] It grabbed attention; it broke through the clutter of the many commercials aired during the Super Bowl; it was memorable; it was discussed by millions of people; and, ultimately, it played an instrumental role in selling truckloads of Macintosh computers. Moreover, it created a unique image for the Mac (short for Macintosh) as described adroitly by one observer.

The Mac is female. Conversely, IBM must be male. IBM is not just male, it is Big Brother male. And Apple is not just female, but New Female. She is strong, athletic, independent, and, most important, liberated. After all, that's what the young athlete is all about. She is, in terms of the 1980s, empowerment and freedom.[5]

Overview

Advertisers in most product categories, including B2B as well as B2C, generally confront an advertising context where audiences are continually bombarded by advertisements. This state of affairs, referred to as advertising *clutter,* means that ad messages must be sufficiently creative to gain the receiver's attention and accomplish even more ambitious goals such as enhancing brand images and motivating prospects to purchase advertised products. The present chapter, which is the first of two to examine the message aspect of advertising, surveys questions such as these: What is advertising creativity? What makes a good advertising message? What are the different types of creative styles, and when and why is each used? What kind of research can be performed as a prelude to developing effective advertising?

First addressed in the chapter is the matter of what makes effective advertising and the related subject of creative advertising. Next covered is the process underlying the formulation of advertising strategy. A third section describes various forms of creative approaches that are widely used by advertising practitioners. A following topic is the concept of means-end chains as a mechanism for bridging the advertiser's creative process with the values that drive consumers' product and brand choices. Finally, the discussion moves away from brand-oriented advertising and examines corporate image and issue advertising.

Creating Effective Advertising

Having in the previous chapter provided an overview of advertising agencies, the creators of advertisements, we turn now to the issue of how the advertising agency and client work together to develop effective advertising campaigns. No simple answer is possible, but toward this end we first must attempt to understand the meaning of *effective advertising*. It is easy, in one sense, to define effective advertising: advertising is effective if it accomplishes the advertiser's objectives. This perspective defines effectiveness from the output side, or in terms of what it accomplishes. It is much more difficult to define effective advertising from an input perspective, or in terms of the composition of the advertisement itself. There are many viewpoints on this issue. Practitioners are broadly split on the matter. For example, a practitioner of direct-mail advertising probably has a different opinion about what constitutes effective advertising than would have Shirley Polykoff, the creator of the Miss Clairol campaign, or Steve Hayden, the inspirational source behind the "1984" Macintosh commercial.

Although it is impractical to provide a singular, all-purpose definition of what constitutes effective advertising, it is possible to talk about general characteristics.[6] At a minimum, good (or effective) advertising satisfies the following considerations:

1. *It must extend from sound marketing strategy.* Advertising can be effective only if it is compatible with other elements of an integrated and well-orchestrated marcom strategy.
2. *Effective advertising must take the consumer's view.* Consumers buy product benefits, not attributes. Therefore, advertising must be stated in a way that relates to the consumer's—rather than the marketer's—needs, wants, and values. An advertising practitioner who specializes in creative thinking has stated the issue in these terms: "Consumers don't want to be bombarded with ads—they want to be inspired by ideas that will change their lives. Ads create transactions. Ideas create transformations. Ads reflect our culture, ideas imagine our future."[7]
3. *Advertising must find a unique way to break through the clutter.* Advertisers continually compete with competitors for the consumer's attention. This is no small task considering the massive number of print advertisements, broadcast commercials, Internet ads, and other sources of information available daily to consumers. Indeed, the situation in television advertising has been characterized as "audiovisual wallpaper"—a sarcastic implication that consumers pay just about as much attention to commercials as they do to the detail in their wallpaper after seeing it for years.[8]
4. *Good advertising should never promise more than it can deliver.* This point speaks for itself, both in terms of ethics and in terms of smart business sense. Consumers learn quickly when they have been deceived and will resent the advertiser. In short, effective advertising does not promise more that the advertised product is capable of delivering.
5. *Good advertising prevents the creative idea from overwhelming the strategy.* The purpose of advertising is to inform and ultimately sell products; the purpose is not to be creative merely for the sake of being clever. It is claimed, though perhaps not fairly, that advertising agencies place excessive emphasis on winning awards at the various ceremonies conducted annually by the ad industry—for example, the Cannes Lions International Advertising Festival in France, the London International Advertising Awards, and the Clio Awards in the United States.

The Role of Creativity

Effective advertising is usually *creative*. Most memorable advertisements make their selling points in an entertaining, creative fashion. But what is creativity? Unfortunately, there is no simple answer to this elusive aspect of advertising.[9] There is some agreement, however, that creative ads share two

JOB OUTLOOK

The creative director oversees the copy chief, art director, and associated staff in developing subject matter and presentation of advertising. College graduates with related experience, a high level of creativity, and strong communication skills should have the best job opportunities. *(Occupational Outlook Handbook, 2004–05 Edition, U.S. DOL, http://www.bls.gov/oco/home.htm)*

features: originality and appropriateness.[10] First, an ad is *original* in the sense that the methods, techniques, and copy are novel for the product category in question. That is, an original ad is somehow out of the ordinary; it differentiates itself from the mass of mediocre advertisements. Advertising that is the same as most other advertising is unable to break through the competitive clutter and grab the consumer's attention. However, originality alone is insufficient. In an entirely different context but nonetheless applicable to advertising, jazz musician Charlie Mingus captured this same idea when stating, "Creativity is more than just being different. Anybody can play weird, that's easy. What's hard is to be as simple as Bach. Making the simple complicated is commonplace, making the complicated simple, awesomely simple, that's creativity."[11]

The second facet of ad creativity, *appropriateness,* means that an advertisement must offer a useful solution to a marketing problem. In an advertising context, the problem, or challenge, is one of achieving objectives such as increasing sales by a specified percentage. An ad that is original but not appropriate may win awards in advertising competitions but will be unlikely to "move the sales dial" by any substantive degree. Creative ads are original while at the same time being useful given the imperatives facing a brand at the time an ad campaign is initiated.

It is easier to give examples of creative advertising than to exactly define it. In addition to the highly creative (and effective!) advertisements presented in the *Marcom Challenge,* the following examples illustrate advertising campaigns that, in the author's opinion, register high marks on both the originality and appropriateness facets of creativity:

- American Family Life Assurance Company—Until the early 2000s, a supplementary insurance company named Aflac was anything but a household name. In fact, that was the problem: despite having invested heavily in advertising for a number of years, most consumers had never heard the name Aflac or little remembered it. Aflac's chief executive officer and chairman knew that a creative advertising campaign was needed to generate the necessary level of brand awareness and recall. Hired for this purpose was, at the time, a little known ad agency—the Kaplan Thaler Group. The creative team assigned to the project generated many ideas for a campaign, but after weeks of creative effort none passed the key test of whether consumers would remember the company for whom the advertising was undertaken.

  Just days before the deadline, a member of the creative team took a long walk during his lunch break and started repeating the name, Aflac, out loud. After hearing himself repeat the name over and over, it dawned on him that he sounded like a quacking duck. With great excitement he returned to his office and, along with his creative teammate, quickly wrote the first spot for an Aflac commercial featuring the now-famous "spokesduck." This creative insight initiated one of advertising's most heralded ad campaigns. Many readers of this text no doubt will recall seeing different Aflac executions, all of which use humor in portraying a frustrated duck that never seems to be noticed. Incorporated seamlessly into dialogue about supplemental insurance in each ad execution, the unnoticed duck simply exclaims, "Aflac!!" in response to questions such as what is supplemental insurance? and what is it called? The ad campaign registered incredible results from its inception and has increased Aflac's sales by over 50 percent![12]
- Nike—Sports shoe and apparel company, Nike, and its advertising agency, Wieden + Kennedy, are known for their original and often captivating advertising. This was typified in 2004 when Wieden + Kennedy created an absorbing campaign for Nike. Professional athletes were shown in various executions playing hockey, volleyball, baseball, bowling, boxing, and so on. You might be wondering, what's the big deal, hundreds of commercials for sporting goods have done the same thing? The brilliance in these ads was the nifty juxtaposition of famous athletes with sports other than those for which they are known.

For example, tennis player Andre Agassi was portrayed playing baseball; quarterback Michael Vick was shown as a hockey player par excellence; six-time Tour de France winner Lance Armstrong was portrayed as an accomplished boxer; baseball pitcher Randy Johnson looked like a professional bowler; and tennis player Serena Williams was shown making a vicious serve in volleyball. As with other Nike commercials, this campaign made the nuanced point that Nike, like the famous athletes who endorse its products, is somehow special and out of the ordinary.[13]

- Honda U.K.—The remarkable engineering that goes into an automobile, the Honda Accord in particular, was celebrated in a two-minute TV commercial introduced in the United Kingdom. The commercial, titled "Cog," itself represented a mechanical wonder and supposedly required over 600 takes before perfection was achieved. Later downloaded to the Internet, the commercial illustrated through a painstaking sequence of events various automobile parts being synchronized in a chain of events reminiscent of watching a kinetic sculpture where a ball rolls down a slide, drops in a tube, spins onto a shelf, flips into a basket, and eventually arrives at the bottom. The advertisement was intended to demonstrate to consumers all the parts and technological marvels that go into making a Honda Accord. Garrison Keillor, the emcee of the American radio program *Prairie Home Companion,* provided the offscreen voice that served to make sense of the intricate visual action in the commercial when simply intoning, "Isn't it nice when things just work?" The "Cog" commercial is clearly the stuff of advertising legend.
- The Apple iPod is a portable digital audio player much in demand by consumers who enjoy listening to music while on the go. With its ability to hold thousands of songs, iPod owners can listen to their favorite tunes whenever and wherever they choose, and without disturbing others—as in the past when people hauled boom boxes around on their shoulders. Although the product is technologically advanced, TV commercials for the iPod were simple in design yet highly creative. Every execution in the iPod campaign featured silhouetted figures against neon backgrounds holding iPods, listening and gyrating to music. The creativity of these ads was due largely to the simplicity of design and the differentiation from typical commercials where identifiable individuals (not silhouetted figures) are shown using products and engaged in dialogue. See Figure 10.1 for an illustration of a silhouetted figure in an iPod commercial.

Advertising Successes and Mistakes

The foregoing discussion has described general features of effective and creative advertising and presented several illustrative campaigns. It will be useful at this point to provide a conceptual framework that identifies the conditions under which advertising campaigns are likely to be successes or failures. Figure 10.2 offers such a framework by conceptualizing advertising's impact as extending from a combination of message convincingness and execution quality.[14]

An advertising message can be thought of as providing the reader, viewer, or listener with a *value proposition.* A **value proposition** is the essence of a message and the reward to the consumer for investing his or her time attending to an advertisement. The reward may come in the form of needed information about a brand or may simply represent an enjoyable experience, such as tens of thousands of people obtained when viewing the "Cog" commercial. Research indicates that starting with a strong selling proposition substantially increases the odds of creating effective advertisements.[15]

Figure 10.1

Illustration of iPod's "Silhouette" Commercial

Courtesy, Apple Computer; Ad Agency: TBWA LA; Photo Credit: Matthew Welch; Model: Katie Malia/Bloc Agency.

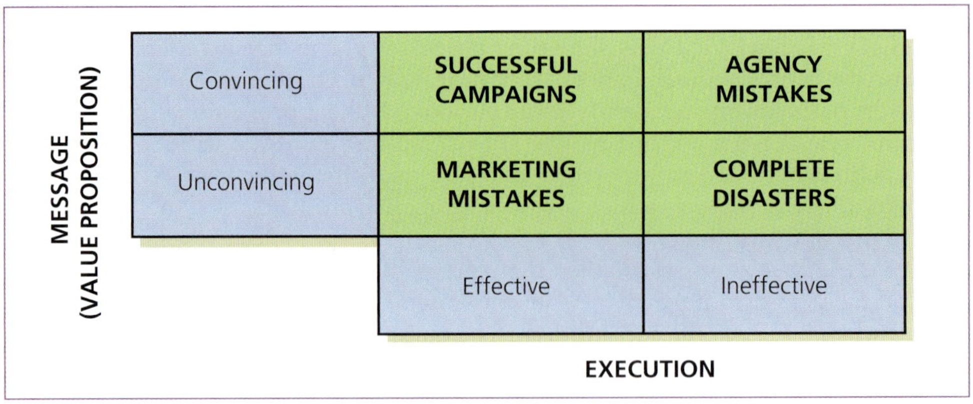

Figure 10.2 Combination of Message Convincingness and Execution Quality

However, though having a convincing message is a necessary condition for creating an effective advertisement, it is insufficient. As shown in Figure 10.2, the ad also must be executed effectively. Hence, advertising messages can be conceptualized in terms of a fourfold classification based on whether value propositions are convincing or unconvincing and if agency executions of these propositions are effective or ineffective: (1) successful campaigns, (2) marketing mistakes, (3) agency mistakes, and (4) complete disasters.

Successful Campaigns. Successful advertising campaigns arise from a combination of having a message founded on a convincing value proposition and an effective (i.e., interesting and engaging) execution. In short, successful campaigns communicate meaningful value propositions in an effective way. Both the brand management team (client side) and the creative team (agency side) have done their work well in this situation.

Marketing Mistakes. The advertising agency may come up with a good, creative execution, but this cannot make up for the absence of a convincing value proposition. *Marketing mistakes* result from brand management's failure to identify a meaningful value proposition that distinguishes the brand from competitive offerings. A bad idea well executed is nonetheless a mistake. An ad agency may be fired when a campaign does not meet expectations, but the fault in this case resides with the brand management team for failing to provide the ad agency with good raw material to work with.

Agency Mistakes. This form of failed ad campaign is due to the ad agency's inability to design an effective execution, even though its brand management client has presented it with a value proposition that should have represented a convincing message. This situation, in short, represents a good idea that has been blown, "defeat stolen from the jaws of victory."

Complete Disasters. Poor value propositions and mediocre executions are the stuff of advertising disasters. Responsibility for failure is evenly distributed between the brand management and creative teams. Disasters can be avoided by conducting research that pretests both the proposition and the executional strategy prior to ever printing or airing a final advertisement. More will be said later about the importance of performing research as input into creative decisions.

How can an agency or its client know in advance—that is, prior to printing or airing an advertisement—whether it is likely to be successful? First, research that examines consumers' product-related needs, expectations, and past experiences should provide the brand manager with a good idea about the likely effectiveness of a particular value proposition. Many advertising agencies in the United Kingdom, the United States, and elsewhere include a position in their organizations called *account planning*. Although the job specifics vary somewhat from agency to agency, *account planners* represent the voice of the customer. Customer research, often of a qualitative nature, is interpreted by account planners and becomes key input into creative advertising development.[16] Second, execution effectiveness can be judged by pretesting advertisements before actually initiating an advertising campaign. Chapter 12 will discuss in detail methods to assess message and execution effectiveness.

Advertising Plans and Strategy

Advertising messages can be developed in an ad hoc fashion without much forethought, or they can be created systematically. Advertising plans provide the framework for the systematic execution of advertising strategies. To appreciate the role of an advertising plan, imagine a soccer team approaching an upcoming game without any idea of how it is going to execute its offense or defense. Without a game plan, the team would have to play in the same spontaneous fashion as do players in a pickup game. Under such circumstances there would be numerous missed assignments and overall misexecution. The team likely would lose unless they played a badly mismatched opponent.

So it is with advertising. Companies compete against opponents who generally are well prepared. This means that a firm must enter the advertising "game" with a clear plan in mind. An advertising plan evaluates a brand's advertising history, proposes where the next period's advertising should head, and justifies the proposed strategy for maintaining or improving a brand's competitive situation.

To put an advertising plan into action requires (1) careful evaluation of customer behavior related to the brand, (2) detailed evaluation of the competition, and (3) a coordinated effort to tie the proposed advertising program to the brand's overall marcom strategy. Because an advertising plan involves a number of steps and details that are beyond the scope of this chapter, attention in this chapter will focus just on the all-important strategy aspect of planning. **Advertising strategy** is what the advertiser says about the brand being advertised. It is the formulation of an advertising message that communicates the brand's value proposition—its primary benefit or how it can solve the consumer's problem.

A Five-Step Program

Formulating an advertising strategy requires that the advertiser and its agency undertake a formal process, such as the following five-step program:[17]

1. Specify the key fact from the customer's viewpoint.
2. State the primary problem, or advertising issue, from brand management's perspective.
3. State the advertising objective.
4. Implement the creative message strategy.
5. Establish mandatory requirements.

Each step in the ad strategy process will be illustrated by considering an advertising campaign undertaken by Holiday Inn, a hotel chain with over 1,000 hotels in the Americas and hundreds more in Europe, the Middle East, Africa, and Asia. Holiday Inn was the first national hotel franchisee organization and the first hotel company to advertise on television some 40 years ago.[18] In a recent advertising effort to demonstrate how accommodating the chain is, a series of television commercials featured an ensemble of a mom, dad, grandma, and quintessential "slacker" (loveable, late-30s Mark), who rather than being out on his own gainfully employed instead lives with his family while supposedly attempting to run a start-up. The various campaign executions featured the slacker making requests from his family for special amenities such as a better bedroom, a fax machine, reward points, and so forth. The coup de grace in every execution was a family member exclaiming, "What do you think this is, a Holiday Inn?" The implication from these hilarious executions is clear: Holiday Inn gives its customers special treatment—the sort expected by the slacker but withheld by his family.

Step 1: Specify the Key Fact

The **key fact** in an advertising strategy is a single-minded statement from the *consumer's point of view* that identifies why consumers are or are not purchasing the product, service, or brand or are not giving it proper consideration.

Research performed for Holiday Inn undoubtedly revealed that many consumers perceived this hotel chain as offering limited amenities in comparison to other similarly priced hotel chains. This perception had to be overcome in order to increase the number of business travelers and family vacationers choosing Holiday Inns over competitive chains.[19]

Step 2: State the Primary Problem

Extending from the key fact, this step states the problem from the *brand management's point of view.* The primary problem may be an image problem, a product perception issue, or a competitive weakness.

Holiday Inn needed to improve its image and change the erroneous perception that it offers fewer amenities (such as kids staying free, in-room restaurant service, reward points, etc.) than competitive hotel chains.

Step 3: State the Communications Objective

This is a straightforward statement about *what effect the advertising is intended to have on the target market.*

Holiday Inn's advertising with slacker Mark and his family was *not* designed to increase awareness of the Holiday Inn name. Most business travelers and family vacationers are fully familiar with this hotel chain that has been in business for over 50 years. Rather, the objective was to clarify misconceptions about the chain—namely, that it does not offer a full range of services—and to increase room occupancy rates.

Step 4: Implement the Creative Message Strategy

Creative message strategy, sometimes also called the *creative platform,* represents the guts of the overall advertising strategy. The creative platform for a brand is summarized in a single statement called a *value proposition* (see the previous section) or *positioning statement.* A *positioning statement* is the key idea that encapsulates what a brand is intended to stand for in its target market's mind and with consideration of how competitors have attempted to position their brands. As discussed back in Chapter 5, a positioning statement for a brand represents how we want customers and prospects to think and feel about our brand. These thoughts and feelings should stand out in comparison to competitive offerings and motivate the customer or prospect to want to try our brand.

© Robert W. Ginn/PhotoEdit

Implementing creative message strategy requires (1) defining the target market, (2) identifying the primary competition, (3) choosing the positioning statement, and (4) offering reasons why.

Define the Target Market. You will recall from the discussion in Chapter 4 that the target market for a brand's advertising strategy and related marketing program can be defined in terms of demographics, geodemographics, psychographics, or *product-usage* characteristics (behavior graphics).

Holiday Inn's target market consists of two groups: (1) frequent business travelers who cannot afford or wish not to pay higher prices at more expensive hotel chains, but nonetheless desire a full range of services unlike the limited offerings at inexpensive outlets; and (2) family vacationers who desire more amenities than those provided by the low-price chains but also wish to economize on their lodging expenditures, including free lodging for their children. Both groups likely are value-oriented and consider it important to get their money's worth when choosing lodging outlets. Perhaps they also like to be pampered somewhat and thus are receptive to a hotel that offers some amenities in comparison to a no-frills, low-budget option.

Identify the Primary Competition. Who are the primary competitors in the segment the brand is attempting to tap, and what are their relative advantages and disadvantages? Answering this question enables an advertiser to know exactly how to position a brand against consumers' perceptions of competitive brands' advantages and disadvantages.

Holiday Inn's primary competitors likely are other mid-priced chains such as Courtyard by Marriott, Best Western, and Radisson Hotels. Holiday Inn's research perhaps revealed that its target audience thought these competitive hotels offered greater amenities.

Choose the Positioning Statement. This aspect of the creative platform, as previously described, amounts to selecting a brand's primary benefit or major selling idea. In most cases, it is a direct or implicit promise in the form of a consumer benefit or solution to a problem.

The primary benefit to business travelers and family vacationers is Holiday Inn's promise of a complete range of amenities comparable to those provided by other mid-level hotels but far superior to the limited offerings of low-end lodging chains.

Offer Reasons Why. These are the facts supporting the positioning statement. In some instances advertisers can back up advertising claims with factual information that is relevant, informative, and interesting to consumers. Many times it is impossible to prove or support the promise being made, such as when the promise is symbolic or psychological. In these instances, advertisers turn to authority figures, experts, or celebrities to support the implicit advertising promise.

Holiday Inn's promise in the series of Mark-the-slacker commercials is that it offers all the services most any traveler would want when choosing a relatively inexpensive hotel.

Step 5: Establish Mandatory Requirements

The final step in formulating an advertising strategy involves the mandatory requirements that must be included in an ad. Mandatory requirements are those imposed by corporate officers as a matter of policy and tradition or perhaps, in some instances, due to regulatory dictates—for example, when advertising prescription drugs to consumers, side effects must be listed. Non-regulatory mandatory requirements remind the advertiser to include, for example, the corporate slogan or logo or a standard tag line at the bottom of a print ad or end of a commercial. (See the *IMC Focus* for discussion of advertising slogans.)

In sum, advertising strategy lays out the details for the upcoming advertising campaign. It insists on a disciplined approach to analyzing the brand, the consumer, and the competition. A single-minded benefit, or positioning statement, is the outcome. The strategy becomes a blueprint, road map, or guide to subsequent advertising efforts. Every proposed tactical decision is evaluated in terms of whether it is compatible with the strategy.

Constructing a Creative Brief

A systematic approach to creative advertising makes sense in theory, but ultimately the people who write advertising copy and create visual imagery—so-called creatives—must summon their full talents to develop effective advertising. Creatives often complain that marketing research reports and other such directives excessively constrain their opportunities for full creative expression. On the other hand, one cannot forget that advertising is a business with an obligation to sell products. Even though research has shown that advertising copy is based on copywriters' own implicit theories of how advertising works on consumers, they do not have the luxury to create for the mere sake of engaging in a creative pursuit.[20] Their ultimate purpose is to write advertising copy that affects consumers' expectations, attitudes, and eventually purchase behavior (sooner rather than later, it is hoped).

How Well Do You Know Advertising Slogans?

imc focus

Slogans, or tag lines, have always played an important role in advertising. Effective slogans encapsulate a brand's key positioning and value proposition and provide consumers with a memory tag for distinguishing one brand from another. Some slogans have been used with success for decades, as evidenced in the following list **(A)** of what some would regard as the top slogans of modern marketing. See if you can match the slogan with its company. (Answers are provided at the bottom.)

These famous slogans aside, it appears that current advertising slogans may be less effective, certainly less memorable, than are these famous slogans. A recent survey of 500 people determined that only 5 percent could correctly identify even half of the slogans in use by 29 advertisers. Only 3 of 29 slogans were correctly identified by more than 50 percent of the surveyed respondents. The following table **(B)** presents the slogans, the companies or brands using the slogans, and the percentages of correct identification.

(A)

Slogan		Company	
1. __"A diamond is forever."	6. __"Good to the last drop."	A. Maxwell House (1915)*	F. Morton Salt (1911)
2. __"Just do it."	7. __"Breakfast of Champions."	B. Wheaties (1935)	G. Clairol (1964)
3. __"The pause that refreshes."	8. __"Does she . . . or doesn't she?"	C. Wendy's (1984)	H. Coca-Cola (1929)
4. __"Tastes great, less filling."	9. __"When it rains it pours."	D. De Beers (1950)	I. Avis (1962)
5. __"We try harder."	10. __"Where's the beef?"	E. Miller Lite (1974)	J. Nike (1988)

*Slogan's date of inception

(B)

Company or Brand	Slogan	Percentage Correct Identification	Company or Brand	Slogan	Percentage Correct Identification
Allstate	"You're in good hands."	87%	Coca-Cola	"Real."	5
State Farm	"Like a good neighbor."	70	Dr Pepper	"Be you."	5
Wal-Mart	"Always low price. Always."	67	General Electric	"Imagination at work."	5
General Electric	"We bring good things to life."	39	Heineken	"It's all about the beer."	4
Sprite	"Obey your thirst."	35	Michelob Ultra	"Lose the carbs. Not the taste."	4
Taco Bell	"Think outside the bun."	34	Sears	"Good life. Great price."	4
McDonald's	"I'm loving it."	33	Chrysler	"Inspiration comes standard."	3
Capital One	"What's in your wallet?"	27	Corona	"Miles away from ordinary."	3
Gatorade	"Is it in you?"	19	Arby's	"What are you eating today?"	2
Chevrolet	"An American revolution."	17	Miller	"Good call."	1
J. C. Penney	"It's all inside."	15	Buick	"The sprit of American style."	1
Nissan	"Shift."	12	Kmart	"Right here, right now."	1
Toyota	"Get the feeling."	11	Staples	"That was easy."	0
Budweiser	"True."	10	Wendy's	"It's better here."	0
Sierra Mist	"Yeah, it's kinda like that."	6			

Sources: The table of matching slogans is from Deborah L. Vence, "The Test of Time," *Marketing News,* December 15, 2004, 8–9. The table with 29 brand slogans is from Becky Ebenkamp, "Slogans' Heroes, Zeroes," *Brandweek,* October 25, 2004, 17.

(A) Answers: 1, D; 2, J; 3, H; 4, E; 5, I; 6, A; 7, B; 8, G; 9, F; 10, C.

The work of copywriters and other creative advertising practitioners is directed by a framework known as a **creative brief**, which is a document designed to channel copywriters' and other creatives' efforts toward a solution that will serve the interests of the client. The term *brief* is used to mean that a client for an advertising project (such as a brand management team) is informing, or briefing, an advertising agency of the client's needs and expectations for a proposed advertising campaign. The creative brief represents an informal pact between client and advertising agency that represents agreement on what an advertising campaign is intended to accomplish.

Although creative briefs vary in terms of their degree of specificity, most briefs would minimally include requests for answers to the following questions:

Background. The initial question that must be addressed is *What is the background to this job?* The answer to this question requires a brief explanation regarding why the advertising agency is being asked to perform a certain advertising job. What is it that the client wishes to achieve with the campaign? For example, the purpose may be to launch a new brand, gain back lost sales from a competitor, or introduce a new version of an established product. Part of the background explanation would include analyses of the competitive environment and cultural dynamics related to the product category that could influence the brand's success potential.

Target Audience. *Whom do we need to reach with the ad campaign?* This is a precise description of the exemplary target market. With knowledge of the behaviorgraphic, psychographic, demographic, or geodemographic characteristics of the intended customer (see Chapter 4), creatives have a specific target at which to direct their efforts. This is as essential in advertising as it is in certain athletic events. For example, the late golf sage Harvey Penick offered the following advice to pupils trying to improve their golf games: "Once you address the golf ball, hitting it has got to be the most important thing in your life at that moment. Shut out all thoughts other than picking out a target and taking dead aim at it."[21] His point to golfers about taking "dead aim" is also applicable to advertising creatives: you can't hit a target unless you know where to aim!

Thoughts and Feelings. *What do members of the target audience currently think and feel about our brand?* Here is where research and account planning are needed as the foundation for the advertising job. The advice here is to perform research *prior* to developing creative advertisements. With the assistance of account planners in interpreting research results, ad creatives are then prepared to design research-based advertising that speaks to the target audience in terms of their known thoughts and feelings about the brand rather than relying on mere suppositions. Sure, effective ads can be created absent any formal research (recall the Aflac ad and how it came about); however, the odds of success are much improved if formal research precedes creative activity.

Objectives and Measures. *What do we want the target audience to think or feel about the brand, and what measurable effects is the advertising designed to accomplish?* This guideline simply reminds everyone what the client wants the advertising to accomplish. It calls for a short statement about the crucial feelings or thoughts that the advertisement should evoke in its intended audience. For example, the ad might be designed to move the audience emotionally, to make them feel deserving of a better lifestyle, or to get them to feel anxious about a currently unsafe course of behavior. Is there a current perception that needs to be changed? For example, if a large number of consumers in the target market consider the brand overpriced, how can we change that perception and convince them that the brand actually is a good value due to its superior quality? Knowing this, creatives can then design appropriate advertisements to achieve that objective. Given multiple objectives, it is desirable to prioritize them from most to least important.

Also, though not a typical practice in the ad industry when constructing creative briefs, it is desirable to indicate not only what objectives are to be accomplished but also how achievement of these objectives will be measured. By specifying measures in advance, client and agency are on the proverbial same page when follow-up research is performed to assess whether the advertising campaign has actually accomplished what it was designed to do.[22]

Behavioral Outcome. *What do we want the target audience to do?* Beyond thoughts and feelings, this guideline focuses on the specific action that the advertising campaign is designed to motivate in the target audience. The advertising might be intended to get prospects to request further information, to go online to participate in a sweepstake or contest, to contact a salesperson, or to go to a retail outlet within the next week to take advantage of a limited-time sales opportunity.

Positioning. *What is the brand positioning?* Copywriters are reminded that their creative work must reflect the brand's positioning statement. The brand management team must clearly articulate the brand's meaning, or what it is to stand for in the audience's collective mind.

Message and Medium. *What general message is to be created and what medium is most appropriate for reaching the target audience?* This guideline identifies the most differentiating and motivating message about the brand that can be delivered to the target audience. It should focus on brand benefits rather than product features. Because credibility and believability are key to getting the audience to accept the message proposition, this section of the creative brief supports the proposition with evidence about product features that back up the claimed benefits. Copywriters are required to work within this context but still have the freedom to be creative. With respect to the appropriate medium, it is the client's job in concert with the ad agency to identify what medium (or media) is (are) best for reaching the target audience. Creatives are told exactly what they are being asked to produce—perhaps a series of TV commercials along with supporting magazine ads.

Strategy. *What is the strategy?* The response to this question articulates a specific advertising strategy to accomplish the job. This strategy statement gives copywriters an understanding of how their creative work must fit into an overall marcom strategy that includes elements other than advertising. For example, the strategy statement may indicate that in addition to advertising, a new brand will be launched with a series of major events, an aggressive buzz-building campaign, and online promotions to encourage consumer trial.

Nitty-Gritty Details. *When and how much?* This section of a creative brief identifies the *deadline* for when the advertising job is to be presented to the client for approval and specifies the *budget* for production of creative deliverables such as finished TV commercials.

In sum, the creative brief is a document prepared by a brand management team (the client) perhaps working with an advertising agency's account executive and is intended to both inspire creatives and channel their efforts. A truly valuable creative brief requires that the document be developed with a full understanding of the client's advertising needs. It also necessitates the acquisition of market research data that inform the agency about the competitive environment and about consumers' current perceptions of the to-be-advertised brand and its competition.

Alternative Styles of Creative Advertising

By the very nature of advertising and the process that goes into message development, there are innumerable ways to devise creative advertisements.[23] Several relatively distinct creative styles have evolved over the years and represent the bulk of contemporary advertising.[24] Table 10.1 summarizes six styles and groups them into three categories: functionally oriented, symbolically or experientially oriented, and product category dominance.

The student may recall the discussion of positioning in Chapter 5 in which distinctions were made among functional, symbolic, and experiential needs or benefits. These same distinctions are maintained in the present explanation of different

Table 10.1
Styles of Creative Advertising

Functional Orientation	Symbolic or Experiential Orientation	Category-Dominance Orientation
• Unique selling proposition	• Brand image • Resonance • Emotional	• Generic • Preemptive

styles of creative advertising. *Functionally oriented* advertising appeals to consumers' needs for tangible, physical, and concrete benefits. *Symbolically or experientially oriented* advertising strategies are directed at psychosocial needs. The *category-dominance* strategies (generic and preemptive in Table 10.1) do not necessarily use any particular type of appeal to consumers but are designed to achieve an advantage over competitors in the same product category. Finally, it is important to note that, as is the case with most categorization schemes, the alternative styles covered in the following sections sometimes have "fuzzy borders" when applied to specific advertising executions. In other words, distinctions are sometimes very fine rather than perfectly obvious, and a particular advertising execution may simultaneously use multiple creative approaches.

Unique Selling Proposition Creative Style

With the **unique selling proposition (USP) style**, an advertiser makes a superiority claim based on a unique product attribute that represents a *meaningful, distinctive consumer benefit.* The main feature of USP advertising is identifying an important difference that makes a brand unique and then developing an advertising claim that competitors either cannot make or have chosen not to make. The translation of the unique product feature into a relevant consumer benefit provides the USP. The USP approach is best suited for a company with a brand that possesses a relatively lasting competitive advantage, such as a maker of a technically complex item or a provider of a sophisticated service.

The Gillette Sensor razor used a USP when claiming that it is "the only razor that senses and adjusts to the individual needs of your face." The Dodge Caravan had a USP, if only temporarily, when it was able to claim that it was "the first and the only minivan with a driver's air bag." NicoDerm CQ's USP is contained in the claim that this product is the only nicotine patch "you can wear for 24 hours." An Allegra advertisement included a USP in its claim that "only Allegra has fexofenadine for effective nondrowsy relief of seasonal allergy symptoms." Prescription drug Flonase uses a comparative advertising method (more of which will be discussed in the following chapter) in claiming that only it—but not Zyrtec, Clarinex, Claritin, or Allegra—is "approved [by the Food and Drug Administration] to relieve nasal symptoms caused by indoor allergies, outdoor allergies and nonallergic irritants." Dyson is promoted as the only vacuum cleaner "not to lose suction."

In many respects the USP style is *the* optimum creative technique, because it gives the consumer a clearly differentiated reason for selecting the advertiser's brand over competitive offerings. If a brand has a truly meaningful advantage over competitive offerings, then advertising should exploit that advantage. The only reason USP advertising is not used more often is that brands in many product categories are pretty much homogeneous, or at parity with one another. They have no unique physical advantages to advertise and therefore are forced to use strategies favoring the more symbolic, psychological end of the strategy continuum.

Brand Image Creative Style

Whereas the USP strategy is based on promoting physical and functional differences between the advertiser's brand and competitive offerings, the **brand image style** involves *psychosocial,* rather than physical differentiation. Advertising attempts to develop an image or identity for a brand by associating the brand with *symbols.* In imbuing a brand with an image, advertisers draw meaning from the culturally constituted world (that is, the world of artifacts and symbols) and transfer that meaning to their brands. In effect, the well-known properties of the everyday world come to reside in the unknown properties of the advertised brand.[25]

Developing an image through advertising amounts to giving a brand a *distinct identity,* or *personality.* This is especially important for brands that compete in product categories where there is little physical differentiation and all brands are relatively homogeneous (bottled water, soft drinks, cigarettes, blue jeans, etc.). Thus, Pepsi at one time was referred to as the soft drink for the "new generation." Mountain Dew has consistently presented itself as a hip, outrageous brand for teens. The quintessential case of brand image advertising is perhaps the Marlboro cigarette campaign, which has been ongoing for a half century. This campaign is replete with images of cowboys. The cowboy—iconic of open ranges, freedom, and individuality—has by virtue of the advertising campaign become attached to the Marlboro brand, which now has acquired some of the meaning represented in the cowboy image itself. Cowboys are equated with freedom and individuality; Marlboro is equated with cowboys; hence, by association, Marlboro itself has come to represent the qualities of the cowboy life.

Brand image advertising is *transformational* (versus informational) in character. That is, **transformational advertising** associates the experience of using an advertised brand with a unique set of psychological characteristics that typically would *not* be associated with the brand experience to the same degree without exposure to the advertisement. Such advertising is transforming (versus informing) by virtue of endowing brand usage with a particular experience that is different from using any similar brand. As the result of repeated advertising, the brand becomes associated with its advertising and the people, scenes, or events in those advertisements.[26] Transformational advertisements contain two notable characteristics: (1) they make the experience of using the brand richer, warmer, more exciting, or more enjoyable than what would be the case based solely on an objective description of the brand, and (2) they connect the experience of using the brand so tightly with the experience of the advertisement that consumers cannot remember the brand without recalling the advertising experience. Marlboro cigarettes and cowboys, for example, are inextricably woven together in many consumers' cognitive structures.[27] Guinness beer and Michael Power also are inseparable in African consumers' minds. (See the *Global Focus* for discussion of the Michael Power advertising campaign.)

Resonance Creative Style

When used in an advertising context, the term *resonance* is analogous to the physical notion of noise resounding off an object. In a similar fashion, an advertisement resonates (*patterns*) the audience's life experiences. A resonant advertising strategy extends from psychographic research and structures an advertising campaign to pattern the prevailing lifestyle orientation of the intended market segment.

Resonant advertising does *not* focus on product claims or brand images but rather seeks to present circumstances or situations that find counterparts in the real or imagined experiences of the target audience. Advertising based on this strategy attempts to match "patterns" in an advertisement with the target audience's stored experiences. For example, Unilever's Dove brand of soap introduced a campaign that associated the brand with "real" women—that is, actual women who are gray, freckled, wrinkled, plump, and imperfect, but nonetheless beautiful—rather than as highly attractive models who are depicted in ads without imperfections and whose beauty is typically unachievable. The imperfections of real women resonate with the target audience who better identify with flawed than flawless beauty insofar as the former is real but the latter manufactured.

Another advertisement that illustrates the use of resonance is one for Quick-Step laminate floors that shows a typical family of four seated at a kitchen table,

A Brand Image for Guinness Beer

global focus

Guinness beer, the famous brand from Ireland, is known throughout much of the world and has long been the preferred beverage among Irish consumers. But things have changed in recent years. Many younger Irish are not especially fond of Guinness, and sales volume in Ireland has been declining by an average annual rate of 3 percent—due in large part to competitors' efforts to steal share through price discounting and also to a swing in preference toward increased wine consumption. Confronted with this disturbing situation, the makers of Guinness have increased advertising activity in other countries in order to grow the brand and offset sales declines at home. One growth area is the African continent, where substantially more Guinness is consumed than in Ireland!

One reason for the growing consumption of Guinness in Africa is the success of an advertising campaign built around a fictional international journalist named Michael Power. The Power character was created by ad agency Saatchi and Saatchi, which introduced the action hero in five-minute action-adventure ads. Power is portrayed in these ads overcoming obstacles through his inner strength, quick thinking, and perseverance rather than by brute force. In addition to his intellect, Power is stylish, physically fit, athletic, and friendly. He is often shown in advertisements enjoying a Guinness with his friends. In Africa, Michael Power and Guinness have images that are inextricably linked.

It is little surprise that Guinness has enjoyed much success throughout the huge African continent and has considerable remaining growth potential.

SOURCES: Susanna Howard, "Guinness Pours Hopes on Africa," *Wall Street Journal Online*, October 27, 2003, http://online.wsj.com; Bill Britt, "Guinness Unspools Feature Film," *Madison+Vine Online*, February 26, 2003, http://adage.com/madisonandvine.

with none of their feet touching the floor. The exaggeration of actual sitting behavior is designed to convey the notion that families with hardwood floors are continually concerned about scratching the surface varnish or denting the wood. Quick-Step laminate floors are touted as "unlike hardwoods" in their ability to "stand up to the wear and tear of everyday living." The ad thus patterns everyday experiences by relating to people's uneasiness about damaging their home flooring.

Emotional Creative Style

Emotional advertising is the third form of symbolically or experientially oriented advertising. Much contemporary advertising aims to reach the consumer at a visceral level through the use of emotional strategy.[28] Many advertising practitioners and scholars recognize that products often are bought on the basis of emotional factors and that appeals to emotion can be very successful if used appropriately and with the right brands. The use of emotion in advertising runs the gamut of positive and negative emotions, including appeals to romance, nostalgia, compassion, excitement, joy, fear, guilt, disgust, and regret.[29] The following chapter will treat several of these emotions—humor, sex, fear, and guilt—in some detail.

Though the emotional strategy can be used when advertising virtually any brand, emotional advertising seems to work especially well for product categories that naturally are associated with emotions (e.g., foods, jewelry, cosmetics, fashion apparel, soft drinks, and long-distance telephoning). For example, the Nestlé Toll House advertisement (Figure 10.3) appeals to the interrelated emotions of parental love, joy, and nostalgia.

Figure 10.3

Illustration of Emotional Advertising Style

Nestlé USA, Inc.

Generic Creative Style

An advertiser employs a **generic style** when making a claim that could be made by any company that markets a brand in that product category. The advertiser makes *no* attempt to differentiate its brand from competitive offerings or to claim superiority. This strategy is most appropriate for a brand that *dominates a product category.* In such instances, the firm making a generic claim will enjoy a large share of any primary demand stimulated by advertising.

For example, Campbell's dominates the prepared-soup market in the United States, selling nearly two-thirds of all soup. Any advertising that increases overall soup sales naturally benefits Campbell's. This explains the "Soup is good food" campaign used by Campbell's in years past. This advertising extolled the virtues of eating soup without arguing why people should buy Campbell's soup. Campbell's subsequently followed this campaign with another one that simply declared, "Never underestimate the power of soup." Along similar lines, AT&T's "Reach out and touch someone" campaign, which encouraged more long-distance calling, was a wise strategy in light of this company's one-time grip on the long-distance telephoning market—now, of course, much reduced due to intense competition in the telecommunications industry.

Preemptive Creative Style

The **preemptive style**, a second category-dominance technique, is employed when an advertiser makes a generic-type claim but does so with an *assertion of superiority.* This approach is most often used by advertisers in product or service categories where there are few, if any, functional differences among competitive brands. Preemptive advertising is a clever strategy when a meaningful superiority claim is made because it effectively precludes competitors from saying the same thing. Any branch of the military service could claim that they enable recruits to "be all you can be," but no other branch could possibly make such a claim after the Army adopted this as its unique statement. The huge JP Morgan Chase, which resulted from the merger of Chase Manhattan and Chemical banks, undertook a $45 million advertising campaign shortly after the merger that referred to Chase as "the Relationship Company." In clear recognition of the value of preemption, the chief marketing officer for Chase justified the campaign by stating, "the idea is to stamp that word [*relationship*] on our brand enough to preempt the use of it by anyone else in the category."[30]

The maker of Visine eyedrops advertised that this brand "gets the red out." All eyedrops are designed to get the red out, but by making this claim first, Visine made a dramatic statement that the consumer will associate only with Visine. No other company could subsequently make this claim for fear of being labeled a mimic. An advertisement for Hanes Smooth Illusions panty hose used a smart preemptive claim in comparing that brand to "liposuction without surgery." Another clever preemptive campaign was introduced by Nissan Motor some years ago with its advertising of the Maxima. Preceding the campaign, the Maxima competed against models such as the Ford Taurus and the Toyota Cressida in the upper-middle segment of the industry. To avoid stiff price competition and price rebates, Nissan wanted a more upscale and high-performance image for the Maxima. Based on extensive research, Maxima's advertising agency devised a clever preemptive claim touting the Maxima as the "four-door sports car." Of course, other sedans have four doors, but Maxima preempted sports car status for itself with this one clever claim. Its sales immediately increased by 43 percent over the previous year despite a price increase.[31]

A final illustration of the preemptive strategy is Citibank's advertising campaign directed at creating awareness for identity theft. In a series of television executions, identity thieves were shown "occupying" the personas of their victims. For example, out of the mouth of an elderly woman comes the voice of a male thief who stole her credit card and made purchases under her assumed identity.

Although any financial institution could have taken the lead in promoting the importance of protecting against identity theft, none could now do so after Citibank had preempted that advertising landscape.

Section Summary

Six general creative styles have been discussed and categorized as functional, symbolic or experiential, or category-dominance oriented. These alternatives provide a useful aid to understanding the different approaches available to advertisers and the factors influencing the choice of creative style. It would be incorrect to think of these approaches as pure and mutually exclusive. Because there is some unavoidable overlap, it is possible that an advertiser may consciously or unconsciously use two or more styles simultaneously.

In fact, some advertising experts contend that advertising is most effective when it reflects both ends of the creative advertising continuum—that is, by addressing both functional product benefits and symbolic or psychosocial benefits. A New York advertising agency provided evidence in partial support of the superiority of combined benefits over using only functional appeals. The agency tested 168 television commercials, 47 of which contained both functional and psychosocial appeals and 121 of which contained functional appeals only. Using recall and persuasion measures, the agency found that the ads containing a combination of functional and psychosocial appeals outperformed the functional-only ads by a substantial margin.[32]

Finally, it is important to recognize that whatever creative style is chosen, it must be clearly positioned in the customer's mind. That is, effective advertising must establish a *clear meaning of what the brand is and how it compares to competitive offerings.* Effective positioning requires that a company be fully aware of its competition and exploit competitive weaknesses. A brand is positioned in the consumer's mind relative to competition. The originators of the positioning concept contend that successful companies must be "competitors oriented," look for weak points in their competitors' positions, and then launch marketing attacks against those weak points.[33] These same management consultants claim that many marketing people and advertisers are in error when operating under the assumption that marketing and advertising are a battle of products. Their contrary position is this:

There are no best products. All that exists in the world of marketing are perceptions in the minds of the customer or prospect. The perception is the reality. Everything else is an illusion.[34]

This perhaps is a bit overstated, but the important point is that how good (or prestigious, dependable, sexy, etc.) a brand is depends more on what people think than on objective reality. And what people think is largely a function of effective advertising that creates a USP, builds an attractive image, or otherwise differentiates the brand from competitive offerings and lodges the intended meaning securely in the customer's mind.

Means-End Chaining and the Method of Laddering as Guides to Creative Advertising Formulation

The preceding discussion emphasized, if only implicitly, that the consumer (or customer in the case of B2B marketing) should be the foremost determinant of advertising messages. The notion of a means-end chain provides a useful framework for understanding the relationship between consumers or customers and advertising messages. A means-end chain represents the linkages among brand *attributes,* the *consequences* obtained from using the brand, and the *personal values* that the consequences reinforce.[35] These linkages represent a means-end chain because the consumer sees the brand and its attributes as a *means* for achieving a desired *end,* namely, the acquisition of desirable consequences (or avoidance of undesirable consequences) and the valued end state resulting from these consequences. Schematically, the means-end chain is as follows:

[Attributes → Consequences] → {Values}

[Means] → {End}

Attributes are features or aspects of advertised brands. In the case of automobiles, for example, attributes include size, storage capacity, engine performance, aesthetic features, and so on. **Consequences** are what consumers hope to receive (*benefits*) or avoid (*detriments*) when consuming brands. Increased status, convenience, performance, safety, and resale value are positive consequences associated with automobiles (benefits), whereas breakdowns, mishandling, and poor resale value are negative consequences that consumers wish to avoid (detriments). In sum, the important thing to appreciate is that attributes reside in brands, whereas consequences are experienced by consumers as a result of brand acquisition and usage.

Values represent those enduring beliefs people hold regarding what is important in life.[36] They pertain to end states that people desire in their lives, they transcend specific situations, and they guide selection or evaluation of behavior.[37] In general, values determine the relative desirability of consequences and serve to organize the meanings for products and brands in consumers' cognitive structures.[38]

Values represent the starting point, the catalyst, and the source of motivation for many aspects of human behavior. Consumer behavior, like other facets of behavior, involves the pursuit of valued states, or outcomes. Brand attributes and their consequences (benefits and detriments) are not sought per se, but rather are desired as means to achieving valued end states. From the consumer's perspective, the *ends* (values) drive the *means* (attributes and their consequences). Let's now examine more fully the values that energize human behavior.

The Nature of Values

Psychologists have conducted extensive research on values and constructed numerous value typologies. This chapter takes the view that 10 basic values adequately represent the important human values that are shared by people in a wide variety of culturally diverse countries. Table 10.2 lists these 10 values.[39] Research identified these values based on studies conducted in 20 culturally diverse countries: Australia, Brazil, Estonia, Finland, Germany, Greece, Holland, Hong Kong, Israel, Italy, Japan, New Zealand, the People's Republic of China, Poland, Portugal, Spain, Taiwan, the United States, Venezuela, and Zimbabwe. People in these countries shared the same values, each of which is now briefly described:[40]

1. *Self-direction.* Independent thought and action is the defining goal of this value type. It includes the desire for freedom, independence, choosing one's own goals, and creativity.
2. *Stimulation.* This value derives from the need for variety and achieving an exciting life.
3. *Hedonism.* Enjoying life and receiving pleasure are fundamental to this value type.
4. *Achievement.* Enjoying personal success through demonstrating competence according to social standards is the defining goal of this value type. Being regarded as capable, ambitious, intelligent, and influential are different aspects of the achievement value.

Table 10.2
Ten Universal Values

1. Self-direction	6. Security
2. Stimulation	7. Conformity
3. Hedonism	8. Tradition
4. Achievement	9. Benevolence
5. Power	10. Universalism

SOURCE: Reprinted from *Advances in Experimental Social Psychology,* vol 25, Shalom H. Schwartz, "Universals in the Content and Structure of Values: Theoretical Advances and Empirical Tests in 20 Countries," pp. 1–65, 1992, with permission from Elsevier.

5. *Power.* The power value entails the attainment of social status and prestige along with control or dominance over people and resources (wealth, authority, social power, and recognition).
6. *Security.* The essence of this value type is the longing for safety, harmony, and the stability of society. This value includes concern for personal and family safety and even national security. (For people in the United States, the valuation of security increased prominently after the September 11, 2001, terrorist attacks on the World Trade Center and the Pentagon. Many marketers and politicians have exploited this need. Likewise, the unimaginable horror of the tsunami in Southeast Asia in December 2004 has elevated the security value to unparalleled heights in this region.)
7. *Conformity.* Self-discipline, obedience, politeness, and, in general, the restraint of actions and impulses that are likely to upset or harm others and violate social norms are at the root of this value type.
8. *Tradition.* This value encompasses respect, commitment, and acceptance of the customs that one's culture and religion impose.
9. *Benevolence.* The motivational goal of benevolence is the preservation and enhancement of the welfare of one's family and friends. It includes being honest, loyal, helpful, a true friend, and loving in a mature manner.
10. *Universalism.* Universalism represents a life goal whereby individuals are motivated to understand, appreciate, tolerate, and protect the welfare of all people and of nature. It incorporates notions of world peace, social justice, equality, unity with nature, environmental protection, and wisdom.

Which Values Are Most Relevant to Advertising?

The 10 values just presented are apt descriptions of human psychology around the world. It is important to note, however, that they apply to all aspects of life and not to consumer behavior per se. Consequently, all 10 values are not equally important to consumers and thus not equally applicable to advertisers in their campaign-development efforts. Before reading on, take a few moments to review the 10 values and identify those that you consider most applicable to advertising and consumption.

If you are like me, you will have concluded that the first six values—self-direction through security—apply to many advertising and consumption situations, whereas the last four are less typical drivers of much consumer behavior. These latter four values certainly are applicable under select advertising situations (e.g., advertising efforts by nonprofit organizations such as churches and charitable organizations) and perhaps even more so in the East than in the West, but they do not typify usual consumer behavior for most products and services. Hence, in concluding our discussion of values, you should realize that self-direction, stimulation, hedonism, achievement, power, and security are the valued end states that drive the bulk of consumer behavior and thus are the goals to which advertisers must appeal.

Table 10.3
A MECCAS Model Conceptualization of Advertising Strategy

Component	Definition
Value orientation	The end level (value) to be focused on in the advertising; it serves as the driving force for the advertising execution.
↑ ***Brand consequences***	The major positive consequences, or benefits of using the brand, that the advertisement verbally or visually communicates to consumers.
↑ ***Brand attributes***	The brand's specific attributes or features that are communicated as a means of supporting the consequence(s) of using the brand.
↑ ***Creative strategy and leverage point***	The overall scenario for communicating the value orientation and the manner (leverage point) by which the advertisement will tap into, reach, or activate the key value that serves as the ad's driving force.

SOURCE: Adapted from Thomas J. Reynolds and Jonathan Gutman, "Advertising Is Image Management," *Journal of Advertising Research* 24 (February/March 1984), 27–36. Reprinted with permission from *Journal of Advertising Research,* © Copyright 1984, by the Advertising Research Foundation.

Advertising Applications of Means-End Chains: The MECCAS Model

The creation of effective advertisements demands that brand managers possess a clear understanding of what people value from product categories and specific brands. Because consumers differ in what they value from a particular brand, it is meaningful to discuss values only at the market segment level. A brand advertiser, armed with knowledge of segment-level values, is in a position to know what brand attributes and consequences to emphasize to a particular market segment as the means by which that brand can help consumers achieve a valued end state. A formal model, called **MECCAS**—an acronym for *m*eans-*e*nd *c*onceptualization of *c*omponents for *a*dvertising *s*trategy—provides a procedure for applying the concept of means-end chains to the creation of advertising messages.[41]

Figure 10.4
MECCAS Illustration for *Self-Direction* Value

DaimlerChrysler Corporation

Table 10.3 presents and defines the various levels of the MECCAS model. Note that the components include a *value orientation, brand consequences* and *brand attributes,* and a *creative strategy and leverage point* that provide the structure for presenting the advertising message and the means for tapping into or activating the value orientation.[42] The *value orientation* represents the consumer value or end level on which the advertising strategy focuses and can be thought of as the *driving force* behind the advertising execution. Every other component is geared toward achieving the end level. Please study the remaining definitions carefully in Table 10.3 before moving on to the illustrative applications of the MECCAS approach that are described next.

The following sections apply the MECCAS framework in analyzing six advertisements, one for each of the first six values shown in Table 10.2. It is important to note that these applications are the author's post hoc interpretations. It is unknown whether the advertisers in these cases actually performed formal means-end analyses in developing their ads. Nonetheless, these analyses will provide an enhanced understanding of how the means-end logic (attributes → consequences → values) can be translated into the design of actual advertisements.

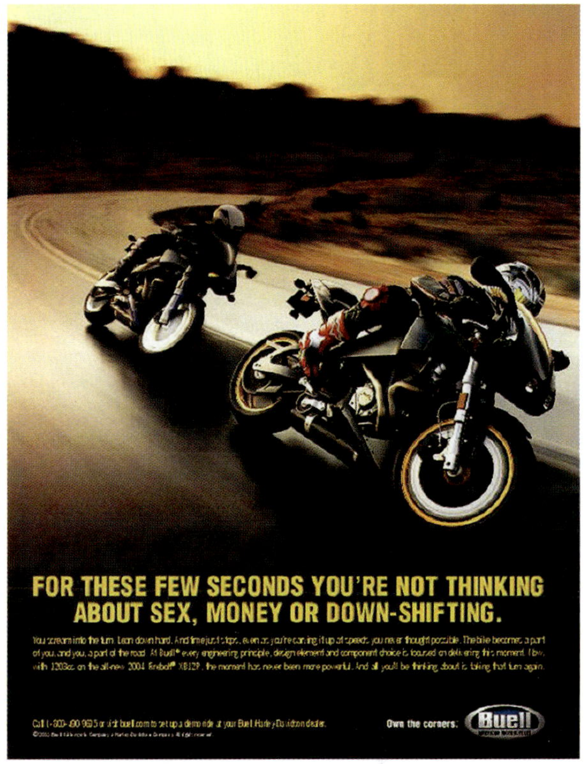

Figure 10.5
MECCAS Illustration for *Stimulation* Value

Self-Direction and the PT Turbo Automobile

The self-direction value includes the desire for freedom, independence, and choosing one's own goals. The value orientation serving as the driving force in the PT Turbo advertisement (Figure 10.4) is an unadorned appeal to consumers' need to reject conformity (see the ad's headline), which represents an appeal to those consumers who desire to freely choose and be unconstrained by the dictates of social pressures.

Stimulation and the Buell Motorcycle

The need for variety and achieving an exciting life is the essence of the stimulation value. The advertisement for the Buell motorcycle (Figure 10.5) appeals to this value by showing two riders in full racing form on an open road. The headline accentuates the appeal to excitement in stating, "For these few seconds you're not thinking about sex, money or down-shifting." In other words, buy a Buell and let it rip!

Figure 10.6
MECCAS Illustration for *Hedonism* Value

Hedonism and Millstone Coffee

Fundamental to this value is enjoying life and receiving pleasure. The ad in Figure 10.6 shows a delectable shot of Millstone French vanilla coffee in the foreground and a bowl of similarly flavored ice cream in the background. The spigot protruding from the ice cream subtly leverages the implication that Millstone coffee is infused with the scrumptious flavor of French vanilla ice cream. Coffee is a product closely allied with enjoying life's little pleasures, but this advertisement takes this form of self-indulgence to a higher level than ordinary for ads in this category.

Achievement and Odyssey Putters

In an appeal to competence, ambition, and accomplishment—the elements of achievement desired by all golfers—the advertisement in Figure 10.7 includes a prominent picture of one Odyssey putter (the two-ball putter) and inserts visuals of five other putters in boxes below. (The two-ball putter undoubtedly was chosen due to its greater attention-grabbing power than any of the other putters.) The leverage point for the core achievement value is the verbal copy at the bottom left of the ad that states, "Put a DFX Putter in your hands. And teach this game a lesson." Only golfers who have

Callaway Golf Company

Figure 10.7

MECCAS Illustration for *Achievement* Value

struggled from lost strokes due to poor putting can fully appreciate this ad, but, of course, the ad is directed at golfers who desire to become more accomplished and competent so as to "teach [the game of golf] a lesson."

Power and the U.S. Army

As a valued end state, power entails the attainment of social status and prestige along with control or dominance over people and resources (e.g., authority, social power, and recognition). The ad in Figure 10.8 for the U.S. Army appeals to the desire among some young men and women to enjoy the power and prestige of rank and the authority to lead others. The leverage point in the ad is the shining beacon overlaid with the bar of a second lieutenant and the corresponding statement that "to wear it is to be there when someone needs a guide." This appeal to power might be thought of as an appeal to humane power (the desire to serve, lead, and guide) rather than authoritarian power (to command and dominate). Whatever the form of power, this ad encourages young people to enroll in Army ROTC programs by appealing to the value they place on achieving recognition and gaining control.

Security and Brita Water Filters

Personal and family safety are aspects of the security value pertinent to the ownership and consumption of many products. The advertisement for the Brita water filter (Figure 10.9) doesn't offer descriptions of specific attributes in the copy other than claiming that "only Brita has a 2-stage filter." Personal and family safety is the consequence that results from this attribute. The leverage point for the valued end state of security is apparent in the visual of rusty pipes and the headline stating, "Your tap water's been through a lot." The coup de grace for the ad appears below the visual in the statement that "[because Brita has a 2-stage filter] even if there's sediment in your pipes, it won't get in you."

Figure 10.8

MECCAS Illustration for *Power* Value

U.S. Army Cadet Command

Identifying Means-End Chains: The Method of Laddering

Laddering is a research technique that has been developed to identify linkages between attributes (A), consequences (C), and values (V). The method is termed *laddering* because it leads to the construction of a hierarchy, or ladder, of relations between a brand's attributes or consequences (the means) and consumer values (the end). **Laddering** involves in-depth, one-on-one interviews that typically last between 30 minutes to more than one hour. In contrast to surveys, the method of laddering attempts to get at the root, or deep, reasons that individual consumers buy certain products and brands.[43]

An interviewer first determines which attributes are most important in the product category to the interviewee and, from there, attempts to identify the linkages in the interviewee's mind from attributes to consequences and from consequences to abstract values. In conducting a laddering interview, the interviewer refers the interviewee to a specific attribute and then, through directed probes, attempts to detect how the interviewee links that attribute with more abstract consequences and how the consequences are

Figure 10.9 MECCAS Illustration for *Security* Value

linked with even more abstract values. After linkages for the first attribute are exhausted, the interviewer moves on to the next salient attribute, and then the next, until all important attributes have been explored; this typically ranges from between three and seven attributes. Probing is accomplished with questions such as the following:[44]

- Why is that [particular attribute] important to you?
- How does that help you out?
- What do you get from that?
- Why do you want that?
- What happens to you as a result of that?

Let us illustrate the method of laddering with the advertisement for the U.S. Army in Figure 10.8. Imagine that an interviewer asks a potential ROTC enrollee why it might be important to her to enroll in an ROTC program. Her response is, "I would like to lead." A follow-up probe by the interviewer ("Why do you want that?") results in this prospect claiming that "it is important that I accomplish something of myself in life." In response to a prompt of "why is that important to you?" she comments, "I want my parents to be proud of me. I want them to see that I'm just as capable as my big brother. I think becoming a second lieutenant in the Army will show that I'm a capable and competent person."

We see in this hypothetical description that enrolling in an ROTC program is linked in this young woman's mind with the opportunity to become an officer and lead others. This consequence is, in turn, linked to the achievement value and the resulting satisfaction from having proud parents. The advertisement in Figure 10.8 apparently is based on the view that there is a market segment of college students who see the Army as an opportunity to realize their ambitions, achieve recognition, and perhaps make others proud of their accomplishments.

Practical Issues in Identifying Means-End Chains

In conclusion, the important point to remember about the MECCAS approach is that it provides a systematic procedure for linking the advertiser's perspective (i.e., a brand with attributes that have desirable and undesirable consequences) with the consumer's perspective (the pursuit of products and brands to achieve desired end states, or values). Effective advertising does not focus on product attributes and consequences per se; rather, it is directed at showing how the advertised brand will benefit the consumer and enable him or her to achieve what he or she most desires in life—self-determination, stimulation, hedonism, and the other values listed in Table 10.2. Products and brands vary in terms of which values they are capable of satisfying; nonetheless, all are capable of fulfilling some value(s), and it is the role of sophisticated advertising to identify and access those values. Advertising and other forms of marketing communications are most relevant to the consumer and thus most effective for the advertised brand when they are based on strong linkages between the right set of attributes, consequences, and values.[45]

All said, it is pertinent to note that the means-end approach and the method of laddering are not without critics. The primary criticisms are several: First, it is claimed that the laddering method "forces" interviewees to identify hierarchies among attributes, consequences, and values that may actually not have existed before the interview and absent the interviewer's directive probes. Second, it is suggested that consumers may possess clear-cut linkages between attributes and consequences but not necessarily between consequences and values. Finally, laddering is criticized on grounds that the ultimate hierarchy constructed is a crude aggregation of A → C → V chains from multiple individuals into a single chain that represents the input into a MECCAS model.[46]

These criticisms are not unfounded, but the reality is that all methods for creative strategy development in advertising have their imperfections. The value of laddering is that it forces advertisers to identify how consumers relate product attributes to more abstract states such as benefits and values. This systematic approach thereby ensures that advertising emphasis will be placed on communicating benefits and implying valued end states rather than focusing on attributes per se. It is likely for some product categories and particular brands that consumers do not possess clear linkages between brand consequences and values. So, although the means-end chain may entail only A → C links rather than the full set of A → C → V links, the systematic laddering procedure serves its purpose by encouraging creative personnel to focus on product benefits rather than attributes.

Corporate Image and Issue Advertising

The type of advertising discussed to this point is commonly referred to as brand-oriented advertising. Such advertising focuses on a specific brand and attempts ultimately to influence consumers to purchase the advertiser's brand.

Another form of advertising, termed **corporate advertising**, focuses not on specific brands but on a corporation's overall image or on economic or social issues relevant to the corporation's interests. This form of advertising is prevalent.[47] Consistent spending on corporate advertising can serve to boost a corporation's equity, much in the same fashion that product-oriented advertising is an investment in the brand equity bank. Two somewhat distinct forms of corporate advertising are discussed in the following sections: (1) image advertising and (2) issue, or advocacy, advertising.[48]

Corporate Image Advertising

Corporate image advertising attempts to increase a firm's name recognition, establish goodwill for the company and its products, or identify itself with some meaningful and socially acceptable activity. This type of corporate advertising is concerned with creating favorable images among audiences such as consumers, stockholders, employees, suppliers, and potential investors. Such advertising asks for no specific action from the target audience(s) other than a favorable attitude toward the corporation and passive approval for the company's activities.[49] For example, a General Motors advertisement for hybrid-powered buses does not promote any specific General Motors vehicle but rather, like other corporate image advertisements, attempts to enhance the company's image by associating it with fuel efficiency and conservation.

In general, research has found that executives regard name identity and image building to be the two most important functions of corporate advertising.[50] Corporate image advertising is directed at more than merely trying to make consumers feel good about a company. Companies are increasingly using the image of their firms to enhance sales and financial performance.[51] Research has shown that a positive corporate image can favorably affect consumers' product evaluations, especially when the purchase decision is risky.[52] Corporate advertising that does not contribute to increased sales and profits is difficult to justify in today's climate of accountability.

Photodisc Green/Getty Images

Corporate Issue (Advocacy) Advertising

The other form of corporate advertising is issue, or advocacy, advertising. When using **issue advertising**, a company takes a position on a controversial social issue of public importance with the intention of swaying public opinion.[53] It does so in a manner that supports the company's position and best interests while expressly or implicitly challenging the opponent's position and denying the accuracy of their facts.[54]

Issue advertising is a topic of considerable controversy.[55] Business executives are divided on whether this form of advertising represents an effective allocation of corporate resources. Critics question the legitimacy of issue advertising and challenge its status as a tax-deductible expenditure. Since further discussion of these points is beyond the scope of this chapter, the interested reader is encouraged to review the sources contained in the last endnote.[56]

Summary

The chapter examined creative advertising, advertising strategy formulation, creative strategies, means-end models, and corporate image and issue advertising. An important initial question asks, what are the general characteristics of effective advertising? Discussion points out that effective advertising must (1) extend from sound marketing strategy, (2) take the consumer's view, (3) break through the competitive clutter, (4) never promise more than can be delivered, and (5) prevent the creative idea from overwhelming the strategy.

Creative advertising formulation involves a multistep process. The strategy is initiated by specifying the key fact that advertising should convey to the target market. This key fact is translated, in step 2, into the primary marketing problem. Extending from this problem statement is the selection of specific communications objectives. The guts of advertising strategy consists, in step 4, of designing the creative message strategy. This involves selecting the target market, identifying the primary competition, and choosing the primary benefit to emphasize. The last step in the process involves ensuring that the advertisement meets all corporate and divisional requirements.

The next major subject covered in this chapter were the alternative forms of creative advertising that are in wide use. Six specific creative styles—unique selling proposition, brand image, resonance, emotional, generic, and preemptive—were described and illustrated with examples.

The chapter then turned to the concept of means-end chains and the MECCAS framework (means-end conceptualization of components for advertising strategy) that is used in designing actual advertisements and campaigns. Means-end chains and MECCAS models provide bridges between product attributes and the consequences to the consumer of realizing product attributes (the means) and the ability of these consequences to satisfy consumption-related values (the end). MECCAS models provide an organizing framework for developing creative ads that simultaneously consider attributes, consequences, and values.

The final subject discussed was corporate advertising. A distinction was made between conventional product- and brand-oriented strategy and advertising that focuses on facilitating corporate goodwill, enhancing a corporation's overall image, and advocating matters of economic or social significance that are relevant to a corporation. Two forms of corporate advertising, image and issue (advocacy) advertising, were described.

Discussion Questions

1. The *Marcom Challenge* presented two advertisements regarded among the greatest in advertising history. These illustrations are very old and predate the birth of most readers of this text. From the years you have been aware of TV

commercials, identify two or three campaigns that you regard as "great" advertising.

2. Early in the chapter when discussing the point that effective advertising must take the consumer's view, the following quotation was presented: "Consumers don't want to be bombarded with ads—they want to be inspired by ideas that will change their lives. Ads create transactions. Ideas create transformations. Ads reflect our culture, ideas imagine our future." What, in your opinion, does this quote mean?
3. When discussing the creative advertising style known as unique selling proposition, or USP, it was claimed that in many respects the USP style is *the* optimum creative technique. Explain whether you agree or disagree with this assertion.
4. Several examples of brand image advertisements were offered in the chapter. Identify two additional examples of advertisements that appear to be using the brand image, or transformational, creative style.
5. One requirement for effective advertising is the ability to break through competitive clutter. Explain what this means, and provide several examples of advertising methods that successfully accomplish this.
6. Select a magazine or newspaper advertisement, and apply the MECCAS model to interpret the ad. In other words, describe what you consider to be the ad's value orientation, its leverage point, and so on.
7. Explain the differences between the USP and brand image creative styles, and indicate the specific conditions under which each is more likely to be used. Provide one illustration of each creative style, using examples other than those used in the text.
8. Using the laddering procedure that was described in the chapter, select a product category of your choice, interview one individual (preferably not a close friend), and construct that person's hierarchical map, or ladder, for *two* product attributes that are important to that person. In other words, after first determining the two product attributes (or features) that this person considers most important in making a choice among brands in the product category you have selected, use the types of probing questions listed in the chapter to see how this individual mentally connects product attributes with consequences, and how, in turn, these consequences extend into valued end states. Be persistent!
9. Some critics contend that advocacy, or issue, advertising should not be treated as a legitimate tax-deductible expenditure. Present and justify your opinion on this matter.
10. Select two advertising campaigns that have been on television for some time, and describe in detail what you think their creative message styles are.
11. Along the lines of the Holiday Inn case described in the chapter, select an advertising campaign, and reconstruct in detail your interpretation of all the steps in the campaign's advertising strategy.

ENDNOTES

1. Based on an interview by Paula Champa in "The Moment of Creation," *Agency,* May/June 1991, 32.
2. For additional reading on this famous advertisement, see James B. Twitchell, *20 Ads That Shook the World: The Century's Most Groundbreaking Advertising and How It Changed Us All* (New York: Crown Publishers, 2000), 118–125.
3. Based on Bradley Johnson, "The Commercial, and the Product, That Changed Advertising," *Advertising Age,* January 10, 1994, 1, 12–14.
4. Bob Garfield, "Breakthrough Product Gets Greatest TV Spot," *Advertising Age,* January 10, 1994, 14; "The Most Famous One-Shot Commercial Tested Orwell, and Made History for Apple Computer," *Advertising Age,* November 11, 1996, A22.
5. Twitchell, *20 Ads That Shook the World,* 190.
6. The following points are a mixture of the author's views and perspectives presented by A. Jerome Jewler, *Creative Strategy in Advertising* (Belmont, Calif.: Wadsworth, 1985), 7–8; and Don E. Schultz and Stanley I. Tannenbaum, *Essentials of Advertising Strategy* (Lincolnwood, IL: NTC Business Books, 1988), 9–10.
7. Joey Reiman, "Selling an Idea for $1 Million," *Advertising Age,* July 5, 2004, 15.

8. Stan Freberg, "Irtnog Revisited," *Advertising Age,* August 1, 1988, 32.
9. For interesting discussion on creativity and the creative process in advertising, review the following sources: Jaafar El-Murad and Douglas C. West, "The Definition and Measurement of Creativity: What Do We Know?" *Journal of Advertising Research* 44 (June 2004), 188–201; Vincent J. Blasko and Michael P. Mokwa, "Paradox, Advertising and the Creative Process," in *Current Issues and Research in Advertising,* ed. J. H. Leigh and C. R. Martin, Jr. (Ann Arbor: Graduate School of Business Administration, University of Michigan, 1989), 351–366; and Jacob Goldenberg, David Mazursky, and Sorin Solomon, "Creative Sparks," *Science* 285 (September 1999), 1495–1496.
10. Scott Koslow, Sheila L. Sasser, and Edward A. Riordan, "What Is Creative to Whom and Why? Perceptions in Advertising Agencies," *Journal of Advertising Research* 43 (March 2003), 96–110.
11. Lou Centlivre, "A Peek at the Creative of the '90s," *Advertising Age,* January 18, 1988, 62.
12. Linda Kaplan Thaler and Robin Koval, *Bang! Getting Your Message Heard in a Noisy World* (New York: Currency Doubleday, 2003), 24.
13. Some of the ideas for this description are inspired by the eloquent comments of Bob Garfield in his review of the Nike commercials, *Advertising Age,* April 5, 2004, 37.
14. This framework is from the world-famous management consulting firm, McKinsey & Company, in an undated document supplied to me by a company that had secured McKinsey's services.
15. Research by rsc, a company that specializes in advertising research, reports that starting with a strong selling proposition leads to effective advertising about 70 percent of the time. This was reported in the company's newsletter, "Better Practices in Advertising," Issue 1, July 2002, 1.
16. An interesting article on account planning, and the difference in its application in the United Kingdom and the United States, is Christopher E. Hackley, "Account Planning: Current Agency Perspectives on an Advertising Enigma," *Journal of Advertising Research* 43 (June 2003), 235–245.
17. Adapted from Don E. Schultz, Dennis Martin, and William P. Brown, *Strategic Advertising Campaigns* (Lincolnwood, Ill.: NTC Business Books, 1987), 240–245.
18. These details are from Holiday Inn's Web site (http://www.holiday-inn.com).
19. The author has taken liberties in surmising the situation that encouraged Holiday Inn to undertake its advertising campaign.
20. Arthur J. Kover, "Copywriters' Implicit Theories of Communication: An Exploration," *Journal of Consumer Research* 21 (March 1995), 596–611.
21. Harvey Penick with Bud Shrake, *Harvey Penick's Little Red Book* (New York: Simon & Schuster, 1992), 45.
22. Don E. Schultz brought this idea to the author's attention in "Determine Outcomes First to Measure Efforts," *Marketing News,* September 1, 2003, 7.
23. A good review of the literature along with the presentation of an insightful message strategy model are provided by Ronald E. Taylor, "A Six-Segment Message Strategy Wheel," *Journal of Advertising Research* 39 (November/December 1999), 7–17.
24. The following discussion represents an adaptation of Charles F. Frazer, "Creative Strategy: A Management Perspective," *Journal of Advertising* 12, no. 4 (1983), 36–41. For other perspectives on creative strategies, see Henry A. Laskey, Ellen Day, and Melvin R. Crask, "Typology of Main Message Strategies for Television Commercials," *Journal of Advertising* 18, no. 1 (1989), 36–41; and Taylor, "A Six-Segment Message Strategy Wheel."
25. Grant McCracken, "Culture and Consumption: A Theoretical Account of the Structure and Movement of the Cultural Meaning of Consumer Goods," *Journal of Consumer Research* 13 (June 1986), 74.
26. Christopher P. Puto and William D. Wells, "Informational and Transformational Advertising: The Differential Effects of Time," in *Advances in Consumer Research,* vol. 11, ed. Thomas C. Kinnear (Provo, Utah: Association for Consumer Research, 1984), 638–643. See also David A. Aaker and Douglas M. Stayman, "Implementing the Concept of Transformational Advertising," *Psychology & Marketing* 9 (May/June 1992), 237–253.
27. Puto and Wells, "Informational and Transformational Advertising," 638.
28. Frazer ("Creative Strategy") refers to this as *affective strategy,* but *emotional strategy* is more descriptive and less subject to alternative interpretations.
29. For a variety of perspectives on the use of emotion in advertising, see Stuart J. Agres, Julie A. Edell, and Tony M. Dubitsky, *Emotion in Advertising: Theoretical and Practical Explorations* (New York: Quorum Books, 1990).
30. Terry Lefton, "Cutting to the Chase," *Brandweek,* April 7, 1997, 47.
31. This description is based on "Four-Door Sports Car," *1990 Winners of the Effie Gold Awards: Case Studies in Advertising Effectiveness* (New York: American Marketing Association of New York and the American Association of Advertising Agencies, 1991), 124–131.
32. Kim Foltz, "Psychological Appeal in TV Ads Found Effective," *Adweek,* August 31, 1987, 38. Please note that this research referred to rational rather than functional appeals, but rational is essentially equivalent to functional.
33. Jack Trout and Al Ries, "The Positioning Era: A View Ten Years Later," *Advertising Age,* July 16, 1979, 39–42.
34. Al Ries and Jack Trout, *The 22 Immutable Laws of Marketing* (New York: Harper Business, 1993), 19.
35. A recent book summarizes much of the thinking on the topic of mean-end chains. See Thomas J. Reynolds and Jerry C. Olson, *Understanding Decision Making: The Means-End Approach to Marketing and Advertising Strategy* (Mahwah, NJ: Erlbaum, 2001). See also Jonathan Gutman, "A Means-End Chain Model Based on Consumer Categorization Processes," *Journal of Marketing* 46 (spring 1982), 60–72; Thomas J. Reynolds and Jonathan Gutman, "Advertising Is Image Management," *Journal of Advertising Research* 24 (February/March 1984), 27–36; Thomas J. Reynolds and Jonathan Gutman, "Laddering Theory, Method, Analysis, and Interpretation," *Journal of Advertising Research* 28 (February/March 1988), 11–31; and Thomas J. Reynolds and Alyce Byrd Craddock, "The Application of MECCAS Model to the Development and Assessment of Advertising Strategy: A Case Study," *Journal of Advertising Research* 28 (April/May 1988), 43–59.

36. For further discussion of cultural values, see Lynn R. Kahle, Basil Poulos, and Ajay Sukhdial, "Changes in Social Values in the United States during the Past Decade," *Journal of Advertising Research* 28 (February/March 1988), 35–41; Sharon E. Beatty, Lynn R. Kahle, Pamela Homer, and Shekhar Misra, "Alternative Measurement Approaches to Consumer Values: The List of Values and the Rokeach Value Survey," *Psychology and Marketing* 2, no. 3 (1985), 181–200; Wagner A. Kamakura and Jose Afonso Mazzon, "Value Segmentation: A Model for the Measurement of Values and Value Systems," *Journal of Consumer Research* 18 (September 1991), 208–218; and Wagner A. Kamakura and Thomas P. Novak, "Value-System Segmentation: Exploring the Meaning of LOV," *Journal of Consumer Research* 19 (June 1992), 119–132.
37. Shalom H. Schwartz, "Universals in the Content and Structure of Values: Theoretical Advances and Empirical Tests in 20 Countries," *Advances in Experimental Social Psychology* 25 (1992), 4.
38. J. Paul Peter and Jerry C. Olson, *Consumer Behavior: Marketing Strategy Perspectives* (Homewood, Ill.: Irwin, 1990).
39. Schwartz, "Universals in the Content and Structure of Values."
40. These descriptions are based on ibid., 5–12.
41. Jerry Olson and Thomas J. Reynolds, "Understanding Consumers' Cognitive Structures: Implications for Advertising Strategy," in *Advertising and Consumer Psychology*, ed. L. Percy and A. Woodside (Lexington, Mass.: Lexington Books, 1983), 77–90.
42. The language used in Table 10.3 is adapted from that employed in the various writings of Gutman, Reynolds, and Olson such as those cited in endnote 35. It is the author's experience that students are confused with the terminology originally used. The present terminology is more user friendly without doing a disservice to the original MECCAS conceptualization.
43. Brain Wansink, "Using Laddering to Understand and Leverage a Brand's Equity," *Qualitative Market Research: An International Journal* 6 no. 2, 111–118.
44. Thomas J. Reynolds, Clay Dethloff, and Steven J. Westberg, "Advancements in Laddering," in Thomas J. Reynolds and Jerry C. Olson, *Understanding Decision Making*, 91–118.
45. Thomas J. Reynolds and David B. Whitlark, "Applying Laddering Data to Communications Strategy and Advertising Practice," *Journal of Advertising Research* 35 (July/August 1995), 9.
46. See John R. Rossiter and Larry Percy, "The a-b-e Model of Benefit Focus in Advertising," in Thomas J. Reynolds and Jerry C. Olson, *Understanding Decision Making*, 183–213; and Joel B. Cohen and Luk Warlop, "A Motivational Perspective on Means-End Chains," in Thomas J. Reynolds and Jerry C. Olson, *Understanding Decision Making*, 389–412.
47. David W. Schumann, Jan M. Hathcote, and Susan West, "Corporate Advertising in America: A Review of Published Studies on Use, Measurement, and Effectiveness," *Journal of Advertising* 20 (September 1991), 35–56. This article provides a thorough review of corporate advertising and is must reading for anyone interested in the topic. For evidence of the increase in corporate advertising, see Mercedes M. Cardona, "Corporate-Ad Budgets At Record High: ANA Survey," *Advertising Age*, April 27, 1998, 36.
48. This distinction is based on a classification by S. Prakash Sethi, "Institutional/Image Advertising and Idea/Issue Advertising As Marketing Tools: Some Public Policy Issues," *Journal of Marketing* 43 (January 1979), 68–78. Sethi actually labels the two subsets of corporate advertising as "institutional/image" and "idea/issue." For reading ease they are shortened here to image versus issue advertising.
49. Ibid.
50. Charles H. Patti and John P. McDonald, "Corporate Advertising: Process, Practices, and Perspectives (1970–1989)," *Journal of Advertising* 14, no. 1 (1985), 42–49.
51. Lewis C. Winters, "Does It Pay to Advertise to Hostile Audiences with Corporate Advertising?" *Journal of Advertising Research* 28 (June/July 1988), 11–18.
52. Zeynep Gürhan-Canli and Rajeev Batra, "When Corporate Image Affects Product Evaluations: The Moderation Role of Perceived Risk," *Journal of Marketing Research* 41 (May 2004), 197–205.
53. Bob D. Cutler and Darrel D. Muehling, "Advocacy Advertising and the Boundaries of Commercial Speech," *Journal of Advertising* 18, no. 3 (1989), 40.
54. Sethi, "Institutional/Image Advertising," 70.
55. For discussion of the First Amendment issues surrounding the use of advocacy advertising, see Cutler and Muehling, "Advocacy Advertising and the Boundaries of Commercial Speech"; and Kent R. Middleton, "Advocacy Advertising, The First Amendment and Competitive Advantage: A Comment on Cutler & Muehling," *Journal of Advertising* 20 (June 1991), 77–81.
56. Louis Banks, "Taking on the Hostile Media," *Harvard Business Review* (March/April 1978), 123–130; Barbara J. Coe, "The Effectiveness Challenge in Issue Advertising Campaigns," *Journal of Advertising* 12, no. 4 (1983), 27–35; David Kelley, "Critical Issues for Issue Ads," *Harvard Business Review* (July/August 1982), 80–87; Ward Welty, "Is Issue Advertising Working?" *Public Relations Journal* (November 1981), 29. For an especially thorough and insightful treatment of issue advertising, particularly with regard to the measurement of effectiveness, see Karen F. A. Fox, "The Measurement of Issue/Advocacy Advertising," in *Current Issues and Research in Advertising*, vol. 9, ed. James H. Leigh and Claude R. Martin, Jr. (Ann Arbor: Division of Research, Graduate School of Business Administration, University of Michigan, 1986), 61–92.

CHAPTER 11

Selecting Message Appeals and Picking Endorsers

Marcom Challenge: Subway Versus McDonald's

Consider all the thoughts and feelings you have stored in memory about two fast-food restaurant chains: McDonald's and Subway. The bigger chain, McDonald's, is known for its standard fare of menu items including Big Macs, french fries, cheeseburgers, and, more recently, some healthy alternatives such as salads and all-white-meat Chicken McNuggets. McDonald's is the world's top fast-food company with more than 30,000 restaurants in over 100 countries. Its total sales in one recent year exceeded $17 billion.[1] McDonald's lost a lot of momentum in the early 2000s, but starting in 2003 sales rebounded—due in large part to an upgraded menu and increased emphasis on healthier alternative food items. The "I'm lovin' it" ad campaign also played a meaningful role in propelling sales growth.

The other fast-food chain, Subway, is known for its customized sandwiches that are prepared to order and are available in 6- or 12-inch options with a variety of meats, vegetables, condiments, and breads from which to choose. Subway is one of McDonald's major competitors, though their menus are distinct. Subway has approximately 21,000 outlets in 75 countries. Subway's sales in a recent year totaled $468 million, which is a pittance compared to McDonald's, but which, from McDonald's perspective, nonetheless poses a formidable challenge.

Starting in late 2004 and extending into 2005, Subway began an aggressive comparative advertising campaign to steal even more customers from McDonald's. The campaign featured the well-known spokesperson, Jared Fogle, who in previous years lost over 200 pounds on a Subway-sandwich "diet." Jared and Subway are virtually inseparable in many consumers' minds. The ad campaign presented Jared front and center comparing Subway and McDonald's products. For example, in one execution he cautioned consumers about eating McDonald's Chicken Selects because they have substantially more fat grams than Subway's sweet onion chicken teriyaki sandwich. In another execution, he pointed out that a certain Subway sandwich has only one-half the total calories of a Big Mac.

This hard-hitting campaign obviously was designed to counter McDonald's increasing success with healthy alternative food items. Subway compared itself against McDonald's in hopes of clearly demonstrating to consumers that Subway is the clear choice when matters of fat-gram consumption and caloric intake enter into the restaurant choice process.

A couple of the issues touched on here—namely, the use of an endorser, Jared, and the application of comparative advertising—are among the many topics covered in the present chapter. Also, the initial section dealing with enhancing consumers' motivation, opportunity, and ability to process advertising messages is related to this vignette inasmuch as Subway's use of a readily recognized endorser and application of a dramatic comparison with better-known McDonald's are well-known tactics for increasing the audience's motivation to attend to and process advertisements.

© Susan Van Etten

CHAPTER OBJECTIVES

1
Appreciate the efforts undertaken by advertisers to enhance the consumer's motivation, opportunity, and ability to process ad messages.

2
Describe the role of endorsers in advertising.

3
Explain the requirements for an effective endorser.

4
Appreciate the factors that enter into the endorser-selection decision.

5
Discuss the role of Q Scores in selecting celebrity endorsers.

6
Describe the role of humor in advertising.

7
Explain the logic underlying the use of appeals to fear in advertising.

8
Understand the nature of appeals to guilt in advertising.

9
Discuss the role of sex appeals, including the downside of such usage.

10
Explain the meaning of subliminal messages and symbolic embeds.

11
Appreciate the role of music in advertising.

12
Understand the function of comparative advertising and the considerations that influence the use of this form of advertising.

Overview

As pointed out repeatedly in the prior chapter, advertisers continually face the challenges of dealing with ad clutter and audiences that often are disengaged and uninterested in the advertiser's message. To be effective, advertising must break through the clutter and provide the audience with sufficient motivation to pay attention and engage in higher order processing of ad messages. Effective advertising, as noted in the prior chapter, is usually creative, and creative ads tend to be both original and appropriate. They provide a meaningful message and often do so in an entertaining manner.

The present chapter surveys some of the common approaches that are used in creating advertising messages. First examined is the issue of how advertisers increase consumers' motivation, opportunity, and ability to process advertising messages. The next major section examines the widespread use of endorsers in advertising. The third section appraises five types of messages that are prevalent in advertising: (1) humor, (2) appeals to fear, (3) appeals to guilt, (4) sex appeals, and (5) subliminal messages. The chapter concludes with reviews of music's role in advertising and the pros and cons of using comparative advertisements.

Where possible, an attempt is made to identify *generalizations* about the creation of effective advertising messages. It is important to realize, however, that generalizations are not the same as scientific laws or principles. These higher forms of scientific truth (such as Einstein's general theory of relativity and Newton's law of gravity) have not been established in the realm of advertising for several reasons: First, the buyer behavior that advertising is designed to influence is complex, dynamic, and variable across situations, which consequently makes it difficult to arrive at straightforward explanations of how advertising elements operate in all situations and across all types of market segments. (Recall in this context the *Marcom Challenge* in Chapter 9 that posed the question, "Is advertising rocket science?") Second, advertisements are themselves highly varied entities that differ in numerous respects rather than just in terms of their use of humor, or sex, or appeals to fear, or any other single dimension. This complexity makes it difficult to draw specific conclusions about any particular feature of advertising. Third, because products differ in terms of technological sophistication and ability to involve consumers, and in various other respects, it is virtually impossible to identify advertising approaches that are universally effective across all products, services, and situations.

Thus, the findings presented and the conclusions drawn should be considered tentative rather than definitive. In accordance with the philosopher's advice, "seek simplicity and distrust it,"[2] it would be naive and misleading to suggest that any particular advertising technique will be successful under all circumstances. Rather, the effectiveness of any message format depends on conditions such as the nature of the competition, the character of the product, the degree of brand equity and market leadership, the advertising environment, and the extent of consumer involvement. Throughout the text we have emphasized the importance of this "it depends" mind-set, and it is important that you bring such an orientation to your reading of the following sections.

Enhancing Processing Motivation, Opportunity, and Ability

It is well known that there is no single way to influence people to form favorable attitudes toward brands or to act in ways desired by marketing communicators. Rather, the appropriate influence strategy depends both on *consumer characteristics* (their motivation, opportunity, and ability to process marcom messages) and on *brand strengths.* If consumers are interested in learning about a product, and a company's brand has clear advantages over competitive brands, then the persuasion tactic to be taken is obvious: *design a message telling people explicitly why your brand is superior.* The result should be equally clear: consumers likely will be swayed by your arguments, which will lead to a relatively enduring attitude change and a strong chance they will select your brand over competitive offerings.[3]

However, the reality is that brands in most product categories are similar, and, because of this, consumers generally are not anxious to devote mental effort toward processing messages that provide little new information. Thus, the marketing communicator, faced with this double whammy (only slightly involved consumers and a me-too brand), has to find ways to enthuse consumers sufficiently such that they will listen to or read the communicator's message. Hence, anything marketing communicators can do to enhance the MOA factors (motivation, opportunity, and ability) likely will result in increased communication effectiveness.

Figure 11.1 provides a framework for the following discussion of how marketing communicators can enhance the MOA factors.[4] Each of six strategies will be systematically discussed and illustrated with examples. At the risk of redundancy, it is important once again to emphasize that it cannot be assumed that consumers will attend to marcom messages and process them just because they are printed, broadcast, or disseminated through some other medium. Rather, it is essential that

Figure 11.1

Enhancing Consumers' Motivation, Opportunity, and Ability to Process Brand Information

I. Enhance Consumers' MOTIVATION to . . .

A. Attend to the message by . . .

- Appealing to hedonic needs (appetite appeals, sex appeals)
- Using novel stimuli (unusual pictures, different ad formats, large number of scenes)
- Using intense or prominent cues (action, loud music, colorful ads, celebrities, large pictures)
- Using motion (complex pictures; edits and cuts)

B. Process brand information by . . .

- Increasing relevance of brand to self (asking rhetorical questions, using fear appeals, using dramatic presentations)
- Increasing curiosity about the brand (opening with suspense or surprise, using humor, presenting little information in the message)

II. Enhance Consumers' OPPORTUNITY to . . .

A. Encode information by . . .

- Repeating brand information
- Repeating key scenes
- Repeating the ad on multiple occasions

B. Reduce processing time by . . .

- Creating Gestalt processing (using pictures and imagery)

III. Enhance Consumers' ABILITY to . . .

A. Access knowledge structures by . . .

- Providing a context (employing verbal framing)

B. Create knowledge structures by . . .

- Facilitating exemplar-based learning (using concretizations, demonstrations, and analogies)

SOURCE: Adapted from Deborah J. MacInnis, Christine Moorman, and Bernard J. Jaworski, "Enhancing and Measuring Consumers' Motivation, Opportunity, and Ability to Process Brand Information from Ads," *Journal of Marketing* 55 (October 1991), 36. Reprinted with permission from Journal of Marketing, published by the American Marketing Association.

U.S. Potato Board

Figure 11.2

An Appeal to Informational Needs

special efforts be made to increase consumers' motivation, opportunity, and ability to process messages. Please carefully examine Figure 11.1 before proceeding so that you have a general appreciation of the topics that will be discussed hereafter.

Motivation to Attend to Messages

Figure 11.1 shows that one of the communicator's objectives is to increase the consumer's motivation to *attend to* the message and *process* brand information. This section discusses just the attention component; the following section will consider the processing element.

There are two forms of attention: voluntary and involuntary.[5] **Voluntary attention** is engaged when consumers devote attention to an advertisement or other marcom message that is perceived as *relevant to their current purchase-related goals.* In other words, messages are voluntarily attended to if they are perceived as pertinent to our needs. Marketing communicators attract voluntary attention by appealing to consumers' informational or hedonic needs. **Involuntary attention**, on the other hand, occurs when attention is captured by the use of attention-gaining techniques rather than by the consumer's inherent interest in the topic at hand. Novel stimuli, intense or prominent cues, complex pictures, and, in the case of broadcast ads, edits and cuts of the sort one sees with MTV-like videos are some of the techniques used to attract attention that otherwise would not be given.

Appeals to Informational and Hedonic Needs

Consumers are most likely to attend to messages that serve their informational needs and those that make them feel good and bring pleasure (that is, those that serve their hedonic needs). Regarding *informational needs,* consumers are attracted to those stimuli that supply relevant facts and figures. A student who wants to move out of a dormitory and into an apartment, for example, will be on the lookout for information pertaining to apartments. Classified ads and overheard conversations about apartments will be attended to even when the apartment seeker is not actively looking for information. As another illustration, consider the advertisement in Figure 11.2 for potatoes placed by the U.S. Potato Board, a trade association. The information value of this ad is best appreciated in the context of the time it was printed, when many American consumers were eschewing potatoes while on low-carbohydrate diets (e.g., Atkins and South Beach). The ad informatively points out that the "healthy potato" is "good for you" and is recommended by experts "as part of a healthy, balanced diet." Detailed nutritional information is provided on the nutrition facts label superimposed on the illustrated potato. (Note also the tape measure surrounding the potato to suggest a small waist.)

Figure 11.3

An Appeal to Hedonic Needs

Procter & Gamble; Ad Agency: Grey Worldwide; Art Director: Caren Josephs; Background Photography: Getty Images; Photograph of child: © 2004 Stacie Isabella Turk.

Hedonic needs are satisfied when consumers attend to messages that make them feel good and serve their pleasure needs. People are most likely to attend to those messages that have become associated with good times, enjoyment, and things we value in life. For example, the use of children (Figure 11.3), warm family scenes, and sex or romance appeals are just some of the commonly used attention-gaining techniques widely used in advertisements. Similarly, advertisements for appetizing food products are especially likely to be noticed when people are hungry (Figure 11.4). For this reason, many restaurant and fast-food marketers advertise on the radio during the after-work rush hour. Fast-food advertisers also promote their products on late-night television for the same reason. Needless to say, the best time to reach consumers with a message is just at the time they are experiencing a need for the product category in which the brand resides.

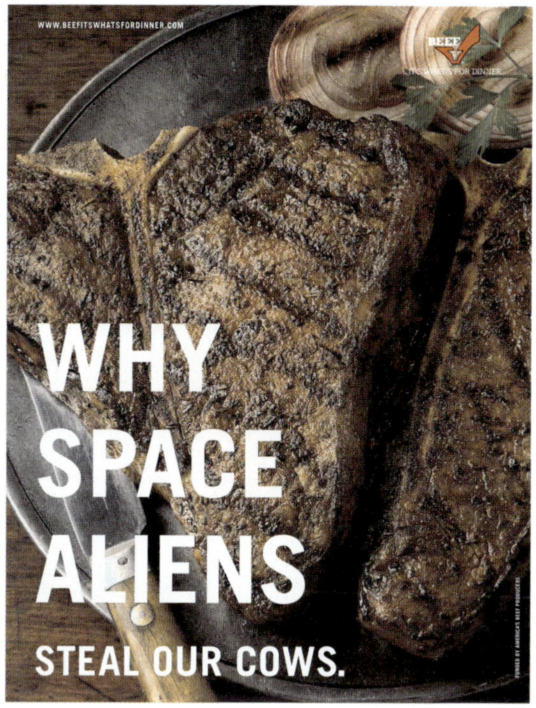

Figure 11.4
Another Appeal to Hedonic Needs

Use of Novel Stimuli

There are innumerable ways marketing communicators use novelty to attract involuntary attention. In general, **novel messages** are *unusual, distinctive,* or *unpredictable.* Such stimuli tend to produce greater attention than those that are familiar and routine. This can be explained by the behavioral concept of *human adaptation.* People adapt to the conditions around them: as a stimulus becomes more familiar, people become desensitized to it. Psychologists refer to this as *habituation.* For example, if you drive past a billboard on the way to school or work each day, you probably notice it less on each occasion. If the billboard were removed, you probably would notice it was no longer there. In other words, we notice by exception.

Examples of novelty abound. Consider, for example, an advertisement for Sauza Conmemorativo tequila. This incredibly eye-catching magazine advertisement, which is not shown here, simply shows an old, full-bearded man wearing a brimmed hat. Most conspicuous, however, is the fact that the broadly smiling man has a mouth with only a single tooth! Imprinted above his mouth is the statement, "This man has one cavity." The ad personifies novelty insofar as most ads show "beautiful people." This eye-catching ad and its use of an old, virtually toothless man is a humorous attempt to catch attention and make a point that is accentuated below the old man's face: "Life is Harsh—Your tequila shouldn't be."

Figure 11.5
Using Novelty to Attract Attention

Figure 11.5 for Glad's Press'n Seal wrap further illustrates the use of novelty to gain the reader's attention. Notice that the ad layout "forces" the reader's eye flow from the unusual, and thus novel, shot of an Eskimo grasping a speared fish shrouded in plastic wrap down to the package, brand name, and minimal body copy. This example represents a key point: the effective use of novelty involves not just attracting attention but also *directing* that attention to key visual and verbal information.

Use of Intense or Prominent Cues

Intense and prominent cues (those that are louder, more colorful, bigger, brighter, etc.) increase the probability of attracting attention. This is because it is difficult for consumers to avoid such stimuli, thus leading to involuntary attention. One need only walk through a shopping mall, department store, or supermarket and observe the various packages, displays, sights, sounds, and smells to appreciate the special efforts marketing communicators take to attract attention. Also, the use of celebrities in advertisements is a sure way of gaining attention due to their general appeal to select audiences. (A subsequent section will discuss in detail the use of celebrities.)

Advertisements, too, utilize intensity to attract attention. For example, the advertisement for Ziploc containers (Figure 11.6)

Figure 11.6

Using an Intense Stimulus to Attract Attention

uses the intense, vibrant colors of a hummingbird and a hibiscus flower to attract the magazine reader's attention and encourage comprehension of the ad's straightforward message: "One simple press of [Ziploc's Snap 'n Seal lids] and you know it's secure."

Using Motion

Advertisers sometimes employ motion to both attract and direct consumer attention to the brand name and to pertinent ad copy. (Motion obviously is used in TV commercials, which is an inherently dynamic medium. However, the issue is more germane in the case of print advertising—magazines and newspapers—which is a static form of advertising display. Hence, artistic and photographic techniques are employed that produce a semblance of movement, though nothing is of course actually moving.) Falling objects (e.g., a flipping coin), people appearing to be running, and automobiles in motion are some of the techniques used in print ads to attract attention. A couple riding in an open-top convertible automobile (Figure 11.7) is an effective attention getter for the advertised product, Norwegian Cruise Line, and is used in making the point that Norwegian Cruise Line departure points are relatively close—"a short trip to the ship."

Motivation to Process Messages

Enhanced processing motivation means that the ad receiver has increased interest in reading or listening to the ad message to determine what it has to say that might be of relevance. Among other desirable outcomes, increased processing motivation has been shown to strengthen the impact of brand attitudes on purchase intentions.[6] To enhance consumers' motivation to process brand information, marketing communicators do two things: (1) enhance the *relevance* of the brand to the consumer and (2) enhance *curiosity* about the brand. Methods for enhancing brand relevance include the use of *rhetorical questions, fear appeals* (discussed later in the chapter in a separate section), and *dramatic presentation* to increase the significance of the brand to consumers' self-interests.[7]

Figure 11.7

Using Motion to Attract Attention

Enhancing curiosity about a brand can be accomplished by using *humor,* presenting *little information* in the message (and thereby encouraging the consumer to think about the brand), or opening a message with *suspense* or *surprise.* The ad for the Pur water filtration system (Figure 11.8) uses surprise to effectively "pull the reader in" and draw attention to this product. The use of surprise (have you ever seen a shopping cart overloaded with gallons of bottled water?) attracts the reader's attention and gives him or her reason to further examine this advertisement. From initially looking at the shopping cart, albeit briefly, the reader's attention next is drawn to the headline ("Don't let the price of bottled water pile up on you.") and then to the picture of a Pur water filtration system attached to a standard water faucet. More information that explains why Pur is a good alternative to purchasing bottled water is provided below the brand name and logo. All in all, this is an effective advertisement that uses the unexpected, or surprise, to capture the magazine reader's attention.

Opportunity to Encode Information

Marketing messages have no chance of effectiveness unless consumers comprehend information about the brand and incorporate it with information related to the product category in their existing memory structure. Hence, the communicator's goal is to get consumers to *encode* information and, toward this end, to make it as simple and quick as possible for them to do so. The secret to facilitating encoding is *repetition:* the marketing communicator should repeat brand information, repeat key scenes, and repeat the advertisement on multiple occasions. Through repetition consumers have an increased opportunity to encode the important information the communicator wishes to convey. This is why we see advertisements repeated night after night on TV, sometimes to excess. But advertisers know that repetition is required to get their point across.

Figure 11.8

Using Suspense or Surprise to Enhance Processing Motivation

Opportunity to Reduce Processing Time

Opportunity to process is further enhanced if the communicator takes extra measures to *reduce the time* required of the consumer to read, listen to, and ultimately discern the meaning of a marcom message. The use of pictures and imagery create a form of total-message processing (or gestalt) whereby the consumer can readily encode the totality of the message rather than having to process information bit by bit. This is in line with the old aphorism that a picture is worth a thousand words. Consider a minimalist advertisement for Crown Royal whisky that simply shows a picture of a snake-encircled bottle of Crown Royal, with the rhetorical question, "Tempted?" written beside it. The ad uses the Garden of Eden and Adam and Eve story—through minimal verbal copy and distinct imagery—to convey the notion that readers of the ad will themselves be tempted to partake of Crown Royal's "coveted fruit."

Ability to Access Knowledge Structures

A brand-based *knowledge structure* represents the associative links in the consumer's long-term memory between the brand and thoughts, feelings, and beliefs about that brand. In general, people are most able to process new information that relates to something they already know or understand. For example, if one knows a lot about computers, then information presented in computer language is readily comprehended. The marketing communicator's task is to enable consumers either to *access* existing knowledge structures or to *create* new knowledge structures.

To facilitate consumer accessing of knowledge structures, marketing communicators need to *provide a context* for the text or pictures. *Verbal framing* is one way of providing a context. This means that pictures in an ad are placed in the context of, or framed with, appropriate words or phrases so ad receivers can better understand brand information and the key selling point of the marcom message. In an advertisement for DuPont's Teflon brand of scratch-resistant coatings, attention is drawn to the incongruous image of a skillet filled with copper wiring, tacks, and shards of glass. Most consumers believe that nonstick skillets can be easily damaged when scratched with sharp objects. Against this prevailing knowledge structure and in view of the incongruous visual, ad copy is required to clarify this image. The limited copy simply points out that DuPont Teflon coatings are scratch resistant and encourages readers to visit their Web site (http://teflon.com) for further information.

Ability to Create Knowledge Structures

Sometimes marketing communicators need to *create* knowledge structures for information they want consumers to have about their brands. This is accomplished by facilitating *exemplar-based learning.* An *exemplar* is a specimen or model of a particular concept or idea. By using concretizations, demonstrations, or analogies, the marketing communicator can facilitate learning by appealing to exemplars. Consider, for example, the concept of freshness. We all know what freshness means, but it is a rather abstract concept that is difficult to verbalize. That is, it is difficult to explain what freshness means without resorting to an example. Diet Pepsi's brand managers faced this situation when introducing to consumers the practice of "freshness dating"—that is, printing on the soft-drink container the final date up to which the beverage remained fresh. If you were Diet Pepsi's brand manager, what grocery products might you use to exemplify freshness? Their choice was to use pictures of products that people routinely inspect for freshness (squeeze an orange, pinch a loaf of bread) and, by analogy, communicate the idea that consumers should check arrows on Diet Pepsi cans to ensure that the contents are not outdated. The advertisement (Figure 11.9) for Nature Made vitamins uses the analogy that this brand of vitamins is not *just* a vitamin any more than the famous Mona Lisa portrait is *just* a picture.

Concretizations

Concretizing is used extensively in advertising to facilitate both consumer learning and retrieval of brand information. **Concretizing** is based on the straightforward idea that it is easier for people to remember and retrieve *tangible* rather than abstract information. Claims about a brand are more concrete (versus abstract) when they are made perceptible, palpable, real, evident, and vivid. Concretizing is accomplished by using concrete words and examples. Here are some illustrations:

1. An advertisement for Johnson's baby powder positioned the brand to be capable of making the user's body feel "as soft as the day you were born." To concretize this claim, a series of age-regression scenes revealed, first, a shot of a woman in her 30s, then a shot as she looked in her 20s, next as an early teenager, and finally as a baby. Accompanying music was played throughout to the lyrics "Make me, make me your baby." This beautiful and somewhat touching ad made concrete Johnson's claim that its baby powder will make the user feel "as soft as the day [he or she was] born."
2. The makers of Anacin tablets needed a concrete way to present that brand as "strong pain relief for splitting headaches." The idea of a splitting headache was concretized by showing a hard-boiled egg splitting with accompanying sound effects.
3. Tinactin, a treatment for athlete's foot, concretized its relief properties by showing a person's pair of feet literally appearing to be on fire (representing the fiery sensation of athlete's foot), which is "extinguished" by an application of Tinactin.
4. To convey the notion that Purina brand Hi Pro dog food will recharge an active dog and keep it running, a magazine ad portrayed the brand in the form of a battery, which is a widely recognized apparatus for charging electrical objects. In effect, the battery in this symbolic concretization conveyed pictorially the more abstract claim contained in the ad's body copy.
5. To establish in consumers' minds that Tums E-X is "twice as strong as Rolaids," the commercial showed a sledgehammer behind Tums and a regular-sized hammer behind Rolaids. The commercial then showed the sledgehammer driving in a nail twice as quickly as the regular hammer, thus concretizing Tums' claim.

Figure 11.9 The Use of Analogy to Create a Knowledge Structure

Courtesy, Nature Made; Ad Agency: Carryon Communication.

Heaven Hill Distilleries, Inc.

Figure 11.10
Facilitating Exemplar-Based Learning with Concretization

6. Another Tums advertisement claimed in its headline that "scientific studies find Tums to be the purest form of calcium available." This claim was concretized with the visual display of a package of Tums inside an empty milk bottle, an exemplar of calcium, and with the juxtaposed words *calcium* and *Tums* forming the new word *Calciums*.
7. Finally, an advertisement for Evan Williams bourbon (Figure 11.10) uses the before-and-after notion of coal transforming into a diamond to illustrate that aging this brand for seven years leads to a smoother taste—"The longer you wait, the better it gets."

Section Summary

The foregoing discussion has emphasized that advertisers, along with other marketing communicators, benefit from enhancing consumers' motivation, opportunity, and ability to process marketing messages. A variety of communication devices enables advertisers to achieve their goals in the hopes of influencing consumers' brand-related attitudes, purchase intentions, and, ultimately, their behavior. Anything the advertiser can do to enhance consumers' MOA factors—motivation, opportunity, and ability to attend to and process ad messages—will benefit your brand's equity and increase the odds that consumers will purchase your brand rather than a competitive offering. As previously mentioned, one way to increase consumers' motivation to attend to ad messages is by using celebrities. The following section examines this prospect in detail.

The Role of Endorsers in Advertising

Advertised brands frequently receive endorsements from a variety of popular public figures. It has been estimated that approximately one-sixth of ads worldwide feature celebrities.[8] In addition to celebrity endorsements, products also receive the explicit or tacit support of noncelebrities.

Celebrity Endorsers

Television stars, movie actors, famous athletes, and even dead personalities are widely used to endorse products. Advertisers and their agencies are willing to pay huge salaries to celebrities who are liked and respected by target audiences and who will, it is hoped, favorably influence consumers' attitudes and behavior toward the endorsed brands. For the most part, such investments are justified. For example, stock prices have been shown to rise when companies announce celebrity endorsement contracts[9] and to fall when negative publicity reaches the media about a celebrity who endorses one of the company's brands.[10]

Top celebrities receive enormous payments for their endorsement services. For example, in a recent year golfer Tiger Woods earned $70 million from endorsement deals with multiple companies.[11] To put this amount of money in perspective, a person earning a not-so-paltry annual income of $100,000 would have to work 700 years at that salary to earn as much as Tiger Woods receives in a single year from his endorsement activities! Other American athletes who are highly paid for their endorsements include basketball players LeBron James ($35 million in endorse-

Controversial Uses of LeBron James in Singapore and China

global focus

Graffiti in Singapore

This country, known for its exceptional cleanliness and tidiness, took umbrage at a strategy undertaken by Nike to create buzz among Singapore's basketball-crazed youth. Nike representatives pasted posters of NBA basketball star LeBron James over the ad panels of 700 Singaporean bus stops. The strategy was designed, in the words of a Nike spokeswoman, "to do something naughty . . . to disrupt the neat environment of Singapore and stay in line with the street-feel of this LeBron James basketball campaign." Considering the chapter's earlier discussion of MOA factors, this campaign undoubtedly had substantial ability to enhance Singaporean's motivations to attend to and process these poster-style advertising messages, but at the expense of irritating a subset of Singapore's citizenry who were offended by an American company insensitive to their desire to preserve the country's immaculate public spaces.

Kung Fu in China

In a TV commercial broadcast in the Peoples' Republic of China for the Air Zoom LeBron II brand of sneakers, LeBron James is shown in a video-style setting battling and defeating an animated kung fu master, a pair of dragons, and two women dressed in traditional Chinese clothing. The commercial, which was based on films featuring Bruce Lee of martial arts fame, was banned after a few airings on local Chinese stations and on China's national sports channel. The Chinese government took great offense with this commercial, which it considered blasphemous to the national practices and culture of China. The Administration for Radio, Film and Television claimed that the advertisement "violates regulations that mandate that all advertisements in China should uphold national dignity and interest and respect the motherland's culture."

In response to both of these advertising efforts, one can only reflect: What were the marcom people at Nike thinking? Did their desire to recruit new customers in countries consumed with enthusiasm for basketball overwhelm their common sense and cultural sensitivity? Corporate insensitivities such as these make it easy to understand why the widespread epithet "ugly American" is hard to shake.

Sources: The Singapore description is based on Rukmini Callimachi, "Nike Graffiti Ads in Singapore Spark Controversy," FOXSports.com, November 26, 2004 http://msn.foxsports.com. The China case is adapted from Audra Ang, "China Bans Nike Commercial as Insult to National Dignity," USATODAY.com, December 6, 2004 http://www.usatoday.com.

ments) and Shaquille O'Neal ($14 million); football player Peyton Manning ($9.5 million); cyclist Lance Armstrong ($16.5 million); tennis players Andre Agassi ($24.5 million), Serena Williams ($15 million), and Venus Williams ($14 million); and golfer Phil Mickelson ($14 million).[12] (See the *Global Focus* insert for a discussion of controversies surrounding Nike's usage of LeBron James in Asia.)

Typical-Person Endorsers

A frequent advertising approach is to show regular people—that is, noncelebrities—using or endorsing products. In addition to being much less expensive than celebrities, typical-person endorsers avoid the potential backlash from using "beautiful people" who may be resented for possessing atypical physical attractiveness or other individual traits.[13] Also, real people who have personally experienced the benefits of using a particular brand possess a degree of credibility that likely is unsurpassed. For example, the Subway chain of sandwich shops (see *Marcom Challenge*) experienced a sales boom when the product was endorsed by previously unknown Jared, who was advertised to have lost 245 pounds while subsisting on a diet of Subway sandwiches. Subway also used twin brothers, Herman and Sherman Smith, who lost over 200 combined pounds on the Subway "diet."

Many advertisements that portray typical-person users often include *multiple people* rather than a single individual. Is there any reason why multiple sources should be more effective than a single source? In fact, there is: the act of portraying more than one person seems to increase the likelihood an advertisement will generate higher levels of message involvement and correspondingly greater message-related thought. In turn, greater elaboration increases the odds that compelling message arguments will favorably influence attitudes.[14]

Endorser Attributes: The TEARS Model

Now that a distinction has been made between the two general types of advertising endorsers, it is important to formally describe endorser attributes and the role they play in facilitating communications effectiveness. Extensive research has demonstrated that two general attributes, *credibility* and *attractiveness,* contribute to an endorser's effectiveness, and that each consists of more distinct subattributes.[15] To facilitate the student's memory with respect to endorser characteristics, we use the acronym *TEARS* to represent five discrete attributes: *t*rustworthiness and *e*xpertise are two dimensions of credibility, whereas physical *a*ttractiveness, *r*espect, and *s*imilarity (to the target audience) are components of the general concept of attractiveness. Table 11.1 lists and defines all five attributes.

Credibility: The Process of Internalization

In its most basic sense, credibility refers to the tendency to believe or trust someone. When an information source, such as an endorser, is perceived as credible, audience attitudes are changed through a psychological process called *internalization.* **Internalization** occurs when the receiver accepts the endorser's position on an issue as his or her own. An internalized attitude tends to be maintained even if the source of the message is forgotten or if the source switches to a different position.[16]

Two important subattributes of endorser credibility are trustworthiness and expertise. **Trustworthiness**, the *T* in the TEARS model, refers to the honesty, integrity, and believability of a source. Though expertise and trustworthiness are not mutually exclusive, often a particular endorser is perceived as highly trustworthy but not especially expert. Endorser trustworthiness simply reflects the fact that prospective endorsers of a brand vary in the degree to which audience members have faith in what they have to say. An endorser's trustworthiness rests on the audience's perception of his or her endorsement motivations. If consumers believe that an endorser is motivated purely by self-interest, that endorser will be less persuasive than someone regarded as having nothing to gain by endorsing the brand.

A celebrity earns the audience's trust through the life he or she lives professionally (on the screen, on the sports field, in public office, etc.) and personally, as revealed to the general public via the mass media. (To demonstrate this point to yourself, spend a moment to rank four living ex-presidents of the United States—George Bush Sr., Jimmy Carter, Bill Clinton, and Gerald Ford—in terms of how trustworthy you perceive them to be. If one or another is not at the top of your list, is it due to his personal life or his actual job performance?) Advertisers capitalize on the value of trustworthiness by selecting endorsers who are widely regarded as being honest, believable, and dependable people.[17]

In general, endorsers must establish that they are not attempting to manipulate the audience and that they are objective in their presentations. By doing so,

Table 11.1

The Five Components in the TEARS Model of Endorser Attributes

T = Trustworthiness	The property of being perceived as believable, dependable—as someone who can be trusted.
E = Expertise	The characteristic of having specific skills, knowledge, or abilities with respect to the endorsed brand.
A = Physical attractiveness	The trait of being regarded as pleasant to look at in terms of a particular group's concept of attractiveness.
R = Respect	The quality of being admired or even esteemed due to one's personal qualities and accomplishments.
S = Similarity (to the target audience)	The extent to which a endorser matches an audience in terms of characteristics pertinent to the endorsement relationship (age, gender, ethnicity, etc.).

they establish themselves as trustworthy and, therefore, credible. Also, an endorser has a greater likelihood of being perceived as trustworthy the more he or she matches the audience in terms of distinct characteristics such as gender and ethnicity. When a spokesperson matches the audience's ethnicity, for example, spokesperson trustworthiness is enhanced, which, in turn, promotes more favorable attitudes toward the advertised brand.[18]

The second aspect of endorser credibility is expertise, the *E* component of the TEARS model. **Expertise** refers to the knowledge, experience, or skills possessed by an endorser as they relate to the endorsed brand. Hence, athletes are considered to be experts when it comes to the endorsement of sports-related products. Models are similarly perceived as possessing expertise with regard to beauty-enhancing products and fashion items. Successful businesspeople are regarded as experts in matters of managerial practices. For example, Donald Trump, due to his extensive business background in commercial real estate transactions and otherwise, would be regarded as high in expertise in business matters and thus was a logical choice when the creators of *The Apprentice* TV program put that show together. (In your opinion is Trump also high in trustworthiness?) Expertise is a perceived rather than an absolute phenomenon. Whether an endorser is indeed an expert is unimportant; all that matters is how the target audience perceives the endorser. An endorser who is perceived as an expert on a given subject is more persuasive in changing audience opinions pertaining to his or her area of expertise than an endorser who is not perceived as an expert.

Attractiveness: The Process of Identification

The second general attribute that contributes to endorser effectiveness, **attractiveness**, means more than simply physical attractiveness—although that can be a very important attribute—and includes any number of virtuous characteristics that consumers may perceive in an endorser: intellectual skills, personality properties, lifestyle characteristics, athletic prowess, and so on. When consumers find something in an endorser that they consider attractive, persuasion occurs through **identification**. That is, when consumers perceive a celebrity endorser to be attractive, they *identify with* the endorser and are likely to adopt the endorser's attitudes, behaviors, interests, or preferences.

The TEARS model identifies three subcomponents of the general concept of attractiveness: *physical attractiveness, respect*, and *similarity*. That is, an endorser is regarded as attractive—in the general sense of this concept—to the extent that he or she is considered physically attractive, respected for reasons other than physical attractiveness, or regarded as similar to the target audience in terms of any characteristic that is pertinent to a particular endorsement relationship. Perceived attractiveness can be achieved via any one of these attributes and does *not* require that a celebrity encompass all simultaneously; however, it goes without saying that a celebrity who possesses the entire "package" of attractiveness attributes would represent awesome endorsement potential.

First, **physical attractiveness**—the *A* component in the TEARS model—is a key consideration in many endorsement relationships.[19] Perhaps no better illustration of this is possible than tennis player Anna Kournikova's success as an endorser. Ms. Kournikova has earned over $10 million per year in endorsement deals, which is an incredible feat in view of the fact that she has never won an event on the professional tennis circuit. Fellow Russian, Maria Sharapova, probably has an even better product endorsement career facing her in view of the fact that she is a highly accomplished tennis player in addition to being physically appealing. There is a good reason why advertising agents and their brand management clients often select highly attractive celebrities to endorse products: research has supported the intuitive expectation that physically attractive endorsers produce more favorable evaluations of ads and advertised brands than do less attractive communicators.[20]

Respect, the *R* in the TEARS model, is the second component of the overall attractiveness attribute. **Respect** represents the quality of being admired or even esteemed due to one's personal qualities and accomplishments. Whereas a celebrity's physical attractiveness may be considered the "form" aspect of the overall attractiveness attribute, respect is the "function" or substantive element. Sometimes function trumps form, even in brand-endorser relations.

Celebrities are respected for their acting ability, athletic prowess, appealing personalities, their stands on important societal issues (the environment, political issues, war and peace, etc.), and any number of other qualities. Perhaps ex-boxer Muhammad Ali personifies the respect dimension more than any other celebrity in the world—both for his incredible skills in the ring and his stand on political and social issues outside the ring. Soccer player David Beckham also scores high on the respect dimension, which explains why he is one of the world's best paid celebrity endorsers. The secret to his endorser success has been described as due to "his ability to function as a one-size-fits-all vessel for his fans' hopes and dreams."[21] I suppose this means that everyone likes Beckham for whatever positive qualities they choose to project onto him.

Individuals who are respected also generally are liked, and it is this respect qua likeability factor that can serve to enhance a brand's equity when a respected or liked celebrity endorser enters into an endorsement relationship with the brand. In some sense, the brand acquires some semblance of the characteristics that are admired in the celebrity who endorses the brand. For example, Gatorade and Michael Jordan are inextricably linked in the minds of many consumers. Tiger Woods and Nike golf equipment also are somewhat indistinct, as are Jared Fogel and Subway. In sum, when a respected or liked celebrity enters into an extended endorser relationship with a brand, the respect for or liking of the celebrity may extend to the brand with which he or she is linked, thus enhancing a brand's equity via the positive effect on consumers' brand-related beliefs and attitudes.

Similarity, the third attractiveness component and the *S* in the TEARS model, represents the degree to which an endorser matches an audience in terms of characteristics pertinent to the endorsement relationship—age, gender, ethnicity, and so on. Similarity is an important attribute for the mere fact that people tend to better like individuals who share with them common features or traits. This, of course, is reminiscent of the aphorism that "birds of a feather flock together."

As it applies to the domain of brand-celebrity relationships, the importance of similarity implies that it typically is desirable for a celebrity to match his or her endorsed brand's target audience in terms of pertinent demographic and psychographic characteristics. There is some evidence that a matchup between endorser and audience similarity is especially important when the product or service in question is one where audience members are *heterogeneous* in terms of their taste and attribute preferences. For example, because people differ greatly in terms of what they like in restaurants, plays, and movies, a spokesperson perceived to be similar to the audience is expected to have the greatest effect in influencing their attitudes and choices. On the other hand, when preferences among audience members are relatively *homogeneous* (such as might be expected with services such as plumbing, dry cleaning, and auto repair), the matchup between spokesperson and audience similarity is not that important. Rather, it is the spokesperson's *experience* or *expertise* with the product or service that appears to have the greatest influence in shaping the audience's attitudes and subsequent behavior.[22]

Endorser Selection Considerations: The "No Tears" Approach

The preceding section described the attributes of celebrities that are important in determining their effectiveness as endorsers. The TEARS model identified five attributes that were grouped under the two general components of credibility and attractiveness. Now let us turn to the issue of how brand managers and their advertising agencies actually select particular endorsers to align with their brands. In a takeoff on the TEARS acronym, endorser selection is described here as the "no-tears" approach. Compared with the prior usage of TEARS, which was merely an acronym combining the first letter of five endorser attributes, the current lowercase usage is applied in the real sense of the word *tears*. In other words, the current discussion is directed at identifying how brand managers and their agencies actually go about selecting celebrities so as to avoid the grief (metaphorically, the tears) from making an unwise decision.

Advertising executives use a variety of factors in selecting celebrity endorsers. The following appear to be the most important: (1) celebrity and audience matchup, (2) celebrity and brand matchup, (3) celebrity credibility, (4) celebrity attractiveness, (5) cost considerations, (6) a working ease or difficulty factor, (7) an endorsement saturation factor, and (8) a likelihood-of-getting-into-trouble factor.[23]

1. Celebrity and Audience Matchup

Perhaps most fundamentally, an endorser must match up well with the endorsed brand's target market. The first question a brand manager must pose when selecting an endorser is, "Will the target market positively relate to this endorser?" Shaquille O'Neal, LeBron James, Allen Iverson, and other National Basketball Association (NBA) superstars who endorse basketball shoes match up well with the predominantly teenage audience who aspire to slam dunk the basketball, block shots, intercept passes, and sink 25-foot jump shots. Sarah Jessica Parker (of *Sex and the City* stardom) matches well with many members of the Gap's target audience of fashion-conscious consumers. Can you think of any endorser relations where the match between celebrity and audience seems inappropriate?

2. Celebrity and Brand Matchup

Advertising executives require that the celebrity's behavior, values, appearance, and decorum be compatible with the image desired for the advertised brand. For example, the chief marketing officer at cosmetics firm Elizabeth Arden explained the choice of supermodel and actress Catherine Zeta-Jones in these terms: "Catherine has [a] great career and family, she's a mom, and she has a timeless beauty, which is exactly the image we want to project."[24]

If a brand has a wholesome image or wants to project this particular attribute, then the celebrity endorser should personify wholesomeness. For example, NBA players Tim Duncan, Kevin Garnett, and Tracy McGrady were signed by German athletic shoemaker Adidas to endorse that brand because they all are modest individuals with wholesome images. Comparatively, a brand intentionally casting itself with a "bad boy" image would select entirely different endorsers. Again using the NBA, Allen Iverson or Vince Carter fit well with this latter image. Suppose a brand manager wished to enhance a brand's equity by portraying the brand as incomparable in terms of durability, dependability, and consistency. Who better to personify these characteristics than, say, Cal Ripken, the Baltimore Orioles baseball player who played in 2,632 consecutive baseball games prior to retiring.

3. Celebrity Credibility

A celebrity's credibility is a primary reason for selecting a celebrity endorser. People who are trustworthy and perceived as knowledgeable about the product category are best able to convince others to undertake a particular course of action. We discussed the two components of credibility, trustworthiness and expertise, in the TEARS model, so further discussion is unnecessary at this point other than to direct your attention to Table 11.2, which identifies the importance ratings of various factors in terms of whether an endorsement will influence consumers' opinions of an endorsed product.

Table 11.2

The Importance of Various Endorser-Related Factors on Consumer's Opinion of Product

Endorser-related factors	Percentage of respondents rating factor as *very* or *extremely* important*
Doesn't use drugs.	66%
Is good role model for kids.	64
Has never been arrested.	54
Has a good family life.	51
Actually uses product in real life.	49
Is/was very successful in his/her sport.	36
Plays/played sport I follow.	30
Plays/played for one of my favorite teams.	30
Is religious.	27
Has been playing or played the sport for a long time.	25
Is someone I would like to be like.	21
Was born in America.	12
Is hottest new star in his/her sport.	14
Is good looking/stylish.	13
Is same gender as me.	8
Came to America from another country.	3

*Response options included "not at all important," "somewhat important," "important," "very important," and "extremely important."

Source: Adapted from a study of 610 people age 18 and older reported in James Tenser, "Endorser Qualities Count More Than Ever," *Advertising Age,* November 8, 2004, S–2, 4.

4. Celebrity Attractiveness

In selecting celebrity spokespeople, advertising executives evaluate different aspects that can be lumped together under the general label *attractiveness.* As discussed earlier in the TEARS model, attractiveness is multifaceted and does not include just physical attractiveness. It also is important to note that advertising executives generally regard attractiveness as subordinate in importance to credibility and endorser matchup with the audience and with the brand.

5. Cost Considerations

How much it will cost to acquire a celebrity's services is an important consideration but one that should not dictate the final choice. Everything else held constant, a less costly celebrity will be selected over a more costly alternative. But, of course, everything else is not held constant. Hence, as with any managerial decision when selecting among alternatives, brand managers must perform a cost-benefit analysis to determine whether a more expensive celebrity can be justified in terms of a proportionately greater return on investment. This, unfortunately, is not a simple calculation because it is difficult to project the revenue stream that will be obtained from using a particular celebrity endorser. Difficulty aside, management must attempt to calculate the alternative returns on investment given multiple options of celebrities who would appropriately fit with a brand's desired image and its target market.

6. Working Ease or Difficulty Factor

Some celebrities are relatively easy to work with, whereas others are simply difficult—stubborn, noncompliant, arrogant, temperamental, inaccessible, or otherwise unmanageable. Brand managers and their advertising agencies would prefer to avoid the "hassle factor" of dealing with individuals who are unwilling to flex their schedules, hesitant to participate with a brand outside of celebrity-restricted bounds, or otherwise difficult to work with.

7. Saturation Factor

Another key consideration, certainly not as important as the previous factors but one that nonetheless has to be evaluated, is the number of other brands the celebrity is endorsing. If a celebrity is overexposed—that is, endorsing too many products—his or her perceived credibility may suffer.[25]

8. The Trouble Factor

A final consideration is an evaluation of the likelihood that a celebrity will get into trouble after an endorsement relation is established. The potential that a celebrity may get into trouble is a matter of considerable concern to brand managers and ad agencies. Suppose a celebrity is convicted of a crime or has his or her image blemished in some way during the course of an advertising campaign. What are the potential negative implications for the endorsed brand? Frankly, there are no simple answers to this provocative question, and researchers are just beginning to explore the issue in a sophisticated fashion.[26]

In the meantime, many advertisers and advertising agencies are reluctant to use celebrity endorsers. Their concern is not without justification. Consider some of the celebrity-related incidents making news in recent years and during past decades: (1) Basketball player Kobe Bryant was convicted, though subsequently acquitted, of a rape charge in Colorado. Shortly thereafter, McDonald's Corporation refused to renew Bryant as a spokesperson, as did a much smaller Italian company that makes Nutella chocolate-hazelnut spread. (2) Swimmer and Olympic gold-medalist Michael Phelps was arrested on a DUI (drive-under-the-influence) charge after returning from the Olympics in Athens. (3) Track star Marion Jones' reputation was tarnished by an investigation into allegations that she had used performance-enhancing drugs. (4) Baseball player Jason Giambi admitted to using performance-enhancing drugs, and home-run-hitting phenomenon Barry Bonds was accused of doing the same. (5) Boxer Mike Tyson—an active endorser before a series of mishaps—was convicted on a rape charge and served a prison sentence (not to mention the fact that he bit a chunk out of opponent Evander Holyfield's ear during a match following his prison sentence). (6) Actress Cybill Shepherd had a lucrative endorsement deal with the beef industry but embarrassed the industry by revealing to the press that she avoided eating beef. (7) Entertainer Michael Jackson was arraigned on child-molestation charges, though subsequently exonerated. (8) Tennis player Jennifer Capriati's promising career was sidetracked at an early age with emotional problems and allegations of drug abuse. She later mounted a successful comeback, but her endorsement deals pale in comparison to those of tennis stars such as the Williams sisters, Serena and Venus. (9) Ex–football player and actor O. J. Simpson was indicted for, but not convicted of, murder.

Due to the risks of such incidents after the consummation of multimillion-dollar celebrity endorsement contracts, there has been increased scrutiny in selecting celebrity endorsers. No selection procedure is fail-safe, however, and it is for this reason that some advertisers and their agencies avoid celebrity endorsements altogether. An alternative is to use the "endorsements" of celebrities who are no longer living. Dead celebrities are well known and respected by consumers in the target audiences to whom they appeal, and, best of all, their use in advertising is virtually risk free inasmuch as they cannot engage in behaviors that will sully their reputations and resonate adversely to the brands they posthumously endorse.

The Role of Q Scores

Needless to say, the selection of high-priced celebrity endorsers is typically undertaken with considerable thought on the part of brand managers and their advertising agencies. Their selection process is facilitated with *Performer Q Scores* that are commercially available from a New York–based firm called Marketing

Evaluations. For reasons that will shortly become apparent, the *Q* in Q Score signifies *quotient*.

Marketing Evaluations obtains Q Scores for approximately 1,500 public figures (entertainers, athletes, and other famous personages) by mailing questionnaires to a representative national panel of individuals. Panel participants are asked two straightforward questions for each person: (1) have you heard of this person? (a measure of *familiarity*); and (2) if so, do you rate him or her poor, fair, good, very good, or one of your favorites? (a measure of *popularity*). The calculation of each performer's Q score, or quotient, is accomplished by determining the percentage of panel members who respond that a particular performer is "one of my favorites" and then dividing that number by the percentage who indicate that they have heard of that person. In other words, the popularity percentage is divided by the familiarity percentage, and the quotient is that person's Q Score. This rating simply reveals the proportion of a group that is familiar with a person and who regard that person as one of their favorites.

For example, results from a survey by Marketing Evaluations revealed that Bill Cosby was known by 95 percent of people surveyed and considered a favorite by 45 percent. Hence, his Q Score (which is expressed without a decimal point) is reported as 47 (i.e., 45 divided by 95 is roughly 47). Comparatively, in this same survey, Roseanne Barr had a Q Score of only 16, which was obtained by dividing the 15 percent of respondents who considered her one of their favorites by the 93 percent who were familiar with her.[27] It comes as little surprise that advertisers have not flocked to Roseanne to sign her up to endorse their products.

Q Scores provide useful information to brand managers and advertising agencies, but there is more to selecting a celebrity to endorse a brand than simply scouring through the pages of Q Scores. Subjective judgment ultimately comes into play in determining whether a prospective celebrity endorser matches well with the brand image and its intended target market.

The Role of Humor in Advertising

Politicians, actors and actresses, public speakers, professors, and indeed all of us at one time or another use humor to create a desired reaction. Advertisers also turn to humor in the hopes of achieving various communication objectives—gaining attention, guiding consumer comprehension of product claims, influencing attitudes, enhancing recall of advertised claims, and, ultimately, creating customer action. The use of humor in advertising is extensive, representing approximately 25 percent of all television advertising in the United States and more than 35 percent in the United Kingdom.[28]

A study based on a sampling of television advertisements from four countries (Germany, Korea, Thailand, and the United States) determined that humorous advertisements in all of these countries generally involve the use of *incongruity resolution*.[29] Humor in U.S. magazine and radio advertising also typically employs incongruity resolution.[30] Incongruity exists when the meaning of an ad is not immediately clear. Baffled by the incongruity, the consumer is provoked to understand the ad's meaning and resolve the incongruity. When the meaning is eventually determined—as, for example, when the humor in an ad is detected—a feeling of *surprise* is experienced, and it is this sensation of surprise that generates a humorous response.[31] In turn, this humorous response can elicit a favorable attitude toward the advertisement and perhaps toward the advertised brand itself.[32]

The Advair advertisement in Figure 11.11 illustrates the use of humor. The prominent visual depicts a dance scene featuring a "cool" dog wearing sunglasses and a diamond-studded collar along with the statement "Go. Boogie." The subtle humor in this ad results from appreciating the conversational usage of the phrase "I feel like a dog," an expression applied when one does not feel good. Asthma sufferers, the audience toward which this ad is directed, certainly feel like dogs when not taking medicine or when their asthma medicine is not working well. The incongruity resolution in this ad thus occurs when one recognizes that he or she, upon taking Advair, will become a "happy dog" who can enjoy life and engage in those activities refrained from when in the condition of "feeling like a dog." Although humor is used relatively infrequently in magazine advertising compared with TV and radio, the Advair advertisement illustrates the use of humor in the magazine medium.[33]

Figure 11.11

The Use of Humor in Magazine Advertising

Whether humor is generally effective and what kinds of humor are most successful are matters of some debate among advertising practitioners and scholars.[34] A survey determined that advertising agency executives consider humor to be especially effective for attracting attention and creating brand awareness.[35] A thorough review of research on the effects of humor leads to the following tentative generalizations:[36]

- Humor is an effective method for attracting attention to advertisements.
- Humor enhances liking of both the advertisement and the advertised brand.
- Humor does not necessarily harm comprehension and may in fact increase memory for advertising claims if the humor is relevant to the advertised brand.[37]
- Humor does not offer an advantage over nonhumor at increasing persuasion.
- Humor does not enhance source credibility.
- The nature of the product affects the appropriateness of using humor. Specifically, humor is used more successfully with established rather than new products. Humor also is more appropriate for products that are more feeling-oriented, or experiential, and those that are not very involving (such as inexpensive consumer packaged goods).

When used correctly and in the right circumstances, humor can be an extremely effective advertising technique. A complication of using humor in advertising is that humorous appeals vary in their effectiveness across demographic groups and even among individuals. For example, men and women are not equally attentive to humorous ads.[38] In addition to demographic differences in responsiveness to humor, research evidence also shows that humorous ads are more effective than nonhumorous ads *only when consumers' evaluations of the advertised brand are already positive.* When prior evaluations are negative toward the advertised brand, humorous ads have been shown to be less effective than nonhumorous ads.[39] This finding has a counterpart in interpersonal relations: when you like someone, you are more likely to consider his or her attempt at humor to be funny than if you do not like that person. Finally, it also has been found that individuals who have a higher *need for humor* (i.e., the tendency to seek out amusement, wit, and nonsense) are more responsive to humorous ads than are those with a lower need on this personality trait.[40]

In sum, humor in advertising can be an extremely effective device for accomplishing a variety of marketing communications objectives. Nonetheless, advertisers should *proceed cautiously* when contemplating the use of humor. First, the effects of humor can differ due to differences in audience characteristics—what strikes some people as humorous is not at all funny to others.[41] Second, the definition of what is funny in one country or region of a country is not necessarily the same in another. Finally, a humorous message may be so distracting to an audience that receivers ignore the message content. There is indeed a fine line in advertising between entertaining (via humor) and providing information sufficient to influence attitudes and behavior. Thus, advertisers should carefully research their intended market segments before venturing into humorous advertising. Please read the *IMC Focus* for a discussion of how the Holiday Inn ad with slacker Mark (discussed in the previous chapter) was created.

Appeals to Consumer Fears

The chapter earlier discussed that marketing communicators employ a variety of techniques to enhance consumers' information-processing motivation, opportunity, or ability. As would be expected, the appeal to fear is especially effective as a means of enhancing motivation. The unfortunate fact is that consumers in the 21st century live in a world where the threat of terrorism is ever present, natural disasters occur occasionally such as the horrific tsunami in countries surrounding the Indian Ocean, and crime and health-related problems abound. It is estimated that nearly 15 million Americans suffer from irrational fears and that anxiety disorders afflict approximately 13 percent of adults.[42]

Advertisers, realizing that people have fears, rational as well as irrational, attempt to motivate consumers to process information and to take action by appealing to their fears. Appeals to fears in advertising identify the negative consequences of either: (1) *not using the advertised brand* or (2) *engaging in unsafe behavior* (such as drinking and driving, smoking, using drugs, eating unhealthy foods, driving without seat belts, and engaging in unprotected sex).[43]

Fear-Appeal Logic

The underlying logic is that appeals to consumer fears will stimulate audience involvement with a message and thereby promote acceptance of the message arguments. The appeal to consumer fears may take the form of *social disapproval* or *physical danger.* For example, mouthwashes, deodorants, toothpastes, and other products appeal to fears when emphasizing the social disapproval we may suffer if our breath is not fresh, our underarms are not dry, or our teeth are not cavity free. Smoke detectors, automobile tires, unsafe sex, driving under the influence of alcohol and other drugs, and being uninsured are a sampling of products and themes used by advertisers to induce fear of physical danger or impending problems. Health-care ads frequently appeal to fears, and advertising agencies justify the use of these appeals with logic such as, "Sometimes you have to scare people to save their lives."[44]

Appropriate Intensity

Aside from the basic ethical issue of whether fear should be used at all, the fundamental issue for advertisers is determining *how intense* the threat should be. Should the advertiser employ a slight threat merely to get the consumer's attention, or should a heavy threat be used so the consumer cannot possibly miss the point the advertiser wishes to make? Although numerous studies have been performed, the fact remains that there still is no consensus on what threat intensity is optimal. There is, however, some consistency in the demonstration that the more an audience experiences fear from an advertised threat, the more likely it is that they will be persuaded to take the recommended action.[45]

Selection of the "Mark" Character in Holiday Inn's Campaign

imc focus

You will recall the Holiday Inn advertising campaign described in the previous chapter, which was presented as an exemplar of clever and creative advertising. That campaign featured various executions of an ensemble of a mom, dad, grandma, and quintessential slacker Mark, who in his late 30s still lives with his family rather than being out on his own gainfully employed. In various executions Mark is portrayed imposing various demands on the family—for amenities such as more space, the family TV, and computer data ports. The coup de grace in every execution is a family member exclaiming, "What do you think this is, a Holiday Inn?"

To those of us who possess no acting ability or cinematic expertise, the Holiday Inn advertisements may appear to be simple little productions. However, as with creating a great movie, the secret is in having a good script *and* proper casting. The casting of Mark was key to the success of the Holiday Inn campaign. The potential for a successful ad campaign came first from the key phrase, "What do you think this is, a Holiday Inn?" The idea for using this phrase originated with the ad agency's copywriter and art director, who had heard the phrase as kids from their own parents when failing to pick up clothes or toys. Once they had this phrase as the campaign centerpiece, they decided that an ensemble cast with a mom, dad, grandma, and slacker Mark would be the constant from one commercial execution to the next.

Casting Mark became an incredible challenge. One candidate after another was rejected because he just didn't seem right for the role. In fact, after many casting failures, there was some question as to whether the concept could be pulled off successfully. Near the point of moving on to another campaign idea, the ad agency's director recalled a guy he had filmed in New Orleans, a downcast street clown named Ross Brockley. After pursuing Brockley, the agency learned that he had given up his stand-up comedy gig and moved back to his native Nebraska. After several phone conversations, the ad agency (Fallon McElligott) was able to convince Ross to consider playing Mark in the Holiday Inn ads. The rest is history: Ross Brockley was offered and accepted the role of Mark and will undoubtedly become one of the comedic legends in advertising lore. His semiconfused mannerisms, slow speech pattern, and he-just-doesn't-get-it demeanor are absolutely perfect for the role of Mark. It is difficult to imagine any other actor who would have been more perfect for this role.

Some readers may recall seeing Brockley more recently in the TV series, *Pilot Season.* Brockley played the character, Russ Chockley, who was cast as a reclusive actor-turned-farmer

Source: Adapted from Paula Champa, "Wake-Up Calls," *Agency* (fall 2001), 6–7. © 2001.

In general, it appears that the degree of threat intensity that is effective in evoking fear in an audience depends in large part on *how much relevance* a topic has for an audience—the greater the relevance, the lower the threat intensity that is needed to activate a response. In other words, people who are highly involved in a topic can be motivated by a relatively "light" appeal to fear, whereas a more intense level of threat is required to motivate uninvolved people.[46]

To illustrate the relation between threat intensity and issue relevance, let us compare a low-threat campaign for Michelin tires with the much more intense appeal of campaigns designed to discourage drinking and driving. A long-standing Michelin advertising campaign contained a series of television commercials that showed adorable babies sitting on or surrounded by tires. These commercials were subtle reminders (low levels of threat) for parents to consider buying Michelin tires to ensure their children's safety. A low level of threat is all that is needed in this situation to evoke fear, because safety for their children is the most relevant concern for most parents.

Consider, by comparison, the level of threat needed to reach high school students and other young people who are the target of public service announcements that attempt to discourage drinking and driving. The last thing many young people want to hear is what they should or should not be doing. Hence, although safety is relevant to most everyone, it is less relevant to young people who consider themselves invulnerable. Consequently, very intense appeals to fear are needed to impress on high schoolers the risk in which they place themselves and their friends when drinking and driving.[47]

The Related Case of Appeals to Scarcity

Advertisers and other persuasion agents appeal to scarcity when emphasizing in their messages that things become more desirable when they are in great demand but short supply.[48] Simply put, an item that is rare or becoming rare is more valued. Salespeople and advertisers use this tactic when encouraging people to buy immediately with appeals such as "Only a few are left," "We won't have any more in stock by the end of the day," and "They're really selling fast."

The theory of **psychological reactance** helps explain why scarcity works.[49] This theory suggests that people react against any efforts to reduce their freedom or choices. Removed or threatened freedom and choices are perceived as even more desirable than previously. Thus, when products are made to seem less available, they become more valuable in the consumer's mind. Of course, appeals to scarcity are not always effective. But if the persuader is credible and legitimate, then an appeal may be effective if it activates a response such as "Not many of this product remain, so I'd better buy now and pay whatever it takes to acquire it."

Perhaps nowhere in the world is scarcity more used as an influence tactic than in Singapore. In the Hokkien dialect of Chinese, the word *kiasu* means the "fear of losing out." Singaporeans, according to a lecturer in the philosophy department at National University, will take whatever they can secure, even if they are not sure they really want it.[50] Many Singaporeans apparently share a herd mentality—no one wants to be different. Marketers, needless to say, have exploited this cultural characteristic to sell all types of products. For example, a Singapore automobile dealership announced that it was moving its location and offered for sale 250 limited-edition BMW 316i models, priced at $78,125 for a manual transmission and $83,125 for an automatic. All 250 models were sold within four days, and the dealer was forced to order another 100, which were quickly sold even though delivery was unavailable for months.

The *kiasu* mentality makes Singaporeans virtually "sitting ducks" for users of the scarcity tactic. However, Singaporean consumers, like consumers everywhere, are only susceptible to such a persuasion tactic in those situations in which there is in fact scarcity. Consumers otherwise would become skeptical of such transparent attempts to mislead them and reject such blatant efforts to sell products by using deceit.

Appeals to Consumer Guilt

Like appeals to fear, appeals to guilt attempt to trigger negative emotions. People feel guilty when they break rules, violate their own standards or beliefs, or behave irresponsibly.[51] Appeals to guilt are powerful because they motivate emotionally mature individuals to undertake responsible action leading to a reduction in the level of guilt. Advertisers and other marketing communicators appeal to guilt and attempt to persuade prospective customers by asserting or implying that feelings of guilt can be relieved by using the promoted product.[52] An analysis of a broad spectrum of magazines revealed that about one 1 of 20 ads contains an appeal to guilt.[53] Consider, for example, the magazine advertisement for Veterinary Pet Insurance (Figure 11.12), a company that markets insurance for the coverage of unexpected pet accidents or illness. The headline surrounding the photo of the rather sad-looking dog puts the pet owner on a guilt trip of sorts when stating, "She'll never know you can't afford the treatment. But you will." This advertisement represents an appeal to anticipatory guilt. That is, the ad attempts to induce a sense of guilt in the reader by suggesting that one would have failed to take proper care of his or her pet if he or she were unable to pay for veterinary treatment.

Evidence, albeit limited, suggests that appeals to guilt are ineffective if advertisements containing guilt appeals *lack credibility* or advertisers are perceived as having *manipulative intentions.* When ads are perceived as lacking credibility or attempting to manipulate the receiver, feelings of guilt are mitigated rather than increased.[54] Thus, appeals to guilt when the advertising is perceived as lacking in credibility or being manipulative have little opportunity to positively influence beliefs, attitudes, or message-relevant behaviors. As stated at the beginning of the chapter, it is important for the student to realize the "it depends" nature of advertising. In this case, whether ads appealing to guilt are effective depends in large part on perceived ad credibility and manipulative intent.

Advertisement Provided Courtesy of Veterinary Pet Insurance Co./DVM Insurance Agency

Figure 11.12

An Appeal to Guilt

The Use of Sex in Advertising

Whereas the previous two sets of advertising appeals—to fear and guilt—are fundamentally negative (i.e., people generally avoid these two emotions), the use of sex in advertising appeals to something that people generally approach rather than avoid. Sex appeals in advertising are used frequently and with increasing explicitness. Products such as soft drinks, alcoholic beverages, cosmetics, automobiles, and many others use sex appeals in hopes of drawing attention to advertisements and making their sales pitch.

Whereas the use of such explicit sex was unthinkable not many years ago, it now represents part of the advertising landscape.[55] The trend is not restricted to the United States; indeed, sexual explicitness is more prevalent and more overt elsewhere—for example, in Brazil and certain European countries.

What Role Does Sex Play in Advertising?

Actually, it has several potential roles.[56] First, sexual material in advertising acts to attract and hold attention for a longer period, often by featuring attractive models in provocative poses.[57] This is called the *stopping-power role* of sex.[58] An advertising campaign for Three Olives vodka typifies this role. Each execution in this campaign portrays an attractive, seductively posed female model in a huge martini glass. Placed conspicuously beside the model-filled martini glass is a rhetorical question (recall the earlier discussion of rhetorical questions in the context of MOA factors): "What's in your martini?" There is clear double entendre contained in this question, on the one hand suggesting that Three Olives should be the vodka in your glass, and, on the other, intimating that by drinking Three Olives one is likely to attract beautiful women.

A second potential role is to *enhance recall* of message points. Research suggests, however, that sexual content or symbolism will enhance recall only if it is appropriate to the product category and the creative advertising execution.[59] Sexual appeals produce significantly better recall when the advertising execution has an appropriate relationship with the advertised product.[60]

A third role performed by sexual content in advertising is to *evoke emotional responses*, such as feelings of arousal and even lust.[61] These reactions can increase an ad's persuasive impact, with the opposite occurring if the ad elicits negative feelings such as disgust, embarrassment, or uneasiness.[62] The advertisement for the Three Olives brand of vodka described previously probably was designed to arouse feelings in the target audience of predominantly young and middle-aged men. The appeal to lust is typified by a Diet Coke television commercial that was aired in the 1990s in which a group of voyeuristic women is shown watching with palpable pleasure from their office building a sexy worker at a nearby construction site taking off his shirt and then opening a Diet Coke.

Whether sexual content elicits a positive or negative reaction depends on the *relevance* of the sexual content to the advertised subject matter. An interesting marketing experiment tested this by varying magazine ads for two products, a ratchet wrench set (a product for which sexual appeal is irrelevant) and a body oil (a relevant sex-appeal product). The study also manipulated three versions of dress for the female model who appeared in the ads: in the *demure* model version, she was shown fully clothed in a blouse and slacks; in the *seductive* model version, she wore the same clothing as in the demure version, but the blouse was completely unbuttoned and knotted at the bottom, exposing some midriff and cleavage; and in the *nude* model version, she was completely undressed. Study findings revealed that the seductive model and body oil combination was perceived most favorably by all respondents. Females regarded the nude model and ratchet set as least appealing.[63] This study was conducted over two decades ago, and it is uncertain whether the same findings would be obtained in the sexually more explicit society in which we now live.

Sexual content stands little chance of being effective unless it is directly relevant to an advertisement's primary selling point. When used appropriately, however, sexual content is capable of eliciting attention, enhancing recall, and creating a favorable association with the advertised product.

The Potential Downside of Sex Appeals in Advertising

The presentation to this point has indicated that when used appropriately, sex appeals in advertising can be effective. The discussion would be incomplete, however, without mentioning the potential hazards of using sex appeals. There is evidence to suggest that the use of explicit sexual illustrations in advertisements may interfere with consumers' processing of message arguments and reduce message comprehension.[64] Moreover, many people are offended by advertisements that portray women (and men) as brainless sex objects. For example, an outcry ensued in response to an advertisement for Old Milwaukee beer featuring the so-called Swedish Bikini Team—a boat full of beautiful Scandinavian-looking women wearing blue bikinis who appeared out of nowhere in front of a group of fishermen. Female employees of Stroh Brewery Company, the makers of Old Milwaukee, sued their employer, claiming that the advertisement created an atmosphere conducive to sexual harassment in the workplace.[65] Regardless of the merits of this particular case, the general point is that sex in advertising can be demeaning to females (and males) and, for this reason, should be used cautiously.

A TV advertisement for Miller Lite beer (dubbed "Catfight") perhaps typifies the questionable use of sexual content in advertising. (This ad was previously discussed in the *IMC Focus* in Chapter 6.) The ad, which was created by the Ogilvy & Mather advertising agency, aired on many occasions during NFL games in the 2002–2003 football season. You may recall seeing the ad, which portrayed two attractive and bosomy women literally ripping each other's clothes off in a swimming pool and later in wet cement as they supposedly fought over whether Miller Lite beer was the beer of choice because it was "better tasting" than other light beers or because it was "less filling." This ad doubtlessly caught the attention of millions of men (and women) who view NFL football, and perhaps aroused emotions and aided brand name recall. Whether or not the ad achieved positive objectives for the makers of Miller Lite, it raises distinct ethical issues about advertising propriety.

The fact remains that many people—men as well as women—are offended by advertisements that portray women (and men) as brainless sex objects. The use of sex in advertising is a matter of concern to people and advertising regulators throughout the world.[66] Sex in advertising can be demeaning to females (and males) and, for this reason, should be used cautiously. Three categories of indecency include advertisements that are sexist or sexy, or that sexually objectify their models. *Sexist ads* are those that demean one sex in comparison with the other, particularly through sex-role stereotyping (e.g., portraying women as "dumb blondes"); *sexy ads* use sexual imagery or suggestiveness; and *sexual objectification* occurs when ads use women (or men, as in the Diet Coke ad mentioned previously) as decorative or attention-getting objects with little or no relevance to the product category. It would seem that the Miller Lite "Catfight" commercial is guilty of sexual objectification.

Another example of sexual objectification was an advertisement for Wolverine boots (not shown here). This ad, which was directed at men, revealed a sultry female wearing only the skimpiest of a bikini bottom as she rested in the sand on her knees against an ocean backdrop. She wore no bikini top, but instead had a pair of Wolverine boots draped over her shoulders by their tied-together strings to strategically cover her breasts. Immediately under the boots was the key ad claim (the *leverage point* in MECCAS terminology from the prior chapter): "The Only Time You'll Want to Take Our Boots Off." This statement, which represents an indirect assertion that Wolverine boots are extremely comfortable and implies that male magazine readers would like to see the model bare breasted, is open to critical challenge on the grounds that the same point could be effectively made in many ways without resorting to the objectification of women. On the other hand, many men—the target audience—likely may react favorably to this ad and regard it as appropriate and inoffensive. Obviously, all parties to advertising do not share equivalent views on what is proper.

The Gillette Company

Figure 11.13

An Appropriate Use of Partial Nudity in Advertising

In concluding this section, it should be noted that "showing skin" in advertisements does not necessarily equate with being sexist or sexually objectifying men or women. For example, the ad for Gillette's Satin Care Spicy Green Tea Shave Gel (Figure 11.13) represents an appealing, attention-getting portrayal of a woman in a context that is appropriate to the advertised brand.

Subliminal Messages and Symbolic Embeds

The word *subliminal* refers to the presentation of stimuli at a rate or level that is below the conscious threshold of awareness. One example is self-help audiotapes (such as tapes to help one quit smoking) that play messages at a decibel level indecipherable to the naked ear. Stimuli that cannot be perceived by the conscious senses may nonetheless be perceived subconsciously. This possibility has generated considerable concern from advertising critics and has fostered much speculation from researchers. The reason for the concern is clear: surveys have shown that a large percentage of American people believe that subliminal methods are used by advertisers.[67] Representatives of the advertising community, however, disavow the widespread use of subliminal advertising.[68]

The original outcry occurred nearly 50 years ago in response to a researcher who claimed to have increased the sales of Coca-Cola and popcorn in a New Jersey movie theater by using subliminal messages. At five-second intervals during the movie *Picnic,* subliminal messages saying "Drink Coca-Cola" and "Eat Popcorn" appeared on the screen for a mere 1/3,000 second. Although the naked eye could not possibly have seen these messages, the researcher, James Vicary, claimed that sales of Coca-Cola and popcorn increased 58 percent and 18 percent, respectively.[69] Though Vicary's research is scientifically meaningless because he failed to use proper experimental procedures, the study nonetheless raised public concerns about subliminal advertising and led to congressional hearings.[70] Federal legislation was never enacted, but since then subliminal advertising has been the subject of concern by advertising critics, a matter of embarrassment for advertising practitioners, and an issue of theoretical curiosity to advertising scholars.[71]

The fires of controversy were fueled again in the 1970s and 80s with the publication of three provocatively titled books: *Subliminal Seduction, Media Sexploitation,* and *The Clam Plate Orgy.*[72] The author of these books, Wilson Key, claimed subliminal advertising techniques are used extensively and have the power to influence consumers' choice behaviors.

A Cautious Challenge

Many advertising practitioners and marcom scholars discount Key's arguments and vehemently disagree with his conclusions. Part of the difficulty in arriving at clear answers as to who's right and who's wrong stems from the fact that commentators differ in what they mean by subliminal advertising. In fact, there are three distinct forms of subliminal stimulation. A first form presents *visual stimuli* at a very rapid rate by means of a device called a *tachistoscope* (say, at 1/3,000 second as in Vicary's research). A second form uses *accelerated speech* in auditory messages. The third form involves the *embedding of hidden symbols* (such as sexual images or words) in print advertisements.[73]

This last form, *embedding,* is what Key has written about and is the form that advertising researchers have studied. However, it is important to remember that embeds (for example, the word *sex* airbrushed into an advertisement) are not truly subliminal since they are visible to the naked eye. Nonetheless, the remaining discussion of subliminal messages is restricted to the practice of embedding.

To better appreciate embedding, consider an advertisement for Edge shaving gel that ran in magazines a number of years ago. This ad featured a picture of a lathered-up man with a look of near ecstasy on his face and a prominent shot of the Edge shaving gel can grasped in his fingertips. Below his lips was a scene of a nude woman on her back with knees raised, a portrayal of an attractive blond woman's face, and a scene of a sexy male on a surfboard surfing through a water tunnel. Aside from the Freudian symbolism associated with the water tunnel and the look of ecstasy on the man's face, the ad also included three vague nude figures airbrushed into the shaving lather above the man's lip.

Are embedded symbols in advertisements effective? To answer this we first need to examine the process that would have to operate for embedding to influence consumer choice behavior. The Edge shaving gel advertisement provides a useful vehicle for motivating this discussion. The first step in the process requires that the consumer consciously or subconsciously process the embedded symbol (the nude figures in the Edge magazine ad). Second, as the result of processing the cue, the consumer would have to develop a greater desire for Edge shaving gel than he had before seeing the ad. Third, because advertising is done at the brand level and because advertisers are interested in selling their brands and not just any brand in the product category, effective symbolic embedding would require that consumers develop a desire for the specific brand, Edge in this case, rather than just any brand in the category. Finally, the consumer would need to transfer the desire for the advertised brand into actual purchase behavior.

Is there evidence to support this chain of events? Despite a few limited studies on the issue, there are a variety of practical problems that *probably prevent embedding from being effective in a realistic marketing context.*[74] Perhaps the major reason why embedding in advertising has little effect is because the images have to be concealed to preclude detection by consumers. Many consumers would resent such tricky advertising efforts if they knew they existed. Thus, precluding detection from consumers means that embedding is a relatively weak technique compared with more vivid advertising representations. Because the majority of consumers devote relatively little time and effort in processing advertisements, a weak stimulus means that most consumers would not be influenced much.[75]

Even if consumers did attend to and encode sexual embeds under natural advertising conditions, there remains serious doubt that this information would have sufficient impact to affect product or brand choice behavior. Standard (supraliminal) advertising information itself has a difficult time influencing consumers. Would subliminal information be any more effective? For example, would men choose Edge shaving gel just because they consciously or subconsciously spotted a nude woman in the advertisement for that product? Unfortunately, positions are mixed on this issue. Let's briefly examine a perspective arguing why subliminal advertising cannot work, and then consider the alternative possibility that under select conditions it might influence purchase behavior.

A Dissenting Perspective

This perspective argues that subliminal advertising is ineffective due to the use of weak stimuli, such as subtle embeds or barely audible sounds. The following quote sums up this viewpoint. Please note that the quote acknowledges subliminal perception *is* a bona fide phenomenon (i.e., extensive research has demonstrated that people are capable of perceiving stimuli in the absence of conscious awareness of those stimuli), but the weak effects of subliminal stimuli are nullified under actual market circumstances where, for example, many brands compete for the consumer's attention at the point of purchase.

A century of psychological research substantiates the general principle that more intense stimuli have a greater influence on people's behavior than weaker ones. While subliminal perception is a bona fide phenomenon, the effects obtained are subtle and obtaining them typically requires a carefully structured context. Subliminal stimuli are usually so weak that the recipient is not just unaware of the stimulus but is also oblivious to the fact that he/she is being stimulated. As a result, the potential effects of subliminal stimuli are easily nullified by other ongoing stimulation in the same sensory channel or by attention being focused on another modality. These factors pose serious difficulties for any possible marketing application.[76]

The Possibility That Subliminal Stimuli May Influence Brand Choice

As discussed back in Chapter 3 in the context of advertising ethics, there is growing evidence that much human behavior is not under conscious control but rather occurs virtually automatically (without cognitive intervention). Communicators can, for example, activate—or prime—subconscious thoughts in people using subtle techniques and subliminal messages. For subconscious priming to be effective, the primed topic must be compatible with the individual's current need states. In other words, one cannot be subliminally induced to act in a certain way unless he or she has a need to act in that way.[77] Moreover, a primed need does not remain an active driver of judgments and behavior over the long run, but is limited in its length of influence. Hence, an advertiser may subliminally activate a certain thought or feeling relating to a brand, but the consumer would not act on that thought or feeling if he or she is not presently in the market to purchase a product that relates to it. In general, it would be expected that mass-media advertising would have little effectiveness in this regard given that exposure to ads and purchase decisions typically are separated in time. However, as noted in Chapter 3, point-of-purchase advertising (e.g., in-store radio programming) may provide an opportune (albeit unethical) medium for subliminally priming consumers into purchasing products and brands.

The Functions of Music in Advertising

Music has been an important component of the advertising landscape virtually since the beginning of recorded sound. Jingles, background music, popular tunes, and classical arrangements are used to attract attention, convey selling points, set an emotional tone for an advertisement, and influence listeners' moods. Well-known entertainers, nonvocal musical accompaniment, and unknown vocalists are used extensively in promoting everything from fabric softeners to automobiles. A Celine Dion song, "I Drove All Night," was featured in a series of Chrysler commercials. Famous rocker Bob Dylan's "Love Sick" was introduced in commercials for Victoria's Secret. Chevrolet launched a major advertising campaign around songs that cited Chevy or Chevy products, including tunes from the Beach Boys ("409"), Don McLean ("American Pie"), Elton John ("Crocodile Rock"), and Prince ("Little Red Corvette").[78]

Many advertising practitioners and scholars think that music performs a variety of useful communications functions. These include *attracting attention,* putting consumers in a *positive mood,* making them *more receptive to message arguments,* and even *communicating meanings* about advertised products.[79] Consider, for example, the use of music in a famous Pepsi advertisement. The antics of a Coke delivery man in a supermarket are captured by a security camera. While the famous Hank Williams song, "Your Cheatin' Heart," plays in the background, the deliveryman approaches a Pepsi cooler that is adjacent to his own Coca-Cola cooler. The delivery man is shown sneaking a look at the Pepsi cooler, opening it, and then removing a can of Pepsi—at which time dozens of Pepsi cans cascade to the floor with a huge noise that catches the attention of shoppers, much to the deliveryman's chagrin. This classic advertisement is an outstanding attention getter that subtly conveys the message that perhaps Pepsi *is* better than Coke. The ad would not have been nearly as effective without the music, "Your Cheatin' Heart," being played in the background.

Music's role in advertising has received relatively little formal inquiry from marketing academics.[80] However, brief review of one study demonstrates the potential influence that music can have.[81] Using classical conditioning procedures, music represented the unconditioned stimulus in an effort to influence experimental subjects' preference for a ballpoint pen, which represented the conditioned stimulus. An *unconditioned stimulus* (US) is one that evokes pleasant feelings or thoughts in people. A *conditioned stimulus* (CS) is one that is emotionally or cognitively neutral prior to the onset of a conditioning experiment. In simple terms, classical conditioning is achieved when the pairing of US and CS results in a transfer of feeling from the US (music in the present case) to the CS (the ballpoint pen).

Experimental subjects in this study were informed that an advertising agency was trying to select music for use in a commercial for a ballpoint pen. Subjects then listened to music while they viewed slides of the pen. The positive US for half the subjects was music from the movie *Grease,* and the negative US for the remaining subjects was classical Asian Indian music. The simple association between the music and the pen influenced product preference—nearly 80 percent of the subjects exposed to the *Grease* music chose the advertised pen, whereas only 30 percent of the subjects exposed to the Asian Indian music chose the advertised pen.[82]

The Role of Comparative Advertising

As alluded to in the *Marcom Challenge,* the practice in which advertisers *directly* or *indirectly* compare their products against competitive offerings, typically claiming that the promoted item is superior in one or several important purchase considerations, is called **comparative advertising**. Comparative ads vary both with regard to the explicitness of the comparisons and with respect to whether the target of the comparison is named or referred to in general terms.[83]

Salespeople have always used comparative messages in arguing the advantages of their products over competitors'. Likewise, print advertisers (i.e., newspapers and magazines) have used comparative claims for decades. It was not until the early 1970s, however, that television commercials in the United States began making direct-comparison claims. Since then all media have experienced notable increases in the use of comparative advertising. In some countries (e.g., Belgium, Hong Kong, and Korea) it is illegal to use comparative advertising; and with the exception of the United States and Great Britain, advertising comparisons are used infrequently in those countries where this form of advertising is legal.[84]

To better appreciate comparative advertising, it will be useful to examine a couple of examples. The ad in Figure 11.14 for Clorox Clean-Up compares itself *directly* against competitor Mr. Clean. Using an interesting graphic, the ad indicates that Clorox Clean-Up can remove tough stains such as wine spills, whereas Mr. Clean cannot. Consider now the *indirect* comparison advertisement for Allegra in Figure 11.15. Without mentioning any competitive brands, this ad shows graphically and comments that a dose of Allegra "lasts up to 4 times longer than one dose of most OTC [over-the-counter] allergy medicines."

Figure 11.14

Illustration of a Direct Comparison Advertisement

Is Comparative Advertising More Effective?

In deciding whether to use a comparative advertisement rather than a more conventional noncomparative format, an advertiser must confront questions such as the following:[85]

- How do comparative and noncomparative advertisements match up in terms of impact on brand awareness, consumer comprehension of ad claims, and credibility?
- Do comparative and noncomparative ads differ with regard to effects on brand preferences, buying intentions, and purchase behavior?
- How do factors such as consumer brand preference and the advertiser's competitive position influence the effectiveness of comparative advertising?
- Under what specific circumstances should an advertiser use comparative advertising?

Researchers have performed numerous studies that have examined the processes by which comparative advertising operates, the results it produces, and how its effects contrast with those from noncomparative ads.[86] Findings are at times inconclusive and even contradictory. Lack of definitive results is to be expected, however, because advertising is a complex phenomenon that varies from situation to situation in terms of executional elements, audience demographics, media characteristics, and other factors. However, a major review of research that has tested comparative versus noncomparative advertising suggests the following tentative conclusions:[87]

- Comparative advertising is better at enhancing brand name recall.
- Comparative advertising promotes better recall of message arguments.

Figure 11.15

Illustration of an Indirect Comparison Advertisement

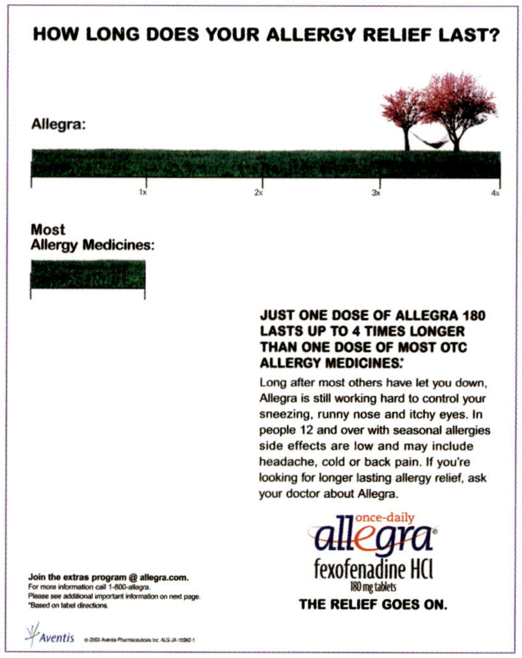

- Comparative advertising is perceived, however, as somewhat less believable than noncomparative advertising.
- Comparative advertising is responsible for generating more favorable attitudes toward the sponsoring brand, especially when the brand is a new (versus established) brand.
- Comparative advertising generates stronger intentions to purchase the sponsored brand.
- Comparative advertising generates more purchases.

It is obvious from this list that a variety of advantages accrue to the use of comparative versus noncomparative advertising. However, as is always the case, one form of advertising is *not* universally superior to another under all circumstances. The following section identifies some specific issues that should be considered when deciding whether to use a comparative advertisement.

Considerations Dictating the Use of Comparative Advertising

Situational Factors

Characteristics of the audience, media, message, company, and product all play important roles in determining whether comparative advertising will be more effective than noncomparative advertising. For example, comparative advertisements seem to be evaluated less favorably by people holding a prior preference for the comparison brand (the brand that the advertised brand is compared against) than by those without a prior preference for that brand.

Distinct Advantages

Comparative advertising is particularly effective for promoting *brands that possess distinct advantages* relative to competitive brands.[88] When a brand has a distinct advantage over competitive brands, comparative advertising provides a powerful method to convey this advantage. The advertisement for Clorox Clean-Up (Figure 11.14) typifies this situation. Relative to noncomparative advertising, comparative advertising has also been shown to increase the perceived similarity between a challenger brand in a product category and the category leader.[89]

The Credibility Issue

The effectiveness of comparative advertising increases when comparative claims are made to appear *more credible.* There are various ways to accomplish this: (1) have an independent research organization support the superiority claims, (2) present impressive test results to back up the claims, and (3) use a trusted endorser as the spokesperson.

Assessing Effectiveness

Because comparative advertisements make claims for an advertised brand relative to another brand and because consumers encode this comparative information in a relative fashion, *measurement techniques* in assessing the effectiveness of comparative advertising are most sensitive when questions are worded in a relative fashion. This is, for maximal sensitivity, the question context, or wording, should match the consumer's encoding mind-set. For example, with reference to the Allegra advertisement (Figure 11.15), there are two alternative questions that could be framed to ascertain whether consumers perceive Allegra as an effective brand in treating seasonal allergies: (1) How likely is it that the effects of Allegra are long lasting? (*nonrelative* framing) or (2) How likely is it that Allegra is longer lasting than most other over-the-counter allergy medicines? (*relative* framing). Research has shown that relative framing does a better job of assessing consumers' beliefs after their exposure to comparative advertisements.[90]

Summary

This chapter discusses three general topics. The first major section focused on methods used by advertisers to enhance an audience's motivation, opportunity, and ability to process ad messages. This section included descriptions and illustrations of advertising efforts to heighten consumers' motivation to attend to and process messages, measures to augment consumers' opportunity to encode information and reduce processing time, and techniques used to increase consumers' ability to access knowledge structures and create new structures.

The second major section dealt with the role of endorsers in advertising. The TEARS model (*t*rustworthiness, *e*xpertise, physical *a*ttractiveness, *r*espect, and *s*imilarity) provided a convenient acronym for thinking about the endorser attributes that play major roles in determining their effectiveness. The following factors appear to be the most important ones used by brand managers in actually selecting celebrity endorsers: (1) celebrity and audience matchup, (2) celebrity and brand matchup, (3) celebrity credibility, (4) celebrity attractiveness, (5) cost considerations, (6) a working ease or difficulty factor, (7) an endorsement saturation factor, and (8) a likelihood-of-getting-into-trouble factor. Discussion of celebrity and typical-person endorsers indicates that endorsers have an influence on consumers via the attributes of credibility and attractiveness. Credibility functions via the process of internalization, whereas attractiveness operates through an identification mechanism.

Finally several sections were devoted to a variety of message appeals in advertising. Widely used advertising techniques discussed in this chapter include humor, appeals to fear, appeals to guilt, sex appeals, subliminal messages, the use of music, and comparative advertisements. Discussion covers empirical research and indicates the factors involved in selecting each of these message elements.

Discussion Questions

1. Using the concepts of attractiveness, expertise, and trustworthiness, explain what makes Tiger Woods an effective (and extremely well paid!) endorser. Do the same for Maria Sharapova.
2. Presented early in the chapter was a quote from philosopher Alfred North Whitehead stating, "Seek simplicity and distrust it." What does this quote mean in terms of the effectiveness of particular advertising appeals, such as the use of humor?
3. Locate examples of magazine advertisements that illustrate each of the following: (a) an effort to increase consumers' motivation to process brand information, and (b) an attempt to enhance consumers' opportunity to encode information. Justify why your chosen examples are good illustrations.

4. Locate two advertisements that illustrate exemplar-based learning, and provide explanations as to how the chosen advertisements facilitate exemplar-based learning.
5. Attractiveness as an attribute of endorsers includes but is not restricted to physical attractiveness. Many would regard British soccer star David Beckham (*Bend It Like Beckham*) as attractive. In what ways other than physical attractiveness might he be considered attractive?
6. Considering the likelihood-of-getting-into-trouble factor, identify three entertainment or sports celebrities that you, as a brand manager, would be reluctant to have endorse your brand for fear they would get into some sort of trouble.
7. Comedian and TV actor Bill Cosby for many years endorsed Jell-O pudding. Suppose you were brand manager for Jell-O and tasked with coming up with a replacement for Mr. Cosby. Who would you select? Justify the rationale behind your choice.
8. Infomercials are long commercials that generally last from 30 to 60 minutes. These commercials typically are aired during fringe times and frequently promote products such as diet aids, balding cures, and exercise products. These infomercials often use endorsements from physicians and other health professionals to buttress claims about the promoted brand's efficacy. Using concepts from this chapter, explain why health professionals are used in this form of advertising.
9. You have probably seen a number of public service announcements along the lines of those described in the fear appeals section to discourage drinking and driving. In your opinion, is this form of advertising effective in altering the behavior of people your age? Be specific in justifying your answer.
10. The fear of getting AIDS should be relevant to many college students. Accordingly, would you agree that a relatively weak fear appeal should suffice in influencing students to either abstain from sexual relations or practice safe sex? If you disagree, then how can you reconcile your disagreement with the degree-of-relevance explanation?
11. Identify three or four products for which you feel appeals to guilt might be a viable approach to persuading consumer acceptance of a brand. What kinds of products do not lend themselves to such appeals? Explain why you feel these products would be inappropriate.
12. Consumers occasionally find television commercials to be humorous and enjoyable. Some advertising pundits claim that such commercials may capture attention but are frequently ineffective in selling products. What is your viewpoint on this issue? Justify your position.
13. Identify two or three television commercials that you consider humorous. Is the use of humor appropriate for the brands advertised in these commercials and given their likely target audiences? Justify your responses.
14. Identify several TV commercials or magazine ads that use sex appeals. Describe each advertisement and then explain whether an appeal to sex is appropriate or inappropriate for the brand.
15. Too much sex is used in advertising. Comment.
16. The article titled "Understanding Jingles and Needledrop: A Rhetorical Approach to Music in Advertising" (see endnote 79) suggests that music in commercials communicates specific meanings to listeners and viewers. In other words, music "speaks" to people by conveying a sense of speed, excitement, sadness, nostalgia, and so on. Identify two commercials in which music communicates a specific emotion or other state or action to consumers, and identify this emotion, state, or action.
17. Photocopy one or two examples of comparative advertisements from magazines. Analyze each ad in terms of why you think the advertiser used a comparative-advertising format and whether you think the advertisement is effective. Justify your position.

ENDNOTES

1. Sales and chain-size statistics for both McDonald's and Subway are from Zack Gonzales, Hoover's Online (http://www.hoovers.com) as of January 5, 2005. Accessed January 5, 2005.
2. This quote is attributable to British mathematician and philosopher Alfred North Whitehead. The original source is unknown to this author.
3. Richard E. Petty and John T. Cacioppo, *Attitudes and Persuasion: Classic and Contemporary Approaches* (Dubuque, Iowa: Wm. C. Brown Company, 1981). See also Richard E. Petty, Rao H. Unnava, and Alan J. Strathman, "Theories of Attitude Change," in *Handbook of Consumer Behavior,* ed. T. S. Robertson and H. H. Kassarjian (Englewood Cliffs, N.J.: Prentice Hall, 1991), 241–280.
4. The ensuing discussion is based on the work of Deborah J. MacInnis, Christine Moorman, and Bernard J. Jaworski, "Enhancing and Measuring Consumers' Motivation, Opportunity, and Ability to Process Brand Information from Ads," *Journal of Marketing* 55 (October 1991), 32–53.
5. James R. Bettman, Mary Frances Luce, and John W. Payne, "Constructive Consumer Choice Processes," *Journal of Consumer Research* 25 (December 1998), 193; Daniel Kahneman, *Attention and Effort* (Englewood Cliffs, NJ: Prentice Hall, 1973).
6. Scott B. MacKenzie and Richard A. Spreng, "How Does Motivation Moderate the Impact of Central and Peripheral Processing on Brand Attitudes and Intentions?" *Journal of Consumer Research* 18 (March 1992), 519–529.
7. For reading on the role and effectiveness of rhetorical questions in advertising, see a series of articles by Edward F. McQuarrie and David Glen Mick: "Figures of Rhetoric in Advertising Language," *Journal of Consumer Research* 22 (March 1996), 424–438; "Visual Rhetoric in Advertising: Text Interpretive, Experimental and Reader Response Analyses," *Journal of Consumer Research* 26 (June 1999), 37–54; and "Visual and Verbal Rhetorical Figures under Directed Processing versus Incidental Exposure to Advertising," *Journal of Consumer Research* 29 (March 2003), 579–587. See also Rohini Ahluwalia and Robert E. Burnkrant, "Answering Questions about Questions: A Persuasion Knowledge Perspective for Understanding the Effects of Rhetorical Questions," *Journal of Consumer Research* 31 (June 2004), 26–42.
8. Erin White, "Found in Translation?" *Wall Street Journal Online,* September 20, 2004, http://online.wsj.com.
9. Jagdish Agrawal and Wagner A. Kamakura, "The Economic Worth of Celebrity Endorsers: An Event Study Analysis," *Journal of Marketing* 59 (July 1995), 56–62.
10. Therese A. Louie, Robert L. Kulik, and Robert Johnson, "When Bad Things Happen to the Endorsers of Good Products," *Marketing Letters* 12 (February 2001), 13–24.
11. "They're in the Money: The Fortunate 50," *Sports Illustrated,* May 17, 2004, 64–65.
12. Ibid.
13. Amanda Bower, "Highly Attractive Models in Advertising and the Women Who Loathe Them: The Implications of Negative Affect for Spokesperson Effectiveness," *Journal of Advertising* 30 (fall 2001), 51–64; Amanda Bower and Stacy Landreth, "Is Beauty Best? Highly Versus Normally Attractive Models in Advertising," *Journal of Advertising* 30 (spring 2001), 1–12.
14. David J. Moore and Richard Reardon, "Source Magnification: The Role of Multiple Sources in the Processing of Advertising Appeals," *Journal of Marketing Research* 24 (November 1987), 412–417.
15. It is important to note that although the present discussion is framed in terms of endorser characteristics, more general treatment of the topic refers to source characteristics. For a classic treatment of the subject, see Herbert C. Kelman, "Processes of Opinion Change," *Public Opinion Quarterly* 25 (spring 1961), 57–78. For a more current treatment, see Daniel J. O'Keefe, *Persuasion Theory and Research* (Newbury Park, Calif.: Sage, 1990), chap. 8.
16. Richard E. Petty, Thomas M. Ostrom, and Timothy C. Brock, eds., *Cognitive Responses in Persuasion* (Hillsdale, N.J.: Lawrence Erlbaum Associates, 1981), 143.
17. It has been demonstrated, however, that under select conditions, a less trustworthy, though expert, source may be more effective than an equally expert but more trustworthy source. This is because people tend to elaborate more on persuasive arguments presented by less (versus more) trustworthy sources and form attitudes that both are held more strongly and are relatively more resistant to change. See Joseph R. Priester and Richard E. Petty, "The Influence of Spokesperson Trustworthiness on Message Elaboration, Attitude Strength, and Advertising Effectiveness," *Journal of Consumer Psychology* 13, no. 4 (2003), 408–421.
18. Rohit Deshpande and Douglas Stayman, "A Tale of Two Cities: Distinctiveness Theory and Advertising Effectiveness," *Journal of Marketing Research* 31 (February 1994), 57–64.
19. For information about how to measure attractiveness, see Roobina Ohanian, "Construction and Validation of a Scale to Measure Celebrity Endorsers' Perceived Expertise, Trustworthiness, and Attractiveness," *Journal of Advertising* 19, no. 3 (1990), 39–52.
20. W. Benoy Joseph, "The Credibility of Physically Attractive Communicators: A Review," *Journal of Advertising* 11, no. 3 (1982), 15–24; Lynn R. Kahle and Pamela M. Homer, "Physical Attractiveness of the Celebrity Endorser: A Social Adaptation Perspective," *Journal of Consumer Research* 11 (March 1985), 954–961. However, empirical evidence is mixed as to whether an attractive endorser benefits a brand only when there is a good matchup between the endorser and the brand or whether, alternatively, attractive endorsers are more beneficial for a brand regardless of how well the endorser matches with the brand. For discussion, review the following two articles: Brian D. Till and Michael Busler, "The Match-Up Hypothesis: Physical Attractiveness, Expertise, and the Role of Fit on Brand Attitude, Purchase Intent and Brand Beliefs," *Journal of Advertising* 29 (fall 2000), 1–14; Michael A. Kamins, "An Investigation into the 'Match-Up' Hypothesis in Celebrity Advertising: When Beauty May Be Only Skin Deep," *Journal of Advertising* 19, no. 1 (1990), 4–13. See also John D. Mittelstaedt, Peter C. Riesz, and William J. Burns, "Why Are Endorsements Effective? Sorting Among Theories of Product and Endorser Effects," *Journal of Current Issues and Research in Advertising* 22 (spring 2000), 55–66.
21. Grant Wahl, "Big Bend," *Sports Illustrated,* June 23, 2003, 65.

22. Lawrence Feick and Robin A. Higie, "The Effects of Preference Heterogeneity and Source Characteristics on Ad Processing and Judgments about Endorsers," *Journal of Advertising* 21 (June 1992), 9–24.
23. Two studies have addressed this issue: B. Zafer Erdogan, Michael J. Baker, and Stephen Tagg, "Selecting Celebrity Endorsers: The Practitioner's Perspective," *Journal of Advertising Research* 41 (May/June 2001), 39–48; Alan R. Miciak and William L. Shanklin, "Choosing Celebrity Endorsers," *Marketing Management* 3 (winter 1994), 51–59.
24. Christine Bittar, "Cosmetic Changes Beyond Skin Deep," *Brandweek,* May 17, 2004, 20.
25. Carolyn Tripp, Thomas D. Jensen, and Les Carlson, "The Effects of Multiple Product Endorsements by Celebrities on Consumers' Attitudes and Intentions," *Journal of Consumer Research* 20 (March 1994), 535–547.
26. For example, see Therese A. Louie and Carl Obermiller, "Consumer Response to a Firm's Endorser (Dis)Association Decisions," *Journal of Advertising* 31 (winter 2002), 41–52; Louie, Kulik, and Johnson, "When Bad Things Happen"; and Brian D. Till and Terence A. Shimp, "Endorsers in Advertising: The Case of Negative Celebrity Information, *Journal of Advertising* 27 (spring 1998), 67–82.
27. David Finkle, "Q-Scores: The Popularity Contest of the Stars," *Wall Street Journal,* June 7, 1992, in special section ("Themes of the Times"), 1.
28. Marc Weinberger and Harlan Spotts, "Humor in U.S. Versus U.K. TV Advertising," *Journal of Advertising* 18, no. 2 (1989), 39–44. For further discussion of differences between American and British advertising, see Terence Nevett, "Differences between American and British Television Advertising: Explanations and Implications," *Journal of Advertising* 21 (December 1992), 61–71.
29. Dana L. Alden, Wayne D. Hoyer, and Chol Lee, "Identifying Global and Culture-Specific Dimensions of Humor in Advertising: A Multinational Analysis," *Journal of Marketing* 57 (April 1993), 64–75.
30. Harlan E. Spotts, Marc G. Weinberger, and Amy L. Parsons, "Assessing the Use and Impact of Humor on Advertising Effectiveness: A Contingency Approach," *Journal of Advertising* 26 (fall 1997), 17–32; Karen Flaherty, Marc G. Weinberger, and Charles S. Gulas, "The Impact of Perceived Humor, Product Type, and Humor Style in Radio Advertising," *Journal of Current Issues and Research in Advertising* 26 (spring 2004), 25–36.
31. Josephine L. C. M. Woltman Elpers, Ashesh Mukherjee, and Wayne D. Hoyer, " Humor in Television Advertising: A Moment-to-Moment Analysis," *Journal of Consumer Research* 31 (December 2004), 592–598.
32. For a formal theoretical account, see Dana L. Alden, Ashesh Mukherjee, and Wayne D. Hoyer, "The Effects of Incongruity, Surprise and Positive Moderators on Perceived Humor in Television Advertising," *Journal of Advertising* 29 (summer 2000), 1–16.
33. Differences in the use of humor across advertising media are demonstrated in Marc G. Weinberger, Harlan Spotts, Leland Campbell, and Amy L. Parsons, "The Use and Effect of Humor in Different Advertising Media," *Journal of Advertising Research* 35 (May/June 1995), 44–56.
34. A thorough review of the issues is provided in two valuable reviews: Paul Surgi Speck, "The Humorous Message Taxonomy: A Framework for the Study of Humorous Ads," *Current Issues and Research in Advertising,* vol. 3, ed. J. H. Leigh and C. R. Martin, Jr. (Ann Arbor: Graduate School of Business Administration, University of Michigan, 1991), 1–44; Marc G. Weinberger and Charles S. Gulas, "The Impact of Humor in Advertising: A Review," *Journal of Advertising* 21 (December 1992), 35–59.
35. Thomas J. Madden and Marc G. Weinberger, "Humor in Advertising: A Practitioner View," *Journal of Advertising Research* 24, no. 4 (1984), 23–29.
36. Based on Weinberger and Gulas, "The Impact of Humor in Advertising: A Review," 56–57.
37. For discussion on this point, see H. Shanker Krishnan and Dipankar Chakravarti, "A Process Analysis of the Effects of Humorous Advertising Executions on Brand Claims Memory," *Journal of Consumer Psychology* 13, no. 3 (2003), 230–245.
38. Thomas J. Madden and Marc G. Weinberger, "The Effects of Humor on Attention in Magazine Advertising," *Journal of Advertising* 11, no. 3 (1982), 4–14.
39. Amitava Chattopadhyay and Kunal Basu, "Humor in Advertising: The Moderating Role of Prior Brand Evaluation," *Journal of Consumer Research* 27 (November 1990), 466–476.
40. Thomas W. Cline, Moses B. Altsech, and James J. Kellaris, "When Does Humor Enhance or Inhibit Ad Responses? The Moderating Role of the Need for Humor," *Journal of Advertising* 32 (fall 2003), 31–46.
41. See Yong Zhang, "Responses to Humorous Advertising: The Moderating Effect of Need for Cognition," *Journal of Advertising* 25 (spring 1996), 15–32; also, Flaherty, Weinberger, and Gulas, "The Impact of Perceived Humor, Product Type, and Humor Style in Radio Advertising."
42. Marianne Szegedy-Maszak, "Conquering Our Phobias: The Biological Underpinnings of Paralyzing Fears," *U.S. News & World Report,* December 6, 2004, 67–74.
43. Please note that there is a related advertising form referred to as "shock advertising" that does not appeal to fear per se but which deliberately intends to startle and even offend its audience. Tentative research on this topic has demonstrated that shock advertising is perhaps even better than appeals to fear in activating attention and encouraging the audience to engage in message-relevant behaviors. See Darren W. Dahl, Kristina D. Frankenberger, and Rajesh V. Manchanda, "Does It Pay to Shock? Reactions to Shocking and Nonshocking Advertising Content among University Students," *Journal of Advertising Research* 43 (September 2003), 268–280.
44. This is a quote from Jerry Della Femina, a well-known advertising agency executive and former copywriter. Cited in Emily DeNitto, "Healthcare Ads Employ Scare Tactics," *Advertising Age,* November 7, 1994, 12.
45. Herbert J. Rotfeld, "Fear Appeals and Persuasion: Assumptions and Errors in Advertising Research," *Current Issues and Research in Advertising,* vol. 11, ed. J. H. Leigh and C. R. Martin, Jr. (Ann Arbor: Graduate School of Business Administration, University of Michigan, 1988), 21–40.
46. Peter Wright, "Concrete Action Plans in TV Messages to Increase Reading of Drug Warnings," *Journal of Consumer Re-*

search 6 (December 1979), 256–269. For an explanation of the psychological mechanism by which fear-intensity operates, see Punam Anand Keller and Lauren Goldberg Block, "Increasing the Persuasiveness of Fear Appeals: The Effect of Arousal and Elaboration," *Journal of Consumer Research* 22 (March 1996), 448–459.

47. For further reading on the use of appeals to fear in antidrinking-and-driving campaigns, see Karen Whitehill King and Leonard N. Reid, "Fear Arousing Anti-Drinking and Driving PSAs: Do Physical Injury Threats Influence Young Adults?" *Current Issues and Research in Advertising*, vol. 12, ed. J. H. Leigh and C. R. Martin, Jr. (Ann Arbor: Graduate School of Business Administration, University of Michigan, 1990), 155–175. Other relevant articles on fear appeals include John F. Tanner, James B. Hunt, and David R. Eppright, "The Protection Motivation Model: Normative Model of Fear Appeals," *Journal of Marketing* 55 (July 1991), 36–45; Tony L. Henthorne, Michael S. LaTour, and Rajan Natarajan, "Fear Appeals in Print Advertising: An Analysis of Arousal and Ad Response," *Journal of Advertising* 22 (June 1993), 59–70; and James T. Strong and Khalid M. Dubas, "The Optimal Level of Fear-Arousal in Advertising: An Empirical Study," *Journal of Current Issues and Research in Advertising* 15 (fall 1993), 93–99.
48. Robert B. Cialdini, *Influence: Science and Practice,* 2nd ed. (Glenview, Ill.: Scott, Foresman, 1988).
49. Jack W. Brehm, *A Theory of Psychological Reactance* (New York: Academic Press, 1966). See also Mona Clee and Robert Wicklund, "Consumer Behavior and Psychological Reactance," *Journal of Consumer Research* 6 (March 1980), 389–405.
50. Ian Stewart, "Public Fear Sells in Singapore," *Advertising Age,* October 11, 1993, I8. Singaporeans even make fun of themselves regarding their *kiasu* behavior. "Mr. Kiasu" is a popular comic book character, and a small cottage industry has sprung up around the character.
51. Carroll E. Izard, *Human Emotions* (New York: Plenum, 1977).
52. Robin Higie Coulter and Mary Beth Pinto, "Guilt Appeals in Advertising: What Are Their Effects?" *Journal of Applied Psychology* 80 (December 1995), 697–705; Bruce A. Huhmann and Timothy P. Brotherton, "A Content Analysis of Guilt Appeals in Popular Magazine Advertisements," *Journal of Advertising* 26 (summer 1997), 35–46.
53. Huhmann and Brotherton, "A Content Analysis of Guilt Appeals in Popular Magazine Advertisements," 36.
54. June Cotte, Robin A. Coulter, and Melissa Moore, "Enhancing or Disrupting Guilt: The Role of Ad Credibility and Perceived Manipulative Intent," *Journal of Business Research* 58 (March 2005), 361–368.
55. A content analysis of magazine advertising indicates that the percentage of ads with sexual content had not changed over a two-decade period. What changed, however, was that sexual illustrations had become more overt. Female models were more likely than male models to be portrayed in nude, partially nude, or suggestive poses. See Lawrence Soley and Gary Kurzbard, "Sex in Advertising: A Comparison of 1964 and 1984 Magazine Advertisements," *Journal of Advertising* 15, no. 3 (1986), 46–54.
56. For a variety of perspectives on the role of sex in advertising, see Tome Reichert and Jacqueline Lambiase, eds., *Sex in Advertising: Perspectives on the Erotic Appeal* (Mahwah, NJ: Lawrence Erlbaum, 2003).
57. Robert S. Baron, "Sexual Content and Advertising Effectiveness: Comments on Belch et al. (1981) and Caccavale et al. (1981)," in *Advances in Consumer Research,* vol. 9, ed. Andrew Mitchell (Ann Arbor, Mich.: Association for Consumer Research, 1982), 428.
58. B. G. Yovovich, "Sex in Advertising—The Power and the Perils," *Advertising Age,* May 2, 1983, M4.
59. Larry Percy, "A Review of the Effect of Specific Advertising Elements upon Overall Communication Response," in *Current Issues and Research in Advertising,* vol. 2, ed. J. H. Leigh and C. R. Martin, Jr. (Ann Arbor: Graduate School of Business Administration, University of Michigan, 1983), 95.
60. David Richmond and Timothy P. Hartman, "Sex Appeal in Advertising," *Journal of Advertising Research* 22 (October/November 1982), 53–61.
61. Michael S. LaTour, Robert E. Pitts, and David C. Snook-Luther, "Female Nudity, Arousal, and Ad Response: An Experimental Investigation," *Journal of Advertising* 19, no. 4 (1990), 51–62.
62. Baron, "Sexual Content and Advertising Effectiveness," 428.
63. Robert A. Peterson and Roger A. Kerin, "The Female Role in Advertisements: Some Experimental Evidence," *Journal of Marketing* 41 (October 1977), 59–63.
64. Jessica Severn, George E. Belch, and Michael A. Belch, "The Effects of Sexual and Non-sexual Advertising Appeals and Information Level on Cognitive Processing and Communication Effectiveness," *Journal of Advertising* 19, no. 1 (1990), 14–22.
65. Ira Teinowitz and Bob Geiger, "Suits Try to Link Sex Harassment Ads," *Advertising Age,* November 18, 1991, 48.
66. A study of consumers in Denmark, Greece, New Zealand, and the United States revealed consistent criticism of sexist role portrayals. See Richard W. Pollay and Steven Lysonski, "In the Eye of the Beholder: International Differences in Ad Sexism Perceptions and Reactions," *Journal of International Consumer Marketing* 6, vol. 2 (1993), 25–43.
67. Three surveys have demonstrated this fact. For the most recent review of these surveys, see Martha Rogers and Kirk H. Smith, "Public Perceptions of Subliminal Advertising: Why Practitioners Shouldn't Ignore This Issue," *Journal of Advertising Research* 33 (March/April 1993), 10–18.
68. Martha Rogers and Christine A. Seiler, "The Answer Is No: A National Survey of Advertising Industry Practitioners and Their Clients about Whether They Use Subliminal Advertising," *Journal of Advertising Research* 34 (March/April 1994), 36–45.
69. This description is adapted from Martin P. Block and Bruce G. Vanden Bergh, "Can You Sell Subliminal Messages to Consumers?" *Journal of Advertising* 14, no. 3 (1985), 59.
70. Vicary himself acknowledged that the study that initiated the original furor over subliminal advertising was based on too small an amount of data to be meaningful. See Fred Danzig, "Subliminal Advertising—Today It's Just Historic Flashback for Researcher Vicary," *Advertising Age,* September 17, 1962, 42, 74.
71. For example, see Sharon E. Beatty and Del I. Hawkins, "Subliminal Stimulation: Some New Data and Interpretation," *Journal of Advertising* 18, no. 3 (1989), 4–8.
72. Wilson B. Key, *Subliminal Seduction: Ad Media's Manipulation of a Not So Innocent America* (New York: Signet, 1972); *Media Sexploitation* (New York: Signet, 1976); *The Clam Plate Orgy: And*

Other Subliminal Techniques for Manipulating Your Behavior (New York: Signet, 1980). Key has since written *The Age of Manipulation: The Con in Confidence, the Sin in Sincere* (New York: Holt, 1989).

73. For a sophisticated treatment of visual imagery and symbolism in advertising (though not dealing with subliminal advertising per se), see Linda M. Scott, "Images in Advertising: The Need for a Theory of Visual Rhetoric," *Journal of Consumer Research* 21 (September 1994), 252–273.
74. Ronnie Cuperfain and T. K. Clarke, "A New Perspective of Subliminal Perception," *Journal of Advertising* 14, no. 1 (1985), 36–41; Myron Gable, Henry T. Wilkens, Lynn Harris, and Richard Feinberg, "An Evaluation of Subliminally Embedded Sexual Stimuli in Graphics," *Journal of Advertising* 16, no. 1 (1987), 26–31; William E. Kilbourne, Scott Painton, and Danny Ridley, "The Effect of Sexual Embedding on Responses to Magazine Advertisements," *Journal of Advertising* 14, no. 2 (1985), 48–56.
75. For discussion of the practical difficulties with implementing subliminal advertising and the questionable effectiveness of this advertising technique, see Timothy E. Moore, "Subliminal Advertising: What You See Is What You Get," *Journal of Marketing* 46 (spring 1982), 41; and Joel Saegert, "Why Marketing Should Quit Giving Subliminal Advertising the Benefit of the Doubt," *Psychology & Marketing* 4 (summer 1987), 107–120.
76. Moore, "Subliminal Advertising: What You See Is What You Get," 46.
77. For an accessible treatment on the issue of automatic, or noncontrolled motivation and behavior, see John A. Bargh, "Losing Consciousness: Automatic Influences on Consumer Judgment, Behavior, and Motivation," *Journal of Consumer Research* 29 (September 2002), 280–285. See also John A. Bargh and Tanya L. Chartrand, "The Unbearable Automaticity of Being," *American Psychologist* 54 (July 1999), 462–479.
78. Vanessa O'Connell, "GM Sings Tunes Inspired by Its Chevrolet Brand," *Wall Street Journal Online,* October 1, 2002, http://online.wsj.com.
79. Very good reviews of music's various advertising functions are available in Gordon C. Bruner II, "Music, Mood, and Marketing," *Journal of Marketing* 54 (October 1990), 94–104; Linda M. Scott, "Understanding Jingles and Needledrop: A Rhetorical Approach to Music in Advertising," *Journal of Consumer Research* 17 (September 1990), 223–236; James J. Kellaris, Anthony D. Cox, and Dena Cox, "The Effect of Background Music on Ad Processing: A Contingency Explanation," *Journal of Marketing* 57 (October 1993), 114–125; and Kineta Hung, "Framing Meaning Perceptions with Music: The Case of Teaser Ads," *Journal of Advertising* 30 (fall 2001), 39–50.
80. Though not described in this chapter, the following studies are recommended reading: Deborah J. MacInnis and C. Whan Park, "The Differential Role of Characteristics of Music on High- and Low-Involvement Consumers' Processing of Ads," *Journal of Consumer Research* 18 (September 1991), 161–173; James J. Kellaris and Robert J. Kent, "The Influence of Music on Consumers' Temporal Perceptions: Does Time Fly When You're Having Fun?" *Journal of Consumer Psychology* 1, no. 4 (1992), 365–376; James J. Kellaris and Robert J. Kent, "An Exploratory Investigation of Responses Elicited by Music Varying in Tempo, Tonality, and Texture," *Journal of Consumer Psychology* 2, no. 4 (1993), 381–402; Michelle L. Roehm, "Instrumental vs. Vocal Versions of Popular Music in Advertising," *Journal of Advertising Research* 41 (May/June 2001), 49–58.
81. Gerald J. Gorn, "The Effects of Music in Advertising on Choice Behavior: A Classical Conditioning Approach," *Journal of Marketing* 46 (winter 1982), 94–101.
82. A replication of this study failed to obtain supporting evidence, thereby calling into question the ability to generalize from Gorn's prior research. See James J. Kellaris and Anthony D. Cox, "The Effects of Background Music in Advertising," *Journal of Consumer Research* 16 (June 1989), 113–118.
83. See Darrell D. Muehling, Donald E. Stem, Jr., and Peter Raven, "Comparative Advertising: Views from Advertisers, Agencies, Media, and Policy Makers," *Journal of Advertising Research* 29 (October/November 1989), 38–48.
84. Naveen Donthu, "A Cross-Country Investigation of Recall of and Attitude toward Comparative Advertising," *Journal of Advertising* 27 (summer 1998), 111–122.
85. These questions are adapted from Stephen B. Ash and Chow-Hou Wee, "Comparative Advertising: A Review with Implications for Further Research," in *Advances in Consumer Research,* vol. 10, ed. R. P. Bagozzi and A. M. Tybout (Ann Arbor, Mich.: Association for Consumer Research, 1983), 374.
86. A sampling of significant comparative advertising research includes the following: Cornelia Droge and Rene Y. Darmon, "Associative Positioning Strategies through Comparative Advertising: Attribute versus Overall Similarity Approaches," *Journal of Marketing Research* 24 (November 1987), 377–388; Cornelia Pechmann and David W. Stewart, "The Effects of Comparative Advertising on Attention, Memory, and Purchase Intentions," *Journal of Consumer Research* 17 (September 1990), 180–191; Cornelia Pechmann and S. Ratneshwar, "The Use of Comparative Advertising for Brand Positioning: Association versus Differentiation," *Journal of Consumer Research* 18 (September 1991), 145–160; Cornelia Pechmann and Gabriel Esteban, "Persuasion Processes Associated with Direct Comparative and Noncomparative Advertising and Implications for Advertising Effectiveness," *Journal of Consumer Psychology* 2, no. 4 (1993), 403–432; Randall L. Rose, Paul W. Miniard, Michael J. Barone, Kenneth C. Manning, and Brian D. Till, "When Persuasion Goes Undetected: The Case of Comparative Advertising," *Journal of Marketing Research* 30 (August 1993), 315–330; Shailendra Pratap Jain, Bruce Buchanan, and Durairaj Maheswaran, "Comparative Versus Noncomparative Advertising: The Moderating Impact of Prepurchase Attribute Verifiability," *Journal of Consumer Psychology* 9, no. 4 (2000), 201–212; Shi Zhang, Frank R. Kardes, and Maria L. Cronley, "Comparative Advertising: Effects of Structural Alignability on Target Brand Evaluations," *Journal of Consumer Psychology* 12, no. 4 (2002), 303–312; Michael J. Barone, Kay M. Palan, and Paul W. Miniard, "Brand Usage and Gender as Moderators of the Potential Deception Associated with Partial Comparative Advertising," *Journal of Advertising* 33 (spring 2004), 19–28.
87. Dhruv Grewal, Sukuman Kavanoor, Edward F. Fern, Carolyn Costley, and James Barnes, "Comparative Versus Noncomparative Advertising: A Meta-Analysis," *Journal of Marketing* 61 (October 1997), 1–15.

88. Terence A. Shimp and David C. Dyer, "The Effects of Comparative Advertising Mediated by Market Position of Sponsoring Brand," *Journal of Advertising* 7, no. 3 (1978), 13–19.
89. Gerald J. Gorn and Charles B. Weinberg, "The Impact of Comparative Advertising on Perception and Attitude: Some Positive Findings," *Journal of Consumer Research* 11 (September 1984), 719–727.
90. Rose, Miniard, Barone, Manning, and Till, "When Persuasion Goes Undetected: The Case of Comparative Advertising"; Paul W. Miniard, Randall L. Rose, Michael J. Barone, and Kenneth C. Manning, "On the Need for Relative Measures When Assessing Comparative Advertising Effects," *Journal of Advertising* 22 (September 1993), 41–57. For an alternative explanation of why relative framed messages are more effective, see Zhang, Kardes, and Cronley, "Comparative Advertising: Effects of Structural Alignability on Target Brand Evaluations."

CHAPTER 12

Assessing Ad Message Effectiveness

Marcom Challenge: What Makes an Advertisement Watchable?

Research by a global advertising research company, Millward Brown, has explored the issue framed in the title to this Marcom Challenge. In their studies of thousands of TV commercials in the United States, Europe, and elsewhere, Millward Brown has determined that commercials classified as *watchable*—that is, ads that both involve the viewer and are enjoyable to watch—are much more likely than ordinary ads to be remembered and are substantially more likely to drive sales.[1] But what makes one commercial more watchable than another? Based on Millward Brown's research, here are some of the characteristics that distinguish watchable from less-watchable commercials:

Humor. Ads that are funny are much more likely to be watchable. Humor in advertising increases both viewer involvement and enjoyment. For example, Wendy's Spicy Chicken Sandwich commercial: the sandwich is so hot that customers will drink water from anywhere to put out the fire – a man drinks water from his water-bed, or a woman plunges her head into a fish tank.

Music. Music is featured prominently in slightly over 50 percent of commercials that are classified as watchable; comparatively, ordinary commercials emphasize music only about 20 percent of the time.

Voice-Overs. Watchable ads include continuous voice-overs rarely (only about 10 percent of the time), whereas ordinary ads often use this technique (about 50 percent of the time). Watchable ads tend to use voice-overs only at the end of commercials.

Pace. Watchable ads are more likely to be fast paced compared to ordinary ads.

Celebrities. Watchable ads use celebrities considerably more often than ordinary ads. Celebrities are excellent attention-getters and can be chosen to attract a specific age group, economic status, etc.

Cute Things. Commercials that include children or animals—babies sleeping, playing, learning to walk, or the Iams dog food puppies, romping, nipping, and napping—tend to be more watchable, primarily because these "cute things" increase viewing enjoyment if not necessarily involvement.

For TV commercials to be successful, it is critical that the viewer's attention be captured and maintained. Many commercials initiate involuntary attention by using loud sounds or flashing lights, but these do not necessarily increase viewer involvement or enjoyment. Moreover, other commercials may be enjoyable to view, but may not be particularly involving or link the message well with the advertised brand. The concept of watchability is relatively new in advertising. Its point of emphasis is that an effective, impactful commercial must be both involving and enjoyable. This then takes us to the subject of the present chapter: advertising research is needed to test commercials both before they are printed or aired (pretesting research) and after they appear in magazines and newspapers or on television and radio (posttesting research). Advertisers cannot assume that creative executions will be effective; rather, they must test ads for effectiveness. Watchability is just one of various indicators of advertising effectiveness.

Associated Press. M&M MARS

CHAPTER OBJECTIVES

1

Explain the rationale and importance of message research.

2

Describe the various research techniques used to measure consumers' recognition and recall of advertising messages.

3

Illustrate measures of physiological arousal to advertisements.

4

Explicate the role of persuasion measurement, including pre- and posttesting of consumer preference.

5

Explain the meaning and operation of single-source measures of advertising effectiveness.

6

Examine some key conclusions regarding television advertising effectiveness.

Overview of Advertising Research

The two preceding chapters examined the role of advertising creativity (Chapter 10) and explored the role of endorsers and forms of advertising executions—humor, sex appeals, appeals to guilt, and so on (Chapter 11). A well-defined value proposition is the key to advertising effectiveness, but there are "different ways to skin the cat"; that is, different types of creative advertising strategies (e.g., USP, brand image, and generic) and different message strategies can accomplish the all-important marcom objectives that were described back in Chapter 6. In short, brand managers and their advertising agencies have many options when creating advertising messages.

At the same time, the brand management team is responsible for researching whether proposed advertisements stand a good chance of being successful *prior* to investing money in printing or airing ads. It would, in other words, be presumptuous at best or even foolhardy to assume that a proposed advertisement will be successful absent any research-based evidence. The demand for *accountability* that is prevalent throughout business (recall the discussion back in Chapter 2) necessitates that ads be tested before they are placed in media and then again during or after the period in which they have been printed or broadcast.

Sound business practice requires that efforts be made to determine whether advertising expenditures are justified, especially considering the amount of money that is invested in advertising both in the United States and worldwide. Accordingly, a significant amount of time and money are spent on testing message effectiveness. This chapter surveys some of the most important techniques used in the advertising research business.

It's Not Easy or Inexpensive

Measuring message effectiveness is a difficult and expensive task. Nonetheless, the value gained from undertaking the effort typically outweighs the drawbacks. In the absence of formal research, most advertisers would not know whether proposed ad messages are going to be effective or whether ongoing advertising is doing a good job, nor could they know what to change to improve future advertising efforts. Advertising research enables management to increase advertising's contribution toward achieving marketing goals and yielding a reasonable return on investment.

Contemporary message research traces its roots to the 19th century, when measures of recall and memory were obtained as indicators of print advertising effectiveness.[2] Today, most national advertisers would not even consider airing a television commercial or placing a magazine advertisement without testing it first. A survey of the largest advertisers and advertising agencies in the United States determined that more than 80 percent of the respondents from each group pretest television commercials before airing them on a national basis.[3] Interestingly, these commercials typically are tested in a preliminary form rather than as finished versions. The purpose of testing commercials in rough form is to enable an economic means of screening out bad ideas at significantly lower expense than is necessitated in developing finished commercials.[4] Research has shown that results from testing prefinished commercials closely parallel those from tests performed on finalized commercials.[5] The *IMC Focus* briefly describes the various prefinished forms in which TV commercials typically are tested.

What Does Advertising Research Involve?

Due to growing calls for advertising accountability, advertising research in its various forms is more prevalent and essential than ever.[6] Advertising research encompasses a variety of purposes, methods, measures, and techniques. Broadly speaking, we can distinguish two general forms of ad research: measures of *media*

Testing TV Commercials in Prefinished Form

imc focus

An advertising agency works from a creative brief that has been developed in conjunction with the client-side brand management team. As described in Chapter 10, the creative brief is a document designed to inspire copywriters by channeling their creative efforts toward a solution that will serve the interests of the client. The creative brief represents an informal pact between client and advertising agency that secures agreement on what an advertising campaign is intended to accomplish. Among other features, the creative brief identifies the brand positioning, the overall marketing strategy for the brand, and a statement of the brand's key value proposition. Working from this brief, copywriters and other agency personnel develop two or more creative executions that are considered suitable for accomplishing agreed-on objectives. However, rather than immediately producing a finished commercial, which can easily cost $500,000 or more, it is practical and cost-efficient to test the advertising concept in a prefinished form. There are five prefinished forms that are tested in television commercial research. The form furthest removed from a finished commercial is the storyboard, whereas the other forms become more like a produced commercial as we progress from the animatics form to the liveamatics version. Each is briefly described here.

1. *Storyboards:* This prefinished version presents a series of key visual frames and the corresponding script of the audio. The sequence of visual frames is literally pasted on a poster-type board, which thus accounts for the storyboard name. The storyboard version, unlike a dynamic commercial, is completely static. Drawings of people replace the actual actors or celebrities who ultimately will appear in the finished commercial. Testing of storyboards often is done in focus group settings with small groups of consumers.
2. *Animatics:* This is a film or videotape of a sequence of drawings with simultaneous playing of audio to represent a proposed commercial. The animatic version maintains the primitive nature of the storyboard but incorporates an element of dynamism by videotaping the sequence of drawings.
3. *Photomatics:* A sequence of photographs is filmed or videotaped and accompanied by audio to represent a proposed commercial. This version is increasingly realistic inasmuch as photographs of real people are displayed rather than, as in the case of storyboards or animatics, merely shown as drawn renderings of real people.
4. *Ripomatics* (also called *steal-o-matics*): Footage is taken from existing commercials and spliced together to represent the proposed commercial. Hence, the ripomatics version captures the realism of an actual commercial but does not entail the huge expense associated with filming an original commercial.
5. *Liveamatics:* This prefinished version entails filming or videotaping live talent to represent the proposed commercial. This version is the closest to a finished commercial, but it does not fully represent the actual settings or talent that will be used in the finished commercial.

SOURCES: Adapted from David Olson, "Principles of Measuring Advertising Effectiveness," American Marketing Association, http://www.marketingpower.com (accessed October 14, 2004), and Karen Whitehill King, John D. Pehrson, and Leonard N. Reid, "Pretesting TV Commercials: Methods, Measures, and Changing Agency Roles," *Journal of Advertising* 22 (September 1993), 85–97.

effectiveness and those of *message effectiveness.* Subsequent chapters will address the matter of media effectiveness; the present chapter focuses exclusively on measuring message effectiveness.

Achieving brand awareness, conveying copy points, influencing attitudes, creating emotional responses, and affecting purchase choices are the various foci of message research. In short, **message research** is undertaken to test the effectiveness of advertising messages. (Message research also is called *copy research,* or *copy testing,* but these terms are too limiting inasmuch as message research involves testing all aspects of advertisements, not just the verbal copy material.)

There are four stages at which ad message research might be conducted: (1) at the copy development stage; (2) at the "rough" stage (i.e., in prefinished form such as animatics and photomatics; see *IMC Focus*); (3) at the final production stage, but prior to placing the ad in magazines, on TV, or in other media; and (4) after the ad has been run in media.[7] In other words, advertising research involves both *pretesting* messages during developmental stages (prior to actual placement in advertising media) and *posttesting* messages for effectiveness after they have been aired or printed. Pretesting is performed to eliminate ineffective ads before they are ever run, while posttesting is conducted to determine whether messages have achieved established objectives.

Sometimes research is done under natural advertising conditions and other times in simulated or laboratory situations. Measures of effectiveness range from paper-and-pencil instruments (such as attitude scales) to physiological devices (e.g., pupillometers that measure eye movement). It should be clear that there is no single encompassing form of message research. Rather, measures of advertising effectiveness are as varied as the questions that advertisers and their agencies want answered.

Industry Standards for Message Research

Message-based research, or copy testing, is in wide use. Yet, it may be a bit sobering to note that much message-based research is not of the highest caliber. Sometimes it is unclear exactly what the research is attempting to measure, measures often fail to satisfy the basic requirements of sound research, and results have little to say about whether tested ads stand a good chance of being effective.

Members of the advertising research community have been mindful of these problems and have sought a higher standard of performance from advertising researchers. A major document, called **Positioning Advertising Copy Testing (PACT)**, was formulated by leading U.S. advertising agencies to remedy the problem of mediocre or flawed advertising research. The document is directed primarily at television advertising but is relevant to the testing of advertising in all media.

The PACT document consists of nine message-testing principles.[8] More than mere pronouncements, these principles represent useful guides to how advertising research should be conducted. It is unnecessary that you attempt to commit these principles to memory; rather, your objective in reading the following principles should be to simply appreciate what constitutes good message research practice. (Please note that the developers of the PACT principles referred to copy testing rather than message research. The descriptions that follow retain the use of copy testing, though as noted previously, message research is a more apt label.)

Principle 1

A good copy testing system needs to provide measurements that are *relevant to the advertising objectives.* The specific objective(s) that an advertising campaign is intended to accomplish (such as creating brand awareness, influencing brand image, or creating warmth) should be the first consideration in determining the methods to assess advertising effectiveness. For example, if the objective for a particular campaign is to evoke strong emotional reactions, a measure of recall would be patently inappropriate.

Principle 2

A good copy testing system is one that *requires agreement about how the results will be used in advance of each specific test.* Specifying the use of research results before data collection ensures that all parties involved (advertiser, agency, and research firm) agree on the research goals and reduces the chance of conflicting interpretations of test results. This principle's intent is to encourage the use of decision rules or action standards that, before actual testing, establish the test results that must be achieved for the test advertisement to receive full media distribution.

Principle 3

A good copy testing system provides *multiple measurements,* because single measurements are generally inadequate to assess the totality of an ad's performance. The process by which advertisements influence customers is complex, so multiple measures are more likely than single measures to capture the various advertising effects.

Principle 4

A good copy testing system is based on *a model of human response to communications*—the reception of a stimulus, the comprehension of the stimulus, and the response to the stimulus. Because advertisements vary in the impact they are intended to achieve, a good copy testing system is capable of answering questions that are patterned to the underlying model of behavior. For example, if consumers purchase a particular product for primarily emotional reasons, then message research should use a suitable measure of emotional response rather than simply measuring recall of copy points. It is interesting to note that message research has historically focused excessively on the rational, cognitive aspect of human behavior and given insufficient attention to emotions and feelings—factors that are increasingly being recognized by scholars and practitioners as just as important, if not more influential, than cognition in driving consumer behavior.[9]

Principle 5

A good copy testing system allows for consideration of *whether the advertising stimulus should be exposed more than once.* This principle addresses the issue of whether a single test exposure (showing an ad or commercial to consumers only once) provides a sufficient test of potential impact. Because multiple exposures are often required for advertisements to accomplish their full effect, message research should expose a test ad to respondents on two or more occasions when the communications situation calls for such a procedure.[10] For example, a single-exposure test is probably insufficient to determine whether an advertisement successfully conveys a complex benefit. On the other hand, a single exposure may be adequate if an advertisement is designed solely to create name awareness for a new brand.

Principle 6

A good copy testing system recognizes that a more finished piece of copy can be evaluated more soundly; therefore, a good system requires, at minimum, that *alternative executions be tested in the same degree of finish.* Test results typically vary depending on the degree of finish, as, for example, when testing a photomatic or ripomatic version of a television commercial (see the *IMC Focus*). Sometimes the amount of information lost from testing a less-than-finished ad is inconsequential; sometimes it is critical.

Principle 7

A good copy testing system *provides controls to avoid the bias normally found in the exposure context.* The context in which an advertisement is contained (e.g., the clutter or lack of clutter in a magazine) will have a substantial impact on how the ad is received, processed, and accepted. For this reason, copy testing procedures should attempt to duplicate the eventual context of an advertisement or commercial.

Principle 8

A good copy testing system is one that takes into account *basic considerations of sample definition.* This typically requires that the sample be representative of the target audience to which test results are to be generalized and that the sample size be sufficiently large to permit reliable statistical conclusions.

Principle 9

Finally, a good copy testing system is one that can *demonstrate reliability and validity.* Reliability and validity are basic requirements of any research endeavor. As applied to message research, a reliable test is one that yields consistent results each time an advertisement is tested, and a valid test is one that is predictive of marketplace performance.

The foregoing principles establish a high set of standards for the advertising research community, and should be viewed as mandatory if advertising effectiveness is to be tested in a meaningful way.

What Do Brand Managers and Ad Agencies Want to Learn from Message Research?

As established back in Chapter 2, marcom efforts are directed at enhancing brand equity with the expectation that enhanced equity will lead ultimately to increases in brand sales and market share. You will recall from the discussion in Chapter 2 that brand equity from the consumer's perspective consists of two elements: *brand awareness* and *brand image.* Advertising's role is thus to augment brand awareness, alter the brand-based attribute and benefit associations that constitute a brand's image, and ultimately effect increases in a brand's sales and market share. Hence, message research is needed to provide diagnostic information about an advertisement's prospective equity-enhancing and sales-expanding potential (pretesting research) and to determine whether finalized advertisements actually accomplished these goals (posttesting research).

Before proceeding, it is important to note that members of the advertising community have attempted for many years to ascertain which measures of advertising best predict advertising effectiveness. Particularly notable is a major study funded by the influential Advertising Research Foundation (ARF) that assessed which of 35 different measures best predict the sales effectiveness of television commercials.[11] Although representing a heroic effort, results from ARF's Copy Research Validity Project are both inconclusive and controversial.[12] Probably the only definitive conclusion that can be made is that *no one measure is always most appropriate or universally best.* Each brand-advertising situation requires a careful assessment of the objectives that advertising is intended to accomplish and then the use of research methods that are appropriate for determining whether these objectives have been accomplished.

Given the scope of advertising research techniques in use, it would be impossible in this chapter to provide an exhaustive treatment. Literally dozens of methods for measuring message effectiveness have appeared over the years, and many companies specialize in measuring advertising effectiveness—firms such as the Starch Readership Service, the Bruzzone Research Company, Millward Brown, Ameritest, Gallup & Robinson, Mapes and Ross, Ipsos-ASI, Research Systems Corporation, and so on.

What Kind of Measures Are Used in Message Research?

Broadly speaking, message research comes in two general forms: qualitative and quantitative. We first will describe qualitative research somewhat briefly, but then devote primary attention to quantitative methods. This is not because the latter is more important; rather, the simple fact is that quantitative research has dominated in the ad industry and has a more established history of use in comparison to qualitative procedures.

Qualitative Message Research

This form of research is called *qualitative* because it is not based on producing numerical results and statistical analyses related to advertising copy and people's responses to that copy. Rather, qualitative research is concerned with generating insights into and interpretations of those advertising elements that influence people's responses to advertisements. Focus groups represent one form of qualitative ad research. For example, panels of focus group participants are presented with a storyboard version of a proposed new commercial, and then with the probing of a moderator are urged to share their thoughts and feelings about the commercial.

There are more sophisticated forms of qualitative advertising research that seek to better understand the meaning consumers derive from advertisements and the mental models that drive their thinking and behavior. One such method is the Zaltman Metaphor Elicitation Technique, which is referred to by its initials ZMET.[13]

This technique is based on several underlying premises, such as the fact that most human communication involves nonverbal elements (pictures, scenes, and music), that people's thoughts and feelings occur nonverbally as images, and that metaphors are the key mechanism for tapping into people's thoughts and feelings.[14] (A **metaphor** is based on the idea that people understand and experience things in terms of other things. For example, we refer to someone as having "eagle eyes" to mean he or she has keen sight; we sometimes characterize products as "lemons" to suggest they are fatally flawed. Hence, "eagle eyes" and "lemons" are metaphors that stand for something else.) Metaphors serve to both reveal people's thoughts and shape them as well. By understanding the metaphors people use when thinking about brands, it is possible to apply this insight in developing advertising copy that resonates with people's brand-relevant thoughts and feelings.

The details about how a ZMET is implemented are beyond the scope of this text. (Please refer to the articles cited in endnote 13 for specifics.) Many readers will have been exposed to ZMET in a prior course in marketing research. In any event, the important takeaway from this brief discussion is that qualitative research such as the Zaltman Metaphor Elicitation Technique can be invaluable as input into developing advertising copy. Hence, unlike the quantitative techniques that follow, ZMET is used as a basis for developing advertising copy rather than for testing that copy.

Quantitative Message Research

Quantitative message research is concerned with measuring the effects an advertisement may have (pretest research) or has had (posttest research). The following sections discuss some of the more popular methods in use by national advertisers. Two key points are needed before proceeding. It first is important to realize that many advertisers—especially smaller companies and organizations—do *not* conduct any advertising research, in either testing proposed advertising copy or testing ads that have been printed or aired in the form of, say, finished newspaper ads or TV commercials. The excuse given is that there is not sufficient time or funding to perform the research. Frankly, this is a bit lame given that the cost of making a mistake (for example, airing bad commercials) is far greater than the cost in terms of both time and money of testing ad copy. I would go so far as to say that no ad should ever be placed in media prior to conducting at least "quick and dirty" research, though more formal research is preferable.

A second preliminary point that will set the stage for the detailed presentation of quantitative message research methods is contained in this quote:

Measurement is the first step that leads to control and eventually to improvement. If you can't measure something, you can't understand it. If you can't understand it, you can't control it. If you can't control it, you can't improve it.[15]

The point of this quote is that advertising research is crucial in order to measure the effects that advertisements have so that improvements can be made on a continual basis.

What exactly does quantitative message research measure? To address this question, it will be helpful to return to one of the previously discussed copy testing principles. PACT principle 4 stated that a good copy testing measurement system is based on a model of human response to communications. In other words, before determining precisely what to measure, it is essential to know which types of responses advertising is capable of eliciting. Think about it for a while. What effects might advertising have? *Have you thought about it?* Well, advertisements can have a variety of effects, including the following: (1) creating brand awareness; (2) teaching prospective customers about brand features and benefits; (3) forging emotional connections with people; (4) influencing purchase-relevant beliefs and positively (or negatively!) affecting attitudes toward advertised brands; (5) shifting people's preferences from one brand to another, and, ultimately; (6) encouraging trial and repeat purchase behavior.

Advertising has the ability to influence people in a variety of ways. Brand managers, their ad agencies, and research vendors can effectively measure the impact of advertising only by first determining what effect an advertising campaign is designed to accomplish. That determined, it then is a matter of conducting research to measure whether the campaign has accomplished the outcomes for which it was created. As the previous quote stated, if you can't measure, you can't control. And if you can't control, you can't influence.

As a matter of convenience (and some necessary simplification), we will categorize message research into four groups of measures: (1) recognition and recall, (2) physiological arousal, (3) persuasion, and (4) sales response. The intent is to provide a representative sampling of the primary measurement techniques that brand managers and their ad agencies use for measuring advertising effectiveness. These general categories and the specific measures contained within each category are summarized in Table 12.1. In brief, measures of *recognition and recall* assess whether advertising has successfully influenced brand awareness and influenced brand-related thoughts and feelings. Measures of *physiological arousal* provide unobtrusive indicators of whether advertisements have emotionally aroused consumers. Measures of *persuasive impact* represent prebehavioral indicators of whether an advertisement is likely to influence purchase intentions and behavior. Finally, measures of *sales response* determine specifically whether an advertising campaign has affected consumers' purchases of an advertised brand.

Measures of Recognition and Recall

After exposure to an advertisement, consumers may experience varying degrees of awareness, the most basic of which is simply noticing an ad without processing specific elements. Advertisers intend, however, for consumers to heed specific parts, elements, or features of an ad and associate those with the advertised brand.[16] Recognition and recall both represent elements of consumers' memories for advertising information, but *recognition measures,* which can be equated with multiple-choice test questions, tap a more superficial level of memory compared with *recall measures,* which are similar to essay questions.[17] It will also be noted

Table 12.1
Illustrative Message Research Methods

Measures of Recognition and Recall
- Starch Readership Service (magazines)
- Bruzzone tests (TV)
- Burke day-after recall testing (TV)

Measures of Physiological Arousal
- Psychogalvanometer
- Pupillometer

Measures of Persuasion
- Ipsos-ASI Next*TV method
- rsc's ARS Persuasion method

Measures of Sales Response (single-source systems)
- IRI's BehaviorScan
- Nielsen's ScanTrack

from the discussion of brand equity in Chapter 2 that recognition is a lower level of brand awareness than recall. In other words, brand managers want consumers not only to recognize a brand name and its attributes or benefits but also to freely recall this information from memory without any cues or reminders.

Several commercial research firms provide advertisers with information on how well their ads perform in terms of generating awareness, which typically is assessed with recognition or recall measures. Three services are described in the following sections: Starch Readership Service (magazine recognition), Bruzzone tests (television recognition), and Burke day-after recall tests (television recall).[18]

Starch Readership Service

Starch Readership Service, a testing service of a company named Roper ASW, measures the primary objective of a *magazine ad*—namely, to be seen and read. Starch examines reader awareness of advertisements in consumer magazines and business publications. Over 75,000 advertisements are studied annually based on interviews with more than 100,000 people involving more than 140 publications. Sample sizes range from 100 to 150 individuals per issue, with most interviews conducted in respondents' homes or, in the case of business publications, in offices or places of business. Interviews are conducted during the early life of a publication. Following a suitable waiting period after the appearance of a publication to give readers an opportunity to read or look through their issue, interviewing commences and continues for a full week (for a weekly publication), two weeks (for a biweekly), or three weeks (for a monthly publication).

Starch interviewers locate eligible readers of each magazine issue studied. An eligible reader is one who has glanced through or read some part of the issue prior to the interviewer's visit and who meets the age, sex, and occupation requirements set for the particular magazine. Once eligibility is established, interviewers turn the pages of the magazine, inquiring about each advertisement being studied. Respondents are first asked, "Did you see or read any part of this advertisement?" If a respondent answers "Yes," a prescribed questioning procedure is followed to determine the respondent's awareness of various parts of the ad (illustrations, headline, etc.). Respondents are then classified as *noted, associated, read-some,* or *read-most* readers according to these specific definitions:[19]

- *Noted* is the percentage of people interviewed who remembered having previously seen the advertisement in the issue being studied.
- *Associated* is the percentage of people interviewed who not only noted the ad but also saw or read some part of it that clearly indicated the name of the brand or advertiser.
- *Read some* is the percentage of people interviewed who read any part of the ad's copy.
- *Read most* is the percentage of people interviewed who read half or more of the written material in the ad.

For each magazine advertisement that has undergone a Starch analysis, indices are developed for that ad's noted, associated, read-some, and read-most scores. Two sets of indices are established: one index compares an advertisement's scores against the average scores for *all ads* in the magazine issue, and the second (called the Adnorm index) compares an advertisement's scores against other ads in the *same product category* as well as with the same size (e.g., full-page) and color classifications (e.g., four-color). Hence, an advertisement that achieves an average value receives an index of 100. By comparison, a score of 130, for example, would mean that a particular ad scored 30 percent above comparable ads, whereas a score of 70 would indicate it scored 30 percent below comparable ads.

Figures 12.1 and 12.2 illustrate two Starch-rated advertisements from an issue of *Sports Illustrated* magazine. The first example (Figure 12.1) is an ad for the Kia

Figure 12.1 Starch-Rated Advertisement for the Kia Sorento

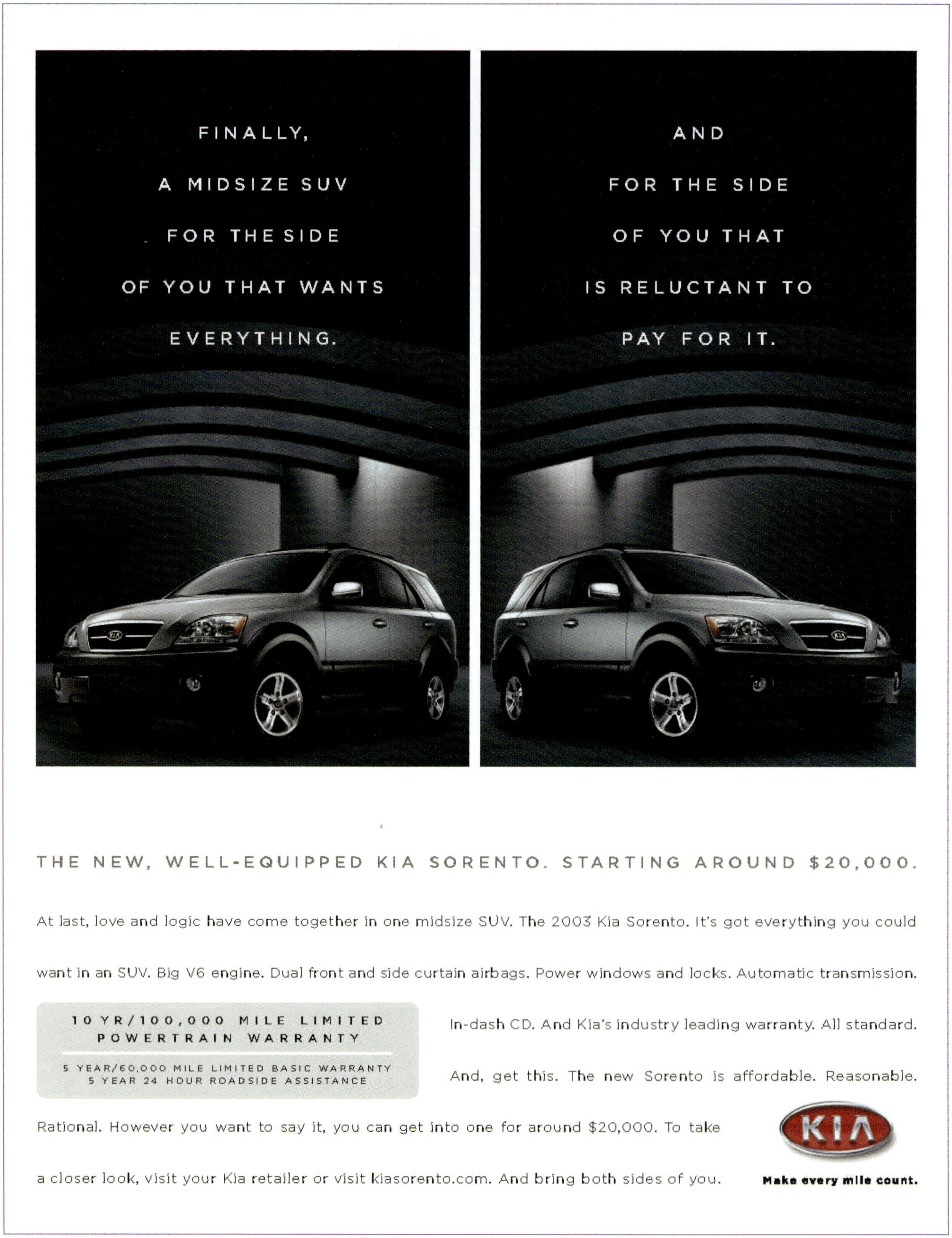

Courtesy of KIA Motors America, Inc.

Sorento that contains a large amount of body copy. The Starch Readership scores for this ad reflect that 39 percent of the respondents remembered having previously seen (or *noted*) the ad, 37 percent *associated* it, 27 percent *read some* of it, and 10 percent *read most* of the body copy contained in this ad. (For readers who are experienced with the Starch procedure, please note that Starch used to attach little yellow labels on advertisements to indicate these percentages, but it no longer affixes these labels; rather, scores are provided in a separate report.) The second illustration (Figure 12.2) is for Jose Cuervo Especial tequila, which, in light of the discussion in the prior chapter, is an obvious sex-oriented appeal to attract attention and perhaps create an emotional bond with the brand, especially in view of *Sports Illustrated*'s audience of predominantly male readers. Containing virtually no body copy other than the three-word headline ("Pursue your daydreams."), this ad's noted, associated, read-some, and read-most scores are substantially higher than the corresponding scores for the Sorento at 58, 54, 39, and 39 percent, respectively. (See the *Global Focus* insert for interesting commentary about developments in tequila marketing.)

NOP Worldwide

Figure 12.2

Starch-Rated Advertisement for Jose Cuervo Especial Tequila

A basic assumption of the Starch procedure is that respondents in fact do remember whether they saw a particular ad in a specific magazine issue. The Starch technique has sometimes been criticized because in so-called bogus ad studies that use prepublication or altered issues, respondents report having seen ads that actually never ran. The company that conducts Starch studies, Roper ASW, does not consider such studies valid and claims that the bogus studies have not adhered to proper procedures for qualifying issue readers and questioning respondents. Research demonstrates that when properly interviewed, most respondents are able to identify the ads they have seen or read in a specific issue with a high degree of accuracy; according to this research, false reporting of ad noting is minimal.[20]

Due to the inherent frailties of people's memories, it is almost certain that Starch scores do *not* provide exact percentages but rather are biased to some degree by people reporting they have seen or read an ad when in fact they have not. Another potential source of bias is people reporting they have *not* seen an ad when, in fact, they have. Nonetheless, it is not exact scores that are critical but rather comparisons between scores for the same ad placed in different magazines or comparative scores among different ads placed in the same magazine issue. For example, the Kia Sorento ad in Figure 12.1 obtained index scores (called Adnorm index scores) of 72 (noted), 74 (associated), 73 (read some), and 59 (read most). These indices mean that this ad performed 28 percent worse than the average noted score (an index of 100 indicates an average-performing ad; hence 100 – 72 = 28 percent worse), for all of the advertisements of similar size and color in this particular issue of *Sports Illustrated,* 26 percent worse than the median associated score, 27 percent worse than the median read-some score, and 41 percent worse than the median read-most score. It is obvious that this ad was a below-average performer. Comparatively, the Adnorm indices for the Jose Cuervo Especial tequila ad (Figure 12.2) are 107 (noted), 108 (associated), 105 (read some), and 229 (read most). Compared to similarly sized advertisements, the somewhat evocative Jose Cuervo ad performed slightly above average in terms of noted, associated, and read-some scores but dramatically above average with respect to its read-most score. Because Starch has been performing these studies since the 1920s and

Is What's Good for Vodka Good for Tequila?

global focus

The distilled spirits industry is more dynamic than most, probably because the age group composed of the most trendsetters, perhaps ages 25–39, is constantly losing members and gaining others as people age, and new generations typically differ from their predecessors. Trends in liquor consumption seem to shift every generation or so in lockstep with cultural developments that influence what's hot and what's not, what's hip and what's mundane. For example, consumption of Scotch whiskey increased for a while during the go-go days of the Internet boom in the 1990s with young professionals finding this drink compatible with cigar smoking, male bonding, and activities of this nature that were popular at the time. Consumption of "white" liquors (e.g., vodka) increased when more traditional "brown" liquors (Scotch, bourbon, etc.) were perceived as "dad's drink," excessively masculine, and passé.

Vodka is perhaps the one liquor that has for the past several decades been the steadiest performer among distilled spirits products. This, no doubt, is due in large part to advertising campaigns such as Absolut's that created hip images for brands and thus the entire product category. Vodka marketers also have been willing to augment the product by adding flavorful tastes (citron, lemon, vanilla, etc.) to a product that has little taste of its own. These added flavors have made vodka a more palatable drink and broadened the market by catering to consumers with multiple taste preferences.

Tequila marketers now seem poised to ape what their more successful vodka competitors have done. Even without any changes at all, tequila sales are on the rise. Between 1997 and 2004, sales volume increased by over 40 percent. Tequila marketers, perhaps including Jose Cuervo, which dominates the market in the United States with over 40 percent market share, are in the process of adding flavors in an effort to expand the market. For example, a Las Vegas company called Tukys imports tequila in bulk from Mexico and then mixes it with flavors in the United States. Tukys introduced a line of tequila mixed with flavors such as watermelon, lime, coffee, strawberry, and orange.

Only time will tell whether Tukys' effort and similar undertakings by other tequila marketers will substantially augment sales in this category. Ethicists have good reason to be concerned that such marketing gimmicks serve to recruit younger people to a product category they otherwise might avoid due to a taste perceived as too harsh. Beyond this, and strictly from a strategic marketing perspective, a possible downside to flavoring tequila is that this could fundamentally change consumer perceptions of tequila—from a traditional drink with a strong Mexican heritage and a distinct taste created by fermenting blue agave plants, a spiky-leafed member of the lily family, to a faddish beverage consumed by non-traditionalists and those who don't appreciate the product's long and cherished heritage. Comparatively, can you imagine distillers in Scotland adding flavors to Scotch whiskey—say, vanilla Scotch, butterscotch Scotch, cherry Scotch, or whatever? It's virtually unthinkable, isn't it?

SOURCE: Adapted from James Arndofer, "Tequila Tries a Flavor Shot to Maintain Sales," *Advertising Age,* January 10, 2005, 4, 36.

has compiled a wealth of baseline data, or norms, advertisers and media planners can make informed decisions concerning the relative merits of different magazines and informed judgments regarding the effectiveness of particular advertisements.

Bruzzone Tests

The Bruzzone Research Company (BRC) provides advertisers with a test of consumer *recognition* of television commercials along with their evaluations of these commercials. Historically, BRC mailed a set of photoboard commercials to a random sample of households and encouraged responses by providing a nominal monetary incentive. Starting in the late 1990s, BRC's data collection turned to the Internet and away from mailed distribution, as testing commercials online proved more efficient, less costly, and equally valid to the mailing procedure.[21]

In its standard testing procedure, BRC e-mails 15 commercials to a sample of online users. For each tested commercial, respondents first see this question: "Do you remember seeing this commercial on TV?" This question is followed by a series of six key scenes from the commercial and corresponding script. Immediately below the six-scene presentation are three response options: "Yes," "No," and "Not Sure." Respondents who respond "Yes" (that they do remember seeing this commercial) continue answering a series of questions about the commercial. (Those who answer "No" or "Not Sure" skip to the next tested commercial.) Importantly, anything that identifies the advertiser (such as mentioning the brand name in the script) is removed, so that those who noticed the commercial can indicate whether they remember the name of the advertised brand. (For a demonstration of BRC's online testing procedure, go to http://www.bruzzone-research.com/online_demoQ.htm.)

An illustrative Bruzzone test is shown in Figure 12.3.[22] This commercial—titled "Thanking the Troops" and sponsored by Anheuser-Busch—aired first on the 2005 Super Bowl and was tested by BRC shortly after that football spectacular. Perusal of the six key scenes reveals that this commercial involved an airport setting in which passengers awaiting flights give a standing ovation to U.S. troops who are en route to their plane.

After indicating whether they recall having seen this commercial, respondents subsequently are asked to indicate how interested they are in the commercial and how it makes them feel about the advertised brand (Budweiser). Respondents also are requested to describe their feelings by checking any of 27 adjectives that, in their opinion, characterize the commercial—items such as amusing, appealing, believable, clever, and so on. Following these ratings, respondents indicate whether it is appropriate for the advertiser (Anheuser-Busch in this case) to air this commercial. They then make known how much they liked the commercial (from "Liked it a lot" to "Disliked it a lot") and whether they remember which brand was being advertised—Coors, Budweiser, Heineken, or "Don't know."

Figure 12.3

Key Scenes and Questions from BRC's Test of the "Thanking the Troops" Commercial

Because BRC has performed hundreds of such tests (between 1992 and 2005 BRC tested nearly 700 ads aired on the 14 Super Bowls played during this period), it has established norms for average commercial performance against which a newly tested commercial can be compared. BRC's Advertising Response Model (ARM) links responses to the 27 descriptive adjectives to consumers' attitudes toward both the advertisement and the advertised product, and ultimately to the overall impact of the ad. Figure 12.4 presents the ARM analysis for Anheuser-Busch's "Thanking the Troops" commercial for its Budweiser brand.

Notice first in the upper-right corner the color coding for this analysis. Specifically, adjectives coded in yellow indicate that the commercial performed

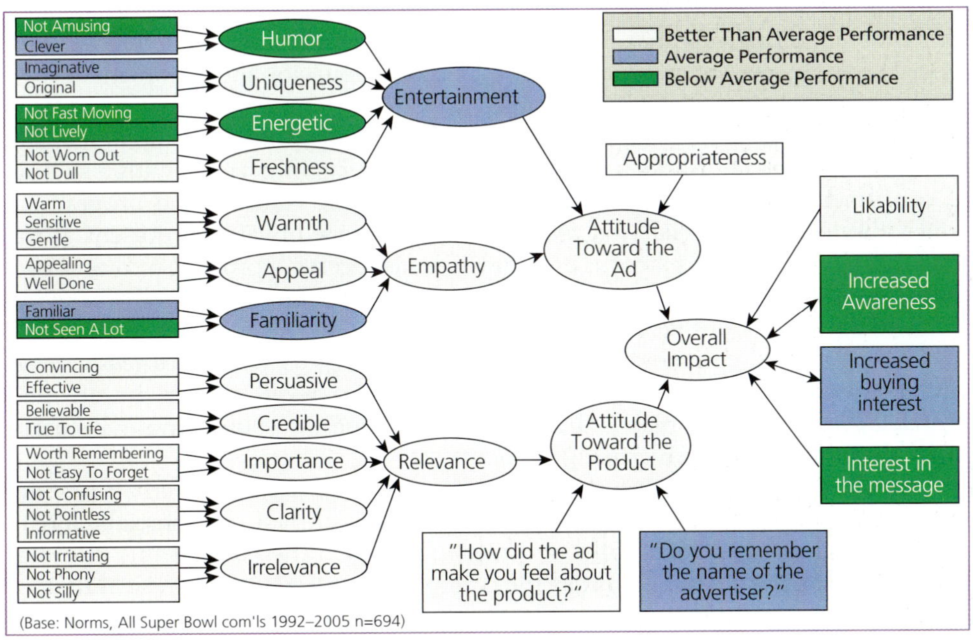

Figure 12.4

Advertising Response Model (ARM) for the "Thanking the Troops" Commercial better than average (compared to BRC norms), words coded in light blue reveal average performance, and those adjectives coded in red indicate below-average performance. A review of Figure 12.4 shows that the Anheuser-Busch commercial scored above average on indicators of uniqueness, freshness, warmth, persuasiveness, credibility, importance, and clarity. At the same time, the ad performed below average on humor (it wasn't intended to be humorous) and energy (it was an intentionally subdued ad). Moving from left to right on Figure 12.4, it further can be seen that the ad performed at just an average level in terms of entertainment value but above average in terms of empathy and relevance. As a result, the ad scored above average in terms of both attitude toward the ad and attitude toward the product. In turn, this commercial's overall impact was above average.

The president of BRC, Don Bruzzone, described this commercial as one of the top-performing commercials aired during the 2005 Super Bowl, virtually tied with two other commercials in the number of consumers who recognized it, remembered which brand it was for, and liked it. Although most Super Bowl ads are funnier and more energetic than Anheuser-Busch's "Thanking the Troops" commercial, hardly any of the 2005 Super Bowl commercials had the overall impact that this commercial exhibited.

In sum, BRC testing provides a valid prediction of actual marketplace performance along with being relatively inexpensive compared with other copy testing methods. Because a Bruzzone test cannot be implemented until after a finished TV commercial has actually been aired, it does not provide a before-the-fact indication of whether a commercial should be aired in the first place. Nevertheless, BRC's testing offers important information for evaluating a commercial's effectiveness and whether it should continue to run.

Day-After Recall Testing

Various companies test advertisements to determine whether viewers have been sufficiently influenced to recall having seen the advertisement in a magazine or on television. For example, Gallup & Robinson and Mapes & Ross are two well-known research companies that provide recall testing of ads placed in *print media.* Ipsos-ASI and Burke Marketing Research are notable firms that test consumer recall of *television commercials.* The following discussion focuses on Burke's procedure inasmuch as day-after recall testing and Burke are virtually inseparable in many people's minds. (It is only fair to note, however, that Burke performs many forms of marketing research other than day-after recall testing.) A later section describes the Ipsos-ASI method in the context of persuasion measurement.

Burke's day-after recall (DAR) procedure tests commercials that have been aired as part of normal television programming. The day following the first airing of a new commercial, Burke's telephone staff conducts interviews with a sample of consumers. The sample includes individuals who watched the program in which the test commercial was placed and who were physically present at the time the commercial was aired. These individuals receive a product or brand cue, are asked whether they saw the test commercial in question, and then are asked to recall all they can about it.

For each tested commercial, Burke reports findings as (1) *claimed-recall scores,* which indicate the percentage of respondents who recall seeing the ad; and (2) *related-recall scores,* which indicate the percentage of respondents who accurately describe specific advertising elements.

Advertisers and agencies use this information, along with verbatim statements from respondents, to assess the effectiveness of test commercials and to identify a commercial's strengths and weaknesses. On the basis of this information, a decision is made to advertise the commercial nationally, to revise it first, or possibly even to drop it.

The Recall Controversy

Considerable controversy has surrounded the use of DAR testing.[23] For example, Coca-Cola executives reject recall as a valid measure of advertising effectiveness because, in their opinion, recall simply measures whether an ad is received but not whether the message is accepted.[24] It also is known that measures of recall are biased in favor of younger consumers. This is to say that recall scores deteriorate with age progression.[25] Third, there is mounting evidence that the recall scores generated by advertisements are not predictive of sales performance; that is, regardless of which measure of recall is used, the evidence suggests that sales levels do not increase with increasing levels of recallability.[26]

Finally, there is some evidence that DAR testing significantly *understates the memorability* of commercials that employ *emotional or feeling-oriented themes* and is biased in favor of rational or thought-oriented commercials.[27] Research has even demonstrated a negative correlation between how well consumers recall ads and how much they like them.[28] In testing the assertion that DAR testing is biased against emotionally oriented commercials, the advertising agency Foote, Cone and Belding (FCB) conducted a study that compared three thinking and three feeling commercials. The six commercials were tested with two methods: the standard DAR measurement described previously and a *masked-recognition test.* The latter test involves showing a commercial to respondents on one day, telephoning them the next, requesting that they turn on their television sets to a given station where the commercial is shown once again (but this time *masked,* i.e., without any brand identification), and then asking them to identify the brand. FCB defines correct brand-name identification by this masked-recognition procedure as *proven recognition,* or *true remembering.*[29]

The results from FCB's research, shown in Table 12.2, demonstrate clearly the bias in day-after recall procedures against emotional, feeling commercials. It can be seen that the thinking commercials (coded A, D, and E in Table 12.2) perform only slightly better under masked-recognition measurement than under the standard DAR test. For example, commercial A obtained a DAR score of 49 percent and a masked-recognition score of 56 percent, thereby yielding a ratio of 114 percent (i.e., 56/49). In fact, as shown in Table 12.2, the average ratio for the three thinking commercials is 119 percent. This indicates that an average of only 19 percent more people recognized the advertised brand when prompted again by seeing the product advertised with the brand masked compared with recalling the brand entirely from memory.

Table 12.2

Day-After Recall Versus Masked-Recognition Research Findings

	Day-After Recall	Masked Recognition	Ratio of Masked Recognition to Recall
Thinking Commercials			
A	49%	56%	114
D	24	32	133
E	21	24	114
Average	31	37	119
Feeling Commercials			
B	21%	37%	176
C	25	36	144
F	10	23	230
Average	19	32	168

Comparatively, Table 12.2 shows that the feeling commercials (B, C, and F) performed considerably better under masked-recognition than under day-after recall procedures. Overall, the masked-recognition method reveals that proven recognition for the three feeling commercials is 68 percent higher than the day-after recall scores (i.e., their average ratio of masked recognition to recall is 168 percent).

These results clearly suggest that day-after recall tests may be biased against emotional, or feeling, commercials. A different research method, such as masked recognition, is needed when testing whether this type of commercial accomplishes suitable levels of awareness. Also, it is important that advertising research measure the emotions and feelings that advertisements evoke in people. The following section discusses the role of physiological measurement toward this end.

Emotional Reaction Measured via Physiological Arousal

Researchers have increasingly recognized that advertisements that positively influence receivers' feelings and emotions can be extremely successful for certain products and situations. Research has shown that ads that are better liked—often because they elicit positive emotions—are more likely to be remembered and to persuade.[30] Along with the trend toward more advertising directed at emotions, there has been a corresponding increase in efforts to measure consumers' affective and emotional reactions to advertisements.[31] Advertising researchers have used various physiological testing devices to measure these reactions. These include such techniques as using the galvanometer (which measures minute levels of perspiration in response to emotional arousal) and pupillometric tests (which measure pupil dilation).

Psychologists have concluded that these physiological functions are indeed sensitive to psychological processes of concern in advertising.[32] Physiological functions such as galvanic skin response and pupil dilation can be measured unobtrusively and without conscious consumer reaction, because these functions are controlled by the autonomic nervous system. The *autonomic nervous system* consists of the nerves and ganglia that furnish blood vessels, the heart, smooth muscles, and glands. Because individuals have little voluntary control over the autonomic nervous system, advertising researchers use changes in physiological functions to indicate the actual, unbiased amount of arousal resulting from advertisements.

To appreciate the potential value of such physiological measurement, consider the case of the Jose Cuervo Especial advertisement (Figure 12.2) that promotes the advertised brand by placing it in the context of a young couple in a provocative embrace along with the suggestive headline, "Pursue your daydreams." During pretesting of this ad, some people may respond that they really find it appealing. Others, when asked what they think of it, may indicate that they dislike the ad because they consider it too sexually suggestive and gratuitous. Still others may even feign aggravation to make (what they perceive to be) a favorable impression on the interviewer. That is, the latter group may actually enjoy the ad but say otherwise in response to an interviewer's query, thereby disguising their true evaluation. Here is where measures of physiological arousal have a potential role to play in advertising research—namely, to prevent self-monitoring of feelings and biased responses to standard paper-and-pencil measures.

The Galvanometer

The **galvanometer** (also referred to as the psychogalvanometer) is a device for measuring *galvanic skin response,* or *GSR.* (*Galvanic* refers to electricity produced by a chemical reaction.) When the consumer's autonomic nervous system is activated by some element in an advertisement, a physical response occurs in the sweat glands located in the palms and fingers. These glands open to varying degrees depending on the intensity of the arousal, and skin resistance drops when the sweat glands open. By sending a very fine electric current through one finger and out the other and completing the circuit through an instrument called a *galvanometer,* testers are able to measure both the degree and the frequency with which an advertisement activates emotional responses. Simply, the galvanometer indirectly assesses the degree of emotional response to an advertisement by measuring minute amounts of perspiration.

There is evidence to indicate that galvanic skin response is a valid indicator of the amount of warmth generated by an advertisement.[33] Many companies have found the galvanometer to be a useful tool for assessing the potential effectiveness of advertisements, direct-mail messages, package copy, and other marcom messages. Advertising research practitioners who use the galvanometer claim that it is a *valid* predictor (see PACT principle 9) of an advertisement's ability to *motivate* consumer purchase behavior.[34] Indeed, in recognition of the galvanometer's ability to reveal an advertisement's motivational properties, practitioners refer to GSR research as the Motivational Response Method, or MRM.

The Pupillometer

Pupillometric tests in advertising are conducted by measuring respondents' pupil dilation as they view a television commercial or focus on a printed advertisement. Respondents' heads are in a fixed position to permit continuous electronic measurement of changes in pupillary responses. Responses to specific elements in an advertisement are used to indicate positive reaction (in the case of greater dilation) or negative reaction (smaller relative dilation). Although not unchallenged, there has been scientific evidence since the late 1960s to suggest that pupillary responses are correlated with people's arousal to stimuli and perhaps even with their likes and dislikes.[35]

Measures of Persuasion

Measures of persuasion are used when an advertiser's objective is to influence consumers' attitudes toward and preference for the advertised brand. Firms that perform this type of research include, among others, Ipsos-ASI and rsc. The following sections describe, first, the Ipsos-ASI Next*TV method, and then rsc's ARS Persuasion method is explained in detail. More discussion is devoted to the latter advertising research procedure because rsc has done a particularly outstanding job in documenting its commercial service. (Parenthetically, it may have occurred to you that companies in the advertising research business have strange names. Actually, these names are no stranger than are the names of well-known companies such as IBM or AT&T. The research companies' names just seem strange because you probably were unfamiliar with them prior to reading this chapter.)

The Ipsos-ASI Next*TV Method

Ipsos is a French company that purchased ASI Market Research, an American company, in 1998. This international firm (which goes by Ipsos-ASI, The Advertising Research Company) performs various forms of advertising research in more than 50 countries. One of its most important advertising research services is the Next*TV method. This method tests television commercials in consumers' homes. Here is how the procedure works:

1. The company recruits consumers by informing them that their task, if they agree to participate, is to evaluate a television program. This is actually a disguise because the real purpose of the research is to evaluate consumer responses to advertisements that are embedded in a TV program.
2. The company mails to a national sample of consumers a videotape that contains a 30-minute TV program (such as a situation comedy) and in which are embedded television commercials. This procedure essentially replicates the actual prime-time viewing context.
3. Consumers are instructed to view the program (and, implicitly, the embedded advertising) from the videotape. The viewing context is thus actual, in-home viewing, the same as when consumers view any television advertising under natural viewing conditions.
4. One day after viewing the videotaped TV program (and advertisements), Ipsos-ASI personnel contact sampled consumers and measure their reactions to the TV program (in concert with the original disguise) and to the advertisements, which, of course, is the primary objective.
5. Ipsos-ASI then measures message recall and persuasion. Persuasion is measured by assessing consumers' attitudes toward advertised brands, their shift in brand preferences, and their brand-related buying intentions and purchase frequency.

Ipsos-ASI Next*TV employs the same basic methodology around the world. The in-home videotape methodology provides a number of advantages. First, the in-home exposure makes it possible to measure advertising effectiveness in a natural environment. Second, by embedding test advertisements in actual programming content along with other advertisements, it is possible to assess the ability of TV commercials to break through the clutter, gain the viewer's attention, and influence message recallability and persuadability. Third, by measuring recall one day after exposure, Ipsos-ASI can determine how well tested commercials are remembered after this delay period. Fourth, the videotape technology allows the use of representative national sampling. Finally, by providing several alternative measures of persuasion, the Next*TV method allows brand managers and their ad agencies to select the measures that best meet their specific needs.

The ARS Persuasion Method

Research Systems Company (which goes simply by rsc) is one of the most active message-testing research suppliers. This company tests individual selling propositions as well as entire television commercials. Commercials are tested at varying stages of completion ranging from rough-cut (e.g., animatics or photomatics) to finished form. Rsc's testing procedure is called the ARS Persuasion method, where ARS stands for Advertising Research System. The ARS testing procedure is as follows:

Commercials are exposed in regular ARS test sessions to [800 to 1,000] men and women (aged 16+) drawn randomly from [eight] metropolitan areas and invited to preview typical television material. Each test commercial and other unrelated commercials are inserted into the television programs. While at the central location, a measurement of ARS Persuasion is made by obtaining brand preferences before and after exposure to the pro-

grams. The ARS Persuasion measure is the percent of respondents choosing the test product over competition after exposure to the TV material minus the percent choosing the test product before exposure.[36]

In other words, the ARS Persuasion method first has respondents indicate which brands they would prefer to receive among various product categories if their names were selected in a drawing to win a "basket" of free items (the *premeasure*). Among the list of products and brands is a "target brand" for which, unbeknownst to respondents, they subsequently will be exposed to a commercial that is being tested. After exposure to a television program, within which is embedded the test commercial, respondents again indicate which brands they would prefer to receive if their names were selected in a drawing (the *postmeasure*). The ARS Persuasion score simply represents the postmeasure percentage of respondents preferring the target brand minus the premeasure percentage who prefer that brand (see the following equation). A positive score indicates that the test commercial has shifted preference *toward* the target brand and reinforced brand preference among pre-choosers.

ARS Persuasion Score = Post % for target brand – Pre % for target brand (Equation 12.1)

Research Systems Corporation has tested over 30,000 commercials in its 30-year history, and from these tests it has been able to establish—albeit not without challenge[37]—that its ARS Persuasion scores predict the magnitude of actual sales performance when commercials are aired. That is, higher-scoring commercials generate greater sales volume and larger market share gains.

Predictive Validity of ARS Persuasion Scores

Based on the results of 332 commercials that were tested in seven countries—including Belgium, Germany, Mexico, and the United States—principals at rsc have demonstrated how ARS Persuasion scores relate to changes in market share.[38] A total of 148 brands (some with multiple commercials tested) representing 76 product categories were involved in the analysis. All 332 commercials were tested under the procedures described previously, and then market-share levels under actual in-market circumstances were compared during a period after advertising commenced for the brands versus a period prior to any advertising. Hence, the key issue is whether ARS Persuasion scores accurately predict the magnitude of market-share gain (or loss) following advertising. In other words, are the scores that rsc generates from its laboratory testing predictive of actual marketplace performance? This obviously is a validity issue as described previously under PACT principle 9. Results from these 332 tests are presented in Table 12.3. This global validation revealed that ARS Persuasion scores are predictive of market-share changes, yielding, in fact, a high correlation coefficient ($r = 0.71$) and an impressive coefficient of determination ($r^2 = .51$).

Table 12.3

Rsc's Global Validation Study: ARS Persuasion Scores and In-Market Results

ARS Persuasion Score Range	Average Share Change	Percentage of Ads Achieving Share-Point Difference of:			
		0.0+	0.5+	1.0+	2.0+
<2.0	−0.2	47%	12%	2%	0%
2.0 – 2.9	0.0	53	19	6	0
3.0 – 3.9	0.5	80	46	26	6
4.0 – 6.9	0.8	80	58	33	9
7.0 – 8.9	1.6	100	87	56	36
9.0 – 11.9	2.2	100	97	72	49
12.0+	5.4	100	100	94	83

SOURCE: "Summary of the ARS Group's Global Validation and Business Implications 2004 Update," June 2004, 17.

To fully understand what these results reveal, let us carefully examine the first row in Table 12.3. This row includes all commercials that received very low (less than 2.0) ARS Persuasion scores, and implies that commercials scoring less than 2.0 are probably incapable of driving market-share gains. In fact, as shown under the "Average Share Change" column, commercials scoring less than 2.0 on the ARS Persuasion measure experienced, on average, *losses* of 0.2 market-share points. Looking at the next four columns reveals that for those commercials yielding ARS Persuasion scores of less than 2.0, only 47 percent were able to maintain market share or yield some small incremental growth. Comparatively, 53 percent (i.e., 100 – 47) of these low-scoring commercials actually suffered market-share losses! Moreover, only 2 percent of these low-scoring commercials generated gains of one full market-share point or more.

At the other extreme, 100 percent of the highly effective commercials (i.e., those with ARS Persuasion scores of 12.0 or higher) yielded positive share gains. Indeed, all 100 percent of these high-performance commercials produced gains of 0.5 share points or better, with 94 percent yielding gains of at least 1.0 share point, and 83 percent providing gains of at least 2.0 share points. The average gain in market-share points for commercials receiving ARS Persuasion scores of 12.0+ was an impressive 5.4.

Let us examine one additional row of data, specifically, that for commercials receiving ARS Persuasion scores in the middle range of 4.0 to 6.9. Commercials in this range yielded an average gain of 0.8 market-share points. Eighty percent of the commercials in this range either maintained or increased their brands' market shares, with 58 percent of the commercials yielding share gains of 0.5 share points or greater, 33 percent producing gains of 1.0 full share point or more, and 9 percent generating gains of 2.0 or more share points. Entries for the other ranges can be interpreted in a similar fashion.

It is apparent from these 332 test cases that ARS Persuasion scores are valid predictors of in-market performance. In sum, the higher the ARS Persuasion score, the greater the likelihood that a tested commercial will produce positive sales gains when the focal brand is advertised under real-world, in-market conditions. This global study thus informs advertisers that they should not place advertising weight behind commercials that have tested poorly. Table 12.3 reveals, in fact, that commercials with a 2.0 or lower ARS Persuasion score most likely will not produce a positive share gain, and that a large percentage (i.e., 100 – 53 = 47 percent) of those scoring in the 2.0 to 2.9 range also are likely to suffer share losses. It is only when commercials test in the 3.0 to 3.9 range or higher that meaningful share gains can be anticipated.

Research Systems Corporation has, of course, a vested interest in reporting that its testing system provides accurate predictions of marketplace performance; nonetheless, the fact that articles authored by rsc principals have been published in peer-reviewed journals (e.g., the *Journal of Advertising Research*) authenticates their conclusions. Moreover, advertising scholars have provided independent endorsement of rsc's ARS Persuasion technique.[39]

Measures of Sales Response (Single-Source Systems)

Determining the sales impact of advertising is—as discussed in Chapters 2, 6, and 9—a most difficult task. However, research procedures now are available—especially in the case of consumer packaged goods (CPG) products available in supermarkets, drugstores, and mass merchandise outlets—that are able to assess the effects an advertising campaign has on a brand's sales. (Please note that discussion will be limited to advertising, but the major providers of single-source systems discussed in this section also offer procedures for testing the sales-generating effects of other marketing-mix variables such as sales promotions and point-of-purchase materials.)

So-called single-source systems (SSSs) have evolved to measure the effects of advertising on sales. SSSs became possible with the advent of three technological developments: (1) *electronic television meters,* (2) *optical laser scanning* of universal product codes (UPC symbols), and (3) *split-cable* technology. **Single-source systems** gather purchase data from panels of households using optical scanning equipment and merge them with household demographic characteristics and, most important, with information about causal marketing variables, such as advertisements, that influence household purchases. The following sections describe two major single-source systems: ACNielsen's ScanTrack and IRI's BehaviorScan.

ACNielsen's ScanTrack

There are two very interesting characteristics of ScanTrack's data-collection procedure. First, and most important, ScanTrack collects purchase data by having its hundreds of panel households use *handheld scanners.* These scanners are located in panel members' homes, usually mounted to a kitchen or pantry wall. Upon returning from a shopping trip, ScanTrack panelists are directed to record purchases of *every bar-coded product purchased* regardless of the store where purchased—a major grocery chain, independent supermarket, mass merchandiser, or wholesale club.[40]

A second distinguishing characteristic of ScanTrack is that panel members also use their handheld scanners to enter any coupons used and to record all store deals and in-store features that influenced their purchasing decisions. Each panel member transmits purchases and other data to Nielsen every week by calling a toll-free number and holding up the scanner to a phone, which records the data via a series of electronic beeps. ACNielsen's ScanTrack has provided advertisers and their agencies with invaluable information about the short- and long-term effects of advertising.

IRI's BehaviorScan

Information Resources Inc. (IRI) pioneered single-source data collection when it introduced its BehaviorScan service a generation ago. IRI operates BehaviorScan panel households in five markets around the United States: Pittsfield, Massachusetts; Eau Claire, Wisconsin; Cedar Rapids, Iowa; Midland, Texas; and Grand Junction, Colorado. (IRI also has BehaviorScan panels in many other countries.) These small cities were chosen because they are located far enough from television stations that residents must depend on *cable TV* to receive good reception. Moreover, grocery stores and drugstores in these cities are equipped with optical scanning devices that read UPC symbols from packages and thereby record exactly which product categories and brands panel households purchase.

In each market, approximately 3,000 households are recruited to participate in a BehaviorScan panel, and about one-third of these households are equipped with electronic meters attached to TV sets. Panel members are eligible for prize drawings as remuneration for their participation. Because each BehaviorScan household has an identification card that is presented at the grocery store checkout on every shopping occasion, IRI knows precisely which items each household purchases by merely linking up optically scanned purchases with ID numbers. (Starting in 2002, IRI also began supplying panel members with handheld scanners to record purchases in stores other than traditional grocery stores, such as mass merchandise outlets and supercenters. This enabled IRI's BehaviorScan procedure to provide coverage of all retail outlets, as does ACNielsen's ScanTrack method.) Panel members also provide IRI with detailed demographic information, including family size, income level, number of televisions owned, the types of newspapers and magazines read, and who in the household does most of the shopping. (Please note that ACNielsen's ScanTrack procedure also collects this type of information.) IRI then combines all these data into a *single source* and thereby determines which households purchase which products and brands and how responsive they are to advertising and other purchase-causing variables. Thus, single-source data consist of (1) household demographic information; (2) household purchase behavior; and (3) household exposure to (or, more technically, the opportunity to see, or OTS) new television commercials that are tested under real-world, or *in-market,* test conditions.

The availability of cable TV enables IRI (with the cooperation of cable companies and advertisers) to intercept a cable signal before it reaches households, *split the signal,* and send different advertisements to two panels of households (test versus control). Hence, the split-cable feature and optically scanned purchase data enable IRI to know which commercial each household had an opportunity to see and how much of the advertised brand the household purchases.

Weight Versus Copy Tests

IRI's BehaviorScan procedure enables testing of television commercial effectiveness. Two types of tests are offered: weight tests and copy tests. In both types of tests, a test commercial is aired in, say, two BehaviorScan markets for up to a full year. With *weight tests,* panel households are divided into test and control groups. The identical commercial is transmitted to both groups, but the number of gross rating points (GRPs), or weight, is varied between the groups during the course of the test period. Any difference between the groups' aggregate purchase behavior for the tested brand is obviously attributable to the advertising weight differential between the two groups.

The second form of testing, *copy tests,* holds the amount of weight constant but varies commercial content. That is, a test group is exposed during the course of the testing period to a new commercial, whereas a control group has an opportunity to see either a public service announcement (PSA) or an old commercial for the same brand inserted in place of the new commercial. Regardless of the type of test, aggregating purchase data across all households in each of the two groups simplifies determining whether differences in advertising copy or weight generate differences in purchase behavior.

The Testing Procedure

To better understand how BehaviorScan's single-source data can be used to show the relationship between advertising and sales activity, consider a situation in which a manufacturer of a new snack food is interested in testing the effectiveness of a television commercial promoting this brand. BehaviorScan would do the following: (1) select, say, two markets in which to conduct the test (perhaps Midland, Texas and Grand Junction, Colorado); (2) stock the manufacturer's brand in all grocery stores and perhaps drugstores located in these markets; (3) selectively broadcast a new commercial for the brand using special split-cable television so approximately one-half of the panel members in each market are exposed either to the new commercial or to PSAs; (4) record electronically (via optical scanners) grocery purchases made by all panel members; and (5) compare the purchase behavior of the two groups of panel members who were potentially exposed to the new commercial versus PSAs.

If the advertising is effective, a greater proportion of the panel members exposed to the test commercial should buy the promoted item than those only exposed to the PSAs. The percentage of panel members who undertake a trial purchase behavior would thereby indicate the effectiveness of the new television commercial, and the percentage that make a repeat purchase would indicate how much the brand is liked.

Some Major Conclusions about Television Advertising

The previous sections have discussed various measures of advertising effectiveness, including rsc's ARS Persuasion method and single-source systems for assessing the sales effectiveness of TV commercials (ScanTrack and BehaviorScan). The extensive testing performed by rsc has played a significant role in enhancing our understanding of the strengths and limitations of television advertising. Research evidence presented by rsc with support from academic circles justifies including a major section devoted to this topic.

Four major conclusions can be drawn from rsc's research that has used the ARS Persuasion method with respect to what it takes for television advertising to successfully enhance a brand's sales performance: (1) ad copy must be distinctive, (2) ad weight without persuasiveness is insufficient, (3) the selling power of advertising wears out over time, and (4) advertising works quickly if it works at all.[41]

Conclusion 1—All Commercials Are Not Created Equal: Ad Copy Must Be Distinctive

What is distinctive ad copy? Research by rsc has shown that commercials having *strong selling propositions* are distinctive and thereby tend to achieve higher ARS Persuasion scores. What determines whether a commercial has a strong selling proposition? Research indicates that any differentiating information concerning a new brand or a new feature of an existing brand gives a selling proposition a significantly higher chance of a superior score.[42] Although commercials for new brands and those with new features are more persuasive on average, advertising for established brands also can be very persuasive via *brand differentiation*—that is, by distinguishing the advertised brand from competitive offerings and providing consumers with a distinctive reason to buy it.[43] The photoboard version of a Mentadent ProCare toothbrush television commercial (Figure 12.5) illustrates an advertisement that obtained a high ARS Persuasion score of 11.2 because the ad contained the strong selling proposition that this toothbrush has a flexible handle that allows gentle brushing.

The foregoing discussion has illustrated a key advertising principle: effective advertising must be persuasive and distinctive, or, stated alternatively, it must possess a strong selling proposition. Appreciation of this point necessitates rigorous testing of proposed advertisements prior to committing any media dollars to their airing or printing. Reminiscent of the classic parental admonition to young children to "look before you cross the street," a similar exhortation can be made to advertisers when formulating advertising messages: "Test before you air or print!" To put it bluntly, it is foolhardy to invest money in a media campaign without first having ensured that the advertising message is fully capable of shifting brand preference toward the advertised brand. It is for this reason that sophisticated advertisers should always pretest proposed advertisements prior to printing or airing them.

Figure 12.5

Illustration of a Commercial With a Strong Selling Proposition

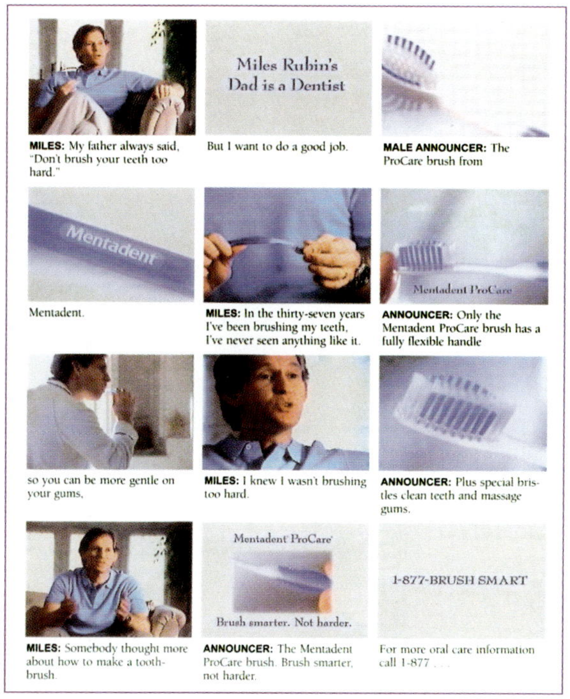

Church & Dwight

Evidence from Frito-Lay's Copy Tests

To test the effectiveness of television commercials for its various brands of salted snack and cookie brands, marketing researchers and brand managers at Frito-Lay commissioned IRI to perform 23 split-panel experiments in BehaviorScan markets over a four-year period.[44] All 23 experiments were copy (versus weight) tests that involved comparing one group of households who were exposed to advertising for a Frito-Lay brand (advertising households) against another group that had no opportunity to see the advertising (control households). Each of the 23 tests was conducted in at least two BehaviorScan markets and lasted a full year. In addition to the advertising versus no-advertising condition, Frito-Lay's BehaviorScan tests also were classified in terms of (1) whether the tested brand was a new brand (e.g., SunChips) or an established brand (e.g., Ruffles); and (2) whether sales for the brand were relatively large (e.g., Doritos) or small (e.g., Rold Gold).

The objective in conducting these tests was to determine whether sales volume would be greater in households exposed to advertisements for Frito-Lay brands versus those households that had no opportunity to be exposed to television commercials for these brands. Results from the 23 Frito-Lay BehaviorScan tests are summarized in Table 12.4.

The first notable observation from Table 12.4 is that advertising for 57 percent of the 23 tested brands generated significant increases in sales volume during the one-year test duration. (Though not shown in Table 12.4, the average gain in sales volume between the advertising versus no-advertising household panels was 15 percent across the 12 advertisements that yielded significant sales increases.) A second key finding shown in Table 12.4 is that advertising for the small sales-volume brands was much more effective in driving sales gains than was advertising for the large brands. In fact, of the 12 small brands tested, 83 percent, or 10 brands, experienced significant increases in sales as a result of their one-year advertising efforts. A third important finding is that advertising for 88 percent of the new brands generated significant sales gains, whereas only 40 percent of the established brands resulted in sales gains from advertising.

The 23 BehaviorScan tests of Frito-Lay brands reveal that advertising is not always effective; indeed, it was effective in slightly more than one-half of the tests. Importantly, this research supports the finding that advertising generally is effective only when it provides distinctive, newsworthy information, such as when introducing new brands or line extensions.

Table 12.4

BehaviorScan Tests of Advertising Effectiveness for 23 Frito-Lay Brands

	Established Brands	New Brands	Total
Large Brands	13% (n=8)*	67% (n=3)	27% (n=11)
Small Brands	71 (n=7)	100 (n=5)	83 (n=12)
Total	40 (n=15)	88 (n=8)	57 (n=23)

*Table entries are to be interpreted as follows: A total of eight (out of 23) tests involved large, established brands. Of the eight tests conducted with this particular combination of brands, only one test, or 13 percent, detected a statistically significant increase in sales volume in those households exposed to advertising compared to the no-advertising control households.

Conclusion 2—More Is Not Necessarily Better: Weight Is Not Enough

Fully appreciating this second major conclusion requires that we first understand the concept of advertising "weight." This concept will be covered more in the next several chapters, but for now, ad *weight* should be understood as meaning the number of *gross rating points,* or *GRPs,* that support an advertising campaign. More GRPs equate to more advertising weight. Obviously, advertising weight and spending also correlate—the more people you want to reach and the more often you wish to reach them, the higher will be the advertising weight and the cost.

Given this background, we now consider a second important conclusion about advertising effectiveness—namely, that the amount of advertising weight invested in a brand does *not* by itself provide a good predictor of sales performance. In other words, merely increasing advertising weight does not directly translate into better performance for a brand. Advertising copy *must also be distinctive and persuasive* (as previously established) for advertising to have a positive impact on a brand's sales and market share. An advertising practitioner perhaps said it best when stating that "airing ineffective advertising is like being off-air; it just costs more."[45] It cannot be overemphasized that unpersuasive, nondistinctive advertising is not worth airing or printing.

This conclusion receives support from a landmark study that analyzed numerous tests based on BehaviorScan single-source data. A well-known advertising scholar and his colleagues determined that when advertisements are unpersuasive, there is no more likelihood of achieving sales volume increases even when doubling and tripling TV advertising weight.[46]

The virtual independence between advertising weight and sales is clearly demonstrated in Table 12.5. The results presented in this table are based on studies

Table 12.5

Relations Among Advertising Weight, Persuasion Scores, and Sales

Test Number	Weight Difference	ARS Persuasion Score	Sales Difference
1	334 GRPs	−1.3	NSD*
2	4,200	0.6	NSD
3	406	1.8	NSD
4	1,400	2.6	NSD
5	695	2.7	NSD
6	800	2.8	NSD
7	2,231	3.5	NSD
8	1,000	3.6	NSD
9	900	3.7	NSD
10	1,800	4.0	NSD
11	947	4.2	NSD
12	820	4.3	NSD
13	1,364	4.4	NSD
14	1,198	4.4	NSD
15	583	5.9	SD†
16	1,949	6.7	SD
17	580	7.0	SD
18	778	7.7	SD
19	1,400	9.0	SD
20	860	9.3	SD

*NSD: Purchases of the advertised brand were *not* significantly different between the two split-cable panels at a 90 percent confidence level.

†SD: Purchases of the advertised brand were significantly different between the two split-cable panels at a 90 percent confidence level.

SOURCE: Margaret Henderson Blair, "An Empirical Investigation of Advertising, Wearin and Wearout," *Journal of Advertising Research* 27 (December 1987/January 1988), 45–50. Reprinted with permission from the *Journal of Advertising Research,* ©1987, by the Advertising Research Foundation.

using single-source data for various brands of CPGs. The data in Table 12.5 are derived from *weight tests* whereby two panels of households had an opportunity to see the identical commercial for a particular brand, but the amount of spending, or weight, was varied between the two panels. These households' subsequent purchases of the advertised brand are later compared based on purchase data acquired via optical scanning devices in grocery stores.

Table 12.5 presents data from 20 weight tests, each involving an actual marketplace examination of advertising's influence on the sales of a branded grocery product. In each test, there are two key features of the advertising effort. First is the number of GRPs, or weight, used to advertise the brand; in Table 12.5 this is expressed as the *weight difference* between the two panels of households. A difference of zero would mean that an identical amount of advertising weight (in terms of GRPs) was aired during the test period to both groups of households. The second key advertising feature is the ARS Persuasion score that the test commercial obtained in each test. These scores range from a low of –1.3 (test 1) to a high of 9.3 (test 20). Finally, for each reported test, the last column indicates whether a statistically significant sales difference occurred between the two panels.

Thus, test 8, for example, shows a weight difference of 1,000 GRPs between the two panels. However, the tested commercial in this case received a below-average ARS Persuasion score of 3.6. Given this combination of a heavy weight difference between the two panels but a relatively unpersuasive commercial, the result was no significant difference (NSD) in sales between the two panels of households at the end of the full-year testing period. In other words, heavy advertising weight was unable to compensate for an unpersuasive commercial.

Now let us examine test 15, in which the weight difference between the two panels of households amounted to 583 GRPs. However, the new commercial in this test received an ARS Persuasion score of 5.9. The result: a significant difference (SD) in sales was recorded when the tested brand was advertised with a moderately persuasive commercial.

Table 12.5 also demonstrates that no significant sales differences are obtained even in instances of huge weight differences such as in tests 2 (a 4,200 GRP difference) and 7 (a 2,231 GRP difference). These two tests corresponded (at the time of the research) with annual ad expenditures of $21 million and $11 million, yet no differential sales response materialized after a full year. Comparatively, notice in tests 15 through 20 that significant sales differences *are* observed even when the weight differences are relatively small compared with the weight differences in tests 2 and 7. Hence, it can be concluded that the primary determinant of sales differences in these tests was the *persuasiveness* of the tested commercials. Whenever the ARS Persuasion score was 5.9 or greater, significant sales differences were detected at the end of the test; in all instances in which the ARS Persuasion score was below 5.9, no significant sales differences were obtained.

Provided these results generalize beyond the tested commercials, the implication is that a commercial's persuasiveness is absolutely critical: persuasiveness, and not mere advertising weight, is the prime determinant of whether an advertising campaign will translate into improved sales performance. Indeed, investing advertising in unpersuasive commercials is akin to throwing money away. Advertising weight is important, but only if a commercial presents a persuasive story.[47]

Campbell Soup Company Findings

Research conducted by rsc for the Campbell Soup Company provides additional evidence regarding the importance of commercial persuasiveness.[48] Figure 12.6 presents the results of rsc's testing of various commercials for an undisclosed Campbell Soup Company brand, which we will assume to be V8 vegetable juice.

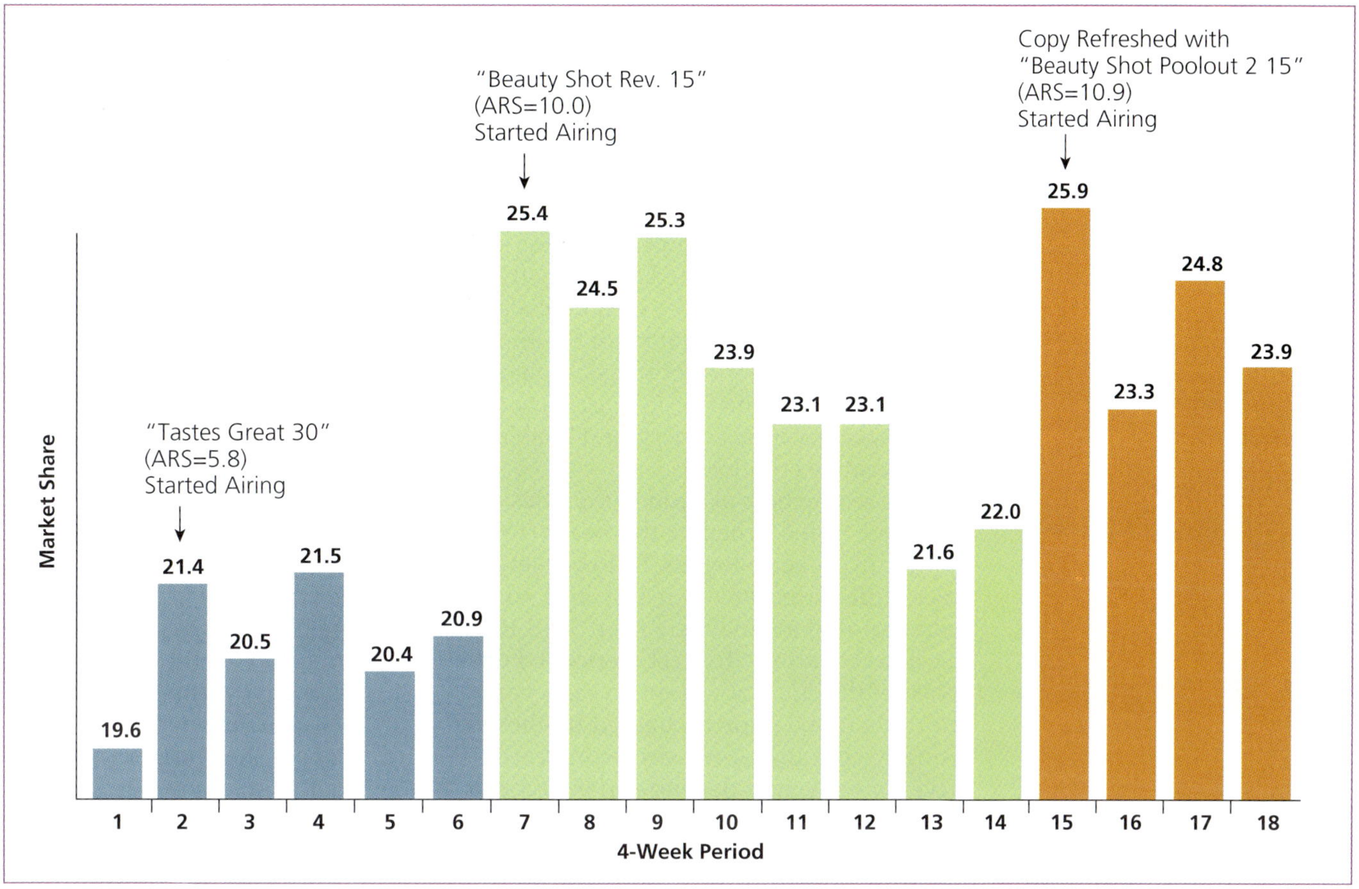

Used with permission from the ARS Group

Figure 12.6

The Role of Sales-Effective Advertising for an Undisclosed Campbell Soup Brand

Note that the horizontal axis is broken into 18 four-week periods, and that the vertical axis of the graph depicts this brand's market shares. It can be seen that V8's market share during the first four-week period was 19.6.

Notice next that a new commercial (titled "Tastes Great 30," with the *30* signifying a 30-second commercial) was aired during the second four-week period. This commercial, when tested by rsc, received an ARS Persuasion score of 5.8. Shortly after airing this new commercial, V8's market share jumped from 19.6 to 21.4—an increase of nearly 2 share points. Thereafter, V8's market share varied from a low of 20.4 (period 5) to a high of 21.5 (period 4). Then in period 7, when a new commercial started airing ("Beauty Shot Revised 15"), V8's market share jumped by an incredible 4.5 share points to 25.4.

Notice how this result correlates to the strength of the new commercial, which obtained an ARS Persuasion score of 10.0. Over the next several months, the market share for V8 fell to 22.0 (period 14). Then in period 15 another new commercial began airing ("Beauty Shot Poolout 2 15"). This commercial, which obtained an ARS Persuasion score of 10.9, immediately increased V8's sales to a 25.9 market share. By period 18 the share had declined to a 23.9, but compared with the initial share of 19.6 in period 1, this still represented a gain of 4.3 share points in slightly more than a year—a substantial market-share gain by any standard in an established product category. These results indicate that persuasive commercials can have a rather dramatic effect in increasing market share.

The Relationship between Media Weight and Creative Content

Beyond rsc's results with the ARS Persuasion method, important research from the academic front has provided further insight into the conditions under which additional advertising weight does or does not increase a brand's sales.[49] This research program tested 47 actual TV commercials that were drawn from a variety of mature product categories for familiar brands (i.e., brands in categories such as frozen entrees, snack chips, and long-distance dialing services). Each of the 47 commercials was classified as to whether its tone and content primarily included (1) *rational information* (i.e., commercials conveying details about product features and benefits); (2) *heuristic appeals* (i.e., commercials employing credible or trustworthy endorsers, and those using pictures or music to convey information about the advertised brand); or (3) *affectively based cues* (i.e., commercials using warmth appeals, captivating scenery, and likable music—all of which are capable of generating positive emotions).

The researchers examined the sales results of *weight tests* for these 47 commercials and tested whether the heavy weight differences between groups of consumers exposed to higher- or lower-levels of advertising weight led to significant sales differences between test and control groups. (The higher-weight groups were exposed to anywhere from 50 to 100 percent more commercials for a particular brand during the test period.) Further and importantly, they also tested whether the effect of weight on sales varied as a function of advertising content. In short, then, the issue addressed by these researchers was whether greater advertising weight uniformly drives increased sales or whether the effect of increased advertising weight depends on the type of creative content in a commercial.

The very important finding from this research is that increased advertising weight led to significant increases in sales for consumers exposed to greater amounts of advertising weight *only* for commercials using *affectively based cues.* For commercials employing rational information or heuristic appeals, no significant sales gains were realized when the amount of advertising weight was increased substantially. It seems, then, that commercials using affectively based cues respond positively to greater advertising weight because this type of commercial evokes positive feelings in consumers; comparatively, commercials containing rational information or heuristic appeals grow tiresome more quickly and may even turn consumers off with repeated showings.

It is important to realize that this research included only commercials drawn from mature product categories and included only familiar brands. The results possibly do not generalize to commercials for new product categories or new brands in mature categories. In either event, heavy advertising weight thrown behind informative advertisements (i.e., those supplying rational information or using heuristic appeals) may *not* serve very well to drive sales. On the other hand, putting more weight behind ads using affectively based cues (i.e., emotional ads) may well increase sales rather substantially.

Conclusion 3—All Good Things Must End: Advertising Eventually Wears Out

Another important lesson learned from the previous presentation of the Campbell's V8 case, as well as supported by abundant other evidence, is that advertising ultimately *wears out* and hence must be periodically refreshed to maintain or increase a brand's sales.[50] Research in the academic community as well as by practitioners has convincingly demonstrated that with the accumulation of GRPs for a brand, the persuasive power of that brand's advertising declines over time.[51] This is referred to as **wearout**, the result of which is diminished effectiveness of advertising as GRPs accumulate over time. Interestingly, *familiar brands* (i.e., those for which consumers have direct usage experience or have learned about the brand via information from marcom messages) have been shown to wear out more slowly than unfamiliar brands.[52] This suggests that stronger brands—that is, those with greater equity (recall discussion in Chapter 2)—can continue to use creative executions for a longer period of time, need to refresh advertising less frequently, and thus obtain a bigger bang for the advertising buck. The old saying that "knowledge begets knowledge" has a counterpart in this context, namely that "success begets more success"—that is, familiar brands that possess greater brand equity enjoy increased marcom effectiveness by postponing the onset of advertising wearout.

The moral from conclusion 3 is that it is important to periodically retest commercials (using, for example, the ARS Persuasion measurement) to determine how much persuasive power remains in a commercial. When the persuasive power falls into the 3.0 to 3.9 range or even below (see Table 12.3), it probably is time to replace the commercial with a new or revised execution.

Conclusion 4—Don't Be Stubborn: Advertising Works Quickly or Not at All

Due to the difficulty of precisely determining what effect advertising has on sales, in many instances advertisers initiate an advertising campaign and then stick with it for a number of months. Even though there may be no initial evidence that advertising is moving the sales dial, there is a tendency among some advertisers to "hang in there," hoping that with repeated exposures (increased weight) the advertising will eventually achieve positive results. Thoughts such as "Let's not drop the campaign too quickly" or "We just have to be patient" oftentimes are applied to sustain a questionable advertising campaign.

Insight into the issue of how long an advertiser should stick with an ad campaign is available from the previously discussed findings from Frito-Lay's series of 23 BehaviorScan copy tests. Though not apparent in Table 12.4, a fourth notable result from the Frito-Lay BehaviorScan testing is that in all 12 (of 23) cases where advertisements for Frito-Lay brands drove significant sales increases, the effects occurred within the first six months. More dramatically, in 11 of the 12 tests with significant sales gains, the increased sales occurred within the first three months! In other words, when advertising works, it works relatively quickly or not at all.

The moral underlying this last conclusion is that although there is some virtue to being patient, there is a difference between being patient and stubborn. Sometimes advertisers have to accept the fact that an advertising campaign simply is not driving sales increases. The economic concept of *sunk costs* is relevant in this context. That concept, in particular, informs us that decisions should not be made with respect to past expenditures but in terms of future prospects. Costs sunk in the past cannot justify continuing with something that is not producing sales gains. Wise decision makers simply have to be prepared to walk away from past mistakes (such as ill-advised advertising campaigns), accept the fact that past expenditures are sunk, strive not to repeat the same mistake in the future, and, in the vernacular, strive not to throw good money after bad.

Summary

Though difficult and often expensive, measuring message effectiveness is essential for advertisers to better understand how well their ads are performing and which changes they need to make to improve performance. Message-based research evaluates the effectiveness of advertising messages. Dozens of techniques for measuring advertising effectiveness have evolved over the years. The reason for this diversity is that advertisements perform various functions and multiple methods are needed to test different indicators of advertising effectiveness.

Starch Readership Service, Bruzzone tests, and day-after recall tests are techniques for measuring recognition and recall. Physiological measures such as galvanic skin response and pupil dilation are used to assess emotional arousal activated by advertisements. The Ipsos-ASI Next*TV method is a videotape, in-home system for measuring consumer reactions to television commercials. Rsc's ARS Persuasion testing is used to measure preference shifts employing a pre- and postmeasurement of consumer preference for a brand before and after they have seen an advertisement for that brand. The impact of advertising on actual purchase behavior is assessed with single-source data collection systems (IRI's BehaviorScan and Nielsen's ScanTrack) that obtain optical-scanned purchase data from household panels and then integrate them with television-viewing behavior and other marketing variables.

No single technique for measuring advertising effectiveness is ideal, nor is any particular technique appropriate for all occasions. The choice of technique depends on the specific objective an advertising campaign is intended to accomplish. Moreover, multiple measurement methods are usually preferable to single techniques to answer the diversity of questions that are typically involved in attempts to assess advertising effectiveness.

The final major section presents conclusions about TV commercial effectiveness based on research that has measured advertising persuasiveness, explored the role of increasing advertising weight, examined the impact of creative copy, and determined whether these advertising factors generate meaningful sales gains. Four major conclusions are that: (1) ad copy must be distinctive in order to drive sales gains; (2) more advertising weight does not necessarily equate to increased sales; (3) advertising eventually wears out; and (4) if advertising is going to work, it will achieve its positive effect relatively quickly.

Discussion Questions

1. It is desirable that measurements of advertising effectiveness focus on sales response rather than on some precursor to sales, yet measuring sales response to advertising is typically difficult. What complicates the measurement of sales response to advertising? To answer this question, please return to Chapter 6 and the section on using sales as an objective for marcom programs.
2. PACT principle 2 states that a good copy testing system should establish how results will be used in advance of each copy test. Explain the specific meaning and importance of this copy testing principle. Construct an illustration of an anticipated result lacking a sufficient action standard and one with a suitable standard.
3. What's the distinction between the pre- and posttesting forms of advertising research? Which in your opinion is more important? Be sure to justify your response.
4. The Bruzzone test is based on a measure of recognition in comparison to day-after recall testing, which, of course, is based on a recall measure. Present an argument as to why the Bruzzone recognition measurement might be more appropriate than the recall measurement in attempting to determine the effectiveness of television commercials. To facilitate your discussion, consider the difference between multiple-choice testing (a form of recognition measurement) and essay testing (a form of recall measurement).
5. Please offer your interpretation of the following quote presented earlier in the chapter: "If you can't measure something, you can't understand it. If you can't understand it, you can't control it. If you can't control it, you can't improve it."

6. If you were an account executive in an advertising agency, what would you tell clients to convince them to use (or not to use) the Starch Readership Service?
7. A test of television advertising effectiveness performed by BehaviorScan will cost you, as brand manager of a new brand of cereal, over $250,000. Why might this be a prudent investment in comparison to spending $50,000 to perform an awareness study?
8. Assume that several years from now, after you have graduated college and begun a career, you open your mail one day and find a letter from Information Resources Inc. (IRI) requesting you to become a BehaviorScan panel member. Would you have any reservations about agreeing to do this? Assume that the letter is from ACNielsen, instead of IRI, requesting your participation in ScanTrack. What would be your reservations, if any, in this case?
9. Select three recent television commercials for well-known brands, identify the objective(s) each appears to be attempting to accomplish, and then propose a procedure for how you would go about testing the effectiveness of each commercial. Be specific.
10. Television commercials are tested in various stages of completion, including storyboards, animatics, photomatics, ripomatics, liveamatics, and finished commercials. What reservations might you have concerning the ability to project results from testing prefinished commercials to actual marketplace results with real commercials? Be specific and refer to the PACT principles where appropriate.
11. What are your thoughts about the value (or lack of value) of using measures of physiological response such as the galvanometer?
12. Turn to Table 12.3 and inspect the row in that table having an ARS Persuasion score range of 7.0 to 8.9. With that particular row in mind, interpret the entries under each of the four columns of share-point differences. For example, what is the specific interpretation of 56 percent under the column heading *1.0+*?
13. Compare and contrast the Ipsos-ASI Next*TV measure with rsc's ARS Persuasion method.
14. In the context of the discussion of single-source data, explain the difference between weight tests and copy tests. Illustrate your understanding of the difference between these two types of tests by designing a hypothetical weight test and then a copy test for the same brand.
15. With reference to Frito-Lay's copy tests in Table 12.4, the results reveal that of the 23 commercials tested, only 57 percent of the tests generated significant differences in sales between the split panels tested. Assume that Frito-Lay's results are applicable to television advertising in general. What is your general conclusion from this key finding?
16. Offer an explanation as to why, in general, increasing advertising weight (more GRPs) is an insufficient means of increasing brand sales?
17. Explain your understanding of why in the case of mature products with familiar brands, greater advertising weight is effective in increasing sales only when affective cues are used in advertising the brand.
18. Offer an explanation as to why in your opinion commercials for familiar brands with strong equities wear out less rapidly than is the case for unfamiliar brands.

ENDNOTES

1. These facts and the remaining comments are adapted from Nigel Hollis, "Understanding the Power of Watchability Can Strengthen Advertising Effectiveness," *Marketing Research* spring 2004, 22–26.
2. Karen Whitehill King, John D. Pehrson, and Leonard N. Reid, "Pretesting TV Commercials: Methods, Measures, and Changing Agency Roles," *Journal of Advertising* 22 (September 1993), 85–97.
3. Ibid.
4. John Kastenholz, Charles Young, and Tony Dubitsky, "Rehearse Your Creative Ideas in Rough Production to Optimize Ad Effectiveness." Paper presented at the Advertising Research Foundation Convention, New York City, April 26–28, 2004.
5. Ibid.

6. William A. Cook and Theodore F. Dunn, "The Changing Face of Advertising Research in the Information Age: An ARF Copy Research Council Survey," *Journal of Advertising Research* 36 (January–February 1996), 55–71.
7. This description is based on Allan L. Baldinger in the *Handbook of Marketing Research* (Thousand Oaks, CA: Sage, forthcoming).
8. Material for this section is extracted from the PACT document, which is published in its entirety in the *Journal of Advertising* 11, no. 4 (1982), 4–29.
9. See, for example, Bruce F. Hall, "A New Model for Measuring Advertising Effectiveness," *Journal of Advertising Research* 42 (April 2002), 23–31.
10. Herbert E. Krugman, "Why Three Exposures May Be Enough," *Journal of Advertising Research* 12 (December 1972), 11–14.
11. Russell I. Haley and Allan L. Baldinger, "The ARF Copy Research Validity Project," *Journal of Advertising Research* 31 (March/April 1991), 11–32.
12. John R. Rossiter and Geoff Eagleson, "Conclusions from the ARF's Copy Research Validity Project," *Journal of Advertising Research* 34 (May/June 1994), 19–32.
13. Gerald Zaltman and Robin Higie Coulter, "Seeing the Voice of the Customer: Metaphor-Based Advertising Research," *Journal of Advertising Research* 35 (July/August 1995), 35–51; Robin A. Coulter, Gerald Zaltman, and Keith S. Coulter, "Interpreting Consumer Perceptions of Advertising: An Application of the Zaltman Metaphor Elicitation Technique," *Journal of Advertising* 30 (winter 2001), 1–21.
14. Zaltman and Coulter, "Seeing the Voice of the Customer: Metaphor-Based Advertising Research."
15. A quote attributable to H. James Harrington, chairman of the board of Emergence Technology Ltd., as presented in Amy Miller and Jennifer Cioffi, "Measuring Marketing Effectiveness and Value: The Unisys Marketing Dashboard," *Journal of Advertising Research* 44 (September 2004), 238.
16. Ivan L. Preston, "The Association Model of the Advertising Communication Process," *Journal of Advertising* 11, no. 2 (1982), 3–15.
17. For an in-depth discussion of the differences between recognition and recall measures, see Erik du Plessis, "Recognition versus Recall," *Journal of Advertising Research* 34 (May/June 1994), 75–91.
18. For further details on other services, see David W. Stewart, David H. Furse, and Randall P. Kozak, "A Guide to Commercial Copytesting Services," in *Current Issues and Research in Advertising*, ed. James H. Leigh and Claude R. Martin, Jr. (Ann Arbor: Division of Research, Graduate School of Business, University of Michigan, 1983), 1–44; and Surendra N. Singh and Catherine A. Cole, "Advertising Copy Testing in Print Media," in *Current Issues and Research in Advertising*, ed. James H. Leigh and Claude R. Martin, Jr. (Ann Arbor: Division of Research, Graduate School of Business, University of Michigan, 1988), 215–284.
19. These definitions are derived from Roper ASW, as available in any Starch Readership Report prepared by this research firm.
20. D. M. Neu, "Measuring Advertising Recognition," *Journal of Advertising Research* 1 (1961), 17–22. For an alternative view, see George M. Zinkhan and Betsy D. Gelb, "What Starch Scores Predict," *Journal of Advertising Research* 26 (August/September 1986), 45–50.
21. Donald E. Bruzzone, "Tracking Super Bowl Commercials Online," *ARF Workshop Proceedings*, October 2001, 35–47.
22. Appreciation for this illustration is extended to Mr. R. Paul Shellenberg, director of sales, and Mr. Donald E. Bruzzone, president, of Bruzzone Research Company, Alameda, Calif.
23. The value of commercial recall testing, and Burke's DAR in particular, have been questioned by Joel S. Dubow, "Point of View: Recall Revisited: Recall Redux," *Journal of Advertising Research* 34 (May/June 1994), 92–106.
24. "Recall Not Communication: Coke," *Advertising Age*, December 26, 1983, 6.
25. Joel S. Dubow, "Advertising Recognition and Recall by Age—Including Teens," *Journal of Advertising Research* 35 (September/October 1995), 55–60.
26. Leonard M. Lodish et al., "How T.V. Advertising Works: A Meta-Analysis of 389 Real World Split Cable T.V. Advertising Experiments," *Journal of Marketing Research* 32 (May 1995), 135. See also John Philip Jones and Margaret H. Blair, "Examining 'Conventional Wisdoms' about Advertising Effects with Evidence from Independent Sources," *Journal of Advertising Research* 36 (November/December 1996), 42.
27. John J. Kastenholz and Chuck E. Young, "The Danger in Ad Recall Tests," *Advertising Age*, June 9, 2003, 24; Jack Honomichl, "FCB: Day-After-Recall Cheats Emotion," *Advertising Age*, May 11, 1981, 2; David Berger, "A Retrospective: FCB Recall Study," *Advertising Age*, October 26, 1981, S36, S38.
28. John Kastenholz, Chuck Young, and Graham Kerr, "Does Day-After Recall Testing Produce Vanilla Advertising?," *Admap*, June 2004, 34–36; Lisa Sanders and Jack Neff, "Copy Tests Under Fire from New Set of Critics," *Advertising Age*, June 9, 2003, 6.
29. Honomichl, "FCB," 82.
30. Steven P. Brown and Douglas M. Stayman, "Antecedents and Consequences of Attitude toward the Ad: A Meta-Analysis," *Journal of Consumer Research* 19 (June 1992), 34–51; Haley and Baldinger, "The ARF Copy Research Validity Project"; David Walker and Tony M. Dubitsky, "Why Liking Matters," *Journal of Advertising Research* 34 (May/June 1994), 9–18.
31. Judie Lannon, "New Techniques for Understanding Consumer Reactions to Advertising," *Journal of Advertising Research* 26 (August/September 1986), RC6–RC9; Judith A. Wiles and T. Bettina Cornwell, "A Review of Methods Utilized in Measuring Affect, Feelings, and Emotion in Advertising," in *Current Issues and Research in Advertising*, ed. James H. Leigh and Claude R. Martin, Jr. (Ann Arbor: Division of Research, Graduate School of Business, University of Michigan, 1991), 241–275.
32. Paul J. Watson and Robert J. Gatchel, "Autonomic Measures of Advertising," *Journal of Advertising Research* 19 (June 1979), 15–26.
33. For an especially thorough and insightful report on the galvanometer, see Priscilla A. LaBarbera and Joel D. Tucciarone, "GSR Reconsidered: A Behavior-Based Approach to Evaluating and Improving the Sales Potency of Advertising," *Journal of Advertising Research* 35 (September/October 1995), 33–53.
34. Ibid.
35. For a detailed discussion of pupil dilation and other physiological measures, see Joanne M. Klebba, "Physiological Measures of Research: A Review of Brain Activity, Electrodermal Response, Pupil Dilation, and Voice Analysis Methods and Studies," in *Current Issues and Research in Advertising*, ed.

James H. Leigh and Claude R. Martin, Jr. (Ann Arbor: Division of Research, Graduate School of Business, University of Michigan, 1985), 53–76. See also John T. Cacioppo and Richard E. Petty, *Social Psychophysiology* (New York: The Guilford Press, 1983).

36. Anthony J. Adams and Margaret Henderson Blair, "Persuasive Advertising and Sales Accountability: Past Experience and Forward Validation," *Journal of Advertising Research* 32 (March/April 1992), 25. Note: This quotation actually indicated that 1,000 respondents are drawn from four metropolitan areas. However, subsequent company newsletters and reports indicate that 800 to 1,000 respondents are randomly selected from eight metropolitan areas.
37. Leonard M. Lodish, "J. P. Jones and M. H. Blair on Measuring Advertising Effects—Another Point of View," *Journal of Advertising Research* 37 (September/October 1997), 75–79.
38. "Summary of the ARS Group's Global Validation and Business Implications 2004 Update," June 2004; The ARS Group, Evansville, IN. Note that an earlier validation study undertaken by the ARS Group was published in the following source: Margaret Henderson Blair and Michael J. Rabuck, "Advertising Wearin and Wearout: Ten Years Later: More Empirical Evidence and Successful Practice," *Journal of Advertising Research* 38 (September/October 1998), 1–13.
39. For example, John Philip Jones, "Quantitative Pretesting for Television Advertising," in John Philip Jones, ed., *How Advertising Works: The Role of Research* (Newbury Park, CA: Sage Publications 1998), 160–169.
40. Information for this description is from Andrew M. Tarshis, "The Single Source Household: Delivering on the Dream," *AIM* (a Nielsen publication) 1, no. 1 (1989).
41. These conclusions are based on Margaret Henderson Blair and Karl E. Rosenberg, "Convergent Findings Increase Our Understanding of How Advertising Works," *Journal of Advertising Research* 34 (May/June 1994), 35–45. Of course, other research by practitioners and academics converge on these general conclusions.
42. Scott Hume, "Selling Proposition Proves Power Again," *Advertising Age,* March 8, 1993, 31.
43. Lee Byers and Mark Gleason, "Using Measurement for More Effective Advertising," *Admap,* May 1993, 31–35.
44. Dwight R. Riskey, "How T.V. Advertising Works: An Industry Response," *Journal of Marketing Research* 34 (May 1997), 292–293. For more complete reporting on the effectiveness of TV advertising, see Lodish et al., "How T.V. Advertising Works: A Meta-Analysis of 389 Real World Split Cable T.V. Advertising Experiments," 125–139; and Leonard M. Lodish et al., "A Summary of Fifty-Five In-Market Experimental Estimates of the Long-Term Effect of TV Advertising," *Marketing Science* 14, no. 3 (1995), G133–G140.
45. The quote is from Jim Donius as cited in Don Bruzzone, "The Top 10 Insights about Measuring the Effect of Advertising," Bruzzone Research Company Newsletter, October 28, 1998, principle 8.
46. Lodish et al., "How T.V. Advertising Works," 128.
47. Compared with the results presented in Table 12.5, research by Lodish et al. does not demonstrate a strong relationship between commercial persuasiveness and sales. See Table 11 in "How T.V. Advertising Works," 137.
48. Adams and Blair, "Persuasive Advertising and Sales Accountability."
49. Deborah J. MacInnis, Ambar G. Rao, and Allen M. Weiss, "Assessing When Increased Media Weight of Real-World Advertisements Helps Sales," *Journal of Marketing Research* 39 (November 2002), 391–407.
50. Lodish et al.'s findings also support this conclusion. See "How T.V. Advertising Works."
51. For review, see Connie Pechmann and David W. Stewart, "Advertising Repetition: A Critical Review of Wearin and Wearout," *Current Issues and Research in Advertising* 11 (1988), 285–330; David W. Stewart, "Advertising Wearout: What and How You Measure Matters," *Journal of Advertising Research* 39 (September/October 1999), 39–42; Blair and Rabuck, "Advertising Wearin and Wearout"; and MacInnis, Rao, and Weiss, "Assessing When Increased Media Weight of Real-World Advertisements Helps Sales."
52. Margaret C. Campbell and Kevin Lane Keller, "Brand Familiarity and Advertising Repetition Effects," *Journal of Consumer Research* 30 (September 2003), 292–304.

CHAPTER 13

Planning for and Analyzing Advertising Media

Marcom Challenge: Is Super Bowl Advertising Worth the Expense?

The cost of placing a 30-second commercial on the National Football League Super Bowl increased from $400,000 in 1984 to $2.4 million in 2005. One may wonder whether the sizable investment in this television extravaganza can be justified, especially considering that 30-second spots on the top-rated prime-time television programs sell for a fraction of that cost, typically in the range of $100,000–$350,000 (as of 2005).

Media planners at a company that specializes in media selection questioned whether the Super Bowl represented a prudent buy and proposed another way to spend the amount of money equivalent to purchasing a 30-second Super Bowl spot.[1] They developed an alternative media plan that consisted of (1) buying advertising time on all network programs aired at the same time on Tuesday evening; (2) securing advertising time on all network programs aired at the same time on Sunday evening (e.g., Sunday night movies); and (3) purchasing a final single spot from the Fox network's Saturday night programming. (The Tuesday and Sunday night buys are called *roadblocks* because advertising purchased on all network programs aired simultaneously acts, metaphorically, as a roadblock to ensure that all consumers viewing TV at this time will be exposed to the brand's advertising.) This alternative media plan was able to secure 13 prime-time advertising spots, or a total time of 6.5 minutes, compared with purchasing a single 30-second ad on the Super Bowl. Comparative GRPs (gross rating points) for the Super Bowl media buy and the alternative plan are as follows:

Group	Super Bowl GRPs	Alternative 13-Spot GRPs	13-Spot Advantage Over Super Bowl
Adults, 18–49	40	65	162%
Adults, 25–54	42	78	186%
Men, 18–49	46	63	137%
Men, 25–54	48	68	142%

Whereas a single 30-second ad on the Super Bowl provided 40 GRPs based on the 18-to-49 age group, 42 GRPs based on the 25-to-54 group, and so on, the equivalently priced 13 spots yielded considerably more GRPs. For example, for all adults ages 25 to 54, the 78 GRPs from the 13 prime-time spots were 86 percent greater than the 42 GRPs generated by the Super Bowl advertisement.

Hence, one can conclude that advertisers should not advertise on the Super Bowl but rather would be better served by investing their advertising money elsewhere. Correct? Not necessarily! One also needs to factor in the all-important issue of advertising *impact*. People react with a relatively unenthusiastic response to advertisements placed on the programs contained in the alternative (13-spot) media buy. Comparatively, advertisements placed on the Super Bowl are, like the program itself, a special event. Consumers look forward to new, dramatic advertisements and often talk about the ads well after the Super Bowl is completed. In fact, evidence indicates that people enjoy watching TV commercials on the Super Bowl. One survey determined that a sample of women indicated their favorite aspect of the Super Bowl is viewing the ads rather than watching the game.[2] Because journalists comment about Super Bowl advertisements in magazines and newspapers, and on the Internet, advertisers receive a secondary form of brand contact. In short, all advertising does not have equivalent impact. When planners are buying advertising media, considerations, often subjective, other than mere comparisons of cost and rating points have to be factored into the decision.

Reuters/Pierre Ducharme/Landov

CHAPTER OBJECTIVES

1

Describe the major factors used in segmenting target audiences for media planning purposes.

2

Explain the meaning of reach, frequency, gross rating points, target rating points, effective reach, and other media concepts.

3

Discuss the logic of the three-exposure hypothesis and its role in media and vehicle selection.

4

Describe the use of the efficiency index procedure for media selection.

5

Distinguish the differences among three forms of advertising allocation: continuous, pulsed, and flighted schedules.

6

Explain the principle of recency and its implications for allocating advertising expenditures over time.

7

Perform cost-per-thousand calculations.

8

Interpret the output from computerized media models.

9

Review actual media plans.

Overview

The previous three chapters have examined the message component of advertising strategy. Though effective messages are essential for successful advertising, these messages are of little use unless advertising media are selected that will effectively reach the intended target audience. This chapter and the following three are devoted to media considerations. The present chapter explores the media planning process and the various factors that go into making media-selection decisions. The next chapter, Chapter 14, examines the traditional print and broadcast media—magazines, newspapers, television, and radio. Chapter 15 focuses on online media (wired and wireless), while Chapter 16 examines alternative advertising media (e.g., product placements in movies and cinema advertising).

Some Useful Terminology: Media Versus Vehicles

Before proceeding, it is important that we introduce some useful terminology. Advertising practitioners distinguish between advertising *media* and *vehicles.* **Media** are the general communication methods that carry advertising messages—that is, television, magazines, newspapers, and so on. **Vehicles** are the specific broadcast programs or print choices in which advertisements are placed. For example, television is a specific medium, and *American Idol, CBS Evening News,* and *Monday Night Football* are vehicles for carrying television advertisements. Magazines are another medium, and *Time, Business Week, Ebony,* and *Cosmopolitan* are vehicles in which magazine ads are placed. Each medium and each vehicle has a set of unique characteristics and virtues. Advertisers attempt to select those media and vehicles that are most compatible with the advertised brand in reaching its target audience and conveying the intended message.

Messages and Media: A Hand-in-Glove Relation

It is important to appreciate the fact that ad message and media considerations are inextricably related. Media and messages represent a hand-in-glove relationship, where each must be compatible with the other. It has been said that advertising creatives "can't move until they deal with a media strategist."[3] Creatives and media specialists must team up to design advertisements that effectively and efficiently deliver the right brand concept to the intended target audience. Indeed, advertising practitioners agree that reaching a specific audience effectively is the most important consideration in selecting advertising media.[4]

Advertisers are placing more emphasis than ever on media planning, and media planners have achieved a level of unparalleled stature.[5] This is because an advertising message can be effective only when placed in the media and vehicles that best reach the target audience at a justifiable expense. The choice of media and vehicles is, in many respects, the most complicated of all marketing communications decisions due to the variety of decisions that must be made. In addition to determining which general media categories to use (television, radio, magazines, newspapers, outdoor, Internet, or alternative media), the media planner must also pick specific vehicles within each medium and decide how to allocate the available budget among the various media and vehicle alternatives. Additional decisions involve choosing geographical advertising locations and determining how to distribute the budget over time. The complexity of media selection is made clear in the following commentary:

An advertiser considering a simple monthly magazine schedule, out of a pool of 30 feasible publications meeting editorial environment and targeting requirements, must essentially consider over one billion schedules when narrowing the possibilities down to the few *feasible alternatives that maximize campaign goals within budget constraints. Why over one billion possible schedules? There are two outcomes for each monthly schedule, either to use a particular publication or not to do so. Therefore, the total number of possible schedules equals two raised to the 30th power (i.e., $2^{30} = 1,073,741,800$). . . . Now imagine how the options explode when one is also considering 60 prime time and 25 daytime broadcast television network programs, 12 cable television networks, 16 radio networks, 4 national newspapers, and 3 newspaper supplements, with each vehicle having between 4.3 [i.e., the average number of weeks in a month] and perhaps as many as 20 or more possible insertions per month.*[6]

Selecting and Buying Media and Vehicles

It will be useful to examine how the advertising industry makes buying decisions related to media and vehicles. As discussed in Chapter 9, traditional full-service advertising agencies have historically been responsible for both creating advertising messages for their clients' brands and planning and buying media time and space in which to place those messages. However, a recent and dramatic change has occurred in the manner in which media planning is performed. An event that rocked the advertising industry was General Motors' (GM) decision to consolidate in a single company its media planning and buying for its many automobile brands. Whereas in the past media planning and buying took place in each advertising agency that represented each GM brand, now *all* media planning is done in a single company under an organization referred to as GM Planworks. This unit handles media planning amounting annually to approximately $3 billion. By consolidating media planning and buying, GM achieves significant cost savings for its various brands.[7]

Other major corporations have followed GM's lead in "unbundling" media planning from creative services. Unilever moved its $700 million U.S. media buying clout from its various ad agencies to a single media buyer. Likewise, Kraft Foods consolidated its $800 million North American media planning and buying account into a single media planner and buyer.

Needless to say, traditional full-service advertising agencies have criticized these moves. Their claim is that creative services and media planning go hand in hand, and that the symbiotic relation between these services is damaged when ad agencies are relegated to just creating ad messages while independent firms are fully responsible for planning media selection. A top official of a major ad agency had this to say.

You can't keep compartmentalizing each aspect of an account. Many of the insights we get come from the media side, and that informs the creative side and vice versa. I have a hard time believing that [ad agencies] can be as effective without that kind of close relationship.[8]

By comparison, the chief executive officer of a media planning company presented a counterperspective.

Separating media buying and planning [from creative] can be beneficial to clients who work in a multi-brand environment. Even though GM has different car lines, with different goals and strategies, there's something to be said for bringing all the planning operations together into one centralized location. It gives them an opportunity to apply learning and strategic thinking across the portfolio in a way that's faster and more efficient.[9]

There obviously are arguments on both sides of the issue, yet the proverbial genie is now out of the bottle. The historical role of the all-powerful full-service advertising agency has diminished. Perhaps of greatest significance is that this development accentuates the importance of the media planning aspect of the advertising process. Creating effective advertising messages is critical, but it is essential also that these messages be placed in the right media and vehicles.

The Media-Planning Process

Media planning is the design of a strategy that shows how investments in advertising time and space will contribute to the achievement of marketing objectives. The challenge in media planning is determining how best to *allocate* the fixed advertising budget for a particular planning period (say, a fiscal year or four-week period) among ad media, across vehicles within media, and over time. As shown in Figure 13.1, media planning involves coordinating three levels of strategy: marketing, advertising, and media strategy. The overall *marketing strategy* (consisting of target market identification and marketing mix selection) provides the impetus and direction for the choice of both advertising and media strategies. The *advertising strategy*—involving advertising objectives, budget, and message and media strategies—thus extends naturally from the overall marketing strategy.

Consider, for example, a *hypothetical* new sport-utility vehicle (SUV) named the *Esuvee.* (Before reading on, please read the *IMC Focus* to appreciate the reason for the Esuvee name.) Let us assume that the name Esuvee was selected for a new SUV model that is to be marketed to young males on the grounds that this vehicle is less likely to roll over than are competitive models purchased by this demographic group. Assume further that outdoor-oriented men represent the Esuvee's primary target market and that prospective owners desire practicality along with a carefree, adventuresome image in an SUV. The media strategy for the Esuvee naturally must extend from the manufacturer's strategy to sell approximately 50,000 Esuvees at retail.

Media strategy is inextricably related to the other aspects of advertising strategy (see Figure 13.1). Let us assume that the Esuvee had received a $15 million advertising budget for 2006. Suppose further that the objective was to create brand awareness for the Esuvee among targeted consumers and convey the desired image. Advertising strategy decisions simultaneously impose constraints on media strategy ($15 million is the maximum amount that could be spent on the 2006 Esuvee campaign) and provide direction for media selection.

The media strategy itself consists of four sets of interrelated activities (see Figure 13.1).

1. Selecting the target audience
2. Specifying media objectives

Figure 13.1
Model of the Media-Planning Process

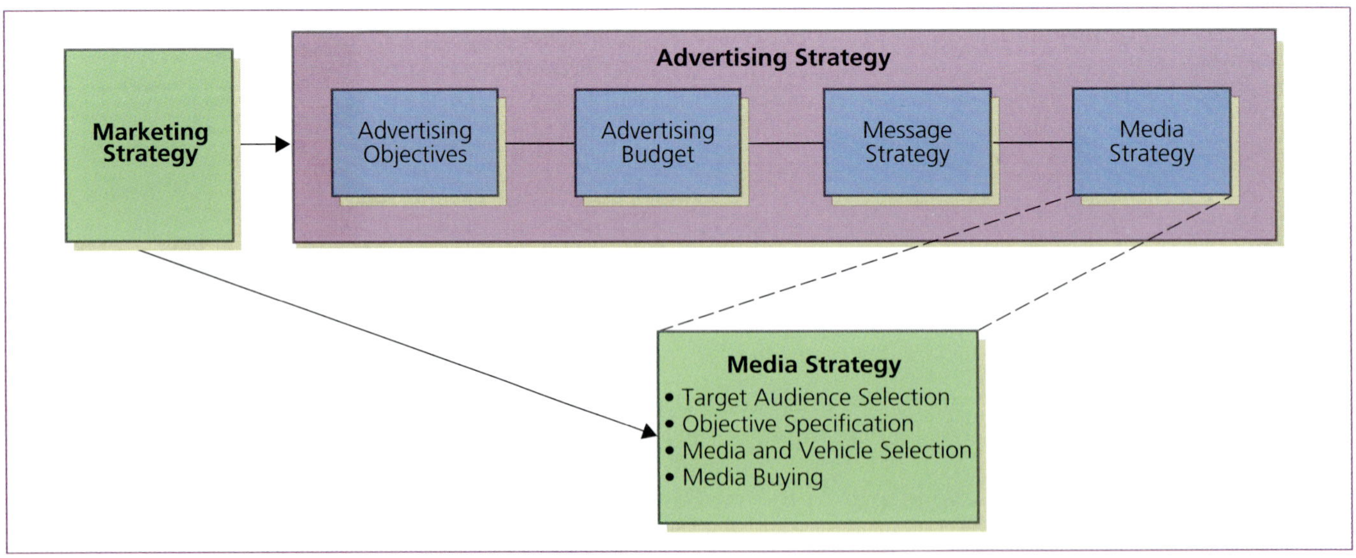

Esuvee and SUV Safety

imc focus

Sport-utility vehicles (SUVs) represent about 25 percent of all vehicles on U.S. roads. Unfortunately, young males between the ages of 17 and 27 are 2.5 times more likely to die in an SUV accident.

To combat the tragic reality that this statistic represents, the 50 American states and the District of Columbia, Puerto Rico, and the U.S. Virgin Islands joined forces and launched a year-long, $27 million safety campaign aimed primarily at young drivers. The campaign focused on four key tips for improving SUV safety:

1. Handling—Because SUVs have a higher center of gravity than passenger cars, there is a greater risk of rollover resulting from speeding, abrupt maneuvers, aggressiveness, and so on.
2. Loading—Overloading SUVs can raise the center of gravity and increase the likelihood of rollover accidents.
3. Properly inflating and maintaining tires—As with all vehicles, improper tire size, pressure, and maintenance may increase the chances of a rollover.
4. Wearing seat belts—Eighty percent of deaths in SUV rollovers occur because occupants are unbelted.

The safety campaign needed a concrete way to demonstrate to young males the importance of safe SUV operation. The centerpiece of the campaign and the element that made the driving tips tangible and prominent (i.e., *concrete*) was the campaign's mascot (a 16-foot-long, 10-foot-wide, and 12-foot-tall "beast" named Esuvee). In one TV commercial, for example, a rodeo-type setting was created in which a young male was shown attempting to ride Esuvee. The rider was abruptly dumped in the dirt because he wasn't wearing a seatbelt. A subsequent, seat-belted rider did not suffer the same unceremonious outcome.

In addition to television commercials, print ads, and a dedicated Web site, events were staged throughout the year in contexts that attracted young males. Connecticut's attorney general made especially clear the case for the ESUVEE campaign in commenting that "smart drivers can save lives with some simple steps: avoid speeding, sudden maneuvers, and overloading. Our education campaign targets young men, who may be most vulnerable and most difficult to reach. If you think this message is hype, look at the numbers—thousands of young Americans killed in rollover crashes every year."

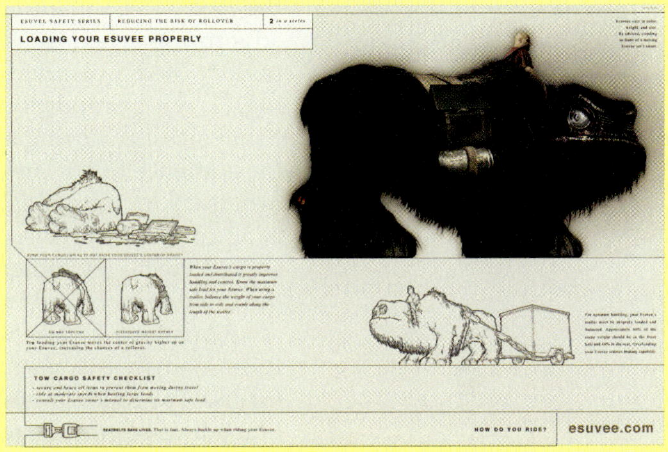

Source: "How Do You Ride? What Everyone Needs to Know about SUV Safety," used with permission from Peppercom Strategic Communications

3. Selecting media categories and vehicles
4. Buying media

The following sections discuss the first three activities in detail. Media buying is discussed only in passing because it is a specialized topic better suited for an elective course one might take as part of a communications or journalism major.

Selecting the Target Audience

Effective media strategy requires, first, that the target audience be pinpointed. Failure to precisely define the audience results in wasted exposures; that is, some nonpurchase candidates are exposed to advertisements, whereas prime candidates are missed. Four major types of information are used in segmenting target audiences for media strategy purposes: (1) buyographics, (2) geographics, (3) demographics, and (4) lifestyle/psychographics. Product usage information (buyographics), when available, generally provides the most meaningful basis for determining which target audience(s) should be pinpointed for receiving an advertising message.[10] Geographic, demographic, and psychographic considerations are typically combined to define the target audience. For example, the target audience for the Esuvee might be defined in terms such as the following: men between the ages of 18 and 49 (a demographic variable), who have incomes exceeding $45,000 (also demographic), who enjoy the outdoors (psychographic), and are carefree and adventurous (psychographic). A target audience defined in such specific terms has obvious implications for both message and media strategy. For example, magazines and TV programs that appeal to outdoor enthusiasts who are adventurous and carefree would effectively reach the Esuvee's target audience.

Specifying Media Objectives

Having pinpointed the audience to whom advertising messages will be directed, the next media-planning consideration involves specifying the *objectives* that an advertising schedule is designed to accomplish during the planned advertising period. Media planners, in setting objectives, confront issues such as the following: (1) what proportion of a target audience do we want to reach with our advertising message during a specified period, (2) how frequently do we need to expose the audience to our message during this period, (3) how much total advertising is necessary to accomplish the reach and frequency objectives, (4) how should we allocate the advertising budget over time, (5) how close to the time of purchase should the target audience be exposed to our advertising message, and (6) what is the most economically justifiable way to accomplish the other objectives?

Practitioners have technical terms they associate with each of these six objectives, namely (1) *reach,* (2) *frequency,* (3) *weight,* (4) *continuity,* (5) *recency,* and (6) *cost.* The following sections treat each objective as a separate matter. A later section addresses their interdependence.

Reach

Advertising managers and media specialists generally regard reaching specific audiences efficiently as the most important consideration when selecting media and vehicles.[11] The issue of reach deals with getting an advertising message heard or seen by the targeted audience. More precisely, **reach** represents the *percentage of the target audience* that is exposed, *at least once,* during a specified time frame to the *vehicles* in which our advertising message is inserted. The time frame used by the majority of media planners is a *four-week period.* (Thus, there are 13 four-week media-planning periods during a full year.) Some media specialists also use the single week as the planning period.

Regardless of the length of the planning period—whether one week, four weeks, a full year, or some other length of time—reach represents the percentage of all target customers who have an *opportunity to see or hear* the advertiser's message one or more times during this time period. (Advertising people use the expression *opportunity to see,* or *OTS,* to refer to all advertising media, whether visual or auditory.) Advertisers never know for sure whether members of their target audiences actually see or hear an advertising message. (How possibly could that be known?) Advertisers only know which media vehicles the target audience is exposed to. From these vehicle exposure data, it then can be inferred that people have had an opportunity to see the advertising message carried in the vehicles.

Other terms used by media planners for describing reach are *1+* (read "one-plus"), *net coverage,* and *unduplicated audience.* Later it will become clear why these terms are interchangeable with *reach.*

Determinants of Reach

Several factors can increase the reach that is achieved with a particular media schedule: (1) use multiple media, (2) diversify vehicles within each medium, and (3) vary the dayparts in the case of radio and TV advertising. Each of these determinants is now explained.

Generally speaking, more prospective customers are reached when a media schedule allocates a fixed advertising budget among *multiple media* rather than to a single medium. For example, if the Esuvee were advertised only on network television, its advertisements would reach fewer people than if it also were advertised on cable TV, in magazines, on the radio, and in national newspapers. If an advertiser were to advertise a brand only in, say, newspapers, it would miss 40 percent of the adult population in the United States which does not regularly read a daily newspaper. Likewise, advertising only on select TV programs would miss people who do not view those particular programs. Hence, using multiple media increases the odds of reaching a greater proportion of the target audience. In general, the more media options used, the greater the chances that an advertising message will come into contact with people whose media habits differ.

A second factor influencing reach is the *number and diversity of media vehicles used*. For example, if Esuvee's media planners were to choose to advertise this SUV in, say, just a single magazine (e.g., *Sports Illustrated*) rather than in a variety of magazines, far fewer consumers would be reached by the advertising effort. Having just read this paragraph, it should be obvious—at least in hindsight—that an ad campaign that uses different vehicles within each medium will better cover the intended audience than focusing exclusively on a single or limited number of vehicles. Again using *Sports Illustrated* for an example, if Esuvee were advertised only in that particular magazine, the ad campaign would fail to reach all people in the target audience who do *not* read that magazine.

Third, reach can be increased by *diversifying the dayparts* used to advertise a brand. For example, network television advertising during prime time and cable television advertising during fringe times would reach more potential automobile purchasers than advertising exclusively during prime time.

In sum, reach is an important consideration when developing a brand's media schedule. Advertisers wish to reach the highest possible proportion of the target audience that the budget permits. However, reach by itself is an inadequate objective for media planning because it tells nothing about *how often* target customers need to be exposed to the brand's advertising message for it to accomplish its goals. Therefore, frequency of advertising exposures must also be considered.

Frequency

Frequency signifies the number of times, on average, during the media-planning period that members of the target audience are exposed to the media *vehicles* that carry a brand's advertising message. Frequency actually represents a media schedule's *average frequency*, but media people use the term *frequency* as a shorthand way of referring to average frequency.

To better understand the concept of frequency and how it relates to reach, consider the simplified example in Table 13.1. This example provides information about 10 hypothetical members of the target audience for the Esuvee and their exposure to *Sports Illustrated* magazine over four consecutive weeks. (We are assuming for purposes of this simplified example that *Sports Illustrated* is the sole vehicle used for advertising the Esuvee.) Member A, for example, is exposed to *Sports Illustrated* on two occasions, weeks two and three. Member B is exposed to *Sports Illustrated* all four weeks. Member C is never exposed to this magazine during the four-week

Table 13.1

Hypothetical Frequency Distribution for the Esuvee Advertised in *Sports Illustrated* Magazine

	Target Audience Member										
Week	**A**	**B**	**C**	**D**	**E**	**F**	**G**	**H**	**I**	**J**	**Total Exposures**
1		X		X	X		X		X		5
2	X	X			X		X		X		5
3	X	X		X				X		X	5
4		X		X		X	X			X	5
Total Exposure	2	4	0	3	2	1	3	1	2	2	

Summary Statistics			
Frequency Distribution (*f*)	**Percentage *f***	**Percentage *f*+**	**Audience Members**
0	10%	100%	C
1	20	90	F, H
2	40	70	A, E, I, J
3	20	30	D, G
4	10	10	B

Reach (1+ exposures) = 90
Frequency = 2.2
GRPs = 200

period. Member D is exposed three times, in weeks one, three, and four, and so on for the remaining six members of Esuvee's mini audience. Notice in the last column of Table 13.1 that for each week, only 5 of 10 households (50 percent) are exposed to *Sports Illustrated* and thus have an opportunity to see an Esuvee advertisement placed in this vehicle. This reflects the fact that a single vehicle (in this case, *Sports Illustrated*) rarely reaches the full target audience.

The Concept of Frequency Distribution

Presented at the bottom of Table 13.1 are the frequency distribution and summary reach and frequency statistics for the Esuvee's media schedule. A *frequency distribution* represents the percentage of audience members (labeled "Percentage *f*" in Table 13.1) who are exposed *f* times (where $f = 0, 1, 2, 3,$ or 4) to the *Sports Illustrated* magazine and thus who have an opportunity to see ads for Esuvee carried in that magazine. The cumulative frequency column (labeled "Percentage *f*+ ") indicates the percentage of the 10-member audience that has been exposed *f* or more times to *Sports Illustrated* magazine during this four-week period (again, $f = 0, 1, 2, 3,$ or 4).

For example, the percentage exposed at least two times is 70 percent. Note carefully that for any value of *f*, the percentage in the Percentage *f*+ column simply represents the summation from the Percentage *f* column of that value plus all greater values. Reading from the Percentage *f* column in Table 13.1, you will see that the percentage of target audience members exposed exactly two times is 40 percent (namely, audience members A, E, I, and J). The percentage exposed exactly three times is 20 percent (members D and G). And the percentage exposed four times is 10 percent (member B). Hence, the cumulative percentage of audience members exposed two or more times (i.e., the percentage *f*+ when $f = 2$) is 70 percent ($40 + 20 + 10 = 70$).

With this background, we now are in a position to illustrate how both frequency and reach are calculated. It can be seen in Table 13.1 that 90 percent of the 10 audience members for the Esuvee advertisement have been exposed to one or more ads during the four-week advertising period. (Reading from the Percentage *f* + column, with $f = 1$, it can be seen that the 1+ cumulative percentage is 90.) This figure, 90 percent, represents the *reach* for this advertising effort. Please note that advertising practitioners drop the percent sign when referring to reach and simply refer to the number. In this case, reach equals 90.

Frequency is the average of the frequency distribution. In this situation, frequency equals 2.2. That is, 20 percent are reached one time, 40 percent are reached two times, 20 percent are reached three times, and 10 percent four times. Or, arithmetically, average frequency (or simply, frequency) equals

$$\frac{(1 \times 20) + (2 \times 40) + (3 \times 20) + (4 \times 10)}{90} = \frac{200}{90} = 2.2$$

This hypothetical situation thus indicates that 90 percent of the Esuvee's target audience is reached by the advertising schedule and that they are exposed an average of 2.2 times during the four-week advertising schedule in *Sports Illustrated.* This value, 2.2, represents this simplified media schedule's frequency. (The exact frequency actually is 2.22; however, media practitioners conventionally round frequency figures to a single decimal place.) Please note carefully that the sum of all frequencies (the numerator in the previous calculation) is divided by the reach figure (reach = 90) to obtain frequency.

Weight

A third objective involved in formulating media plans is determining how much advertising volume (termed *weight* by practitioners) is required to accomplish advertising objectives. Different metrics are used in determining an advertising schedule's weight during a specific advertising period. This section describes three weight metrics: gross ratings, target ratings, and effective ratings. First, however, it will be useful to explain the meaning of ratings.

What Are Ratings?

The concept of ratings has a unique meaning in the advertising industry unlike the meaning used in everyday talk. When people typically use the word *rating,* they are referring to a judgment about something. For example, a movie (or a restaurant, CD, etc.) might be rated on a five-star scale from terrible (= 1 star) to wonderful (= 5 stars). However, in the context of advertising, the term *ratings* simply refers to the percentage of an audience that has an *opportunity to see* an advertisement placed in that vehicle. Let us illustrate the meaning of ratings using television as an example. As of 2005, the ACNielsen company, which is well-known in the area of measuring television ratings, estimated that there were approximately 109.6 million households in the United States who had television sets. Therefore, a single **rating point** during this period represents 1 percent (1,096,000) of all television households.

Suppose, for example, that during one week in 2005, say February 14 to February 20, a TV program named *Medium* had roughly 12 million households tuned in. *Medium*'s ratings during that week would thus be 10.9 (i.e., 12 ÷ 109.6), which would indicate in a straightforward fashion that about 11 percent of all TV households viewed *Medium* during the week of February 14 to February 20, 2005. This, quite simply, is the meaning of ratings.

Gross Rating Points (GRPs)

Notice at the bottom of Table 13.1 that Esuvee's ad schedule in *Sports Illustrated* yields 200 GRPs. **Gross rating points**, or **GRPs**, reflect the gross weight that a particular advertising schedule has delivered. The term *gross* is the key. GRPs indicate the total coverage, or *duplicated audience,* exposed to a particular advertising schedule. Compare these terms with the alternative terms given earlier for *reach*—that is, *net coverage* and *unduplicated audience.*

Returning to our hypothetical example of an advertisement for the Esuvee in *Sports Illustrated,* the reach was 90, meaning that nine of the 10 households in our mini audience were exposed to at least a single issue of *SI* magazine. The gross rating points in this example amount to 200 GRPs because audience members were exposed multiple times (2.22 times on average) to the vehicles that carried the Esuvee advertisement during the four-week ad schedule.

It should be apparent from this discussion that GRPs represent the arithmetic product of reach times frequency.

$$\begin{aligned} \text{GRPs} &= \text{Reach (R)} \times \text{Frequency (F)} \\ &= 90 \times 2.22 \\ &= 200 \end{aligned}$$

By simple algebraic manipulation the following additional relations are obtained:

$$R = \text{GRPs} \div F$$
$$F = \text{GRPs} \div R$$

Determining GRPs in Practice

In advertising practice, media planners make media purchases by deciding how many GRPs are needed to accomplish established objectives. However, because the frequency distribution and reach and frequency statistics are unknown before the fact (i.e., at the time when the media schedule is determined), media planners need some other way to determine how many GRPs will result from a particular schedule.

There is, in fact, a simple way to make this determination. GRPs are ascertained by simply summing the ratings obtained from the individual vehicles included in a prospective media schedule. Remember, gross rating points are nothing more than *the sum of all vehicle ratings in a media schedule.* For example, during the week of March 21 to March 27, 2005, the 10 most highly rated TV programs were as follows:

Program	Network	Household Rating
American Idol—Tuesday	Fox	15.9
Desperate Housewives	ABC	14.4
American Idol—Wednesday	Fox	12.3
CSI: Miami	CBS	12.3
American Idol—Special	Fox	12.1
Survivor	CBS	10.9
CSI: NY	CBS	10.7
NCAA Basketball—Eastern Regional Championship	CBS	10.4
House	Fox	10.4
Two and a Half Men	CBS	10.4

SOURCE: Nielsen Top 10 TV Ratings: Broadcast TV Programs © Nielsen Media Research, http://www.nielsenmedia.com.

Suppose by chance that an advertiser had placed a single ad on each of these TV programs during the week of March 21–27, 2005. This being the case, the advertiser would have accumulated 119.8 GRPs when advertising in these particular programs (15.9 + 14.4 + … + 10.4 = 119.8). In short, the gross ratings generated by a particular media schedule simply equal the sum of the individual ratings obtained across all vehicles included in that schedule.

Target Rating Points (TRPs)

A slight but important variant of GRPs is the notion of target rating points. **Target rating points**, or **TRPs**, adjust vehicle ratings to reflect just those individuals *who* *match the advertiser's target audience.* Returning to the Esuvee example, let us assume that the advertising target for this SUV model is primarily men between the ages of 18 and 49 who have incomes of $45,000 or more. Considering the 10 TV programs listed previously, assume that, as a matter of simplicity, only 35 percent of the total audience exposed to each of these programs actually match Esuvee's target market. Hence, although placing a single ad in each of these programs yields 119.8 *gross* rating points, this same schedule produces only 41.9 *target* rating points (i.e., 119.8 × .35 = 41.9). It should be obvious from this simple illustration that GRPs represent some degree of wasted coverage insofar as some audience members fall outside the target audience the advertiser wishes to reach. Comparatively, target rating points, TRPs, represent a better indicator of a media schedule's *nonwasted weight.* GRPs equal gross weight, some of which is wasted; TRPs equal net weight, none of which is wasted.

The Concept of Effective Reach

Alternative media schedules are usually compared in terms of the number of GRPs (or TRPs) that each generates. It is important to realize, however, that a greater number of GRPs (or TRPs) does not necessarily indicate superiority. Consider, for example, two alternative media plans, X and Z, both of which require the same budget. Plan X generates 95 percent reach and an average frequency of 2.0, thereby yielding 190 GRPs. (Note again that reach is defined as the proportion of the audience exposed one or more times to advertising vehicles during the course of a typically four-week campaign.) Plan Z provides for 166 GRPs from a reach of 52 percent and a frequency of 3.2. Which plan is better? Plan X is clearly superior in terms of total GRPs and reach, but Plan Z has a higher frequency level. If the brand in question requires a greater number of exposures for the advertising to achieve effectiveness, then Plan Z may be superior even though it yields fewer GRPs. By the way, the same comparison would apply as well if this example were in terms of TRPs rather than GRPs.

It is for the reason suggested in the preceding comparison that many advertisers and media planners have become critical of the GRP and TRP concepts, contending that "it rests on the very dubious assumption that every exposure is of equal value, that the 50th exposure is the same as the tenth or the first."[12] Although the GRP concept remains very much a part of media planning, the advertising industry has turned away from the exclusive use of "raw" advertising weight toward a concept of media *effectiveness.*[13] The determination of media effectiveness takes into consideration *how often* members of the target audience have an opportunity to be exposed to advertising messages for the focal brand. The terms *effective reach* and *effective frequency* often are used interchangeably by media practitioners to capture the idea that an effective media schedule delivers a sufficient but not excessive number of ads to the target audience. Although either term is acceptable, hereafter we will simply refer to *effective reach.*

Effective reach is based on the idea that an advertising schedule is effective only if it does not reach members of the target audience *too few* or *too many* times during the media scheduling period, which, as noted previously, is typically a four-week period. In other words, there is a theoretical optimum range of exposures to an advertisement with minimum and maximum limits. But what constitutes too few or too many exposures? This, unfortunately, is one of the most complicated issues in all of advertising. The only statement that can be made with certainty is, "It depends!"

It depends, in particular, on considerations such as the level of consumer awareness of the advertised brand, its competitive position, the audience's degree of loyalty to the brand, message creativity and novelty, and the objectives that advertising is intended to accomplish for the brand. In fact, high levels of weekly exposure to a brand's advertising may be unproductive for loyal consumers because of a leveling off of ad effectiveness.[14] Specifically, brands with higher market shares and greater customer loyalty typically require *fewer* advertising exposures to achieve minimal levels of effectiveness. Likewise, it would be expected that distinctive advertising campaigns require *fewer* exposures to accomplish their objectives. The higher up the hierarchy of effects the advertising is attempting to move the consumer, the *greater* the number of exposures needed to achieve minimal effectiveness. For example, more exposures probably would be needed to convince consumers that the Esuvee provides the dual advantages of practicality and excitement than merely to make them aware that there is a brand named Esuvee.

How Many Exposures Are Needed?

It follows from the foregoing discussion that the minimum and maximum numbers of effective exposures can be determined only by conducting sophisticated research. Because research of this nature is time-consuming and expensive, advertisers and media planners generally have used rules of thumb in place of research in determining exposure effectiveness. Advertising industry thinking on this matter has been heavily influenced by the so-called **three-exposure hypothesis**, which addresses the *minimum* number of exposures needed for advertising to be effective. Its originator, an advertising practitioner named Herbert Krugman, argued that a consumer's initial exposure to a brand's advertising initiates a response of "what is it?" The second exposure triggers a response of "what of it?" And the third exposure and those thereafter are merely reminders of the information that the consumer already has learned from the first two exposures.[15] This hypothesis, which was based on little empirical data and a lot of intuition, has virtually become gospel in the advertising industry. Many advertising practitioners have interpreted the three-exposure hypothesis to mean that media schedules are *ineffective* when they deliver average frequencies of *fewer than three exposures* to the vehicle in which a brand's advertisement is placed.

Although there is some intuitive appeal to the notion that frequencies of fewer than three are insufficient, this interpretation of the three-exposure hypothesis is too literal and also fails to recognize that Krugman's hypothesis had in mind three exposures to an advertising *message* and not three exposures to vehicles carrying the message.[16] The difference is that vehicle exposure, or what we previously referred to as *opportunity to see* an ad *(OTS)*, is not tantamount to advertising exposure. A reader of a magazine issue certainly will be exposed to some advertisements in that issue, but the odds are that he or she will not be exposed to all, or even most, of the dozens of advertisements placed in that issue. Likewise, a viewer of a TV program will probably miss some of the commercials placed during a 30- or 60-minute program. Hence, the number of consumers who actually are exposed to any particular advertising message carried in a vehicle—what Krugman had in mind—is less than the number of people who are exposed to the vehicle that carries the message.

Aside from this general misunderstanding of the three-exposure hypothesis, it must also be recognized that no specific number of minimum exposures—whether 3, 7, 17, or any other number—is absolutely correct for all advertising situations. It cannot be overemphasized that what is effective (or ineffective) for one product or brand may not necessarily be so for another. "There is no magic number, no comfortable '3+' level of advertising exposures that works, even if we refer to advertising exposure rather than OTS."[17]

Effective Reach Planning in Advertising Practice

The mostly widely accepted view among media planners is that *fewer than three exposures* during a four-week media schedule is generally considered ineffective, while *more than 10 exposures* during this period is considered excessive. The range of effective reach, then, can be thought of as *three to 10 exposures* during a designated media-planning period.

The use of effective reach rather than gross rating points as the basis for media planning can have a major effect on overall media strategies. In particular, effective reach planning generally leads to using *multiple media* rather than depending exclusively on television, which is often the strategy when using the GRP criterion. Prime-time television is especially effective in terms of generating high levels of reach (1+ exposures) but may be deficient in terms of achieving effective reach (3+ exposures). Thus, the use of effective reach as the decision criterion often involves giving up some of prime-time television's reach to obtain greater frequency (at the same total cost) from other media.

This is illustrated in Table 13.2, which compares four media plans involving different combinations of media expenditures from an annual advertising budget of $12 million.[18] Plan A allocates 100 percent of the $12 million budget to network television advertising, plan B allocates 67 percent to television and 33 percent to network radio, plan C splits the budget between network television and magazines, and plan D allocates 67 percent to television and 33 percent to outdoor advertising.

Notice first that plan A (the use of network television only) leads to the lowest levels of reach, effective reach, frequency, and GRPs. An even split of network television and magazines (plan C) generates an especially high level of reach (91 percent), while combinations of network television with network radio (plan B) and network television with outdoor advertising (plan D) are especially impressive in terms of frequency, GRPs, and the percentage of consumers exposed three or more times.

More to the point, notice that the network-television-only plan compared with the remaining plans yields far fewer GRPs and considerably fewer effective rating points (ERPs). (Please note that in Table 13.2 ERPs equal the product of effective reach, or 3+ exposures, times frequency; plan A, for example, yields 81 ERPs, i.e., 29 × 2.8 = 81.) Plan D, which combines 67 percent network television and 33 percent outdoor advertising, is especially outstanding in terms of the numbers of GRPs and ERPs generated. This is because outdoor advertising is seen frequently as people travel to and from work and engage in other activities.

Should we conclude from this discussion that plan D is the best and plan A is the worst? Not necessarily! Clearly, the impact from seeing one billboard advertisement is generally far less than being exposed to a captivating television commercial. This illustration points out a fundamental aspect of media planning: *subjective factors* also must be considered when allocating advertising dollars. Superficially, the numbers do favor plan D. However, judgment and past experience may favor plan A on the grounds that the only way to effectively advertise

Table 13.2

Alternative Media Plans Based on a $12 Million Annual Budget and Four-Week Media Analysis

	Plan A: TV (100%)	Plan B: TV (67%), Radio (33%)	Plan C: TV (50%), Magazines (50%)	Plan D: TV (67%), Outdoor (33%)
Reach (1+ exposures)	69%	79%	91%	87%
Effective reach (3+ exposures)	29%	48%	53%	61%
Frequency	2.8	5.5	3.2	6.7
GRPs	193	435	291	583
ERPs	81	264	170	409
Cost per GRP	$62,176	$27,586	$41,237	$20,583
Cost per ERP	$148,148	$45,455	$70,588	$29,340

SOURCE: Adapted from "The Muscle in Multiple Media," *Marketing Communications,* December 1983, 25.

this particular product is by presenting dynamic action shots of people consuming and enjoying the product. Only television could satisfy this requirement. Other media (radio, magazines, and outdoor advertising) may be used to complement the key message driven home by TV ads. (The strengths and limitations of each of these ad media are discussed in the following chapter.)

It is useful to return again to a point established in Chapter 6: *it is better to be vaguely right than precisely wrong*. Reach, frequency, effective reach, GRPs, and TRPs are precise in their appearance but, in application, if used blindly, may be precisely wrong. Discerning decision makers never rely on numbers to make decisions for them. Rather, the numbers should be used solely as additional inputs into a decision that ultimately involves insight, wisdom, and judgment.

An Alternative Approach: Frequency Value Planning

Advertising scholars have proposed an alternative approach to the three-exposure doctrine.[19] The objective of *frequency value planning* is to select that media schedule (from a set of alternative schedules) that generates the most exposure value per GRP—or, stated differently, select that media plan that provides a "bigger bang for the buck." Frequency value planning is an approach that attempts to get the most out of an advertising investment in the sense of selecting the most *efficient* advertising schedule. The following implementation steps are involved:

Step 1. Estimate the *exposure utility* for each level of vehicle exposure, or OTS, that a schedule produces.[20] Exposure utility represents the worth, or value, of each additional opportunity for audience members to see an ad for a brand during the period of an advertising schedule. Table 13.3 lists OTSs (from 0 to 10+) and their corresponding exposure utilities. (Please note that these utilities are not invariant across all situations but have to be determined uniquely for each brand-advertising situation.) It can be seen that 0 vehicle exposures has, of course, an exposure utility of 0. One exposure adds the greatest amount of utility, assumed here to be 0.50 units; a second OTS contributes 0.13 additional units of utility (for an overall utility of 0.63); a third exposure contributes 0.09 more units to the second exposure (for an overall utility of 0.72 units); and so on. One can readily see that this utility function reflects decreasing marginal utility with each additional OTS. At an OTS of 10, the maximum utility of 1.00 is achieved. Hence, this illustration proposes that OTSs in excess of 10 offer no additional utility. By graphing the utilities in Table 13.3, one can readily see that the function is nonlinear and concave to the origin. In other words, each additional exposure contributes decreasing utility.

Step 2. Estimate the *frequency distribution* of the various media schedules that are under consideration. Computer programs, such as the program discussed later in the chapter, are available for this purpose. Table 13.4 shows the distributions for

Table 13.3

Exposure Utilities for Different OTS Levels

OTS	Exposure Utility
0	0.00
1	0.50
2	0.63
3	0.72
4	0.79
5	0.85
6	0.90
7	0.94
8	0.97
9	0.99
10+	1.00

two alternative media schedules. Reading in Table 13.4 from columns B (Schedule 1) and D (Schedule 2), it can be seen that 15 percent of the target audience is estimated to be exposed zero times to Schedule 1 (8 percent exposed zero times to Schedule 2), 11.1 percent of the target audience is estimated to be exposed exactly one time to Schedule 1 (21.0 percent are exposed one time to Schedule 2), 12.5 percent of the audience exposed exactly two times to Schedule 1 (17.6 percent to Schedule 2), 13.2 percent three times to Schedule 1 (13.6 percent to Schedule 2), and so on.

Step 3. Estimate the *OTS value at each OTS level.*[21] Entries in the *OTS value* columns in Table 13.4 (column C for Schedule 1, column E for Schedule 2) are calculated at each OTS level (OTS = 1, 2, 3, ... , 10+) by simply taking the arithmetic product of the Exposure Utility at each OTS level times the Percentage of Target column. Hence, at an OTS of one exposure, the exposure value is $0.5 \times 11.1 = 5.55$ for Schedule 1 and $0.5 \times 21.0 = 10.5$ for Schedule 2. At an OTS of two exposures, the exposure value is $0.63 \times 12.5 = 7.875$ (Schedule 1) and $0.63 \times 17.6 = 11.088$ (Schedule 2), and so on.

Step 4. Determine the *total value across all OTS levels.* After calculating the value at each OTS level, the *total value* is obtained by simply summing the individual exposure values ($5.55 + 7.875 + 9.504 + \ldots + 10.5 = 66.481$ for Schedule 1). The total value for Schedule 2 is virtually identical at 66.482.

Step 5. Develop an *index of exposure efficiency.* This index is calculated by dividing each schedule's *total value* by the number of *GRPs* produced by that schedule. Total GRPs are determined from the data in Table 13.4 in the same way they were identified earlier from the data in Table 13.1. Specifically, Schedule 1's total of 398.6 GRPs (see bottom of Table 13.4) is calculated as $(1 \times 11.1) + (2 \times 12.5) + (3 \times 13.2) + \ldots + (10 \times 10.5)$. (You should ensure that you understand this by calculating the GRPs for Schedule 2.) The index of exposure efficiency for Schedule 1 is 0.167 (i.e., $66.481 \div 398.6$), whereas the index value for Schedule 2 is 0.199 (i.e., $66.482 \div 333.8$).

What can be concluded from these calculations? With higher index values representing greater *efficiency,* it should be clear that Schedule 2 in Table 13.4 is the more efficient media schedule. That is, Schedule 2 has a higher efficiency index

Table 13.4

Frequency Distributions and Valuations of Two Media Schedules

		Schedule 1		Schedule 2	
OTS	(A) Exposure Utility	(B) Percentage of Target	(C) OTS Value (A × B)	(D) Percentage of Target	(E) OTS Value (A × D)
0	0.00	15.0%	0.000	8.0%	0.000
1	0.50	11.1	5.550	21.0	10.500
2	0.63	12.5	7.875	17.6	11.088
3	0.72	13.2	9.504	13.6	9.792
4	0.79	11.0	8.690	10.9	8.611
5	0.85	8.4	7.140	8.6	7.310
6	0.90	6.3	5.670	6.6	5.940
7	0.94	5.0	4.700	5.2	4.888
8	0.97	3.9	3.783	3.9	3.783
9	0.99	3.1	3.069	3.0	2.970
10+	1.00	10.5	10.500	1.6	1.600
Total Value:			66.481		66.482
GRPs:			398.6		333.8
Index of Exposure Efficiency (Value/GRPs):			0.167		0.199

than Schedule 1 because Schedule 2 accomplishes an equivalent exposure value (66.482 versus 66.481) but with fewer GRPs and hence less expense. Moreover, whereas Schedule 1 reaches a high percentage of the target audience 10 or more times (i.e., OTS = 10+ = 10.5 percent), Schedule 2 focuses more on reaching the audience at least one time rather than wasting, expenditures on reaching the audience 10 or more times (OTS = 1+ = 92 percent for Schedule 2, compared with Schedule 1's 1+ of 85 percent).

Although this method of frequency value planning is theoretically sounder than the three-exposure heuristic, the latter is embedded in advertising practice whereas the former was introduced more recently. The implication is not that this newer procedure should be dismissed out of hand; the point, instead, is that advertising practice has not as yet widely adopted the approach. It is only fair to note that the difficulty with implementing frequency value planning is in estimating exposure utilities, such as those presented in Table 13.3. There simply is no easy way to estimate exposure utilities, which thus accounts for why many media planners prefer to employ rules of thumb.

Continuity

Continuity involves the matter of how advertising should be allocated during the course of an advertising campaign. The fundamental issue is this: should the media budget be distributed uniformly throughout the period of the advertising campaign, should it be spent in a concentrated period to achieve the most impact, or should some other schedule between these two extremes be used? As always, the determination of what is best depends on the specifics of the situation. In general, however, a uniform advertising schedule may suffer from too little advertising weight at any one time. A heavily concentrated schedule, on the other hand, can suffer from excessive exposures during the advertising period and a complete absence of advertising at all other times.

Advertisers have three general alternatives related to allocating the budget over the course of the campaign: *continuous, pulsing,* and *flighting* schedules. To understand the differences among these three scheduling options, consider the advertising decision faced by a local dairy company that markets various dairy-based products. Figure 13.2 shows how advertising allocations might differ from month to month depending on the use of continuous, pulsing, or flighting schedules. Assume the annual advertising budget available to this marketer is $3 million.

Continuous Schedule

In a **continuous advertising schedule**, an equal or relatively equal number of ad dollars are invested throughout the campaign. The illustration in panel A of Figure 13.2 shows an extreme case of continuous advertising in which the advertiser allocates the $3 million advertising budget in equal amounts of exactly $250,000 for all 12 months throughout the year.

Such an advertising allocation would make sense only if dairy products were consumed in essentially equal quantities throughout the year. However, though dairy products are consumed year-round, consumption is particularly high during May, June, July, and August when people increasingly eat ice cream, which is an especially important product in this dairy company's product line and one for which sales are especially sensitive to advertising support. This calls for a *discontinuous* allocation of advertising dollars throughout the year.

Pulsing

In a pulsing advertising schedule, some advertising is used during every period of the campaign, but the amount of advertising varies from period to period. In panel B of Figure 13.2, a pulsing schedule for this dairy company shows that

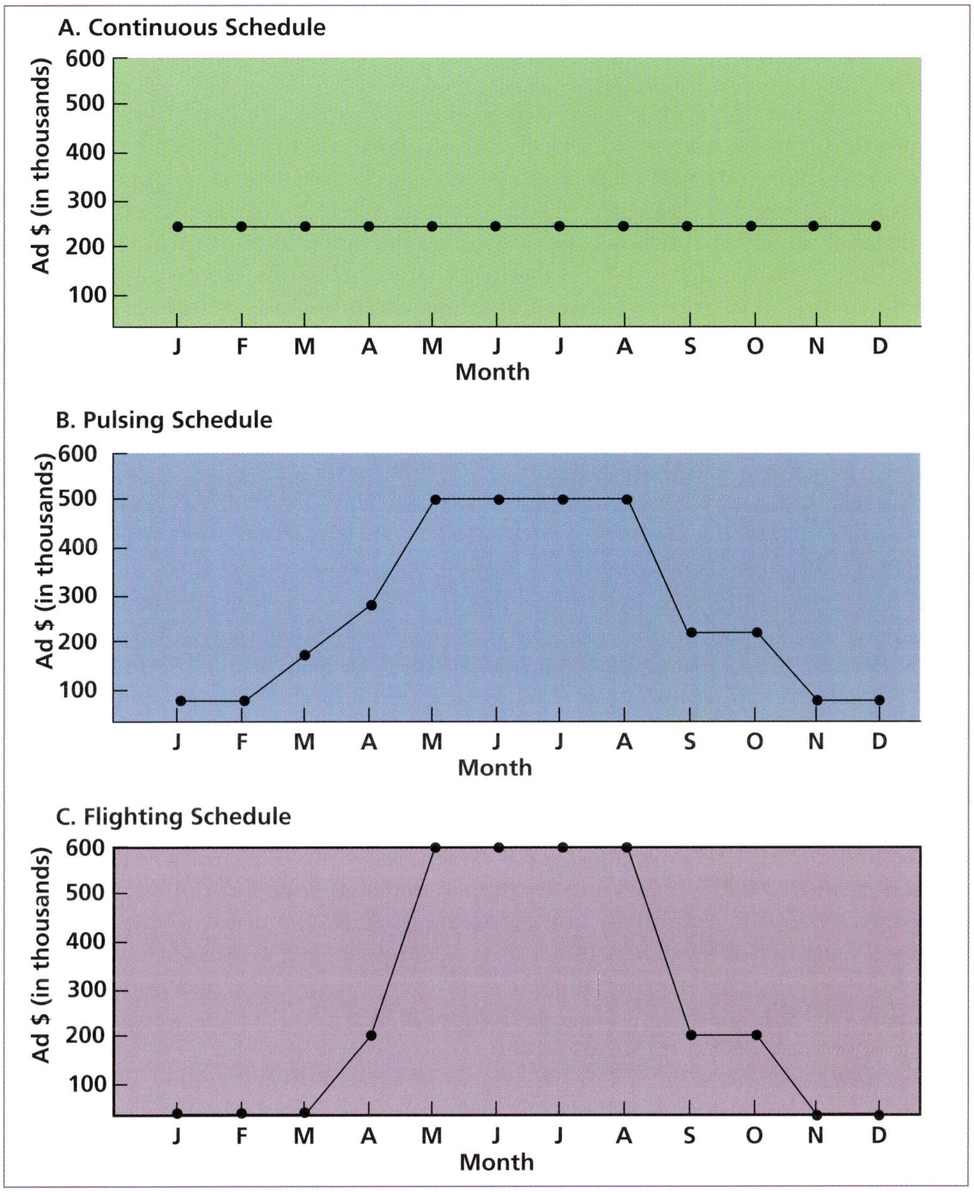

Figure 13.2

Continuous, Pulsing, and Flighting Advertising Schedules for a Brand of Ice Cream

its advertising is especially heavy during the high ice cream–consumption months of May through August (spending $500,000 each month) but the company nonetheless advertises in every month throughout the year. The minimum advertising expenditure is $50,000 even in the relatively low ice cream–sales months of January, February, November, and December.

© Taxi/Getty Images

Flighting

In a flighting schedule, the advertiser varies expenditures throughout the campaign and allocates *zero* expenditures in some months. As demonstrated in panel C of Figure 13.2, the dairy company allocates $600,000 to each of the four high ice cream–consumption months (May through August), $200,000 each to moderately ice cream–consumption months (April, September, and October), but zero dollars to the five low-consumption months (January, February, March, November, and December).

Thus, pulsing and flighting are similar in that they both involve *differential levels of advertising expenditures* throughout the year, but the schedules differ in that some advertising takes place during every period with pulsing but not with flighting. The following analogies may help to eliminate any confusion between pulsing and flighting. *Pulsing* in advertising is similar to an individual's heartbeat or pulse. One's pulse changes continuously between some lower and upper bounds but is always present in a living person. Comparatively, a *flighting* schedule is like an airplane, which at times is on the ground but at different altitudes when in flight. Thus, a pulsed advertising schedule is always beating (some advertising is placed in every ad period), whereas a flighted schedule soars at times to very high levels but is nonexistent on other occasions.

Recency Planning (a.k.a. The Shelf-Space Model)

Some advertising practitioners argue that flighted and pulsed advertising schedules are necessitated by the tremendous increases in media costs, especially the expense of network television advertising. Few advertisers, according to the logic of discontinuous ad scheduling (i.e., flighted or pulsed schedules), can afford to advertise consistently heavily throughout the year. According to this argument, advertisers are forced to advertise only at select times—namely, during periods when there is the greatest chance of accomplishing communication and sales objectives. This argument further holds that during periods when advertising is undertaken, there should be *sufficient frequency* to justify the advertising effort. In other words, the argument favoring discontinuous advertising (pulsing or flighting) goes hand in hand with the goal of achieving effective reach (3+) during any advertising period in which a brand manager chooses to have an advertising presence.

At first blush, the logic of discontinuous scheduling appears unassailable. However, the prudence of this argument has been challenged in recent years, most forcefully by Erwin Ephron, a New York media specialist. Ephron and his supporters assert that the advertising industry has failed to prove the value of the effective reach (3+) criterion for allocating advertising budgets and that this dubious criterion leads inappropriately to flighted allocations. Ephron has formulated an argument favoring continuous advertising that he terms the *principle of recency,* also called the *shelf-space model* or the *theory of effective weekly planning.*[22]

Because flighting is an on-and-off advertising proposition, consider by analogy what would happen to a brand's sales if retail shelves were out of stock for that brand during various times throughout the year. The brand obviously would experience zero sales during those periods of stock-outs when the shelves were empty. Sales would be obtained only during those times when the shelves held some amount of the brand. This, in a sense, is the way it is with flighted advertising schedules: the "shelves" are empty during certain periods (when no advertising is being run) and full during others.

The **recency principle**, or *shelf-space model,* is built on three interrelated ideas: (1) that consumers' *first exposure* to an advertisement for a brand is the most powerful; (2) that advertising's primary role is to influence brand choice, and that advertising does indeed influence choice for the *subset of consumers who are in the market* for the product category at the time a brand in that category advertises; and (3) that achieving a *high level of weekly reach* for a brand should be emphasized over acquiring heavy frequency. Let's examine all three ideas.

The Powerful First Exposure

Empirical evidence (albeit somewhat tentative) has demonstrated that the first exposure to advertising has a greater effect on sales than do additional exposures.[23] (The utility function given previously in Table 13.3 was based on the logic that the first exposure has the greatest impact.) Using single-source data, which was covered in Chapter 12, an advertising researcher produced provocative findings based on an extensive study of 142 brands representing 12 product categories (detergents, bar soaps, shampoos, ice cream, peanut butter, ground coffee, etc.). The researcher demonstrated that the first advertising exposure for these brands generated the highest proportion of sales and that additional exposures added very little to the first.[24]

Influencing Brand Choice

The concept of recency planning is based on the idea that consumer needs determine advertising effects. Advertising is especially effective when it occurs *close to the time when consumers are in the market for a particular product.* There is, in other words, a window of advertising opportunity for capturing the consumer's selection of the advertised brand versus other brands in the product category. "Advertising's job is to influence the purchase. Recency planning's job is to place the message in that window."[25]

Though recency planning is based on the idea that the first advertising exposure is the most powerful, this does not mean that a single exposure is sufficient. The point instead is that in the short-term additional exposures are likely to be wasted on consumers who are not in the market for the product. The logic, in other words, is that a brand can achieve greater sales volume by reaching more consumers a single time during an advertising period (a reach objective) rather than reaching fewer consumers more often (a frequency objective).

The advertising budget is not necessarily lower with recency planning; rather, the budget is allocated differently than is a flighted advertising budget. In particular, recency planning allocates the budget over more weeks throughout the year and invests less weight (fewer GRPs or TRPs) during the weeks in which advertising is undertaken. Recency planning uses *one week,* rather than four weeks, as the planning period and attempts to reach as many target consumers as possible in as many weeks as the budget will permit.

Optimizing Weekly Reach

Accordingly, it can be argued that media planners should devise schedules that are geared toward providing a continuous (or near continuous) presence for a brand with the objective of optimizing *weekly reach* rather than effective reach as embodied in the three-exposure hypothesis. The logic of recency planning can be summarized as follows:

1. Contrary to the three-exposure hypothesis, which has been interpreted to mean that advertising must *teach* consumers about brands (therefore requiring multiple exposures), the recency principle, or shelf-space model, assumes that the role of advertising is *not* to teach but to influence consumers' *brand selection.* "Unless it's a new brand, a new benefit, or a new use, there is not much learning involved."[26] Hence, the purpose of most advertising is to remind us of, reinforce, or evoke earlier messages rather than to teach consumers about product benefits or uses.
2. With the objective of influencing brand selection, advertising must therefore reach consumers when they are ready to buy a brand. The purpose of advertising by this logic is to "rent the shelf" so as to ensure a brand presence close to the time when consumers make purchase decisions. *Out of sight, out of mind* is a key advertising principle.
3. Advertising messages are most effective when they are *close to the time of purchase,* and a single advertising exposure is effective if it reaches consumers close to the time when they are making brand-selection decisions.
4. The cost effectiveness of a single exposure is approximately *three times greater* than the value of subsequent exposures.[27]

5. Hence, rather than concentrating the advertising budget to achieve multiple exposures only at select times throughout the year, planners should allocate the budget to *reach more consumers more often.*
6. In a world without budget constraints, the ideal advertising approach would be to achieve a weekly reach of 100 (i.e., to reach 100 percent of the target audience at least one time) and to sustain this level of reach for all 52 weeks of the year. Such a schedule would yield 5,200 weekly reach points. Because most advertisers cannot afford to sustain such a constant level of advertising, the next best approach is to *reach as high a percentage of the target audience as possible for as many weeks as possible.* This goal can be accomplished by (1) using 15-second TV commercials as well as more expensive 30-second spots; (2) spreading the budget among cheaper media (e.g., radio) rather than spending exclusively on television advertising; and (3) buying cheaper TV programs (cable, syndicated) rather than exclusively prime-time network programs. All of these strategies free up advertising dollars and permit an advertising schedule that will reach a high percentage of the target audience continuously rather than sporadically.

Toward Reconciliation: It Depends!

The concept of scheduling media to achieve a continuous rather than sporadic presence has considerable appeal. However, no single approach is equally effective for all brands. The logic of recency planning recognizes this when suggesting (in the first point previously) that for new brands, new benefits, or different ways of using a brand, the advertising objective indeed may be to teach rather than merely remind. Another advertising executive summarizes the issue well.

We've always believed that the first exposure is the most powerful, yet we don't want to have hard and fast rules. Every brand is a different situation. The leader in a category has different frequency needs than a competitor with less market share. It's not fair to say every brand has the same need for frequency.[28]

As a student it may be somewhat disconcerting to receive "mixed signals" such as these. Assuredly, it would be easier if there were hard-and-fast rules or straightforward principles that said, "Here is how you should do it." Advertising practice, unfortunately, is not as simple as this. We repeat a theme that has been emphasized at different points throughout the text: what works best depends on the specific circumstances facing a brand. If the brand is *mature* and well established, then effective weekly reach (the shelf-space model) is probably an appropriate way to allocate the advertising budget. On the other hand, if the brand is *new,* or if *new benefits or uses* for the brand have been developed, or if the advertising *message is complex,* then the budget should be allocated in a manner that achieves the frequency necessary to teach consumers about brand benefits and uses. In other words, when any of these latter conditions prevail, a flighted ad schedule is more appropriate than a weekly reach schedule.

These opposing viewpoints about how advertising works can be distinguished as the "strong" and "weak" models of advertising.[29] The *strong model* takes the position that advertising is important because it teaches consumers about brands and encourages trial purchases leading to the prospect of repeat buying. The *weak model* contends that most advertising messages are not important to consumers and that consumers do not learn much from advertising. This is because advertising usually is for brands that consumers already know about. In this case, advertising merely serves to *remind* consumers about brands they already know.

A reconciliation between these opposing viewpoints comes from appreciating the fact that advertising at any time *does* have influence on a relatively small percentage of consumers, and these are the consumers who happen to be in the market for the product at the time of the advertising. For example, a newspaper advertisement announcing a retailer's special sale for a particular brand of television may encourage store traffic and purchases from the relatively small subset of consumers who, at this time, need a new television set. Most consumers, however, do not need a new television set at this particular time. It thus may be said that advertising achieves its effectiveness "through a chance encounter with a ready consumer."[30]

Should it be concluded from this discussion that a single advertising exposure is all that is necessary and that advertising time and space should be scheduled so that recency is optimized and frequency is neglected? Absolutely not. Rather, what you should understand is that the specific advertising situation dictates whether emphasis on reach or frequency is more important. Brands familiar to consumers require less frequency, whereas new or relatively unfamiliar brands require higher levels of frequency. Brands that employ complex messages (e.g., containing technical details or subtle claims) also generally require more frequency.[31]

Cost Considerations

Media planners attempt to allocate the advertising budget in a cost-efficient manner subject to satisfying other objectives. One of the most important and universally used indicators of media efficiency is the cost-per-thousand criterion. Cost per thousand (abbreviated **CPM**, with the *M* representing the Roman numeral for 1,000) is the cost of reaching 1,000 people. The measure can be refined to mean the cost of reaching 1,000 members of the target audience, excluding those people who fall outside the target market. This refined measure is designated **CPM-TM**.

CPM and CPM-TM are calculated by dividing the cost of an advertising insertion by a vehicle's circulation within the total market (CPM) or in just the target market (CPM-TM):

CPM = Cost of ad ÷ Number of total contacts (expressed in thousands)
CPM-TM = Cost of ad ÷ Number of target market contacts (expressed in thousands)

The term *contacts* is used here in a general sense to include any type of advertising audience (television viewers, magazine readers, radio listeners, etc.).

Illustrative Calculations

To illustrate how CPM and CPM-TM are calculated, consider the following unconventional advertising situation. During Saturday football games at a major university, a local airplane advertising service flies messages on a trailing device that extends behind the plane. The cost is $500 per message. The football stadium holds 80,000 fans and is filled to capacity every Saturday. Hence, the CPM in this situation is $6.25, which is the cost per message ($500) divided by the number of thousands of people (80) who potentially are exposed to (i.e., have an opportunity to see, or OTS) an advertising message trailing from the plane.

Now assume that a new student bookstore uses the airplane advertising service to announce its opening to the 20,000 students who are in attendance at the game. Because the target market in this instance is only a fraction of the total audience, CPM-TM is a more appropriate cost-per-thousand statistic. CPM-TM in this instance is $25 ($500 ÷ 20)—which of course is four times higher than the CPM statistic because the target audience is one-fourth the size of the total audience.

To further illustrate how CPM and CPM-TM are calculated, consider a more conventional advertising situation. Suppose an advertiser promoted its brand on the reality program *American Idol,* and that during this particular week *American Idol*'s Nielsen rating is 16.7, meaning that viewers in approximately 18.3 million households had an OTS for any commercial aired on that program. At a cost of $658,333 for a 30-second commercial on Wednesday evening airings of *American Idol* during the 2005 season, the CPM is as follows:

Total viewership = 18,303,200 Households
Cost of 30-second commercial = $658,333
CPM = $658,333 ÷ 18,303.2
= $35.97

If we assume that the advertised brand's target market consists only of girls and women between the ages of 13 and 34 and that this submarket represents 70 percent of the total audience—or 12,812,240 girls and women who view *American Idol*—then the CPM-TM is

$$\text{CPM-TM} = \$658{,}333 \div 12{,}812.24 = \$51.38$$

Use with Caution!

The CPM and CPM-TM statistics are useful for comparing the *cost-efficiency* of different advertising vehicles. They must be used cautiously, however, for several reasons. First, these are measures of cost-efficiency—not of effectiveness. A particular vehicle may be extremely efficient but totally ineffective because it: (1) reaches the wrong audience (if CPM is used rather than CPM-TM) or (2) is inappropriate for the product category and brand advertised. By analogy, a Volkswagen Beetle may be more efficient in terms of miles-per-gallon than a large pickup truck but less effective for one's purposes.[32]

A second limitation of CPM and CPM-TM measures is their lack of comparability across media. As is emphasized in the following chapter, the various media perform unique roles and are therefore priced differently. A lower CPM for radio does not mean that buying radio time is better than buying a more expensive (CPM-wise) television schedule.

Finally, CPM statistics can be misused unless vehicles within a particular medium are compared on the same basis. For example, the CPM for an advertisement placed on daytime television is lower than that for a prime-time program, but this represents a case of comparing apples with oranges. The proper comparison would be between two daytime programs or between two prime-time programs rather than across dayparts. Similarly, it would be inappropriate to compare the CPM for a black-and-white magazine ad against a four-color magazine ad unless the two ads are considered equal in terms of their ability to present the brand effectively.

The Necessity of Making Trade-Offs

Various media-planning objectives—reach, frequency, weight, continuity, recency, and cost—have now been discussed in some detail. Each was introduced without direct reference to the other objectives. It is important to recognize, however, that these objectives are actually somewhat at odds with one another. That is, given a fixed advertising budget (e.g., $15 million for the Esuvee), the media planner cannot simultaneously optimize reach, frequency, and continuity objectives. Tradeoffs must be made because media planners operate under the constraint of fixed advertising budgets. Hence, optimizing one objective (e.g., minimizing CPM or maximizing GRPs) requires the sacrifice of other objectives. This simply is due to the mathematics of constrained optimization: multiple objectives cannot simultaneously be optimized when constraints (like limited budgets) exist.

For example, with a fixed advertising budget, the media planner can choose to maximize reach or frequency but not both. With increases in reach, frequency is sacrificed and vice versa—if you want to reach more people, you cannot reach them as often with a fixed advertising budget; if you want to reach them more often, you cannot reach as many. This discussion may remind you of a lesson you learned in basic statistics about the trade-off between committing Type I (alpha) and Type II (beta) errors while holding sample size constant. That is, with a fixed sample size, decisions to decrease a Type I error (say, from .05 to .01) must inevitably result in an increase in the Type II error and vice versa.

As an advertising practitioner "you can't have your cake and eat it too." The brand manager faced with an advertising budget constraint, which always is the case, must decide whether frequency is more important (the three-exposure hypothesis) or reach is more imperative (the recency principle).

Thus, each media planner must decide what is best given the particular circumstances surrounding the advertising decision facing his or her brand. As previously discussed, achieving *effective reach* (3+ exposures) is particularly important when brands are new or when established brands have new benefits or uses. In these circumstances, the task of advertising is to *teach* consumers, and part of teaching is *repetition.* The more complex the message, the greater the need for repetition to convey the message effectively. However, for established brands that already are well known by consumers, the advertising task is more one of *reminding* consumers about the brand. The ad budget in this situation is best allocated to achieve the maximum level of *reach.*

Media-Planning Software

On top of the difficult task of making intelligent tradeoffs among sometimes opposing objectives (reach, frequency, etc.), there literally are thousands, if not millions, of possible advertising schedules that could be selected depending on how the various media and media vehicles are combined. Fortunately, this daunting task is facilitated by the availability of computerized models to assist media planners in selecting media and vehicles. These models essentially attempt to optimize an objective function (e.g., selecting a schedule that yields the greatest level of reach or the highest frequency), subject to satisfying constraints such as not exceeding the upper limit on the advertising budget. A computer algorithm searches through the possible solutions and selects the specific media schedule that optimizes the objective function and satisfies all specified constraints.

Comprehensive media-scheduling programs allow the user to evaluate all major advertising media categories and subcategories and to find optimum schedules based on selecting multiple vehicles from within a single advertising medium and combining plans across multiple media. However, it will be assumed here that magazines are the only medium under consideration. Using for illustration purposes a hypothetical $1.5 million magazine campaign for the Esuvee during its introductory advertising month of June 2006, the following steps are involved:

Step 1. Develop a *media database.* This initial aspect of media planning entails three activities: (1) select prospective advertising vehicles, (2) specify their ratings, and (3) and identify individual vehicle cost. Table 13.5 illustrates the essential information contained in the media database for the Esuvee. (Parenthetically, the *Global Focus* insert provides a source on the Internet for obtaining useful information about media vehicles in countries around the world. Be sure to visit this Web site to see the wealth of available information.)

Step 2. Select the *criterion for schedule optimization.* Media-schedule optimization alternatives include maximizing reach (1+), effective reach (3+), frequency, and GRPs. In the illustration to follow, *maximizing reach* has been selected as the optimizing criterion for Esuvee's June 2006 campaign.

Step 3. Specify *constraints.* These include (1) determining a *budget constraint* for the media planning period, and (2) identifying *the maximum number of ad insertions for each vehicle.* The magazine budget constraint for June 2006 has been set at $1.5 million. The computer algorithm is being "told," in other words, to generate a solution that maximizes reach but spends no more than $1.5 million to accomplish this objective. In addition to the overall budget constraint, magazine-insertion

Searching for Media Options Around the Globe

global focus

Suppose you are interested in learning about news media in any city and state in the United States. Perhaps your interest goes beyond the United States and you wish to know what news media and advertising outlets may be available in most any city in the world. How would you learn, for example, what newspapers are available in Moscow, or what TV stations exist in Barcelona? Fortunately, there is an independent site on the Internet, named the Kidon Media-Link (http://www.kidon.com/media-link), that makes this information available. Kidon provides direct links to various news sources (and potential advertising outlets) at its Web site. One simply goes to the Kidon Media-Link home page, selects the continent where a city of interest is located, identifies the country, navigates to the desired city, and then inspects available media. Indeed, up-to-date news is provided at the media outlets available in that city. It is worth your time to access Kidon Media-Link and learn more about this interesting resource that provides direct links to media throughout the globe.

constraints also are identified in Table 13.5. The purpose of these insertion constraints is to assure that the optimum solution does not recommend inserting more ads in a particular publication than can be run during the four-week scheduling period. As can be seen in Table 13.5, with only three exceptions (*ESPN Magazine, The Sporting News,* and *Sports Illustrated*), all remaining magazines are issued only once per month. Hence, the maximum number of insertions is set at *1*. Though advertisers sometimes run multiple ads for a brand in the same magazine issue, the simplifying assumption made here is that not more than one ad for the Esuvee should be placed in any particular magazine per issue.

Step 4. Seek out the optimum media schedule according to the specified objective function and subject to satisfying the budget and number-of-insertion constraints. The following illustration reveals how this is accomplished.

Table 13.5

Media Database for the Esuvee, June 2006

Magazine	Rating	4C/Open Cost*	Maximum Insertions**
American Hunter	7.0	$ 29,830	1
American Rifleman	8.7	44,470	1
Bassmaster	8.8	34,855	1
Car & Driver	10.8	149,350	1
Ducks Unlimited	2.9	24,925	1
ESPN Magazine	15.6	148,750	2
Field & Stream	18.7	101,600	1
Game & Fish	5.8	20,540	1
Guns & Ammo	13.5	30,780	1
Hot Rod	18.5	72,790	1
Maxim	24.6	179,000	1
Men's Fitness	9.5	49,425	1
Men's Health	18.3	121,425	1
Motor Trend	14.5	127,155	1
North American Hunter	10.5	27,210	1
Outdoor Life	15.7	55,700	1
The Sporting News	10.7	49,518	4
Sports Illustrated	44.3	226,000	4

*4C/open stands for a full-page, four-color ad purchased without a quantity discount. Cost information is from *Marketer's Guide to Media*, 27 (New York: VNU Business Publications USA, 2004), 149–152.

**Maximum insertions are based on how frequently a magazine is published. *The Sporting News* and *Sports Illustrated* are published weekly, which thus would enable one ad in each of the weeks during the four-week scheduling period. With the exception of *ESPN Magazine*, which is published every other week, all other magazines under consideration are published monthly.

Hypothetical Illustration: Esuvee's June 2006 Magazine Schedule

Let's assume that a media planner for the Esuvee is in the process of choosing the optimal four-week schedule—during the June 2006 introduction of the Esuvee—from among magazines considered appropriate for reaching males, ages 18 to 49, who have household incomes of $45,000 or greater, and who are outdoor-oriented (i.e., they like to hunt, fish, cycle, camp, etc.). As of 2006 there were approximately 67 million American males ages 18 to 49. On the assumption that only 40 percent of this group satisfies the Esuvee's income target of $45,000 or greater, the target market is reduced to 26.8 million prospective customers for the Esuvee (i.e., .4 × 67 million). All subsequent planning is based on this estimate.

The Esuvee Database

The media planner has prepared a database consisting of 18 magazines considered suitable for reaching the target audience (see Table 13.5). These magazines were selected because they are read predominantly by male readers who engage in outdoor activities such as hunting, fishing, and cycling and who have household incomes of $45,000 or greater.

The second key input was magazine ratings. Ratings (see the second column in Table 13.5) were determined by dividing each magazine's audience size by the size of Esuvee's target market, which was estimated as 26.8 million potential customers.[33] Next, costs (the third column) were designated according to the price charged by each magazine for a one-time placement of a full-page, four-color advertisement. Finally, maximum insertions (the last column) were based on each magazine's publication cycle. Fifteen of the 18 magazines are published once per month, whereas *ESPN Magazine* is published bimonthly and *Sporting News* and *Sports Illustrated* are published weekly. Hence, only one ad each can be placed during the four-week period in 15 of the magazines, whereas it is possible to place up to two ads in *ESPN Magazine* and up to four ads each in *Sporting News* and *Sports Illustrated.*

The Objective Function and Constraints

The information in Table 13.5 was input into a computerized media scheduling program.[34] With this information, the program was instructed to maximize reach (1+) without exceeding a budget of $1.5 million for this four-week introductory advertising campaign. Earlier it was indicated that the first-year advertising budget for the Esuvee totaled $15 million. The media planner has decided to invest $1.5 million in magazine advertising in the introductory month and another $4.5 million on TV advertising during this month. The remainder of the budget, $9 million, will be allocated throughout the remainder of 2006. (To simplify the discussion, only the magazine component of the media schedule is described here.)

The Optimal Schedule

Had advertisements been placed in all 18 magazines listed in Table 13.5 (including multiple insertions in the three magazines—*ESPN Magazine, Sports Illustrated,* and *Sporting News*—where multiple insertions were permissible), the total advertising cost would have amounted to nearly $2.5 million. This amount would have been unacceptable, however, because a $1.5 million budget constraint was imposed on magazine advertising in June 2006. It thus was necessary to make a selection from these magazines such that the budget constraint was met and the goal to maximize reach was satisfied. This is precisely what media-scheduling algorithms accomplish. Given 18 magazines with different numbers of maximum insertions in each, there are numerous combinations of magazines that could be selected. However, in a matter of seconds, the scheduling algorithm identified the single combination of magazines that would maximize reach for an expenditure of $1.5 million or less. The solution is displayed in Table 13.6.

Table 13.6 shows that the optimal schedule consists of four ads in *Sporting News,* two ads in *Sports Illustrated,* and one ad each in 13 other magazines. (Three magazines—*Car & Driver, ESPN Magazine,* and *Motor Trend*—were not included in the final solution. Perusal of Table 13.5 reveals that these magazines are relatively expensive in view of the ratings delivered.) The total cost of this schedule is $1,422,622, which is just under, by $77,378, the specified upper limit of $1.5 million. Note that the inclusion of any single additional advertisement would have exceeded the imposed budget limit. The least expensive magazine of the three that are not included is *Motor Trend* at a cost of $127,155. Had an advertisement been placed in this magazine (or in *Car & Driver* or *ESPN Magazine*), the total cost would

Table 13.6

ADplus Magazine Schedule for the Esuvee, June 2006

	Frequency (*f*) Distributions				
		Vehicle		Message	
	f	%*f*	%*f*+	%*f*	%*f*+
XYZ Ad Agency	0	27.8	100.0	53.9	100.0
Esuvee SUV	1	5.1	72.2	2.7	46.1
June 2006	2	10.3	67.1	6.0	43.4
Target: 26,800,000	3	14.7	56.8	9.2	37.4
Males/18–49/$45K HHI/Outdoor	4	15.2	42.1	9.9	28.2
Message/Vehicle = 52.5%	5	11.7	26.9	7.8	18.4
	6	7.3	15.1	5.0	10.5
	7	4.1	7.8	2.9	5.5
	8	2.2	3.7	1.5	2.6
	9	1.0	1.5	0.7	1.1
	10+	0.5	0.5	0.4	0.4

Summary Evaluation	Vehicle	Message
Reach (1+)	72.2%	46.1%
Effective reach (3+)	56.8%	37.4%
Gross rating points (GRPs)	293.9	193.8
Average frequency (F)	4.1	4.2
Gross impressions (000s)	78,765.2	51,928.7
Cost-per-thousand (CPM)	$18.32	$27.78
Cost-per-rating point (CPP)	$4,909	$7,445

Vehicle List	Rating	Ad Cost	CPM-MSG	Ads	Total Cost	Mix
Guns & Ammo	13.5	$ 30,780	$16.20	1	$ 30,780	2.1%
North American Hunter	10.5	27,210	18.42	1	27,210	1.9
Game & Fish	5.8	20,540	25.17	1	20,540	1.4
Outdoor Life	15.7	55,700	25.22	1	55,700	3.9
Hot Rod	18.5	72,790	27.96	1	72,790	5.0
Bassmaster	8.8	34,855	28.15	1	34,855	2.4
American Hunter	7.0	29,830	30.29	1	29,830	2.1
The Sporting News	10.7	49,518	32.89	4	198,072	13.7
Sports Illustrated	44.3	226,000	36.26	2	452,000	31.3
American Rifleman	8.7	44,470	36.33	1	44,470	3.1
Men's Fitness	9.5	49,425	36.98	1	49,425	3.4
Field & Stream	18.7	101,600	38.62	1	101,600	7.0
Men's Health	18.3	121,425	47.16	1	121,425	8.4
Maxim	24.6	179,000	51.72	1	179,000	12.4
Ducks Unlimited	2.9	24,925	61.09	1	24,925	1.7
		Totals:	$27.78	19	$1,442,622	100.0%

have exceeded the budget constraint of $1,500,000. The solution in Table 13.6 is *the* optimum solution for maximizing reach subject to satisfying the budget constraint.

Interpretation of the Solution

Let us carefully examine the data in Table 13.6. Notice first that the boxed section in the upper left-hand corner provides pertinent details about the media schedule (ad agency, client name, planning period, target size, target description, and message-to-vehicle ratio). The only explanation needed is in regard to the message-to-vehicle ratio, which is shown as equaling 52.5 percent. This value represents the likelihood that consumers who are exposed to the magazine vehicle *also* will be exposed to the advertising message within it. In other words, the expectation is that only slightly more than 50 percent of consumers exposed to any particular magazine in the Esuvee's schedule will actually attend an Esuvee ad inserted in these magazines. This ratio, although a rough estimate, was obtained from a survey of media directors who were asked to identify the message-to-vehicle ratios they employ for different media categories.[35] The corresponding ratios for television, radio, and newspapers have been estimated at 32 percent, 16 percent, and 16 percent, respectively.[36] These ratios mean that roughly one of three TV viewers and one of six radio listeners and newspaper readers are expected to attend any particular advertisement contained in each medium. These ratios are, of course, imperfect estimates that are not applicable to every advertising situation. For example, people watching the NFL Super Bowl are probably much more likely to view advertisements than normally is the case.

The next pertinent information to observe in Table 13.6 is the vehicle and message *frequency distributions*. Conceptually these are identical, but the percentages in the message distribution are lower for the reasons described in the previous paragraph. To interpret the *vehicle distribution*, recall the earlier discussion (Table 13.1) of the 10-household market for the Esuvee advertised in *Sports Illustrated* magazine. It will be helpful to review the concepts of (1) exposure level *(f)*; (2) frequency distribution, or percentage of audience exposed at each level of *f* (Percentage *f*); and (3) cumulative frequency distribution (Percentage *f*+). When *f* equals zero, the Percentage *f* and Percentage *f*+ values in Table 13.6 are 27.8 and 100, respectively. This is to say that the 27.8 percent of the 26.8 million target audience members for the Esuvee will *not* be exposed to any of the 15 magazines that made it into the optimal solution and that are listed at the bottom of Table 13.6. The cumulative frequency when *f* equals zero is of course 100—that is, 100 percent of the audience members will be exposed zero or more times to magazine vehicles in Esuvee's four-week advertising schedule.

Note further that Percentage *f* and Percentage *f*+ are 5.1 and 72.2 when *f* equals 1. That is, the media algorithm estimates that 5.1 percent of the target audience will be exposed to *exactly* one of the 15 magazines, and 72.2 percent of the audience will be exposed to one or more of the magazines during this four-week period in June 2006. Note carefully under the summary evaluation in the middle of Table 13.6 that vehicle *reach* equals 72.2 percent. With reach defined as the percentage of the target audience exposed one or more times (i.e., 1+), the level of reach is determined merely by identifying the corresponding value in the Percentage *f*+ column, which, when *f* equals 1, is 72.2 percent. It should also be clear that because 27.8 percent of the audience is exposed zero times, the complement of this value (100 – 27.8 = 72.2 percent) is the percentage of the audience exposed one or more times—that is, the percentage of the audience reached.

Hence, this optimum schedule yields a *vehicle reach* of 72.2, which is the maximum level of reach that any combination of the 18 magazines included in the database (Table 13.5) could achieve within a budget constraint of $1.5 million.

This optimal vehicle schedule produces 293.9 *GRPs*. These GRPs, by the way, are calculated simply by multiplying the ratings for each magazine by the number of ads placed in that magazine [(*Guns & Ammo* = 13.5 × 1) + (*North American Hunter* = 10.5 × 1) + … (*Ducks Unlimited* = 2.9 × 1) = 293.9 GRPs].

Further, this magazine schedule during June 2006 is estimated to reach the audience an average of 4.1 times (see *average frequency* under the summary evaluation in Table 13.6). Having defined earlier that frequency = GRPs ÷ reach, you can readily calculate that frequency = 293.9 ÷ 72.2 = 4.0706, which is rounded in Table 13.6 to 4.1.

Effective reach (i.e., 3+) is 56.8 percent. That is, nearly 57 percent of the total audience are exposed to three or more vehicles. This value is obtained, of course, by reading across from $f = 3$ to the corresponding *percentage f+* column.

The *cost per thousand (CPM)* is $18.32. This value is calculated as follows: (1) audience size is 26,800,000; (2) 72.2 percent—or 19,349,600 of the audience members—are reached by the schedule of magazines shown in Table 13.6; (3) each person reached is done so on average 4.0706 times (in Table 13.6, frequency is presented only to a single decimal point and is rounded up to 4.1); (4) the number of gross impressions, which is the number of people reached multiplied by the average number of times they are reached, is thus 78,765,200 (see summary evaluation in Table 13.6); (5) the *total cost* of this media schedule is $1,422,622 (see the bottom of the Total Cost column in Table 13.6); and (6) hence, the CPM is $1,442,622 ÷ 78,765.2 = $18.32.

Finally, the *cost per rating point (CPP)* is $4,909. This is calculated simply by dividing total cost by the number of GRPs produced (i.e., $1,442,622 ÷ 293.9 GRPs).

Does Table 13.6 present a good media schedule? In terms of reach, the schedule is the best of all possible schedules that could have been produced from the various combinations of 18 magazines that were input into the media scheduling algorithm and subject to a $1.5 million budget constraint. No other combination from among these magazines could have exceeded this schedule's vehicle reach of 72.2 percent. Note carefully, however, that this *opportunity to see* (OTS) the advertisement for Esuvee is not tantamount to having actually seen the advertisement. Indeed, it can be seen under the *message* frequency distribution that the advertising message for Esuvee is estimated to reach only 46.1 percent of the audience one or more times. Such an achievement would be inadequate were it not for the fact, as earlier noted, that television advertising is to be run simultaneously with the magazine schedule. The combination of these media can be expected to produce much more impressive numbers and to achieve Esuvee's introductory advertising objectives.

There's No Substitute for Judgment and Experience

It is critical to emphasize that media models such as what has just been illustrated do not make the ultimate scheduling decision. All they can do is efficiently perform the calculations needed to determine which single media schedule will optimize some objective function such as maximizing reach or GRPs. Armed with the answer, it is up to the media planner to determine whether the media schedule satisfies other, nonquantitative objectives such as those described in the following chapter.

Now that fundamental issues in media scheduling have been identified, it will be useful to consider several actual media plans. First discussed is an award-winning plan for Diet Dr Pepper. Next presented is the plan used to introduce the Saab 9–5 luxury automobile. The final plan is for two brands of Olympus cameras. These three media plans are presented here as a matter of general appreciation. The objective is for students to gain deeper understanding of the considerations that go into developing media plans and the specific architecture of such plans. It certainly is not the intent that students attempt to commit this material to memory.

The Diet Dr Pepper Plan

An award-winning advertising campaign for Diet Dr Pepper developed by the Young & Rubicam advertising agency nicely illustrates a media schedule for a consumer packaged good.[37] Although this is not a current schedule, which explains why the following description is framed in past tense, the fundamentals are as applicable now as when the schedule was implemented.

© Susan Van Etten

Campaign Target and Objectives

The target audience for Diet Dr Pepper consisted primarily of adults ages 18 to 49 who were present or prospective diet soft-drink consumers. The objectives for the Diet Dr Pepper advertising campaign (titled "The Taste You've Been Looking For") were as follows:

1. To increase Diet Dr Pepper sales by 4 percent and improve its growth rate to at least 1.5 times that of the diet soft-drink category.
2. To heighten consumers' evaluations of the key product benefit and image factors that influence brand choice in this category: it is refreshing, tastes as good as regular Dr Pepper, is a good product to drink at any time, and is a fun brand to drink.
3. To enhance those key brand-personality dimensions that differentiate Diet Dr Pepper from other diet drinks—particularly that Diet Dr Pepper is a unique, clever, fun, entertaining, and interesting brand to drink.

Creative Strategy

The creative strategy for Diet Dr Pepper positioned the brand as "tasting more like regular Dr Pepper." This was a key claim based on research revealing that nearly 60 percent of initial trial users of Diet Dr Pepper were motivated by the desire to have a diet soft drink that tasted like regular Dr Pepper. The cornerstone of the campaign entailed the heavy use of 15-second commercials, which historically had not been used by major soft-drink brands, Coca-Cola and Pepsi-Cola, which instead preferred the entertainment value of longer commercials. The aggressive use of 15-second commercials enabled Diet Dr Pepper to simply convey its key taste claim ("Tastes more like regular Dr Pepper") and differentiate the brand from competitive diet drinks. Moreover, by employing cheaper 15-second commercials, it was possible to buy considerably more commercial spots and hence achieve greater reach, frequency, and GRPs for the same advertising budget. Diet Dr Pepper's advertising expenditures for the year totaled $20.3 million.

Media Strategy

The advertising schedule for Diet Dr Pepper generated a total of 1,858 GRPs, with a cumulative *annual* reach of 95 and frequency of 19.6. These media-weight values were accomplished with the national media plan summarized as a flowchart in Table 13.7.

Each of the 12 months and the week-beginning dates (Mondays) are listed across the top of the chart. Table entries reflect the GRPs achieved by each TV vehicle for each weekly period based on targeted adults in the age category 18 to 49. The first entry, a 41 for the *NFL Championship Games,* indicates that 41 gross rating points were produced by placing advertisements for Diet Dr Pepper during the football games televised the week beginning January 17. Ten additional GRPs were garnered by placing an ad on the *Road to the Super Bowl* program that aired during the week of January 24.

It can be seen that the Diet Dr Pepper media plan consisted of (1) placing advertisements during professional and college football games (the SEC stands for Southeastern Conference); (2) sponsoring various special events (e.g., the *Country Music Awards* and golfing events); and (3) continuously advertising during prime

Table 13.7

Media Plan for Diet Dr Pepper

ADULTS 18–49 GRPs	JAN					FEB				MAR				APR				MAY					JUN			
	27	3	10	17	24	31	7	14	21	28	7	14	21	28	4	11	18	25	2	9	16	23	30	6	13	20
SPORTS																										
NFL Championship Games				41																						
Road to the Superbowl					10																					
FOX "Game of the Week"																										
NBC "Game of the Week"																										
NBC Thanksgiving Game																										
ABC Monday Night Football																										
4Q Sports Total				41	10																					
SEC Championship Game																										
SEC-CFA Regular Game																										
SEC Thanksgiving Game																										
SEC Local/Conference Fee																										
SEC Sponsorship Total																										
TOTAL SPORTS				41	10																					
EVENTS																										
McDonald's Golf Classic																				1						
Daytime Emmy Awards																						23				
Country Music Awards																			32							
Garth Brooks Special																			12							
Michael Bolton Sponsorship																										
May Event Print																				17		18				
JC Penney LPGA Golf																										
Harvey Penick Special																							1			
Diners Club Golf																										
TOTAL EVENTS																			61	18	17	41	1			
CONTINUITY																										
Prime			53			53				53		54		34	35			35				35				35
May Event Prime Scatter																			29		28					
Late Night			6		5					5				3					3			4				
Syndication			14			14				13				8				8				8				8
Cable			13			14					14			11				11				11				
TOTAL CONTINUITY			86	126	15	86	81			85		68		56	57		54		86	28	86		58			43
Integration-to-date																										
Total Diet Plan			86	126	15	86	81			85		68		56	57		54		147	46	103	127	59			43
A18-49 GRPs/Week																										
Amount Over Budget																										
A18-49 GRPs/Month	227					167				238				167				477					102			
A18-49 GRPs/Quarter	632													746												

time, on late-night television (e.g., *David Letterman*), on syndicated programs, and on cable stations.

At the bottom of Table 13.7 is a summary of GRPs broken down by week (e.g., 86 GRPs during the week beginning January 10), month (e.g., 227 GRPs during January), and quarter (e.g., 632 GRPs produced during the first quarter, January through March). It can be seen that the media schedule was *flighted* insofar as

ADULTS 18–49 GRPs	JUL					AUG				SEP				OCT					NOV				DEC			
	27	4	11	18	25	1	8	15	22	29	5	12	19	26	3	10	17	24	31	7	14	21	28	5	12	19
SPORTS																										
NFL Championship Games																										
Road to the Superbowl																										
FOX "Game of the Week"														28							24			25		
NBC "Game of the Week"																13				22				20		
NBC Thanksgiving Game																						22				
ABC Monday Night Football																22		20	10	24						25
4Q Sports Total														28		35		20	10	46	24	22		45		25
SEC Championship Game																								33		
SEC-CFA Regular Game															8											
SEC Thanksgiving Game																						6				
SEC Local/Conference Fee																										
SEC Sponsorship Total															8							6		33		
TOTAL SPORTS														28	8	35		20	10	46	24	28		78		25
EVENTS																										
McDonald's Golf Classic																										
Daytime Emmy Awards																										
Country Music Awards																										
Garth Brooks Special																										
Michael Bolton Sponsorship																										
May Event Print																										
JC Penney LPGA Golf																										
Harvey Penick Special																										
Diners Club Golf																										
TOTAL EVENTS																										
CONTINUITY																										
Prime	25				25				26																	
May Event Prime Scatter																										
Late Night																										
Syndication																										
Cable																										
TOTAL CONTINUITY	25				25				26																	
Integration-to-date																										
Total Diet Plan	25				25				26					28	8	35		20	10	46	24	28		78		15
A18-49 GRPs/Week																										
Amount Over Budget																										
A18-49 GRPs/Month	75					51				52				91					108				103			
A18-49 GRPs/Quarter	**178**													**302**												

advertisements were placed during approximately two-thirds of the 52 weeks with no advertising during the remaining weeks. In sum, the media schedule was designed to highlight Diet Dr Pepper during a variety of special events and to maintain continuity throughout the year with prime-time network advertising and less expensive support on syndicated and cable programming.

Saab 9-5's Media Plan

The 9–5 model represented Saab's first entry in the luxury category and was designed to compete against well-known high-equity brands including Mercedes, BMW, Volvo, Lexus, and Infiniti. Despite being a unique automobile company—with a respected background in airplane manufacturing—Saab had done relatively little to enhance its brand image in the United States. Saab suffered from both a low level of consumer awareness and a poorly defined brand image.

Campaign Target and Objectives

Prior to the introduction of the 9–5 model, Saab's product mix had historically attracted younger consumers. Achieving success for its new luxury sedan required that the advertising appeal to upscale families and relatively affluent older consumers.

The introductory advertising campaign was designed to achieve the following objectives: (1) generate excitement for the new 9–5 model line; (2) increase overall awareness for the Saab name; (3) encourage consumers to visit dealers and test-drive the 9–5; and (4) retail 11,000 units of the 9–5 during the introductory year.

Creative Strategy

The Saab 9–5 was positioned as a luxury automobile capable of delivering an ideal synthesis of performance and safety. Creative advertising executions portrayed

Table 13.8
Media Plan for the Saab 9–5

	JAN				FEB				MAR					APR				MAY					JUN			
	29	5	12	19	26	2	9	16	23	2	9	16	23	30	6	13	20	27	4	11	18	25	1	8	15	22
Network TV					74 wk														95 wk							
Network Cable					40 wk														60 wk							
Magazines																										
Newspapers																										
USA Today																										
3 PBW (2X)														1X		1X										
SPBW (1X)															1X											
PBW (12X)																										
T Page (58X)		1X		1X	1X	1X		1X		2X	2X	2X	2X	2X	2X	2X	2X	2X	1X	1X		1X		1X		1X
1/4 PBW (8X)												4X	2X	2X												
Wall Street Jrnl																										
3 PBW (2X)														1X		1X										
SPBW (1X)															1X											
PBW (12X)																										
4 col x 14" (63X)		1X	1X		1X	1X	1X		1X	2X	2X	2X	2X	2X	2X	2X	2X	2X	1X	1X	1X	1X	1X	1X	1X	1X
4 col x 8" (8X)												2X	4X	2X												
Interactive																										

Legend:

1X, 2X, etc. = Number of insertions per week placed in *USA Today* or WSJ (1X = one insertion, 2X - two insertions, etc.)

3 PBW = 3 pages black & white magazine ad

SPBW = Spread page B&W (ad runs across 2 pages like a centerfold)

Saab as a premium European luxury manufacturer and were designed to have a hint of mystery and wit. An intensive media campaign was needed to deliver the creative executions and achieve the company's three advertising objectives.

Media Strategy

An integrated media campaign was designed to generate high levels of reach and frequency among the target group of older and financially well-off consumers and ultimately to sell at retail 11,000 Saab 9–5 vehicles. The media schedule is presented in Table 13.8. It first will be noted that TV advertising started in January, which was before the 9–5's introduction in April. Network and cable TV advertising ran from mid-January through early February and then again throughout May following the 9–5's introduction. Notice that the initial network TV campaign accumulated 74 GRPs for each of three weeks (the weeks beginning January 19, January 26, and February 2) and that accompanying advertising on cable TV amassed 40 GRPs for each of these same three weeks. Following the 9–5's introduction, the May television schedule accumulated 95 and 60 GRPs, respectively, on network and cable TV. Or, in other words, a total of 620 television GRPs [$(95 \times 4) + (60 \times 4)$] were purchased in May.

Table 13.8 further reveals that magazine advertising for the Saab 9–5 started in late January and continued for the remainder of the year without interruption. A variety of magazines was used to reach Saab's designated market for the 9–5. These included automotive magazines (e.g., *Car & Driver* and *Road & Track*), sports publications (e.g., *Ski* and *Tennis*), home magazines (e.g., *Martha Stewart Living* and *Architectural Digest*), business magazines (e.g., *Money, Forbes,* and *Working*

	JUL				AUG					SEP				OCT				NOV					DEC			
	29	6	13	20	27	3	10	17	24	31	7	14	21	28	5	12	19	26	2	9	16	23	30	7	14	21
Network TV																										
Network Cable																										
Magazines																										
Newspapers																										
USA Today																										
3 PBW (2X)																										
SPBW (1X)																										
PBW (12X)														1X	3X	2X					3X	1X	2X			
T Page (58X)		1X	1X	1X	1X	1X	1X	1X	1X	1X	1X	1X	2X	1X		1X	2X	2X	2X	2X		1X	1X	2X	2X	1X
1/4 PBW (8X)																										
Wall Street Jrnl																										
3 PBW (2X)																										
SPBW (1X)																										
PBW (12X)														1X	2X	2X	1X				2X	1X	2X	1X		
4 col x 14" (63X)	1X	2X	1X	1X	1X	1X	1X	1X	1X	1X		1X	2X	1X	1X	1X	1X	2X	2X	2X	1X	1X	1X	1X	2X	1X
4 col x 8" (8X)																										
Interactive																										

PBW = 1-page black & white
T Page = An odd shaped add placement
1/4 PBW = 1/4 page B&W
Interactive = Internet banner ad placed on *The Wall Street Journal Interactive Edition*

Women), and general interest publications (e.g., *Time* and *New York Magazine*). National newspaper advertising in *USA Today* and the *Wall Street Journal* also ran throughout the year. And finally, Internet banner advertising ran continuously throughout the introductory year.

Olympus Camera Media Plan

The camera business has become increasingly competitive and diverse with new players entering the industry on a regular basis.[38] Where at one time it was primarily only Kodak, Canon, Olympus, and Nikon who dominated the industry, now firms such as Sony and Hewlett Packard also compete for the buying public's camera purchases. The modern camera industry is now one of sophisticated consumer electronics rather than simply point-and-click devices. To successfully transition the company's camera business into the broader world of consumer electronics, executives at Olympus realized the company would need to implement a marketing communications program that would change both consumer and retailer perceptions of Olympus—a change from the belief that Olympus is merely a point-and-click camera maker to the perception that it is a major player in designer electronics. The shift began in earnest when Olympus asked The Martin Agency to develop a media campaign for introducing two new brands, the Stylus Verve and the m:robe.

Campaign Objectives

The first product, Stylus Verve, had all of the features of Olympus' flagship Stylus Digital line, but was uniquely designed and available in six colors. To make the jump even more substantial, Olympus introduced a wholly new product to the market in early 2005, the m:robe—an MP3 player and camera all in one. The Martin Agency's job was to create a media plan that would serve to successfully introduce the Stylus Verve and the m:robe and, at the same time, to facilitate the shift in marketplace perceptions that Olympus was a maker of designer electronics items and not merely cameras.

The Strategy

A high-impact, event-driven media strategy was developed to meet these objectives. Overall, the idea was to place the Olympus message in media that people talk about, that get ink, that generate buzz, that yield free media coverage, that have longevity, and that are influential. Moreover, it was important that the selected media reach both males and females and be suitable for Olympus' key, fourth-quarter selling season running from October through December.

Olympus' current sponsorships of the U.S. Tennis Open and Olympus Fashion Week allowed for the perfect kick off in August 2004 and wrap-up in February 2005. Having these two events already in place allowed for the high-impact, event-driven media to fill the gap.

Media and Vehicles

TV programs were selected to deliver high viewership and to satisfy the criteria previously mentioned. Considered especially suitable were high-impact and widely viewed programs that aired only once a year. Ads for the Stylus Verve were placed in programs such as the *World Series*, the *American Music Awards, Macy's Thanksgiving Day Parade*, and *Dick Clark's Rockin' New Years Eve*. The m:robe was launched in the ultimate high-profile program, the *Super Bowl*, followed by *The Grammys*. Network cable added frequency and continuity to the network TV schedule. Ad placements on E! and ESPN complimented and extended the entertainment and sporting events. The addition of programs such as *Sex and the City* and *Friends* rounded out the TV schedule and further served to generate buzz for the Verve and m:robe.

In addition to TV spots, magazine issues such as *People*'s "Sexiest Man Alive," *Sports Illustrated*'s "Sportsman of the Year," and *Time*'s "Person of the Year" carried four-page gatefold ads for the Stylus Verve. These special magazine issues reach millions of consumers who are exposed to ad messages in a positive context. Moreover, these special issues have a "life of their own" when people talk, for example, about whether they agree with *People*'s choice of the sexiest man alive. As part of the m:robe launch, the biggest magazine issue of the year, *Sports Illustrated*'s "Swimsuit" edition, was utilized, along with *Rolling Stone*'s "Richest Rock Stars" issue, a perfect tie in with the music aspect of the product.

Out of home (OOH) also played a role using a combination of impact units purchased within four key Olympus markets and in-theater advertising in the top-25 markets. High-impact OOH units were selected based on high-traffic areas, as well as proximity to key Olympus retailers. A five-week flight of in-theater advertising starting Thanksgiving weekend capitalized on the heavy holiday movie traffic. Additionally, an online element of highly visible brand placements and sponsorships was developed for both the Stylus Verve and the m:robe. The chosen sites had to be contextually relevant for the target and included high-traffic areas on the Web featuring entertainment and sporting events—for example, E! Online for entertainment and Fox Sports for its coverage of Worlds Series baseball and the National Football League.

However, for m:robe, the online element went beyond just Web-site advertising and entered a whole new dimension. With the m:robe propelling Olympus into the consumer electronics category, the online element needed to express the m:robe experience and help define its points of differentiation from competitive brands, while helping support ad placements on the Super Bowl. To achieve these objectives, a non-branded interactive Web site was developed featuring the pop-lockin' dance moves that would later be viewed as the focus of the Olympus Super Bowl spots. (Pop locking is a stylized form of dancing in which people, or animated characters, tense up, or pop their muscles quickly, and lock out their joints. The "robot" dance is one form of pop locking.)

The interactive Web site allowed users to make the Web-site characters pop lock or see themselves pop lock by uploading a picture of their head to the Web site. This Web site was passed along to friends and family, getting picked up on blogs and other Web sites in the process. Once the units on the Super Bowl aired, the previously unbranded Web site (http://www.poplockin.com) was changed to Olympus Groove (http://www.olympusgroove.com) and became the official site of m:robe. Users could still dance, but the site now became an online community for m:robe users.

Table 13.9 presents a flowchart of the 2004–2005 media plan for Olympus' Stylus Verve and m:robe brands. Because the plan was not bought specifically in terms of generating designated levels of gross ratings, no point totals are presented. Please note the diversity of media used (sponsored events, national TV, print, online, in-theater, and OOH) and the various vehicles used in each medium. This was a truly integrated media plan that generated impressive results.

Results

The Stylus Verve advertising campaign launched during the U.S. Tennis Open in August and concluded with New Years. During this period, unaided awareness of Olympus increased by 23 percent. The advertising also contributed to an increase in consumers believing that Olympus was trendy and innovative. The m:robe launch raised awareness of Olympus as a player in the digital music category from 0 percent to 5 percent, which was on par with the more established iRiver brand; moreover, 20 percent of the respondents to an advertising tracking study

Table 13.9

2004–05 Media Plan for Olympus' Stylus Verve and m:robe Brands

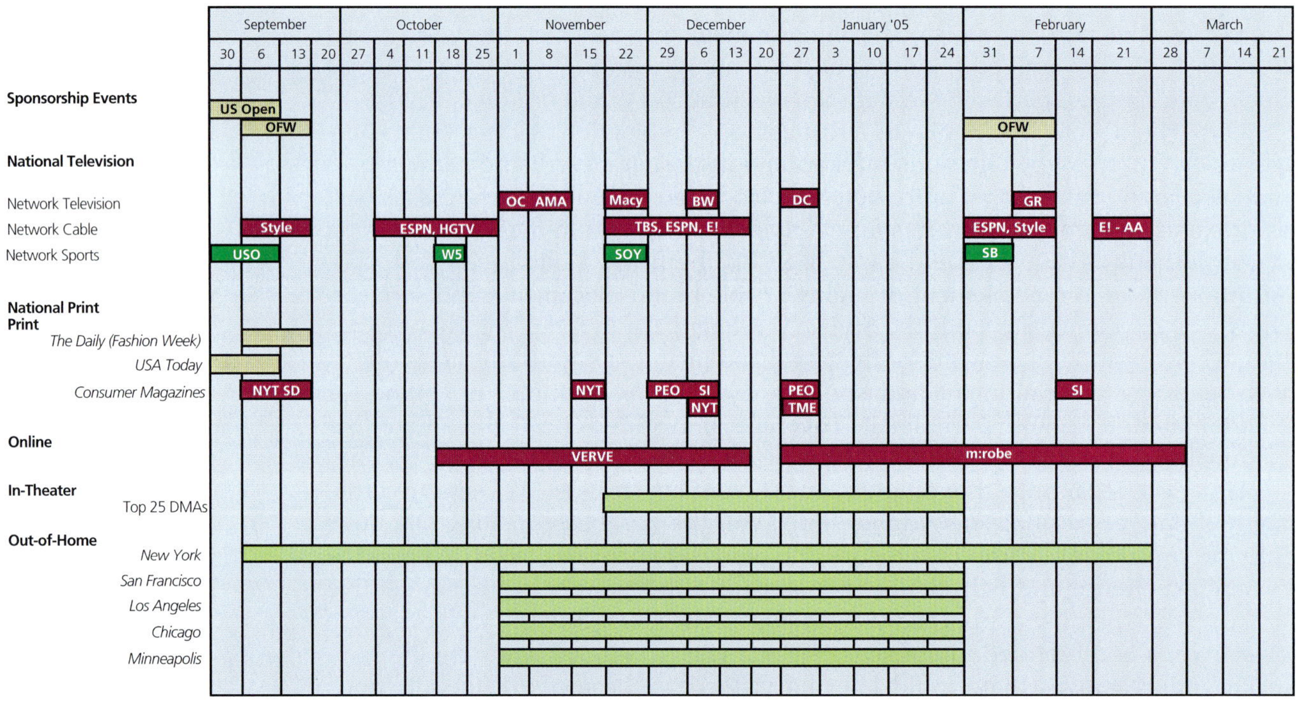

Television Event Programs

US Open on CBS
Style Network - Fashion Week Coverage (Sept and Feb)
ESPN: NFL and high-profile programming
HGTV: High-profile prime and weekend day
World Series Game #3
The OC Premiere
American Music Awards
Macy's Parade
Sports Illustrated Sportsman of the Year on FOX
Barbara Walter's 25 Most Intruiging People
Dick Clark's Rockin New Year's Eve
Super Bowl coverage on ESPN
Super Bowl
Grammy Awards
Academy Awards on E!
TBS: Seinfeld, Friends, Everybody Loves Raymond, Sex and the City
ESPN: NFL and high-profile programming
E! / Style bonus: Entertainment/high-profile programming

Consumer Magazines

NYT = New York Times
SD = Time Style & Design
PEO = People Magazine
SI = Sports Illustrated
TME = Time Magazine

indicated that they believe Olympus offers good quality features. This compares favorably with Apple's iPod score of 17 percent on this same feature. The online components saw equally successful results: LiquidTreat, an online design newsletter (http://www.liquidtreat.com), and Maxim Online (http://www.maximonline.com) listed poplockin' (http://www.poplockin.com) as their "Site of the Week." The Super Bowl increased traffic to Olympus Groove (http://www.olympusgroove.com) and OlympusAmerica (http://www.olympusamerica.com) by over 400 percent, and post-Grammy's traffic jumped over 700 percent. Retailer perceptions were also greatly influenced when the Super Bowl media buy was announced as part of m:robe's product launch at the 2005 Consumer Electronic Show, generating press coverage in *USA Today* and the *Wall Street Journal.*

Summary

Selection of advertising media and vehicles is one of the most important and complicated of all marketing communications decisions. Media planning must be coordinated with marketing strategy and with other aspects of advertising strategy. The strategic aspects of media planning involve four steps: (1) selecting the target audience toward which all subsequent efforts will be directed; (2) specifying media objectives, which typically are stated in terms of reach, frequency, gross rating points (GRPs), or effective rating points (ERPs); (3) selecting general media categories and specific vehicles within each medium; and (4) buying media.

Media and vehicle selection are influenced by a variety of factors; most important are target audience, cost, and creative considerations. Media planners select media vehicles by identifying those that will reach the designated target audience, satisfy budgetary constraints, and be compatible with and enhance the advertiser's creative message. There are numerous ways to schedule media insertions over time, but media planners have typically used some form of pulsed or flighted schedule whereby advertising is on at times, off at others, but never continuous. The principle of recency, also referred to as the shelf-space model of advertising, challenges the use of flighted advertising schedules and purports that weekly efficient reach should be the decision criterion of choice because this approach ensures that advertising will be run at the time when consumers are making brand selection decisions.

The chapter provided detailed explanations of the various considerations used by media planners in making advertising media decisions. These included the concepts of reach, frequency, gross rating points (GRPs), effective rating points (ERPs), and cost and continuity considerations. Media vehicles within the same medium are compared in terms of cost using the cost-per-thousand criterion.

The chapter included a detailed discussion of a computerized media-selection model. This model requires information about vehicle cost, ratings, maximum number of insertions, and a budget constraint and then maximizes an objective function subject to that budget. Optimization criteria include maximizing reach (1+), effective reach (3+), frequency, or GRPs.

The chapter concluded with descriptions of media plans for Diet Dr Pepper, the Saab 9–5, and the Styles Verve and m:robe brands of Olympus cameras.

Discussion Questions

1. Why is target audience selection the critical first step in formulating a media strategy?
2. Compare and contrast TRPs and GRPs as media selection criteria?
3. Why is reach also called *net coverage* or *unduplicated audience*?
4. A television advertising schedule produced the following vehicle frequency distribution:

f	Percentage *f*	Percentage *f*+
0	31.4	100.0
1	9.3	68.6
2	7.1	59.4
3	6.0	52.2
4	5.2	46.2
5	4.6	41.0
6	4.1	36.4
7	3.7	32.3
8	3.4	28.5
9	3.1	25.1
10+	22.0	22.0

   (a) What is the reach for this advertising schedule?
   (b) What is the effective reach?
   (c) How many GRPs does this schedule generate?
   (d) What is the frequency for this schedule?
5. Assume that the TV advertising schedule in question 4 cost $2 million and generated 240 million gross impressions. What are the CPM and CPP?
6. A publication called the *$ Ad Summary* (also generally known as *Leading National Advertisers,* or *LNA*) is an invaluable source for determining how much money brands invest in advertising. Go to your library and find the most recent version of *LNA.* Identify the advertising expenditures and the media used in advertising the following brands: Mountain Dew, Pantene Shampoo, and Nike footwear.
7. With reference to the three-exposure hypothesis, explain the difference between three exposures to an advertising message versus three exposures to an advertising vehicle.
8. When an advertiser uses the latter, what implicit assumption is that advertiser making?
9. Describe in your own words the fundamental logic underlying the principle of recency (or what also is referred to as the shelf-space model of advertising). Is this model always the best model to apply in setting media allocations over time?
10. A TV program has a rating of 17.6. With approximately 109.6 million television households in the United States as of 2005, what is that program's CPM if a 30-second commercial costs $600,000? Now assume that an advertiser's target audience consists only of people ages 25 to 54, which constitutes 62 percent of the program's total audience. What is the CPM-TM in this case?

11. Which is more important for an advertiser: maximizing reach or maximizing frequency? Explain in detail.
12. In the output presented in Table 13.6, the message-to-vehicle ratio equals 52.5 percent. Explain in your own words precisely what this means. Why is the ratio for TV lower than this?
13. Reach will be lower for an advertised brand if the entire advertising budget during a four-week period is devoted to advertising exclusively on a single program than if the same budget is allocated among a variety of TV programs. Why is this so?
14. Following are the ratings and number of ad insertions on five cable TV programs designated as C1 through C5: C1 (rating = 7; insertions = 6); C2 (rating = 4; insertions = 12); C3 (rating = 3; insertions = 20); C4 (rating = 5; insertions = 10); C5 (rating = 6; insertions = 15). How many GRPs would be obtained from this cable TV advertising schedule?
15. Assume that in Canada there are 30 million TV households. A particular prime-time TV program aired at nine o'clock in the evening and had a *rating* of 18.5 and a 32 *share*. At the nine o'clock airtime, how many TV sets were tuned into this or another program? (Hint: Ratings are based on total households, whereas share is based on just the households that have their TV sets on at a particular time, in this case at nine o'clock at night. Because the numerator value remains constant in both the calculation of ratings and share values, by simple algebraic manipulation you can determine from the rating information the number of households with their sets on.)

ENDNOTES

1. Rob Frydlewicz, "Missed Super Bowl? Put Your Bucks Here," *Advertising Age,* January 30, 1995, 18.
2. Joe Mantese, "Majority Prefer Super Bowl Ads, Socializing Vs. the Game Itself," *MediaDailyNews,* February 7, 2005.
3. Thom Forbes, "Consumer Central: The Media Focus Is Changing—And So Is the Process," *Agency,* winter 1998, 38.
4. Karen Whitehill King and Leonard N. Reid, "Selecting Media for National Accounts: Factors of Importance to Agency Media Specialists," *Journal of Current Issues and Research in Advertising* 19 (fall 1997), 55–64.
5. Kate Maddox, "Media Planners in High Demand," *BtoB,* November 8, 2004, 24; Ave Butensky, "Hitting the Spot," *Agency,* winter 1998, 26.
6. Kent M. Lancaster, "Optimizing Advertising Media Plans Using ADOPT on the Microcomputer," working paper, University of Illinois, December 1987, 2–3. (Note that in the last line of this quote Lancaster actually used 30 rather than 20 possible insertions. I have changed it to 20 so as not to create confusion with the earlier reference to "30 feasible publications.")
7. Laura Freeman, "Taking Apart Media," *Agency,* winter 2001, 20–25.
8. Ibid., 22.
9. Ibid., 23.
10. Henry Assael and Hugh Cannon, "Do Demographics Help in Media Selection?" *Journal of Advertising Research* 19 (December 1979), 7–11; Hugh M. Cannon and G. Russell Merz, "A New Role for Psychographics in Media Selection," *Journal of Advertising* 9, no. 2 (1980), 33–36, 44.
11. Karen Whitehill King, Leonard N. Reid, and Wendy Macias, "Selecting Media for National Advertising Revisited: Criteria of Importance to Large-Company Advertising Managers," *Journal of Current Issues and Research in Advertising* 26 (spring 2004), 59–68.
12. A quote from advertising consultant Alvin Achenbaum cited in B. G. Yovovich, "Media's New Exposures," *Advertising Age,* April 13, 1981, S7.
13. One study found that more than 80 percent of advertising agencies use effective reach as a criterion in media planning.

See Peggy J. Kreshel, Kent M. Lancaster, and Margaret A. Toomey, "How Leading Advertising Agencies Perceive Effective Reach and Frequency," *Journal of Advertising* 14, no. 3 (1985), 32–38.

14. Gerard J. Tellis, "Advertising Exposure, Loyalty, and Brand Purchase: A Two-Stage Model of Choice," *Journal of Marketing Research* 25 (May 1988), 134–144.
15. Herbert E. Krugman, "Why Three Exposures May Be Enough," *Journal of Advertising Research* 12, no. 6 (1972), 11–14.
16. This point is made especially forcefully by Hugh M. Cannon and Edward A. Riordan, "Effective Reach and Frequency: Does It Really Make Sense?" *Journal of Advertising Research* 34 (March/April 1994), 19–28.
17. Ibid., 24.
18. Adapted from "The Muscle in Multiple Media," *Marketing Communications,* December 1983, 25.
19. Cannon and Riordan, "Effective Reach and Frequency," 25–26. The following illustration is adapted from this source.
20. The original authors of this procedure referred to it as exposure value rather than utility, but this use of *value* gets confused with the later use of *value.*
21. A procedure for estimating these values is available in Hugh M. Cannon, John D. Leckenby, and Avery Abernethy, "Beyond Effective Frequency: Evaluating Media Schedules Using Frequency Value Planning," *Journal of Advertising Research* 42 (November/December 2002), 33–47.
22. Erwin Ephron, "More Weeks, Less Weight: The Shelf-Space Model of Advertising," *Journal of Advertising Research* 35 (May/June 1995), 18–23. See also Ephron's various writings archived at his Web site, Ephron on Media (http://www.ephrononmedia.com).
23. Ibid., 5–18. See also John Philip Jones, "Single-Source Research Begins to Fulfill Its Promise," *Journal of Advertising Research* 35 (May/June 1995), 9–16; Lawrence D. Gibson, "What Can One TV Exposure Do?" *Journal of Advertising Research* 36 (March/April 1996), 9–18; and Kenneth A. Longman, "If Not Effective Frequency, Then What?" *Journal of Advertising Research* 37 (July/August 1997), 44–50.
24. Jones, "Single-Source Research Begins to Fulfill Its Promise." Despite these findings, which have had considerable impact on the advertising community, there is some counterevidence suggesting that Jones' research results are not solely the result of advertising exposure but in fact are correlated with sales promotion activity. In other words, what may appear to be the exclusive impact of successful advertising may actually be due at least in part to a brand's sales promotion activity (such as couponing or cents-off dealing) that takes place at the same time that advertising for the brand is running on television. Until research evidence is more definitive on this matter, a reasonable conclusion is that Jones' measure of advertising effectiveness is interesting but perhaps simplistic in the absence of proper experimental or statistical controls for sales promotions, price changes, and other potential determinants of a brand's sales volume. For counterperspectives to Jones' claims, see Gary Schroeder, Bruce C. Richardson, and Avu Sankaralingam, "Validating STAS Using BehaviorScan," *Journal of Advertising Research* 37 (July/August 1997), 33–43. For another challenge, see Gerard J. Tellis and Doyle L. Weiss, "Does TV Advertising Really Affect Sales? The Role of Measures, Models, and Data Aggregation," *Journal of Advertising* 24 (fall 1995), 1–12.
25. Erwin Ephron, "What Is Recency?," Ephron on Media, http://www.ephrononmedia.com.
26. Ephron, "More Weeks, Less Weight: The Shelf-Space Model of Advertising," 19.
27. Ibid., 20.
28. A quote from Joanne Burke, senior vice president worldwide media research director, TN Media, New York, in Laurie Freeman, "Effective Weekly Planning Gets a Boost," *Advertising Age* (July 24, 1995), S8, S9.
29. Erwin Ephron, "Recency Planning," *Journal of Advertising Research* 37 (July/August 1997), 61–65.
30. Ibid., 61.
31. For elaboration on these points, see Gerard J. Tellis, "Effective Frequency: One Exposure or Three Factors?" *Journal of Advertising Research* 37 (July/August 1997), 75–80.
32. This analogy is adapted from Charles H. Patti and Charles F. Frazer, *Advertising: A Decision-Making Approach* (Hinsdale, IL: Dryden Press, 1988), 369.
33. To construct Table 13.5, magazine audience sizes were based on the larger of the estimated audience sizes provided by Simmons and MRI. Figures were obtained from *Marketer's Guide to Media: 2004,* vol. 27 (New York: VNU Business Publications USA, 2004), 164–168. Because many of the readers of these magazines do not satisfy the income requirement of $45,000 or are not within the 18–49 age category targeted for the *Esuvee,* each magazine's total audience size was arbitrarily reduced by 50 percent prior to being divided by the target audience size of 26.8 million.
34. The program is ADplus, which was developed by Kent Lancaster and is distributed by Telmar Information Services Corp., 470 Park Ave. South, 15th Floor, New York, NY 10016 (phone: 212-725-3000). It is noteworthy that a newer version of ADplus is available from Telmar under the name InterMix. However, when I ran the program using the database provided in Table 13.5, it generated a perverse solution (i.e., a solution I know to be wrong). Requests were made of the program developer, Kent Lancaster, to aid me in determining why the program generated an inappropriate solution. Unfortunately, he was unable to be of assistance. Accordingly, my faith in InterMix is diminished and I have chosen to use its predecessor, ADplus. Newer versions of ADplus, or of InterMix, may generate somewhat different solutions than are presented here (see Table 13.6). Professor Lancaster informed me that the InterMix uses "heuristic procedures," and apparently the "heuristics" have changed over time. In any event, the results presented in Table 13.6 are for illustration purposes only and are intended to simply explain how the various media diagnostics (reach, frequency, etc.) are generated.

35. Kent M. Lancaster, Peggy J. Kreshel, and Joya R. Harris, "Estimating the Impact of Advertising Media Plans: Media Executives Describe Weighting and Timing Factors," *Journal of Advertising* 15 (September 1986), 21–29, 45.
36. Kent Lancaster, *ADplus for Multi-media Advertising Planning* (Gainesville, FL: Media Research Institute, Inc., 1990), 18.
37. The following descriptions are based on a summary of a Diet Dr Pepper's advertising campaign prepared by Young & Rubicam. Appreciation for these materials is extended to Chris Wright-Isak and John T. O'Brien.
38. Appreciation is extended to Dr. Lauren Tucker of the Martin Agency (Richmond, VA) for facilitating my access to this media plan. I also greatly appreciate the assistance of Ms. Lori Baker of the Martin Agency in providing me with the plan discussed in this section. The description provided herein is an adaptation of the plan provided by Ms. Baker in April 2005.

CHAPTER 14

Using Traditional Advertising Media

Marcom Challenge: Does TV Deliver *ROI* for Mature Brands?

Television as an advertising medium has undergone rather dramatic changes in the past decade or so. The average television household now has upwards of 90 or more TV channels from which to choose, which means that advertisements simply do not reach the large numbers of consumers they once did. Beyond this audience fractionalization, people have many more entertainment options to divert their attention away from watching TV. Then to further complicate matters for advertisers, the number of households owning personal video recorders such as TiVo is continually increasing, and the owners of these devices often use them to completely skip or fast-forward through commercials. Finally, the cost of TV advertising continues to increase, which means that ads placed on television must be even more effective than in the past to yield a positive return on investment (ROI).

Against this backdrop, an important study—referred to as the Deutsche Bank report—was released in 2004 that presented data showing that a high percentage of the advertisements for *mature brands* in the consumer packaged goods (CPG) category do not yield positive *ROIs*.[1] The study used marketing-mix modeling, which was briefly described in Chapter 2, to assess TV advertising's short- and long-term effectiveness for 23 well-known CPG brands—some of which are mature (e.g., Coca-Cola classic, Campbell's soup, and Heinz ketchup) and some that are relatively new (e.g., Swiffer, Mach3 razors and blades, and Crest Whitestrips). Results indicated that only 5 of the 23 brands examined (22 percent) enjoyed positive *ROI* from TV advertising in the short term (i.e., less than one year), whereas 12 of the 23 brands (52 percent) yielded positive *ROIs* in the long term. Newer brands and those representing meaningful new products were substantially more likely to yield positive returns than were mature brands.

This latter finding—that new brands perform better than mature brands—should come as no surprise in view of the previous discussion in Chapter 12, where it was emphasized that TV advertising generally is effective only when the advertising is persuasive and provides distinctive, newsworthy information, such as when introducing new brands.

The takeaway from this discussion of the Deutsche Bank report should not be that television advertising is necessarily a wasted investment—and hopefully not, considering the amount that companies spend on it (for example, as shown previously in Table 9.1, 33 companies each invested over $1 billion in a recent year on advertising in the United States. The biggest ad spender,

General Motors, spent nearly $3.5 billion during that single year!). What instead should be gleaned from these comments, along with those in Chapter 12, is that advertisers must have something reasonably important to say about their brands and that commercials must be presented in an attention-getting, creative fashion if there is to be a reasonable likelihood that investments in TV commercials will deliver positive *ROIs.*

Associated Press AP

CHAPTER OBJECTIVES

1. Describe the four major traditional advertising media.
2. Discuss newspaper advertising and its strengths and limitations.
3. Evaluate magazine advertising and its strengths and limitations.
4. Discuss radio advertising and its strengths and limitations.
5. Discuss television advertising and its strengths and limitations.

Overview

This chapter focuses on the four major mass advertising media: newspapers, magazines, radio, and television. The following sections are devoted to each of these four major media, with primary emphasis devoted to exploring each medium's strengths and limitations. A few words of caution are in order before proceeding. In particular, it might be tempting to play a count-'em game when examining each medium's strengths and limitations. That is, the reader might erroneously conclude that one medium is superior to another simply because more advantages and fewer limitations are listed. But this assuredly is not the intent of the following discussions.

The overall value or worth of an advertising medium depends on the advertiser's specific needs in a particular situation and the overall budget available for advertising a brand. No advertising medium is always best. The value or worth of a medium depends on the circumstances confronting a brand at a particular time: its advertising objective, the target market toward which this objective is aimed, and the available budget. An analogy will clarify this point. Suppose someone asked you, "What type of restaurant is best?" An immediate single answer is difficult to offer because you undoubtedly would recognize that what is best depends on your particular needs on a specific dining occasion. In some circumstances price and speed of service are of the essence, and restaurants like McDonald's would win out by these criteria. On other occasions ambiance rules the day, and a classy French restaurant might be considered ideal. In yet another situation you may be looking for a balance between dining elegance and a reasonable price and favor a middle-of-the-road eating establishment. In sum, there is no such thing as a universally "best" restaurant.

The same is true of advertising media. Which medium is "best" depends entirely on the advertiser's objectives, the creative needs, the competitive challenge, and budget availability. The best medium, or combination of media, is determined not by counting advantages and limitations but by conducting a careful examination of the advertised brand's needs and resources.

The presentation of ad media progresses in the following order: first covered are the two print media, newspapers and magazines. Then examined are the broadcast media, radio and television. Advertising in the United States in these four media totaled approximately $150 billion in a recent year. Newspapers commanded approximately 32 percent of this total, magazines slightly over 8 percent, radio about 14 percent, and television nearly 46 percent.[2]

Newspapers

Newspapers in the United States reach approximately 56 million households in the United States during the week and about 59 million on Sundays.[3] *USA Today* (2.22 million daily circulation), the *Wall Street Journal* (2.11 million), and the *New York Times* (1.12 million) are the three largest U.S. newspapers in terms of daily circulation.[4] Newspapers historically had been the leading advertising medium, but television surpassed newspapers as the medium that receives the greatest amount of advertising expenditures. This is partially attributable to the fact that newspaper readership has been on a constant decline for a number of years.

Local advertising is clearly the mainspring of newspapers. However, newspapers have become more active in their efforts to increase national advertising.

These efforts have been facilitated by the Newspaper Advertising Bureau (NAB), a nonprofit sales and research organization. The NAB offers a variety of services that assist both newspapers and national advertisers by simplifying the task of buying newspaper space and by offering discounts that make newspapers a more attractive medium.

Buying Newspaper Space

A major problem in the past when buying newspaper space, especially for advertisers that purchased space from newspapers in many cities, was that newspaper page size and column space varied, thereby preventing an advertiser from preparing a single advertisement to fit every newspaper. Analogously, imagine what it would be like to advertise on television if, rather than having fixed 15-, 30-, or 60-second commercials for all networks and local stations, some local stations ran only 28-second commercials, while others preferred 23-second, 16-second, or 11-second commercials. Buying time on television would be nightmarish for advertisers. So it was in buying newspaper space until the advertising industry adopted a standardized system known as the **Standardized Advertising Unit (SAU) system**. The implementation of the SAU system made it possible for advertisers to purchase any one of 56 standard ad sizes to fit the advertising publishing parameters of all newspapers in the United States.

Under this system, advertisers prepare advertisements and purchase space in terms of column widths and depth in inches. There are six column *widths:*

1 column: $2\frac{1}{16}$ inches
2 columns: $4\frac{1}{4}$ inches
3 columns: $6\frac{7}{16}$ inches
4 columns: $8\frac{5}{8}$ inches
5 columns: $10\frac{13}{16}$ inches
6 columns: 13 inches

Space *depth* varies in size from 1 inch to 21 inches. Thus, an advertiser can purchase an ad as small as 1 inch by $2\frac{1}{16}$ inches or as large as 13 inches by 21 inches with numerous in-between combinations of column widths and depths in inches. A chosen size for a particular advertisement can then be run in newspapers throughout the country. Space rates can be compared from newspaper to newspaper and adjusted for circulation differences. For example, the daily SAU column-inch rate for the *Chicago Tribune* (circulation: 681,000) is $580, whereas the same rate in the competitive *Chicago Sun-Times* (circulation: 482,000) is $575.[5] On the surface, the *Sun-Times* is cheaper than the *Tribune,* but when adjusted to a per-thousand-readers basis, the cost per thousand (CPM) of procuring a column inch in the *Tribune* is approximately $0.85 (i.e., $580 ÷ 681) compared with a cost of about $1.19 (i.e., $575 ÷ 482) to advertise in the *Sun-Times.* Hence, it is actually cheaper to advertise in the *Tribune.* Of course, the advertiser must observe audience characteristics, newspaper image, and other factors when making an advertising decision rather than considering only cost.

The choice of an advertisement's position must also be considered when buying newspaper space. Space rates apply only to advertisements placed *ROP* (run of press), which means that the ad appears in any location, on any page, at the discretion of the newspaper. Premium charges may be assessed if an advertiser has a preferred space positioning, such as at the top of the page in the financial section. Whether premium charges are actually assessed is a matter of negotiation between the advertiser and the newspaper.

© Susan Van Etten

Newspaper Advertising's Strengths and Limitations

As with all advertising media, newspaper advertising has various strengths and limitations (see Table 14.1).

Newspaper Advertising's Strengths

Because people read newspapers for news, they are in the *right mental frame to process advertisements* that present news of store openings, new products, sales, and so forth.

Mass audience coverage, or broad reach, is a second strength of newspaper advertising. Coverage is not restricted to specific socioeconomic or demographic groups but rather extends across all strata. However, newspaper readers on average are more economically upscale than television viewers. College graduates are more likely to read a newspaper than the population at large. Because economically advantaged consumers are comparatively light TV viewers, newspaper advertising provides a relatively inexpensive medium for reaching these consumers. Special interest newspapers also reach large numbers of potential consumers. For example, the vast majority of college students read a campus newspaper.

Flexibility is perhaps the greatest strength of newspapers. National advertisers can adjust copy to match the specific buying preferences and peculiarities of localized markets. Local advertisers can vary copy through in-paper inserts targeted to specific zip codes. In addition, advertising copy can be placed in a newspaper section that is compatible with the advertised product. Retailers of wedding accessories advertise in the bridal section, providers of financial services advertise in the business section, sporting goods stores advertise in the sports section, and so forth. A second facet of newspaper flexibility is that this medium enables advertisers to design an ad of a variety of sizes, as compared to all other mass media where few size or length options are possible.

The *ability to use detailed copy* is another of newspaper advertising's strengths. Detailed product information and extensive editorial passages are used in newspaper advertising to an extent unparalleled by any other medium.

Timeliness is a final significant strength of newspaper advertising. Short lead times (the time between placing an ad and having it run) permit advertisers to tie in advertising copy with local market developments or newsworthy events. Advertisers can develop copy or make copy changes quickly and thereby take advantage of dynamic marketplace developments.

Newspaper Advertising's Limitations

Clutter is a problem in newspapers, as it is in all of the other major media. A reader perusing a newspaper is confronted with large numbers of ads, all of which compete for the reader's limited time and only a subset of which receive the reader's attention. It is noteworthy, however, that a national survey of consumers revealed

Table 14.1

Newspaper Advertising's Strengths and Limitations

Strengths	Limitations
Audience in appropriate mental frame to process messages	Clutter
Mass audience coverage	Not a highy selective medium
Flexibility	Higher rates for occasional advertisers
Ability to use detailed copy	Mediocre reproduction quality
Timeliness	Complicated buying for national advertisers
	Changing composition of readers

that they perceived newspapers as being significantly less cluttered with advertisements than television, radio, and magazines.[6]

A second limitation of newspaper advertising is that newspapers are *not a highly selective medium.* Newspapers are able to reach broad cross sections of people but, with few exceptions (such as campus newspapers), are unable to reach specific groups of consumers effectively. Media specialists consider newspapers to fare poorly in comparison to network television in efficiently targeting specific audiences.[7]

Occasional users of newspaper space (such as national advertisers who infrequently advertise in newspapers) *pay higher rates* than do heavy users (such as local advertisers) and have difficulty in securing preferred, non-ROP positions. In fact, newspapers' price lists (called *rate cards*) show higher rates for national than local advertisers.

Newspapers generally offer a *mediocre reproduction quality.* For this and other reasons, newspapers are not generally known to enhance a product's perceived quality, elegance, or snob appeal, as can magazines and television.

Buying difficulty is a particularly acute problem in the case of the national advertiser who wishes to secure newspaper space in multiple markets. On top of the high rates charged to national advertisers is the fact that each newspaper must be contacted individually. Fortunately, as mentioned previously, the NAB has made great strides toward facilitating the purchase of newspaper space by national advertisers.

A final significant problem with newspaper advertising involves the *changing composition of newspaper readers.* While most everyone used to read a daily newspaper, readership has declined progressively during the past generation. The most faithful newspaper readers are individuals age 45 and older, but the large and attractive group of consumers age 30 to 44 are reading daily newspapers less frequently than ever. Daily newspaper readership in this age group has fallen dramatically in recent decades.

Magazines

Although considered a mass medium, there are literally hundreds of special-interest magazines, each appealing to audiences that manifest specific interests and lifestyles. In fact, Standard Rate and Data Service (now known simply as SRDS Media Solutions), a company that tracks information for the magazine industry (as well as for most other media), identifies well over 2,500 consumer magazines in dozens of specific categories, such as automotive (e.g., *Motor Trend*); general editorial (e.g., the *New Yorker*); sports (e.g., *Sports Illustrated*); women's fashions, beauty, and grooming (e.g., *Glamour*); and many others. In addition to consumer magazines, hundreds of other publications are classified as farm magazines or business publications. Advertisers obviously have numerous options when selecting magazines to promote their products. Advertisers and media planners turn to SRDS (http://www.srds.com) to obtain information on standardized ad rates, contact information, reader profiles and other information, which facilitates media planning and buying.

Buying Magazine Space

A number of factors influence the choice of magazine vehicles in which to advertise. Most important is selecting magazines that reach the type of people who constitute the advertiser's target market. However, because the advertiser typically can choose from several alternative vehicles to satisfy the target market objective, cost considerations also play an extremely important role.

Advertisers that are interested in using the magazine medium can acquire a wealth of data about the composition of a magazine's readership in terms of demographic profiles. This information is provided in each magazine's *media kit* that is made available to ad agencies and prospective advertisers. Media kits for many magazines can be found online. For example, Figure 14.1 presents the demographic profile for *Sports Illustrated* based on data compiled by Mediamark Research Inc. (MRI) for fall 2004. The median age of *Sports Illustrated*'s readership is 38.8 with a median household income of $62,845. Also presented in Figure 14.1 are specific breakdowns by age, education, occupation, household income, and geographic region. For each demographic grouping, the first column contains audience size expressed in thousands, the second column presents percentage breakdowns for each demographic subgroup, and the last column indexes each percentage against that group's proportionate population representation. For example, 41.2 percent of *Sports Illustrated*'s readers fall in the age group of 35–54, 26.7 percent are employed in professional and managerial positions, 40.4 percent have household incomes of $75,000 or more, and 32.8 percent of *Sports Illustrated*'s readers are located in the South. Note carefully, however, that though the greatest number of readers are from the South, readers in this region are below their proportionate population representation (index = 91; see last column), whereas individuals living in the North Central region of the United States are proportionately more likely to read *Sports Illustrated* (index = 113).

Another demographic profile (of *Cosmopolitan* readers) is provided in Figure 14.2. Several interesting observations can be gleaned from this figure. For example, women in the age category 18–24 constitute about 32 percent of *Cosmopolitan*'s readers, but the index of 258 reveals that this age group represents this magazine's read-

Figure 14.1

Sports Illustrated Magazine's Demographic Profile

	Audience (in thousands)	Composition (%)	Index
Age			
18–24	3,757	18.7	145
25–34	4,701	23.4	127
35–54	8,263	41.2	104
55–64	1,996	10.0	77
Median Age	38.8		
Education			
Attended/Graduated College+	12,239	61.0	118
Occupation			
Professional	2,858	14.3	113
Management/Business/Finance	2,497	12.5	126
Professional/Managerial	5,354	26.7	118
Sales/Office	3,097	15.4	97
Natural Resource/Construction/Maintenance	2,013	10.0	153
Other Employed	4,943	24.6	130
Household Income (HHI)			
$75,000+	8,102	40.4	131
$50,000+	12,332	61.5	120
$40,000+	14,275	71.2	117
$30,000+	16,303	81.3	113
<$30,000	3,751	18.7	67
Median HHI	$62,845		
Geographic Region			
Northeast	3,718	18.5	97
North Central	5,140	25.6	113
South	6,580	32.8	91
West	4,618	23.0	104

SOURCE: *Sports Illustrated,* MRI Fall 2004, http://sportsillustrated.cnn.com/adinfo/si/mriabc.html

	Audience (in thousands)	Composition (%)	Index
Age			
Total Women	14,083	85.3	164
18–24	4,483	31.8	258
25–34	3,697	26.3	147
35–49	3,927	27.9	92
Median Age	31.4		
Education			
Attended/Graduated College+	9,203	65.3	126
Employment			
Total Employed	10,157	72.1	126
Full-Time	7,555	53.6	124
Marital Status			
Single	5,899	41.9	197
Married	5,559	39.5	72
Divorced/Widowed/Separated	2,625	18.6	77
Individual Employment Income (IEI)			
$20,000+	6,322	44.9	121
$25,000+	5,275	37.5	121
Median IEI	$26,053		
Household Income (HHI)			
$30,000+	10,958	77.8	113
$40,000+	9,319	66.2	115
Median HHI	$58,015		

SOURCE: *Cosmopolitan,* MRI Fall 2004, http://www.cosmopolitan.com.

Figure 14.2
Cosmopolitan Magazine's Demographic Profile

ership by 2.58 times greater than this age group's proportionate population representation. In short, *Cosmopolitan* attracts a younger readership base. Moreover, approximately 42 percent of *Cosmopolitan*'s readers are single, and, again, with an index of 197, far exceed single people's proportionate representation in the U.S. population. Finally, because many of *Cosmopolitan*'s readers are young and single, their median individual employment income is relatively low at $26,053; however, being fashion conscious, it is likely that a large percentage of the *Cosmopolitan* reader's disposable income goes toward purchasing the products advertised in this magazine.

Media kits also provide prospective advertisers with pertinent cost information in the form of *rate cards.* A partial rate card for *Cosmopolitan* magazine is presented in Figure 14.3. This card includes advertising rates for different page sizes (full page, two-thirds page, half page, one-third page, etc.), and for four-color, two-color, and black-and-white (B&W) ads. For example, an advertiser would pay $175,900 to place a full-page, four-color ad in *Cosmopolitan* on a one-time (open) rate basis. However, as is typical in magazines' price policies, cumulative discounts are available based on the number of pages advertised in *Cosmopolitan*

	4-Color	2-Color	B&W
Full Page	$175,900	$158,300	$140,700
2/3 Page	131,900	118,700	105,500
1/2 Page	118,700	106,900	95,000
1/3 Page	88,000	79,200	70,400
1/6 Page	70,400	63,300	56,300
Bleed Page	202,285	182,045	161,805
Second Cover	224,300		
Third Cover	193,500		
Fourth Cover	237,500		

SOURCE: *Cosmopolitan,* MRI 2005, http://www.cosmopolitan.com. Courtesy of Mediamark Research Inc.

Figure 14.3
Partial Rate Card for *Cosmopolitan* Magazine (2005 rates; rate base = 2,900,000)

during 12 consecutive months. Cumulative quantity discounts provide clear incentives for advertisers to maintain continuity with a particular magazine.

Although every magazine has its own media kit, advertisers and their agencies do not have to contact each magazine to obtain them. SRDS compiles media kits and then makes them available (of course, for a fee) to advertisers and their agencies. Also, rate cards can be obtained online by simply conducting a search such as inputting "Cosmopolitan media kit" into Google. Information for each magazine (or *book* as they are referred to in the advertising industry) includes editorial features, rates, readership profiles, circulation, and contact information.

The CPM measure introduced in the previous chapter and discussed earlier in the context of the newspaper medium is used by advertisers to compare different magazine buys. CPM information for each magazine is available from two syndicated magazine services: Mediamark Research Inc. (MRI) and Simmons Market Research Bureau (SMRB). These services provide CPM figures for general reader categories (e.g., total men) and also break out CPMs for subgroups (e.g., men ages 18 to 49, male homeowners). These more specific subgroupings enable the advertiser to compare different magazine vehicles in terms of cost per thousand for reaching the target market (or *CPM-TM*) rather than only in terms of gross CPMs. Cost-per-thousand data are useful in making magazine vehicle selection decisions, but many other factors must be taken into account.

Magazine Advertising's Strengths and Limitations

Magazine advertising too has both strengths and limitations, depending on the advertisers' needs and resources (see Table 14.2).

Magazine Advertising's Strengths

Some magazines reach *very large audiences.* For example, magazines like *Better Homes & Gardens, TV Guide, Reader's Digest, Sports Illustrated,* and *Time* have total audiences that exceed 25 million readers.

However, the ability to pinpoint specific audiences (termed *selectivity*) is the feature that most distinguishes magazine advertising from other media. If a potential market exists for a product, there most likely is at least one periodical that reaches that market. Selectivity enables an advertiser to achieve effective, rather than wasted, exposure. This translates into more efficient advertising and lower costs per 1,000 target customers.

Magazines are also noted for their *long life.* Unlike other media, magazines often are used for reference and kept around the home (and barber shops, and beauty salons, and dentists' and doctors' offices, etc.) for weeks. Magazine subscribers sometimes pass along their copies to other readers, further extending a magazine's life.

In terms of qualitative considerations, magazines as an advertising medium are exceptional with regard to elegance, quality, beauty, prestige, and snob appeal. These features result from the *high level of reproduction quality* and from the sur-

Table 14.2

Magazine Advertising's Strengths and Limitations

Strengths	Limitations
Some magazines reach large audiences	Not intrusive
Selectivity	Long lead times
Long life	Clutter
High reproduction quality	Somewhat limited geographic options
Ability to present detailed information	Variability of circulation patterns by market
Ability to convey information authoritatively	
High involvement potential	

rounding editorial content that often transfers to the advertised product. For example, food items advertised in *Bon Appetit* always look elegant, furniture items in *Better Homes & Gardens* look tasteful, and clothing items in *Cosmopolitan* and *Gentlemen's Quarterly (GQ)* appear especially fashionable.

Magazines are also a particularly good source for providing *detailed product information* and for conveying this information with a *sense of authority.* That is, because the editorial content of magazines often includes articles that themselves represent a sense of insight, expertise, and credibility, the advertisements carried in these magazines convey a similar sense of authority, or correctness.

A final and especially notable feature of magazine advertising is its creative ability to get consumers *involved in ads* or, in a sense, to attract readers' interest and to encourage them to think about the advertised brands. This ability is due to the self-selection and reader-controlled nature of magazines compared with more intrusive media such as radio and television. A cute, albeit unintentional, portrayal of this ability appeared in the *Family Circus* comic strip, which typically presents the thoughts of preschool-age children as they contemplate the world around them. This particular strip opens with Billy saying to his sister, Dolly, "I'll tell you the difference between TV, radio, and books. . . . TV puts stuff into your mind with pictures and sound. You don't even hafta think." In the next box he states, "Radio puts stuff into your mind with just sounds and words. You make up your own pictures." And in the final section, Billy proclaims, "Books are quiet friends! They let you make up your own pictures and sounds. They make you *think*."[8] Substitute the word *magazines* for *books,* and you have a pretty good characterization of the power of magazine advertising.

Magazine Advertising's Limitations

Several limitations are associated with magazine advertising. First, unlike TV and radio, which by their very nature infringe on the attention of the viewer and listener, magazine advertising is *not intrusive;* readers control whether to be exposed to a magazine ad.

A second limitation is *long lead times.* In newspapers and the broadcast media, it is relatively easy to change ad copy on fairly short notice and in specific markets. Magazines, by comparison, have long closing dates that require advertising materials to be on hand for weeks in advance of the actual publication date. For example, for four-color ads the closing dates for the following sampling of magazines are shown in parentheses: *Better Homes & Gardens* (eight weeks), *Cosmopolitan* (seven weeks), *Sports Illustrated* (five weeks), and *Time* (four weeks).

© Susan Van Etten

As with other advertising media, *clutter* is a problem with magazine advertising. In certain respects clutter is a worse problem with magazines than, say, television, because readers can become engrossed in editorial content and skip over advertisements so as not to have their reading disrupted.

Magazine advertising also provides *fewer geographic options* than do other media, although some large circulation magazines such as *Sports Illustrated* provide considerable selectivity. For example, *Sports Illustrated* offers advertising rates for seven key regions, all 50 states, and 33 metropolitan areas. An advertiser could choose to advertise in *Sports Illustrated* only in the Cleveland, Ohio, area, say, and in so doing pay $17,614 for a full-page, four-color ad. (This rate is for 2005.)

A final limitation of magazine advertising is variability in circulation patterns from market to market. *Rolling Stone,* for example, is read more in metropolitan than rural areas. Hence, advertisers who are interested, say, in reaching young males would not be very successful in reaching nonmetropolitan readers. This would necessitate placing ads

JOB OUTLOOK

In addition to courses in business, marketing, and consumer behavior, prospective market and survey researchers should take courses such as economics, psychology, English, and sociology. Quantitative skills are vital to researchers, so courses in mathematics, statistics, sampling theory and survey design, and computer science are extremely helpful. *(Occupational Outlook Handbook, 2004–05 Edition, U.S. DOL, http://www.bls.gov/oco/home.htm)*

in one or more magazines other than *Rolling Stone*, which would up the total cost of the media buy. Radio, TV, or both might better serve the advertiser's needs and provide more uniform market coverage.

Magazine Audience Measurement

When selecting magazine vehicles, it is critical for advertisers to know the audience size reached by candidate magazines. Determining the size of a particular magazine's readership might seem an easy task. All one need do is tally the number of people who subscribe to a magazine, right? Unfortunately, it is not that simple; several complicating factors make subscription counting an inadequate way of determining a magazine's readership. First, magazine subscriptions are collected through a variety of intermediaries, making it difficult to obtain accurate lists of who subscribes to which magazines. Second, magazines often are purchased from newsstands, supermarkets, and other retail outlets rather than through subscriptions, thus completely eliminating knowledge of who purchases which magazines. Third, magazines that are available in public locations such as doctors' offices, barber shops, and beauty salons are read by numerous people and not just the subscriber. Finally, individual magazine subscribers often share issues with other people.

For all these reasons, the number of subscriptions to a magazine and the number of people who actually read the magazine are not equivalent. Fortunately, two previously mentioned services—MRI and Simmons—specialize in measuring magazine readership and determining audience size. These two companies offer very similar, yet competitive, services.

In brief, both services take large, national probability samples and query respondents to identify their media consumption habits (e.g., which magazines they read) and determine their purchase behaviors for an extensive variety of products and brands. Statisticians then employ inference procedures to generalize sample results to the total population. Advertisers and media planners use the readership information along with detailed demographic and product and brand usage data to evaluate the absolute and relative value of different magazines.

Advantages aside, not all is perfect in the world of magazine audience measurement. At least three notable problems are recognized: (1) respondents to readership surveys are asked to rate numerous magazines (and other media), which can lead to fatigue and hasty or faulty responses; (2) sample sizes often are small, especially for small-circulation magazines, which leads to high margins of sampling error when generalizing to the total population; and (3) sample composition may be unrepresentative of audience readership.[9] Also, because these two readership services use different research methods, their results often are discrepant. Consider, for example, Simmons' versus MRI's estimates for the following magazines: *Ebony* (17.38 million versus 10.42 million), *Golf Digest* (9.20 million versus 5.69 million), and *House & Garden* (20.73 million versus 12.96 million).[10] In percentage terms and using the smaller estimate as the base, these differences are 66.8, 61.7, and 60 percent, respectively. Media planners thus confront the challenge of determining which service is right or whether both are wrong in their estimates of audience size.[11]

Using Simmons and MRI Reports

Despite these problems, media planners must make the most of the audience estimates and readership profiles generated by Simmons and MRI. Both of these companies produce annual reports of product and brand usage data and detailed media information. Using bottled water and seltzer as an illustration, Table 14.3

Table 14.3 Illustration of a Skeleton MRI Report for Bottled Water

Adults	Total '000	A '000	B % Down	C % Across	D Index
Total	197,462	46,248	100.0	23.4	100
Men	94,827	19,536	42.2	20.6	88
Women	102,635	26,711	57.8	26.0	111
Graduated College	43,406	11,933	25.8	27.5	117
Graduated High School	66,168	14,726	31.8	22.3	95
18–24	24,807	7,640	16.5	30.8	131
25–34	40,154	11,150	24.1	27.8	119
35–44	44,393	12,058	26.1	27.2	116
45–54	33,700	7,982	17.3	23.7	101
55–64	22,149	3,979	8.6	18.0	77
65 or over	32,260	3,438	7.4	10.7	46
Northeast	39,284	9,572	20.7	24.4	104
North Central	46,039	8,960	19.4	19.5	83
South	69,564	14,865	32.1	21.4	91
West	42,574	12,851	27.8	30.2	129
Radio: Classic Rock	21,275	5,699	12.3	26.8	114
Radio: Classical	3,128	919	2.0	29.4	125
Radio: Country	38,490	8,925	19.3	23.2	99
Radio: Adult Contemporary	41,362	11,674	25.2	28.2	121
Radio: Modern Rock	9,465	3,039	6.6	32.1	137

SOURCE: Mediamark Reporter (Mediamark Research Inc., Spring 1999). http://www.mediamark.com

provides a pared-down report that will be useful for explaining the construction and interpretation of Simmons and MRI reports.[12] For ease of exposition, we will hereafter refer to the bottled-water and seltzer category simply as "bottled water."

MRI and Simmons reports are structurally equivalent to the data contained in Table 14.3. Each of the detailed tables in these reports present cross-tabulations of demographic segments or media by product or brand usage. Table 14.3 presents usage of bottled water delineated by gender, educational status, age groupings, geographic region, and radio vehicles. The table is to be interpreted as follows:

1. The first row (Total) shows the occurrence of bottled-water purchases in the total U.S. population. Thus, of the 197,462,000 adults living in the United States at the time of data collection, 46,248,000 (see column A), or 23.4 percent (see column C, % Across), purchased bottled water at least once in recent months.
2. Each set of detailed entries shows the estimate in four different ways (denoted as columns A, B, C, and D) for the product category (bottled water in this case), and the specified population grouping:
   a. Column A presents the estimate of *total product users* (expressed in thousands). For example, of the 46,248,000 product users, 19,536,000 are men and 26,711,000 are women.
   b. Column B (% Down) represents the *composition of buyers* in each demographic group. For example, the 26,711,000 female users of bottled water represent 57.8 percent of all product users; that is, 26,711,000 ÷ 46,248,000 = 57.8 percent. Please note that each value in column B (% Down) is calculated by dividing the column A value for a particular row by the total value in column A (i.e., 46,248,000).

c. Column C (% Across) reflects each demographic group's *coverage* with respect to the particular product category. For example, female purchasers of bottled water (26,711,000) represent 26.0 percent of the 102,635,000 women who live in the United States.
d. Column D (Index) is a measure of the particular demographic group compared with the total population. For example, 26.0 percent of women are bottled-water purchasers compared with 23.4 percent of all adults. (See the % Across figure in the top, or Total, row). The index is a calculation of this relationship: (26.0 ÷ 23.4) x 100 = 111. This index indicates that women are 11 percent more likely than the general population to purchase bottled water. Men, with an index of 88, are disproportionately less likely to purchase bottled water.

The educational status, age, and radio listenership data can be interpreted in an analogous fashion. Regarding age, it can be seen that proportionately the greatest consumption of bottled water is by consumers in the 18-to-24 (index = 131), 25-to-34 (index = 119), and 35-to-44 (index = 116) age categories. Comparatively, consumers in the older age categories are less likely to purchase bottled water. Does this mean that bottled-water marketers should cater only to the younger age groups and neglect the others? Probably not. For example, although people ages 45 to 54 (index = 101) are proportionately less likely than the younger age groups to consume bottled water, there are, nonetheless, a total of nearly eight million people in this age group who *do* consume bottled water. It thus would make little sense to disregard such a large number of consumers simply because the index number is barely greater than 100. Although prudent bottled-water marketers would not neglect these older consumers, the index numbers in Table 14.3 suggest that less media emphasis, or weight, should be directed at older consumers than the weight targeted at the younger consumers.

Turning to the radio data in Table 14.3, it can be seen that listeners of country radio stations have the lowest index number (index = 99) compared with the index numbers for listeners of the other four types of radio programming, which range from 114 for classic rock to 137 for modern rock. How might an advertiser use these data? Looking just at index numbers, modern rock stations represent the best choice for bottled-water ads, but the index number conveys only part of the story.[13] Note carefully that a bottled-water advertisement placed on modern rock stations would potentially reach only a few more than three million bottled-water purchasers. There would be relatively little wasted coverage with this vehicle, but not many bottled-water purchasers would be reached. Comparatively, an advertisement placed on adult contemporary stations would have a chance of reaching nearly 11.7 million potential bottled-water consumers. Although a smaller percentage of the listeners of adult contemporary stations purchase bottled water compared with the percentage of modern rock listeners, advertisements placed on adult contemporary stations reach a far greater number of actual and potential bottled-water consumers.

In using media data supplied in MRI and Simmons reports, the advertiser must weigh various pieces of information to make intelligent media selection decisions. This includes (1) the size of the potential audience that a vehicle might reach, (2) the attractiveness of its coverage as revealed by the total product purchasers exposed to that vehicle (column A) and compared with other media (column D), (3) its cost compared with other vehicles, and (4) its appropriateness for the advertised brand. It thus should be apparent that making intelligent advertising-vehicle decisions cannot be reduced to simply comparing index numbers. These numbers are merely input into a judgment that a careful decision maker must make after considering all of the available information. Finally, there is evidence that media planners too often use MRI and Simmons data in a simplistic manner that fails to fully utilize all information provided by these reports.[14]

Radio

Radio is a nearly ubiquitous medium: there are over 11,000 commercial radio stations in the United States; almost 100 percent of all homes have radios; most homes have several; virtually all cars have a radio; more than 50 million radios are purchased in the United States each year; and radio in the United States reaches about 94 percent of all persons age 12 or older.[15] These impressive figures indicate radio's strong potential as an advertising medium. Although radio has always been a favorite of local advertisers, regional and national advertisers have increasingly recognized radio's advantages as an ad medium.

Buying Radio Time

Radio advertisers are interested in reaching target customers at a reasonable expense while ensuring that the station format is compatible with a brand's image and its creative message strategy. Several considerations influence the choice of radio vehicle. *Station format* (classical, progressive, country, top-40, talk, and so forth) is a major consideration. Certain formats are obviously most appropriate for particular products and brands.

A second consideration is the *choice of geographic areas to cover.* National advertisers buy time from stations whose audience coverage matches the advertiser's geographic areas of interest. This typically means locating stations in preferred metropolitan statistical areas (MSAs) or in so-called areas of dominant influence (ADIs), which number approximately 200 in the United States and correspond to the major television markets.

A third consideration in buying radio time is the *choice of daypart.* Radio dayparts include the following:

Morning drive:	5 A.M. to 10 A.M.
Midday:	10 A.M. to 3 P.M.
Afternoon drive:	3 P.M. to 7 P.M.
Evening:	7 P.M. to Midnight
Late night:	Midnight to 7 A.M.

Rate structures vary depending on the attractiveness of the daypart; for example, morning and afternoon drive times are more expensive than midday and late night dayparts. Information about rates and station formats is available in *Spot Radio Rates and Data,* a source published by SRDS Media Solutions.

Radio Advertising's Strengths and Limitations

This section examines the advantages and also explores some of the problems with radio advertising (see the summary in Table 14.4).

Table 14.4

Radio Advertising's Strengths and Limitations

Strengths	Limitations
Ability to reach segmented audiences	Clutter
Intimacy	No visuals
Economy	Audience fractionalization
Short lead times	Buying difficulties
Transfer of imagery from TV	
Use of local personalities	

Radio Advertising's Strengths

The first major strength of radio is that it is second only to magazines in its *ability to reach segmented audiences.* An extensive variety of radio programming enables advertisers to pick specific formats and stations to be optimally compatible with both the composition of their target audience and their creative message strategies. Radio can be used to pinpoint advertisements to specific groups of consumers: teens, Hispanics, sports fanatics, news addicts, jazz enthusiasts, conservatives, and so on. As noted earlier, there are over 11,000 commercial radio stations in the United States, and these stations are formatted to cater to special listening interests. The *Global Focus* insert talks about the status of radio stations in China and indicates that the absence of distinct formats has prevented many major global advertisers from investing heavily in this ad medium.

A second major advantage of radio advertising is its *ability to reach prospective customers on a personal and intimate level.* Local store merchants and radio announcers can be extremely personable and convincing. Their messages sometimes come across as if they are personally speaking to each audience member. A top-level advertising agency representative metaphorically described radio as a "universe of private worlds" and a "communication between two friends."[16] In other words, people select radio stations in much the same way that they select personal friends. People listen to those radio stations with which they closely identify. Because of this, radio advertising is likely to be received when the customer's mental frame is most conducive to persuasive influence. Radio advertising, then, is a personal and intimate form of friendly persuasion.

Economy is a third advantage of radio advertising. In terms of target audience CPM, radio advertising is considerably cheaper than other mass media. Over the past several decades, radio's CPM has increased less than any other advertising medium.

Another relative advantage of radio advertising is *short lead times.* Because radio production costs are typically inexpensive and scheduling deadlines are short, copy changes can be made quickly to take advantage of important developments and changes in the marketplace. For example, a sudden weather change may suggest an opportunity to advertise weather-related products. A radio spot can be prepared quickly to accommodate the needs of the situation. Radio advertising copy can be changed swiftly in response to changing inventory levels and special events and holidays.

A very important advantage of radio advertising is its ability to *transfer images from television advertising.* A memorable television advertising campaign that has been aired frequently effects in consumers a mental association between the sight and sound elements in the commercial. This mental image can then be transferred to a radio commercial that uses the TV sound or some adaptation of it. The radio commercial thus evokes in listeners a mental picture of the TV ad—much in the fashion that Billy described in the *Family Circus* cartoon mentioned earlier. The advertiser effectively gains the advantage of TV advertising at the lower cost of radio.[17]

A final strength of radio advertising is its ability to avail itself of the reputations and the sometimes bigger-than-life persona of *local personalities.* Snapple Natural Beverages, for example, gained much of its early success when it started advertising on a New York radio show hosted by the highly controversial Howard Stern. Snapple later regained lost momentum when it signed up conservative talk-show host Rush Limbaugh to promote its Snapple Diet Iced Tea.

Radio Advertising's Limitations

Radio's foremost limitation, one it shares with other ad media, is that it is *cluttered* with competitive commercials and other forms of noise, chatter, and interference. Radio listeners frequently switch stations, especially on their car radios, to avoid

The (Sorry) State of Radio Advertising in China

global focus

As a controlled economy that only in recent years has moved toward a rapidly developing market economy, China has been slow to develop radio as a major advertising medium. This in large part is due to the historical control of radio by the Chinese government and the treatment of this medium as a propaganda vehicle. Whereas nearly two-thirds of Chinese advertising expenditures are allocated to television, only about 2 percent of ad expenditures are directed toward radio advertising. Media buyers refrain from purchasing airtime on Chinese radio stations because most of China's 1,500 stations do not have pure formats such as all-talk, all-classical music, or whatever. Another reason that many advertisers refrain from airing ads on Chinese radio is that there is no formal monitoring system in place, which means that advertisers have no assurance that the ads they buy are actually broadcast.

One development that is likely to lead to increased radio advertising is the rapid growth in passenger cars in China, from 4.1 million vehicles in 2003 to an estimated 10.4 million by 2009. With millions of Chinese drivers riding in their cars and listening to radios, it is only a matter of time before radio stations develop pure formats that specifically cater to people's listening interests. When that time arrives, advertisers will be able to direct their ads to the individuals who are most likely to buy their products and specific brands.

SOURCE: Adapted from Geoffrey A. Fowler, "Why Advertisers Are Tuning in to Chinese Radio," *Wall Street Journal Online*, April 28, 2004, http://online.wsj.com.

commercials.[18] The irritation of having to listen to one commercial after another partially explains why many people have turned to iPods and other brands of portable digital-audio players as an alternative to radio listening. The iPod's growing popularity has been shown, in fact, to be correlated with reduced radio ratings. So-called AQH ratings, which measure the number of people tuned to radio during an average quarter hour (AQH) as a percentage of the population, fell by almost 6 percent between 2000 and 2004, with the ratings decline among the college-aged demographic (18–24) even greater at 11 percent.[19]

A second limitation is that radio is the only major medium that is *unable to employ visualizations.* However, radio advertisers attempt to overcome the medium's visual limitation by using sound effects and choosing concrete words to conjure up mental images in the listener. It is important to note that many advertising campaigns use radio as a supplement to other media rather than as a stand-alone medium. This reduces radio's task from one of creating visual images to one of *reactivating images* that already have been created via television or magazines. On the other hand, information-based advertising campaigns do not necessarily require visualizations, and radio under such circumstances is fully capable of delivering brand-based information—for example, a mortgage company's interest rate, a special sale at a local department store, or the location of an automobile repair shop.

A third problem with radio advertising results from a high degree of *audience fractionalization.* On the one hand, selectivity is a major advantage of radio advertising, but at the same time the advertiser is unable to reach a diverse audience because each radio station and program has its own unique set of audience demographics and interests.

A final limitation is the *difficulty of buying radio time.* This problem is particularly acute in the case of the national advertiser that wishes to place spots in different markets throughout the country. With over 11,000 commercial radio stations operating in the United States, buying time is complicated by unstandardized rate structures that include a number of combinations of fixed and discount rates. One prospect that may offset this problem is the growth of the fledgling satellite radio industry. Companies such as Sirius Satellite Radio and XM Satellite Radio Holdings can broadcast nationally (even internationally) and thus offer advertisers an opportunity to reach large audiences and pay a single rate for the purchased airtime. XM Satellite Radio is predicting it will have 20 million subscribers by 2010.[20]

Radio Audience Measurement

Radio audiences are measured both nationally and locally. Arbitron is the major company at both the national and the local levels involved with measuring radio listenership and audience demographics. At the national level, Arbitron owns a service that goes by the acronym RADAR, which stands for Radio's All Dimension Audience Research. The RADAR service produces radio-listening estimates by recruiting 70,000 individuals age 12 and older, who, during a one-week period, make diary entries that identify their daily listening behavior, including the radio stations they listened to, the time of day they listened to each station, and their location when they listened (e.g., in the car, at home, or at work). RADAR's research provides ratings estimates for network radio programming and audience demographic characteristics. Advertisers use this information to select network programming that matches their intended target audiences.

At the local level, there used to be two major research services that measured radio audience sizes: Birch Scarborough Research and Arbitron. However, in the early 1990s Birch discontinued operations, leaving Arbitron the sole supplier of local radio ratings data. Arbitron measures listening patterns in over 250 markets located throughout the United States. Arbitron researchers obtain data in each market from 250 to 13,000 randomly selected individuals age 12 or older. Respondents are compensated for maintaining diaries of their listening behavior for a seven-day period. Subscribers to the Arbitron service (thousands of radio stations, advertisers, and agencies) receive reports that detail people's listening patterns, their station preferences, and their demographic breakdowns. This information is invaluable to advertisers and their agencies for purposes of selecting radio stations whose listener compositions match the advertiser's target market.

At the time of this writing (in early 2005), there is a new radio-audience measurement service from a company called Navigauge that may eventually challenge Arbitron. Navigauge's service is designed to measure radio-listening behavior exclusively in motor vehicles by using a continuous tracking device that provides moment-by-moment detection of which specific stations vehicle drivers are tuned into.[21] Arbitron itself is in the process of attempting to get away from the paper-diary method of data collection by having people in test markets carry pager-like meters throughout the day. More will be said about this subsequently in the context of measuring TV viewing insofar as Arbitron is collaborating with the king of TV-audience measurement, Nielsen, to measure people's away-from-home listening (radio) and their viewing (TV) habits.

Television

Television is practically ubiquitous in the United States and throughout the rest of the industrialized world. Television sets are present in slightly more than 98 percent of all American households, which amounted to 109.6 million TV households in the United States by late 2004.[22] As an advertising medium, television is uniquely personal and demonstrative, yet it is also expensive and subject to considerable competitive clutter. Consumers consider television the most cluttered of all ad media.[23]

Before we elaborate on television's specific strengths and weaknesses, it first will be instructive to examine two specific aspects of television advertising: (1) the different programming segments, or so-called dayparts; and (2) the alternative outlets for television commercials (network, spot, syndicated, cable, and local).

Television Programming Dayparts

Advertising costs, audience characteristics, and programming appropriateness vary greatly at different times of the day. Like radio, these times of day are referred to as dayparts. There are seven TV dayparts, with the following shown for Eastern Standard Time:

Early morning:	5 A.M. to 9 A.M.
Daytime:	9 A.M. to 4 P.M.
Early fringe:	4 P.M. to 7 P.M.
Prime access:	7 P.M. to 8 P.M.
Prime time:	8 P.M. to 11 P.M.
Late fringe:	11 P.M. to 2 A.M.
Overnight:	2 A.M. to 5 A.M.

The three major dayparts are daytime, fringe time, and prime time, each of which has its own strengths and weaknesses.

Daytime

The period that begins with the early morning news shows and extends to 4:00 P.M. is known as *daytime.* Early daytime appeals first to adults with news programs and then to children with special programs designed for them. Afternoon programming—with its special emphasis on soap operas, talk shows, and financial news—appeals primarily to people working at home, retirees, and, contrary to the stereotype, even young males. Indeed, research reveals that single men between the ages of 18 and 34 view soap operas such as *All My Children, As the World Turns,* and *The Young and the Restless.* Males apparently watch this form of entertainment as an escape from everyday life and, interestingly, as a way of acquiring gossip-type information for aiding conversations with women.[24]

Fringe Time

The period preceding and following prime time is known as *fringe time.* Early fringe starts with afternoon reruns and is devoted primarily to children but becomes more adult oriented as prime time approaches. Late fringe appeals primarily to young adults.

Prime Time

The period between 8:00 P.M. and 11:00 P.M. (or between 7:00 P.M. and 10:00 P.M. in some parts of the United States) is known as *prime time.* The best and most expensive programs are scheduled during this period. Audiences are largest during prime time. Table 14.5 indicates the average prime-time audience size for the four major U.S. networks, which ranges from 13.6 million viewers on average for CBS down to 9.5 million viewers for ABC. Interestingly, the total audience size garnered

Table 14.5

Average Prime-Time Audience (in millions) for Four Major Networks (9/22/03–4/18/04)

Network	Estimated Viewers (in millions)
ABC	9.5
CBS	13.6
Fox	9.8
NBC	10.9
Total	43.8

SOURCE: Nielsen Media Research, reported in "Stiff Competition: TV Has Seen Better Days," *Marketing News,* December 15, 2004, 8.

AP Photo/Jennifer Szymaszek

by these four major networks is about 44 million; comparatively, the total audience size during the 1994–1995 period was just over 62 million. This decline of 29 percent reflects the continuing trend wherein network TV is capturing smaller audiences, whereas cable TV's audience base continues to grow.[25]

The networks naturally charge the highest rates for prime-time advertising. Popular prime-time programs sometimes reach as many as 20 million households. Advertisers pay dearly to reach the huge numbers of households that popular prime-time programs deliver. The five highest-priced programs for the 2004 television season are shown in Table 14.6, where it can be seen that the cost for a single 30-second commercial placed on these programs ranges from a low of $409,877 (*The Apprentice*) to a high of $658,333 (*American Idol,* Wednesday broadcast). Please note that these advertising prices are for just the five most expensive TV programs. Most 30-second commercials broadcast on prime-time TV during the 2004 season were in the range of $50,000 to $300,000.

Network, Spot, Syndicated, Cable, and Local Advertising

Television messages are transmitted by local stations, which are either locally owned cable television systems or affiliated with the six commercial networks (ABC, CBS, NBC, Fox, UPN, and WB) or with an independent cable network (such as TBS, Turner Broadcasting System). This arrangement of local stations and networks allows for different ways of buying advertising time on television.

Network Television Advertising

Companies that market products nationally often use network television to reach potential customers throughout the country. The advertiser, typically working through an advertising agency, purchases desired time slots from one or more of the networks and advertises at these times on all local stations that are affiliated with the network. The cost of such advertising depends on the time of day when an ad is aired, the popularity of the television program in which the ad is placed, and the time of year—advertising rates are typically highest in the fourth quarter (October through December) when more people are inside watching television and ratings are at their peak. The average cost for all 30-second prime-time television commercials during each of the four quarters in one recent year were as follows: first quarter (January–March), $165,700; second quarter (April–June), $180,800; third quarter (July–September), $150,600; and fourth quarter (October–December), $212,000.[26]

Table 14.6
The Five Highest Priced TV Programs

Show	Network	Price
American Idol (Wed.)	Fox	$658,333
American Idol (Tues.)	Fox	620,000
ER	NBC	479,250
Survivor: Vanuatu	CBS	412,833
The Apprentice	NBC	409,877

Source: Claire Atkinson, "'Idol' Tops TV Price Chart," *Advertising Age*, September 27, 2004, 1. Reprinted with permission from *Advertising Age*. Copyright, Crain Communications Inc. 2004.

Network television advertising, although expensive in terms of per-unit cost, can be a cost-efficient means to reach mass audiences. Consider a 30-second commercial that costs $300,000 and reaches 15 percent of the 109.6 million American households with TV sets, or about 16.44 million households. Although $300,000 is a lot to pay for 30 seconds of commercial time, reaching 16.44 million households means that the advertiser would have paid approximately only $18.25 to reach every 1,000 households.

Network advertising is inefficient, and in fact unfeasible, if the national advertiser chooses to concentrate efforts only on select markets. For example, some brands, though marketed nationally, are directed primarily at consumers in certain geographic locales. In this case, it would be wasteful to invest in network advertising, which would reach many areas where target audiences are not located.

Spot Television Advertising

The national advertiser's alternative to network advertising is *spot advertising*. As the preceding discussion intimated and as the name suggests, this type of advertising is placed (spotted) only in selected markets.

Spot advertising is particularly desirable when a company rolls out a new brand market by market before it achieves national distribution, when a marketer needs to concentrate on particular markets due to poor performance in these markets or because of aggressive competitive efforts, or when a company's product distribution is limited to one or a few geographical regions. Also, spot advertising is useful even for those advertisers who use network advertising but need to supplement the national coverage with greater amounts of advertising in select markets that have particularly high brand potential. Greater use of spot television advertising is harmonious with the growing practices of regional-oriented marketing and geodemographic segmentation of consumer markets, such as was discussed in Chapter 4.

Syndicated Advertising

Syndicated programming occurs when an independent company—such as Buena Vista Television Advertising Sales (an affiliate of the Walt Disney Company) and Sony Pictures Television—markets a TV show to as many network-affiliated or cable television stations as possible. Because an independent firm markets syndicated programs to individual television stations, the same syndicated program will appear on, say, NBC stations in some markets and on ABC or CBS stations in other markets.

Syndicated programs are either original productions or shows that first appeared on network television and are subsequently shown as reruns. During a recent television season, the five most costly syndicated programs (and their costs per 30-second commercial) were *Friends* ($179,320), *Seinfeld* ($154,118), *Entertainment Tonight* ($110,693), *Everybody Loves Raymond* ($104,597), and *Will & Grace* ($104,303). Prices for 30-second commercials on most syndicated programs typically range between $12,000 and $80,000.[27]

Cable Advertising

Unlike network television, which is free to all owners of television sets, cable television requires users to subscribe (pay a fee) to a cable service and have their sets specially wired to receive signals via satellite or other means. Though cable television has been available since the 1940s, only in recent decades have advertisers turned to cable as a valuable advertising medium. Growing numbers of major national companies now advertise on cable TV. Cable television's household penetration increased from less than 25 percent of all households in 1980 to a current level of about 84 percent of U.S. households with television sets.[28] Advertising spending on cable TV is climbing steadily.

Cable advertising is attractive to national advertisers for several reasons. First, because cable networks focus on narrow areas of viewing interest (so-called narrowcasting), advertisers are able to reach more *finely targeted audiences* (in terms of demographics and psychographics) than when using network, syndicated, or spot advertising. Indeed, cable stations are available to reach almost any imaginable viewing preference. A brand marketer can select cable stations that appeal to a variety of specific viewing interests such as cooking and eating (Food Network); golfing (Golf Channel); sports in general (ESPN and ESPN2); music entertainment (Country Music Television, MTV, MuchMusic, and VH1); nature, science, and animal life (Animal Planet, Discovery Channel, and Outdoor Life Network); general education (the History Channel and Travel Channel); and so forth.

A second reason that cable advertising appeals to national advertisers is that high network advertising prices and declining audiences have compelled advertisers to *experiment with media alternatives* such as cable. A third factor behind cable advertising's growth is the *demographic composition of cable audiences.* Cable subscribers are more economically upscale and younger than the population as a whole. By comparison, the heaviest viewers of network television tend to be somewhat economically downscale. It is little wonder that the relatively upscale characteristics of cable viewers have great appeal to many national advertisers.

Local Television Advertising

Television advertising historically was dominated by national advertisers, but local advertisers have turned to television in ever greater numbers. Local advertisers often find that the CPM advantages of television along with the ability to demonstrate products justify the TV medium. Many local advertisers are using cable stations to an unprecedented degree. In fact, the growth rate in local cable advertising is faster than other ad media.[29]

Television Advertising's Strengths and Limitations

Like the other forms of media, advertising on television has a number of strengths and limitations (see the summary in Table 14.7).

Television Advertising's Strengths

Beyond any other consideration, television possesses the unique capability to *demonstrate a product in use.* No other medium can reach consumers simultaneously through both auditory and visual senses. Viewers can see and hear a product being used, identify with the product's users, and imagine using the product.

Television also has *intrusion value* unparalleled by other media. That is, television advertisements engage one's senses and attract attention even when one would prefer not to be exposed to an advertisement. In comparison, it is much easier to avoid a magazine or newspaper ad by merely flipping the page, or to avoid a radio ad by changing channels. But it is often easier to sit through a television commercial rather than to attempt to avoid it either physically or mentally. Of

Table 14.7

Television Advertising's Strengths and Limitations

Strengths	Limitations
Demonstration ability	Rapidly escalating cost
Intrusion value	Erosion of viewing audiences
Ability to generate excitement	Audience fractionalization
One-on-one reach	Zipping and zapping
Ability to use humor	Clutter
Effective with sales force and trade	
Ability to achieve impact	

course, as will be discussed shortly, remote controls and digital video recorders (also called *personal video recorders*) have made it easier for viewers to avoid television commercials via *zipping* and *zapping*.

A third relative advantage of television advertising is its combined *ability to provide entertainment and generate excitement*. Advertised products can be brought to life or made to appear even bigger than life. Products advertised on television can be presented dramatically and made to appear more exciting and less mundane than perhaps they actually are.

Television also has the unique ability to *reach consumers one on one*, as is the case when a spokesperson or endorser espouses the merits of a particular product. Like a sales presentation, the interaction between spokesperson and consumer takes place on a personal level.

More than any other medium, television is *able to use humor* as an effective advertising strategy. As discussed in a previous chapter, many of the most memorable commercials are those using a humorous format.

In addition to its effectiveness in reaching ultimate consumers, television advertising also is *effective with a company's sales force and the trade*. Salespeople find it easier to sell new or established brands to the trade when a major advertising campaign is planned. The trade has added incentive to increase merchandise support (e.g., through advertising features and special display space) for a brand that is advertised on television.

In the final analysis, the greatest relative advantage of television advertising is its *ability to achieve impact*, that is, the ability to activate consumers' awareness of ads and enhance their receptiveness to sales messages.

Television Advertising's Limitations

As an advertising medium, television suffers from several distinct problems. First, and perhaps most serious, is the *rapidly escalating advertising cost*. The cost of network television advertising has more than tripled over the past two decades. A dramatic illustration of this is the increasing cost of buying advertising time during the Super Bowl. In 1975 a 30-second commercial cost $110,000. By 2005, 30 years later, the average price for placing a 30-second ad on Super Bowl XXXIX was $2.4 million! (For more on Super Bowl advertising, see the *IMC Focus*.) In addition to the cost of buying airtime, it is very costly to produce television commercials. The *average* cost of making a national 30-second commercial was $372,000 in a recent year.[30]

A second problem is the *erosion of television viewing audiences*. Syndicated programs, cable television, the Internet, and other leisure and recreational alternatives have diminished the number of people viewing network television. The four major networks' share of television audiences during prime time fell from over 90 percent around 1980 to only about 60 percent today. Program *ratings* have consistently fallen over the past 40 years. Whereas the most popular programs used to have ratings in the 50s (meaning that more than 50 percent of all television households were tuned in to these programs), the top-rated programs now rarely exceed a rating of 20. For example, *Gunsmoke* was the top-rated program from 1957 to 1961 with ratings consistently around 40. From 1972 to 1976 *All in the Family* was the leading program with ratings above 30.

Today it is rare for a show to have a rating above 18. For example, the 10 top-rated programs during the week of January 24–30, 2005, are shown in Table 14.8. The highest rated program, *American Idol* (Tuesday broadcast), had a rating of 15.8, and the two programs tied for the tenth top rating, *Numb3rs* and *Without a Trace*, had ratings slightly below 10.[31] Ratings on network television continue to slide.

There also has been substantial *audience fractionalization*. Advertisers cannot expect to attract large homogeneous audiences when advertising on any particular program due to the great amount of program selection now available to television viewers.

imc focus

The Super Bowl football game, which pits the winners of the National and American conferences of the National Football League, is for many Americans the most important sporting event of the year. Super Bowl Sunday, which occurs annually in late January or early February, has been described as the third or fourth largest "holiday" celebrated in America. People throw parties and consume large quantities of food and drink while watching the clash of professional football teams. This event is one of the few remaining television spectaculars that can be described as mass television. The sponsoring TV network is able to command huge prices for 30-second commercials because advertisers know they can reach nearly 90 million people with an advertisement placed on this single program. Advertising rates have basically doubled in the past decade, from $1,130,577 in 1995 to $2,210,400 in 2005 (both cost figures have been adjusted for inflation to 2000 dollars).

Interestingly, the price for a 30-second ad fell slightly in 2001 and then again in 2002 to approximately $2,000,000. The dot-com crash of 2000 and the recession of 2001 probably explained the declining prices for Super Bowl ads. Since 2002, prices have steadily inched up. The following table provides detailed statistics for every Super Bowl from its inception in 1967 through 2001. It is worth noting that the prices for each year have been adjusted for inflation and are presented in constant 2000 dollars. For example, the actual price of a 30-second commercial during Super Bowl XXXIX in 2005 was $2,400,000, which, when adjusted for inflation, amounts to $2,210,400 in 2000 dollars.

Sources: Claire Atkinson, "Super Bowl: It's a Big (Ad) Deal," *Advertising Age,* January 3, 2005, 10 (ratings for 2002–2004 are provided in this source; all other ratings are from the following sources); Richard Linnett and Wayne Friedman, "No Gain," *Advertising Age,* January 15, 2001, 43; Wayne Friedman, "Second Down," *Advertising Age,* September 3, 2001, 3, 22. The 2005 rating is from "Super Bowl Ratings Down from '04," CBSNews.com, February 7, 2005 (accessed June 7, 2005). Reprinted with permission from *Advertising Age.* Copyright, Crain Communications Inc.

Year	Price (adjusted for inflation to 2000 dollars)	Rating (% of U.S. households tuned to Super Bowl)
1967	$216,665	23.0%
1968	267,362	36.8
1969	316,901	36.0
1970	347,264	39.4
1971	306,311	39.9
1972	353,493	44.2
1973	401,645	42.7
1974	373,957	41.6
1975	352,286	42.4
1976	378,515	42.3
1977	460,604	44.4
1978	488,888	47.2
1979	526,868	47.1
1980	575,030	46.3
1981	614,707	44.4
1982	615,995	49.1
1983	691,968	48.6
1984	746,246	46.4
1985	800,651	46.4
1986	864,644	48.3
1987	872,117	45.8
1988	873,880	41.9
1989	937,923	43.5
1990	922,800	39.0
1991	1,012,041	41.9
1992	982,466	40.3
1993	1,013,529	45.1
1994	1,046,356	45.5
1995	1,130,577	41.3
1996	1,207,967	46.0
1997	1,288,224	43.3
1998	1,374,172	44.5
1999	1,654,742	40.2
2000	2,100,000	43.3
2001	2,050,000	41.1
2002	1,824,380*	40.4
2003	2,172,801*	40.7
2004	2,144,750*	41.4
2005	2,210,400*	43.4

*The actual costs of Super Bowl advertising from 2002 to 2005 were deflated to 2000 dollars using the Gross Domestic Product Deflator Inflation Calculator, http://www1.jsc.nasa.gov/bu2/inflateGDP.html. Values for the remaining years (from 1967 to 2001) were already calculated from the 2001 source materials presented in the source documentation.

Fourth, when watching TV programs, viewers spend much of their time switching from station to station, zapping or zipping commercials. *Zapping* occurs when viewers switch to another channel when commercials are aired, prompting one observer to comment (only partially with tongue in cheek) that the remote control "zapper" is the greatest threat to capitalism since Karl Marx.[32] Research reveals that perhaps as much as one-third of the potential audience for a TV commercial may be lost to zapping.[33] Although zapping is extensive, one intriguing study presented evidence suggesting that commercials that are zapped are

Table 14.8

Top-10 Prime-Time Broadcast TV Programs (for week of 1/24/05–1/30/05)

Rank*	Program	Network	Rating**	Total Viewers***
1	American Idol-Tuesday	Fox	15.8	28,062,000
2	American Idol-Wednesday	Fox	15.2	26,568,000
3	CSI: Crime Scene Investigation	CBS	14.0	21,821,000
4	ER	NBC	13.0	19,751,000
5	CBS Sunday Movie	CBS	12.4	18,667,000
6	CSI: NY	CBS	11.5	17,560,000
7	Cold Case	CBS	10.6	16,694,000
8	CSI: Miami	CBS	10.3	14,957,000
9	Medium	NBC	10.2	15,776,000
10	Numb3rs	CBS	9.9	15,456,000
10	Without A Trace	CBS	9.9	14,547,000

*Based on household rating percentage from Nielsen Media Research's National People Meter sample.

**As of September 20, 2004, there were an estimated 109.6 million TV households. A single rating point represents 1 percent, or 1,096,000 households.

***Total viewers includes all persons over the age of two.

actively processed prior to being zapped and may have a more positive effect on brand purchase behavior than commercials that are not zapped.[34] This provocative prospect certainly requires further support before being accepted as fact.

In addition to zapping, television viewers also engage in zipping. *Zipping* takes place when ads that have been recorded along with program material using a video cassette recorder or a digital video recorder (of the TiVo variety) are fast-forwarded (zipped through) when the viewer watches the prerecorded material. Research has shown that zipping is extensive.[35] Digital, or personal, video recorders (DVRs or PVRs), which are essentially VCRs with the storage powers of personal computers, make zipping behavior easier than ever. PVRs from companies such as TiVo and ReplayTV allow viewers to fast-forward past commercials by simply pushing a skip button that fast-forwards in 30-second intervals, which, by no coincidence, is the standard length of a TV commercial.

An estimated 7 percent of American households (about 7.7 million) had DVRs as of early 2005,[36] and it is projected that by 2007 anywhere from a low estimate of 32.6 million to a high estimate of 45.9 million households will have DVRs.[37] Many DVR owners use the technology to fast-forward through commercials or skip them all together. One study found that nearly 60 percent of males skip commercials and an even greater percentage of females, nearly 70 percent, do the same.[38] Fast-forwarding through commercials is particularly high (upwards of 75 percent) when programs are prerecorded for later viewing; however, fast-forwarding of commercials drops considerably (to a level below 20 percent) when people watch live programs.[39] The implication is clear: commercials are more likely to be watched during live programs, which perhaps explains why programs such as *American Idol* command such premium prices.

As the penetration of DVRs increases, many advertisers may switch to media other than television for concern that TV simply isn't delivering the eyeballs that are being paid for. However, it is important to note that research conducted by Procter & Gamble came to the conclusion that consumers fast-forwarding through ads with DVRs recall those ads at about the same level as do people who see the ad at normal speed in real time.[40] Nonetheless, other indicators of advertising effectiveness (feelings of warmth, likeability, overall persuasion) may be negatively affected when fast-forwarding, which thus makes it inappropriate to conclude that "TiVo-ing" does not diminish commercial effectiveness.

Clutter is a fifth serious problem with television advertising. Clutter refers to the growing amount of nonprogram material, including public service messages and promotional announcements for stations and programs, but especially commercials. In fact, out of every broadcast hour of prime-time television, nonprogram content ranges slightly over 15 minutes among the six major TV networks, or more than 25 percent of the time.[41] As noted earlier, consumers perceive television to be the most cluttered of all major advertising media. Clutter has been created by the network's increased use of promotional announcements to stimulate audience viewing of heavily promoted programs and by advertisers' increased use of shorter commercials. Whereas 60-second commercials once were prevalent, the duration of the vast majority of commercials today is only 30 or 15 seconds.[42] The effectiveness of television advertising has suffered from the clutter problem, which creates a negative impression among consumers about advertising in general, turns viewers away from the television set, and perhaps reduces advertising recognition and recall.[43]

Infomercials

Discussion of television advertising would not be complete without at least a brief mention of the *infomercial*. Introduced to television in the early 1980s, the long commercial, or **infomercial**, is an alternative to the conventional, short form of television commercial. By comparison, infomercials are full-length commercial segments run on television that typically last 28 to 30 minutes and combine product news and entertainment. Infomercials account for nearly one-fourth of the programming time for most cable stations. Marketers' increased use of infomercials extends from two primary factors: First, technologically complicated products and those that require detailed explanations benefit from the long commercial format. Second, the infomercial format is in lockstep with increasing demands for marketing accountability insofar as most orders obtained from infomercials occur within 24 hours or so after an infomercial is aired.[44] Due to the rapid response, it is very easy to determine whether infomercials are moving the sales dial; comparatively, such rapid sales response is rarely the case with most products advertised via traditional commercials.

In the early years, infomercials were restricted primarily to unknown companies selling skin-care products, balding treatments, exercise equipment, and other such products. However, the growing respectability of this form of advertising has encouraged a number of consumer goods companies to promote their brands via infomercials. Well-known infomercial users include Avon, Braun, Clairol, Chrysler, Estée Lauder, Hoover, Pioneer, Procter & Gamble, and Sears. Manufacturers of consumer durables are increasingly using infomercials. For example, General Motors' Chevrolet division featured famous baseball star Cal Ripken Jr. in an infomercial touting its Silverado pickup truck. Philips Consumer Electronics used a 30-minute infomercial in marketing its digital video disc (DVD) player. Consider the following successful infomercial application by Kodak.

Kodak introduced a 30-minute infomercial to promote its new DC210 zoom digital camera. Up to that time Eastman Kodak had little sales and profit to show for the $500 million it had invested in digital imaging. The infomercial, which cost nearly $400,000 to produce, included a toll-free number that invited viewers to request a $175 coupon that was good toward the purchase of the camera and other Kodak products at retail locations. Follow-up research indicated that approximately one out of 12 callers who received the discount coupon ordered the camera at a retail outlet, an impressive statistic in view of the fact that the DC210's retail price was $899 at the time of the promotion. Retail sales in cities where the DC210 infomercials were aired exceeded by 80 percent sales of this brand in cities without infomercials. Moreover, retail selling time was substantially reduced insofar as consumers already were presold by the infomercial. Kodak officials concluded that the infomercial was a cost-effective way to introduce consumers to the advantages of digital imaging.[45]

Numerous advertisers have found infomercials on television to be an extremely effective tool for moving merchandise. This long-form commercial is apparently here to stay. Although consumers have complaints with infomercials (e.g., that some make false claims and are deceptive),[46] this form of long commercial appears to be especially effective for consumers who are brand and price conscious and who place high importance on shopping convenience.[47]

Brand Placements in Television Programs

Returning to our earlier discussion of advertising clutter along with consumers' responses in the form of zipping and zapping behavior, many observers fear that television advertising is no longer as effective as it used to be. (Recall the discussion of the Deutsche Bank study in the *Marcom Challenge.*) Brand managers and network television executives have responded to consumers' zipping and zapping behavior by borrowing from the movie industry and finding a way to circumvent TV viewers' fondness for avoiding commercials. Have you noticed brands appearing more often in television programs? This is not by happenstance; rather, brand managers are paying to get prominent placements for their brands—precisely as they have done in placing their products in movies. The widely viewed *Survivor* program perhaps epitomizes the use of product placements, perhaps to the point where TV viewers now realize that the brands placed in *Survivor* episodes are little more than thinly disguised commercials.

Brand placements represent a growing form of marketing communications. Placements occur not just in TV programs and movies but also in music videos, video games, and even in novels.[48] Compared with movie placements, brand appearances in TV programs have the advantages of (1) much larger audiences; (2) more frequent exposure; and (3) global reach, especially when programs are rerun around the world under syndication.[49]

It perhaps goes without saying that brand placements on TV can be very effective provided the brand is displayed in a context that appropriately matches the brand's image. The downside with placements in TV programs is that brand managers relinquish the full control available to them by comparison when providing the final approval for TV commercials. Interestingly, the more people feel a sense of connection with a TV program—that is, they identify with a program's characters, issues, and images—the higher their recall of brands that are placed in that program.[50] This obviously implies that TV programs that create a heightened sense of connectedness among their audiences are more effective vehicles in which to place brands in comparison to programs that fail to achieve high levels of connectedness.

Television Audience Measurement

As noted earlier, a 30-second commercial on prime-time television for national airing can cost as much as $2,400,000 (for a Super Bowl spot in 2005) or less than $100,000. Of course, the cost of advertising on spot television (i.e., non-national) is considerably cheaper inasmuch as the market covered is much smaller. Also, advertising on cable stations and syndicated programs typically is cheaper than on network TV, again due to smaller audience sizes. Whatever the case, the reason for the disparity in commercial costs is *ratings*. Generally speaking, higher-rated programs command higher prices. Because prices and ratings go hand in hand, the accurate measurement of program audience size—the basis on which ratings are determined—is a critically important, multimillion-dollar industry. Advertising researchers continually seek ways to measure more accurately the size of TV program audiences. In the following discussion we will distinguish network (national) and local audience measurement. Inherent in this distinction is whether audience-size data are collected via electronic technology (so-called people meters) or with paper diaries.

National (Network) Audience Measurement: Nielsen's People Meter Technology

The *people meter,* by Nielsen Media Research, represents perhaps the most important (and controversial!) research innovation since the advent of television audience measurement.[51] Nielsen uses the people meter technology by outfitting a national sample of households with TV set–top boxes that require consumers to punch a button to record their viewing. Only 5,100 households (of 109.6 million TV households in the United States as of 2004) are currently included in Nielsen's sample, though this is expected to increase to 10,000 households by 2006. The box has eight buttons for family members and two additional buttons for visitors (see Figure 14.4). A family member (or visitor) is requested to push his or her designated numerical button each time he or she selects a particular program. The meter automatically records which programs are being watched, which family members are in attendance, and how many households are watching. These data are then statistically extrapolated to all households to arrive at estimates of each program's ratings on a given occasion, such as *American Idol* on a particular Tuesday. Information from each household's people meter is fed daily into a central computer via telephone lines, although typically only about 80 percent of the 5,100 households actually transmit data to Nielsen.[52] This viewing information is then combined with each household's demographic profile to provide a single source of data about audience size and composition.

You might be wondering, why would anyone take the time to push a button on every occasion they sit down to watch TV? In actuality, it is likely that some portion of the participating households and household members are not especially faithful in pushing their button(s) to identify they are viewing TV. However, because Nielsen compensates participating households—up to $600 for a two-year period—many participants feel obligated to perform the task for which they are being paid, albeit modestly.

People meters likely are here to stay in one form or another, and probably so is the controversy surrounding their use. The major networks, which pay Nielsen more than $10 million annually for its data, are growing increasingly critical of Nielsen's data. They claim that Nielsen undercounts major segments of the population, especially young people and viewers watching TV outside the home.

Local Audience Measurement: Nielsen's Diary Panels

The 5,100 households (soon to be 10,000) on which Nielsen's network audience measurement is based are scattered around the United States. For example, in the city where I am located (Columbia, South Carolina—a metropolitan area with over 500,000 residents and one of the top-100 TV markets in the United States), there may be only 50 or fewer households that are included in Nielsen's national sample. Obviously, there are many more households represented in much larger markets (New York City, Los Angeles, Chicago, etc.), but fewer in smaller markets. Considering just Columbia, South Carolina, for illustration, it should be obvious that the 50 or so households included as part of Nielsen's national people meter sample are far too few to draw statistically reliable estimates of TV viewing in the Columbia market.

Given this statistical fact, Nielsen has used an alternative data collection procedure for estimating TV program ratings in local markets. In particular, Nielsen has since the 1950s used

Figure 14.4
Nielsen People Meter

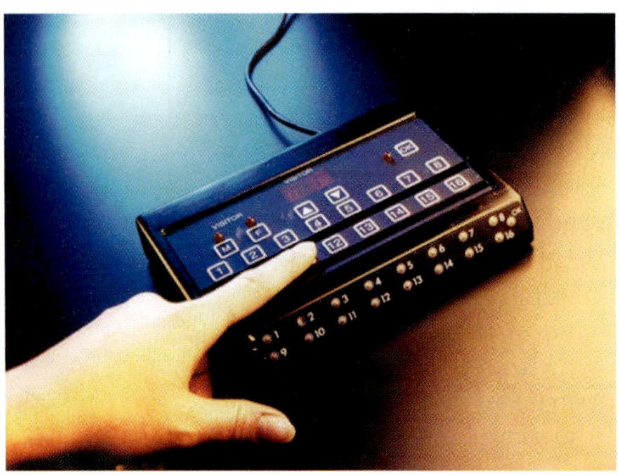

Nielsen Media Research

paper diaries to collect information regarding audience viewing habits and the composition of households that view particular programs. **Paper diaries** of TV viewing behavior are filled out by a sample of 375,000 households from local markets throughout the United States. Each of these households completes a 20-page diary four times a year—February, May, July, and November, which are the months of the year known in the TV industry as "sweep" periods. Randomly selected households in 210 markets throughout the United States fill out the diaries. The diaries are delineated for each day of the week into 15-minute chunks. Participating households identify which household member(s) watch which TV programs during each 15-minute chunk.[53] You might be thinking, who would take the time to faithfully record their viewing behavior? Needless to say, this measurement system is imperfect because some participating households do not perform a careful job in recording who watched what. Further, over 10 percent of households return diaries with substantial sections blank or containing impossible-to-read entries due to illegible handwriting.

Local Audience Measurement: Nielsen's Local People Meters

It is for these reasons that the TV industry has insisted on a superior method of measuring viewing behavior in local markets. Enter the local people meter technology. *Local people meters* (LPMs) are the same devices used by Nielsen for its national audience measurement. Compared to paper diaries, which collect crucial viewing and demographic information only during the four sweep months, LPMs provide media buyers with daily feedback about audience size and composition for particular programs.

At the time of this writing, the LPM procedure is being tested in the Boston market and soon will be introduced in 10 major markets throughout the United States. These 10 markets—Boston, Chicago, Los Angeles, New York, San Francisco, Dallas–Fort Worth, Detroit, Philadelphia, Washington DC, and Atlanta—represent approximately 30 percent of all TV households in the United States.

Measuring Away-from-Home Viewers (and Listeners)

As noted earlier in the context of Arbitron's radio audience measurement service, Arbitron and Nielsen are collaborating in an attempt to measure people's radio listening and TV viewing when they are *away from home.*[54] Needless to say, much radio listening and TV viewing occur outside the home. For example, millions of college students listen to radios and watch TV in their dorms, but the traditional Arbitron and Nielsen measuring systems do not include this group in their samples. Likewise, people often consume radio and TV while at bars and restaurants; when they are exercising in gyms; while working in offices, stores, and factories; and so on. Yet the traditional Arbitron (radio) and Nielsen (TV) systems miss these out-of-home listening and viewing experiences. Nielsen and Arbitron are involved in a pilot project at the time of this writing to count away-from-home listeners and viewers.

Testing began in Wilmington, Delaware, and then expanded to nearby Philadelphia. A sample of 1,500 people in Philadelphia carry *portable people meters* (PPMs) that are about the size of a pager. These meters are capable of detecting inaudible codes that are embedded in radio and TV programs and thus are able to track the exact radio and TV programs that people have been exposed to, regardless of the location of that exposure. Only time will tell whether the PPM technology is feasible and economical, but most people in the advertising industry look forward to the prospect of having more complete information about away-from-home listening and viewing to supplement the in-home audience measurements. Importantly, in the Philadelphia testing only about 10 percent of households recruited to participate in the PPM test were willing to do so. This compares with typical acceptance rates ranging from 30 to 40 percent for Nielsen's in-home people meter procedure.[55]

The Challengers Have Come and Gone

Nielsen is often criticized for its monopoly powers because it is the only major service involved with estimating national and local TV audiences. It is interesting to note that Arbitron, of radio-audience measurement fame, introduced a service in the early 1990s called ScanAmerica to compete with Nielsen's rating system. However, within two years Arbitron discontinued the service due to lack of industry support. Another company named Statistical Research Inc. worked on developing its own TV measurement system called SMART, standing for Systems for Measuring and Reporting Television, but that company also discontinued the initiative due to lack of financial support. The challengers have come and gone. Nielsen, with all its imperfections, is the sole basis on which TV audiences are measured and program ratings (and thus advertising costs) are determined.

Summary

Excluding out-of-home advertising (covered in Chapter 8) and Internet advertising (covered in Chapter 15), there are four major media available to media planners: newspapers and magazines (print media), and radio and television (broadcast media). Each medium has unique qualities with both strengths and weaknesses. This chapter provides a detailed analysis of each medium. Newspapers provide mass audience coverage and reach readers who are in the appropriate mental frame to process messages. But newspapers suffer from high clutter and limited selectivity, among other limitations. Magazines enable advertisers to reach selective audiences and to present detailed information in an involving manner. This medium lacks intrusiveness, however, and also experiences considerable clutter. Radio also has the ability to reach segmented audiences and is economical. Clutter and the lack of visuals are notable weaknesses. Finally, television is an intrusive medium that is able to generate excitement, demonstrate brands in use, and achieve impact. Television advertising suffers from clutter, audience fractionalization, and high cost.

In addition to examining each medium's strengths and limitations, the chapter also examined how media space and time are purchased. Another major point of focus was the measurement of audience size and composition for each medium. Specific coverage included Mediamark Research Inc. and the Simmons Market Research Bureau in the area of magazine measurement, the Arbitron service in the case of radio audience measurement, and Nielsen Media Research on the matter of measuring TV audiences. Detailed discussion of Nielsen's people meter system—including local people meters (LPMs) and portable people meters (PPMs)—was provided along with mention of its historical paper diary method for measuring local audiences.

Discussion Questions

1. What are the advantages and disadvantages of cable television advertising? Why are more national advertisers turning to cable television as a viable advertising medium?
2. Assume you are brand manager for a new product line of book bags designed for college students. These bags come in each university's school colors and are imprinted with the school's mascot. Assume you have five million dollars to invest in a two-month magazine advertising campaign (July and August). Which magazines would you choose for this campaign? Justify your choices.

3. Assume you are a manufacturer of various jewelry items. Graduation rings for high school students are among the most important items in your product line. You are in the process of developing a media strategy aimed specifically at high school students. With an annual budget of $10 million, what media and specific vehicles would you use? How would you schedule the advertising over time?
4. Examine a copy of the most recent *Spot Radio Rates and Data* available in your library and compare the advertising rates for three or four of the radio stations in your hometown or university community.
5. Pick your favorite clothing store in your university community (or hometown), and justify the choice of one radio station that the clothing store should select for its radio advertising. Do not feel constrained by what the clothing store may be doing already; focus instead on what you think is most important. Be certain to make explicit all criteria used in making your choice and all radio stations considered.
6. Magazine A is read by 11,000,000 people and costs $52,000 for a full-page, four-color advertisement. Magazine B reaches 15,000,000 readers and costs $68,000 for a full-page, four-color advertisement. Holding all other factors constant, in which magazine would you choose to advertise and why?
7. Go online and see if you can locate a current (as of January of the present year) rate card for your favorite magazine. Carefully study this rate card and summarize your observations regarding price differentials for, say, black-and-white ads versus four-color ads of the same page size. (If you can't locate a rate card for your favorite magazine, find one for your next favorite, and so on.)
8. Radio is the only major medium that is nonvisual. Is this a major disadvantage? Thoroughly justify your response.
9. Will, in your opinion, portable digital-audio players (e.g., Apple's iPod) eventually replace radio?
10. One marketer made the following assertion: "Infomercials are junk. I wouldn't waste my money advertising on this medium." What is your response to her contention?
11. Members of the advertising community often claim that people meters are flawed. What are some of the reasons why people meters may not yield precise information about the number of households tuned into a specific television program or provide accurate demographic information of the people who actually do view a particular program?
12. Locate a recent SMRB or MRI publication in your library, and select a product used by large numbers of consumers (soft drinks, cereal, candy bars, etc.). Pick out the index numbers for the 18–24, 25–34, 35–44, 45–54, 55–64, and 65 and older age categories. Show how the index numbers were calculated. Also, identify some magazines that would be especially suitable for advertising to the *heavy users* of your selected product category.
13. With the following data, fill in the empty blanks:

Age Range	Total '000	A '000	B % Down	C % Across	D Index
All Adults	169,557	49,639	100.0	29.3	100
18–24	14,859	6,285	_____	_____	_____
25–34	38,494	10,509	_____	_____	_____

14. Based exclusively on the data in question 13, if you were an advertiser deciding whether to advertise your brand just to people ages 18 to 24, just to the 25-to-34 age group, or to both age groups, what would be your decision? Provide a detailed rationale for your decision.
15. Why, in your opinion, is viewership of cable TV growing rather dramatically at the expense of network TV?

16. What effect, in your view, will personal video recorders (of the TiVo variety) have on television advertising effectiveness, say, 10 years from now?
17. What are your thoughts about brand placements in TV programs? Do you find these placements irritating or do you accept them as simply part of the programming landscape? Do you think they influence your attitudes toward advertised brands and purchase behavior?
18. Offer your thoughts about the likelihood that portable people meters (PPMs) will serve to effectively track people's listening and viewing behaviors when they are away from home.

ENDNOTES

1. Jack Neff, "TV Doesn't Sell Package Goods," *Advertising Age,* May 24, 2004, 1, 30.
2. *Marketer's Guide to Media,* 2004, vol. 27 (New York: VNU Business Media, Inc.), 12.
3. Ibid., 182.
4. "Top 50 Newspapers by Circulation," *Advertising Age,* November 8, 2004, 16.
5. *Marketer's Guide to Media,* 184.
6. Michael T. Elliott and Paul Surgi Speck, "Consumer Perceptions of Advertising Clutter and Its Impact across Various Media," *Journal of Advertising Research* 38 (January/February 1998), 29–41.
7. Karen Whitehill King, Leonard N. Reid, and Margaret Morrison, "Large-Agency Media Specialists' Opinions on Newspaper Advertising for National Accounts," *Journal of Advertising* 26 (summer 1997), 1–18. This article indicates that ad agencies consider newspapers to be less effective as an advertising medium in most all respects compared with network television.
8. Bill Keane, *The Family Circus,* August, 9, 1992.
9. Stephen M. Blacker, "Magazines Need Better Research," *Advertising Age,* June 10, 1996, 23; Erwin Ephron, "Magazines Stall At Research Crossroads," *Advertising Age,* October 19, 1998, 38.
10. *Marketer's Guide to Media,* 158, 160.
11. For additional information on magazine audience measurement, see Thomas C. Kinnear, David A. Horne, and Theresa A. Zingery, "Valid Magazine Audience Measurement: Issues and Perspectives," in *Current Issues and Research in Advertising,* ed. James H. Leigh and Claude R. Martin, Jr. (Ann Arbor: Division of Research, Graduate School of Business, University of Michigan, 1986), 251–270.
12. The following information is based on Mediamark Reporter (Mediamark Research Inc., March 2000).
13. For an interesting critique of making vehicle selection decisions based exclusively on index numbers, see Theodore F. D'Amico, "Magazines' Secret Weapon: Media Selection on the Basis of Behavior, as Opposed to Demography," *Journal of Advertising Research* 39 (November/December 1999), 53–60.
14. Kevin J. Clancy, Paul D. Berger, and Thomas L. Magliozzi, "The Ecological Fallacy: Some Fundamental Research Misconceptions Corrected," *Journal of Advertising Research* 43 (December 2003), 370–380, especially 377–379.
15. Special advertising section to *Adweek, Brandweek,* and *Mediaweek* by the Radio Advertising Bureau in 2000; also, *Marketer's Guide to Media,* 66.
16. Burt Manning, "Friendly Persuasion," *Advertising Age,* September 13, 1982, M8.
17. For further reading on the nature and value of imagery in advertising, see Paula Fitzgerald Bone and Pam Scholder Ellen, "The Generation and Consequences of Communication-Evoked Imagery," *Journal of Consumer Research* 19 (June 1992), 93–104; and Darryl W. Miller and Lawrence J. Marks, "Mental Imagery and Sound Effects in Radio Commercials," *Journal of Advertising* 21 (December 1992), 83–93.
18. A thorough study of this behavior was conducted by Avery M. Abernethy, "The Accuracy of Diary Measures of Car Radio Audiences: An Initial Assessment," *Journal of Advertising* 18, no. 3 (1989), 33–49.
19. Abbey Klaassen, "iPod Threatens $20B Radio-ad Biz," *Advertising Age,* January 24, 2005, 1, 57.
20. "Sirius Satellite, Radio Rival XM Gain Subscribers," *Wall Street Journal Online,* December 28, 2004, http://online.wsj.com.
21. Nat Ives, "A Radio Challenge to Arbitron," *New York Times,* August 23, 2004, http://www.nytimes.com.
22. "Top Ten Primetime Broadcast TV Programs," Nielsen's Top 10 TV Ratings: Broadcast Programs, http://www.nielsenmedia.com/ratings/broadcast_programs.html.
23. Elliott and Speck, "Consumer Perceptions of Advertising Clutter and Its Impact across Various Media."
24. Cynthia M. Frisby, "Reaching the Male Consumer by Way of Daytime TV Soap Operas," *Journal of Advertising Research* 42 (March/April 2002), 56–64.
25. Statistics in this paragraph are from Nielsen Media Research as reported in "Stiff Competition: TV Has Seen Better Days," *Marketing News,* December 15, 2004, 8.
26. *Marketer's Guide to Media,* 25.
27. Wayne Friedman, "Familiar Friends Tops in Syndie Pricing," *Advertising Age,* January 20, 2003, 25.
28. *Marketer's Guide to Media,* 48.
29. Ellen Sheng, "Local Cable Advertising Heats Up As Viewership Further Fragments," *Wall Street Journal Online,* December 15, 2004, http://online.wsj.com.
30. Joe Mandese, "Amid Media Price Inflation, TV Production Costs Also Soar, Pose Threat to Addressability," *MediaPost's MediaDailyNews,* October 13, 2004, http://www.mediapost.com/news_main.cfm.
31. "Top Ten Primetime Broadcast TV Programs."
32. "The Toughest Job in TV," *Newsweek,* October 3, 1988, 72; Dennis Kneale, "'Zapping' of TV Ads Appears Pervasive," *Wall Street Journal,* April 25, 1988, 21.

33. John J. Cronin, "In-Home Observations of Commercial Zapping Behavior," *Journal of Current Issues and Research in Advertising* 17 (fall 1995), 69–76.
34. Fred S. Zufryden, James H. Pedrick, and Avu Sankaralingam, "Zapping and Its Impact on Brand Purchase Behavior," *Journal of Advertising Research* 33 (January/February 1993), 58–66.
35. John J. Cronin and Nancy E. Menelly, "Discrimination vs. 'Zipping' of Television Commercials," *Journal of Advertising* 21 (June 1992), 1–7.
36. Jonathan B. Weinbach, "Penalty for Holding . . . the Remote!" *Wall Street Journal Online,* February 4, 2005, http://online.wsj.com.
37. Megan Larson, "To Each His Own," *Adweek Magazines Special Report,* May 3, 2004, SR30.
38. "Study: DVR Users Skip Live Ads, Too," *Brandweek,* October 18, 2004, 7.
39. Erwin Ephron, "Live TV Is Ready for Its Closeup," *Advertising Age,* March 22, 2004, 19.
40. Jack Neff, "P&G Study: PVR Ad Recall Similar to TV," *Advertising Age,* March 17, 2003, 4.
41. Andrew Green, "Clutter Crisis Countdown," *Advertising Age,* April 21, 2003, 22.
42. For an interesting article that compares the effectiveness of 15- and 30-second commercials, see Surendra N. Singh and Catherine A. Cole, "The Effects of Length, Content, and Repetition on Television Commercial Effectiveness," *Journal of Marketing Research* 30 (February 1993), 91–104.
43. Whether advertising clutter has adverse effects on brand name recall and message memorability is a matter of some dispute. For somewhat different accounts, see Tom J. Brown and Michael L. Rothschild, "Reassessing the Impact of Television Advertising Clutter," *Journal of Consumer Research* 20 (June 1993), 138–146; Robert J. Kent and Chris T. Allen, "Does Competitive Clutter in Television Advertising 'Interfere' with the Recall and Recognition of Brand Names and Ad Claims?" *Marketing Letters* 4, no. 2 (1993), 175–184; Robert J. Kent and Chris T. Allen, "Competitive Interference in Consumer Memory for Advertising: The Role of Brand Familiarity," *Journal of Marketing* 58 (July 1994), 97–105; and Robert J. Kent, "Competitive Clutter in Network Television Advertising: Current Levels and Advertiser Response," *Journal of Advertising Research* 35 (January/February 1995), 49–57.
44. Jim Edwards, "The Art of the Infomercial," *Brandweek,* September 3, 2001, 14–18.
45. "Digital Profits: A Case Study of Kodak's Infomercial," *Infomercial and Direct Response Television Sourcebook '98,* a supplement to *Adweek Magazines,* 20–21.
46. Paul Surgi Speck, Michael T. Elliott, and Frank H. Alpert, "The Relationship of Beliefs and Exposure to General Perceptions of Infomercials," *Journal of Current Issues and Research in Advertising* 14 (spring 1997), 51–66.
47. Research has indicated that infomercial shoppers are impulsive; see Naveen Donthu and David Gilliland, "Observations: The Infomercial Shopper," *Journal of Advertising Research* 36 (March/April 1996), 69–76. There is countervailing evidence that challenges the claim that infomercial shoppers are particularly impulsive; see Tom Agee and Brett A. S. Martin, "Planned or Impulse Purchases? How to Create Effective Infomercials," *Journal of Advertising Research* 41 (November/December 2001), 35–42.
48. James A. Karrh, "Brand Placement: A Review," *Journal of Current Issues and Research in Advertising,* 20 (fall 1998), 31–50.
49. Rosellina Ferraro and Rosemary J. Avery, "Brand Appearance on Prime-Time Television," *Journal of Current Issues and Research in Advertising,* 22 (fall 2000), 1–16.
50. Cristel Antonia Russell, Andrew T. Norman, and Susan E. Heckler, "The Consumption of Television Programming: Development and Validation of the Connectedness Scale," *Journal of Consumer Research* 31 (June 2004), 150–161.
51. For a technical analysis of the reliability of people-meter measurement, see Roland Soong, "The Statistical Reliability of People Meter Ratings," *Journal of Advertising Research* 28 (February/March 1988), 50–56.
52. Emily Nelson and Sarah Ellison, "Nielsen's Feud with TV Networks Shows Scarcity of Marketing Data," *Wall Street Journal Online,* October 29, 2003, http://online.wsj.com.
53. These details are from Brooks Barnes, "For Nielsen, Fixing Old Ratings System Causes New Static," *Wall Street Journal Online,* September 16, 2004, http://online.wsj.com.
54. Joan Fitzgerald, "Evaluating Return on Investment of Multimedia Advertising with a Single-Source Panel: A Retail Case Study," *Journal of Advertising Research* 44 (September/October 2004), 262–270.
55. Wayne Friedman, "People Meter Pilots 'Need More Work'," *Advertising Age,* June 23, 2003, 59.

CHAPTER 15

Employing the Internet for Advertising

Marcom Challenge: In a Zero-Sum Environment, Gains for Online Advertising Are Losses for Traditional Media

You will recall from Chapter 14 that the traditional advertising media include broadcast (television and radio) and print media (magazines and newspapers). Throughout most of the twentieth century, these four media commanded the bulk of marketing communicators' advertising budgets. Magazines and newspapers dominated through most of the first half of the past century, but with radio's advent as a broadcast medium in the early 1920s and television's ascendancy by the 1950s, a major change in the advertising landscape had occurred. Though newspaper advertising remained a dominant advertising medium into the 1980s, television continued to capture an ever-growing portion of media expenditures. It could be argued that television's heyday as an advertising medium has now passed with marketers' unceasing endeavors to identify advertising outlets that are less cluttered, more precise in targeting prospective customers, and more economical. Television's loss (along with the ad revenue losses experienced by other major media) is largely due to the arrival of the Internet as a viable advertising medium. In short, the purveyors of advertising media live in a zero sum world.

The concept of *zero sum* captures the idea that any gain for one constituent in a competitive environment represents a loss for another. The media environment is generally of this nature: marketers' increased advertising expenditures on, say, television generally result in their decreased spending in other media such as magazines and radio. Today, the "800-pound gorilla" in the media world is online advertising. Forrester Research, an independent technology research company, reports that in 2005 nearly half of all marketers increased funding for online advertising while decreasing spending in traditional media such as magazines, newspapers, and postal mail. Moreover, Forrester Research forecasts that by 2010 online advertising and promotional spending will rival the combined spending allocated to cable and satellite TV and radio.[1]

According to another survey of over 2,000 Web users, consumers' Internet usage continues to grow at the expense of the traditional media: TV, radio, magazines, and newspapers. Sixty-one percent of the respondents to the survey indicated they now spend more time on the Internet than they did the previous year. Given the zero-sum character of time available for media consumption, 36 percent of the respondents indicated watching television less, 34 percent expend less time reading magazines, 30 percent have reduced their newspaper reading, and 27 percent have cut their radio listening.[2]

It is virtually axiomatic that marketers chase eyeballs wherever they happen to be located and place their advertising expenditures in those media where consumers allocate their time. The statistics thus indicate that the eyeballs are increasingly being devoted to consumption of online media, and marketers, accordingly, are allocating greater portions of their marcom budgets to online media while reducing spending in the traditional media.

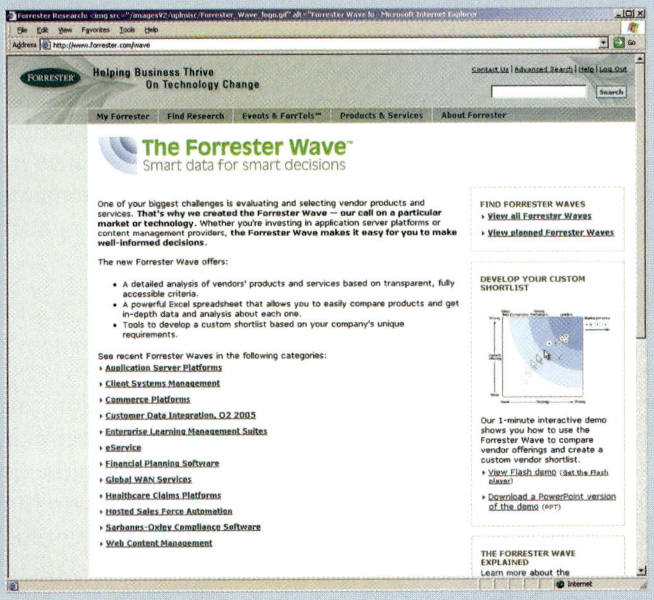

Courtesy, Forrester Research, Inc.

CHAPTER OBJECTIVES

1

Appreciate the magnitude, nature, and potential for Internet advertising.

2

Be familiar with the two key features of Internet advertising: individualization and interactivity.

3

Understand how Internet advertising differs from advertising in conventional mass-oriented advertising media, as well as how the same fundamentals apply to both general categories of ad media.

4

Understand the various forms of Internet advertising: display ads, rich media, e-mail advertising, Web logs, search engine advertising, and advertising via behavioral targeting.

5

Appreciate the importance of measuring Internet advertising effectiveness and the various metrics used for this purpose.

Overview

The Internet performs a multifaceted marketing function, serving as a mechanism for building demand, conducting transactions, filling orders, providing customer service, and serving as a versatile advertising medium. However, this chapter is *not* about e-commerce in general but rather is restricted to looking at the Internet as a rapidly growing advertising medium. It is important to recognize that the Internet's exact role as an advertising medium is in a state of flux: new technologies are continually emerging, and marketers are experimenting with varied uses of online advertising. This chapter's objective is to present coverage of most aspects of Internet advertising, hoping that students will fully appreciate the changes occurring and the uncertainties of what exactly the future might bring. Nonetheless, upon completing this chapter, you will have developed an appreciation of the scope and potential of the Internet as a viable advertising medium—a medium that undoubtedly will continue to steal advertising dollars from the traditional ad media.

Traditional advertising media, such as those covered in the previous chapter (television, radio, magazines, and newspaper), have served advertisers' needs for generations. In recent years, however, there have been increased efforts on the part of advertisers and their agencies to locate new media that are less costly, less cluttered, and potentially more effective than the established media. Some observers have gone so far as to claim that traditional advertising is on its deathbed.[3] The contention is that online advertising is superior to traditional media because it provides consumers with virtually full control over the commercial information they choose to receive or avoid. The Internet is claimed to be a better communications medium due to its versatility and superiority at targeting customers.[4] Most agree, however, that the Internet is nothing more than a potentially key element of IMC programs and not a replacement for conventional media.[5]

Dating back only to 1994, the World Wide Web has become an important medium for Internet advertising. Though at the time of this writing the Internet commands less than 5 percent of advertising revenue in the United States, surveys reveal that it accounts for about 14 percent of America's media usage.[6] As of 2004, slightly over 150 million Americans were active Internet users.[7] Online advertising spending in the United States amounted to over $9.6 billion in 2004, and is estimated to grow to $26 billion by 2010.[8] Perhaps the most dramatic indicator of the Internet's growth as an advertising medium is the fact that advertising revenue generated by search engine companies Google and Yahoo! virtually equaled in 2005 the combined prime-time ad revenues garnered by the big-three television networks in the United States—ABC, CBS, and NBC.[9]

The Two i's of the Internet: Individualization and Interactivity

Individualization and interactivity (the Internet's two *i*'s) are key features of the Internet and of advertising in that medium.[10] *Individualization* refers to the fact that the Internet user has control over the flow of information. This feature leads, in turn, to the ability to target advertisements and promotions that are relevant to the consumer. *Interactivity,* which is intertwined with individualization, allows for users to select the information they perceive as relevant and for brand managers to build relationships with customers via two-way communication. We now elaborate on the importance of the Internet's interactivity feature.

Traditional advertising media vary in the degree to which they are able to generate mental activity from consumers. Nonetheless, all these media engage the consumer in a relatively passive fashion: the consumer listens to or sees information about the advertised brand, but he or she has limited control over the amount or rate of information received. What you see (or hear) is what you get. There is action but no interaction. Whereas action involves a flow in one direction (from advertiser *to* consumer), interaction entails reciprocal behavior. This idea of *reciprocity* generally defines the nature of interactive media.

Interactive advertising enables the user (who no longer is a "receiver" in the traditional, passive model of communications) to *control the amount or rate of information* that he or she wishes to acquire from a commercial message. The user can choose to devote one second or 15 minutes to a message. He or she is, for all intents and purposes, involved in a "conversation" with the commercial message at a subvocal level. A request for additional information occurs with the push of a button, the touch of a screen, or the click of a mouse. In all instances, the user and source of commercial information are engaged in a give-and-take exchange of information—communications intercourse rather than mere transmission and reception. By analogy, a North American football quarterback and receivers are somewhat equivalent to the traditional media: the quarterback throws the ball, and the receivers attempt to catch it. Comparatively, in British rugby, players toss the ball back and forth as they advance downfield—each player both passes and receives; their relation is analogous to the give-and-take reciprocity that defines interactive advertising.[11]

JOB OUTLOOK

Familiarity with word processing and database applications also is important for many positions. Computer skills are vital because marketing, product promotion, and advertising on the Internet are increasingly common. (*Occupational Outlook Handbook, 2004–05 Edition, U.S. DOL, http://www.bls.gov/oco/home.htm*)

The Internet is undeniably a more interactive advertising medium than most. Nonetheless, it is important to note that the Internet as a medium for advertising is not homogeneous; rather, there are a variety of different forms of online advertising. These range from e-mail and banner advertisements, which typically offer relatively little opportunity or desire for interaction, to ads encountered when one actively searches a product category or topic (referred to as search engine ads that appear as sponsored links when one conducts, say, a Google search), which generate more interaction.

The Internet Compared with Other Ad Media

In the early days of the World Wide Web (roughly from 1994 to 1999), many businesspeople thought the Internet would be an advertising panacea—a means of reaching millions of customers worldwide with ad messages in a way that would allow for greater accountability than would traditional media. The assumption was that people would be interested in receiving Internet ads and that the advertising would be effective in creating brand awareness, influencing attitudes and purchase intentions, and driving sales. The notion that the Internet was dramatically different from conventional ad media was as simplistic as the corresponding idea of a "new economy" that assumed that dot-com companies played under rules different from the conventional microeconomic principles that for generations have explained the requirements for success in the "old economy."

As covered in the previous chapter, each of the major advertising media has its unique set of advantages and disadvantages. Each ad medium is capable of achieving particular advertising objectives at a cost to the advertiser. In planning for and selecting a single advertising medium or, more likely, a portfolio of integrated media, the advertiser's objective is to achieve against the target market necessary objectives for the brand as inexpensively as possible. (Recall our mantra presented initially in Chapter 1: all marketing communications should be (1) directed to a particular *target market,* (2) clearly *positioned,* (3) created to achieve a *specific objective,* and (4) undertaken to accomplish the objective *within budget constraint.*)

From the discussion in the previous chapter, it should be obvious that no advertising medium is perfect for all purposes. The Internet is no exception, contrary to the early hype. It can be argued, in fact, that the Internet's interactivity feature may represent a disadvantage rather than an advantage. According to this argument, the Internet user is in a "leaning forward" mind-set compared with, say, the TV viewer who is "leaning back." In other words, whereas the TV viewer is casually watching TV programs and advertisements in a relaxed mood (leaning back, so to speak), the Internet user is goal driven and on a mission to obtain information (leaning forward). In this mind-set, banner ads, pop-ups, and unsolicited e-mail messages simply represent an interruption, an obstacle to the user's primary mission for connecting to the Internet.[12] Advertisements seen while in a leaning-forward mission mind-set are actively avoided and thus can have little possible effect, beyond perhaps mere brand identification. Of course, Internet advertising comes in several forms and generalizations such as these are not necessarily appropriate to all. We direct our attention now to the various forms of Internet ads and their unique characteristics.

Internet Advertising Formats

Internet advertisers use a variety of advertising formats. Table 15.1 lists the various forms of Internet advertising that are described in this chapter. The largest form of online advertising—paid search, or search engine advertising—commands about 40 percent of all Internet advertising. Other forms of online advertising are much smaller in terms of revenue generated. The following presentation provides a current treatment of online advertising formats. It is important to appreciate, however, that any sweeping and definitive claims would be misleading, because Internet advertising is so new, with a history dating back slightly more than a decade. Imagine, by comparison, the futility in the mid-1950s of providing a definitive treatment about the nature and effectiveness of TV advertising. Only with time have we come to know how TV advertising performs and what its strengths and limitations are. Similarly, more time is needed before conclusive statements are possible about online advertising.

Table 15.1
Internet Advertising Formats

- Web Sites
- Display or Banner Ads
- Rich Media Formats
  - Pop-Ups
  - Interstitials
  - Superstitials
  - Video Ads
- Web Logs
  - Blogs
  - Podcasts
- E-mail
  - Opt-in Versus Spam
  - E-zines
  - Wireless E-mail Advertising
  - Mobile Phones and Text Messaging
- Search Engine Advertising
  - Keyword-Matching Advertising
  - Content-Targeted Advertising
- Advertising via Behavioral Targeting

Web Sites

Before discussing specific online advertising formats, it will be useful to briefly discuss Web sites. On the one hand, a company's Web site is itself an advertisement for the company. However, beyond being a form of advertising, Web sites represent a venue for generating and transacting exchanges between organizations and their customers. Web sites can be considered the centerpiece of companies' online advertising efforts, with other advertising formats (e.g., banners, e-mail, and paid searches) simply serving to drive traffic to their Web sites. Hence, Web sites are key to successfully integrated online advertising programs. It serves little utility to drive prospects to a bad Web site—that is, one that is difficult to navigate, provides little useful information, is unattractive, or fails to offer entertainment value.

The Web site for a brand is an invaluable advertising medium for conveying information about the brand, its character, and its promotional offerings. Perhaps the major difference between Web sites and other online ad formats is that users seek out Web sites in a goal-oriented fashion (e.g., to learn more about a company or brand, to play a game, or to register for a contest), whereas the other online formats typically are "stumbled upon accidentally."[13] Research has shown, for example, that

Courtesy, LUCASFILM LTD.

half of all new-vehicle buyers visit Web sites prior to going to automobile dealerships; moreover, people who visit these Web sites spend, on average, about five hours online shopping for new vehicles.[14]

The advertising value of a Web site is well documented in a recent study that found that site visitations for newly released movies play a prominent role in predicting box office performance. Specifically, the greater the number of unique (not repeat) visits to a new movie's Web site, the more people actually see the movie in a cinema.[15]

A small-town retailer was fond of saying that "merchandise well displayed is half sold," implying, of course, that attractively displayed items capture the shopper's attention and invite purchase.[16] The same advice applies to Web-site construction: attractive and user-friendly sites invite usage and revisits. Research on the "look" of Web pages is in its infancy, but there is some tentative evidence that Web pages designed with relatively simple backgrounds (i.e., without a lot of color and animation) might be better liked than more complex pages. In a study using a state lottery as the focal Web site, it was learned that the most complex background produced the least favorable attitudes toward the advertised service and the weakest purchase intentions.[17] It would be foolhardy to generalize this finding to other products, but it does suggest that too many bells and whistles in a Web site may serve to distract attention away from the key message arguments on which involved consumers form their attitudes toward advertised products and services.

Because consumers visit Web sites with the objective of acquiring useful information or being entertained, it follows that Web sites are of most value when they fulfill consumers' goal-seeking needs by providing useful information rather than attempting to dazzle with excessive graphic cleverness. The architect's advice that "form follows function" certainly applies to the Web site as an online advertising tool. It has been demonstrated, for example, that the background color of a Web page affects the perceived speed of a download. That is, more relaxing colors (such as blue and green) are perceived to download more quickly than exciting colors (such as red and yellow).[18]

Display or Banner Ads

The most popular advertising format in the Internet's short advertising history has been the static advertisement known as a display, or banner, ad. This format can be considered analogous to a static print ad in a magazine or newspaper. Banner ads are a staple of Internet advertising. These are typically small, static ads placed in frequently visited Web sites. Banner ads on the Internet are ubiquitous. Click-through rates (CTRs) to banner ads are very low, averaging less than 0.3 percent. Banner ads for B2B companies receive somewhat higher CTRs than do those for B2C companies.[19] In other words, online users pay attention and solicit information from only a small percentage of all the Internet banner ads to which they are exposed. (Remember, exposure is necessary for but not equivalent to attention. Exposure merely indicates that the consumer has had a chance to see an advertisement.) Although the mere exposure to a banner ad can have some value in enhancing brand awareness, the low CTRs largely reduce the effectiveness of banner ads much beyond being noticed.

Research has found that CTRs are a function of brand familiarity, with brands that consumers know best receiving substantially higher CTRs than unfamiliar brands.[20] Importantly, but not particularly surprisingly, this same research revealed that CTRs decrease with multiple exposures to banner ads for familiar brands, whereas the rates increase with more exposures to ads for unfamiliar brands. New and relatively unknown brands thus need to produce a banner-ad media schedule that allows for multiple exposures. Established brands, on the other hand, may not experience increased CTRs with multiple exposures. This, however, does not necessarily imply that established brands do not benefit from banner advertising. On the contrary, such brands may achieve increasing levels of brand awareness—culminating in top-of-mind awareness, or TOMA, even though consumers choose not to click through to the brand's Web site. (The student may recall the discussion of brand awareness back in Chapter 2, where a brand awareness pyramid portrayed a progression from brand unawareness, to brand recognition, to brand recall, and, ideally, ultimately to TOMA.) Banner advertising, along with other communications elements in an IMC program, can serve to facilitate increasing levels of brand awareness and thus enhance brand equity.

Because CTRs are trivially small, online advertisers have turned to new technology and larger ad sizes to grab the online surfer's attention. Many of these changes and the standardization of banner sizes have been facilitated by the efforts of the Internet Advertising Bureau (IAB), a trade association that is a leader in the Internet advertising industry. The IAB endorsed seven new Internet ad formats, labeled Internet marketing units (IMUs). These seven new IMUs compare with the earlier full banner, the size of which was 468 x 60 pixels (28,080 square pixels).

Table 15.2 contrasts the new IMUs against this original full banner. This table makes it clear that the new IMUs are generally considerably larger than the original full banner ad. It is likely that the larger ad sizes increase attention and thus CTRs. A study conducted by a research firm for the IAB determined that the skyscraper and large rectangle IMUs were more than three to six times as effective in increasing brand awareness and favorable message associations as the 468 x 60 standard banner IMU.[21]

In addition to increasing the size and differentiating the shapes of banner ads, Internet advertisers, like the savvy conventional advertisers who preceded them, have turned increasingly to *customer targeting* as a means of increasing CTRs and achieving their objectives for brand equity enhancement.[22] With improved tracking technology, it has become possible to determine more about Internet surfers' consumer behavior and then to tailor the specific banner ads that surfers are exposed to. This is accomplished with electronic files (called *cookies*) that track users' online behavior. The following quote illustrates how cookies enable Internet advertisers to direct ads that are compatible with Internet users' product-usage interests:

If a golfer clicks on an ad for a golf magazine, that click is recorded. The next time our golf-loving Web surfer goes online, an ad server detects him or her, finds a golf banner and serves it up. By isolating that user, Internet ad companies can sell targeted golf-related advertising. The user doesn't have to go back to the same site to get the targeted ad, either. The ad-server companies [e.g., DoubleClick, 24/7 Media, Engage Technologies] sign up hundreds of client Web sites onto their ad networks, which enables the ad servers to follow users from Web site to Web site.[23]

Table 15.2

Types and Sizes of Internet Marketing Units (IMUs)

Type and Size of IMU (pixel size)	Square Pixels	Size Differential Versus Full Banner
Full Banner (468 × 60)	28,800	——
Skyscraper (120 × 600)	72,000	156%
Wide Skyscraper (160 × 600)	96,000	242
Rectangle (180 × 150)	27,000	–4
Medium Rectangle (300 × 250)	75,000	167
Large Rectangle (336 × 280)	94,080	235
Vertical Rectangle (240 × 400)	96,000	242
Square Pop-Up (250 × 250)	62,500	123

DoubleClick, one of the more prominent Internet companies, has over 100 million user profiles that advertisers can use for targeting their ads. These profiles are created when users register for something online or make online purchases. Often a profile contains detailed demographic information, including the profiled user's age, gender, and income. Needless to say, these user profiles represent a marvelous advertising tool, and, at the same time, create the potential for invasion of users' privacy.[24] In an Internet advertising variation on the well-known principle of physics that for every action there is an equally strong and opposing reaction, many consumers avoid Web ads by downloading ad-blocking software. Of course, nothing in life comes for free. Consumers receive free television programming because advertisers subsidize this freedom. Likewise, if ad-killing software becomes widely used, Internet users may have to pay for the Web content that we presently enjoy at no cost.

Rich Media: Pop-Ups, Interstitials, Superstitials, and Video Ads

It was only a matter of time before Internet advertisers began using online formats that were more dynamic than banners in their use of motion, sights, and sounds. This newer form of online advertising is referred to as *rich media,* and includes pop-up ads, interstitials, superstitials, and now even video advertisements. There has been a natural progression, in other words, from the relatively dull and inanimate form of banner advertising to the attention-gaining, albeit annoying, animated form of online advertising. These rich media formats might even be compared to the low-budget ads on cable TV that use fast-talking salespeople, elevated noise levels, and dynamic movements to gain viewers' attention.

Let us briefly distinguish rich media formats. **Pop-ups** are ads that appear in a separate window that materializes on the screen seemingly out of nowhere while a selected Web page is loading. **Interstitials**—based on the word *interstitial,* which describes the space that intervenes between things—are, by comparison, ads that appear *between* (rather than within, as is the case with pop-ups) two content Web pages. In short, both pop-up ads and interstitials are obtrusive, but in different ways. The difference between pop-ups and interstitials is more than trite, as described compellingly in this quote:

First, unlike pop-ups, interstitials do not interrupt the user's interactive experience because they tend to run while the user waits for a page to download. Users, however, have less control over interstitials because there is no "exit" option to stop or delete an interstitial, which is common among pop-ups. In other words, with interstitials, users have to wait until the entire ad has run.[25]

Superstitials are short, animated ads that play over or on top of a Web page. Finally, **online video ads**, also referred to as streaming video, are audio-video ads that are similar to standard 30-second TV commercials but are often shortened to 10 or 15 seconds and compressed into manageable file sizes. With more households having access to broadband connection to the Internet, video ads are now feasible—unlike with dial-up connection, which was much too slow in downloading audio-video files.

Pop-up ads, interstitials, and superstitials, though often a source of irritation, are effective attention getters. Internet advertisers, like advertisers in all other media, have to fight through the clutter to find ways to attract and hold the online user's attention. Bigger ads, ads popping up, and ads that offer sounds, animation, and movement are just some of the ways that have been devised to accomplish these objectives. These formats are more eye-catching and memorable than are standard (i.e., static) banner ads and yield higher CTRs.

However, in their effort to gain attention, rich media advertising formats also create great levels of annoyance among Internet users. One study determined that whereas only about 10 percent of respondents indicate they are "very annoyed" with TV ads, over 80 percent of these respondents revealed considerable annoyance with pop-ups.[26] Advertisers have accordingly cut back in their use of pop-up ads, though interstitials, superstitials, and video ads are widely used.

Web Logs

You may recall that the topic of Web logs, or *blogs,* was introduced in Chapter 7 when discussing the role of the Internet in creating buzz and disseminating word-of-mouth information. Brief additional discussion will be provided in this section. It was estimated as of early 2005 that 31.6 million hosted blogs had been created on services such as Blogger, BlogSpot, LiveJournal, Xanga, and MSN Spaces. The number of hosted blogs is expected to grow to over 50 million by the end of 2005.[27] Upwards of 40 thousand new blogs appear daily![28]

Blogs are, in a manner of speaking, "everyman's" way of communicating with others and establishing digital communities wherein individuals, mostly of like mind, can exchange their views on issues of personal relevance. It is in this context that products and brands are sometimes discussed. It is here where companies can endeavor to further enhance the equity of their brands and perhaps even to generate additional business. The importance of blogs to businesses has been stated in a direct and convincing fashion in the pages of *BusinessWeek* magazine:

Go ahead and bellyache about blogs. But you cannot afford to close your eyes to them, because they're simply the most explosive outbreak in the information world since the Internet itself. And they're going to shake up just about every business—including yours. It doesn't matter whether you're shipping paper clips, pork bellies, or videos of Britney in a bikini, blogs are a phenomenon that you cannot ignore, postpone, or delegate. Given the changes barreling down upon us, blogs are not a business elective. They're a prerequisite.[29]

It is likely that small businesses may benefit most from blogging, in large part due to the fact that blogs published by small businesses may better connect with prospective customers on an intellectual or emotional level and also appear less commercial and thus more credible. Much of the appeal of blogs is that a company can communicate directly with prospective customers, who in turn can become active communicators through their own posted comments. The interactive feature of the Internet that was described at the beginning of the chapter is perhaps realized better by blogs than any other form of online advertising.

Blogs as an Advertising Format

Brand marketers can develop their own blogs or simply place advertisements on blogs that are appropriate for the advertiser's brand. For example, Google offers a service that enables small ads to be placed on blog sites. Only after a blog visitor clicks on the ad is revenue generated. Advertisers can turn to Blogads (http://blogads.com), which is a network of bloggers who accept advertising; the network matches advertisers with appropriate blogs at which to place their advertisements. Advertisers purchase ads through Blogads on a weekly or monthly basis at a cost ranging from $10 up to $3,000 for highly popular blogs.[30]

Though the numbers indicate that blogging is growing at an epidemic rate, this does not necessarily mean that blogs represent a viable advertising medium. The value of blogs to their producers and consumers is the community created and the opportunity for a free and honest exchange of ideas. Because advertising is often perceived as less than fully objective and is seen by many as an intrusion, the purpose for producing and consuming blogs may be antithetical with using blogs as an advertising vehicle. In short, it is doubtful that blogs represent a major advertising opportunity.

The Special Case of Podcasting

Whereas traditional blogs are written documents, *podcasting* is an audio version of blogging. Podcasts, which are derived from the name iPod, are MP3 audio files that are available for free online and are accompanied by written blogs. **Podcasting** is a way of publishing sound files to the Internet, allowing users to subscribe to a feed and receive new audio files automatically. In effect, podcasters self-produce radio-type programs. Consumers subscribe to podcasts using a special form of so-called aggregator software that periodically checks for and downloads new content, which then is playable on computers and digital audio players. KarmaBanque, for example, is a podcast that provides a unique view on business and financial matters. Podcasting enables advertisers the opportunity to target messages to consumers who share similar lifestyle characteristics as revealed by their self-selection to particular podcasts.[31] For further reading about podcasting, go online to Podcasting Avenue (http://podcasters.blogspot.com).

E-mail Advertising

The primary reason many people use the Internet is to send and receive e-mail messages. With millions of people online and the numbers substantially increasing each year, it is little wonder that marketing communicators have turned to e-mail as a viable advertising medium. *E-mail advertising* is simply the use of the Internet for sending commercial messages. However, as with any other advertising medium, there is no such thing as a single type of e-mail message; rather, e-mail messages appear in many forms, ranging from pure-text documents to more sophisticated versions that use all the audio-video powers of the Internet. Oftentimes firms send e-mail messages and encourage recipients to pass along the messages to their personal distribution list of other people. See the *Global Focus* insert for an application of e-mail advertising designed to build buzz.

Expenditures on e-mail advertising in the United States amounted to slightly less than $300 million in 2005, which is dramatically less than what was predicted only a few years ago.[32] The fact of the matter is that the bloom is off the e-mail advertising rose. Seen at one time as a substitute for postal mail and telemarketing, e-mail is not nearly as effective as originally expected because many marketers have simply "spoiled the commons." This expression, in the event you don't remember it from a basic economics course (also termed the *tragedy of the commons*), refers to the excessive and damaging use of what effectively amounts to a free resource. Common grazing land for cattle represents the classic case of spoiling the commons. Imagine a situation where a large field is available for all farmers in a community to feed their cattle. All is well as long as not too many animals graze the field and the grass can naturally replace itself at a rate faster than it is consumed. But if there are too many cattle grazing the field, the grass can't recover rapidly enough and in the long term the field may become bare—certainly unable to support the number of cattle grazing it. In short, the commons have been spoiled.

This, unfortunately, has been the case with e-mail advertising. Too many messages are sent, and too many represent *spam,* or junk mail, rather than messages received from companies for whom the recipient has some interest. Indeed, it is estimated that approximately two-thirds of all commercial e-mail messages repre-

Nescafé's Viral E-mail Effort in Argentina

global focus

Café con Leche, which is a mixture of coffee with milk, is marketed by Nescafé in Argentina and some other countries. Given a very small budget for marketing the brand in Argentina, it was necessary for Nescafé to come up with a clever marcom strategy. The plan devised involved the use of e-mails to create brand buzz. (Recall that Chapter 7 discussed buzz building in some detail.) Users of Café con Leche who were known to be technology savvy and frequent forwarders of e-mail messages were recruited. The request made of these men and women, all in the 25-to-45 age group, was to pass along a commercial message for Café con Leche to at least 15 other people. The spot focused on two young women who were preparing an iced coffee with Café con Leche. Also included was a link to a Web site containing a virtual kitchen. Visitors to the site could click on ingredients located in cupboards and a refrigerator while following recipes to create coffee shakes with ice cream and to mix Café con Leche with rum or other ingredients. The intent, of course, was to increase user involvement with the brand and to demonstrate its variety of uses.

Within only a month of the launch of the campaign, the e-mail message was forwarded 100,000 times. Moreover, upwards of 20 percent of visitors to the Web site responded to a survey by providing information about the brand and its uses. Beyond this specific application, which was unique at the time for Argentina, one may question why anyone would be willing to forward e-mail messages to other people. The fact is that all Internet users receive e-mails that encourage us to pass them along to others. Why are people willing to pass messages along? Research has determined that the major motives for passing e-mail messages along are because people enjoy doing so and find it entertaining and possibly of help to others.

Sources: Charles Newbery, "Nescafé Builds Buzz Via Viral E-Mail Effort," *Advertising Age*, May 2, 2005, 24; Joseph E. Phelps, Regina Lewis, Lynne Mobilio, David Perry, and Niranjan Raman, "Viral Marketing or Electronic Word-of-Mouth Advertising: Examining Consumer Responses and Motivations to Pass Along Email," *Journal of Advertising Research* 44 (December 2004), 333–348.

sent spam.[33] Unspoiling the e-mail advertising commons is possible only by gaining recipients' permission to send them e-mail ads.

Opt-In E-mailing Versus Spam

Opt-in e-mailing is the practice of marketers asking for and receiving consumers' permission to send them messages on particular topics. The consumer has agreed, or opted-in, to receive messages on topics of interest rather than receiving messages that are unsolicited. Imagine, for example, that a hypothetical consumer is interested in purchasing a digital camera and visits a Web site that appeared when she conducted a Google search for "digital cameras." While logged into this Web site, which was quite informative, she received a query that asked whether she would be interested in receiving more information about photographic equipment. She replied, "Yes," and provided her e-mail address as well as other information. The Web site electronically recorded her "permission granted" and, unknown to the unsuspecting shopper, sold her name and e-mail address to a broker that specializes in compiling lists. This list broker, in turn, sold her name and e-mail address to companies that market photographic equipment and supplies. Our hypothetical Internet user's name and e-mail address eventually appeared on a variety of lists, and she received regular e-mail messages for photographic equipment and supplies.

In theory, opt-in e-mailing serves both the marketer's and the consumer's interests. However, frequency and quantity of e-mail messages can become intrusive as more and more companies have access to your name and areas of interest. Consumers feel especially violated when the e-mail messages deal with topics that are tangential to their primary interests. For example, when granting the original Web site permission to send photography-related messages, our unsuspecting consumer may have been interested only in information about digital cameras, when in fact she subsequently was bombarded with messages involving more aspects of photography and more photography products than she ever could have imagined. She knew not what she had opted for—some of the information received was relevant, most was not.

Although this example may appear to cast a negative evaluation of opt-in e-mail, the fact remains that advertisers who send messages to individuals whose interests are known, if only somewhat broadly, increase their odds of providing consumers with relevant information. Moreover, sophisticated marketers are using a more detailed opt-in procedure so they can better serve both their own needs for accurate targeting and consumers' needs for relevant information. For example, a consumer might say, "Send me information about men's clothes; but I don't have any kids, so don't send me anything about kids' clothiers. And I want to hear from you only once a month."[34]

Compare this with the practice of sending unsolicited e-mail messages, a practice pejoratively referred to as *spam*. As you may know, Spam is a brand of canned, processed meat that people love to joke about. For whatever reason, Internet users and pundits began using the word *spam* in reference to unsolicited and unwanted commercial e-mail messages. Such messages offer little prospect that recipients will do much more than click on and then rapidly click off these unsolicited messages. It could be argued that spam at least has a chance of influencing brand awareness, perhaps much like may happen when the consumer is perusing a magazine and unintentionally comes across an ad for a product in which he or she has little interest. However, whereas the consumer expects to see ads in magazines and realizes that this is part of the "cost of entry," the consumer does not, at least at the present time, expect to receive unsolicited e-mail messages. Hence, any brand awareness gain a marketer might obtain from e-mailing unsolicited messages is likely to be offset by the negative reaction consumers have to this form of advertising.

Anti-spam legislation under the rubric CAN-SPAM has been passed in the United States, and regulations against unsolicited e-mail are even more stringent in Europe. The spam problem represents a bothersome intrusion for consumers and also presents an economic cost to legitimate marketers that use commercial e-mail messages as an honest way of conducting business. In an effort to curtail spamming, the Federal Trade Commission has recommended to Congress a rewards program that pays anywhere from $100,000 to $250,000 as incentives for people to turn in spammers.[35]

Phishing

Perhaps even more troubling than spam is a related illegal e-mailing practice known as *phishing*. **Phishing** takes place when criminals send e-mail messages appearing to be from legitimate corporations and direct recipients to phony Web sites that are designed to look like companies' actual Web sites. These phony Web sites attempt to extract personal data from people such as their credit card and ATM numbers. Pronounced like *fishing*, the practice of phishing has the same intent—to cast line with hopes of hooking some suckers. Not only are consumers injured when their identities are stolen, but brand equity also suffers when thieves masquerade as legitimate businesses.

E-mail Magazines (E-zines)

A growing form of e-mail advertising known as *e-zines*, or sponsored e-mail, is the distribution of free magazine-like publications. E-zines typically are distributed on a local rather than national basis, and are available in most major U.S. cities. These publications tend to focus on trendy issues such as entertainment, fashion, and food and beverages. Most e-zines include a relatively small number of ads that link readers to the Web sites of stores and brands. In order to boost the credibility of their publications, e-zine editors clearly identify advertisements and avoid mentioning advertisers' products in editorial copy.[36] E-zines enable advertisers to reach highly targeted audiences and to deliver credible advertising messages that are clearly designated as such.

The Special Case of Wireless E-mail Advertising

Laptops with wireless modems, personal digital assistants, cellular phones, and pagers are invaluable tools for millions of businesspeople and consumers around the globe. These mobile appliances enable people to remain connected to the Web without being tethered to a wired laptop or desktop PC. Needless to say, advertisers would like to reach businesspeople and consumers on their wireless devices just as much as they covet contacting them when they are electronically wired into the Internet. This section discusses the nature and future of wireless advertising. Because wireless advertising is in its infancy, the following comments are necessarily somewhat speculative.

The growth of wireless advertising was made possible with the advent of wireless fidelity technology, commonly referred to as Wi-Fi. **Wi-Fi** is a technology that enables computers and other wireless devices such as cell phones to connect to the Internet via low-power radio signals instead of cables. Hence, users can have Internet access at base stations, or so-called hotspots, that are Wi-Fi equipped.

Companies that advertise via the Internet will have greater access to millions of consumers who, before wireless-enabled Internet access, could be reached only in their homes or offices at times separated from the occasion during which consumers were actually in the marketplace to make product and brand selections. Now consumers can be contacted at or close to the point of purchase where advertising can have greater impact in influencing brand choice. For example, it is one thing to receive an advertising message at home late at night several days prior to, say, going to the mall to casually shop. That advertising received in advance of the shopping trip may be forgotten prior to making product and brand choices. Comparatively, imagine sitting in a mall at a comfortable bench surfing the Web wirelessly and being exposed to an ad announcing a sale at a store located only 100 yards away. This advertising is likely to be substantially more effective than that received at a time and point separated from the buying decision. Wi-Fi has a huge future as an advertising medium for contacting business customers and everyday consumers.

Locating Hotspots

A challenge for Internet users is to locate hotspots where wireless Internet connection is possible. Now available are small and inexpensive Wi-Fi finders that facilitate locating hotspots. For example, a product called WiFi Seeker requires users to simply push a button and a light sweeping past four bars indicates when a Wi-Fi signal is detected. The WiFi Seeker also is useful for identifying the best place in a home or business for locating a base station.[37] Some cities such as Philadelphia have installed citywide Wi-Fi technology enabling Internet access virtually anywhere. Companies have developed inexpensive portable devices that make it possible for users to set up temporary Wi-Fi networks at locations of their choice. These devices (e.g., Apple Computer's AirPort Express) simply require that one have access to a high-speed Internet connection such as a DSL line; then by plugging the device into the connecting line a hotspot is created. A company called RaySat Inc. has developed a satellite antenna that turns moving vehicles into rolling hotspots.[38]

Mobile Phones and Text Messaging

Cellular phones, or mobile phones, are nearly ubiquitous. As of 2005, there were 180 million mobile phone subscribers in the United States and hundreds of millions more around the world.[39] Worldwide manufacturers shipped approximately 700 million mobile phones in 2005, and by 2008 shipments are expected to increase to nearly 900 million.[40] Most of these phones are equipped with Wi-Fi technology, which allows users virtually unlimited access to the Internet via their mobile phones.

© Dennis MacDonald/PhotoEdit

Americans until recently have used their mobile phones primarily as talking devices, but Europeans and Asians have for years used these phones for transmitting *text messages*. Americans are following suit. Short Message System (SMS) allows users to send and receive text messages on their mobile phones of up to 160 characters in length. Multimedia Messaging Service (MMS) is a more advanced technology that permits transmitting messages along with graphics and sound. In a sense, the mobile phone is emerging into what amounts almost to a small laptop computer. Indeed, mobile phones are being dubbed the *third screen*, meaning that TV (the first screen), computers (the second screen), and now mobile phones are common audiovisual devices for receiving information, entertainment, and advertisements.

The growing numbers of mobile phone users indicate considerable potential for advertisers to reach people through these devices. Younger consumers are especially viable targets. It is estimated that about 75 percent of teens ages 15 to 19 and 90 percent of people in their early 20s use their cell phones for text messaging on a regular basis.[41] Perhaps the more important issue, however, is whether people want to be contacted by advertisers. Because mobile phones are highly personal items (i.e., they go with us everywhere and often are in constant contact with our bodies), many critics of wireless advertising (as well as advertisers themselves) are concerned that unwanted messages represent an invasion of privacy. Feeling invaded, recipients of undesired advertisements may immediately delete the intruding item and hold negative feelings toward the offending advertiser—"How dare you send me a message for a product or service about which I have absolutely no interest!"

In addition to privacy invasion, others are skeptical about wireless advertising's future on the grounds that advertising is antithetical to the reasons that people own mobile phones in the first place. The argument, in other words, is that people own mobile phones for reasons of enhancing time utilization and increasing work-related productivity while away from the workplace or home, and the last thing they want while using these devices is to receive unwanted, interrupting advertising messages. Another potential limit on the immediate future of effective wireless advertising is that the small screens on mobile phones limit the space for presenting creative advertising messages.

It would seem, based on the downside arguments just noted, that advertising on mobile phones has distinct limitations. Only the future will tell for sure. It is certain at the present time, however, that many advertisers much desire the opportunity to reach prospective customers via their mobile phones. Another certainty is that successful text messaging from marketers must be based on an opt-in model, where message recipients have absolutely indicated their interest in receiving certain types of messages via mobile phones. Wireless ad recipients must, in other words, have complete *control* over the advertising content they are willing to receive as well as when and where they receive ad messages. Advertisers must secure the wireless device user's permission to send him or her ad messages and make the user a quid pro quo: if you grant me (the advertiser) permission to send messages to you regularly, say once a week, I will provide you with useful information on topics of interest to you. Such an arrangement benefits the interests of both advertiser and consumer and thus provides an opportunity for the advertising community to profit from ads placed on mobile phones.

Many who are skeptical of a successful future for mobile phone advertising nonetheless believe this ad medium may have value for local retailers such as restaurants, entertainment complexes, and various service operations. Retail outlets can send promotional offers, price discounts, and other pertinent information to consumers who are in the vicinity of the retailer's store. This is made possible by positioning systems (similar to the Global Positioning Satellite) that pinpoint a mobile phone user's location to a particular retail outlet within 100 feet or less (30.5 meters or less). For example, Jiffy Lube, the retail chain offering quick oil changes, tested the use of wireless advertisements in San Francisco. Recipients received oil change reminders on their pagers or cell phones whenever they passed a Jiffy Lube franchise and were promised an attractive discount if they came in for an oil change during nonpeak times.[42]

In the final analysis, mobile phones offer a potentially attractive advertising medium, but there are notable problems that may or may not be overcome. It is clear that spamming mobile phone users is totally ineffective and that successful advertisers must gain the user's permission and allow him or her control over message content and how often, when, and where message receipt is acceptable. The next several years will provide us with a rearview-mirror perspective on whether wireless advertising is merely a passing fad or a viable, long-term advertising medium.

Search Engine Advertising

There are thousands of companies with Web sites on the Internet promoting their goods and services and encouraging prospective customers to place orders. The competition is intense with many other firms promoting their own offerings. All of these competitors face the challenge of first getting prospective customers to visit their Web sites, and only subsequently can they hope to convert these Web surfers into actual purchasers. In view of the competitive intensity, how does a marketing organization attract prospective customers to its Web site? Well, of course, all of the previously discussed Internet advertising tools (display ads, rich media, e-mail, etc.) play a role in attracting people to Web sites. For the most part, however, these tools have limited ability to draw traffic to Web sites, this due in large part to the fact that most Internet users do not click through to Web sites that are encountered via intrusive banner ads, pop-ups, e-mail messages, and so on. There has to be a better way, and in fact there is. This better way is described with various terms such as *search engine marketing, search engine advertising, keyword search,* or simply *search. Search engine advertising* is the term preferred here insofar as the text focuses on marcom and advertising rather than all aspects of marketing. Further, the acronym for search engine advertising, SEA, nicely captures the idea that keywords are strategically placed in the Internet "sea" in hopes they will be found by the surfers located in this cyberspace sea.

The Fundamentals of Search Engine Advertising

So what does search engine advertising (SEA) entail? First, by way of numbers, it is the fastest growing form of Internet advertising and, based on the latest available data, SEA commanded 40 percent of the $9.6 billion U.S. marketers spent on online advertising.[43] A second key to understanding SEA is the realization that Internet search engines include a variety of well-known services that people use when seeking information as they perform what can be referred to as *natural searches*—for example, one enters the expression "inexpensive book bags" when searching online for items of this sort. Among the best-known search engines are Google, Yahoo! Search, MSN Search, and Ask Jeeves. Google and Yahoo! Search are the most used search engines and together account for over three-quarters of all searches.[44]

A third critical element of SEA is that this form of advertising attempts to place messages in front of people precisely when their

natural search efforts indicate they apparently are interested in buying a particular good or service. In this context, you might remember reading in Chapter 13 the following statement: Advertising achieves its effectiveness "through a chance encounter with a ready consumer."[45] Search engine advertising is, in many respects, the optimum form of advertising for purposes of increasing the chances of encountering ready consumers! That is, as described next in the context of "keywords," SEA places ads exactly where customers who are interested in particular goods or services are searching. In terms of the hierarchy of effects, such as discussed in Chapter 6, SEA can move people to action or serve equity-enhancing purposes in addition to performing a sales-generating role. The *IMC Focus* insert discusses SEA's equity-enhancement role.

A fourth key feature of SEA, and probably the most important, is the concept of *keywords.* **Keywords** are specific words and short phrases that describe the nature, attributes, and benefits of a marketer's offering. For example, suppose a consumer was performing an online search to locate a really specific product such as a *navy blue sports coat.* In performing a natural search for such an item, one consumer might input the expression "navy blue sports coat," another consumer when searching for the same item may simply input "blue blazer," yet another may enter "dress jacket." In other words, there are many ways that different consumers might perform searches for the same item. When I entered "navy blue sports coat" into the Google search line, slightly fewer than 1,000 matches were returned. Of most relevance to the present discussion, the right side of the Google results page listed eight sponsored links. These links were for companies that paid Google to advertise their Web sites. For example, the first two links were for Sierra Trading Post (http://www.sierratradingpost.com) and Shopping.com (http://shopping.com). Clicking through to the Web sites for these two companies led me to learn that both companies offer multiple products for sale, of which navy blue sports coats are just one of many. Please note that a future attempt to repeat this search would undoubtedly yield different results.

Now, from the perspective of a company that sells sports coats, it would be useful to have an ad for its product appear whenever consumers enter into a search engine any expression that might relate to navy blue sports coats. In other words, when natural search results are returned by Google, Yahoo! Search, Ask Jeeves, or any other search engine, companies would like to have their Web sites listed as sponsored links. Why so? Well, as mentioned previously, when I entered "navy blue sports coat," nearly 1,000 items were returned. Because each Google page lists only 10 items and considering that most people will look into maybe only about five pages, this means that over 950 potential items—including your company's listing—would never be seen unless it appeared somewhere on the first five pages of search results. Because advertising is all about increasing the odds that ready consumers will have a chance encounter with *your ad* (not just any ad), your task as an Internet advertiser is to increase the odds of that happening. Sponsored links to natural searches serve beautifully to accomplish this objective. The foregoing description can be summarized in the series of steps listed in Figure 15.1.

Figure 15.1

The Role of Keywords in Increasing the Odds That Ready Consumers Encounter Your Ad

Step 1: Prospective purchasers of a specific good or service perform natural search using one or more search engines to locate that item.

Step 2: Matches to Internet shopper's search are generated by Google or another search engine.

Step 3: Alongside the matches are sponsored links that correspond to the keyword(s) entered by the shopper.

Step 4: These sponsored links appear because companies offering the searched item purchased corresponding keywords from the search engine company.

Step 5: Shoppers may click through to a sponsored Web site and purchase a desired item or, at least, consider this Web site for future purchases.

Enhancing Brand Equity via Search Engine Advertising

imc focus

Search engine advertising has been dominated by sellers of goods and services such as Internet auctioneer eBay. For many firms the purpose of SEA is to generate quick sales. Firms, especially those operating in the B2B realm, are now using search ads not to generate immediate sales but rather to build brand awareness and improve brand images, or, in other words, to enhance brand equity. The computer chip maker Intel, for example, buys search ads that appear as sponsored links when Web surfers type any of nearly 10,000 keywords or phrases—such as "computer chips," "laptop computers," and "mobile computing." For example, at the time this material was written, users conducting a search for "mobile computing" saw an Intel ad appear on the right side of the search results as a sponsored link. Clicking on this link, searchers were taken to an animated Web site that promoted Intel's chips for laptop computers. Intel claimed that these search ads yielded positive results even when no immediate sales occurred. For example, many businesspeople download technical reports supplied by Intel that describe the merits of its products. This information can serve to influence future purchases of Intel products.

Pitney Bowes, a B2B marketer like Intel, also used to use search ads to sell its products online. It now is purchasing search ads increasingly as a means of enhancing its brand equity by driving prospective customers to its Web site where they can obtain technical reports on topics such as business security. Senior executives, who are difficult to reach via other forms of traditional and Internet advertising, are responsive to ads and Web sites that provide them with useful information.

SOURCE: Adapted from Kevin J. Delaney, "Your Ad Here, 10 Words Max," *Wall Street Journal Online*, March 24, 2005, http://online.wsj.com.

Purchasing Keywords and Selecting Content-Oriented Web Sites

There actually are two forms of search engine advertising available to online advertisers. One form, as described already, is keyword search (also called *keyword-matching*), and the other involves placing ads on content-oriented Web sites that provide appropriate contexts in which to advertise a particular type of product. Each form of SEA is described using Google's advertising services for illustration. Google is selected for illustration rather than another search engine insofar as it is by far the leading search engine.

Keyword-Matching Advertising

To become a sponsored link to Internet shoppers' search results, interested advertisers must bid for and purchase keywords from search engine services such as Google. For example, the obvious keywords that a sports coat advertiser might employ to attract consumers to its Web site would include terms and phrases such as "sports coats," "blazers," "blue blazer," "blue sports coat," "blue sports jacket," "wool sports coat," "moderately priced blazers," and so forth. Google has a keyword advertising program called AdWords.

Interested students can learn more about AdWords by reviewing the demonstration for that program at https://adwords.google.com. One will discover from the demonstration that prospective advertisers bid for keywords by indicating how much they are willing to pay each time an Internet shopper clicks on their Web site when it appears as a sponsored link. Options range from five cents to $100 for each click through. This is termed the *cost-per-click*, or simply CPC. The higher an advertiser's bid, the more prominent the placement of the advertiser's sponsored link. That is, the highest bidder per keyword receives the top placement, the second highest bidder the second placement, and so on. When purchasing keywords, advertisers also indicate the top amount they are willing to budget each day. So for example, if an advertiser is willing to pay only 20 cents per CPC for a keyword and specifies a daily budget limit of $30, then that advertiser could receive a maximum of 150 click throughs to its Web site on a given day.

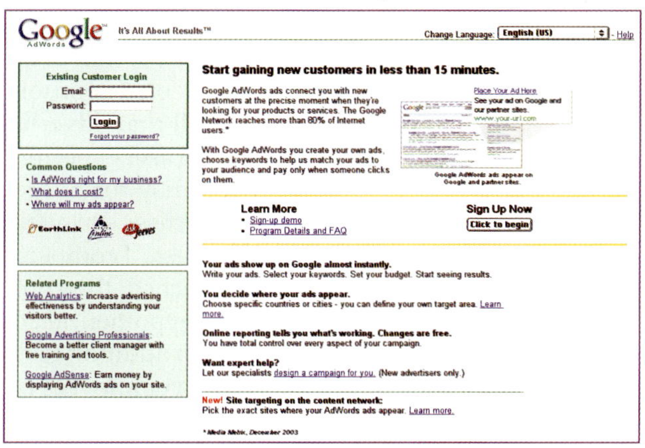

The keyword advertiser also can specify the country where ads are to be sponsored and particular local areas where ads are to be targeted. For example, advertisers of services provided in local communities are interested in reaching only people located in particular communities and surrounding areas. Google's AdWords program also provides advertisers with performance reports that indicate which keywords are generating the most click throughs and how much each keyword costs on average. Advertisers can then decide to drop usage of underperforming keywords or rebid how much they are willing to pay to use these words or phrases.

Content-Targeted Advertising

In addition to its AdWords service, Google has another program called AdSense. With this program, Google enables Internet advertisers to run ads on Web sites other than Google's own site. Advertisers specify the sites on which they want their ads to appear rather than picking keywords that are tied to Internet surfers' natural search behavior (as described previously for the AdWords program). Advertisers pay Google to run ads on selected Web sites, and then Google pays these Web sites about 80 percent of the revenue generated from advertisers.[46] In a sense, Google operates as an ad agency placing ads on other Web sites, taking as commission about 20 percent of the revenue and allowing the content-oriented Web sites to earn the bulk of the ad-placement cost.

This form of SEA is particularly attractive to marketers of products that people typically do not search for using keywords. For example, most people would not perform searches for staple products such as bread and milk; purchasing keywords for these products would likely yield few productive results. However, advertisers of these products could benefit greatly by placing ads on content-oriented Web sites that are devoted to matters of health and fitness. People who go to such Web sites might then encounter ads for bread or milk touting these products' health-related benefits. For example, at the time of this writing, widely circulated reports appeared in various media about the weight-loss benefits of drinking at least 24 ounces of milk daily along with undertaking a regular exercise regimen. The trade association responsible for promoting milk could take advantage of this publicity by placing ads on various health-oriented Web sites and linking the ads to media reports describing milk's weight-loss benefits.

In summary, SEA with programs such as Google's AdWords and AdSense provide Internet advertisers with ways to place their ads in places where prospective customers are searching and thus to increase the odds of encountering ready consumers. The advantages are clear (cost efficiency, pinpointed targeting, and quick and easy assessment of ad effectiveness), yet SEA is not without problems.

SEA Is Not without Problems

The major problem with search engine advertising, especially the keyword-matching variety, is that of click fraud. **Click fraud** occurs when a competitor or other party clicks on a sponsored link repeatedly in order to foul up advertising effectiveness. Recall that advertisers pay for sponsored links on a cost-per-click basis, and that advertisers specify an upper limit on how much they are willing to budget daily. You may further recall that at 20 cents per click and with a daily limit of $30, the advertiser can achieve a total of only 150 click throughs on a given day. That being the case, a competitor could repeatedly click on a sponsored link until the 150 limit is reached, thus precluding any legitimate click throughs from happening. As such, our hypothetical advertiser would receive zero benefit from its modest investment.

In addition to competitors engaging in click fraud, this practice also takes place when employees of content-oriented Web sites repeatedly click on advertised Web sites so as to increase the revenue paid to them by a search engine such as Google.

Again, advertisers suffering from fraudulent click throughs receive no benefit from their advertising. So-called bot software programs (short for *robot*) are used to automatically click on ads repeated times, thereby generating a lot of revenue for Web sites and wasting advertisers' honest investment that is intended to enhance their brand images and drive sales.

Estimates of the magnitude of click fraud range from 5 percent to 20 percent.[47] The magnitude of the problem prompted a top executive at Google to describe click fraud as "the biggest threat to the Internet economy" and to encourage that something be done as quickly as possible to curtail the problem before it threatens the SEA business model.[48]

Advertising via Behavioral Targeting

This form of online advertising was introduced back in Chapter 4 when discussing marcom targeting more generally. It was pointed out that companies such as Revenue Science and Tacoda Systems track Internet users' surfing behaviors and provide this information to advertisers that wish to target prospective customers based on their online search behavior. For example, a prospective furniture company could employ the services of Tacoda Systems to identify people who frequently visit Web sites that provide furniture-related content. (It is technologically simple to identify Web users' site-selection behavior by inserting cookies on computers to indicate which Web sites have been visited.) Having identified prospective furniture purchasers—as revealed by their Internet search habits—a furniture advertiser could then serve up ads to these people whenever they subsequently visit furniture-related Web sites. Because unlike with content-oriented SEA where the advertiser must pay for every person who has an opportunity to see the advertiser's message, with behavioral targeting only those consumers known to be interested in furniture would receive ads from our hypothetical furniture marketer. By being selective, it would be possible for this advertiser to place ads on many more Web sites than it could afford when employing a relatively indiscriminate content-oriented campaign.

The essence of online behavioral targeting is thus a matter of directing online advertisements to just those individuals who most likely are interested—as indicated by their online site-selection behavior—in making a purchase decision for a particular product category. Many argue that behavioral targeting takes Internet advertising to a level higher than that provided by SEA. In fact, one practitioner has dubbed behavioral targeting "search [engine advertising] on steroids."[49]

As always is the case with any form of advertising, behavioral targeting is not without its disadvantages. The most notable of these is that this form of targeting can be viewed as an invasion of people's privacy. Simply, many people feel violated knowing that their Web-search behavior is being closely tracked.

Measuring Internet Ad Effectiveness

A major concern for Internet advertisers is *measuring* the effectiveness of their advertising placements. This is, of course, precisely the same concern that brand managers have when advertising in conventional media, as was mentioned in the previous chapter when discussing audience measurement in the context of each of the major conventional media. You will recall, for example, the services available for magazine audience measurement (Mediamark Research Inc. and Simmons Market Research Bureau), radio audience measurement (Arbitron's RADAR service), and television audience measurement (Nielsen's people meters). In every instance, these audience measurement services have been developed to determine as precisely as possible the numbers of readers, listeners, or viewers of particular advertising vehicles and to identify their demographic characteristics. With the conventional media as a benchmark, the student can easily appreciate that Internet advertisers have precisely the same measurement concerns: How many people clicked through a particular Web ad? What are the demographic characteristics of these people? How many visited a particular Web site? What actions were taken following click throughs or site visits.

The Tools of Internet Audience Measurement

Three primary methods of Internet audience measurement are in use: (1) analysis of server log files, (2) surveys of sample users using recall measurement, and (3) electronic measurement of a sample of Internet users.[50] Each of these measurement methods is briefly discussed. *Log-file analysis* involves examining server log files. When a file is requested from a particular Web site, its computer server records the request in a so-called log file along with any subsequent actions taken by the Web user. Hence, the primary advantage of log file analysis is that it effectively provides a census of all user activity at a particular Web site. The downside of this analysis, however, is that it tracks machines and provides no information about the people who request particular files. Another drawback of this type of analysis is the difficulty of distinguishing individual users from the computer programs, called *robots* and *spiders,* that companies create to automatically surf the Internet and covertly gather competitive information.

The second tool, *surveys of sample users using recall measures,* involves the use of survey methods (telephone interviews, mail questionnaires, or in-person interviews) to obtain information about consumers' Web-site use along with their demographic and perhaps psychographic characteristics. The objective is, of course, to relate Web-site use as recalled from memory by interviewees to their demographic and psychographic characteristics. The problems with this method include the fact that: (1) memories are fallible, (2) people overstate their use of popular Web sites and understate their use of less popular sites, and (3) people often provide responses that involve putting themselves in a positive light rather than necessarily revealing their true Internet use (socially desirable responding). These limitations are not unique to Internet usage measurement. You will recall from the previous chapter that radio and magazine audience measurements also use survey techniques and thus suffer from the same deficiencies.

Electronic measurement of a sample of users is possibly the most valuable tool for assessing Internet usage activity. Software meters are installed in the computers of a large sample of Internet users, and this software records electronically precisely how each sampled user actually uses the Internet. Statistical procedures are used to draw inferences from the electronically metered sample to the population of Internet users. Companies such as Media Metrix and Nielsen Media Research are among the best-known researchers using electronic measurement. Nielsen, for example, attaches software tracking meters to the computers of a panel of 30,000 randomly selected Internet users.[51] These meters allow Nielsen to record everything the sampled users do online—which sites they visit, how long they stay at each site, which ad banners they click on, and so on. This information is sent instantly to a central database, which enables Nielsen to prepare periodic reports on Internet traffic and usage. Because each panel member provides Nielsen with information about gender, educational level, income, household size, geographic location, and other pertinent data, it subsequently is possible for Nielsen to link this demographic information with use of particular Web sites. The characteristics of users of particular Web sites thus are acquired from this electronic metering, and brand managers can then target ads to Web sites that best match the demographic characteristics of the brand's target market.

Metrics for Measuring Internet Ad Performance

The word *metric* refers, in general, to a unit of measurement. As applied in the present context, the issue is one of which particular indicators are most appropriate for assessing the effectiveness of Web sites and ads placed in these sites. Thinking of Web sites as a type of advertising *vehicle,* as that term was used in the previous chapter when discussing traditional ad media, the measurement issue is one of assessing the worth or effectiveness of Web-site vehicles. In actuality, a wide variety of metrics are used because advertisers have different measurement objectives. There are at least four general objectives, as follows, for assessing Website advertising effectiveness and (in parentheses) a variety of metrics that can be used to indicate whether the objective has been accomplished:[52]

1. The *exposure value or popularity* of a Web site or Internet ad (e.g., number of users exposed to an ad, number of unique visitors, and click-through rate)
2. The ability of a site to *attract and hold users' attention* and the *quality of customer relationships* (e.g., average time per visit, number of visits by unique visitors, and average interval between user visits)
3. The *usefulness* of Web sites (e.g., proportion of repeat visitors)
4. The *ability to target users* (e.g., profile of Web-site visitors and visitors' previous Web-site search behavior)

It should be apparent that many metrics are used to assess the effectiveness of Web sites and the ads placed on those sites. Because detailed discussion of these metrics is beyond the scope of this text, brief discussion is devoted to just three widely used metrics: click-through rates, cost per thousand impressions, and cost per action.

Click-through rates, as mentioned several times already, simply represent the percentage of people who are exposed to, say, an Internet-delivered ad and actually clicked their mouse on it. The click-through percentage has continued to decline, especially for banner ads, and many in the advertising community have become disenchanted with this metric—though some claim that banner ads can have a positive effect on brand awareness even if Internet users do not click through to learn more about the advertised brand.

Cost per thousand impressions (CPM) is a simple alternative to click-through rates that assesses how much (on a per-thousand-impressions basis) it costs to place an ad on a particular Web site. The only information revealed by the CPM metric is what it costs (again, on a per-thousand-impressions basis) to have an ad come into potential contact with the eyeballs of Internet users. This measure captures Internet users' *opportunity to see* (OTS) an ad but provides no information about the actual effect of an advertisement.

Use of the CPM metric is beginning to give way to the cost-per-action, or CPA, metric. The *action* in cost-per-action refers to determining the number of users who actually click on a display or rich-media ad, visit a brand's Web site, register their names on the brand's site, or purchase the advertised brand. Many advertisers prefer to pay for Internet advertising on a CPA rather than a CPM basis. The terms of purchasing Internet advertising on a CPA basis vary greatly, with higher prices paid for actions involving actual purchases or actions closer to purchase (such as registering for free samples of a brand) compared with merely clicking on a banner ad.

In the final analysis it should be apparent that there is no such thing as perfect measurability—for the Internet or for that matter any other advertising medium. The difficulty of determining how effective is an ad medium is illustrated, in the extreme, by the following set of questions: "Consider the Nike logo on Tiger Woods's baseball cap: Does it make you more likely to buy a pair of the company's shoes? If so, would you admit it to a surveyor? Would you admit it to yourself? Would you even know it?"[53]

Summary

This chapter has covered a variety of online advertising media. Table 15.1 structured the discussion by identifying specific forms of Internet advertising. Online advertising spending in the United States amounted to over $9.6 billion in 2004 and is expected to grow to as much as $26 billion by 2010. In comparison to most other advertising media, the Internet possesses the two key features of individualization and interactivity. These features allow users to control the information they receive and the amount of time and effort devoted to processing advertising messages.

The bulk of the chapter discussed various forms of Internet advertising media. First, Web sites were considered the centerpiece of companies' online advertising efforts, with other advertising formats (e.g., banners, e-mail, and paid searches) serving to drive traffic to companies' sites. Display, or banner, ads are the most popular form of Internet advertising, though click-through rates are notoriously low. Because CTRs to displays are trivially small, online advertisers have turned to new technology and larger ad sizes to grab the online surfer's attention. Rich-media formats such as pop-ups, interstitials, superstitials, and video ads have experienced increased usage due to their ability to attract attention. The downside of rich-media ads is that Internet users find them intrusive and annoying.

Web logs (blogs) were described as a potential advertising vehicle, but one with an uncertain future in view of the fact that users' reasons for blogging is antithetical to the role and purpose of advertising. The ubiquity of blogs, including the radio-type version known as *podcasts,* makes this an attractive prospect for advertisers, but only time will tell whether advertising on blogs is an economically viable option. It simply is too early to know.

E-mail advertising has fallen in importance due to the "spoiling of the commons" resulting from excessive spamming and phishing. Permission-based, or opt-in, e-mail is an effort to legitimize the use of e-mail advertising, but many consumers simply do not like being advertised to on the Internet. E-mail magazines (e-zines) represent a more acceptable advertising medium, insofar as ads are clearly labeled for what they are, which explains why this form of sponsored e-mail is on the rise. Also, given the huge increase in wireless devices such as Wi-Fi–enabled laptops, personal digital assistants, and mobile phones, advertisers covet the opportunity to reach people when they are away from their homes and workplaces. Again, only time will tell whether, for example, mobile phones represent a viable advertising medium.

Search engine advertising (SEA) is the form of Internet advertising that commands the largest advertising investment in capturing about 40 percent of all online ad expenditures. The fundamental concept underlying SEA is that advertisements can be located where consumers and B2B customers are searching. In other words, SEA increases the odds of encountering the ready consumer. Two forms of SEA are widely used: keyword matching and placing ads on content-oriented Web sites that match the advertiser's offering.

Behavioral targeting is a final form of Internet advertising discussed in this chapter. This form of advertising directs ads just to those individuals who most likely are interested in purchasing a particular good or service as indicated by their past online site-selection behavior. Many argue that behavioral targeting takes Internet advertising to a level higher than even SEA. In fact, one practitioner has dubbed behavioral targeting as search engine advertising on steroids.

The final topic discussed was measuring Internet ad effectiveness. Log-file analysis, surveys to measure recall, and electronic measurement were described as the tools of Internet audience measurement. Explained also were three specific metrics for measuring ad performance, namely, click-through rates, cost per thousand impressions, and cost per action.

Discussion Questions

1. As noted in the text, some observers have gone so far as to claim that traditional advertising is on its deathbed and will eventually be supplanted by Internet advertising. What are your views on this?
2. Provide an interpretation of the meaning and importance for advertisers of the Internet's two *i*'s, individualization and interactivity. Use your own words and ideas rather than merely feeding back what is described in the text.
3. The text described the Internet user as being in a "leaning-forward" mind-set compared with, say, the TV viewer who is "leaning back." Explain what this means and why the distinction is advantageous or problematic for Internet advertisers.
4. Describe your typical response behavior to Internet ads. That is, do you often click on banner ads? What's your reaction to pop-ups, interstitials, and superstitials?
5. Can banner ads be effective if less than 0.3 percent of all people click through these ads? Use the consumer processing model from Chapter 5 to frame your response.
6. Do you believe that Internet companies' use of cookies invades your privacy? Would you favor legislation that prevents the use of this technology? If such a law were passed, what would be the downside from the consumer's perspective?
7. Have you personally downloaded ad-blocking software onto your computer? What are the implications of this practice if millions of consumers had ad-blocking software loaded on their PCs and other Internet appliances?
8. The following set of questions was quoted in the chapter in reference to the Nike logo on Tiger Woods's baseball cap: Does it make you more likely to buy a pair of the company's shoes? If so, would you admit it to a surveyor? Would you admit it to yourself? Would you even know it? What implications do these questions (and their answers) hold for measuring Internet advertising effectiveness?
9. The Cookie Central Web site (http://www.cookiecentral.com) is dedicated to explaining exactly what cookies are and what they can do. Visit this site and present a discussion on how cookies can be and are used to compile lists for behavioral targeting purposes.
10. What has been your personal experience with e-mail advertising? Are you part of any opt-in lists whereby you receive regular (say once a week) e-mail messages? What proportion of the e-mail messages do you receive on a daily basis that you would consider spam?
11. One virtue of e-mail advertising is that different messages for the same product or service can be mailed to various customer groups who differ with respect to pertinent buyographic, demographic, or other characteristics. This ability to "mass customize" messages should increase marcom effectiveness, yet a cynic might look at this practice as a bit deceptive—somehow saying different things about your product to different audiences seems misleading. What is your view on this?
12. E-mail advertising is claimed to be very effective for viral marketing purposes—that is, buzz generation. This is accomplished by requesting an e-mail recipient to forward the message to a friend. Return to the discussion of buzz generation in Chapter 7 along with the *Global Focus* insert in the present chapter, and then present your views on the effectiveness of the e-mail viral marketing practice. In other words, explain what makes e-mail buzz generation effective or not.
13. Behavioral targeting was characterized as search engine advertising on steroids. Explain what the practitioner who used this clever expression had in mind.

14. From the perspective of an advertiser for a product such as cereal, compare and contrast the strengths and weaknesses of the two forms of search engine advertising: keyword-matching versus content-targeted advertising.
15. It was claimed when discussing e-mail advertising that advertisers using this medium may be accused of spoiling the commons. Explain what this means and then indicate whether you agree or disagree with this statement.
16. What, in your view, is the potential of using blogs as an advertising medium?
17. What, in your view, is the potential of using mobile phones as an advertising medium?

ENDNOTES

1. *US Online Marketing Forecast: 2005 to 2010,* Forrester Research, Inc., May 2005, http://www.centerformediaresearch.com.
2. Gavin O'Malley, "BURST!: Internet Continues Snagging Eyeballs from TV," MediaPost Publications, http://publications.mediapost.com.
3. Roland T. Rust and Richard W. Oliver, "Notes and Comments: The Death of Advertising," *Journal of Advertising* 23 (December 1994), 71–77. See also Roland T. Rust and Sajeev Varki, "Rising from the Ashes of Advertising," *Journal of Business Research* 37 (November 1996), 173–181.
4. For example, Rafi A. Mohammed, Robert J. Fisher, Bernard J. Jaworski, and Aileen M. Cahill, *Internet Marketing: Building Advantage in a Networked Economy* (New York: McGraw-Hill, 2002), 370.
5. Ibid., 375.
6. Stephen Baker, "The Online Ad Surge," *BusinessWeek,* November 22, 2004, 76–82.
7. Kate Fitzgerald, "Debate Grows Over Net Data," *Advertising Age,* March 15, 2004, 4, 78.
8. The 2004 figure is from "Interactive Advertising Revenues Grow Nearly 33% As 2004 Totals $9.6 Billion," Internet Advertising Bureau, April 28, 2005, http://www.iab.net/news/pr_2005_4_27.asp. The 2010 forecast is from Wendy Davis, "Forrester: Online Ad Spend to Reach $14.7 Billion in 2005," *Online Media Daily,* May 4, 2005, http://publications.mediapost.com/index.cfm?
9. Kris Oser, "New Ad Kings: Yahoo, Google," *Advertising Age,* April 25, 2005, 1, 50.
10. Mohammed et al., *Internet Marketing: Building Advantage in a Networked Economy,* 371.
11. For more formal treatments of the concept of interactivity, see the following sources: Yuping Liu and L. J. Shrum, "What Is Interactivity and Is It Always Such a Good Thing? Implications of Definition, Person, and Situation for the Influence of Interactivity on Advertising Effectiveness," *Journal of Advertising* 31 (winter 2002), 53–64; Sally J. McMillan and Jang-Sun Hwang, "Measures of Perceived Interactivity: An Exploration of the Role of Direction of Communication, User Control, and Time in Shaping Perceptions of Interactivity," *Journal of Advertising* 31 (fall 2002), 29–42; and Yuping Liu, "Developing a Scale to Measure the Interactivity of Websites," *Journal of Advertising Research* 43 (June 2003), 207–216.
12. The ideas in this paragraph are adapted from Terry Lefton, "The Great Flameout," *The Industry Standard,* March 19, 2001, 75–78.
13. Shelly Rodgers and Esther Thorson, "The Interactive Advertising Model: How Users Perceive and Process Online Ads," *Journal of Interactive Advertising* 1 (fall 2000), http://jiad.org/vol1/no1/Rodgers/index.html.
14. Jean Halliday, "Half Hit Web before Showrooms," *Advertising Age,* October 4, 2004, 76.
15. Fred Zufryden, "New Film Website Promotion and Box-Office Performance," *Journal of Advertising Research* 40 (January/April 2000), 55–64.
16. I learned this advice from my dear late father, who worked in retailing for many years. I'm not sure whether this was his own wisdom or whether it can be attributed to another source.
17. Julie S. Stevenson, Gordon C. Bruner II, and Anand Kumar, "Webpage Background and Viewer Attitudes," *Journal of Advertising Research* 40 (January/April 2000), 29–34. See also Gordon C. Bruner II, and Anand Kumar, "Web Commercials and Advertising Hierarchy-of-Effects," *Journal of Advertising Research* 40 (January/April 2000), 35–42. The latter article involves research using a non-student sample and provides interesting refinement concerning the role of Web-page complexity.
18. Gerald J. Gorn, Amitava Chattopadhyay, Jaideep Sengupta, and Shashank Tripathi, "Waiting for the Web: How Screen Color Affects Time Perception," *Journal of Marketing Research* 41 (May 2004), 215–225.
19. Ritu Lohtia, Naveen Donthus, and Edmund K. Hershberger, "The Impact of Content and Design Elements on Banner Advertising Click-through Rates," *Journal of Advertising Research* 43 (December 2003), 410–418.
20. Micael Dahlen, "Banner Advertisements through a New Lens," *Journal of Advertising Research* 41 (July/August 2001), 23–30.
21. "Interactive Advertising Bureau/Dynamic Logic Ad Unit Effectiveness Study," Interactive Advertising Bureau, March/June 2001, http://www.iab.net.
22. For an interesting application, see Lee Sherman and John Deighton, "Banner Advertising: Measuring Effectiveness and Optimizing Placement," *Journal of Interactive Marketing* 15 (spring 2001), 60–64.
23. Alex Frangos, "How It Works: The Technology Behind Web Ads," *Wall Street Journal Online,* April 23, 2001, http://online.wsj.com.
24. For reading on privacy and ethical issues in interactive marketing, see the special issue of *Journal of Public Policy & Marketing* 19 (spring 2000), 1–73.

25. Rodgers and Thorson, "The Interactive Advertising Model: How Users Perceive and Process Online Ads."
26. Jack Neff, "Spam Research Reveals Disgust with Pop-up Ads," *Advertising Age,* August 25, 2003, 1, 21.
27. Tobi Elkin, "Just an Online Minute . . . BlogNation," May 4, 2005, minute@mediapost.com, http://www.mediapost.com, accessed May 4, 2005.
28. Stephen Baker and Heather Green, "Blogs Will Change Your Business," *BusinessWeek,* May 2, 2005, 57–67.
29. Baker and Green, "Blogs Will Change Your Business," 57.
30. Jessica Mintz, "Many Advertisers Find Blogging Frontier Is Still Too Wild," *Wall Street Journal Online,* March 25, 2005, http://online.wsj.com.
31. Albert Maruggi, "Podcasting Offers a Sound Technique," *Brandweek,* May 2, 2005, 21.
32. The current estimate is from eMarketer, April 2004, as reproduced in "E-Mail Advertising Spending in the U.S., 2000–2005," *BtoB's Interactive Marketing Guide,* 2005, 14.
33. "DoubleClick's 2004 Consumer Email Study," DoubleClick, October 2004, http://www.doubleclick.com.
34. Jane E. Zarem, "Predicting the Next Email Business Model," *1to1 Magazine,* May/June 2001, 23.
35. "FTC Recommends Bounty to Nab Spammers," *Wall Street Journal Online,* September 16, 2004, http://online.wsj.com.
36. Elizabeth Weinstein, "Retailers Tap E-Zines to Reach Niche Audiences," *Wall Street Journal Online,* April 28, 2005, http://online.wsj.com.
37. David LaGesse, "Hunting for the Hottest Wi-Fi Spots," *U.S. News and World Report,* August 2, 2004, 84.
38. Don Clark, "Wi-Fi Access to Be Offered in Cars," *Wall Street Journal Online,* January 5, 2005, http://online.wsj.com.
39. Kathleen M. Joyce, "Missing the Medium," *Promo,* August 2004, 37–43.
40. Roger O. Crockett, "iPod Killers?," *BusinessWeek,* April 25, 2005, 64.
41. Jyoti Thottam, "How Kids Set the (Ring) Tone," *Time,* April 4, 2005, 38–45.
42. Jeff Green, "Leveraging the Lube Job," *Brandweek,* July 17, 2000, 48–50.
43. "Interactive Advertising Revenues Grow Nearly 33% As 2004 Totals $9.6 Billion."
44. Danny Sullivan, "Nielsen NetRatings Search Engine Ratings," Search Engine Watch, April 22, 2005, http://searchenginewatch.com.
45. Erwin Ephron, "Recency Planning," *Journal of Advertising Research* 37 (July/August 1997), 61.
46. Kevin J. Delaney, "Google to Target Brands in Revenue Push," *Wall Street Journal Online,* April 25, 2005, http://online.wsj.com.
47. Ibid.
48. Ibid.
49. Richard Karpinski, "Behavioral Targeting," *i.Intelligence,* spring 2004, 16.
50. Steve Coffey, "Internet Audience Measurement: A Practitioner's View," *Journal of Interactive Advertising* 1 (spring 2001), http://jiad.org/vol1/no2/coffey/index.html. Much of the following discussion is based on this article.
51. This discussion is based on Chris Warren, "Tools of the Trade," *Critical Mass,* fall 1999, 22–27.
52. Subodh Bhat, Michael Bevans, and Sanjit Sengupta, "Measuring Users' Web Activity to Evaluate and Enhance Advertising Effectiveness," *Journal of Advertising* 31 (fall 2002), 97–106. This source identified a fifth objective (comarketing success) that is not listed here.
53. Rob Walker, "The Holy Grail of Internet Advertising, the Ability to Measure Who Is Clicking on the Message, Is Under Assault," *New York Times,* August 27, 2001, C4.

CHAPTER 16
Using Other Advertising Media

Marcom Challenge: Some Definitions Encapsulating This Chapter

Clutter—A state or condition of confusion or disorderliness

Direct—Proceeding to a target by the shortest route

Precision—The state or quality of being exact

Ingenuity—The quality of being clever or skillful in producing or designing something

The preceding terms and their definitions are relevant for appreciating the various forms of "other" advertising media that are described in this chapter. The text up to this chapter has reviewed the major forms of mass-media and online advertising. The present chapter explores a number of other media that provide alternatives to the better known and more traditional advertising media.

These other media—direct advertising through the postal service; advertising messages delivered in the form of videotapes, CD-ROMs, and DVDs; yellow pages advertising; videogame advertising (a.k.a. adver-gaming); product placements in movies, in songs, and elsewhere; cinema advertising; and so on—are increasingly being used to avoid the *clutter* problem that characterizes the mass media.

Clutter, as defined previously, is a state of confusion or disorderliness. The traditional media and the Internet represent a disorderly state for individual advertisers inasmuch as their attempts to capture the viewer's or listener's attention is offset by the efforts of hundreds of other advertisers to accomplish the same goal. Any advertiser's message is easily lost amid the confusion caused by consumers being inundated by one advertisement after another.

Some of these other media, though not necessarily all, reach the target market via a *direct* route rather than through an intermediary such as a television network. For example, postal advertising and audio-video advertising (for example, via CD-ROMs and DVDs) are direct forms of advertising. Direct advertising provides advertisers with a means of targeting messages to a target market that has been selected with *precision*. This is to say that direct advertising results in fewer wasted exposures and thus more efficient delivery of advertising messages.

But accomplishing precision is not limited to advertising delivered via direct channels. For example, product placements inserted in movies and in music recordings enable advertisers to reach desired target audiences with greater precision than is typically the case when placing ads in the context of TV programs, in newspapers, or in other mass media. This is because the audiences for particular movies and the fans of individual recording artists tend to share many lifestyle and demographic characteristics.

Finally, the advertiser's choice of other ad media is limited only by the lack of *ingenuity.* With skill and cleverness, advertisers can use any of an endless number of ad media to reach target audiences efficiently and effectively. Virtually any blank surface can become a channel for delivering ad messages. For example, advertisements are placed on vehicles (buses and taxis), in restrooms, in the sky (skywriting), in sporting venues, in shopping malls, and even as temporary tattoos on peoples' foreheads and on other body parts. The options are virtually limitless, bounded only by the lack of ingenuity.

© Robert Brenner/PhotoEdit

CHAPTER OBJECTIVES

1

Explain why postal mail advertising is an efficient and effective ad medium.

2

Understand p-mail's five distinctive features compared to mass forms of advertising.

3

Appreciate the role of database marketing, data mining, and lifetime-value analysis.

4

Understand the role of audio-video advertising.

5

Appreciate the value of yellow-pages advertising.

6

Recognize the growth and role of video-game advertising (adver-gaming).

7

Appreciate branded entertainment and brand placements in various venues (movies, TV, etc.).

8

Understand the role of cinema advertising and Web films.

9

Appreciate the potential value of various other ad media.

Overview

This chapter, as the title suggests, deals with the general topic of other advertising media. The vague term *other media* is used here to include all forms of advertising that were *not* previously covered and will not be subsequently treated in this text. As such, mass-media advertising via traditional media such as television and magazines (the topic of Chapter 14) and Internet advertising (Chapter 15) are excluded. Word-of-mouth advertising and buzz generation (Chapter 7) are outside the scope of the present chapter. Also, out-of-home advertising, external store signage, and point-of-purchase advertising (Chapter 8) were previously covered. Finally, advertising via sales promotion vehicles such as freestanding inserts (Chapter 18) and advertising that takes place at sponsored events and in support of worthy causes (Chapter 20) are covered in subsequent chapters.

Now that we know which topics aren't covered in the present chapter, it will be useful to overview the topics that are examined. Table 16.1 facilitates this discussion. It can be seen that "other" forms of advertising are broadly delineated along two dimensions: whether the advertising is direct or indirect, and whether it is delivered to homes and workplaces or at any of a virtually infinite number of public venues. *Direct advertising* is delivered to individuals' homes or workplaces typically via postal mail in the form of print materials (e.g., direct mail and catalogs) or in a digital or electronic form such as DVDs and CD-ROMs. *Indirect advertising* is delivered either to homes and workplaces (e.g., via the Yellow Pages and in video games) or at a variety of public venues. The fact is that advertisements can be delivered in virtually any public environment in which messages can be printed, sung, blared, or announced. Ads appear on blimps, restroom walls, T-shirts, buses and bus stops, shopping carts, store floors, race cars, boats, athletes' apparel, and signs that trail behind small airplanes. Advertisements also appear as product placements in movies and television programs. These "special purpose" media are minor, albeit growing, in relation to the traditional advertising media and the rapidly growing Internet medium.

Direct Advertising

Postal Mail Advertising

The prior chapter discussed advertising on the Web in its various forms, including discussion of e-mail advertising. This section of the chapter includes detailed coverage of nonelectronic mail advertising, or postal mail. **Postal mail advertising**,

Table 16.1
Framework for Various Forms of "Other" Advertising

	Advertising Directed to Private Venues (Homes and Workplaces)	Advertising Delivered at Private and Public Venues
Direct Advertising	• Postal mail delivery • Video ads (VCRs, CD-ROMs, and DVDs)	Not applicable
Indirect Advertising	• Yellow pages • Video games	• Brand placements in movies, TV programs, and songs • Cinema advertising and Web films • Virtual signage • Miscellaneous alternative media

or, for short, *p-mail* in parallel to e-mail, refers to any advertising matter delivered by the postal service to the person whom the marketer wishes to influence. These advertisements can take the form of letters, postcards, programs, calendars, folders, catalogs, videocassettes, blotters, order blanks, price lists, menus, and so on.

At least four factors account for the widespread use of p-mail by B2B as well as B2C marketers. First, the *rising cost of television advertising* and *increasing audience fragmentation* have led many advertisers to reduce investments in the television medium. Second, p-mailing enables *unparalleled targeting* of messages to desired prospects. Why? Because, according to one expert, it is "a lot better to talk to 20,000 prospects than 2 million suspects."[1] Third, increased emphasis on *measurable advertising results* has encouraged advertisers to use the medium—namely, p-mail—that most clearly identifies how many prospects purchased the advertised product. Fourth, many *consumers have favorable attitudes* toward mail advertisements and would be disappointed if they could not get direct mail offers and catalogs.

Illustration of a Successful P-mail Campaign

A direct-mail campaign for the Saab 9–5 typifies effective p-mailing.[2] The Saab 9–5 represented Saab's first entry in the luxury category and was designed to compete against well-known high-equity brands, including Mercedes, BMW, Volvo, Lexus, and Infiniti. A total of 200,000 consumers, including 65,000 current Saab owners and 135,000 prospects, were targeted with the objective of encouraging them to test-drive the 9–5. The Martin Agency of Richmond, Virginia, developed an IMC strategy, prominent among which were multiple p-mailings. The effort was designed to engage prospects in a dialogue about the new 9–5 and to learn more about their automobile purchase interests. Mailings provided prospects with brand details and made an appealing offer for them to test-drive the 9–5. Names of the most qualified prospects were then fed to dealers for follow-up.

The Martin Agency designed four mailings: (1) an initial mailing announced the new Saab 9–5, provided a photo of the car, and requested recipients to complete a survey of their automobile purchase interests and needs; (2) a subsequent qualification mailing provided respondents to the first mailing with product information addressing their specific purchase interests (performance, safety, versatility, etc.) and offered a test-drive kit as an incentive for returning an additional survey; (3) a third mailing included a special issue from *Road & Track* magazine that was devoted to the Saab 9–5's product development process; and (4) a final test-drive kit mailing extended an offer for recipients to test-drive the 9–5 for three hours and also provided an opportunity for prospects to win an all-expenses-paid European driving adventure (through Germany, Italy, and Sweden) as incentive for test-driving the 9–5.

An outbound telemarketing campaign was conducted as a follow-up to the p-mailings. Telephone calls were made to all people who responded to the initial mailings as well as to all prospects who had automobile leases or loans that were expiring. These callings reinforced the European test-drive offer and set up times for local dealers to call back to schedule test-drives. The direct marketing effort for the 9–5 was fabulously successful. Of the 200,000 initial prospects who were contacted by the introductory mailing, 16,000 indicated interest in test-driving the 9–5 (an 8 percent response rate), and more than 2,200 test-drives were scheduled.

P-mail's Distinctive Features

P-mail expenditures are huge. In the United States alone, more than $50 billion is annually invested in p-mailing.[3] These expenditures include B2B as well as B2C direct mailings. The recent growth in p-mailing is largely attributable to many marketers' concern with e-mail limitations resulting from spam issues and firewall protection. Because the vast majority of e-mailings never get delivered or are instantaneously deleted on the assumption they are spam, or junk, many marketing people now regard p-mail as a more efficient form of direct marketing and a better ROI. P-mailing offers five distinctive features as compared to mass forms of advertising efforts: targetability, measurability, accountability, flexibility, and efficiency:

- *Targetability.* P-mail is capable of targeting a precisely defined group of people. For example, The Martin Agency selected just 200,000 consumers to receive mailings for the Saab 9–5. These included 65,000 current Saab owners and 135,000 prospects who satisfied income and car ownership requirements, and other hurdles.
- *Measurability.* It is possible with p-mail to determine exactly how effective the advertising effort was because the marketer knows how many mailings were sent and how many people responded. This enables ready calculations of cost per inquiry and cost per order. As previously noted, more than 2,200 consumers signed up for test-drives of the Saab 9–5. Proprietary dealer sales data reveal how many of the initial 200,000 mailings resulted in purchases.
- *Accountability.* As has been repeatedly pointed out in this text, marcom practitioners are increasingly being required to justify the results of their communications efforts. P-mailing simplifies this task because results can be readily demonstrated (as in the case of the Saab 9–5) and brand managers can justify budget allocations to p-mail.
- *Flexibility.* Effective p-mail can be produced relatively quickly (compared with, say, producing a TV commercial), so it is possible for a company to launch a p-mail campaign that meets changing circumstances. For example, if inventory levels are excessive, a quick postcard or letter may serve to reduce the inventory. P-mail also offers the advantage of permitting the marketer to test communications ideas on a small-scale basis quickly and out of the view of competitors. Comparatively, a mass-media effort cannot avoid the competition's eyes. P-mail also is flexible in the sense that it has no constraints in terms of form, color, or size (other than those imposed by cost and practical considerations). It also is relatively simple and inexpensive to change p-mail ads. Compare this with the cost of changing a television commercial.
- *Efficiency.* P-mail makes it possible to direct communications efforts only to a highly targeted group, such as the 200,000 consumers who received mailings for the Saab 9–5. The cost-efficiency resulting from such targeting is considerable compared with mass-advertising efforts.

An alleged disadvantage of p-mail is its *expense.* On a cost-per-thousand (CPM) basis, p-mail typically is more expensive than other media. For example, the CPM for a particular mailing may be as high as $200 to $300, whereas a magazine's CPM might be as low as $4. However, compared with other media, p-mail is much less wasteful and will usually produce the highest percentage of responses. Thus, on a *cost-per-order basis,* p-mail is often a better bargain.

Perhaps the major problem with p-mail is that many people consider it excessively *intrusive and invasive of privacy.* Consumers are accustomed to receiving massive quantities of mail and so have been "trained" to accept the voluminous amount of p-mail received. It is not the amount of mail that concerns most people but the fact that virtually any business or other organization can readily obtain their names and addresses.

What Functions Can P-mail Accomplish?

Research and practical experience indicate that p-mail campaigns can achieve the following functions, all of which are straightforward and thus require no explanation:[4]

1. Increase sales and usage from current customers
2. Sell products and services to new customers
3. Build traffic at a specific retailer or Web site

4. Stimulate product trial with promotional offers and incentives
5. Generate leads for a sales force
6. Deliver product-relevant information and news
7. Gather customer information that can be used in building a database
8. Communicate with individuals in a relatively private manner and thereby minimize the likelihood of competitive detection; in other words, p-mail advertising, unlike mass advertising, reaches the customer and prospects under competitors' radar screens

Who Uses P-mail Advertising?

All types of marketers use p-mail as a strategically important advertising medium. Some automobile manufacturers, for example, budget as much as 10 percent of their advertising expenditures to p-mail, with car companies' mailing expenditures in the United States alone having exceeded $70 million in a recent year.[5] Both B2B companies and marketers of consumer goods have turned increasingly to p-mailing as an advertising option. Packaged goods companies such as Ralston Purina, Kraft, Gerber Products, Sara Lee, Quaker Oats, and Procter & Gamble are some of the primary users of p-mailings. P-mailing by firms such as these is especially valuable for introducing new brands and distributing product samples.

The Special Case of Catalogs

Catalog marketing, though a form of direct mail, deserves a separate discussion due to its distinctiveness and importance. Cataloging is a huge enterprise, with more than 16 billion catalogs distributed in a recent year.[6] Name a product, and at least one company is probably marketing that item by catalog. The growth rate for catalog sales in the United States has exceeded that enjoyed by fixed-site retailers. Various factors account for this. From the *marketer's perspective,* catalog selling provides an efficient and effective way to reach prime prospects. From the *consumer's perspective,* shopping by catalog offers several advantages: (1) catalog shopping saves time because people do not have to find parking spaces and deal with in-store crowds; (2) catalog buying appeals to consumers who are fearful of shopping due to concerns about crime; (3) catalogs allow people the convenience of making purchase decisions at their leisure and away from the pressure of a retail store; (4) the availability of toll-free 800 numbers and online Web sites, credit-card purchasing, and liberal return policies make it easy for people to order from catalogs; (5) consumers are confident purchasing from catalogs because merchandise quality and prices often are comparable, or even superior, to what is available in stores; and (6) guarantees are attractive.

Illustrative of this last point, consider the policy of L. L. Bean, the famous retailer from Maine:

> *All of our products are guaranteed to give 100 percent satisfaction in every way. Return anything purchased from us at any time if it proves otherwise. We will replace it, refund your purchase price or credit your credit card, as you wish. We do not want you to have anything from L.L. Bean that is not completely satisfactory.*

Although catalog marketing is pervasive, the growth rate has subsided for several reasons: First, industry observers note that the novelty of catalog

© Susan Van Etten

scanning has worn off for many consumers. Second, as typically is the case when a product or service reaches maturity, the costs of catalog marketing have increased dramatically. A primary reason is that firms have incurred the expenses of developing more attractive catalogs and compiling better mailing lists in an effort to outperform their competitors. Costs have been further strained by third-class postal rate increases in recent years and sharp increases in paper prices.

Some catalog companies have responded to the slowdown by sending out even more catalogs than they mailed in the past. Other companies have scaled back their efforts. Marginal companies have dropped out, which invariably is the case when an industry reaches maturity. Many catalog companies have found it unprofitable to remain in the catalog business, but the best companies continue to flourish. In their efforts to achieve steady growth, some U.S. catalogers have expanded to markets overseas, and European catalogers have made inroads into the U.S. market. For example, Lands' End opened a distribution center in Japan and mass mails catalogs to consumers in that country. Lands' End also is actively pursuing German consumers, which is understandable in view of the fact that mail order accounts for nearly 6 percent of overall retail sales in Germany compared with 3 percent in the United States. L. L. Bean mails catalogs to more than 100 countries, although nearly 70 percent of its international sales comes from Japan alone.

European catalogers have also intensified their marketing efforts in the attractive U.S. market. The strongest European catalogers are huge concerns that offer a vast array of merchandise—everything from clothing and furniture to consumer electronics and appliances. U.S. catalogers, by comparison, tend to concentrate on specialty lines of merchandise. European catalogs are massive, ranging in size from 700 to 1,300 pages. Most European catalog companies are experienced international marketers. For instance, the French cataloger La Redoute earns a substantial percentage of its sales in other countries, as does Otto Versand, a German cataloger.

Database Marketing

Successful direct mailing necessitates the availability of computer databases and the *addressability* inherent in the databases. That is, databases enable contacts with present or prospective customers who can be accessed by companies whose databases contain postal and electronic addresses along with the buyographic, geographic, demographic, and, perhaps, psychographic data of the nature previously described in this text (Chapter 4). Direct advertising, in comparison to broadcast advertising, does not deal with customers as a mass but rather creates individual relationships with each customer or prospective customer. The following analogy aptly pits addressable media against broadcast media: "Broadcast media send communications; addressable media send and receive. Broadcasting targets its audience much as a battleship shells a distant island into submission; addressable media initiate conversations."[7]

An up-to-date database provides firms with a number of assets, including the ability to direct advertising efforts to those people who represent the best prospects for the company's products or services, to offer varied messages to different groups of customers, to create long-term relationships with customers, to enhance advertising productivity, and to calculate the lifetime value of a customer or prospect. Due to the importance of customer lifetime value, the following section focuses on this fifth database asset.

Lifetime-Value Analysis

A key feature of database marketing is the need to consider each address contained in a database from a lifetime-value perspective. That is, each present or prospective customer is viewed as not just an address but rather as a *long-term asset*. **Customer lifetime value** is the *net present value* (NPV) of the profit that a company stands to realize on the average new customer during a given number of years. This concept is best illustrated using the data in Table 16.2.[8]

	Year 1	Year 2	Year 3	Year 4	Year 5
Revenue					
A Customers	1,000	400	180	90	50
B Retention rate	40%	45%	50%	55%	60%
C Average yearly sales	$150	$150	$150	$150	$150
D Total revenue	$150,000	$60,000	$27,000	$13,500	$7,500
Costs					
E Cost percentage	50%	50%	50%	50%	50%
F Total costs	$75,000	$30,000	$13,500	$6,750	$3,750
Profits					
G Gross profit	$75,000	$30,000	$13,500	$6,750	$3,750
H Discount rate	1	1.2	1.44	1.73	2.07
I NPV profit	$75,000	$25,000	$9,375	$3,902	$1,812
J Cumulative NPV profit	$75,000	$100,000	$109,375	$113,277	$115,088
K Lifetime value per customer	$75.00	$100.00	$109.38	$113.28	$115.09

Table 16.2

Customer Lifetime-Value Analysis

Assume, for illustration purposes, that a retailer has a database of 1,000 customers (see the intersection of row A and Year 1 column in Table 16.2). The analysis examines the NPV of each customer over a five-year period. Row B, the *retention rate,* indicates the likelihood that people will remain customers of this particular retailer during a five-year period. Hence, 40 percent of 1,000 customers in Year 1 will continue to be customers in Year 2, or, in other words, 400 of the initial 1,000 customers will be remaining in Year 2 (see intersection of row A and the Year 2 column). Forty-five percent of these 400 customers, or 180 customers, will remain into Year 3, and so on.

Row C indicates that the *average yearly sales* in Years 1 through 5 are constant at $150. That is, customers on average spend $150 at this particular retail establishment. Thus, the *total revenue,* row D, in each of the five years is simply the product of rows A and C. For example, the 1,000 customers in Year 1 who spend on average $150 produce $150,000 of total revenue.

Row E reflects the cost of selling merchandise to the store's customers. For simplification it is assumed that the cost is 50 percent of revenue. Total costs in each year, row F, are thus calculated by simply multiplying the values in rows D and E.

Gross profit, row G, is calculated by subtracting total costs (row F) from total revenue (row D). The *discount rate,* row H, is a critical component of NPV analysis and requires some discussion. This rate reflects the idea that money received in future years is not equivalent in value to money received today. This is because money received today, say $100, can be immediately invested and begin earning interest. Over time, the $100 grows more valuable as interest accumulates and compounds. Delaying the receipt of money thus means giving up the opportunity to earn interest. This being the case, $100 received in the future, say in three years, is worth less than the same amount received today. Some adjustment is needed to equate the value of money received at different times. This adjustment is called the *discount rate* and can be expressed as:

$$D = (1 + i)^n$$

where D is the discount rate, i is the interest rate, and n is the number of years before the money will be received. The discount rate given in row H of Table 16.2 assumes an interest rate of 20 percent. Thus, the discount rate in Year 3 is 1.44, because the retailer will have to wait two years (from Year 1) to receive the profit that will be earned in Year 3. That is:

$$(1 + 0.2)^2 = 1.44$$

The *NPV profit,* row I, is determined by simply taking the reciprocal of the discount rate (i.e., $1 \div D$) and multiplying the gross profit, row G, by that reciprocal. For example, in Year 3, the reciprocal of 1.44 is 0.694, which implies that the present value of $1 received two years later is only about $0.69 at an interest rate of 20 percent. Thus, the NPV of the $13,500 gross profit to be earned in Year 3 is $9,375. (You should perform the calculation for Years 4 and 5 to ensure that you understand the derivation of NPV. Recall that the reciprocal of a particular value, such as 1.44, is calculated by dividing that value into 1.)

The *cumulative NPV profit,* row J, simply sums the NPV profits across the years. This summation reveals that the cumulative NPV profit to our hypothetical retailer, who had 1,000 customers in Year 1, of whom 50 remain after five years, is $115,088. Finally, row K, the *lifetime value per customer,* shows the average worth of each of the 1,000 people who were customers of our hypothetical retailer in Year 1. The average lifetime value of each of these customers, expressed as NPV over a five-year period, is thus $115.09.

Now that you understand the concept of *lifetime-value analysis,* we can turn to more strategic concerns. The key issue is this: what can a database marketer do to enhance the average customer's lifetime value? There are five ways to augment lifetime value:[9]

1. Increase the *retention rate.* The more customers a firm has and the longer they are retained, the greater the lifetime value. It therefore behooves marketers and advertisers to focus on retention rather than just acquisition. Database marketing is ideally suited for this purpose, because it enables regular communication with customers (through newsletters, frequency programs, and so on) and relationship building. Customer relationship management (CRM) is a widespread marketing practice—a practice justified by the ability to enhance the lifetime value of the average customer.
2. Increase the *referral rate.* Positive relations created with existing customers can influence others to become customers through the positive word of mouth expressed by a company's satisfied users.
3. Enhance the average *purchase volume per customer.* Existing customers can be encouraged to purchase more of a brand by augmenting their brand loyalty. Product satisfaction and capable management of customer relations are means to building the base of loyal customers.
4. Cut *direct costs.* By altering the channel of distribution via direct marketing efforts, a firm may be able to cut costs and hence increase profit margins.
5. Reduce *marketing communications costs.* Effective database marketing can lead to meaningful reductions in marketing communications expenses because direct advertising often is more productive than mass-media advertising.

The Practice of Data Mining

Databases can be massive in size with millions of addresses and dozens of variables for each database entrant. The availability of high-speed computers and inexpensive computer software has made it possible for companies to literally mine their databases for the purpose of learning more about customers' buying behavior. The goal of **data mining** is to discover hidden facts contained in databases. Sophisticated data miners look for *revealing relations* among the variables contained in a database for purposes of using these relationships to better target prospective customers, develop cooperative marketing relations with other companies, and otherwise better understand who buys what, and when, how often, and along with what other products and brands they make their purchases.

Consider, for example, a credit card company that mines its huge database and learns that its most frequent and largest-purchase users are disproportionately more likely than the average credit card user to vacation in exotic locations. The company could use this information to design a promotional offering that has an exotic vacation site as the grand prize. A furniture chain mining its database learns that families with two or more children rarely make major furniture purchases within two years of buying a new automobile. Armed with this information, the chain could acquire automobile purchase lists and then direct advertisements to households that have *not* purchased a new automobile for two or more years. These examples are purely illustrative, but they provide a sense of how databases can be mined and used for making strategic advertising and promotional decisions.

Another use of databases is to segregate a company's customer list by the *recency* (R) of a customer's purchase, the *frequency* (F) of purchases, and the *monetary value* (M) of each purchase. Companies typically assign point values to accounts based on these classifications. Each company has its own customized procedure for point assignment (i.e., its own R-F-M formula), but in every case more points are assigned to more recent, more frequent, and more expensive purchases. The R-F-M system offers tremendous opportunities for database manipulation and mail targeting. For example, a company might choose to send out free catalogs only to accounts whose point totals exceed a certain amount.

Another application of the R-F-M categories is for a company to divide customers into equal-sized groupings such as quartiles (four equal-sized groups) or quintiles (five equal-sized groups) for each of the R, F, and M categories. Hence, with respect to recency of purchase, the first quintile would consist of the top one-fifth of the customer database who have most recently purchased from the company, and the last quintile would include the bottom one-fifth of customers who have least recently purchased the company's products. Likewise, customers' purchase frequencies also would be delineated into five equal quintiles, ranging from the top (most frequent purchasers) to bottom quintiles (least frequent purchasers). Finally, customers' amount of purchases of the company's products would be grouped into five equal-sized quintiles. These quintile delineations of the R-F-M categories would thus lead to 125 total combinations (each combination is known as a *cell*) of customer groupings—that is, 5 recency quintiles x 5 frequency quintiles x 5 monetary-value quintiles. Cell 1 would include customers who have purchased the company's products most recently, have purchased most frequently, and have spent the most amount in purchasing from the company, while cell 125 would include customers who have purchased products least recently, have purchased least frequently, and have spent the least amount in purchasing from the company. Customers in the 123 intermediate cells would fall between these two extremes.

Having delineated all customers into one of 125 cells, a company can then test the effectiveness of a proposed p-mailing using the following procedure:

1. Take a representative random sample of customers from each of the 125 cells.
2. Distribute a catalog, brochure, or other p-mailing to the sampled customers from each of the 125 cells. This mailing would encourage recipients to purchase the company's advertised product(s).
3. Provide sufficient time for sampled customers to respond to the mail offering.
4. After sufficient time has elapsed (based on past mailing experience), determine the response rate and average expenditure for each of the 125 R-F-M cells.
5. Project these statistics to the full membership of each of the 125 groupings.
6. Based on these response rate and average expenditure projections, and with knowledge of the cost of distributing the mailing to all customers in each group, calculate whether distributing the mailing to *all* customers in a particular cell would be a profitable proposition.
7. Based on the sample results, mail the catalog, brochure, or other piece only to those cells in which the potential revenue from the customers outstrips the mailing expense.

It should be clear from this description that testing of the sort just described can be performed to determine which customers in a company's database represent the best prospects for future mailings. Based on these results, a decision is made to mail, say, a catalog to those database entrants who occupy a select subset of the R-F-M cells, namely, the most profitable cells. In the absence of testing a proposed new mailing, a company would be taking a "shot in the dark" if it were to mail its catalog to all customers in its database. The testing procedure represents a systematic approach that likely will produce a more profitable outcome compared with blanketing a mailing to all database occupants.

Audio-Video Advertising

Whereas the prior discussion of direct advertising has focused primarily on print forms of direct advertising, a second general form of direct advertising is the use of electronic devices to present audiovisual advertising messages that have been captured in the form of videotapes, CD-ROMs, or DVDs. This form of advertising involves capturing key visual and audio information about a brand and distributing the information to business customers or final consumers for projection on computer monitors or television screens. Although there is limited research to verify the effectiveness of audio-video advertising, firms in this industry maintain (albeit not without self-interest) that video advertising is both more effective and less expensive than print advertising delivered via direct mail. It is claimed that business customers and consumers are less likely to throw away an unsolicited audiovisual message than they are a brochure or other printed material and that videos are more persuasive. Although unverified in a scientific sense, it stands to reason that video advertising is potentially more entertaining than comparable print advertising and thus more effective in gaining attention and influencing memorability of an advertising message.

Companies are increasingly using the audiovisual medium to present consumers and B2B customers with detailed product information. Consider, for example, the valuable use of CD-ROMs and DVDs to market new automobiles and vacation spots. When used for the introduction of new automobiles, a car company can provide detailed product information as well as show scenes of the product in use and illustrations of the "typical" purchaser of the new car.

Imagine also how a tourist destination might effectively use CD-ROM and DVD advertising. When a prospective tourist requests information, a disc could be mailed out that would contain the sights (video as well as still pictures) and sounds (music, wildlife and outdoor sounds, etc.) of the area and would present this information in a newsworthy and entertaining fashion. CD-ROMs and DVDs also have considerable potential in the area of B2B marketing. Audio-video presentations of new products can be mailed to prospective customers, who are encouraged to call for additional information or to arrange a personal sales visit.

Indirect Forms of Advertising

As previously portrayed in Table 16.1, indirect advertising can be broadly distinguished as being directed to *homes* and *workplaces* (private venues) or disseminated in a wide variety of *private* and *public venues.* Yellow-pages and video-game advertising directed to homes and workplaces are covered first, and then a variety of public-venue forms of indirect advertising are examined.

Advertising Directed to Homes and Workplaces

Yellow-Pages Advertising

Advertising in the yellow pages is not a substitute for but a complement to other advertising media when used in an IMC program. This old advertising medium, with a past as a static form of communication in the pages of telephone directories, is seeing a new life with the creation of online yellow pages. The yellow pages is an advertising medium that consumers turn to when they are seeking a product or service supplier and are prepared to make a purchase.

The yellow pages—the online version (e.g., http://www.yellowpages.com and http://www.superpages.com) as well as the traditional print volume—represent a huge advertising medium with annual revenues exceeding $15 billion.[10] Over 7,000 localized yellow-pages directories are distributed annually to hundreds of millions of consumers. There are currently more than 4,000 headings for different product and service listings. Local businesses place the majority of yellow-pages ads, but national advertisers also are frequent users of the yellow pages. For example, the following national companies in a recent year all invested over $20 million advertising in the yellow pages: ServiceMaster ($51 million), U-Haul ($38 million), State Farm Insurance ($35 million), and Budget and Ryder ($20.5 million).[11]

Who Uses the Yellow Pages? Although most people use the yellow pages at one time or another, heavy users tend to fall most heavily in the 25-to-49 age category, are college educated, and have relatively high household incomes ($60,000 and up).[12] Some of the major reasons for using yellow pages include saving time spent shopping around for information, saving energy and money, finding information quickly, and learning about products and services. In a typical week, an estimated 60 percent of all American adults use the yellow pages at least once.

Distinguishing Features of Yellow-Pages Advertising. The yellow pages differ from other ad media in several respects.[13] First, whereas consumers often avoid exposure to advertisements in other media, customers actively seek out ads in the yellow pages. Second, the advertiser largely determines the quality of ad placement in the yellow pages by the actions it takes. For example, by placing a large ad, the advertiser receives prized placement (i.e., placement earlier in the sequence of ads under a particular category) than do purchasers of small ads; also, companies that are long-time yellow-pages advertisers receive the best ad placements.

A third distinguishing feature of yellow-pages advertising is that there are clear-cut limits on possible creative executions. That is, when advertising in the yellow pages, advertisers have fewer creative options available than when advertising in other media. It is noteworthy, however, that now advertisers in the yellow pages have greater color and graphic options available than solely using black print against a yellow background. Research indicates that the use of color and higher-quality graphics have positive effects in attracting attention, signaling product quality, and even increasing the likelihood that the advertised brand will be selected over competitive options.[14]

A fourth distinguishing characteristic of yellow-pages advertising is the method of purchase. Whereas advertising in mass media such as TV, radio, magazines, and newspapers allows for frequent adjustments in the creative execution and budget allocations, yellow-pages advertisements are purchased for a full year and thus cannot be changed in either purchase amount or creative execution.

Overall, the yellow pages is a valuable advertising medium, especially for local advertisers in their efforts to attract new customers and to reach past customers.

Video-game Advertising (a.k.a. Adver-gaming)

Brand managers and marcom practitioners are continually looking for alternatives to mass-media advertising, especially TV, and seeking ways to get their messages before difficult-to-reach consumers such as young males. Electronic games (*video games*) provide an excellent advertising medium for this purpose. These games typically are available on game consoles or online, and marketers either customize their own games or incorporate their brands into existing games (a form of product placement). The producers of video games now actively pursue tie-ins with brand marketers, who pay for advertising space within the games.

It is easy to understand why video games represent a potentially valuable ad medium considering that popular games sell millions of units, and users of these games play for an average of 40 hours before growing tired of them.[15] Moreover, JupiterResearch, a technology research firm, expects over 60 million game players by 2009, with 40 percent of those in the 18-to-34 age category.[16] Although in the early years of this technology video games were most played by young males, today nearly 40 percent of game players are girls and women.[17]

An Illustration of Adver-Gaming. DaimlerChrysler sought a way to effectively advertise the company's Wrangler Rubicon brand in its Jeep line. In an appeal to the young males representing the primary target for this brand, Wrangler's brand team commissioned a video game—named *Jeep 4x4: Trail of Life*—that gave players an opportunity to "drive" the Wrangler up steep inclines and across rivers. It only took six months for 250,000 game players to download the Jeep game and provide their names and addresses to DaimlerChrysler. (Regarding the discussion earlier in the chapter about database marketing, note that these names and addresses would become part of DaimlerChrysler's ever-growing database.) Hundreds of the limited-edition Wrangler Rubicons, priced at $29,000, were sold to people who played the game. The marketing people at DaimlerChrysler were able to determine this, of course, by comparing dealer sales records with the name and address information supplied by people who played the *4x4: Trail of Life* game.[18]

Nielsen to Measure Video-game Audiences. Expenditures on adver-gaming, somewhere in the $1 billion vicinity at the time of this writing, are minuscule in comparison to those on TV and other mass media. Nevertheless, in anticipation of continued growth, Nielsen (of TV ratings fame) has developed a service to measure video-game audiences. Nielsen employs a small monitor (somewhat akin to the set-top boxes used in TV measurement) to measure game-playing behavior. For example, an inaudible audio signal was coded into the *Tony Hawk's Underground 2* game that is played online, and Nielsen's monitoring system was alerted each time game players viewed product placements for the Chrysler Jeep.[19] Measures of viewers' recall of ads placed in games and their reactions to these ads will require telephone surveying and perhaps personal interviewing.

Advertising Delivered at Private and Public Venues

Presented in this context are several forms of advertising: branded entertainment (i.e., product placements in movies, on TV, and in other media), cinema advertising and Web films, virtual signage, and miscellaneous modes of ad delivery.

Branded Entertainment: Brand Placements in Movies and Other Media

The practice of what typically is referred to as *product placement*—but which more appropriately should be dubbed *brand placement* inasmuch as marketers promote specific brands, not products in general—has risen in recent years to unprecedented heights. It has been estimated that brand-placement spending in the United States exceeded $4 billion in 2005.[20] Interestingly, there is little scientific evidence regarding the effectiveness of brand placements.[21] Most of the evidence is anecdotal, and the discussion in this section will be in that vein.

In their efforts to present brand messages in a manner that does not appear blatant, marketers seek opportunities to have their brands mentioned in positive contexts—including movies, TV programs, books, songs, and so on. Brand placement activity is perfectly aligned with one of the five key features of IMC introduced in Chapter 1, namely that the customer represents the starting point for all marcom decisions. The essence of this principle, as it relates to media selection, is that marketing communicators should seek opportunities to present brand messages in positive contexts where potential customers naturally *place themselves.* People go to movies, watch TV programs, listen to music, and so on; hence, all of these venues are potentially attractive contexts in which to present brand messages. This then is the general rationale for so-called branded entertainment, namely, that brand messages placed in entertainment events are conveyed in a covert fashion compared to traditional advertising's overt approach and that brand placements do not come across as advertisements.

By way of comparison with traditional mass-media advertising, brand placements in movies, TV programs, and elsewhere have certain distinct advantages as well as disadvantages. First, in terms of advantages, brand placements generally are less intrusive than advertisements and thus less likely to be avoided. Second, because consumers, especially younger people, often dislike being marketed to, brand placements are less likely to be summarily rejected as just another persuasive attempt. Third, when a brand is appropriately connected with the plot of a movie (or TV program, song, etc.) and with the characters in that entertainment event, there is a strong potential for the placement to buttress or even augment a brand's image and to build an emotional connection with the target audience. Finally, a prominent placement can create a memorable association that serves to enhance consumers' memories (recognition and recall) of a brand and thus possibly their chances of selecting it from among competitive options.

On the downside, marcom practitioners lose control of how their brands are positioned when movie and TV directors make the decision of how exactly brands are placed in an entertainment event. Whereas an advertisement is a perfectly controlled context for a brand, when a brand is placed in, say, a movie, the control of the positioning is to some degree lost to the movie's director. Another disadvantage of brand placements is the difficulty of measuring their effectiveness and their ROI. Third, prices of brand placements are spiraling upward, and many brand managers consider the cost unreasonably high. For example, 79 percent of major marketers surveyed in a poll conducted by the Association of National Advertisers believe branded-entertainment deals are overpriced.[22]

In sum, brand placements offer many potential advantages, but these do not come free of cost. We now discuss specific forms of brand placements: in movies, on TV, and in songs.

Brand Placements in Movies. Brand placements in movies date back to the 1940s, yet the frequency of occurrence is greater now than ever. It is virtually impossible to attend a movie without seeing various well-known brands (Coca-Cola, Nike, Apple, Ford, etc.) appearing in these movies. For example, the movie *Sahara,* which just opened at the time this chapter was being written, featured nearly 20 brands—including Apple, Budweiser, Coca-Cola, Intel, Jeep, Mercedes, Ray-Ban, Samsung, and *USA Today.* Interested readers can see the brands that are featured in favorite films by going to the following Web site: http://www.brandchannel.com/brandcameo_films.asp. This source has been tracking brand placements in movies since the early 2000s. It also includes a section that identifies which brands are placed in the most films.

Do brand placements work? Public evidence of whether such "advertising" is effective is limited. There is evidence, however, that brand awareness and recall increase with more prominent placements.[23] It would seem that advertisers have little to lose and much to gain when using this form of supplemental marketing communications. The typical price for a brand placement ranges from as low as $25,000 to into the millions.[24] For example, Ford invested millions to have its Jaguar, Aston Martin, and Thunderbird brands featured in the James Bond movie *Die Another Day.*

Several factors determine how much a brand placement is worth and thus how much it should cost a brand marketer to place a brand in a particular movie.[25] A first determinant is the amount of time the brand gets on screen. Placements in which a brand is in the foreground of a scene and in which the brand logo is clearly seen are more valuable to a brand and lead to higher prices than instances in which the brand is in the background and the logo is difficult to detect. Second, brand placements are more valuable (and thus should be priced higher) when characters in the movie use the brand and perhaps mention it and exclaim its virtues. A third determinant of a placement's value is whether the brand appears during an important plot point in the movie (if it does, the placement is worth more). In short, the more time a brand placement receives, the more tightly it is woven into the movie's plot, and the more the brand and key movie characters are connected, the more valuable the placement is and the higher the price to be paid for garnering the placement.

Based on a large global study conducted by a major advertising media company (over 11,000 interviews conducted with consumers from 20 countries), younger consumers appear to be the most responsive to brand placements in movies.[26] Compared to older age groups, 16-to-24 year olds were the most likely to *notice* brand placements in movies (57 percent) and to *consider trying* the brands seen in films (41 percent). The comparative notice and consider-trying statistics for 35-to-44 year olds were 49 percent and 28 percent and, for 45-to-54 year olds, 43 percent and 22 percent. Perhaps the most interesting finding from this study was the difference across countries in the percentages of consumers saying they would try a brand if they saw it in a film. The percentages for a subset of countries were Mexico (53 percent), Singapore (49 percent), India (35 percent), Hong Kong (33 percent), the United States (26 percent), Finland (14 percent), Denmark (14 percent), the Netherlands (9 percent), and France (8 percent). Consumers from the latter four countries objected to brand placements because they are considered as interfering with the film-making process.

For a discussion of the problems and opportunities with brand placements when movies are exported overseas, see the *Global Focus.*

Brand Placements in TV Programs. The topic of brand placements in TV programs was briefly mentioned in Chapter 14 when discussing television as a mass-advertising medium. A few additional comments are appropriate at this time. Brand-placement spending on television is even greater than in movies, accounting for nearly 60 percent of brand-placement expenditures in 2005.[27] The substantial increase in brand placements on TV has been concurrent with the growth of reality television programming. Programs such as *Survivor* and *The Apprentice* represent near-perfect contexts in which to place brands and provide brand managers with an alternative form of exposure to the traditional 30-second commercial. Of course, brand placements are not limited just to reality shows. Brand placements can be observed on most successful TV programs. Even reruns of TV sitcoms are being digitally remastered to include brands in scenes where they did not exist when initially produced.[28]

Brand marketers are attempting to get their brands integrated into TV programs in as seamless a fashion as possible. For example, Agent Jack Bauer, the daring Counter Terrorist Unit character on Fox network's *24,* always drives a Ford F-150 truck. Jack and the truck are inseparable. The truck appears in the program not as a prop, but as a natural element of the action-packed program. Likewise, brands such as Coca-Cola and Campbell's soup are featured in *American Dreams,*

Dubbing in Brands to Fit the Needs of Different Countries

global focus

Interestingly, as much as 60 percent of the revenue produced by Hollywood movies is generated in non-U.S. markets. This raises a very interesting challenge as well as an opportunity: what does a movie studio do when a brand placed in a movie is unavailable in another country where the rights to the movie are sold? Movie studios used to sell product-placement rights only on a single occasion to advertisers interested primarily in exposure to U.S. audiences. Now they have turned to dubbing product placements to accommodate advertisers' efforts to reach audiences in other countries. This has been made possible as movies increasingly are being shot with digital cameras rather than with 35 mm film.

In *Spider-Man 2,* for example, the U.S. version featured a Dr Pepper logo on the refrigerator in the pizza shop where Spider-Man (Peter Parker as played by Tobey Maguire) works. However, when Sony Pictures was unable to interest the marketers of Dr Pepper in paying for overseas brand placements, the rights were sold to Mirinda (a fruit-flavored soft drink marketed by PepsiCo outside the United States). Mirinda's brand then appeared on the pizza shop refrigerator in 60 countries where *Spider-Man 2* was distributed.

In the Warner Bros. movie *Looney Tunes: Back in Action,* Sprint Corp. bought only the U.S. product-placement rights in that its wireless service isn't available outside the United States. So where the U.S. release shows a close-up of the red Sprint logo on a cell phone, in the international release of the movie, the orange square logo of Orange (a unit of France Telecom SA) replaces the Sprint logo. In another cell phone placement, Cingular Wireless is the brand appearing in *Charlie's Angels: Full Throttle,* but just in the United States. In the movie's international release, T-Mobile (a unit of Deutsche Telekom AG) is dubbed in place of Cingular.

Dubbing logos in international releases of U.S. films has enabled movie studios to increase revenue generation from brand placements. At the same time, this practice has been criticized as another effort to turn movies into glorified infomercials.

SOURCE: Adapted from Charles Goldsmith, "Dubbing in Product Plugs," *Wall Street Journal Online,* December 6, 2004, http://online.wsj.com.

a program about a Philadelphia family during the Vietnam era and its struggles during this tumultuous time to keep four children grounded in the parents' traditional Catholic values while simultaneously allowing them to experiment with the rapid sociocultural changes being ushered in during this period. Brands embedded in this program stand to be perceived as both traditional and modern—a fine line between two potentially contradictory value schemes, but nonetheless a position that many brands would hope to occupy in their appeal to multiple age groups.

Brand Placements in Books and Songs. The previous sections have discussed brand placements in movies and TV programs. In actuality, brand placement activity has become universal. Books often mention specific brands in the context of describing their protagonists' lifestyles, which, needless to say, can represent positive plugs for brands when real or fictional characters are themselves perceived positively. (What brand marketer would want to see a brand associated with a dastardly character or "loser"?) When listening to songs, one often hears references to specific brands. Hip-hop artists are especially active promoters of brands. As one observer has noted, "These brands are part of the artists' lives, and what they're selling is a lifestyle."[29]

Cinema Advertising and Web Films

In addition to placements of brands *in* movies, the movie theater has in recent years itself become a medium for placing advertising messages *prior to* featured films. Expenditures on cinema advertising are trivial in comparison, say, to TV advertising, amounting to only about $350 million in a recent year. Research has demonstrated that, at least in its infancy, consumers are not antagonized by cinema advertisements.[30] Younger consumers are more positively disposed toward cinema advertising than older individuals, which makes for an attractive proposition for brand marketers given the difficulties of reaching the younger demographic group with traditional advertising media. The prospect that cinema advertising has a bright future is perhaps best evidenced by the fact that Nielsen

Figure 16.1
An Advertisement Directed at Prospective Cinema Advertisers

Media Research has introduced Nielsen Cinema, which is an in-theater audience measurement service that will be used by cinema companies and advertisers for buying and selling cinema advertising. Figure 16.1 is an advertisement from Regal CineMedia Corporation directed at prospective movie advertisers. The ad points out that movie advertising is especially valuable for reaching young audiences and that it delivers high levels of brand recall.

Another film-related advertising medium is *Web films.* This form of advertising involves producing short films that feature the advertised brand and are available on the Internet for free viewing. BMW introduced this advertising genre when in 2000 it presented Clive Owen as "The Driver" in five films titled *Ambush, Chosen, The Follow, Star,* and *Powder Keg.*[31] The Driver appeared in each action-packed film driving a different BMW vehicle, all of which served to portray BMW vehicles in the most positive light. American Express created its own Web films that featured Seinfeld and Superman in an extension of an advertisement involving these characters that first aired on a Super Bowl program. In another illustration of Web films, Dr. Martens (known for its hip boots) has attempted to regain the glory of its 1990s success years by investing $10 million in the production of six films, each telling the story of individuals with unique jobs or avocations. A company spokesperson justified the choice of Web films by saying that this medium enables Dr. Martens to reach its target of 18–35 men and women and to present an authentic and honest message that parallels the brand's image.[32]

Virtual Signage

Largely unbeknownst to television viewers, the brand logos sometimes seen on sports fields, tennis courts, and other venues actually are not there. That is, computer technology is used to "paint" advertisers' logos at these venues. Attendees at a sporting event cannot see the signs because the logos are not physically present, but television viewers have no idea that what they are viewing is merely a computer-generated image rather than a "real" sign. Virtual signs have been used in boxing, football, tennis, baseball, and basketball venues. These signs enable advertisers to use state-of-the-art graphics to attract and hold viewer attention during the actual playing of a sporting event. Advertisers in the United States have enthusiastically embraced virtual signage as a potentially promising advertising medium, but in Europe regulators such as the European Broadcasting Union have categorically banned virtual advertising from events in which it holds broadcasting rights.[33]

Figure 16.2
3M's Post-it Notes as an Advertising Medium

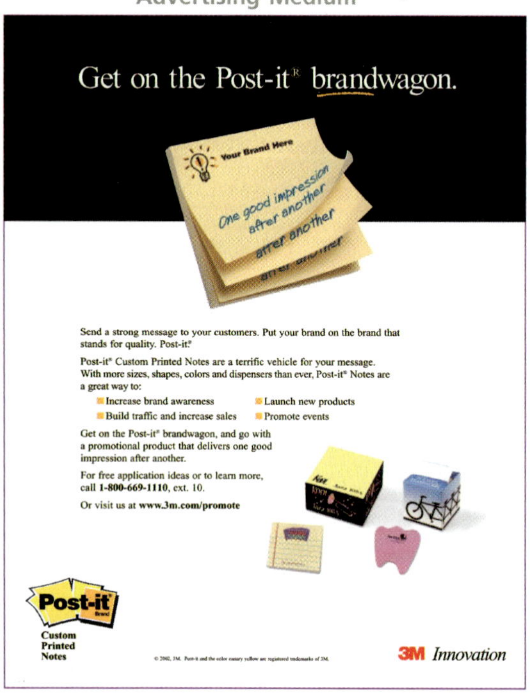

Some Additional Alternative Media

Following is a discussion of a potpourri of alternative media, all of which have minor but potentially useful roles to play as part of an integrated marcom effort. Creative advertisers find many ways to reach customers using alternative media. For example, Figure 16.2 is an advertisement from 3M Company that is directed at advertising agencies and their clients. On reading the advertisement you will see that 3M is suggesting that Post-it Notes can be used as a powerful advertising medium that will reach potential customers day after day, note after note. Figure 16.3 is a photo taken at a professional football stadium (the Carolina Panthers stadium in Charlotte, North Carolina), showing a cup holder emblazoned with an advertisement for Coca-Cola.[34] Why let the space go to waste when it can be sold as an advertising outlet?

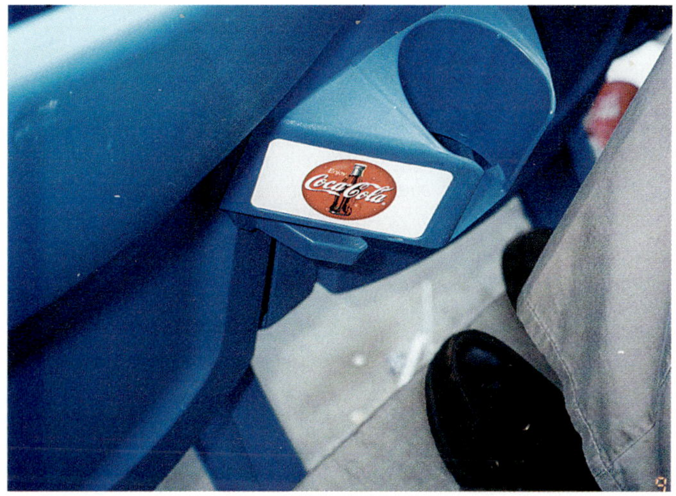

Figure 16.3

A Football Stadium's Cup Holders as an Advertising Medium

Advertisers have even turned to using restroom space as a venue to convey their messages. Since its introduction, Axe deodorant from Unilever has been advertised in public restrooms in major U.S. markets. A company spokesman justified this choice by saying that Axe is a brand that "is about helping a guy attract women," and that guys are in the right mind-set to accept ad messages for a brand such as Axe during their restroom interludes when frequenting bars.[35]

An enterprising firm called The Fruit Label Company has used apples and other fruit and vegetable items to carry mini-ads for movies and other products. Levi Strauss & Co. advertised Levi's 501 jeans on the back covers of Marvel and DC comics, an excellent medium because these two comic-book companies combined sell more than 10 million copies of their comic books every month. The comics provided Levi Strauss & Co. with an outlet for reaching the notoriously difficult-to-reach segment of boys ages 12 to 17.

Another interesting ad medium is skywriting. A company named Skytypers—with bases in California, Florida, and New York—"writes" sky messages in the form of white cloud formations. At a recent U.S. Open tennis tournament in Flushing Meadows, New York, tennis patrons saw messages for brands such as Heineken, Dunkin' Donuts, GEICO, and Song Airways. A message of 25 to 30 letters costs between $25,000 and $30,000 and can be seen by upwards of 2.5 million people in the 400-square-mile area surrounding the site of the U.S. Open.[36] See the *IMC Focus* for another description of a fascinating advertising medium.

In conclusion, this brief discussion of alternative media has been intended merely to demonstrate that the imagination, along with good taste, are the only limits to the choice of advertising media. These examples illustrate rather vividly that virtually any blank surface can be converted into space for an advertisement. In the final analysis, we must be mindful of the advice about IMC presented in Chapter 1: contact brand users wherever and whenever possible, use all appropriate touch points to convey messages that will increase brand awareness and augment images, and be sure to integrate messages across all touch points to assure they all speak with a single voice. Multiple media are to little avail if their messages are inconsistent or possibly even in conflict.

The Human Body as an Ad Medium

imc focus

As noted previously, virtually any location or space represents a potential advertising medium. Advertisers are limited only by their ingenuity in selecting settings in or on which to place their ads. Perhaps the last frontier in advertising space was breached when advertisers began using the human body as an ad medium. People's bodies now represent a form of billboard for ad messages. Foreheads seem to be the preferred spot for tattoo ads. A British company, for example, pays students the equivalent of about $8 an hour to walk up and down busy streets with their foreheads temporarily imprinted with brand names. The company has a group of about 1,000 students who are willing to serve as walking billboards.

Tattoo advertising also has appeared in the United States. A Massachusetts-based firm borrowed the forehead-tattooing idea from Great Britain and introduced it in that state and elsewhere. Dunkin' Donuts ran a forehead tattoo promotion in conjunction with the National Collegiate Athletic Association (NCAA) March Madness basketball tourney. One hundred students from 10 universities in Boston, Massachusetts; Illinois; Georgia; and Florida earned between $50 and $100 per day to walk around their campuses with the Dunkin' Donuts logo tattooed on their foreheads.

In another campaign tied to the famous Boston Marathon, approximately 1,000 students were tattooed with a slogan for Reebok shoes exclaiming, "The Pain Train is Coming" (in reference to fictional Terry Tate who, at the time, was Reebok's iconic endorser).

Whether tattoo advertising is a fad or has some staying power is unknown at this time. One prospect is that there are more people willing to have their bodies serve as tattooed billboards than there are companies who are interested in using this advertising medium. One need only go online to an eBay auction to see that there are various individuals auctioning off their bodies as venues for temporary or even permanent brand-name tattoos. For example, at the time of writing this section, one auctioneer was offering to *permanently* tattoo his shaven head for any nonvulgar brand—at an asking price of $50,000. He had yet to receive any bids.

SOURCE: Details about the British campaign and those for Dunkin' Donuts and Reebok are from Arundhati Parmar, "Maximum Exposure," *Marketing News*, September 15, 2003, 6, 8.

Summary

This chapter has devoted coverage to a variety of "other" advertising media. Table 16.1 structured the discussion by delineating these other ad options into direct and indirect media. In addition to this breakdown, alternative media also were classified as being directed primarily to homes and workplaces or to public venues. Direct advertising via postal mail (p-mail) received the most extensive coverage in view of its widespread usage and huge investment in this medium.

Direct advertising is increasingly being viewed as a critical component of successful IMC programs. Indeed, for many firms direct advertising is the cornerstone of their communications efforts. The increased sophistication of database marketing has been largely responsible for the growing use and effectiveness of direct advertising. Major advances in computer technology have made it possible for companies to maintain huge databases containing millions of prospects and customers. An up-to-date database allows targeting of messages to prime prospects, provides for an ability to vary message content to different groups, enhances advertising productivity, enables the determination of a customer's lifetime value, and affords an opportunity to build long-term relations with customers. The availability of high-speed computers and inexpensive computer software has made it possible for companies to literally mine their databases for the purpose of learning more about customers' buying behavior. Sophisticated data miners look for revealing relations that can be used to target prospective customers, develop cooperative marketing relations, and otherwise better understand who buys what, and when, how often, and along with what other products and brands they make their purchases.

Two forms of indirect advertising that are directed mostly at homes and workplaces are yellow-pages advertising and video-game advertising (also known as adver-gaming). The yellow pages (online as well as in print form) is virtually a must for local advertisers in their quest to attract prospective customers and repeat purchases. Adver-gaming is a new but rapidly growing form of advertising that appeals mostly to young men but increasingly to girls and women who also are avid gamers.

There are a variety of other forms of indirect advertising that reach consumers primarily in public venues outside homes and workplaces. Brand placements in movies, on TV, and in songs is another rapidly growing ad medium. These placements provide advertisers with an opportunity to reach consumers in a rather covert fashion (in comparison to traditional advertising, which, in a manner of speaking, is "in your face") and to portray brands positively by connecting them with entertainment plots and characters.

Another interesting development in the search for alternative advertising media is the recent growth of cinema advertising. Most theaters now show a few commercials prior to presenting the featured movie. These ads oftentimes are the same ones shown on TV. The appeal of this medium is that it captures the attention of a young demographic group that is difficult to reach via traditional media. Moreover, shown prior to the commencement of the feature film, cinema advertising is not as disruptive as are TV commercials. Another form of cinematic advertising is the recent emergence of Web films. These typically are short films made available online at no cost to the viewer. Web films are entertaining and attract viewers by buzz-building word of mouth. The films often are exciting and portray the featured brand in a fashion that holds positive associations for the featured brand—such as BMW automobiles or Dr Martens' boots.

Discussion Questions

1. Virtually any space is a potential medium for a marketer's advertisement. Please identify several novel forms of advertising media that go beyond the "other" media described in this chapter. Describe the target for each of these novel media, and offer an explanation as to why, in your opinion, each novel medium is effective or ineffective.
2. Can you recall any prominent brand placements in movies you have seen lately? What were these placements? Were the products "positioned" in positive or negative contexts? How successful, in your opinion, were these placements?
3. Have you ever viewed a CD-ROM or DVD advertisement? If so, what are your views on why this form of advertising was or was not effective?
4. Describe your use, if any, of yellow-pages advertising in recent weeks.
5. Assume you are the proprietor of a sports bar in a community of, say, 250,000 people. Can you offer any good reasons for *not* advertising your business in the yellow pages?
6. Four types of "graphics" are used in compiling databases: buyographics, demographics, geographics, and psychographics. Provide one illustrative variable that a catalog marketer of men's or women's clothing (your choice) might include in its database for each of these "graphics."
7. Explain the meaning and importance of database "addressability."
8. The section describing database assets included the claim that an up-to-date database allows a marketing organization to create long-term relationships with customers. What does this mean?
9. Assume you are a direct marketer for a line of merchandise imprinted with the logos of major universities. These items are targeted to the fans and supporters of university athletic programs. Detail how you would compile an appropriate

mailing list, one that would reach people who are most likely to purchase the logo merchandise. Use your college or university for illustration.

10. Following is a lifetime-value analysis framework similar to that presented in the chapter. Perform the calculations necessary to complete row K:

	Year 1	Year 2	Year 3	Year 4	Year 5
Revenue					
A Customers	2,000	____	____	____	____
B Retention rate	30%	40%	55%	65%	70%
C Average yearly sales	$250	$250	$250	$250	$250
D Total revenue	____	____	____	____	____
Costs					
E Cost percentage	50%	50%	50%	50%	50%
F Total costs	____	____	____	____	____
Profits					
G Gross profit	____	____	____	____	____
H Discount rate	1	1.15	____	____	____
I NPV profit	____	____	____	____	____
J Cumulative NPV profit	____	____	____	____	____
K Lifetime value per customer	____	____	____	____	____

11. Assume that, 10 years after graduating from your university or college, you are appointed to your school's Athletics Oversight Committee. The chair of the committee suggests that it would be useful to know the lifetime value of the average football season-ticket holder. Describe how you might go about estimating the average ticket holder's lifetime value over the first five years starting with the year that he or she first purchases season tickets. Refer to Table 16.2 to assist you with this analysis. Make whatever assumptions you deem necessary and then conduct the analysis. Your analysis obviously would be facilitated by using a spreadsheet program such as Microsoft Excel.
12. Your college or university no doubt has an organizational unit that is responsible for marketing merchandise to alumni and other customers—items emblazoned with your school's logo, such as sweatshirts, T-shirts, caps, cups, and so on. Assume that the merchandising unit in your school does *not* have an up-to-date computerized database. Explain how you would go about putting together such a database. What specific information would you maintain in your computerized database for each customer? How would you use this information?
13. As a consumer who probably has spent considerable time perusing the pages of different catalogs, provide your perspective on the value of catalogs to you. Why would you (or why would you not) purchase from a catalog company?
14. What are your views on adver-gaming? Respond to this question by commenting about this advertising practice both from the perspective of advertisers and from the viewpoint of game players.
15. Brand placements in movies, on TV, and in songs represent a subtle, even covert, way to present a brand message. Traditional advertising, by comparison, is, in a manner of speaking, "in your face." One therefore could argue that traditional advertising is a more honest form of communications than the practice of branded entertainment. What are your views on this? Might one argue that brand placements are even a bit deceitful?
16. Visit http://www.brandchannel.com/brandcameo_films.asp and identify a movie that you either have seen or are at least familiar with. Examine the

brands that have been placed in that movie and comment on why you think these brands chose to be placed in that particular movie.

17. What are your views on the effectiveness of brand placements in songs?
18. What are your views on both the appropriateness and the effectiveness of placing advertisements in restrooms?

ENDNOTES

1. Don Schultz as quoted in Gary Levin, "Going Direct Route," *Advertising Age,* November 18, 1991, 37.
2. Information provided by The Martin Agency, Richmond, VA.
3. An industry expert in forecasting advertising expenditures, Robert Coen, estimated that slightly more than $48 billion was spent on direct mail in 2003 and that expenditures would grow to approximately $51 billion in 2004. Carol Krol, "Return to Spending," *BtoB,* October 11, 2004, 25.
4. This list is slightly adapted from one provided by the United States Postal Service in a CD-ROM titled "How to Develop and Execute a Winning Direct Mail Campaign," circa 2001, http://www.usps.com.
5. Jean Halliday, "Driving Sales Directly," *Advertising Age,* October 22, 2001, 22.
6. Eric Yoder, "Driving Value from the Catalogue Customer," *1to1 Magazine,* November/December 2001, 31–35.
7. Robert C. Blattberg and John Deighton, "Interactive Marketing: Exploiting the Age of Addressability," *Sloan Management Review* (fall 1991), 5.
8. There are more sophisticated approaches to lifetime-value analysis, but this example contains all the elements essential to understanding the fundamentals of the approach.
9. Arthur M. Hughes, *Strategic Database Marketing* (Chicago: Probus, 1994), 17.
10. Joel J. Davis, "Section One: Industry Overview," *Understanding Yellow Pages,* http://www.ypa-academics.org/UYPII/section1.html.
11. Ibid.
12. Joel J. Davis, "Section Five: Consumer Dynamics," *Understanding Yellow Pages,* http://www.ypa-academics.org/UYPII/section5.html.
13. Avery M. Abernethy and David N. Laband, "The Customer Pulling Power of Different-sized Yellow Pages Advertisements," *Journal of Advertising Research* 42 (May/June 2002), 66–72.
14. For details see Karen V. Fernandez and Dennis L. Rosen, "The Effectiveness of Information and Color in Yellow Page Advertising," *Journal of Advertising* 29 (summer 2000), 61–73; Gerald L. Lohse and Dennis L. Rosen, "Signaling Quality and Credibility in Yellow Pages Advertising: The Influence of Color and Graphics on Choice," *Journal of Advertising* 30 (summer 2001), 73–85.
15. Kenneth Hein, "Getting in the Game," *Brandweek,* February 17, 2004, 26–28.
16. Suzanne Vranica, "Y&R Bets on Videogame Industry," *Wall Street Journal Online,* May 11, 2004, http://online.wsj.com.
17. Ronald Grover, Cliff Edwards, Ian Rowley, and Moon Ihlwan, "Game Wars," *BusinessWeek,* February 28, 2005, 60–66.
18. Kevin J. Delaney, "Ads in Videogames Pose a New Threat to Media Industry," *Wall Street Journal Online,* July 28, 2004, http://online.wsj.com.
19. Kevin J. Delaney, "Videogame Makers Borrow TV's Tactics for Selling Ads," *Wall Street Journal Online,* October 18, 2004, http://online.wsj.com.
20. Marc Graser, "Product-Placement Spending Poised to Hit $4.25 Billion in '05," *Advertising Age,* April 4, 2005, 16.
21. For an exception, see Cristel Antonia Russell, "Investigating the Effectiveness of Product Placements in Television Shows: The Role of Modality and Plot Connection Congruence on Brand Memory and Attitude," *Journal of Consumer Research* 29 (December 2002), 306–318. For coverage of practitioners' views on brand placement, see James A. Karrh, Kathy Brittain McKee, and Carol J. Pardun, "Practitioners' Evolving Views on Product Placement Effectiveness," *Journal of Advertising Research* 43 (June 2003), 138–149.
22. Abbey Klaasen, "Marketers Fear Being Fleeced at Corner of Madison and Vine," *Advertising Age,* March 28, 2005, 3, 124.
23. Ibid. See also, Emma Johnstone and Christopher A. Dodd, "Placements As Mediators of Brand Salience within a UK Cinema Audience," *Journal of Marketing Communications* 6 (September 2000), 141–158; and Alain d'Astous and Francis Chartier, "A Study of Factors Affecting Consumer Evaluations and Memory of Product Placements in Movies," *Journal of Current Issues and Research in Advertising* 22 (fall 2000), 31–40.
24. Pola B. Gupta and Kenneth R. Lord, "Product Placement in Movies: The Effect of Prominence and Mode on Audience Recall," *Journal of Current Issues and Research in Advertising* 20 (spring 1998), 47–60.
25. Adapted from Brian Steinberg, "Product Placement Pricing Debated," *Wall Street Journal Online,* November 19, 2004, http://online.wsj.com.
26. Emma Hall, "Young Consumers Receptive to Movie Product Placements," *Advertising Age,* March 29, 2004, 8.
27. Graser, "Product-Placement Spending Poised to Hit $4.25 billion in '05."
28. Patricia Odell, "Rewriting Placement History," *Promo,* March 2005, 8.
29. Quoting Ryan Berger, a trend spotter, in T. L. Stanley, "Cool Consumption Good Fit for Hip-Hop," *Advertising Age,* July 12, 2004, 16.
30. "The Power of In-Cinema Marketing," Special advertising section of *Advertising Age,* Spring 2005, C1.

31. For full descriptions, see Youngme Moon, "BMW Films, Harvard Business School Case 9-502-046," May 15, 2002.
32. Alice Cuneo, "Dr. Martens Targets Teens with Web Films," *Advertising Age,* September 13, 2004, 14.
33. Kimberley A. Strassel, "Virtual Ads Vie for Field Position, But Regulators Move to Stop Them," *Wall Street Journal Online,* October 17, 1997, http://online.wsj.com.
34. I include this photo in honor of my late, great friend, John Kuhayda, and to his dear wife Patty and family. John was the embodiment of integrity and loyalty. Every moment we spent together was one of joy. His "dash" was too short but full of substance and character. He will always be my Padna, the Champ.
35. Lisa Sanders, "More Marketers Have to Go to the Bathroom," *Advertising Age,* September 20, 2004, 53.
36. Michael Applebaum, "Look, Up in the Sky: Brands!" *Brandweek,* September 13, 2004, 42.

PART 5
Promotion Management, Marketing-Oriented Public Relations, and Sponsorships

Part Five includes four chapters that cover trade- and consumer-oriented sales promotions along with the marketing aspect of public relations and the use of sponsorships and events. *Chapter 17* overviews sales promotions by explaining the targets of promotional efforts, the reasons underlying the rapid growth of promotions, and sales promotion's capabilities and limitations. The chapter also examines trade-oriented promotions, describing the most widely used forms of trade promotions and discussion of forward buying, diverting, and the advent of manufacturer-oriented everyday low pricing. Efficient consumer response, category management, and account-specific marketing also receive prominent treatment. The chapter concludes with a discussion of nine empirical generalizations about trade and consumer promotions.

Two forms of consumer-oriented sales promotions, sampling and couponing, are the subjects of *Chapter 18*. The various forms of sampling programs and three major sampling initiatives are discussed (targeting, innovative distribution methods, and sampling's ROI). The second topic in Chapter 18, couponing, includes treatment of the various forms of coupons, the economic implications of couponing, and the process of coupon redemption and misredemption.

Chapter 19 continues coverage of consumer-oriented promotions by examining various promotions other than sampling and couponing. Each of the following promotional programs receives coverage: premiums, price-off promotions, bonus packs, promotional games, rebates/refunds, and sweepstakes/contests. The chapter concludes with a three-step procedure for evaluating sales promotion ideas and suggestions for conducting a post-mortem analysis.

Chapter 20, on marketing-oriented public relations and sponsorships, includes a discussion of the historically entrenched practice of reactive public relations, as well as the more recent practice of proactive public relations. A special section is devoted to negative publicity, including the issue of how to handle rumors and urban legends. The last major section covers both cause marketing and event marketing—the two specific aspects of sponsorship marketing. Coverage includes discussion of the specific factors that a company should consider when selecting an event to sponsor—factors such as image match-up, target audience fit, clutter, and economic viability. The benefits of cause-oriented marketing are detailed, and factors that should be considered when selecting a cause to support are reviewed.

CHAPTER 17

Sales Promotion and the Role of Trade Promotions

Marcom Challenge: It's a Matter of Power—Nike Versus Foot Locker

A theme presented throughout this chapter is that the role of sales promotions, especially trade-oriented promotions, is largely a function of the relative *power* between manufacturers and retailers. Power, in a dictionary sense, describes the strength, might, or force that one entity has relative to another. In the marketplace, power involves the ability of one channel member to command or control another. Greater power relative to another is achieved with increased economic or non-economic (e.g., informational) resources. The competitive marketplace virtually necessitates that companies amass power in order to flourish, if not only to simply survive. Greater power means that one participant in a market relationship—such as a manufacturer or a retailer—has increased ability to influence the nature of the relationship and the terms of sale between the two parties. Weak trade partners have terms of sale imposed on them, whereas more powerful partners can, at the extreme, dictate terms of sale. Wal-Mart, for example, is a mega-powerful retailer that is well known for commanding its suppliers to produce products that meet Wal-Mart's price and non-price requirements.

A recent episode in the athletic footwear industry illustrates another application of power, when a major power clash transpired between two industry giants—Nike, a manufacturer, and Foot Locker, a retailer. This collision occurred when the CEO of Foot Locker became infuriated at Nike's rigid terms of sale being imposed on Foot Locker (and other retail buyers) in both the selection of which of Nike's shoes Foot Locker would carry in its stores and in how the shoes would be priced. Due to its industry dominance and power position, Nike requires retailers to buy all types of Nike shoes, not just the particular models that retailers would like to cherry pick as most appropriate for their clientele. Also, Nike provides retailers lower markups on Nike shoes in comparison to the markups permitted by other athletic footwear makers.

Angered by Nike's rigid terms and power politics, Foot Locker's CEO announced it would cut Nike orders by 15 percent to 25 percent per year, or between $150 million and $250 million annually. What was Nike's response to Foot Locker's power play? On the one hand, you might think that Nike would relax its rigid terms so as to appease Foot Locker and prevent the huge loss of business. On the other hand, Nike could respond in kind by making its own power move. That, in fact, is exactly the course of action undertaken: Nike slashed its planned shipments to Foot Locker by $400 million (40 percent of the previous year's shipments) and withheld its most highly demanded shoes from being sold in Foot Locker stores. One power move trumped by another! A former Foot Locker executive opined that Foot Locker's CEO made the mistake of thinking that Nike is as dependent on his company as Foot Locker is reliant on Nike. "They've taught Foot Locker a lesson they'll never forget."[1]

© Susan Van Etten

CHAPTER OBJECTIVES

1

Understand the nature and purpose of sales promotions.

2

Know the factors that account for the increased investment in promotions, especially those that are trade oriented.

3

Recognize the tasks that promotions can and cannot accomplish.

4

Appreciate the objectives of trade-oriented promotions and the factors critical to building a successful trade promotion program.

5

Comprehend the various forms of trade allowances and the reasons for their use.

6

Be aware of forward buying and diverting and how these practices emerge from manufacturers' use of off-invoice allowances.

7

Appreciate the role of everyday low pricing (EDLP) and pay-for-performance programs as means of reducing forward buying and diverting.

8

Recognize the concept and practice known as efficient consumer response (ECR).

9

Appreciate the practice of category management.

10

Understand nine empirical generalizations about promotions.

Overview

The objective of this chapter and the two that follow is to provide a thorough introduction to sales promotion's role in the overall marcom function. This chapter introduces the topic of sales promotions and then examines the role of trade-oriented promotions. The following two chapters extend this introduction by analyzing promotion's job in influencing the actions of consumers.

What Exactly Is Sales Promotion?

It first will be useful to clarify some terminology. Whereas marketing academics typically refer to the term *sales promotions,* practitioners truncate the expression to simply *promotions.* This contrast between academia and practice probably originated because one of the elements of the marketing mix (product, place, price, and *promotion*) is applied by academics in reference to *all* forms of marketing communications (advertising, sales promotions, public relations, personal selling, etc.) and not to sales promotions per se. Thus, in the pursuit of precise terminology, academics separate the specific practice of sales promotions from the more inclusive notion of promotion *in toto.* Practitioners need not concern themselves with this distinction and thus use the more efficient term *promotions* in reference to what professors call *sales promotions.* Distinction noted, this text uses the term *promotion* in lieu of or interchangeably with *sales promotion.*

By definition, **promotion** refers to any *incentive* used by a manufacturer to induce the *trade* (wholesalers, retailers, or other channel members) or *consumers* to buy a brand and to encourage the *sales force* to aggressively sell it. Retailers and not-for-profit organizations also use promotional incentives to encourage desired behaviors from their consumers and clientele—shop at this store rather than a competitor's, buy this brand rather than another, purchase larger quantities, donate now rather than later, become a season-ticket holder, and so on. The incentive is *additional to the basic benefits* provided by the brand and *temporarily changes its perceived price or value.*[2]

The italicized features require comment. First, by definition, promotions involve incentives (i.e., bonuses or rewards) that are designed to encourage trade customers or end-user consumers to purchase a particular brand sooner, more frequently, or in larger quantities, or to engage in some other behavior that will benefit the manufacturer or retailer that offers the promotion. Second, these incentives (allowances, rebates, sweepstakes, coupons, premiums, and so on) are additions to—not substitutes for—the basic benefits a purchaser typically acquires when buying a particular product or service. Third, the target of the incentive is the trade, consumers, the sales force, or all three parties. Finally, the incentive changes a brand's perceived price or value, but only temporarily. This is to say that a sales promotion incentive for a particular brand applies to a single purchase or perhaps several purchases during a period, but not to every purchase a trade customer or consumer would make over an extended time.

In contrast to advertising, which typically, though not always, is relatively long term in orientation and best suited to enhancing buyer attitudes and augmenting brand equity, promotion is more *short-term oriented* and capable of influencing *behavior* (rather than just attitudes or intentions). Indeed, the academically oriented term *sales promotion* precisely captures this short-term, behavioral orientation insofar as promotions are designed to promote purchases, which from the brand promoter's perspective are sales. Promotion has the character of urgency in its injunction to act *now* because tomorrow is too late.[3] Promotion has the power to influence behavior because it offers the buyer superior value in the short term and can make buyers feel better about the buying experience.[4]

It also is important to note at this point that although consumer packaged goods (CPG) companies are the biggest users of promotions, all types of companies use promotional incentives. For example, restaurants offer coupons and other forms of price discounts, and sometimes provide free desserts when a special entrée is purchased. Online companies offer free shipping for orders above a certain monetary amount. Furniture stores provide free gifts when selected items are purchased. And automobile companies regularly offer rebates and cheap financing to attract purchasers. In fact, a recent study of rebate programs concluded that automobile manufacturers' frequent use of rebates positively impacts revenue in the short run but has a negative effect on profits in the long run.[5]

In an unconventional yet increasingly practiced form of promotion by not-for-profit organizations, a major state university wrote letters to hundreds of high school students who had been named National Merit Semifinalists and offered the following:

*If you attain **finalist** status in the National Merit competition, we will offer you, upon admission to the university, a Presidential Scholarship that will pay the value of tuition for four years as well as on-campus housing during your freshman year. You will also receive a University National Merit Scholarship of at least $1,000 . . . if, as a finalist, you do not receive another National Merit sponsored scholarship. In addition, you will receive $2,000 for use in summer research or study abroad. If you list [name of university] as your college of choice with the National Merit Scholarship Corporation, you also will receive a free laptop computer when you enroll.*

Though not your typical $1 coupon, free sample, or mail-in premium, this offer attempts to induce an action (enroll at this particular university) that is no different than efforts brand managers employ to encourage purchases of their brands. The point is clear: promotions are used universally.

Promotion Targets

To appreciate more fully the role of promotion, consider the following promotion from Schering-Plough, a leader in the foot-care category. Schering-Plough markets two well-known foot-care brands: Lotrimin AF and Tinactin. To gain greater trade support for these brands and to generate excitement and enthusiasm among its own sales force of 152 people, Schering-Plough introduced the "Howwe Gosell" promotion. (This promotional label plays on the name of the famous sportscaster, the late Howard Cosell, who gained celebrity for his outspoken personality and quirky mannerisms while announcing major sporting events, especially boxing matches featuring Muhammad Ali, and football games on *Monday Night Football*.) The promotion appealed to Schering-Plough's sales force to be part of the "team" coached by Howwe Gosell, who encouraged his "players" (the sales force) on to a victory ending in higher sales of Lotrimin AF and Tinactin. In keeping with the football motif, salespeople received "playbooks" and had a chance to score points that would earn them National Football League merchandise or expense-paid trips to the Super Bowl. The result: Tinactin and Lotrimin AF gained 19 percent and 14 percent, respectively, in sales volume during the promotional period. Howwe Gosell was a topic of much discussion among the sales force, and the trade devoted more display space to these brands than they had ever previously enjoyed.[6]

© Susan Van Etten

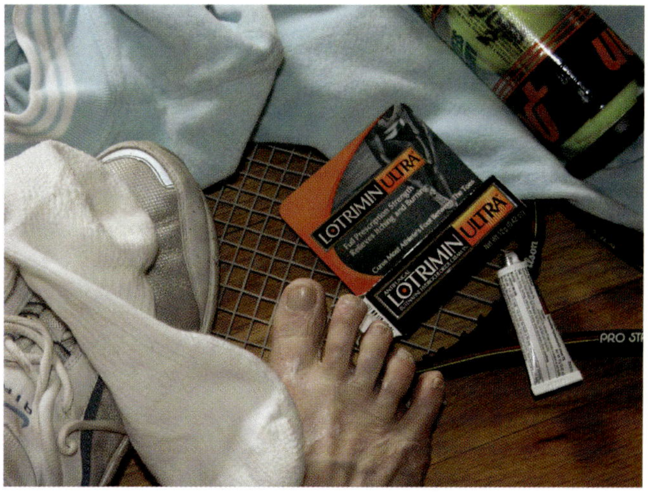

For Schering-Plough's foot-care brands to achieve their marketing objectives (sales volume and market share), several things had to happen: First, Schering-Plough's *sales force* had to enthusiastically and aggressively sell these brands to the trade. Second, *retailers* had to be encouraged to allocate sufficient store space to the brands and provide merchandising support to enable them to stand out, if only temporarily, from competitive brands. Third, consumers needed reasons for selecting Lotrimin AF and Tinactin over competitive foot-care brands. The promotion was extremely effective in appealing to all three groups.

All three groups—the sales force, retailers, and consumers—are targets of sales promotional efforts (see Figure 17.1). First, trade- and consumer-oriented sales promotions provide the manufacturer's sales force with the necessary tools for aggressively and enthusiastically selling to wholesale and retail buyers. In other words, salespeople have an incentive to put special selling emphasis behind a promoted brand; they are, in other words, *encouraged* to actively sell those brands that are being promoted.

A promotion undertaken by a manufacturer also can encourage retail salespeople to devote more attention to the manufacturer's brands. Consider a promotion undertaken by Packard Bell, which at one time was a top brand in home PC sales, only to lose its commanding presence to Dell, Gateway, and Hewlett-Packard / Compaq. In an effort to regain some of its lost market share, Packard Bell designed an innovative program to influence the retail salespeople in electronic and computer stores to emphasize Packard Bell computers to prospective purchasers. After acquiring a mailing list of names and home addresses, Packard Bell mailed retail salespeople a series of three interactive CD-ROMs that were packaged as takeout food items (a pizza box, Chinese food container, and a chicken bucket). These food items were appropriately themed to the takeout eating habits of the targeted group of youthful male salespeople. Each CD-ROM contained information about the latest features of Packard Bell computers along with interesting supplemental segments, including movie trailers, classic TV advertising spots, and music videos. The "Home Delivery" program was a major success. Follow-up research determined that 95 percent of the targeted salespeople wanted to receive more CD-ROMs; 64 percent reported having viewed the CD-ROMs on multiple occasions; and, of greatest significance, 70 percent of the salespeople acknowledged that their perceptions of Packard Bell had improved after viewing the CD-ROMs and that they recommended Packard Bell PCs more often than before.[7] (See the *Global Focus* insert for another example of how a sales promotion can incentivize retail salespeople.)

A second target of sales promotion efforts is the trade, including wholesalers but especially retailers. Various types of allowances, discounts, contests, and advertising support programs are used in a forward thrust from manufacturers to

Figure 17.1
Brand-Level Promotional Imperatives

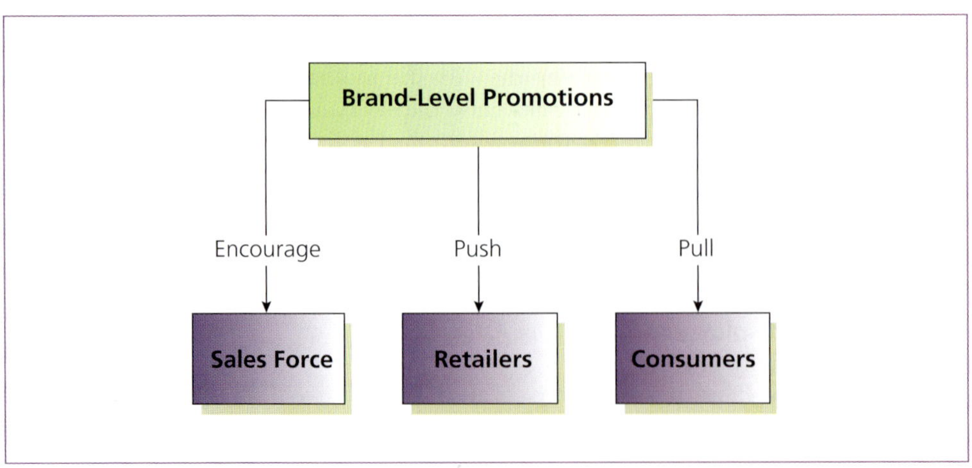

Driving Sales for Fiat in Brazil

global focus

Fiat Automobiles of Brazil had redesigned its Marea sedan and station wagon and was looking for an exciting promotion. A promotion agency was employed to create a program that would achieve two key objectives: (1) encourage prospective customers to test drive the Marea, and (2) motivate salespeople to develop thorough product knowledge.

One of the Marea's top new features was a redesigned CD player. With this feature in mind, the promotion agency began the process of developing a campaign targeted mostly to males age 35 and older. The client, Fiat, wanted a promotional campaign that would create buzz; encourage nearly 20,000 consumers to test-drive the Marea; and, ultimately, sell a lot of cars.

The creative promotional program centered on the giveaway of a CD containing the music of two well-known and respected Brazilian singers, Milton Nascimento and Gilberto Gil. CDs were distributed via direct mail to targeted consumers and also through inserts in magazines that reached the demographic group. Accompanying advertising copy pointed out to recipients that it was important that they bring their free CDs with them when visiting a Fiat dealership. Dealer visits were encouraged by promoting the fact that CD recipients would receive free concert tickets and an opportunity to win a new Marea automobile.

On arriving at a dealership and requesting a test-drive, a salesperson would insert the customer's free CD into the Marea's CD player. Near the end of the test-drive, the salesperson would switch the CD to the final track. This track, unbeknownst to the customer, contained an audio code that was compared with a printed code located under the driver-side visor. The customer became an automatic winner of a new Marea if the CD code matched the printed code under the visor. Of course, only one person won the car. However, everyone who took a test-drive received free concert tickets. They also were entered into a sweepstakes that provided everyone an opportunity to win a second Marea.

The promotional program also included an incentive to energize dealer salespeople. One part of the program involved "mystery shoppers" trained by Fiat who visited dealerships to test salespeople and managers on their technical knowledge of the Marea and their customer service skills. Salespeople and managers judged as having impeccable knowledge and sales skills received cash prizes. Additionally, each month during the course of the year, top-performing salespeople and managers earned additional cash prizes. At the campaign's end, top performers received paid vacations to Brazil's luxurious Comandatuba Island.

All told, more than 22,000 CD recipients visited dealerships to take test-drives in the redesigned Marea. Incredibly, 3,000, or nearly 14 percent, actually purchased a Marea—which is an extremely high conversion rate. In the final analysis, the Marea experienced a 20 percent sales increase during the promotional period, attributable in large part to a promotion that appealed to the target market and also incentivized dealerships and their salespeople.

SOURCE: Adapted from "A Real Gasser," *Promo,* January 2002, 27. Used with permission from *Promo.*

trade accounts (referred to as *push* efforts) that provide retailers with reasons for stocking, displaying, advertising, and perhaps placing the promoted brand on a price-discounted deal. Third, the use of consumer-oriented promotions (e.g., coupons, samples, premiums, cents-off deals, sweepstakes, and contests) serve to *pull* a brand through the channel by providing consumers with a special reason to purchase a promoted brand on a trial or repeat basis.

Increased Budgetary Allocations to Promotions

Advertising spending as a percentage of total marketing communications expenditures has declined in recent years, while promotion spending has steadily increased. Media advertising expenditures as a proportion of total marketing communications expenditures used to average over *40 percent* of companies' budgets. However, beginning about a quarter century ago and continuing today, media advertising's portion of the total marcom budget has fallen to less than one-quarter. In fact, one recent report estimates that for CPGs trade promotions command 54 percent of total U.S. marcom expenditures, that consumer promotions capture 28.5 percent of the total, and that consumer advertising achieves only 17.5 percent of the total.[8] Why have firms shifted money from advertising and into promotions, especially trade-oriented promotions? The following section examines the major reasons underlying this shift.

Factors Accounting for the Shift

Several factors account for why CPG brand managers have shifted budgetary allocations increasingly toward a greater proportion of trade promotions. However, before we describe the reasons for this shift, it first will be beneficial to briefly review the concepts of *push* and *pull* marketing strategies.

Push and *pull* (as these terms were used in Figure 17.1) are physical metaphors characterizing the promotional activities manufacturers undertake to encourage channel members (the trade) to handle and merchandise brands and consumers to purchase them. **Push** involves a *forward thrust* of effort, metaphorically speaking, whereby a manufacturer directs personal selling, trade advertising, and trade-oriented promotions to wholesalers and retailers. Through this combination of sales influence, advertising, and, perhaps especially, promotions in the form of allowances and other deals, manufacturers "push" channel members to increase their inventories of the manufacturer's brand versus competitive brands. **Pull**, on the other hand, entails a *backward tug*, again speaking metaphorically, from consumers to retailers. This tug, or pull, is the result of a manufacturer's successful advertising and consumer promotion efforts that encourage consumers to prefer, at least in the short term, the manufacturer's brand versus competitive offerings.

Table 17.1 illustrates the differences between push- and pull-oriented promotional strategies based on two companies' allocations of $30 million among different promotional activities. Company X emphasizes a *push strategy* by allocating most of its promotional budget to personal selling and trade promotions aimed at retail customers. Company Y, on the other hand, uses a *pull strategy* by investing the vast majority of its budget in consumer advertising.

It is important to recognize that pushing and pulling are *not* mutually exclusive activities. Both efforts occur simultaneously. Manufacturers promote to consumers (creating pull) *and* to trade members (accomplishing push). The issue is not *which strategy to use* but rather *which to emphasize.* Effective marketing communications involves a *combination of forces:* exerting push to the trade and creating pull from consumers.

Historically, at least through the 1970s, the emphasis in CPG marketing was on promotional pull (such as company Y's budget in Table 17.1). Manufacturers advertised heavily, especially on network television, and literally forced retailers to handle their brands by creating consumer demand for those heavily advertised items. However, over the past generation, pull-oriented marketing has become less effective due in large part to the splintering of the mass media and audience fractionalization as discussed in Chapter 14. Along with this reduced effectiveness has come an increase in the use of push-oriented sales promotion practices (such as company X's budget in Table 17.1).

Increased investment in sales promotion, especially trade-oriented promotions, has gone hand in hand with the growth in push marketing. Major developments

Table 17.1
Push and Pull Strategies

	Company X (PUSH)	Company Y (PULL)
Personal Selling to Retailers	$13,500,000	$6,000,000
Sales Promotion to Retailers	12,000,000	150,000
Advertising to Retailers	2,400,000	300,000
Advertising to Consumers	1,800,000	20,550,000
Sales Promotion to Consumers	300,000	3,000,000
TOTAL	$30,000,000	$30,000,000

Table 17.2

Developments Underlying the Growth in Promotions

- Shift in manufacturer versus retailer balance of power
- Increased brand parity and price sensitivity
- Reduced brand loyalty
- Splintered mass market and reduced media effectiveness
- Emphasis on short-term results in corporate reward structures
- Responsive consumers

that have given rise to sales promotion are summarized in Table 17.2 and discussed hereafter. It is important to emphasize at this point that these developments are interdependent rather than separate and distinct. Hence, there is no particular order of importance implied by the listing in Table 17.2.

Balance-of-Power Shift

Until roughly 1980, national manufacturers of CPG products generally were more powerful and influential than the supermarkets, drugstores, and mass merchandisers that carried the manufacturers' brands. The reason was twofold. First, manufacturers were able to create consumer *pull* by virtue of heavy network television advertising, thus effectively requiring retailers to handle their brands whether retailers wanted to or not. Second, retailers did little research of their own and, accordingly, were dependent on manufacturers for information such as whether a new product would be successful. A manufacturer's sales representative could convince a buyer to carry a new product using test-market results suggesting a successful product introduction.

The balance of power began shifting when network television dipped in effectiveness as an advertising medium and, especially, with the advent of optical scanning equipment. Armed with a steady flow of data from optical scanners, retailers now know virtually on a real-time basis which products are selling and which advertising and promotion programs are working. Retailers no longer need to depend on manufacturers for data. Instead, retailers use the facts they now possess to demand terms of sale rather than merely accepting manufacturers' terms. The consequence for manufacturers is that for every promotional dollar used to support retailers' advertising or merchandising programs, one less dollar is available for the manufacturer's own advertising. Needless to say, retailers are *not* always more powerful than manufacturers, as indicated in the *Marcom Challenge* where a manufacturer (Nike) was more powerful than its recalcitrant retailer (Foot Locker) and accordingly dictated the terms of sale.

Increased Brand Parity and Price Sensitivity

In earlier years when truly new products were being offered to the marketplace, manufacturers could effectively advertise unique advantages over competitive offerings. As product categories have matured, however, most new offerings represent only slight changes from existing products, thus resulting, more often than not, in greater similarities between competitive brands. With fewer distinct product differences, consumers have grown more reliant on price and price incentives (coupons, cents-off deals, refunds, etc.) as ways of differentiating parity brands. Because concrete advantages are often difficult to obtain, both manufacturers and retailers have turned increasingly to promotion as a means of achieving temporary advantages over competitors.

Reduced Brand Loyalty

Consumers probably are less loyal than they once were. This is partly due to the fact that brands have grown increasingly similar, thereby making it easier for consumers to switch among brands. Also, marketers have effectively trained consumers to expect that at least one brand in a product category will always be on deal with a coupon, cents-off offer, or refund; hence, many consumers rarely purchase brands other than those on deal. (The term **deal** refers to any form of sales promotion that delivers a *price reduction* to consumers. Retailer discounts, manufacturer cents-off offers, and the ubiquitous coupon are the most common forms of deals.)

One team of researchers investigated the impact that deal promotions have on consumers' price sensitivity using eight years of data for a nonfood brand in the CPG category. These researchers determined that price promotions make consumers more price sensitive in the long run. Moreover, increased use of price promotions serves, for all intents and purposes, to "train" consumers to search for deals. Nonloyal consumers are especially likely to be conditioned by marketers' use of price deals.[9] Research also reveals that the use of coupons by brands in the liquid detergent category (brands such as Wisk, Era, and Bold) resulted in increased consumer price sensitivity and reduced brand loyalty.[10]

The upshot of heightened dealing activity is that marketers have created a "monster" in the form of consumers' desire for deals. Reduced loyalty and increased brand-switching behavior have resulted, requiring more dealing activity to feed the monster's insatiable appetite. A major international study of sales promotion activities in Germany, Japan, the United Kingdom, and the United States investigated the effects of price-related promotions (such as cents-off deals and coupons) on a brand's sales *after* a promotional period is over. The dramatic finding from this research, which examined dozens of brands in 25 consumer goods categories, is that these promotions have virtually *no impact* on a brand's long-term sales or on consumers' repeat buying loyalty. No strong aftereffects occurred because extra sales for the promoted brands came almost exclusively from a brand's long-term customer base. In other words, the people who normally buy a brand are the ones who are most responsive to the brand's price promotion. Hence, price promotions effectively serve to induce consumers to buy on deal what they would have bought at regular prices anyway. In sum, although price-related promotions typically result in immediate and huge sales spikes, these short-term gains generally do not positively influence long-term brand growth.[11]

Splintering of the Mass Market and Reduced Media Effectiveness

Advertising *efficiency* is directly related to the degree of homogeneity in consumers' consumption needs and media habits. The greater their homogeneity, the less costly it is for mass advertising to reach target audiences. However, as consumer lifestyles have diversified and advertising media have narrowed in their appeal, mass-media advertising's efficiency has weakened. On top of this, advertising effectiveness has declined with simultaneous increases in ad clutter and escalating media costs. These combined forces have influenced many brand managers to devote proportionately larger budgets to promotions at the expense of advertising.

Short-Term Orientation and Corporate Reward Structures

Sales promotions go hand in hand with the brand management system, which is the dominant organizational structure in CPG firms. The reward structure in firms organized along brand manager lines emphasizes *short-term sales response* rather than slow, long-term growth. In other words, brand managers' performances are assessed on an annual basis or even quarter-by-quarter. And sales promotion is incomparable when it comes to generating quick sales response. In fact, the majority of packaged-good brand sales are associated with some kind of promotional deal.[12]

Consumer Responsiveness

A final force that explains the shift toward sales promotion at the expense of advertising is that consumers respond favorably to money-saving opportunities and other value-adding promotions. Consumers would not be responsive to promotions unless there was something in it for them—and, in fact, there is. All promotion techniques provide consumers with *rewards* (benefits, incentives, or inducements) that encourage certain forms of behavior desired by brand managers. These rewards, or benefits, are both utilitarian and hedonic.[13] Consumers using sales promotions receive *utilitarian*, or functional, benefits of (1) monetary savings (e.g., when using coupons); (2) reduced search and decision costs (e.g., by simply availing themselves of a promotional offer and not thinking about other alternatives); and (3) improved product quality, because price reductions allow consumers to buy superior brands they might not otherwise purchase.

Consumers also obtain *hedonic*, nonfunctional benefits when taking advantage of sales promotion offers, including (1) a sense of being a wise shopper when taking advantage of sales promotions;[14] (2) a need for stimulation and variety when, say, trying brands they otherwise might not purchase if it were not for attractive promotions; and (3) entertainment value when, for example, consumers compete in promotional contests or participate in sweepstakes.

An Unintended Consequence of Growth: New Accounting Rules

In view of the major increase in sales promotions over the past quarter century, especially trade-oriented promotions, the organization responsible for establishing accounting standards in the United States—the Financial Accounting Standards Board (FASB)—reexamined how sales promotion expenditures should be handled on business organizations' income statements. Promotion expenditures historically were treated in exactly the same fashion as advertising expenditures, namely, as current expenses that were deducted from top-line revenue. However, a unit of FASB called the Emerging Issues Task Force proposed new accounting regulations (EITF 00-14 and 00-25) that went into effect in late 2001. EITF 00-14 and 00-25 require that those sales promotions used as a form of *price discount*—including promotions directed to retailers (e.g., off-invoice and slotting allowances, both of which are discussed later in this chapter) as well as to consumers (e.g., couponing expenditures and loyalty programs)—must now be treated as reductions in sales revenue. Some companies (e.g., Procter & Gamble [P&G] and Unilever) have long accounted for promotion expenditures in the way proposed by these new accounting regulations, but most firms did not, which thus created an apples and oranges situation when comparing top-line revenue figures. FASB's regulations were designed to create an apples-versus-apples environment by placing all firms on equal footing in how they account for price-oriented sales promotions. It is estimated that adherence to these new accounting rules will cut reported net sales for CPG companies by 8.5 percent on average.[15]

Table 17.3 presents simplified income statements to illustrate the effect of this accounting change. For illustrative purposes, consider that a firm has $50 million in sales revenue, that cost of goods sold equals $20 million, general and administrative expenses total $10 million, sales promotion expenditures amount to $8 million, and advertising expenditures equal $5 million. Under the historical (pre-EITF 00-14 and 00-25) accounting procedures, top-line revenue would be recorded at the full amount of $50 million, and sales promotion expenditures along with the other expenses would be deducted from this amount to yield a bottom-line profit of $7 million (see entries under the "old" accounting procedure in Table 17.3).

Table 17.3

Illustration of "Old" and "New" Accounting Procedures

	"Old" Accounting Procedure	"New" Accounting Procedure
Revenue	$50,000,000	$42,000,000
Cost of Goods Sold	20,000,000	20,000,000
G&A Expenses	10,000,000	10,000,000
Sales Promotion	8,000,000	NA*
Advertising	5,000,000	5,000,000
Total Expenses	43,000,000	35,000,000
Pretax Profit	$ 7,000,000	$ 7,000,000

* The $8,000,000 spent on sales promotions has been deducted from the top line.

Under the "new" (post-EITF 00-14 and 00-15) accounting procedure and assuming identical expenditures, the bottom-line profit would remain at $7 million. Notice in Table 17.3, however, that the difference between the "old" and "new" procedures is in the amount recorded for the top-line revenue—specifically, $50 million under the "old" procedure compared to $42 million for the "new" procedure ($50 million sales minus $8 million promotion expenditures).

You might be thinking that this is no big deal insofar as the change in accounting procedures really has had no impact on the bottom-line figure. The significance of the change, however, is that it better reflects "true" levels of sales revenue, which was the intent of the FASB's regulations. In other words, when sales promotions represent little more than a price discount, the amount of discount should not be treated as revenue, which under the old accounting system served to inflate actual revenue and to mislead financial analysts, stockholders, and other parties regarding a firm's actual revenue generation. Moreover, sales forces compensated on the basis of top-line results were overcompensated because revenue itself was overstated. Hence, under the new accounting rules, price-discounting promotions are appropriately treated as direct reductions from sales revenue rather than as indirect expense reductions.

Although it is too early to know with any certainty what impact, if any, this change in accounting rules will have on brand managers' allocations of marcom funds to sales promotions, it is possible to conjecture that their behavior may be altered somewhat in order to "protect" the top line. In other words, knowing that every dollar of price-discounting promotion is immediately deducted from the revenue line, brand managers may move relatively more money into advertising or into other forms of sales promotions other than price discounts. Only time will tell, but this change in accounting standards likely is not a trivial development in terms of managerial behavior with respect to allocating marcom budgets.

What Are Sales Promotion's Capabilities and Limitations?

Trade and consumer promotions are capable of accomplishing certain objectives and not others. Table 17.4 summarizes these "can" and "cannot" capabilities, each of which is discussed hereafter.[16]

What Promotions Can *Accomplish*

Promotions cannot work wonders but are well-suited to accomplishing the following tasks.

Table 17.4

Tasks That Promotions Can and Cannot Accomplish

Sales Promotions *Can*

- Stimulate sales force enthusiasm for a new, improved, or mature product
- Invigorate sales of a mature brand
- Facilitate the introduction of new products to the trade
- Increase on- and off-shelf merchandising space
- Neutralize competitive advertising and sales promotions
- Obtain trial purchases from consumers
- Hold current users by encouraging repeat purchases
- Increase product usage by loading consumers
- Preempt competition by loading consumers
- Reinforce advertising

Sales Promotions *Cannot*

- Compensate for a poorly trained sales force or for a lack of advertising
- Give the trade or consumers any compelling long-term reason to continue purchasing a brand
- Permanently stop an established brand's declining sales trend or change the basic nonacceptance of an undesired product

Stimulate Sales Force Enthusiasm for a New, Improved, or Mature Product

There are many exciting and challenging aspects of personal selling; there also are times when the job can become dull, monotonous, and unrewarding. For example, imagine what it would be like to repeatedly call on a customer if you never had anything new or different to say about your brands or the marketing efforts that support them. Maintaining enthusiasm would be difficult, to say the least. Exciting sales promotions give salespeople persuasive ammunition when interacting with buyers; they revive enthusiasm and make the salesperson's job easier and more enjoyable. A case in point is the previously described Howwe Gosell promotion for Schering-Plough's two foot-care brands, Lotrimin AF and Tinactin.

Invigorate Sales of a Mature Brand

Promotions can invigorate sales of a mature product that requires a shot in the arm. Promotions cannot, however, reverse the sales decline for an undesirable product or brand. Consider, for example, a promotion undertaken by Bazooka bubble gum in Latin America, where, as in the United States, Bazooka bubble gum comes wrapped with a Bazooka Kid comic strip. The character in this comic strip is known to children in Argentina, Paraguay, and Uruguay as *El Pibe Bazooka.* Bazooka commanded over 40 percent of the gum market in these countries, but its share had fallen by more than 10 points due to an onslaught of competitors. The maker of Bazooka gum, Cadbury, turned to its promotion agency for ideas to offset competitive inroads. The agency devised a promotion that led to temporarily replacing *El Pibe Bazooka* with Secret Clues that, when placed under a decoder screen, would reveal keys to "Bazooka Super Treasure." More than 150 million Secret Clues hit the market, and three million decoder screens were made available to kids through magazine and newspaper inserts and at candy stands and schools. After buying Bazooka and placing a Secret Clue under a decoder screen, kids learned immediately whether they would receive instant-win prizes such as T-shirts, soccer balls, and school bags. Kids could also enter a Super Treasure sweepstakes by mailing in 10 proofs of purchase. Top prizes included multimedia computers for winners and their schools along with stereo systems, TVs, bicycles, and other attractive items.

Courtesy, TOPPS, Inc.

Consumer response was so overwhelming that Bazooka experienced distribution problems within several weeks of initiating the promotion. Bazooka sales increased by 28 percent and gained back about seven share points. This successful promotion demonstrates the power of sales incentives that catch the imagination of a receptive target market. Kids were encouraged to buy Bazooka gum to win instant prizes and to purchase the brand on repeated occasions to become eligible for very attractive sweepstakes awards.[17]

Facilitate the Introduction of New Products to the Trade

To achieve sales and profit objectives, marketers continually introduce new products and add new brands to existing categories. Promotions to wholesalers and retailers are typically necessary to encourage the trade to handle new offerings, which practitioners refer to as *stock-keeping units*, or SKUs. In fact, many retailers refuse to carry additional SKUs unless they receive extra compensation in the form of off-invoice allowances, display allowances, and slotting allowances. (Each of these various forms of allowances is discussed later in the chapter.)

Increase On- and Off-Shelf Merchandising Space

Trade-oriented promotions, often in conjunction with consumer promotions, enable a manufacturer to obtain extra shelf space or more desirable space for a temporary period. This space may be in the form of extra facings on the shelf or off-shelf space in a gondola or an end-of-aisle display.[18] As established in Chapter 8 in the discussion of point-of-purchase materials, preferred shelf space plays an important role in lifting a brand's sales volume.

Neutralize Competitive Advertising and Sales Promotions

Sales promotions can effectively offset competitors' advertising and promotion efforts. For example, one company's 50-cent coupon loses much of its appeal when a competitor simultaneously comes out with a $1 coupon. As previously described, Bazooka's promotion in Argentina, Paraguay, and Uruguay offset competitors' promotions and won back lost market share.

Obtain Trial Purchases from Consumers

Marketers depend on free samples, coupons, and other sales promotions to encourage trial purchases of new brands. Many consumers would never try new products or previously untried brands without these promotional inducements. Consider the following creative promotion that was extraordinarily successful in introducing a new line of lightbulbs in England.

Although consumers worldwide use massive quantities of lightbulbs, many people consider the brand name not all that important when selecting lightbulbs, because they assume that lightbulbs are essentially commodities—one bulb is as good (or bad) as the next. Against this perception Philips Lighting attempted to create a differential advantage for its brand when introducing the Softone line of colored bulbs. But after more than a decade of marketing the brand, it had achieved a loyal following only among a small and predominantly older group of consumers. With a surge in home improvement activity in England in the late 90s, Philips attempted one more time to build demand for its Softone line—especially among younger families, who might become loyal product users for years.

This was quite a challenge considering that TV advertising was unable to adequately convey the subtle colors of Softone bulbs. It therefore was necessary to use some form of promotion to build brand awareness among the target segment and encourage trial purchase behavior—leading, hopefully, to repeat purchasing among loyal brand users. Philips hired a promotion agency to create a campaign that would achieve the dual awareness-building and trial-generating objectives. And, the available budget was approximately only $2 million.

The agency developed a program based on what it described as a "ludicrously simple idea." Certain households were selected to receive bags, each of which contained an information brochure, a coupon, and a brief questionnaire. The attractive brochure described the product's benefits and emphasized the mood-generating ability of colored lightbulbs. The coupon was for 50 pence (approximately 75 cents) off the purchase of a bulb. Bags were distributed just to households targeted based on a combination of their demographic and psychographic characteristics that made them prime prospects for purchasing the product. The distribution crews placed the bags in mailboxes. (Parenthetically, this would be illegal in the United States, which permits only the U.S. Postal Service to use mailboxes; such a restriction does not exist in England.)

You will note that the bags did *not* contain lightbulbs. Rather, a response sheet inside the bags asked recipients if they were interested in receiving a free bulb and, if so, which of seven colors they wanted. Interested households were instructed to hang the bag with the completed questionnaire on their outside doorknob. Then, that same evening distribution crews inspected each household's response sheet and slipped the preferred-color lightbulb into the bag.

A total of two million bags were distributed. Of these, 700,000 households requested a free bulb—for a response rate of 35 percent. Follow-up surveys revealed that over 50 percent of bulb recipients actually used the bulbs. A total of 160,000 coupons were redeemed, which at 8 percent is an incredibly high redemption level—as you will see in the following chapter. Sales in the six-month period following this special promotion doubled the prior average. Moreover, a subsequent bag distribution campaign was three times more efficient than the inaugural effort by focusing on neighborhoods near key retail accounts. This simple program illustrates how creative and strategically sound promotions can be highly successful in generating trial purchase behavior.[19]

Hold Current Users by Encouraging Repeat Purchases

Brand switching is a fact of life faced by all brand managers. The strategic use of certain forms of promotion can encourage at least short-run repetitive purchasing. Premium programs, refunds, sweepstakes, and various continuity programs (all described in Chapter 19) are useful promotions for encouraging repeat purchasing.

Increase Product Usage by Loading Consumers

The effect of many deal-oriented promotions is to encourage consumer *stockpiling*—that is, to influence consumers to purchase more of a particular brand than they normally would to take advantage of the deal. Research has found that when readily stockpiled items (e.g., canned goods, paper products, and soap) are promoted with a deal, purchase quantity increases—or stated alternatively, the consumption rate accelerates—by a substantial magnitude in the *short term*.[20]

© Susan Van Etten

This practice prompts a critical question: do these short-term increases resulting from consumer stockpiling actually lead to *long-term* consumption increases of the promoted product category or do they merely represent *borrowed future sales*? An important study found that price promotions do not increase category profitability but simply serve to shift short-term sales revenue from one brand to another. That is, sales gains in the short term induced by consumer stockpiling were offset by reduced demand in the long term.[21] This finding thus suggests that price-oriented promotions may encourage consumers to load up in the short term, but that this short-term *loading* simply steals purchases that otherwise would have been made during subsequent periods.

Please note that the foregoing finding is based on research involving a single product—namely, a nonfood item (probably a brand from the household cleaning category) that could not be disclosed by the researchers due to the manufacturer's proprietary concerns. Can this finding be generalized, or is the result idiosyncratic to this particular product category? No simple answer is possible, and, as usual, it depends on the circumstances surrounding a specific brand and promotional event. Other researchers, however, have provided tentative evidence that establishes when the practice of loading might have positive long-term effects. These researchers have determined that loading does increase consumers' product usage, especially when usage-related thoughts about a product are vivid in the consumer's memory. For example, people will not necessarily consume more soup just because they have stockpiled above-average quantities. However, if soup is on their minds (due to the presence of an advertising campaign touting soup's versatility), consumption is likely to increase. Also, products that are regularly visible (such as perishable items placed in the front of the refrigerator) are likely to receive greater use when consumers have stockpiled quantities of such products.[22]

This finding receives additional support from research that has examined the impact of consumer inventory levels on the amount of usage for two product categories, ketchup and yogurt. Researchers predicted that consumption of yogurt would be more sensitive to inventory level because unlike ketchup, yogurt can be consumed at different times of the day and under a variety of circumstances (with meals, as a snack, etc.). Their results supported this expectation as the amount of yogurt consumption, but not ketchup, was influenced by the quantity of yogurt available in consumers' refrigerators—more yogurt, more (than normal) consumption; more ketchup, no more (than normal) consumption.[23]

Although no simple conclusion is available at this stage of research, the empirical evidence suggests that marketer's price-oriented deals that encourage stockpiling promote increased long-term consumption for some product categories but not others. The evidence suggests two conditions when increased consumption occurs from stockpiling. First, when stockpiled products are *physically visible* to consumers as well as perishable, the effect may be to encourage increased short-term consumption without stealing sales from future periods. Second, consumers seem to increase their consumption rate of stockpiled products when the product is *convenient to consume* compared with when it requires preparation. Hence, it would be expected that snack foods would be consumed more rapidly when larger quantities are available in the household than would, say, a product such as pasta that has to be prepared.[24]

On the other hand, the use of price deals that lead consumers to stockpile products like ketchup and household cleaning products may simply serve to increase product purchasing in the short term without increasing long-term consumption. Consumers, in effect, stockpile these items when they go on deal but do not increase normal product usage. Thus, we would tentatively conclude that price dealing is a useful offensive weapon (that is, for purposes of increasing total consumption) only for items such as yogurt, cookies, and salty snacks, whereas products such as ketchup should be price promoted only for defensive reasons such as offsetting competitive efforts that attempt to steal market share.

Preempt Competition by Loading Consumers

When consumers are loaded with one company's brand, they are temporarily out of the marketplace for competitive brands. Hence, one brand's promotion serves to preempt sales of competitive brands.

Reinforce Advertising

A final can-do capability of sales promotion is to reinforce advertising. An advertising campaign can be strengthened greatly by a well-coordinated sales promotion effort.

The relationship between advertising and promotion is two way. On the one hand, an exciting promotion can reinforce advertising's impact. On the other, advertising is increasingly being used as a communications mechanism for delivering promotional offerings. It is estimated, in fact, that upwards of one-third of all media advertisements (TV, print, Internet, etc.) carry a promotional message.[25] The growing importance of promotion-oriented advertising is evidenced by the fact that promotion agencies are increasingly responsible for creating advertisements—a role historically of the traditional full-service advertising agency.

What Promotions Cannot Accomplish

As with other marketing communications elements, there are limits to what sales promotions are capable of accomplishing. Particularly notable are the following three limitations.

Inability to Compensate for a Poorly Trained Sales Force or for a Lack of Advertising

When suffering from poor sales performance or inadequate growth, some companies consider promotion to be the solution. However, promotions will provide at best a *temporary fix* if the underlying problem is due to a poor sales force, a lack of brand awareness, a weak brand image, or other maladies that only proper sales management and advertising efforts can overcome.

Inability to Give the Trade or Consumers Any Compelling Long-Term Reason to Continue Purchasing a Brand

The trade's decision to continue stocking a brand and consumers' repeat purchasing are based on continued satisfaction with the brand. Satisfaction results from the brand's meeting profit objectives (for the trade) and providing benefits (for consumers). Promotions cannot compensate for a fundamentally flawed or mediocre brand unless the promotions offset the flaws by offering superior value to the trade and consumers.

Inability to Permanently Stop an Established Brand's Declining Sales Trend or Change the Basic Nonacceptance of an Undesired Product

Declining sales of a brand over an extended period indicate poor product performance or the availability of a superior alternative. Promotions cannot reverse the basic nonacceptance of an undesired brand. A declining sales trend can be reversed only through product improvements or perhaps an advertising campaign that breathes new life into an aging brand. Promotions used in combination with advertising efforts or product improvements may reverse the trend, but sales promotion by itself would be a waste of time and money when a brand is in a state of permanent decline.

The Role of Trade Promotions

With the shift in power from manufacturers to retailers, and with brands from competitive manufacturers becoming increasingly indistinct, retailers have pressured the manufacturers that supply them to also provide attractive price discounts and other forms of promotional dollars. Consider the case of Clorox. In the late 1990s The Clorox Company acquired a firm named First Brands. One of First Brands' most important products was the line of plastic items (wraps and bags) under the Glad brand name. Clorox thought it could quickly boost sales of Glad products insofar as First Brands had previously invested virtually nothing in media advertising behind the brand and had instead relied almost exclusively on consumer promotions (primarily coupons) and heavy trade promotion spending.

Clorox's strategy was to cut Glad's consumer and trade price promotions and to invest heavily in mass-media advertising. Clorox cut trade promotion spending on Glad both in 1999 and then again in 2000. Much to Clorox's surprise and frustration, competitors did not follow suit by also cutting trade promotions on their own brands. How did retailers react? They withdrew merchandise support, and Glad sales fell dramatically—as did Clorox's stock price, which dropped by about 20 percent in the two years after acquiring First Brands.

With declining market share and a sagging stock price, Clorox responded in the only way it could: it returned to couponing and trade promotion spending. Though Clorox's long-term strategy is to build Glad's brand equity via increased advertising spending and new product introductions, the fact remains that its effort to cut trade-promotion spending was rebuffed by large, powerful retailers. As previously discussed, the power of retailers continues to grow relative to that of manufacturers. As one observer noted, "Without unique products and strong advertising, package-goods brands have little choice but to pay up to maintain shelf space, especially as consolidation makes retailers more powerful."[26]

As indicated earlier in the chapter, trade promotions represent over half of every manufacturer dollar invested in advertising and promoting new and existing products. Manufacturers' trade promotions are directed at wholesalers, retailers, and other marketing intermediaries (rather than at consumers). A manufacturer's consumer-oriented advertising and promotions are likely to fail unless trade promotions have succeeded in influencing channel intermediaries to stock adequate quantities. The special incentives offered by manufacturers to their distribution channel members are then expected to be passed through to consumers in the form of price discounts offered by retailers, often stimulated by advertising support and special displays. As we will see later, however, this does not always occur.

Even though trade promotions do not always work the way they are designed to, manufacturers have legitimate objectives for using trade-oriented promotions.[27] In particular, these objectives include the following:

1. Introducing new or revised products
2. Increasing distribution of new packages or sizes
3. Building retail inventories
4. Maintaining or increasing the manufacturer's share of shelf space
5. Obtaining displays outside normal shelf locations
6. Reducing excess inventories and increasing turnover
7. Achieving product features in retailers' advertisements
8. Countering competitive activity
9. Selling as much as possible to final consumers

Ingredients for a Successful Trade Promotion Program

To accomplish these myriad objectives, several ingredients are critical to building a successful trade promotion program.[28]

Financial Incentive

A manufacturer's trade promotion must offer wholesalers, retailers, and other channel intermediaries increased profit margins, increased sales volume, or both.

Correct Timing

Trade promotions are appropriately timed when they are (1) tied in with a seasonal event during a time of growing sales (such as candy sales during Valentine's

Day, Halloween, and Christmas); (2) paired with a consumer-oriented sales promotion; or (3) used strategically to offset competitive promotional activity.

Minimize the Retailer's Effort and Cost

The more effort and expense required, the less likely it is that retailers will cooperate in a program they see as benefiting the manufacturer but not themselves.

Quick Results

The most effective trade promotions are those that generate immediate sales or increases in store traffic. (As you will see in the next chapter, *instant gratification* is an important motivator of consumer responses to consumer-oriented promotions. This same motive applies to retailers as well.)

Improve Retailer Performance

Promotions are effective when they help the retailer do a better selling job or improve merchandising methods as, for example, by providing retailers with improved displays.

Trade Allowances

This major type of trade-oriented promotions, **trade allowances**, is used by manufacturers, in theory, to reward wholesalers and retailers for performing activities in support of the manufacturer's brand. These allowances, also called *trade deals,* encourage retailers to stock the manufacturer's brand, discount the brand's price to consumers, feature it in advertising, or provide special display or other point-of-purchase support.

By using trade allowances, manufacturers hope to accomplish two interrelated objectives: (1) increase purchases of the manufacturer's brand by wholesalers and retailers, and (2) augment consumers' purchases of the manufacturer's brand from retailers. This latter objective is based on the expectations that consumers are receptive to price reductions and that retailers will in fact *pass along to consumers* the discounts they receive from manufacturers.

These expectations do not always become reality. Retailers often take advantage of allowances without performing the services for which they receive credit. In fact, a study of trade promotion spending by ACNielsen revealed that 70 percent of surveyed manufacturers rated the value they received from trade promotion spending as fair or poor—only 30 percent responded that the value was "good" or "excellent."[29] Moreover, the vast majority of retailers think that trade promotions should serve to increase sales and profits of entire product categories without concern for whether a manufacturer's specific brand benefits from the trade promotion.[30]

There is, in short, a substantial rift between manufacturers and retailers over the matter of which party trade promotions are intended to benefit. Manufacturers use trade promotions, of course, to advance their brands' sales and profit performance. Retailers, on the other hand, tend to regard trade dollars as an opportunity for increasing their profit margins and thus boosting bottom lines. This schism is easy to understand because parties to economic transactions often have conflicting objectives yet depend on each other for success.

Major Forms of Trade Allowances

Three major forms of trade allowances are (1) off-invoice allowances, (2) bill-back allowances, and (3) slotting allowances. As we will see in the following discussion, manufacturers use off-invoice and bill-back allowances as a matter of choice, but slotting allowances are imposed on them by retailers.

Off-Invoice Allowances

The most frequently used form of trade allowance is an off-invoice allowance, which represents a manufacturer's *temporary price reduction* to the trade on a particular brand. **Off-invoice allowances** are, as the name suggests, deals offered periodically to the trade that permit retailers to deduct a fixed amount from the invoice—*merely by placing an order* during the period which the manufacturer is "dealing" a brand. (A slight variant is a deal that provides the trade with free goods for orders meeting or exceeding required quantities.) In offering an off-invoice allowance, the manufacturer's sales force informs retail buyers that a discount of, say, 15 percent can be deducted from the invoice amount for all quantities purchased during the specified deal period. Many manufacturers of CPGs provide off-invoice allowances at regularly scheduled intervals, which for many brands is one four-week period during every 13-week business quarter. This means that many brands are on off-invoice deals approximately 30 percent of the year.

A manufacturer in using an off-invoice allowance does so with the expectation that retailers will purchase more of the manufacturer's brand during the deal period than they normally would and, to rapidly sell off excess inventories, will pass the deals on to consumers in the form of reduced prices—which thus should spur consumers' purchasing of the manufacturer's price-reduced brand. However, as previously stated, retailers do not always comply with this expectation and, in fact, are typically not contractually bound to pass along discounted prices to consumers. Rather, retailers receive an off-invoice allowance (of, say, 15 percent) when purchasing the manufacturer's brand but often they do not discount their selling prices to consumers or they reduce prices by substantially less than the full 15 percent.[31] Manufacturers estimate that retailers pass through to consumers only about one-half of the trade funds that they provide to retailers. Later on we will discuss two undesirable offshoots of off-invoice allowances—*forward buying* and *diverting*—but first it will be useful to discuss the other two major forms of trade allowances, bill-back and slotting allowances.

Bill-Back Allowances

Another form of trade allowance is the so-called bill-back allowance. Retailers receive allowances for featuring the manufacturer's brand in advertisements (**bill-back *ad* allowances**) or for providing special displays (**bill-back *display* allowances**). As the expression indicates, retailers do *not* deduct bill-back allowances directly from the invoice by virtue of ordering products (as is the case with off-invoice allowances) but rather *must earn the allowances* by performing designated advertising or display services in behalf of the manufacturer's brand. The retailer effectively bills (i.e., charges) the manufacturer for the services rendered, and the manufacturer pays an allowance to the retailer for the services received.

To illustrate, assume that the sales force for the Campbell Soup Company informs retailers that during October they will receive a 5 percent discount on all cases of V8 juice purchased during this period provided they run newspaper advertisements in which V8 juice is prominently featured. With proof of having run feature ads in newspapers, retailers then would bill Campbell Soup for a 5 percent advertising allowance. Similarly, Campbell Soup's sales force could offer a 2 percent display allowance whereby retailers could receive an additional 2 percent discount on all purchases of V8 juice during the deal period for displaying V8 juice in prime locations.

Courtesy of Campbell Soup Company

Slotting Allowances

Slotting allowances are the fees manufacturers pay retailers for access to the slot, or location, that the retailer must make available in its distribution center to accommodate the manufacturer's new brand. This form of trade allowance applies specifically to the situation where a manufacturer attempts to get one of its brands—typically a new brand—accepted by retailers.[32] Also called a *stocking allowance* or *street money,* a slotting allowance is *not* something manufactures of branded products choose to offer retailers. To the contrary, retailers impose slotting allowances on manufacturers. Retailers demand this fee of manufacturers supposedly to compensate them for added costs incurred when taking a new brand into distribution and placing it on the shelf. It should be obvious that manufacturers and retailers hold somewhat differing views regarding the appropriateness and value of the slotting-allowance practice.[33] The following discussion examines many of the key issues.[34]

When first used back in the 1960s, slotting allowances compensated retailers for the *real costs* of taking on a new stock-keeping unit, or SKU. The cost at that time averaged $50 per SKU per *account.* However, slotting allowances now can cost as much as $300 per SKU and represent a healthy profit margin for retailers. You probably are thinking, "This sounds like bribery." You also may be wondering, "Why do manufacturers tolerate slotting allowances?" Let's examine each issue.

First, slotting allowances are indeed a form of bribery. The retailer that demands slotting allowances denies the manufacturer shelf space unless the manufacturer is willing to pay the up-front fee—the slotting allowance—to acquire that space for its new brand. Second, manufacturers tolerate slotting allowances because they are confronted with a classic dilemma: either they pay the fee and eventually recoup the cost through profitable sales volume, or they refuse to pay the fee and in so doing accept a fate of not being able to successfully introduce new brands. The expression "Between a rock and a hard place" appropriately describes the reality of slotting allowances from the manufacturer's perspective.

In certain respects, slotting allowances are a *legitimate cost* of doing business. When, for example, a large, multistore supermarket chain takes on a new brand, it incurs several added expenses. These expenses arise because the chain must make space for that new brand in its distribution center, create a new entry in its computerized inventory system, possibly redesign store shelves, and notify individual stores about the new SKU. In addition to these expenses, the chain takes the risk that the new brand will fail. This is a likely result in the grocery industry, where at least half of all new brands are failures. Hence, the slotting allowance provides the retailer with what effectively amounts to an insurance policy against the prospects that a brand will fail.

It is questionable, however, whether the actual expenses incurred by retailers are anywhere near the slotting allowances they charge. Actual charges are highly variable. Some supermarkets charge as little as $5 per store to stock a new item, while others charge as much as $300 per item per store. Large companies can afford to pay slotting allowances, because their volume is sufficient to recoup the expense. However, brands with small consumer franchises are frequently unable to afford these fees. Smaller manufacturers thus are placed at a competitive disadvantage when attempting to gain distribution for their new products.

How, you might be wondering, are retailers able to impose expensive slotting fees on manufacturers? The reason is straightforward: as noted earlier in the chapter, the balance of power has shifted away from manufacturers and toward retailers. Power means being able to call the shots, and increasing numbers of retailers are doing this. It might be said that retailers are calling the shots to control the slots. Also, CPG manufacturers have hurt their own cause by introducing thousands of new brands each year, most of which are trivial variants of existing products rather than distinct new offerings with meaningful profit opportunities for retailers and many of which ultimately fail. As such, every manufacturer competes against every other manufacturer for limited shelf space, and slotting allowances are simply a mechanism used by retailers to exploit the competition among manufacturers. Furthermore, many grocery retailers find it easy to rationalize slotting allowances on the grounds that their net profit margins in selling groceries are minuscule (typically 1 percent to 1.5 percent) and that slotting allowances enable them to earn returns comparable to those earned by manufacturers.

Further understanding of the rationale and dynamics underlying slotting allowances is possible by making a comparison with apartment prices in any college community. When units are abundant, different apartment complexes compete aggressively with one another and rental prices are forced downward to the benefit of students. On the other hand, when apartments are scarce (which typically is the case in most college communities), prices often are inflated. The result: you may be forced to pay exorbitant rent to live in a second-rate, albeit conveniently located, apartment.

© Susan Van Etten

This is also the case in today's marketing environment. Each year retailers are confronted with requests to stock thousands of new brands (consider these new brands equivalent to potential tenants). The amount of shelf space (the number of apartments) is limited because relatively few new stores are being built. Hence, retailers are able to command slotting allowances (charge higher rent), and manufacturers are willing to pay the higher rent to "live" in desirable locations.

What can a manufacturer do to avoid paying slotting allowances? Sometimes nothing. But powerful manufacturers such as P&G and Kraft, for example, are less likely to pay slotting fees than are weaker national and particularly regional manufacturers. Retailers know that P&G's and Kraft's new brands probably will be successful. This is because P&G and Kraft invest substantially in research to develop meaningful new products; they spend heavily on advertising to create consumer demand for these products; and they use extensive consumer promotions (e.g., sampling and couponing) to create strong consumer pull for their brands. Another way to avoid paying slotting allowances is simply to refuse to pay them and, if need be, to accept the consequence of being refused shelf space by some, if not most, retail chains.

Whereas slotting allowances represent a form of *entry fee* for getting a new brand into a grocery chain's distribution center, some retail chains charge manufacturers a fee for having unsuccessful brands removed from their distribution centers. These **exit fees** could just as well be called *deslotting allowances.* Here is how they operate: when introducing a new brand to a retail chain, the manufacturer and chain enter into a contractual arrangement. This arrangement stipulates the average volume of weekly product movement during a specified period that must be achieved for the manufacturer's brand to be permitted to remain in the chain's distribution center. Then, if the brand has not met the stipulated average weekly movement, the chain will issue a deslotting charge. This charge, or exit fee, is intended to cover the handling costs for the chain to remove the item from its distribution center.

This practice may seem to be a marketplace application of the old saying about having salt rubbed into a wound. However, it really represents the fact that retailers, especially in the supermarket industry, no longer are willing to pay for manufacturers' new-product mistakes. There clearly is some economic logic to deslotting charges. Indeed, these charges are another form of insurance policy to protect retail chains from slow-moving and unprofitable brands. To continue the apartment rental analogy, a deslotting charge operates in much the same fashion as the stipulation between apartment owner and tenant regarding property damage. If as a tenant you damage an apartment, the apartment owner is fully justified in forfeiting all or part of your rental deposit. As such, your deposit provides the apartment owner with an insurance policy against your potential negligence. This is precisely how an exit fee, or deslotting charge, operates.

In the final analysis, the issue of slotting allowances is extremely complicated. Manufacturers have legitimate reasons for not wanting to pay slotting allowances, but retailers have justification for charging them. Can both sides be right? Is the practice of slotting allowances a case of free-market competition working at its best, or at its worst? Simple answers are unavailable because the "correct" answer depends largely on which perspective—manufacturer's or retailer's—one takes on the matter.[35]

And in the middle of this battle are government regulators, who have the responsibility of ensuring that the practice of slotting allowances does not reduce competition or harm consumers by forcing them to pay higher prices or limiting their options because smaller manufacturers are unable to gain shelf space for their new products. One regulatory agency, the Bureau of Alcohol, Tobacco, Firearms and Explosives, passed a ruling that prohibits the use of slotting fees in the marketing of alcohol products.[36] However, no prohibitions exist for the many other product categories where slotting allowances are charged. Although the Federal Trade Commission continues to investigate whether slotting allowances need to be regulated, it has not as yet issued any regulation against retailers charging these fees.[37] In the meantime, slotting allowances remain for manufacturers an additional cost of introducing new products and an additional source of revenue for retailers. The power struggle goes on!

Undesirable Consequences of Off-Invoice Allowances: Forward Buying and Diverting

Manufacturers' off-invoice allowances make considerable sense in theory, but in practice many retailers do not perform the services necessary to earn the allowances they receive from manufacturers. Large retail chains are particularly likely to take advantage of manufacturers' allowances without passing the savings along to consumers. A major reason is that large chains, unlike smaller chains, are able to merchandise their own *private brands.* Because private brands can be sold at lower prices than manufacturers' comparable brands, large chains are able to use private brands to satisfy the needs of price-sensitive consumers while selling manufacturers' brands at their normal prices and pocketing the trade allowance as extra profit.

A second major problem with manufacturers' off-invoice allowances is that they often induce retailers to *stockpile* products to take advantage of the temporary price reductions. Forward buying and diverting are two interrelated practices used by retailers, especially those in the grocery trade, to capitalize on manufacturers' trade allowances. Table 17.5 illustrates these practices.[38]

Table 17.5
Illustration of Forward Buying and Diverting

1. In preparation for a huge promotional event in 2006 surrounding the Cinco de Mayo celebration of Mexican independence on May 5, Beauty Products Inc.—a hypothetical manufacturer of personal-care products—extends an off-invoice offer to grocery chains in the Los Angeles area. This promotion is a 15 percent off-invoice allowance on all orders placed for SynActive shampoo (a hypothetical brand) during the week beginning April 3, 2006, and extending through the week beginning April 24, 2006.
2. Assume that FB&D Supermarkets of Los Angeles orders 15,000 cases of SynActive shampoo—many more cases than it typically would sell in its own stores during any four-week period. Beauty Products Inc. has offered the 15 percent off-invoice allowance to FB&D Supermarkets with the expectation that FB&D will reduce SynActive's retail price to consumers by as much as 15 percent during the week of Cinco de Mayo festivities.
3. FB&D sells at the discounted price only 3,000 of the 15,000 cases purchased. (The remaining cases include some that are forward bought and some that will be diverted.)
4. FB&D resells 5,000 cases of SynActive at a small profit margin to Opportunistic Food Brokers—a company that services grocery retailers throughout the West. (This is the practice of diverting.)
5. FB&D later sells the remaining 7,000 cases of SynActive to shoppers in its own stores but at the regular, full price. (These 7,000 cases represent forward buys.)

Forward Buying

As earlier noted, manufacturers' trade allowances are typically available for four weeks of each business quarter (which translates to about 30 percent of the year). During these deal periods, retailers buy larger quantities than needed for normal inventory and warehouse the excess volume, thereby avoiding purchasing the brand at its full price during the remaining 70 percent of the time when a deal is not offered. Retailers often purchase enough products on one deal to carry them over until the manufacturer's next regularly scheduled deal. This is the practice of **forward buying**, which, for obvious reasons, is also called *bridge buying*—the amount of inventory purchased during one deal period bridges all the way to the next deal period. Approximately 75 percent of all leading grocer retailers practice forward buying.[39]

When a manufacturer marks down a product's price by, say, 15 percent, retail chains commonly stock up with a 10- to 12-week supply. A number of manufacturers sell 80 percent to 90 percent of their volume on deal. It is estimated that forward buying costs manufacturers between 0.5 percent and 1.1 percent of retail prices, which translates into hundreds of millions of dollars annually.[40]

The practice of forward buying has given rise to computer models that enable retail buyers to estimate the profit potential from a forward buy and the optimum number of weeks of inventory to purchase. The models take into consideration the amount of savings from a deal and then incorporate into their calculations the various added costs from forward buying. These added costs include warehouse storage expenses, shipping costs, and the cost of tying up money in inventory when that money could be used to earn a better return in some other manner. Retailers, when forward buying, balance savings from reduced purchasing costs against the added expenses of the kind just noted.

It may appear that forward buying benefits all parties to the marketing process, but this is not the case. First, as previously mentioned, a substantial portion of retailers' *savings from forward buying often are not passed on to consumers.* Second, forward buying leads to *increased distribution* costs because wholesalers and retailers pay greater carrying charges by holding inventories of large quantities of forward-bought items. In fact, the average grocery product takes up to 12 weeks from the time it is shipped by a manufacturer until it reaches retail store shelves. This delay obviously is not due to transit time but rather reflects storage time in wholesalers' and retailers' warehouses from stockpiling surplus quantities of forward-bought items. Third, manufacturers experience *reduced margins* due to the price discounts they offer as well as the increased costs they incur.

A notable case in point is the situation that confronted Campbell Soup Company with massive forward buying of its chicken noodle soup when that product was placed on trade deal. As much as 40 percent of its annual chicken noodle soup production was sold to wholesalers and retailers in just six weeks when this product was on deal. Because wholesalers and retailers forward-bought chicken noodle soup in large quantities, Campbell had to schedule extra work shifts and pay overtime to keep up with the accelerated production and shipping schedules. After years of falling prey to forward buying, Campbell implemented a *bill-and-hold program* whereby it invoices (bills) the retailer as soon as the retailer places a forward-bought order but delays shipping (holds) the order until desired quantities are requested by the retailer. This program smoothed out Campbell's production and shipping schedules by allowing retailers to purchase large amounts at deal prices while delaying shipments until inventory was needed. The bill-and-hold program has not eliminated forward buying, but the negative consequences for Campbell Soup Company have been reduced.

Diverting

Diverting occurs when a manufacturer *restricts a deal to a limited geographical area* rather than making it available nationally. In Table 17.5, SynActive shampoo is available only in Los Angeles as part of Beauty Products Inc.'s participation in the

Cinco de Mayo festivities. The manufacturer intends for only retailers in that area (such as FB&D Supermarkets) to benefit from the deal. However, what happens with diverting is that retailers take advantage of the opportunity by buying abnormally large quantities at the deal price and then selling off, at a small profit margin, the excess quantities through food brokers in other geographical areas. (Finance people would label diverting an application of *arbitrage* behavior.) Over 50 percent of retailers acknowledge engaging in the practice of diverting.

Retailers blame manufacturers for offering irresistible deals and argue that they must take advantage of the deals in any way legally possible to remain competitive with other retailers. Manufacturers could avoid the diverting problem by placing brands on *national deal* only. This solution is more ideal than practical, however, since regional marketing efforts are expanding, and local deals and regional marketing go hand in hand. Further complicating the problem is that products intended for foreign markets sometimes are diverted back into a domestic market.

There are other negative consequences of diverting. First, product quality potentially suffers due to delays in getting products from manufacturers to retail shelves. For example, Tropicana requires its chilled juices to be stored between 32 and 36 degrees. If unrefrigerated for a few hours because of careless diverting practices, the product can go bad, and consumers may form negative impressions of the brand. A second and potentially more serious problem could result from product tampering—such as the infamous Tylenol incident in the early 1980s, when seven Chicago residents died from this brand being laced with cyanide by a mentally ill person. In the event of product tampering, it would be difficult, if not impossible, to identify exactly where a diverted brand may have been shipped.

Don't Blame Retailers

The preceding discussion has perhaps made it seem that retailers are villains when engaging in the practice of forward buying and diverting. This would be an unfair representation of retail buyers who are simply taking advantage of an opportunity that is provided by manufacturers offering attractive trade deals. One retail executive explains his company's forward buying and diverting actions in this fashion: "We are very aggressive when it comes to buying at the best price. We have to be. If we don't, somebody else will."[41] In other words, retailers are simply exhibiting rational behavior when they forward buy and divert. The opportunity to increase profits is provided to retailers by manufacturers' indiscriminate off-invoice allowances, and smart retailers take advantage of the break.

If Nobody Is at Fault, Then What's the Problem?

In brief, the problem is that the present system is wasteful and inefficient. The overall level of costs throughout the distribution system is higher than it could be in a more "ideal" world where costs are better managed and inefficiencies are removed. What the ideal world might look like is the topic to which we now turn. It needs to be stated in advance that the "ideal" world may be just that, as business reality involves inherent conflicts between trading partners such as manufacturers and retailers. The concept of win-win situations is great in theory but not easy to implement in practice. Zero-sum thinking often rules ("What you gain is what I lose."), and it is for this reason that concessions and compromises give way to "get yours"–type behavior.

Efforts to Rectify Trade Allowance Problems

Because trade allowances spawn inefficiencies, create billions of added dollars in distribution costs, are often economically unprofitable for manufacturers, and perhaps inflate prices to consumers, a variety of efforts have been undertaken to fundamentally alter the way business is conducted, especially in the grocery industry.[42] The following sections are devoted to five notable developments that hold important implications for trade allowances. Two of these represent major changes in the interrelations between manufacturers and retailers (namely, the efficient consumer response and category management movements), whereas the final three reflect more specific practices on the part of manufacturers (everyday low pricing, pay-for-performance programs, and account-specific marketing).

Efficient Consumer Response (ECR)

Efficient consumer response (ECR) is a broad-based concept of business management that is oriented toward enhancing efficiencies and reducing costs in the grocery industry. Kurt Salmon Associates, a consulting firm, issued a report that estimated that some $30 billion, or 10 percent of total grocery sales, is wasted. This waste, according to the Salmon report, is due to inefficient ordering procedures, maintenance of excessive inventories, and inefficient promotional practices. The report argued that billions of dollars could be saved if ECR were fully implemented throughout the distribution chain. The objective of ECR is to improve efficiencies in the grocery industry between all parties (manufacturers, wholesalers, brokers, and retailers) and reduce costs for everyone, especially the final consumer. ECR also includes the objective of reducing the huge expenditures on trade promotion. Although many of the ECR initiatives go beyond the scope of this chapter, several features are noteworthy:

1. *Improved product replenishment practices.* The objective is to move products more efficiently from manufacturers' production facilities to retailers' shelves. *Electronic data interchange* (EDI) between manufacturers and retailers is a major means of reducing the time and cost of order fulfillment. EDI essentially entails constant electronic exchanges between trading partners: retailers are able to maintain minimal inventory levels because manufacturers ship required product quantities just in time to replenish depleting inventories. For example, the fully coordinated EDI system between Procter & Gamble and Wal-Mart allows Wal-Mart to carry minimal levels of P&G brands with the assurance that additional quantities of brands like Tide detergent and Pringles chips will be replenished as needed. Another example is the relation between Costco stores and Kimberly-Clark Corporation, which manufactures Huggies disposable diapers. A contractual relationship between these two entities turns responsibility for stock replenishment over to Kimberly-Clark. Costco shares detailed data about individual store sales of diapers, and Kimberly-Clark uses this information to determine precisely when new inventories should be shipped.
2. *Reduced trade promotions.* The objective is to minimize inventory costs in the system, and this necessitates reducing drastically the practices of forward buying and diverting. Everyday low pricing and pay-for-performance programs, as discussed later, represent major steps in this direction.
3. *Improved product introductions.* The objective is for manufacturers to bring to market new products meeting consumer needs rather than simply introduce slight variations on existing offerings. Fewer, more meaningful product introductions likely would substantially cut slotting allowances and exit fees.

In sum, the ultimate objective of ECR is to reduce wasteful practices that lead to excessive prices for consumers and diminished profits for manufacturers, wholesalers, and retailers. As with all revolutions, it will be a matter of years before the benefits of ECR are anywhere close to being fully realized.[43]

Category Management

Manufacturers produce different product lines among which the individual brands in each line constitute a group, or category. Likewise, retailers merchandise multiple brands that compete in each of many categories. A grocery store, for example, has categories of detergents, breakfast cereals, and pain relievers; an appliance dealer has kitchen appliances, video devices, computer equipment, and audio equipment. Although manufacturers and retailers both work with categories, their interests are not necessarily equivalent. Whereas manufacturers are concerned with the profitability of their individual brands, retailers are more interested in the overall profitability of a product category. With growing retailer power, manufacturers have been forced to market their brands with greater concern for the retailer's broader category interests rather than focusing exclusively on the profitability of their own brands.

Category management involves the working relationship between manufacturers and retailers and attempts to find ways whereby both parties can be more profitable. The implementation of category management means that retailers and manufacturers must work together, share market intelligence, and develop strategies that are mutually beneficial. Category managers from both the manufacturer and the retailer sides of business jointly plan and execute merchandising programs, promotion deals, and advertising executions that are agreeable to both parties and improve the performance for both.

Figure 17.2 presents five interrelated stages involved in the actual process of implementing category management. Although both manufacturers and retailers must individually conduct these same five activities, the following discussion presents the manufacturer's perspective:[44]

1. *Reviewing the category:* A manufacturer would initiate a category management program by conducting a thorough study of the product category. After carefully defining the category (e.g., soft drinks) and its subcategories (e.g., colas, noncolas, regular, and diet), the manufacturer must gather information pertaining to category sales volume and growth rate, sales by type of retail outlet, household purchasing patterns, and comparisons of the performances of the manufacturer's brands and its competitors'. By acquiring these data, the manufacturer can identify growth opportunities and develop new or modified marketing strategies that capitalize on the opportunities.
2. *Targeting consumers:* This stage requires the manufacturer to acquire an in-depth understanding of the typical consumer in the product category. The consumer is profiled with respect to relevant demographic characteristics (e.g., income level and age) and examined with respect to their product-purchase and usage patterns (Where do they shop? How much do they typically purchase?), lifestyles (What activities do they participate in?), and media preferences. Armed with this information, a manufacturer is prepared to know a brand's potential in specific stores and to make intelligent decisions about the choice of advertising media, promotions, and product offerings.
3. *Merchandise planning:* This stage entails developing a detailed strategy for the best mix of brands for each retail account within a particular category. The manufacturer recommends to the retailer an optimum mix of brands, prices, and shelf-space allocation that will enable the retailer to achieve desired volume and profit goals within the category. Sophisticated software applications enable manufacturers to assist retailers in developing product-stocking programs, called *planograms,* that designate the specific products and brands that the store should stock to best appeal to the consumers in its trade area.

Figure 17.2
The Five Stages of Category Management

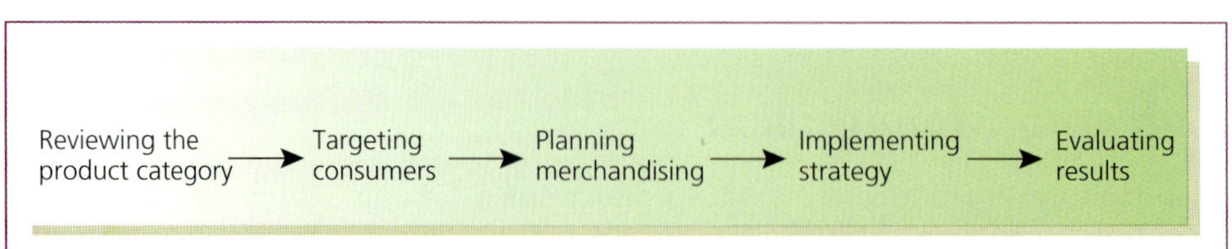

4. *Implementing the strategy:* Results from the first three stages provide the content for an ongoing interaction between the manufacturer's sales team and a retail chain's category buyer. Merchandising plans are the foundation for the sales team's recommendations to the retailer concerning appropriate product mix, pricing, promotions, and shelf-space allocations for the category. The sales team also explains how the manufacturer's advertising program will target the retailer's consumers and thus generate business for the retailer.
5. *Evaluating results:* Effective implementation of category management programs requires that manufacturers answer this key question: did the strategies proposed for the retail account achieve their objectives? If the program has not achieved these objectives, answering this question will direct manufacturers and retailers to alter their strategies; if objectives have been achieved, the prudence of continuing with the previously proposed strategy will be reinforced.

In sum, manufacturers are able to undertake category management programs that are mutually beneficial to themselves and their retail accounts. Sophisticated software applications backed by careful study of consumer behavior, competitor actions, and market developments enable manufacturers and retailers to formulate merchandising programs that suit the needs of all parties: retailers, manufacturers, and consumers.

Everyday Low Pricing (EDLP)

Manufacturers lose billions of dollars every year to inefficient and ineffective trade deals stemming from the trade's practice of forward buying and diverting. It is for this reason that the powerful P&G, under the leadership of then chief executive officer Edwin Artzt, undertook a bold move in the 1990s to break the practice of forward buying and diverting. P&G introduced a new form of pricing called *everyday low pricing*, or EDLP, which the company also refers to as *value pricing*—signifying its desire to compete on the basis of providing product values and not mere price savings. Because some retailers also practice everyday low prices, we will distinguish between "back-door" EDLP as used by manufacturers from the "front-door" variety practiced by retailers.[45] Our interest is with the back-door variety of EDLP, which for clarity's sake we label EDLP(M) to stand for manufacturers' use of EDLP.

EDLP(M) is a form of pricing whereby a manufacturer charges the same price for a particular brand day in and day out. In other words, rather than charging *high-low prices*—that is, regular, or "high," prices for a period followed by off-invoice, or "low," prices for a shorter period—EDLP(M) involves charging the same price over an extended period. Because no off-invoice allowances are offered the trade under this pricing strategy, wholesalers and retailers have no reason to engage in forward buying or diverting. Hence, their profit is made from selling merchandise rather than from buying it.

© Susan Van Etten

How Has P&G Fared?

Researchers examined the effects of P&G's value pricing initiative over the first six years of its implementation.[46] The analysis encompassed a total of 24 product categories and 118 brands in these categories. From the year prior to P&G's implementation of value pricing through the first six years of the practice, P&G's advertising expenditures and net prices both increased by approximately 20 percent. During this same period, its expenditures on trade deals decreased by nearly 16 percent, and coupon spending was reduced by about 54 percent.

What was the effect of these changes? P&G *lost* about 18 percent market share on average across the 24 product categories analyzed. Value pricing clearly was a disaster for P&G, right? In actuality, it was not.

Although P&G suffered a significant decline in market share (due largely to competitors' retaliatory increases in promotional deals while P&G was cutting its own dealing activity), at the same time its overall profits *increased* by virtue of cutting trade deals and coupon activity and increasing net prices.[47] It could be argued that it is unwise ever to relinquish market share; however, in the final analysis, giving up market share can be justified if the share that remains generates greater profitability than what was obtained with a larger but less profitable share. Over the long haul, the bottom line (profits) is a more telling indicator of firm success than is the top line (sales).

What Have Other Manufacturers Done?

Manufacturers less powerful than P&G have found it difficult to convert to a pure system of everyday low pricing. Even P&G has experienced resistance and has deviated from a pure EDLP pricing with some brands such as laundry detergents. Three major reasons account for why many retailers resist manufacturers' EDLP pricing initiatives. First, those retailers that established distribution infrastructures necessary to practice forward buying have resisted EDLP(M) pricing.[48] Second, there is some evidence that EDLP(M) pricing benefits the manufacturers that price their products in this fashion more than it does the retailers that pay EDLP(M) rather than high-low prices. Finally, it also has been argued that EDLP(M) pricing takes some of the excitement out of retailing. With EDLP(M) pricing, the retailer charges the same price to consumers day after day. Comparatively, with high-low pricing, there are periods when retailers are able to advertise attractive price savings, which breaks the monotony of never varying the retail price. Although in the long term the consumer realizes no savings from high-low pricing, in the short term it may be exciting to receive an appealing discount.

Although pricing practices by manufacturers remain somewhat in a state of flux, it appears that a pure EDLP(M) pricing system will not dominate. Some combination of EDLP(M) pricing along with periodic promotional funds provided to the trade by manufacturers is the pricing system most likely to endure.

Pay-for-Performance Programs

As noted earlier, many trade promotions, especially in the grocery industry, are unprofitable for manufacturers because they merely shift future buying to the present when the trade engages in forward buying and diverting. Manufacturers, accordingly, have a strong incentive to devise an alternative system to the traditional off-invoice allowance. One such system is so-called pay-for-performance programs. The *IMC Focus* insert offers an explanation from the vantage point of one manufacturer, Nestlé, as to why there is a need to shift trade spending in this direction.

Rewarding Selling Rather Than Buying

As the name suggests, **pay-for-performance** is a form of trade allowance that rewards retailers for performing the primary function that justifies a manufacturer's offering a trade allowance—namely, *selling increased quantities of the manufacturer's brand to consumers.* In other words, pay-for-performance programs are designed to reward retailers for *selling* the manufacturer's brand supported with a trade allowance rather than for merely buying the brand at an off-invoice price.

One form of pay-for-performance programs is called *scanner-verified trade promotions* or *scan downs.* This name is based on the idea that retail sales volume for a trade-supported brand is recorded via optical scanning devices at the point of sale. Scan downs entail three key facets:[49]

1. A manufacturer agrees with a retailer on a period during which the retailer receives an allowance for all quantities of a promoted brand that are *sold to*

Pay-for-Performance at Nestlé

imc focus

There is an old country music song by a singer named Jerry Reed about a disputatious divorce settlement. One line in the song, which also is the song's title, states, "She got the goldmine, [and] I got the shaft." Like the offended party in Jerry Reed's song, many manufacturers believe they are getting the shaft when it comes to trade promotions. Their sense is that retailers grab the trade dollars without performing any duties that serve the manufacturer's interests.

Marketing officials at Nestlé are fed up with spending trade dollars that serve little useful purpose. Accordingly, promotional contracts with retailers now emphasize the minimum duties retailers must perform to receive Nestlé's trade dollars, duties such as reducing retail prices for a specified period of time, featuring Nestlé's brands in retailers' circulars, and providing special displays. Retailers that fail to meet Nestlé's contractual requirements will not receive promotional funds, or, at the extreme, Nestlé will simply withdraw its brands from noncomplying retailers' stores.

consumers at the designated deal price (e.g., an item that regularly sells to consumers at $1.99 per unit is to be reduced to $1.79).

2. The retailer's own scanning data *verify the exact amount* of the promoted brand that has been sold during this period at the deal price (e.g., 5,680 units at $1.79 each).
3. The *manufacturer pays the retailer quickly*, say within five days, at the designated allowance for the quantity sold. The manufacturer would reimburse the retailer for the reduced margin in selling a certain number of units (e.g., 5,680 units at a reduced margin of $0.20, or $1,136) and compensate the retailer for the amount of the trade allowance (e.g., 5,680 units at $0.05 each, or $284; thus, the manufacturer would mail a check to the retailer totaling $1,420).

A Win-Win-Win Situation

Scanner-verified programs provide an incentive to the retailer only for the items sold at discount to consumers during the agreed-on time period. Thus unlike off-invoice allowances, manufacturers using scan downs do *not* pay for allowances where no benefit is received. Rather, manufacturers compensate retailers only for those items that are sold to consumers at discounted prices. Hence, this form of pay-for-performance program benefits all parties: consumers, retailers, and manufacturers. Consumers win by receiving reduced prices; retailers win by obtaining allowances for moving increased quantities of manufacturers' promoted brands; and manufacturers win by increasing sales of their brands, if only temporarily, by reducing prices to consumers. By comparison, when using off-invoice allowances, manufacturers have no assurance that the off-invoice allowances given to retailers will be passed on to consumers.

In theory, then, with pay-for-performance programs, everyone wins. The rub, however, is that retailers do not win as much as they do with "gain without pain" off-invoice programs that offer rewards and require no effort other than placing an order. It is for this reason that pay-for-performance programs are embraced more heartily by manufacturers than by retailers. It also is for this reason that large, powerful manufacturers (such as Nestlé in the *IMC Focus*) sometimes need to take dramatic steps such as discontinuing selling their brands to retailers failing to perform the duties that serve the manufacturer's promoted brand.

Pay-for-performance programs are a natural correlate to the efficient consumer response (ECR) initiative that was previously discussed. Only time will tell whether these programs become widely implemented. The technological infrastructure is available in the United States to support this form of trade promotion, and well-known companies such as ACNielsen and Information Resources Inc. make it possible by serving, for a fee, as *scanning agents*. Scanning agents profit from performing the following functions: (1) *collecting* scanner data from retailers, (2) *verifying* the amount of product movement that meets the manufacturer's promotional requirements and warrants compensation, (3) *paying* the retailer, and (4) *collecting* funds from the manufacturer along with a commission for services rendered.

Customizing Promotions: Account-Specific Marketing

Account-specific marketing, also called *co-marketing,* is a descriptive term that characterizes promotional and advertising activity that a manufacturer *customizes* to specific retail accounts. To appreciate this practice fully, it is necessary to place it in the context of the off-invoice allowance promotion, which is a temporary price reduction that is offered to *all* accounts. With off-invoice programs, a manufacturer's promotion dollars are anything but customized to the needs of specific retail accounts. On the other hand, account-specific marketing, or co-marketing, directs promotion dollars to specific retail customers and develops in concert with the retailer an advertising or promotion program that simultaneously serves the manufacturer's brand, the retailer's volume and profit requirements, and the consumer's needs. Local radio tie-in advertising and loyalty programs using retailers' shopper databases are especially popular account-specific practices.

Some Examples

When introducing its expensive Photosmart photography system—a photo-scanning-and-printing system for home computers—Hewlett-Packard (HP) developed co-marketing arrangements with a small number of retailers. HP selected prime consumer prospects in each retailer's trade area and mailed invitations customized to appear as if they were from the retailer, not HP. Prospective purchasers were invited to see an in-store demonstration and receive a chance to win a free Photosmart system.

SPAM and SPAM derived terms are trademarks of Hormel Foods, LLC and are used with permission by Hormel Foods. MONTY PYTHON'S SPAMALOT™ is a musical stage play written by Eric Idle and John DuPrez, produced by Spamalot LLC. Logo used by permission of Spamalot LLC.

An illustration from the CPG category is Hormel Foods' account-specific effort with the SPAM® Family of Products (the canned-meat product). To boost sales and to lure new consumers to the brand, Hormel Foods introduced the "SPAM Stuff" continuity program. Following in the footsteps of Marlboro, Kool-Aid, and Pepsi, all of which had previously launched "stuff" programs, Hormel Foods offered consumers points toward the acquisition of free items (such as beanbag characters, boxer shorts, mouse pads, mugs, and T-shirts) with each purchase of SPAM products. In addition to offering "freebies" to encourage consumers to try SPAM products, Hormel Foods developed some account-specific programs to draw the trade's attention to the brand. Retailers were provided with SPAM advertising materials (called *ad slicks*) for their advertising flyers. They also received local advertising support for promoting SPAM on the radio and in newspapers. To further excite retailer participation, Hormel Foods offered one supermarket per region with a "SPAM Day" promotion for the best in-store display. Winning stores received "SPAM-wear" for employees and customers, free SPAMBURGER hamburgers grilled in the store's parking lot, and personal appearances by SPAM Cans characters.

It would also be understandable if you were to consider this promotional program somewhat goofy. This surely is a lighthearted attempt on the part of Hormel Foods to increase interest in SPAM from both consumers and retailers. Silly as it may seem, programs like this often are effective in encouraging retailers to devote greater attention to a brand (e.g., provide increased display space) and to entice consumers to purchase the brand more regularly.

What Does the Future Hold?

Account-specific marketing is a relatively recent innovation. First introduced by marketers in the packaged goods field, the practice has spread to companies that manufacture and market soft goods (e.g., apparel items) and durable items such as the HP Photosmart system. Because account-specific marketing requires a lot of effort in both development and implementation and is costly, the future of this practice is uncertain. It appears that interest among packaged goods companies has peaked already.[50] The future will depend on results. As always, the proof is in the pudding. Account-specific marketing will increase in those industries where and for those companies whose programs yield increased results but decrease where the returns fail to justify the efforts. Because powerful retailers benefit from well-designed account-specific programs (oftentimes programs that they develop and then sell to manufacturers, who pay for the programs' implementation), it is likely that co-marketing is here to stay.

Generalizations about Promotions

The foregoing discussion has referred to research evidence regarding how promotions work and the objectives accomplished. Researchers—especially during the past two decades—have vigorously studied the functioning and effectiveness of sales promotions. Empirical efforts have enabled researchers to draw some tentative conclusions. These conclusions, more formally termed *empirical generalizations,* represent consistent evidence regarding different facets of promotion performance. Nine empirical generalizations are noteworthy (see Table 17.6).[51]

Generalization 1: Temporary retail price reductions substantially increase sales—but only in the short term.

The evidence is clear that temporary retail price reductions generally result in substantial increases in short-term sales. These short-term sales increases are termed *sales spikes.* These spikes in the short term generally occur, however, at the expense

Table 17.6

Nine Generalizations about Promotions

1. Temporary retail price reductions substantially increase sales.
2. The greater the frequency of deals, the lower the height of the deal spike.
3. The frequency of deals changes the consumer's reference price.
4. Retailers pass through less than 100 percent of trade deals.
5. Higher-market-share brands are less deal elastic.
6. Advertised promotions can result in increased store traffic.
7. Feature advertising and displays operate synergistically to influence sales of discounted brands.
8. Promotions in one product category affect sales of brands in complementary and competitive categories.
9. The effects of promoting higher- and lower-quality brands are asymmetric.

Source: Adapted from Robert C. Blattberg, Richard Briesch, and Edward J. Fox, "How Promotions Work," *Marketing Science* 14 (No. 3, 1995), G122–G132.

of some reduction in consumer purchases of the promoted brand either preceding or following the promotional period.[52] Moreover, the effects of retail price promotions are short lived. For example, one study examined price promotions for various brands in the soup and yogurt categories—the former representing a storable product and the latter a perishable—and found that the effect these promotions had on consumers' purchase likelihood, brand choice, and purchase quantity lasted only a matter of several weeks and did not alter consumers' long-term purchase behavior.[53]

Generalization 2: The greater the frequency of deals, the lower the height of the deal spike.

When manufacturers (and thus retailers) offer frequent deals, consumers learn to anticipate the likelihood of future deals, and thus their responsiveness to any particular deal is diminished. In short, infrequent deals generate greater spikes, whereas frequent deals generate less dramatic sales increases. The psychology of deal responsiveness also entails the issue of *reference prices*. When deals are frequently offered, the consumer's internal reference price (i.e., the price the consumer expects to pay for a particular brand) is lowered, thus making the deal price less attractive and generating less responsiveness than would be the case if the deal were offered less frequently.

Generalization 3: The frequency of deals changes the consumer's reference price.

A corollary to the preceding generalization is that frequent deals on a brand tend to reduce consumers' price expectation, or reference price, for that brand. This lowering of a brand's reference price has the undesirable consequence of lowering the brand's equity and thus the seller's ability to charge premium prices. Taken together, generalizations 2 and 3 indicate that excessive dealing has the undesirable effects of both reducing a brand's reference price and diminishing consumer responsiveness to any particular deal.

Generalization 4: Retailers pass through less than 100 percent of trade deals.

The simple reality is that manufacturers' trade deals, which typically are offered to retailers in the form of off-invoice discounts, are not always passed on to consumers. Though a manufacturer offers, say, a 15 percent off-invoice allowance, perhaps only 60 percent of retailers will extend this allowance to consumers as lower retail prices. There is no legal obligation for retailer's to pass through trade discounts. Retailers choose to pass along discounts only if their profit calculus leads them to the conclusion that greater profits can be earned from passing discounts to consumers rather than from directly "pocketing" the discounts. It is for this reason that manufacturers increasingly are implementing pay-for-performance programs.

Generalization 5: Higher-market-share brands are less deal elastic.

Suppose that a brand's price is reduced at retail by 20 percent and that sales volume increases by 30 percent. This would represent an elasticity coefficient of

1.5 (i.e., 30 ÷ 20), a value indicating that the increase in the quantity demanded is proportionately one and one-half times greater than the reduction in price. Generalization 5 suggests that for brands holding larger market shares, the deal elasticity coefficient generally is smaller than for smaller-share brands. The reason is straightforward: smaller-share brands have proportionately more customers to gain when they are placed on deal, whereas larger-share brands have fewer remaining customers. In short, a larger-share brand when placed on deal gains "less bang for the promotional buck" compared with a smaller-share brand.

Generalization 6: Advertised promotions can result in increased store traffic.

On balance the research suggests that store traffic benefits from brand-dealing activity. When exposed to a retailer's advertising featuring brands on deal, some consumers will switch stores, if only temporarily, so as to take advantage of attractive deals from stores other than those in which they most regularly shop. Retailers refer to this temporary store-switching behavior as consumer "cherry picking," an apt metaphor. Interestingly, research has demonstrated that cherry-picking shopping behavior increases with increases in family size, when the head of household is a senior citizen, when a family does not have a working woman in the household, and with decreases in family income. All of these variables suggest that cherry-picking is greater when the opportunity cost of visiting multiple stores is reduced—for example, it is less costly in terms of time expenditure for a retired senior citizen to visit multiple stores to avail him- or herself of price discounts than it is for a younger, employed person.[54] This same research further revealed that cherry pickers save on average approximately 5 percent per item across all purchases.

Generalization 7: Feature advertising and displays operate synergistically to influence sales of discounted brands.

When brands are placed on price deal, sales generally increase (see generalization 1). When brands are placed on price deal and are advertised in the retailers' advertised features, sales increase even more (see generalization 6). When brands are placed on price deal, are feature advertised, and receive special display attention, sales increase by substantially more. In other words, the combined effects of advertising and display positively interact to boost a dealt brand's retail sales. (This point was made previously in Chapter 8 in a slightly different manner when discussing point-of-purchase advertising.)

Generalization 8: Promotions in one product category affect sales of brands in complementary and competitive categories.

An interesting thing often happens when a brand in a particular product category is promoted—namely, sales for brands in complementary and competitive categories are affected. For example, when Tostitos tortilla chips are promoted, sales of complementary salsa brands likely increase. On the other hand, sales of brands in the competitive potato chip category could be expected to decrease as tortilla-chip purchases by consumers reduce their selection of potato chips.

Generalization 9: The effects of promoting higher- and lower-quality brands are asymmetric.

When a higher-quality brand is promoted, say, via a substantial price reduction, there is a tendency for that brand to attract switchers and thus steal sales from lower-quality brands.[55] However, a lower-quality brand on promotion is proportionately less likely to attract switchers from higher-quality brands. In other words, switching behavior is *asymmetric*—the proportion of switchers drifting from low- to high-quality brands, when the latter is on deal, is higher than the proportion moving in the other direction when a low-quality brand is on deal.[56]

Summary

Sales promotion was introduced in this first of three chapters devoted to the topic. The precise nature of sales promotion was described. Promotion was explained as having three targets: the trade (wholesalers and retailers), consumers, and a company's own sales force. The chapter proceeded to discuss the reasons for a significant trend toward increased investment in promotions vis-à-vis advertising. This shift is part of the movement from pull- to push-oriented marketing, particularly in the case of CPGs. Underlying factors include a balance-of-power transfer from manufacturers to retailers, increased brand parity and growing price sensitivity, reduced brand loyalty, splintering of the mass market and reduced media effectiveness, a growing short-term orientation, and favorable consumer responsiveness to sales promotions.

The chapter also detailed the specific tasks that promotions can and cannot accomplish. For example, promotions cannot give the trade or consumers compelling long-term reasons to purchase. However, promotions are ideally suited for generating trial-purchase behavior, facilitating the introduction of new products, gaining shelf space for a brand, encouraging repeat purchasing, and performing a variety of other tasks. Also discussed were nine empirical generalizations about sales promotions.

Following this general introduction, the chapter presented the topic of trade-oriented sales promotions and described its various forms. Trade-oriented promotions represent on average over 50 percent of CPG companies' promotional budgets. These programs perform a variety of objectives. Trade allowances, or trade deals, are offered to retailers for performing activities that support the manufacturer's brand. Manufacturers find allowance promotions attractive for several reasons: they are easy to implement, can successfully stimulate initial distribution, are well accepted by the trade, and can increase trade purchases during the allowance period. However, two major disadvantages of trade allowances, especially of the off-invoice variety, are that they often are not passed along by retailers to consumers and may induce the trade to stockpile a product in order to take advantage of the temporary price reduction. This merely shifts business from the future to the present. Two prevalent practices in current business are forward buying and diverting. Another form of trade deal, called a *slotting allowance,* applies to new-product introductions. Manufacturers of grocery products typically are required to pay retailers a slotting fee for the right to have their product carried by the retailer. Exit fees, or deslotting charges, are assessed to manufacturers whose products do not achieve prearranged levels of sales volume.

To reduce forward buying and diverting, some manufacturers have revised their method of pricing products. P&G is most notable in this regard for introducing what it calls *value pricing,* or what others refer to as *everyday low pricing by a manufacturer,* or EDLP(M). This method of pricing eliminates the historical practice of periodically offering attractive trade deals and instead charges the same low price at all times. Another major development in the grocery industry that is aimed at curtailing forward buying and diverting is the implementation of pay-for-performance programs, which also are called *scanner-verified systems,* or *scan downs.* With this method of trade allowance, retailers are compensated for the amount of a manufacturer's brand that they sell to consumers, rather than according to how much they purchase from the manufacturer (as is the case with off-invoice allowances). Pay-for-performance programs and everyday low pricing are both part of the paradigm shift in the grocery industry known as *efficient consumer response* (ECR). Category management is another development that is designed to create better working relations between manufacturers and retailers and to increase efficiency in their relations.

Discussion Questions

1. The term *promotional inducement* has been suggested as an alternative to *sales promotion.* Explain why this term is more descriptive than the established one.
2. Describe the factors that have accounted for sales promotion's rapid growth. Do you expect a continued increase in the use of promotion throughout the following decade?
3. Why, in your opinion, is the Internet a good medium for offering sales promotions to consumers?
4. Explain in your own words the meaning of push- versus pull-oriented promotional strategies. Using for illustration a well-known supermarket brand of your choice, explain which elements of this brand's marcom mix embody push and which embody pull.
5. Assume you are the vice president of marketing of a large, well-known CPG company (e.g., P&G, Unilever, or Johnson & Johnson). What steps might you take to restore a balance of power favoring your company in its relations with retailers?
6. Are promotions able to reverse a brand's temporary sales decline or a permanent sales decline? Be specific.
7. How can a manufacturer's use of trade- and consumer-oriented promotions generate enthusiasm and stimulate improved performance from the sales force?
8. Generalization 5 in the chapter claimed that higher-market-share brands are less deal elastic. Construct a realistic example to illustrate your understanding of this empirical generalization.
9. Generalization 8 asserted that promotions in one product category affect sales of brands in complementary and competitive categories. Tostitos tortilla chips were used as an example of this generalization. Provide examples of two additional brands and the complementary and competitive product categories that likely would be affected by promotions for your two illustrative brands.
10. Assume you are the marketing manager of a company that manufactures a line of paper products (tissues, napkins, etc.). Your current market share is 7 percent, and you are considering offering retailers an attractive bill-back allowance for giving your brand special display space. Comment on this promotion's chances for success.
11. In your own words, explain the practices of forward buying and diverting. Also, describe the advantages and disadvantages of bill-and-hold programs.
12. Assume you are a buyer for a large supermarket chain and that you have been asked to speak to a group of marketing students at a nearby university. During the question-and-answer session following your comments, a student makes the following statement: "My father works for a grocery product manufacturer, and he says that slotting allowances are nothing more than a form of larceny!" How would you defend your company's practice to this student?

13. Explain why selling private brands often enables large retail chains to pocket trade deals instead of passing their reduced costs along to consumers in the form of lower product prices.
14. In your own words, explain why EDLP(M) pricing diminishes forward buying and diverting.
15. In your own words, discuss how pay-for-performance programs, or scan downs, would, if widely implemented, virtually eliminate forward buying and diverting.

ENDNOTES

1. Adapted from Maureen Tkacik, "In a Clash of the Sneaker Titans, Nike Gets Leg Up on Foot Locker," *Wall Street Journal Online,* May 13, 2003, http://online.wsj.com.
2. This definition combines the author's thoughts with those from two sources: Roger A. Strang, "Sales Promotion Research: Contributions and Issues" (unpublished paper presented at the AMA/MSI/PMAA Sales Promotion Workshop, Babson College, May 1983); and James H. Naber, James Webb Young address (University of Illinois, Urbana–Champaign, October 21, 1986).
3. Jacques Chevron, "Branding and Promotion: Uneasy Cohabitation," *Brandweek,* September 14, 1998, 24.
4. Pierre Chandon, Brian Wansink, and Gilles Laurent, "A Benefit Congruency Framework of Sales Promotion Effectiveness," *Journal of Marketing* 64 (October 2000), 65–81. Robert M. Schindler, "Consequences of Perceiving Oneself as Responsible for Obtaining a Discount: Evidence for Smart-Shopper Feelings," *Journal of Consumer Psychology* 7, no. 4 (1998), 371–392.
5. Koen Pauwels, Jorge Silva-Risso, Shuba Srinivasan, and Dominique M. Hanssens, "New Products, Sales Promotions, and Firm Value: The Case of the Automobile Industry," *Journal of Marketing* 68 (October 2004), 142–156.
6. Kellie Krumplitsch, "Promotion Explosion: The Reggie Awards," *Brandweek,* April 4, 1994, 29, 32.
7. Tobi Elkin, "Packard Bell Delivers," *Brandweek,* March 2, 1998, R3–R6.
8. This estimate is from the marketing consulting firm, Cannondale Associates, as cited in "Upward Bound," *Promo,* April 2004, AR3–AR5.
9. Carl F. Mela, Sunil Gupta, and Donald R. Lehmann, "The Long-Term Impact of Promotion and Advertising on Consumer Brand Choice," *Journal of Marketing Research* 34 (May 1997), 248–261.
10. Purushottam Papatla and Lakshman Krishnamurthi, "Measuring the Dynamic Effects of Promotions on Brand Choice," *Journal of Marketing Research* 33 (February 1996), 20–35.
11. A. S. C. Ehrenberg, Kathy Hammond, and G. J. Goodhardt, "The After-Effects of Price-Related Consumer Promotions," *Journal of Advertising Research* 34 (July/August 1994), 11–21.
12. Robert C. Blattberg and Scott A. Neslin, "Sales Promotion: The Long and the Short of It," *Marketing Letters* 1, no. 1 (1989), 81–97.
13. Chandon, Wansink, and Laurent, "A Benefit Congruency Framework of Sales Promotion Effectiveness," 65–81. The following discussion of benefits is based on a typology provided by these authors. See Table 1 on pages 68–69. Another insightful perspective along similar lines is provided in Figure 2 of Kusum L. Ailawadi, Scott A. Neslin, and Karen Gedenk, "Pursuing the Value-Conscious Consumer: Store Brands Versus National Brand Promotions," *Journal of Marketing* (January 2001), 71–89.
14. Research indicates that consumers who take advantage of promotional deals feel good about themselves for being "smart shoppers" and that these feelings are particularly strong when consumers have a sense of being personally responsible for availing themselves of a deal. See Robert M. Schindler, "Consequences of Perceiving Oneself as Responsible for Obtaining a Discount: Evidence of Smart-Shopper Feelings," *Journal of Consumer Psychology* 7 (4), 371–392.
15. Jack Neff, "Accounting by New Rules," *Advertising Age,* July 15, 2002, 4.
16. This discussion is guided by Charles Fredericks, Jr., "What Ogilvy & Mather Has Learned about Sales Promotion," *The Tools of Promotion* (New York: Association of National Advertisers, 1975); and Don E. Schultz and William A. Robinson, *Sales Promotion Management* (Lincolnwood, Ill.: NTC Business Books, 1986), chap. 3.
17. Amie Smith and Al Urbanski, "Excellence x 16," *Promo,* December 1998, 136.
18. A facing is a row of shelf space. Brands typically are allocated facings proportionate to their profit potential to the retailer. Manufacturers must pay for extra facings by offering display allowances or providing other inducements that increase the retailer's profit.
19. "Adventures in Light Bulbs," *Promo,* December 2000, 89.
20. Chakravarthi Narasimhan, Scott A. Neslin, and Subrata K. Sen, "Promotional Elasticities and Category Characteristics," *Journal of Marketing* 60 (April 1996), 17–30. See also Sandrine Macé and Scott A. Neslin, "The Determinants of Pre- and Post-promotion Dips in Sales of Frequently Purchased Goods," *Journal of Marketing Research* 41 (August 2004), 339–350.
21. Carl F. Mela, Kamel Jedidi, and Douglas Bowman, "The Long-Term Impact of Promotions on Consumer Stockpiling Behavior," *Journal of Marketing Research* 35 (May 1998), 250–262.
22. Brian Wansink and Rohit Deshpande, "'Out of Sight, Out of Mind': Pantry Stockpiling and Brand-Usage Frequency," *Marketing Letters* 5, no. 1 (1994), 91–100.
23. Kusum L. Ailawadi and Scott A. Neslin, "The Effect of Promotion on Consumption: Buying More and Consuming It Faster," *Journal of Marketing Research* 35 (August 1998), 390–398.
24. Pierre Chandon and Brian Wansink, "When Are Stockpiled Products Consumed Faster? A Convenience-Salience Framework of Postpurchase Consumption Incidence and Quantity," *Journal of Marketing Research* 39 (August 2002), 321–335.
25. Betsy Spethmann, "Value Ads," *Promo,* March 2001, 74–79.

26. Jack Neff, "Clorox Gives in on Glad, Hikes Trade Promotion," *Advertising Age*, November 27, 2000, 22.
27. These objectives are adapted from a consumer promotion seminar conducted by Ennis Associates and sponsored by the Association of National Advertisers (New York, undated). See also Chakravarthi Narasimhan, "Managerial Perspectives on Trade and Consumer Promotions," *Marketing Letters* 1, no. 3 (1989), 239–251.
28. Don E. Schultz and William A. Robinson, *Sales Promotion Management* (Lincolnwood, Ill.: NTC Business Books, 1986), 265–266.
29. "ACNielsen Study Finds Trade Promotion Disconnect Between Manufacturers and Retailers" (http://www.acnielsen.co.nz/news.asp?newsID=221).
30. This study is by Cannondale Associates as reported in Christopher W. Hoyt, "You Cheated, You Lied," *Promo*, July 1997, 64.
31. For a technical treatment regarding the profit implications of a retailer's decision to pass through a manufacturer's allowance, see Rajeev K. Tyagi, "A Characterization of Retailer Response to Manufacturer Trade Deals," *Journal of Marketing Research* 36 (November 1999), 510–516.
32. The term *slotting allowances* was originally used only with reference to new products, but the term has over time become a catchall expression for all efforts by manufacturers to gain retailer support for its brands.
33. These differences are placed in stark contrast in Table 3 of William L. Wilkie, Debra M. Desrochers, and Gregory T. Gundlach, "Marketing Research and Public Policy: The Case of Slotting Fees," *Journal of Public Policy & Marketing* 21 (fall 2002), 275–288.
34. For a more complete treatment of the issue, including the presentation of survey results from both manufacturers and retailers, see Paul N. Bloom, Gregory T. Gundlach, and Joseph P. Cannon, "Slotting Allowances and Fees: Schools of Thought and the Views of Practicing Managers," *Journal of Marketing* 64 (April 2000), 92–108.
35. See Wilkie, Desrochers, and Gundlach, "Marketing Research and Public Policy" for further discussion of the economic and, especially, public policy issues attendant to the practice of slotting allowances.
36. For an insightful discussion, see Gregory T. Gundlach and Paul N. Bloom, "Slotting Allowances and the Retail Sale of Alcohol Beverages," *Journal of Public Policy & Marketing* 17 (fall 1998), 173–184.
37. See David Balto, "Recent Legal and Regulatory Developments in Slotting Allowances and Category Management," *Journal of Public Policy & Marketing* 21 (fall 2002), 289–294.
38. This illustration is adapted from Zachary Schiller, "Not Everyone Loves a Supermarket Special," *Business Week*, February 17, 1992, 64.
39. Christopher W. Hoyt, "Retailers and Suppliers Are Still Miles Apart," *Promo*, February 1996, 49.
40. Robert D. Buzzell, John A. Quelch, and Walter J. Salmon, "The Costly Bargain of Trade Promotion," *Harvard Business Review* 68 (March/April 1990), 145.
41. Jon Berry, "Diverting," *Adweek's Marketing Week*, May 18, 1992, 22.
42. An insightful demonstration of why trade allowances are unprofitable is provided in Magid M. Abraham and Leonard M. Lodish, "Getting the Most out of Advertising and Promotion," *Harvard Business Review* 68 (May/June 1990), 50–60.
43. For a fuller account of the ECR "movement," see Barbara E. Kahn and Leigh McAlister, *Grocery Revolution: The New Focus on the Consumer* (Reading, MA: Addison-Wesley, 1997), ch. 6.
44. The discussion is adapted from *Category Management* (Northbrook, IL: Nielsen Marketing Research, 1992), especially 112–121.
45. For discussion of everyday low pricing by retailers, see Stephen J. Hoch, Xavier Dreze, and Mary E. Purk, "EDLP, Hi-Lo, and Margin Arithmetic," *Journal of Marketing* 58 (October 1994), 16–27.
46. Kusum L. Ailawadi, Donald R. Lehmann, and Scott A. Neslin, "Market Response to a Major Policy Change in the Marketing Mix: Learning from Procter & Gamble's Value Pricing Strategy," *Journal of Marketing* 65 (January 2001), 44–61.
47. This conclusion is based on profit estimations made in ibid., 57.
48. Kenneth Craig Manning, "Development of a Theory of Retailer Response to Manufacturers' Everyday Low Cost Programs" (Ph.D. dissertation, University of South Carolina, 1994).
49. Kerry E. Smith, "Scan Down, Pay Fast," *Promo*, January 1994, 58–59; "The Proof Is in the Scanning," *Promo*, February 1995, 15.
50. Betsy Spethmann, "Wake Up and Smell the Co-Marketing," *Promo*, August 1998, 43–47.
51. The following discussion is based on the outstanding synthesis of the literature provided by Robert C. Blattberg, Richard Briesch, and Edward J. Fox, "How Promotions Work," *Marketing Science* 14, no. 3 (1995), G122–G132. The order of generalizations presented here is adapted from Blattberg et al.'s presentation. Please refer to this article for coverage of the specific studies on which the generalizations are based.
52. Harald J. van Heerde, Peter S. H. Leeflang, and Dick R. Wittink, "The Estimation of Pre- and Postpromotion Dips with Store-Level Scanner Data," *Journal of Marketing Research* 37 (August 2000), 383–395.
53. Koen Pauwels, Dominique M. Hanssens, and S. Siddarth, "The Long-Term Effects of Price Promotions on Category Incidence, Brand Choice, and Purchase Quantity," *Journal of Marketing Research* 39 (November 2002), 421–439.
54. Edward J. Fox and Stephen J. Hoch, "Cherry-Picking," *Journal of Marketing* 69 (January 2005), 46–62.
55. What appears to be an asymmetric effect due to brand quality may actually be due to market share. In other words, smaller-market-share brands, which in many product categories are of lower quality, are able to attract more brand switchers compared to larger-market-share brands simply because small-share brands have proportionately greater numbers of consumers to attract from large-share brands than the latter have to recruit from small-share brands. For evidence relating to this issue, see Raj Sethuraman and V. Srinivasan, "The Asymmetric Share Effect: An Empirical Generalization on Cross-Price Effects," *Journal of Marketing Research* 39 (August 2002), 379–386.
56. For a review of interesting experimental research on this issue, see Stephen M. Nowlis and Itamar Simonson, "Sales Promotions and the Choice Context as Competing Influences on Decision Making," *Journal of Consumer Psychology* 9, no. 1 (2000), 1–16.

CHAPTER 18

Consumer-Oriented Promotions: Sampling and Couponing

Marcom Challenge: Sampling and Couponing to College Students

Try to recall your first few days on campus as a freshman. Life was great: You had money in your pocket, possibly saved up from working in the summer. You felt absolutely no school-related pressure in that first week before the beginning of classes. It was exciting seeing all the new people, few of whom were from your high school, many from other states and different countries. Life was good. However, one thing that may have surprised you this first week in college was that your campus may have looked like a shopping mall with people trying to get you to sign up for any of several credit cards, different wireless phone programs, and perhaps other items. Also, you may have been surprised to receive a sampler pack of free items at the bookstore. Or perhaps you received coupons for discounts at local merchants. Your new campus was not much different than what you had always experienced, especially if you are an American-born student, namely, your campus was yet another venue for promoting products and hawking wares.

Marketers do indeed covet the opportunity to reach and influence college-age students. College campuses are an ideal venue for sampling and couponing products, largely because students' buying preferences are probably more open to influence than later in life. Marketers in a recent year spent almost $40 million on mobile tours to campuses where they gave away free samples and coupons. Commercial research indicates that nearly two-thirds of students who receive a sampled product subsequently purchase that item. It is little wonder that more than two million Campus Trial Paks are annually distributed in bookstores at nearly 900 campuses around the United States. For example, in one recent year—perhaps your freshman year—SpongeBob SquarePants boxes included free samples of brands such as Clearasil, Vicks NyQuil, Clairol Herbal Essences shampoo, and, of course, the nearly ubiquitous AOL CD-ROMs. Products also are sampled on days of hosted events such as FHM Comedy Fest and the mtvU Campus Invasion Tour. Sampling of products builds excitement for the events as well as for the brands that are given to students.

The big-box electronics retailer, Best Buy, is one of the sponsors of the Comedy Fest and mtvU tour. In addition to offering samples of brands, Best Buy uses these events as a prime opportunity to acquaint students with its stores. One particularly effective strategy is providing students with attractive coupons for redemption at Best Buy stores. Beyond merely offering coupons, at select universities Best Buy even buses students to its closest available store.[1]

Another method of campus advertising is on mouse pads. According to New Age Marketing, MousepAD-vertising, mouse pads promote products and services by reaching millions of college Internet users whenever they log on to the Internet in their classrooms, libraries, computer labs, dorms, etc.—places where advertising was often previously restricted.

CHAPTER OBJECTIVES

1

Appreciate the objectives of consumer-oriented sales promotions.

2

Recognize that many forms of promotions perform different objectives for marketers.

3

Know the role of sampling, the forms of sampling, and the trends in sampling practice.

4

Be aware of the role of couponing, the types of coupons, and the developments in couponing practice.

5

Understand the coupon redemption process and misredemption.

6

Appreciate the role of promotion agencies.

Overview

This chapter introduces the many consumer-oriented sales promotions that are part of the brand manager's arsenal when attempting to influence desired behaviors from present and prospective customers. Building on the base developed in Chapter 17, which introduced the general topic of promotions and then focused on trade-oriented promotions, the present chapter devotes exclusive coverage to *consumer-oriented promotions.* The practices of sampling and couponing receive primary attention in this chapter; the subsequent chapter then explores additional forms of consumer-oriented promotions.

Before proceeding, it is appropriate to reiterate some advice that was provided in Chapter 1 and repeated elsewhere in the text. That guidance involved the relations among target markets, brand positioning, objectives, and budgets and was summarized in the form of the following mantra:

All marketing communications should be (1) directed to a particular ***target market****, (2) clearly* ***positioned****, (3) created to achieve a* ***specific objective****, and (4) undertaken to accomplish the objective* ***within budget constraint****.*

This counsel, when considered in the context of consumer promotions, simply advises that target marketing and brand positioning are the starting points for all decisions. With a precise target and clear positioning, the brand manager is in a position to specify the objective(s) a particular promotion program is (are) designed to accomplish. The manager also must work diligently to ensure that promotion spending does not exceed the budget constraint. This is the challenge that brand managers face when using consumer-oriented promotions to achieve strategic objectives.

Why Use Consumer Promotions?

In almost every product category, whether durable products or consumer packaged goods (CPGs), there are several brands available to wholesalers and retailers (the trade) to choose among and for consumers ultimately to select or reject for personal or family consumption. As a brand manager, your objective is to get your brand adequately placed in as many retail outlets as possible and to ensure that the brand moves off the shelves with frequency sufficient to keep retailers satisfied with its performance and to achieve your own profit objectives. This requires that you get consumers to try your brand and, hopefully, to become regular versus only occasional purchasers.

Your competitors have identical goals. They are attempting to garner the support of the same wholesalers and retailers that you desire and activate trial purchases and achieve purchase regularity from the consumers you also covet. Their gain is your loss. It is a vicious zero-sum game in the battle for trade customers and final consumers. You are unwilling to make it easy for your competitors, and they are not inclined to make your life a proverbial bed of roses.

Though the stakes pale in comparison, brand managers—like their counterparts in the military—are constantly attacking, counterattacking, and defending their turf against competitive inroads. Advertising plays a major role in this battle, flying above the day-to-day action, in a manner of speaking, and dropping persuasive bombs. Sales promotion, on the other hand, is analogous to an army's ground troops, who are engaged in the "dirty work" of fighting off the competition and engaging in hand-to-hand battle. Advertising alone is insufficient; promotion by itself is inadequate. Together they can make a formidable opponent.

Now, in answer to the question opening this section (Why use consumer promotions?), the short response is that promotions are used because they accomplish goals that advertising by itself cannot. Consumers oftentimes need to be *induced* to buy now rather than later, to buy your brand rather than a competitor's, to buy more rather than less, and to buy more frequently. Sales promotions are uniquely suited to achieving these imperatives. Whereas advertising makes consumers aware of your brand and promotes a positive image, promotions serve to *consummate the transaction.*

Before proceeding, a final preliminary point is in order. This actually is a personal request regarding your study of this chapter and the following. In particular, as a consumer living in a market-oriented society who is exposed daily to the commonplace practice of marketers inundating us with many forms of promotions (coupons, samples, sweepstakes, games, rebates, etc.), you may think you already understand everything you need to know about these ordinary topics. Without a doubt, you do know a lot about promotions—at least at an experiential level. Yet, just as you are aware of Einstein's theory of relativity ($E = mc^2$), you probably do not actually understand the theory in a sophisticated fashion. Though promotions are trivial in comparison to Einstein's theory, the point I am attempting to make is that you probably also do not understand sales promotions beyond a relatively superficial level. It is my wish that you study the material in this and the following chapter with the goal of *really* understanding why the various types of promotions are used and which unique objectives each is designed to accomplish. Sophisticated brand managers do not simply reach into a "bag" and pick out any promotional tool as if the multiple forms of promotions are completely interchangeable. Rather, each is chosen to accomplish strategic objectives to a degree better than alternative options, given the budget constraint.

Brand Management Objectives and Consumer Rewards

What objectives do brand managers hope to accomplish by using consumer-oriented promotions, and why are consumers receptive to samples, coupons, contests, sweepstakes, cents-off offers, and other promotional efforts? Answers to these interrelated questions will provide us with a useful framework for understanding why particular forms of promotions are useful in view of the goal that must be accomplished for a brand at a given point in time.

Brand Management Objectives

The overarching objective of consumer-oriented promotions is to promote increased sales (sales promotion = promoting sales). Subsidiary to this overarching goal and in concert with trade-oriented promotions (the subject of the prior chapter), consumer promotions are capable of achieving various sales-influencing objectives for "our" brand:[2]

- Gaining trade support for inventorying increased quantities of our brand during a limited period and providing superior display space for our brand during this period
- Reducing brand inventory for a limited period when inventories have grown to an excessive level due to slow sales caused by economic conditions or effective competitive actions
- Providing the sales force with increased motivation during a promotional period to gain greater distribution for our brand, better display space, or other preferential treatment vis-à-vis competitive brands
- Protecting our customer base against competitors' efforts to steal them away
- Introducing new brands to the trade and to consumers
- Entering new markets with established brands

- Promoting trial purchases among consumers who have never tried our brand or achieving retrial from those who have not purchased our brand for an extended period
- Rewarding present customers for continuing to purchase our brand
- Encouraging repeat purchasing of our brand and reinforcing brand loyalty
- Enhancing our brand's image
- Increasing advertising readership
- Facilitating the process of continually expanding the list of names and addresses in our database

As can be seen, consumer promotions are used to accomplish a variety of objectives, with the ultimate goal of driving increased sales of our brand. Consumer promotions, when done effectively, can serve to gain the trade's support, inspire the sales force to improve performance, and, most important for present purposes, motivate consumers to commit a trial purchase of our brand and, ideally, to purchase it with greater frequency and perhaps even in larger quantities.

To simplify matters, the discussions of specific forms of consumer-oriented promotions in this and the following chapter focus primarily on objectives directed at *influencing consumer behavior* rather than initiating trade or sales-force action. We will focus on three general categories of objectives: (1) generating trial purchases, (2) encouraging repeat purchases, and (3) reinforcing brand images.

Some sales promotions (such as samples and coupons) are used primarily for *trial impact.* A brand manager employs these promotional tools to prompt nonusers to try a brand for the first time or to encourage retrial from prior users who have not purchased the brand for perhaps extended periods. At other times, managers use promotions to hold onto their current customer base by rewarding them for continuing to purchase the promoted brand or loading them with a stockpile of the manufacturer's brand so they have no need, at least in the short run, to switch to another brand. This is sales promotions' *repeat-purchase objective.* Sales promotions also can be used for *image reinforcement* purposes. For example, the careful selection of the right premium object or appropriate sweepstakes prize can serve to bolster a brand's image.

Consumer Rewards

Consumers would not be responsive to sales promotions unless there was something in it for them—and, in fact, there is. All promotion techniques provide consumers with *rewards* (benefits, incentives, or inducements) that encourage certain forms of behavior desired by brand managers. These rewards, or benefits, are both utilitarian and hedonic.[3] Consumers who use sales promotions receive various *utilitarian,* or functional, benefits: (1) obtaining monetary savings (e.g., when using coupons); (2) reducing search and decision costs (e.g., by simply availing themselves of a promotional offer and not having to think about other alternatives); and (3) obtaining improved product quality made possible by a price reduction that allows consumers to buy superior brands they might not otherwise purchase. Consumers also obtain *hedonic* benefits when taking advantage of sales promotion offers: (1) accomplishing a sense of being a wise shopper when taking advantage of sales promotions; (2) achieving a need for stimulation and variety when, say, trying a brand one otherwise might not purchase if it were not for an attractive promotion; and (3) obtaining entertainment value when, for example, the consumer competes in a promotional contest or participates in a sweepstakes. Consumer promotions also perform an *informational function* by influencing consumer beliefs about a brand—for example, by suggesting the brand is of higher quality than previously thought because it is copromoted with another brand that is itself widely regarded as being high quality.[4]

The rewards consumers receive from sales promotions sometimes are immediate, while at other times they are delayed. An *immediate reward* is one that delivers monetary savings or some other form of benefit as soon as the consumer performs a marketer-specified behavior. For example, you potentially obtain immediate pleasure when you try a free food item or beverage that has been sampled in a supermarket or a club store such as Costco or Sam's Club. *Delayed rewards* are those that follow the behavior by a period of days, weeks, or even longer. For example, you may have to wait six or eight weeks before a mail-in premium item can be enjoyed.

Generally speaking, consumers are more responsive to immediate rewards than they are to delayed rewards. Of course, this is in line with the natural human preference for *immediate gratification.*

Classification of Promotion Methods

It is insightful to consider each consumer-oriented promotion technique in terms of its brand management objective and its consumer reward. Table 18.1 presents a six-cell typology that was constructed by cross-classifying the two forms of consumer rewards (immediate versus delayed) with the three objectives for using promotions (generating trial purchases, encouraging repeat purchases, and reinforcing brand image).

Cell 1 includes three promotion techniques—samples, instant coupons, and shelf-delivered coupons—that encourage *trial purchase* behavior by providing consumers with an immediate reward. The reward is either monetary savings, in the case of instant coupons, or a free product, in the case of samples. Media- and mail-delivered coupons, free-with-purchase premiums, and scanner-delivered coupons—all found in **cell 2**—are some of the techniques that generate consumer trial yet delay the reward. Coupons along with samples are the topics of the present chapter, while premiums and other forms of consumer-oriented promotions are covered in the following chapter.

Table 18.1

Major Consumer-Oriented Promotions

Consumer Reward	Brand Management Objective: Generating Trial Purchases	Brand Management Objective: Encouraging Repeat Purchases	Brand Management Objective: Reinforcing Brand Image
Immediate	**Cell 1** • Samples 18* • Instant coupons 18 • Shelf-delivered coupons 18	**Cell 3** • Price-offs 19 • Bonus packs 19 • In-, on-, and near-pack premiums 19 • Games 19	**Cell 5**
Delayed	**Cell 2** • Scanner-delivered coupons 18 • Media- and mail-delivered coupons 18 • Online coupons 18 • Mail-in premiums 19 • Free-with-purchase premiums 19	**Cell 4** • In- and on-pack coupons 18 • Rebates and refunds 19 • Phone cards 19 • Continuity programs 19	**Cell 6** • Self-liquidating premiums 19 • Sweepstakes and contests 19

* Indicates the chapter, either Chapter 18 or 19, in which this form of sales promotion is covered.

Cells 3 and 4 contain promotional tools that are intended to encourage *repeat purchases* from consumers. Marketing communicators design these techniques to reward a brand's existing customers and to keep them from switching to competitive brands—in other words, to encourage repeat purchasing. Immediate reward tools, in **cell 3**, include price-offs; bonus packs; in-, on-, and near-pack premiums; and games. Delayed reward techniques, listed in **cell 4**, include in- and on-pack coupons, refund and rebate offers, phone cards, and continuity programs.

Building a brand's image is primarily the task of advertising; however, sales promotion tools may support advertising efforts by *reinforcing a brand's image.* By nature, these techniques are incapable of providing consumers with an immediate reward; therefore, **cell 5** is vacant. **Cell 6** contains self-liquidating premiums and two promotional tools, contests and sweepstakes, that, if designed appropriately, can reinforce or even strengthen a brand's image in addition to performing other tasks. (See the *Global Focus* insert for an interesting contest for M&M's candies.)

Caution Is in Order!

It is important to reemphasize that the classification of promotional tools in Table 18.1 is necessarily simplified. First, the table classifies each technique with respect to the *primary* objective it is designed to accomplish. It is important to recognize, however, that promotions are capable of accomplishing more than a single objective. For example, bonus packs (cell 3) are classified as encouraging repeat purchasing, but first-time triers also occasionally purchase brands that offer extra volume. The various forms of coupons located in cells 1 and 2 are designed primarily to encourage triers and to attract switchers from other brands. In actuality, however, most coupons are redeemed by current purchasers rather than by new buyers. In other words, though intended to encourage trial purchasing and switching, coupons also invite repeat purchasing by rewarding present customers for continuing to purchase "our" brand.

Second, the tools in Table 18.1 are categorized under the primary objective each is designed to accomplish *toward consumers.* It is important to recognize, however, that manufacturers use consumer-oriented sales promotions also to *leverage trade support.* For example, when a manufacturer informs retailers that a certain brand will be sampled during a designated period, the manufacturer is virtually assured that retailers will purchase extra quantities of that brand and possibly provide additional display space. In other words, consumer-oriented promotions can influence trade behavior as well as consumer action.

Finally, note that two techniques, coupons and premiums, are found in more than one cell. This is because these techniques achieve different objectives depending on the specific form of *delivery vehicle.* Coupons delivered through the media (newspapers, magazines, and online) or in the mail offer a form of delayed reward, whereas instant coupons that are peeled from a package at the point of purchase offer an immediate reward. Similarly, premium objects that are delivered in, on, or near a product's package provide an immediate reward, while those requiring mail delivery yield a reward only after some delay.

Sampling

The baby food division of H. J. Heinz Company developed a rather revolutionary product idea: a powdered, instant baby food. Although Heinz's management was optimistic about instant baby food, they knew consumers would resist trying the product because of a natural inertia regarding dramatic product shifts and the fear of treating their babies as guinea pigs. A further complication was the difficulty of communicating the product's benefits by advertising alone. Heinz needed a way to persuade mothers to try instant baby food. The solution was to employ the

M&M's Global Color Vote

global focus

Masterfoods, the owner of M&M's candies, has in recent years conducted contests asking consumers to vote for their preferred new M&M's color. In a recent contest, 10 million votes were cast by people from more than 200 countries in choosing among pink, purple, or aqua as their preferred new M&M's color. TV and print ads and an Internet campaign were undertaken to drum up the vote, and in the United States special events were conducted to increase enthusiasm. For example, a voting day was held at Wal-Mart stores, which generated 600,000 votes, and National Association for Stock Car Auto Racing (NASCAR) enthusiasts also voted at racing events.

And the winner? Purple garnered over 40 percent of the worldwide vote and barely eked out aqua, which earned just short of 40 percent of the votes. Pink came in last with not quite 20 percent. But, of course, Masterfoods did not conduct this contest simply to find out which color consumers most like. The company's hope, instead, was that the contest would increase enthusiasm for M&M's and grow sales volume. And that is exactly what happened. Sales growth of 21 percent was enjoyed in the United States. Sales in Mexico were up 16 percent, while sales in Canada increased over the previous year by 5 percent. M&M's product movement also was up in Europe and the Asia-Pacific region.

Source: Adapted from Mike Beirne, "Getting Out the Vote, Globally," *Brandweek*, March 17, 2003, R15.

services of a company that specializes in delivering samples to mothers of newborn infants. This form of sampling avoided waste distribution and gave mothers firsthand experience with preparing and feeding their babies instant food. Many sample recipients became loyal users.

This case illustrates the power of sampling as a promotional technique. Most practitioners agree that sampling is the *premier sales promotion device for generating trial usage.* In fact, some observers believe that sample distribution is almost a necessity when introducing *truly* new products. Sampling is effective because it provides consumers with an opportunity to personally experience a new brand. It allows an active, hands-on interaction with the sampled brand rather than a passive encounter, as is the case with the receipt of promotional techniques such as coupons.

By definition, **sampling** includes any method used to deliver an actual- or trial-sized product to consumers. The vast majority of manufacturers use sampling as part of their marcom programs for purposes of generating trial or retrial and leveraging trade support. Brand managers in the United States invest more than $1.5 billion annually on product sampling.[5]

Various distribution methods are used to deliver samples either alone (*solo* sampling) or in cooperation with other brands (*co-op* sampling):

- *Direct mail:* Samples are mailed to households targeted by demographic characteristics or in terms of geodemographics (as discussed in Chapter 4).
- *Newspapers and magazines:* Samples often are included in magazines and newspapers. The newspaper is an increasingly attractive medium for broad-scale sampling, especially when considering that 55 million American households receive daily newspapers and nearly 60 million receive Sunday papers. This is a cost-efficient form of sampling for reaching a mass audience.
- *Door-to-door sampling by distribution crews:* This form of sampling allows considerable targeting and possesses advantages such as lower cost and short lead times between when a sampling request is made by a brand manager and when samples are ultimately delivered by the sampling company. Companies that specialize in door-to-door sampling target household selection to fit the client's needs. Samples can be distributed just in blue-collar neighborhoods, Hispanic areas, or in any other locale where residents match the sampled brand's target market.
- *On- or in-pack sampling:* This method uses the package of another product to serve as the sample carrier. Figure 18.1 is an advertisement from a company called Co-op Promotions that specializes in this form of promotion. The ad indicates that Nuprin pain reliever was sampled in Ace bandages and that the

Figure 18.1

On- and In-Pack Sampling

Molly McButter brand was sampled in Success Rice. The complementary nature between each brand pair is obvious, which is a key requirement of this form of tie-in promotion.

- *High-traffic locations and events:* Shopping centers, movie theaters, airports, and special events offer valuable forums for sample distribution. More will be said about this form of sampling in a later discussion of creative forms of sampling.
- *Sampling at unique venues:* Brand managers and their promotion agencies sometimes choose unique locations for sampling products that are especially appropriate for people at a certain stage of life, referred to as life's *change points.* Sampling to college students at the beginning of a new school year (see *Marcom Challenge*) is one illustration of change-point sampling. Marriage offices are another change-point for reaching newlyweds. Newlywed kits containing various products are sometimes presented to couples when they apply for marriage licenses. The rationale for this sampling location is based on the fact that newlyweds in the United States spend in excess of $70 billion for their households in the first year after marriage.[6]
- *In-store sampling:* Demonstrators provide product samples in grocery stores and other retail outlets for trial while consumers are shopping. It is understandable that in-store sampling is the most frequent form of sampling when considering that this distribution mode offers samples to consumers where and when their purchase decisions can be influenced most immediately. A toy store such as Toys "R" Us, for example, would be an appropriate outlet for reaching moms and kids, and Blockbuster is an excellent venue for delivering samples to teens and young adults.
- *Internet sampling:* Brand managers are increasingly distributing samples online. They typically employ the services of companies that specialize in online sample delivery, companies such as StartSampling and TheFreeSite.com. We return to online sampling in a later discussion of creative delivery methods.

Major Sampling Practices

Brand managers have distributed free samples for generations. Historically, however, many sampling efforts were unsophisticated and wasteful. In particular, there was a tendency to use mass-distribution outlets in getting sampled products in the hands of as many people as possible. Sophisticated sampling now insists on three prudent practices: (1) targeting rather than mass distributing samples, (2) using innovative distribution methods where appropriate, and (3) undertaking efforts to measure sampling's return on investment.

Targeting Sample Recipients

Sampling services that specialize in precision distribution (targeting) have emerged in recent years. For example, one sampling specialist aims for children under the age of 8 by distributing samples at zoos, museums, and other locations that appeal to young children and their parents. It reaches children and teens (ages 9 to 17) at venues such as little league baseball fields, movie theaters, and skating centers. Young adults (ages 18 to 24) receive samples at colleges and universities, malls, beaches, and concerts. Airports, shopping centers, and high-density retail districts are good sites for homing in on adults ages 25 to 54.

Newlyweds, as mentioned previously, receive free samples when applying for marriage licenses.

Another form of targeting is delivering samples to consumers who are either product nonusers or users of competitive brands. The Gillette Company, for example, mailed 400,000 Sensor razors to men who use competitive wet razors.

How would you reach high school males? This is one of the most inaccessible markets because they are not particularly heavy television viewers or magazine readers. MarketSource, another company that specializes in targeted sample distribution, developed a program that connected with teenage males by distributing gift packages of product samples (such as shaving cream, razors, mouthwash, and candy) at tuxedo rental shops. Recipients picked up their sample pack when they arranged to rent a prom tuxedo.

Suppose you wanted to reach young children with free samples. Where would you gain access to this group? Distributors hand out sample packs at stores such as Toys "R" Us. One sampling executive describes the advantage of this form of targeting sampling in these terms:

When you're giving your product to customers in Toys "R" Us, you can bet with 99 percent accuracy you're reaching families with children under 12 or grandparents with grandchildren that age. You don't have that kind of certainty of reach with other [forms of marketing communications].[7]

How might you reach urban residents? Lafayette Jones, president of a company that specializes in delivering samples to African-Americans and Latinos, has established a network of several thousand African-American and Latino churches through which samples are distributed. Ministers in these churches often present sample bags to members of the congregation. Jones's company also distributes samples to urban residents through a large network of beauty salons and barber shops.[8]

A final illustration of targeted sampling involves the distribution of Benadryl anti-itch cream conducted a few years ago by Warner-Lambert, then makers of Benadryl (since merged under the Pfizer name). Warner-Lambert wanted to develop a sampling program that would contact victims of itching caused by mosquito bites, heat rash, poison ivy, and so on. The objective was to approach prospective consumers at "point-of-itch" locations where they would be most receptive to learning about the virtues of Benadryl. The company considered sampling at retail lawn-and-garden departments but eliminated that prospect as not quite satisfying its point-of-itch objective. It eventually came up with the clever idea of sampling at KOA Kampground—locations where people camp, enjoy the outdoors, and . . . itch. Twenty-five million people visit KOA Kampgrounds every year. During a two-summer period Warner-Lambert distributed six million Benadryl samples to 550 campgrounds, thereby achieving effective and cost-efficient sample distribution.[9]

All of the foregoing illustrations indicate that almost any group of consumers can be selectively sampled. Probably the only limitation to selective sampling is the absence of creativity!

Using Creative Distribution Methods

Companies are applying numerous creative ways to get sample merchandise into the hands of targeted consumers. One company distributed samples of Chunky candy bars to consumers stuck in rush-hour traffic. Progresso Soup, marketed by The Pillsbury Company (now owned by General Mills), employed a fleet of "Soupermen" to deliver cups of hot soup from backpack dispensers to consumers in cold-weather cities such as Cleveland, Chicago, Detroit, and Pittsburgh. From October through March, sampling teams visited consumers in these cities at sporting events, races, outdoor shows, and other locales—all of which represented ideal locations for getting consumers to try cups of hot Progresso soup.

Guinness Import Company sampled its unique beer using tractor trailers equipped with dozens of taps. These trailers traveled to Irish music festivals in cities such as New York, Chicago, and San Francisco. According to a company spokesperson, Guinness invested in the trailers because it regards hands-on sampling at special events as a good opportunity to create a unique brand usage experience and to avoid the clutter of mass-media advertising.

Another example of creative sampling is provided by the Marie Callender's brand of frozen foods owned by ConAgra Frozen Foods. West of the Rocky Mountains, Marie Callender's is a name well known for home-style restaurants. The line of frozen foods under the Marie Callender's name performed well in western markets, but in the Midwest and eastern markets, sales were sluggish because the Marie Callender's name in these markets had no preestablished brand equity as it had in the West. ConAgra decided it would have to aggressively sample Marie Callender's frozen foods to establish the name and generate trade and consumer enthusiasm.

ConAgra developed a clever way to sample its line of Marie Callender's frozen foods. Old Airstream trailers were purchased and converted into retro Marie Callender's Mobile Diners. The trailers were sent to six markets: Chicago, Detroit, Grand Rapids, Milwaukee, Pittsburgh, and New England. Samples of Marie Callender's entrees were distributed to more than 100,000 consumers in these markets. Live radio broadcasts and in-store point-of-purchase banners announced the diner visits. As a result of the sampling program, key retail accounts in the six-market area ordered ConAgra's Marie Callender's frozen foods, and consumers demonstrated their receptiveness to this new brand through trial and repeat purchasing.[10]

The famous Ben & Jerry's Homemade ice cream offers another illustration of creative sampling. After Ben & Jerry's was purchased by Unilever, the brand managers decided to sample the product to increase its market penetration and to convert new users from competitive brands. But how do you sample ice cream? It could be done in supermarkets, but that venue somehow doesn't quite fit with Ben & Jerry's image. Obviously, unlike most other products, sampling through the mail also is out of the question. Given these product-sampling limitations, Ben & Jerry's marketing team decided to sample Ben & Jerry's ice cream at a special event titled "Urban Pasture," which was designed specifically for that purpose, and invited fans to "stop and taste the ice cream."

Requiring the event to match Ben & Jerry's upscale, pastoral image, the promotion planners created an "Urban Pasture" motif complete with cow manikins, banners, lounge chairs, live bands, and, of course, free ice cream. The event toured 13 major U.S. cities, including Boston, Chicago, Los Angeles, and New York. The "Urban Pasture" set up in each city included a main stage from which music was played, and ice-cream-scooping matches were hosted by sports and entertainment celebrities, with the winner at each tour stop receiving the opportunity to select a charity to receive an attractive donation—clearly in line with the brand's philanthropic image. Each "pasture" was up for a single day, but sampling crews remained in each city for at least an additional week during which they sampled Ben & Jerry's ice cream from cow-bedecked buses.

In addition to giving away more than one million samples of the ice cream during the entire tour, a sweepstakes also was run at each tour stop, whereby winners received a month-long lease on a large recreational vehicle along with spending money and a year's supply of Ben & Jerry's ice cream. Also at each site, coupons were distributed and participants had an opportunity to receive T-shirts, ball caps, travel mugs, and other premium items. All in all, the promotional events in 13 cities for Ben & Jerry's Homemade ice cream increased consumer interest in the brand, encouraged subsequent trial purchasing, and undoubtedly influenced some consumers to become loyal repeat purchasers.[11]

The promotion agency for Nivea for Men skin-care products, Maya Marketing, devised a clever method to sample this product to male consumers. Street teams distributed samples of Nivea products at almost 800 rail and subway stations across the United States. The brand enjoyed a 100 percent increase in sales in large part due to this creative sampling program.[12] (A final illustration of creative sampling is presented in the *IMC Focus* insert.)

The most recent method used to creatively sample brands is the Internet. As noted earlier, a number of specialized companies have entered this business to serve as online sampling portals for the CPG companies they represent. Interested consumers are driven to online sampling sites and register to receive free samples for brands that interest them. Samples are then mailed in a timely fashion. Because mailing represents a major cost element, it is estimated that online sampling costs are perhaps three times greater than sampling in stores or at special events.[13] The justification for this added expense is that people who go online to request a particular sample generally are really interested in that brand—and eventually may purchase it—in comparison, say, to people who receive a sample at an event. Hence, online sampling may be less wasteful than alternative forms of sampling. Though representing a useful way to distribute samples, it is doubtful that online sampling will displace alternative sampling methods.

Estimating Return on Investment

As previously detailed in Chapter 2, marketing communicators are increasingly being held accountable for their decisions. Financial officers, senior marketing executives, and chief executives are demanding evidence that investments in advertising and promotions can be justified by the profits they return. Return on investment (ROI) is a tool that can be used to assess whether an investment in a sampling program is cost justified. Table 18.2 lays out the straightforward steps in applying an ROI analysis to a sampling investment.[14] Please read carefully the systematic procedure described in Table 18.2.

Table 18.2

Calculating the ROI for a Sampling Investment

- Step 1: *Determine the total cost of sampling,* which includes the cost of the sample goods plus the costs of distribution—mailing, door-to-door distribution, and so on. Assume, for example, that the cost of distributing a trial-sized unit is $0.60 and that 15,000,000 units are distributed; hence, the total cost is $9 million.
- Step 2: *Calculate the profit per unit* by determining the average number of annual uses of the product and multiplying this by the per-unit profit. Assume, for example, that on average six units of the sampled product are purchased per year and that the profit per unit is $1. Thus, each user promises the company a profit potential of $6 when they become users of the sampled brand.
- Step 3: *Calculate the number of converters* needed for the sampling program to break even. (Converters are individuals who after sampling a brand become users.) Given the cost of the sampling program ($9 million) and the profit potential per user ($6), the number of conversions needed in this case to break even is 1,500,000 (i.e., $9 million divided by $6). This number represents a 10 percent conversion rate just to break even (i.e., 1,500,000 divided by 15,000,000).
- Step 4: *Determine the effectiveness of the sampling.* For a sampling to be successful, the conversion rate must exceed the break-even rate with gains in the 10 to 16 percent range. In this case, this would mean a minimum of 1,650,000 people must become users after trying the sampled brand (i.e., 1,500,000 times 1.1) to justify the sampling cost and yield a reasonable profit from the sampling investment.

Sampling Toilet Tissue

imc focus

This is a bit of a sensitive topic, but it's part of life, so let's deal with it. If you were brand manager of a line of toilet tissue and thought sampling would benefit the brand, how would you provide consumers with free samples? Obviously, many of the traditional sampling methods would be inappropriate due to the high cost of sending out, say, millions of rolls of tissue. Think about it before reading on, what would you do?

Brand managers of P&G's Charmin brand faced precisely this challenge. They had tried various sampling methods, such as giving away rolls to discharged hospital patients, but without much success in building brand volume. Then someone hit upon the idea of sampling Charmin at outdoor events. The company manufactured a fleet of tractor-trailer mounted bathrooms (see Figure 18.2) and conducted the Charmin Potty Palooza tour at events such as state fairs and Oktoberfests. Each trailer was equipped with running water, wall-papered walls, faux-wood floors, Charmin toilet tissue, and various samples of P&G's other brands—Safeguard soap, Bounty paper towels, and Pampers diapers—along with changing tables.

As described by Charmin's brand manager, "[Toilet tissue] is a category that consumers don't think much about. To break through that and understand the benefits of Charmin Ultra, you really need to try it." P&G's research indicated a 14 percent increase in Charmin sales among people who used P&G's Potty Palooza facilities.

SOURCE: Adapted from Jack Neff, "P&G Brings Potty to Parties," *Advertising Age*, February 17, 2003, 22.

When Should Sampling Be Used?

Promotion managers use sampling to induce consumers to try either a brand that is new or one that is moving into a different market. While it is important to encourage trial usage for new brands, sampling is not appropriate for all new or improved products. Ideal circumstances include the following:[15]

1. Either when a new or improved brand is either *demonstrably superior* to other brands or when it has *distinct relative advantages* over brands that it is intended to replace. If a brand does not possess superiority or distinct advantages, it probably is not economically justifiable to give it away.
2. When the product concept is so innovative that it is *difficult to communicate by advertising alone.* The earlier example of Heinz instant baby food illustrates this point, as do the examples of sampling Ben & Jerry's Homemade ice cream and Charmin toilet tissue (see *IMC Focus* and Figure 18.2). In general, sampling enables consumers to learn about product advantages that marketers would have difficulty convincing them of via advertising alone. Procter & Gamble (P&G) sampled its new line of olestra-made Fat Free Pringles to lunchtime crowds in 20 major cities. The brand management team knew that consumers had to experience for themselves that this fat-free version of Pringles tasted virtually the same as regular Pringles chips.
3. When promotional budgets *can afford to generate consumer trial quickly.* If generating quick trial is not essential, then cheaper trial-impacting promotional tools such as coupons should be used.

Figure 18.2

Sampling Charmin via a Fleet of Tractor Trailers

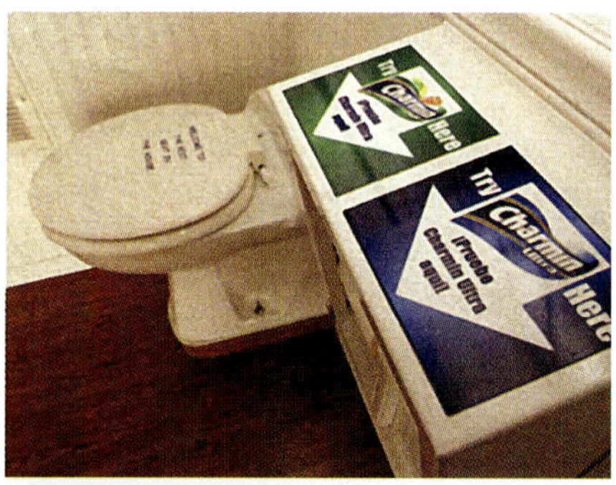

Sampling Problems

There are several problems with the use of sampling. First, sampling is expensive. Second, mass mailings of samples can be mishandled by the postal service or other distributors. Third, samples distributed door to door or in high-traffic locations may suffer from wasted distribution and not reach the hands of the best potential customers. Fourth, in- or on-package sampling excludes consumers who do not buy the carrying brand. Fifth, in-store sampling often fails to reach sufficient numbers of consumers to justify its expense.

A sixth problem with samples is that consumers may misuse them. Consider the case of Sun Light dishwashing liquid, a product of Lever Brothers. This product, which smells like lemons, was extensively sampled some years ago to more than 50 million households. Unfortunately, nearly 80 adults and children claimed that they became ill after consuming the product, having mistaken the dishwashing liquid for lemon juice! According to a Lever Brothers' marketing research director at the time of the sampling, there is always a potential problem of misuse when a product is sent to homes rather than purchased with prior product knowledge at a supermarket.[16]

A final sampling problem, pilferage, can result when samples are distributed through the mail. A case in point occurred in Poland shortly after the Iron Curtain separating eastern from western Europe was literally and symbolically demolished with the fall of Communist dominion in the East. P&G mailed 580,000 samples of Vidal Sassoon Wash & Go shampoo to consumers in Poland, the first ever mass mailing of free samples in that country. The mailing was a big hit—so big, in fact, that about 2,000 mailboxes were broken into. The shampoo samples, although labeled "Not for sale," turned up on open markets and were in high demand at a price of 60 cents each. P&G paid nearly $40,000 to the Polish Post, Poland's mail service, to deliver the samples. In addition to the cost of distribution, P&G paid thousands more to have mailboxes repaired.[17]

Due to its expense and because of waste and other problems, the use of sampling fell out of favor for a period of time as many marketers turned to less expensive promotions, especially couponing. However, with the development of creative solutions and innovations, brand managers and their promotion agencies have again become enthusiastic about sampling. Sampling has become more efficient in reaching specific target groups, its results are readily measurable, and the rising costs of media advertising have increased its relative attractiveness.

Couponing

A **coupon** is a promotional device that rewards consumers for purchasing the coupon-offering brand by providing either *cents-off savings* or *free merchandise.* Cents-off savings often are as high as $1 or more. For example, S. C. Johnson & Son offered a $10 coupon for its Grab-it floor sweeper starter kit. As an alternative to price-discounting coupons, free-merchandise offers typically come in the form of "buy one, get one free" in which the free item typically is another unit of the same brand (see Figure 18.3).

Coupons are delivered through newspapers; magazines; freestanding inserts; direct mail; in or on packages; online; and at the point of purchase by package, shelf, and electronic delivery devices. It is important to appreciate the fact that not all delivery methods have the same objective. *Instant coupons* (that is, those that can be peeled from packages at the point of purchase) provide immediate rewards to consumers and encourage trial purchases as well as repeat buying from loyal consumers (see Table 18.1). *Mail- and media-delivered coupons* delay the reward, although they also generate trial purchase behavior. Before discussing these specific coupon delivery modes in detail, it first will be instructive to examine pertinent developments in coupon use.

Couponing Background

Approximately 250 billion coupons are distributed annually in the United States, and coupon promotions cost U.S. marketers about $7 billion annually.[18] Nearly all

Figure 18.3 A Buy One Get One Free Coupon Offer

Courtesy, Wm. Wrigley Jr. Company

CPG marketers issue coupons. The use of coupons is not, however, restricted to packaged goods. For example, General Motors Corporation mailed coupons valued as high as $1,000 to its past customers in hopes of encouraging them to purchase new cars. Surveys indicate that virtually all American consumers use coupons at least on occasion. However, research has established that consumers vary greatly in terms of their psychological inclination to use coupons and that this coupon proneness is predictive of actual coupon redemption behavior.[19]

The appeal of coupons is not limited to American consumers. A major international study found that consumers in every country included in the survey valued coupons. Although vastly more coupons are distributed in the United States than elsewhere, redemption rates (the percentage of all distributed coupons that are taken to stores for price discounts) are higher in most other countries. However, couponing in some countries is virtually nonexistent or in the fledgling stage. For example, in Germany the government limits the face value of coupons to 1 percent of a product's value, which effectively eliminates this form of promotion in that country for CPGs. Only a small amount of couponing occurs in France because the few chains that control the retail grocery market in that country generally oppose the use of coupons. Couponing activity in Japan is in the early stages following the lifting of government restrictions.

Coupon Distribution Methods

The method of coupon distribution preferred by brand managers is the *freestanding insert* (FSI). FSIs, which are inserts most often appearing in Sunday newspapers, account for approximately 87 percent of all coupons distributed in the United States.[20] The other media for coupon distribution are handouts at stores and other locations, magazines and newspapers, product packages, direct mail, and the Internet.

Another major trend in coupon distribution has been the establishment of *cooperative coupon programs.* These are programs in which a service distributes coupons for a single company's multiple brands or brands from multiple companies. Two such service companies—Valassis and SmartSource—are responsible for distributing the billions of FSI coupons in separate inserts in newspapers around the United States. Both Valassis and SmartSource distribute coupons every Sunday throughout the year and represent literally hundreds of different brands and companies. P&G has its own FSI insert program (P&G brandSAVER) that is distributed in Sunday newspapers every four weeks. Valpak Direct Marketing Systems is a cooperative program for distributing coupons by direct mail.

Economic Impact

The extensive use of couponing has not occurred without criticism. Some critics contend that coupons are wasteful and may actually increase prices of consumer goods. Whether coupons are wasteful and inefficient is debatable. However, it is undeniable that coupons are an expensive proposition. For a better understanding of coupon costs, consider the case of a coupon with a $1 face value. (The *face value* is the amount paid to the consumer when he or she redeems the coupon at a retail checkout along with a purchase of the brand for which the coupon is offered.) The actual cost of this coupon is considerably more than $1. In fact, the actual cost, as shown in Table 18.3, is substantially more at $1.59. As can be seen from the table, the major cost element is the face value of $1 that is deducted from the purchase price. But the marketers offering this coupon incur several other costs: (1) a hefty distribution and postage charge (40 cents), (2) a handling fee that is paid to retailers for their trouble (8 cents), (3) a misredemption charge resulting from fraudulent redemptions (estimated at 7 cents), (4) internal preparation and processing costs (2 cents), and (5) a redemption cost (2 cents). The actual cost of $1.59 per redeemed coupon is 59 percent greater than the face value of $1. Assume a marketer distributes 40 million

Table 18.3
Full Coupon Cost

1. Face value	$1.00
2. Distribution and postage cost	.40
3. Handling charge	.08
4. Consumer misredemption cost	.07
5. Internal preparation and processing cost	.02
6. Redemption cost	.02
Total Cost	$1.59

SOURCE: Adapted from an analysis performed by the McKinsey & Co. consulting firm.

of these FSI coupons and that 2 percent, or 800,000, are redeemed. The total cost of this coupon "drop" would thus amount to $1,272,000. It should be apparent that coupon activity requires substantial investment to accomplish desired objectives.

Obviously, programs that aid in reducing costs, such as cooperative couponing and online delivery, are eagerly sought. Coupons are indeed costly, some are wasteful, and other promotional devices may be better. However, the extensive use of coupons suggests either that there are a large number of incompetent brand managers or that better promotional tools are not available or are economically infeasible. The latter explanation is the more reasonable when considering how the marketplace operates. If a business practice is uneconomical, it will not continue to be used for long. When a better business practice is available, it will replace the previous solution. Conclusion: it appears that coupons are used extensively because marketers have been unable to devise more effective and economical methods for accomplishing the trial-generating objectives that coupons accomplish.

Is Couponing Profitable?

There is evidence that those households most likely to redeem coupons are also the most likely to buy the brand in the first place. Moreover, most consumers revert to their pre-coupon brand choice immediately after redeeming a competitive brand's coupon.[21] Hence, when consumers who redeem would have bought the brand anyway, the effect of couponing, at least on the surface, is merely to increase costs and reduce the per-unit profit margin. However, the issue is more involved than this. Although it is undeniable that most coupons are redeemed by current brand users, competitive dynamics force companies to continue offering coupons to prevent *present consumers from switching* to other brands that do offer coupons or other promotional deals.

Couponing is a fact of life that will continue to remain an important part of marketing in North America and elsewhere. The real challenge for promotion managers is to continually seek ways to increase couponing profitability, to target coupons to consumers who may not otherwise purchase their brands, and to reward consumers for remaining loyal to their brands.

The following sections describe the major forms of couponing activity, the objectives each is intended to accomplish, and the innovations designed to increase couponing profitability. The presentation of couponing delivery methods follows the framework presented earlier in Table 18.1. It will be worthwhile to revisit Table 18.1 so as to better understand the specific couponing methods that follow.

Point-of-Purchase Couponing

As discussed in Chapter 8 in the context of point-of-purchase advertising, approximately 70 percent of purchase decisions are made while shoppers are in the store. It thus makes sense to deliver coupons at the point where decisions are made.

Point-of-purchase coupons come in three forms: instant, shelf-delivered, and electronically delivered by optical scanner.

Instantly Redeemable Coupons

Most coupon distribution methods have delayed impact on consumers because the coupon is received in the consumer's home and held for a period of time before it is redeemed. **Instantly redeemable coupons** (IRCs) are *peelable* from the package and are designed to be removed by the consumer and redeemed at checkout along with a purchase of the brand carrying the coupon. This form of coupon represents an *immediate reward* that can spur the consumer to undertake a trial purchase of the promoted brand (see cell 1 in Table 18.1). Instant coupons provide a significant price reduction and an immediate point-of-purchase incentive for consumers.

Although the instant coupon is a minor form of couponing, it has emerged in recent years as an alternative to price-off deals (in which every package must be reduced in price). The redemption level for instant coupons is considerably higher than the level for other couponing techniques. Whereas the dominant couponing method, FSIs, generates an average redemption level of approximately 1.5 percent (i.e., on average about 15 out of every 1,000 households that receive FSIs actually redeem them at stores), the average redemption rate for instant coupons is about 30 percent.[22] One would think that most purchasers would remove instant coupons at the time of making a purchase so as to receive the savings, but obviously the majority do not take advantage of these instant coupons.

A study compared the effectiveness of instantly redeemable coupons against freestanding inserts in generating sales for a brand of body wash. The FSI coupons and IRCs had face values of either 50 cents or $1. Each coupon type and value combination (that is, 50-cent FSI coupon, $1 FSI coupon, 50-cent IRC, or $1 IRC) was placed on the body wash brand in each of two markets for a two-month period. Recorded sales data revealed that the IRCs out-performed FSI coupons of equal value. Moreover, the 50-cent IRC increased sales volume by 23 percent more than the $1 FSI coupon![23] This obviously is a counterintuitive finding that requires explanation.

A spokesperson for the company that conducted this research said his company had no idea why the 50-cent IRC out-performed the $1 FSI coupon. However, research from the academic front offers an answer. One study found that a 75-cent coupon was not considered any more attractive than a 40-cent coupon.[24] A more directly relevant study determined that higher-value coupons *signal* higher prices to consumers.[25] This is especially true when consumers are unfamiliar with a brand. In this situation, high coupon values may scare off consumers by suggesting, or signaling, that these brands are high priced.

Perhaps the $1 FSI coupon for the body wash implied to prospective customers that the brand must be high priced or it could not otherwise justify offering such an attractive coupon. This being the case, they would not have removed the FSI coupon for later redemption. Comparatively, the 50-cent IRC was available to consumers at the point of purchase where the brand's actual price was also available. They had no reason to expect a high price; rather, they saw an opportunity to receive an attractive discount by simply peeling the coupon and presenting it to the clerk when checking out.

Ironically, higher-valued coupons may attract primarily current brand users who know the brand's actual price and realize the deal offered by the attractive coupon, whereas potential switchers from other brands may be discouraged by a higher-valued coupon if to them it signals a high price. This, of course, is particularly problematic in the use of FSIs, a form of coupon received away from the point of purchase and that, as a matter of practicality, include only the coupon value but not the brand's regular price. Such is not the case, however, with IRCs.

© Susan Van Etten

It would be unwise to draw sweeping generalizations from this single study based on only one product category (body wash), but the intriguing finding suggests that IRCs are capable of outperforming FSIs. Only with additional research will we know whether this finding holds up for other products.

Shelf-Delivered Coupons

Shelf-delivered coupon devices are attached to the shelf alongside coupon-sponsoring brands. A red device (referred to as the "instant coupon machine") is the best known among several shelf-delivered couponing services. Consumers interested in purchasing a particular brand can pull a coupon from the device and then redeem it when checking out. The average redemption rate for shelf-delivered coupons is approximately 9 percent to 10 percent.[26]

Scanner-Delivered Coupons

There are several electronic systems for dispensing coupons at the point of purchase. Best known among these is a service from Catalina Marketing Corporation that is available in thousands of stores nationwide. Catalina offers two programs, one called Checkout Coupon and the other Checkout Direct. The Checkout Coupon program delivers coupons based on the particular brands a shopper has purchased. Once the optical scanner records that the shopper has purchased a *competitor's brand,* a coupon from the participating manufacturer is dispensed. By targeting competitors' customers, Catalina's Checkout Coupon program ensures that the manufacturer will reach people who buy the product category but are not currently purchasing the manufacturer's brand. The redemption rate is approximately 8 percent.[27]

The other couponing program from Catalina, called Checkout Direct, enables marketers to deliver coupons only to consumers who satisfy the coupon-sponsoring manufacturer's specific targeting requirements. The Checkout Direct program allows the coupon user to target consumers with respect to their purchase pattern for a particular product (e.g., direct coupons only to consumers who purchase toothpaste at least once every six weeks) or based on the amount of product usage (e.g., deliver coupons only to heavy users of the product). When shoppers who satisfy the coupon-sponsor's requirement make a purchase (as indicated by their check-cashing ID number), a coupon for the sponsoring brand is automatically dispensed for use on the shopper's next purchase occasion.

Frito-Lay used the Checkout Direct system to increase trial purchases of its new Baked Lay's brand. Frito-Lay's brand managers targeted super-heavy users of healthier snack foods such as its own Baked Tostitos. Based on optical scanner data that records and stores consumers' past purchase data, the Checkout Direct system was programmed to issue coupons for Baked Lay's only to those consumers who purchased "better-for-you" snacks at least eight times during the past 12 months. When these consumers checked out, the scanner triggered a coupon for Baked Lay's. In excess of 40 percent of the coupons were redeemed, and the repeat-purchase rate was a very impressive 25 percent.[28]

Both Catalina programs are used to encourage trial purchasing. However, because coupons are distributed to consumers when they are checking out of a store and cannot be used until their next visit, the reward is *delayed*—unlike the instant or shelf-delivered coupons. Nevertheless, these scanner-delivered couponing methods are effective and cost-efficient because they provide a way to carefully target coupon distribution. Targeting, in the case of Checkout Coupon, is directed at competitive-brand users and, in the case of Checkout Direct, is aimed at users who satisfy a manufacturer's prescribed product-usage requirements.

Mail- and Media-Delivered Coupons

These coupon-delivery modes initiate trial purchase behavior by offering consumers *delayed* rewards. Mail-delivered coupons represent about 2 percent of all manufacturer-distributed coupons. Mass-media modes (newspapers and magazines) are clearly dominant, carrying about 90 percent of all coupons—the bulk of which is in the form of freestanding inserts in Sunday newspapers.

Mail-Delivered Coupons

Marketers typically use mail-delivered coupons to introduce new or improved products. Mailings can be either directed at a broad cross section of the market or targeted to specific geodemographic segments. Mailed coupons achieve the *highest household penetration.*

Coupon distribution via magazines and newspapers reaches fewer than 60 percent of all homes, whereas mail can reach as high as 95 percent. Moreover, direct mail achieves the *highest redemption rate* (3.5 percent) of all mass-delivered coupon techniques.[29] There also is empirical evidence to suggest that direct-mail coupons *increase the amount of product purchases,* particularly when coupons with higher face values are used by households that own their homes, have larger families, and are more educated.[30]

The major disadvantage of direct-mailed coupons is that they are *relatively expensive* compared with other coupon-distribution methods. Another disadvantage is that direct mailing is especially inefficient and expensive for brands enjoying a high market share. This is because a large proportion of the coupon recipients may already be regular users of the coupon brand, thereby defeating the primary purpose of generating trial purchasing. The inefficiencies of mass mailing account for the rapid growth of efforts to target coupons to narrowly defined audiences such as users of competitive brands.

FSIs and Other Media-Delivered Coupons

As earlier noted, approximately 87 percent of all coupons distributed in the United States are via freestanding inserts in Sunday newspapers. The cost per thousand for freestanding inserts is only about 50 percent to 60 percent of that for direct-mail coupons, which largely explains why FSIs are the dominant coupon-delivery mode. Another advantage of FSIs is that they perform an extremely important *reminder function* for the consumer who peruses the Sunday inserts, clips coupons for brands he or she intends to buy in the coming week, and then redeems these at a later date.[31] Finally, there is some evidence that FSIs also perform an *advertising function.* That is, when perusing the Sunday inserts, consumers are exposed to FSI "advertisements" and are somewhat more likely to purchase promoted brands even without redeeming coupons.[32] This comes as no great surprise because FSI coupons often are extremely eye-catching "advertisements."

Research has shown that attractive pictures in FSIs are particularly effective when viewers of the FSI are loyal to a brand other than the one featured in the FSI. In this situation, consumers, loyal as they are to another brand, are not motivated to process arguments about a nonpreferred brand featured in the FSI. Hence, the use of attractive pictures (versus message arguments) is necessary to enhance consumer attitudes, if only temporarily, and increase the odds that consumers will clip the FSI coupon.[33]

In addition to FSIs, coupons also are distributed in magazines and as part of the regular (noninsert) newspaper page. Redemption rates for coupons distributed in magazines and newspapers average less than 1 percent.[34] A second problem with magazine- and newspaper-delivered coupons is that they do not generate much trade interest. Finally, coupons delivered via magazines and newspapers are particularly susceptible to misredemption. The latter issue is so significant to all parties involved in couponing that it deserves a separate discussion later.

In- and On-Pack Coupons

In- and on-pack coupons are included either inside a product's package or as part of a package's exterior. This form of couponing should not be confused with the previously discussed instant, or peelable, coupon. Whereas IRCs are removable at the point of purchase and redeemable for that particular item while the shopper is in the store, an in- or on-pack coupon cannot be removed until it is in the shopper's home to be redeemed on a subsequent purchase occasion. This form of couponing thus affords consumers with a *delayed* reward that is designed more for encouraging *repeat* than trial purchases (see cell 4 in Table 18.1).

A coupon for one brand often is promoted by another brand. For example, General Mills promoted its brand of granola bars by placing cents-off coupons in cereal boxes. Practitioners call this practice *crossruffing,* a term borrowed from bridge and bridge-type card games where partners alternate trumping one another when they are unable to follow suit.

Though marketers use crossruffing to create trial purchases or to stimulate purchase of products, such as granola bars, that are not staple items, in- and on-pack coupons carried by the same brand are generally intended to stimulate *repeat purchasing.* That is, once consumers have exhausted the contents of a particular package, they are more likely to repurchase that brand if an attractive inducement, such as a cents-off coupon, is available immediately. A package coupon has *bounce-back value,* so to speak. An initial purchase, the bounce, may stimulate another purchase, the bounce back, when a hard-to-avoid inducement such as an in-package coupon is made available.[35]

A major advantage of in- and on-pack coupons is that there are virtually no distribution costs. Moreover, redemption rates are much higher because most of the package-delivered coupons are received by brand users. The average redemption rate for in-pack coupons is around 6 percent to 7 percent, whereas the redemption rate for on-pack coupons is slightly less than 5 percent.[36] Limitations of package-delivered coupons are that they offer delayed value to consumers, do not reach nonusers of the carrying brand, and do not leverage trade interest due to the delayed nature of the offer.

Online Couponing

A number of Internet sites now distribute coupons. Although representing a very small percentage of all coupons distributed (less than 1 percent), online couponing is growing in popularity. Consumers print the coupons on their home (or work) printers, and then, as with other modes of coupon delivery, redeem the printed coupon along with the purchased item at checkout.

Allowing consumers to print their own coupons creates considerable potential for fraud because it leaves open the possibility that consumers will manipulate the face value and print multiple copies. Moreover, computer savvy criminals download coupon files and scan coupons into their computers, and then change the bar codes, dates, amounts, and even the sponsoring brand.[37] To avoid this problem, some online couponing services allow the consumer to select the brands for which he or she would like to receive coupons, and then actual coupons are mailed. It is too early to predict whether online couponing will continue to grow in popularity, especially since some retailers such as Wal-Mart refuse to accept Internet coupons. However, unless companies are able to curtail the substantial amount of online couponing fraud, it is likely that online couponing will not experience significant growth.

The Coupon Redemption Process and Misredemption

Coupon misredemption is a long-standing and widespread problem and assuredly is not limited to Internet couponing. The best way to understand how misredemption occurs is to examine the redemption process. A graphic of the process is provided in Figure 18.4.

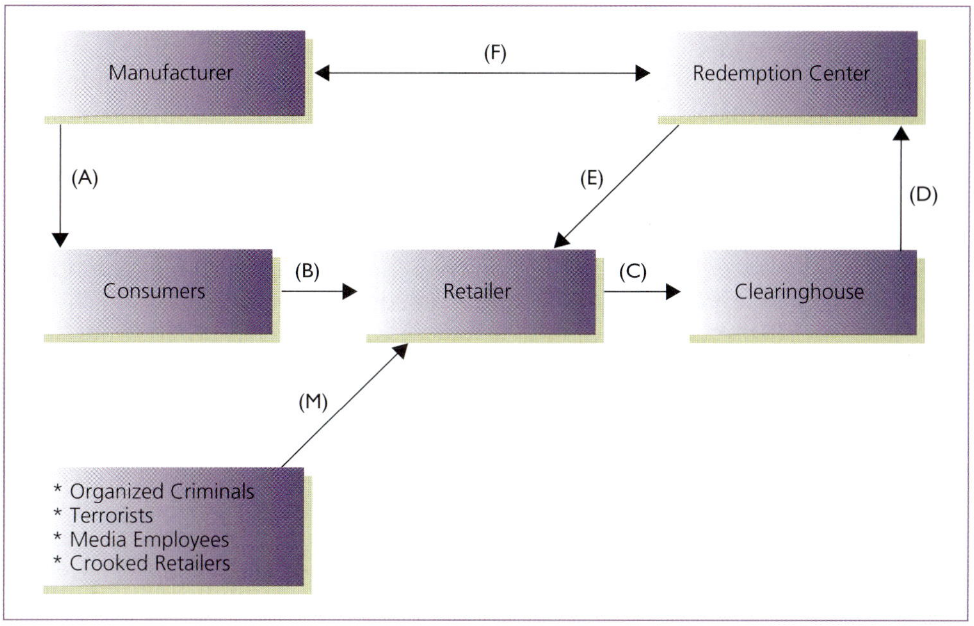

Figure 18.4

Coupon Redemption and Misredemption Process

The Process

The process begins with a manufacturer distributing coupons to consumers via FSIs, direct mail, or any of the other distribution modes previously described (see path A in Figure 18.4). Consumers collect coupons, take them to the store, and present them to a checkout clerk, who subtracts each coupon's face value from the shopper's total purchase cost (path B). For the shopper to be entitled to the coupon discount, certain conditions and restrictions must be met: (1) he or she must buy the merchandise specified on the coupon in the size, brand, and quantity directed; (2) only one coupon can be redeemed per item; (3) cash may not be given for the coupon; and (4) the coupon must be redeemed before the expiration date. (Some coupon misredemption occurs because consumers present coupons that do not meet these requirements.)

Retailers, in turn, redeem the coupons they have received to obtain reimbursement from the manufacturers that sponsored the coupons. Retailers typically hire another company, called a *clearinghouse,* to sort and redeem the coupons in return for a fee (path C). The two major clearinghouses in the United States are Carolina Manufacturer's Service (CMS) and Nielsen Coupon Clearing House (NCH). Clearinghouses, acting on behalf of a number of retail clients, consolidate coupons before forwarding them. Clearinghouses maintain control by ensuring that their clients sold products legitimately in the amounts they submitted for redemption.

Clearinghouses forward the coupons to *redemption centers* (path D), which serve as agents of coupon-issuing manufacturers. A redemption center pays off on all properly redeemed coupons (path E) and then is compensated for its services by the manufacturer (path F). If a center questions the validity of certain coupons, it may go to its client, a manufacturer, for approval on redeeming suspected coupons.

The system is not quite as clear-cut as it may appear from this description. Some large retailers act as their own clearinghouses, some manufacturers serve as their own redemption centers, and some independent firms, such as NCH, offer both clearinghouse and redemption-center services.

However, regardless of the specific mechanism by which a coupon is ultimately redeemed (or misredeemed), the retailer is reimbursed for the amount of the *face value* paid to the consumer and for payment of a handling charge, which currently is 8 cents per coupon. Herein rests the potential for misredemption: an unscrupulous person could thus make a profit of $1.08 from a coupon with a face value of $1. One thousand such misredeemed coupons are worth $1,080! Exacerbating the potential for misredemption is the fact that many coupons now have face values worth as much as $1 or more.

The Consequences

Estimates of the misredemption rate have ranged from a low of 15 percent to a high of 40 percent. Many brand managers have assumed a 20 to 25 percent rate of misredemption when budgeting for coupon events. However, a recent study found that past estimates of coupon misredemption have been inflated. It now appears that fraudulent coupon redemption is, on average, closer to 3 or 4 percent rather than the 20 to 25 percent assumed previously.[38] Although the magnitude of misredemption has been reduced by imposing tighter controls on coupon redemption at all stages of the redemption process, a 3 to 4 percent misredemption level nevertheless represents millions of dollars lost by manufacturers.

The Participants

Now with an understanding of the redemption process and consequences, how does misredemption occur and who participates in it? Misredemption occurs at every level of the redemption process. Sometimes *consumers* present coupons that have expired, coupons for items not purchased, or coupons for a smaller-sized product than that specified by the coupon. Some *clerks* take coupons to the store and exchange them for cash without making a purchase. At the *store management* level, retailers may boost profits by submitting extra coupons in addition to those redeemed legitimately. A dishonest retailer can buy coupons on the black market, age them in a clothes dryer, mix them with legitimate coupons, and then mail in the batch for redemption. Shady *clearinghouses* engage in misredemption by combining illegally purchased coupons with real ones and certifying the batch as legitimate.

The major source of coupon misredemption is large-scale *professional misredeemers* (see path M, standing for misredemption, in Figure 18.4). These professional misredeemers either: (1) recruit the services of actual retailers to serve as conduits through which coupons are misredeemed or (2) operate phony businesses that exist solely for the purpose of redeeming huge quantities of illegal coupons. Illegal coupons typically are obtained by removing FSIs from Sunday newspapers.

The following examples illustrate organized misredemption efforts. The proprietor of Wadsworth Thriftway store in Philadelphia illegally submitted in excess of 1.5 million coupons valued at more than $800,000.[39] The top three executives of the Sloans Supermarket in New York were indicted for their role in a 20-year operation that led to $3.5 million in coupon misredemption.[40] Another Philadelphian acted as a middleman between charities, from which he purchased coupons in bulk, and a supermarket employee, who submitted them for repayment by manufacturers or their redemption centers. The middleman earned $200,000 from the couponing scam before he was arrested.[41] Five operators of Shop n' Bag supermarkets in Philadelphia bought nearly 12 million coupons for only 20 percent to 30 percent of their face value and then redeemed them prior to being arrested.[42] And finally, according to the *New York Post,* Mideastern terrorists misredeemed perhaps up to $100 million by funneling illegally redeemed coupons through minimarts and Hispanic bodegas.[43]

The Role of Promotion Agencies

As discussed in Chapter 9, brand managers typically employ the services of advertising agencies to create advertising messages, buy advertising media, and perform other services related to a brand's advertising function. Though less well known than their ad agency counterparts, brand managers also hire specialized promotion agencies to perform sales promotion functions. These agencies—again like their advertising agency counterparts—work with brand managers in formulating promotion strategies and implementing tactical programs.

Assume, for example, that the brand manager of a hypothetical brand of shampoo, SynActive, believes that this new brand needs to be sampled in trial-sized bottles to facilitate high levels of trial-purchase behavior. The promotion also will include coupons in the box containing the trial-size sample. Further, an introductory advertising campaign in magazines will include an attractive sweepstakes offer to draw attention to the ad and enhance consumer involvement with the brand. The brand manager determines that it will be best to use the services of a promotion agency that can expertly design a sampling program that efficiently targets sample distribution to young consumers and a sweepstakes program that would appeal to this age group.

The Rise of the Online Promotion Agency

In addition to traditional promotion agencies, which traditionally have emphasized programs using off-line media and in-store distribution, there is a new generation of promotion agencies that emphasize online promotions. The Internet has become an increasingly important venue for conducting promotions. Coupons, sweepstakes offers, online promotional games, free sample offerings, and online continuity programs are just some of the promotions that are virtually ubiquitous on the Web. These programs are effective because they enable marketers to target promotions to preferred consumers, to deliver the programs relatively inexpensively, and to measure results with greater precision than what is possible with other marketing programs. Promotion agencies are a valuable resource for brand managers in both planning strategically sound promotions and carrying through their implementation.

Summary

This chapter focused on consumer-oriented promotions. The various sales promotion tools available to marketers were classified in terms of whether the reward offered consumers is immediate or delayed and whether the manufacturer's objective is to achieve trial impact, encourage repeat purchases, or reinforce brand images. Specific sales promotion techniques are classified as falling into one of six general categories (see Table 18.1).

The first and most critical requirement for a successful sales promotion is that it be based on clearly defined objectives. Second, the program must be designed with a specific target market in mind. It should also be realized that many consumers, perhaps most, desire to maximize the rewards gained from participating in a promotion while minimizing the amount of time and effort invested. Consequently, an effective promotion, from a consumer-response perspective, must make it relatively easy for consumers to obtain their rewards, and the size of the reward must be sufficient to justify the consumers' efforts. A third essential ingredient for effective sales promotions is that programs must be developed with the interests of retailers in mind—not just those of the manufacturer.

The bulk of the chapter was devoted to two of the major forms of consumer-oriented sales promotions: sampling and couponing. It was pointed out that sampling is the premier promotion for generating trial usage of a new brand. The various methods of distributing samples were presented, and it was emphasized that regardless of distribution method, three practices are necessary for sampling success: (1) targeting rather than mass distributing samples, (2) using innovative distribution methods where appropriate, and (3) undertaking efforts to measure sampling's return on investment. The specific circumstances when sampling is appropriately used were discussed, and various problems with sampling were identified.

The second major type of promotion, couponing, was described in terms of the magnitude of usage and types of distribution methods (via freestanding inserts, direct mail, and optical scanners, at the point of purchase, on the Internet, etc.). The growing role of online couponing was identified. A major section described the coupon-redemption process and in this context discussed the act of coupon misredemption.

Discussion Questions

1. Why are immediate (versus delayed) rewards more effective in inducing the consumer behaviors desired by a brand marketer? Use a specific, concrete illustration from your own experience to support your answer.
2. One of the major trends in product sampling is selective sampling of targeted groups. Assume you work for a company that has just developed a candy bar that tastes almost as good as other candy bars but has far fewer calories. Marketing research has identified the target market as economically upscale consumers, ages primarily 25 to 54, who reside in suburban and urban areas. Explain specifically how you might selectively sample your new product to approximately two million such consumers.
3. Compare and contrast sampling and media-delivered coupons in terms of objectives, consumer impact, and overall roles in marketing communications strategies.
4. A packaged-goods company plans to introduce a new bath soap that differs from competitive soaps by virtue of a distinct new fragrance. Should sampling be used to introduce the product?
5. A manufacturer of golf balls introduced a new brand that supposedly delivered greater distance than competitively priced balls. However, in accordance with restrictions established by the governing body that regulates golf balls and other golfing equipment and accessories, this new ball when struck by a driver travels on average only a couple of yards farther than competitive brands. The manufacturer identified a list of two million golfers and mailed a single golf ball to each. In view of what you have learned about sampling in this chapter, comment on the advisability of this sampling program.
6. Present your personal views concerning the number of coupons distributed annually in the United States. Is widespread couponing in the best interest of consumers?
7. Rather than offering discounts in the form of coupons, why don't brand managers simply reduce the prices of their brands?
8. Using Table 18.3 as a rough guide, calculate the full cost per redeemed coupon given the following facts: (1) face value = 75 cents, (2) 20 million coupons distributed at $7 per thousand, (3) redemption rate = 3 percent, (4) handling cost = 8 cents, and (5) misredemption rate = 5 percent.
9. Go through a Sunday newspaper and select three FSIs. Analyze each in terms of what you think are the marketer's objectives in using this particular promotion. Don't restrict your chosen FSIs to just those offering coupons.
10. Assume you are brand manager of Mountain State Bottled Water. This new brand competes in a product category with several well-known brands. Your marketing communications objective is to generate trial purchases among predominantly younger and better-educated consumers. Propose a promotion that would accomplish this objective. Assume that your promotion is purely experimental and that it will be undertaken in a small city of only 250,000 people. Also assume that: (1) you cannot afford product sampling; (2) you will not advertise the promotion; and (3) your budget for this experimental promotion is $5,000. What would you do?
11. A concluding section of the chapter indicated that promotion agencies have become an increasingly important resource for brand managers in planning and executing promotional programs. One could argue that the fees brand managers pay for the services of promotion agencies might better be spent elsewhere—for example, on increased advertising levels. Present arguments both in favor of and in opposition to hiring promotion agencies.

ENDNOTES

1. Adapted from Tim Parry, "College Try," *Promo,* September 2004, 23–25.
2. Though the following discussion is based mostly on the author's prior writing and thinking on the topic, these points are influenced by descriptions obtained from various practitioners.
3. Pierre Chandon, Brian Wansink, and Gilles Laurent, "A Benefit Congruency Framework of Sales Promotion Effectiveness," *Journal of Marketing* 64 (October 2000), 65–81. The following discussion of benefits is based on a typology provided by these authors. See their Table 1 on pages 68–69.
4. The idea that consumer promotions perform an informational role receives prominent attention in Priya Raghubir, J. Jeffrey Inman, and Hans Grande, "The Three Faces of Consumer Promotions," *California Management Review* 46 (summer 2004), 23–42.
5. Lorin Cipolla, "Instant Gratification," *Promo,* April 2004, AR33.
6. Sarah Ellison and Carlos Tehada, "Young Couples Starting Out Are Every Marketer's Dream," *Wall Street Journal Online,* January 30, 2003, http://online.wsj.com.
7. "Sampling Wins Over More Marketers," *Advertising Age,* July 27, 1992, 12.
8. Lafayette Jones, "A Case for Ethnic Sampling," *Promo,* October 2000, 41–42.
9. David Vaczek, "Points of Switch," *Promo,* September 1998, 39–40.
10. Stephanie Thompson, "Mobile Marie," *Brandweek,* March 2, 1998, R11.
11. Adapted from Betsy Spethmann, "Branded Moments," *Promo,* September 2000, 83–98.
12. Cipolla, AR35.
13. Dan Hanover, "We Deliver," *Promo,* March 2001, 43–45.
14. Adapted from Glenn Heitsmith, "Gaining Trial," *Promo,* September 1994, 108; and "Spend a Little, Get a Lot," *Trial and Conversion III: Harnessing the Power of Sampling Special Advertising Supplement* (New York: Promotional Marketing Association, Inc., 1996–1997), 18.
15. Charles Fredericks, Jr., "What Ogilvy & Mather Has Learned about Sales Promotion," *The Tools of Promotion* (New York: Association of National Advertisers, 1975). Although this is an old source, the wisdom still holds true today.
16. Lynn G. Reiling, "Consumers Misuse Mass Sampling for Sun Light Dishwashing Liquid," *Marketing News,* September 3, 1982, 1, 2.
17. Maciek Gajewski, "Samples: A Steal in Poland," *Advertising Age,* November 4, 1991, 54.
18. "Clipping Path," *Promo,* April 2004, AR7.
19. Donald R. Lichtenstein, Richard G. Netemeyer, and Scot Burton, "Distinguishing Coupon Proneness from Value Consciousness: An Acquisition-Transaction Utility Theory Perspective," *Journal of Marketing* 54 (July 1990), 54–67. For a detailed treatment of factors that influence consumers' coupon-redemption behavior, see also Banwari Mittal, "An Integrated Framework for Relating Diverse Consumer Characteristics to Supermarket Coupon Redemption," *Journal of Marketing Research* 31 (November 1994), 533–544. See also Judith A. Garretson and Scot Burton, "Highly Coupon and Sales Prone Consumers: Benefits Beyond Price Savings," *Journal of Advertising Research* 43 (June 2003), 162–172.
20. "Clipping Path," AR7.
21. Kapil Bawa and Robert W. Shoemaker, "The Effects of a Direct Mail Coupon on Brand Choice Behavior," *Journal of Marketing Research* 24 (November 1987), 370–376.
22. Daniel Shannon, "Still a Mighty Marketing Mechanism," *Promo,* April 1996, 86.
23. "Checkout: Instant Results," *Promo,* October 1998, 75.
24. Kapil Bawa, Srini S. Srinivasan, and Rajendra K. Srivastava, "Coupon Attractiveness and Coupon Proneness: A Framework for Modeling Coupon Redemption," *Journal of Marketing Research* 34 (November 1997), 517–525.
25. Priya Raghubir, "Coupon Value: A Signal for Price?" *Journal of Marketing Research* 35 (August 1998), 316–324.
26. Russ Bowman and Paul Theroux, *Promotion Marketing* (Stamford, CT: Intertec Publishing Corporation, 2000), 24.
27. Ibid.
28. "When the Chips Are Down," *Promo* Magazine Special Report, April 1998, S7.
29. Bowman and Theroux.
30. Kapil Bawa and Robert W. Shoemaker, "Analyzing Incremental Sales from a Direct Mail Coupon Promotion," *Journal of Marketing Research* 53 (July 1989), 66–78.
31. Erwin Ephron, "More Weeks, Less Weight: The Shelf-Space Model of Advertising," *Journal of Advertising Research* 35 (May/June 1995), 18–23.
32. Srini S. Srinivasan, Robert P. Leone, and Francis J. Mulhern, "The Advertising Exposure Effect of Free Standing Inserts," *Journal of Advertising* 24 (spring 1995), 29–40.
33. France Leclerc and John D. C. Little, "Can Advertising Copy Make FSI Coupons More Effective?" *Journal of Marketing Research* 34 (November 1997), 473–484.
34. Bowman and Theroux.
35. For a technical analysis of the role of crossruffing, see Sanjay K. Dhar and Jagmohan S. Raju, "The Effects of Cross-Ruff Coupons on Sales and Profits," *Marketing Science* 44 (November 1998), 1501–1516.
36. Bowman and Theroux. It is noteworthy that one clearinghouse, CMS, estimates the on-pack redemption rate at 4.7 percent, whereas the other, NCH, estimates it at 11.5 percent. This latter figure seems out of line and perhaps is a misprint.
37. Karen Holt, "Coupon Crimes," *Promo,* April 2004, 23–26, 70; Jack Neff, "Internet Enabling Coupon Fraud Biz," *Advertising Age,* October 20, 2003, 3.
38. "A Drop in the Crime Rate," *Promo,* December 1997, 12.
39. Cecelia Blalock, "Another Retailer Nabbed in Coupon Misredemption Plot," *Promo,* December 1993, 38.
40. Ibid.
41. Cecelia Blalock, "Tough Sentence for Coupon Middle Man," *Promo,* June 1993, 87.
42. "Clipped, Supermarket Owners Charged with Coupon Fraud," *Promo,* May 1997, 14.
43. "Report: Coupon Scams Are Funding Terrorism," *Promo,* August 1996, 50. This issue was also the subject of testimony before the Senate Judiciary Technology, Terrorism, and Government Information Subcommittee, Feb. 24, 1998.

CHAPTER 19

Consumer-Oriented Promotions: Premiums and Other Promotional Methods

Marcom Challenge: Luring College Students with Perks

The previous chapter was introduced by discussing the use of sampling and couponing on college campuses. This chapter continues that theme by considering other promotions used by colleges and universities to recruit new students and gain favor with the student body. It used to be that the difference between attending one university or another boiled down to differences in financial incentives (a.k.a. scholarship money or financial aid) offered by competing institutions. But now that most schools provide financial assistance (over 80 percent of private-school students receive some form of financial aid), the distinguishing factor involves other forms of promotional perks. (Needless to say, colleges and universities differ with respect to their academic quality; however, many students have choices among several schools that have similar academic reputations; hence, the decision sometimes comes down to which school offers more attractive prequisites and provides other special services for a fee.) Following is a listing of some of the perks and special services that are offered at schools of higher education in the United States:[1]

- New York University offers free theater tickets and movie screenings.
- Many universities, including Duke and Northwestern, offer free cell phones and cable TV.
- Freshmen at Emory University receive free tickets to Atlanta Braves baseball games and are even escorted to games.
- At Bryn Mawr students can borrow video cameras without a charge.
- Ohio University offers free computers, printers, and microwave/refrigerator combination appliances.
- Northwestern University upgraded its Internet system so students could watch cable TV on their computers, receiving as many as 10 channels.
- Virginia Tech offers its students unlimited Internet access.

Sales promotion practices are alive and well on college campuses, just as they are elsewhere in society. Interestingly, students in many institutions have grown accustomed to the offering of perks and regard these "extras" as a form of entitlement.

Some perks at such universities include state-of-the-art recreational facilities. For example, Baylor University has a 52-foot climbing wall, and centers at some big schools include deluxe private health clubs with saunas, steam rooms, whirlpools, sprays, and slides, with staff to lead programs from karate to yoga. Georgia Tech has a $45 million recreation complex about the size of a basketball colosseum, with a pool and water slide, hot tub, and sun deck.[2]

At the University of Wisconsin, Oshkosh, students get massages, pedicures and manicures, and Washington State University claims to have the largest Jacuzzi in the west, capable of holding 53 people. At Indiana University of Pennsylvania, students can play one of 52 golf courses from around the world on room-sized golf simulators, using real balls and clubs.[3] Other schools are relying on clever methods to attract students, including reality shows and sending birthday cards to prospective students.[4]

However, some students and their parents are concerned that these non-academic accoutrements may diminish the quality of the educational experience by encouraging students to spend excessive time having fun rather than getting down to business and doing what is needed to make the most of a college education. After reading the above list of perks, you may feel yourself ripped off if your college or university is not offering similar freebies. Consider, however, that many perks are offered by private institutions that charge much higher tuitions than most public colleges and universities.

CHAPTER OBJECTIVES

1

Understand the role of premiums, the types of premiums, and the developments in premium practice.

2

Recognize the role of price-off promotions and bonus packages.

3

Be aware of the role of rebates and refund offers.

4

Know the differences among sweepstakes, contests, and games, and the reasons for using each form of promotion.

5

Understand the role of continuity programs.

6

Appreciate retailer-driven promotions.

7

Evaluate the potential effectiveness of sales promotion ideas, and appraise the effectiveness of completed promotional programs.

Overview

This chapter picks up where Chapter 18 left off. In particular, the present chapter discusses major forms of consumer-oriented promotions other than sampling and couponing, which, of course, were the focus of the prior chapter. To again frame the subsequent discussion, Table 18.1 is repeated in this chapter as Table 19.1. The presentation proceeds as follows: first discussed is the use of product *premiums* (cells 2, 3, 4, and 6 in Table 19.1); second is *price-off promotions* (cell 3); third, *bonus packs* (cell 3); fourth, *games* (cell 3); fifth, *rebates and refunds* (cell 4); sixth, *continuity programs* (cell 4); and, seventh, *sweepstakes and contests* (cell 6). Three additional topics will follow the discussion of specific promotional tools: (1) overlay and tie-in promotions, (2) retailer-driven promotions, and (3) techniques for evaluating sales promotion ideas.

It again is important to emphasize that each of the various promotional techniques covered in this chapter performs a unique role and is therefore appropriately used to achieve limited objectives. This chapter conveys each tool's role and identifies, where appropriate, unique limitations or problems associated with using each tool. It again will be useful to peruse Table 19.1 before proceeding with your study of the various types of promotions.

Premiums

Many B2B firms as well as consumer-oriented companies use premiums. Broadly defined, **premiums** are articles of merchandise or services (e.g., travel) offered as a form of gift by manufacturers to induce action on the part of the sales force, trade representatives, or consumers. Our focus in this chapter is on premiums' consumer-oriented role.

Consumer-oriented premiums represent a versatile promotional tool, possessing the ability to generate trial purchases, encourage repeat purchasing, and reinforce brand images. Brand managers use several forms of premium offers to motivate desired consumer behaviors: (1) free-with-purchase premiums; (2) mail-in

Table 19.1
Major Consumer-Oriented Promotions

Consumer Reward	Brand Management Objective: Generating Trial Purchases	Encouraging Repeat Purchases	Reinforcing Brand Image
Immediate	**Cell 1** • Samples • Instant coupons • Shelf-delivered coupons	**Cell 3** • Price-offs • Bonus packs • In-, on-, and near-pack premiums • Games	**Cell 5**
Delayed	**Cell 2** • Scanner-delivered coupons • Media- and mail-delivered coupons • Online coupons • Mail-in premiums • Free-with-purchase premiums	**Cell 4** • In- and on-pack coupons • Rebates and refunds • Phone cards • Continuity programs	**Cell 6** • Self-liquidating premiums • Sweepstakes and contests

offers; (3) in-, on-, and near-pack premiums; and (4) self-liquidating offers. These forms of premiums perform somewhat different objectives. Free-with-purchase and mail-in offers are useful primarily for generating brand *trial* or *retrial.* In-, on-, and near-pack premiums serve *customer-holding purposes* by rewarding present consumers for continuing to purchase a liked or preferred brand. And self-liquidators perform a combination of *customer-holding* and *image-reinforcement* functions.

Free-with-Purchase Premiums

Free-with-purchase premiums (also called *free-gift-with-purchase premiums*) are provided by both marketers of durable goods and consumer packaged goods (CPG) brands. As shown in Table 19.1, this form of premium typically represents a delayed reward to consumers that is primarily designed to generate *trial purchases.* Examples of this type of free-with-purchase premium include an offer from Michelin to receive a $100-retail-value emergency roadside kit with the purchase of four Michelin tires. Compaq offered a free Rio 600 digital audio player with the purchase of select computer models. Volkswagen gave away Apple iPods with purchases of New Beetle automobiles. Attractive premiums such as these might provide indecisive consumers with an added reason to purchase the premium-offering brand rather than a competitive option. All of these examples represent *immediate* rewards inasmuch as consumers receive the premium items at the time of purchasing the brands sponsoring the promotions.

CPG firms also offer free-with-purchase premiums. For example, offers of free music (digital downloads) represent an especially hot form of premium offering. Pepsi-Cola offered 100 million free iTune downloads in an under-the-cap promotion for Pepsi, Diet Pepsi, and Sierra Mist. Purchasers of these brands searched under the cap for redemption codes that permitted free downloading of songs from Apple's iTunes Music Store, a typical value of about 99 cents per song. Purchasers had a one-in-three chance of winning a redemption code. Pepsi-Cola extended the initial under-the-cap promotion the following year by automatically entering people who downloaded songs into a sweepstakes program that gave them a chance of winning hundreds of iPods.[2]

Research has shown that the perceived value of a premium item, or gift, depends on the value of the brand that is offering the gift. In particular, the identical item was perceived to be of lower value when it was offered as a free gift by a lower- versus higher-priced brand.[3] This finding buttresses the point made in the previous chapter that sales promotions perform an *informational role* in addition to utilitarian and hedonic functions. This is to say that sales promotions provide signaling information used by consumers to judge product quality and value. An important implication of this finding is that brands used as gift items must be cautious that their images are not damaged by the sponsoring brand. The adage "Beware of the company you keep" is as applicable in the premium-partners context as it is in social relations.

© Susan Van Etten

Mail-In Offers

By definition, a **mail-in offer** is a premium in which consumers receive a free item from the sponsoring manufacturer in return for submitting a required number of proofs of purchase. As shown in Table 19.1, this form of premium represents a *delayed reward* to consumers that is primarily designed to generate *trial purchases* (cell 2). For example, Vaseline Intensive Care lotion offered a free watch when consumers purchased one bottle of this brand and submitted a proof of purchase and $2 for shipping and handling. However, this type of premium may

ConAgra Brands, Inc.

Figure 19.1

Illustration of a Mail-In Premium

also stimulate repeat purchasing when requiring more proofs of purchase than can be acquired on a single purchase occasion. Illustratively, ConAgra Foods Inc., the makers of brands such as Chef Boyardee canned pasta and Hunt's SnackPack pudding, offered free movie tickets for multiple proofs of purchase of these brands (see Figure 19.1, upper right-hand corner).

Perhaps as few as 2 percent to 4 percent of consumers who are exposed to free mail-in offers actually take advantage of these opportunities. However, mail-in premiums can be effective if the premium item is appealing to the target market. See the *Global Focus* insert for a really clever promotion that used a mail-in premium.

In-, On-, and Near-Pack Premiums

In- and on-pack premiums offer a free item inside or attached to a package or make the package itself the premium item. For example, in a delightful promotional program for Cap'n Crunch cereal, the box was labeled "Christmas Crunch," and Cap'n Horatio Crunch (the brand's cartoon-character icon) was shown on the package dressed as Santa Claus. The package advertised a free Christmas tree ornament inside the box—a premium offer with much appeal to small children during the holiday season. In general, in- and on-package premiums offer consumers immediate value and thereby encourage increased product consumption from consumers who like or prefer the premium-offering brand (see Table 19.1, cell 3).

This form of premium is not restricted to children. For example, Ralston Purina offered tiny sports car models in about 11 million boxes of six cereal brands. Ten of these boxes contained scale-model red Corvettes. Lucky consumers turned in the models for real Corvettes.

Near-pack premiums provide the retail trade with specially displayed premium pieces that retailers then give to consumers who purchase the promoted product. Near-pack premiums are less expensive because additional packaging is not required. Furthermore, near-pack premiums can build sales volume in stores that put up displays and participate fully.

Self-Liquidating Offers

Self-liquidating offers (known as SLOs by practitioners) are named for the fact that the consumer mails in a stipulated number of proofs of purchase along with sufficient money to cover the manufacturer's purchasing, handling, and mailing costs of the premium item. In other words, the actual cost of the premium is paid for by consumers; from the manufacturer's perspective the item is cost-free, or, in other words, self-liquidating. Attractive self-liquidating offers can serve to enhance a brand's image (cell 6 in Table 19.1)—by associating the brand with a positively valued premium item—and also can encourage repeat purchasing by requiring multiple proofs of purchase to be eligible for the premium offer. SLOs are often used by brand managers as a complement to sweepstakes offers. The combination of these two promotions enhances consumer interest in and interaction with the brand.

Gerber employed an SLO promotion when offering the Gerber Keepsake Millennium Cup. With 12 Gerber baby food proofs of purchase and $8.95, consumers received a cup engraved with their child's name and birth date. This item at retail likely would have sold for around $25. Many parents could be expected to have purchased Gerber exclusively until they acquired the requisite number of proofs of purchase.

General Mills employed two forms of premium promotions for its child-oriented cereals (see Figure 19.2). First, an in-pack premium, as described pre-

Barq's Root Beer and Russian Knickknacks

global focus

Barq's root beer is a regional soft drink brand that was founded in New Orleans. Nearly a hundred years after its founding, Barq's remained a small-share brand with a limited advertising and promotion budget. In the early 1990s Barq's decided to promote the brand in commemoration of the 15th anniversary of Elvis Presley's death. Barq's vice president of marketing thought up a great premium idea that would involve purchasing an old Cadillac that had been owned by Elvis, cutting it into thousands of small pieces, and offering each piece to a different consumer as part of a mail-in premium requiring multiple proofs of purchase of Barq's root beer. There was only one problem with this premium idea: the administrators of the Presley estate demanded a $1 million licensing fee, which exceeded tenfold Barq's budget for the promotion.

Unable to afford this, Barq's marketing vice president scrambled to find a replacement. Just about this time the Soviet government collapsed. Seeing the news on TV, the vice president hit immediately on the idea of a replacement for the failed Elvis promotion: "The Soviet Union Going Out of Business Sale." Mind you, this had all taken place within a month or less—decision-making on the run, so to speak. With a meager $70,000 in his possession, Rick Hill, Barq's marketing vice president, boarded a plane to Russia to purchase ex-Soviet Union memorabilia. Unable to find legitimate businesspersons from whom to purchase ex-Soviet items, Hill turned to members of the Soviet Mafia. Within two weeks he spent the $70,000 acquiring 4,000 pounds of ex-Soviet stuff (Russian nesting dolls, Lenin Day pins, military medals, etc.) that was shipped back to the United States. Barq's offered one randomly chosen Soviet knickknack with a 12-pack proof of purchase and 50 cents postage and handling charge. This last-minute, desperate promotion achieved incredible results: 5 percent of all consumers eligible for the promotion actually took advantage of it, and sales increased 30 percent versus the comparable period the previous year. This mail-in premium promotion also received the industry's top promotion award for the year. The moral of the story: a creative promotion that is of high topical interest and captures the public's imagination can be extremely successful.

SOURCE: Adapted from Rod Taylor, "From Russia with Root Beer," *Promo,* June 2003, 143–144.

viously, was offered by making available five different DVDs in 10 million boxes of its various cereal brands. This form of in-pack premium is an excellent way of encouraging repeat purchasing. A second form of premium appears in the upper left-hand corner of Figure 19.2. Parents could send in $4.99 and receive a Strawberry Shortcake watch for their child. This self-liquidating offer could serve to enhance the image of General Mills' various cereal brands by creating an association in children's minds between General Mills' cereal brands and this much-admired cartoon character.

It is interesting to note that very few consumers ever send for a premium. Companies expect only 0.1 percent of self-liquidators to be redeemed. A circulation of 20 million, for example, would be expected to produce only about 20,000 redemptions. Industry specialists generally concur that the most important consideration in developing a self-liquidating offer is that the premium be appealing to the target audience and represent a meaningful value. It is generally assumed that consumers look for a savings of at least 50 percent of the suggested retail price.

Figure 19.2

Illustration of Both In-Pack and Self-Liquidating Premium Offers

Courtesy of General Mills

Phone Cards

Phone cards represent a rather unique type of premium offer. This form of promotion incentive is classified in Table 19.1 as performing a *repeat-purchasing* objective and providing consumers with a *delayed reward* (cell 4). This is a bit of a simplification insofar as phone cards also are capable of generating trial purchases and reinforcing brand images. Although a variety of phone cards are available, the most common type offers a preset amount of long-distance calling time. Phone cards are lightweight and easy to mail, provide an inexpensive promotional tool, and are perceived as useful by consumers. Marketers also are able to collect information from consumers, who typically are required to answer a few questions before their cards are activated.[4]

What Makes a Good Premium Offer?

It is undeniable that consumers enjoy gifts, like to receive something for free, and are responsive to offers for premium objects that are attractive and valuable. However, brand managers must be careful to select premiums that are suitable in view of the objectives that are intended to be accomplished during the promotional period. In other words, as previously established, the various forms of premiums serve somewhat different objectives. As always, the choice of premium object and delivery method should be based on an explicit detailing of which objective is to be accomplished. Also, managers must be circumspect in choosing premium items that are congenial with the brand's image and appropriate for the target market.

Price-Offs

Price-off promotions (also called *cents-off* or *price packs*) entail a reduction (typically ranging from 10 to 25 percent) in a brand's regular price. A price-off is clearly labeled as such on the package. This type of promotion is effective when the marketer's objective is any of the following: (1) to reward present brand users; (2) to get consumers to purchase larger quantities of a brand than they normally would (i.e., to load them), thereby effectively preempting the competition; (3) to establish a repeat-purchase pattern after initial trial; (4) to ensure that promotional dollars do, in fact, reach consumers (no such assurance is possible with trade allowances); (5) to obtain off-shelf display space when such allowances are offered to retailers; and (6) to provide the sales force with an incentive to obtain retailer support. Although price-off promotions perform multiple objectives, this text classifies price-offs as primarily representing a form of *immediate reward* for consumers to encourage *repeat purchasing* (cell 3 in Table 19.1).

Price-offs cannot reverse a downward sales trend, produce a significant number of new users, or attract as many trial users as samples, coupons, or premium packs. Furthermore, *retailers often dislike price-offs* because they create inventory and pricing problems, particularly when a store has a brand in inventory at both the price-off and the regular prices. Yet despite trade problems, price-offs have strong consumer appeal.

FTC Price-Off Regulations

Manufacturers cannot indiscriminately promote their brands with continuous or near-continuous price-off labeling. To do so would deceive consumers into thinking the brand is on sale when in fact the announced sale price is actually the regular price.

The Federal Trade Commission controls price-off labeling with the following regulations:[5]

1. Price-off labels may only be used on brands already in distribution with established retail prices.
2. There is a limit of three price-off label promotions per year per brand size.
3. There must be a hiatus of at least 30 days between price-off label promotions on any given brand size.
4. No more than 50 percent of a brand's volume over a 12-month period may be generated from price-off label promotions.
5. The manufacturer must provide display materials to announce the price-off label offer.
6. The dealer is required to show the regular shelf price in addition to the new price reflecting the price-off label savings.

Bonus Packs

Bonus packs are extra quantities of a product that a company gives to consumers at the regular price. Listerine mouthwash provided consumers with a free 250-milliliter bottle along with the purchase of a 1.7-liter bottle. Carnation offered consumers 25 percent more hot cocoa mix at the regular price. Flex-A-Min, a product designed to enhance joint flexibility, offered 33 percent more tablets for free. Golf ball manufacturers on occasion reward consumers with an extra pack of three balls when they purchase a dozen.

Table 19.1 classifies this form of promotion as providing consumers with an *immediate reward* and, for manufacturers, primarily serving a *repeat purchase* objective (cell 3). In other words, consumers most likely to avail themselves of a bonus offer are present brand users. A bonus quantity (at no extra price) thus rewards them for their purchase loyalty and encourages repeat purchasing.

Bonus packs are sometimes used as an *alternative to price-off deals* when the latter are either overused or resisted by the trade. The extra value offered to the consumer is readily apparent and for that reason can be effective in *loading current users* and thereby removing them from the market—a defensive tactic that is used against aggressive competitors.

Games

Promotional games represent a growing form of promotion that is being increasingly used in lieu of sweepstakes and contests. Games provide consumers with an *instant reward* and, for marketers, serve primarily to encourage *repeat purchasing* from existing brand users (cell 3 in Table 19.1). An instant-win game promotion is shown in Figure 19.3 for Fisher Boy. Here the consumer looks inside specially marked packages to see if they have won a home theater system or other prize. In general, promotional games are capable of creating excitement, stimulating brand interest, and reinforcing brand loyalty.

Game promotions often involve the placement of winning numbers under package lids. Coca-Cola, for example, offered consumers a chance to win $1 million and a role in a movie from Universal Studios, along with thousands of other smaller prizes, if the consumer opened a can containing winning numbers. V8 vegetable juice had a look-under-the-cap contest in which winners received trips to famous resorts. Orville Redenbacher's popcorn offered consumers who were lucky enough to select specially marked packages of this brand a Mitsubishi home theater system (50 winners) as the first prize, DVD players as the second prize (50 winners), and VCRs as the third prize (50 winners). Please note that almost invariably, games are marketed with claims of "instant win" to appeal to consumers' natural preference for instant gratification.

Figure 19.3

Illustration of a Game Promotion

High Liner Foods USA, Inc.

Avoiding Snafus

Brand managers and the promotion firms they recruit to execute games have to be extremely careful to ensure that a game does not go awry. There have been a number of celebrated snafus in the conduct of promotional games. For example, a Pepsi bottler in the Philippines offered a one-million-peso grand prize (which at the time was equivalent to approximately $36,000) to holders of bottle caps with the number *349* printed on them. To the bottler's (and PepsiCo's) great chagrin, a computer error (by the printer that produced the game numbers) created 500,000 bottle caps with the winning number *349* imprinted—making

PepsiCo liable for approximately $18 billion! The botched promotion created mayhem for PepsiCo, including attacks on Pepsi trucks and bottling plants and anti-Pepsi rallies. Pepsi's sales plummeted in the Philippines, and market share fell by nine points. To resolve the problem, PepsiCo paid consumers with winning caps $19 apiece. More than 500,000 Filipinos collected about $10 million. The Filipino justice department excused PepsiCo from criminal liability and dismissed thousands of lawsuits.[6]

PepsiCo blew it again in a game conducted in the United States. Contestants participated in a spell-your-surname event with letters printed on bottle caps. Because very few caps bore vowels, PepsiCo assumed that only a small number of people would win. What the game planners failed to realize, however, was that many Asian names contain only consonants (such as Ng).[7]

The Beatrice Company's Monday Night Football promotion illustrates another failed game. Contestants scratched silver-coated footballs off cards to reveal numbers, hoping to win the prize offered if the numbers on the cards matched the number of touchdowns and field goals scored in the weekly Monday night National Football League game. Game planners intended the chances of getting a match to be infinitesimal. However, to Beatrice's great surprise, a salesman for rival Procter & Gamble (P&G) put in a claim for a great deal more money than Beatrice had planned on paying out. A computer buff, the salesman cracked the game code and determined that 320 patterns showed up repeatedly in the cards. By scratching off just one line, he could determine which numbers were underneath the rest. With knowledge of the actual number of touchdowns and field goals scored on a particular Monday night, he would start scratching cards until winning numbers were located. He enlisted friends to assist in collecting and scratching the cards. Thousands of cards were collected, mostly from Beatrice salespeople. The P&G salesman and friends identified 4,000 winning cards worth $21 million in prize money! Beatrice discontinued the game and refused to pay up.[8]

This section would be incomplete without discussing a major scandal that rocked the promotions industry in 2001. Brand managers for McDonald's restaurants and Simon Marketing, a company hired to run a summer promotion for McDonald's, created a Monopoly-type game that was to provide customers with millions of dollars in promotional prizes. Unfortunately, there was a major problem in the game's execution. An employee in charge of game security at Simon Marketing allegedly stole winning tickets and distributed them to various friends and accomplices, who obtained approximately $13 million in prize money. After learning of the theft and informing the Federal Bureau of Investigation, McDonald's immediately introduced a different promotional game run by another promotional agency so as to make good on its promise to customers and restore its credibility. Apparently, the Simon Marketing employee who ripped off McDonald's had for several years been stealing winning game tickets from other games. A spokesperson for the Promotion Marketing Association, the trade association for the industry, characterized this debacle as a "black eye" for the promotion marketing industry. The moral is clear: promotional games can go awry, and brand managers must go to extreme lengths to protect the integrity of the games that are designed to build, not bust, relationships with customers.[9]

Rebates and Refunds

A **rebate** (also called a *refund*) refers to the practice in which manufacturers give *cash discounts* or reimbursements to consumers who submit proofs of purchase. Unlike coupons, which the consumer redeems at retail checkouts, rebates are mailed with proofs of purchase to manufacturers, and, unlike premiums, the consumer receives a cash refund with a rebate rather than a gift item. Marketers are fond of rebates because they provide an alternative to the use of coupons and stimulate increased consumer purchasing. Rebate offers can reinforce brand loyalty, provide the sales force with something to talk about, and enable the manufacturer to flag the package with a potentially attractive deal.

© Robert Brenner/PhotoEdit

Refund offers are used by both CPG companies and durable goods companies. For example, Enfamil offered a $4 rebate on its infant formula product. With rising gas prices following the start of the war in Iraq, credit card companies offered rebates on gasoline purchases. Uniroyal provided a $40 mail-in rebate with the purchase of four Tiger Paw tires. Automobile companies are among the major users of rebate programs. It is not unusual for automobile companies to offer rebates amounting to as much as $3,000 or $4,000 per vehicle. American automobile companies have relied on rebates for years, and now European manufacturers are increasingly using rebates when marketing their cars in the United States. As is illustrated in the *IMC Focus*, even realtors are beginning to use rebates.

Rebates offer consumers *delayed* rather than immediate value, since the consumer must wait to receive the reimbursement. In using these programs, manufacturers achieve customer-holding objectives by encouraging consumers to make multiple purchases (in the case of CPG items) or by rewarding previous users with a cash discount for again purchasing the manufacturer's brand. Rebate offers also attract switchers from competitive brands who avail themselves of attractive discount offers.

For CPG brands, rebates require consumers to acquire rebate slips at retail sites or to go online to designated sites and download appropriate forms. There is some evidence indicating that consumers are more responsive to online than offline (via traditional retail outlets) rebate and refund offers.[10]

Phantom Discounts

Perhaps the major reason manufacturers are using rebates more now than ever is that many consumers never bother to redeem them. Thus, when using rebates, manufacturers get the best of both worlds—they stimulate consumer purchases of rebated items without having to pay out the rebated amount because most consumers do not undertake the effort to mail in rebate forms. Hence, rebates can be thought of as a form of *phantom discount*.[11] It is for this reason consumer advocates often condemn manufacturers' use of rebates.

One may wonder why consumers purchase rebated items but then fail to take the time to submit forms to receive the rebate amount. Academic research offers an explanation. It appears that at the time of brand choice, consumers tend to exaggerate the benefit to be obtained from a rebate relative to the future effort required to redeem a rebate offer.[12] In other words, it seems that many consumers engage in a form of self-deception when purchasing rebated merchandise. They find rebate offers attractive and on that basis decide to purchase particular brands. Yet later on at home they are unwilling to commit the time and effort to send in the rebate form, or simply forget to do so.

Are manufacturers exploiting consumers when offering rebates, or are consumers to be blamed for their own inaction? This should make for interesting class discussion.

The Use of Rebates by an Enterprising Realtor

imc focus

Let's suppose you just received your license to sell home real estate and that you're anxious to differentiate yourself from the literally hundreds of other realtors against whom you will have to compete. Frankly, in an old and highly marketing-oriented industry, most competitive-advantage tricks already have been discovered. One really has to be enterprising to gain a leg up on your counterparts in the industry who want to make money just as badly as you do.

However, Daniel Rubén Odio-Páez was a bit more enterprising than other realtors operating in the Virginia suburbs of Washington, DC. Having just received his realtor's license and deciding to work for a very small agency rather than a large chain that would restrict his latitude, Mr. Odio came up with the idea of offering rebates to his home-buying clients. He offered to give clients two-thirds of his own commission on the purchase of a new home, or one-third of his commission when purchasing an older home. Exactly how much would Odio rebate to his clients? Assume a new home cost $500,000, Mr. Odio's commission of 3 percent would thus yield him $15,000 of which two-thirds ($10,000) would be rebated to the home purchaser and one-third ($5,000) would be his to retain.

You might be thinking, How could a realtor justify giving away two-thirds of his commission? Odio explains it this way: "I'm happy to make [a 1 percent commission] for two hours of my time." This is to say that this neophyte realtor estimated that in many instances he would need to expend only a couple of hours helping his clients negotiate purchase agreements with home sellers and participating in the final closing after the transaction had been consummated. His implicit decision calculus was that by giving away two-thirds of his commission in rebates he could increase his business more than threefold and thereby be better off than if he were to retain all 100 percent of the commission. Stated differently, assuming an average new home selling price of $500,000 in the Northern Virginia market, Odio would receive $5,000 for each house sold after rebating $10,000 to his clients. Had he sold the same house without giving away the rebate, he would have received the full $15,000 commission. Hence, he would have to sell exactly three homes with rebates to equal selling one home without rebates. Mr. Odio's calculus obviously led him to believe that rebates would increase his selling business more than threefold compared to not offering rebates.

As a newbie in the industry, offering rebates gave him a unique way to build his business and to gain tons of free publicity. The potential downside of his rebating practice is that other realtors might be forced into offering their own rebates. A "rebate war" would serve well the interests of home buyers but would have devastating implications on realtors' earnings. Mr. Odio obviously was betting that other realtors would not follow his lead.

SOURCE: Adapted from James R. Hagerty, "Young Realtor's Brash Pitch: I Give Rebates," *Wall Street Journal Online*, July 6, 2004, http://online.wsj.com.

Rebate Fraud

Rebate fraud occurs by manufacturers, retailers, and consumers themselves. Manufacturers commit fraud when promoting rebate offers but then failing to fulfill them when consumers submit rebate slips with accompanying proof of purchase. Retailers sometimes advertise attractive rebates but then do not disclose (or disclose only in fine print) that the rebates will not arrive for several months or that the consumer must purchase another item to be eligible for the rebate. For example, a retail advertisement may claim that a computer has a $400 rebate offer but neglect to mention that the consumer must sign up for three years of Internet service to receive it.[13]

It is not just marketers that engage in misleading or fraudulent rebating practices. Consumers undertake their own form of rebate-related fraud. There is, in fact, a huge amount of fraud associated with bogus claims paid out to "professional" rebaters. Fraud occurs when professionals acquire their own cash registers, generate phony cash-register receipts, and send them on to manufacturers to collect refund checks without making the required product purchases. Other scam artists use computers to design phony UPC symbols, which they mail to manufacturers as evidence of purchases they actually have not made. Of course, these professionals do not send in just single refund requests; rather, they submit requests under multiple names and then have refund checks mailed to different post office boxes.

Two promotions illustrate this fraudulent practice.[14] One manufacturer ran a $3 refund offer requiring submission of a UPC to be eligible for the refund. Three out of four refund requests had the same misprinted UPC number on them. Investigators determined that *Moneytalk,* a former refunding magazine, had misprinted the product's UPC number in one of its issues. In a second case, a manufacturer's rebate forms were available in stores before its product reached store shelves. Nonetheless, this did not deter 2,200 rebate requests from flowing in immediately—all accompanied by bogus cash-register receipts and UPC numbers.

Postal authorities and marketers are taking aggressive efforts to curtail refunding fraud. Many marketers are beginning to state on their refund and rebate forms that they will not send checks to post office boxes. Others are stating that checks will be mailed only to the return address listed on the envelope. Because organized refund redeemers use computers to generate mailing and return address labels, manufacturers are further deterring fraud by stipulating on their refund and rebate forms that printed mailing labels are prohibited.

Sweepstakes and Contests

Sweepstakes and contests are widely used forms of sales promotions. Though sweepstakes, or sweeps, and contests differ in how they are executed, both offer consumers the opportunity to win cash, merchandise, or travel prizes.

Sweepstakes

In a **sweepstakes**, winners are determined purely *on the basis of chance.* Accordingly, proofs of purchase cannot be required as a condition for entry. A sweepstakes from Nabisco is illustrative. In a promotion for various Nabisco brands (e.g., Fig Newtons, Chips Ahoy, and Wheat Thins), consumers are encouraged to enter a sweepstakes online at NabiscoWorld.com (http://www.nabiscoworld.com) and register for the grand prize: a spa vacation for two in Honolulu. Durable good marketers also employ sweepstakes promotions, as illustrated in Figure 19.4 for the Buell motorcycle "Slay the Dragon II" sweep.

Sweepstakes represent a very popular promotional tool. Indeed, approximately three-quarters of packaged-goods marketers use sweepstakes, and nearly one-third of households participate in at least one sweepstakes every year.[15] Compared with many other sales promotion techniques, sweepstakes are relatively inexpensive, simple to execute, and are able to accomplish a variety of marketing objectives. In addition to reinforcing a brand's image and attracting attention to advertisements, well-designed sweepstakes can promote increased brand distribution at retail, augment sales-force enthusiasm, and reach specific groups through a prize structure that is particularly appealing to consumers in the group. Because sweeps require less effort from consumers and generate greater participation, brand managers much prefer this form of promotion over contests.

The effectiveness and appeal of a sweepstakes is generally limited if the sweepstakes is used alone. However, when tied in with advertising, point-of-purchase displays, and other promotional tools, sweepstakes can work effectively to produce significant results.

Figure 19.4
A Sweepstakes Offer for a Durable Good Brand

Courtesy, Buell Motorcycle Company

Contests

In a **contest**, the participant must act according to the rules of the contest and may or may not be required to submit proofs of purchase.

Brand managers at Hershey's Syrup created a contest that appealed to soccer moms and their children. The contest simply required submission of an action photo of a 6- to 17-year-old child or teen playing soccer along with an original store receipt with the purchase price of a 24-ounce bottle of Hershey's Syrup circled. This promotion associated Hershey's Syrup with the sport of soccer that is beloved by millions of families and also encouraged brand purchasing so as to allow the consumer to participate in the contest and thus become eligible to win any of numerous prizes. A contest such as this fits with the brand's wholesome image and matches the interests of many consumers in its target market.

Contests sometimes require participants to do more than simply send in a photo, as was the case with the contest for Hershey's Syrup. For example, Dickies, a manufacturer of work clothes, required entrants to nominate someone for the "American Worker of the Year" award and to explain in 100 words or less their reasons why the nominee deserves this recognition. A promotion for Sun-Maid raisins required entrants to create an original recipe that used at least one-half cup of raisins and could be prepared in 20 minutes or less. Pillsbury (maker of dessert baking mixes and frostings) required entrants to explain in 50 words or less, "What upcoming event would you like the Pillsbury Doughboy to help you celebrate and why?" Contests such as these typically include a coupon as part of the offer to encourage brand purchase and stimulate greater consumer interaction with the brand.

The makers of Motrin® IB ran an *Extreme Makeover: Home Edition* contest whereby participants could win an extreme makeover of their homes valued at $50,000 (Figure 19.5). The contest required participants to send a photo of their homes and write an essay regarding why their homes were worthy of an extreme makeover. This contest appropriately related Motrin to the successful TV program *Extreme Makeover: Home Edition* in claiming that Motrin IB (Ibuprofen) is *Home Edition*'s "partner in pain relief."

Online Sweeps and Contests

Online promotional events are growing in importance. Most companies now direct consumers to register online to participate in a sweepstakes or contest. Online sweeps and contests (along with online games) appeal to consumers and also further the interest of brands by creating awareness, building consumer interaction with the brand, and enabling the expansion of a brand's opt-in e-mail database. You can go to the Web sites of some of your favorite brands and see that almost every one offers some form of online sweeps, contest, or game.

Continuity Promotions

Promotions sometimes reward consumers' repeat purchasing of a particular brand by awarding points leading to reduced prices or free merchandise. It is obvious from this description why continuity promotions also are referred to as *loyalty* or *point* programs. Frequent-flyer programs by airlines and frequent-guest programs by hotels represent one form of loyalty program. Flyers and hotel guests accumulate points that can be redeemed eventually for free flights and lodging. These programs encourage consumers to stick with a particular airline or hotel to accumulate requisite numbers of points as quickly as possible. Renaissance Hotels, for example, provided 1,000 bonus miles per stay plus three extra miles for every U.S. dollar spent. These points were added to hotel guests frequent-flyer point totals with designated airlines.

Figure 19.5 Illustration of a Promotional Context

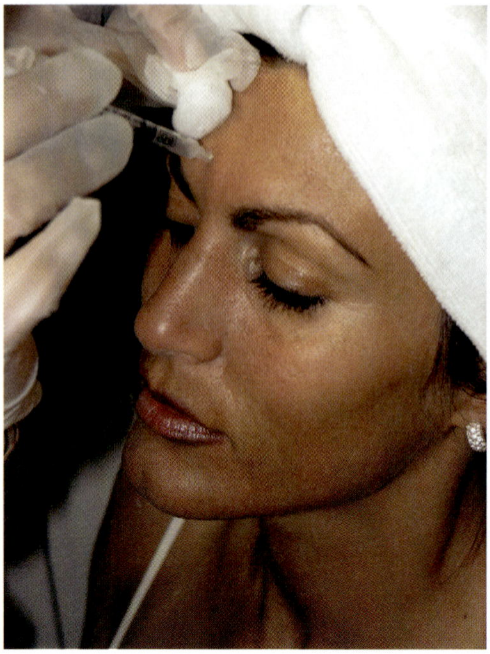

© Susan Van Etten

In a novel application of a loyalty program, Medicis Pharmaceutical—maker of Restylane, an antiwrinkle skin filler product that costs between $500 and $750 per treatment—introduced a program to encourage women to get injections every six months, which is the time period after which the effects of the product wear off. With each subsequent appointment, the consumer accumulates gifts that grow in value with every follow-up injection—worth $375 after the fourth follow-up injection. This program obviously is designed to encourage repeat business. Many first-time users of cosmetic-enhancement products get injections of products such as Restylane or Botox on impulse, but then do not return for follow-up treatments. Medicis Pharmaceutical has designs of encouraging repeat business with this interesting program.[16]

Pfizer, maker of erectile dysfunction product Viagra, introduced the Value Card loyalty program whereby users after every six prescriptions of Viagra are filled receive the seventh free. The marketing director for Viagra explained the program as a way of building long-term relations with customers.[17]

In general, continuity programs reward consumers for purchasing a particular brand repeatedly. The program need not be based on point accumulation and instead may simply require a certain number of purchases to be eligible for prizes. For example, Budget Rent A Car ran a continuity promotion whereby renters received free Bollé ski goggles with five car rentals from Budget.

Consumers who are already loyal to a brand that offers a point program or other continuity plan are rewarded for what they would have done anyway—namely, buy a preferred brand on a regular basis. In such a case, a point program does not encourage repeat purchasing; it does, however, serve to cement a relation with the consumer that is strong already. On the other hand, point programs can encourage consumers whose loyalty is divided among several brands to purchase more frequently the brand that awards promotion points or rewards repeat purchases in some other fashion. This is perhaps where continuity programs have the greatest value.

Overlay and Tie-In Promotions

Discussion to this point has concentrated on individual sales promotions. In practice, promotions often are used in combination to accomplish objectives that could not be achieved by using a single promotional tool. Furthermore, these techniques, individually or in conjunction with one another, are used oftentimes to promote simultaneously two or more brands either from the same company or from different firms.

The simultaneous use of *two or more sales promotion techniques* is called an **overlay**, or *combination,* program. The *simultaneous promotion of multiple brands in a single promotional effort* is called a **tie-in**, or *group,* promotion. In other words, *overlay* refers to the use of multiple promotional tools, whereas *tie-in* refers to the promotion of multiple brands from the same or different companies. Overlay programs and tie-ins often are used together, as the following sections illustrate.

Overlay Programs

Media clutter, as noted repeatedly in past chapters, is an ever-present problem facing marketers. When used individually, promotion tools (particularly coupons) may never be noticed by consumers. A combination of tools, such as the use of a coupon offer with another promotional device, increases the likelihood that consumers will attend to a promotional message and process the promotion offer. In addition, the joint use of several techniques in a well-coordinated promotional program equips the sales force with a strong sales program and provides the trade with an attractive incentive to purchase in larger quantities (in anticipation of enhanced consumer response) and to increase display activity. Nearly all the illustrative figures used previously in the chapter have overlaid a coupon with a refund, sweepstakes, contest, or other promotional offer.

Tie-In Promotions

Growing numbers of companies use tie-ins (group promotions) to generate increased sales, to stimulate trade and consumer interest, and to gain optimal use of their promotional budgets. Tie-in promotions are cost-effective because the cost is shared among multiple brands. Two or more brands, either from the same company (intracompany tie-ins) or from different companies (intercompany tie-ins) are involved in a tie-in. For example, Figure 19.6 illustrates a tie-in promotion between Orville Redenbacher's popcorn and 7-Up soft drinks. Tie-in relationships between complementary brands from different companies are being used with increasing regularity. For example, a freestanding insert showed a breakfast plate of Black Label bacon (from Hormel) and Grands! biscuits (from Pillsbury). The FSI (see Figure 19.7) included coupons for each brand. These companies shared the cost of producing and distributing this FSI offer.

Figure 19.6

Illustration of a Tie-In Promotion

Implementation Problems

Tie-in promotions are capable of accomplishing useful objectives, but not without potential problems. Promotion lead time—the amount of time required to plan and execute a promotion—is lengthened because two or more entities have to coordinate their separate promotional schedules. Furthermore, creative conflicts and convoluted messages may result from each partner trying to receive primary attention for its product or service.

To reduce problems as much as possible and to accomplish objectives, it is important that: (1) the profiles of each partner's customers be similar with regard to pertinent demographic or other consumption-influencing characteristics; (2) the partners' images should reinforce each other (e.g., Hormel and Pillsbury both are well-known brands with images of consistently high quality); and (3) the partners must be willing to cooperate rather than imposing their own interests to the detriment of the other partner's welfare.

Figure 19.7

Illustration of Another Tie-In Promotion

Retailer Promotions

Discussion to this point has focused on manufacturer promotions that are directed at consumers. Retailers also design promotions for their present and prospective customers. These retailer-inspired promotions are created for purposes of increasing store traffic, offering shoppers attractive price discounts or other deals, and building customer loyalty.

Retail Coupons

Couponing is a favorite promotion among many retailers in the grocery, drug, and mass-merchandise areas of business. Some grocery retailers hold special "coupon days" when they redeem manufacturer coupons at

Figure 19.8
Illustration of a Retailer's Loyalty-Card Program

double or even triple their face value. For example, a grocery store on a "triple-coupon day" would deduct $1.50 from the consumer's bill when he or she submits a manufacturer's coupon with a face value of 50 cents. Retailers typically limit their double- or triple-discount offers to manufacturer coupons having face values of 99 cents or less.

Frequent-Shopper Programs

A number of retailers offer their customers frequent-shopper cards that entitle shoppers to discounts on select items purchased on any particular shopping occasion. For example, in a Wednesday advertising flyer, one grocery retailer offered its cardholders savings such as $2.99 on the purchase of two Mrs. Paul's fish fillets, $1.25 when buying two cans of Minute Maid juice, and $1.70 with the purchase of Freschetta pizza. Customers receive these savings on submitting their frequent-shopper cards to checkout clerks, who scan the card number and deduct savings from the shopper's bill when discounted items are scanned. These frequent-shopper cards encourage repeat purchasing from a particular retail chain. Because they are designated with labels such as "VIC" (very important customer), they also serve to elevate the shopper's sense of importance to a store. Finally, frequent-shopper card programs provide retailers with valuable databases containing information on shopper demographics and purchase habits.

In another form of loyalty program, some retailers provide customers with plastic cards that are presented to clerks for automatic scanning with every purchase made from that particular store. For example, Dick's Sporting Goods is a retail chain that specializes, as the name suggests, in a wide variety of sporting goods products. Dick's has a "Score Card" program (see Figure 19.8) whereby customers submit their cards with every purchase and accumulate points enabling discounts on subsequent purchases. This is a perfect application of a loyalty, or rewards, program—one in which earning points fits perfectly with the point-scoring athletic games whose equipment and apparel is featured in this retail chain's stores.

Special Price Deals

Many retailers use a variety of creative ways of reducing prices on a temporary basis. For example, Goody's—a regional discount apparel chain—runs a periodic price-discounting promotion in which paper shopping bags are mailed out to shoppers—paper bags of the sort that one sees in grocery stores. The bags are printed with statements such as, "20% off everything you can stuff in this bag." The deal is offered on a one-day-only basis and then repeated again at different times throughout the year. The value of a special-pricing program such as this is that it creates excitement on the part of customers, while at the same time not requiring blanket price reductions for all customers—just those who bring their bags to the store on the designated date.

Samples and Premiums

Sampling is another form of retailer-based sales promotion that is in wide use. Although many instances of store sampling represent joint programs between stores and manufacturers, retailers are sampling their own store or private label products increasingly. Club stores such as Costco are famous for providing a variety of food samples on any given purchase occasion. Such promotions serve to increase sales of the sampled items and also possess an entertainment-type value that enhances the shopping experience.

Stores also offer premiums to encourage purchases of select items. For example, Lowe's Companies, a major retail chain in the home-improvement industry, partnered with Omaha Steaks, a supplier of premium meat products, with the objective of increasing sales of gas grills priced at more than $150. The giveaway of steaks and burgers increased Lowe's grill sales by 35 percent in participating stores.

Evaluating Sales Promotion Ideas

It should be apparent by this point that numerous alternatives are available to manufacturers and retailers when planning sales promotions. There also are a variety of objectives that effective promotion programs are able to achieve. The combination of numerous alternatives and diverse objectives leads to a staggering array of possibilities. A systematic procedure for selecting the type of sales promotion is therefore essential. The following sections outline procedures for appraising potential promotions during the idea stage and then, after they have run, for evaluating their effectiveness.

A Procedure for Evaluating Promotion Ideas

The following straightforward, three-step procedure directs a brand manager in determining which promotion ideas and approaches have the best chance of succeeding.[18]

Step 1: Identify the Objectives

The most basic yet important step toward successful consumer-oriented promotions is the clear identification of the specific objective(s) that is (are) to be accomplished. Objectives should be specified as they relate both to the trade and to ultimate consumers; for example, objectives may be to generate trial, to load consumers, to preempt competition, to increase display space, and so on.

In this first step, the promotional planner must commit the objectives to writing and state them specifically and in measurable terms. For example, "to increase sales" is too general. In comparison, the objective "to increase display space by 25 percent over the comparable period last year" is specific and measurable.

Step 2: Achieve Agreement

Everyone involved in a brand's marketing must agree with the objectives developed. Failure to achieve agreement on objectives results in various decision makers (such as the advertising, sales, and brand managers) pushing for different programs because they have different goals in mind. Also, in line with the following step, a promotion program can more easily be evaluated in terms of a specific objective than can a vague generalization.

JOB OUTLOOK

For marketing, sales, and promotions management positions, some employers prefer a bachelor's or master's degree in business administration with an emphasis on marketing. In highly technical industries, such as computer and electronics manufacturing, a bachelor's degree in engineering or science, combined with a master's degree in business administration, is preferred. *(Occupational Outlook Handbook, 2004–05 Edition, U.S. DOL, http://www.bls.gov/oco/home.htm)*

Step 3: Evaluate the Idea

With specific objectives established and agreement achieved, the following five-point evaluation system can be used to rate alternative sales promotion ideas:

1. *Is the idea a good one?* Every idea should be evaluated against the promotion's objectives. For example, if increasing product trial is the objective, a sample or a coupon would be rated favorably, whereas a sweepstakes would flunk this initial evaluation.
2. *Will the promotion idea appeal to the target market?* A contest, for example, might have great appeal to children but for certain adult groups have disastrous results. In general, remember that the target market represents the benchmark against which all proposals should be judged.

3. *Is the idea unique, or is the competition doing something similar?* The prospects of receiving interest from both the trade and the consumers depend on developing promotions that are not ordinary. Creativity is every bit as important to the success of promotions as it is with advertising.
4. *Is the promotion presented clearly so that the intended market will notice, comprehend, and respond positively to the promotion?* Sales promotion planners should start with one fundamental premise: most consumers are unwilling to spend much time and effort figuring out how a promotion works. It is critical to a promotion's success that instructions be user-friendly. Let consumers know quickly and clearly what the offer is and how to respond to it.
5. *Is the proposed idea cost-effective?* This requires an evaluation of whether the proposed promotion will achieve the intended objectives at an affordable cost. Sophisticated promotion planners cost out alternative programs and know in advance the likely bottom-line payoff from a promotion.

Postmortem Analysis

The previous section described a general procedure for evaluating proposed promotion ideas while they are in the planning stage, before actual implementation. It would be useful to also have a way of evaluating a promotional program after it has been implemented. Such evaluation would be useful for future planning purposes, especially if the evaluation becomes part of brand management's "institutional memory" rather than discarded shortly after the evaluation is completed. A seasoned practitioner in the promotion industry has proposed judging completed promotion programs in terms of five characteristics: expense, efficiency, execution ease, equity enhancement, and effectiveness.[19]

Expense

A promotion program's expense is the sum of the direct outlays invested in the promotion. Typical cost elements include the expense to create the promotion, costs to advertise it, and payouts for coupons redeemed, refunds paid, game prizes awarded, and so on.

Efficiency

Efficiency represents a promotion's *cost per unit moved.* The efficiency metric is calculated simply by dividing the total cost of the completed promotion by the total units sold during the promotional period.

Execution Ease

This represents the total time and effort that went into the planning and execution of a promotion. Obviously, everything else held constant, promotions that require less time and effort are preferred.

Equity Enhancement

This criterion cannot be measured objectively but involves a subjective assessment of whether a promotion has enhanced a brand's image or possibly even detracted from it. A sweepstakes offer, for example, may serve to enhance a brand's equity by associating it with, say, a prestigious grand prize. A self-liquidating premium may accomplish the same goal. Comparatively, a game may be inappropriate for some brands by virtue of appearing tacky. As always, the evaluation depends on the brand positioning and target-market situation.

Effectiveness

A promotion's effectiveness can best be assessed by determining the total units of the promoted item that were sold during the promotional period.

Combining the Individual Factors

Having evaluated a completed promotion program along the five "E" dimensions just noted, it would be helpful if the individual evaluations could be combined into a single score. This can be done simply enough by using a straightforward model that weights each of the five factors in importance and then summates the products of each factor's score by its weight. A model such as the following could be used:

$$\text{Program } j\text{'s Score} = \sum_{i=1}^{5} (E_{ij} \times W_i)$$

where,

Program j = A just-completed promotional program (one of many potential promotional programs that have been run and subsequently evaluated).

E_{ij} = Evaluation of the jth promotional program on the ith evaluation factor (i.e., the efficiency factor, the executional ease factor, etc.).

W_i = Weight, or relative importance, of the ith factor in determining promotion success. (Note that the weight component is subscripted just with an i, and not also a j, because the weights are constant across program evaluations. Comparatively, evaluations of the individual factors, E_{ij}, require a j subscript to reflect the likelihood of varying evaluations across different promotional programs.)

Table 19.2 illustrates this straightforward model.[20] Consider a company that has run three promotional programs during a particular year. On completion, each program was evaluated with respect to the five evaluative criteria (expense, efficiency, etc.) on 10-point scales, with 1 indicating poor performance and 10 reflecting an excellent execution on each evaluative criterion. Notice also in Table 19.2 that the five criteria have been weighted as follows: Expense = .2, Efficiency = .1, Execution Ease = .1, Equity Enhancement = .3, and Effectiveness = .3. These weights sum to 1 and reflect the relative importance *to this particular brand manager* of the five factors. (Relative importance of these factors will obviously vary across different brands, depending on each brand's image, the company's financial standing, and so on.)

Given this particular set of weights and evaluations, it can be concluded that program 1 was the least successful of the three promotions, whereas program 3 was the most successful. These evaluations can thus be archived for reference by

Table 19.2

Evaluation of Three Completed Promotional Programs

Program *j*	Expense *Weight = .2*	Efficiency *Weight = .1*	Execution Ease *Weight = .1*	Equity Enhancement *Weight = .3*	Effectiveness *Weight = .3*	Total Score
Program 1	7	6	7	5	9	6.9
Program 2	9	8	8	7	8	7.9
Program 3	8	9	8	10	9	9.0

future brand managers. Eventually, norms can be established for specifying the average effectiveness level achieved by different types of promotions (samples, coupon programs, rebates, etc.).

Of course, Table 19.2 is purely illustrative. However, in actual promotion situations it is possible for brand managers to formally evaluate promotions, provided that the procedure for evaluating each criterion is clearly articulated, systematically implemented, and consistently applied (as best as possible) to all promotions that are appraised. The point to be appreciated is that the model on which Table 19.2 is based is suggestive of how promotional programs *can* be evaluated.

Intelligent brand managers must develop their own models to accommodate their brand's specific needs, but the point to be emphasized is that this can be accomplished with the application of thought and effort. The alternative to having a formalized evaluation system, such as the one proposed here, is simply to run promotion events and then never to evaluate their success. Can you imagine as a student what it would be like to take courses but never to receive grades, never to be evaluated? How would you know how well you have done? How would your institution know whether grading standards have changed over the years? Like it or not, evaluation is essential. Good business practice requires it. The issue is not whether to evaluate promotions but how to do it in a valid and reliable manner.

Summary

This chapter focused on consumer-oriented promotions other than sampling and couponing. Specific topics addressed include the use of product premiums, price-off promotions, bonus packs, games, rebates and refunds, continuity programs, and sweepstakes and contests.

The discussion of premiums included the various forms of premium offers: free-with-purchase premiums; mail-in offers; in-, on-, and near-pack premiums; self-liquidating offers; and phone cards as a special form of premium. Also described were the specific conditions necessary to execute a successful premium promotion.

Price-off promotions, which typically entail a reduction ranging from 10 to 25 percent of a brand's regular price, were described as a form of sales promotion that provides consumers with an immediate reward and serves marketers by encouraging repeat purchasing. The Federal Trade Commission's specific regulations regarding price-off promotions were presented.

Bonus packs provide consumers with extra quantities of a promoted brand for free (e.g., 25 percent more than the regular size). This form of promotion represents an immediate reward for consumers and serves to encourage repeat purchasing by rewarding consumers for their loyalty to a brand.

Games are frequently used as a means of increasing consumer enthusiasm and involvement with a brand, and in so doing perform a repeat-purchasing function by providing consumers with an instant reward. The implementation of games is fraught with the potential for snafus, so brand managers and their promotion agencies must exercise caution when using this form of promotion.

Rebate and refund programs are used by CPG and durable-goods companies as a means of offering consumers a cash discount—but, of course, only if they go to the effort of redeeming the rebate offer. Marketers are fond of rebates because they provide an alternative to the use of coupons and stimulate consumer purchase behavior. Rebate offers can reinforce brand loyalty, provide the sales force with something to talk about, and enable the manufacturer to flag the package with a potentially attractive deal. Because most consumers never redeem rebates, this form of promotion is referred to as a *phantom discount*. Consumers, in a sense, self-deceive themselves in buying a brand to take advantage of the rebate offer but then do not undertake the necessary effort to redeem the rebate within the period allotted by the brand marketer.

Both sweepstakes and contests offer consumers the opportunity to win cash, merchandise, or travel prizes. Unlike other forms of sales promotions, sweeps and contests serve primarily image-enhancement purposes rather than generating trial usage or encouraging repeat-purchase behavior. Where sweeps require no effort on the part of the consumer other than mere entry via mail or more frequently online, contests necessitate that the consumer write an essay or perform another function. Sweeps generate much higher responses from consumers than contests and thus are preferred.

Continuity promotions are used by many marketers to encourage brand loyalty and repeat-purchase behavior. These include the ubiquitous frequent-flyer programs offered by airlines, frequent-guest offerings from hotels, and many variants of these well-known programs. For example, the erectile dysfunction product, Viagra, offered its purchasers a free seventh prescription after six purchases.

Overlay and tie-in promotions involve the use of two or more sales promotion techniques in combination with one another (an overlay, or combination, program) or the simultaneous promotion of multiple brands in a single promotional effort (a tie-in, or group, promotion). Both types of joint promotions are widely used as a means of spreading promotional dollars among multiple brands or companies and achieving greater impact from every promotional offering.

The chapter concluded by discussing various forms of retailer-driven promotions and procedures for testing promotions, whether undertaken by manufacturers or retailers. First discussed was a three-step procedure for testing promotion ideas prior to their implementation; then described was a method for conducting a postmortem analysis of completed promotions. This latter analysis involves evaluating what can be referred to as the five "E" factors related to promotion success: expense, efficiency, execution ease, equity enhancement, and effectiveness.

Discussion Questions

1. Present a position on the following statement (voiced by a student who read a previous edition of this textbook): "I can't understand why in Table 19.1 mail-in premiums are positioned as accomplishing just a trial-impact function. It would seem that this form of promotion also accomplishes repeat-purchasing objectives."

2. Your company markets hot dogs, bologna, and other processed meats. You wish to offer a self-liquidating premium that would cost consumers approximately $25, would require five proofs of purchase, and would be appropriately themed to your product category during the summer months. Your primary market segment consists of families with school-age children crossing all socioeconomic strata. Suggest two premium items and justify your choices.
3. What is the purpose of the Federal Trade Commission price-off regulations?
4. Compare bonus packs and price-off deals in terms of consumer impact.
5. How can sales promotion reinforce a brand's image? Is this a major objective of sales promotion?
6. Compare sweepstakes, contests, and games in terms of how they function and their relative effectiveness.
7. Your company markets antifreeze. Sales to consumers take place in a very short period, primarily September through December. You want to tie in a promotion between your brand and the brand of another company that would bring more visibility to your brand and encourage retailers to provide more shelf space. Recommend a partner for this tie-in promotion and justify the choice.
8. Have you participated in online promotions, and, if so, what has been your experience? Considering just a single online promotion that you participated in and considering yourself representative of the brand's target market, do you think the promotion accomplished its objective?
9. What are your thoughts regarding the future of online promotions?
10. Visit a local grocery store and identify five instances of sales promotions. Describe each promotion and comment on the objectives that promotion was intended to accomplish for the sponsoring brand or for the retailer.
11. Have you ever participated in some form of loyalty program? What has been your experience? For example, do you think the program served to increase your repeat business with the sponsoring brand?

ENDNOTES

1. Adapted from Elizabeth Bernstein, "Colleges Use Perks from Cable to Cellphones to Lure Students," *Wall Street Journal Online,* April 11, 2003, http://online.wsj.com.
2. Amy Johannes, "Music Premiums Top Charts," *Promo,* February 2005, 13.
3. Priya Raghubir, "Free Gift with Purchase: Promoting or Discounting the Brand?" *Journal of Consumer Psychology* 14 (1 & 2), 2004, 181–186.
4. John Palmer, "Still on the Line," *Promo,* December 2000, 73–76.
5. *Consumer Promotion Seminar Fact Book* (New York: Association of National Advertisers, undated), 7.
6. Glenn Heitsmith, "Botched Pepsi Promotion Prompts Terrorist Attacks," *Promo,* September 1993, 10.
7. Laurie Baum, "How Beatrice Lost at Its Own Game," *BusinessWeek,* March 2, 1987, 66.
8. Ibid.
9. For further reading, see Bob Sperber and Karen Benezra, "A Scam to Go?" *Brandweek,* August 27, 2001, 4, 10; Kat MacArthur, "McSwindle," *Advertising Age,* August 27, 2001, 1, 22, 23; Donald Silberstein, "Managing Promotional Risk," *Promo,* October 2001, 57; "Arch Enemies," *Promo,* December 2001, 17.
10. "Walking the Tightrope," *Promo,* March 2001, 48–51.
11. William M. Bulkeley, "Rebates' Appeal to Manufacturers: Few Consumers Redeem Them," *Wall Street Journal Online,* February 10, 1998, http://online.wsj.com.
12. Dilip Soman, "The Illusion of Delayed Incentives: Evaluating Future Effort-Money Transactions," *Journal of Marketing Research* 35 (November 1998), 427–437.
13. Ira Teinowitz and Tobi Elkin, "FTC Cracks Down on Rebate Offers," *Advertising Age,* July 3, 2000, 29.

14. Kerry J. Smith, "Postal Inspectors Target Rebate Fraud," *Promo,* April 1994, 13.
15. "Healthy, Wealthy, and Wiser," *Promo's 8th Annual SourceBook 2001,* 38–39.
16. Rhonda L. Rundle, "A New Wrinkle in Rewards Programs," *Wall Street Journal Online,* March 2, 2005, http://online.wsj.com.
17. Rich Thomaselli, "Pfizer Introduces Viagra Loyalty Program," *Advertising Age,* April 19, 2004, 3, 59.
18. Adapted from Don E. Schultz and William A. Robinson, *Sales Promotion Management* (Lincolnwood, Ill.: NTC Business Books, 1986), 436–445.
19. Sara Owens, "A Different Kind of E-marketing," *Promo,* May 2001, 53–54.
20. This table is an adaptation of ibid., 53.

CHAPTER 20

Marketing-Oriented Public Relations and Sponsorships

Marcom Challenge: The Smell of Bowling Alleys—Beer, Smoke, Musty Shoes, and Scented Bowling Balls

Bowling alleys are places where many people rarely if ever visit, because they frankly don't find these venues very appealing. Rented shoes, used bowling balls, lingering tobacco smoke, and the smell of stale beer are just some of the unforgettable images people associate with bowling alleys. This perhaps explains why there are fewer than three million bowlers in the United States, only about half as many as there were less than a generation ago.

One aspect of bowling alleys is about to change. The *Wall Street Journal,* in a March 2005 article discussed, of all things, a new product line of scented bowling balls.[1] The following day a similar article appeared in my local newspaper. "What's going on?", I thought. "Why would these multiple articles about scented bowling balls be appearing simultaneously in the news media?" I went online and googled "scented bowling balls." My query received nearly 1,500 hits. Apparently, the idea of a scented bowling ball had caught the imagination of a lot of journalists. Stories about this specialty line of bowling balls were being aired and printed around the country. Millions of people were learning about this new product very quickly, some of whom undoubtedly would seek additional information and possibly contemplate immediate purchases.

In the event that scented bowling balls are news to you, let me provide a few details. These bowling balls were invented by a company named Storm Products, Inc., located in Utah. Because bowling balls are made from shaped urethane, the technology of scenting is quite simple: just add scents to the chemical mix prior to shaping the bowling balls. Storm Products' first scented ball was grape. Now each of this company's many varieties of scented balls has its own unique name: the X Factor Ace (wintergreen), the Atomic Charge (cranberry), Fear Factor (plum), Eraser Banshee (piña colada), and so on.

Storm Products' scented bowling balls cost $150 to $250 and are said to have a soothing effect on bowlers. In fact, some users of these balls believe that the particular smell of their scented ball enables them to relax when approaching the lane, and enhances their concentration. There is a scientific explanation for this. In a nutshell, olfaction, the sense of smell, is known to be related to people's memories, their felt emotions, and their mood states. You undoubtedly remember certain smells that are attached to pleasant or unpleasant memories of your past. These memories are so vivid that upon contact with the particular scent your mind races back to a situation, an event, or a person with which you associate the scent. Some smells put you in a positive mood, because you associate the smells with pleasant circumstances or perhaps with a much-cherished person. Other smells may place you in a negative mood due to their association in your memory with unpleasant situations. Of course, a bowler selecting a particular scent for his or her ball likely would choose one that is associated with past positive experiences and memories. Hence, as the bowler steps up to the lane and raises the ball close to his or her nose in preparation of rolling it down the alley, it is possible that the scent of his or her ball unconsciously activates something in the brain that serves to elevate the bowler's mood and perhaps calm the nerves.

But what, you may be wondering, do scented bowling balls have to do with the topic of this chapter. Read on; an explanation will be offered in short order.

CHAPTER OBJECTIVES

1

Appreciate the nature and role of marketing public relations (MPR).

2

Understand the differences between proactive and reactive MPR.

3

Understand the types of commercial rumors and how to control them.

4

Be aware of event sponsorships and how to select appropriate events.

5

Recognize the nature and role of cause-oriented marketing.

Overview

This chapter explores the multiple roles performed by the public relations aspect of an integrated marketing communications program. Also examined are the related topics of event sponsorship and cause-related marketing as part of the more general practice known as *sponsorship marketing*. These growing aspects of IMC are conceptually aligned with public relations and in some organizations are administratively treated as part of the public relations department.

Public relations, or PR, is an organizational activity involved with fostering goodwill between a company and its various publics. PR efforts are aimed at various corporate constituencies, including employees, suppliers, stockholders, governments, the public, labor groups, citizen action groups, and consumers. As just described, PR involves relations with *all* of an organization's relevant publics. In other words, most PR activities do *not* involve marketing per se but rather deal with general management concerns. This more encompassing aspect of public relations can be called *general PR*.

Our concern in this chapter is only with the narrow aspect of public relations involving an organization's interactions with consumers. The marketing-oriented aspect of public relations is called *marketing public relations*, or MPR for short.[2]

Though general PR historically played a relatively minor marcom role, MPR is performing an increasingly important function. Whereas advertising messages are paid for by identified sponsors and are regarded by consumers as direct attempts to influence their attitudes and behaviors, MPR messages come across not as advertisements but as unbiased reports from journalists. An MPR message in comparison with an advertisement assumes a mantle of *credibility*. MPR messages also are considerably less expensive than advertisements because the airtime or newspaper space is provided free of charge by the newspaper, magazine, radio, or television station that prints or airs the message. Hence, for the dual reasons of high credibility and low expense, MPR messages (and thus the PR departments that produce them) have achieved a more prominent position in firms' IMC efforts. MPR performs a particularly important role in *new-product introductions* and in overall brand-building efforts.

Is It Time to Say Goodbye to Advertising? Probably Not!

The role that PR, or MPR, should play in a firm's marcom program has been a matter of no small debate over the years. Most marcom practitioners and brand managers have historically believed that MPR's role is specialized and limited. Some critics contend that MPR is too difficult to control and measure. However, a provocative book titled *The Fall of Advertising & the Rise of PR* has challenged prevailing beliefs and argued for an expanded role for PR.[3] The book's authors—a father and daughter team, Al and Laura Ries—contend that public relations and its major tool, publicity, represent the most important instrument in the marketer's tool bag. Their thesis is that new products can be introduced with little if any advertising and, instead, that a brand's marketing communicators can get the job done with creative and powerful public relations. They use as anecdotal evidence the success of well-known brands such as eBay, PlayStation, Starbucks, The Body Shop, Palm, and BlackBerry—all of which were introduced without large advertising budgets and focused instead on publicity and word-of-mouth buzz.

Let us return to scented bowling balls (please read the *Marcom Challenge* if you haven't already). Do you think that Storm Products needed to heavily advertise these balls in order to achieve success? Probably not. Getting publicity releases published and aired around the country served to inform millions of people about this unique and fun new product. In brand equity terms, publicity would have created high levels of product awareness and piqued bowlers' interest in scented bowling balls. Then, those early purchasers of scented balls would have further spread the word via the buzz accompanying something as strangely original as a scented bowling ball. (It would really be worthwhile for you to return to Chapter 7 for a brief review of the section on creating buzz.) With reference to buzz creation in Chapter 7, the discussion about designing products to be unique or visible under "Igniting Explosive Self-Generating Demand" should make it clear that scented bowling balls are both highly unique and highly visible ("smellable"). Hence, news about this product would have spread rapidly once the media started talking about it and initial product adopters began showing off their scented bowling balls. MPR accomplished the awareness-building job and piqued prospective purchasers' interest. Advertising would have been relatively unnecessary.

But let's fast-forward a short time, say, six months, after the barrage of initial publicity. How now will the product's uniqueness remain on the minds of potential purchasers? Why would prospective purchasers have a compelling reason to purchase Storm's brand of scented bowling balls rather than competitive brands introduced later, especially if these brands have a lower price point? Surely, the news media would have little interest in telling additional stories about scented bowling balls—that would be yesterday's news. Returning to the book (*The Fall of Advertising & the Rise of PR*), Ries and Ries have a point when stating that PR (or what we're calling *MPR*), is invaluable for introducing new products.

However, two very important qualifications to the Ries and Ries claim must be acknowledged: First, all new products cannot, contrary to their omnibus claim, rely on publicity for successful introductions. Considering that most new products are *not* high in uniqueness or visibility, the news media are not interested in presenting free publicity for these mundane products. Only a small subset of products (such as scented bowling balls) captures the imagination of the media. Hence, widespread publicity simply is not an option for ordinary products. Marketing communicators therefore must create the news themselves, and that means investing in advertising to create brand awareness and build positive brand images. In short, brand-equity creation via MPR is restricted to that subset of truly unique products and brands.

Second, even for those truly unique new products that can benefit from MPR, it is only a matter of time before free publicity no longer is available. At that point, the brand-equity-maintenance responsibility falls squarely on advertising's shoulders. After the newsworthiness wears off, advertising is absolutely necessary to maintain brand interest.

Marketing public relations, or MPR, can be extremely effective and substantially less costly than advertising, but it is not a panacea. My best advice is that marketing practitioners should not default to advertising as the marcom tool of first choice. Instead, public relations should be first considered insofar as it is a cheaper, more credible, and potentially more impactful means of accomplishing marcom objectives. However, and it's a critical however, one should not be blind to the fact that publicity simply cannot be generated for products that are mundane. That being the case, brand managers must turn to advertising as the tool of second resort. If you are introducing scented bowling balls, you can obtain a lot of free impressions from the media. MPR is great in this case; go for it! If you are introducing, say, a new line of unscented bowling alley floor wax (boring!), don't kid yourself—the media likely will be unwilling to devote space or airtime to this product, so advertising and personal selling will be needed to build brand awareness.

Let us turn now to a deeper exploration of MPR.

The MPR Aspect of General Public Relations

Marketing-oriented public relations, MPR, is an increasingly important component in companies' marcom programs. A recent survey of senior marketing managers determined that MPR registers very high for purposes of increasing brand awareness, providing credibility, reaching purchase influencers, and educating consumers.[4]

MPR can be further delineated as involving both proactive and reactive initiatives. **Proactive MPR** is a tool for communicating a brand's merits and is used typically in conjunction with other marcom tools such as advertising and promotions. Dictated by a company's marketing objectives, proactive MPR is offensively rather than defensively oriented and opportunity seeking rather than problem solving.

Reactive MPR, by comparison, describes the conduct of public relations in response to outside influences. It is undertaken as a result of external pressures and challenges brought by competitive actions, shifts in consumer attitudes, changes in government policy, or other external influences. Reactive MPR deals most often with influences having negative consequences for an organization. Reactive MPR attempts to repair a company's reputation, prevent market erosion, and regain lost sales.

Proactive MPR

The major role of proactive MPR is in the area of product introductions or product revisions. Proactive MPR is integrated with other IMC tools to give a product additional exposure, newsworthiness, and credibility. This last factor, *credibility,* largely accounts for the effectiveness of proactive MPR. Whereas advertising is oftentimes suspect—because we question advertisers' motives, knowing they have a personal stake in influencing us—product announcements by a newspaper editor or television broadcaster are notably more believable. Consumers are less likely to question the motivation underlying an editorial-type endorsement.

Publicity is the major tool of proactive MPR. Like advertising, the fundamental purposes of marketing-oriented publicity are to enhance a brand's equity in a twofold manner: (1) facilitating brand awareness and (2) augmenting brand image by forging in customers' minds strong and favorable associations with the brand. Three widely used forms of publicity are product releases, executive-statement releases, and feature articles.

Product releases announce new products, provide relevant information about product features and benefits, and inform interested listeners and readers how additional information can be obtained. Product releases are often published in the product section of trade magazines (i.e., publications that cater to specific industries) and in general interest business publications such as *BusinessWeek, Forbes, Fortune,* and the *Wall Street Journal.* Product releases also are reprinted in the business or consumer news section of consumer magazines and in local, national (e.g., *USA Today*), or international newspapers (e.g., the *International Herald Tribune*).

Audiovisual product releases have gained wide usage in recent years. For example, Hershey introduced its new Hershey's Kisses with almonds by showing a 6-foot, 500-pound replica of a Hershey's Kiss covered in gold sequins and foil being dropped from a Times Square building in New York City, reminiscent of New Year's Eve. Hershey's PR agency videotaped the event, distributed tapes to New York networks, and the same evening the event was seen on TV by millions of Americans. For less than $100,000, Hershey's new product received tremendous exposure.

Executive-statement releases are news releases quoting chief executive officers and other corporate executives. Unlike a product release, which is restricted to describing a new or modified product, an executive-statement release may address a wide variety of issues relevant to a corporation's publics, such as those illustrated in the following list:

- Statements about industry developments and trends
- Forecasts of future sales
- Views on the economy
- Comments on research and development or market research findings
- Announcements of new marketing programs launched by the company
- Views on foreign competition or global developments
- Comments on environmental issues

JOB OUTLOOK

PR specialists work as advocates for businesses and organizations to maintain positive relationships with the public. They help organizations and the public adapt to each other by understanding attitudes and concerns of consumers, employees, and various other groups, and work to improve communication with these groups and with the media. *(Occupational Outlook Handbook, 2004–05 Edition, U.S. DOL, http://www.bls.gov/oco/home.htm)*

Whereas product releases are typically published in the business and product sections of newspapers and magazines, executive-statement releases are published in the news section. This location carries with it a significant degree of credibility. Note that any product release can be converted into an executive-statement release by changing the way it is written.

Feature articles are detailed descriptions of products or other newsworthy programs that are written by a PR firm for immediate publication or airing by print or broadcast media or distribution via appropriate Internet sites. Materials such as these are inexpensive to prepare, yet they can provide companies with tremendous access to many potential customers—as was the case with Storm Products' scented bowling balls.

Many newspapers often publish feature articles about new products that are of likely interest to the paper's readers. For example, the "do it yourself" section of a local newspaper recently published a product release for the Skil cordless screwdriver. Although this release appeared to be written by a local columnist, to the trained eye it obviously was a product release prepared by Skil's PR agency and likely was published in dozens, if not hundreds, of local newspapers. The opening paragraph and an accompanying photo of the product immediately captured the reader's attention when stating, "Don't be deceived by the size of Skil's palm-sized cordless screwdriver. The tool has a bigger punch than you'd expect." Later in the release the do-it-yourselfer's interest was really piqued with the claim "But here's the real beauty of the tool: charge the battery, stick the screwdriver in a drawer, and it will hold the charge for two years. So it's ready to work whenever you are." It is easy to imagine that thousands of readers of this product release searched for a Skil cordless screwdriver on their next trip to their favorite store carrying products such as this.

Reactive MPR

Unanticipated marketplace developments can place an organization in a vulnerable position that demands reactive MPR. In simple terms, bad things happen and unanticipated events sometimes occur that require a public relations response. In the sports realm, for example, the National Basketball Association suffered terrible embarrassment after a melee broke out in a game between the Detroit Pistons and the Indiana Pacers. Several players even went into the stands and exchanged blows with fans. Major League Baseball in the same year, 2004, experienced the humiliating disclosure that some of the league's most successful and celebrated players had allegedly used steroids. Only time will tell whether the fortunes of these two major U.S. sports organizations will suffer from these shameful episodes.

In the corporate domain, Firestone tires—made by Firestone, a U.S. subsidiary of Japan's Bridgestone Corporation—was the focus of negative publicity when Ford Explorer SUVs fitted with Firestone tires experienced numerous rollover accidents. The particular tire in question was eventually recalled, but both Firestone and the Explorer were subjected to intense public scrutiny and even scorn. Vioxx, the arthritis and acute-pain medication made by the pharmaceutical giant, Merck & Co., was withdrawn from worldwide distribution in late 2004 after a scientific study revealed that patients taking Vioxx for 18 months or longer had double the risk of suffering heart attacks or strokes compared to a control group taking a placebo. With 2003 Vioxx sales of $2.5 billion, this withdrawal had significant financial implications for Merck, and the negative publicity surrounding Merck's failure to withdraw the product even sooner could have damaging long-term implications for the Vioxx brand and for Merck overall.

In general, the most dramatic factors underlying the need for reactive MPR are product defects and failures. Following are some illustrations of crises that have received widespread media attention. The ordering is chronological and ranges from an event occurring as far back as the early 1980s to those happening recently.

Product Tamperings: Tylenol and Sudafed

In 1982, seven people in the Chicago area died from cyanide poisoning after ingesting Tylenol capsules. Many analysts predicted that Tylenol would never regain its previously sizable market share. Some observers even questioned whether Johnson & Johnson ever would be able to market anything under the Tylenol name.

Johnson & Johnson's handling of the Tylenol tragedy was nearly brilliant. Rather than denying a problem existed, J&J acted swiftly by removing Tylenol from retail shelves. Spokespersons appeared on television and cautioned consumers not to ingest Tylenol capsules. A tamperproof package was designed, setting a standard for other companies. As a final good-faith gesture, J&J offered consumers free replacements for products they had disposed of in the aftermath of the Chicago tragedy. Tylenol regained its market share shortly after this campaign began.

In a tragic replay of the Tylenol case, two people in the state of Washington died in 1991 after ingesting cyanide-laced Sudafed capsules. Following Tylenol's lead, Burroughs Wellcome Company, Sudafed's maker, immediately withdrew the product from store shelves, suspended advertising, established an 800-number phone line for consumer inquiries, and offered a $100,000 reward for information leading to the arrest of the product tamperer. Burrough Wellcome's quick and effective response reportedly resulted in only a brief sales slump for Sudafed.

The Perrier Case

Perrier was the leading brand of bottled water in the United States until 1990 when Source Perrier, the manufacturer, announced that traces of a toxic chemical, benzene, had been found in some of its products. Perrier recalled 72 million bottles from U.S. supermarkets and restaurants and subsequently withdrew the product from distribution elsewhere in the world. The total cost of the global recall was estimated to have exceeded $150 million. Perrier's sales in the United States declined by 40 percent, and Evian replaced it as the leading imported bottled water. Perrier's business has never fully recovered. For another case of defective bottled water, see the *Global Focus* description of Coca-Cola's Dasani brand in the United Kingdom.

The Pepsi Hoax

PepsiCo was the target of a hoax when a New Orleans man contacted the Cable News Network (CNN) and alleged that he had found a syringe in a can of Diet Pepsi. This was only the first of several reported contaminations from different geographical areas. PepsiCo officials, knowing the reports were false and that the Diet Pepsi bottling process was completely safe, reacted to the negative publicity

Negative Publicity for Coca-Cola's Dasani in the United Kingdom

global focus

Unlike European brands of bottled water such as Evian and Perrier that come from mineral springs, Coca-Cola's Dasani brand is tap water that undergoes a rigid filtering process to remove chlorine and mineral particles. After these are removed, a mineral mix is added to the purified water to provide a fresh taste. Although Dasani is a success in North America, it was new to the European continent as of 2004. Coca-Cola chose the United Kingdom as the launching point for its planned European "invasion." First off, the brand received negative press from British tabloids, which harshly criticized Coca-Cola for marketing filtered tap water rather than the spring water that Europeans have grown to expect. This negative press may have doomed the brand from the outset, but the coup de grace came when Coke recalled Dasani after testing revealed that its bottled water had excessive levels of a chemical (bromate) that increases the risk of cancer after long-term exposure. The problem apparently resulted from adding calcium chloride to the water in compliance with the United Kingdom's regulation that all brands of bottled water contain calcium. Coke's batch of calcium chloride apparently contained unexpectedly high levels of bromide, and excessive levels of bromide's derivative, bromate, formed during production.

This incident put a rapid halt to Coke's plans to market Dasani globally. Although capable of marketing a variety of smaller brands in different countries, the company had hoped to gain the economies of scale that only a high-equity brand can provide. In light of this contamination problem, some observers believe Coke should drop Dasani in Europe and introduce another brand in its stead.

SOURCES: Adapted from Chad Terhune and Deborah Ball, "Dasani Recall Hurts Coke's Bid to Boost Water Sales in EU," *Wall Street Journal Online,* March 22, 2004, http://online.wsj.com; Chad Terhune, Betsy McKay, and Deborah Ball, "Coke Table Dasani Plans in Europe," *Wall Street Journal Online,* March 25, 2004, http://online.wsj.com.

by using the media. A video showing the bottling process of PepsiCo products was released shortly after the initial news broke and was seen by an estimated 187 million viewers. It demonstrated the remote possibility that a foreign object, especially something as large as a syringe, could be inserted in cans in the less than one second they are open for filling and capping. That same day, PepsiCo's president and chief executive officer appeared on ABC's *Nightline* along with the commissioner of the Food and Drug Administration (FDA). PepsiCo's chief executive officer assured viewers that the Diet Pepsi can was 99.9 percent safe, and the FDA commissioner warned consumers of the penalties for making false claims.

Two days later, the FDA commissioner noted at a news conference that "it is simply not logical to conclude that a nationwide tampering has occurred" and that the FDA was "unable to confirm even one case of tampering." These statements were later broadcast over national TV along with a video news release showing a consumer inserting a syringe into a Diet Pepsi can. She had been caught by the store's surveillance camera. With this exposure, the crisis was essentially over.

PepsiCo ran nationwide newspaper advertisements to assuage any residual consumer fears. The headlines to these full-page ads read, "Pepsi is pleased to announce . . . nothing." The ads proceeded to inform readers that "those stories about Diet Pepsi were simply a hoax. Plain and simple, not true." Although volume case sales dropped slightly during the period immediately following the hoax, sales returned to normal in a matter of weeks.

Coke in Europe

An accident in a Coca-Cola bottling plant in Belgium in 1999 introduced some tainted carbon dioxide into bottles of Coke, and European consumers, mostly in Belgium, reported becoming ill after drinking the product. Coca-Cola's initial response was to deny that its product was at fault, which prompted a public outcry in reaction to this corporate denial and created feelings among consumers that Coca-Cola officials did not care about their health and safety. Media throughout Europe wrote articles asserting that Coca-Cola products had poisoned consumers. Senior officers at Coca-Cola eventually got the message, and its PR people were put to work to offset the considerable damage to Coke's brand equity and profitability. Among other initiatives, the company hired thousands of Belgians to distribute coupons to grocery store shoppers for free 1.5-liter bottles. This incident resulted in millions of dollars of lost revenue, much more than likely would have been lost had the company responded more quickly and apologetically.[5]

Coke and Pepsi in India

As is well known, India is a huge country with a population exceeding one billion. Though historically India has not been a huge market for soft drinks, the market size is growing along with a rapidly increasing middle class. Coke and Pepsi, as well as many other consumer-goods marketers, see India as having huge growth potential. Unfortunately for Coke and Pepsi, an Indian environmental group released a report in 2003 claiming that its laboratory tests revealed that pesticide residues in various soft-drink brands bottled by Coke and Pepsi were at least 30 times higher than acceptable limits in Europe. Shortly after the report became public, sales of these two major soft-drink brands fell by over 30 percent.[6] Officials at both companies denied that their pesticide-related standards are any different in India than elsewhere. Nonetheless, India's supreme court issued a ruling that both Coke and Pepsi must provide warning labels on their soft-drink containers that indicate the level of pesticide residue. In view of this publicity disaster, it will be a major challenge for both companies to restore the trust Indian consumers had in these high-equity brands.

Corporate Response and Crisis Management

As the previous examples illustrate, product crises and negative publicity can hit a company at any time. The lesson to be learned is that quick and positive responses to negative publicity are imperative. Negative publicity is something to be dealt with head-on, not denied. When done effectively, reactive MPR can virtually save a brand or a company. A corporate response immediately following negative publicity can lessen the damage that will result, damage such as a diminution in the public's confidence in a company and its products or a major loss in sales and profits.

And in the era of the Internet, a company's brand image can be tarnished virtually immediately as the result of a product failure, defect, contamination problem, or any other form of negative marketing-related news. Consider the Firestone/Ford Explorer debacle that was mentioned previously. In the wake of news that its 15-inch tires fitted on Ford Explorer SUVs were responsible, at least in part, for hundreds of rollovers and more than 200 deaths, Bridgestone/Firestone issued a massive recall. This was *not* the first major recall of Firestone tires; in fact, nearly a quarter of a century earlier (in 1978) Firestone recalled hundreds of thousands of faulty tires. The damage was relatively minimal in that earlier time, however, perhaps because consumers were unaware of the severity of the problem and due to the hiring of highly respected actor Jimmy Stewart, who appeared in multiple TV commercials publicizing the brand's long history as a successful and trusted company.

Let's now move the calendar forward to August 2000 and Bridgestone/Firestone's recall of 6.5 million Firestone tires in that year. Newspapers, network television, and other media constantly reported one rollover accident after another. Officials at Ford denied that that company was at fault and placed the blame squarely on the shoulders of Bridgestone/Firestone. Consumer groups such as the Tire Action Group immediately had a presence on the Internet, and people in chat rooms routinely discussed the Ford Explorer's rollover accidents and the potential fault of Firestone's tires.

With the near-viral proliferation of information made possible via the Internet, it is difficult for companies to control the spread of negative information. According to some observers, the Internet magnifies consumer concerns, thus making it especially difficult to manage bad publicity in the Internet age. Although Bridgestone/Firestone was incredibly slow to respond to the negative publicity being disseminated, Ford realized the power of the Internet and created a banner ad that it placed on about 200 Web sites with the potential of reaching millions of people. The ad invited viewers to click through to Ford's recall site, which included information about the specific tire models included in the recall, the tire models that were appropriate for replacement, and locations of authorized replacement dealers. The site also provided press releases from Ford and a statement from the company's chief executive officer claiming that Ford does not take lightly its customers' safety and trust.

Whereas Bridgestone/Firestone was slow to react to the negative publicity, Ford adroitly took advantage of the speed and impact of the Internet to offset negative publicity directed toward it. Perhaps the Ford Explorer was itself not free of blame for the numerous rollover accidents, but due in large part to Ford's PR efforts, the general public placed the blame almost exclusively on Firestone. A consultancy firm reported that Firestone's score on a reputation index had plummeted by an amount never before registered in its research on company and brand reputations.[7]

Just as Ford used the Internet to its advantage in offsetting bad publicity about Firestone tires and the Explorer's rollover accidents, other company's faced with negative publicity must also avail themselves of the power of this medium. One observer has compared the spread of negative product news via the Internet as equivalent to "reverse viral marketing."[8] To offset this "virus," companies can use the Internet to convey their own news in hopes of partially offsetting the negative information about their brands. This is especially important in the present era of great skepticism where consumers have grown increasingly cynical of corporations due to the shenanigans of companies such as Adelphia, Enron, Tyco, WorldCom, and others.

It is important to note, however, that not all consumers are equally swayed by negative publicity about a brand or company. In particular, consumers who hold more positive evaluations of a company are more likely to challenge negative publicity about that company and thus are less likely to experience diminished evaluations following negative publicity. On the other hand, those who are less loyal are especially susceptible to the adverse effects of negative publicity.[9]

The Special Case of Rumors and Urban Legends

You have heard them and probably helped spread them since you were a child in elementary school. They are often vicious and malicious. Sometimes they are just comical. Almost always they are false. We are talking about rumors and urban legends. As a technical aside, urban legends and rumors capture slightly different phenomena. Whereas urban legends are a form of rumor, they go beyond rumor by transmitting a story involving the use of irony; that is, urban legends convey subtle messages that are in contradiction of what is literally expressed in the story context.[10] As a case in point, consider the "Gucci Kangaroo" legend:

Have you heard about the American tourists who were driving in the outback of Australia? They had been drinking, and it seems that their car hit a kangaroo. Thinking the kangaroo to be dead, the tourists decided to take a gag photograph. They hastily propped the kangaroo up against a fence and dressed it in the driver's Gucci jacket. They proceeded to take photographs of the well-dressed marsupial. Well, it seems that the kangaroo had merely been stunned rather than dead. All of a sudden he revived and jumped away wearing the man's jacket, which also contained the driver's license, money, and airline ticket.[11]

Technical distinction noted, we need not get hung up differentiating between the more general case of rumors and the specific instance of urban legends. Hereafter we will refer simply to rumors in a sense that encompasses urban legends. It further is noteworthy that our interest involves only those rumors that involve products, brands, stores, or other objects of marketing practice.[12] A variety of Internet Web sites focus on rumors and urban legends, and many of these refer to products, technological developments, and even specific brands. For a review of many types of urban legends, go to Urban Legends Reference Pages (http://www.snopes.com) and see legends related to business and specific products such as automobiles and computers.

Commercial rumors are widely circulated but unverified propositions about a product, brand, company, store, or other commercial target.[13] Rumors are probably the most difficult problem faced by public relations personnel. What makes rumors so troublesome is that they spread like wildfire and almost always state or imply something very undesirable, and possibly repulsive, about the target of the rumor.[14] For example, the rumor spread quickly around the United States that because Mountain Dew is colored with a dye (Yellow 5), drinking the product lowers a man's sperm count. Though untrue, this urban legend influenced teenager's soft-drink consumption behavior, with some actually consuming more Mountain Dew than normal as a means of birth control and others consuming less for fear that later in life they would not be able to have children.[15]

Consider also the case of the persistent rumor and urban legend that for years surrounded Procter & Gamble (P&G). The rumor involved P&G's famous man-in-the-moon logo, which was claimed to be a symbol of the devil. According to the rumormongers, when the stars in the old logo were connected, the number *666* (a symbol of the Antichrist) was formed. Also, the curls in the man-in-the-moon's beard also supposedly formed *666* when held up to a mirror.

Although nonsensical, this rumor spread throughout the Midwest and South. P&G eventually decided to drop the old logo and change to a new one. The new logo retains the 13 stars, which represent the original U.S. colonies, but eliminates the curly hairs in the beard that appeared to form the number *666*.

Following are some other rumors and urban legends you may have heard at one time or another. Many of these are from the past and none are true, but all have been widely circulated:

- McDonald's Corporation makes sizable donations to the Church of Satan.
- Wendy's hamburgers contain something other than beef, namely red worms. (Other versions of this rumor have substituted McDonald's or Burger King as the target.)
- Pop Rocks (a carbonated candy made by General Foods) explode in your stomach when mixed with soda.
- Bubble Yum chewing gum contains spider eggs.
- A woman while shopping in a Kmart store was bitten by a poisonous snake when trying on a coat imported from Taiwan.
- A boy and his date stopped at a Kentucky Fried Chicken (KFC) restaurant on their way to a movie. Later the girl became violently ill, and the boy rushed her to the hospital. The examining physician said the girl appeared to have been poisoned. The boy went to the car and retrieved an oddly shaped half-eaten piece from the KFC bucket. The physician recognized it to be the remains of a rat. It was determined that the girl died from consuming a fatal amount of strychnine from the rat's body.[16]
- In what is referred to as the "Gerber Myth," thousands of consumers sent letters to a post office box in Minneapolis following a rumor circulating on the Internet (as well as in church bulletins and day-care centers) that Gerber, a baby food company, was giving away $500 savings bonds as part of a lawsuit settlement. Complying with the rumor's advice, parents mailed copies of their

child's birth certificate and Social Security card to the Minneapolis address. For a period of time, the post office box received daily between 10,000 and 12,000 pieces of Gerber Myth mail.

The preceding examples illustrate two basic types of commercial rumors: conspiracy and contamination.[17] **Conspiracy rumors** involve supposed company policies or practices that are threatening or ideologically undesirable to consumers. For example, a conspiracy rumor circulated in New Orleans claiming that the founder of the Popeyes restaurant chain, Al Copeland, supported a reprehensible politician known to have Ku Klux Klan and Nazi connections. Copeland immediately called a press conference, vehemently denied any connections with the politician, and offered a $25,000 reward for information leading to the source of the rumor. This swift response squashed the rumor before it gained momentum.[18]

Another example of a conspiracy rumor involved the little-known Brooklyn Bottling Corporation. This company introduced an inexpensive line of soft drinks under the name Tropical Fantasy. Tropical Fantasy quickly gained sales momentum and was heading toward becoming the top-selling brand in small grocery stores in many northeastern markets. But then rumor peddlers went to work. Leaflets started appearing in low-income neighborhoods warning consumers away from Tropical Fantasy and claiming that the brand was manufactured by the Ku Klux Klan and contained stimulants that would sterilize African-American men. Angry Tropical Fantasy drinkers threatened distributors with baseball bats and threw bottles at delivery trucks. Some stores stopped accepting shipments. Sales of Tropical Fantasy plummeted.[19] One can only wonder whether an employee of a competitive brand may have started this malicious rumor.

Contamination rumors deal with undesirable or harmful product or store features. For example, a rumor started in Reno, Nevada, that the Mexican imported beer Corona was contaminated with urine. A beer distributor in Reno who handled Heineken, a competitive brand, actually had initiated the rumor. Corona sales fell by 80 percent in some markets. The rumor was hushed when an out-of-court settlement against the Reno distributor required a public statement declaring that Corona was not contaminated.

What Is the Best Way to Handle a Rumor?

When confronted with a rumor, some companies believe that doing nothing is the best way to handle it. This cautious approach is apparently based on the fear that an antirumor campaign will call attention to the rumor itself. An expert on rumors claims that rumors are like fires, and, like fires, time is the worst enemy. His advice is to not merely hope that a rumor will simmer down but to combat it swiftly and decisively to put it out![20] An antirumor media campaign needs to be launched as quickly as possible.

An antirumor campaign would minimally involve the following activities: (1) deciding on the specific points in the rumor that need to be refuted; (2) emphasizing that the conspiracy or contamination rumor is untrue and unfair; (3) picking appropriate media and vehicles for delivering the antirumor message; and (4) selecting a credible spokesperson (such as a scientist, a government official as in the case of the Pepsi hoax described previously, a civic leader, or a respected theologian) to deliver the message on the company's behalf.[21]

Sponsorship Marketing

Sponsorships represent a rapidly growing aspect of marketing communications, and are considered by most marketing executives as an important marketing tool; indeed, more than two-thirds of chief marketing officers who responded to a recent survey indicated that event sponsorship is a vital marketing function.[22]

© Associated Press/AP

Sponsorships involve investments in events or causes for the purpose of achieving various corporate objectives, especially ones related to enhancing brand equity and augmenting sales. The following definition captures the practice of sponsorship marketing:

> *[S]ponsorship involves two main activities: (1) an exchange between a sponsor [such as a brand] and a sponsee [such as a sporting event] whereby the latter receives a fee and the former obtains the right to associate itself with the activity sponsored and (2) the marketing of the association by the sponsor. Both activities are necessary if the sponsorship fee is to be a meaningful investment.*[23]

Event sponsorships range from supporting athletic events (such as golf and tennis tournaments, college football bowl games, the Olympics, extreme sports such as snowboarding, and soccer) to underwriting rock concerts and supporting festivals and fairs. Cause-oriented sponsorships typically involve supporting causes deemed to be of interest to some facet of society, such as environmental protection and wildlife preservation.

At least five factors account for the growth in sponsorships:[24]

1. By attaching their names to special events and causes, companies are able to avoid the clutter inherent in advertising media. For example, Visa USA sponsors the Triple Crown of horse racing consisting of the Kentucky Derby, the Preakness Stakes, and the Belmont Stakes. Visa's vice president of marketing justified this choice on grounds that horse racing is an uncluttered area, thus allowing Visa to receive primary attention from consumers. It is noteworthy, however, that some extensively sponsored events such as the National Association for Stock Car Auto Racing (NASCAR), have become highly cluttered.
2. Sponsorships help companies respond to consumers' changing media habits. For example, with the decline in network-television viewing, sponsorships offer a potentially effective and cost-efficient way to reach customers.
3. Sponsorships help companies gain the approval of various constituencies, including stockholders, employees, and society at large.
4. Relationships forged between a brand and a sponsored event can serve to enhance a brand's equity, both by increasing consumers' awareness of the brand and by enhancing its image.[25]
5. The sponsorship of special events and causes enables marketers to target their communications and promotional efforts to specific geographic regions or to specific demographic and lifestyle groups. For example, Columbia Sportswear Company was one of the sponsors of the 2005 Albuquerque International Balloon Fiesta. This event attracts thousands of photographers and other enthusiasts and is thus an ideal venue for creating a strong, positive link with Columbia Sportswear.

Now that we have provided an overview of the general features of sponsorship marketing, the following sections detail the practice of event and cause-oriented sponsorships, respectively.

Event Sponsorships

Though relatively small compared to the two major components of the marcom mix—that is, advertising and promotions—expenditures on event sponsorship are increasing. Worldwide, brand marketers are estimated to spend around $50 billion on event sponsorships in 2006.[26] U.S. marketers alone will spend more than $10 billion on events in that same year.[27] Well over half of this amount goes toward sponsoring various sporting events such as motor sports (e.g., NASCAR), golf and tennis, professional sports leagues and teams, and the Olympics.[28] Companies also sponsor entertainment events and tours, festivals and fairs, the arts, and cultural institutions.

Thousands of companies invest in some form of **event sponsorship**, which is defined as a form of brand promotion that ties a brand to a meaningful athletic, entertainment, cultural, social, or other type of high-interest public activity. Event marketing is distinct from advertising, promotion, point-of-purchase merchandising, or public relations, but it generally incorporates elements from all these communications tools.

Selecting Sponsorship Events

Marketers sponsor events for purposes of developing relationships with consumers, enhancing brand equity, and strengthening ties with the trade. Successful event sponsorships require a meaningful *fit* among the brand, the event, and the target market. Budget Rent A Car, for example, oriented much of its marketing communications efforts toward women, who are the key decision makers on car rentals, both as business and leisure travelers and as coordinators of company travel. Accordingly, Budget became a major sponsor of women's professional sports leagues such as the Ladies Professional Golf Association and the Women's Tennis Association.

What specific factors should a company consider when selecting an event? The following points identify the key issues to consider when evaluating whether an event represents a suitable association for a brand:[29]

1. *Image matchup*—Is the event consistent with the brand image, and will it benefit the image? The Coleman Company, a maker of grills and other outdoor equipment, sponsors NASCAR races, fishing tournaments, and country-music festivals. All these events appropriately match Coleman's image and also represent appropriate venues for its target customers. Unionbay, a jeans and sportswear brand, along with soft-drink brand Mountain Dew and snowboard maker Burton, sponsored the U.S. Open Snowboarding Championships. It would seem that this event matches perfectly the images of all three brands.
2. *Target audience fit*—Does the event offer a strong likelihood of reaching the desired target audience? Wal-Mart stores and General Mills' Hamburger Helper brand are two of the sponsors of fishing competitions, which might seem like a limited event for these brands to sponsor until it is pointed out that there are more than 50 million Americans who are active fishermen (and women).[30] The Old Navy chain of retail clothing stores has sponsored Major League Soccer. The demographics of Old Navy's typical customer match well the characteristics of consumers who both participate in soccer and view it live or on television. H. J. Heinz Company's frozen pizza-topped snack, Bagel Bites, has sponsored ESPN's winter and summer X Games (X stands for *extreme sports*) in an appeal to teenagers. This event is just behind the Olympic Games in its appeal to 6- to 17-year-olds. Professional bull riding holds a tour that visits more than 70 cities annually. Cowboys from Australia, Brazil, Canada, and the United States compete on the bull-riding tour, and millions of TV viewers and event attendees are loyal followers. Sponsoring companies' products that match well with the demographic and lifestyle profiles of bull-riding enthusiasts include Anheuser-Busch Bud Light, Carhartt work clothing, DeWalt tools, Jack Daniel's whiskey, Wrangler jeans, and Dickies line of work and casual clothing.
3. *Sponsor misidentification*—Is this event one that the competition has previously sponsored, and therefore is there a risk of being perceived as "me-too-istic" and confusing the target audience as to the sponsor's identity? Sponsor misidentification is not a trivial issue. For example, Coca-Cola paid $250 million to be the official soft drink of the National Football League (NFL) for a

five-year period. After sponsoring the NFL for several years, a general survey (not about Coca-Cola per se) asked football fans to name brands that sponsor the NFL. Thirty-five percent of the respondents named Coke as an NFL sponsor. Unfortunately (for Coca-Cola), another 34 percent falsely identified Pepsi-Cola as a sponsor![31]

4. *Clutter*—As with most every marcom communications medium, an event sponsor typically competes for signage and attention from every other company that sponsors the event. It obviously makes little sense to sponsor an event unless live participants and television viewers are likely to notice your brand and associate it with the event that it is paying to sponsor. NASCAR, for example, attracts a large number of sponsors due to the extraordinary growth rate in fan interest. However, recognizing the problem with sponsorship clutter, one observer noted that unless a brand is a prime NASCAR sponsor it easily "can get lost on the bumper."[32]
5. *Complement other marcom elements*—Does the event complement existing sponsorships and fit with other marcom programs for the brand? Many brands sponsor multiple events. In the spirit of integrated marketing communications, it is important that these events "speak with a single voice." (If the notion of speaking with a single voice is unclear, please refer back to the IMC discussion in Chapter 1.)
6. *Economic viability*—This last point raises the all-important issue about budget constraints. Companies that sponsor events must support the sponsorships with adequate advertising, point-of-purchase materials, and publicity.[33] One professional in the sponsorship arena uses the rule of thumb that two to three times the cost of a sponsorship must be spent in properly supporting it and offers the following advice:

A sponsorship is an opportunity to spend money. But like a car without gasoline, sponsorship without sufficient funds to maximize it goes nowhere. Therein lies the biggest secret to successfully leveraging sponsorship: It's not worth spending money for rights fees unless you are prepared to properly support it.[34]

Creating Customized Events

Some firms develop their own events rather than sponsoring existing events. For example, managers of the Kibbles 'n Bits brand of dog food developed the "Do Your Bit for Kibbles and Bits" tour that covered 33 U.S. cities during a three-month period. The event involved having consumers in each of these cities enter their dogs into a competition to determine which dog would be picked for the brand's next TV commercial based on the quality of tricks the dog would perform to receive Kibbles 'n Bits food. More than 11,000 people attended the event, and 2,500 dogs were entered into the competition. The Kibbles 'n Bits brand gained anywhere from one to four share points in key markets during this event.[35]

In general, there are two major reasons that brand managers choose to customize their own events rather than sponsor events conducted by another organization. First, having a customized event provides a brand total control over the event. This eliminates externally imposed timing demands or other constraints and also removes the problem of clutter from too many other sponsors. Also, the customized event is developed to match perfectly the brand's target audience and to maximize the opportunity to enhance the brand's image and sales. A second reason for the customization trend is that there is a good chance that a specially designed event is more effective but less costly than a preexisting event.

It would be simplistic to conclude that brand managers or higher-level marketing executives should eschew sponsoring well-known and prestigious events. Sponsoring the Olympics or another major sporting or entertainment event can greatly enhance a brand's image and boost sales volume. Indeed, successfully achieving a strong link with an event that is highly valued means that the event's stature may transfer at least in some small part to the sponsoring brand. However, achieving such an outcome requires that a strong, durable, and positive link be established between the sponsoring brand and the event. All too often individual brands are swamped by larger and better-known sponsoring brands and no solid or durable link is formed. This being the case, it is doubtful that the sponsorship represents a good return on investment.[36]

Ambushing Events

In addition to increased customization, a number of companies engage in what is called *ambush marketing*, or simply *ambushing*. **Ambushing** takes place when companies that are *not* official sponsors of an event undertake marketing efforts to convey the impression that they are.[37] For example, research following a past summer Olympics in Atlanta determined that 72 percent of respondents to a survey identified Visa as an official sponsor of the Olympic Games and that 54 percent named American Express as a sponsor. As a matter of fact, Visa paid $40 million to sponsor the Olympics, whereas American Express simply advertised heavily during the telecast of the Olympics.[38]

One may question whether it is ethical to ambush a competitor's sponsorship of an event, but a counterargument can easily be made that ambushing is simply a financially prudent way of offsetting a competitor's effort to obtain an advantage over your company or brand. (The ethical aspects of ambushing would make for interesting class discussion.)

Measuring Success

Whether participating as an official sponsor of an event, customizing your own event, or ambushing a competitor's sponsorship, the results from all these efforts must be measured to determine effectiveness. As always, *accountability* is the key. Sponsorships cannot be justified unless there is proof that brand equity and financial objectives are being achieved. Many critics have claimed that sponsorship arrangements often involve little more than managerial ego trips—that is, key executives sponsor high-profile events as a means of meeting famous athletes or entertainers and gaining great tickets and luxurious accommodations. Whether this cynical perspective is correct is beyond this text to resolve, but the point to be emphasized is that a brand's welfare cannot be compromised by executive caprice.

As always, measuring whether an event has been successful requires, first, that the brand marketer specify the objective(s) that the sponsorship is intended to accomplish. Second, to measure results, there has to be a baseline against which to compare some outcome measure. This baseline is typically a premeasure of brand awareness, brand associations, or attitudes prior to sponsoring an event. Third, it is necessary to measure the same variable (awareness, associations, etc.) after the event to determine whether there has been a positive change from the baseline premeasure.

The metrics used to measure sponsorship effectiveness are typically straightforward. The measure most frequently used by companies is a simple head count of how many people attended an event.[39] The total cost of the event is then divided by the number of attendees to obtain a measure of efficiency; this measure is useful for comparison against the per-capita costs of other sponsorships. Other frequently used measures include tracking sales volume following an event, determining how many hits to the brand's Web site occurred postevent, and counting the number of samples or coupons that were distributed.

Cause-Related Marketing

A relatively minor but important aspect of overall sponsorships, cause-related marketing involves an amalgam of public relations, sales promotion, and corporate philanthropy. As of 2004, American marketers spent $1 billion on cause-related marketing.[40] **Cause-related marketing (CRM)** entails alliances that companies form with *nonprofit organizations* to promote their mutual interests. Companies wish to enhance their brands' images and sales, whereas nonprofit partners obtain additional funding by aligning their causes with corporate sponsors. Though CRM was initiated in the United States in the early 1980s, companies throughout the world have become active participants in supporting causes.

There are several varieties of cause-related practices, but the most common form of CRM arrangement involves a company contributing to a designated cause every time the customer undertakes some action that supports the company and its brands. The company's contribution is, in other words, contingent on the customer performing a behavior (such as buying a product or redeeming a coupon) that benefits the firm. Obviously, firms aligning themselves with particular causes do so partially with philanthropic intentions but also with interest in enhancing their brands' images and, frankly, selling more products, preferably at higher prices. As always, whether cause-related alignments accomplish these goals depends very much on the specifics of the situation—in this case, the nature of the product involved and the magnitude of the contribution offered.[41]

The following examples illustrate how cause-related marketing operates.

- Whirlpool Corporation's KitchenAid division has been a supporter of the Susan G. Komen Breast Cancer Foundation. In a unique program, Whirlpool donated $50 to the foundation for every purchase of a pink mixer (pink being the symbol for breast cancer awareness) that was purchased via the company's Web site or a toll-free telephone number. The $50 donation represented a generous 17 percent of the revenue Whirlpool obtained for this special-colored mixer priced at $289.99.
- General Mills' Yoplait brand yogurt also supports the Susan G. Komen Breast Cancer Foundation. In its Save Lids to Save Lives promotion, Yoplait made a 10-cent contribution to the Komen Foundation for every lid that consumers mailed back to the company (see Figure 20.1).
- In another breast cancer CRM program, Lee Jeans conducted Lee National Denim Day. Individuals were urged to wear jeans to work on one particular day in October and to donate $5 to the Susan G. Komen Breast Cancer Foundation.
- The *IMC Focus* on page 594 provides a more detailed description of another program that is aligned with the Susan G. Komen Breast Cancer Foundation, namely, Georgia-Pacific's Quilts of Inspiration program.
- In support of the Share Our Strength program that is dedicated to reducing hunger and poverty, Tyson Foods donated more than 12 million pounds of chicken and other food products. For every package purchased, Tyson donated a pound of chicken, beef, or pork to the Share Our Strength program—up to three million pounds (see Figure 20.2).
- The Campbell Soup Company has for more than a quarter century sponsored the Labels for Education program, which helps schools obtain classroom supplies by asking families to collect labels from various Campbell's brands. Since the program began, Campbell has contributed items worth at least $100 million to schools and organizations in exchange for the millions of labels submitted.
- For each Heinz baby food label mailed in by consumers, H. J. Heinz Company contributed 6 cents to a hospital near the consumer's home.
- Nabisco Brands donated $1 to the Juvenile Diabetes Research Foundation for each certificate that was redeemed with a Ritz-brand proof of purchase.
- Hershey donated 25 cents to local children's hospitals for each Hershey coupon redeemed.

Figure 20.1
Yoplait's Save Lids to Save Lives CRM Program

Figure 20.2 Tyson's Share Our Strength CRM Program

Georgia Pacific's Quilts of Inspiration CRM Program

imc focus

Georgia-Pacific, the maker of Quilted Northern Ultra bath tissue (among many other products), wanted a strategic way to differentiate itself from other brands that compete in this mundane product category, where product functionality and price are typically the primary purchase considerations. How, beyond appeals to pure functionality or price, could this brand be looked upon as different, in a positive way, than other brands? For example, would it be possible to create a positive emotional response?

Enter a role for cause-related marketing. The brand management team for Quilted Northern made the strategic decision to link the brand with the Susan G. Komen Breast Cancer Foundation by using a CRM program along with other marcom initiatives. During a six-month period in 2004, Georgia-Pacific's Quilts of Inspiration program teamed with a TV program, *The View,* and conducted a sweepstakes promotion that invited participants to submit quilt blocks containing inspirational messages for women affected by breast cancer. A total of 1,422 blocks were submitted during the six-month period, including 71 from celebrities. The quilt formed from these blocks was unveiled on *The View* and subsequently auctioned online to benefit the Komen Foundation.

For its part, Georgia-Pacific contributed 50 cents for every Quilted Northern Ultra UPC that consumers mailed in. GP promised to donate up to $500,000 annually in its role to fight breast cancer. Although the sales gain certainly cannot be attributed exclusively or even primarily to the CRM program, the case volume for this brand of bath tissue rose over 25 percent and increased its market share by nearly a full share point. It would appear that this campaign represents a classic win-win-win situation. That is, the Komen Foundation benefited by receipts up to $500,000; Georgia-Pacific gained by increasing sales and market share; and consumers were rewarded by knowing they were contributing to an important cause when submitting a UPC from the purchase of Quilted Northern Ultra.

SOURCE: Adapted from Chuck Stogel, "G-P Rolls Out Pink Carpet for Breast Cancer Effort," *Brandweek,* March 7, 2005, R16.

- Reynolds Metals Company, a maker of aluminum foil and other food packaging products, contributed 5 cents to local Meals on Wheels programs every time any of three Reynolds brands was purchased.
- Domino's Pizza teamed with Easter Seals in an ambitious CRM effort. Twenty-eight million Domino's Pizza box tops offered customers a coupon worth up to $10 toward the purchase of the electronic game called SimCity 3000. When redeeming coupons, consumers were required to send in $5 donations to Easter Seals.

The Benefits of CRM

Cause-related marketing is corporate philanthropy based on profit-motivated giving. In addition to helping worthy causes, corporations satisfy their own tactical and strategic objectives when undertaking cause-related efforts. By supporting a deserving cause, a company can (1) enhance its corporate or brand image, (2) thwart negative publicity, (3) generate incremental sales, (4) increase brand awareness, (5) broaden its customer base, (6) reach new market segments, and (7) increase a brand's retail merchandising activity.[42]

Research reveals that consumers have favorable attitudes toward cause-related marketing efforts. According to the 2004 Cone Corporate Citizenship Study, the vast majority of Americans (72 percent) think it is acceptable for companies to involve a cause in their marketing. Moreover, an even larger proportion of respondents to this survey (86 percent) indicated that they would be likely to switch from one brand to another of equal quality and price if the other brand associates itself with a cause. This latter percentage takes on added significance when noting that in 1993, the first year Cone conducted its Corporate Citizenship Study, the percentage of consumers indicating they would switch brands to a brand supporting a cause was only 66 percent.[43]

On the downside, about one-half of the sample in another study expressed negative attitudes toward CRM; this negativity is due in large part to consumers' cynicism about the sponsoring firm's self-serving motive.[44] Research has revealed that brands may not benefit from CRM efforts if their support is perceived as having an ulterior motive rather than authentic concern about the sponsored cause.[45] Also, consumers are distrustful of CRM programs that are vague in terms of exactly how much will be donated to the cause, and, in fact, the majority of CRM offers are abstract and unclear about the amount of contribution (e.g., "a portion of the proceeds will be donated").[46] In comparison with some ambiguous offers, the illustrations of CRM programs are perfectly clear as to how much will be donated. The illustrations are notable for their clarity and thus should earn consumers' respect rather than displeasure.

It's a Matter of Fit

How should a company decide which cause to support? Although there are many worthy causes, only a subset is relevant to the interests of any brand and its target audience. Selecting an appropriate cause is a matter of fitting the brand to a cause that is naturally related to the brand's attributes, benefits, or image and also relates closely to the target market's interests. When there is a natural congruence between the sponsor and the cause, the sponsoring brand benefits in terms of being perceived as more socially responsible and is looked upon more favorably.[47] The absence of a close fit can suggest to consumers that the brand is sponsoring a cause merely for self-serving reasons. Campbell Soup Company's Labels for Education program beautifully matches the target audience of children and their parents who consume Campbell's branded products. In fact, the same can be said of all of the illustrative examples of CRM programs provided previously.

Accountability

In the final analysis, brand marketers are obligated to show that their CRM efforts yield sufficient return on investment or achieve other important, nonfinancial objectives. Corporate philanthropy is wonderful, but cause-related marketing is not needed for this purpose—companies can contribute to worthy causes without tying the contribution to consumers' buying a particular brand.[48] However, when employing a cause-related marketing effort, a company intends to accomplish marketing goals (such as improved sales or enhanced image) rather than merely exercising its philanthropic aspirations. Hence, a CRM effort should be founded on specific objectives—just the same as any marcom campaign. Research—such as a pre- and posttest, as described for event sponsorships—is absolutely essential to determine whether a CRM effort has achieved its objective and is thereby strategically and financially accountable.

Courtesy of Campbell Soup Company

Colgate-Palmolive applied a straightforward formula in measuring the effectiveness of one of its sponsorships in which the CRM program was based on consumers redeeming FSI coupons. Using scanner data, Colgate compared product sales in the three weeks following a coupon drop with the average sales for the preceding six months. The difference between these two sales figures was multiplied by the brand's net profit margin, and the event's cost on a per-unit basis was subtracted to determine the incremental profit.[49] This procedure has the virtue of being logically sound and easy to implement.

Summary

This chapter covered two major topics: marketing public relations and sponsorship marketing. Public relations (PR) entails a variety of functions and activities that are directed at fostering harmonious interactions with an organization's publics (customers, employees, stockholders, governments, and so forth). An important distinction was made between general public relations (general PR), which deals with overall managerial issues and problems (such as relations with stockholders and employees), and marketing public relations (MPR). The chapter focused on MPR.

MPR consists of proactive MPR and reactive MPR. Proactive MPR is an increasingly important tool in addition to advertising and promotions for enhancing a brand's equity and market share. Proactive MPR is dictated by a company's marketing objectives. It seeks opportunities rather than solves problems. Reactive MPR, on the other hand, responds to external pressures and typically deals with changes that have negative consequences for an organization. Handling negative publicity and rumors are two areas in which reactive PR is most needed.

The other major topic covered in this chapter was sponsorship marketing. Sponsorships involve investments in events and causes to achieve various corporate objectives. Event marketing is a rapidly growing facet of marketing communications. Though small in comparison with advertising and other major promotional elements, expenditures on event promotions are estimated to exceed $10 billion in 2006. Event marketing is a form of brand promotion that ties a brand to a meaningful athletic, cultural, social, or other type of high-interest public activity or entertainment. Event marketing is growing because it provides companies with alternatives to the cluttered mass media, an ability to segment consumers on a local or regional basis, and opportunities for reaching narrow lifestyle groups whose consumption behavior can be tied to the event.

Cause-related marketing (CRM) is a relatively minor aspect of overall sponsorship but a practice that is growing in importance. Although there are several varieties of CRM programs, the distinctive feature of the most common form of CRM is that a company's contribution to a designated cause is linked to customers engaging in revenue-producing exchanges with the firm. Cause-related marketing serves corporate interests while helping worthy causes. Well-conducted CRM programs represent a win-win-win situation for corporate sponsors, the causes that are sponsored, and the consumers who engage in behaviors that generate funds for a worthy cause.

Discussion Questions

1. Select a brand of your choice, preferably one that you really like and purchase regularly. Assuming that this brand is not presently involved in a cause sponsorship, propose a nonprofit organization with which your chosen brand might align itself. Also, devise a specific CRM program for this brand that would enhance the brand's sales volume and contribute to the cause.
2. Assume you are the owner of a restaurant in your college or university community. A rumor about your business has circulated claiming that your head chef has AIDS. Your business is falling off. Explain precisely how you would combat this rumor.
3. What are the advantages of publicity compared with advertising?
4. Some marketing practitioners consider publicity to be too difficult to control and measure. Evaluate these criticisms.

5. Some marketing people claim that any news about a brand, negative or positive, is good as long as it enables the brand to get noticed and encourages people to talk about the brand. Do you agree that negative publicity is always good? Under what conditions might it *not* be good?
6. Many homeowners perform a chore each spring (or even more often) that involves refreshing the landscaping surrounding their homes by covering the ground around plants and other ornamental vegetation with some form of mulch. Over time the mulch either washes away or fades in color, thus requiring periodic refreshment. In view of the aggravation and expense of this periodic task, a long-term solution has been devised. In particular, companies are now offering mulch made from recycled vehicle tires that is shaped and colored to look like natural mulch. This unnatural mulch has the advantage of lasting for up to 10 years because it doesn't fade in the sun or wash or blow away as easily as does natural mulch. On the other hand, the upfront expense is about three times greater than when landscaping with natural mulch. All said, how might you use proactive MPR to create some inexpensive brand exposure and incremental sales for artificial mulch made from recycled tires?
7. Assume you are the director of your college or university's athletic department. A major story hits the news claiming that several of your athletes received inappropriate assistance writing term papers. Supposing the story is untrue (in other words, that this is nothing but a rumor), how would you handle this negative publicity?
8. Faced with the rumor about Corona beer being contaminated with urine (see the discussion earlier in the chapter), what course of action would you have taken if the Heineken distributor in Reno had not been identified as starting the rumor? In other words, if the source of the rumor were unknown, what steps would you have taken?
9. Classify the various rumors presented in the text (e.g., P&G's logo and McDonald's/Church of Satan connection) as either conspiracy or contamination rumors.
10. Describe two or three commercial rumors, or urban legends, other than those mentioned in the chapter. Identify each as either a conspiracy or a contamination rumor. Describe how you think these rumors started and why people apparently consider them newsworthy enough to pass along. (You might want to locate an urban legend Internet site for ideas. See, for example, http://www.snopes.com.)
11. Is ambushing unethical or just smart, hard-nosed marketing?
12. In 1999, the year after Mark McGwire had slugged a record-smashing 70 home runs—a record broken three years later by Barry Bonds—the coffee chain Starbucks contributed $5,000 to child-literacy causes for each home run McGwire hit. Explain why this is or is not, in your opinion, a good CRM program from Starbucks' perspective.

ENDNOTES

1. Jonathan Eig, "For That Sweet Smell of Success, Try Scented Bowling Balls," *Wall Street Journal Online,* March 14, 2005, http://online.wsj.com.
2. The dividing line between marketing PR and general PR is not perfectly clear. For further discussion, see Philip J. Kitchen and Danny Moss, "Marketing and Public Relations: The Relationship Revisited," *Journal of Marketing Communications* 1 (June 1995), 105–118.
3. Al Ries and Laura Ries, *The Fall of Advertising & the Rise of PR* (New York: HarperBusiness, 2002).
4. Paul Holmes, "Senior Marketers Are Sharply Divided about the Role of PR in the Overall Mix," *Advertising Age,* January 24, 2005, C1.
5. Amie Smith, "Coke's European Resurgence," *Promo,* December 1999, 91.

6. Joanna Slater, "Coke, Pepsi Fight Charges of Product Contamination," *Wall Street Journal Online,* August 15, 2003, http://online.wsj.com.
7. Jean Halliday, "Firestone's Dilemma: Can This Brand Be Saved?" *Advertising Age,* September 4, 2000, 1, 54; William H. Holstein, "Guarding the Brand Is Job 1," *U.S. News & World Report,* September 11, 2000; Karen Lundegaard, "The Web @ Work? / Ford Motor Company," *Wall Street Journal Online,* October 16, 2000, http://online.wsj.com.
8. Dana James quoting PR man Jack Bergen in "When Your Company Goes Code Blue," *Marketing News,* November 6, 2000, 1, 15.
9. Rohini Ahluwalia, Robert E. Burnkrant, and H. Rao Unnava, "Consumer Response to Negative Publicity: The Moderating Role of Commitment," *Journal of Marketing Research* 37 (May 2000), 203–214. For another related finding, see Niraj Dawar and Madan M. Pillutla, "Impact of Product-Harm Crises on Brand Equity: The Moderating Role of Consumer Expectations," *Journal of Marketing Research* 37 (May 2000), 215–226.
10. For an insightful discussion of urban legends and an interesting experiment testing factors influencing the likelihood that legends will be transmitted, see D. Todd Donavan, John C. Mowen, and Goutam Chakraborty, "Urban Legends: The Word-of-Mouth Communication of Morality Through Negative Story Content," *Marketing Letters* 10 (February 1999), 23–34.
11. Ibid.
12. Donavan et al.'s content analysis of 100 urban legends revealed that 45 percent included product references, 12 percent involved warnings about innovations and technology, and 10 percent identified specific brands.
13. This definition is adapted from Fredrick Koenig, *Rumor in the Marketplace: The Social Psychology of Commercial Hearsay* (Dover, Mass.: Auburn House, 1985), 2.
14. For a review of the academic literature related to rumors as well as inspection of three interesting studies, see Michael A. Kamins, Valerie S. Folkes, and Lars Perner, "Consumer Responses to Rumors: Good News, Bad News," *Journal of Consumer Psychology* 6, no. 2 (1997), 165–187.
15. Ellen Joan Pollock, "Why Mountain Dew Is Now Grist for Fertile Teen Gossip," *Wall Street Journal Online,* October 14, 1999, http://online.wsj.com.
16. These rumors, all of which are false, have been in circulation at one time or another since the 1970s. All are thoroughly documented and analyzed in Koenig's fascinating book, *Rumor in the Marketplace.*
17. Koenig, *Rumor in the Marketplace,* 19.
18. Amy E. Gross, "How Popeyes and Reebok Confronted Product Rumors," *Adweek's Marketing Week,* October 22, 1990, 27.
19. "A Storm over Tropical Fantasy," *Newsweek,* April 22, 1991, 34.
20. Koenig, *Rumor in the Marketplace,* 167.
21. These recommendations are adapted from ibid., 172–173.
22. Kate Maddox, "Report Finds Most CMOs View Events as 'Vital'," *BtoB,* March 14, 2005, 6.
23. T. Bettina Cornwell and Isabelle Maignan, "An International Review of Sponsorship Research," *Journal of Advertising* 27 (spring 1998), 11.
24. The first three factors are adapted from Meryl Paula Gardner and Phillip Joel Shuman, "Sponsorship: An Important Component of the Promotions Mix," *Journal of Advertising* 16, no. 1 (1987), 11–17.
25. T. Bettina Cornwell, Donald P. Roy, and Edward A. Steinard II, "Exploring Managers' Perceptions of the Impact of Sponsorship on Brand Equity," *Journal of Advertising* 30 (summer 2001), 41–42.
26. Kevin Clancy and Dan Belmont, "Are the Olympics Really Worth It?" *Brandweek,* August 9, 2004, 25.
27. Patricia Odell, "Crowd Control," *Promo,* January 2005, 23.
28. For an interesting report on the effectiveness of sponsoring NASCAR events, see Stephen W. Pruitt, T. Bettina Cornwell, and John M. Clark, "The NASCAR Phenomenon: Auto Racing Sponsorship and Shareholder Wealth," *Journal of Advertising Research* 44 (September/October 2004), 281–296. Relatedly, for a report on the effectiveness of sponsoring professional sports stadiums, see John M. Clar, T. Bettina Cornwell, and Stephen W. Pruitt, "Corporate Stadium Sponsorships, Signaling Theory, Agency Conflicts, and Shareholder Wealth," *Journal of Advertising Research* 42 (November/December 2002), 16–32.
29. Adapted from Mava Heffler, "Making Sure Sponsorships Meet All the Parameters," *Brandweek,* May 16, 1994, 16.
30. Robert Marich, "Hunters, Anglers Lure the Big Bucks," *Advertising Age,* February 14, 2005, S-8.
31. James Crimmins and Martin Horn, "Sponsorship: From Management Ego Trip to Marketing Success," *Journal of Advertising Research* 36 (July/August 1996), 11–21.
32. Sam Walker, "NASCAR Gets Coup as Anheuser Is Set to Raise Sponsorship Role," *Wall Street Journal Online,* November 13, 1998, http://online.wsj.com.
33. For one illustration of the importance of adequately promoting event sponsorships, see Pascale G. Quester and Beverley Thompson, "Advertising and Promotion Leverage on Arts Sponsorship Effectiveness," *Journal of Advertising Research* 41 (January/February 2001), 33–47.
34. Heffler, "Making Sure Sponsorships Meet All the Parameters."
35. Wayne D'Orio, "The Main Event," *Promo,* May 1997, 19.
36. You may want to examine the following two articles that address the issue of whether Olympic sponsorship is a prudent financial investment: Kathleen Anne Farrell and W. Scott Frame, "The Value of Olympic Sponsorships: Who Is Capturing the Gold?" *Journal of Market Focused Management* 2 (1997), 171–182. For a more positive perspective, see Anthony D. Miyazaki and Angela G. Morgan, "Assessing Market Value of Event Sponsoring: Corporate Olympic Sponsorships," *Journal of Advertising Research* 41 (January/February 2001), 9–15.
37. Dennis M. Sandler and David Shani, "Olympic Sponsorship vs. 'Ambush' Marketing: Who Gets the Gold?" *Journal of Advertising Research* 29 (August/September 1989), 9–14.
38. David Shani and Dennis Sandler, "Counter Attack: Heading Off Ambush Marketers," *Marketing News,* January 18, 1999, 10.
39. This is based on a survey of event marketing conducted by the magazine *Promo* and published in Patricia Odell, "Crowd Control," *Promo,* January 2005, 22–29.
40. Betsy Spethmann, "A Feel for the Neighborhood," *Promo,* February 2005, 20.
41. Michal Strahilevitz, "The Effects of Product Type and Donation Magnitude on Willingness to Pay More for a Charity-Linked Brand," *Journal of Consumer Psychology* 8, no. 3 (1999), 215–241.
42. P. Rajan Varadarajan and Anil Menon, "Cause-Related Marketing: A Coalignment of Marketing Strategy and Corporate Philanthropy," *Journal of Marketing* 52 (July 1988), 58–74.

43. "2004 Cone Corporate Citizenship Study Results," Cause Marketing Forum, December 8, 2004, http://www.causemarketingforum.com.
44. Deborah J. Webb and Lois a Mohr, "A Typology of Consumer Responses to Cause-Related Marketing: From Skeptics to Socially Concerned," *Journal of Public Policy & Marketing* 17 (fall 1998), 239–256.
45. Lisa R. Szykman, Paul N. Bloom, and Jennifer Blazing, "Does Corporate Sponsorship of a Socially-Oriented Message Make a Difference? An Investigation of the Effects of Sponsorship Identity on Responses to an Anti-Drinking and Driving Message," *Journal of Consumer Psychology* 14, nos. 1&2 (2004), 13–20.
46. John W. Pracejus, G. Douglas Olsen, and Norman R. Brown, "On the Prevalence and Impact of Vague Quantifiers in the Advertising of Cause-Related Marketing (CRM)," *Journal of Advertising* 32 (winter 2003–2004), 19–28.
47. Satya Menon and Barbara E. Kahn, "Corporate Sponsorships of Philanthropic Activities: When Do They Impact Perception of Sponsor Brand?," *Journal of Consumer Psychology* 13, no. 3 (2003), 316–327; Nora J. Rifon, Sejung Marina Choi, Carrie S. Trimble, and Hairong Li, "Congruence Effects in Sponsorship: The Mediating Role of Sponsor Credibility and Consumer Attributions of Sponsor Motive," *Journal of Advertising* 33 (spring 2004), 29–42.
48. It has been argued that cause-related marketing may serve to enhance a company's goodwill but may not improve a company's ability to compete. See Michael E. Porter and Mark R. Kramer, "The Competitive Advantage of Corporate Philanthropy," *Harvard Business Review* (December 2002), 5–16.
49. Gary Levin, "Sponsors Put Pressure on for Accountability," *Advertising Age,* June 21, 1993, S1.

GLOSSARY

A

Achievers One of eight VALS segments of American adult consumers. Motivated by the desire for achievement, Achievers have goal-oriented lifestyles and a deep commitment to career and family. See also **Believers, Experiencers, Innovators, Makers, Strivers, Survivors,** and **Thinkers**.

Account-specific marketing A descriptive term that characterizes promotional and advertising activity that a manufacturer customizes to specific retail accounts; also called *co-marketing*.

Active synthesis The second stage of perceptual encoding, active synthesis involves a more refined perception of a stimulus than simply an examination of its basic features. The context of the situation in which information is received plays a major role in determining what is perceived and interpreted.

Advertising strategy A plan of action guided by corporate and marketing strategies which determine the following: how much can be invested in advertising; at what markets advertising efforts need to be directed; how advertising must be coordinated with other marketing elements; and, to some degree, how advertising is to be executed.

Affordability method An advertising budgeting method that sets the budget by spending on advertising those funds that remain after budgeting for everything else.

Ambushing An activity that takes place when companies that are not official sponsors of an event undertake marketing efforts to convey the impression that they are.

Attention A stage of information processing in which the consumer focuses cognitive resources on and thinks about a message to which he or she has been exposed.

Attractiveness An attribute that includes any number of virtuous characteristics that receivers may perceive in an endorser. The general concept of attractiveness consists of three related ideas: *similarity, familiarity,* and *liking*.

Attributes In the means-end conceptualization of advertising strategy, attributes are features or aspects of the advertised product or brand.

Awareness class The first step in product adoption. Four marketing-mix variables influence the awareness class: samples, coupons, advertising, and product distribution.

B

Baby boom The birth of 75 million Americans between 1946 and 1964.

Believers One of eight VALS segments of American adult consumers. Believers are motivated by ideals. They are conservative, conventional people with concrete beliefs based on traditional, established codes: family, religion, community, and the nation. See also **Achievers, Experiencers, Innovators, Makers, Strivers, Survivors,** and **Thinkers**.

Bill-back allowances A form of trade allowance in which retailers receive allowances for featuring the manufacturer's brand in advertisements (bill-back ad allowances) or for providing special displays (bill-back display allowances).

Bonus pack Is a form of sales promotion whereby extra quantities of the product are provided to consumers at the brand's regular price.

Brand Is a company's particular offering of a product, service, or other consumption object. Brands represent the focus of marcom efforts.

Brand image style A creative advertising style that involves psychosocial rather than physical differentiation. The advertiser attempts to develop an image for a brand by associating it with symbols.

Buzz creation The systematic and organized effort to encourage people to talk favorably about a particular item (a product, service, or specific brand) and to recommend its usage to others who are part of their social network.

C

Category management A system established by Procter & Gamble whereby category managers who have direct profit responsibility manage a company's various product categories.

Cause-related marketing (CRM) A relatively narrow aspect of overall sponsorship which involves an amalgam of public relations, sales promotion, and corporate philanthropy. The distinctive feature of CRM is that a company's contribution to a designated cause is linked to customers' engaging in revenue-producing exchanges with the firm.

Cells 1 through 6 Sales promotions are classified into six categories, or cells, based on the manufacturer's objective in using a promotion—whether generating trial purchasing, encouraging repeat buying, or enhancing a brand's image—and the type of reward offered consumers (immediate or delayed).

Click fraud When a competitor or other party clicks on a sponsored link repeatedly in order to foul up advertising effectiveness.

Commercial rumor A widely circulated but unverified proposition about a product, brand, company, store, or other commercial target.

Comparative advertising The practice in which advertisers directly or indirectly compare their products against competitive offerings, typically claiming the promoted item is superior in one or several important purchase considerations. Comparative ads vary both with regard to the explicitness of the comparisons and with respect to whether their target of comparison is named or referred to in general terms.

Compatibility Is the degree to which an innovation is perceived to fit into a person's way of doing things; in general, a new product/brand is more compatible to the extent that it matches consumers' needs, personal values, beliefs, and past consumption practices.

Competitive parity method A budgeting method that sets the advertising budget by basically following what competitors are doing. Also called the **match-competitors method**.

Complexity The degree of perceived difficulty of an innovation. The more difficult an innovation is to understand or use, the slower the rate of adoption.

Comprehension The ability to understand and create meaning out of stimuli and symbols.

Concretizing A marketing approach based on the idea that it is easier for people to remember and retrieve *tangible* rather than *abstract* information.

Consequences In the means-end conceptualization of advertising strategy, consequences represent the desirable or undesirable results from consuming a particular product or brand.

Conspicuity The ability of a sign to capture attention; those signage characteristics that enable walkers or drivers and their passengers to distinguish a sign from its surrounding environment. This requires that a sign be of sufficient size and the information on it be clear, concise, legible, and distinguishable from the competing signage.

Conspiracy rumors Unconfirmed statements that involve supposed company policies or practices that are threatening or ideologically undesirable to consumers.

Contact Potential message delivery channels capable of reaching target customers and presenting the communicator's brand in a favorable light. Interchangeable term with **touch point**.

Contamination rumors Unconfirmed statements dealing with undesirable or harmful product or store features.

Contest A form of consumer-oriented sales promotion in which consumers have an opportunity to win cash, merchandise, or travel prizes. Winners become eligible by solving the specified contest problem.

Continuity A media planning consideration that involves how advertising should be allocated during the course of an advertising campaign.

Continuous advertising schedule In a continuous schedule, a relatively equal number of ad dollars are invested in advertising throughout the campaign.

Corporate advertising Advertising that focuses on specific products or brands in a corporation's overall image or on economic/social issues relevant to the corporation's interests.

Corporate image advertising A specific form of corporate advertising that attempts to gain name recognition for a company, establish goodwill for it and its products, or identify itself with some meaningful and socially acceptable activity.

Corrective advertising Advertising based on the premise that a firm that misleads consumers should have to use future advertisements to rectify any deceptive impressions it has created in consumers' minds. Its purpose is to prevent a firm from continuing to deceive consumers rather than to punish the firm.

Coupon A promotional device that provides cents-off savings to consumers upon redeeming the coupons.

CPM An abbreviation for cost per thousand, in which the *M* represents the Roman numeral for 1,000. CPM is the cost of reaching 1,000 people.

CPM-TM A refinement of CPM that measures the cost of reaching 1,000 members of the target market, excluding those people who fall outside of the target market.

Creative brief The work of copywriters is directed by this framework, which is a document designed to inspire copywriters by channeling their creative efforts toward a solution that will serve the interests of the client.

Customer lifetime value The net present value (NPV) of the profit that a company stands to realize on the average new customer during a given number of years.

D

Data mining Involves the process of searching databases to extract information and discover potentially hidden but useful facts about past, present, and prospective customers.

Deal Refers to any form of sales promotion that delivers a price reduction to consumers. Retailer discounts, manufacturer cents-off offers, and the ubiquitous coupon are the most common forms of deals.

Diffusion process The process by which an innovation is communicated and adopted throughout the marketplace. In contrast to the individual-level adoption process, it is the process of spreading out; as time passes, a new product is adopted by increasingly greater numbers of people.

Diverting Occurs when a manufacturer restricts a deal to a limited geographical area rather than making it available nationally, which results in retailers buying abnormally large quantities at the deal price and then selling off, at a small profit margin, the excess quantities through brokers in other geographical areas.

Dual-coding theory The idea that pictures are represented in memory in verbal as well as visual form, whereas words are less likely to have visual representations.

E

EDLP(M) pricing This is a form of pricing whereby a manufacturer charges the same price for a particular brand day in and day out. Rather than charging high-low prices (regular, or "high," prices for a period followed by off-invoice, or "low," prices for a shorter period), EDLP(M) involves charging the same price over an extended period.

Effective reach The idea that an advertising schedule is effective only if it does not reach members of the target audience too few or too many times during the media scheduling period, typically a four-week period. In other words, there is a theoretical optimum range of exposures to an advertisement with minimum and maximum limits. Also called *effective frequency*.

Efficient consumer response (ECR) A broad-based concept of business management oriented toward altering industry practices to enhance efficiencies and reduce costs.

Elasticity Is a measure of how responsive the demand for a brand is as a function of changes in marketing variables such as price and advertising.

Encoding specificity principle A principle of cognitive psychology, which states that information recall is enhanced when the context in which people attempt to retrieve information is the same or similar to the context in which they originally encoded the information.

Encoding variability hypothesis A hypothesis contending that people's memories for information are enhanced when multiple pathways, or connections, are created between the object to be remembered and the information about the object that is to be remembered.

Ethics In the context of marketing communications involves matters of right and wrong, or *moral,* conduct.

Event sponsorship A form of brand promotion that ties a brand to a meaningful cultural, social, athletic, or other type of high-interest public activity.

Executive-statement release A news release quoting CEOs and other corporate executives.

Exit fee A *deslotting charge* to cover the handling costs for a chain to remove an item from its distribution center.

Experiencers One of eight VALS segments of American adult consumers. Experiencers are motivated by self-expression. As young, enthusiastic, and impulsive consumers, Experiencers quickly become enthusiastic about new possibilities but are equally quick to cool. See also **Achievers, Believers, Innovators, Makers, Strivers, Survivors,** and **Thinkers**.

Experiential needs Needs representing desires for products that provide sensory pleasure, variety, and stimulation.

Expertise The knowledge, experience, or skills possessed by an endorser as they relate to the communications topic.

Exposure In marketing terms, signifies that consumers come in contact with the marketer's message.

F

Feature analysis The initial stage of perceptual encoding whereby a receiver examines the basic features of a stimulus (brightness, depth, angles, etc.) and from this makes a preliminary classification.

Feature article A detailed description of a product or other newsworthy programs that are written by a PR firm for immediate publication or airing by print or broadcast media or distribution via appropriate Internet sites.

Forward buying The practice whereby retailers take advantage of manufacturers' trade deals by buying larger quantities than needed for normal inventory. Retailers often buy enough product on one deal to carry them over until the manufacturer's next scheduled deal; hence, forward buying also is called *bridge buying*.

Free-with-purchase premium This form of premium is typically provided by durable-good brands and involves free merchandise with the purchase of the brand.

Frequency The number of times, on average, within a four-week period that members of the target audience are exposed to the advertiser's message. Also called *average frequency*.

Functional needs Those needs involving current consumption-related problems, potential problems, or conflicts.

G

Galvanometer A device (also referred to as a psychogalvanometer) for measuring *galvanic skin response* or *GSR*. The galvanometer indirectly assesses the degree of emotional response to an advertisement by measuring minute amounts of perspiration.

Generation X (Gen X) To avoid overlap with the baby boomer generation and Generation Y, this text defines Generation X as people born between 1965 and 1981. See also **Baby boom** and **Generation Y**.

Generation Y (Gen Y) To avoid overlap with the preceding generation, Generation X, this text defines Generation Y as people born between 1982 and 1994. See also **Generation X**.

Generic style A creative advertising style in which the advertiser makes a claim about its brand that could be made by any company that markets the product.

Gross rating points (GRPs) A statistic that represents the mathematical product of reach multiplied by frequency. The number of GRPs indicates the total weight of advertising during a time frame, such as a four-week period. The number of GRPs indicates the gross coverage or duplicated audience that is exposed to a particular advertising schedule.

H

Hedonic needs Needs such as pleasure satisfied by messages that make people feel good. People are most likely to attend those stimuli that have become associated with rewards and that relate to those aspects of life that they value highly.

Hierarchy of effects A model predicated on the idea that advertising moves people from an initial stage of unawareness about a product/brand to a final stage of purchasing that product/brand.

I

Identification The process whereby the source attribute of attractiveness influences message receivers, that is, receivers perceive a source to be attractive and therefore identify with the source and adopt the attitudes, behaviors, interests, or preferences of the source.

Infomercial A form of television advertising that serves as an innovative alternative to the conventional form of short television commercial. Infomercials are full-length commercial segments run on cable (and sometimes network) television that typically last 30 minutes and combine product news and entertainment.

Innovators One of eight VALS segments of American adult consumers. Innovators are successful, sophisticated, take-charge people with high self-esteem. Because they have such abundant resources, they exhibit all three primary motivations (i.e., ideals, achievement, and self-expression) in varying degrees. See also **Achievers, Believers, Experiencers, Makers, Strivers, Survivors,** and **Thinkers**.

In-pack premium Is a premium item provided inside the package of the brand that offers the free item as a promotional inducement.

Instantly redeemable coupons Are coupons that are peelable from a brand's package and are to be removed by the consumer and redeemed at checkout.

Integrated marketing communications (IMC) A communications process that entails the planning, integration, and implementation of diverse forms of marcom (advertisements, sales promotions, publicity releases, events, etc.) that are delivered over time to a brand's targeted customers and prospects.

Intense and prominent cues Cues that are louder, more colorful, bigger, brighter, and so on, thereby increasing the probability of attracting attention.

Internalization The source attribute of credibility influences message receivers via a process of internalization; that is, receivers perceive a source to be credible and therefore accept the source's position or attitude as their own. Internalized attitudes tend to be maintained even when the source of the message is forgotten and even when the source switches to a new position.

Interstitials A form of Internet advertising in which messages appear between two content Web pages rather than within a Web page as is the case with pop-up ads.

Involuntary attention One of the forms of attention that requires little or no effort on the part of the message receiver; the stimulus intrudes upon a person's consciousness even though he or she does not want it to. See also **Voluntary attention**.

Issue advertising A form of corporate advertising that takes a position on a controversial social issue of public importance. It does so in a manner that supports the company's position and best interests. Also called *advocacy advertising*. See also **Corporate image advertising**.

K

Key fact A single-minded statement in an advertising strategy, from the consumer's point of view, that identifies why consumers are or are not purchasing the product, service, or brand or are not giving it proper consideration.

Keywords One of the features of search engine advertising (SEA), keywords are specific words and short phrases that describe the nature, attributes, and benefits of a marketer's offering.

L

Laddering A marketing research technique that has been developed to identify linkages between attributes, consequences, and values. It involves in-depth, one-on-one interviews using primarily a series of directed probes.

M

Mail-in offer Is a premium in which consumers receive a free item from the sponsoring manufacturer in return for submitting a required number of proofs of purchase.

Makers One of eight VALS segments of American adult consumers. Makers are motivated by self-expression. They express themselves and experience the world by working on it—building a house, raising children, fixing a car, or canning vegetables—and have enough skill and energy to carry out their projects successfully. See also **Achievers, Believers, Experiencers, Innovators, Strivers, Survivors,** and **Thinkers**.

Marcom objectives The goals that the various marcom elements aspire to individually or collectively achieve during a scope of time such as a business quarter or fiscal year. Objectives provide the foundation for all remaining decisions.

Market mavens Individuals who have information about many kinds of products, places to shop, and other facets of markets, and who initiate discussions with consumers and respond to requests from consumers for market information.

Match-competitors method Also called the **competitive parity method**, this advertising budgeting procedure sets the ad budget for a brand by basically following what competitors are doing.

Mature consumers Also called *seniors,* mature consumers are the approximately 66 million consumers aged 55 and older. They are wealthier and more willing to spend than ever before, and they control nearly 70 percent of the net worth of all U.S. households.

Meaning The set of internal responses and resulting predispositions evoked within a person when presented with a sign or stimulus object.

MECCAS An acronym for Means-End Conceptualization of Components for Advertising Strategy, a model for applying the concept of means-end chains to the creation of advertising messages.

Media The general communication methods that carry advertising messages, that is—television, magazines, newspapers, and so on.

Media planning An approach that involves the process of designing a scheduling plan that shows how advertising time and space will contribute to the achievement of marketing objectives.

Message research Also known as *copy testing*, message research is a technique that tests the effectiveness of creative messages. Copy testing involves both pretesting a message during its development stages and posttesting the message for effectiveness after it has been aired or printed.

Metaphor A form of figurative language that applies a word or a phrase to a concept or an object, such as a brand, that it does not literally denote to suggest a comparison with the brand (e.g., Budweiser is "the king of beers").

Middle age Is the age range starting at age 35 and ending at age 54 at which point maturity is reached.

N

Near-pack premium A premium offer that provides the retail trade with specially displayed premium pieces that retailers then give to consumers who purchase the promoted brand.

Novel messages Are those that are unusual, distinctive, or unpredictable. Such messages tend to produce greater attention than those that are familiar and routine.

O

Objective-and-task method A budgeting method that establishes the advertising budget by determining the communication tasks that need to be established. See also **Percentage-of-sales method**.

Observability The degree to which other people can observe one's ownership and use of a new product. The more a consumption behavior can be sensed by other people, the more observable it is and typically the more rapid is its rate of adoption.

Off-invoice allowance A deal offered periodically to the trade that literally permits wholesalers and retailers to deduct a fixed amount from the invoice.

Online video ads Also referred to as *streaming video,* these are audio-video Internet ads that are similar to standard 30-second TV commercials but are often shortened to 10 or 15 seconds and compressed into manageable file sizes.

On-pack premium Is a premium item that is attached to the package of the brand that offers the free item as a promotional inducement.

Opinion leader Is a person who frequently influences other individuals' attitudes and behavior related to new products. They inform other people (followers) about new products, reduce followers' perceived risk in purchasing new products, and confirm decisions that followers have already made.

Opt-in e-mailing Is the practice of marketers' asking for and receiving consumers' permission to send them messages on a particular topic. The consumer agrees (opts-in) to receive messages on topics of interest rather than receiving messages that are unsolicited.

Overlay program The use of two or more sales promotion techniques in combination with one another; also called *combination program*.

P

Paper diaries ACNielsen's alternative data collection procedure (as opposed to the electronic people meter) for estimating TV program ratings in local markets throughout the United States. Participating households complete a 20-page diary four times a year, during sweep months.

Pay-for-performance programs A form of trade allowance that rewards retailers for performing the primary function that justifies a manufacturer's offering a trade allowance—namely, selling increased quantities of the manufacturer's brands to shoppers.

Percentage-of-sales method A budgeting method that involves setting the budget as a fixed percentage of past or anticipated (typically the latter) sales volume. See also **Objective-and-task method**.

Perceptual encoding The process of interpreting stimuli, which includes two stages: feature analysis and active synthesis.

Phishing An illegal e-mailing practice related to spam in which criminals send email messages appearing to be from legitimate corporations and direct recipients to phony Web sites that are designed to look like companies' actual Web sites. These phony Web sites attempt to extract personal data from people such as their credit card and ATM numbers.

Physical attractiveness Is a key consideration in many endorsement relationships and involves an endorser's beauty, athleticism, and sexuality.

P-mail advertising P-mail, which is structurally equivalent to e-mail and is shorthand for "postal," refers to any advertising matter a company sends via the postal service.

Podcasting An audio version of blogging and a way of publishing sound files to the Internet, podcasting allows users to subscribe to a feed and receive new audio files automatically. Consumers subscribe to podcasts using a special form of so-called aggregator software that periodically checks for and downloads new content, which then is playable on computers and digital audio players.

Pop-up ads Are a form of Internet advertising in which ads appear in a separate window that materializes on the screen seemingly out of nowhere when a selected Web page is loading.

Positioning The key feature, benefit, or image that a brand stands for in the target audience's collective mind.

Positioning Advertising Copy testing (PACT) A set of nine copy testing principles developed by leading U.S. advertising agencies.

Positioning statement The key idea that encapsulates what a brand is intended to stand for in its target market's mind.

Preemptive style A creative advertising style in which the advertiser that makes a particular claim effectively prevents competitors from making the same claim for fear of being labeled a copycat.

Premiums Articles of merchandise or services offered by manufacturers to induce action on the part of the sales force, trade representatives, or consumers.

Price-off promotion Also called cents-off or price packs, this form of sales promotion entails a reduction, typically ranging from 10 to 25 percent, in a brand's regular price.

Proactive MPR A form of marketing PR that is offensively rather than defensively oriented and opportunity-seeking rather than problem solving. See also **Reactive MPR**.

Product release A publicity tool that announces a new product, provides relevant information about product features and benefits, and informs interested listeners/readers how additional information can be obtained.

Promotion Refers to any *incentive* used by a manufacturer to induce the *trade* (wholesalers, retailers, or other channel members) and/or *consumers* to buy a brand and to encourage the *sales force* to aggressively sell it.

Psychographics Information about consumers' attitudes, values, motivations, and lifestyles that relate to buying behavior in a particular product category.

Psychological reactance A theory that suggests that people react against any efforts to reduce their freedoms or choices. When products are made to seem less available, they become more valuable in the consumer's mind.

Pull Marketing efforts directed to ultimate consumers with the intent of influencing their acceptance of the manufacturer's brand. Manufacturers hope that the consumers will then encourage retailers to handle the brand. Typically used in conjunction with *push*.

Push A manufacturer's selling and other promotional efforts directed at gaining trade support from wholesalers and retailers for the manufacturer's product.

R

Rating points Ratings points are the foundation for concepts such as effective, gross, and target rating points. A single rating point simply represents one percent of a designated group or an entire population that is exposed to a particular advertising vehicle such as a TV program.

Reach The percentage of an advertiser's target audience that is exposed to at least one advertisement over an established time frame (a four-week period represents the typical time frame for most advertisers). Reach represents the number of target customers who see or hear the advertiser's message one or more times during the time period. Also called *net coverage, unduplicated audience,* or *cumulative audience (cume)*.

Reactive MPR Marketing undertaken as a result of external pressures and challenges brought by competitive actions, changes in consumer attitudes, or other external influences. It typically deals with changes that have negative consequences for the organization. See also **Proactive MPR**.

Rebate Manufacturers give cash discounts or reimbursements to consumers who submit proofs of purchase when purchasing the manufacturer's brand. Unlike coupons, which the consumer redeems at retail checkouts, rebates/refunds are mailed with proofs of purchase to manufacturers.

Recency principle Known also as the shelf-space model for media planning, this principle is based on the idea that achieving a high level of weekly reach for a brand should be emphasized over acquiring heavy frequency.

Relationship An enduring link between a brand and its customers. Successful relationships between customers and brands lead to repeat purchasing and perhaps even loyalty toward a brand.

Relative advantage The degree to which an innovation is perceived as better than an existing idea or object in terms of increasing comfort, saving time or effort, and increasing the immediacy of reward.

Repeater class This third stage in the adoption process is influenced by four marketing-mix variables: advertising, price, distribution, and product satisfaction.

Respect Is an endorser characteristic that represents the quality of being admired or esteemed due to one's personal qualities and accomplishments.

Revenue premium The revenue differential between a branded item and a corresponding private labeled item.

ROMI The idea of *return on investment* (ROI), which is well known in accounting, finance, or managerial economics circles, is referred to in marketing circles as ROMI, or *return on marketing investment*.

S

Sales-to-advertising response function The relationship between money invested in advertising and the response, or output, of that investment in terms of revenue generated.

Sampling The use of various distribution methods to deliver actual- or trial-size products to consumers. The purpose is to initiate trial-usage behavior.

Self-liquidating offer Known as SLOs by practitioners, this form of premium requires consumers to mail in a stipulated number of proofs of purchase along with sufficient money to cover the manufacturer's purchasing, handling, and mailing costs of the premium item.

Self-regulation Regulation of advertising by advertisers themselves rather by state or federal government bodies.

Semiotics The study of signs and the analysis of meaning-producing events. This perspective sees meaning as a constructive process.

Share of market (SOM) Represents a brand's proportion of overall product category sales.

Share of voice (SOV) Represents a brand's proportion of overall advertising expenditures in a product category.

Sign Something physical and perceivable by our senses that represents or signifies something (the referent) to somebody (the interpreter) in some context.

Similarity Represents the degree to which an endorser matches an audience in terms of characteristics such as age, gender, and ethnicity that are pertinent to the quality of an endorsement relationship.

Single-source systems (SSSs) Systems that gather purchase data from panels of households using optical scanning equipment and merge it with household demographic characteristics and, most important, with information about causal marketing variables that influence household purchases.

Slotting allowance The fee a manufacturer pays a supermarket or other retailer to get that retailer to handle the manufacturer's new product. The allowance is called slotting in reference to the slot, or location, that the retailer must make available in its warehouse to accommodate the manufacturer's product.

Standardized Advertising Unit (SAU) system A system adopted in the 1980s, making it possible for advertisers to purchase any one of 56 standard ad sizes to fit the advertising publishing parameters of all newspapers in the United States.

Strivers One of eight VALS segments of American adult consumers. Strivers are trendy and fun loving. Because they are motivated by achievement, Strivers are concerned about the opinions and approval of others. Money defines success for Strivers, who don't have enough of it to meet their desires. See also **Achievers, Believers, Experiencers, Innovators, Makers, Survivors,** and **Thinkers**.

Superstitials Are short, animated Internet ads that play over or on top of a Web page.

Survivors One of eight VALS segments of American adult consumers. Survivors live narrowly focused lives. With few resources with which to cope, they often believe that the world is changing too quickly. They are comfortable with the familiar and are primarily concerned with safety and security. Because they must focus on meeting needs rather than fulfilling desires, Survivors do not show a strong primary motivation. See also **Achievers, Believers, Experiencers, Innovators, Makers, Strivers,** and **Thinkers**.

Sweepstakes A form of consumer-oriented sales promotion in which winners receive cash, merchandise, or travel prizes. Winners are determined purely on the basis of chance.

Symbolic needs Internal consumer needs such as the desire for self-enhancement, role position, or group membership.

Synergy When multiple methods, used in combination with one another, yield more positive communication results than do the tools used individually.

T

Target rating points (TRPs) An adaptation of gross rating points (GRPs), TRPs adjust a vehicle's rating to reflect just those individuals who match the advertiser's target audience.

Thinkers One of eight VALS segments of American adult consumers. Thinkers are motivated by ideals. They are mature, satisfied, comfortable, and reflective people who value order, knowledge, and responsibility. See also **Achievers, Believers, Experiencers, Innovators, Makers, Strivers,** and **Survivors**.

Three-exposure hypothesis This addresses the *minimum* number of exposures needed for advertising to be effective.

Tie-in The simultaneous promotion of multiple brands in a single sales-promotion effort; also called *joint promotion*.

Touch point See **Contact**.

Trade allowances Also called trade deals, these allowances are used by manufacturers to reward wholesalers and retailers for performing activities in support of the manufacturer's brand such as featuring the brand in retail advertisements or providing special display space.

Transformational advertising Brand image advertising that associates the experience of using an advertised brand with the unique set of psychological characteristics that would not typically be associated with the brand experience to the same degree without exposure to the advertisement.

Trialability The extent to which an innovation can be used on a limited basis. Trialability is tied closely to the concept of perceived risk. In general, products that lend themselves to trialability are adopted at a more rapid rate.

Trier class The group of consumers who actually try a new product; the second step in which an individual becomes a new brand consumer. Coupons, distribution, and price are the variables that influence consumers to become triers.

Trustworthiness The honesty, integrity, and reliability of a source.

U

Unfair advertising Is a legal term to define advertising acts or practices that cause or are likely to cause substantial injury to consumers, which is not reasonably avoidable by consumers themselves and not outweighed by countervailing benefits to consumers or competition.

Unique selling proposition (USP) style A creative advertising style that promotes a product attribute that represents a meaningful, distinctive consumer benefit.

V

Values In the means-end conceptualization of advertising strategy, values represent important beliefs that people hold about themselves and that determine the relative desirability of consequences.

Value proposition Is the essence of an advertisement or other marcom message and the reward to the consumer for investing his or her time attending the message.

Vehicles The specific broadcast programs or print choices in which advertisements are placed.

VIEW Is an acronym that can be used when evaluating four general features of a particular package: visibility, information, emotional appeal, and workability.

Voluntary attention One of three forms of attention that occurs when a person willfully notices a stimulus. See also **Involuntary attention**.

W

Wearout Refers to the ultimately diminished effectiveness of advertising over time.

Wi-Fi Short for *wireless fidelity,* this technology enables computers and other wireless devices such as cell phones to connect to the Internet via low-power radio signals instead of cables. Hence, users can have Internet access at base stations, or so-called hotspots, that are Wi-Fi equipped.

NAME INDEX

T

U

V

W

Y

Z

SUBJECT INDEX

B

C

H

I

J

N

O

P

Q

R

S

T

U

V

W